THE COLLINS
POCKET REFERENCE
SPANISH
DICTIONARY

SPANISH·ENGLISH   ENGLISH·SPANISH

HarperCollins*Publishers*

First published 1990

© William Collins Sons & Co. Ltd. 1990

First reprint 1990

ISBN 0 00 433257-1

Printed and bound by
Collins Manufacturing, Glasgow

INTRODUCTION

This dictionary of Spanish and English is designed to provide the user with wide-ranging and up-to-date coverage of the two languages, and is ideal for both school and reference use.

A special feature of Collins dictionaries is the comprehensive 'signposting' of meanings on both sides of the dictionary, guiding the user to the most appropriate translation for a given context. We hope you will find this dictionary easy and pleasant to consult for all your study and reference needs.

ABREVIATURAS

ABBREVIATIONS

adjetivo, locución adjetiva	a	adjective, adjectival phrase
abreviatura	ab(b)r	abbreviation
adverbio, locución adverbial	ad	adverb, adverbial phrase
administración, lengua administrativa	ADMIN	administration
agricultura	AGR	agriculture
América Latina	AM	Latin America
anatomía	ANAT	anatomy
arquitectura	ARQ, ARCH	architecture
astrología, astronomía	ASTRO	astrology, astronomy
el automóvil	AUT(O)	the motor car and motoring
aviación, viajes aéreos	AVIAT	flying, air travel
biología	BIO(L)	biology
botánica, flores	BOT	botany
inglés británico	Brit	British English
química	CHEM	chemistry
lengua familiar (! vulgar)	col(!)	colloquial usage (! particularly offensive)
comercio, finanzas, banca	COM(M)	commerce, finance, banking
informática	COMPUT	computers
conjunción	conj	conjunction
construcción	CONSTR	building
compuesto	cpd	compound element
cocina	CULIN	cookery
economía	ECON	economics
electricidad, electrónica	ELEC	electricity, electronics
enseñanza, sistema escolar y universitario	ESCOL	schooling, schools and universities
España	Esp	Spain
especialmente	esp	especially
exclamación, interjección	excl	exclamation, interjection
femenino	f	feminine
lengua familiar (! vulgar)	fam(!)	colloquial usage (! particularly offensive)
ferrocarril	FERRO	railways
uso figurado	fig	figurative use
fotografía	FOTO	photography
(verbo inglés) del cual la partícula es inseparable	fus	(phrasal verb) where the particle is inseparable
generalmente	gen	generally
geografía, geología	GEO	geography, geology
geometría	GEOM	geometry
infinitivo	inf	infinitive
informática	INFORM	computers
invariable	inv	invariable
irregular	irg	irregular
lo jurídico	JUR	law
América Latina	LAm	Latin America
gramática, lingüística	LING	grammar, linguistics
masculino	m	masculine

ABREVIATURAS ABBREVIATIONS

matemáticas	MAT(H)	mathematics
medicina	MED	medical term, medicine
masculino/femenino	m/f	masculine/feminine
lo militar, ejército	MIL	military matters
música	MUS	music
sustantivo, nombre	n	noun
navegación, náutica	NAUT	sailing, navigation
sustantivo numérico	num	numeral noun
complemento	obj	(grammatical) object
	o.s.	oneself
peyorativo	pey, pej	derogatory, pejorative
fotografía	PHOT	photography
fisiología	PHYSIOL	physiology
plural	pl	plural
política	POL	politics
participio de pasado	pp	past participle
prefijo	pref	prefix
preposición	prep	preposition
pronombre	pron	pronoun
psicología, psiquiatría	PSICO, PSYCH	psychology, psychiatry
	pt	past tense
sustantivo no empleado en el plural	q	collective (uncountable) noun, not used in plural
química	QUIM	chemistry
ferrocarril	RAIL	railways
religión, lo eclesiástico	REL	religion, church service
	sb	somebody
enseñanza, sistema escolar y universitario	SCOL	schooling, schools and universities
singular	sg	singular
España	Sp	Spain
	sth	something
sujeto	su(b)j	(grammatical) subject
subjuntivo	subjun	subjunctive
sufijo	suff	suffix
tauromaquia	TAUR	bullfighting
también	tb	also
técnica, tecnología	TEC(H)	technical term, technology
telecomunicaciones	TELEC, TEL	telecommunications
televisión	TV	television
imprenta, tipografía	TIP, TYP	typography, printing
inglés norteamericano	US	American English
verbo	vb	verb
verbo intransitivo	vi	intransitive verb
verbo pronominal	vr	reflexive verb
verbo transitivo	vt	transitive verb
zoología, animales	ZOOL	zoology
marca registrada	®	registered trademark
indica un equivalente cultural	≈	introduces a cultural equivalent

SPANISH PRONUNCIATION

Consonants

b	[b, ß]	boda, bomba, labor	see notes on v below
c	[k]	caja	c before a, o or u is pronounced as in cat
ce, ci	[θe, θi]	cero cielo	c before e or i is pronounced as in thin
ch	[tʃ]	chiste	ch is pronounced as ch in chair
d	[d, ð]	danés ciudad	at the beginning of a phrase or after l or n, d is pronounced as in English. In any other position it is pronounced like th in the
g	[g, ɣ]	gafas paga	g before a, o or u is pronounced as in gap, if at the beginning of a phrase or after n. In other positions the sound is softened
ge, gi	[xe, xi]	gente girar	g before e or i is pronounced similar to ch in Scottish loch
h		haber	h is always silent in Spanish
j	[x]	jugar	j is pronounced similar to ch in Scottish loch
ll	[ʎ]	talle	ll is pronounced like the lli in million
ñ	[ɲ]	niño	ñ is pronounced like the ni in onion
q	[k]	que	q is pronounced as k in king
r, rr	[r, rr]	quitar garra	r is always pronounced in Spanish, unlike the silent r in dancer. rr is trilled, like a Scottish r
s	[s]	quizás isla	s is usually pronounced as in pass, but before b, d, g, l, m or n it is pronounced as in rose
v	[b, ß]	vía dividir	Spanish v and b are pronounced in the same way. At the beginning of a phrase or after m or n they are pronounced as b in boy. In any other position the sound is softened and the lips do not meet
z	[θ]	tenaz	z is pronounced as th in thin

f, k, l, m, n, p, t and x are pronounced as in English.

Vowels

a	[a]	p**a**t**a**	not as long as *a* in f**a**r. When followed by a consonant in the same syllable (i.e. in a closed syllable), as in am**a**nte, the *a* is short, as in b**a**t
e	[e]	m**e**	like *e* in th**e**y. In a closed syllable, as in g**e**nte, the *e* is short as in p**e**t
i	[i]	p**i**no	as in m**ea**n or mach**i**ne
o	[o]	l**o**	as in l**o**cal. In a closed syllable, as in c**o**ntrol, the *o* is short as in c**o**t
u	[u]	l**u**nes	as in r**u**le. It is silent after *q*, and in g**u**e, g**u**i, unless marked g**ü**e, g**ü**i e.g. antig**ü**edad, when it is pronounced like *w* in w**o**lf

Semivowels

i, y	[j]	b**i**en	pronounced like *y* in **y**es
		h**i**elo	
		yunta	
u	[w]	h**u**evo	unstressed *u* between consonant and vowel is pronounced like *w* in **w**ell. See also notes on *u* above
		f**u**ente	
		antig**ü**edad	

Diphthongs

ai, ay	[ai]	b**ai**le	as *i* in r**i**de
au	[au]	**au**to	as *ou* in sh**ou**t
ei, ey	[ei]	bu**ey**	as *ey* in gr**ey**
eu	[eu]	d**eu**da	both elements pronounced independently [e]+[u]
oi, oy	[oi]	h**oy**	as *oy* in t**oy**

Stress

The rules of stress in Spanish are as follows:

(a) when a word ends in a vowel or in *n* or *s*, the second last syllable is stressed: pat**a**ta, pat**a**tas, c**o**me, c**o**men
(b) when a word ends in a consonant other than *n* or *s*, the stress falls on the last syllable: par**e**d, habl**a**r
(c) when the rules set out in a and b are not applied, an acute accent appears over the stressed vowel: com**ú**n, geograf**í**a, ingl**é**s

In the phonetic transcription, the symbol ['] precedes the syllable on which the stress falls.

PRONUNCIACIÓN INGLESA

Vocales y diptongos

	Ejemplo inglés	*Ejemplo español/explicación*
ɑ:	f**a**ther	Entre *a* de p**a**dre y *o* de n**o**che
ʌ	b**u**t, c**o**me	*a* muy breve
æ	m**a**n, c**a**t	Con los labios en la posición de *e* en p**e**na se pronuncia el sonido *a* parecido a la *a* de c**a**rro
ə	f**a**ther, **a**go	Vocal neutra parecida a una *e* u *o* casi mudas
ə:	b**i**rd, h**ea**rd	Entre *e* abierta, y *o* cerrada, sonido alargado
ɛ	g**e**t, b**e**d	Como en p**e**rro
ɪ	**i**t, b**i**g	Más breve que en s**i**
i:	t**ea**, s**ee**	Como en f**i**no
ɔ	h**o**t, w**a**sh	Como en t**o**rre
ɔ:	s**aw**, **a**ll	Como en p**o**r
u	p**u**t, b**oo**k	Sonido breve, más cerrado que b**u**rro
u:	t**oo**, y**ou**	Sonido largo, como en **u**no
aɪ	fl**y**, h**igh**	Como en fr**ai**le
au	h**ow**, h**ou**se	Como en p**au**sa
ɛə	th**ere**, b**ear**	Casi como en v**ea**, pero el segundo elemento es la vocal neutra [ə]
eɪ	d**ay**, ob**ey**	*e* cerrada seguida por una *i* débil
ɪə	h**ere**, h**ear**	Como en man**ía**, mezclándose el sonido *a* con la vocal neutra [ə]
əu	g**o**, n**o**te	[ə] seguido por una breve *u*
ɔɪ	b**oy**, **oi**l	Como en v**oy**
uə	p**oor**, s**ure**	*u* bastante larga más la vocal neutra [ə]

Consonantes

	Ejemplo inglés	*Ejemplo español/explicación*
b	*b*ig, lob*b*y	Como en tum*b*a
d	men*d*e*d*	Como en con*d*e, an*d*ar
g	*g*o, *g*et, bi*g*	Como en *g*rande, *g*ol
dʒ	*g*in, *j*u*dg*e	Como en la *ll* andaluza y en *G*eneralitat (catalán)
ŋ	si*ng*	Como en ví*n*culo
h	*h*ouse, *h*e	Como la jota hispanoamericana
j	*y*oung, *y*es	Como en *y*a
k	*c*ome, mo*ck*	Como en *c*aña, Es*c*ocia
r	*r*ed, t*r*ead	Se pronuncia con la punta de la lengua hacia atrás y sin hacerla vibrar
s	*s*and, ye*s*	Como en ca*s*a, *s*esión
z	ro*s*e, *z*ebra	Como en des*d*e, mi*s*mo
ʃ	*sh*e, ma*ch*ine	Como en *ch*ambre (francés), ro*x*o (portugués)
tʃ	*ch*in, ri*ch*	Como en *ch*ocolate
v	*v*alley	Como en f, pero se retiran los dientes superiores vibrándolos contra el labio inferior
w	*w*ater, *wh*ich	Como en la *u* de h*u*evo, p*u*ede
ʒ	vi*s*ion	Como en *j*ournal (francés)
θ	*th*ink, my*th*	Como en re*c*eta, *z*apato
ð	*th*is, *th*e	Como en la *d* de habla*d*o, verda*d*

p, f, m, n, l, t iguales que en español
El signo * indica que la r final escrita apenas se pronuncia en inglés británico cuando la palabra siguiente empieza con vocal. El signo ['] indica la sílaba acentuada.

A

a |a| *prep* (*a + el = al*) **1** (*dirección*) to; **fueron ~ Madrid/Grecia** they went to Madrid/Greece; **me voy ~ casa** I'm going home **2** (*distancia*): **está ~ 15 km de aquí** it's 15 kms from here **3** (*posición*): **estar ~ la mesa** to be at table; **al lado de** next to, beside; *ver tb* **puerta 4** (*tiempo*): **~ las 10/~ medianoche** at 10/midnight; **~ la mañana siguiente** the following morning; **~ los pocos días** after a few days; **estamos ~ 9 de julio** it's the ninth of July; **~ los 24 años** at the age of 24; **al año/~ la semana** (*AM*) a year/week later **5** (*manera*): **~ la francesa** the French way; **~ caballo** on horseback; **~ oscuras** in the dark **6** (*medio, instrumento*): **~ lápiz** in pencil; **~ mano** by hand; **cocina ~ gas** gas stove **7** (*razón*): **~ 30 ptas el kilo** at 30 pesetas a kilo; **~ más de 50 km/h** at more than 50 kms per hour **8** (*dativo*): **se lo di ~ él** I gave it to him; **vi al policía** I saw the policeman; **se lo compré ~ él** I bought it from him **9** (*tras ciertos verbos*): **voy ~ verle** I'm going to see him; **empezó ~ trabajar** he started working *o* to work **10** (+ *infinitivo*): **al verle, le reconocí inmediatamente** when I saw him I recognized him at once; **el camino ~ recorrer** the distance we (*etc*) have to travel; **¡~ callar!** keep quiet!; **¡~ comer!** let's eat!

abad, esa |a'βað, 'ðesa| *nm/f* abbot/ abbess; **~ía** *nf* abbey.

abajo |a'βaxo| *ad* (*situación*) (down) below, underneath; (*en edificio*) downstairs; (*dirección*) down, downwards; **~ de** *prep* below, under; **el piso de ~** the downstairs flat; **la parte de ~** the lower part; **¡~ el gobierno!** down with the government!; **cuesta/río ~** downhill/ downstream; **de arriba ~** from top to bottom; **el ~ firmante** the undersigned; **más ~** lower *o* further down.

abalorios |aβa'lorjos| *nmpl* (*chucherías*) trinkets.

abalanzarse |aβalan'θarse| *vr*: **~ sobre** *o* **contra** to throw o.s. at.

abanderado |aβande'raðo| *nm* standard bearer.

abandonado, a |aβando'naðo, a| *a* der-

elict; (*desatendido*) abandoned; (*desierto*) deserted; (*descuidado*) neglected.

abandonar |aβando'nar| *vt* to leave; (*persona*) to abandon, desert; (*cosa*) to abandon, leave behind; (*descuidar*) to neglect; (*renunciar a*) to give up; (*INFORM*) to quit; **~se** *vr*: **~se a** to abandon o.s. to; **abandono** *nm* (*acto*) desertion, abandonment; (*estado*) abandon, neglect; (*renuncia*) withdrawal, retirement; **ganar por ~** to win by default.

abanicar |aβani'kar| *vt* to fan; **abanico** *nm* fan; (*NAUT*) derrick.

abaratar |aβara'tar| *vt* to lower the price of // *vi*, **~se** *vr* to go *o* come down in price.

abarcar |aβar'kar| *vt* to include, embrace; (*AM*) to monopolize.

abarrotado, a |aβarro'taðo, a| *a* packed.

abarrote |aβa'rrote| *nm* packing; **~s** *nmpl* (*AM*) groceries, provisions; **~ro, a** *nm/f* (*AM*) grocer.

abastecer |aβaste'θer| *vt* to supply; **abastecimiento** *nm* supply.

abasto |a'βasto| *nm* supply; (*abundancia*) abundance; **no dar ~ a** to be unable to cope with.

abatido, a |aβa'tiðo, a| *a* dejected, downcast.

abatimiento |aβati'mjento| *nm* (*depresión*) dejection, depression.

abatir |aβa'tir| *vt* (*muro*) to demolish; (*pájaro*) to shoot *o* bring down; (*fig*) to depress; **~se** *vr* to get depressed; **~se sobre** to swoop *o* pounce on.

abdicación |aβðika'θjon| *nf* abdication.

abdicar |aβði'kar| *vi* to abdicate.

abdomen |aβ'ðomen| *nm* abdomen.

abecedario |aβeθe'ðarjo| *nm* alphabet.

abedul |aβe'ðul| *nm* birch.

abeja |a'βexa| *nf* bee.

abejorro |aβe'xorro| *nm* bumblebee.

aberración |aβerra'θjon| *nf* aberration.

abertura |aβer'tura| *nf* = **apertura**.

abeto |a'βeto| *nm* fir.

abierto, a *pp de* **abrir** // |a'βjerto, a| *a* open; (*AM*) generous.

abigarrado, a |aβiɣa'rraðo, a| *a* multicoloured.

abismal |aβis'mal| *a* (*fig*) vast, enormous.

abismar |aβis'mar| *vt* to humble, cast down; **~se** *vr* to sink; **~se en** (*fig*) to be plunged into.

abismo |a'βismo| *nm* abyss.

abjurar [aβxu'rar] *vi*: ~ de to abjure, for-swear.

ablandar [aβlan'dar] *vt* to soften // *vi*, ~se *vr* to get softer.

abnegación [aβneɣa'θjon] *nf* self-denial.

abnegado, a [aβne'ɣaðo, a] *a* self-sacrificing.

abocado, a [aβo'kaðo, a] *a*: ~ verse ~ al desastre to be heading for disaster.

abochornar [aβotʃor'nar] *vt* to embarrass; ~se *vr* to get flustered; (*BOT*) to wilt.

abofetear [aβofete'ar] *vt* to slap (in the face).

abogacía [aβoɣa'θia] *nf* legal profession; (*ejercicio*) practice of the law.

abogado, a [aβo'ɣaðo, a] *nm/f* lawyer; (*notario*) solicitor; (*en tribunal*) barrister (*Brit*), attorney (*US*); ~ defensor defence lawyer *o* attorney (*US*).

abogar [aβo'ɣar] *vi*: ~ por to plead for; (*fig*) to advocate.

abolengo [aβo'leŋgo] *nm* ancestry, line-age.

abolición [aβoli'θjon] *nf* abolition.

abolir [aβo'lir] *vt* to abolish; (*cancelar*) to cancel.

abolladura [aβoʎa'ðura] *nf* dent.

abollar [aβo'ʎar] *vt* to dent.

abominable [aβomi'naβle] *a* abominable.

abominación [aβomina'θjon] *nf* abomination.

abonado, a [aβo'naðo, a] *a* (*deuda*) paid(-up) // *nm/f* subscriber.

abonar [aβo'nar] *vt* (*deuda*) to settle; (*terreno*) to fertilize; (*idea*) to endorse; ~se *vr* to subscribe; **abono** *nm* payment; fertilizer; subscription.

abordar [aβor'ðar] *vt* (*barco*) to board; (*asunto*) to broach.

aborigen [aβo'rixen] *nm/f* aborigine.

aborrecer [aβorre'θer] *vt* to hate, loathe.

abortar [aβor'tar] *vi* (*malparir*) to have a miscarriage; (*deliberadamente*) to have an abortion; **aborto** *nm* miscarriage; abortion.

abotagado, a [aβota'ɣaðo, a] *a* swollen.

abotonar [aβoto'nar] *vt* to button (up), do up.

abovedado, a [aβoβe'ðaðo, a] *a* vaulted, domed.

abrasar [aβra'sar] *vt* to burn (up); (*AGR*) to dry up, parch.

abrazadera [aβraθa'ðera] *nf* bracket.

abrazar [aβra'θar] *vt* to embrace, hug.

abrazo [a'βraθo] *nm* embrace, hug; un ~ (*en carta*) with best wishes.

abrebotellas [aβreβo'teʎas] *nm inv* bottle opener.

abrecartas [aβre'kartas] *nm inv* letter opener.

abrelatas [aβre'latas] *nm inv* tin (*Brit*) *o* can opener.

abreviar [aβre'βjar] *vt* to abbreviate; (*texto*) to abridge; (*plazo*) to reduce;

abreviatura *nf* abbreviation.

abridor [aβri'ðor] *nm* bottle opener; (*de latas*) tin (*Brit*) *o* can opener.

abrigar [aβri'ɣar] *vt* (*proteger*) to shelter; (*suj: ropa*) to keep warm; (*fig*) to cherish.

abrigo [a'βriɣo] *nm* (*prenda*) coat, over-coat; (*lugar protegido*) shelter.

abril [a'βril] *nm* April.

abrillantar [aβriʎan'tar] *vt* to polish.

abrir [a'βrir] *vt* to open (up) // *vi* to open; ~se *vr* to open (up); (*extenderse*) to open out; (*cielo*) to clear; ~se paso to find *o* force a way through.

abrochar [aβro'tʃar] *vt* (*con botones*) to button (up); (*zapato, con broche*) to do up.

abrumar [aβru'mar] *vt* to overwhelm; (*sobrecargar*) to weigh down.

abrupto, a [a'βrupto, a] *a* abrupt; (*empinado*) steep.

absceso [aβs'θeso] *nm* abscess.

absentismo [aβsen'tismo] *nm* absentee-ism.

absolución [aβsolu'θjon] *nf* (*REL*) absolution; (*JUR*) acquittal.

absoluto, a [aβso'luto, a] *a* absolute; en ~ *ad* not at all.

absolver [aβsol'βer] *vt* to absolve; (*JUR*) to pardon; (: *acusado*) to acquit.

absorbente [aβsor'βente] *a* absorbent; (*interesante*) absorbing.

absorber [aβsor'βer] *vt* to absorb; (*embeber*) to soak up.

absorción [aβsor'θjon] *nf* absorption; (*COM*) takeover.

absorto, a [aβ'sorto, a] *pp de* **absorber** // *a* absorbed, engrossed.

abstemio, a [aβs'temjo, a] *a* teetotal.

abstención [aβsten'θjon] *nf* abstention.

abstenerse [aβste'nerse] *vr*: ~ (de) to abstain *o* refrain (from).

abstinencia [aβsti'nenθja] *nf* abstinence; (*ayuno*) fasting.

abstracción [aβstrak'θjon] *nf* abstrac-tion.

abstracto, a [aβs'trakto, a] *a* abstract.

abstraer [aβstra'er] *vt* to abstract; ~se *vr* to be *o* become absorbed.

abstraído, a [aβstra'iðo, a] *a* absent-minded.

absuelto, a [aβ'swelto] *pp de* **absolver**.

absurdo, a [aβ'surðo, a] *a* absurd.

abuelo, a [a'βwelo, a] *nm/f* grandfather/mother; ~s *nmpl* grandparents.

abulia [a'βulja] *nf* lethargy.

abultado, a [aβul'taðo, a] *a* bulky.

abultar [aβul'tar] *vt* to enlarge; (*aumentar*) to increase; (*fig*) to exagger-ate // *vi* to be bulky.

abundancia [aβun'danθja] *nf*: una ~ de plenty of; **abundante** *a* abundant, plentiful; **abundar** *vi* to abound, be plentiful.

aburguesarse [aβurɣe'sarse] *vr* to

become middle-class.

aburrido, a |aβu'rriðo, a| *a* (*hastiado*) bored; (*que aburre*) boring; **aburrimiento** *nm* boredom, tedium.

aburrir |aβu'rrir| *vt* to bore; ~**se** *vr* to be bored, get bored.

abusar |aβu'sar| *vi* to go too far; ~ **de** to abuse; **abuso** *nm* abuse.

abusivo, a |aβu'siβo, a| *a* (*precio*) exorbitant.

abyecto, a |aβ'jekto, a| *a* wretched, abject.

A.C. *abr* (= *Año de Cristo*) A.D.

a/c *abr* (= *al cuidado de*) c/o.

acá |a'ka| *ad* (*lugar*) here; ¿**de cuándo** ~? since when?

acabado, a |aka'βaðo, a| *a* finished, complete; (*perfecto*) perfect; (*agotado*) worn out; (*fig*) masterly // *nm* finish.

acabar |aka'βar| *vt* (*llevar a su fin*) to finish, complete; (*consumir*) to use up; (*rematar*) to finish off // *vi* to finish, end; ~**se** *vr* to finish, stop; (*terminarse*) to be over; (*agotarse*) to run out; ~ **con** to put an end to; ~ **de llegar** to have just arrived; ~ **por hacer** to end (up) by doing; ¡**se acabó!** it's all over!; (¡*basta!*) that's enough!

acabóse |aka'βose| *nm*: **esto es el** ~ this is the last straw.

academia |aka'ðemja| *nf* academy; **académico, a** *a* academic.

acaecer |akae'θer| *vi* to happen, occur.

acalorado, a |akalo'raðo, a| *a* (*discusión*) heated.

acalorarse |akalo'rarse| *vr* (*fig*) to get heated.

acampar |akam'par| *vi* to camp.

acanalar |akana'lar| *vt* to groove; (*ondular*) to corrugate.

acantilado |akanti'laðo| *nm* cliff.

acaparar |akapa'rar| *vt* to monopolize; (*acumular*) to hoard.

acariciar |akari'θjar| *vt* to caress; (*esperanza*) to cherish.

acarrear |akarre'ar| *vt* to transport; (*fig*) to cause, result in.

acaso |a'kaso| *ad* perhaps, maybe // *nm* chance; (**por**) **si** ~ (just) in case.

acatamiento |akata'mjento| *nm* respect; (*de la ley*) observance.

acatar |aka'tar| *vt* to respect, obey.

acatarrarse |akata'rrarse| *vr* to catch a cold.

acaudalado, a |akauða'laðo, a| *a* well-off.

acaudillar |akauði'ʎar| *vt* to lead, command.

acceder |akθe'ðer| *vi*: ~ **a** (*petición etc*) to agree to; (*tener acceso a*) to have access to; (*INFORM*) to access.

accesible |akθe'siβle| *a* accessible.

acceso |ak'θeso| *nm* access, entry; (*camino*) access, approach; (*MED*) attack, fit.

accesorio, a |akθe'sorjo, a| *a, nm* accessory.

accidentado, a |akθiðen'taðo, a| *a* uneven; (*montañoso*) hilly; (*azaroso*) eventful // *nm/f* accident victim.

accidental |akθiðen'tal| *a* accidental; **accidentarse** *vr* to have an accident.

accidente |akθi'ðente| *nm* accident.

acción |ak'θjon| *nf* action; (*acto*) action, act; (*COM*) share; (*JUR*) action, lawsuit; ~ **ordinaria/preferente** ordinary/preference share; **accionar** *vt* to work, operate; (*INFORM*) to drive.

accionista |akθjo'nista| *nm/f* shareholder, stockholder.

acebo |a'θeβo| *nm* holly; (*árbol*) holly tree.

acechanza |aθe'tʃanθa| *nf* = **acecho**.

acechar |aθe'tʃar| *vt* to spy on; (*aguardar*) to lie in wait for; **acecho** *nm*: **estar al acecho (de)** to lie in wait (for).

aceitar |aθei'tar| *vt* to oil, lubricate.

aceite |a'θeite| *nm* oil; (*de oliva*) olive oil; ~**ra** *nf* oilcan; **aceitoso, a** *a* oily.

aceituna |aθei'tuna| *nf* olive.

acelerador |aθelera'ðor| *nm* accelerator.

acelerar |aθele'rar| *vt* to accelerate.

acelga |a'θelɣa| *nf* chard, beet.

acento |a'θento| *nm* accent; (*acentuación*) stress.

acentuar |aθen'twar| *vt* to accent; to stress; (*fig*) to accentuate.

acepción |aθep'θjon| *nf* meaning.

aceptable |aθep'taβle| *a* acceptable.

aceptación |aθepta'θjon| *nf* acceptance; (*aprobación*) approval.

aceptar |aθep'tar| *vt* to accept; (*aprobar*) to approve.

acequia |a'θekja| *nf* irrigation ditch.

acera |a'θera| *nf* pavement (*Brit*), sidewalk (*US*).

acerado, a |aθe'raðo, a| *a* steel; (*afilado*) sharp; (*fig: duro*) steely; (: *mordaz*) biting.

acerbo, a |a'θerβo, a| *a* bitter; (*fig*) harsh.

acerca |a'θerka|: ~ **de** *prep* about, concerning.

acercar |aθer'kar| *vt* to bring *o* move nearer; ~**se** *vr* to approach, come near.

acerico |aθe'riko| *nm* pincushion.

acero |a'θero| *nm* steel.

acérrimo, a |a'θerrimo, a| *a* (*partidario*) staunch; (*enemigo*) bitter.

acertado, a |aθer'taðo, a| *a* correct; (*apropiado*) apt; (*sensato*) sensible.

acertar |aθer'tar| *vt* (*blanco*) to hit; (*solución*) to get right; (*adivinar*) to guess // *vi* to get it right, be right; ~ **a** to manage to; ~ **con** to happen *o* hit on.

acertijo |aθer'tixo| *nm* riddle, puzzle.

acervo |a'θerβo| *nm* heap; ~ **común** undivided estate.

aciago, a |a'θjaɣo, a| *a* ill-fated, fateful.

acicalar [aθika'lar] *vt* to polish; (*persona*) to dress up; ~se *vr* to get dressed up.

acicate [aθi'kate] *nm* spur.

acidez [aθi'ðeθ] *nf* acidity.

ácido, a ['aθiðo, a] *a* sour, acid // *nm* acid.

acierto *etc vb ver* **acertar** // [a'θjerto] *nm* success; (*buen paso*) wise move; (*solución*) solution; (*habilidad*) skill, ability.

aclamación [aklama'θjon] *nf* acclamation; (*aplausos*) applause.

aclamar [akla'mar] *vt* to acclaim; (*aplaudir*) to applaud.

aclaración [aklara'θjon] *nf* clarification, explanation.

aclarar [akla'rar] *vt* to clarify, explain; (*ropa*) to rinse // *vi* to clear up; ~se *vr* (*explicarse*) to understand; ~se la garganta to clear one's throat.

aclaratorio, a [aklara'torjo, a] *a* explanatory.

aclimatación [aklimata'θjon] *nf* acclimatization; **aclimatar** *vt* to acclimatize; **aclimatarse** *vr* to become acclimatized.

acné [ak'ne] *nm* acne.

acobardar [akoβar'ðar] *vt* to intimidate.

acodarse [ako'ðarse] *vr*: ~ en to lean on.

acogedor, a [akoxe'ðor, a] *a* welcoming; (*hospitalario*) hospitable.

acoger [ako'xer] *vt* to welcome; (*abrigar*) to shelter; ~se *vr* to take refuge.

acogida [ako'xiða] *nf* reception; refuge.

acolchar [akol'tʃar] *vt* to pad; (*fig*) to cushion.

acometer [akome'ter] *vt* to attack; (*emprender*) to undertake; **acometida** *nf* attack, assault.

acomodado, a [akomo'ðaðo, a] *a* (*persona*) well-to-do.

acomodador, a [akomoða'ðor, a] *nm/f* usher(ette).

acomodar [akomo'ðar] *vt* to adjust; (*alojar*) to accommodate; ~se *vr* to conform; (*instalarse*) to install o.s.; (*adaptarse*): ~se (a) to adapt to (to).

acomodaticio, a [akomoða'tiθjo, a] *a* (*pey*) accommodating, obliging; (*manejable*) pliable.

acompañar [akompa'ɲar] *vt* to accompany; (*documentos*) to enclose.

acondicionar [akondiθjo'nar] *vt* to arrange, prepare; (*pelo*) to condition.

acongojar [akongo'xar] *vt* to distress, grieve.

aconsejar [akonse'xar] *vt* to advise, counsel; ~se *vr*: ~se con to consult.

acontecer [akonte'θer] *vi* to happen, occur; **acontecimiento** *nm* event.

acopio [a'kopjo] *nm* store, stock.

acoplamiento [akopla'mjento] *nm* coupling, joint; **acoplar** *vt* to fit; (*ELEC*) to connect; (*vagones*) to couple.

acorazado, a [akora'θaðo, a] *a* armour-

plated, armoured // *nm* battleship.

acordar [akor'ðar] *vt* (*resolver*) to agree, resolve; (*recordar*) to remind; ~se *vr* to agree; ~se (de algo) to remember sth; **acorde** *a* (*MUS*) harmonious; **acorde con** (*medidas etc*) in keeping with // *nm* chord.

acordeón [akorðe'on] *nm* accordion.

acordonado, a [akorðo'naðo, a] *a* (*calle*) cordoned-off.

acorralar [akorra'lar] *vt* to round up, corral.

acortar [akor'tar] *vt* to shorten; (*duración*) to cut short; (*cantidad*) to reduce; ~se *vr* to become shorter.

acosar [ako'sar] *vt* to pursue relentlessly; (*fig*) to hound, pester.

acostar [akos'tar] *vt* (*en cama*) to put to bed; (*en suelo*) to lay down; (*barco*) to bring alongside; ~se *vr* to go to bed; to lie down.

acostumbrado, a [akostum'braðo, a] *a* usual; ~ a used to.

acostumbrar [akostum'brar] *vt*: ~ a uno a algo to get sb used to sth // *vi*: ~ (a) hacer to be in the habit of doing; ~se *vr*: ~se a to get used to.

acotación [akota'θjon] *nf* marginal note; (*GEO*) elevation mark; (*de límite*) boundary mark; (*TEATRO*) stage direction.

ácrata ['akrata] *a, nm/f* anarchist.

acre ['akre] *a* (*sabor*) sharp, bitter; (*olor*) acrid; (*fig*) biting // *nm* acre.

acrecentar [akreθen'tar] *vt* to increase, augment.

acreditar [akreði'tar] *vt* (*garantizar*) to vouch for, guarantee; (*autorizar*) to authorize; (*dar prueba de*) to prove; (*COM: abonar*) to credit; (*embajador*) to accredit; ~se *vr* to become famous.

acreedor, a [akree'ðor, a] *a*: ~ a worthy of // *nm/f* creditor.

acribillar [akriβi'ʎar] *vt*: ~ a balazos to riddle with bullets.

acrimonia [akri'monja], **acritud** [akri'tuð] *nf* acrimony.

acróbata [a'kroβata] *nm/f* acrobat.

acta ['akta] *nf* certificate; (*de comisión*) minutes *pl*, record; ~ de nacimiento/de matrimonio birth/marriage certificate; ~ notarial affidavit.

actitud [akti'tuð] *nf* attitude; (*postura*) posture.

activar [akti'βar] *vt* to activate; (*acelerar*) to speed up.

actividad [aktiβi'ðað] *nf* activity.

activo, a [ak'tiβo, a] *a* active; (*vivo*) lively // *nm* (*COM*) assets *pl*.

acto ['akto] *nm* act, action; (*ceremonia*) ceremony; (*TEATRO*) act; en el ~ immediately.

actor [ak'tor] *nm* actor; (*JUR*) plaintiff // *a*: parte ~a prosecution.

actriz [ak'triθ] *nf* actress.

actuación [aktwa'θjon] *nf* action; (*comportamiento*) conduct, behaviour; (*JUR*) proceedings *pl*; (*desempeño*) performance.

actual [ak'twal] *a* present(-day), current; **~idad** *nf* present; **~idades** *nfpl* news *sg*; **en la ~idad** at present; (*hoy día*) nowadays.

a. de J.C. *abr* (= *antes de Jesucristo*) B.C.

actualizar [aktwali'θar] *vt* to update, modernize.

actualmente [aktwal'mente] *ad* at present; (*hoy día*) nowadays.

actuar [ak'twar] *vi* (*obrar*) to work, operate; (*actor*) to act, perform // *vt* to work, operate; **~ de** to act as.

actuario, a [ak'twarjo, a] *nm/f* clerk; (*COM*) actuary.

acuarela [akwa'rela] *nf* watercolour.

acuario [a'kwarjo] *nm* aquarium; **A~** Aquarius.

acuartelar [akwarte'lar] *vt* (*MIL: disciplinar*) to confine to barracks.

acuático, a [a'kwatiko, a] *a* aquatic.

acuciar [aku'θjar] *vt* to urge on.

acuclillarse [akukli'ʎarse] *vr* to crouch down.

acuchillar [akutʃi'ʎar] *vt* (*TEC*) to plane (down), smooth.

acudir [aku'ðir] *vi* (*asistir*) to attend; (*ir*) to go; **~ a** (*fig*) to turn to; **~ en ayuda de** to go to the aid of.

acuerdo *etc vb ver* **acordar** // [a'kwerðo] *nm* agreement; **¡de ~!** agreed!; **de ~ con** (*persona*) in agreement with; (*acción, documento*) in accordance with; **estar de ~** to be agreed, agree.

acumular [akumu'lar] *vt* to accumulate, collect.

acuñar [aku'nar] *vt* (*moneda*) to mint; (*frase*) to coin.

acuoso, a [a'kwoso, a] *a* watery.

acurrucarse [akurru'karse] *vr* to crouch; (*ovillarse*) to curl up.

acusación [akusa'θjon] *nf* accusation; **acusar** *vt* to accuse; (*revelar*) to reveal; (*denunciar*) to denounce.

acuse [a'kuse] *nm*: **~ de recibo** acknowledgement of receipt.

acústico, a [a'kustiko, a] *a* acoustic // *nf* (*de una sala etc*) acoustics *pl*.

achacar [atʃa'kar] *vt* to attribute.

achacoso, a [atʃa'koso, a] *a* sickly.

achantar [atʃan'tar] *vt* (*fam*) to scare, frighten; **~se** *vr* to back down.

achaque *etc vb ver* **achacar** // [a'tʃake] *nm* ailment.

achicar [atʃi'kar] *vt* to reduce; (*humillar*) to humiliate; (*NAUT*) to bale out.

achicoria [atʃi'korja] *nf* chicory.

achicharrar [atʃitʃa'rrar] *vt* to scorch, burn.

adagio [a'ðaxjo] *nm* adage; (*MUS*) adagio.

adaptación [aðapta'θjon] *nf* adaptation.

adaptador [aðapta'ðor] *nm* (*ELEC*) adapter.

adaptar [aðap'tar] *vt* to adapt; (*acomodar*) to fit.

adecuado, a [aðe'kwaðo, a] *a* (*apto*) suitable; (*oportuno*) appropriate.

adecuar [aðe'kwar] *vt* to adapt; to make suitable.

adelantado, a [aðelan'taðo, a] *a* advanced; (*reloj*) fast; **pagar por ~** to pay in advance.

adelantamiento [aðelanta'mjento] *nm* advance, advancement; (*AUTO*) overtaking.

adelantar [aðelan'tar] *vt* to move forward; (*avanzar*) to advance; (*acelerar*) to speed up; (*AUTO*) to overtake // *vi*, **~se** *vr* to go forward, advance.

adelante [aðe'lante] *ad* forward(s), ahead // *excl* come in!; **de hoy en ~** from now on; **más ~** later on; (*más allá*) further on.

adelanto [aðe'lanto] *nm* advance; (*mejora*) improvement; (*progreso*) progress.

adelgazar [aðelɣa'θar] *vt* to thin (down) // *vi* to get thin; (*con régimen*) to slim down, lose weight.

ademán [aðe'man] *nm* gesture; **ademanes** *nmpl* manners; **en ~ de** as if to.

además [aðe'mas] *ad* besides; (*por otra parte*) moreover; (*también*) also; **~ de** besides, in addition to.

adentrarse [aðen'trarse] *vr*: **~ en** to go into, get inside; (*penetrar*) to penetrate (into).

adentro [a'ðentro] *ad* inside, in; **mar ~** out at sea; **tierra ~** inland.

adepto, a [a'ðepto, a] *nm/f* supporter.

aderezar [aðere'θar] *vt* (*ensalada*) to dress; (*comida*) to season; **aderezo** *nm* dressing; seasoning.

adeudar [aðeu'ðar] *vt* to owe; **~se** *vr* to run into debt.

adherirse [aðe'rirse] *vr*: **~ a** to adhere to; (*partido*) to join.

adhesión [aðe'sjon] *nf* adhesion; (*fig*) adherence.

adición [aði'θjon] *nf* addition.

adicionar [aðiθjo'nar] *vt* to add.

adicto, a [a'ðikto, a] *a*: **~ a** addicted to; (*dedicado*) devoted to // *nm/f* supporter, follower; (*toxicómano etc*) addict.

adiestrar [aðjes'trar] *vt* to train, teach; (*conducir*) to guide, lead; **~se** *vr* to practise; (*enseñarse*) to train o.s.

adinerado, a [aðine'raðo, a] *a* wealthy.

adiós [a'ðjos] *excl* (*para despedirse*) goodbye!, cheerio!; (*al pasar*) hello!

aditivo [aði'tiβo] *nm* additive.

adivinanza [aðiβi'nanθa] *nf* riddle; **adivinar** *vt* to prophesy; (*conjeturar*) to guess; **adivino, a** *nm/f* fortune-teller.

adj *abr* (= *adjunto*) encl.

adjetivo [aðxe'tiβo] *nm* adjective.
adjudicación [aðxuðika'θjon] *nf* award; adjudication.
adjudicar [aðxuði'kar] *vt* to award; ~se *vr*: ~se algo to appropriate sth.
adjuntar [aðxun'tar] *vt* to attach, enclose; **adjunto, a** *a* attached, enclosed // *nm/f* assistant.
administración [aðministra'θjon] *nf* administration; (*dirección*) management; **administrador, a** *nm/f* administrator; manager(ess).
administrar [aðminis'trar] *vt* to administer; **administrativo, a** *a* administrative.
admirable [aðmi'raβle] *a* admirable.
admiración [aðmira'θjon] *nf* admiration; (*asombro*) wonder; (*LING*) exclamation mark.
admirar [aðmi'rar] *vt* to admire; (*extrañar*) to surprise; ~se *vr* to be surprised.
admisible [aðmi'siβle] *a* admissible.
admisión [aðmi'sjon] *nf* admission; (*reconocimiento*) acceptance.
admitir [aðmi'tir] *vt* to admit; (*aceptar*) to accept.
admonición [aðmoni'θjon] *nf* warning.
adobar [aðo'βar] *vt* (*CULIN*) to season.
adobe [a'ðoβe] *nm* adobe, sun-dried brick.
adoctrinar [aðoktri'nar] *vt*: ~ en to indoctrinate with.
adolecer [aðole'θer] *vi*: ~ de to suffer from.
adolescente [aðoles'θente] *nm/f* adolescent, teenager.
adonde [a'ðonðe] *conj* (to) where.
adónde [a'ðonðe] *ad* = **dónde**.
adopción [aðop'θjon] *nf* adoption.
adoptar [aðop'tar] *vt* to adopt.
adoptivo, a [aðop'tiβo, a] *a* (*padres*) adoptive; (*hijo*) adopted.
adoquín [aðo'kin] *nm* paving stone.
adorar [aðo'rar] *vt* to adore.
adormecer [aðorme'θer] *vt* to put to sleep; ~se *vr* to become sleepy; (*dormirse*) to fall asleep.
adornar [aðor'nar] *vt* to adorn.
adorno [a'ðorno] *nm* adornment; (*decoración*) decoration.
adosado, a [aðo'saðo, a] *a*: casa adosada semi-detached house.
adquiero *etc vb ver* **adquirir**.
adquirir [aðki'rir] *vt* to acquire, obtain.
adquisición [aðkisi'θjon] *nf* acquisition.
adrede [a'ðreðe] *ad* on purpose.
adscribir [aðskri'βir] *vt* to appoint.
adscrito *pp de* **adscribir**.
aduana [a'ðwana] *nf* customs *pl*.
aduanero, a [a'ðwa'nero, a] *a* customs *cpd* // *nm/f* customs officer.
aducir [aðu'θir] *vt* to adduce; (*dar como prueba*) to offer as proof.
adueñarse [aðwe'narse] *vr*: ~ de to take possession of.

adulación [aðula'θjon] *nf* flattery.
adular [aðu'lar] *vt* to flatter.
adulterar [aðulte'rar] *vt* to adulterate // *vi* to commit adultery.
adulterio [aðul'terjo] *nm* adultery.
adúltero, a [a'ðultero, a] *a* adulterous // *nm/f* adulterer/adulteress.
adulto, a [a'ðulto, a] *a, nm/f* adult.
adusto, a [a'ðusto, a] *a* stern; (*austero*) austere.
advenedizo, a [aðβene'ðiðo, a] *nm/f* upstart.
advenimiento [aðβeni'mjento] *nm* arrival; (*al trono*) accession.
adverbio [að'βerβjo] *nm* adverb.
adversario, a [aðβer'sarjo, a] *nm/f* adversary.
adversidad [aðβersi'ðað] *nf* adversity; (*contratiempo*) setback.
adverso, a [að'βerso, a] *a* adverse.
advertencia [aðβer'tenθja] *nf* warning; (*prefacio*) preface, foreword.
advertir [aðβer'tir] *vt* to notice; (*avisar*): ~ a uno de to warn sb about o of.
Adviento [að'βjento] *nm* Advent.
advierto *etc*, **advirtiendo** *etc vb ver* **advertir**.
adyacente [aðja'θente] *a* adjacent.
aéreo, a [a'ereo, a] *a* aerial.
aerobic [ae'roβik] *nm* aerobics *sg*.
aerodeslizador [aeroðesliθa'ðor], **aerodeslizante** [aeroðesli'θante] *nm* hovercraft.
aeromozo, a [aero'moθo, a] *nm/f* (*AM*) air steward(ess).
aeronáutica [aero'nautika] *nf* aeronautics *sg*.
aeronave [aero'naβe] *nm* spaceship.
aeroplano [aero'plano] *nm* aeroplane.
aeropuerto [aero'pwerto] *nm* airport.
aerosol [aero'sol] *nm* aerosol.
afabilidad [afaβili'ðað] *nf* friendliness; **afable** *a* affable.
afamado, a [afa'maðo, a] *a* famous.
afán [a'fan] *nm* hard work; (*deseo*) desire.
afanar [afa'nar] *vt* to harass; (*fam*) to pinch; ~se *vr*: ~se por hacer to strive to do; **afanoso, a** *a* (*trabajo*) hard; (*trabajador*) industrious.
afear [afe'ar] *vt* to disfigure.
afección [afek'θjon] *nf* (*MED*) disease.
afectación [afekta'θjon] *nf* affectation; **afectado, a** *a* affected; **afectar** *vt* to affect.
afectísimo, a [afek'tisimo, a] *a* affectionate; ~ suyo yours truly.
afectivo, a [afek'tiβo, a] *a* (*problema etc*) emotional.
afecto [a'fekto] *nm* affection; **tenerle ~ a uno** to be fond of sb.
afectuoso, a [afek'twoso, a] *a* affectionate.
afeitar [afei'tar] *vt* to shave; ~se *vr* to shave.

afeminado, a [afemi'naðo, a] *a* effeminate.

aferrado, a [afe'rraðo, a] *a* stubborn.

aferrar [afe'rrar] *vt* to grasp; *(barco)* to moor // *vi* to moor.

Afganistán [afganis'tan] *nm* Afghanistan.

afianzamiento [afjanθa'mjento] *nm* strengthening; security; **afianzar** *vt* to strengthen; to secure; **afianzarse** *vr* to become established.

afición [afi'θjon] *nf* fondness, liking; **la ~** the fans *pl*; **pinto por ~** I paint as a hobby; **aficionado, a** *a* keen, enthusiastic; *(no profesional)* amateur; **ser ~ a algo** to be very keen on *o* fond of sth // *nm/f* enthusiast, fan; amateur.

aficionar [afiθjo'nar] *vt*: **~ a uno a algo** to make sb like sth; **~se vr: ~se a algo** to grow fond of sth.

afiche [a'fitʃe] *nm* (*AM*) poster.

afilado, a [afi'laðo, a] *a* sharp.

afilar [afi'lar] *vt* to sharpen.

afiliarse [afi'ljarse] *vr* to affiliate.

afín [a'fin] *a* *(parecido)* similar; *(conexo)* related.

afinar [afi'nar] *vt* (*TEC*) to refine; *(MUS)* to tune // *vi* to play/sing in tune.

afincarse [afin'karse] *vr* to settle.

afinidad [afini'ðað] *nf* affinity; *(parentesco)* relationship; **por ~** by marriage.

afirmación [afirma'θjon] *nf* affirmation; **afirmar** *vt* to affirm, state; *(reforzar)* to strengthen; **afirmativo, a** *a* affirmative.

aflicción [aflik'θjon] *nf* affliction; *(dolor)* grief.

afligir [afli'xir] *vt* to afflict; *(apenar)* to distress; **~se vr** to grieve.

aflojar [aflo'xar] *vt* to slacken; *(desatar)* to loosen, undo; *(relajar)* to relax // *vi* to drop; *(bajar)* to go down; **~se vr** to relax.

aflorar [aflo'rar] *vi* to come to the surface, emerge.

afluente [aflu'ente] *a* flowing // *nm* tributary.

afluir [aflu'ir] *vi* to flow.

afmo, a *abr* (= *afectísimo(a) suyo(a)*) Yours.

afónico, a [a'foniko, a] *a*: **estar ~** to have a sore throat; to have lost one's voice.

aforo [a'foro] *nm* (*de teatro etc*) capacity.

afortunado, a [afortu'naðo, a] *a* fortunate, lucky.

afrancesado, a [afranθe'saðo, a] *a* francophile; *(pey)* Frenchified.

afrenta [a'frenta] *nf* affront, insult; *(deshonra)* dishonour, shame.

África ['afrika] *nf* Africa; **~ del Sur** South Africa; **africano, a** *a*, *nm/f* African.

afrontar [afron'tar] *vt* to confront; *(poner cara a cara)* to bring face to face.

afuera [a'fwera] *ad* out, outside; **~s nfpl** outskirts.

agachar [aɣa'tʃar] *vt* to bend, bow; **~se vr** to stoop, bend.

agalla [a'ɣaʎa] *nf* (*ZOOL*) gill; **~s nfpl** (*MED*) tonsillitis *sg*; (*ANAT*) tonsils; **tener ~s** *(fam)* to have guts.

agarradera [aɣarra'ðera] *nf* (*AM*), **agarradero** [aɣarra'ðero] *nm* handle; **~s npl** pull *sg*, influence *sg*.

agarrado, a [aɣa'rraðo, a] *a* mean, stingy.

agarrar [aɣa'rrar] *vt* to grasp, grab; (*AM*) to take, catch; *(recoger)* to pick up // *vi* (*planta*) to take root; **~se vr** to hold on (tightly).

agarrotar [aɣarro'tar] *vt* (*lío*) to tie tightly; *(persona)* to squeeze tightly; *(reo)* to garrotte; **~se vr** (*motor*) to seize up; (*MED*) to stiffen.

agasajar [aɣasa'xar] *vt* to treat well, fête.

agencia [a'xenθja] *nf* agency; **~ inmobiliaria** estate (*Brit*) *o* real estate (*US*) agent's (office); **~ matrimonial** marriage bureau; **~ de viajes** travel agency.

agenciarse [axen'θjarse] *vr* to obtain, procure.

agenda [a'xenda] *nf* diary.

agente [a'xente] *nm* agent; *(de policía)* policeman; **~ femenino** policewoman; **~ inmobiliario** estate agent (*Brit*), realtor (*US*); **~ de bolsa** stockbroker; **~ de seguros** insurance agent.

ágil ['axil] *a* agile, nimble; **agilidad** *nf* agility, nimbleness.

agitación [axita'θjon] *nf* (*de mano etc*) shaking, waving; *(de líquido etc)* stirring; (*fig*) agitation.

agitar [axi'tar] *vt* to wave, shake; *(líquido)* to stir; (*fig*) to stir up, excite; **~se vr** to get excited; *(inquietarse)* to get worried *o* upset.

aglomeración [aɣlomera'θjon] *nf*: **~ de tráfico/gente** traffic jam/mass of people.

aglomerar [aɣlome'rar] *vt*, **aglomerarse** *vr* to crowd together.

agnóstico, a [aɣ'nostiko, a] *a*, *nm/f* agnostic.

agobiar [aɣo'βjar] *vt* to weigh down; *(oprimir)* to oppress; *(cargar)* to burden.

agolparse [aɣol'parse] *vr* to crowd together.

agonía [aɣo'nia] *nf* death throes *pl*; (*fig*) agony, anguish.

agonizante [aɣoni'θante] *a* dying.

agonizar [aɣoni'θar] *vi* (*tb*: **estar agonizando**) to be dying.

agosto [a'ɣosto] *nm* August.

agotado, a [aɣo'taðo, a] *a* *(persona)* exhausted; *(libros)* out of print; *(acabado)* finished; (*COM*) sold out.

agotador, a [aɣota'ðor, a] *a* exhausting.

agotamiento [aɣota'mjento] *nm* exhaustion.

agotar [aɣo'tar] *vt* to exhaust; *(consumir)* to drain; *(recursos)* to use up, deplete; ~se *vr* to be exhausted; *(acabarse)* to run out; *(libro)* to go out of print.

agraciado, a [aɣra'θjaðo, a] *a* *(atractivo)* attractive; *(en sorteo etc)* lucky.

agraciar [aɣra'θjar] *vt* (*JUR*) to pardon; *(con premio)* to reward.

agradable [aɣra'ðaβle] *a* pleasant, nice.

agradar [aɣra'ðar] *vt*: él me agrada I like him.

agradecer [aɣraðe'θer] *vt* to thank; *(favor etc)* to be grateful for; **agradecido, a** *a* grateful; ¡muy ~! thanks a lot!; **agradecimiento** *nm* thanks *pl*; gratitude.

agradezco *etc vb ver* **agradecer.**

agrado [a'ɣraðo] *nm*: ser de tu *etc* ~ to be to your *etc* liking.

agrandar [aɣran'dar] *vt* to enlarge; *(fig)* to exaggerate; ~se *vr* to get bigger.

agrario, a [a'ɣrarjo, a] *a* agrarian, land *cpd*; *(política)* agricultural, farming.

agravante [aɣra'βante] *a* aggravating // *nf*: con la ~ de que ... with the further difficulty. that ...

agravar [aɣra'βar] *vt* *(pesar sobre)* to make heavier; *(irritar)* to aggravate; ~se *vr* to worsen, get worse.

agraviar [aɣra'βjar] *vt* to offend; *(ser injusto con)* to wrong; ~se *vr* to take offence; **agravio** *nm* offence; wrong; *(JUR)* grievance.

agredir [aɣre'ðir] *vt* to attack.

agregado [aɣre'ɣaðo] *nm* aggregate; *(persona)* attaché.

agregar [aɣre'ɣar] *vt* to gather; *(añadir)* to add; *(persona)* to appoint.

agresión [aɣre'sjon] *nf* aggression.

agresivo, a [aɣre'siβo, a] *a* aggressive.

agriar [a'ɣrjar] *vt* to (turn) sour; ~se *vr* to turn sour.

agrícola [a'ɣrikola] *a* farming *cpd*, agricultural.

agricultor, a [aɣrikul'tor, a] *nm/f* farmer.

agricultura [aɣrikul'tura] *nf* agriculture, farming.

agridulce [aɣri'ðulθe] *a* bittersweet; *(CULIN)* sweet and sour.

agrietarse [aɣrje'tarse] *vr* to crack; *(piel)* to chap.

agrimensor, a [aɣrimen'sor, a] *nm/f* surveyor.

agrio, a ['aɣrjo, a] *a* bitter.

agronomía [aɣrono'mia] *nf* agronomy, agriculture.

agropecuario, a [aɣrope'kwarjo, a] *a* farming *cpd*, agricultural.

agrupación [aɣrupa'θjon] *nf* group; *(acto)* grouping.

agrupar [aɣru'par] *vt* to group.

agua ['aɣwa] *nf* water; *(NAUT)* wake; *(ARQ)* slope of a roof; ~s *nfpl* (*de piedra*) water *sg*, sparkle *sg*; *(MED)* water *sg*, urine *sg*; *(NAUT)* waters; ~s abajo/arriba downstream/upstream; ~ bendita/destilada/potable holy/distilled/drinking water; ~ caliente hot water; ~ corriente running water; ~ de colonia eau de cologne; ~ mineral **(con/sin gas)** (fizzy/non-fizzy) mineral water; ~s jurisdiccionales territorial waters; ~s mayores excrement *sg*.

aguacate [aɣwa'kate] *nm* avocado pear.

aguacero [aɣwa'θero] *nm* (heavy) shower, downpour.

aguado, a [a'ɣwaðo, a] *a* watery, watered down // *nf* (*AGR*) watering place; *(NAUT)* water supply; *(ARTE)* watercolour.

aguafiestas [aɣwa'fjestas] *nm/f inv* spoilsport, killjoy.

aguafuerte [aɣwa'fwerte] *nm o f* etching.

aguamanil [aɣwama'nil] *nm* *(jofaina)* washbasin.

aguanieve [aɣwa'njeβe] *nf* sleet.

aguantar [aɣwan'tar] *vt* to bear, put up with; *(sostener)* to hold up // *vi* to last; ~se *vr* to restrain o.s.; **aguante** *nm* *(paciencia)* patience; *(resistencia)* endurance.

aguar [a'ɣwar] *vt* to water down.

aguardar [aɣwar'ðar] *vt* to wait for.

aguardiente [aɣwar'ðjente] *nm* brandy, liquor.

aguarrás [aɣwa'rras] *nm* turpentine.

agudeza [aɣu'ðeθa] *nf* sharpness; *(ingenio)* wit.

agudizar [aɣuði'θar] *vt* *(crisis)* to make worse; ~se *vr* to get worse.

agudo, a [a'ɣuðo, a] *a* sharp; *(voz)* high-pitched, piercing; *(dolor, enfermedad)* acute.

agüero [a'ɣwero] *nm*: buen/mal ~ good/bad omen.

aguijar [aɣi'xar] *vt* to goad; *(incitar)* to urge on // *vi* to hurry along.

aguijón [aɣi'xon] *nm* sting; *(fig)* spur; **aguijonear** *vt* = **aguijar.**

águila ['aɣila] *nf* eagle; *(fig)* genius.

aguileño, a [aɣi'leɲo, a] *a* *(nariz)* aquiline; *(rostro)* sharp-featured.

aguinaldo [aɣi'naldo] *nm* Christmas box.

aguja [a'ɣuxa] *nf* needle; *(de reloj)* hand; *(ARQ)* spire; *(TEC)* firing-pin; ~s *nfpl* (*ZOOL*) ribs; *(FERRO)* points.

agujerear [aɣuxere'ar] *vt* to make holes in.

agujero [aɣu'xero] *nm* hole.

agujetas [aɣu'xetas] *nfpl* stitch *sg*; *(rigidez)* stiffness *sg*.

aguzar [aɣu'θar] *vt* to sharpen; *(fig)* to incite.

ahí [a'i] *ad* there; de ~ que so that, with the result that; ~ llega here he comes; por ~ that way; *(allá)* over there; 200 o por ~ 200 or so.

ahijado, a |ai'xaðo, a| *nm/f* godson/daughter.

ahinco |a'inko| *nm* earnestness.

ahíto, a |a'ito, a| *a*: **estoy ~** I'm full up.

ahogar |ao'ɣar| *vt* to drown; (*asfixiar*) to suffocate, smother; (*fuego*) to put out; **~se** *vr* (*en el agua*) to drown; (*por asfixia*) to suffocate.

ahogo |a'oɣo| *nm* breathlessness; (*fig*) financial difficulty.

ahondar |aon'dar| *vt* to deepen, make deeper; (*fig*) to study thoroughly // *vi*: **~ en** to study thoroughly.

ahora |a'ora| *ad* now; (*hace poco*) a moment ago, just now; (*dentro de poco*) in a moment; **~ voy** I'm coming; **~ mismo** right now; **~ bien** now then; **por ~** for the present.

ahorcar |aor'kar| *vt* to hang; **~se** *vr* to hang o.s.

ahorita |ao'rita| *ad* (*fam*) right now.

ahorrar |ao'rrar| *vt* (*dinero*) to save; (*esfuerzos*) to save, avoid; **ahorro** *nm* (*acto*) saving; (*frugalidad*) thrift; **ahorros** *nmpl* savings.

ahuecar |awe'kar| *vt* to hollow (out); (*voz*) to deepen; **~se** *vr* to give o.s. airs.

ahumar |au'mar| *vt* to smoke, cure; (*llenar de humo*) to fill with smoke // *vi* to smoke; **~se** *vr* to fill with smoke.

ahuyentar |aujen'tar| *vt* to drive off, frighten off; (*fig*) to dispel.

airado, a |ai'raðo, a| *a* angry; **airar** *vt* to anger; **airarse** *vr* to get angry.

aire |'aire| *nm* air; (*viento*) wind; (*corriente*) draught; (*MUS*) tune; **~s** *nmpl*: **darse ~s** to give o.s. airs; **al ~ libre** in the open air; **~ acondicionado** air conditioning; **airoso, a** *a* windy; draughty; (*fig*) graceful.

aislado, a |ais'laðo, a| *a* isolated; (*incomunicado*) cut-off; (*ELEC*) insulated.

aislar |ais'lar| *vt* to isolate; (*ELEC*) to insulate.

ajar |a'xar| *vt* to spoil; (*fig*) to abuse.

ajardinado, a |axarði'naðo, a| *a* landscaped.

ajedrez |axe'ðreθ| *nm* chess.

ajeno, a |a'xeno, a| *a* (*que pertenece a otro*) somebody else's; **~ a** foreign to; **~ de** free from, devoid of.

ajetreado, a |axetre'aðo, a| *a* busy.

ajetreo |axe'treo| *nm* bustle.

ají |a'xi| *nm* chili, red pepper; (*salsa*) chili sauce.

ajo |'axo| *nm* garlic.

ajorca |a'xorka| *nf* bracelet.

ajuar |a'xwar| *nm* household furnishings *pl*; (*de novia*) trousseau; (*de niño*) layette.

ajustado, a |axus'taðo, a| *a* (*tornillo*) tight; (*cálculo*) right; (*ropa*) tight (-fitting); (*DEPORTE: resultado*) close.

ajustar |axus'tar| *vt* (*adaptar*) to adjust; (*encajar*) to fit; (*TEC*) to engage;

(*IMPRENTA*) to make up; (*apretar*) to tighten; (*concertar*) to agree (on); (*reconciliar*) to reconcile; (*cuenta, deudas*) to settle // *vi* to fit.

ajuste |a'xuste| *nm* adjustment; (*COSTURA*) fitting; (*acuerdo*) compromise; (*de cuenta*) settlement.

al |al| = **a** + **el**, *ver* **a**.

ala |'ala| *nf* wing; (*de sombrero*) brim; (*futbolista*) winger.

alabanza |ala'Banθa| *nf* praise.

alabar |ala'Bar| *vt* to praise.

alacena |ala'θena| *nf* kitchen cupboard (*Brit*), kitchen closet (*US*).

alacrán |ala'kran| *nm* scorpion.

alado, a |a'laðo, a| *a* winged.

alambique |alam'bike| *nm* still.

alambrada |alam'braða| *nf*, **alambrado** |alam'braðo| *nm* wire fence; (*red*) wire netting.

alambre |a'lambre| *nm* wire; **~ de púas** barbed wire; **alambrista** *nm/f* tightrope walker.

alameda |ala'meða| *nf* (*plantío*) poplar grove; (*lugar de paseo*) avenue, boulevard.

álamo |'alamo| *nm* poplar; **~ temblón** aspen.

alano |a'lano| *nm* mastiff.

alarde |a'larðe| *nm* show, display; **hacer ~ de** to boast of.

alargador |alarɣa'ðor| *nm* (*ELEC*) extension lead.

alargar |alar'ɣar| *vt* to lengthen, extend; (*paso*) to hasten; (*brazo*) to stretch out; (*cuerda*) to pay out; (*conversación*) to spin out; **~se** *vr* to get longer.

alarido |ala'riðo| *nm* shriek.

alarma |a'larma| *nf* alarm.

alarmante |alar'mante| *a* alarming.

alazán |ala'θan| *nm* sorrel.

alba |'alßa| *nf* dawn.

albacea |alßa'θea| *nm/f* executor/executrix.

albahaca |al'ßaka| *nf* basil.

Albania |al'ßanja| *nf* Albania.

albañal |alßa'nal| *nm* drain, sewer.

albañil |alßa'nil| *nm* bricklayer; (*cantero*) mason.

albarán |alßa'ran| *nm* (*COM*) delivery note, invoice.

albaricoque |alßari'koke| *nm* apricot.

albedrío |alße'ðrio| *nm*: **libre ~** free will.

alberca |al'ßerka| *nf* reservoir; (*AM*) swimming pool.

albergar |alßer'ɣar| *vt* to shelter.

albergue *etc vb ver* **albergar** // |al'ßerɣe| *nm* shelter, refuge; **~ de juventud** youth hostel.

albóndiga |al'ßondiɣa| *nf* meatball.

albor |al'ßor| *nm* whiteness; (*amanecer*) dawn; **~ada** *nf* dawn; (*diana*) reveille; **~ear** *vi* to dawn.

albornoz |alßor'noθ| *nm* (*de los árabes*) burnous; (*para el baño*) bathrobe.

alborotar |alβoro'tar| *vi* to make a row // *vt* to agitate, stir up; ~**se** *vr* to get excited; (*mar*) to get rough; **alboroto** *nm* row, uproar.

alborozar |alβoro'θar| *vt* to gladden; ~**se** *vr* to rejoice.

alborozo |alβo'roθo| *nm* joy.

albricias |al'βriθjas| *nfpl*: ¡~! good news!

álbum |'alβum| (*pl* ~**s**, ~**es**) *nm* album; ~ **de recortes** scrapbook.

albumen |al'βumen| *nm* egg white, albumen.

alcachofa |alka'tʃofa| *nf* artichoke.

alcalde, esa |al'kalde, esa| *nm/f* mayor(ess).

alcaldía |alkal'dia| *nf* mayoralty; (*lugar*) mayor's office.

alcance *etc vb ver* **alcanzar** // |al'kanθe| *nm* reach; (*COM*) adverse balance.

alcancía |alkan'θia| *nf* money box.

alcantarilla |alkanta'riʎa| *nf* (*de aguas cloacales*) sewer; (*en la calle*) gutter.

alcanzar |alkan'θar| *vt* (*algo: con la mano, el pie*) to reach; (*alguien: en el camino etc*) to catch up (with); (*autobús*) to catch; (*suj: bala*) to hit, strike // *vi* (*ser suficiente*) to be enough; ~ **a hacer** to manage to do.

alcaparra |alka'parra| *nf* caper.

alcatraz |alka'traθ| *nm* gannet.

alcayata |alka'jata| *nf* hook.

alcázar |al'kaθar| *nm* fortress; (*NAUT*) quarter-deck.

alcoba |al'koβa| *nf* bedroom.

alcohol |al'kol| *nm* alcohol; ~ **metílico** methylated spirits *pl* (*Brit*), wood alcohol (*US*); **alcohólico, a** *a*, *nm/f* alcoholic.

alcoholímetro |alko'limetro| *nm* Breathalyser ® (*Brit*), drunkometer (*US*).

alcoholismo |alko'lismo| *nm* alcoholism.

alcornoque |alkor'noke| *nm* cork tree; (*fam*) idiot.

aldaba |al'daβa| *nf* (door) knocker.

aldea |al'dea| *nf* village; ~**no, a** *a* village *cpd* // *nm/f* villager.

ale |'ale| *excl* come on!, let's go!

aleación |alea'θjon| *nf* alloy.

aleatorio, a |alea'torjo, a| *a* random.

aleccionar |alekθjo'nar| *vt* to instruct; (*adiestrar*) to train.

alegación |aleɣa'θjon| *nf* allegation; **alegar** *vt* to allege; (*JUR*) to plead // *vi* (*AM*) to argue.

alegato |ale'ɣato| *nm* (*JUR*) allegation; (*AM*) argument.

alegoría |aleɣo'ria| *nf* allegory.

alegrar |ale'ɣrar| *vt* (*causar alegría*) to cheer (up); (*fuego*) to poke; (*fiesta*) to liven up; ~**se** *vr* (*fam*) to get merry *o* tight; ~**se de** to be glad about.

alegre |a'leɣre| *a* happy, cheerful; (*fam*) merry, tight; (*chiste*) risqué, blue; **alegría** *nf* happiness; merriment.

alejamiento |alexa'mjento| *nm* removal; (*distancia*) remoteness.

alejar |ale'xar| *vt* to remove; (*fig*) to estrange; ~**se** *vr* to move away.

alemán, ana |ale'man, ana| *a*, *nm/f* German // *nm* (*LING*) German.

Alemania |ale'manja| *nf*: ~ **Occidental/Oriental** West/East Germany.

alentador, a |alenta'ðor, a| *a* encouraging.

alentar |alen'tar| *vt* to encourage.

alergia |a'lerxja| *nf* allergy.

alero |a'lero| *nm* (*de tejado*) eaves *pl*; (*de carruaje*) mudguard.

alerta |a'lerta| *a*, *nm* alert.

aleta |a'leta| *nf* (*de pez*) fin; (*de ave*) wing; (*de foca, DEPORTE*) flipper; (*AUTO*) mudguard.

aletargar |aletar'ɣar| *vt* to make drowsy; (*entumecer*) to make numb; ~**se** *vr* to grow drowsy; to become numb.

aletear |alete'ar| *vi* to flutter.

alevín |ale'βin|, **alevino** |ale'βino| *nm* fry, young fish.

alevosía |aleβo'sia| *nf* treachery.

alfabeto |alfa'βeto| *nm* alphabet.

alfalfa |al'falfa| *nf* alfalfa, lucerne.

alfarería |alfare'ria| *nf* pottery; (*tienda*) pottery shop; **alfarero, a** *nm/f* potter.

alféizar |al'feiðar| *nm* window-sill.

alférez |al'fereθ| *nm* (*MIL*) second lieutenant; (*NAUT*) ensign.

alfil |al'fil| *nm* (*AJEDREZ*) bishop.

alfiler |alfi'ler| *nm* pin; (*broche*) clip; (*pinza*) clothes peg.

alfiletero |alfile'tero| *nm* needlecase.

alfombra |al'fombra| *nf* carpet; (*más pequeña*) rug; **alfombrar** *vt* to carpet; **alfombrilla** *nf* rug, mat.

alforja |al'forxa| *nf* saddlebag.

alforza |al'forθa| *nf* pleat.

algarabía |alɣara'βia| *nf* (*fam*) gibberish.

algarrobo |alɣa'rroβo| *nm* carob tree.

algas |'alɣas| *nfpl* seaweed.

algazara |alɣa'θara| *nf* din, uproar.

álgebra |'alxeβra| *nf* algebra.

álgido, a |'alxiðo| *a* icy, chilly; (*momento etc*) crucial, decisive.

algo |'alɣo| *pron* something; anything // *ad* somewhat, rather; ¿~ **más?** anything else?; (*en tienda*) is that all?; **por ~ será** there must be some reason for it.

algodón |alɣo'ðon| *nm* cotton; (*planta*) cotton plant; ~ **de azúcar** candy floss (*Brit*), cotton candy (*US*); ~ **hidrófilo** cotton wool (*Brit*), absorbent cotton (*US*).

algodonero, a |alɣoðo'nero, a| *a* cotton *cpd* // *nm/f* cotton grower // *nm* cotton plant.

alguacil |alɣwa'θil| *nm* bailiff; (*TAUR*) mounted official.

alguien |'alɣjen| *pron* someone, somebody; (*en frases interrogativas*) anyone, anybody.

alguno, a |al'ɣuno, a| *a* (*delante de nm*:

algún some; (después de n): **no tiene talento alguno** he has no talent, he doesn't have any talent // pron (alguien) someone, somebody; **algún que otro libro** some book or other; **algún día iré** I'll go one o some day; **sin interés** ~ without the slightest interest; ~ **que otro** an occasional one; ~**s piensan** some (people) think.

alhaja [a'laxa] nf jewel; (tesoro) precious object, treasure.

alhelí [ale'li] nm wallflower, stock.

aliado, a [a'ljaðo, a] a allied.

alianza [a'ljanθa] nf alliance; (anillo) wedding ring.

aliar [a'ljar] vt to ally; ~**se** vr to form an alliance.

alias ['aljas] ad alias.

alicates [ali'kates] nmpl pliers; ~ **de uñas** nail clippers.

aliciente [ali'θjente] nm incentive; (atracción) attraction.

alienación [aljena'θjon] nf alienation.

aliento [a'ljento] nm breath; (respiración) breathing; **sin** ~ breathless.

aligerar [alixe'rar] vt to lighten; (reducir) to shorten; (aliviar) to alleviate; (mitigar) to ease; (paso) to quicken.

alimaña [ali'maɲa] nf pest.

alimentación [alimenta'θjon] nf (comida) food; (acción) feeding; (tienda) grocer's (shop); **alimentador** nm: **alimentador de papel** sheet-feeder; **alimentar** vt to feed; (nutrir) to nourish; **alimentarse** vr to feed.

alimenticio, a [alimen'tiθjo, a] a food cpd; (nutritivo) nourishing, nutritious.

alimento [ali'mento] nm food; (nutrición) nourishment; ~**s** nmpl (JUR) alimony sg.

alineación [alinea'θjon] nf alignment; (DEPORTE) line-up.

alinear [aline'ar] vt to align; ~**se** vr (DEPORTE) to line up; ~**se en** to fall in with.

aliñar [ali'ɲar] vt (CULIN) to season; **aliño** nm (CULIN) dressing.

alisar [ali'sar] vt to smooth.

aliso [a'liso] nm alder.

alistarse [alis'tarse] vr to enlist; (inscribirse) to enrol.

aliviar [ali'βjar] vt (carga) to lighten; (persona) to relieve; (dolor) to relieve, alleviate.

alivio [a'liβjo] nm alleviation, relief.

aljibe [al'xiβe] nm cistern.

alma ['alma] nf soul; (persona) person; (TEC) core.

almacén [alma'θen] nm (depósito) warehouse, store; (MIL) magazine; (AM) shop; (grandes) **almacenes** nmpl department store sg; **almacenaje** nm storage; **almacenaje secundaria** (INFORM) backing storage.

almacenar [almaθe'nar] vt to store, put

in storage; (proveerse) to stock up with; **almacenero** nm warehouseman, (AM) shopkeeper.

almanaque [alma'nake] nm almanac.

almeja [al'mexa] nf clam.

almendra [al'mendra] nf almond; **almendro** nm almond tree.

almiar [al'mjar] nm haystack.

almíbar [al'miβar] nm syrup.

almidón [almi'ðon] nm starch; **almidonar** vt to starch.

almirantazgo [almiran'taθɣo] nm admiralty.

almirante [almi'rante] nm admiral.

almirez [almi'reθ] nm mortar.

almizcle [al'miθkle] nm musk.

almohada [almo'aða] nf pillow; (funda) pillowcase; **almohadilla** nf cushion; (TEC) pad; (AM) pincushion.

almohadón [almoa'ðon] nm large pillow; bolster.

almorranas [almo'rranas] nfpl piles, haemorrhoids.

almorzar [almor'θar] vt: ~ **una tortilla** to have an omelette for lunch // vi to (have) lunch.

almuerzo etc vb ver **almorzar** // [al'mwerθo] nm lunch.

alocado, a [alo'kaðo, a] a crazy.

alojamiento [aloxa'mjento] nm lodging(s) (pl); (viviendas) housing.

alojar [alo'xar] vt to lodge; ~**se** vr to lodge, stay.

alondra [a'londra] nf lark, skylark.

alpargata [alpar'ɣata] nf rope-soled sandal, espadrille.

Alpes ['alpes] nmpl: **los** ~ the Alps.

alpinismo [alpi'nismo] nm mountaineering, climbing; **alpinista** nm/f mountaineer, climber.

alpiste [al'piste] nm birdseed.

alquilar [alki'lar] vt (suj: propietario: inmuebles) to let, rent (out); (: coche) to hire out; (: TV) to rent (out); (suj: alquilador: inmuebles, TV) to rent; (: coche) to hire; '**se alquila casa**' 'house to let (Brit) o to rent' (US).

alquiler [alki'ler] nm renting; letting; hiring; (arriendo) rent; hire charge; ~ **de automóviles** car hire; **de** ~ for hire.

alquimia [al'kimja] nf alchemy.

alquitrán [alki'tran] nm tar.

alrededor [alreðe'ðor] ad around, about; ~**es** nmpl surroundings; ~ **de** prep around, about; **mirar a su** ~ to look (round) about one.

alta ['alta] nf ver **alto**.

altanería [altane'ria] nf haughtiness, arrogance; **altanero, a** a arrogant, haughty.

altar [al'tar] nm altar.

altavoz [alta'βoθ] nm loudspeaker; (amplificador) amplifier.

alteración [altera'θjon] nf alteration;

(*alboroto*) disturbance.

alterar |alte'rar| *vt* to alter; to disturb; ~se *vr* (*persona*) to get upset.

altercado |alter'kaðo| *nm* argument.

alternar |alter'nar| *vt* to alternate // *vi,* ~se *vr* to alternate; (*turnar*) to take turns; ~ con to mix with; **alternativo, a** *a* alternative; (*alterno*) alternating // *nf* alternative; (*elección*) choice; **alterno, a** *a* alternate; (*ELEC*) alternating.

Alteza |al'teθa| *nf* (*tratamiento*) Highness.

altibajos |alti'βaxos| *nmpl* ups and downs.

altiplanicie |altipla'niθje| *nf,* **altiplano** |alti'plano| *nm* high plateau.

altisonante |altiso'nante| *a* high-flown, high-sounding.

altitud |alti'tuð| *nf* height; (*AVIAT, GEO*) altitude.

altivez |alti'βeθ| *nf* haughtiness, arrogance; **altivo, a** *a* haughty, arrogant.

alto, a |'alto, a| *a* high; (*persona*) tall; (*sonido*) high, sharp; (*noble*) high, lofty // *nm* halt; (*MUS*) alto; (*GEO*) hill; (*AM*) pile // *ad* (*de sitio*) high; (*de sonido*) loud, loudly // *nf* (certificate of) discharge // *excl* halt!; **la pared tiene 2 metros de ~** the wall is 2 metres high; **en alta mar** on the high seas; **en voz alta** in a loud voice; **las altas horas de la noche** the small *o* wee hours; **en lo ~ de** at the top of; **pasar por ~** to overlook; **dar de alta** to discharge.

altoparlante |altopar'lante| *nm* (*AM*) loudspeaker.

altura |al'tura| *nf* height; (*NAUT*) depth; (*GEO*) latitude; **la pared tiene 1.80 de ~** the wall is 1 metre 80cm high; **a estas ~s** at this stage; **a estas ~s del año** at this time of the year.

alubia |a'luβja| *nf* French bean, kidney bean.

alucinación |aluθina'θjon| *nf* hallucination; **alucinar** *vi* to hallucinate // *vt* to deceive; (*fascinar*) to fascinate.

alud |a'luð| *nm* avalanche; (*fig*) flood.

aludir |alu'ðir| *vi:* ~ a to allude to; **darse por aludido** to take the hint.

alumbrado |alum'braðo| *nm* lighting; **alumbramiento** *nm* lighting; (*MED*) childbirth, delivery.

alumbrar |alum'brar| *vt* to light (up) // *vi* (*MED*) to give birth.

aluminio |alu'minjo| *nm* aluminium (*Brit*), aluminum (*US*).

alumno, a |a'lumno, a| *nm/f* pupil, student.

alunizar |aluni'θar| *vi* to land on the moon.

alusión |alu'sjon| *nf* allusion.

alusivo, a |alu'siβo, a| *a* allusive.

aluvión |alu'βjon| *nm* alluvium; (*fig*) flood.

alverja |al'βerxa| *nf* (*AM*) pea.

alza |'alθa| *nf* rise; (*MIL*) sight.

alzada |al'θaða| *nf* (*de caballos*) height; (*JUR*) appeal.

alzamiento |alθa'mjento| *nm* (*aumento*) rise, increase; (*acción*) lifting, raising; (*mejor postura*) higher bid; (*rebelión*) rising; (*COM*) fraudulent bankruptcy.

alzar |al'θar| *vt* to lift (up); (*precio, muro*) to raise; (*cuello de abrigo*) to turn up; (*AGR*) to gather in; (*IMPRENTA*) to gather; ~se *vr* to get up, rise; (*rebelarse*) to revolt; (*COM*) to go fraudulently bankrupt; (*JUR*) to appeal.

allá |a'ʎa| *ad* (*lugar*) there; (*por ahí*) over there; (*tiempo*) then; ~ **abajo** down there; **más ~** further on; **más ~ de** beyond; **¡~ tú!** that's your problem!

allanamiento |aʎana'mjento| *nm:* ~ **de morada** burglary.

allanar |aʎa'nar| *vt* to flatten, level (out); (*igualar*) to smooth (out); (*fig*) to subdue; (*JUR*) to burgle, break into; ~se *vr* to fall down; ~se a to submit to, accept.

allegado, a |aʎe'xaðo, a| *a* near, close // *nm/f* relation.

allí |a'ʎi| *ad* there; ~ **mismo** right there; **por ~** over there; (*por ese camino*) that way.

ama |'ama| *nf* lady of the house; (*dueña*) owner; (*institutriz*) governess; (*madre adoptiva*) foster mother; ~ **de casa** housewife; ~ **de cría** *o* **de leche** wet-nurse; ~ **de llaves** housekeeper.

amabilidad |amaβili'ðað| *nf* kindness; (*simpatía*) niceness; **amable** *a* kind; nice; **es Vd muy** ~ that's very kind of you.

amaestrado, a |amaes'traðo, a| *a* (*animal: en circo etc*) performing.

amaestrar |amaes'trar| *vt* to train.

amagar |ama'xar| *vt, vi* to threaten; (*DEPORTE, MIL*) to feint; **amago** *nm* threat; (*gesto*) threatening gesture; (*MED*) symptom.

amalgama |amal'xama| *nf* amalgam; **amalgamar** *vt* to amalgamate; (*combinar*) to combine, mix.

amamantar |amaman'tar| *vt* to suckle, nurse.

amanecer |amane'θer| *vi* to dawn // *nm* dawn; **el niño amaneció afiebrado** the child woke up with a fever.

amanerado, a |amane'raðo, a| *a* affected.

amansar |aman'sar| *vt* to tame; (*persona*) to subdue; ~se *vr* (*persona*) to calm down.

amante |a'mante| *a:* ~ **de** fond of // *nm/f* lover.

amapola |ama'pola| *nf* poppy.

amar |a'mar| *vt* to love.

amarar |ama'rar| *vi* (*avión*) to land (on the sea).

amargado, a [amar'γaðo, a] *a* bitter.

amargar [amar'γar] *vt* to make bitter, *(fig)* to embitter; **~se** *vr* to become embittered.

amargo, a [a'marγo, a] *a* bitter; **amargura** *nf* bitterness.

amarillento, a [amari'ʎento, a] *a* yellowish; *(tez)* sallow; **amarillo, a** *a, nm* yellow.

amarrar [ama'rrar] *vt* to moor; *(sujetar)* to tie up.

amarras [a'marras] *nfpl*: **soltar ~** to set sail.

amartillar [amarti'ʎar] *vt (fusil)* to cock.

amasar [ama'sar] *vt (masa)* to knead; *(mezclar)* to mix, prepare; *(confeccionar)* to concoct; **amasijo** *nm* kneading; mixing; *(fig)* hotchpotch.

amateur ['amatur] *nm/f* amateur.

amatista [ama'tista] *nf* amethyst.

amazona [ama'θona] *nf* horsewoman; **A~s** *nm*: **el A~s** the Amazon.

ambages [am'baxes] *nmpl*: **sin ~** in plain language.

ámbar ['ambar] *nm* amber.

ambición [ambi'θjon] *nf* ambition; **ambicionar** *vt* to aspire to; **ambicioso, a** *a* ambitious.

ambidextro, a [ambi'ðekstro, a] *a* ambidextrous.

ambientación [ambjenta'θjon] *nf (CINE, TEATRO etc)* setting; *(RADIO)* sound effects.

ambiente [am'bjente] *nm (tb fig)* atmosphere; *(medio)* environment.

ambigüedad [ambiγwe'ðað] *nf* ambiguity; **ambiguo, a** *a* ambiguous.

ámbito ['ambito] *nm (campo)* field; *(fig)* scope.

ambos, as ['ambos, as] *apl, pron pl* both.

ambulancia [ambu'lanθja] *nf* ambulance.

ambulante [ambu'lante] *a* travelling *cpd*, itinerant.

ambulatorio [ambula'torjo] *nm* state health-service clinic.

ameba [a'meβa] *nf* amoeba.

amedrentar [ameðren'tar] *vt* to scare.

amén [a'men] *excl* amen; **~ de** besides.

amenaza [ame'naθa] *nf* threat.

amenazar [amena'θar] *vt* to threaten // *vi*: **~ con hacer** to threaten to do.

amenguar [amen'ɣwar] *vt* to diminish; *(fig)* to dishonour.

amenidad [ameni'ðað] *nf* pleasantness.

ameno, a [a'meno, a] *a* pleasant.

América [a'merika] *nf* America; **~ del Norte/del Sur** North/South America; **~ Central/Latina** Central/Latin America; **americano, a** *a, nm/f* American // *nf* coat, jacket.

amerizar [ameri'θar] *vi (avión)* to land (on the sea).

ametralladora [ametraʎa'ðora] *nf* machine gun.

amianto [a'mjanto] *nm* asbestos.

amigable [ami'γaβle] *a* friendly.

amígdala [a'miɣðala] *nf* tonsil, **amigdalitis** *nf* tonsillitis.

amigo, a [a'miɣo, a] *a* friendly // *nm/f* friend; *(amante)* lover; **ser ~ de algo** to be fond of sth; **ser muy ~s** to be close friends.

amilanar [amila'nar] *vt* to scare; **~se** *vr* to get scared.

aminorar [amino'rar] *vt* to diminish; *(reducir)* to reduce; **~ la marcha** to slow down.

amistad [amis'tað] *nf* friendship; **~es** *nfpl* friends; **amistoso, a** *a* friendly.

amnesia [am'nesja] *nf* amnesia.

amnistía [amnis'tia] *nf* amnesty.

amo ['amo] *nm* owner; *(jefe)* boss.

amodorrarse [amoðo'rrarse] *vr* to get sleepy.

amolar [amo'lar] *vt (perseguir)* to annoy.

amoldar [amol'dar] *vt* to mould; *(adaptar)* to adapt.

amonestación [amonesta'θjon] *nf* warning; **amonestaciones** *nfpl* marriage banns.

amonestar [amones'tar] *vt* to warn; *(REL)* to publish the banns of.

amontonar [amonto'nar] *vt* to collect, pile up; **~se** *vr* to crowd together; *(acumularse)* to pile up.

amor [a'mor] *nm* love; *(amante)* lover; **hacer el ~** to make love.

amoratado, a [amora'taðo, a] *a* purple.

amordazar [amorða'θar] *vt* to muzzle; *(fig)* to gag.

amorfo, a [a'morfo, a] *a* amorphous, shapeless.

amorío [amo'rio] *nm (fam)* love affair.

amoroso, a [amo'roso, a] *a* affectionate, loving.

amortajar [amorta'xar] *vt* to shroud.

amortiguador [amortiɣwa'ðor] *nm* shock absorber; *(parachoques)* bumper; **~es** *nmpl (AUTO)* suspension *sg*.

amortiguar [amorti'ɣwar] *vt* to deaden; *(ruido)* to muffle; *(color)* to soften.

amortización [amortiθa'θjon] *nf (de deuda)* repayment; *(de bono)* redemption.

amotinar [amoti'nar] *vt* to stir up, incite (to riot); **~se** *vr* to mutiny.

amparar [ampa'rar] *vt* to protect; **~se** *vr* to seek protection; *(de la lluvia etc)* to shelter; **amparo** *nm* help, protection; **al amparo de** under the protection of.

amperio [am'perjo] *nm* ampère, amp.

ampliación [amplja'θjon] *nf* enlargement; *(extensión)* extension; **ampliar** *vt* to enlarge; to extend.

amplificación [amplifika'θjon] *nf* enlargement; **amplificador** *nm* amplifier.

amplificar [amplifi'kar] *vt* to amplify.

amplio, a ['ampljo, a] *a* spacious; *(de falda etc)* full; *(extenso)* extensive; *(ancho)* wide; **amplitud** *nf* spaciousness; extent; *(fig)* amplitude.

ampolla [am'poʎa] *nf* blister; *(MED)* ampoule.

ampuloso, a [ampu'loso, a] *a* bombastic, pompous.

amputar [ampu'tar] *vt* to cut off, amputate.

amueblar [amwe'βlar] *vt* to furnish.

amurallar [amura'ʎar] *vt* to wall up *o* in.

anacronismo [anakro'nismo] *nm* anachronism.

ánade ['anaðe] *nm* duck.

anadear [anaðe'ar] *vi* to waddle.

anales [a'nales] *nmpl* annals.

analfabetismo [analfaβe'tismo] *nm* illiteracy; **analfabeto, a** *a, nm/f* illiterate.

analgésico [anal'xesiko] *nm* painkiller, analgesic.

análisis [a'nalisis] *nm inv* analysis.

analista [ana'lista] *nm/f (gen)* analyst.

analizar [anali'θar] *vt* to analyse.

analogía [analo'xia] *nf* analogy.

analógico, a [ana'loxiko, a] *a (INFORM)* analog; *(reloj)* analogue *(Brit)*, analog *(US)*.

análogo, a [a'naloɣo, a] *a* analogous, similar (*a* to).

ananá(s) [ana'na(s)] *nm* pineapple.

anaquel [ana'kel] *nm* shelf.

anarquía [anar'kia] *nf* anarchy; **anarquismo** *nm* anarchism; **anarquista** *nm/f* anarchist.

anatomía [anato'mia] *nf* anatomy.

anca ['anka] *nf* rump, haunch; **~s** *nfpl (fam)* behind *sg*.

anciano, a [an'θjano, a] *a* old, aged // *nm/f* old man/woman // *nm/f* elder.

ancla ['ankla] *nf* anchor; **~dero** *nm* anchorage; **anclar** *vi* to (drop) anchor.

ancho, a ['antʃo, a] *a* wide; *(falda)* full; *(fig)* liberal // *nm* width; *(FERRO)* gauge; **ponerse ~** to get conceited; **estar a sus anchas** to be at one's ease.

anchoa [an'tʃoa] *nf* anchovy.

anchura [an'tʃura] *nf* width; *(extensión)* wideness.

andaderas [anda'ðeras] *nfpl* baby walker *sg*.

andadura [anda'ðura] *nf* gait; *(de caballo)* pace.

Andalucía [andalu'θia] *nf* Andalusia; **andaluz, a** *a, nm/f* Andalusian.

andamio [an'damjo], **andamiaje** [anda'mjaxe] *nm* scaffold(ing).

andar [an'dar] *vt* to go, cover, travel // *vi* to go, walk, travel; *(funcionar)* to go, work; *(estar)* to be // *nm* walk, gait, pace; **~se** *vr* to go away; **~ a pie/a caballo/en bicicleta** to go on foot/on horseback/by bicycle; **~ haciendo algo** to be doing sth; **¡anda!**, *(sorpresa)* go on!; **anda por o en los 40** he's about 40.

andariego, a [anda'rjeɣo, a] *a (itinerante)* wandering.

andén [an'den] *nm (FERRO)* platform; *(NAUT)* quayside; *(AM: de la calle)* pavement *(Brit)*, sidewalk *(US)*.

Andes ['andes] *nmpl:* **los ~** the Andes.

Andorra [an'dorra] *nf* Andorra.

andrajo [an'draxo] *nm* rag; **~so, a** *a* ragged.

andurriales [andu'rrjales] *nmpl* wilds *npl*.

anduve, anduviera *etc vb ver* **andar**.

anécdota [a'nekðota] *nf* anecdote, story.

anegar [ane'ɣar] *vt* to flood; *(ahogar)* to drown; **~se** *vr* to drown; *(hundirse)* to sink.

anejo, a [a'nexo, a] *a, nm* = **anexo**.

anemia [a'nemja] *nf* anaemia.

anestésico [anes'tesiko] *nm* anaesthetic.

anexar [anek'sar] *vt* to annex; *(documento)* to attach; **anexión** *nf,* **anexionamiento** *nm* annexation; **anexo, a** *a* attached // *nm* annexe.

anfibio, a [an'fiβjo, a] *a* amphibious // *nm* amphibian.

anfiteatro [anfite'atro] *nm* amphitheatre; *(TEATRO)* dress circle.

anfitrión, ona [anfi'trjon, ona] *nm/f* host(ess).

ángel ['anxel] *nm* angel; **~ de la guarda** guardian angel; **tener ~** to be charming; **angélico, a, angelical** *a* angelic(al).

angina [an'xina] *nf (MED)* inflammation of the throat; **~ de pecho** angina; **tener ~s** to have tonsillitis.

anglicano, a [angli'kano, a] *a, nm/f* Anglican.

angosto, a [an'gosto, a] *a* narrow.

anguila [an'gila] *nf* eel; **~s** *nfpl (NAUT)* slipway *sg*.

angula [an'gula] *nf* elver, baby eel.

ángulo ['angulo] *nm* angle; *(esquina)* corner; *(curva)* bend.

angustia [an'gustja] *nf* anguish; **angustiar** *vt* to distress, grieve.

anhelante [ane'lante] *a* eager; *(deseoso)* longing.

anhelar [ane'lar] *vt* to be eager for; to long for, desire // *vi* to pant, gasp; **anhelo** *nm* eagerness; desire.

anidar [ani'ðar] *vi* to nest.

anillo [a'niʎo] *nm* ring; **~ de boda** wedding ring.

ánima ['anima] *nf* soul; **las ~s** the Angelus (bell) *sg*.

animación [anima'θjon] *nf* liveliness; *(vitalidad)* life; *(actividad)* activity; bustle.

animado, a [ani'maðo, a] *a* lively; *(vivaz)* animated; **animador, a** *nm/f (TV)* host(ess), compère; *(DEPORTE)* cheerleader.

animadversión [animaðßer'sjon] *nf* ill-will, antagonism.

animal [ani'mal] *a* animal; *(fig)* stupid // *nm* animal; *(fig)* fool; *(bestia)* brute.

animar [ani'mar] *vt (BIO)* to animate,

give life to; (*fig*) to liven up, brighten up, cheer up; (*estimular*) to stimulate; ~se *vr* to cheer up; to feel encouraged; (*decidirse*) to make up one's mind.

ánimo ['animo] *nm* (*alma*) soul; (*mente*) mind; (*valentía*) courage // *excl* cheer up!

animoso, a [ani'moso, a] *a* brave; (*vivo*) lively.

aniquilar [aniki'lar] *vt* to annihilate, destroy.

anís [a'nis] *nm* aniseed; (*licor*) anisette.

aniversario [aniβer'sarjo] *nm* anniversary.

anoche [a'notʃe] *ad* last night; antes de ~ the night before last.

anochecer [anotʃe'θer] *vi* to get dark // *nm* nightfall, dark; al ~ at nightfall.

anodino, a [ano'ðino, a] *a* dull, anodyne.

anomalía [anoma'lia] *nf* anomaly.

anonimato [anoni'mato] *nm* anonymity.

anónimo, a [a'nonimo, a] *a* anonymous; (*COM*) limited // *nm* (*carta*) anonymous letter; (: *maliciosa*) poison-pen letter.

anormal [anor'mal] *a* abnormal.

anotación [anota'θjon] *nf* note; annotation.

anotar [ano'tar] *vt* to note down; (*comentar*) to annotate.

anquilosamiento [ankilosa'mjento] *nm* (*fig*) paralysis; stagnation.

ansia ['ansja] *nf* anxiety; (*añoranza*) yearning; **ansiar** *vt* to long for.

ansiedad [ansje'ðað] *nf* anxiety.

ansioso, a [an'sjoso, a] *a* anxious; (*anhelante*) eager; ~ de o por algo greedy for sth.

antagónico, a [anta'ɣoniko, a] *a* antagonistic; (*opuesto*) contrasting; **antagonista** *nm/f* antagonist.

antaño [an'taɲo] *ad* long ago, formerly.

Antártico [an'tartiko] *nm*: el ~ the Antarctic.

ante ['ante] *prep* before, in the presence of; (*encarado con*) faced with // *nm* (*piel*) suede; ~ todo above all.

anteanoche [antea'notʃe] *ad* the night before last.

anteayer [antea'jer] *ad* the day before yesterday.

antebrazo [ante'βraθo] *nm* forearm.

antecedente [anteθe'ðente] *a* previous // *nm* antecedent; ~s *nmpl* record *sg*; background *sg*.

anteceder [anteθe'ðer] *vt* to precede, go before.

antecesor, a [anteθe'sor, a] *nm/f* predecessor.

antedicho, a [ante'ðitʃo, a] *a* aforementioned.

antelación [antela'θjon] *nf*: con ~ in advance.

antemano [ante'mano]: de ~ *ad* beforehand, in advance.

antena [an'tena] *nf* antenna; (*de*

televisión *etc*) aerial.

anteojo [ante'oxo] *nm* eyeglass; ~s *nmpl* (*AM*) glasses, spectacles.

antepasados [antepa'saðos] *nmpl* ancestors.

antepecho [ante'petʃo] *nm* guardrail, parapet; (*repisa*) ledge, sill.

anteponer [antepo'ner] *vt* to place in front; (*fig*) to prefer.

anteproyecto [antepro'jekto] *nm* preliminary sketch; (*fig*) blueprint.

anterior [ante'rjor] *a* preceding, previous; ~idad *nf*: con ~idad a prior to, before.

antes ['antes] *ad* (*con prioridad*) before // *prep*: ~ de before // *conj*: ~ de ir/de que te vayas before going/before you go; ~ bien (*but*) rather; dos días ~ two days before o previously; no quiso venir ~ she didn't want to come any earlier; tomo el avión ~ que el barco I take the plane rather than the boat; ~ que yo before me; lo ~ posible as soon as possible; cuanto ~ mejor the sooner the better.

antesala [ante'sala] *nf* anteroom.

antiaéreo, a [antia'ereo, a] *a* anti-aircraft.

antibalas [anti'βalas] *a inv*: chaleco ~ bullet-proof jacket.

antibiótico [anti'βjotiko] *nm* antibiotic.

anticiclón [antiθi'klon] *nm* anticyclone.

anticipación [antiθipa'θjon] *nf* anticipation; con 10 minutos de ~ 10 minutes early.

anticipado, a [antiθi'paðo, a] *a* (in) advance.

anticipar [antiθi'par] *vt* to anticipate; (*adelantar*) to bring forward; (*COM*) to advance; ~se *vr*: ~se a su época to be ahead of one's time.

anticipo [anti'θipo] *nm* (*COM*) advance.

anticonceptivo, a [antikonθep'tiβo, a] *a*, *nm* contraceptive.

anticongelante [antikonxe'lante] *nm* antifreeze.

anticuado, a [anti'kwaðo, a] *a* out-of-date, old-fashioned; (*desusado*) obsolete.

anticuario [anti'kwarjo] *nm* antique dealer.

anticuerpo [anti'kwerpo] *nm* (*MED*) antibody.

antídoto [an'tiðoto] *nm* antidote.

antiestético, a [anties'tetiko, a] *a* unsightly.

antifaz [anti'faθ] *nm* mask; (*velo*) veil.

antigualla [anti'ɣwaʎa] *nf* antique; (*reliquia*) relic.

antiguamente [antiɣwa'mente] *ad* formerly; (*hace mucho tiempo*) long ago.

antigüedad [antiɣwe'ðað] *nf* antiquity; (*artículo*) antique; (*rango*) seniority.

antiguo, a [an'tiɣwo, a] *a* old, ancient; (*que fue*) former.

antílope [an'tilope] *nm* antelope.

antillano, a [anti'ʎano, a] *a*, *nm/f* West

Indian.

Antillas [an'tiʎas] *nfpl*: las ~ the West Indies.

antinatural [antinatu'ral] *a* unnatural.

antipatía [antipa'tia] *nf* antipathy, dislike; **antipático, a** *a* disagreeable, unpleasant.

antirrobo [anti'rroβo] *a inv* (*alarma etc*) anti-theft.

antisemita [antise'mita] *a* anti-Semitic // *nm/f* anti-Semite.

antiséptico, a [anti'septiko, a] *a* antiseptic // *nm* antiseptic.

antítesis [an'titesis] *nf inv* antithesis.

antojadizo, a [antoxa'ðiθo, a] *a* capricious.

antojarse [anto'xarse] *vr* (*desear*): se me antoja comprarlo I have a mind to buy it; (*pensar*): se me antoja que I have a feeling that.

antojo [an'toxo] *nm* caprice, whim; (*rosa*) birthmark; (*lunar*) mole.

antología [antolo'xia] *nf* anthology.

antorcha [an'tortʃa] *nf* torch.

antro ['antro] *nm* cavern.

antropófago, a [antro'pofaɣo, a] *a, nm/f* cannibal.

antropología [antropolo'xia] *nf* anthropology.

anual [a'nwal] *a* annual; ~idad [anwali'ðað] *nf* annuity.

anuario [a'nwarjo] *nm* yearbook.

anudar [anu'ðar] *vt* to knot, tie; (*unir*) to join; ~se *vr* to get tied up.

anulación [anula'θjon] *nf* annulment; (*cancelación*) cancellation.

anular [anu'lar] *vt* (*contrato*) to annul, cancel; (*ley*) to revoke, repeal; (*suscripción*) to cancel // *nm* ring finger.

anunciación [anunθja'θjon] *nf* announcement; A~ (*REL*) Annunciation.

anunciante [anun'θjante] *nm/f* (*COM*) advertiser.

anunciar [anun'θjar] *vt* to announce; (*proclamar*) to proclaim; (*COM*) to advertise.

anuncio [a'nunθjo] *nm* announcement; (*señal*) sign; (*COM*) advertisement; (*cartel*) poster.

anzuelo [an'θwelo] *nm* hook; (*para pescar*) fish hook.

añadidura [aɲaði'ðura] *nf* addition, extra; por ~ besides, in addition.

añadir [aɲa'ðir] *vt* to add.

añejo, a [a'ɲexo, a] *a* old; (*vino*) mellow.

añicos [a'ɲikos] *nmpl*: hacer ~ to smash, shatter.

añil [a'ɲil] *nm* (*BOT, color*) indigo.

año ['aɲo] *nm*; ¡Feliz A~ Nuevo! Happy New Year!; tener 15 ~s to be 15 (years old); los ~s 80 the eighties; ~ bisiesto/escolar leap/school year; el ~ que viene next year.

añoranza [aɲo'ranθa] *nf* nostalgia;

(*anhelo*) longing.

apabullar [apaβu'ʎar] *vt* (*tb fig*) to crush, squash.

apacentar [apaθen'tar] *vt* to pasture, graze.

apacible [apa'θiβle] *a* gentle, mild.

apaciguar [apaθi'ɣwar] *vt* to pacify, calm (down).

apadrinar [apaðri'nar] *vt* to sponsor, support; (*REL*) to be godfather to.

apagado, a [apa'ɣaðo, a] *a* (*volcán*) extinct; (*color*) dull; (*voz*) quiet; (*sonido*) muted, muffled; (*persona*: *apático*) listless; estar ~ (*fuego, luz*) to be out; (*RADIO, TV etc*) to be off.

apagar [apa'ɣar] *vt* to put out; (*ELEC, RADIO, TV*) to turn off; (*sonido*) to silence, muffle; (*sed*) to quench.

apagón [apa'ɣon] *nm* blackout; power cut.

apalabrar [apala'βrar] *vt* to agree to; (*contratar*) to engage.

apalear [apale'ar] *vt* to beat, thrash; (*AGR*) to winnow.

apañar [apa'ɲar] *vt* to pick up; (*asir*) to take hold of, grasp; (*reparar*) to mend, patch up; ~se *vr* to manage, get along.

aparador [apara'ðor] *nm* sideboard; (*escaparate*) shop window.

aparato [apa'rato] *nm* apparatus; (*máquina*) machine; (*doméstico*) appliance; (*boato*) ostentation; ~ de facsímil facsimile (machine), fax; ~so, a *a* showy, ostentatious.

aparcamiento [aparka'mjento] *nm* car park (*Brit*), parking lot (*US*).

aparcar [apar'kar] *vt, vi* to park.

aparear [apare'ar] *vt* (*objetos*) to pair, match; (*animales*) to mate; ~se *vr* to make a pair; to mate.

aparecer [apare'θer] *vi*, **aparecerse** *vr* to appear.

aparejado, a [apare'xaðo, a] *a* fit, suitable; llevar *o* traer ~ to involve.

aparejo [apa'rexo] *nm* preparation; harness; rigging; (*de poleas*) block and tackle.

aparentar [aparen'tar] *vt* (*edad*) to look; (*fingir*): ~ tristeza to pretend to be sad.

aparente [apa'rente] *a* apparent; (*adecuado*) suitable.

aparezco *etc vb ver* **aparecer**.

aparición [apari'θjon] *nf* appearance; (*de libro*) publication; (*espectro*) apparition.

apariencia [apa'rjenθja] *nf* (*outward*) appearance; en ~ outwardly, seemingly.

apartado, a [apar'taðo, a] *a* separate; (*lejano*) remote // *nm* (*tipográfico*) paragraph; ~ (*de correos*) post office box.

apartamento [aparta'mento] *nm* apartment, flat (*Brit*).

apartamiento [aparta'mjento] *nm* separation; (*aislamiento*) remoteness, isolation; (*AM*) apartment, flat (*Brit*).

apartar [apar'tar] *vt* to separate; (*quitar*)

to remove; (*MINEROLOGIA*) to extract; ~se *vr* to separate, part; (*irse*) to move away; to keep away.

aparte [a'parte] *ad* (*separadamente*) separately; (*además*) besides // *nm* aside; (*tipográfico*) new paragraph.

apasionado, a [apasjo'naðo, a] *a* passionate; biassed, prejudiced.

apasionar [apasjo'nar] *vt* to excite; le apasiona el fútbol she's crazy about football; ~se *vr* to get excited.

apatía [apa'tia] *nf* apathy.

apático, a [a'patiko, a] *a* apathetic.

apátrida [a'patrida] *a* stateless.

Apdo *abr* (= *Apartado* (*de Correos*)) PO BOX.

apeadero [apea'ðero] *nm* halt, stop, stopping place.

apearse [ape'arse] *vr* (*jinete*) to dismount; (*bajarse*) to get down o out; (*AUTO, FERRO*) to get off o out.

apechugar [apetʃu'xar] *vr*: ~ con algo to face up to sth.

apedrear [apeðre'ar] *vt* to stone.

apegarse [ape'xarse] *vr*: ~se a to become attached to; **apego** *nm* attachment, devotion.

apelación [apela'θjon] *nf* appeal.

apelar [ape'lar] *vi* to appeal; ~ a (*fig*) to resort to.

apellidar [apeʎi'ðar] *vt* to call, name; ~se *vr*: se **apellida Pérez** her (sur)name's Pérez.

apellido [ape'ʎiðo] *nm* surname.

apenar [ape'nar] *vt* to grieve, trouble; (*AM: avergonzar*) to embarrass; ~se *vr* to grieve; (*AM*) to be embarrassed.

apenas [a'penas] *ad* scarcely, hardly // *conj* as soon as, no sooner.

apéndice [a'pendiθe] *nm* appendix; **apendicitis** *nf* appendicitis.

apercibirse [aperθi'βirse] *vr*: ~ de to notice.

aperitivo [aperi'tiβo] *nm* (*bebida*) aperitif; (*comida*) appetizer.

apero [a'pero] *nm* (*AGR*) implement; ~s *nmpl* farm equipment *sg*.

apertura [aper'tura] *nf* opening; (*POL*) liberalization.

apesadumbrar [apesaðum'brar] *vt* to grieve, sadden; ~se *vr* to distress o.s.

apestar [apes'tar] *vt* to infect // *vi*: ~ (a) to stink (of).

apetecer [apete'θer] *vt*: ¿te apetece una tortilla? do you fancy an omelette?; **apetecible** *a* desirable; (*comida*) appetizing.

apetito [ape'tito] *nm* appetite; ~so, a *a* appetizing; (*fig*) tempting.

apiadarse [apja'ðarse] *vr*: ~ de to take pity on.

ápice ['apiθe] *nm* apex; (*fig*) whit, iota.

apilar [api'lar] *vt* to pile o heap up; ~se *vr* to pile up.

apiñarse [api'narse] *vr* to crowd o press

together.

apio ['apjo] *nm* celery.

apisonadora [apisona'ðora] *nf* (*máquina*) steamroller.

aplacar [apla'kar] *vt* to placate; ~se *vr* to calm down.

aplanar [apla'nar] *vt* to smooth, level; (*allanar*) to roll flat, flatten.

aplastar [aplas'tar] *vt* to squash (flat); (*fig*) to crush.

aplatanarse [aplata'narse] *vr* to get lethargic.

aplaudir [aplau'ðir] *vt* to applaud.

aplauso [a'plauso] *nm* applause; (*fig*) approval, acclaim.

aplazamiento [aplaθa'mjento] *nm* postponement.

aplazar [apla'θar] *vt* to postpone, defer.

aplicación [aplika'θjon] *nf* application; (*esfuerzo*) effort.

aplicado, a [apli'kaðo, a] *a* diligent, hard-working.

aplicar [apli'kar] *vt* (*ejecutar*) to apply; ~se *vr* to apply o.s.

aplique *etc vb ver* aplicar // [a'plike] *nm* wall light.

aplomo [a'plomo] *nm* aplomb, self-assurance.

apocado, a [apo'kaðo, a] *a* timid.

apocamiento [apoka'mjento] *nm* timidity; (*depresión*) depression.

apocarse [apo'karse] *vr* to feel small o humiliated.

apodar [apo'ðar] *vt* to nickname.

apoderado [apoðe'raðo] *nm* agent, representative.

apoderar [apoðe'rar] *vt* to authorize, empower; (*JUR*) to grant (a) power of attorney to; ~se *vr*: ~se de to take possession of.

apodo [a'poðo] *nm* nickname.

apogeo [apo'xeo] *nm* peak, summit.

apolillarse [apoli'ʎarse] *vr* to get moth-eaten.

apología [apolo'xia] *nf* eulogy; (*defensa*) defence.

apoltronarse [apoltro'narse] *vr* to get lazy.

apoplejía [apople'xia] *nf* apoplexy, stroke.

apoquinar [apoki'nar] *vt* (*fam*) to fork out, cough up.

aporrear [aporre'ar] *vt* to beat (up).

aportar [apor'tar] *vt* to contribute // *vi* to reach port; ~se *vr* (*AM*) to arrive, come.

aposentar [aposen'tar] *vt* to lodge, put up; **aposento** *nm* lodging; (*habitación*) room.

apósito [a'posito] *nm* (*MED*) dressing.

apostar [apos'tar] *vt* to bet, stake; (*tropas etc*) to station, post // *vi* to bet.

apostilla [apos'tiʎa] *nf* note, comment.

apóstol [a'postol] *nm* apostle.

apóstrofo [a'postrofo] *nm* apostrophe.

apostura [apos'tura] *nf* neatness; (*elegancia*) elegance.

apoyar [apo'jar] *vt* to lean, rest; (*fig*) to support, back; (*fig*) *vr*: ~**se en** to lean on; **apoyo** *nm* (*gen*) support; backing, help.

apreciable [apre'θjaßle] *a* considerable; (*fig*) esteemed.

apreciación [apreθja'θjon] *nf* appreciation; (*COM*) valuation.

apreciar [apre'θjar] *vt* to evaluate, assess; (*COM*) to appreciate, value.

aprecio [a'preθjo] *nm* valuation, estimate; (*fig*) appreciation.

aprehender [apreen'der] *vt* to apprehend, detain; **aprehensión** *nf* detention, capture.

apremiante [apre'mjante] *a* urgent, pressing.

apremiar [apre'mjar] *vt* to compel, force // *vi* to be urgent, press; **apremio** *nm* urgency.

aprender [apren'der] *vt*, *vi* to learn.

aprendiz, a [apren'diθ, a] *nm/f* apprentice; (*principiante*) learner; ~**aje** *nm* apprenticeship.

aprensión [apren'sjon] *nm* apprehension, fear; **aprensivo, a** *a* apprehensive.

apresar [apre'sar] *vt* to seize; (*capturar*) to capture.

aprestar [apres'tar] *vt* to prepare, get ready; (*TEC*) to prime, size; ~**se** *vr* to get ready.

apresurado, a [apresu'raðo, a] *a* hurried, hasty; **apresuramiento** *nm* hurry, haste.

apresurar [apresu'rar] *vt* to hurry, accelerate; ~**se** *vr* to hurry, make haste.

apretado, a [apre'taðo, a] *a* tight; (*escritura*) cramped.

apretar [apre'tar] *vt* to squeeze; (*TEC*) to tighten; (*presionar*) to press together, pack // *vi* to be too tight.

apretón [apre'ton] *nm* squeeze; ~ **de manos** handshake.

aprieto [a'prjeto] *nm* squeeze; (*dificultad*) difficulty, jam; **estar en un** ~ to be in a fix.

aprisa [a'prisa] *ad* quickly, hurriedly.

aprisionar [aprisjo'nar] *vt* to imprison.

aprobación [aproßa'θjon] *nf* approval.

aprobar [apro'ßar] *vt* to approve (of); (*examen, materia*) to pass // *vi* to pass.

apropiación [apropja'θjon] *nf* appropriation.

apropiado, a [apro'pjaðo, a] *a* appropriate.

apropiarse [apro'pjarse] *vr*: ~ **de** to appropriate.

aprovechado, a [aproße'tʃaðo, a] *a* industrious, hardworking; (*económico*) thrifty; (*pey*) unscrupulous; **aprovechamiento** *nm* use; exploitation.

aprovechar [aproße'tʃar] *vt* to use; (*explotar*) to exploit; (*experiencia*) to profit from; (*oferta, oportunidad*) to take advantage of // *vi* to progress, improve; ~**se** *vr*: ~**se de** to make use of; to take advantage of; **¡que aproveche!** enjoy your meal!

aproximación [aproksima'θjon] *nf* approximation; (*de lotería*) consolation prize; **aproximado, a** *a* approximate.

aproximar [aproksi'mar] *vt* to bring nearer; ~**se** *vr* to come near, approach.

apruebo *etc vb ver* **aprobar.**

aptitud [apti'tuð] *nf* aptitude.

apto, a ['apto, a] *a* suitable.

apuesto, a [a'pwesto, a] *a* neat, elegant // *nf* bet, wager.

apuntador [apunta'ðor] *nm* prompter.

apuntalar [apunta'lar] *vt* to prop up.

apuntar [apun'tar] *vt* (*con arma*) to aim at; (*con dedo*) to point at o to; (*anotar*) to note (down); (*TEATRO*) to prompt; ~**se** *vr* (*DEPORTE*: *tanto, victoria*) to score; (*ESCOL*) to enrol.

apunte [a'punte] *nm* note.

apuñalar [apuɲa'lar] *vt* to stab.

apurado, a [apu'raðo, a] *a* needy; (*difícil*) difficult; (*peligroso*) dangerous; (*AM*) hurried, rushed.

apurar [apu'rar] *vt* (*agotar*) to drain; (*recursos*) to use up; (*molestar*) to annoy; ~**se** *vr* (*preocuparse*) to worry; (*darse prisa*) to hurry.

apuro [a'puro] *nm* (*aprieto*) fix, jam; (*escasez*) want, hardship; (*vergüenza*) embarrassment; (*AM*) haste, urgency.

aquejado, a [ake'xaðo, a] *a*: ~ **de** (*MED*) afflicted by.

aquel, aquella, aquellos, as [a'kel, a'keʎa, a'keʎos, as] *a* that; (*pl*) those.

aquél, aquélla, aquéllos, as [a'kel, a'keʎa, a'keʎos, as] *pron* that (one); (*pl*) those (ones).

aquello [a'keʎo] *pron* that, that business.

aquí [a'ki] *ad* (*lugar*) here; (*tiempo*) now; ~ **arriba** up here; ~ **mismo** right here; ~ **yace** here lies; **de** ~ **a siete días** a week from now.

aquietar [akje'tar] *vt* to quieten (down), calm (down).

ara ['ara] *nf*: **en** ~**s de** for the sake of.

árabe ['araße] *a, nm/f* Arab // *nm* (*LING*) Arabic.

Arabia [a'raßja] *nf*: ~ **Saudí** o **Saudita** Saudi Arabia.

arado [a'raðo] *nm* plough.

Aragón [ara'ɣon] *nm* Aragon; **aragonés, esa** *a, nm/f* Aragonese.

arancel [aran'θel] *nm* tariff, duty; ~ **de aduanas** customs (duty).

arandela [aran'dela] *nf* (*TEC*) washer.

araña [a'raɲa] *nf* (*ZOOL*) spider; (*lámpara*) chandelier.

arañar [ara'ɲar] *vt* to scratch.

arañazo [ara'ɲaθo] *nm* scratch.

arar [a'rar] *vt* to plough, till.

arbitraje [arßi'traxe] *nm* arbitration.

arbitrar [arβi'trar] *vt* to arbitrate in; (*DEPORTE*) to referee // *vi* to arbitrate.

arbitrariedad [arβitraɾje'ðað] *nf* arbitrariness; (*acto*) arbitrary act; **arbitrario, a** *a* arbitrary.

arbitrio [ar'βitrjo] *nm* free will; (*JUR*) adjudication, decision.

árbitro ['arβitro] *nm* arbitrator; (*DEPORTE*) referee; (*TENIS*) umpire.

árbol ['arβol] *nm* (*BOT*) tree; (*NAUT*) mast; (*TEC*) axle, shaft; **arbolado, a** *a* wooded; (*camino etc*) tree-lined // *nm* woodland.

arboladura [arβola'ðura] *nf* rigging.

arbolar [arβo'lar] *vt* to hoist, raise.

arboleda [arβo'leða] *nf* grove, plantation.

arbusto [ar'βusto] *nm* bush, shrub.

arca ['arka] *nf* chest, box.

arcada [ar'kaða] *nf* arcade; (*de puente*) arch, span; ~s *nfpl* retching *sg*.

arcaico, a [ar'kaiko, a] *a* archaic.

arce ['arθe] *nm* maple tree.

arcén [ar'θen] *nm* (*de autopista*) hard shoulder; (*de carretera*) verge.

arcilla [ar'θiʎa] *nf* clay.

arco ['arko] *nm* arch; (*MAT*) arc; (*MIL, MUS*) bow; ~ **iris** rainbow.

archipiélago [artʃi'pjelaɣo] *nm* archipelago.

archivador [artʃiβa'ðor] *nm* filing cabinet.

archivar [artʃi'βar] *vt* to file (away); **archivo** *nm* file, archive(s) (*pl*).

arder [ar'ðer] *vi* to burn; **estar que arde** (*persona*) to fume.

ardid [ar'ðið] *nm* ploy, trick.

ardiente [ar'ðjente] *a* burning, ardent.

ardilla [ar'ðiʎa] *nf* squirrel.

ardor [ar'ðor] *nm* (*calor*) heat; (*fig*) ardour; ~ **de estómago** heartburn.

arduo, a ['arðwo, a] *a* arduous.

área ['area] *nf* area; (*DEPORTE*) penalty area.

arena [a'rena] *nf* sand; (*de una lucha*) arena.

arenal [are'nal] *nm* (*arena movediza*) quicksand.

arengar [aren'gar] *vt* to harangue.

arenisca [are'niska] *nf* sandstone; (*cascajo*) grit.

arenoso, a [are'noso, a] *a* sandy.

arenque [a'renke] *nm* herring.

arete [a'rete] *nm* earring.

argamasa [arɣa'masa] *nf* mortar, plaster.

Argel [ar'xel] *nm* Algiers; ~**ia** *nf* Algeria; **argelino, a** *a, nm/f* Algerian.

Argentina [arxen'tina] *nf*: (**la**) **A**~ Argentina.

argentino, a [arxen'tino, a] *a* Argentinian; (*de plata*) silvery // *nm/f* Argentinian.

argolla [ar'ɣoʎa] *nf* (large) ring.

argot [ar'ɣo] (*pl* ~**s**) *nm* slang.

argucia [ar'ɣuθja] *nf* subtlety, sophistry.

argüir [ar'ɣwir] *vt* to deduce; (*discutir*) to argue; (*indicar*) to indicate, imply; (*censurar*) to reproach // *vi* to argue.

argumentación [arɣumenta'θjon] *nf* (line of) argument.

argumentar [arɣumen'tar] *vt, vi* to argue.

argumento [arɣu'mento] *nm* argument; (*razonamiento*) reasoning; (*de novela etc*) plot; (*CINE, TV*) storyline.

aria ['arja] *nf* aria.

aridez [ari'ðeθ] *nf* aridity, dryness.

árido, a ['ariðo, a] *a* arid, dry; ~**s** *nmpl* dry goods.

Aries ['arjes] *nm* Aries.

ariete [a'rjete] *nm* battering ram.

ario, a ['arjo, a] *a* Aryan.

arisco, a [a'risko, a] *a* surly; (*insociable*) unsociable.

aristócrata [aris'tokrata] *nm/f* aristocrat.

aritmética [arit'metika] *nf* arithmetic.

arma ['arma] *nf* arm; ~**s** *nfpl* arms; ~ **blanca** blade, knife; (*espada*) sword; ~ **de fuego** firearm; ~**s cortas** small arms.

armadillo [arma'ðiʎo] *nm* armadillo.

armado, a [ar'maðo, a] *a* armed; (*TEC*) reinforced // *nf* armada; (*flota*) fleet.

armadura [arma'ðura] *nf* (*MIL*) armour; (*TEC*) framework; (*ZOOL*) skeleton; (*FISICA*) armature.

armamento [arma'mento] *nm* armament; (*NAUT*) fitting-out.

armar [ar'mar] *vt* (*soldado*) to arm; (*máquina*) to assemble; (*navío*) to fit out; ~**la**, ~ **un lío** to start a row, kick up a fuss.

armario [ar'marjo] *nm* wardrobe.

armatoste [arma'toste] *nm* (*mueble*) monstrosity; (*máquina*) contraption.

armazón [arma'θon] *nf o m* body, chassis; (*de mueble etc*) frame; (*ARQ*) skeleton.

armería [arme'ria] *nf* (*museo*) military museum; (*tienda*) gunsmith's.

armiño [ar'miɲo] *nm* stoat; (*piel*) ermine.

armisticio [armis'tiθjo] *nm* armistice.

armonía [armo'nia] *nf* harmony.

armónica [ar'monika] *nf* harmonica.

armonioso, a [armo'njoso, a] *a* harmonious.

armonizar [armoni'θar] *vt* to harmonize; (*diferencias*) to reconcile // *vi*: ~ **con** (*fig*) to be in keeping with; (*colores*) to tone in with, blend.

arnés [ar'nes] *nm* armour; **arneses** *nmpl* harness *sg*.

aro ['aro] *nm* ring; (*tejo*) quoit; (*AM: pendiente*) earring.

aroma [a'roma] *nm* aroma, scent.

aromático, a [aro'matiko, a] *a* aromatic.

arpa ['arpa] *nf* harp.

arpía [ar'pia] *nf* shrew.

arpillera [arpi'ʎera] *nf* sacking, sackcloth.

arpón [ar'pon] *nm* harpoon.

arquear [arke'ar] *vt* to arch, bend; ~se *vr* to arch, bend; **arqueo** *nm* (*gen*) arching; (*NAUT*) tonnage.

arqueología [arkeolo'xia] *nf* archaeology; **arqueólogo, a** *nm/f* archaeologist.

arquero [ar'kero] *nm* archer, bowman.

arquetipo [arke'tipo] *nm* archetype.

arquitecto [arki'tekto] *nm* architect; **arquitectura** *nf* architecture.

arrabal [arra'ßal] *nm* suburb; (*AM*) slum; ~es *nmpl* outskirts.

arraigado, a [arrai'yaðo, a] *a* deep-rooted; (*fig*) established.

arraigar [arrai'yar] *vt* to establish // *vi*, ~se *vr* to take root; (*persona*) to settle.

arrancar [arran'kar] *vt* (*sacar*) to extract, pull out; (*arrebatar*) to snatch (away); (*INFORM*) to boot; (*fig*) to extract // *vi* (*AUTO, máquina*) to start; (*ponerse en marcha*) to get going; ~ de to stem from.

arranque *etc vb ver* **arrancar** // [a'rranke] *nm* sudden start; (*AUTO*) start; (*fig*) fit, outburst.

arras ['arras] *nfpl* pledge *sg*, security *sg*.

arrasar [arra'sar] *vt* (*aplanar*) to level, flatten; (*destruir*) to demolish.

arrastrado, a [arras'traðo, a] *a* poor, wretched; (*AM*) servile.

arrastrar [arras'trar] *vt* to drag (along); (*fig*) to drag down, degrade; (*suj: agua, viento*) to carry away // *vi* to drag, trail on the ground; ~se *vr* to crawl; (*fig*) to grovel; **llevar algo arrastrado** to drag sth along.

arrastre [a'rrastre] *nm* drag, dragging.

arrayán [arra'jan] *nm* myrtle.

arre ['arre] *excl* gee up!

arrear [arre'ar] *vt* to drive on, urge on // *vi* to hurry along.

arrebatado, a [arreßa'taðo, a] *a* rash, impetuous; (*repentino*) sudden, hasty.

arrebatar [arreßa'tar] *vt* to snatch (away), seize; (*fig*) to captivate; ~se *vr* to get carried away, get excited.

arrebato [arre'ßato] *nm* fit of rage, fury; (*éxtasis*) rapture.

arreglado, a [arre'ylaðo, a] *a* (*ordenado*) neat, orderly; (*moderado*) moderate, reasonable.

arreglar [arre'ylar] *vt* (*poner orden*) to tidy up; (*algo roto*) to fix, repair; (*problema*) to solve; ~se *vr* to reach an understanding; **arreglárselas** (*fam*) to get by, manage.

arreglo [a'rreylo] *nm* settlement; (*orden*) order; (*acuerdo*) agreement; (*MUS*) arrangement, setting.

arremangar [arreman'gar] *vt* to roll up, turn up; ~se *vr* to roll up one's sleeves.

arremeter [arreme'ter] *vt* to attack, assault.

arrendador, a [arrenda'ðor, a] *nm/f* landlord/lady.

arrendamiento [arrenda'mjento] *nm* letting; (*alquilar*) hiring; (*contrato*) lease; (*alquiler*) rent; **arrendar** *vt* to let, lease; to rent; **arrendatario, a** *nm/f* tenant.

arreo [a'rreo] *nm* adornment; ~s *nmpl* harness *sg*, trappings.

arrepentimiento [arrepenti'mjento] *nm* regret, repentance.

arrepentirse [arrepen'tirse] *vr* to repent; ~ de to regret.

arrestar [arres'tar] *vt* to arrest; (*encarcelar*) to imprison; **arresto** *nm* arrest; (*MIL*) detention; (*audacia*) boldness, daring; **arresto domiciliario** house arrest.

arriar [a'rrjar] *vt* (*velas*) to haul down; (*bandera*) to lower, strike; (*un cable*) to pay out.

arriba [a'rrißa] ♦ **1** *ad* (*posición*) above; desde ~ from above; ~ de todo at the very top, right on top; **Juan está** ~ Juan is upstairs; lo ~ **mencionado** the aforementioned

2 (*dirección*): calle ~ up the street

3: de ~ **abajo** from top to bottom; **mirar a uno de** ~ **abajo** to look sb up and down

4: para ~: de 5000 pesetas para ~ from 5000 pesetas up(wards)

♦ *a*: de ~: el piso de ~ the upstairs flat (*Brit*) o apartment; la parte de ~ the top o upper part

♦ *prep*: ~ de (*AM*) above; ~ de 200 pesetas more than 200 pesetas

♦ *excl*: ¡~! up!; ¡manos ~! hands up!; ¡~ España! long live Spain!

arribar [arri'ßar] *vi* to put into port; (*llegar*) to arrive.

arribista [arri'ßista] *nm/f* parvenu(e), upstart.

arriendo *etc vb ver* **arrendar** // [a'rrjendo] *nm* = **arrendamiento**.

arriero [a'rrjero] *nm* muleteer.

arriesgado, a [arrjes'yaðo, a] *a* (*peligroso*) risky; (*audaz*) bold, daring.

arriesgar [arrjes'yar] *vt* to risk; (*poner en peligro*) to endanger; ~se *vr* to take a risk.

arrimar [arri'mar] *vt* (*acercar*) to bring close; (*poner de lado*) to set aside; ~se *vr* to come close o closer; ~se a to lean on.

arrinconar [arrinko'nar] *vt* (*colocar*) to put in a corner; (*enemigo*) to corner; (*fig*) to put on one side; (*abandonar*) to push aside.

arrobado, a [arro'ßaðo, a] *a* entranced, enchanted.

arrodillarse [arroði'ʎarse] *vr* to kneel (down).

arrogancia [arro'yanθja] *nf* arrogance; **arrogante** *a* arrogant.

arrojar [arro'xar] *vt* to throw, hurl; (*humo*) to emit, give out; (*COM*) to yield, produce; ~se *vr* to throw o hurl o.s.

arrojo [a'rroxo] *nm* daring.

arrollador, a [arroʎa'ðor, a] *a* crushing, overwhelming.

arrollar [arro'ʎar] *vt* (*AUTO etc*) to run over, knock down; (*DEPORTE*) to crush.

arropar [arro'par] *vt* to cover, wrap up; ~se *vr* to wrap o.s. up.

arrostrar [arros'trar] *vt* to face (up to); ~se *vr*: ~se con uno to face up to sb.

arroyo [a'rrojo] *nm* stream; (*de la calle*) gutter.

arroz [a'rroθ] *nm* rice; ~ con leche rice pudding.

arruga [a'rruɣa] *nf* fold; (*de cara*) wrinkle; (*de vestido*) crease.

arrugar [arru'ɣar] *vt* to fold; to wrinkle; to crease; ~se *vr* to get creased.

arruinar [arrwi'nar] *vt* to ruin, wreck; ~se *vr* to be ruined, go bankrupt.

arrullar [arru'ʎar] *vi* to coo // *vt* to lull to sleep.

arrumaco [arru'mako] *nm* (*caricia*) caress; (*halago*) piece of flattery.

arsenal [arse'nal] *nm* naval dockyard; (*MIL*) arsenal.

arsénico [ar'seniko] *nm* arsenic.

arte ['arte] *nm* (*gen m en sg y siempre f en pl*) art; (*maña*) skill, guile; ~s *nfpl* arts.

artefacto [arte'fakto] *nm* appliance; (*ARQUEOLOGIA*) artefact.

arteria [ar'terja] *nf* artery.

artesanía [artesa'nia] *nf* craftsmanship; (*artículos*) handicrafts *pl*; **artesano, a** *nm/f* artisan, craftsman/woman.

ártico, a ['artiko, a] *a* Arctic // *nm*: el A~ the Arctic.

articulación [artikula'θjon] *nf* articulation; (*MED, TEC*) joint; **articulado, a** *a* articulated; jointed.

articular [artiku'lar] *vt* to articulate; to join together.

artículo [ar'tikulo] *nm* article; (*cosa*) thing, article; ~s *nmpl* goods.

artífice [ar'tifiθe] *nm/f* artist, craftsman/woman; (*fig*) architect.

artificial [artifi'θjal] *a* artificial.

artificio [arti'fiθjo] *nm* art, skill; (*artesanía*) craftsmanship; (*astucia*) cunning.

artillería [artiʎe'ria] *nf* artillery.

artillero [arti'ʎero] *nm* artilleryman, gunner.

artimaña [arti'maɲa] *nf* trap, snare; (*astucia*) cunning.

artista [ar'tista] *nm/f* (*pintor*) artist, painter; (*TEATRO*) artist, artiste; **artístico, a** *a* artistic.

artritis [ar'tritis] *nf* arthritis.

arveja [ar'βexa] *nf* (*AM*) pea.

arzobispo [arθo'βispo] *nm* archbishop.

as [as] *nm* ace.

asa ['asa] *nf* handle; (*fig*) lever.

asado [a'saðo] *nm* roast (meat); (*AM*) barbecue.

asador [asa'ðor] *nm* spit.

asadura [asa'ðura] *nf* entrails *pl*, offal.

asalariado, a [asala'rjaðo, a] *a* paid, salaried // *nm/f* wage earner.

asaltador, a [asalta'ðor, a], **asaltante** [asal'tante] *nm/f* assailant.

asaltar [asal'tar] *vt* to attack, assault; (*fig*) to assail; **asalto** *nm* attack, assault; (*DEPORTE*) round.

asamblea [asam'blea] *nf* assembly; (*reunión*) meeting.

asar [a'sar] *vt* to roast.

asbesto [as'βesto] *nm* asbestos.

ascendencia [asθen'denθja] *nf* ancestry; (*AM*) ascendancy; **de ~ francesa** of French origin.

ascender [asθen'der] *vi* (*subir*) to ascend, rise; (*ser promovido*) to gain promotion // *vt* to promote; ~ a to amount to; **ascendiente** *nm* influence // *nm/f* ancestor.

ascensión [asθen'sjon] *nf* ascent; la A~ (*REL*) the Ascension.

ascenso [as'θenso] *nm* ascent; (*promoción*) promotion.

ascensor [asθen'sor] *nm* lift (*Brit*), elevator (*US*).

ascético, a [as'θetiko, a] *a* ascetic.

asco ['asko] *nm*: ¡qué ~! how revolting *o* disgusting!; **el ajo me da ~** I hate *o* loathe garlic; **estar hecho un ~** to be filthy.

ascua ['askwa] *nf* ember; **estar en ~s** to be on tenterhooks.

aseado, a [ase'aðo, a] *a* clean; (*arreglado*) tidy; (*pulcro*) smart.

asear [ase'ar] *vt* to clean, wash; to tidy (up).

asediar [ase'ðjar] *vt* (*MIL*) to besiege, lay siege to; (*fig*) to chase, pester; **asedio** *nm* siege; (*COM*) run.

asegurado, a [aseɣu'raðo, a] *a* insured; **asegurador, a** *nm/f* insurer.

asegurar [aseɣu'rar] *vt* (*consolidar*) to secure, fasten; (*dar garantía de*) to guarantee; (*preservar*) to safeguard; (*afirmar, dar por cierto*) to assure, affirm; (*tranquilizar*) to reassure; (*tomar un seguro*) to insure; ~se *vr* to assure o.s., make sure.

asemejarse [aseme'xarse] *vr* to be alike; ~ a to be like, resemble.

asentado, a [asen'taðo, a] *a* established, settled.

asentar [asen'tar] *vt* (*sentar*) to seat, sit down; (*poner*) to place, establish; (*alisar*) to level, smooth down *o* out; (*anotar*) to note down // *vi* to be suitable, suit.

asentir [asen'tir] *vi* to assent, agree; ~ con la cabeza to nod (one's head).

aseo [a'seo] *nm* cleanliness; ~s *nmpl* toilet *sg* (*Brit*), cloakroom *sg* (*Brit*), restroom *sg* (*US*).

aséptico, a |a'septiko, a| a germ-free, free from infection.

asequible |ase'kiβle| a (precio) reasonable; (meta) attainable; (persona) approachable.

aserradero |aserra'ðero| nm sawmill; **aserrar** vt to saw.

aserrín |ase'rrin| nm sawdust.

asesinar |asesi'nar| vt to murder; (POL) to assassinate; **asesinato** nm murder; assassination.

asesino, a |ase'sino. a| nm/f murderer, killer; (POL) assassin.

asesor, a |ase'sor. a| nm/f adviser, consultant.

asesorar |aseso'rar| vt (JUR) to advise, give legal advice to; (COM) to act as consultant to; ~se con o de to take advice from, consult; ~ía vf (cargo) consultancy; (oficina) consultant's office.

asestar |ases'tar| vt (golpe) to deal, strike; (arma) to aim; (tiro) to fire.

asfalto |as'falto| nm asphalt.

asfixia |as'fiksja| nf asphyxia, suffocation.

asfixiar |asfik'sjar| vt to asphyxiate, suffocate; ~se vr to be asphyxiated, suffocate.

asgo etc vb ver **asir**.

así |a'si| ad (de esta manera) in this way, like this, thus; (aunque) although; (tan pronto como) as soon as; ~ que so; ~ como as well as; ~ y todo even so; ¿no es ~? isn't it?, didn't you? etc; ~ de grande this big.

Asia |'asja| nf Asia; **asiático, a** a, nm/f Asian, Asiatic.

asidero |asi'ðero| nm handle.

asiduidad |asiðwi'ðað| nf assiduousness; **asiduo, a** a assiduous; (frecuente) frequent // nm/f regular (customer).

asiento |a'sjento| nm (mueble) seat, chair; (de coche, en tribunal etc) seat; (localidad) seat, place; (fundamento) site; ~ delantero/trasero front/back seat.

asignación |asiɣna'θjon| nf (atribución) assignment; (reparto) allocation; (sueldo) salary; ~ (semanal) pocket money.

asignar |asiɣ'nar| vt to assign, allocate.

asignatura |asiɣna'tura| nf subject; course.

asilado, a |asi'laðo. a| nm/f inmate; (POL) refugee.

asilo |a'silo| nm (refugio) asylum, refuge; (establecimiento) home, institution; ~ político political asylum.

asimilación |asimila'θjon| nf assimilation.

asimilar |asimi'lar| vt to assimilate.

asimismo |asi'mismo| ad in the same way, likewise.

asir |a'sir| vt to seize, grasp.

asistencia |asis'tenθja| nf audience; (MED) attendance; (ayuda) assistance;

asistente nm/f assistant; los ~s those present.

asistido, a |asis'tiðo. a| a: ~ por ordenador computer-assisted.

asistir |asis'tir| vt to assist, help // vi: ~ a to attend, be present at.

asma |'asma| nf asthma.

asno |'asno| nm donkey; (fig) ass.

asociación |asoθja'θjon| nf association; (COM) partnership; **asociado, a** a associate // nm/f associate; (COM) partner.

asociar |aso'θjar| vt to associate.

asolar |aso'lar| vt to destroy.

asolear |asole'ar| vt to put in the sun; ~se vr to sunbathe.

asomar |aso'mar| vt to show, stick out // vi to appear; ~se vr to appear, show up; ~ la cabeza por la ventana to put one's head out of the window.

asombrar |asom'brar| vt to amaze, astonish; ~se vr (sorprenderse) to be amazed; (asustarse) to get a fright; **asombro** nm amazement, astonishment; (susto) fright; **asombroso, a** a astonishing, amazing.

asomo |a'somo| nm hint, sign.

aspa |'aspa| nf (cruz) cross; (de molino) sail; en ~ X-shaped.

aspaviento |aspa'βjento| nm exaggerated display of feeling; (fam) fuss.

aspecto |as'pekto| nm (apariencia) look, appearance; (fig) aspect.

aspereza |aspe'reθa| nf roughness; (agrura) sourness; (de carácter) surliness; **áspero, a** a rough; bitter, sour; harsh.

aspersión |asper'sjon| nf sprinkling.

aspiración |aspira'θjon| nf breath, inhalation; (MUS) short pause; aspiraciones nfpl aspirations.

aspiradora |aspira'ðora| nf vacuum cleaner, Hoover ®.

aspirante |aspi'rante| nm/f (candidato) candidate; (DEPORTE) contender.

aspirar |aspi'rar| vt to breathe in // vi: ~ a to aspire to.

aspirina |aspi'rina| nf aspirin.

asquear |aske'ar| vt to sicken // vi to be sickening; ~se vr to feel disgusted; **asqueroso, a** a disgusting, sickening.

asta |'asta| nf lance; (arpón) spear; (mango) shaft, handle; (ZOOL) horn; a media ~ at half mast.

astado, a |as'taðo. a| a horned // nm bull.

asterisco |aste'risko| nm asterisk.

astilla |as'tiʎa| nf splinter; (pedacito) chip; ~s nfpl firewood sg.

astillero |asti'ʎero| nm shipyard.

astringente |astrin'xente| a, nm astringent.

astro |'astro| nm star.

astrología |astrolo'xia| nf astrology; **as-**

trólogo, a *nm/f* astrologer.

astronauta [astro'nauta] *nm/f* astronaut.

astronave [astro'naβe] *nm* spaceship.

astronomía [astrono'mia] *nf* astronomy; **astrónomo, a** *nm/f* astronomer.

astucia [as'tuθja] *nf* astuteness; (*ardid*) clever trick; **astuto, a** *a* astute; (*taimado*) cunning.

asueto [a'sweto] *nm* holiday; (*tiempo libre*) time off *q*.

asumir [asu'mir] *vt* to assume.

asunción [asun'θjon] *nf* assumption; (*REL*): A~ Assumption.

asunto [a'sunto] *nm* (*tema*) matter, subject, (*negocio*) business.

asustar [asus'tar] *vt* to frighten; ~se *vr* to be/become frightened.

atacar [ata'kar] *vt* to attack.

atadura [ata'ðura] *nf* bond, tie.

atajo [a'taxo] *nm* short cut; (*DEPORTE*) tackle.

atañer [ata'ɲer] *vi*: ~ a to concern.

ataque *etc vb ver* atacar // [a'take] *nm* attack; ~ **cardíaco** heart attack.

atar [a'tar] *vt* to tie, tie up.

atardecer [atarðe'θer] *vi* to get dark // *nm* evening; (*crepúsculo*) dusk.

atareado, a [atare'aðo, a] *a* busy.

atascar [atas'kar] *vt* to clog up; (*obstruir*) to jam; (*fig*) to hinder; ~se *vr* to stall; (*cañería*) to get blocked up; **atasco** *nm* obstruction; (*AUTO*) traffic jam.

ataúd [ata'uð] *nm* coffin.

ataviar [ata'βjar] *vt* to deck, array; ~se *vr* to dress up.

atavío [ata'βio] *nm* attire, dress; ~s *nmpl* finery *sg*.

atemorizar [atemori'θar] *vt* to frighten, scare; ~se *vr* to get scared.

Atenas [a'tenas] *n* Athens.

atención [aten'θjon] *nf* attention; (*bondad*) kindness // *excl* (be) careful!, look out!

atender [aten'der] *vt* to attend to, look after // *vi* to pay attention.

atenerse [ate'nerse] *vr*: ~ a to abide by, adhere to.

atentado [aten'taðo] *nm* crime, illegal act; (*asalto*) assault; ~ **contra la vida de uno** attempt on sb's life.

atentamente [atenta'mente] *ad*: Le saluda ~ Yours faithfully.

atentar [aten'tar] *vi*: ~ a o **contra** to commit an outrage against.

atento, a [a'tento, a] *a* attentive, observant; (*cortés*) polite, thoughtful.

atenuante [ate'nwante] *a* attenuating, extenuating.

atenuar [ate'nwar] *vt* to attenuate; (*disminuir*) to lessen, minimize.

ateo, a [a'teo, a] *a* atheistic // *nm/f* atheist.

aterciopelado, a [aterθjope'laðo, a] *a* velvety.

aterido, a [ate'riðo, a] *a*: ~ **de frío** frozen stiff.

aterrador, a [aterra'ðor, a] *a* frightening.

aterrar [ate'rrar] *vt* to frighten; to terrify; ~se *vr* to be frightened; to be terrified.

aterrizaje [aterri'θaxe] *nm* (*AVIAT*) landing.

aterrizar [aterri'θar] *vi* to land.

aterrorizar [aterrori'θar] *vt* to terrify.

atesorar [ateso'rar] *vt* to hoard, store up.

atestado, a [ates'taðo, a] *a* packed // *nm* (*JUR*) affidavit.

atestar [ates'tar] *vt* to pack, stuff; (*JUR*) to attest, testify to.

atestiguar [atesti'γwar] *vt* to testify to, bear witness to.

atiborrar [atiβo'rrar] *vt* to fill, stuff; ~se *vr* to stuff o.s.

ático ['atiko] *nm* attic; ~ **de lujo** penthouse (flat (*Brit*) o apartment).

atildar [atil'dar] *vt* to criticize; ~se *vr* to spruce o.s. up.

atinado, a [ati'naðo, a] *a* (*sensato*) wise; (*correcto*) right, correct.

atisbar [atis'βar] *vt* to spy on; (*echar una ojeada*) to peep at.

atizar [ati'θar] *vt* to poke; (*horno etc*) to stoke; (*fig*) to stir up, rouse.

atlántico, a [at'lantiko, a] *a* Atlantic // *nm*: el (**océano**) A~ the Atlantic (Ocean).

atlas ['atlas] *nm* atlas.

atleta [at'leta] *nm* athlete; **atlético, a** *a* athletic; **atletismo** *nm* athletics *sg*.

atmósfera [at'mosfera] *nf* atmosphere.

atolondramiento [atolondra'mjento] *nm* bewilderment; (*insensatez*) silliness.

atollar [ato'ʎar] *vi*, **atollarse** *vr* to get stuck; (*fig*) to get into a jam.

atómico, a [a'tomiko, a] *a* atomic.

atomizador [atomiθa'ðor] *nm* atomizer; (*de perfume*) spray.

átomo ['atomo] *nm* atom.

atónito, a [a'tonito, a] *a* astonished, amazed.

atontado, a [aton'taðo, a] *a* stunned; (*bobo*) silly, daft.

atontar [aton'tar] *vt* to stun; ~se *vr* to become confused.

atormentar [atormen'tar] *vt* to torture; (*molestar*) to torment; (*acosar*) to plague, harass.

atornillar [atorni'ʎar] *vt* to screw on o down.

atracador, a [atraka'ðor, a] *nm/f* robber.

atracar [atra'kar] *vt* (*NAUT*) to moor; (*robar*) to hold up, rob // *vi* to moor; ~se *vr*: ~se (**de**) to stuff o.s. (with).

atracción [atrak'θjon] *nf* attraction.

atraco [a'trako] *nm* holdup, robbery.

atractivo, a [atrak'tiβo, a] *a* attractive // *nm* attraction; (*belleza*) attractiveness.

atraer [atra'er] *vt* to attract.

atragantarse [atraɣan'tarse] *vr*: ~ (**con**)

to choke (on); **se me ha atragantado el chico** I can't stand the boy.

atrancar [atran'kar] vt (puerta) to bar, bolt.

atrapar [atra'par] vt to trap; (resfriado etc) to catch.

atrás [a'tras] ad (movimiento) back(wards); (lugar) behind; (tiempo) previously; **ir hacia ~** to go back(wards); **to go to the rear; estar ~** to be behind o at the back.

atrasado, a [atra'saðo, a] a slow; (pago) overdue, late; (país) backward.

atrasar [atra'sar] vi to be slow; **~se** vr to remain behind; (tren) to be o run late; **atraso** nm slowness; lateness, delay; (de país) backwardness; **atrasos** nmpl arrears.

atravesar [atraβe'sar] vt (cruzar) to cross (over); (traspasar) to pierce; to go through; (poner al través) to lay o put across; **~se** vr to come in between; (intervenir) to interfere.

atravieso etc vb ver **atravesar**.

atrayente [atra'jente] a attractive.

atreverse [atre'βerse] vr to dare; (insolentarse) to be insolent; **atrevido, a** a daring; insolent; **atrevimiento** nm daring; insolence.

atribución [atriβu'θjon] nf: **atribuciones** (POL) powers; (ADMIN) responsibilities.

atribuir [atriβu'ir] vt to attribute; (funciones) to confer.

atribular [atriβu'lar] vt to afflict, distress.

atributo [atri'βuto] nm attribute.

atrocidad [atroθi'ðað] nf atrocity, outrage.

atropellar [atrope'ʎar] vt (derribar) to knock over o down; (empujar) to push (aside); (AUTO) to run over, run down; (agraviar) to insult; **~se** vr to act hastily; **atropello** nm (AUTO) accident; (empujón) push; (agravio) wrong; (atrocidad) outrage.

atroz [a'troθ] a atrocious, awful.

atto, a abr = **atento**.

atuendo [a'twendo] nm attire.

atún [a'tun] nm tuna.

aturdir [atur'ðir] vt to stun; (de ruido) to deafen; (fig) to dumbfound, bewilder.

atusar [atu'sar] vt to smooth (down).

audacia [au'ðaθja] nf boldness, audacity; **audaz** a bold, audacious.

audible [au'ðiβle] a audible.

audición [auði'θjon] nf hearing; (TEATRO) audition.

audiencia [au'ðjenθja] nf audience; A~ (JUR) High Court.

auditor [auði'tor] nm (JUR) judge-advocate; (COM) auditor.

auditorio [auði'torjo] nm audience; (sala) auditorium.

auge ['auxe] nm boom; (clímax) climax.

augurar [auɣu'rar] vt to predict; (presagiar) to portend.

augurio [au'ɣurjo] nm omen.

aula ['aula] nf classroom; (en universidad etc) lecture room.

aullar [au'ʎar] vi to howl, yell.

aullido [au'ʎiðo] nm howl, yell.

aumentar [aumen'tar] vt to increase; (precios) to put up; (producción) to step up; (con microscopio, anteojos) to magnify // vi, **~se** vr to increase, be on the increase; **aumento** nm increase; rise.

aun [a'un] ad even; **~ así** even so; **~ más** even o yet more.

aún [a'un] ad: **~ está aquí** he's still here; **~ no lo sabemos** we don't know yet; **¿no ha venido ~?** hasn't she come yet?

aunque [a'unke] conj though, although, even though.

aúpa [a'upa] excl come on!

aureola [aure'ola] nf halo.

auricular [auriku'lar] nm (TEL) earpiece, receiver; **~es** nmpl headphones.

aurora [au'rora] nf dawn.

auscultar [auskul'tar] vt (MED: pecho) to listen to, sound.

ausencia [au'senθja] nf absence.

ausentarse [ausen'tarse] vr to go away; (por poco tiempo) to go out.

ausente [au'sente] a absent.

auspicios [aus'piθjos] nmpl auspices; (protección) protection sg.

austeridad [austeri'ðað] nf austerity; **austero, a** a austere.

austral [aus'tral] a southern // nm monetary unit of Argentina.

Australia [aus'tralja] nf Australia; **australiano, a** a, nm/f Australian.

Austria ['austrja] nf Austria; **austríaco, a** a, nm/f Austrian.

autenticar [autenti'kar] vt to authenticate; **auténtico, a** a authentic.

auto ['auto] nm (JUR) edict, decree; (: orden) writ; (AUTO) car; **~s** nmpl (JUR) proceedings; (: acta) court record sg.

autoadhesivo [autoaðe'siβo] a self-adhesive; (sobre) self-sealing.

autobiografía [autoβjoɣra'fia] nf autobiography.

autobús [auto'βus] nm bus.

autocar [auto'kar] nm coach (Brit), (passenger) bus (US).

autóctono, a [au'toktono, a] a native, indigenous.

autodefensa [autoðe'fensa] nf self-defence.

autodeterminación [autoðetermina'θjon] nf self-determination.

autoescuela [autoes'kwela] nf driving school.

autógrafo [au'toɣrafo] nm autograph.

automación [automa'θjon] nf = **automatización**.

autómata [au'tomata] nm automaton.

automático, a [auto'matiko, a] a automatic // nm press stud.

automatización [automatiθa'θjon] *nf* automation

automotor, triz [automo'tor, 'triθ] *a* self-propelled // *nm* diesel train.

automóvil [auto'moβil] *nm* (motor) car (*Brit*), automobile (*US*); **automovilismo** *nm* (*actividad*) motoring; (*DEPORTE*) (sports)car racing; **automovilista** *nm/f* motorist, driver; **automovilístico, a** *a* (*industria*) car *cpd*.

autonomía [autono'mia] *nf* autonomy; **autónomo, a, autonómico, a** (*Esp POL*) *a* autonomous.

autopista [auto'pista] *nf* motorway (*Brit*), freeway (*US*).

autopsia [au'topsja] *nf* autopsy, post-mortem.

autor, a [au'tor, a] *nm/f* author.

autoridad [autori'ðað] *nf* authority; **autoritario, a** *a* authoritarian.

autorización [autoriθa'θjon] *nf* authorization; **autorizado, a** *a* authorized; (*aprobado*) approved.

autorizar [autori'θar] *vt* to authorize; (*aprobar*) to approve.

autorretrato [autorre'trato] *nm* self-portrait.

autoservicio [autoser'βiθjo] *nm* (*tienda*) self-service shop (*Brit*) *o* store (*US*); (*restaurante*) self-service restaurant.

autostop [auto'stop] *nm* hitch-hiking; **hacer ~** to hitch-hike; **~ista** *nm/f* hitch-hiker.

autosuficiencia [autosufi'θjenθja] *nf* self-sufficiency.

autovía [auto'βia] *nf* ≈ A-road (*Brit*), state highway (*US*).

auxiliar [auksi'ljar] *vt* to help // *nm/f* assistant; **auxilio** *nm* assistance, help; **primeros auxilios** first aid *sg*.

Av *abr* (= *Avenida*) Av(e).

aval [a'βal] *nm* guarantee; (*persona*) guarantor.

avalancha [aβa'lantʃa] *nf* avalanche.

avance [a'βanθe] *nm* advance; (*pago*) advance payment; (*CINE*) trailer.

avanzar [aβan'θar] *vt, vi* to advance.

avaricia [aβa'riθja] *nf* avarice, greed; **avaricioso, a** *a* avaricious, greedy.

avaro, a [a'βaro, a] *a* miserly, mean // *nm/f* miser.

avasallar [aβasa'ʎar] *vt* to subdue, subjugate.

Avda *abr* (= *Avenida*) Av(e).

ave ['aβe] *nf* bird; **~ de rapiña** bird of prey.

avecinarse [aβeθi'narse] *vr* (*tormenta*, *fig*) to be on the way.

avellana [aβe'ʎana] *nf* hazelnut; **avellano** *nm* hazel tree.

avemaría [aβema'ria] *nm* Hail Mary, Ave Maria.

avena [a'βena] *nf* oats *pl*.

avenida [aβe'niða] *nf* (*calle*) avenue.

avenir [aβe'nir] *vt* to reconcile; **~se** *vr* to come to an agreement, reach a compromise.

aventajado, a [aβenta'xaðo, a] *a* outstanding.

aventajar [aβenta'xar] *vt* (*sobrepasar*) to surpass, outstrip.

aventar [aβen'tar] *vt* to fan, blow; (*grano*) to winnow.

aventura [aβen'tura] *nf* adventure; **aventurado, a** *a* risky; **aventurero, a** *a* adventurous.

avergonzar [aβerɣon'θar] *vt* to shame; (*desconcertar*) to embarrass; **~se** *vr* to be ashamed; to be embarrassed.

avería [aβe'ria] *nf* (*TEC*) breakdown, fault.

averiado, a [aβe'rjaðo, a] *a* broken down; '**~**' 'out of order'.

averiguación [aβeriɣwa'θjon] *nf* investigation; (*descubrimiento*) ascertainment.

averiguar [aβeri'ɣwar] *vt* to investigate; (*descubrir*) to find out, ascertain.

aversión [aβer'sjon] *nf* aversion, dislike.

avestruz [aβes'truθ] *nm* ostrich.

aviación [aβja'θjon] *nf* aviation; (*fuerzas aéreas*) air force.

aviador, a [aβja'ðor, a] *nm/f* aviator, airman/woman.

aviar [a'βjar] *vt* to prepare; **estar aviado** (*fig*) to be in a mess.

avicultura [aβikul'tura] *nf* poultry farming.

avidez [aβi'ðeθ] *nf* avidity, eagerness; **ávido, a** *a* avid, eager.

avinagrado, a [aβina'ɣraðo, a] *a* sour, acid.

avinagrarse [aβina'ɣrarse] *vr* to go *o* turn sour.

avío [a'βio] *nm* preparation; **~s** *nmpl* gear *sg*, kit *sg*.

avión [a'βjon] *nm* aeroplane; (*ave*) martin; **~ de reacción** jet (plane).

avioneta [aβjo'neta] *nf* light aircraft.

avisar [aβi'sar] *vt* (*advertir*) to warn, notify; (*informar*) to tell; (*aconsejar*) to advise, counsel; **aviso** *nm* warning; (*noticia*) notice.

avispa [a'βispa] *nf* wasp.

avispado, a [aβis'paðo, a] *a* sharp, clever.

avispero [aβis'pero] *nm* wasp's nest.

avispón [aβis'pon] *nm* hornet.

avistar [aβis'tar] *vt* to sight, spot.

avituallar [aβitwa'ʎar] *vt* to supply with food.

avivar [aβi'βar] *vt* to strengthen, intensify; **~se** *vr* to revive, acquire new life.

axila [ak'sila] *nf* armpit.

axioma [ak'sjoma] *nm* axiom.

ay [ai] *excl* (*dolor*) ow!, ouch!; (*aflicción*) oh!, oh dear!; **¡~ de mí!** poor me!

aya ['aja] *nf* governess; (*niñera*) nanny.

ayer |a'jer| *ad, nm* yesterday; **antes de ~** the day before yesterday.

ayo |'ajo| *nm* tutor.

ayote |a'jote| *nm* (*AM*) pumpkin.

ayuda |a'juða| *nf* help, assistance // *nm* page; **ayudante, a** *nm/f* assistant, helper; (*ESCOL*) assistant; (*MIL*) adjutant.

ayudar |aju'ðar| *vt* to help, assist.

ayunar |aju'nar| *vi* to fast; **ayunas** *nfpl:* **estar en ayunas** (*no haber comido*) to be fasting; (*ignorar*) to be in the dark; **ayuno** *nm* fasting.

ayuntamiento |ajunta'mjento| *nm* (*consejo*) town (*o* city) council; (*edificio*) town (*o* city) hall.

azabache |aθa'βatʃe| *nm* jet.

azada |a'θaða| *nf* hoe.

azafata |aθa'fata| *nf* air stewardess.

azafrán |aθa'fran| *nm* saffron.

azahar |aθa'ar| *nm* orange/lemon blossom.

azar |a'θar| *nm* (*casualidad*) chance, fate; (*desgracia*) misfortune, accident; **por ~** by chance; **al ~** at random.

azogue |a'θoɣe| *nm* mercury.

azoramiento |aθora'mjento| *nm* alarm; (*confusión*) confusion.

azorar |aθo'rar| *vt* to alarm; **~se** *vr* to get alarmed.

Azores |a'θores| *nfpl:* **las ~** the Azores.

azotar |aθo'tar| *vt* to whip, beat; (*pegar*) to spank; **azote** *nm* (*látigo*) whip; (*latigazo*) lash, stroke; (*en las nalgas*) spank; (*calamidad*) calamity.

azotea |aθo'tea| *nf* (flat) roof.

azteca |aθ'teka| *a, nm/f* Aztec.

azúcar |a'θukar| *nm* sugar; **azucarado, a** *a* sugary, sweet.

azucarero, a |aθuka'rero, a| *a* sugar *cpd* // *nm* sugar bowl.

azucena |aθu'θena| *nf* white lily.

azufre |a'θufre| *nm* sulphur.

azul |a'θul| *a, nm* blue.

azulejo |aθu'lexo| *nm* tile.

azuzar |aθu'θar| *vt* to incite, egg on.

B

B.A. *abr* (= *Buenos Aires*) B.A.

baba |'baβa| *nf* spittle, saliva; **babear** *vi* to drool, slaver.

babel |ba'βel| *nm o f* bedlam.

babero |ba'βero| *nm* bib.

babor |ba'βor| *nm* port (side).

baboso, a |ba'βoso, a| *a* (*AM fam*) silly.

babucha |ba'βutʃa| *nf* slipper.

baca |'baka| *nf* (*AUTO*) luggage *o* roof rack.

bacalao |baka'lao| *nm* cod(fish).

bacinica |baθi'nika| *nf,* **bacinilla** |baθi'niʎa| *nf* chamber pot.

bacteria |bak'terja| *nf* bacterium, germ.

báculo |'bakulo| *nm* stick, staff.

bache |'batʃe| *nm* pothole, rut; (*fig*) bad patch.

bachillerato |batʃiʎe'rato| *nm* (*ESCOL*) school-leaving examination (*Brit*), bachelor's degree (*US*), baccalaureate (*US*).

bagaje |ba'ɣaxe| *nm* baggage, luggage.

bagatela |baɣa'tela| *nf* trinket, trifle.

Bahama |ba'ama|: **las (Islas) ~** the Bahamas.

bahía |ba'ia| *nf* bay.

bailar |bai'lar| *vt, vi* to dance; **~ín, ina** *nm/f* (*ballet*) dancer; **baile** *nm* dance; (*formal*) ball.

baja |'baxa| *nf ver* **bajo.**

bajada |ba'xaða| *nf* descent; (*camino*) slope; (*de aguas*) ebb.

bajamar |baxa'mar| *nf* low tide.

bajar |ba'xar| *vi* to go down, come down; (*temperatura, precios*) to drop, fall // *vt* (*cabeza*) to bow, bend; (*escalera*) to go down, come down; (*precio, voz*) to lower; (*llevar abajo*) to take down; **~se** *vr* to get out of; to get off; **~ de** (*coche*) to get out of; (*autobus*) to get off.

bajeza |ba'xeθa| *nf* baseness *q*; (*una ~*) vile deed.

bajío |ba'xio| *nm* shoal, sandbank; (*AM*) lowlands *pl.*

bajo, a |'baxo, a| *a* (*mueble, número, precio*) low; (*piso*) ground; (*de estatura*) small, short; (*color*) pale; (*sonido*) faint, soft, low; (*voz: en tono*) deep; (*metal*) base; (*humilde*) low, humble // *ad* (*hablar*) softly, quietly; (*volar*) low // *prep* under, below, underneath // *nm* (*MUS*) bass // *nf* drop, fall; (*MIL*) casualty; **~ la lluvia** in the rain; **dar de baja** (*soldado*) to discharge; (*empleado*) to dismiss, sack.

bajón |ba'xon| *nm* fall, drop.

bala |'bala| *nf* bullet.

baladí |bala'ði| *a* trivial.

baladronada |balaðro'naða| *nf* (*dicho*) boast, brag; (*hecho*) piece of bravado.

balance |ba'lanθe| *nm* (*COM*) balance; (: *libro*) balance sheet; (: *cuenta general*) stocktaking.

balancear |balanθe'ar| *vt* to balance // *vi,* **~se** *vr* to swing (to and fro); (*vacilar*) to hesitate; **balanceo** *nm* swinging.

balanza |ba'lanθa| *nf* scales *pl,* balance; **~ comercial** balance of trade; **~ de pagos** balance of payments; (*ASTROLOGIA*) **B~** Libra.

balar |ba'lar| *vi* to bleat.

balaustrada |balaus'traða| *nf* balustrade; (*pasamanos*) banisters *pl.*

balazo |ba'laθo| *nm* (*golpe*) shot; (*herida*) bullet wound.

balbucear |balβuθe'ar| *vi, vt* to stammer, stutter; **balbuceo** *nm* stammering, stuttering.

balbucir |balβu'θir| *vi, vt* to stammer, stutter.

balcón [bal'kon] *nm* balcony.

baldar [bal'dar] *vt* to cripple.

balde ['balde] *nm* bucket, pail; **de ~** *ad* (for) free, for nothing; **en ~** *ad* in vain.

baldío, a [bal'dio, a] *a* uncultivated; (*terreno*) waste // *nm* waste land.

baldosa [bal'dosa] *nf* (*azulejo*) floor tile; (*grande*) flagstone.

Baleares [bale'ares] *nfpl*: **las (Islas) ~** the Balearic Islands.

balido [ba'liðo] *nm* bleat, bleating.

balín [ba'lin] *nm* pellet; **balines** *nmpl* buckshot *sg*.

balística [ba'listika] *nf* ballistics *pl*.

baliza [ba'liθa] *nf* (*AVIAT*) beacon; (*NAUT*) buoy.

balneario, a [balne'arjo, a] *a*: **estación balnearia** (bathing) resort // *nm* spa, health resort.

balón [ba'lon] *nm* ball.

baloncesto [balon'θesto] *nm* basketball.

balonmano [balon'mano] *nm* handball.

balonvolea [balombo'lea] *nm* volleyball.

balsa ['balsa] *nf* raft; (*BOT*) balsa wood.

bálsamo ['balsamo] *nm* balsam, balm.

baluarte [ba'lwarte] *nm* bastion, bulwark.

ballena [ba'ʎena] *nf* whale.

ballesta [ba'ʎesta] *nf* crossbow; (*AUTO*) spring.

ballet [ba'le] *nm* ballet.

bambolear [bambole'ar] *vi*, **bambolearse** *vr* to swing, sway; (*silla*) to wobble; **bamboleo** *nm* swinging, swaying; wobbling.

bambú [bam'bu] *nm* bamboo.

banana [ba'nana] *nf* (*AM*) banana; **banano** *nm* (*AM*) banana tree.

banca ['banka] *nf* (*asiento*) bench; (*COM*) banking.

bancario, a [ban'karjo, a] *a* banking *cpd*, bank *cpd*.

bancarrota [banka'rrota] *nf* bankruptcy; **hacer ~** to go bankrupt.

banco ['banko] *nm* bench; (*ESCOL*) desk; (*COM*) bank; (*GEO*) stratum; **~ de crédito/de ahorros** credit/savings bank; **~ de arena** sandbank; **~ de hielo** iceberg.

banda ['banda] *nf* band; (*pandilla*) gang; (*NAUT*) side, edge; **la B~ Oriental** Uruguay; **~ sonora** soundtrack.

bandada [ban'daða] *nf* (*de pájaros*) flock; (*de peces*) shoal.

bandeja [ban'dexa] *nf* tray.

bandera [ban'dera] *nf* (*de tela*) flag; (*estandarte*) banner.

banderilla [bande'riʎa] *nf* banderilla.

banderín [bande'rin] *nm* pennant, small flag.

banderola [bande'rola] *nf* banderole; (*MIL*) pennant.

bandido [ban'diðo] *nm* bandit.

bando ['bando] *nm* (*edicto*) edict, proclamation; (*facción*) faction; **los ~s** the banns.

bandolero [bando'lero] *nm* bandit, brigand.

banquero [ban'kero] *nm* banker.

banqueta [ban'keta] *nf* stool; (*AM*: *en la calle*) pavement (*Brit*), sidewalk (*US*).

banquete [ban'kete] *nm* banquet; (*para convidados*) formal dinner.

banquillo [ban'kiʎo] *nm* (*JUR*) dock, prisoner's bench; (*banco*) bench; (*para los pies*) footstool.

bañador [bapa'ðor] *nm* swimming costume (*Brit*), bathing suit (*US*).

bañar [ba'par] *vt* to bath, bathe; (*objeto*) to dip; (*de barniz*) to coat; **~se** *vr* (*en el mar*) to bathe, swim; (*en la bañera*) to bath, have a bath.

bañera [ba'pera] *nf* bath(tub).

bañero [ba'pero] *nm* lifeguard.

bañista [ba'pista] *nm/f* bather.

baño ['bapo] *nm* (*en bañera*) bath; (*en río*) dip, swim; (*cuarto*) bathroom; (*bañera*) bath(tub); (*capa*) coating.

baptista [bap'tista] *nm/f* Baptist.

baqueta [ba'keta] *nf* (*MUS*) drumstick.

bar [bar] *nm* bar.

barahúnda [bara'unda] *nf* uproar, hubbub.

baraja [ba'raxa] *nf* pack (of cards); **barajar** *vt* (*naipes*) to shuffle; (*fig*) to jumble up.

baranda [ba'randa], **barandilla** [baran'diʎa] *nf* rail, railing.

baratija [bara'tixa] *nf* trinket.

baratillo [bara'tiʎo] *nm* (*tienda*) junkshop; (*subasta*) bargain sale; (*conjunto de cosas*) secondhand goods *pl*.

barato, a [ba'rato, a] *a* cheap // *ad* cheap, cheaply.

baraúnda [bara'unda] *nf* = **barahúnda**.

barba ['barβa] *nf* (*mentón*) chin; (*pelo*) beard.

barbacoa [barβa'koa] *nf* (*parrilla*) barbecue; (*carne*) barbecued meat.

barbaridad [barβari'ðað] *nf* barbarity; (*acto*) barbarism; (*atrocidad*) outrage; **una ~** (*fam*) loads *pl*; **¡qué ~!** (*fam*) how awful!

barbarie [bar'βarje] *nf*, **barbarismo** [barβa'rismo] *nm* barbarism, savagery; (*crueldad*) barbarity.

bárbaro, a ['barβaro, a] *a* barbarous, cruel; (*grosero*) rough, uncouth // *nm/f* barbarian // *ad*: **lo pasamos ~** (*fam*) we had a great time; **¡qué ~!** (*fam*) how marvellous!; **un éxito ~** (*fam*) a terrific success; **es un tipo ~** (*fam*) he's a great bloke.

barbecho [bar'βetʃo] *nm* fallow land.

barbero [bar'βero] *nm* barber, hairdresser.

barbilampiño [barβilam'pipo] *a* cleanshaven, smooth-faced; (*fig*) inexperienced.

barbilla [bar'βiʎa] *nf* chin, tip of the chin.

barbo ['barβo] *nm*: **~ de mar** red mullet.

barbotar |barßo'tar|, **barbotear**
|barßote'ar| *vt, vi* to mutter, mumble.
barbudo, a |bar'ßuðo, a| *a* bearded.
barca |'barka| *nf* (small) boat; ~
pesquera fishing boat; ~ de pasaje
ferry; **~za** *nf* barge; **~za** de des-
embarco landing craft.
Barcelona |barθe'lona| *nf* Barcelona.
barcelonés, esa |barθelo'nes, esa| *a* of *o*
from Barcelona.
barco |'barko| *nm* boat; (*buque*) ship; ~
de carga cargo boat.
barítono |ba'ritono| *nm* baritone.
barman |'barman| *nm* barman.
Barna. *abr* = **Barcelona.**
barniz |bar'niθ| *nm* varnish; (*en la loza*)
glaze; (*fig*) veneer; **~ar** *vt* to varnish;
(*loza*) to glaze.
barómetro |ba'rometro| *nm* barometer.
barquero |bar'kero| *nm* boatman.
barquillo |bar'kiʎo| *nm* cone, cornet.
barra |'barra| *nf* bar, rod; (*de un bar,
café*) bar; (*de pan*) French loaf;
(*palanca*) lever; ~ de carmín *o* de labios
lipstick.
barraca |ba'rraka| *nf* hut, cabin.
barranca |ba'rranka| *nf* ravine, gully;
barranco *nm* ravine; (*fig*) difficulty.
barrena |ba'rrena| *nf* drill; **barrenar** *vt*
to drill (through), bore; **barreno** *nm*
large drill.
barrer |ba'rrer| *vt* to sweep; (*quitar*) to
sweep away.
barrera |ba'rrera| *nf* barrier.
barriada |ba'rrjaða| *nf* quarter, district.
barricada |barri'kaða| *nf* barricade.
barrido |ba'rriðo| *nm*, **barrida** |ba'rriða|
nf sweep, sweeping.
barriga |ba'rriɣa| *nf* belly; (*panza*)
paunch; **barrigón, ona, barrigudo, a** *a*
potbellied.
barril |ba'rril| *nm* barrel, cask.
barrio |'barrjo| *nm* (*vecindad*) area,
neighborhood (*US*); (*en las afueras*) suburb; ~ chino red-light district.
barro |'barro| *nm* (*lodo*) mud; (*objetos*)
earthenware; (*MED*) pimple.
barroco, a |ba'rroko, a| *a, nm* baroque.
barrote |ba'rrote| *nm* (*de ventana*) bar.
barruntar |barrun'tar| *vt* (*conjeturar*) to
guess; (*presentir*) to suspect; **barrunto**
nm guess; suspicion.
bartola |bar'tola|: a la ~ *ad*: tirarse a la
~ to take it easy, be lazy.
bártulos |'bartulos| *nmpl* things, belong-
ings.
barullo |ba'ruʎo| *nm* row, uproar.
basamento |basa'mento| *nm* base,
plinth.
basar |ba'sar| *vt* to base; **~se** *vr*: **~se** en
to be based on.
basca |'baska| *nf* nausea.
báscula |'baskula| *nf* (platform) scales
pl.
base |'base| *nf* base; a ~ de on the basis

of; (*mediante*) by means of; ~ de datos
(*INFORM*) database.
básico, a |'basiko, a| *a* basic.
basílica |ba'silika| *nf* basilica.
bastante |bas'tante| ♦ *a* **1** (*suficiente*)
enough; ~ dinero enough *o* sufficient
money; **~s** libros enough books
2 (*valor intensivo*): ~ gente quite a lot
of people; tener ~ calor to be rather hot
♦ *ad*: ~ bueno/malo quite good/rather
bad; ~ rico pretty rich; (lo) ~
inteligente (como) para hacer algo
clever enough *o* sufficiently clever to do
sth.
bastar |bas'tar| *vi* to be enough *o*
sufficient; **~se** *vr* to be self-sufficient; ~
para to be enough to; ¡basta! (that's)
enough!
bastardilla |bastar'ðiʎa| *nf* italics *pl.*
bastardo, a |bas'tarðo, a| *a, nm/f*
bastard.
bastidor |basti'ðor| *nm* frame; (*de
coche*) chassis; (*TEATRO*) wing; **entre
~es** (*fig*) behind the scenes.
basto, a |'basto, a| *a* coarse, rough; **~s**
nmpl (*NAIPES*) ≈ clubs.
bastón |bas'ton| *nm* stick, staff; (*para
pasear*) walking stick.
basura |ba'sura| *nf* rubbish (*Brit*), gar-
bage (*US*).
basurero |basu'rero| *nm* (*hombre*) dust-
man (*Brit*), garbage man (*US*); (*lugar*)
dump; (*cubo*) (rubbish) bin (*Brit*), trash
can (*US*).
bata |'bata| *nf* (*gen*) dressing gown; (*cu-
bretodo*) smock, overall; (*MED, TEC etc*)
lab(oratory) coat.
batalla |ba'taʎa| *nf* battle; de ~ for
everyday use.
batallar |bata'ʎar| *vi* to fight.
batallón |bata'ʎon| *nm* battalion.
batata |ba'tata| *nf* (*AM*) sweet potato.
bate |'bate| *nm* bat; **~ador** *nm* (*AM*)
batter, batsman.
batería |bate'ria| *nf* battery; (*MUS*)
drums *pl*; ~ de cocina kitchen utensils
pl.
batido, a |ba'tiðo, a| *a* (*camino*) beaten,
well-trodden // *nm* (*CULIN*): ~ (de leche)
milk shake.
batidora |bati'ðora| *nf* beater, mixer; ~
eléctrica food mixer, blender.
batir |ba'tir| *vt* to beat, strike; (*vencer*)
to beat, defeat; (*revolver*) to beat, mix;
~se *vr* to fight; ~ palmas to clap,
applaud.
batuta |ba'tuta| *nf* baton; llevar la ~
(*fig*) to be the boss, be in charge.
baúl |ba'ul| *nm* trunk; (*AUTO*) boot
(*Brit*), trunk (*US*).
bautismo |bau'tismo| *nm* baptism,
christening.
bautizar |bauti'θar| *vt* to baptize, chris-
ten; (*fam: diluir*) to water down;
bautizo *nm* baptism, christening.

bayeta |ba'jeta| nf floorcloth.
hayo, a |'bajo, a| a bay // nf borry.
bayoneta |bajo'neta| nf bayonet.
baza |'baθa| nf trick; **meter ~** to butt in.
bazar |ba'θar| nm bazaar.
bazofia |ba'θofja| nf pigswill (Brit), hogwash (US); (libro etc) trash.
beato, a |be'ato, a| a blessed; (piadoso) pious.
bebé |be'ße| nm baby.
bebedero |beße'ðero| nm (para animales) drinking trough.
bebedizo, a |beße'ðiθo, a| a drinkable // nm potion.
bebedor, a |beße'ðor, a| a hard-drinking.
beber |be'ßer| vt, vi to drink.
bebida |be'ßiða| nf drink.
beca |'beka| nf grant, scholarship.
befarse |be'farse| vr: ~ de algo to scoff at sth.
beldad |bel'dað| nf beauty.
Belén |be'len| nm Bethlehem; **b~** nm (de navidad) nativity scene, crib.
belga |'belɣa| a, nm/f Belgian.
Bélgica |'belxika| nf Belgium.
Belice |be'liθe| nm Belize.
bélico, a |'beliko, a| a (actitud) warlike; **belicoso, a** a (guerrero) warlike; (agresivo) aggressive, bellicose.
beligerante |belixe'rante| a belligerent.
bellaco, a |be'Aako, a| a sly, cunning // nm villain, rogue; **bellaquería** nf (acción) dirty trick; (calidad) wickedness.
belleza |be'Aeθa| nf beauty.
bello, a |'beAo, a| a beautiful, lovely; Bellas Artes Fine Art.
bellota |be'Aota| nf acorn.
bemol |be'mol| nm (MUS) flat; **esto tiene ~es** (fam) this is a tough one.
bencina |ben'θina| nf (AM: gasolina) petrol (Brit), gasoline (US).
bendecir |bende'θir| vt to bless.
bendición |bendi'θjon| nf blessing.
bendito, a |ben'dito, a| pp de **bendecir** // a holy; (afortunado) lucky; (feliz) happy; (sencillo) simple // nm/f simple soul.
benedictino, a |benedik'tino, a| a, nm Benedictine.
beneficencia |benefi'θenθja| nf charity.
beneficiar |benefi'θjar| vt to benefit, be of benefit to; **~se** vr to benefit, profit; **~io, a** nm/f beneficiary.
beneficio |bene'fiθjo| nm (bien) benefit, advantage; (ganancia) profit, gain; **~so, a** a beneficial.
benéfico, a |be'nefiko, a| a charitable.
beneplácito |bene'plaθito| nm approval, consent.
benevolencia |beneßo'lenθja| nf benevolence, kindness; **benévolo, a** a benevolent, kind.
benigno, a |be'niɣno, a| a kind; (suave)

mild; (MED: tumor) benign, non-malignant.
beodo, a |be'oðo, a| a drunk.
berenjena |beren'xena| nf aubergine (Brit), eggplant (US).
Berlín |ber'lin| n Berlin; **berlinés, esa** a of o from Berlin // nm/f Berliner.
bermejo, a |ber'mexo, a| a red.
berrear |berre'ar| vi to bellow, low.
berrido |be'rriðo| nm bellow(ing).
berrinche |be'rrintʃe| nm (fam) temper, tantrum.
berro |'berro| nm watercress.
berza |'berθa| nf cabbage.
besamel |besa'mel| nf (CULIN) white sauce, bechamel sauce.
besar |be'sar| vt to kiss; (fig: tocar) to graze; **~se** vr to kiss (one another); **beso** nm kiss.
bestia |'bestja| nf beast, animal; (fig) idiot; **~ de carga** beast of burden.
bestial |bes'tjal| a bestial; (fam) terrific; **~idad** nf bestiality; (fam) stupidity.
besugo |be'suɣo| nm sea bream; (fam) idiot.
besuquear |besuke'ar| vt to cover with kisses; **~se** vr to kiss and cuddle.
betún |be'tun| nm shoe polish; (QUIMICA) bitumen.
biberón |biße'ron| nm feeding bottle.
Biblia |'bißlja| nf Bible.
bibliografía |bißljoɣra'fia| nf bibliography.
biblioteca |bißljo'teka| nf library; (mueble) bookshelves pl; **~ de consulta** reference library; **~rio, a** nm/f librarian.
B.I.C. nf abr (= Brigada de Investigación Criminal) CID (Brit), FBI (US).
bicarbonato |bikarßo'nato| nm bicarbonate.
bici |'biθi| nf (fam) bike.
bicicleta |biθi'kleta| nf bicycle, cycle.
bicho |'bitʃo| nm (animal) small animal; (sabandija) bug, insect; (TAUR) bull.
bidé |bi'ðe| nm bidet.
bien |bjen| ♦ nm 1 (bienestar) good; **te lo digo por tu ~** I'm telling you for your own good; **el ~ y el mal** good and evil 2 (posesión): **~es** goods; **~es de consumo** consumer goods; **~es inmuebles o raíces/~es muebles** real estate sg/ personal property sg
♦ ad 1 (de manera satisfactoria, correcta etc) well; **trabaja/come ~** she works/eats well; **contestó ~** he answered correctly; **me siento ~** I feel fine; **no me siento ~** I don't feel very well; **se está ~ aquí** it's nice here
2 (frases): **hiciste ~ en llamarme** you were right to call me
3 (valor intensivo) very; **un cuarto ~ caliente** a nice warm room; **~ se ve que ...** it's quite clear that ...

4: estar ~: estoy muy bien aquí I feel very happy here; está bien que vengan it's alright for them to come; ¡está bien! lo haré oh alright, I'll do it
5 (de buena gana): yo ~ que iría pero ... I'd gladly go but ...
♦ excl: ¡~! (aprobación) O.K!; ¡muy ~! well done!
♦ a inv (matiz despectivo): niño ~ rich kid; gente ~ posh people
♦ conj **1**: ~ ... ~: ~ en coche ~ en tren either by car or by train
2: no ~ (esp AM): no ~ llegue te llamaré as soon as I arrive I'll call you
3: si ~ even though; ver tb más.

bienal [bje'nal] a biennial.

bienaventurado, a [bjenaßentu'raðo, a] a (feliz) happy, fortunate.

bienestar [bjenes'tar] nm well-being, welfare.

bienhechor, a [bjene'tʃor, a] a beneficent // nm/f benefactor/benefactress.

bienvenida [bjembe'niða] nf welcome; dar la ~ a uno to welcome sb.

bienvenido [bjembe'niðo] excl welcome!

bife ['bife] nm (AM) steak.

bifurcación [bifurka'θjon] nf fork.

bigamia [bi'vamja] nf bigamy; **bígamo, a** a bigamous // nm/f bigamist.

bigote [bi'vote] nm moustache; **bigotudo, a** a with a big moustache.

bikini [bi'kini] nm bikini; (CULIN) toasted ham and cheese sandwich.

bilingüe [bi'lingwe] a bilingual.

billar [bi'ʎar] nm billiards sg; (lugar) billiard hall; (mini-casino) amusement arcade.

billete [bi'ʎete] nm ticket; (de banco) banknote (Brit), bill (US); (carta) note; ~ sencillo, ~ de ida solamente de ida y vuelta single (Brit) o one-way (US) ticket/return (Brit) o round-trip (US) ticket; ~ de 20 libras £20 note.

billetera [biʎe'tera] nf, **billetero** [biʎe'tero] nm wallet.

billón [bi'ʎon] nm billion.

bimensual [bimen'swal] a twice monthly.

bimotor [bimo'tor] a twin-engined // nm twin-engined plane.

binóculo [bi'nokulo] nm pince-nez.

biografía [bjovra'fia] nf biography; **biógrafo, a** nm/f biographer.

biología [bjolo'xia] nf biology; **biológico, a** a biological; **biólogo, a** nm/f biologist.

biombo ['bjombo] nm (folding) screen.

biopsia [bi'opsja] nf biopsy.

birlar [bir'lar] vt (fam) to pinch.

Birmania [bir'manja] nf Burma.

bis [bis] excl encore! // ad: viven en el 27 ~ they live at 27a.

bisabuelo, a [bisa'ßwelo, a] nm/f great-grandfather/mother.

bisagra [bi'savra] nf hinge.

bisbisar [bisßi'sar], **bisbisear** [bisßise'ar]

vt to mutter, mumble.

bisiesto [bi'sjesto] a: año ~ leap year.

bisnieto, a [bis'njeto, a] nm/f great-grandson/daughter.

bisonte [bi'sonte] nm bison.

bistec [bis'tek], **bisté** [bis'te] nm steak.

bisturí [bistu'ri] nm scalpel.

bisutería [bisute'ria] nf imitation o costume jewellery.

bit [bit] nm (INFORM) bit.

bizcar [biθ'kar] vi to squint.

bizco, a ['biθko, a] a cross-eyed.

bizcocho [biθ'kotʃo] nm (CULIN) sponge cake.

bizquear [biθke'ar] vi to squint.

blanco, a ['blanko, a] a white // nm/f white man/woman, white // nm (color) white; (en texto) blank; (MIL, fig) target // nf (MUS) minim; en ~ blank; noche en ~ sleepless night; estar sin ~ to be broke.

blancura [blan'kura] nf whiteness.

blandir [blan'dir] vt to brandish.

blando, a ['blando, a] a soft; (tierno) tender, gentle; (carácter) mild; (fam) cowardly; **blandura** nf softness; tenderness; mildness.

blanquear [blanke'ar] vt to whiten; (fachada) to whitewash; (paño) to bleach // vi to turn white; **blanquecino, a** a whitish.

blasfemar [blasfe'mar] vi to blaspheme, curse; **blasfemia** nf blasphemy.

blasón [bla'son] nm coat of arms; (fig) honour; **blasonar** vt to emblazon // vi to boast, brag.

bledo ['bleðo] nm: me importa un ~ I couldn't care less.

blindado, a [blin'daðo, a] a (MIL) armour-plated; (antibala) bullet-proof; coche (Esp) o carro (AM) ~ armoured car.

blindaje [blin'daxe] nm armour, armour-plating.

bloc [blok] (pl ~s) nm writing pad.

bloque ['bloke] nm block; (POL) bloc; ~ de cilindros cylinder block.

bloquear [bloke'ar] vt to blockade; **bloqueo** nm blockade; (COM) freezing, blocking.

blusa ['blusa] nf blouse.

boato [bo'ato] nm show, ostentation.

bobada [bo'ßaða], **bobería** [boße'ria] nf foolish action; foolish statement; decir bobadas to talk nonsense.

bobina [bo'ßina] nf (TEC) bobbin; (FOTO) spool; (ELEC) coil.

bobo, a ['boßo, a] a (tonto) daft, silly; (cándido) naïve // nm/f fool, idiot // nm (TEATRO) clown, funny man.

boca ['boka] nf mouth; (de crustáceo) pincer; (de cañón) muzzle; (entrada) mouth, entrance; ~s nfpl (de río) mouth sg; ~ abajo/arriba face down/up; a ~jarro point-blank; se me hace agua la

~ my mouth is watering.

bocacalle [boka'kaʎe] *nf* (entrance to a) street; **la primera** ~ the first turning *o* street.

bocadillo [boka'ðiʎo] *nm* sandwich.

bocado [bo'kaðo] *nm* mouthful, bite; (*de caballo*) bridle; ~ **de Adán** Adam's apple.

bocanada [boka'naða] *nf* (*de vino*) mouthful, swallow; (*de aire*) gust, puff.

bocazas [bo'kaθas] *nm inv* (*fam*) bigmouth.

boceto [bo'θeto] *nm* sketch, outline.

bocina [bo'θina] *nf* (MUS) trumpet; (AUTO) horn; (*para hablar*) megaphone.

bocha ['botʃa] *nf* bowl; ~**s** *nfpl* bowls *sg*.

bochinche [bo'tʃintʃe] *nm* (*fam*) uproar.

bochorno [bo'tʃorno] *nm* (*vergüenza*) embarrassment; (*calor*): **hace** ~ it's very muggy; ~**so, a** *a* muggy; embarrassing.

boda ['boða] *nf* (*tb*: ~**s**) wedding, marriage; (*fiesta*) wedding reception; ~**s de plata/de oro** silver/golden wedding.

bodega [bo'ðexa] *nf* (*de vino*) (wine) cellar; (*depósito*) storeroom; (*de barco*) hold.

bodegón [boðe'xon] *nm* (ARTE) still life.

bofe ['bofe] *nm* (*tb*: ~**s**: *de res*) lights.

bofetada [bofe'taða] *nf*, **bofetón** [bofe'ton] *nm* slap (in the face).

boga ['boxa] *nf*: **en** ~ (*fig*) in vogue.

bogar [bo'xar] *vi* (*remar*) to row; (*navegar*) to sail.

Bogotá [boxo'ta] *n* Bogotá; **bogotano, a** *a* of *o* from Bogotá.

bohemio, a [bo'emjo, a] *a, nm/f* Bohemian.

boicot [boi'kot] (*pl* ~**s**) *nm* boycott; ~**ear** *vt* to boycott; ~**eo** *nm* boycott.

boina ['boina] *nf* beret.

bola ['bola] *nf* ball; (*canica*) marble; (NAIPES) (grand) slam; (*betún*) shoe polish; (*mentira*) tale, story; ~**s** *nfpl* (AM) bolas *sg*; ~ **de billar** billiard ball; ~ **de nieve** snowball.

bolchevique [boltʃe'βike] *a, nm/f* Bolshevik.

boleadoras [bolea'ðoras] *nfpl* (AM) bolas *sg*.

bolera [bo'lera] *nf* skittle *o* bowling alley.

boleta [bo'leta] *nf* (AM: *billete*) ticket; (: *permiso*) pass, permit.

boletería [bolete'ria] *nf* (AM) ticket office.

boletín [bole'tin] *nm* bulletin; (*periódico*) journal, review; ~ **escolar** (*Esp*) school report; ~ **de noticias** news bulletin; ~ **de pedido** application form; ~ **de precios** price list; ~ **de prensa** press release.

boleto [bo'leto] *nm* ticket.

boli ['boli] *nm* (*fam*) Biro ®, pen.

boliche [bo'litʃe] *nm* (*bola*) jack; (*juego*) bowls *sg*; (*lugar*) bowling alley.

bolígrafo [bo'lixrafo] *nm* ball-point pen,

Biro ®.

bolívar [bo'liβar] *nm* monetary unit of Venezuela.

Bolivia [bo'liβja] *nf* Bolivia; **boliviano, a** *a, nm/f* Bolivian.

bolo ['bolo] *nm* skittle; (*píldora*) (large) pill; (**juego de**) ~**s** *nmpl* skittles *sg*.

bolsa ['bolsa] *nf* (*cartera*) purse; (*saco*) bag; (AM) pocket; (ANAT) cavity, sac; (COM) stock exchange; (MINERÍA) pocket; ~ **de agua caliente** hot water bottle; ~ **de aire** air pocket; ~ **de papel** paper bag; ~ **de plástico** plastic bag.

bolsillo [bol'siʎo] *nm* pocket; (*cartera*) purse; **de** ~ pocket(-size).

bolsista [bol'sista] *nm/f* stockbroker.

bolso ['bolso] *nm* (*bolsa*) bag; (*de mujer*) handbag.

bollo ['boʎo] *nm* (*pan*) roll; (*bulto*) bump, lump; (*abolladura*) dent.

bomba ['bomba] *nf* (MIL) bomb; (TEC) pump // *a* (*fam*): **noticia** ~ bombshell // *ad* (*fam*): **pasarlo** ~ to have a great time; ~ **atómica/de humo/de retardo** atomic/smoke/time bomb; ~ **de gasolina** petrol pump.

bombardear [bombarðe'ar] *vt* to bombard; (MIL) to bomb; **bombardeo** *nm* bombardment; bombing.

bombardero [bombar'ðero] *nm* bomber.

bombear [bombe'ar] *vt* (*agua*) to pump (out *o* up); (MIL) to bomb; ~**se** *vr* to warp.

bombero [bom'bero] *nm* fireman.

bombilla [bom'biʎa] *nf* (*Esp*) (light) bulb.

bombín [bom'bin] *nm* bowler hat.

bombo ['bombo] *nm* (MUS) bass drum; (TEC) drum.

bombón [bom'bon] *nm* chocolate.

bonachón, ona [bona'tʃon, ona] *a* good-natured, easy-going.

bonaerense [bonae'rense] *a* of *o* from Buenos Aires.

bonanza [bo'nanθa] *nf* (NAUT) fair weather; (*fig*) bonanza; (MINERÍA) rich pocket *o* vein.

bondad [bon'dað] *nf* goodness, kindness; **tenga la** ~ **de** (please) be good enough to; ~**oso, a** *a* good, kind.

bonito, a [bo'nito, a] *a* pretty; (*agradable*) nice // *nm* (*atún*) tuna (fish).

bono ['bono] *nm* voucher; (FINANZAS) bond.

bonobús [bono'βus] *nm* (*Esp*) bus pass.

boquear [boke'ar] *vi* to gasp.

boquerón [boke'ron] *nm* (*pez*) (kind of) anchovy; (*agujero*) large hole.

boquete [bo'kete] *nm* gap, hole.

boquiabierto, a [bokia'βjerto, a] *a*: **quedar** ~ to be amazed *o* flabbergasted.

boquilla [bo'kiʎa] *nf* (*para riego*) nozzle; (*para cigarro*) cigarette holder; (MUS) mouthpiece.

borbollar [borβo'ʎar], **borbollear**

[borˈβoʎeˈar], **borbotar** [borβoˈtar] vi to bubble.

borbotón [borβoˈton] nm: **salir a borbotones** to gush out.

bordado [borˈðaðo] nm embroidery.

bordar [borˈðar] vt to embroider.

borde [ˈborðe] nm edge, border; (de camino etc) side; (en la costura) hem; **al ~ de** (fig) on the verge o brink of; **ser ~** (Esp: fam) to be a pain (in the neck); **~ar** vt to border.

bordillo [borˈðiʎo] nm kerb (Brit), curb (US).

bordo [ˈborðo] nm (NAUT) side; **a ~** on board.

borinqueño, a [borinˈkenjo, a] a, nm/f Puerto Rican.

borra [ˈborra] nf (pelusa) fluff; (sedimento) sediment.

borrachera [borraˈtʃera] nf (ebriedad) drunkenness; (orgía) spree, binge.

borracho, a [boˈrratʃo, a] a drunk // nm/f (que bebe mucho) drunkard, drunk; (temporalmente) drunk, drunk man/woman.

borrador [borraˈðor] nm (escritura) first draft, rough sketch; (cuaderno) scribbling pad; (goma) rubber (Brit), eraser.

borrajear [borraxeˈar] vt, vi to scribble.

borrar [boˈrrar] vt to erase, rub out.

borrasca [boˈrraska] nf storm.

borrico, a [boˈrriko, a] nm/f donkey/she-donkey; (fig) stupid man/woman.

borrón [boˈrron] nm (mancha) stain.

borroso, a [boˈrroso, a] a vague, unclear; (escritura) illegible.

bosque [ˈboske] nm wood; (grande) forest.

bosquejar [boskeˈxar] vt to sketch; **bosquejo** nm sketch.

bosta [ˈbosta] nf dung; (abono) manure.

bostezar [bosteˈθar] vi to yawn; **bostezo** nm yawn.

bota [ˈbota] nf (calzado) boot; (saco) leather wine bottle.

botánico, a [boˈtaniko, a] a botanical // nm/f botanist // nf botany.

botar [boˈtar] vt to throw, hurl; (NAUT) to launch; (fam) to throw out // vi to bounce.

bote [ˈbote] nm (salto) bounce; (golpe) thrust; (vasija) tin, can; (embarcación) boat; **de ~ en ~** packed, jammed full; **~ salvavidas** lifeboat; **~ de la basura** (AM) dustbin (Brit), trashcan (US).

botella [boˈteʎa] nf bottle.

botica [boˈtika] nf chemist's (shop) (Brit), pharmacy; **~rio, a** nm/f chemist (Brit), pharmacist.

botijo [boˈtixo] nm (earthenware) jug.

botín [boˈtin] nm (calzado) half boot; (polaina) spat; (MIL) booty.

botiquín [botiˈkin] nm (armario) medicine cabinet; (portátil) first-aid kit.

botón [boˈton] nm button; (BOT) bud;

(de florete) tip; **~ de oro** buttercup.

botones [boˈtones] nm inv bellboy (Brit), bellhop (US).

bóveda [ˈboβeða] nf (ARQ) vault.

boxeador [bokseaˈðor] nm boxer.

boxeo [bokˈseo] nm boxing.

boya [ˈboja] nf (NAUT) buoy; (flotador) float.

bozal [boˈθal] nm (de caballo) halter; (de perro) muzzle.

bracear [braθeˈar] vi (agitar los brazos) to wave one's arms.

bracero [braˈθero] nm labourer; (en el campo) farmhand.

bracete [braˈθete]: **de ~** ad arm in arm.

braga [ˈbraγa] nf (cuerda) sling, rope; (de bebé) nappy (Brit), diaper (US); **~s** nfpl (de mujer) panties, knickers (Brit).

bragueta [braˈγeta] nf fly, flies pl.

braille [breil] nm braille.

bramar [braˈmar] vi to bellow, roar; **bramido** nm bellow, roar.

brasa [ˈbrasa] nf live o hot coal.

brasero [braˈsero] nm brazier.

Brasil [braˈsil] nm: **(el) ~** Brazil; **brasileño, a** a, nm/f Brazilian.

bravata [braˈβata] nf boast.

braveza [braˈβeθa] nf (valor) bravery; (ferocidad) ferocity.

bravío, a [braˈβio, a] a wild; (feroz) fierce.

bravo, a [ˈbraβo, a] a (valiente) brave; (bueno) fine, splendid; (feroz) ferocious; (salvaje) wild; (mar etc) rough, stormy // excl bravo!; **bravura** nf bravery; ferocity; (pey) boast.

braza [ˈbraθa] nf fathom; **nadar a la ~** to swim (the) breast-stroke.

brazada [braˈθaða] nf stroke.

brazado [braˈθaðo] nm armful.

brazalete [braθaˈlete] nm (pulsera) bracelet; (banda) armband.

brazo [ˈbraθo] nm arm; (ZOOL) foreleg; (BOT) limb, branch; **luchar a ~ partido** to fight hand-to-hand; **ir del ~** to walk arm in arm.

brea [ˈbrea] nf pitch, tar.

brebaje [breˈβaxe] nm potion.

brecha [ˈbretʃa] nf (hoyo, vacío) gap, opening; (MIL, fig) breach.

brega [ˈbreγa] nf (lucha) struggle; (trabajo) hard work.

breve [ˈbreβe] a short, brief // nf (MUS) breve; **~dad** nf brevity, shortness.

brezal [breˈθal] nm moor(land), heath; **brezo** nm heather.

bribón, ona [briˈβon, ona] a idle, lazy // nm/f (vagabundo) vagabond; (pícaro) rascal, rogue.

bricolaje [brikoˈlaxe] nm do-it-yourself, DIY.

brida [ˈbriða] nf bridle, rein; (TEC) clamp; **a toda ~** at top speed.

bridge [britʃ] nm bridge.

brigada [briˈγaða] nf (unidad) brigade;

(*trabajadores*) squad, gang // *nm* ≈ staff-sergeant, sergeant-major.

brillante |bri'ʎante| *a* brilliant // *nm* diamond.

brillar |bri'ʎar| *vi* (*tb fig*) to shine; (*joyas*) to sparkle.

brillo |'briʎo| *nm* shine; (*brillantez*) brilliance; (*fig*) splendour; **sacar ~ a** to polish.

brincar |brin'kar| *vi* to skip about, hop about, jump about; **está que brinca** he's hopping mad.

brinco |'brinko| *nm* jump, leap.

brindar |brin'dar| *vi*: **~ a o por** to drink (a toast) to // *vt* to offer, present.

brindis |'brindis| *nm* toast; (*TAUR*) (ceremony of) dedication.

brío |'brio| *nm* spirit, dash; **brioso, a** *a* spirited, dashing.

brisa |'brisa| *nf* breeze.

británico, a |bri'taniko, a| *a* British // *nm/f* Briton, British person.

brocal |bro'kal| *nm* rim.

brocha |'brotʃa| *nf* (large) paintbrush; **~ de afeitar** shaving brush.

broche |'brotʃe| *nm* brooch.

broma |'broma| *nf* joke; **en ~** in fun, as a joke; **bromear** *vi* to joke.

bromista |bro'mista| *a* fond of joking // *nm/f* joker, wag.

bronca |'bronka| *nf* row; **echar una ~ a uno** to tick sb off.

bronce |'bronθe| *nm* bronze; **~ado, a** *a* bronze; (*por el sol*) tanned // *nm* (sun)tan; (*TEC*) bronzing.

broncearse |bronθe'arse| *vr* to get a suntan.

bronco, a |'bronko, a| *a* (*manera*) rude, surly; (*voz*) harsh.

bronquitis |bron'kitis| *nf* bronchitis.

brotar |bro'tar| *vi* (*BOT*) to sprout; (*aguas*) to gush (forth); (*MED*) to break out.

brote |'brote| *nm* (*BOT*) shoot; (*MED, fig*) outbreak.

bruces |'bruθes|: **de ~ ad**: **caer o dar de ~** to fall headlong, fall flat.

bruja |'bruxa| *nf* witch; **brujería** *nf* witchcraft.

brujo |'bruxo| *nm* wizard, magician.

brújula |'bruxula| *nf* compass.

bruma |'bruma| *nf* mist; **brumoso, a** *a* misty.

bruñido |bru'niðo| *nm* polish; **bruñir** *vt* to polish.

brusco, a |'brusko, a| *a* (*súbito*) sudden; (*áspero*) brusque.

Bruselas |bru'selas| *n* Brussels.

brutal |bru'tal| *a* brutal.

brutalidad |brutali'ðað| *nf* brutality.

bruto, a |'bruto, a| *a* (*idiota*) stupid; (*bestial*) brutish; (*peso*) gross; **en ~** raw, unworked.

Bs.As. *abr* (= *Buenos Aires*) B.A.

bucal |bu'kal| *a* oral; **por vía ~** orally.

bucear |buθe'ar| *vi* to dive // *vt* to explore; **buceo** *nm* diving; (*fig*) investigation.

bucle |'bukle| *nm* curl.

budismo |bu'ðismo| *nm* Buddhism.

buen |bwen| *am ver* **bueno**.

buenamente |bwena'mente| *ad* (*fácilmente*) easily; (*voluntariamente*) willingly.

buenaventura |bwenaßen'tura| *nf* (*suerte*) good luck; (*adivinación*) fortune.

bueno, a |'bweno, a| ♦ *a* (*antes de nmsg*: **buen**) 1 (*excelente etc*) good; **es un libro ~ o es un buen libro** it's a good book; **hace ~, hace buen tiempo** the weather is *o* it is fine; **el ~ de Paco** good old Paco; **fue muy ~ conmigo** he was very nice *o* kind to me

2 (*apropiado*): **ser bueno/a para** to be good for; **creo que vamos por buen camino** I think we're on the right track

3 (*irónico*): **le di un buen rapapolvo** I gave him a good *o* real ticking off; **¡buen conductor estás hecho!** some *o* a fine driver you are!; **¡estaría ~ que ...!** a fine thing it would be if ...!

4 (*atractivo, sabroso*): **está bueno este bizcocho** this sponge is delicious; **Carmen está muy buena** Carmen is looking good

5 (*saludos*): **¡buen día!, ¡buenos días!** good morning!; **¡buenas (tardes)!** (good) afternoon!; (*más tarde*) (good) evening!; **¡buenas noches!** good night!

6 (*otras locuciones*): **estar de buenas** to be in a good mood; **por las buenas o por las malas** by hook or by crook; **de buenas a primeras** all of a sudden

♦ *excl*: **¡~!** all right!; **~, ¿y qué?** well, so what?

Buenos Aires *nm* Buenos Aires.

buey |bwei| *nm* ox.

búfalo |'bufalo| *nm* buffalo.

bufanda |bu'fanda| *nf* scarf.

bufar |bu'far| *vi* to snort.

bufete |bu'fete| *nm* (*despacho de abogado*) lawyer's office.

buffer |'bufer| *nm* (*INFORM*) buffer.

bufón |bu'fon, ona| *nm* clown.

buhardilla |buar'ðiʎa| *nf* (*desván*) attic.

búho |'buo| *nm* owl; (*fig*) hermit, recluse.

buhonero |buo'nero| *nm* pedlar.

buitre |'bwitre| *nm* vulture.

bujía |bu'xia| *nf* (*vela*) candle; (*ELEC*) candle (power); (*AUTO*) spark plug.

bula |'bula| *nf* (*papal*) bull.

bulbo |'bulßo| *nm* bulb.

bulevar |bule'ßar| *nm* boulevard.

Bulgaria |bul'xarja| *nf* Bulgaria; **búlgaro, a** *a*, *nm/f* Bulgarian.

bulto |'bulto| *nm* (*paquete*) package; (*fardo*) bundle; (*tamaño*) size, bulkiness; (*MED*) swelling, lump; (*silueta*) vague shape; (*estatua*) bust, statue.

bulla ['buʎa] *nf* (*ruido*) uproar; (*de gente*) crowd.

bullicio [bu'ʎiθjo] *nm* (*ruido*) uproar; (*movimiento*) bustle.

bullir [bu'ʎir] *vi* (*hervir*) to boil; (*burbujear*) to bubble; (*mover*) to move, stir.

buñuelo [bu'ɲwelo] *nm* ≈ doughnut (*Brit*), donut (*US*); (*fruta de sartén*) fritter.

BUP [bup] *nm abr* (*Esp* = *Bachillerato Unificado Polivalente*) *secondary education and leaving certificate for 14-17 age group*.

buque ['buke] *nm* ship, vessel.

burbuja [bur'βuxa] *nf* bubble; **burbujear** *vi* to bubble.

burdel [bur'ðel] *nm* brothel.

burdo, a ['burðo, a] *a* coarse, rough.

burgués, esa [bur'ɣes, esa] *a* middle-class, bourgeois; **burguesía** *nf* middle class, bourgeoisie.

burla ['burla] *nf* (*mofa*) gibe; (*broma*) joke; (*engaño*) trick.

burladero [burla'ðero] *nm* (bullfighter's) refuge.

burlador, a [burla'ðor, a] *a* mocking // *nm/f* (*bromista*) joker // *nm* (*libertino*) seducer.

burlar [bur'lar] *vt* (*engañar*) to deceive; (*seducir*) to seduce // *vi*, ~se *vr* to joke; ~se de to make fun of.

burlesco, a [bur'lesko, a] *a* burlesque.

burlón, ona [bur'lon, ona] *a* mocking.

burocracia [buro'kraθja] *nf* civil service; (*pey*) bureaucracy.

burócrata [bu'rokrata] *nm/f* civil servant; (*pey*) bureaucrat.

buromática [buro'matika] *nf* office automation.

burro, a ['burro] *nm/f* donkey/she-donkey; (*fig*) ass, idiot.

bursátil [bur'satil] *a* stock-exchange *cpd*.

bus [bus] *nm* bus.

busca ['buska] *nf* search, hunt // *nm* (*TEL*) bleeper; en ~ de in search of.

buscapleitos [buska'pleitos] *nm/f inv* troublemaker.

buscar [bus'kar] *vt* to look for, search for, seek // *vi* to look, search, seek; se busca secretaria secretary wanted.

buscón, ona [bus'kon, ona] *a* thieving // *nm* petty thief // *nf* whore.

busilis [bu'silis] *nm* (*fam*) snag.

busque *etc vb ver* **buscar**.

búsqueda ['buskeða] *nf* = **busca**.

busto ['busto] *nm* (*ANAT*, *ARTE*) bust.

butaca [bu'taka] *nf* armchair; (*de cine*, *teatro*) stall, seat.

butano [bu'tano] *nm* butane (gas).

buzo ['buθo] *nm* diver.

buzón [bu'θon] *nm* (*en puerta*) letter box; (*en la calle*) pillar box.

C

C. *abr* (= *centígrado*) C; (= *compañía*) Co.

c. *abr* (= *capítulo*) ch.

C/ *abr* (= *calle*) St.

c.a. *abr* (= *corriente alterna*) AC.

cabal [ka'βal] *a* (*exacto*) exact; (*correcto*) right, proper; (*acabado*) finished, complete; ~es *nmpl*: estar en sus ~es to be in one's right mind.

cabalgadura [kaβalɣa'ðura] *nf* mount, horse.

cabalgar [kaβal'ɣar] *vt*, *vi* to ride.

cabalgata [kaβal'ɣata] *nf* procession.

caballa [ka'βaʎa] *nf* mackerel.

caballeresco, a [kaβaʎe'resko, a] *a* noble, chivalrous.

caballería [kaβaʎe'ria] *nf* mount; (*MIL*) cavalry.

caballeriza [kaβaʎe'riθa] *nf* stable; **caballerizo** *nm* groom, stableman.

caballero [kaβa'ʎero] *nm* (*hombre galante*) gentleman; (*de la orden de caballería*) knight; (*trato directo*) sir.

caballerosidad [kaβaʎerosi'ðað] *nf* chivalry.

caballete [kaβa'ʎete] *nm* (*ARTE*) easel; (*TEC*) trestle.

caballito [kaβa'ʎito] *nm* (*caballo pequeño*) small horse, pony; ~s *nmpl* (*en verbena*) roundabout *sg*, merry-go-round.

caballo [ka'βaʎo] *nm* horse; (*AJEDREZ*) knight; (*NAIPES*) queen; ~ de vapor *o* de fuerza horsepower.

cabaña [ka'βaɲa] *nf* (*casita*) hut, cabin.

cabaré, cabaret [kaβa're] (*pl* cabarés, cabarets) *nm* cabaret.

cabecear [kaβeθe'ar] *vt*, *vi* to nod.

cabecera [kaβe'θera] *nf* head; (*de distrito*) chief town; (*IMPRENTA*) headline.

cabecilla [kaβe'θiʎa] *nm/f* ringleader.

cabellera [kaβe'ʎera] *nf* (head of) hair; (*de cometa*) tail.

cabello [ka'βeʎo] *nm* (*tb*: ~s) hair *sg*.

caber [ka'βer] *vi* (*entrar*) to fit, go; caben 3 más there's room for 3 more.

cabestrillo [kaβes'triʎo] *nm* sling.

cabestro [ka'βestro] *nm* halter.

cabeza [ka'βeθa] *nf* head; (*POL*) chief, leader; ~da *nf* (*golpe*) butt; dar ~das to nod off.

cabida [ka'βiða] *nf* space.

cabildo [ka'βildo] *nm* (*de iglesia*) chapter; (*POL*) town council.

cabina [ka'βina] *nf* cabin; (*de camión*) cab; ~ telefónica telephone box (*Brit*) *o* booth.

cabizbajo, a [kaβiθ'βaxo, a] *a* crestfallen, dejected.

cable ['kaβle] *nm* cable.

cabo ['kaβo] *nm* (*de objeto*) end,

extremity; (MIL) corporal; (NAUT) rope, cable; (GEO) cape: al ~ de 3 días after 3 days.

cabra |'kaβra| nf goat.

cabré etc vb ver **caber**.

cabrío, a |ka'βrio, a| a goatish; macho ~ (he-)goat, billy goat.

cabriola |ka'βrjola| nf caper.

cabritilla |kaβri'tiʎa| nf kid, kidskin.

cabrito |ka'βrito| nm kid.

cabrón |ka'βron| nm cuckold; (fam!) bastard (!).

cacahuete |kaka'wete| nm (Esp) peanut.

cacao |ka'kao| nm cocoa; (BOT) cacao.

cacarear |kakare'ar| vi (persona) to boast; (gallina) to crow.

cacería |kaθe'ria| nf hunt.

cacerola |kaθe'rola| nf pan, saucepan.

cacique |ka'θike| nm chief, local ruler; (POL) local party boss; **caciquismo** nm system of dominance by the local boss.

caco |'kako| nm pickpocket.

cacto |'kakto| nm, **cactus** |'kaktus| nm inv cactus.

cacharro |ka'tʃarro| nm earthenware pot; ~s nmpl pots and pans.

cachear |katʃe'ar| vt to search, frisk.

cachemir |katʃe'mir| nm cashmere.

cacheo |ka'tʃeo| nm searching, frisking.

cachete |ka'tʃete| nm (ANAT) cheek; (bofetada) slap (in the face).

cachimba |ka'tʃimba| nf pipe.

cachiporra |katʃi'porra| nf truncheon.

cachivache |katʃi'βatʃe| nm (trasto) piece of junk; ~s nmpl junk sg.

cacho |'katʃo, a| nm (small) bit; (AM: cuerno) horn.

cachondeo |katʃon'deo| nm (fam) farce, joke.

cachondo, a |ka'tʃondo, a| a (ZOOL) on heat; (fam) randy, sexy; (gracioso) funny.

cachorro, a |ka'tʃorro, a| nm/f (perro) pup, puppy; (león) cub.

cada |'kaða| a inv each; (antes de número) every; ~ día each day, every day; ~ dos días every other day; ~ uno/a each one, every one; ~ vez más more and more; uno de ~ diez one out of every ten.

cadalso |ka'ðalso| nm scaffold.

cadáver |ka'ðaβer| nm (dead) body, corpse.

cadena |ka'ðena| nf chain; (TV) channel; trabajo en ~ assembly line work.

cadencia |ka'ðenθja| nf cadence, rhythm.

cadera |ka'ðera| nf hip.

cadete |ka'ðete| nm cadet.

caducar |kaðu'kar| vi to expire; **caduco, a** a expired; (persona) very old.

C.A.E. abr (= cóbrese al entregar) COD.

caer |ka'er| vi, **caerse** vr to fall (down); me cae bien/mal I get on well with him/I can't stand him; ~ en la cuenta to catch on; su cumpleaños cae en viernes her birthday falls on a Friday.

café |ka'fe| (pl ~s) nm (bebida, planta) coffee; (lugar) café // a (color) brown; ~ con leche white coffee; ~ solo black coffee; **cafetal** nm coffee plantation.

cafetería |kafete'ria| nf (gen) café.

cafetero, a |kafe'tero, a| a coffee cpd; ser muy ~ to be a coffee addict // nf coffee pot.

cagar |ka'xar| vt (fam!) to shit (!); to bungle, mess up // vi to have a shit (!).

caída |ka'iða| nf fall; (declive) slope; (disminución) fall, drop.

caiga etc vb ver **caer**.

caimán |kai'man| nm alligator.

caja |'kaxa| nf box; (para reloj) case; (de ascensor) shaft; (COM) cashbox; (donde se hacen los pagos) cashdesk; (: en supermercado) checkout, till; ~ de ahorros savings bank; ~ de cambios gearbox; ~ fuerte, ~ de caudales safe, strongbox.

cajero, a |ka'xero, a| nm/f cashier.

cajetilla |kaxe'tiʎa| nf (de cigarrillos) packet.

cajón |ka'xon| nm big box; (de mueble) drawer.

cal |kal| nf lime.

cala |'kala| nf, (GEO) cove, inlet; (de barco) hold.

calabacín |kalaβa'θin| nm (BOT) baby marrow; (: más pequeño) courgette (Brit), zucchini (US).

calabacita |kalaβa'θita| nf (AM) courgette (Brit), zucchini (US).

calabaza |kala'βaθa| nf (BOT) pumpkin.

calabozo |kala'βoθo| nm (cárcel) prison; (celda) cell.

calado, a |ka'lado, a| a (prenda) lace cpd // nm (NAUT) draught // nf (de cigarrillo) puff.

calamar |kala'mar| nm squid.

calambre |ka'lambre| nm (tb: ~s) cramp.

calamidad |kalami'ðað| nf calamity, disaster.

calamina |kala'mina| nf calamine.

calaña |ka'laɲa| nf model, pattern.

calar |ka'lar| vt (tela) to soak, drench; (penetrar) to pierce, penetrate; (comprender) to see through; (vela, red) to lower; ~se vr (AUTO) to stall; ~se las gafas to stick one's glasses on.

calavera |kala'βera| nf skull.

calcañal |kalka'ɲal|, **calcañar** |kalka'ɲar|, **calcaño** |kal'kaɲo| nm heel.

calcar |kal'kar| vt (reproducir) to trace; (imitar) to copy.

calceta |kal'θeta| nf (knee-length) stocking; hacer ~ to knit.

calcetín |kalθe'tin| nm sock.

calcinar |kalθi'nar| vt to burn, blacken.

calcio |'kalθjo| nm calcium.

calco |'kalko| nm tracing.

calcomanía |kalkoma'nia| nf transfer.

calculadora [kalkula'ðora] *nf* calculator.
calcular [kalku'lar] *vt* (*MAT*) to calculate, compute; ~ que ... to reckon that ...; **cálculo** *nm* calculation.
caldear [kalde'ar] *vt* to warm (up), heat (up).
caldera [kal'dera] *nf* boiler.
calderilla [kalde'riʎa] *nf* (*moneda*) small change.
caldero [kal'dero] *nm* small boiler.
caldo ['kaldo] *nm* stock; (*consomé*) consommé.
calefacción [kalefak'θjon] *nf* heating; ~ **central** central heating.
calendario [kalen'darjo] *nm* calendar.
calentador [kalenta'ðor] *nm* heater.
calentar [kalen'tar] *vt* to heat (up); ~**se** *vr* to heat up, warm up; (*fig*: *discusión etc*) to get heated.
calentura [kalen'tura] *nf* (*MED*) fever, (high) temperature.
calibrar [kali'ßrar] *vt* to gauge, measure; **calibre** *nm* (*de cañón*) calibre, bore; (*diámetro*) diameter; (*fig*) calibre.
calidad [kali'ðað] *nf* quality; **de ~** quality *cpd*; **en ~ de** in the capacity of, as.
cálido, a ['kaliðo, a] *a* hot; (*fig*) warm.
caliente *etc vb ver* **calentar** // [ka'ljente] *a* hot; (*fig*) fiery; (*disputa*) heated; (*fam*: *cachondo*) randy.
calificación [kalifika'θjon] *nf* qualification; (*de alumno*) grade, mark.
calificar [kalifi'kar] *vt* to qualify; (*alumno*) to grade, mark; ~ **de** to describe as.
calizo, a [ka'liθo, a] *a* lime *cpd* // *nf* limestone.
calma ['kalma] *nf* calm; (*pachorra*) slowness.
calmante [kal'mante] *nm* sedative, tranquillizer.
calmar [kal'mar] *vt* to calm, calm down // *vi* (*tempestad*) to abate; (*mente etc*) to become calm.
calmoso, a [kal'moso, a] *a* calm, quiet.
calor [ka'lor] *nm* heat; (~ *agradable*) warmth.
caloría [kalo'ria] *nf* calorie.
calorífero, a [kalo'rifero, a] *a* heat-producing, heat-giving // *nm* heating system.
calumnia [ka'lumnja] *nf* calumny, slander; **calumnioso, a** *a* slanderous.
caluroso, a [kalu'roso, a] *a* hot; (*sin exceso*) warm; (*fig*) enthusiastic.
calvario [kal'ßarjo] *nm* stations *pl* of the cross.
calvicie [kal'ßiθje] *nf* baldness.
calvo, a ['kalßo, a] *a* bald; (*terreno*) bare, barren; (*tejido*) threadbare // *nf* bald patch; (*en bosque*) clearing.
calza ['kalθa] *nf* wedge, chock.
calzado, a [kal'θaðo, a] *a* shod // *nm* footwear // *nf* roadway, highway.
calzador [kalθa'ðor] *nm* shoehorn.

calzar [kal'θar] *vt* (*zapatos etc*) to wear; (*un mueble*) to put a wedge under; ~**se** *vr*: ~**se los zapatos** to put on one's shoes; ¿**qué (número) calza?** what size do you take?
calzón [kal'θon] *nm* (*tb*: **calzones** *nmpl*) shorts *pl*; (*AM*: *de hombre*) pants, (: *de mujer*) panties.
calzoncillos [kalθon'θiʎos] *nmpl* underpants.
callado, a [ka'ʎaðo, a] *a* quiet.
callar [ka'ʎar] *vt* (*asunto delicado*) to keep quiet about, say nothing about; (*persona, opinión*) to silence // *vi*, ~**se** *vr* to keep quiet, be silent; ¡**cállate!** be quiet!, shut up!
calle ['kaʎe] *nf* street; (*DEPORTE*) lane; ~ **arriba/abajo** up/down the street; ~ **de un solo sentido** one-way street.
calleja [ka'ʎexa] *nf* alley, narrow street;
callejear [kaʎexe'ar] *vi* to wander (about) the streets; **callejero, a** *a* street *cpd* // *nm* street map; **callejón** *nm* alley, passage; **callejón sin salida** cul-de-sac; **callejuela** *nf* side-street, alley.
callista [ka'ʎista] *nm/f* chiropodist.
callo ['kaʎo] *nm* callus; (*en el pie*) corn; ~**s** *nmpl* (*CULIN*) tripe *sg*; ~**so, a** *a* horny, rough.
cama ['kama] *nf* bed; (*GEO*) stratum; ~ **individual/de matrimonio** single/double bed.
camada [ka'maða] *nf* litter; (*de personas*) gang, band.
camafeo [kama'feo] *nm* cameo.
cámara ['kamara] *nf* chamber; (*habitación*) room; (*sala*) hall; (*CINE*) cine camera; (*fotográfica*) camera; ~ **de aire** inner tube.
camarada [kama'raða] *nm* comrade, companion.
camarera [kama'rera] *nf* (*en restaurante*) waitress; (*en casa, hotel*) maid.
camarero [kama'rero] *nm* waiter.
camarilla [kama'riʎa] *nf* (*clan*) clique; (*POL*) lobby.
camarín [kama'rin] *nm* dressing room.
camarón [kama'ron] *nm* shrimp.
camarote [kama'rote] *nm* cabin.
cambiable [kam'bjaßle] *a* (*variable*) changeable, variable; (*intercambiable*) interchangeable.
cambiante [kam'bjante] *a* variable.
cambiar [kam'bjar] *vt* to change; (*dinero*) to exchange // *vi* to change; ~**se** *vr* (*mudarse*) to move; (*de ropa*) to change; ~ **de idea** to change one's mind; ~ **de ropa** to change (one's clothes).
cambiazo [kam'bjaθo] *nm*: **dar el ~ a uno** to swindle sb.
cambio ['kambjo] *nm* change; (*trueque*) exchange; (*COM*) rate of exchange; (*oficina*) bureau de change; (*dinero menudo*) small change; **en ~** on the other hand; (*en lugar de*) instead; ~ **de**

dlvlsas foreign exchange; ~ de
velocidades gear lever; ~ de vía points
pl.

cambista [kam'bista] nm (COM)
exchange broker.

camelar [kame'lar] vt (con mujer) to flirt
with; (persuadir) to cajole.

camello [ka'meʎo] nm camel; (fam:
traficante) pusher.

camilla [ka'miʎa] nf (MED) stretcher.

caminante [kami'nante] nm/f traveller.

caminar [kami'nar] vi (marchar) to
walk, go; (viajar) to travel, journey // vt
(recorrer) to cover, travel.

caminata [kami'nata] nf long walk; (por
el campo) hike.

camino [ka'mino] nm way, road;
(sendero) track; a medio ~ halfway
(there); en el ~ on the way, en route; ~
de on the way to; ~ particular private
road.

camión [ka'mjon] nm lorry (Brit), truck
(US); **camionero, a** nm/f lorry o truck
driver.

camioneta [kamjo'neta] nf van, light
truck.

camisa [ka'misa] nf shirt; (BOT) skin; ~
de dormir nightdress; ~ de fuerza
straitjacket; **camisería** nf outfitter's
(shop).

camiseta [kami'seta] nf (prenda) tee-
shirt; (: ropa interior) vest; (de
deportista) top.

camisón [kami'son] nm nightdress, night-
gown.

camorra [ka'morra] nf: armar o buscar
~ to look for trouble, kick up a fuss.

campamento [kampa'mento] nm camp.

campana [kam'pana] nf bell; ~da nf
peal; ~rio nm belfry.

campanilla [kampa'niʎa] nf small bell.

campaña [kam'paɲa] nf (MIL, POL)
campaign.

campechano, a [kampe'tʃano, a] a
(franco) open.

campeón, ona [kampe'on, ona] nm/f
champion; **campeonato** nm champion-
ship.

campesino, a [kampe'sino, a] a country
cpd, rural; (gente) peasant cpd // nm/f
countryman/woman; (agricultor)
farmer.

campestre [kam'pestre] a country cpd,
rural.

camping ['kampin] nm camping; (lugar)
campsite; ir de o hacer ~ to go camping.

campiña [kam'piɲa] nf countryside.

campo ['kampo] nm (fuera de la ciudad)
country, countryside; (AGR, ELEC) field;
(de fútbol) pitch; (de golf) course; (MIL)
camp.

camposanto [kampo'santo] nm
cemetery.

camuflaje [kamu'flaxe] nm camouflage.

cana ['kana] nf ver **cano**.

Canadá [kana'ða] nm Canada;
canadiense a, nm/f Canadian // nf fur-
lined jacket.

canal [ka'nal] nm canal; (GEO) channel,
strait; (de televisión) channel; (de
tejado) gutter; ~ de Panamá Panama
Canal; ~izar vt to channel.

canalón [kana'lon] nm (conducto
vertical) drainpipe; (del tejado) gutter.

canalla [ka'naʎa] nf rabble, mob // nm
swine.

canapé [kana'pe] (pl ~s) nm sofa,
settee; (CULIN) canapé

Canarias [ka'narjas] nfpl: (las Islas) ~
the Canary Islands, the Canaries.

canario, a [ka'narjo, a] a, nm/f (native)
of the Canary Isles // nm (ZOOL) canary.

canasta [ka'nasta] nf (round) basket;
canastilla [-'tiʎa] nf small basket; (de
niño) layette.

canasto [ka'nasto] nm large basket.

cancela [kan'θela] nf gate.

cancelación [kanθela'θjon] nf cancellation.

cancelar [kanθe'lar] vt to cancel; (una
deuda) to write off.

cáncer ['kanθer] nm (MED) cancer; C~
(ASTROLOGIA) Cancer.

canciller [kanθi'ʎer] nm chancellor.

canción [kan'θjon] nf song; ~ de cuna
lullaby; **cancionero** nm song book.

cancha ['kantʃa] nf (de baloncesto, tenis
etc) court; (AM: de fútbol) pitch.

candado [kan'daðo] nm padlock.

candela [kan'dela] nf candle.

candelero [kande'lero] nm (para vela)
candlestick; (de aceite) oil lamp.

candente [kan'dente] a red-hot; (fig:
tema) burning.

candidato, a [kandi'ðato, a] nm/f
candidate.

candidez [kandi'ðeθ] nf (sencillez)
simplicity; (simpleza) naiveté; **cándido,
a** a simple; naive.

candil [kan'dil] nm oil lamp; ~ejas
[-'lexas] nfpl (TEATRO) footlights.

candor [kan'dor] nm (sinceridad) frank-
ness; (inocencia) innocence.

canela [ka'nela] nf cinnamon.

cangrejo [kan'grexo] nm crab.

canguro [kan'guro] nm kangaroo; hacer
de ~ to babysit.

caníbal [ka'nißal] a, nm/f cannibal.

canica [ka'nika] nf marble.

canijo, a [ka'nixo, a] a frail, sickly.

canino, a [ka'nino, a] a canine // nm
canine (tooth).

canjear [kanxe'ar] vt to exchange.

cano, a ['kano, a] a grey-haired, white-
haired // nf white o grey hair; tener
canas to be going grey.

canoa [ka'noa] nf canoe.

canon ['kanon] nm canon; (pensión)
rent; (COM) tax.

canónigo [ka'noniɣo] nm canon.
canonizar [kanoni'θar] vt to canonize.
cansado, a [kan'saðo, a] a tired, weary; (tedioso) tedious, boring.
cansancio [kan'sanθjo] nm tiredness, fatigue.
cansar [kan'sar] vt (fatigar) to tire, tire out; (aburrir) to bore; (fastidiar) to bother; **~se** vr to tire, get tired; (aburrirse) to get bored.
cantábrico, a [kan'taβriko, a] a Cantabrian; **mar C~** ≈ Bay of Biscay.
cantante [kan'tante] a singing // nm/f singer.
cantar [kan'tar] vt to sing // vi to sing; (insecto) to chirp; (rechinar) to squeak // nm (acción) singing; (canción) song; (poema) poem.
cántara ['kantara] nf large pitcher.
cántaro ['kantaro] nm pitcher, jug; **llover a ~s** to rain cats and dogs.
cante ['kante] nm: **~ jondo** flamenco singing.
cantera [kan'tera] nf quarry.
cantidad [kanti'ðað] nf quantity, amount.
cantilena [kanti'lena] nf = **cantinela**.
cantimplora [kantim'plora] nf (frasco) water bottle, canteen.
cantina [kan'tina] nf canteen; (de estación) buffet.
cantinela [kanti'nela] nf ballad, song.
canto ['kanto] nm singing; (canción) song; (borde) edge, rim; (de un cuchillo) back; **~ rodado** boulder.
cantor, a [kan'tor, a] nm/f singer.
canturrear [kanturre'ar] vi to sing softly.
canuto [ka'nuto] nm (tubo) small tube; (fam: droga) joint.
caña ['kaɲa] nf (BOT: tallo) stem, stalk; (carrizo) reed; (vaso) tumbler; (de cerveza) glass of beer; (ANAT) shinbone; **~ de azúcar** sugar cane; **~ de pescar** fishing rod.
cañada [ka'naða] nf (entre dos montañas) gully, ravine; (camino) cattle track.
cáñamo ['kaɲamo] nm hemp.
caño ['kaɲo] nm (tubo) tube, pipe; (de albañal) sewer; (MUS) pipe; (de fuente) jet.
cañón [ka'ɲon] nm (MIL) cannon; (de fusil) barrel; (GEO) canyon, gorge.
cañonera [kaɲo'nera] nf (tb: lancha ~) gunboat.
caoba [ka'oβa] nf mahogany.
caos ['kaos] nm chaos.
cap. abr (= capítulo) ch.
capa ['kapa] nf cloak, cape; (GEO) layer, stratum; **so ~ de** under the pretext of.
capacidad [kapaθi'ðað] nf (medida) capacity; (aptitud) capacity, ability.
capacitación [kapaθita'θjon] nf training.
capar [ka'par] vt to castrate, geld.
caparazón [kapara'θon] nm shell.

capataz [kapa'taθ] nm foreman.
capaz [ka'paθ] a able, capable; (amplio) capacious, roomy.
capcioso, a [kap'θjoso, a] a wily, deceitful.
capellán [kape'ʎan] nm chaplain; (sacerdote) priest.
caperuza [kape'ruθa] nf hood.
capilla [ka'piʎa] nf chapel.
capital [kapi'tal] a capital // nm (COM) capital // nf (ciudad) capital; **~ social** share capital.
capitalismo [kapita'lismo] nm capitalism; **capitalista** a, nm/f capitalist.
capitalizar [kapitali'θar] vt to capitalize.
capitán [kapi'tan] nm captain.
capitanear [kapitane'ar] vt to captain.
capitolio [kapi'toljo] nm capitol.
capitulación [kapitula'θjon] nf (rendición) capitulation, surrender; (acuerdo) agreement, pact; **capitulaciones** (matrimoniales) nfpl marriage contract sg.
capitular [kapitu'lar] vi to come to terms, make an agreement.
capítulo [ka'pitulo] nm chapter.
capó [ka'po] nm (AUTO) bonnet.
capón [ka'pon] nm (gallo) capon.
caporal [kapo'ral] nm chief, leader.
capota [ka'pota] nf (de mujer) bonnet; (AUTO) hood (Brit), top (US).
capote [ka'pote] nm (abrigo: de militar) greatcoat; (: de torero) cloak.
Capricornio [kapri'kornjo] nm Capricorn.
capricho [ka'pritʃo] nm whim, caprice; **~so, a** a capricious.
cápsula ['kapsula] nf capsule.
captar [kap'tar] vt (comprender) to understand; (RADIO) to pick up; (atención, apoyo) to attract.
captura [kap'tura] nf capture; (JUR) arrest; **capturar** vt to capture; to arrest.
capucha [ka'putʃa] nf hood, cowl.
capullo [ka'puʎo] nm (BOT) bud; (ZOOL) cocoon; (fam) idiot.
caqui ['kaki] nm khaki.
cara ['kara] nf (ANAT, de moneda) face; (aspecto) appearance; (de disco) side; (fig) boldness; **~ a** ad facing; **de ~** opposite, facing; **dar la ~** to face the consequences; **¿~ o cruz?** heads or tails?; **¡qué ~ más dura!** what a nerve!
carabina [kara'βina] nf carbine, rifle; (persona) chaperone.
Caracas [ka'rakas] n Caracas.
caracol [kara'kol] nm (ZOOL) snail; (concha) (sea) shell.
caracolear [karakole'ar] vi (caballo) to prance about.
carácter [ka'rakter] (pl **caracteres**) nm character; **tener buen/mal ~** to be good natured/bad tempered.
característico, a [karakte'ristiko, a] a characteristic // nf characteristic.

caracterizar [karakteri'θar] *vt* (*distinguir*) to characterize, typify; (*honrar*) to confer (a) distinction on.

caradura [kara'ðura] *nm/f*: es un ~ he's got a nerve.

carajo [ka'raxo] *nm* (*fam!*): ¡~! shit! (*!*).

caramba [ka'ramba] *excl* good gracious!

carámbano [ka'rambano] *nm* icicle.

caramelo [kara'melo] *nm* (*dulce*) sweet; (*azúcar fundida*) caramel.

carapacho [kara'patʃo] *nm* shell, carapace.

caraqueño, a [kara'keɲo, a] *a, nm/f* of o from Caracas.

carátula [ka'ratula] *nf* (*careta, máscara*) mask; (*TEATRO*): la ~ the stage.

caravana [kara'βana] *nf* caravan; (*fig*) group; (*AUTO*) tailback.

carbón [kar'βon] *nm* coal; **papel** ~ carbon paper; **carboncillo** *nm* (*ARTE*) charcoal; **carbonero, a** *nm/f* coal merchant; **carbonilla** [-'niʎa] *nf* coal dust.

carbonizar [karβoni'θar] *vt* to carbonize; (*quemar*) to char.

carbono [kar'βono] *nm* carbon.

carburador [karβura'ðor] *nm* carburettor.

carcajada [karka'xaða] *nf* (loud) laugh, guffaw.

cárcel [ˈkarθel] *nf* prison, jail; (*TEC*) clamp; **carcelero, a** *a* prison *cpd* // *nm/f* warder.

carcomer [karko'mer] *vt* to bore into, eat into; (*fig*) to undermine; **~se** *vr* to become worm-eaten; (*fig*) to decay; **carcomido, a** *a* worm-eaten; (*fig*) rotten.

cardenal [karðe'nal] *nm* (*REL*) cardinal; (*MED*) bruise.

cárdeno, a [ˈkarðeno, a] *a* purple; (*lívido*) livid.

cardíaco, a [kar'ðiako, a] *a* cardiac, heart *cpd*.

cardinal [karði'nal] *a* cardinal.

cardo [ˈkarðo] *nm* thistle.

carear [kare'ar] *vt* to bring face to face; (*comparar*) to compare; **~se** *vr* to come face to face, meet.

carecer [kare'θer] *vi*: ~ de to lack, be in need of.

carencia [ka'renθja] *nf* lack; (*escasez*) shortage; (*MED*) deficiency.

carente [ka'rente] *a*: ~ de lacking in, devoid of.

carestía [kares'tia] *nf* (*escasez*) scarcity, shortage; (*COM*) high cost.

careta [ka'reta] *nf* mask.

carga [ˈkarɣa] *nf* (*peso, ELEC*) load; (*de barco*) cargo, freight; (*MIL*) charge; (*obligación, responsabilidad*) duty, obligation.

cargado, a [kar'ɣaðo, a] *a* loaded; (*ELEC*) live; (*café, té*) strong; (*cielo*) overcast.

cargamento [karɣa'mento] *nm* (*acción*) loading; (*mercancías*) load, cargo.

cargar [kar'ɣar] *vt* (*barco, arma*) to load; (*ELEC*) to charge; (*COM: algo en cuenta*) to charge; (*INFORM*) to load // *vi* (*MIL: enemigo*) to charge; (*AUTO*) to load (up); (*inclinarse*) to lean; ~ **con** to pick up, carry away; (*peso, fig*) to shoulder, bear; **~se** *vr* (*fam: estropear*) to break; (: *matar*) to bump off.

cargo [ˈkarɣo] *nm* (*puesto*) post, office; (*responsabilidad*) duty, obligation; (*fig*) weight, burden; (*JUR*) charge; **hacerse** ~ **de** to take charge of o responsibility for.

carguero [kar'ɣero] *nm* freighter, cargo boat; (*avión*) freight plane.

Caribe [ka'riβe] *nm*: el ~ the Caribbean; **del** ~ Caribbean.

caribeño, a [kari'βeɲo, a] *a* Caribbean.

caricatura [karika'tura] *nf* caricature.

caricia [ka'riθja] *nf* caress.

caridad [kari'ðað] *nf* charity.

caries [ˈkarjes] *nf inv* (*MED*) tooth decay.

cariño [ka'riɲo] *nm* affection, love; (*caricia*) caress; (*en carta*) love...; **~so, a** *a* affectionate.

caritativo, a [karita'tiβo, a] *a* charitable.

cariz [ka'riθ] *nm*: tener o tomar buen/mal ~ to look good/bad.

carmesí [karme'si] *a, nm* crimson.

carmín [kar'min] *nm* lipstick.

carnal [kar'nal] *a* carnal; **primo** ~ first cousin.

carnaval [karna'βal] *nm* carnival.

carne [ˈkarne] *nf* flesh; (*CULIN*) meat; ~ **de cerdo/cordero/ternera/vaca** pork/lamb/veal/beef.

carné [kar'ne] *nm*: ~ **de conducir** driving licence (*Brit*), driver's license (*US*); ~ **de identidad** identity card.

carnero [kar'nero] *nm* sheep, ram; (*carne*) mutton.

carnet [kar'ne(t)] *nm* = **carné**.

carnicería [karniθe'ria] *nf* butcher's (shop); (*fig: matanza*) carnage, slaughter.

carnicero, a [karni'θero, a] *a* carnivorous // *nm/f* (*tb fig*) butcher; (*carnívoro*) carnivore.

carnívoro, a [kar'niβoro, a] *a* carnivorous.

carnoso, a [kar'noso, a] *a* beefy, fat.

caro, a [ˈkaro, a] *a* dear; (*COM*) dear, expensive // *ad* dear, dearly.

carpa [ˈkarpa] *nf* (*pez*) carp; (*de circo*) big top; (*AM: de camping*) tent.

carpeta [kar'peta] *nf* folder, file.

carpintería [karpinte'ria] *nf* carpentry, joinery; **carpintero** *nm* carpenter.

carraspera [karras'pera] *nf* hoarseness.

carrera [ka'rrera] *nf* (*acción*) run(ning); (*espacio recorrido*) run; (*certamen*) race; (*trayecto*) course; (*profesión*) career; (*ESCOL*) course.

carreta |ka'rreta| *nf* wagon, cart.

carrete |ka'rrete| *nm* reel, spool; (*TEC*) coil.

carretera |karre'tera| *nf* (main) road, highway; ~ **de circunvalación** ring road; ~ **nacional** ≈ A road (*Brit*), state highway (*US*).

carretilla |karre'tiʎa| *nf* trolley; (*AGR*) (wheel)barrow.

carril |ka'rril| *nm* furrow; (*de autopista*) lane; (*FERRO*) rail.

carrillo |ka'rriʎo| *nm* (*ANAT*) cheek; (*TEC*) pulley.

carrizo |ka'rriθo| *nm* reed.

carro |'karro| *nm* cart, wagon; (*MIL*) tank; (*AM: coche*) car.

carrocería |karroθe'ria| *nf* bodywork, coachwork.

carroña |ka'rroɲa| *nf* carrion *q*.

carrusel |karru'sel| *nm* merry-go-round, roundabout.

carta |'karta| *nf* letter; (*CULIN*) menu; (*naipe*) card; (*mapa*) map; (*JUR*) document; ~ **de crédito** credit card; ~ **certificada** registered letter; ~ **marítima** chart; ~ **verde** (*AUTO*) green card.

cartel |kar'tel| *nm* (*anuncio*) poster, placard; (*ESCOL*) wall chart; (*COM*) cartel; ~**era** *nf* hoarding, billboard; (*en periódico etc*) entertainments guide; 'en ~era' 'showing'.

cartera |kar'tera| *nf* (*de bolsillo*) wallet; (*de colegial, cobrador*) satchel; (*de señora*) handbag; (*para documentos*) briefcase; (*COM*) portfolio; **ocupa la ~ de Agricultura** she is Minister of Agriculture.

carterista |karte'rista| *nm/f* pickpocket.

cartero |kar'tero| *nm* postman.

cartilla |kar'tiʎa| *nf* primer, first reading book; ~ **de ahorros** savings book.

cartón |kar'ton| *nm* cardboard.

cartucho |kar'tutʃo| *nm* (*MIL*) cartridge.

casa |'kasa| *nf* house; (*hogar*) home; (*edificio*) building; (*COM*) firm, company; ~ **consistorial** town hall; ~ **de huéspedes** boarding house; ~ **de socorro** first aid post.

casadero, a |kasa'ðero, a| *a* of marrying age.

casado, a |ka'saðo, a| *a* married // *nm/f* married man/woman.

casamiento |kasa'mjento| *nm* marriage, wedding.

casar |ka'sar| *vt* to marry; (*JUR*) to quash, annul; ~**se** *vr* to marry, get married.

cascabel |kaska'ßel| *nm* (small) bell.

cascada |kas'kaða| *nf* waterfall.

cascanueces |kaska'nweθes| *nm inv* nutcrackers.

cascar |kas'kar| *vt*, **cascarse** *vr* to crack, split, break (open).

cáscara |'kaskaɾa| *nf* (*de huevo, fruta seca*) shell; (*de fruta*) skin; (*de limón*) peel.

casco |'kasko| *nm* (*de bombero, soldado*) helmet; (*NAUT: de barco*) hull; (*ZOOL: de caballo*) hoof; (*botella*) empty bottle; (*de ciudad*): **el ~ antiguo** the old part; **el ~ urbano** the town centre.

cascote |kas'kote| *nm* rubble.

caserío |kase'rio| *nm* hamlet; (*casa*) country house.

casero, a |ka'sero, a| *a* (*pan etc*) homemade // *nm/f* (*propietario*) landlord/lady; (*COM*) house agent; **ser muy ~** to be home-loving; **'comida casera'** 'home cooking'.

caseta |ka'seta| *nf* hut; (*para bañista*) cubicle; (*de feria*) stall.

casete |ka'sete| *nm o f* cassette.

casi |'kasi| *ad* almost, nearly; ~ **nada** hardly anything; ~ **nunca** hardly ever, almost never; ~ **te caes** you almost fell.

casilla |ka'siʎa| *nf* (*casita*) hut, cabin; (*TEATRO*) box office; (*AJEDREZ*) square; (*para cartas*) pigeonhole.

casino |ka'sino| *nm* club; (*de juego*) casino.

caso |'kaso| *nm* case; **en ~ de...** in case of...; **el ~ es que** the fact is that; **en ese ~** in that case; **hacer ~ a** to pay attention to; **hacer o venir al ~** to be relevant.

caspa |'kaspa| *nf* dandruff.

cassette |ka'sete| *nm o f* = **casete**.

casta |'kasta| *nf* caste; (*raza*) breed; (*linaje*) lineage.

castaña |kas'taɲa| *nf* chestnut.

castañetear |kastaɲete'ar| *vi* (*dientes*) to chatter.

castaño, a |kas'taɲo, a| *a* chestnut (-coloured), brown // *nm* chestnut tree.

castañuelas |kasta'ɲwelas| *nfpl* castanets.

castellano, a |kaste'ʎano, a| *a* Castilian // *nm* (*LING*) Castilian, Spanish.

castidad |kasti'ðað| *nf* chastity, purity.

castigar |kasti'yar| *vt* to punish; (*DEPORTE*) to penalize; (*afligir*) to afflict; **castigo** *nm* punishment; (*DEPORTE*) penalty.

Castilla |kas'tiʎa| *nf* Castille.

castillo |kas'tiʎo| *nm* castle.

castizo, a |kas'tiθo, a| *a* (*LING*) pure; (*de buena casta*) purebred, pedigree.

casto, a |'kasto, a| *a* chaste, pure.

castor |kas'tor| *nm* beaver.

castrar |kas'trar| *vt* to castrate.

casual |ka'swal| *a* chance, accidental; ~**idad** *nf* chance, accident; (*combinación de circunstancias*) coincidence; **¡qué ~idad!** what a coincidence!

cataclismo |kata'klismo| *nm* cataclysm.

catador |kata'ðor, a| *nm/f* wine taster.

catalán, ana |kata'lan, ana| *a, nm/f* Catalan // *nm* (*LING*) Catalan.

catalizador |kataliθa'ðor| *nm* catalyst.

catálogo |ka'taloxo| *nm* catalogue.

Cataluña |kata'luɲa| nf Catalonia.

catar |ka'tar| vt to taste, sample.

catarata |kata'rata| nf (GEO) waterfall; (MED) cataract.

catarro |ka'tarro| nm catarrh; (constipado) cold.

catástrofe |ka'tastrofe| nf catastrophe.

catedral |kate'ðral| nf cathedral.

catedrático, a |kate'ðratiko, a| nm/f professor.

categoría |katexo'ria| nf category; (rango) rank, standing; (calidad) quality; **de ~** (hotel) top-class.

categórico, a |kate'xoriko, a| a categorical.

catolicismo |katoli'θismo| nm Catholicism.

católico, a |ka'toliko, a| a, nm/f Catholic.

catorce |ka'torθe| num fourteen.

cauce |'kauθe| nm (de río) riverbed; (fig) channel.

caución |kau'θjon| nf bail; **caucionar** vt (JUR) to bail, go bail for.

caucho |'kautʃo| nm rubber; (AM: llanta) tyre.

caudal |kau'ðal| nm (de río) volume, flow; (fortuna) wealth; (abundancia) abundance; **~oso, a** a (río) large; (persona) wealthy, rich.

caudillo |kau'ðiʎo| nm leader, chief.

causa |'kausa| nf cause; (razón) reason; (JUR) lawsuit, case; **a ~ de** because of.

causar |kau'sar| vt to cause.

cautela |kau'tela| nf caution, cautiousness; **cauteloso, a** a cautious, wary.

cautivar |kauti'ßar| vt to capture; (fig) to captivate.

cautiverio |kauti'ßerjo| nm, **cautividad** |kautißi'ðað| nf captivity.

cautivo, a |kau'tißo, a| a, nm/f captive.

cauto, a |'kauto, a| a cautious, careful.

cava |'kaßa| nm champagne-type wine.

cavar |ka'ßar| vt to dig.

caverna |ka'ßerna| nf cave, cavern.

cavidad |kaßi'ðað| nf cavity.

cavilar |kaßi'lar| vt to ponder.

cayado |ka'jaðo| nm (de pastor) crook; (de obispo) crozier.

cayendo etc vb ver **caer**.

caza |'kaθa| nf (acción: gen) hunting; (: con fusil) shooting; (una ~) hunt, chase; (animales) game // nm (AVIAT) fighter.

cazador, a |kaθa'ðor, a| nm/f hunter // nf jacket.

cazar |ka'θar| vt to hunt; (perseguir) to chase; (prender) to catch.

cazo |'kaθo| nm saucepan.

cazuela |ka'θwela| nf (vasija) pan; (guisado) casserole.

cebada |θe'ßaða| nf barley.

cebar |θe'ßar| vt (animal) to fatten (up); (anzuelo) to bait; (MIL, TEC) to prime.

cebo |'θeßo| nm (para animales) feed, food; (para peces, fig) bait; (de arma) charge.

cebolla |θe'ßoʎa| nf onion; **cebollín** nm spring onion.

cebra |'θeßra| nf zebra.

cecear |θeθe'ar| vi to lisp; **ceceo** nm lisp.

cedazo |θe'ðaθo| nm sieve.

ceder |θe'ðer| vt to hand over, give up, part with // vi (renunciar) to give in, yield; (disminuir) to diminish, decline; (romperse) to give way.

cedro |'θeðro| nm cedar.

cédula |'θeðula| nf certificate, document.

CEE nf abr (= Comunidad Económica Europea) EEC.

cegar |θe'xar| vt to blind; (tubería etc) to block up, stop up // vi to go blind; **~se** vr: **~se (de)** to be blinded (by).

ceguera |θe'xera| nf blindness.

ceja |'θexa| nf eyebrow.

cejar |θe'xar| vi (fig) to back down.

celada |θe'laða| nf ambush, trap.

celador, a |θela'ðor, a| nm/f (de edificio) watchman; (de museo etc) attendant.

celda |'θelda| nf cell.

celebración |θeleßra'θjon| nf celebration.

celebrar |θele'ßrar| vt to celebrate; (alabar) to praise // vi to be glad; **~se** vr to occur, take place.

célebre |'θeleßre| a famous.

celebridad |θeleßri'ðað| nf fame; (persona) celebrity.

celeste |θe'leste| a sky-blue; (ASTRO) celestial, heavenly.

celestial |θeles'tjal| a celestial, heavenly.

celibato |θeli'ßato| nm celibacy.

célibe |'θeliße| a, nm/f celibate.

celo |'θelo| nm zeal; (REL) fervour; (ZOOL): **en ~** on heat; **~s** nmpl jealousy sg; **tener ~s** to be jealous.

celofán |θelo'fan| nm cellophane.

celoso, a |θe'loso, a| a (envidioso) jealous; (trabajador) zealous; (desconfiado) suspicious.

celta |'θelta| a Celtic // nm/f Celt.

célula |'θelula| nf cell.

celuloide |θelu'loiðe| nm celluloid.

cementerio |θemen'terjo| nm cemetery, graveyard.

cemento |θe'mento| nm cement; (hormigón) concrete; (AM: cola) glue.

cena |'θena| nf evening meal, dinner.

cenagal |θena'xal| nm bog, quagmire.

cenar |θe'nar| vt to have for dinner // vi to have dinner.

cenicero |θeni'θero| nm ashtray.

cenit |θe'nit| nm zenith.

ceniza |θe'niθa| nf ash, ashes pl.

censo |'θenso| nm census; **~ electoral** electoral roll.

censura |θen'sura| nf (POL) censorship; (moral) censure, criticism.

censurar |θensu'rar| vt (idea) to censure; (cortar: película) to censor.

centella |θen'teʎa| nf spark.

centellear [θente'ear] *vi* (*metal*) to gleam; (*estrella*) to twinkle; (*fig*) to sparkle; **centelleo** *nm* gleam(ing); twinkling; sparkling.

centenar [θente'nar] *nm* hundred.

centenario, a [θente'narjo, a] *a* centenary; hundred-year-old // *nm* centenary.

centésimo, a [θen'tesimo, a] *a* hundredth.

centígrado [θen'tiɣraðo] *a* centigrade.

centímetro [θen'timetro] *nm* centimetre (*Brit*), centimeter (*US*).

céntimo ['θentimo] *nm* cent.

centinela [θenti'nela] *nm* sentry, guard.

centollo [θen'toʎo] *nm* spider crab.

central [θen'tral] *a* central // *nf* head office; (*TEC*) plant; (*TEL*) exchange; ~ **nuclear** nuclear power station.

centralización [θentraliθa'θjon] *nf* centralization.

centralizar [θentrali'θar] *vt* to centralize.

centrar [θen'trar] *vt* to centre.

céntrico, a ['θentriko, a] *a* central.

centrista [θen'trista] *a* centre *cpd*.

centro ['θentro] *nm* centre; ~ **comercial** shopping centre; ~ **juvenil** youth club.

centroamericano, a [θentroameri'kano, a] *a, nm/f* Central American.

ceñir [θe'nir] *vt* (*rodear*) to encircle, surround; (*ajustar*) to fit (tightly); (*apretar*) to tighten.

ceño ['θeno] *nm* frown, scowl; **fruncir el** ~ to frown, knit one's brow.

CEOE *nf abr* (*Esp = Confederación Española de Organizaciones Empresariales*) ≈ CBI (*Brit*), employers' organization.

cepillar [θepi'ʎar] *vt* to brush; (*madera*) to plane (down).

cepillo [θe'piʎo] *nm* brush; (*para madera*) plane.

cera ['θera] *nf* wax.

cerámica [θe'ramika] *nf* ceramics *sg*, pottery.

cerca ['θerka] *nf* fence // *ad* near, nearby, close; ~s *nmpl* foreground *sg*; ~ **de** *prep* near, close to.

cercanía [θerka'nia] *nf* nearness, closeness; ~s *nfpl* outskirts, suburbs.

cercano, a [θer'kano, a] *a* close, near.

cercar [θer'kar] *vt* to fence in; (*rodear*) to surround.

cerciorar [θerθjo'rar] *vt* (*asegurar*) to assure; ~**se** *vr* (*descubrir*) to find out; (*asegurarse*) to make sure.

cerco ['θerko] *nm* (*AGR*) enclosure; (*AM*) fence; (*MIL*) siege.

cerdo ['θerðo] *nm* pig.

cereal [θere'al] *nm* cereal; ~**es** *nmpl* cereals, grain *sg*.

cerebro [θe'reβro] *nm* brain; (*fig*) brains *pl*.

ceremonia [θere'monja] *nf* ceremony; **ceremonial** *a, nm* ceremonial;

ceremonioso, a *a* ceremonious; (*cumplido*) formal.

cereza [θe'reθa] *nf* cherry.

cerilla [θe'riʎa] *nf* (*fósforo*) match.

cernerse [θer'nerse] *vr* to hover.

cernidor [θerni'ðor] *nm* sieve.

cero ['θero] *nm* nothing, zero.

cerrado, a [θe'rraðo, a] *a* closed, shut; (*con llave*) locked; (*tiempo*) cloudy, overcast; (*curva*) sharp; (*acento*) thick, broad.

cerradura [θerra'ðura] *nf* (*acción*) closing; (*mecanismo*) lock.

cerrajero [θerra'xero] *nm* locksmith.

cerrar [θe'rrar] *vt* to close, shut; (*paso, carretera*) to close; (*grifo*) to turn off; (*cuenta, negocio*) to close // *vi* to close, shut; (*la noche*) to come down; ~**se** *vr* to close, shut; ~ **con llave** to lock; ~ **un trato** to strike a bargain.

cerro ['θerro] *nm* hill.

cerrojo [θe'rroxo] *nm* (*herramienta*) bolt; (*de puerta*) latch.

certamen [θer'tamen] *nm* competition, contest.

certero, a [θer'tero, a] *a* (*gen*) accurate.

certeza [θer'teθa], **certidumbre** [θerti'ðumbre] *nf* certainty.

certificado [θertifi'kaðo] *nm* certificate.

certificar [θertifi'kar] *vt* (*asegurar, atestar*) to certify.

cervatillo [θerβa'tiʎo] *nm* fawn.

cervecería [θerβeθe'ria] *nf* (*fábrica*) brewery; (*bar*) public house, pub.

cerveza [θer'βeθa] *nf* beer.

cesación [θesa'θjon] *nf* cessation, suspension.

cesante [θe'sante] *a* redundant.

cesantía [θesan'tia] *nf* unemployment.

cesar [θe'sar] *vi* to cease, stop // *vt* (*funcionario*) to remove from office.

cese ['θese] *nm* (*de trabajo*) dismissal; (*de pago*) suspension.

césped ['θespeð] *nm* grass, lawn.

cesta ['θesta] *nf* basket.

cesto ['θesto] *nm* (large) basket, hamper.

cetro ['θetro] *nm* sceptre.

cfr *abr* (= *confróntese*) cf.

ch... *ver bajo la letra* CH, *después de* C.

Cía *abr* (= *compañía*) Co.

cianuro [θja'nuro] *nm* cyanide.

cicatriz [θika'triθ] *nf* scar; ~**ar** *vt* to heal; ~**arse** *vr* to heal (up), form a scar.

ciclismo [θi'klismo] *nm* cycling.

ciclo ['θiklo] *nm* cycle.

ciclón [θi'klon] *nm* cyclone.

ciego, a ['θjeɣo, a] *a* blind // *nm/f* blind man/woman.

cielo ['θjelo] *nm* sky; (*REL*) heaven; ¡~**s**! good heavens!

ciempiés [θjem'pjes] *nm inv* centipede.

cien [θjen] *num ver* **ciento**.

ciénaga ['θjenaɣa] *nf* marsh, swamp.

ciencia ['θjenθja] *nf* science; ~**s** *nfpl*

(*ESCOL*) science *sg*; ~**-ficción** *nf* science fiction.

cieno ['θjeno] *nm* mud, mire.

científico, a [θjen'tifiko, a] *a* scientific // *nm/f* scientist.

ciento ['θjento], **cien** *num* hundred; **pagar al 10 por** ~ to pay at 10 per cent.

cierne ['θjerne] *nm*: **en** ~ in blossom.

cierre *etc vb ver* **cerrar** // ['θjerre] *nm* closing, shutting; (*con llave*) locking; ~ **de cremallera** zip (fastener).

cierro *etc vb ver* **cerrar**.

cierto, a ['θjerto, a] *a* sure, certain; (*un tal*) a certain: (*correcto*) right, correct; ~ **hombre** a certain man; **ciertas personas** certain *o* some people; **sí, es** ~ yes, that's correct.

ciervo ['θjerβo] *nm* (*ZOOL*) deer; (: *macho*) stag.

cierzo ['θjerθo] *nm* north wind.

cifra ['θifra] *nf* number, numeral; (*cantidad*) number, quantity; (*secreta*) code.

cifrar [θi'frar] *vt* to code, write in code; (*resumir*) to abridge.

cigala [θi'yala] *nf* Norway lobster.

cigarra [θi'yarra] *nf* cicada.

cigarrera [θiya'rrera] *nf* cigar case.

cigarrillo [θiya'rriʎo] *nm* cigarette.

cigarro [θi'yarro] *nm* cigarette; (*puro*) cigar.

cigüeña [θi'ɣweɲa] *nf* stork.

cilíndrico, a [θi'lindriko, a] *a* cylindrical.

cilindro [θi'lindro] *nm* cylinder.

cima ['θima] *nf* (*de montaña*) top, peak; (*de árbol*) top; (*fig*) height.

címbalo ['θimbalo] *nm* cymbal.

cimbrar [θim'brar], **cimbrear** [θimbre'ar] *vt* to brandish; ~**se** *vr* to sway.

cimentar [θimen'tar] *vt* to lay the foundations of; (*fig: fundar*) to found.

cimiento [θi'mjento] *nm* foundation.

cinc [θink] *nm* zinc.

cincel [θin'θel] *nm* chisel; ~**ar** *vt* to chisel.

cinco ['θinko] *num* five.

cincuenta [θin'kwenta] *num* fifty.

cine ['θine] *nm* cinema.

cineasta [θine'asta] *nm/f* (*director de cine*) film director.

cinematográfico, a [θinemato'ɣrafiko, a] *a* cine-, film *cpd*.

cínico, a ['θiniko, a] *a* cynical // *nm/f* cynic.

cinismo [θi'nismo] *nm* cynicism.

cinta ['θinta] *nf* band, strip; (*de tela*) ribbon; (*película*) reel; (*de máquina de escribir*) ribbon; ~ **adhesiva** sticky tape; ~ **magnetofónica** tape; ~ **métrica** tape measure.

cinto ['θinto] *nm* belt.

cintura [θin'tura] *nf* waist.

cinturón [θintu'ron] *nm* belt; ~ **de seguridad** safety belt.

ciprés [θi'pres] *nm* cypress (tree).

circo ['θirko] *nm* circus.

circuito [θir'kwito] *nm* circuit.

circulación [θirkula'θjon] *nf* circulation; (*AUTO*) traffic.

circular [θirku'lar] *a, nf* circular // *vi, vt* to circulate // *vi* (*AUTO*) to drive; '**circule por la derecha**' 'keep (to the) right'.

círculo ['θirkulo] *nm* circle.

circuncidar [θirkunθi'dar] *vt* to circumcise.

circundar [θirkun'dar] *vt* to surround.

circunferencia [θirkunfe'renθja] *nf* circumference.

circunscribir [θirkunskri'ßir] *vt* to circumscribe; ~**se** *vr* to be limited.

circunscripción [θirkunskrip'θjon] *nf* division; (*POL*) constituency.

circunspecto, a [θirkuns'pekto, a] *a* circumspect, cautious.

circunstancia [θirkuns'tanθja] *nf* circumstance.

circunstante [θirkuns'tante] *nm/f* onlooker, bystander.

cirio ['θirjo] *nm* (wax) candle.

ciruela [θi'rwela] *nf* plum; ~ **pasa** prune.

cirugía [θiru'xia] *nf* surgery; ~ **estética** *o* **plástica** plastic surgery.

cirujano [θiru'xano] *nm* surgeon.

cisne ['θisne] *nm* swan.

cisterna [θis'terna] *nf* cistern, tank.

cita ['θita] *nf* appointment, meeting; (*de novios*) date; (*referencia*) quotation.

citación [θita'θjon] *nf* (*JUR*) summons *sg*.

citar [θi'tar] *vt* (*gen*) to make an appointment with; (*JUR*) to summons; (*un autor, texto*) to quote; ~**se** *vr*: **se citaron en el cine** they arranged to meet at the cinema.

cítricos ['θitrikos] *nmpl* citrus fruit(s).

ciudad [θju'ðað] *nf* town; (*más grande*) city; ~**anía** *nf* citizenship; ~**ano, a** *nm/f* citizen.

cívico, a ['θißiko, a] *a* civic.

civil [θi'ßil] *a* civil // *nm* (*guardia*) policeman.

civilización [θißiliθa'θjon] *nf* civilization.

civilizar [θißili'θar] *vt* to civilize.

civismo [θi'ßismo] *nm* public spirit.

cizaña [θi'θaɲa] *nf* (*fig*) discord.

cl. *abr* (= centilitro) cl.

clamar [kla'mar] *vt* to clamour for, cry out for // *vi* to cry out, clamour.

clamor [kla'mor] *nm* (*grito*) cry, shout; (*fig*) clamour, protest.

clandestino, a [klandes'tino, a] *a* clandestine; (*POL*) underground.

clara ['klara] *nf* (*de huevo*) egg white.

claraboya [klara'ßoja] *nf* skylight.

clarear [klare'ar] *vi* (*el día*) to dawn; (*el cielo*) to clear up, brighten up; ~**se** *vr* to be transparent.

clarete [kla'rete] *nm* rosé (wine).

claridad [klari'ðað] *nf* (*del día*) brightness; (*de estilo*) clarity.

clarificar [klarifi'kar] *vt* to clarify.
clarín [kla'rin] *nm* bugle.
clarinete [klari'nete] *nm* clarinet.
clarividencia [klariβi'ðenθja] *nf* clairvoyance; (*fig*) far-sightedness.
claro, a ['klaro, a] *a* clear; (*luminoso*) bright; (*color*) light; (*evidente*) clear, evident; (*poco espeso*) thin // *nm* (*en bosque*) clearing // *ad* clearly // *excl* of course!
clase ['klase] *nf* class; ~ **alta/media/obrera** upper/middle/working class.
clásico, a ['klasiko, a] *a* classical; (*fig*) classic.
clasificación [klasifika'θjon] *nf* classification; (*DEPORTE*) league (table).
clasificar [klasifi'kar] *vt* to classify.
claudia ['klauðja] *nf* greengage.
claudicar [klauði'kar] *vi* (*fig*) to back down.
claustro ['klaustro] *nm* cloister.
cláusula ['klausula] *nf* clause.
clausura [klau'sura] *nf* closing, closure; **clausurar** *vt* (*congreso etc*) to bring to a close.
clavar [kla'βar] *vt* (*clavo*) to hammer in; (*cuchillo*) to stick, thrust; (*tablas etc*) to nail (together).
clave ['klaβe] *nf* key; (*MUS*) clef.
clavel [kla'βel] *nm* carnation.
clavícula [kla'βikula] *nf* collar bone.
clavija [kla'βixa] *nf* peg, dowel, pin; (*ELEC*) plug.
clavo ['klaβo] *nm* (*de metal*) nail; (*BOT*) clove.
claxon ['klakson] (*pl* ~s) *nm* horn.
clemencia [kle'menθja] *nf* mercy, clemency.
cleptómano, a [klep'tomano, a] *nm/f* kleptomaniac.
clerical [kleri'kal] *a* clerical.
clérigo ['kleriɣo] *nm* clergyman.
clero ['klero] *nm* clergy.
cliché [kli'tʃe] *nm* cliché; (*FOTO*) negative.
cliente, a ['kljente, a] *nm/f* client, customer.
clientela [kljen'tela] *nf* clientele, customers *pl*.
clima ['klima] *nm* climate.
climatizado, a [klimati'θaðo, a] *a* air-conditioned.
clínica ['klinika] *nf* clinic; (*particular*) private hospital.
clip [klip] (*pl* ~s) *nm* paper clip.
clorhídrico, a [klo'riðriko, a] *a* hydrochloric.
club [klub] (*pl* ~s *o* ~es) *nm* club; ~ **de jóvenes** youth club.
cm *abr* (= *centímetro, centímetros*) cm.
C.N.T. *abr* (*Esp*) = *Confederación Nacional de Trabajo*.
coacción [koak'θjon] *nf* coercion, compulsion.
coagular [koaɣu'lar] *vt*, **coagularse** *vr*

(*leche, sangre*) to clot; **coágulo** *nm* clot.
coalición [koali'θjon] *nf* coalition.
coartada [koar'taða] *nf* alibi.
coartar [koar'tar] *vt* to limit, restrict.
coba ['koβa] *nf*: **dar ~ a uno** to soft-soap sb.
cobarde [ko'βarðe] *a* cowardly // *nm* coward; **cobardía** *nf* cowardice.
cobaya [ko'βaja] *nf*, **cobayo** [ko'βajo] *nm* guinea pig.
cobertizo [koβer'tiθo] *nm* shelter.
cobertor [koβer'tor] *nm* bedspread.
cobertura [koβer'tura] *nf* cover.
cobija [ko'βixa] *nf* (*AM*) blanket.
cobijar [koβi'xar] *vt* (*cubrir*) to cover; (*abrigar*) to shelter; **cobijo** *nm* shelter.
cobra ['koβra] *nf* cobra.
cobrador, a [koβra'ðor, a] *nm/f* (*de autobús*) conductor/conductress; (*de impuestos, gas*) collector.
cobrar [ko'βrar] *vt* (*cheque*) to cash; (*sueldo*) to collect, draw; (*objeto*) to recover; (*precio*) to charge; (*deuda*) to collect // *vi* to draw one's pay; ~**se** *vr* to recover, get well; **cóbrese al entregar** cash on delivery (COD).
cobre ['koβre] *nm* copper; ~s *nmpl* brass instruments.
cobro ['koβro] *nm* (*de cheque*) cashing; (*pago*) payment; **presentar al ~** to cash.
Coca-Cola ['koka'kola] *nf* ® Coca-Cola ®.
cocaína [koka'ina] *nf* cocaine.
cocción [kok'θjon] *nf* (*CULIN*) cooking; (: *el hervir*) boiling.
cocear [koθe'ar] *vi* to kick.
cocer [ko'θer] *vt*, *vi* to cook; (*en agua*) to boil; (*en horno*) to bake.
cocido [ko'θiðo] *nm* stew.
cocina [ko'θina] *nf* kitchen; (*aparato*) cooker, stove; (*acto*) cookery; ~ **eléctrica/de gas** electric/gas cooker; ~ **francesa** French cuisine; **cocinar** *vt*, *vi* to cook.
cocinero, a [koθi'nero, a] *nm/f* cook.
coco ['koko] *nm* coconut; ~**tero** *nm* coconut palm.
cocodrilo [koko'ðrilo] *nm* crocodile.
coche ['kotʃe] *nm* (*AUTO*) car (*Brit*), automobile (*US*); (*de tren, de caballos*) coach, carriage; (*para niños*) pram (*Brit*), baby carriage (*US*); ~ **celular** Black Maria, prison van; ~ **fúnebre** hearse; **coche-cama** (*pl* **coches-camas**) *nm* (*FERRO*) sleeping car, sleeper.
cochera [ko'tʃera] *nf* garage; (*de autobuses, trenes*) depot.
coche restaurante (*pl* **coches restaurante**) *nm* (*FERRO*) dining car, diner.
cochino, a [ko'tʃino, a] *a* filthy, dirty // *nm/f* pig.
codazo [ko'ðaθo] *nm*: **dar un ~ a uno** to nudge sb.
codear [koðe'ar] *vi* to elbow, nudge; ~**se**

vr: ~se con to rub shoulders with.

codicia |ko'ðiθja| *nf* greed; (*fig*) lust; **codiciar** *vt* to covet; **codicioso, a** *a* covetous.

código |'koðiɣo| *nm* code; ~ **de barras** bar code; ~ **civil** common law.

codillo |ko'ðiʎo| *nm* (*ZOOL*) knee; (*TEC*) elbow (joint).

codo |'koðo| *nm* (*ANAT. de tubo*) elbow; (*ZOOL*) knee.

codorniz |koðor'niθ| *nf* quail.

coerción |koer'θjon| *nf* coercion.

coetáneo, a |koe'taneo, a| *a, nm/f* contemporary.

coexistir |koe(k)sis'tir| *vi* to coexist.

cofradía |kofra'ðia| *nf* brotherhood, fraternity.

coger |ko'xer| *vt* (*Esp*) to take (hold of); (*objeto caído*) to pick up; (*frutas*) to pick, harvest; (*resfriado, ladrón, pelota*) to catch // *vi*: ~ **por el buen camino** to take the right road; ~se *vr* (*el dedo*) to catch; ~se **a algo** to get hold of sth.

cogollo |ko'ɣoʎo| *nm* (*de lechuga*) heart.

cogote |ko'ɣote| *nm* back *o* nape of the neck.

cohabitar |koaβi'tar| *vi* to live together, cohabit.

cohecho |ko'etʃo| *nm* (*acción*) bribery; (*soborno*) bribe.

coherente |koe'rente| *a* coherent.

cohesión |koe'sjon| *nm* cohesion.

cohete |ko'ete| *nm* rocket.

cohibido, a |koi'βiðo, a| *a* (*PSICO*) inhibited; (*tímido*) shy.

cohibir |koi'βir| *vt* to restrain, restrict.

coima |ko'ima| *nf* (*AM*) bribe.

coincidencia |koinθi'ðenθja| *nf* coincidence.

coincidir |koinθi'ðir| *vi* (*en idea*) to coincide, agree; (*en lugar*) to coincide.

coito |'koito| *nm* intercourse, coitus.

coja *etc vb ver* **coger.**

cojear |koxe'ar| *vi* (*persona*) to limp, hobble; (*mueble*) to wobble, rock.

cojera |ko'xera| *nf* lameness; (*andar cojo*) limp.

cojín |ko'xin| *nm* cushion; **cojinete** *nm* small cushion, pad; (*TEC*) ball bearing.

cojo, a *etc vb ver* **coger** // |'koxo, a| *a* (*que no puede andar*) lame, crippled; (*mueble*) wobbly // *nm/f* lame person, cripple.

cojón |ko'xon| *nm*: ¡**cojones!** (*fam!*) shit! (!); **cojonudo, a** *a* (*fam*) great, fantastic.

col |kol| *nf* cabbage; ~es **de Bruselas** Brussels sprouts.

cola |'kola| *nf* tail; (*de gente*) queue; (*lugar*) end, last place; (*para pegar*) glue, gum; **hacer** ~ to queue (up).

colaborador, a |kolaβora'ðor, a| *nm/f* collaborator.

colaborar |kolaβo'rar| *vi* to collaborate.

colada |ko'laða| *nf*: **hacer la** ~ to do the washing.

colador |kola'ðor| *nm* (*de té*) strainer; (*para verduras etc*) colander.

colapso |ko'lapso| *nm* collapse; ~ **nervioso** nervous breakdown.

colar |ko'lar| *vt* (*líquido*) to strain off; (*metal*) to cast // *vi* to ooze, seep (through); ~se *vr* to jump the queue; ~se **en** to get into without paying; (*fiesta*) to gatecrash.

colateral |kolate'ral| *nm* collateral.

colcha |'koltʃa| *nf* bedspread.

colchón |kol'tʃon| *nm* mattress.

colchoneta |koltʃo'neta| *nf* (*en gimnasio*) mattress.

colear |kole'ar| *vi* (*perro*) to wag its tail.

colección |kolek'θjon| *nf* collection; **coleccionar** *vt* to collect; **coleccionista** *nm/f* collector.

colecta |ko'lekta| *nf* collection.

colectivo, a |kolek'tiβo, a| *a* collective, joint // *nm* (*AM*) (small) bus.

colector |kolek'tor| *nm* collector; (*sumidero*) sewer.

colega |ko'leɣa| *nm/f* colleague.

colegial, a |kole'xjal, a| *nm/f* schoolboy/girl.

colegio |ko'lexjo| *nm* college; (*escuela*) school; (*de abogados etc*) association.

colegir |kole'xir| *vt* (*juntar*) to collect, gather; (*deducir*) to infer, conclude.

cólera |'kolera| *nf* (*ira*) anger; (*MED*) cholera; **colérico, a** |ko'leriko, a| *a* irascible, bad-tempered.

colesterol |koleste'rol| *nm* cholesterol.

coleta |ko'leta| *nf* pigtail.

colgante |kol'ɣante| *a* hanging // *nm* (*joya*) pendant.

colgar |kol'ɣar| *vt* to hang (up); (*ropa*) to hang out // *vi* to hang; (*teléfono*) to hang up.

coliflor |koli'flor| *nf* cauliflower.

colilla |ko'liʎa| *nf* cigarette end, butt.

colina |ko'lina| *nf* hill.

colindante |kolin'dante| *a* adjacent, neighbouring.

colindar |kolin'dar| *vi* to adjoin, be adjacent.

colisión |koli'sjon| *nf* collision; ~ **de frente** head-on crash.

colmado, a |kol'maðo, a| *a* full.

colmar |kol'mar| *vt* to fill to the brim; (*fig*) to fulfil, realize.

colmena |kol'mena| *nf* beehive.

colmillo |kol'miʎo| *nm* (*diente*) eye tooth; (*de elefante*) tusk; (*de perro*) fang.

colmo |'kolmo| *nm* height, summit; ¡**es el** ~! it's the limit!

colocación |koloka'θjon| *nf* (*acto*) placing; (*empleo*) job, position; (*situación*) place, position.

colocar |kolo'kar| *vt* to place, put, position; (*dinero*) to invest; (*poner en* *empleo*) to find a job for; ~se *vr* to get a job.

Colombia [ko'lombja] *nf* Colombia; **colombiano, a** *a, nm/f* Colombian.

colonia [ko'lonja] *nf* colony; (*de casas*) housing estate; (*agua de* ~) cologne.

colonización [koloniθa'θjon] *nf* colonization; **colonizador, a** [koloniθa'ðor, a] *a* colonizing // *nm/f* colonist, settler.

colonizar [koloni'θar] *vt* to colonize.

coloquio [ko'lokjo] *nm* conversation; (*congreso*) conference.

color [ko'lor] *nm* colour.

colorado, a [kolo'raðo, a] *a* (*rojo*) red; (*chiste*) rude.

colorante [kolo'rante] *nm* colouring.

colorar [kolo'rar] *vt* to colour; (*teñir*) to dye.

colorear [kolore'ar] *vt* to colour.

colorete [kolo'rete] *nm* blusher.

colorido [kolo'riðo] *nm* colouring.

columna [ko'lumna] *nf* column; (*pilar*) pillar; (*apoyo*) support.

columpiar [kolum'pjar] *vt*, **columpiarse** *vr* to swing; **columpio** *nm* swing.

collar [ko'ʎar] *nm* necklace; (*de perro*) collar.

coma ['koma] *nf* comma // *nm* (MED) coma.

comadre [ko'maðre] *nf* (*madrina*) godmother; (*vecina*) neighbour; (*chismosa*) gossip; ~**ar** *vi* to gossip.

comandancia [koman'danθja] *nf* command.

comandante [koman'dante] *nm* commandant.

comandar [koman'dar] *vt* to command.

comarca [ko'marka] *nf* region.

comba ['komba] *nf* (*curva*) curve; (*cuerda*) skipping rope; **saltar a la** ~ to skip.

combar [kom'bar] *vt* to bend, curve.

combate [kom'bate] *nm* fight; (*fig*) battle; **combatiente** *nm* combatant.

combatir [komba'tir] *vt* to fight, combat.

combinación [kombina'θjon] *nf* combination; (*QUIMICA*) compound; (*bebida*) cocktail; (*plan*) scheme, setup; (*prenda*) slip.

combinar [kombi'nar] *vt* to combine.

combustible [kombus'tiβle] *nm* fuel.

combustión [kombus'tjon] *nf* combustion.

comedia [ko'meðja] *nf* comedy; (*TEATRO*) play, drama.

comediante [kome'ðjante] *nm/f* (comic) actor/actress.

comedido, a [kome'ðiðo, a] *a* moderate.

comedor, a [kome'ðor, a] *nm/f* (*persona*) glutton // *nm* (*habitación*) dining room; (*restaurante*) restaurant; (*cantina*) canteen.

comensal [komen'sal] *nm/f* fellow guest (*o diner*).

comentar [komen'tar] *vt* to comment on;

(*fam*) to discuss.

comentario [komen'tarjo] *nm* comment, remark; (*literario*) commentary; ~**s** *nmpl* gossip *sg*.

comentarista [komenta'rista] *nm/f* commentator.

comenzar [komen'θar] *vt*, *vi* to begin, start, commence; ~ **a hacer algo** to begin *o* start doing sth.

comer [ko'mer] *vt* to eat; (*DAMAS, AJEDREZ*) to take, capture // *vi* to eat; (*almorzar*) to have lunch; ~se *vr* to eat up.

comercial [komer'θjal] *a* commercial; (*relativo al negocio*) business *cpd*.

comerciante [komer'θjante] *nm/f* trader, merchant.

comerciar [komer'θjar] *vi* to trade, do business.

comercio [ko'merθjo] *nm* commerce, trade; (*negocio*) business; (*fig*) dealings *pl*.

comestible [komes'tiβle] *a* eatable, edible; ~**s** *nmpl* food *sg*, foodstuffs.

cometa [ko'meta] *nm* comet // *nf* kite.

cometer [kome'ter] *vt* to commit.

cometido [kome'tiðo] *nm* (*misión*) task, assignment; (*deber*) commitment.

comezón [kome'θon] *nf* itch, itching.

comicios [ko'miθjos] *nmpl* elections.

cómico, a ['komiko, a] *a* comic(al) // *nm/f* comedian; (*de teatro*) (comic) actor/actress.

comida [ko'miða] *nf* (*alimento*) food; (*almuerzo, cena*) meal; (*de mediodía*) lunch.

comidilla [komi'ðiʎa] *nf*: **ser la** ~ **de la ciudad** to be the talk of the town.

comienzo *etc vb ver* **comenzar** // [ko'mjenθo] *nm* beginning, start.

comilona [komi'lona] *nf* (*fam*) blow-out.

comillas [ko'miʎas] *nfpl* quotation marks.

comino [ko'mino] *nm*: **(no) me importa un** ~ I don't give a damn.

comisaría [komisa'ria] *nf* (*de policía*) police station; (*MIL*) commissariat.

comisario [komi'sarjo] *nm* (*MIL etc*) commissary; (*POL*) commissar.

comisión [komi'sjon] *nf* commission.

comité [komi'te] (*pl* ~s) *nm* committee.

como ['komo] *ad* as; (*tal*) like; (*aproximadamente*) about, approximately // *conj* (*ya que, puesto que*) as, since; (*en cuanto*) as soon as; ¡~ **no!** of course!; ~ **no lo haga hoy** unless he does it today; ~ **si** as if; **es tan alto** ~ **ancho** it is as high as it is wide.

cómo ['komo] *ad* how?, why? // *excl* what?, I beg your pardon? // *nm*: **el** ~ **y el porqué** the whys and wherefores.

cómoda ['komoða] *nf* chest of drawers.

comodidad [komoði'ðað] *nf* comfort; **venga a su** ~ come at your convenience.

comodín [komo'ðin] *nm* joker.

cómodo, a ['komoðo, a] *a* comfortable; (*práctico, de fácil uso*) convenient.

compacto, a [kom'pakto, a] *a* compact.

compadecer [kompaðe'θer] *vt* to pity, be sorry for; ~se *vr*: ~se de to pity, be o feel sorry for.

compadre [kom'paðre] *nm* (*padrino*) godfather; (*amigo*) friend, pal.

compañero, a [kompa'ɲero, a] *nm/f* companion; (*novio*) boy/girlfriend; ~ de clase classmate.

compañía [kompa'ɲia] *nf* company.

comparación [kompara'θjon] *nf* comparison; en ~ con in comparison with.

comparar [kompa'rar] *vt* to compare.

comparativo, a [kompara'tiβo, a] *a* comparative.

comparecer [kompare'θer] *vi* to appear (in court).

comparsa [kom'parsa] *nm/f* (*TEATRO*) extra.

compartimiento [komparti'mjento] *nm* (*FERRO*) compartment.

compartir [kompar'tir] *vt* to divide (up), share (out).

compás [kom'pas] *nm* (*MUS*) beat, rhythm; (*MAT*) compasses *pl*; (*NAUT etc*) compass.

compasión [kompa'sjon] *nf* compassion, pity.

compasivo, a [kompa'siβo, a] *a* compassionate.

compatibilidad [kompatiβili'ðað] *nf* compatibility.

compatible [kompa'tiβle] *a* compatible.

compatriota [kompa'trjota] *nm/f* compatriot, fellow countryman/woman.

compendiar [kompen'djar] *vt* to summarize; (*libro*) to abridge; **compendio** *nm* summary; abridgement.

compensación [kompensa'θjon] *nf* compensation.

compensar [kompen'sar] *vt* to compensate.

competencia [kompe'tenθja] *nf* (*incumbencia*) domain, field; (*JUR, habilidad*) competence; (*rivalidad*) competition.

competente [kompe'tente] *a* (*JUR, persona*) competent; (*conveniente*) suitable.

competición [kompeti'θjon] *nf* competition.

competir [kompe'tir] *vi* to compete.

compilar [kompi'lar] *vt* to compile.

complacencia [kompla'θenθja] *nf* (*placer*) pleasure; (*tolerancia excesiva*) complacency.

complacer [kompla'θer] *vt* to please; ~se *vr* to be pleased.

complaciente [kompla'θjente] *a* kind, obliging, helpful.

complejo, a [kom'plexo, a] *a, nm* complex.

complementario, a [komplemen'tarjo,

a] *a* complementary.

completar [komple'tar] *vt* to complete.

completo, a [kom'pleto, a] *a* complete; (*perfecto*) perfect; (*lleno*) full // *nm* full complement.

complicado, a [kompli'kaðo, a] *a* complicated; estar ~ en to be mixed up in.

complicar [kompli'kar] *vt* to complicate.

cómplice ['kompliθe] *nm/f* accomplice.

complot [kom'plo(t)] (*pl* ~s) *nm* plot; (*conspiración*) conspiracy.

componer [kompo'ner] *vt* to make up, put together; (*MUS, LITERATURA, IMPRENTA*) to compose; (*algo roto*) to mend, repair; (*arreglar*) to arrange; ~se *vr*: ~se de to consist of; componérselas para hacer algo to manage to do sth.

comportamiento [komporta'mjento] *nm* behaviour, conduct.

comportarse [kompor'tarse] *vr* to behave.

composición [komposi'θjon] *nf* composition.

compositor, a [komposi'tor, a] *nm/f* composer.

compostura [kompos'tura] *nf* (*composición*) composition; (*reparación*) mending, repair; (*acuerdo*) agreement; (*actitud*) composure.

compra ['kompra] *nf* purchase; ~s *nfpl* purchases, shopping *sg*; ir de ~s to go shopping; **comprador, a** *nm/f* buyer, purchaser.

comprar [kom'prar] *vt* to buy, purchase.

comprender [kompren'der] *vt* to understand; (*incluir*) to comprise, include.

comprensión [kompren'sjon] *nf* understanding; (*totalidad*) comprehensiveness; **comprensivo, a** *a* comprehensive; (*actitud*) understanding.

compresa [kom'presa] *nf*: ~ higiénica sanitary towel (*Brit*) o napkin (*US*).

comprimido, a [kompri'miðo, a] *a* compressed // *nm* (*MED*) pill, tablet.

comprimir [kompri'mir] *vt* to compress; (*fig*) to control.

comprobante [kompro'βante] *nm* proof; (*COM*) voucher; ~ de recibo receipt.

comprobar [kompro'βar] *vt* to check; (*probar*) to prove; (*TEC*) to check, test.

comprometer [komprome'ter] *vt* to compromise; (*exponer*) to endanger; ~se *vr* to compromise o.s.; (*involucrarse*) to get involved.

compromiso [kompro'miso] *nm* (*obligación*) obligation; (*cometido*) commitment; (*convenio*) agreement; (*dificultad*) awkward situation.

compuesto, a [kom'pwesto, a] *a*: ~ de composed of, made up of // *nm* compound.

computador [komputa'ðor] *nm*, **computadora** [komputa'ðora] *nf* computer;

~ central mainframe computer; ~ personal personal computer.

cómputo ['komputo] *nm* calculation.

comulgar [komul'var] *vi* to receive communion.

común [ko'mun] *a* common // *nm*: el ~ the community.

comunicación [komunika'θjon] *nf* communication; (*informe*) report.

comunicado [komuni'kado] *nm* announcement; ~ de prensa press release.

comunicar [komuni'kar] *vt, vi,* **comunicarse** *vr* to communicate; está comunicando (*TEL*) the line's engaged (*Brit*) o busy (*US*); **comunicativo, a** *a* communicative.

comunidad [komuni'ðað] *nf* community.

comunión [komu'njon] *nf* communion.

comunismo [komu'nismo] *nm* communism; **comunista** *a, nm/f* communist.

con [kon] ♦ *prep* 1 (*medio, compañía*) with; comer ~ cuchara to eat with a spoon; atar algo ~ cuerda to tie sth up with string; pasear ~ uno to go for a walk with sb

2 (*a pesar de*): ~ todo, merece nuestros respetos all the same, he deserves our respect

3 (*para* ~): es muy bueno para ~ los niños he's very good with (the) children
4 (*infin*): ~ llegar tan tarde se quedó sin comer by arriving so late he missed out on eating
♦ *conj*: ~ que: será suficiente ~ que le escribas it will be sufficient if you write to her.

conato [ko'nato] *nm* attempt; ~ de robo attempted robbery.

concebir [konθe'ßir] *vt, vi* to conceive.

conceder [konθe'ðer] *vt* to concede.

concejal, a [konθe'xal, a] *nm/f* town councillor.

concejo [kon'θexo] *nm* council.

concentración [konθentra'θjon] *nf* concentration.

concentrar [konθen'trar] *vt,* **concentrarse** *vr* to concentrate.

concepción [konθep'θjon] *nf* conception.

concepto [kon'θepto] *nm* concept.

concertar [konθer'tar] *vt* (*MUS*) to harmonize; (*acordar: precio*) to agree; (: *tratado*) to conclude; (*trato*) to arrange, fix up; (*combinar: esfuerzos*) to coordinate; (*reconciliar: personas*) to reconcile // *vi* to harmonize, be in tune.

concesión [konθe'sjon] *nf* concession.

concesionario [konθesjo'narjo] *nm* (licensed) dealer, agent.

conciencia [kon'θjenθja] *nf* conscience; tener/tomar ~ de to be/become aware of; tener la ~ limpia/tranquila to have a clear conscience.

concienciar [konθjen'θjar] *vt* to make aware; ~se *vr* to become aware.

concienzudo, a [konθjen'θuðo, a] *a* conscientious.

concierto *etc vb ver* **concertar** // [kon'θjerto] *nm* concert; (*obra*) concerto.

conciliar [konθi'ljar] *vt* to reconcile.

concilio [kon'θiljo] *nm* council.

conciso, a [kon'θiso, a] *a* concise.

conciudadano, a [konθjuða'ðano, a] *nm/f* fellow citizen.

concluir [konklu'ir] *vt, vi,* **concluirse** *vr* to conclude.

conclusión [konklu'sjon] *nf* conclusion.

concluyente [konklu'jente] *a* (*prueba, información*) conclusive.

concordar [konkor'ðar] *vt* to reconcile // *vi* to agree, tally.

concordia [kon'korðja] *nf* harmony.

concretar [konkre'tar] *vt* to make concrete, make more specific; ~se *vr* to become more definite.

concreto, a [kon'kreto, a] *a, nm* (*AM*) concrete; en ~ (*en resumen*) to sum up; (*específicamente*) specifically; no hay nada en ~ there's nothing definite.

concurrencia [konku'rrenθja] *nf* turnout.

concurrido, a [konku'rriðo, a] *a* (*calle*) busy; (*local, reunión*) crowded.

concurrir [konku'rrir] *vi* (*juntarse: ríos*) to meet, come together; (: *personas*) to gather, meet.

concursante [konkur'sante] *nm/f* competitor.

concurso [kon'kurso] *nm* (*de público*) crowd; (*ESCOL, DEPORTE, competencia*) competition; (*ayuda*) help, cooperation.

concha ['kontʃa] *nf* shell.

conde ['konde] *nm* count; **condal** *a*: la ciudad condal Barcelona.

condecoración [kondekora'θjon] *nf* (*MIL*) medal.

condecorar [kondeko'rar] *vt* (*MIL*) to decorate.

condena [kon'dena] *nf* sentence.

condenación [kondena'θjon] *nf* condemnation; (*REL*) damnation.

condenar [konde'nar] *vt* to condemn; (*JUR*) to convict; ~se *vr* (*JUR*) to confess (one's guilt); (*REL*) to be damned.

condensar [konden'sar] *vt* to condense.

condesa [kon'desa] *nf* countess.

condescender [kondesθen'der] *vi* to acquiesce, comply.

condición [kondi'θjon] *nf* condition; **condicional** *a* conditional.

condicionar [kondiθjo'nar] *vt* (*acondicionar*) to condition; ~ algo a to make sth conditional on.

condimento [kondi'mento] *nm* seasoning.

condolerse [kondo'lerse] *vr* to sympathize.

condón [kon'don] *nm* condom.

conducir [kondu'θir] *vt* to take, convey; (*AUTO*) to drive // *vi* to drive; (*fig*) to lead; ~se *vr* to behave.

conducta [kon'dukta] *nf* conduct, behaviour.

conducto [kon'dukto] *nm* pipe, tube; (*fig*) channel.

conductor, a [konduk'tor, a] *a* leading, guiding // *nm* (*FISICA*) conductor; (*de vehículo*) driver.

conduje *etc vb ver* **conducir.**

conduzco *etc vb ver* **conducir.**

conectado, a [konek'taðo, a] *a* (*INFORM*) on-line.

conectar [konek'tar] *vt* to connect (up); (*enchufar*) plug in.

conejo [ko'nexo] *nm* rabbit.

conexión [konek'sjon] *nf* connection.

confección [konfe(k)'θjon] *nf* preparation; (*industria*) clothing industry.

confeccionar [konfekθjo'nar] *vt* to make (up).

confederación [konfeðera'θjon] *nf* confederation.

conferencia [konfe'renθja] *nf* conference; (*lección*) lecture; (*TEL*) call.

conferir [konfe'rir] *vt* to award.

confesar [konfe'sar] *vt* to confess, admit.

confesión [konfe'sjon] *nf* confession.

confesionario [konfesjo'narjo] *nm* confessional.

confeti [kon'feti] *nm* confetti.

confiado, a [kon'fjaðo, a] *a* (*crédulo*) trusting; (*seguro*) confident; (*presumido*) conceited, vain.

confianza [kon'fjanθa] *nf* trust; (*aliento, confidencia*) confidence; (*familiaridad*) intimacy, familiarity; (*pey*) vanity, conceit.

confiar [kon'fjar] *vt* to entrust // *vi* to trust.

confidencia [konfi'ðenθja] *nf* confidence.

confidencial [konfiðen'θjal] *a* confidential.

confidente [konfi'ðente] *nm/f* confidant/e; (*policial*) informer.

configurar [konfiɣu'rar] *vt* to shape, form.

confín [kon'fin] *nm* limit; ~**es** *nmpl* confines, limits.

confinar [konfi'nar] *vi* to confine; (*desterrar*) to banish.

confirmar [konfir'mar] *vt* to confirm.

confiscar [konfis'kar] *vt* to confiscate.

confite [kon'fite] *nm* sweet (*Brit*), candy (*US*).

confitería [konfite'ria] *nf* confectionery; (*tienda*) confectioner's (shop).

confitura [konfi'tura] *nf* jam.

conflictivo, a [konflik'tiβo, a] *a* (*asunto, propuesta*) controversial; (*país, situación*) troubled.

conflicto [kon'flikto] *nm* conflict; (*fig*) clash.

confluir [kon'flwir] *vi* (*ríos*) to meet; (*gente*) to gather.

conformar [konfor'mar] *vt* to shape, fashion // *vi* to agree; ~**se** *vr* to conform;

(*resignarse*) to resign o.s.

conforme [kon'forme] *a* alike, similar; (*de acuerdo*) agreed, in agreement // *ad* as // *excl* agreed! // *nm* agreement // *prep*: ~ **a** in accordance with.

conformidad [konformi'ðað] *nf* (*semejanza*) similarity; (*acuerdo*) agreement; (*resignación*) resignation; **conformista** *a, nm/f* conformist.

confortable [konfor'taβle] *a* comfortable.

confortar [konfor'tar] *vt* to comfort.

confrontar [konfron'tar] *vt* to confront; (*dos personas*) to bring face to face; (*cotejar*) to compare // *vi* to border.

confundir [konfun'dir] *vt* (*borrar*) to blur; (*equivocar*) to mistake, confuse; (*mezclar*) to mix; (*turbar*) to confuse; ~**se** *vr* (*hacerse borroso*) to become blurred; (*turbarse*) to get confused; (*equivocarse*) to make a mistake; (*mezclarse*) to mix.

confusión [konfu'sjon] *nf* confusion.

confuso, a [kon'fuso, a] *a* confused.

congelado, a [konxe'laðo, a] *a* frozen; ~**s** *nmpl* frozen food(s); **congelador** *nm*, **congeladora** *nf* (*aparato*) freezer, deep freeze.

congelar [konxe'lar] *vt* to freeze; ~**se** *vr* (*sangre, grasa*) to congeal.

congeniar [konxe'njar] *vi* to get on (*Brit*) *o* along (*US*) well.

congestionar [konxestjo'nar] *vt* to congest; ~**se** *vr*: **se le congestionó la cara** his face became flushed.

congoja [kon'goxa] *nf* distress, grief.

congraciarse [kongra'θjarse] *vr* to ingratiate o.s.

congratular [kongratu'lar] *vt* to congratulate.

congregación [kongreɣa'θjon] *nf* congregation.

congregar [kongre'ɣar] *vt*, **congregarse** *vr* to gather together.

congresista [kongre'sista] *nm/f* delegate, congressman/woman.

congreso [kon'greso] *nm* congress.

conjetura [konxe'tura] *nf* guess; **conjeturar** *vt* to guess.

conjugar [konxu'ɣar] *vt* to combine, fit together; (*LING*) to conjugate.

conjunción [konxun'θjon] *nf* conjunction.

conjunto, a [kon'xunto, a] *a* joint, united // *nm* whole; (*MUS*) band; **en ~** as a whole.

conjurar [konxu'rar] *vt* (*REL*) to exorcise; (*fig*) to ward off // *vi* to plot.

conmemoración [konmemora'θjon] *nf* commemoration.

conmemorar [konmemo'rar] *vt* to commemorate.

conmigo [kon'miɣo] *pron* with me.

conminar [konmi'nar] *vt* to threaten.

conmoción [konmo'θjon] *nf* shock; (*fig*) upheaval; ~ **cerebral** (*MED*) concussion.

conmovedor, a [konmoβe'ðor, a] *a*

touching, moving; (*emocionante*) exciting.

conmover [konmo'ßer] *vt* to shake, disturb; (*fig*) to move.

conmutador [konmuta'ðor] *nm* switch; (*AM TEL*: *centralita*) switchboard; (: *central*) telephone exchange.

cono ['kono] *nm* cone.

conocedor, a [konoθe'ðor, a] *a* expert, knowledgeable // *nm/f* expert.

conocer [kono'θer] *vt* to know; (*por primera vez*) to meet, get to know; (*entender*) to know about; (*reconocer*) to recognize; ~**se** *vr* (*una persona*) to know o.s.; (*dos personas*) to (get to) know each other.

conocido, a [kono'θiðo, a] *a* (well-)known // *nm/f* acquaintance.

conocimiento [konoθi'mjento] *nm* knowledge; (*MED*) consciousness; ~**s** *nmpl* (*personas*) acquaintances; (*saber*) knowledge *sg*.

conozco *etc vb ver* **conocer**.

conque ['konke] *conj* and so, so then.

conquista [kon'kista] *nf* conquest; **conquistador, a** *a* conquering // *nm* conqueror.

conquistar [konkis'tar] *vt* to conquer.

consagrar [konsa'xrar] *vt* (*REL*) to consecrate; (*fig*) to devote.

consciente [kons'θjente] *a* conscious.

consecución [konseku'θjon] *nf* acquisition; (*de fin*) attainment.

consecuencia [konse'kwenθja] *nf* consequence, outcome; (*firmeza*) consistency.

consecuente [konse'kwente] *a* consistent.

consecutivo, a [konseku'tißo, a] *a* consecutive.

conseguir [konse'xir] *vt* to get, obtain; (*sus fines*) to attain.

consejero, a [konse'xero, a] *nm/f* adviser, consultant; (*POL*) councillor.

consejo [kon'sexo] *nm* advice; (*POL*) council.

consenso [kon'senso] *nm* consensus.

consentimiento [konsenti'mjento] *nm* consent.

consentir [konsen'tir] *vt* (*permitir, tolerar*) to consent to; (*mimar*) to pamper, spoil; (*aguantar*) to put up with // *vi* to agree, consent; ~ **que uno haga algo** to allow sb to do sth.

conserje [kon'serxe] *nm* caretaker; (*portero*) porter.

conservación [konserßa'θjon] *nf* conservation; (*de alimentos, vida*) preservation.

conservador, a [konserßa'ðor, a] *a* (*POL*) conservative // *nm/f* conservative.

conservante [konser'ßante] *nm* preservative.

conservar [konser'ßar] *vt* to conserve, keep; (*alimentos, vida*) to preserve; ~**se** *vr* to survive.

conservas [kon'serßas] *nfpl* canned food(s).

conservatorio [konserßa'torjo] *nm* (*MUS*) conservatoire.

considerable [konsiðe'raßle] *a* considerable.

consideración [konsiðera'θjon] *nf* consideration; (*estimación*) respect.

considerado, a [konsiðe'raðo, a] *a* (*atento*) considerate; (*respetado*) respected.

considerar [konsiðe'rar] *vt* to consider.

consigna [kon'sixna] *nf* (*orden*) order, instruction; (*para equipajes*) left-luggage office.

consigo *etc vb ver* **conseguir** // [kon'sixo] *pron* (*m*) with him; (*f*) with her; (*Vd.*) with you; (*reflexivo*) with o.s.

consiguiendo *etc vb ver* **conseguir**.

consiguiente [konsi'xjente] *a* consequent; **por** ~ and so, therefore, consequently.

consistente [konsis'tente] *a* consistent; (*sólido*) solid, firm; (*válido*) sound.

consistir [konsis'tir] *vi*: ~ **en** (*componerse de*) to consist of; (*ser resultado de*) to be due to.

consola [kon'sola] *nf* control panel.

consolación [konsola'θjon] *nf* consolation.

consolar [konso'lar] *vt* to console.

consolidar [konsoli'ðar] *vt* to consolidate.

consomé [konso'me] (*pl* ~**s**) *nm* consommé, clear soup.

consonante [konso'nante] *a* consonant, harmonious // *nf* consonant.

consorcio [kon'sorθjo] *nm* consortium.

conspiración [konspira'θjon] *nf* conspiracy.

conspirador, a [konspira'ðor, a] *nm/f* conspirator.

conspirar [konspi'rar] *vi* to conspire.

constancia [kon'stanθja] *nf* constancy; **dejar** ~ **de** to put on record.

constante [kons'tante] *a, nf* constant.

constar [kons'tar] *vi* (*evidenciarse*) to be clear *o* evident; ~ **de** to consist of.

constatar [konsta'tar] *vt* (*controlar*) to check; (*observar*) to note.

consternación [konsterna'θjon] *nf* consternation.

constipado, a [konsti'paðo, a] *a*: **estar** ~ to have a cold // *nm* cold.

constitución [konstitu'θjon] *nf* constitution; **constitucional** *a* constitutional.

constituir [konstitu'ir] *vt* (*formar, componer*) to constitute, make up; (*fundar, erigir, ordenar*) to constitute, establish.

constitutivo, a [konstitu'tißo, a] *a* constitutive, constituent.

constituyente [konstitu'jente] *a* constituent.

constreñir [konstre'ɲir] *vt* (*restringir*) to restrict.

construcción [konstruk'θjon] *nf* construction, building.

constructor, a [konstruk'tor, a] *nm/f* builder.

construir [konstru'ir] *vt* to build, construct.

construyendo *etc vb ver* **construir**.

consuelo [kon'swelo] *nm* consolation, solace.

cónsul ['konsul] *nm* consul; **consulado** *nm* consulate.

consulta [kon'sulta] *nf* consultation; (*MED*): **horas de ~** surgery hours.

consultar [konsul'tar] *vt* to consult.

consultorio [konsul'torjo] *nm* (*MED*) surgery.

consumar [konsu'mar] *vt* to complete, carry out; (*crimen*) to commit; (*sentencia*) to carry out.

consumición [konsumi'θjon] *nf* consumption; (*bebida*) drink; (*comida*) food; **~ mínima** cover charge.

consumidor, a [konsumi'ðor, a] *nm/f* consumer.

consumir [konsu'mir] *vt* to consume; **~se** *vr* to be consumed; (*persona*) to waste away.

consumismo [konsu'mismo] *nm* consumerism.

consumo [kon'sumo] *nm* consumption.

contabilidad [kontaβili'ðað] *nf* accounting, book-keeping; (*profesión*) accountancy; **contable** *nm/f* accountant.

contacto [kon'takto] *nm* contact; (*AUTO*) ignition.

contado, a [kon'taðo, a] *a*: **~s** (*escasos*) numbered, scarce, few // *nm*: **pagar al ~** to pay (in) cash.

contador [konta'ðor] *nm* (*aparato*) meter; (*AM*: *contante*) accountant.

contagiar [konta'xjar] *vt* (*enfermedad*) to pass on, transmit; (*persona*) to infect; **~se** *vr* to become infected.

contagio [kon'taxjo] *nm* infection; **contagioso, a** *a* infectious; (*fig*) catching.

contaminación [kontamina'θjon] *nf* contamination; (*polución*) pollution.

contaminar [kontami'nar] *vt* to contaminate; (*aire, agua*) to pollute.

contante [kon'tante] *a*: **dinero ~ (y sonante)** cash.

contar [kon'tar] *vt* (*páginas, dinero*) to count; (*anécdota, chiste etc*) to tell // *vi* to count; **~ con** to rely on, count on.

contemplación [kontempla'θjon] *nf* contemplation.

contemplar [kontem'plar] *vt* to contemplate; (*mirar*) to look at.

contemporáneo, a [kontempo'raneo, a] *a, nm/f* contemporary.

contendiente [konten'djente] *nm/f* contestant.

contenedor [kontene'ðor] *nm* container.

contener [konte'ner] *vt* to contain, hold, (*retener*) to hold back, contain; **~se** *vr* to control *o* restrain o.s.

contenido, a [konte'niðo, a] *a* (*moderado*) restrained; (*risa etc*) suppressed // *nm* contents *pl*, content.

contentar [konten'tar] *vt* (*satisfacer*) to satisfy; (*complacer*) to please; **~se** *vr* to be satisfied.

contento, a [kon'tento, a] *a* contented, content; (*alegre*) pleased; (*feliz*) happy.

contestación [kontesta'θjon] *nf* answer, reply.

contestador [kontesta'ðor] *nm*: **~ automático** answering machine.

contestar [kontes'tar] *vt* to answer, reply; (*JUR*) to corroborate, confirm.

contexto [kon'te(k)sto] *nm* context.

contienda [kon'tjenda] *nf* contest.

contigo [kon'tiɣo] *pron* with you.

contiguo, a [kon'tiɣwo, a] *a* (*de al lado*) next; (*vecino*) adjacent, adjoining.

continente [konti'nente] *a, nm* continent.

contingencia [kontin'xenθja] *nf* contingency; (*riesgo*) risk; **contingente** *a, nm* contingent.

continuación [kontinwa'θjon] *nf* continuation; **a ~** then, next.

continuar [konti'nwar] *vt* to continue, go on with // *vi* to continue, go on; **~ hablando** to continue talking *o* to talk.

continuidad [kontinwi'ðað] *nf* continuity.

continuo, a [kon'tinwo, a] *a* (*sin interrupción*) continuous; (*acción perseverante*) continual.

contorno [kon'torno] *nm* outline; (*GEO*) contour; **~s** *nmpl* neighbourhood *sg*, surrounding area *sg*.

contorsión [kontor'sjon] *nf* contortion.

contra ['kontra] *prep, ad* against // *nm inv* **con** // *nf*: **la C~** (*Nicaragua*) the Contras *pl*.

contraataque [kontraa'take] *nm* counter-attack.

contrabajo [kontra'βaxo] *nm* double bass.

contrabandista [kontraβan'dista] *nm/f* smuggler.

contrabando [kontra'βando] *nm* (*acción*) smuggling; (*mercancías*) contraband.

contracción [kontrak'θjon] *nf* contraction.

contrachapado [kontratʃa'paðo] *nm* plywood.

contradecir [kontraðe'θir] *vt* to contradict.

contradicción [kontraðik'θjon] *nf* contradiction.

contradictorio, a [kontraðik'torjo, a] *a* contradictory.

contraer [kontra'er] *vt* to contract; (*limitar*) to restrict; **~se** *vr* to contract; (*limitarse*) to limit o.s.

contragolpe |kontra'xolpe| *nm* backlash.

contraluz |kontra'luθ| *nf*: a ~ against the light.

contramaestre |kontrama'estre| *nm* foreman.

contrapartida |kontrapar'tiða| *nf*: como ~ (de) in return (for).

contrapelo |kontra'pelo|: a ~ *ad* the wrong way.

contrapesar |kontrape'sar| *vt* to counterbalance; (*fig*) to offset; **contrapeso** *nm* counterweight.

contraproducente |kontraproðu'θente| *a* counterproductive.

contrariar |kontra'rjar| *vt* (*oponerse*) to oppose; (*poner obstáculo*) to impede; (*enfadar*) to vex.

contrariedad |kontrarje'ðað| *nf* (*oposición*) opposition; (*obstáculo*) obstacle, setback; (*disgusto*) vexation, annoyance.

contrario, a |kon'trarjo, a| *a* contrary; (*persona*) opposed; (*sentido, lado*) opposite // *nm/f* enemy, adversary; (*DEPORTE*) opponent; **al/por el** ~ on the contrary; **de lo** ~ otherwise.

contrarrestar |kontrarres'tar| *vt* to counteract.

contrasentido |kontrasen'tiðo| *nm*: es un ~ que él ... it doesn't make sense for him to ....

contraseña |kontra'seɲa| *nf* (*INFORM*) password.

contrastar |kontras'tar| *vt* to resist // *vi* to contrast.

contraste |kon'traste| *nm* contrast.

contratar |kontra'tar| *vt* (*firmar un acuerdo para*) to contract for; (*empleados, obreros*) to hire, engage; ~**se** *vr* to sign on.

contratiempo |kontra'tjempo| *nm* setback.

contratista |kontra'tista| *nm/f* contractor.

contrato |kon'trato| *nm* contract.

contravenir |kontraβe'nir| *vi*: ~ a to contravene, violate.

contraventana |kontraβen'tana| *nf* shutter.

contribución |kontriβu'θjon| *nf* (*municipal etc*) tax; (*ayuda*) contribution.

contribuir |kontriβu'ir| *vt, vi* to contribute; (*COM*) to pay (in taxes).

contribuyente |kontriβu'jente| *nm/f* (*COM*) taxpayer; (*que ayuda*) contributor.

control |kon'trol| *nm* control; (*inspección*) inspection, check; ~**ador, a** *nm/f* controller; **controlador aéreo** air-traffic controller.

controlar |kontro'lar| *vt* to control; (*inspeccionar*) to inspect, check.

controversia |kontro'βersja| *nf* controversy.

contundente |kontun'dente| *a* (*instrumento*) blunt; (*argumento, derrota*) overwhelming.

contusión |kontu'sjon| *nf* bruise.

convalecencia |konβale'θenθja| *nf* convalescence.

convalecer |konβale'θer| *vi* to convalesce, get better.

convaleciente |konβale'θjente| *a, nm/f* convalescent.

convalidar |konβali'ðar| *vt* (*título*) to recognize.

convencer |konβen'θer| *vt* to convince; (*persuadir*) to persuade.

convencimiento |konβenθi'mjento| *nm* (*acción*) convincing; (*persuasión*) persuasion; (*certidumbre*) conviction.

convención |konβen'θjon| *nf* convention.

conveniencia |konβe'njenθja| *nf* suitability; (*conformidad*) agreement; (*utilidad, provecho*) usefulness; ~**s** *nfpl* conventions; (*COM*) property *sg*.

conveniente |konβe'njente| *a* suitable; (*útil*) useful.

convenio |kon'βenjo| *nm* agreement, treaty.

convenir |konβe'nir| *vi* (*estar de acuerdo*) to agree; (*ser conveniente*) to suit, be suitable.

convento |kon'βento| *nm* convent.

convenza *etc vb ver* **convencer**.

converger |konβer'xer|, **convergir** |konβer'xir| *vi* to converge.

conversación |konβersa'θjon| *nf* conversation.

conversar |konβer'sar| *vi* to talk, converse.

conversión |konβer'sjon| *nf* conversion.

convertir |konβer'tir| *vt* to convert.

convicción |konβik'θjon| *nf* conviction.

convicto, a |kon'βikto, a| *a* convicted, found guilty; (*condenado*) condemned.

convidado, a |konβi'ðaðo, a| *nm/f* guest.

convidar |konβi'ðar| *vt* to invite.

convincente |konβin'θente| *a* convincing.

convite |kon'βite| *nm* invitation; (*banquete*) banquet.

convivencia |konβi'βenθja| *nf* coexistence, living together.

convocar |konβo'kar| *vt* to summon, call (together).

convulsión |konβul'sjon| *nf* convulsion.

conyugal |konju'βal| *a* conjugal; **cónyuge** |'konjuxe| *nm/f* spouse.

coñac |ko'ɲak| (*pl* ~**s**) *nm* cognac, brandy.

coño |'koɲo| *excl* (*fam!: enfado*) shit! (*!*); (*: sorpresa*) bloody hell! (*!*).

cooperación |koopera'θjon| *nf* cooperation.

cooperar |koope'rar| *vi* to cooperate.

cooperativa |koopera'tiβa| *nf* cooperative.

coordinadora |koorðina'ðora| *nf* (*comité*) coordinating committee.

coordinar [koorði'nar] *vt* to coordinate.

sopa ['kupa] *nf* cup; (*vaso*) glass, (*de árbol*) top; (*de sombrero*) crown; ~s *nfpl* (*NAIPES*) ≈ hearts; (**tomar una**) ~ (to have a) drink.

copia ['kopja] *nf* copy; ~ **de respaldo** *o* **seguridad** (*INFORM*) back-up copy; **copiar** *vt* to copy.

copioso, a [ko'pjoso, a] *a* copious, plentiful.

copla ['kopla] *nf* verse; (*canción*) (popular) song.

copo ['kopo] *nm*: ~ **de nieve** snowflake; ~**s de maíz** cornflakes.

copropietarios [kopropje'tarjos] *nmpl* joint owners.

coqueta [ko'keta] *a* flirtatious, coquettish; **coquetear** *vi* to flirt.

coraje [ko'raxe] *nm* courage; (*ánimo*) spirit; (*ira*) anger.

coral [ko'ral] *a* choral // *nf* (*MUS*) choir // *nm* (*ZOOL*) coral.

coraza [ko'raθa] *nf* (*armadura*) armour; (*blindaje*) armour-plating.

corazón [kora'θon] *nm* heart.

corazonada [koraθo'naða] *nf* impulse; (*presentimiento*) hunch.

corbata [kor'ßata] *nf* tie.

corchete [kor'tfete] *nm* catch, clasp.

corcho ['kortfo] *nm* cork; (*PESCA*) float.

cordel [kor'ðel] *nm* cord, line.

cordero [kor'ðero] *nm* lamb.

cordial [kor'ðjal] *a* cordial; ~**idad** *nf* warmth, cordiality.

cordillera [korði'Åera] *nf* range (of mountains).

Córdoba ['korðoßa] *n* Cordova.

cordón [kor'ðon] *nm* (*cuerda*) cord, string; (*de zapatos*) lace; (*MIL etc*) cordon.

corneta [kor'neta] *nf* bugle.

coro ['koro] *nm* chorus; (*conjunto de cantores*) choir.

corona [ko'rona] *nf* crown; (*de flores*) garland; ~**ción** *nf* coronation; **coronar** *vt* to crown.

coronel [koro'nel] *nm* colonel.

coronilla [koro'niÅa] *nf* (*ANAT*) crown (of the head).

corporación [korpora'θjon] *nf* corporation.

corporal [korpo'ral] *a* corporal, bodily.

corpulento, a [korpu'lento a] *a* (*persona*) heavily-built.

corral [ko'rral] *nm* farmyard.

correa [ko'rrea] *nf* strap; (*cinturón*) belt; (*de perro*) lead, leash.

corrección [korrek'θjon] *nf* correction; (*represión*) rebuke; **correccional** *nm* reformatory.

correcto, a [ko'rrekto, a] *a* correct; (*persona*) well-mannered.

corredizo, a [korre'ðiðo, a] *a* (*puerta etc*) sliding.

corredor, a [korre'ðor, a] *a* running //

nm (*pasillo*) corridor; (*balcón corrido*) gallery; (*COM*) agent, broker // *nm/f* (*DEPORTE*) runner.

corregir [korre'xir] *vt* (*error*) to correct; (*amonestar, reprender*) to rebuke, reprimand; ~**se** *vr* to reform.

correo [ko'rreo] *nm* post, mail; (*persona*) courier; **C~s** Post Office *sg*; ~ **aéreo** airmail.

correr [ko'rrer] *vt* to run; (*viajar*) to cover, travel; (*cortinas*) to draw; (*cerrojo*) to shoot // *vi* to run; (*líquido*) to run, flow; ~**se** *vr* to slide, move; (*colores*) to run.

correspondencia [korrespon'denθja] *nf* correspondence; (*FERRO*) connection.

corresponder [korrespon'der] *vi* to correspond; (*convenir*) to be suitable; (*pertenecer*) to belong; (*tocar*) to concern; ~**se** *vr* (*por escrito*) to correspond; (*amarse*) to love one another.

correspondiente [korrespon'djente] *a* corresponding.

corresponsal [korrespon'sal] *nm/f* correspondent.

corrido, a [ko'rriðo, a] *a* (*avergonzado*) abashed // *nf* (*de toros*) bullfight; **3 noches corridas** 3 nights running; **un kilo** ~ a good kilo.

corriente [ko'rrjente] *a* (*agua*) running; (*fig*) flowing; (*dinero etc*) current; (*común*) ordinary, normal // *nf* current // *nm* current month; ~ **eléctrica** electric current.

corrija *etc vb ver* **corregir**.

corrillo [ko'rriÅo] *nm* ring, circle (of people); (*fig*) clique.

corro ['korro] *nm* ring, circle (of people).

corroborar [korroßo'rar] *vt* to corroborate.

corroer [korro'er] *vt* to corrode; (*GEO*) to erode.

corromper [korrom'per] *vt* (*madera*) to rot; (*fig*) to corrupt.

corrosivo, a [korro'sißo, a] *a* corrosive.

corrupción [korrup'θjon] *nf* rot, decay; (*fig*) corruption.

corsé [kor'se] *nm* corset.

cortacésped [korta'θespeð] *nm* lawn mower.

cortado, a [kor'taðo, a] *a* (*gen*) cut; (*leche*) sour; (*confuso*) confused; (*desconcertado*) embarrassed // *nm* coffee (with a little milk).

cortar [kor'tar] *vt* to cut; (*suministro*) to cut off; (*un pasaje*) to cut out // *vi* to cut; ~**se** *vr* (*turbarse*) to become embarrassed; (*leche*) to turn, curdle; ~**se el pelo** to have one's hair cut.

cortauñas [korta'uɲas] *nm inv* nail clippers *pl*.

corte ['korte] *nm* cut, cutting; (*de tela*) piece, length; **las C~s** the Spanish Parliament; ~ **y confección** dressmaking; ~ **de luz** power cut.

cortedad [korte'ðað] *nf* shortness; *(fig)* bashfulness, timidity.

cortejar [korte'xar] *vt* to court.

cortejo [kor'texo] *nm* entourage; ~ fúnebre funeral procession.

cortés [kor'tes] *a* courteous, polite.

cortesía [korte'sia] *nf* courtesy.

corteza [kor'teθa] *nf* (*de árbol*) bark; (*de pan*) crust.

cortina [kor'tina] *nf* curtain.

corto, a ['korto, a] *a* (*breve*) short; (*tímido*) bashful; ~ de luces not very bright; ~ de vista short-sighted; estar ~ de fondos to be short of funds; ~circuito *nm* short circuit.

corvo, a ['korßo, a] *a* curved.

cosa ['kosa] *nf* thing; (*asunto*) affair; ~ de about; eso es ~ mía that's my business.

cosecha [ko'setʃa] *nf* (*AGR*) harvest; (*de vino*) vintage.

cosechar [kose'tʃar] *vt* to harvest, gather (in).

coser [ko'ser] *vt* to sew.

cosmético, a [kos'metiko, a] *a, nm* cosmetic.

cosquillas [kos'kiʎas] *nfpl:* hacer ~ to tickle; tener ~ to be ticklish.

costa ['kosta] *nf* (*GEO*) coast; C~ Brava Costa Brava; C~ Cantábrica Cantabrian Coast; C~ del Sol Costa del Sol; a toda ~ at any price.

costado [kos'taðo] *nm* side.

costal [kos'tal] *nm* sack.

costar [kos'tar] *vt* (*valer*) to cost; (*necesitar*) to require, need; me cuesta hablarle I find it hard to talk to him.

Costa Rica *nf* Costa Rica; **costarricense, costarriqueño, a** *a, nm/f* Costa Rican.

coste ['koste] *nm* = costo.

costear [koste'ar] *vt* to pay for.

costilla [kos'tiʎa] *nf* rib; (*CULIN*) cutlet.

costo ['kosto] *nm* cost, price; ~ de la vida cost of living; ~so, a *a* costly, expensive.

costra ['kostra] *nf* (*corteza*) crust; (*MED*) scab.

costumbre [kos'tumbre] *nf* custom, habit.

costura [kos'tura] *nf* sewing, needlework; (*zurcido*) seam.

costurera [kostu'rera] *nf* dressmaker.

costurero [kostu'rero] *nm* sewing box *o* case.

cotejar [kote'xar] *vt* to compare.

cotidiano, a [koti'ðjano, a] *a* daily, day to day.

cotización [kotiθa'θjon] *nf* (*COM*) quotation, price; (*de club*) dues *pl*.

cotizar [koti'θar] *vt* (*COM*) to quote, price; ~se *vr:* ~se a to sell at, fetch; (*BOLSA*) to stand at, be quoted at.

coto ['koto] *nm* (*terreno cercado*) enclosure; (*de caza*) reserve.

cotorra [ko'torra] *nf* parrot.

COU [kou] *nm abr* (*Esp*) = Curso de Orientación Universitaria.

coyote [ko'jote] *nm* coyote, prairie wolf.

coyuntura [kojun'tura] *nf* (*ANAT*) joint; (*fig*) juncture, occasion.

coz [koθ] *nf* kick.

cráneo ['kraneo] *nm* skull, cranium.

cráter ['krater] *nm* crater.

creación [krea'θjon] *nf* creation.

creador, a [krea'ðor, a] *a* creative // *nm/f* creator.

crear [kre'ar] *vt* to create, make.

crecer [kre'θer] *vi* to grow; (*precio*) to rise.

creces ['kreθes]: con ~ *ad* amply, fully.

crecido, a [kre'θiðo, a] *a* (*persona, planta*) full-grown; (*cantidad*) large.

creciente [kre'θjente] *a* growing; (*cantidad*) increasing; (*luna*) crescent // *nm* crescent.

crecimiento [kreθi'mjento] *nm* growth; (*aumento*) increase.

credenciales [kreðen'θjales] *nfpl* credentials.

crédito ['kreðito] *nm* credit.

credo ['kreðo] *nm* creed.

crédulo, a ['kreðulo, a] *a* credulous.

creencia [kre'enθja] *nf* belief.

creer [kre'er] *vt, vi* to think, believe; ~se *vr* to believe o.s. (to be); ~ en to believe in; ¡ya lo creo! I should think so!

creíble [kre'ißle] *a* credible, believable.

creído, a [kre'iðo, a] *a* (*engreído*) conceited.

crema ['krema] *nf* cream; (*natillas*) custard.

cremallera [krema'ʎera] *nf* zip (fastener).

crepitar [krepi'tar] *vi* to crackle.

crepúsculo [kre'puskulo] *nm* twilight, dusk.

crespo, a ['krespo, a] *a* (*pelo*) curly.

crespón [kres'pon] *nm* crêpe.

cresta ['kresta] *nf* (*GEO, ZOOL*) crest.

creyendo *vb ver* creer.

creyente [kre'jente] *nm/f* believer.

creyó *etc vb ver* creer.

crezco *etc vb ver* crecer.

cría *etc vb ver* criar // ['kria] *nf* (*de animales*) rearing, breeding; (*animal*) young; *ver tb* crío.

criadero [kria'ðero] *nm* nursery; (*ZOOL*) breeding place.

criado, a [kri'aðo, a] *nm* servant // *nf* servant, maid.

criador [kria'ðor] *nm* breeder.

crianza [kri'anθa] *nf* rearing, breeding; (*fig*) breeding.

criar [kri'ar] *vt* (*amamantar*) to suckle, feed; (*educar*) to bring up; (*producir*) to grow, produce; (*animales*) to breed.

criatura [kria'tura] *nf* creature; (*niño*) baby, (small) child.

criba ['krißa] *nf* sieve; **cribar** *vt* to sieve.

crimen |'krimen| *nm* crime.
criminal |krimi'nal| *a, nm/f* criminal.
crin |krin| *nf (tb:* ~es *nfpl)* mane.
crío, a |'krio, a| *nm/f (fam)* kid.
crisis |'krisis| *nf inv* crisis; ~ **nerviosa** nervous breakdown.
crispar |kris'par| *vt (músculo)* to tense (up); *(nervios)* to set on edge.
cristal |kris'tal| *nm* crystal; *(de ventana)* glass, pane; *(lente)* lens; ~**ino, a** *a* crystalline; *(fig)* clear // *nm* lens of the eye; ~**izar** *vt, vi* to crystallize.
cristiandad |kristjan'dað| *nf* Christendom.
cristianismo |kristja'nismo| *nm* Christianity.
cristiano, a |kris'tjano, a| *a, nm/f* Christian.
Cristo |'kristo| *nm (Dios)* Christ; *(crucifijo)* crucifix.
criterio |kri'terjo| *nm* criterion; *(juicio)* judgement.
criticar |kriti'kar| *vt* to criticize.
crítico, a |'kritiko, a| *a* critical // *nm/f* critic // *nf* criticism.
croar |kro'ar| *vi* to croak.
cromo |'kromo| *nm* chrome.
crónico, a |'kroniko, a| *a* chronic // *nf* chronicle, account.
cronómetro |kro'nometro| *nm (DEPORTE)* stopwatch.
cruce *etc vb ver* **cruzar** // |'kruθe| *nm* crossing; *(de carreteras)* crossroads.
crucificar |kruθifi'kar| *vt* to crucify.
crucifijo |kruθi'fixo| *nm* crucifix.
crucigrama |kruθi'xrama| *nm* crossword (puzzle).
crudo, a |'kruðo, a| *a* raw; *(no maduro)* unripe; *(petróleo)* crude; *(rudo, cruel)* cruel // *nm* crude (oil).
cruel |krwel| *a* cruel; ~**dad** *nf* cruelty.
crujido |kru'xiðo| *nm (de madera etc)* creak.
crujiente |kru'xjente| *a (galleta etc)* crunchy.
crujir |kru'xir| *vi (madera etc)* to creak; *(dedos)* to crack; *(dientes)* to grind; *(nieve, arena)* to crunch.
cruz |kruθ| *nf* cross; *(de moneda)* tails *sg.*
cruzado, a |kru'θaðo, a| *a* crossed // *nm* crusader // *nf* crusade.
cruzar |kru'θar| *vt* to cross; ~**se** *vr (líneas etc)* to cross; *(personas)* to pass each other.
Cruz Roja *nf* Red Cross.
cuaderno |kwa'ðerno| *nm* notebook; *(de escuela)* exercise book; *(NAUT)* logbook.
cuadra |'kwaðra| *nf (caballeriza)* stable; *(AM)* block.
cuadrado, a |kwa'ðraðo, a| *a* square // *nm (MAT)* square.
cuadrar |kwa'ðrar| *vt* to square // *vi:* ~ **con** to square with, tally with; ~**se** *vr (soldado)* to stand to attention.
cuadrilátero |kwaðri'latero| *nm*

cuadrilla |kwa'ðriʎa| *nf* party, group.
cuadro |'kwaðro| *nm* square; *(ARTE)* painting; *(TEATRO)* scene; *(diagrama)* chart; *(DEPORTE, MED)* team; *(POL)* executive; **tela a** ~**s** checked *(Brit)* o chequered *(US)* material.
cuádruplo, a |'kwaðruplo, a|, **cuádruple** |'kwaðruple| *a* quadruple.
cuajar |kwa'xar| *vt* to thicken; *(leche)* to curdle; *(sangre)* to congeal; *(adornar)* to adorn; *(CULIN)* to set; ~**se** *vr* to curdle; to congeal; to set; *(llenarse)* to fill up.
cual |kwal| *ad* like, as // *pron:* **el** ~ *etc* which; *(persona: sujeto)* who; *(: objeto)* whom // *a* such as; **cada** ~ each one; **tal** ~ just as it is.
cuál |kwal| *pron interr* which (one).
cualesquier(a) |kwales'kjer(a)| *pl de* **cualquier(a).**
cualidad |kwali'ðað| *nf* quality.
cualquier |kwal'kjer|, *pl* cualesquier(a) *a (indefinido)* any; ~ **día de éstos** any day now; *(después de n:* ~a): **no es un hombre** ~**a** he isn't an ordinary man, he isn't just anybody; *pron:* ~**a: eso** ~**a lo sabe hacer** anybody can do that; **es un** ~**a** he's a nobody.
cuando |'kwando| *ad* when; *(aún si)* if, even if // *conj (puesto que)* since // *prep:* **yo,** ~ **niño**... when I was a child...; ~ **no sea así** even if it is not so; ~ **más** at (the) most; ~ **menos** at least; ~ **no** if not, otherwise; **de** ~ **en** ~ from time to time.
cuándo |'kwando| *ad* when; ¿**desde** ~?, ¿**de** ~ **acá?** since when?
cuantioso, a |kwan'tjoso, a| *a* substantial.
cuanto, a |'kwanto, a| ♦ *a* **1** *(todo):* **tiene todo** ~ **desea** he's got everything he wants; **le daremos** ~**s ejemplares necesite** we'll give him as many copies as o all the copies he needs; ~**s hombres la ven** all the men who see her
2: unos ~s: **había unos** ~**s periodistas** there were (quite) a few journalists
3 *(+ más):* ~ **más vino bebes peor te sentirás** the more wine you drink the worse you'll feel
♦ *pron:* **tiene** ~ **desea** he has everything he wants; **tome** ~/~**s quiera** take as much/many as you want
♦ *ad:* **en** ~: **en** ~ **profesor** as a teacher; **en** ~ **a mí** as for me; *ver tb* **antes**
♦ *conj* **1:** ~ **más gana menos gasta** the more he earns the less he spends; ~ **más joven se es más se es confiado** the younger you are the more trusting you are
2: en ~: **en** ~ **llegue/llegué** as soon as I arrive/arrived
cuánto, a |'kwanto, a| *a (exclamación)*

what a lot of; (interr: sg) how much?; (: pl) how many? // pron, ad how; (interr: sg) how much?; (: pl) how many?; ¡~a gente! what a lot of people!; ¿~ cuesta? how much does it cost?; ¿a ~s estamos? what's the date?; Señor no sé ~s Mr. So-and-So.

cuarenta [kwa'renta] num forty.

cuarentena [kwaren'tena] nf quarantine.

cuaresma [kwa'resma] nf Lent.

cuartear [kwarte'ar] vt to quarter; (dividir) to divide up; ~se vr to crack, split.

cuartel [kwar'tel] nm (de ciudad) quarter, district; (MIL) barracks pl; ~ general headquarters pl.

cuarteto [kwar'teto] nm quartet.

cuarto, a ['kwarto, a] a fourth // nm (MAT) quarter, fourth; (habitación) room // nf (MAT) quarter, fourth; (palmo) span; ~ de baño bathroom; ~ de estar living room; ~ de hora quarter (of an) hour; ~ de kilo quarter kilo.

cuatro ['kwatro] num four.

cuba ['kuβa] nf cask, barrel.

Cuba ['kuβa] nf Cuba; **cubano, a** a, nm/f Cuban.

cúbico, a ['kuβiko, a] a cubic.

cubierto, a pp de cubrir // [ku'βjerto, a] a covered // nm cover; (en la mesa) place; ~s nmpl cutlery sg // nf cover, covering; (neumático) tyre; (NAUT) deck; a ~ de covered with o in.

cubil [ku'βil] nm den; ~ete nm (en juegos) cup.

cubo ['kuβo] nm cube; (balde) bucket, tub; (TEC) drum.

cubrecama [kuβre'kama] nm bedspread.

cubrir [ku'βrir] vt to cover; ~se vr (cielo) to become overcast.

cucaracha [kuka'ratʃa] nf cockroach.

cuco, a ['kuko, a] a pretty; (astuto) sharp // nm cuckoo.

cucurucho [kuku'rutʃo] nm cornet.

cuchara [ku'tʃara] nf spoon; (TEC) scoop; ~da nf spoonful; ~dita nf teaspoonful.

cucharita [kutʃa'rita] nf teaspoon.

cucharón [kutʃa'ron] nm ladle.

cuchichear [kutʃitʃe'ar] vi to whisper.

cuchilla [ku'tʃiʎa] nf (large) knife; (de arma blanca) blade; ~ de afeitar razor blade.

cuchillo [ku'tʃiʎo] nm knife.

cuchitril [kutʃi'tril] nm hovel; (habitación etc) pigsty.

cuello ['kweʎo] nm (ANAT) neck; (de vestido, camisa) collar.

cuenca ['kwenka] nf (ANAT) eye socket; (GEO) bowl, deep valley.

cuenta etc vb ver contar // ['kwenta] nf (cálculo) count, counting; (en café, restaurante) (COM) account; (de collar) bead; (fig) account; a fin de ~s in the end; caer en la ~ to catch on;

darse ~ de to realize; tener en ~ to bear in mind; echar ~s to take stock; ~ corriente/de ahorros current/savings account; ~kilómetros nm inv ≈ milometer; (de velocidad) speedometer.

cuento etc vb ver contar // ['kwento] nm story.

cuerda ['kwerða] nf rope; (hilo) string; (de reloj) spring; dar ~ a un reloj to wind up a clock.

cuerdo, a ['kwerðo, a] a sane; (prudente) wise, sensible.

cuerno ['kwerno] nm horn.

cuero ['kwero] nm (ZOOL) skin, hide; (TEC) leather; en ~s stark naked; ~ cabelludo scalp.

cuerpo ['kwerpo] nm body.

cuervo ['kwerβo] nm crow.

cuesta etc vb ver costar // ['kwesta] nf slope; (en camino etc) hill; ~ arriba/ abajo uphill/downhill; a ~s on one's back.

cueste etc vb ver costar.

cuestión [kwes'tjon] nf matter, question, issue; (riña) quarrel, dispute.

cueva ['kweβa] nf cave.

cuidado [kwi'ðaðo] nm care, carefulness; (preocupación) care, worry // excl careful!, look out!

cuidadoso, a [kwiða'ðoso, a] a careful; (preocupado) anxious.

cuidar [kwi'ðar] vt (MED) to care for; (ocuparse de) to take care of, look after // vi: ~ de to take care of, look after; ~se vr to look after o.s.; ~se de hacer algo to take care to do sth.

culata [ku'lata] nf (de fusil) butt.

culebra [ku'leβra] nf snake.

culinario, a [kuli'narjo, a] a culinary, cooking cpd.

culminación [kulmina'θjon] nf culmination.

culo ['kulo] nm bottom, backside; (de vaso, botella) bottom.

culpa ['kulpa] nf fault; (JUR) guilt; por ~ de because of, through; tener la ~ (de) to be to blame (for); ~bilidad nf guilt; ~ble a guilty // nm/f culprit.

culpar [kul'par] vt to blame; (acusar) to accuse.

cultivar [kulti'βar] vt to cultivate.

cultivo [kul'tiβo] nm (acto) cultivation; (plantas) crop.

culto, a ['kulto, a] a (cultivado) cultivated; (que tiene cultura) cultured, educated // nm (homenaje) worship; (religión) cult.

cultura [kul'tura] nf culture.

cumbre ['kumbre] nf summit, top.

cumpleaños [kumple'aɲos] nm inv birthday.

cumplido, a [kum'pliðo, a] a complete, perfect; (abundante) plentiful; (cortés) courteous // nm compliment; visita de ~ courtesy call.

cumplidor, a [kumpli'ðor, a] *a* reliable.

cumplimentar [kumplimen'tar] *vt* to congratulate.

cumplimiento [kumpli'mjento] *nm* (*de un deber*) fulfilment; (*acabamiento*) completion.

cumplir [kum'plir] *vt* (*orden*) to carry out, obey; (*promesa*) to carry out, fulfil; (*condena*) to serve; (*años*) to reach, attain // *vi*: ~ **con** (*deberes*) to carry out, fulfil; ~**se** *vr* (*plazo*) to expire; **hoy cumple dieciocho años** he is eighteen today.

cúmulo ['kumulo] *nm* heap.

cuna ['kuna] *nf* cradle, cot.

cundir [kun'dir] *vi* (*noticia, rumor, pánico*) to spread; (*rendir*) to go a long way.

cuneta [ku'neta] *nf* ditch.

cuña ['kuɲa] *nf* wedge.

cuñado, a [ku'ɲaðo, a] *nm/f* brother/sister-in-law.

cuota ['kwota] *nf* (*parte proporcional*) share; (*cotización*) fee, dues *pl*.

cupe, cupiera *etc vb ver* **caber.**

cupo *vb ver* **caber** // ['kupo] *nm* quota.

cupón [ku'pon] *nm* coupon.

cúpula ['kupula] *nf* dome.

cura ['kura] *nf* (*curación*) cure; (*método curativo*) treatment // *nm* priest.

curación [kura'θjon] *nf* cure; (*acción*) curing.

curar [ku'rar] *vt* (*MED: herida*) to treat, dress; (: *enfermo*) to cure; (*CULIN*) to cure, salt; (*cuero*) to tan // *vi*, ~**se** *vr* to get well, recover.

curiosear [kurjose'ar] *vt* to glance at, look over // *vi* to look round, wander round; (*explorar*) to poke about.

curiosidad [kurjosi'ðað] *nf* curiosity.

curioso, a [ku'rjoso, a] *a* curious // *nm/f* bystander, onlooker.

currante [ku'rrante] *nm/f* (*fam*) worker.

currar [ku'rrar], **currelar** [kurre'lar] *vi* (*fam*) to work; **curro** *nm* (*fam*) work, job.

currículo [ku'rrikolo], **currículum** [ku'rrikulum] *nm* curriculum vitae.

cursi ['kursi] *a* (*fam*) pretentious; (: *amanerado*) affected.

cursiva [kur'siβa] *nf* italics *pl*.

curso ['kurso] *nm* course; **en** ~ (*año*) current; (*proceso*) going on, under way.

cursor [kur'sor] *nm* (*INFORM*) cursor.

curtido, a [kur'tiðo, a] *a* (*cara etc*) weather-beaten; (*fig: persona*) experienced.

curtir [kur'tir] *vt* (*cuero etc*) to tan.

curvo, a ['kurβo, a] *a* (*gen*) curved; (*torcido*) bent // *nf* (*gen*) curve, bend.

cúspide ['kuspiðe] *nf* (*GEO*) peak; (*fig*) top.

custodia [kus'toðja] *nf* safekeeping; custody; **custodiar** *vt* (*conservar*) to take care of; (*vigilar*) to guard.

custodio [kus'toðjo] *nm* guardian, keeper.

cutícula [ku'tikula] *nf* cuticle.

cutis ['kutis] *nm inv* skin, complexion.

cutre ['kutre] *a* (*fam: lugar*) grotty; (: *persona*) naff.

cuyo, a ['kujo, a] *pron* (*de quien*) whose; (*de que*) whose, of which; **en** ~ **caso** in which case.

C.V. *abr* (= *caballos de vapor*) H.P.

CH

chabacano, a [tʃaβa'kano, a] *a* vulgar, coarse.

chabola [tʃa'βola] *nf* shack; ~**s** *nfpl* shanty town *sg*.

chacal [tʃa'kal] *nm* jackal.

chacra ['tʃakra] *nf* (*AM*) smallholding.

chacha ['tʃatʃa] *nf* (*fam*) maid.

cháchara ['tʃatʃara] *nf* chatter; **estar de** ~ to chatter away.

chafar [tʃa'far] *vt* (*aplastar*) to crush; (*arruinar*) to ruin.

chal [tʃal] *nm* shawl.

chalado, a [tʃa'lado, a] *a* (*fam*) crazy.

chalé, chalet [tʃa'le] (*pl* **chalés, chalets**) *nm* villa, ≈ detached house.

chaleco [tʃa'leko] *nm* waistcoat, vest (*US*); ~ **salvavidas** life jacket.

chalupa [tʃa'lupa] *nf* launch, boat.

champán [tʃam'pan], **champaña** [tʃam'paɲa] *nm* champagne.

champiñón [tʃampi'ɲon] *nm* mushroom.

champú [tʃam'pu] (*pl* **champúes, champús**) *nm* shampoo.

chamuscar [tʃamus'kar] *vt* to scorch, sear, singe.

chance ['tʃantʃe] *nm* (*AM*) chance.

chancho, a ['tʃantʃo, a] *nm/f* (*AM*) pig.

chanchullo [tʃan'tʃuʎo] *nm* (*fam*) fiddle.

chantaje [tʃan'taxe] *nm* blackmail.

chapa ['tʃapa] *nf* (*de metal*) plate, sheet; (*de madera*) board, panel; (*AM AUTO*) number (*Brit*) *o* license (*US*) plate.

chaparrón [tʃapa'rron] *nm* downpour, cloudburst.

chapotear [tʃapote'ar] *vt* to sponge down // *vi* (*fam*) to splash about.

chapucero, a [tʃapu'θero, a] *a* rough, crude // *nm/f* bungler.

chapurrear [tʃapurre'ar] *vt* (*idioma*) to speak badly.

chapuza [tʃa'puθa] *nf* botched job.

chaqueta [tʃa'keta] *nf* jacket.

charca ['tʃarka] *nf* pond, pool.

charco ['tʃarko] *nm* pool, puddle.

charcutería [tʃarkute'ria] *nf* (*tienda*) shop selling chiefly pork meat products; (*productos*) cooked pork meats *pl*.

charla ['tʃarla] *nf* talk, chat; (*conferencia*) lecture.

charlar [tʃar'lar] *vi* to talk, chat.

charlatán, ana [tʃarla'tan, ana] *nm/f* chatterbox; (*estafador*) trickster.

charol [tʃa'rol] *nm* varnish; (*cuero*) patent leather.

chascarrillo [tʃaska'rriʎo] *nm* (*fam*) funny story.

chasco ['tʃasko] *nm* (*broma*) trick, joke; (*desengaño*) disappointment.

chasis ['tʃasis] *nm inv* chassis.

chasquear [tʃaske'ar] *vt* (*látigo*) to crack; (*lengua*) to click; **chasquido** *nm* (*de lengua*) click; (*de látigo*) crack.

chatarra [tʃa'tarra] *nf* scrap (metal).

chato, a ['tʃato, a] *a* flat; (*nariz*) snub.

chaval, a [tʃa'βal, a] *nm/f* kid, lad/lass.

checo(e)slovaco, a [tʃeko(e)slo'βako, a] *a, nm/f* Czech, Czechoslovak.

Checo(e)slovaquia [tʃeko(e)slo'βakja] *nf* Czechoslovakia.

cheque ['tʃeke] *nm* cheque (*Brit*), check (*US*); ~ **de viajero** traveller's cheque (*Brit*), traveler's check (*US*).

chequeo [tʃe'keo] *nm* (*MED*) check-up; (*AUTO*) service.

chequera [tʃe'kera] *nf* (*AM*) chequebook (*Brit*), checkbook (*US*).

chicano, a [tʃi'kano, a] *a nm/f* chicano.

chicle ['tʃikle] *nm* chewing gum.

chico, a ['tʃiko, a] *a* small, little // *nm/f* (*niño*) child; (*muchacho*) boy/girl.

chícharo ['tʃitʃaro] *nm* (*AM*) pea.

chicharrón [tʃitʃa'rron] *nm* (*pork*) crackling.

chichón [tʃi'tʃon] *nm* bump, lump.

chiflado, a [tʃi'flaðo, a] *a* crazy.

chiflar [tʃi'flar] *vt* to hiss, boo.

chile ['tʃile] *nm* chilli pepper.

Chile ['tʃile] *nm* Chile; **chileno, a** *a, nm/f* Chilean.

chillar [tʃi'ʎar] *vi* (*persona*) to yell, scream; (*animal salvaje*) to howl; (*cerdo*) to squeal; (*puerta*) to creak.

chillido [tʃi'ʎiðo] *nm* (*de persona*) yell, scream; (*de animal*) howl; (*de frenos*) screech(ing).

chillón, ona [tʃi'ʎon, ona] *a* (*niño*) noisy; (*color*) loud, gaudy.

chimenea [tʃime'nea] *nf* chimney; (*hogar*) fireplace.

China ['tʃina] *nf*: (**la**) ~ China.

chinche ['tʃintʃe] *nf* (*insecto*) (bed)bug; (*TEC*) drawing pin (*Brit*), thumbtack (*US*) // *nm/f* nuisance, pest.

chincheta [tʃin'tʃeta] *nf* drawing pin (*Brit*), thumbtack (*US*).

chino, a ['tʃino, a] *a, nm/f* Chinese // *nm* (*LING*) Chinese.

Chipre ['tʃipre] *nf* Cyprus; **chipriota, chipriote** *a, nm/f* Cypriot.

chiquito, a [tʃi'kito, a] *a* very small, tiny // *nm/f* kid.

chiripa [tʃi'ripa] *nf* fluke.

chirriar [tʃi'rrjar] *vi* (*goznes etc*) to creak, squeak; (*pájaros*) to chirp, sing.

chirrido [tʃi'rriðo] *nm* creak(ing), squeak(ing); (*de pájaro*) chirp(ing).

chis [tʃis] *excl* sh!

chisme ['tʃisme] *nm* (*habladurías*) piece of gossip; (*fam: objeto*) thingummyjig.

chismoso, a [tʃis'moso, a] *a* gossiping // *nm/f* gossip.

chispa ['tʃispa] *nf* spark; (*fig*) sparkle; (*ingenio*) wit; (*fam*) drunkenness.

chispeante [tʃispe'ante] *a* sparkling.

chispear [tʃispe'ar] *vi* to spark; (*lloviznar*) to drizzle.

chisporrotear [tʃisporrote'ar] *vi* (*fuego*) to throw out sparks; (*leña*) to crackle; (*aceite*) to hiss, splutter.

chiste ['tʃiste] *nm* joke, funny story.

chistoso, a [tʃis'toso, a] *a* (*gracioso*) funny, amusing; (*bromista*) witty.

chivo, a ['tʃiβo, a] *nm/f* (billy-/nanny-) goat; ~ **expiatorio** scapegoat.

chocante [tʃo'kante] *a* startling; (*extraño*) odd; (*ofensivo*) shocking.

chocar [tʃo'kar] *vi* (*coches etc*) to collide, crash // *vt* to shock; (*sorprender*) to startle; ~ **con** to collide with; (*fig*) to run into, run up against; ¡**chócala**! (*fam*) put it there!

chocolate [tʃoko'late] *a, nm* chocolate.

chochear [tʃotʃe'ar] *vi* to dodder, be senile.

chocho, a ['tʃotʃo, a] *a* doddering, senile; (*fig*) soft, doting.

chófer ['tʃofer], **chofer** [tʃo'fer] *nm* driver.

chollo ['tʃoʎo] *nm* (*fam*) bargain, snip.

choque *etc vb ver* **chocar** // ['tʃoke] *nm* (*impacto*) impact; (*golpe*) jolt; (*AUTO*) crash; (*fig*) conflict.

chorizo [tʃo'riθo] *nm* hard pork sausage, (type of) salami.

chorrear [tʃorre'ar] *vi* to gush (out), spout (out); (*gotear*) to drip, trickle.

chorro ['tʃorro] *nm* jet; (*fig*) stream.

choza ['tʃoθa] *nf* hut, shack.

chubasco [tʃu'βasko] *nm* squall.

chuleta [tʃu'leta] *nf* chop, cutlet.

chulo ['tʃulo] *nm* (*pícaro*) rascal; (*rufián*) pimp.

chupado, a [tʃu'paðo, a] *a* (*delgado*) skinny, gaunt.

chupete [tʃu'pete] *nm* dummy (*Brit*), pacifier (*US*).

chupar [tʃu'par] *vt* to suck; (*absorber*) to absorb; ~**se** *vr* to grow thin.

churro, a ['tʃurro, a] *a* coarse // *nm* (type of) fritter.

chusco, a ['tʃusko, a] *a* funny.

chusma ['tʃusma] *nf* rabble, mob.

chutar [tʃu'tar] *vi* (*DEPORTE*) to shoot (at goal).

D

D. *abr* (= *Don*) Esq.

Da. *abr* = *Doña*.

dactilógrafo, a [dakti'loɣrafo, a] *nm/f* typist.

dádiva ['daðiβa] nf (donación) donation; (regalo) gift: **dadivoso, a** a generous.

dado, a ['daðo, a] pp de **dar** // nm die; ~s nmpl dice; ~ **que** conj given that.

daltónico, a [dal'toniko, a] a colourblind.

dama ['dama] nf (gen) lady; (AJEDREZ) queen; ~s nfpl (juego) draughts.

damasco [da'masko] nm damask.

damnificar [damnifi'kar] vt to harm; (persona) to injure.

danés, esa [da'nes, esa] a Danish // nm/f Dane.

danzar [dan'θar] vt, vi to dance.

dañar [da'ɲar] vt (objeto) to damage; (persona) to hurt; ~**se** vr (objeto) to get damaged.

dañino, a [da'ɲino, a] a harmful.

daño ['daɲo] nm (a un objeto) damage; (a una persona) harm, injury; ~**s y perjuicios** (JUR) damages; **hacer** ~ **a** to damage; (persona) to hurt, injure; **hacerse** ~ to hurt o.s.

dar [dar] ♦ vt 1 (gen) to give; (obra de teatro) to put on; (film) to show; (fiesta) to hold; ~ **algo a uno** to give sb sth o sth to sb; ~ **de beber a uno** to give sb a drink

2 (producir: intereses) to yield; (fruta) to produce

3 (locuciones + n): **da gusto escucharle** it's a pleasure to listen to him; ver tb **paseo** y otros n

4 (+ n: = perífrasis de verbo): **me da pena/asco** it frightens/sickens me

5 (considerar): ~ **algo por descontado/ entendido** to take sth for granted/as read; ~ **algo por concluido** to consider sth finished

6 (hora): **el reloj dio las 6** the clock struck 6 (o'clock)

7: **me da lo mismo** it's all the same to me; ver tb **igual, más**

♦ vi 1: ~ **con**: **dimos con él dos horas más tarde** we came across him two hours later; **al final di con la solución** I eventually came up with the answer

2: ~ **en**: ~ **en** (blanco, suelo) to hit; **el sol me da en la cara** the sun is shining (right) on my face

3: ~ **de sí** (zapatos etc) to stretch, give

♦ ~**se** vr 1: ~**se por vencido** to give up

2 (ocurrir): **se han dado muchos casos** there have been a lot of cases

3: ~**se a**: **se ha dado a la bebida** he's taken to drinking

4: **se me dan bien/mal las ciencias** I'm good/bad at science

5: **dárselas de**: **se las da de experto** he fancies himself o poses as an expert.

dardo ['darðo] nm dart.

dársena ['darsena] nf dock.

datar [da'tar] vi: ~ **de** to date from.

dátil ['datil] nm date.

dato ['dato] nm fact, piece of informa-tion.

deha. abr (– derecha) r.h.

d. de J.C. abr (= después de Jesucristo) A.D.

de [de] prep (de + el = del) **1** (posesión) of; **la casa** ~ **Isabel/mis padres** Isabel's/ my parents' house; **es** ~ **ellos** it's theirs

2 (origen, distancia, con números) from; **soy** ~ **Gijón** I'm from Gijón; ~ **8 a 20** from 8 to 20; **salir del cine** to go out of o leave the cinema; ~ ... **en** ... from ... to ...; ~ **2 en 2** 2 by 2, 2 at a time

3 (valor descriptivo): **una copa** ~ **vino** a glass of wine; **la mesa** ~ **la cocina** the kitchen table; **un billete** ~ **1000 pesetas** a 1000 peseta note; **un niño** ~ **tres años** a three-year-old (child); **una máquina** ~ **coser** a sewing machine; **ir vestido** ~ **gris** to be dressed in grey; **la niña del vestido azul** the girl in the blue dress; **trabaja** ~ **profesora** she works as a teacher; ~ **lado** sideways; ~ **atrás/ delante** rear/front

4 (hora, tiempo): **a las 8** ~ **la mañana** at 8 o'clock in the morning; ~ **día/noche** by day/night; ~ **hoy en ocho días** a week from now; ~ **niño era gordo** as a child he was fat

5 (comparaciones): **más/menos** ~ **cien personas** more/less than a hundred people; **el más caro** ~ **la tienda** the most expensive in the shop; **menos/más** ~ **lo pensado** less/more than expected

6 (causa): **del calor** from the heat; ~ **puro tonto** out of sheer stupidity

7 (tema): about; **clases** ~ **inglés** English classes; **¿sabes algo** ~ **él?** do you know anything about him?; **un libro** ~ **física** a physics book

8 (adjetivo + de + infin): **fácil** ~ **entender** easy to understand

9 (oraciones pasivas): **fue respetado** ~ **todos** he was loved by all

10 (condicional + infin) if; ~ **ser posible** if possible; ~ **no terminarlo hoy** if I etc don't finish it today.

dé vb ver **dar**.

deambular [deambu'lar] vi to stroll, wander.

debajo [de'βaxo] ad underneath; ~ **de** below, under; **por** ~ **de** beneath.

debate [de'βate] nm debate; **debatir** vt to debate.

deber [de'βer] nm duty // vt to owe // vi: **debe (de)** it must, it should; ~**es** nmpl (ESCOL) homework; **debo hacerlo** I must do it; **debe de ir** he should go; ~**se** vr: ~**se a** to be owing o due to.

debido, a [de'βiðo, a] a proper, just; ~ **a** due to, because of.

débil ['deβil] a (persona, carácter) weak; (luz) dim; **debilidad** nf weakness; dim-ness.

debilitar [deβili'tar] vt to weaken; ~**se** vr to grow weak.

debutar [deβu'tar] *vi* to make one's debut.

década ['dekaða] *nf* decade.

decadencia [deka'ðenθja] *nf* (*estado*) decadence; (*proceso*) decline, decay.

decaer [deka'er] *vi* (*declinar*) to decline; (*debilitarse*) to weaken.

decaído, a [deka'iðo, a] *a*: estar ~ (*abatido*) to be down.

decaimiento [dekai'mjento] *nm* (*declinación*) decline; (*desaliento*) discouragement; (*MED: estado débil*) weakness.

decano, a [de'kano, a] *nm/f* (*de universidad etc*) dean.

decapitar [dekapi'tar] *vt* to behead.

decena [de'θena] *nf*: una ~ ten (or so).

decencia [de'θenθja] *nf* (*modestia*) modesty; (*honestidad*) respectability.

decente [de'θente] *a* (*correcto*) seemly, proper; (*honesto*) respectable.

decepción [deθep'θjon] *nf* disappointment.

decepcionar [deθepθjo'nar] *vt* to disappoint.

decidir [deθi'ðir] *vt* (*persuadir*) to convince, persuade; (*resolver*) to decide // *vi* to decide; ~se *vr*: ~se a to make up one's mind to.

décimo, a ['deθimo, a] *a* tenth // *nm* tenth.

decir [de'θir] *vt* (*expresar*) to say; (*contar*) to tell; (*hablar*) to speak // *nm* saying; ~se *vr*: se dice que it is said that; ~ para o entre sí to say to o.s.; querer ~ to mean; ¡dígame! (*TEL*) hello!; (*en tienda*) can I help you?

decisión [deθi'sjon] *nf* (*resolución*) decision; (*firmeza*) decisiveness.

decisivo, a [deθi'siβo, a] *a* decisive.

declamar [dekla'mar] *vt, vi* to declaim.

declaración [deklara'θjon] *nf* (*manifestación*) statement; (*explicación*) explanation.

declarar [dekla'rar] *vt* to declare, state; to explain // *vi* to declare; (*JUR*) to testify; ~se *vr* to propose.

declinar [dekli'nar] *vt* (*gen*) to decline; (*JUR*) to reject // *vi* (*el día*) to draw to a close.

declive [de'kliβe] *nm* (*cuesta*) slope; (*fig*) decline.

decolorarse [dekolo'rarse] *vr* to become discoloured.

decoración [dekora'θjon] *nf* decoration.

decorado [deko'raðo] *nm* (*CINE, TEATRO*) scenery, set.

decorar [deko'rar] *vt* to decorate; **decorativo, a** *a* ornamental, decorative.

decoro [de'koro] *nm* (*respeto*) respect; (*dignidad*) decency; (*recato*) propriety; ~so, a *a* (*decente*) decent; (*modesto*) modest; (*digno*) proper.

decrecer [dekre'θer] *vi* to decrease, diminish.

decrépito, a [de'krepito, a] *a* decrepit.

decretar [dekre'tar] *vt* to decree; **decreto** *nm* decree.

dedal [de'ðal] *nm* thimble.

dedicación [deðika'θjon] *nf* dedication; **dedicar** *vt* (*libro*) to dedicate; (*tiempo, dinero*) to devote; (*palabras: decir, consagrar*) to dedicate, devote; **dedicatoria** *nf* (*de libro*) dedication.

dedo ['deðo] *nm* finger; ~ (del pie) toe; ~ pulgar thumb; ~ índice index finger; ~ mayor o cordial middle finger; ~ anular ring finger; ~ meñique little finger; hacer ~ (*fam*) to hitch (a lift).

deducción [deðuk'θjon] *nf* deduction.

deducir [deðu'θir] *vt* (*concluir*) to deduce, infer; (*COM*) to deduct.

defecto [de'fekto] *nm* defect, flaw; **defectuoso, a** *a* defective, faulty.

defender [defen'der] *vt* to defend.

defensa [de'fensa] *nf* defence // *nm* (*DEPORTE*) defender, back; **defensivo, a** *a* defensive // *nf*: a la defensiva on the defensive.

defensor, a [defen'sor, a] *a* defending // *nm/f* (*abogado* ~) defending counsel; (*protector*) protector.

deficiencia [defi'θjenθja] *nf* deficiency.

deficiente [defi'θjente] *a* (*defectuoso*) defective; ~ en lacking o deficient in; ser un ~ mental to be mentally handicapped.

déficit ['defiθit] (*pl* ~s) *nm* deficit.

definir [defi'nir] *vt* (*determinar*) to determine, establish; (*decidir*) to define; (*aclarar*) to clarify; **definitivo, a** *a* definitive; **en definitiva** definitively; (*en resumen*) in short.

deformación [deforma'θjon] *nf* (*alteración*) deformation; (*RADIO etc*) distortion.

deformar [defor'mar] *vt* (*gen*) to deform; ~se *vr* to become deformed; **deforme** *a* (*informe*) deformed; (*feo*) ugly; (*malhecho*) misshapen.

defraudar [defrau'ðar] *vt* (*decepcionar*) to disappoint; (*estafar*) to cheat; to defraud.

defunción [defun'θjon] *nf* death, demise.

degeneración [dexenera'θjon] *nf* (*de las células*) degeneration; (*moral*) degeneracy.

degenerar [dexene'rar] *vi* to degenerate.

degollar [devo'ʎar] *vt* to behead; (*fig*) to slaughter.

degradar [devra'ðar] *vt* to debase, degrade; ~se *vr* to demean o.s.

degustación [devusta'θjon] *nf* sampling, tasting.

deificar [deifi'kar] *vt* (*persona*) to deify.

dejadez [dexa'ðeθ] *nf* (*negligencia*) neglect; (*descuido*) untidiness, carelessness; **dejado, a** *a* (*negligente*) careless; (*indolente*) lazy.

dejar [de'xar] *vt* to leave; (*permitir*) to allow, let; (*abandonar*) to abandon, for-

sake; (*beneficios*) to produce, yield // *vi*:
~ **de** (*parar*) to stop; (*no hacer*) to fail
to; **no dejes de comprar un billete** make
sure you buy a ticket; ~ **a un lado** to
leave *o* set aside.

dejo ['dexo] *nm* (*LING*) accent.

del [del] = **de** + **el**, *ver* **de**.

delantal [delan'tal] *nm* apron.

delante [de'lante] *ad* in front, (*enfrente*)
opposite; (*adelante*) ahead; ~ **de** in
front of, before.

delantero, a [delan'tero, a] *a* front // *nm*
(*DEPORTE*) forward, striker // *nf* (*de
vestido, casa etc*) front part; (*DEPORTE*)
forward line; **llevar la delantera** (**a uno**)
to be ahead (of sb).

delatar [dela'tar] *vt* to inform on *o*
against, betray; **delator, a** *nm/f* informer.

delegación [deleɣa'θjon] *nf* (*acción,
delegados*) delegation; (*COM*: *oficina*)
office, branch; ~ **de policía** police
station.

delegado, a [dele'ɣaðo, a] *nm/f*
delegate; (*COM*) agent.

delegar [dele'ɣar] *vt* to delegate.

deletrear [deletre'ar] *vt* to spell (out).

deleznable [deleθ'naßle] *a* brittle;
(*excusa, idea*) feeble.

delfín [del'fin] *nm* dolphin.

delgadez [delɣa'ðeθ] *nf* thinness, slim-
ness.

delgado, a [del'ɣaðo, a] *a* thin;
(*persona*) slim, thin; (*tierra*) poor; (*tela
etc*) light, delicate.

deliberación [delißera'θjon] *nf* delibera-
tion.

deliberar [deliße'rar] *vt* to debate, discuss.

delicadeza [delika'ðeθa] *nf* (*gen*)
delicacy; (*refinamiento, sutileza*) refinement.

delicado, a [deli'kaðo, a] *a* (*gen*)
delicate; (*sensible*) sensitive;
(*quisquilloso*) touchy.

delicia [de'liθja] *nf* delight.

delicioso, a [deli'θjoso, a] *a* (*gracioso*)
delightful; (*exquisito*) delicious.

delincuencia [delin'kwenθja] *nf*
delinquency; **delincuente** *nm/f*
delinquent; (*criminal*) criminal.

delineante [deline'ante] *nm/f*
draughtsman/woman.

delinear [deline'ar] *vt* (*dibujo*) to draw;
(*fig, contornos*) to outline.

delinquir [delin'kir] *vi* to commit an
offence.

delirante [deli'rante] *a* delirious.

delirar [deli'rar] *vi* to be delirious, rave.

delirio [de'lirjo] *nm* (*MED*) delirium;
(*palabras insensatas*) ravings *pl*.

delito [de'lito] *nm* (*gen*) crime; (*infracción*) offence.

demacrado, a [dema'krado, a] *a*: **estar
~** to look pale and drawn, be wasted
away.

demagogo, a [dema'ɣoɣo, a] *nm/f*
demagogue.

demanda [de'manda] *nf* (*pedido, COM*)
demand; (*petición*) request; (*JUR*)
action, lawsuit.

demandante [deman'dante] *nm/f*
claimant.

demandar [deman'dar] *vt* (*gen*) to
demand; (*JUR*) to sue, file a lawsuit
against.

demarcación [demarka'θjon] *nf* (*de
terreno*) demarcation.

demás [de'mas] *a*: **los ~ niños** the other
children, the remaining children // *pron*:
los/las ~ the others, the rest (of them);
lo ~ the rest (of it).

demasía [dema'sia] *nf* (*exceso*) excess,
surplus; **comer en ~** to eat to excess.

demasiado, a [dema'sjaðo, a] *a* too, too
much; ~**s** too many // *ad* too, too much;
¡es ~! it's too much!; **¡qué ~!** (*fam*)
great!

demencia [de'menθja] *nf* (*locura*) madness; **demente** *nm/f* lunatic // *a* mad,
insane.

democracia [demo'kraθja] *nf* democracy.

demócrata [de'mokrata] *nm/f* democrat;
democrático, a *a* democratic.

demoler [demo'ler] *vt* to demolish;
demolición *nf* demolition.

demonio [de'monjo] *nm* devil, demon;
¡~s! hell!, damn!; **¿cómo ~s?** how the
hell?

demora [de'mora] *nf* delay; **demorar** *vt*
(*retardar*) to delay, hold back; (*detener*)
to hold up // *vi* to linger, stay on; ~**se** *vr*
to be delayed.

demos *vb ver* **dar**.

demostración [demostra'θjon] *nf* (*de
teorema*) demonstration; (*de afecto*)
show, display.

demostrar [demos'trar] *vt* (*probar*) to
prove; (*mostrar*) to show; (*manifestar*)
to demonstrate; **demostrativo, a** *a*
demonstrative.

demudado, a [demu'ðaðo, a] *a* (*rostro*)
pale.

den *vb ver* **dar**.

denegar [dene'ɣar] *vt* (*rechazar*) to refuse; (*JUR*) to reject.

denigrar [deni'ɣrar] *vt* (*desacreditar, in-
famar*) to denigrate; (*injuriar*) to insult.

denominación [denomina'θjon] *nf*
(*clase*) denomination.

denotar [deno'tar] *vt* (*indicar*) to indicate; (*significar*) to denote.

densidad [densi'ðað] *nf* (*FISICA*)
density; (*fig*) thickness.

denso, a [' denso, a] *a* (*apretado*) solid;
(*espeso, pastoso*) thick; (*fig*) heavy.

dentadura [denta'ðura] *nf* (set of) teeth
pl; ~ **postiza** false teeth *pl*.

dentera [den'tera] *nf* (*sensación desagradable*) the shivers *pl*.

dentífrico, a |den'tifriko. a| a dental // nm toothpaste.

dentista |den'tista| nm/f dentist.

dentro |'dentro| ad inside // prep: ~ de in, inside, within; **mirar por** ~ to look inside; ~ **de tres meses** within three months.

denuncia |de'nunθja| nf (delación) denunciation; (acusación) accusation; (de accidente) report; **denunciar** vt to report; (delatar) to inform on o against.

departamento |departa'mento| nm (sección administrativa) department, section; (AM: piso) flat (Brit), apartment.

departir |depar'tir| vi to converse.

dependencia |depen'denθja| nf dependence; (POL) dependency; (COM) office, section.

depender |depen'der| vi: ~ de to depend on.

dependienta |depen'djenta| nf saleswoman, shop assistant.

dependiente |depen'djente| a dependent // nm salesman, shop assistant.

depilar |depi'lar| vt (con cera) to wax; (cejas) to pluck; **depilatorio** nm hair remover.

deplorable |deplo'raβle| a deplorable.

deplorar |deplo'rar| vt to deplore.

deponer |depo'ner| vt to lay down // vi (JUR) to give evidence; (declarar) to make a statement.

deportar |depor'tar| vt to deport.

deporte |de'porte| nm sport; **deportista** a sports cpd // nm/f sportsman/woman; **deportivo, a** a (club, periódico) sports cpd // nm sports car.

depositante |deposi'tante|, **depositador, a** |deposita'ðor, a| nm/f depositor.

depositar |deposi'tar| vt (dinero) to deposit; (mercaderías) to put away, store; (persona) to confide; ~se vr to settle; ~io, a nm/f trustee.

depósito |de'posito| nm (gen) deposit; (de mercaderías) warehouse, store; (de agua, gasolina etc) tank.

depravar |depra'βar| vt to deprave, corrupt; ~se vr to become depraved.

depreciar |depre'θjar| vt to depreciate, reduce the value of; ~se vr to depreciate, lose value.

depredador, a |depreða'ðor, a| a (ZOOL) predatory // nm (ZOOL) predator.

depresión |depre'sjon| nf depression.

deprimido, a |depri'miðo, a| a depressed.

deprimir |depri'mir| vt to depress; ~se vr (persona) to become depressed.

deprisa |de'prisa| ad quickly, hurriedly.

depuración |depura'θjon| nf purification; (POL) purge; **depurar** vt to purify; (purgar) to purge.

derecha |de'retʃa| nf right(-hand) side; (POL) right; **a la** ~ (estar) on the right; (torcer etc) (to the) right.

derecho, a |de'retʃo, a| a right, right-hand // nm (privilegio) right; (lado) right(-hand) side // ad straight, directly; ~s nmpl (de aduana) duty sg; (de autor) royalties; **tener** ~ **a** to have a right to.

deriva |de'riβa| nf: **ir** o **estar a la** ~ to drift, be adrift.

derivado |deri'βaðo| nm (COM) by-product.

derivar |deri'βar| vt to derive; (desviar) to direct // vi, ~se vr to derive, be derived; (NAUT) to drift.

derramamiento |derrama'mjento| nm (dispersión) spilling; ~ **de sangre** bloodshed.

derramar |derra'mar| vt to spill; (verter) to pour out; (esparcir) to scatter; ~se vr to pour out; ~ **lágrimas** to weep.

derrame |de'rrame| nm (de líquido) spilling; (de sangre) shedding; (de tubo etc) overflow; (pérdida) leakage; (MED) discharge; (declive) slope.

derredor |derre'ðor| ad: **al** o **en** ~ **de** around, about.

derretido, a |derre'tiðo, a| a melted; (metal) molten.

derretir |derre'tir| vt (gen) to melt; (nieve) to thaw; (fig) to squander; ~se vr to melt.

derribar |derri'βar| vt to knock down; (construcción) to demolish; (persona, gobierno, político) to bring down.

derrocar |derro'kar| vt (gobierno) to bring down, overthrow.

derrochar |derro'tʃar| vt to squander; **derroche** nm (despilfarro) waste, squandering.

derrota |de'rrota| nf (NAUT) course; (MIL, DEPORTE etc) defeat, rout; **derrotar** vt (gen) to defeat; **derrotero** nm (rumbo) course.

derrumbar |derrum'bar| vt (edificio) to knock down; ~se vr to collapse.

des vb ver **dar**.

desabotonar |desaβoto'nar| vt to unbutton, undo // vi (flores) to bloom; ~se vr to come undone.

desabrido, a |desa'βriðo, a| a (comida) insipid, tasteless; (persona) rude, surly; (respuesta) sharp; (tiempo) unpleasant.

desabrochar |desaβro'tʃar| vt (botones, broches) to undo, unfasten; ~se vr (ropa etc) to come undone.

desacato |desa'kato| nm (falta de respeto) disrespect; (JUR) contempt.

desacertado, a |desaθer'taðo, a| a (equivocado) mistaken; (inoportuno) unwise.

desacierto |desa'θjerto| nm mistake, error.

desaconsejado, a |desakonse'xaðo, a| a

ill-advised.

desaconsejar [desakonse'xar] *vt* to advise against.

desacorde [desa'korðe] *a* discordant; **estar ~ con algo** to disagree with sth.

desacreditar [desakreði'tar] *vt* (*desprestigiar*) to discredit, bring into disrepute; (*denigrar*) to run down.

desacuerdo [desa'kwerðo] *nm* (*conflicto*) disagreement, discord; (*error*) error, blunder.

desafiar [desa'fjar] *vt* (*retar*) to challenge; (*enfrentarse a*) to defy.

desafilado, a [desafi'laðo, a] *a* blunt.

desafinado, a [desafi'naðo, a] *a*. **estar ~** to be out of tune.

desafinarse [desafi'narse] *vr* to go out of tune.

desafío *etc vb ver* **desafiar** // [desa'fio] *nm* (*reto*) challenge; (*combate*) duel; (*resistencia*) defiance.

desaforado, a [desafo'raðo, a] *a* (*grito*) ear-splitting; (*comportamiento*) outrageous.

desafortunadamente [desafortunaða-'mente] *ad* unfortunately.

desafortunado, a [desafortu'naðo, a] *a* (*desgraciado*) unfortunate, unlucky.

desagradable [desaɣra'ðaßle] *a* (*fastidioso, enojoso*) unpleasant; (*irritante*) disagreeable.

desagradar [desaɣra'ðar] *vi* (*disgustar*) to displease; (*molestar*) to bother.

desagradecido, a [desaɣraðe'θiðo, a] *a* ungrateful.

desagrado [desa'ɣraðo] *nm* (*disgusto*) displeasure; (*contrariedad*) dissatisfaction.

desagraviar [desaɣra'ßjar] *vt* to make amends to; **desagravio** *nm* (*satisfacción*) amends; (*compensación*) compensation.

desagüe [des'aɣwe] *nm* (*de un líquido*) drainage; (*cañería*) drainpipe; (*salida*) outlet, drain.

desaguisado, a [desaɣi'saðo, a] *a* illegal // *nm* outrage.

desahogado, a [desao'ɣaðo, a] *a* (*holgado*) comfortable; (*espacioso*) roomy, large.

desahogar [desao'ɣar] *vt* (*aliviar*) to ease, relieve; (*ira*) to vent; **~se** *vr* (*relajarse*) to relax; (*desfogarse*) to let off steam.

desahogo [desa'oɣo] *nm* (*alivio*) relief; (*comodidad*) comfort, ease.

desahuciar [desau'θjar] *vt* (*enfermo*) to give up hope for; (*inquilino*) to evict; **desahucio** *nm* eviction.

desairar [desai'rar] *vt* (*menospreciar*) to slight, snub; (*cosa*) to disregard.

desaire [des'aire] *nm* (*menosprecio*) slight; (*falta de garbo*) unattractiveness.

desajustar [desaxus'tar] *vt* (*desarreglar*) to disarrange; (*desconcertar*) to throw

off balance; **~se** *vr* to get out of order; (*aflojarse*) to loosen.

desajuste [desa'xuste] *nm* (*de máquina*) disorder; (*situación*) imbalance.

desalentador, a [desalenta'ðor, a] *a* disheartening.

desalentar [desalen'tar] *vt* (*desanimar*) to discourage.

desaliento *etc vb ver* **desalentar** // [desa'ljento] *nm* discouragement.

desaliño [desa'liɲo] *nm* (*negligencia*) slovenliness.

desalmado, a [desal'maðo, a] *a* (*cruel*) cruel, heartless.

desalojar [desalo'xar] *vt* (*expulsar, echar*) to eject; (*abandonar*) to move out of // *vi* to move out.

desamarrar [desama'rrar] *vt* to untie; (*NAUT*) to cast off.

desamor [desa'mor] *nm* (*frialdad*) indifference; (*odio*) dislike.

desamparado, a [desampa'raðo, a] *a* (*persona*) helpless; (*lugar: expuesto*) exposed; (*desierto*) deserted.

desamparar [desampa'rar] *vt* (*abandonar*) to desert, abandon; (*JUR*) to leave defenceless; (*barco*) to abandon.

desandar [desan'dar] *vt*: **~ lo andado** *o* **el camino** to retrace one's steps.

desangrar [desan'grar] *vt* to bleed; (*fig: persona*) to bleed dry; **~se** *vr* to lose a lot of blood.

desanimado, a [desani'maðo, a] *a* (*persona*) downhearted; (*espectáculo, fiesta*) dull.

desanimar [desani'mar] *vt* (*desalentar*) to discourage; (*deprimir*) to depress; **~se** *vr* to lose heart.

desapacible [desapa'θißle] *a* (*gen*) unpleasant.

desaparecer [desapare'θer] *vi* (*gen*) to disappear; (*el sol, la luz*) to vanish; **desaparecido, a** *a* missing; **desaparecidos** *nmpl* (*en accidente*) people missing; **desaparición** *nf* disappearance.

desapasionado, a [desapasjo'naðo, a] *a* dispassionate, impartial.

desapego [desa'peɣo] *nm* (*frialdad*) coolness; (*distancia*) detachment.

desapercibido, a [desaperθi'ßiðo, a] *a* (*desprevenido*) unprepared; **pasar ~** to go unnoticed.

desaplicado, a [desapli'kaðo, a] *a* slack, lazy.

desaprensivo, a [desapren'sißo, a] *a* unscrupulous.

desaprobar [desapro'ßar] *vt* (*reprobar*) to disapprove of; (*condenar*) to condemn; (*no consentir*) to reject.

desaprovechado, a [desaproße'tʃaðo, a] *a* (*oportunidad, tiempo*) wasted; (*estudiante*) slack.

desaprovechar [desaproße'tʃar] *vt* to waste.

desarmar [desar'mar] *vt* (*MIL*, *fig*) to disarm; (*TEC*) to take apart, dismantle; **desarme** *nm* disarmament.

desarraigar [desarrai'ɣar] *vt* to uproot; **desarraigo** *nm* uprooting.

desarreglado, a [desarre'ɣlaðo, a] *a* (*desordenado*) disorderly, untidy.

desarreglar [desarre'ɣlar] *vt* (*desordenar*) to disarrange; (*trastocar*) to upset, disturb.

desarreglo [desa'rreɣlo] *nm* (*de casa*, *persona*) untidiness; (*desorden*) disorder.

desarrollar [desarro'ʎar] *vt* (*gen*) to develop; (*extender*) to unfold; ~se *vr* to develop; (*extenderse*) to open (out); (*FOTO*) to develop; **desarrollo** *nm* development.

desarticular [desartiku'lar] *vt* (*hueso*) to dislocate; (*objeto*) to take apart; (*fig*) to break up.

desaseo [desa'seo] *nm* (*suciedad*) slovenliness; (*desarreglo*) untidiness.

desasir [desa'sir] *vt* to loosen; ~se *vr* to extricate o.s.; ~se de to let go, give up.

desasosegar [desasose'ɣar] *vt* (*inquietar*) to disturb, make uneasy; ~se *vr* to become uneasy.

desasosiego *etc vb ver* desasosegar // [desaso'sjeɣo] *nm* (*intranquilidad*) uneasiness, restlessness; (*ansiedad*) anxiety.

desastrado, a [desas'traðo, a] *a* (*desaliñado*) shabby; (*sucio*) dirty.

desastre [de'sastre] *nm* disaster; **desastroso, a** *a* disastrous.

desatado, a [desa'taðo, a] *a* (*desligado*) untied; (*violento*) violent, wild.

desatar [desa'tar] *vt* (*nudo*) to untie; (*paquete*) to undo; (*separar*) to detach; ~se *vr* (*zapatos*) to come untied; (*tormenta*) to break.

desatascar [desatas'kar] *vt* (*cañería*) to unblock, clear.

desatender [desaten'der] *vt* (*no prestar atención a*) to disregard; (*abandonar*) to neglect.

desatento, a [desa'tento, a] *a* (*distraído*) inattentive; (*descortés*) discourteous.

desatinado, a [desati'naðo, a] *a* foolish, silly; **desatino** *nm* (*idiotez*) foolishness, folly; (*error*) blunder.

desatornillar [desatorni'ʎar] *vt* to unscrew.

desautorizado, a [desautori'θaðo, a] *a* unauthorized.

desautorizar [desautori'θar] *vt* (*oficial*) to deprive of authority; (*informe*) to deny.

desavenencia [desaβe'nenθja] *nf* (*desacuerdo*) disagreement; (*discrepancia*) quarrel.

desaventajado, a [desaβenta'xaðo, a] *a* (*inferior*) inferior; (*poco ventajoso*) disadvantageous.

desayunar [desaju'nar] *vi* to have breakfast // *vt* to have for breakfast; **desayuno** *nm* breakfast.

desazón [desa'θon] *nf* (*angustia*) anxiety; (*fig*) annoyance.

desazonar [desaθo'nar] *vt* (*fig*) to annoy, upset; ~se *vr* (*enojarse*) to be annoyed; (*preocuparse*) to worry, be anxious.

desbandarse [desβan'darse] *vr* (*MIL*) to disband; (*fig*) to flee in disorder.

desbarajuste [desβara'xuste] *nm* confusion, disorder.

desbaratar [desβara'tar] *vt* (*deshacer*, *destruir*) to ruin.

desbloquear [desβloke'ar] *vt* (*negociaciones*, *tráfico*) to get going again; (*COM*: *cuenta*) to unfreeze.

desbocado, a [desβo'kaðo, a] *a* (*caballo*) runaway.

desbordar [desβor'ðar] *vt* (*sobrepasar*) to go beyond; (*exceder*) to exceed // *vi*, ~se *vr* (*río*) to overflow; (*entusiasmo*) to erupt.

descabalgar [deskaβal'ɣar] *vi* to dismount.

descabellado, a [deskaβe'ʎaðo, a] *a* (*disparatado*) wild, crazy.

descabellar [deskaβe'ʎar] *vt* to ruffle; (*TAUR*: *toro*) to give the coup de grace to.

descafeinado, a [deskafei'naðo, a] *a* decaffeinated // *nm* decaffeinated coffee.

descalabro [deska'laβro] *nm* blow; (*desgracia*) misfortune.

descalificar [deskalifi'kar] *vt* to disqualify; (*desacreditar*) to discredit.

descalzar [deskal'θar] *vt* (*zapato*) to take off; **descalzo, a** *a* barefoot(ed); (*fig*) destitute.

descambiar [deskam'bjar] *vt* to exchange.

descaminado, a [deskami'naðo, a] *a* (*equivocado*) on the wrong road; (*fig*) misguided.

descampado [deskam'paðo] *nm* open space.

descansado, a [deskan'saðo, a] *a* (*gen*) rested; (*que tranquiliza*) restful.

descansar [deskan'sar] *vt* (*gen*) to rest // *vi* to rest, have a rest; (*echarse*) to lie down.

descansillo [deskan'siʎo] *nm* (*de escalera*) landing.

descanso [des'kanso] *nm* (*reposo*) rest; (*alivio*) relief; (*pausa*) break; (*DEPORTE*) interval, half time.

descapotable [deskapo'taβle] *nm* (*tb*: **coche** ~) convertible.

descarado, a [deska'raðo, a] *a* (*sin vergüenza*) shameless; (*insolente*) cheeky.

descarga [des'karɣa] *nf* (*ARQ*, *ELEC*, *MIL*) discharge; (*NAUT*) unloading.

descargar [deskar'ɣar] *vt* to unload; (*golpe*) to let fly; ~se *vr* to unburden o.s.; **descargo** nm (COM) receipt; (JUR) evidence.

descarnado, a [deskar'naðo, a] a scrawny; (fig) bare.

descaro [des'karo] nm nerve.

descarriar [deska'rrjar] vt (descaminar) to misdirect; (fig) to lead astray; ~se vr (perderse) to lose one's way; (separarse) to stray; (pervertirse) to err, go astray.

descarrilamiento [deskarrila'mjento] nm (de tren) derailment.

descarrilar [deskarri'lar] vi to be derailed.

descartar [deskar'tar] vt (rechazar) to reject; (eliminar) to rule out; ~se vr (NAIPES) to discard; ~se de to shirk.

descascarillado, a [deskaskari'ʎaðo, a] a (paredes) peeling.

descendencia [desθen'denθja] nf (origen) origin, descent; (hijos) offspring.

descender [desθen'der] vt (bajar: escalera) to go down // vi to descend; (temperatura, nivel) to fall, drop; ~ de to be descended from.

descendiente [desθen'djente] nm/f descendant.

descenso [des'θenso] nm descent; (de temperatura) drop.

descifrar [desθi'frar] vt to decipher; (mensaje) to decode.

descolgar [deskol'ɣar] vt (bajar) to take down; (teléfono) to pick up; ~se vr to let o.s. down.

descolorido, a [deskolo'riðo, a] a faded; (pálido) pale.

descompaginar [deskompaxi'nar] vt (desordenar) to disarrange, mess up.

descompasado, a [deskompa'saðo, a] a (sin proporción) out of all proportion; (excesivo) excessive.

descomponer [deskompo'ner] vt (desordenar) to disarrange, disturb; (TEC) to put out of order; (dividir) to break down (into parts); (fig) to provoke; ~se vr (corromperse) to rot, decompose; (el tiempo) to change (for the worse); (TEC) to break down.

descomposición [deskomposi'θjon] nf (gen) breakdown; (de fruta etc) decomposition.

descompostura [deskompos'tura] nf (TEC) breakdown; (desorganización) disorganization; (desorden) untidiness.

descompuesto, a [deskom'pwesto, a] a (corrompido) decomposed; (roto) broken.

descomunal [deskomu'nal] a (enorme) huge.

desconcertado, a [deskonθer'taðo, a] a disconcerted, bewildered.

desconcertar [deskonθer'tar] vt (confundir) to baffle; (incomodar) to upset, put out; ~se vr (turbarse) to be upset.

desconchado, a [deskon'tʃaðo, a] a (pintura) peeling.

desconcierto etc vb ver desconcertar // [deskon'θjerto] nm (gen) disorder; (desorientación) uncertainty; (inquietud) uneasiness.

desconectar [deskonek'tar] vt to disconnect.

desconfianza [deskon'fjanθa] nf distrust.

desconfiar [deskon'fjar] vi to be distrustful; ~ de to distrust, suspect.

descongelar [deskonxe'lar] vt to defrost; (COM, POL) to unfreeze.

descongestionar [deskonxestjo'nar] vt (cabeza, tráfico) to clear.

desconocer [deskono'θer] vt (ignorar) not to know, be ignorant of; (no aceptar) to deny; (repudiar) to disown.

desconocido, a [deskono'θiðo, a] a unknown // nm/f stranger.

desconocimiento [deskonoθi'mjento] nm (falta de conocimientos) ignorance; (repudio) disregard.

desconsiderado, a [deskonsiðe'raðo, a] a (descuidado) inconsiderate; (insensible) thoughtless.

desconsolar [deskonso'lar] vt to distress; ~se vr to despair.

desconsuelo etc vb ver desconsolar // [deskon'swelo] nm (tristeza) distress; (desesperación) despair.

descontado, a [deskon'taðo, a] a: **dar por ~ (que)** to take (it) for granted (that).

descontar [deskon'tar] vt (deducir) to take away, deduct; (rebajar) to discount.

descontento, a [deskon'tento, a] a dissatisfied // nm dissatisfaction, discontent.

descorazonar [deskoraθo'nar] vt to discourage, dishearten.

descorchar [deskor'tʃar] vt to uncork.

descorrer [desko'rrer] vt (cortinas, cerrojo) to draw back.

descortés [deskor'tes] a (mal educado) discourteous; (grosero) rude.

descoser [desko'ser] vt to unstitch; ~se vr to come apart (at the seams).

descosido, a [desko'siðo, a] a (COSTURA) unstitched; (desordenado) disjointed.

descrédito [des'kreðito] nm discredit.

descreído, a [deskre'iðo, a] a (incrédulo) incredulous; (falto de fe) unbelieving.

descremado, a [deskre'maðo, a] a skimmed.

describir [deskri'ßir] vt to describe; **descripción** [deskrip'θjon] nf description.

descrito [des'krito] pp de describir.

descuartizar [deskwarti'θar] vt (animal) to cut up.

descubierto, a pp de descubrir // [desku'ßjerto, a] a uncovered, bare; (persona) bareheaded // nm (bancario) overdraft; **al ~** in the open.

descubrimiento |dcskuβri'mjcnto| *nm*
(*hallazgo*) discovery; (*revelación*) revelation.

descubrir |dcsku'βrir| *vt* to discover,
find; (*inaugurar*) to unveil; (*vislumbrar*)
to detect; (*revelar*) to reveal, show;
(*destapar*) to uncover; ~se *vr* to reveal
o.s.; (*quitarse sombrero*) to take off
one's hat; (*confesar*) to confess.

descuento *etc vb ver* **descontar** //
|des'kwento| *nm* discount.

descuidado, a |dcskwi'ðaðo. a| *a* (*sin
cuidado*) careless; (*desordenado*) untidy; (*olvidadizo*) forgetful; (*dejado*)
neglected; (*desprevenido*) unprepared.

descuidar |dcskwi'ðar| *vt* (*dejar*) to
neglect; (*olvidar*) to overlook // *vi*, ~se
vr (*distraerse*) to be careless; (*estar
desaliñado*) to let o.s. go; (*des-
prevenirse*) to drop one's guard; ¡des-
cuida! don't worry!; **descuido** *nm*
(*dejadez*) carelessness; (*olvido*)
negligence.

desde |'desðc| ♦ *prep* **1** (*lugar*) from; ~
Burgos hasta mi casa hay 30 km it's 30
kms from Burgos to my house
2 (*posición*): hablaba ~ el balcón she
was speaking from the balcony
3 (*tiempo*: + *ad*, *n*): ~ **ahora** from now
on; ~ la boda since the wedding; ~ niño
since I *etc* was a child; ~ 3 años atrás
since 3 years ago
4 (*tiempo*: + *vb*) since; for; nos
conocemos ~ 1978/hace 20 años we've
known each other since 1978/for 20 years;
no le veo ~ 1983/~ hace 5 años I haven't
seen him since 1983/for 5 years
5 (*gama*): ~ los más lujosos hasta los
más económicos from the most luxurious
to the most reasonably priced
6: ~ luego (que no) of course (not)
♦ *conj*: ~ que: ~ que recuerdo for as
long as *o* ever since I can remember; ~
que llegó no ha salido he hasn't been out
since he arrived.

desdecirse |desðc'θirsc| *vr* to retract; ~
de to go back on.

desdén |des'ðcn| *nm* scorn.

desdeñar |desðc'ɲar| *vt* (*despreciar*) to
scorn.

desdicha |des'ðitʃa| *nf* (*desgracia*) mis-
fortune; (*infelicidad*) unhappiness; **des-
dichado, a** *a* (*sin suerte*) unlucky; (*infeliz*) unhappy.

desdoblar |desðo'βlar| *vt* (*extender*) to
spread out; (*desplegar*) to unfold.

desear |desc'ar| *vt* to want, desire, wish
for.

desecar |desc'kar| *vt*, **desecarse** *vr* to
dry up.

desechar |desc'tʃar| *vt* (*basura*) to throw
out *o* away; (*ideas*) to reject, discard;
desechos *nmpl* rubbish *sg*, waste *sg*.

desembalar |desemba'lar| *vt* to unpack.

desembarazado, a |desemba'raðaðo. a|

a (*libre*) clear, free; (*desenvuelto*) free
and easy.

desembarazar |desembara'θar| *vt*
(*desocupar*) to clear; (*desenredar*) to
free; ~se *vr*: ~se de to free o.s. of, get
rid of.

desembarcar |desembar'kar| *vt*
(*mercancías etc*) to unload // *vi*, ~se *vr*
to disembark.

desembocadura |desemboka'ðura| *nf*
(*de río*) mouth; (*de calle*) opening.

desembocar |desembo'kar| *vi* to flow
into; (*fig*) to result in.

desembolso |desem'bolso| *nm* payment.

desembragar |desembra'xar| *vi* to
declutch.

desemejanza |desemc'xanθa| *nf* dis-
similarity.

desempatar |desempa'tar| *vi* to replay,
hold a play-off; **desempate** *nm*
(*FÚTBOL*) replay, play-off; (*TENIS*) tie-
break(er).

desempeñar |desempc'ɲar| *vt* (*cargo*) to
hold; (*papel*) to perform; (*lo empeñado*)
to redeem; ~se *vr* to get out of debt; ~
un papel (*fig*) to play (a role).

desempeño |desem'pcɲo| *nm* redeem-
ing; (*de cargo*) occupation.

desempleado, a |desemplc'aðo. a| *nm/f*
unemployed person; **desempleo** *nm* unemployment.

desempolvar |desempol'βar| *vt* (*mue-
bles etc*) to dust; (*lo olvidado*) to revive.

desencadenar |desenkaðc'nar| *vt* to un-
chain; (*ira*) to unleash; ~se *vr* to break
loose; (*tormenta*) to burst; (*guerra*) to
break out.

desencajar |desenka'xar| *vt* (*hueso*) to
put out of joint; (*mandíbula*) to dislocate; (*mecanismo, pieza*) to disconnect, disengage.

desencanto |desen'kanto| *nm* disillusion-
ment.

desenchufar |desentʃu'far| *vt* to unplug.

desenfadado, a |desenfa'ðaðo. a| *a*
(*desenvuelto*) uninhibited; (*descarado*)
forward; **desenfado** *nm* (*libertad*) freedom; (*comportamiento*) free and easy
manner; (*descaro*) forwardness.

desenfocado, a |desenfo'kaðo. a| *a*
(*FOTO*) out of focus.

desenfrenado, a |desenfre'naðo. a| *a*
(*descontrolado*) uncontrolled; (*inmode-
rado*) unbridled; **desenfreno** *nm* (*vicio*)
wildness; (*de las pasiones*) lack of self-
control.

desenganchar |desengan'tʃar| *vt* (*gen*)
to unhook; (*FERRO*) to uncouple.

desengañar |desenga'ɲar| *vt* to disillu-
sion; ~se *vr* to become disillusioned;
desengaño *nm* disillusionment; (*decepción*) disappointment.

desenlace |desen'laθc| *nm* outcome.

desenmarañar |desenmara'ɲar| *vt* (*fig*)
to unravel.

desenmascarar |desenmaska'rar| *vt* to unmask.

desenredar |desenre'ðar| *vt* (*pelo*) to untangle; (*problema*) to sort out.

desentenderse |desenten'derse| *vr*: ~ de to pretend not to know about; (*apartarse*) to have nothing to do with.

desenterrar |desente'rrar| *vt* to exhume; (*tesoro, fig*) to unearth, dig up.

desentonar |desento'nar| *vi* (MUS) to sing (*o* play) out of tune; (*color*) to clash.

desentrañar |desentra'ɲar| *vt* (*misterio*) to unravel.

desentumecer |desentume'θer| *vt* (*pierna etc*) to stretch; (DEPORTE) to loosen up.

desenvoltura |desenβol'tura| *nf* (*libertad, gracia*) ease; (*descaro*) free and easy manner.

desenvolver |desenβol'βer| *vt* (*paquete*) to unwrap; (*fig*) to develop; ~se *vr* (*desarrollarse*) to unfold, develop; (*arreglárselas*) to cope.

deseo |de'seo| *nm* desire, wish; ~so, a *a*: estar ~so de to be anxious to.

desequilibrado, a |desekili'βraðo, a| *a* unbalanced.

desertar |deser'tar| *vi* to desert.

desértico, a |de'sertiko, a| *a* desert *cpd*.

desesperación |desespera'θjon| *nf* (*impaciencia*) desperation, despair; (*irritación*) fury.

desesperar |desespe'rar| *vt* to drive to despair; (*exasperar*) to drive to distraction // *vi*: ~ de to despair of; ~se *vr* to despair, lose hope.

desestabilizar |desestaβili'θar| *vt* to destabilize.

desestimar |desesti'mar| *vt* (*menospreciar*) to have a low opinion of; (*rechazar*) to reject.

desfachatez |desfatʃa'teθ| *nf* (*insolencia*) impudence; (*descaro*) rudeness.

desfalco |des'falko| *nm* embezzlement.

desfallecer |desfaʎe'θer| *vi* (*perder las fuerzas*) to become weak; (*desvanecerse*) to faint.

desfasado, a |desfa'saðo, a| *a* (*anticuado*) old-fashioned; **desfase** *nm* (*diferencia*) gap.

desfavorable |desfaβo'raβle| *a* unfavourable.

desfigurar |desfiɣu'rar| *vt* (*cara*) to disfigure; (*cuerpo*) to deform.

desfiladero |desfila'ðero| *nm* gorge.

desfilar |desfi'lar| *vi* to parade; **desfile** *nm* procession.

desfogarse |desfo'ɣarse| *vr* (*fig*) to let off steam.

desgajar |desɣa'xar| *vt* (*arrancar*) to tear off; (*romper*) to break off; ~se *vr* to come off.

desgana |des'ɣana| *nf* (*falta de apetito*) loss of appetite; (*renuencia*) unwillingness; ~**do**, a *a*: estar ~do (*sin apetito*) to have no appetite; (*sin entusiasmo*) to have lost interest.

desgarrador, a |desɣarra'ðor, a| *a* (*fig*) heartrending.

desgarrar |desɣa'rrar| *vt* to tear (up); (*fig*) to shatter; **desgarro** *nm* (*en tela*) tear; (*aflicción*) grief; (*descaro*) impudence.

desgastar |desɣas'tar| *vt* (*deteriorar*) to wear away *o* down; (*estropear*) to spoil; ~se *vr* to get worn out; **desgaste** *nm* wear (and tear).

desgracia |des'ɣraθja| *nf* misfortune; (*accidente*) accident; (*vergüenza*) disgrace; (*contratiempo*) setback; por ~ unfortunately.

desgraciado, a |desɣra'θjaðo, a| *a* (*sin suerte*) unlucky, unfortunate; (*miserable*) wretched; (*infeliz*) miserable.

desgreñado, a |desɣre'ɲaðo, a| *a* dishevelled.

deshabitado, a |desaβi'taðo, a| *a* uninhabited.

deshacer |desa'θer| *vt* (*casa*) to break up; (TEC) to take apart; (*enemigo*) to defeat; (*diluir*) to melt; (*contrato*) to break; (*intriga*) to solve; ~se *vr* (*disolverse*) to melt; (*despedazarse*) to come apart *o* undone; ~se de to get rid of; ~se en lágrimas to burst into tears.

deshecho, a |des'etʃo, a| *a* undone; (*roto*) smashed; estar ~ (*persona*) to be shattered.

desheredar |desere'ðar| *vt* to disinherit.

deshidratar |desiðra'tar| *vt* to dehydrate.

deshielo |des'jelo| *nm* thaw.

deshonesto, a |deso'nesto, a| *a* indecent.

deshonra |des'onra| *nf* (*deshonor*) dishonour; (*vergüenza*) shame; **deshonrar** *vt* to dishonour.

deshora |des'ora|: a ~ *ad* at the wrong time.

deshuesar |deswe'sar| *vt* (*carne*) to bone; (*fruta*) to stone.

desierto, a |de'sjerto, a| *a* (*casa, calle, negocio*) deserted // *nm* desert.

designar |desiɣ'nar| *vt* (*nombrar*) to designate; (*indicar*) to fix.

designio |de'siɣnjo| *nm* plan.

desigual |desi'ɣwal| *a* (*terreno*) uneven; (*lucha etc*) unequal.

desilusión |desilu'sjon| *nf* disillusionment; (*decepción*) disappointment; **desilusionar** *vt* to disillusion; to disappoint; desilusionarse *vr* to become disillusioned.

desinfectar |desinfek'tar| *vt* to disinfect.

desinflar |desin'flar| *vt* to deflate.

desintegración |desinteɣra'θjon| *nf* disintegration.

desinterés |desinte'res| *nm* (*objetividad*) disinterestedness; (*altruismo*) unselfishness.

desistir [desis'tir] vi (renunciar) to stop, desist.

desleal [desle'al] a (infiel) disloyal; (COM: competencia) unfair; ~**tad** nf disloyalty.

desleír [desle'ir] vt (líquido) to dilute; (sólido) to dissolve.

deslenguado, a [deslen'gwaðo, a] a (grosero) foul-mouthed.

desligar [desli'γar] vt (desatar) to untie, undo; (separar) to separate; ~**se** vr (de un compromiso) to extricate o.s.

desliz [des'liθ] nm (fig) lapse; ~**ar** vt to slip, slide; ~**arse** vr (escurrirse: persona) to slip, slide; (coche) to skid; (aguas mansas) to flow gently; (error) to creep in.

deslucido, a [deslu'θiðo, a] a dull; (torpe) awkward, graceless; (deslustrado) tarnished.

deslumbrar [deslum'brar] vt to dazzle.

desmán [des'man] nm (exceso) outrage; (abuso de poder) abuse.

desmandarse [desman'darse] vr (portarse mal) to behave badly; (excederse) to get out of hand; (caballo) to bolt.

desmantelar [desmante'lar] vt (deshacer) to dismantle; (casa) to strip.

desmaquillador [desmakiʎa'ðor] nm make-up remover.

desmayado, a [desma'jaðo, a] a (sin sentido) unconscious; (carácter) dull; (débil) faint, weak.

desmayar [desma'jar] vi to lose heart; ~**se** vr (MED) to faint; **desmayo** nm (MED: acto) faint; (: estado) unconsciousness; (depresión) dejection.

desmedido, a [desme'ðiðo, a] a excessive.

desmejorar [desmexo'rar] vt (dañar) to impair, spoil; (MED) to weaken.

desmembrar [desmem'brar] vt (MED) to dismember; (fig) to separate.

desmemoriado, a [desmemo'rjaðo, a] a forgetful.

desmentir [desmen'tir] vt (contradecir) to contradict; (refutar) to deny // vi: ~ de to refute; ~**se** vr to contradict o.s.

desmenuzar [desmenu'θar] vt (deshacer) to crumble; (carne) to chop; (examinar) to examine closely.

desmerecer [desmere'θer] vt to be unworthy of // vi (deteriorarse) to deteriorate.

desmesurado, a [desmesu'raðo, a] a disproportionate.

desmontar [desmon'tar] vt (deshacer) to dismantle; (tierra) to level // vi to dismount.

desmoralizar [desmorali'θar] vt to demoralize.

desmoronar [desmoro'nar] vt to wear away, erode; ~**se** vr (edificio, dique) to fall into disrepair; (economía) to decline.

desnatado, a [desna'taðo, a] a skimmed.

desnivel [desni'βel] nm (de terreno) unevenness.

desnudar [desnu'ðar] vt (desvestir) to undress; (despojar) to strip; ~**se** vr (desvestirse) to get undressed; **desnudo, a** a naked // nm/f nude; desnudo de devoid o bereft of.

desnutrición [desnutri'θjon] nf malnutrition; **desnutrido, a** a undernourished.

desobedecer [desoβeðe'θer] vt, vi to disobey; **desobediencia** nf disobedience.

desocupado, a [desoku'paðo, a] a at leisure; (desempleado) unemployed; (deshabitado) empty, vacant.

desocupar [desoku'par] vt to vacate.

desodorante [desoðo'rante] nm deodorant.

desolación [desola'θjon] nf (lugar) desolation; (fig) grief.

desolar [deso'lar] vt to ruin, lay waste.

desorden [des'orðen] nm confusion; (político) disorder, unrest.

desorganizar [desorγani'θar] vt (desordenar) to disorganize.

desorientar [desorjen'tar] vt (extraviar) to mislead; (confundir, desconcertar) to confuse; ~**se** vr (perderse) to lose one's way.

desovar [deso'βar] vi (peces) to spawn; (insectos) to lay eggs.

despabilado, a [despaβi'laðo, a] a (despierto) wide-awake; (fig) alert, sharp.

despabilar [despaβi'lar] vt (el ingenio) to sharpen // vi, ~**se** vr to wake up; (fig) to get a move on.

despacio [des'paθjo] ad slowly.

despachar [despa'tʃar] vt (negocio) to do, complete; (enviar) to send, dispatch; (vender) to sell, deal in; (billete) to issue; (mandar ir) to send away.

despacho [des'patʃo] nm (oficina) office; (de paquetes) dispatch; (venta) sale; (comunicación) message.

desparpajo [despar'paxo] nm self-confidence; (pey) nerve.

desparramar [desparra'mar] vt (esparcir) to scatter; (líquido) to spill.

despavorido, a [despaβo'riðo, a] a terrified.

despectivo, a [despek'tiβo, a] a (despreciativo) derogatory; (LING) pejorative.

despecho [des'petʃo] nm spite; a ~ de in spite of.

despedazar [despeða'θar] vt to tear to pieces.

despedida [despe'ðiða] nf (adiós) farewell; (de obrero) sacking.

despedir [despe'ðir] vt (visita) to see off, show out; (empleado) to dismiss; (inquilino) to evict; (objeto) to hurl; (olor etc) to give out o off; ~**se** vr: ~**se** de to say goodbye to.

despegar [despe'xar] vt to unstick // vi (avión) to take off; ~se vr to come loose, come unstuck; **despego** nm detachment.

despegue etc vb ver **despegar** // [des'peɣe] nm takeoff.

despeinado, a [despei'naðo, a] a dishevelled, unkempt.

despejado, a [despe'xaðo, a] a (lugar) clear, free; (cielo) clear; (persona) wide-awake, bright.

despejar [despe'xar] vt (gen) to clear; (misterio) to clear up // vi (el tiempo) to clear; ~se vr (tiempo, cielo) to clear (up); (misterio) to become clearer; (cabeza) to clear.

despellejar [despeʎe'xar] vt (animal) to skin.

despensa [des'pensa] nf larder.

despeñadero [despeɲa'ðero] nm (GEO) cliff, precipice.

desperdicio [desper'ðiθjo] nm (despilfarro) squandering; ~s nmpl (basura) rubbish sg (Brit), garbage sg (US); (residuos) waste sg.

desperezarse [despere'θarse] vr to stretch (o.s.).

desperfecto [desper'fekto] nm (deterioro) slight damage; (defecto) flaw, imperfection.

despertador [desperta'ðor] nm alarm clock.

despertar [desper'tar] vt (persona) to wake up; (recuerdos) to revive; (sentimiento) to arouse // vi, ~se vr to awaken, wake up // nm awakening.

despiadado, a [despja'ðaðo, a] a (ataque) merciless; (persona) heartless.

despido etc vb ver **despedir** // [des'piðo] nm dismissal, sacking.

despierto, a etc vb ver **despertar** // [des'pjerto, a] a awake; (fig) sharp, alert.

despilfarro [despil'farro] nm (derroche) squandering; (lujo desmedido) extravagance.

despistar [despis'tar] vt to throw off the track o scent; (fig) to mislead, confuse; ~se vr to take the wrong road; (fig) to become confused.

desplazamiento [desplaθa'mjento] nm displacement.

desplazar [despla'θar] vt to move; (NAUT) to displace; (INFORM) to scroll; (fig) to oust; ~se vr (persona) to travel.

desplegar [desple'ɣar] vt (tela, papel) to unfold, open out; (bandera) to unfurl; **despliegue** vb etc ver **desplegar** // [des'pljeɣe] nm display.

desplomarse [desplo'marse] vr (edificio, gobierno, persona) to collapse.

desplumar [desplu'mar] vt (ave) to pluck; (fam: estafar) to fleece.

despoblado, a [despo'ßlaðo, a] a (sin

habitantes) uninhabited.

despojar [despo'xar] vt (alguien: de sus bienes) to divest of, deprive of; (casa) to strip, leave bare; (alguien: de su cargo) to strip of.

despojo [des'poxo] nm (acto) plundering; (objetos) plunder, loot; ~s nmpl (de ave, res) offal sg.

desposado, a [despo'saðo, a] a, nm/f newly-wed.

desposeer [despose'er] vt: ~ a uno de (puesto, autoridad) to strip sb of.

déspota ['despota] nm/f despot.

despreciar [despre'θjar] vt (desdeñar) to despise, scorn; (afrentar) to slight; **desprecio** nm scorn, contempt; slight.

desprender [despren'der] vt (separar) to separate; (desatar) to unfasten; (olor) to give off; ~se vr (botón: caerse) to fall off; (: abrirse) to unfasten; (olor, perfume) to be given off; ~se de to follow from; se desprende que it transpires that.

desprendimiento [desprendi'mjento] nm (gen) loosening; (generosidad) disinterestedness; (indiferencia) detachment; (de gas) leak; (de tierra, rocas) landslide.

despreocupado, a [despreoku'paðo, a] a (sin preocupación) unworried, nonchalant; (negligente) careless.

despreocuparse [despreoku'parse] vr to be carefree; ~ de to have no interest in.

desprestigiar [despresti'xjar] vt (criticar) to run down; (desacreditar) to discredit.

desprevenido, a [despreße'niðo, a] a (no preparado) unprepared, unready.

desproporcionado, a [despropor-θjo'naðo, a] a disproportionate, out of proportion.

después [des'pwes] ad afterwards, later; (próximo paso) next; ~ de comer after lunch; **un año ~** a year later; **~ se debatió el tema** next the matter was discussed; **~ de corregido el texto** after the text had been corrected; **~ de todo** after all.

desquite [des'kite] nm (satisfacción) satisfaction; (venganza) revenge.

destacar [desta'kar] vt to emphasize, point up; (MIL) to detach, detail // vi, ~se vr (resaltarse) to stand out; (persona) to be outstanding o exceptional.

destajo [des'taxo] nm: **trabajar a ~** to do piecework.

destapar [desta'par] vt (botella) to open; (cacerola) to take the lid off; (descubrir) to uncover; ~se vr (revelarse) to reveal one's true character.

destartalado, a [destarta'laðo, a] a (desordenado) untidy; (ruinoso) tumbledown.

destello [des'teʎo] nm (de estrella)

twinkle; (de faro) signal light.

destemplado, a [destem'plaðo, a] a (MUS) out of tune; (voz) harsh; (MED) out of sorts; (tiempo) unpleasant, nasty.

desteñir [deste'nir] vt to fade // vi, ~se vr to fade; esta tela no destiñe this fabric will not run.

desternillarse [desterni'ʎarse] vr: ~ de risa to split one's sides laughing.

desterrar [deste'rrar] vt (exilar) to exile; (fig) to banish, dismiss.

destetar [deste'tar] vt to wean.

destierro etc vb ver desterrar // [des'tjerro] nm exile.

destilar [desti'lar] vt to distil; **destilería** nf distillery.

destinar [desti'nar] vt (funcionario) to appoint, assign; (fondos) to set aside (a for).

destinatario, a [destina'tarjo, a] nm/f addressee.

destino [des'tino] nm (suerte) destiny; (de avión, viajero) destination.

destituir [destitu'ir] vt to dismiss.

destornillador [destorniʎa'ðor] nm screwdriver.

destornillar [destorni'ʎar] vt, **destornillarse** vr (tornillo) to unscrew.

destreza [des'treθa] nf (habilidad) skill; (maña) dexterity.

destrozar [destro'θar] vt (romper) to smash, break (up); (estropear) to ruin; (nervios) to shatter.

destrozo [des'troθo] nm (acción) destruction; (desastre) smashing; ~s nmpl (pedazos) pieces; (daños) havoc sg.

destrucción [destruk'θjon] nf destruction.

destruir [destru'ir] vt to destroy.

desuso [des'uso] nm disuse; caer en ~ to become obsolete.

desvalido, a [desβa'liðo, a] a (desprotegido) destitute; (sin fuerzas) helpless.

desvalijar [desβali'xar] vt (persona) to rob; (casa, tienda) to burgle; (coche) to break into.

desván [des'βan] nm attic.

desvanecer [desβane'θer] vt (disipar) to dispel; (borrar) to blur; ~se vr (humo etc) to vanish, disappear; (color) to fade; (recuerdo, sonido) to fade away; (MED) to pass out; (duda) to be dispelled.

desvanecimiento [desβaneθi'mjento] nm (desaparición) disappearance; (de colores) fading; (evaporación) evaporation; (MED) fainting fit.

desvariar [desβa'rjar] vi (enfermo) to be delirious; **desvarío** nm delirium.

desvelar [desβe'lar] vt to keep awake; ~se vr (no poder dormir) to stay awake; (vigilar) to be vigilant o watchful.

desvencijado, a [desβenθi'xaðo, a] a

(silla) rickety; (máquina) broken-down.

desventaja [desβen'taxa] nf disadvantage.

desventura [desβen'tura] nf misfortune.

desvergonzado, a [desβerɣon'θaðo, a] a shameless.

desvergüenza [desβer'ɣwenθa] nf (descaro) shamelessness; (insolencia) impudence; (mala conducta) effrontery.

desvestir [desβes'tir] vt, **desvestirse** vr to undress.

desviación [desβja'θjon] nf deviation; (AUTO) diversion, detour.

desviar [des'βjar] vt to turn aside; (río) to alter the course of; (navío) to divert, re-route; (conversación) to sidetrack; ~se vr (apartarse del camino) to turn aside; (: barco) to go off course.

desvío etc vb ver desviar // [des'βio] nm (desviación) detour, diversion; (fig) indifference.

desvirtuar [desβir'twar] vt, **desvirtuarse** vr to spoil.

desvivirse [desβi'βirse] vr: ~ por (anhelar) to long for, crave for; (hacer lo posible por) to do one's utmost for.

detallar [deta'ʎar] vt to detail.

detalle [de'taʎe] nm detail; (fig) gesture, token; al ~ in detail; (COM) retail.

detallista [deta'ʎista] nm/f retailer.

detener [dete'ner] vt (gen) to stop; (JUR) to arrest; (objeto) to keep; ~se vr to stop; (demorarse): ~se en to delay over, linger over.

detenidamente [deteniða'mente] ad (minuciosamente) carefully; (extensamente) at great length.

detenido, a [dete'niðo, a] a (arrestado) under arrest; (minucioso) detailed // nm/f person under arrest, prisoner.

detergente [deter'xente] nm detergent.

deteriorar [deterjo'rar] vt to spoil, damage; ~se vr to deteriorate; **deterioro** nm deterioration.

determinación [determina'θjon] nf (empeño) determination; (decisión) decision.

determinar [determi'nar] vt (plazo) to fix; (precio) to settle; ~se vr to decide.

detestar [detes'tar] vt to detest.

detonar [deto'nar] vi to detonate.

detrás [de'tras] ad behind; (atrás) at the back; ~ de behind.

detrimento [detri'mento] nm: en ~ de to the detriment of.

deuda ['deuða] nf (condición) indebtedness, debt; (cantidad) debt.

deudor, a [deu'ðor, a] nm/f debtor.

devaluación [deβalwa'θjon] nf devaluation.

devastar [deβas'tar] vt (destruir) to devastate.

devengar [deβen'gar] vt (COM) to accrue, earn.

devoción [deβo'θjon] nf devotion.

devolución [deßolu'θjon] nf (reenvío) return, sending back; (reembolso) repayment; (JUR) devolution.

devolver [deßol'ßer] vt to return; (lo extraviado, lo prestado) to give back; (carta al correo) to send back; (COM) to repay, refund; (visita, la palabra) to return // vi (fam) to be sick.

devorar [deßo'rar] vt to devour.

devoto, a [de'ßoto, a] a devout // nm/f admirer.

devuelto, devuelva etc vb ver **devolver**.

di vb ver **dar; decir**.

día ['dia] nm day; ¿qué ~ es? what's the date?; estar/poner al ~ to be/keep up to date; el ~ de hoy/de mañana today/tomorrow; al ~ siguiente (on) the following day; vivir al ~ to live from hand to mouth; de ~ by day, in daylight; en pleno ~ in full daylight; ~ festivo (Esp) o feriado (AM) holiday; ~ libre day off.

diablo ['djaßlo] nm devil; **diablura** nf prank.

diafragma [dja'fraɣma] nm diaphragm.

diagnosis [djaɣ'nosis] nf inv, **diagnóstico** [djaɣ'nostiko] nm diagnosis.

diagrama [dja'ɣrama] nm diagram; ~ de flujo flowchart.

dialecto [dja'lekto] nm dialect.

dialogar [djalo'ɣar] vi: ~ con (POL) to hold talks with.

diálogo ['djaloɣo] nm dialogue.

diamante [dja'mante] nm diamond.

diana ['djana] nf (MIL) reveille; (de blanco) centre, bull's-eye.

diapositiva [djaposi'tißa] nf (FOTO) slide, transparency.

diario, a ['djarjo, a] a daily // nm newspaper; a ~ daily; de ~ everyday.

diarrea [dja'rrea] nf diarrhoea.

dibujar [dißu'xar] vt to draw, sketch; **dibujo** nm drawing; **dibujos animados** cartoons.

diccionario [dikθjo'narjo] nm dictionary.

dice etc vb ver **decir**.

diciembre [di'θjembre] nm December.

dictado [dik'taðo] nm dictation.

dictador [dikta'ðor] nm dictator; **dictadura** nf dictatorship.

dictamen [dik'tamen] nm (opinión) opinion; (juicio) judgment; (informe) report.

dictar [dik'tar] vt (carta) to dictate; (JUR: sentencia) to pronounce; (decreto) to issue; (AM: clase) to give.

dicho, a ['ditʃo, a] pp de **decir** // a: en ~s países in the aforementioned countries // nm saying.

diecinueve [djeθi'nweße] num nineteen.

dieciocho [djeθi'otʃo] num eighteen.

dieciséis [djeθi'seis] num sixteen.

diecisiete [djeθi'sjete] num seventeen.

diente ['djente] nm (ANAT, TEC) tooth; (ZOOL) fang; (: de elefante) tusk; (de

ajo) clove; hablar entre ~s to mutter, mumble.

diera, dieron etc vb ver **dar**.

diesel ['disel] a: motor ~ diesel engine.

dieta ['djeta] nf diet.

diez [djeθ] num ten.

difamar [difa'mar] vt (JUR: hablando) to slander; (: por escrito) to libel.

diferencia [dife'renθja] nf difference; **diferenciar** vt to differentiate between // vi to differ; **diferenciarse** vr to differ, be different; (distinguirse) to distinguish o.s.

diferente [dife'rente] a different.

diferido [dife'riðo] nm: en ~ (TV etc) recorded.

difícil [di'fiθil] a difficult.

dificultad [difikul'taθ] nf difficulty; (problema) trouble; (objeción) objection.

dificultar [difikul'tar] vt (complicar) to complicate, make difficult; (estorbar) to obstruct.

difundir [difun'dir] vt (calor, luz) to diffuse; (RADIO, TV) to broadcast; ~ una noticia to spread a piece of news; ~se vr to spread (out).

difunto, a [di'funto, a] a dead, deceased // nm/f deceased (person).

diga etc vb ver **decir**.

digerir [dixe'rir] vt to digest; (fig) to absorb.

digital [dixi'tal] a (INFORM) digital.

dignarse [diɣ'narse] vr to deign to.

digno, a ['diɣno, a] a worthy.

digo etc vb ver **decir**.

dije etc vb ver **decir**.

dilatado, a [dila'taðo, a] a dilated; (período) long drawn-out; (extenso) extensive.

dilatar [dila'tar] vt (cuerpo) to dilate; (prolongar) to prolong; (aplazar) to delay.

dilema [di'lema] nm dilemma.

diligencia [dili'xenθja] nf diligence; (ocupación) errand, job; ~s nfpl (JUR) formalities; **diligente** a diligent.

diluir [dilu'ir] vt to dilute.

diluvio [di'lußjo] nm deluge, flood.

dimensión [dimen'sjon] nf dimension.

diminuto, a [dimi'nuto, a] a tiny, diminutive.

dimitir [dimi'tir] vi to resign.

dimos vb ver **dar**.

Dinamarca [dina'marka] nf Denmark; **dinamarqués, esa** a Danish // nm/f Dane.

dinámico, a [di'namiko, a] a dynamic.

dinamita [dina'mita] nf dynamite.

dínamo ['dinamo] nf dynamo.

dineral [dine'ral] nm large sum of money, fortune.

dinero [di'nero] nm money; ~ contante, ~ efectivo cash, ready cash.

dio vb ver **dar**.

dios [djos] nm god; ¡D~ mío! (oh,) my

God!

diosa |'djosa| *nf* goddess.

diploma |di'ploma| *nm* diploma.

diplomacia |diplo'maθja| *nf* diplomacy; (*fig*) tact.

diplomado, a |diplo'maðo, a| *a* qualified.

diplomático, a |diplo'matiko, a| *a* diplomatic // *nm/f* diplomat.

diputado, a |dipu'taðo, a| *nm/f* delegate; (*POL*) ≈ member of parliament (*Brit*), ≈ representative (*US*).

dique |'dike| *nm* dyke.

diré *etc vb ver* **decir.**

dirección |direk'θjon| *nf* direction; (*señas*) address; (*AUTO*) steering; (*gerencia*) management; (*POL*) leadership; ~ **única/prohibida** one-way street/no entry.

directo, a |di'rekto, a| *a* direct; (*RADIO, TV*) live; **transmitir en** ~ to broadcast live.

director, a |direk'tor, a| *a* leading // *nm/f* director; (*ESCOL*) head(teacher) (*Brit*), principal (*US*); (*gerente*) manager(ess); (*PRENSA*) editor; ~ **de cine** film director; ~ **general** managing director.

dirigir |diri'xir| *vt* to direct; (*carta*) to address; (*obra de teatro, film*) to direct; (*MUS*) to conduct; (*comercio*) to manage; ~**se** *vr:* ~**se a** to go towards, make one's way towards; (*hablar con*) to speak to.

dirija *etc vb ver* **dirigir.**

discernir |disθer'nir| *vt* (*distinguir, discriminar*) to discern.

disciplina |disθi'plina| *nf* discipline.

discípulo, a |dis'θipulo, a| *nm/f* disciple.

disco |'disko| *nm* disc; (*DEPORTE*) discus; (*TEL*) dial; (*AUTO*: *semáforo*) light; (*MUS*) record; ~ **compacto/de larga duración** compact disc/long-playing record (L.P.); ~ **de freno** brake disc; (*INFORM*): ~ **flexible/rígido** floppy/hard disk.

disconforme |diskon'forme| *a* differing; **estar** ~ (**con**) to be in disagreement (with).

discordia |dis'korðja| *nf* discord.

discoteca |disko'teka| *nf* disco(theque).

discreción |diskre'θjon| *nf* discretion; (*reserva*) prudence; **comer a** ~ to eat as much as one wishes; **discrecional** *a* (*facultativo*) discretionary.

discrepancia |diskre'panθja| *nf* (*diferencia*) discrepancy; (*desacuerdo*) disagreement.

discreto, a |dis'kreto, a| *a* (*diplomático*) discreet; (*sensato*) sensible; (*reservado*) quiet; (*sobrio*) sober.

discriminación |diskrimina'θjon| *nf* discrimination.

disculpa |dis'kulpa| *nf* excuse; (*pedir perdón*) apology; **pedir** ~**s a/por** to apologize to/for; **disculpar** *vt* to excuse,

pardon; **disculparse** *vr* to excuse o.s.; to apologize.

discurrir |disku'rrir| *vi* (*pensar, reflexionar*) to think, meditate; (*recorrer*) to roam, wander; (*el tiempo*) to pass, flow by.

discurso |dis'kurso| *nm* speech.

discutir |disku'tir| *vt* (*debatir*) to discuss; (*pelear*) to argue about; (*contradecir*) to argue against // *vi* to discuss; (*disputar*) to argue.

disecar |dise'kar| *vt* (*conservar: animal*) to stuff; (: *planta*) to dry.

diseminar |disemi'nar| *vt* to disseminate, spread.

diseño |di'seɲo| *nm* design; (*ARTE*) drawing.

disfraz |dis'fraθ| *nm* (*máscara*) disguise; (*excusa*) pretext; ~**ar** *vt* to disguise; ~**arse** *vr:* ~**arse de** to disguise o.s. as.

disfrutar |disfru'tar| *vt* to enjoy // *vi* to enjoy o.s.; ~ **de** to enjoy, possess.

disgustar |disɣus'tar| *vt* (*no gustar*) to displease; (*contrariar, enojar*) to annoy, upset; ~**se** *vr* to be annoyed; (*dos personas*) to fall out.

disgusto |dis'ɣusto| *nm* (*repugnancia*) disgust; (*contrariedad*) annoyance; (*tristeza*) grief; (*riña*) quarrel; (*avería*) misfortune.

disidente |disi'ðente| *nm* dissident.

disimular |disimu'lar| *vt* (*ocultar*) to hide, conceal // *vi* to dissemble.

disipar |disi'par| *vt* to dispel; (*fortuna*) to squander; ~**se** *vr* (*nubes*) to vanish; (*indisciplinarse*) to dissipate.

disminución |disminu'θjon| *nf* decrease, reduction.

disminuir |disminu'ir| *vt* (*acortar*) to decrease; (*achicar*) to diminish; (*estrechar*) to lessen.

disolver |disol'ßer| *vt* (*gen*) to dissolve; ~**se** *vr* to dissolve; (*COM*) to go into liquidation.

disparar |dispa'rar| *vt, vi* to shoot, fire.

disparate |dispa'rate| *nm* (*tontería*) foolish remark; (*error*) blunder; **decir** ~**s** to talk nonsense.

disparo |dis'paro| *nm* shot.

dispensar |dispen'sar| *vt* to dispense; (*disculpar*) to excuse.

dispersar |disper'sar| *vt* to disperse; ~**se** *vr* to scatter.

disponer |dispo'ner| *vt* (*arreglar*) to arrange; (*ordenar*) to put in order; (*preparar*) to prepare, get ready // *vi*: ~ **de** to have, own; ~**se** *vr:* ~**se para** to prepare to, prepare for.

disponible |dispo'nißle| *a* available.

disposición |disposi'θjon| *nf* arrangement, disposition; (*aptitud*) aptitude; (*INFORM*) layout; **a la** ~ **de** at the disposal of.

dispositivo |disposi'tißo| *nm* device, mechanism.

dispuesto, a pp de **disponer** // |dis'pwesto, a| a (arreglado) arranged; (preparado) disposed

disputar |dispu'tar| vt (discutir) to dispute, question; (contender) to contend for // vi to argue.

disquete |dis'kete| nm floppy disk, diskette.

distancia |dis'tanθja| nf distance.

distanciar |distan'θjar| vt to space out; ~se vr to become estranged.

distante |dis'tante| a distant.

diste, disteis vb ver **dar**.

distinción |distin'θjon| nf distinction; (elegancia) elegance; (honor) honour.

distinguido, a |distin'giðo, a| a distinguished.

distinguir |distin'gir| vt to distinguish; (escoger) to single out; ~se vr to be distinguished.

distinto, a |dis'tinto, a| a different; (claro) clear.

distracción |distrak'θjon| nf distraction; (pasatiempo) hobby, pastime; (olvido) absent-mindedness, distraction.

distraer |distra'er| vt (atención) to distract; (divertir) to amuse; (fondos) to embezzle; ~se vr (entretenerse) to amuse o.s.; (perder la concentración) to allow one's attention to wander.

distraído, a |distra'iðo, a| a (gen) absent-minded; (entretenido) amusing.

distribuir |distriβu'ir| vt to distribute.

distrito |dis'trito| nm (sector, territorio) region; (barrio) district.

disturbio |dis'turβjo| nm disturbance; (desorden) riot.

disuadir |diswa'ðir| vt to dissuade.

disuelto |di'swelto| pp de **disolver**.

DIU nm abr (= dispositivo intrauterino) IUD.

diurno, a |'djurno, a| a day cpd.

divagar |diβa'xar| vi (desviarse) to digress.

diván |di'βan| nm divan.

divergencia |diβer'xenθja| nf divergence.

diversidad |diβersi'ðað| nf diversity, variety.

diversificar |diβersifi'kar| vt to diversify.

diversión |diβer'sjon| nf (gen) entertainment; (actividad) hobby, pastime.

diverso, a |di'βerso, a| a diverse; ~s nmpl sundries; ~s **libros** several books.

divertido, a |diβer'tiðo, a| a (chiste) amusing; (fiesta etc) enjoyable.

divertir |diβer'tir| vt (entretener, recrear) to amuse; ~se vr (pasarlo bien) to have a good time; (distraerse) to amuse o.s.

dividir |diβi'ðir| vt (gen) to divide; (separar) to separate; (distribuir) to distribute, share out.

divierta etc vb ver **divertir**.

divino, a |di'βino, a| a divine.

divirtiendo etc vb ver **divertir**.

divisa |di'βisa| nf (emblema, moneda) emblem, badge; ~**s** nfpl foreign exchange sg.

divisar |diβi'sar| vt to make out, distinguish.

división |diβi'sjon| nf (gen) division; (de partido) split; (de país) partition.

divorciar |diβor'θjar| vt to divorce; ~se vr to get divorced; **divorcio** nm divorce.

divulgar |diβul'xar| vt (desparramar) to spread; (hacer circular) to divulge, circulate; ~se vr to leak out.

DNI nm abr (Esp: = Documento Nacional de Identidad) national identity card.

dobladillo |doβla'ðiʎo| nm (de vestido) hem; (de pantalón: vuelta) turn-up (Brit), cuff (US).

doblar |do'βlar| vt to double; (papel) to fold; (caño) to bend; (la esquina) to turn, go round; (film) to dub // vi to turn; (campana) to toll; ~se vr (plegarse) to fold (up), crease; (encorvarse) to bend.

doble |'doβle| a double; (de dos aspectos) dual; (fig) two-faced // nm double; ~**s** nmpl (DEPORTE) doubles sg // nm/f (TEATRO) double, stand-in; **con sentido** ~ with a double meaning.

doblegar |doβle'xar| vt to fold, crease; ~se vr to yield.

doce |'doθe| num twelve; ~**na** nf dozen.

docente |do'θente| a: **centro/personal** ~ teaching establishment/staff.

dócil |'doθil| a (pasivo) docile; (obediente) obedient.

doctor, a |dok'tor, a| nm/f doctor.

doctrina |dok'trina| nf doctrine, teaching.

documentación |dokumenta'θjon| nf documentation, papers pl.

documento |doku'mento| nm (certificado) document; **documental** a, nm documentary.

dólar |'dolar| nm dollar.

doler |do'ler| vt, vi to hurt; (fig) to grieve; ~se vr (de su situación) to grieve, feel sorry; (de las desgracias ajenas) to sympathize; **me duele el brazo** my arm hurts.

dolor |do'lor| nm pain; (fig) grief, sorrow; ~ **de cabeza** headache; ~ **de estómago** stomachache.

domar |do'mar|, **domesticar** |domesti'kar| vt to tame.

domiciliación |domiθilia'θjon| nf: ~ **de pagos** (COM) standing order.

domicilio |domi'θiljo| nm home; ~ **particular** private residence; ~ **social** (COM) head office; **sin** ~ **fijo** of no fixed abode.

dominante |domi'nante| a dominant; (persona) domineering.

dominar |domi'nar| vt (gen) to dominate; (idiomas) to be fluent in // vi to dominate, prevail; ~se vr to control o.s.

domingo |do'mingo| *nm* Sunday.

dominio |do'minjo| *nm* (*tierras*) domain; (*autoridad*) power, authority; (*de las pasiones*) grip, hold; (*de varios idiomas*) command.

don |don| *nm* (*talento*) gift; ~ Juan Gómez Mr Juan Gomez o Juan Gomez Esq.

donaire |do'naire| *nm* charm.

donar |do'nar| *vt* to donate.

doncella |don'θeʎa| *nf* (*criada*) maid.

donde |'donde| *ad* where // *prep*: el coche está allí ~ el farol the car is over there by the lamppost o where the lamppost is; por ~ through which; en ~ where, in which.

dónde |'donde| *ad interr* where?; ¿a ~ vas? where are you going (to)?; ¿de ~ vienes? where have you come from?; ¿por ~? where?, whereabouts?

dondequiera |donde'kjera| *ad* anywhere; por ~ everywhere, all over the place // *conj*: ~ que wherever.

doña |'doɲa| *nf*: ~ Alicia Alicia; ~ Victoria Benito Mrs Victoria Benito.

dorado, a |do'raðo. a| *a* (*color*) golden; (*TEC*) gilt.

dormir |dor'mir| *vt*: ~ la siesta por la tarde to have an afternoon nap // *vi* to sleep; ~se *vr* to fall asleep.

dormitar |dormi'tar| *vi* to doze.

dormitorio |dormi'torjo| *nm* bedroom; ~ común dormitory.

dorsal |dor'sal| *nm* (*DEPORTE*) number.

dos |dos| *num* two.

dosis |'dosis| *nf inv* dose, dosage.

dotado, a |do'taðo. a| *a* gifted; ~ de endowed with.

dotar |do'tar| *vt* to endow; **dote** *nf* dowry; **dotes** *nfpl* (*talentos*) gifts.

doy *vb ver* **dar**.

drama |'drama| *nm* drama.

dramaturgo |drama'turɣo| *nm* dramatist, playwright.

droga |'droɣa| *nf* drug.

drogadicto, a |droɣa'ðikto. a| *nm/f* drug addict.

droguería |droɣe'ria| *nf* hardware shop (*Brit*) o store (*US*).

ducha |'dutʃa| *nf* (*baño*) shower; (*MED*) douche; **ducharse** *vr* to take a shower.

duda |'duða| *nf* doubt; **dudar** *vt*, *vi* to doubt; **dudoso, a** |du'ðoso. a| *a* (*incierto*) hesitant; (*sospechoso*) doubtful.

duela *etc vb ver* **doler**.

duelo *vb ver* **doler** // |'dwelo| *nm* (*combate*) duel; (*luto*) mourning.

duende |'dwende| *nm* imp, goblin.

dueño, a |'dweɲo. a| *nm/f* (*propietario*) owner; (*de pensión, taberna*) landlord/ lady; (*empresario*) employer.

duermo *etc vb ver* **dormir**.

dulce |'dulθe| *a* sweet // *ad* gently, softly // *nm* sweet; ~**ría** *nf* (*AM*) confectioner's.

dulzura |dul'θura| *nf* sweetness; (*ternura*) gentleness.

duplicar |dupli'kar| *vt* (*hacer el doble de*) to duplicate; ~se *vr* to double.

duque |'duke| *nm* duke; ~**sa** *nf* duchess.

duración |dura'θjon| *nf* duration.

duradero, a |dura'ðero. a| *a* (*tela*) hard-wearing; (*fe, paz*) lasting.

durante |du'rante| *prep* during.

durar |du'rar| *vi* (*permanecer*) to last; (*recuerdo*) to remain.

durazno |du'raθno| *nm* (*AM*: *fruta*) peach; (: *árbol*) peach tree.

durex |'dureks| *nm* (*AM*: *tira adhesiva*) Sellotape ® (*Brit*), Scotch tape ® (*US*).

dureza |du'reθa| *nf* (*calidad*) hardness.

durmiente |dur'mjente| *nm/f* sleeper.

duro, a |'duro. a| *a* hard; (*carácter*) tough // *ad* hard // *nm* (*moneda*) five peseta coin o piece.

E

e |e| *conj* and.

E *abr* (= *este*) E.

ebanista |eβa'nista| *nm/f* cabinetmaker.

ébano |'eβano| *nm* ebony.

ebrio, a |'eβrjo. a| *a* drunk.

ebullición |eβuʎi'θjon| *nf* boiling.

eccema |ek'θema| *nf* (*MED*) eczema.

eclesiástico, a |ekle'sjastiko. a| *a* ecclesiastical.

eclipse |e'klipse| *nm* eclipse.

eco |'eko| *nm* echo; tener ~ to catch on.

ecología |ekolo'xia| *nf* ecology.

economato |ekono'mato| *nm* cooperative store.

economía |ekono'mia| *nf* (*sistema*) economy; (*cualidad*) thrift.

económico, a |ekono'miko. a| *a* (*barato*) cheap, economical; (*persona*) thrifty; (*COM*: *año etc*) financial; (: *situación*) economic.

economista |ekono'mista| *nm/f* economist.

ecuador |ekwa'ðor| *nm* equator; (el) E~ Ecuador.

ecuánime |e'kwanime| *a* (*carácter*) level-headed; (*estado*) calm.

ecuatoriano, a |ekwato'rjano. a| *a*, *nm/f* Ecuadorian.

ecuestre |e'kwestre| *a* equestrian.

echar |e'tʃar| *vt* to throw; (*agua, vino*) to pour (out); (*empleado*: *despedir*) to fire, sack; (*hojas*) to sprout; (*cartas*) to post; (*humo*) to emit, give out // *vi*: ~ a correr/llorar to run off/burst into tears; ~se *vr* to lie down; ~ llave a to lock (up); ~ abajo (*gobierno*) to overthrow; (*edificio*) to demolish; ~ mano a to lay hands on; ~ una mano a uno (*ayudar*) to give sb a hand; ~ de menos to miss.

edad |e'ðað| *nf* age; ¿qué ~ tienes? how

old are you?; **tiene ocho años de** ~ he is eight (years old); **de ~ mediana/ avanzada** middle-aged/advanced in years; **la E~ Media** the Middle Ages.

edición |eði'θjon| *nf* (*acto*) publication; (*ejemplar*) edition.

edicto |e'ðikto| *nm* edict, proclamation.

edificio |eði'fiθjo| *nm* building; (*fig*) edifice, structure.

Edimburgo |eðim'burɣo| *nm* Edinburgh.

editar |eði'tar| *vt* (*publicar*) to publish; (*preparar textos*) to edit.

editor, a |eði'tor, a| *nm/f* (*que publica*) publisher; (*redactor*) editor // *a*; **casa ~a** publishing house, publisher; **~ial** *a* editorial // *nm* leading article, editorial; **casa ~ial** publishing house, publisher.

educación |eðuka'θjon| *nf* education; (*crianza*) upbringing; (*modales*) (good) manners *pl*.

educar |eðu'kar| *vt* to educate; (*criar*) to bring up; (*voz*) to train.

EE. UU. *nmpl abr* = **Estados Unidos.**

efectista |efek'tista| *a* sensationalist.

efectivamente |efektiβa'mente| *ad* (*como respuesta*) exactly, precisely; (*verdaderamente*) really; (*de hecho*) in fact.

efectivo, a |efek'tiβo, a| *a* effective; (*real*) actual, real // *nm*: **pagar en ~** to pay (in) cash; **hacer ~ un cheque** to cash a cheque.

efecto |e'fekto| *nm* effect, result; **~s** *nmpl* (~s *personales*) effects; (*bienes*) goods; (*COM*) assets; **en ~** in fact; (*respuesta*) exactly, indeed.

efectuar |efek'twar| *vt* to carry out; (*viaje*) to make.

eficacia |efi'kaθja| *nf* (*de persona*) efficiency; (*de medicamento etc*) effectiveness.

eficaz |efi'kaθ| *a* (*persona*) efficient; (*acción*) effective.

efusivo, a |efu'siβo, a| *a* effusive; **mis más efusivas gracias** my warmest thanks.

EGB *nf abr* (*Esp ESCOL*) = *Educación General Básica.*

egipcio, a |e'xipθjo, a| *a*, *nm/f* Egyptian.

Egipto |e'xipto| *nm* Egypt.

egoísmo |eɣo'ismo| *nm* egoism.

egoísta |eɣo'ista| *a* egoistical, selfish // *nm/f* egoist.

egregio, a |e'ɣrexjo, a| *a* eminent, distinguished.

Eire |'eire| *nm* Eire.

ej. *abr* (= *ejemplo*) eg.

eje |'exe| *nm* (*GEO, MAT*) axis; (*de rueda*) axle; (*de máquina*) shaft, spindle.

ejecución |exeku'θjon| *nf* execution; (*cumplimiento*) fulfilment; (*actuación*) performance; (*JUR*: *embargo de deudor*) attachment.

ejecutar |exeku'tar| *vt* to execute, carry out; (*matar*) to execute; (*cumplir*) to fulfil; (*MUS*) to perform, (*JUR*: *embargar*) to attach, distrain (on).

ejecutivo, a |exeku'tiβo, a| *a* executive; **el (poder)** ~ the executive (power).

ejemplar |exem'plar| *a* exemplary // *nm* example; (*ZOOL*) specimen; (*de libro*) copy; (*de periódico*) number, issue.

ejemplo |e'xemplo| *nm* example; **por ~** for example.

ejercer |exer'θer| *vt* to exercise; (*influencia*) to exert; (*un oficio*) to practise // *vi* (*practicar*) to practise (*de* as); (*tener oficio*) to hold office.

ejercicio |exer'θiθjo| *nm* exercise; (*período*) tenure; ~ **comercial** financial year.

ejército |e'xerθito| *nm* army; **entrar en el** ~ to join the army, join up.

ejote |e'xote| *nm* (*AM*) green bean.

el, la, los, las, lo |el, la, los, las, lo| ♦ *artículo definido* **1** the; **el libro/la mesa/ los estudiantes** the book/table/students **2** (*con n abstracto: no se traduce*): **el amor/la juventud** love/youth **3** (*posesión: se traduce a menudo por a posesivo*): **romperse el brazo** to break one's arm; **levantó la mano** he put his hand up; **se puso el sombrero** she put her hat on **4** (*valor descriptivo*): **tener la boca grande/los ojos azules** to have a big mouth/blue eyes **5** (*con días*) on; **me iré el viernes** I'll leave on Friday; **los domingos suelo ir a nadar** on Sundays I generally go swimming **6** (*lo + a*): **lo difícil/caro** what is difficult/expensive; (= *cuán*): **no se da cuenta de lo pesado que es** he doesn't realise how boring he is ♦ *pron demostrativo* **1**: **mi libro y el de usted** my book and yours; **las de Pepe son mejores** Pepe's are better; **no la(s) blanca(s) sino la(s) gris(es)** not the white one(s) but the grey one(s) **2**: **lo de**: **lo de ayer** what happened yesterday; **lo de las facturas** that business about the invoices ♦ *pron relativo*: **el que** *etc* **1** (*indefinido*): **el (los) que quiera(n) que se vaya(n)** anyone who wants to can leave; **llévese el que más le guste** take the one you like best **2** (*definido*): **el que compré ayer** the one I bought yesterday; **los que se van** those who leave **3**: **lo que**: **lo que pienso yo/más me gusta** what I think/like most ♦ *conj*: **el que**: **el que lo diga** the fact that he says so; **el que sea tan vago me molesta** his being so lazy bothers me ♦ *excl*: **¡el susto que me diste!** what a fright you gave me! ♦ *pron personal* **1** (*persona: m*) him; (:

f) her; (: *pl*) them; **lo/las** veo I can see him/them
2 (*animal, cosa: sg*) it; (: *pl*) them; **lo** (*o* **la**) veo I can see it; **los** (*o* **las**) veo I can see them
3: **lo** (*como sustituto de frase*): no lo sabía I didn't know; ya lo entiendo I understand now.

él [el] *pron* (*persona*) he; (*cosa*) it; (*después de prep: persona*) him; (: *cosa*) it.

elaborar [elaβo'rar] *vt* (*producto*) to make, manufacture; (*preparar*) to prepare; (*madera, metal etc*) to work; (*proyecto etc*) to work on *o* out.

elasticidad [elastiθi'ðað] *nf* elasticity.

elástico, a [e'lastiko, a] *a* elastic; (*flexible*) flexible // *nm* elastic; (*un ~*) elastic band.

elección [elek'θjon] *nf* election; (*selección*) choice, selection.

electorado [elekto'raðo] *nm* electorate, voters *pl*.

electricidad [elektriθi'ðað] *nf* electricity.

electricista [elektri'θista] *nm/f* electrician.

eléctrico, a [e'lektriko, a] *a* electric.

electrizar [elektri'θar] *vt* to electrify.

electro... [elektro] *pref* electro...; **~cución** *nf* electrocution; **~cutar** *vt* to electrocute; **electrodo** *nm* electrode; **~domésticos** *nmpl* (electrical) household appliances; **~imán** *nm* electromagnet; **~magnético, a** *a* electromagnetic.

electrónico, a [elek'troniko, a] *a* electronic // *nf* electronics *sg*.

electrotecnia [elektro'teknja] *nf* electrical engineering; **electrotécnico, a** *nm/f* electrical engineer.

electrotermo [elektro'termo] *nm* immersion heater.

elefante [ele'fante] *nm* elephant.

elegancia [ele'van̄θja] *nf* elegance, grace; (*estilo*) stylishness.

elegante [ele'vante] *a* elegant, graceful; (*estiloso*) stylish, fashionable.

elegía [ele'xia] *nf* elegy.

elegir [ele'xir] *vt* (*escoger*) to choose, select; (*optar*) to opt for; (*presidente*) to elect.

elemental [elemen'tal] *a* (*claro, obvio*) elementary; (*fundamental*) elemental, fundamental.

elemento [ele'mento] *nm* element; (*fig*) ingredient; **~s** *nmpl* elements, rudiments.

elevación [eleßa'θjon] *nf* elevation; (*acto*) raising, lifting; (*de precios*) rise; (*GEO etc*) height, altitude; (*de persona*) loftiness.

elevar [ele'ßar] *vt* to raise, lift (up); (*precio*) to put up; **~se** *vr* (*edificio*) to rise; (*precios*) to go up; (*transportarse, enajenarse*) to get carried away.

eligiendo *etc vb ver* **elegir.**

elija *etc vb ver* **elegir.**

eliminar [elimi'nar] *vt* to eliminate, remove.

eliminatoria [elimina'torja] *nf* heat, preliminary (round).

elite [e'lite] *nf* elite.

elocuencia [elo'kwenθja] *nf* eloquence.

elogiar [elo'xjar] *vt* to praise, eulogize; **elogio** *nm* praise.

elote [e'lote] *nm* (*AM*) corn on the cob.

eludir [elu'ðir] *vt* (*evitar*) to avoid, evade; (*escapar*) to escape, elude.

ella ['eʎa] *pron* (*persona*) she; (*cosa*) it; (*después de prep: persona*) her; (: *cosa*) it.

ellas ['eʎas] *pron* (*personas y cosas*) they; (*después de prep*) them.

ello ['eʎo] *pron* it.

ellos ['eʎos] *pron* they; (*después de prep*) them.

emanar [ema'nar] *vi*: **~ de** to emanate from, come from; (*derivar de*) to originate in.

emancipar [emanθi'par] *vt* to emancipate; **~se** *vr* to become emancipated, free o.s.

embadurnar [embaður'nar] *vt* to smear.

embajada [emba'xaða] *nf* embassy.

embajador, a [embaxa'ðor, a] *nm/f* ambassador/ambassadress.

embalar [emba'lar] *vt* (*envolver*) to parcel, wrap (up); (*envasar*) to package // *vi* to sprint.

embalsamar [embalsa'mar] *vt* to embalm.

embalse [em'balse] *nm* (*presa*) dam; (*lago*) reservoir.

embarazada [embara'θaða] *a* pregnant // *nf* pregnant woman.

embarazar [embara'θar] *vt* to obstruct, hamper; **~se** *vr* (*aturdirse*) to become embarrassed; (*confundirse*) to get into a mess.

embarazo [emba'raθo] *nm* (*de mujer*) pregnancy; (*impedimento*) obstacle, obstruction; (*timidez*) embarrassment.

embarcación [embarka'θjon] *nf* (*barco*) boat, craft; (*acto*) embarkation, boarding.

embarcadero [embarka'ðero] *nm* pier, landing stage.

embarcar [embar'kar] *vt* (*cargamento*) to ship, stow; (*persona*) to embark, put on board; **~se** *vr* to embark, go on board.

embargar [embar'xar] *vt* (*JUR*) to seize, impound.

embarque *etc vb ver* **embarcar** // [em'barke] *nm* shipment, loading.

embaucar [embau'kar] *vt* to trick, fool.

embeber [embe'ßer] *vt* (*absorber*) to absorb, soak up; (*empapar*) to saturate // *vi* to shrink; **~se** *vr*: **~se en la lectura** to be engrossed *o* absorbed in a book.

embellecer [embeʎe'θer] *vt* to embellish,

beautify.

embestida [embes'tiða] *nf* attack, onslaught; (*carga*) charge; **embestir** *vt* to attack, assault; to charge, attack // *vi* to attack.

emblema [em'blema] *nm* emblem.

embobado, a [embo'ßaðo, a] *a* (*atontado*) stunned, bewildered.

émbolo ['embolo] *nm* (*AUTO*) piston.

embolsar [embol'sar] *vt* to pocket, put in one's pocket.

emborrachar [emborra'tʃar] *vt* to make drunk, intoxicate; ~se *vr* to get drunk.

emboscada [embos'kaða] *nf* (*celada*) ambush.

embotar [embo'tar] *vt* to blunt, dull; ~se *vr* (*adormecerse*) to go numb.

embotellamiento [emboteʎa'mjento] *nm* (*AUTO*) traffic jam.

embotellar [embote'ʎar] *vt* to bottle; ~se *vr* (*circulación*) to get into a jam.

embrague [em'braɣe] *nm* (*tb: pedal de* ~) clutch.

embriagar [embrja'ɣar] *vt* (*emborrachar*) to make drunk; (*alegrar*) to delight; ~se *vr* (*emborracharse*) to get drunk.

embriaguez [embrja'ɣeθ] *nf* (*borrachera*) drunkenness.

embrión [em'brjon] *nm* embryo.

embrollar [embro'ʎar] *vt* (*el asunto*) to confuse, complicate; (*persona*) to involve, embroil; ~se *vr* (*confundirse*) to get into a muddle o mess.

embrollo [em'broʎo] *nm* (*enredo*) muddle, confusion; (*aprieto*) fix, jam.

embromar [embro'mar] *vt* (*burlarse de*) to tease, make fun of.

embrujado, a [embru'xado, a] *a* bewitched; **casa embrujada** haunted house.

embrutecer [embrute'θer] *vt* (*atontar*) to stupefy; ~se *vr* to be stupefied.

embudo [em'buðo] *nm* funnel.

embuste [em'buste] *nm* trick; (*mentira*) lie; (*hum*) fib; ~**ro, a** *a* lying, deceitful // *nm/f* (*tramposo*) cheat; (*mentiroso*) liar; (*hum*) fibber.

embutido [embu'tiðo] *nm* (*CULIN*) sausage; (*TEC*) inlay.

embutir [embu'tir] *vt* (*TEC*) to inlay; (*llenar*) to pack tight, cram.

emergencia [emer'xenθja] *nf* emergency; (*surgimiento*) emergence.

emerger [emer'ɣer] *vi* to emerge, appear.

emigración [emiɣra'θjon] *nf* emigration; (*de pájaros*) migration.

emigrar [emi'ɣrar] *vi* (*personas*) to emigrate; (*pájaros*) to migrate.

eminencia [emi'nenθja] *nf* eminence; **eminente** *a* eminent, distinguished; (*elevado*) high.

emisario [emi'sarjo] *nm* emissary.

emisión [emi'sjon] *nf* (*acto*) emission;

(*COM etc*) issue; (*RADIO, TV: acto*) broadcasting; (: *programa*) broadcast, programme (*Brit*), program (*US*).

emisora [emi'sora] *nf* radio o broadcasting station.

emitir [emi'tir] *vt* (*olor etc*) to emit, give off; (*moneda etc*) to issue; (*opinión*) to express; (*RADIO*) to broadcast.

emoción [emo'θjon] *nf* emotion; (*excitación*) excitement; (*sentimiento*) feeling.

emocionante [emoθjo'nante] *a* (*excitante*) exciting, thrilling.

emocionar [emoθjo'nar] *vt* (*excitar*) to excite, thrill; (*conmover*) to move, touch; (*impresionar*) to impress.

emotivo, a [emo'tißo, a] *a* emotional.

empacar [empa'kar] *vt* (*gen*) to pack; (*en caja*) to bale, crate.

empacho [em'patʃo] *nm* (*MED*) indigestion; (*fig*) embarrassment.

empadronarse [empaðro'narse] *vr* (*POL: como elector*) to register.

empalagoso, a [empala'ɣoso, a] *a* cloying; (*fig*) tiresome.

empalmar [empal'mar] *vt* to join, connect // *vi* (*dos caminos*) to meet, join; **empalme** *nm* joint, connection; junction; (*de trenes*) connection.

empanada [empa'naða] *nf* pie, pasty.

empantanarse [empanta'narse] *vr* to get swamped; (*fig*) to get bogged down.

empañarse [empa'ɲarse] *vr* (*nublarse*) to get misty, steam up.

empapar [empa'par] *vt* (*mojar*) to soak, saturate; (*absorber*) to soak up, absorb; ~se *vr*: ~se de to soak up.

empapelar [empape'lar] *vt* (*paredes*) to paper.

empaquetar [empake'tar] *vt* to pack, parcel up.

emparedado [empare'ðaðo] *nm* sandwich.

empastar [empas'tar] *vt* (*embadurnar*) to paste; (*diente*) to fill.

empaste [em'paste] *nm* (*de diente*) filling.

empatar [empa'tar] *vi* to draw, tie; **empate** *nm* draw, tie.

empecé, empecemos *vb ver* **empezar.**

empedernido, a [empeðer'niðo, a] *a* hard, heartless; (*fijado*) hardened, inveterate.

empedrado, a [empe'ðraðo, a] *a* paved // *nm* paving.

empedrar [empe'ðrar] *vt* to pave.

empeine [em'peine] *nm* (*de pie, zapato*) instep.

empeñado, a [empe'ɲaðo, a] *a* (*persona*) determined; (*objeto*) pawned.

empeñar [empe'ɲar] *vt* (*objeto*) to pawn, pledge; (*persona*) to compel; ~se *vr* (*obligarse*) to bind o.s., pledge o.s.; (*endeudarse*) to get into debt; ~se en to be set on, be determined to.

empeño [em'peɲo] nm (determinación, insistencia) determination, insistence; (cosa prendada) pledge; **casa de ~s** pawnshop.

empeorar [empeo'rar] vt to make worse, worsen // vi to get worse, deteriorate.

empequeñecer [empekeɲe'θer] vt to dwarf; (fig) to belittle.

emperador [empera'ðor] nm emperor.

emperatriz [empera'triθ] nf empress.

empezar [empe'θar] vt, vi to begin, start.

empiece etc vb ver **empezar.**

empiezo etc vb ver **empezar.**

empinar [empi'nar] vt to raise; **~se** vr (persona) to stand on tiptoe; (animal) to rear up; (camino) to climb steeply.

empírico, a [em'piriko, a] a empirical.

emplasto [em'plasto], **emplaste** [em'plaste] nm (MED) plaster.

emplazamiento [emplaθa'mjento] nm site, location; (JUR) summons sg.

emplazar [empla'θar] vt (ubicar) to site, place, locate; (JUR) to summons; (convocar) to summon.

empleado, a [emple'aðo, a] nm/f (gen) employee; (de banco etc) clerk.

emplear [emple'ar] vt (usar) to use, employ; (dar trabajo a) to employ; **~se** vr (conseguir trabajo) to be employed; (ocuparse) to occupy o.s.

empleo [em'pleo] nm (puesto) job; (puestos: colectivamente) employment; (uso) use, employment.

empobrecer [empoβre'θer] vt to impoverish; **~se** vr to become poor o impoverished.

empollar [empo'ʎar] vt, vi (fam) to swot (up); **empollón, ona** nm/f (fam) swot.

emporio [em'porjo] nm emporium, trading centre; (AM: gran almacén) department store.

empotrado, a [empo'traðo, a] a (armario etc) built-in.

emprender [empren'der] vt (empezar) to begin, embark on; (acometer) to tackle, take on.

empresa [em'presa] nf (de espíritu etc) enterprise; (COM) company, firm; **~rio, a** nm/f (COM) manager.

empréstito [em'prestito] nm (public) loan.

empujar [empu'xar] vt to push, shove; **empuje** nm thrust; (presión) pressure; (fig) vigour, drive.

empujón [empu'xon] nm push, shove.

empuñar [empu'ɲar] vt (asir) to grasp, take (firm) hold of.

emular [emu'lar] vt to emulate; (rivalizar) to rival.

en [en] prep **1** (posición) in; (: sobre) on; **está ~ el cajón** it's in the drawer; **~ Argentina/La Paz** in Argentina/La Paz; **~ la oficina/el colegio** at the office/school; **está ~ el suelo/quinto piso** it's on the floor/the fifth floor

2 (dirección) into; **entró ~ el aula** she went into the classroom; **meter algo ~ el bolso** to put sth into one's bag

3 (tiempo) in; on; **~ 1605/3 semanas/invierno** in 1605/3 weeks/winter; **~ (el mes de) enero** in (the month of) January; **~ aquella ocasión/aquella época** on that occasion/at that time

4 (precio) for; **lo vendió ~ 20 dólares** he sold it for 20 dollars

5 (diferencia) by; **reducir/aumentar ~ una tercera parte/un 20 por ciento** to reduce/increase by a third/20 per cent

6 (manera): **~ avión/autobús** by plane/bus; **escrito ~ inglés** written in English

7 (después de vb que indica gastar etc) on; **han cobrado demasiado ~ dietas** they've charged too much to expenses; **se le va la mitad del sueldo ~ comida** he spends half his salary on food

8 (tema, ocupación): **experto ~ la materia** expert on the subject; **trabaja ~ la construcción** he works in the building industry

9 (a + ~ + infinitivo): **lento ~ reaccionar** slow to react.

enajenación [enaxena'θjon] nf, **enajenamiento** [enaxena'mjento] nm alienation; (fig: distracción) absent-mindedness; (: embelesamiento) rapture, trance.

enajenar [enaxe'nar] vt to alienate; (fig) to carry away.

enamorado, a [enamo'raðo, a] a in love // nm/f lover.

enamorar [enamo'rar] vt to win the love of; **~se** vr: **~se de alguien** to fall in love with sb.

enano, a [e'nano, a] a tiny // nm/f dwarf.

enardecer [enarðe'θer] vt (pasiones) to fire, inflame; (persona) to fill with enthusiasm; **~se** vr: **~ por** to get excited about; (entusiasmarse) to get enthusiastic about.

encabezamiento [enkaβeθa'mjento] nm (de carta) heading; (de periódico) head-line; (preámbulo) foreword, preface.

encabezar [enkaβe'θar] vt (movimiento, revolución) to lead, head; (lista) to head, be at the top of; (carta) to put a heading to; (libro) to entitle.

encadenar [enkaðe'nar] vt to chain (together); (poner grilletes a) to shackle.

encajar [enka'xar] vt (ajustar): **~ (en)** to fit (into); (fam: golpe) to give, deal; (entrometer) to insert // vi to fit (well); (fig: corresponder a) to match; **~se** vr: **~se en un sillón** to squeeze into a chair.

encaje [en'kaxe] nm (labor) lace.

encalar [enka'lar] vt (pared) to whitewash.

encallar [enka'ʎar] vi (NAUT) to run aground.

encaminar [enkami'nar] vt to direct,

send; ~se vr: ~se a to set out for.
encandilar [enkandi'lar] vt to dazzle.
encantado, a [enkan'taðo, a] a (hechizado) bewitched; (muy contento) delighted; ¡~! how do you do!, pleased to meet you.
encantador, a [enkanta'ðor, a] a charming, lovely // nm/f magician, enchanter/ enchantress.
encantar [enkan'tar] vt to charm, delight; (hechizar) to bewitch, cast a spell on; **encanto** nm (magia) spell, charm; (fig) charm, delight.
encarcelar [enkarθe'lar] vt to imprison, jail.
encarecer [enkare'θer] vt to put up the price of // vi, ~se vr to get dearer.
encarecimiento [enkareθi'mjento] nm price increase.
encargado, a [enkar'γaðo, a] a in charge // nm/f agent, representative; (responsable) person in charge.
encargar [enkar'γar] vt to entrust; (recomendar) to urge, recommend; ~se vr: ~se de to look after, take charge of.
encargo [en'karγo] nm (pedido) assignment, job; (responsabilidad) responsibility; (recomendación) recommendation; (COM) order.
encariñarse [enkari'narse] vr: ~ con to grow fond of, get attached to.
encarnación [enkarna'θjon] nf incarnation, embodiment.
encarnizado, a [enkarni'θaðo, a] a (lucha) bloody, fierce.
encarrilar [enkarri'lar] vt (tren) to put back on the rails; (fig) to correct, put on the right track.
encasillar [enkasi'λar] vt (tb: fig) to pigeonhole; (actor) to typecast.
encauzar [enkau'θar] vt to channel.
encendedor [enθende'ðor] nm lighter.
encender [enθen'der] vt (con fuego) to light; (incendiar) to set fire to; (luz, radio) to put on, switch on; (avivar: pasiones) to inflame; ~se vr to catch fire; (excitarse) to get excited; (de cólera) to flare up; (el rostro) to blush.
encendido [enθen'diðo] nm (AUTO) ignition.
encerado [enθe'raðo] nm (ESCOL) blackboard.
encerar [enθe'rar] vt (suelo) to wax, polish.
encerrar [enθe'rrar] vt (confinar) to shut in, shut up; (comprender, incluir) to include, contain.
encía [en'θia] nf gum.
encienda etc vb ver **encender**.
encierro etc vb ver **encerrar** // [en'θjerro] nm shutting in, shutting up; (calabozo) prison.
encima [en'θima] ad (sobre) above, over; (además) besides; ~ de (en) on, on top of; (sobre) above, over; (además

de) besides, on top of; por ~ de over; ¿llevas dinero ~? have you (got) any money on you?; se me vino ~ it got on top of me.
encinta [en'θinta] a pregnant.
enclenque [en'klenke] a weak, sickly.
encoger [enko'xer] vt to shrink, contract; (fig: asustar) to scare; ~se vr to shrink, contract; (fig) to cringe; ~se de hombros to shrug one's shoulders.
encolar [enko'lar] vt (engomar) to glue, paste; (pegar) to stick down.
encolerizar [enkoleri'θar] vt to anger, provoke; ~se vr to get angry.
encomendar [enkomen'dar] vt to entrust, commend; ~se vr: ~se a to put one's trust in.
encomiar [enko'mjar] vt to praise, pay tribute to.
encomienda etc vb ver **encomendar** // [enko'mjenda] nf (encargo) charge, commission; (elogio) tribute; ~ postal (AM) parcel post.
encono [en'kono] nm (rencor) rancour, spite.
encontrado, a [enkon'traðo, a] a (contrario) contrary, conflicting; (hostil) hostile.
encontrar [enkon'trar] vt (hallar) to find; (inesperadamente) to meet, run into; ~se vr to meet (each other); (situarse) to be (situated); (entrar en conflicto) to crash, collide; ~se con to meet; ~se bien (de salud) to feel well.
encorvar [enkor'ßar] vt to curve; (inclinar) to bend (down); ~se vr to bend down, bend over.
encrespar [enkres'par] vt (cabellos) to curl; (fig) to anger, irritate; ~se vr (el mar) to get rough; (fig) to get cross, get irritated.
encrucijada [enkruθi'xaða] nf crossroads sg; (empalme) junction.
encuadernación [enkwaðerna'θjon] nf binding.
encuadernador, a [enkwaðerna'ðor, a] nm/f bookbinder.
encuadrar [enkwa'ðrar] vt (retrato) to frame; (ajustar) to fit, insert; (encerrar) to contain.
encubrir [enku'ßrir] vt (ocultar) to hide, conceal; (criminal) to harbour, shelter.
encuentro etc vb ver **encontrar** // [en'kwentro] nm (de personas) meeting; (AUTO etc) collision, crash; (DEPORTE) match, game; (MIL) encounter.
encuesta [en'kwesta] nf inquiry, investigation; (sondeo) (public) opinion poll; ~ judicial post mortem.
encumbrado, a [enkum'braðo, a] a eminent, distinguished.
encumbrar [enkum'brar] vt (persona) to exalt; ~se vr (fig) to become conceited.
encharcado, a [entʃar'kaðo, a] a (terreno) flooded.

enchufar [entʃu'far] *vt* (*ELEC*) to plug in; (*TEC*) to connect, fit together; **enchufe** *nm* (*ELEC*: *clavija*) plug; (: *toma*) socket; (*de dos tubos*) joint, connection; (*fam*: *influencia*) contact, connection; (: *puesto*) cushy job.

endeble [en'deβle] *a* (*argumento*, *excusa*, *persona*) weak.

endemoniado, a [endemo'njaðo, a] *a* possessed (of the devil); (*travieso*) devilish.

enderezar [endere'θar] *vt* (*poner derecho*) to straighten (out); (: *verticalmente*) to set upright; (*fig*) to straighten *o* sort out; (*dirigir*) to direct; ~se *vr* to straighten up.

endeudarse [endeu'ðarse] *vr* to get into debt.

endiablado, a [endja'βlaðo, a] *a* devilish, diabolical; (*hum*) mischievous.

endilgar [endil'var] *vt* (*fam*): ~le algo a uno to lumber sb with sth; ~le un sermón a uno to lecture sb.

endomingarse [endomiŋ'garse] *vr* to dress up, put on one's best clothes.

endosar [endo'sar] *vt* (*cheque etc*) to endorse.

endulzar [endul'θar] *vt* to sweeten; (*suavizar*) to soften.

endurecer [endure'θer] *vt* to harden; ~se *vr* to harden, grow hard.

endurecido, a [endure'θiðo, a] *a* (*duro*) hard; (*fig*) hardy, tough; **estar ~ a algo** to be hardened *o* used to sth.

enemigo, a [ene'miɣo, a] *a* enemy, hostile // *nm/f* enemy.

enemistad [enemis'tað] *nf* enmity.

enemistar [enemis'tar] *vt* to make enemies of, cause a rift between; ~se *vr* to become enemies; (*amigos*) to fall out.

energía [ener'xia] *nf* (*vigor*) energy, drive; (*empuje*) push; (*TEC, ELEC*) energy, power.

enérgico, a [e'nerxiko, a] *a* (*gen*) energetic; (*voz, modales*) forceful.

energúmeno, a [ener'vumeno, a] *nm/f* (*fig fam*) madman/woman.

enero [e'nero] *nm* January.

enfadado, a [enfa'ðaðo, a] *a* angry, annoyed.

enfadar [enfa'ðar] *vt* to anger, annoy; ~se *vr* to get angry *o* annoyed.

enfado [en'faðo] *nm* (*enojo*) anger, annoyance; (*disgusto*) trouble, bother.

énfasis ['enfasis] *nm* emphasis, stress.

enfático, a [en'fatiko, a] *a* emphatic.

enfermar [enfer'mar] *vt* to make ill // *vi* to fall ill, be taken ill.

enfermedad [enferme'ðað] *nf* illness; ~ venérea venereal disease.

enfermera [enfer'mera] *nf* nurse.

enfermería [enferme'ria] *nf* infirmary; (*de colegio etc*) sick bay.

enfermero [enfer'mero] *nm* male nurse.

enfermizo, a [enfer'miθo, a] *a* (*persona*) sickly, unhealthy; (*fig*) unhealthy.

enfermo, a [en'fermo, a] *a* ill, sick // *nm/f* invalid, sick person; (*en hospital*) patient.

enflaquecer [enflake'θer] *vt* (*adelgazar*) to make thin; (*debilitar*) to weaken.

enfocar [enfo'kar] *vt* (*foto etc*) to focus; (*problema etc*) to consider, look at.

enfoque *etc vb ver* **enfocar** // [en'foke] *nm* focus.

enfrentar [enfren'tar] *vt* (*peligro*) to face (up to), confront; (*oponer, carear*) to put face to face; ~se *vr* (*dos personas*) to face *o* confront each other; (*DEPORTE*: *dos equipos*) to meet; ~se a *o* con to face up to, confront.

enfrente [en'frente] *ad* opposite; **la casa de ~** the house opposite, the house across the street; ~ de *prep* opposite, facing.

enfriamiento [enfria'mjento] *nm* chilling, refrigeration; (*MED*) cold, chill.

enfriar [enfri'ar] *vt* (*alimentos*) to cool, chill; (*algo caliente*) to cool down; (*habitación*) to air, freshen; ~se *vr* to cool down; (*MED*) to catch a chill; (*amistad*) to cool.

enfurecer [enfure'θer] *vt* to enrage, madden; ~se *vr* to become furious, fly into a rage; (*mar*) to get rough.

engalanar [engala'nar] *vt* (*adornar*) to adorn; (*ciudad*) to decorate; ~se *vr* to get dressed up.

enganchar [engan'tʃar] *vt* to hook; (*ropa*) to hang up; (*dos vagones*) to hitch up; (*TEC*) to couple, connect; (*MIL*) to recruit; (*fam*: *persona*) to rope in; ~se *vr* (*MIL*) to enlist, join up.

enganche [en'gantʃe] *nm* hook; (*TEC*) coupling, connection; (*acto*) hooking (up); (*MIL*) recruitment, enlistment; (*AM*: *depósito*) deposit.

engañar [enga'ɲar] *vt* to deceive; (*estafar*) to cheat, swindle; ~se *vr* (*equivocarse*) to be wrong; (*disimular la verdad*) to deceive *o* kid o.s.

engaño [en'gaɲo] *nm* deceit; (*estafa*) trick, swindle; (*error*) mistake, misunderstanding; (*ilusión*) delusion; ~so, a *a* (*tramposo*) crooked; (*mentiroso*) dishonest, deceitful; (*aspecto*) deceptive; (*consejo*) misleading.

engarzar [engar'θar] *vt* (*joya*) to set, mount; (*fig*) to link, connect.

engatusar [engatu'sar] *vt* (*fam*) to coax.

engendrar [enxen'drar] *vt* to breed; (*procrear*) to beget; (*fig*) to cause, produce; **engendro** *nm* (*BIO*) foetus; (*fig*) monstrosity; (*idea*) brainchild.

englobar [englo'βar] *vt* (*incluir*) to include, comprise.

engomar [engo'mar] *vt* to glue, stick.

engordar [engor'ðar] *vt* to fatten // *vi* to get fat, put on weight.

engorroso, a [engo'rroso, a] *a* bothersome, trying.

engranaje [engra'naxe] *nm* (*AUTO*) gear.

engrandecer [engrande'θer] *vt* to enlarge, magnify; (*alabar*) to praise, speak highly of; (*exagerar*) to exaggerate.

engrasar [engra'sar] *vt* (*TEC: poner grasa*) to grease; (: *lubricar*) to lubricate, oil; (*manchar*) to make greasy.

engreído, a [engre'iðo, a] *a* vain, conceited.

engrosar [engro'sar] *vt* (*ensanchar*) to enlarge; (*aumentar*) to increase; (*hinchar*) to swell.

enhebrar [ene'βrar] *vt* to thread.

enhorabuena [enora'βwena] *nf* congratulations *pl* // *ad* well and good.

enigma [e'niɣma] *nm* enigma; (*problema*) puzzle; (*misterio*) mystery.

enjabonar [enxaβo'nar] *vt* to soap; (*fam: adular*) to soft-soap; (: *regañar*) to tick off.

enjambre [en'xamβre] *nm* swarm.

enjaular [enxau'lar] *vt* to (put in a) cage; (*fam*) to jail, lock up.

enjuagar [enxwa'ɣar] *vt* (*ropa*) to rinse (out).

enjuague *etc vb ver* **enjuagar** // [en'xwaɣe] *nm* (*MED*) mouthwash; (*de ropa*) rinse, rinsing.

enjugar [enxu'ɣar] *vt* to wipe (off); (*lágrimas*) to dry; (*déficit*) to wipe out.

enjuiciar [enxwi'θjar] *vt* (*JUR: procesar*) to prosecute, try; (*fig*) to judge.

enjuto, a [en'xuto, a] *a* dry, dried up; (*fig*) lean, skinny.

enlace [en'laθe] *nm* link, connection; (*relación*) relationship; (*tb:* ~ **matrimonial**) marriage; (*de carretera, trenes*) connection; ~ **sindical** shop steward.

enlazar [enla'θar] *vt* (*unir con lazos*) to bind together; (*atar*) to tie; (*conectar*) to link, connect; (*AM*) to lasso.

enlodar [enlo'ðar] *vt* to cover in mud; (*fig: manchar*) to stain; (: *rebajar*) to debase.

enloquecer [enloke'θer] *vt* to drive mad // *vi*, ~**se** *vr* to go mad.

enlutado, a [enlu'taðo, a] *a* (*persona*) in mourning.

enmarañar [enmara'ɲar] *vt* (*enredar*) to tangle (up), entangle; (*complicar*) to complicate; (*confundir*) to confuse; ~**se** *vr* (*enredarse*) to become entangled; (*confundirse*) to get confused.

enmarcar [enmar'kar] *vt* (*cuadro*) to frame.

enmascarar [enmaska'rar] *vt* to mask; ~**se** *vr* to put on a mask.

enmendar [enmen'dar] *vt* to emend, correct; (*constitución etc*) to amend; (*comportamiento*) to reform; ~**se** *vr* to reform, mend one's ways; **enmienda** *nf* correction; amendment; reform.

enmohecerse [enmoe'θerse] *vr* (*metal*) to rust, go rusty; (*muro, plantas*) to get mouldy.

enmudecer [enmuðe'θer] *vi*, **enmudecerse** *vr* (*perder el habla*) to fall silent; (*guardar silencio*) to remain silent.

ennegrecer [enneɣre'θer] *vt* (*poner negro*) to blacken; (*oscurecer*) to darken; ~**se** *vr* to turn black; (*oscurecerse*) to get dark, darken.

ennoblecer [ennoβle'θer] *vt* to ennoble.

enojadizo, a [enoxa'ðiθo, a] *a* irritable, short-tempered.

enojar [eno'xar] *vt* (*encolerizar*) to anger; (*disgustar*) to annoy, upset; ~**se** *vr* to get angry; to get annoyed.

enojo [e'noxo] *nm* (*cólera*) anger; (*irritación*) annoyance; ~**so, a** *a* annoying.

enorgullecerse [enorɣuʎe'θerse] *vr* to be proud; ~ **de** to pride o.s. on, be proud of.

enorme [e'norme] *a* enormous, huge; (*fig*) monstrous; **enormidad** *nf* hugeness, immensity.

enraizar [enrai'θar] *vi* to take root.

enredadera [enreða'ðera] *nf* (*BOT*) creeper, climbing plant.

enredar [enre'ðar] *vt* (*cables, hilos etc*) to tangle (up), entangle; (*situación*) to complicate, confuse; (*meter cizaña*) to sow discord among *o* between; (*implicar*) to embroil, implicate; ~**se** *vr* to get entangled, get tangled (up); (*situación*) to get complicated; (*persona*) to get embroiled; (*AM: fam*) to meddle.

enredo [en'reðo] *nm* (*maraña*) tangle; (*confusión*) mix-up, confusion; (*intriga*) intrigue.

enrevesado, a [enreβe'saðo, a] *a* (*asunto*) complicated, involved.

enriquecer [enrike'θer] *vt* to make rich, enrich; ~**se** *vr* to get rich.

enrojecer [enroxe'θer] *vt* to redden // *vi*, ~**se** *vr* (*persona*) to blush.

enrolar [enro'lar] *vt* (*MIL*) to enlist; (*reclutar*) to recruit; ~**se** *vr* (*MIL*) to join up; (*afiliarse*) to enrol.

enrollar [enro'ʎar] *vt* to roll (up), wind (up).

enroscar [enros'kar] *vt* (*torcer, doblar*) to coil (round), wind; (*tornillo, rosca*) to screw in; ~**se** *vr* to coil, wind.

ensalada [ensa'laða] *nf* salad; **ensaladilla (rusa)** *nf* Russian salad.

ensalzar [ensal'θar] *vt* (*alabar*) to praise, extol; (*exaltar*) to exalt.

ensambladura [ensambla'ðura] *nf*, **ensamblaje** [ensam'blaxe] *nm* assembly; (*TEC*) joint.

ensamblar [ensam'blar] *vt* to assemble.

ensanchar [ensan'tʃar] *vt* (*hacer más ancho*) to widen; (*agrandar*) to enlarge, expand; (*COSTURA*) to let out; ~**se** *vr* to get wider, expand; (*pey*) to give o.s.

airs; **ensanche** nm (de calle) widening; (de negocio) expansion.

ensangrentar |ɛnsangren'tar| vt to stain with blood.

ensañar |ɛnsa'ɲar| vt to enrage; ~se vr: ~se con to treat brutally.

ensartar |ɛnsar'tar| vt (cuentas, perlas etc) to string (together).

ensayar |ɛnsa'jar| vt to test, try (out); (TEATRO) to rehearse.

ensayista |ɛnsa'jista| nm/f essayist.

ensayo |ɛn'sajo| nm test, trial; (QUIMICA) experiment; (TEATRO) rehearsal; (DEPORTE) try; (ESCOL, LITERATURA) essay.

ensenada |ɛnse'naða| nf inlet, cove.

enseñanza |ɛnse'naɲθa| nf (educación) education; (acción) teaching; (doctrina) teaching, doctrine.

enseñar |ɛnse'ɲar| vt (educar) to teach; (instruir) to teach, instruct; (mostrar, señalar) to show.

enseres |ɛn'seres| nmpl belongings.

ensillar |ɛnsi'ʎar| vt to saddle (up).

ensimismarse |ɛnsimis'marse| vr (abstraerse) to become lost in thought; (estar absorto) to be lost in thought; (AM) to become conceited.

ensordecer |ɛnsorðe'θer| vt to deafen // vi to go deaf.

ensortijado, a |ɛnsorti'xaðo. a| (pelo) curly.

ensuciar |ɛnsu'θjar| vt (manchar) to dirty, soil; (fig) to defile; ~se vr (mancharse) to get dirty; (fig) to dirty o.s., wet o.s.

ensueño |ɛn'sweɲo| nm (sueño) dream, fantasy; (ilusión) illusion; (soñando despierto) daydream.

entablado |ɛnta'Blaðo| nm (piso) floorboards pl; (armazón) boarding.

entablar |ɛnta'Blar| vt (recubrir) to board (up); (AJEDREZ, DAMAS) to set up; (conversación) to strike up; (JUR) to file // vi to draw.

entablillar |ɛntaBli'ʎar| vt (MED) to (put in a) splint.

entallar |ɛnta'ʎar| vt (traje) to tailor // vi: el traje entalla bien the suit fits well.

ente |'ɛnte| nm (organización) body, organization; (fam: persona) odd character.

entender |ɛnten'der| vt (comprender) to understand; (darse cuenta) to realize; (querer decir) to mean // vi to understand; (creer) to think, believe; ~ de to know all about; ~ algo de to know a little about; ~ en to deal with, have to do with; ~se vr (comprenderse) to be understood; (2 personas) to get on together; (ponerse de acuerdo) to agree, reach an agreement; ~se mal (2 personas) to get on badly.

entendido, a |ɛnten'diðo. a| a (comprendido) understood; (hábil)

skilled; (inteligente) knowledgeable // nm/f (experto) expert // excl agreed!;

entendimiento nm (comprensión) understanding; (inteligencia) mind, intellect; (juicio) judgement.

enterado, a |ɛnte'raðo. a| a well-informed; estar ~ de to know about, be aware of.

enteramente |ɛntera'mente| ad entirely, completely.

enterar |ɛnte'rar| vt (informar) to inform, tell; ~se vr to find out, get to know.

entereza |ɛnte'reθa| nf (totalidad) entirety; (fig: carácter) strength of mind; (: honradez) integrity.

enternecer |ɛnterne'θer| vt (ablandar) to soften; (apiadar) to touch, move; ~se vr to be touched, be moved.

entero, a |ɛn'tero. a| a (total) whole, entire; (fig: recto) honest; (: firme) firm, resolute // nm (COM: punto) point; (AM: pago) payment.

enterrador |ɛnterra'ðor| nm gravedigger.

enterrar |ɛnte'rrar| vt to bury.

entibiar |ɛnti'Bjar| vt (enfriar) to cool; (calentar) to warm; ~se vr (fig) to cool.

entidad |ɛnti'ðað| nf (empresa) firm, company; (organismo) body; (sociedad) society; (FILOSOFIA) entity.

entiendo etc vb ver **entender**.

entierro |ɛn'tjerro| nm (acción) burial; (funeral) funeral.

entomología |ɛntomolo'xia| nf entomology.

entonación |ɛntona'θjon| nf (LING) intonation; (fig) conceit.

entonar |ɛnto'nar| vt (canción) to intone; (colores) to tone; (MED) to tone up // vi to be in tune; ~se vr (engreírse) to give o.s. airs.

entonces |ɛn'tonθes| ad then, at that time; desde ~ since then; en aquel ~ at that time; (pues) ~ and so.

entornar |ɛntor'nar| vt (puerta, ventana) to half close, leave ajar; (los ojos) to screw up.

entorpecer |ɛntorpe'θer| vt (entendimiento) to dull; (impedir) to obstruct, hinder; (: tránsito) to slow down, delay.

entrada |ɛn'traða| nf (acción) entry, access; (sitio) entrance, way in; (INFORM) input; (COM) receipts pl, takings pl; (CULIN) entrée; (DEPORTE) innings sg; (TEATRO) house, audience; (para el cine etc) ticket; (COM): ~s y salidas income and expenditure; (TEC): ~ de aire air intake o inlet; de ~ from the outset.

entrado, a |ɛn'traðo. a| a: ~ en años elderly; una vez ~ el verano in the summer(time), when summer comes.

entrante |ɛn'trante| a next, coming; mes/año ~ next month/year.

entraña [en'traɲa] *nf* (*fig: centro*) heart, core; (*raíz*) root; **~o** *nfpl* (*ANAT*) entrails; (*fig*) heart *sg*; **entrañable** *a* close, intimate.

entrar [en'trar] *vt* (*introducir*) to bring in; (*INFORM*) to input // *vi* (*meterse*) to go in, come in, enter; (*comenzar*): ~ diciendo to begin by saying; **no me entra** I can't get the hang of it.

entre ['entre] *prep* (*dos*) between; (*más de dos*) among(st).

entreabrir [entrea'βrir] *vt* to half-open, open halfway.

entrecejo [entre'θexo] *nm*; **fruncir el ~** to frown.

entrecortado, a [entrekor'taðo, a] *a* (*respiración*) difficult; (*habla*) faltering.

entredicho [entre'ðitʃo] *nm* (*JUR*) injunction; **poner en ~** to cast doubt on; **estar en ~** to be banned.

entrega [en'treɣa] *nf* (*de mercancías*) delivery; (*de novela etc*) instalment.

entregar [entre'ɣar] *vt* (*dar*) to hand (over), deliver; **~se** *vr* (*rendirse*) to surrender, give in, submit; (*dedicarse*) to devote o.s.

entrelazar [entrela'θar] *vt* to entwine.

entremeses [entre'meses] *nmpl* hors d'œuvres.

entremeter [entreme'ter] *vt* to insert, put in; **~se** *vr* to meddle, interfere; **entremetido, a** *a* meddling, interfering.

entremezclar [entremeθ'klar] *vt*, **entremezclarse** *vr* to intermingle.

entrenador, a [entrena'ðor, a] *nm/f* trainer, coach.

entrenarse [entre'narse] *vr* to train.

entrepierna [entre'pjerna] *nf* crotch.

entresacar [entresa'kar] *vt* to pick out, select.

entresuelo [entre'swelo] *nm* mezzanine, entresol.

entretanto [entre'tanto] *ad* meanwhile, meantime.

entretejer [entrete'xer] *vt* to interweave.

entretener [entrete'ner] *vt* (*divertir*) to entertain, amuse; (*detener*) to hold up, delay; (*mantener*) to maintain; **~se** *vr* (*divertirse*) to amuse o.s.; (*retrasarse*) to delay, linger; **entretenido, a** *a* entertaining, amusing; **entretenimiento** *nm* entertainment, amusement; (*mantenimiento*) upkeep, maintenance.

entrever [entre'βer] *vt* to glimpse, catch a glimpse of.

entrevista [entre'βista] *nf* interview; **entrevistar** *vt* to interview; **entrevistarse** *vr* to have an interview.

entristecer [entriste'θer] *vt* to sadden, grieve; **~se** *vr* to grow sad.

entrometer [entrome'ter] *vt etc* = **entremeter** *etc*.

entroncar [entron'kar] *vi* to be connected *o* related.

entumecer [entume'θer] *vt* to numb,

benumb; **~se** *vr* (*por el frío*) to go *o* become numb; **entumecido, a** *a* numb, stiff.

enturbiar [entur'βjar] *vt* (*el agua*) to make cloudy; (*fig*) to confuse; **~se** *vr* (*oscurecerse*) to become cloudy; (*fig*) to get confused, become obscure.

entusiasmar [entusjas'mar] *vt* to excite, fill with enthusiasm; (*gustar mucho*) to delight; **~se** *vr*: **~se con** *o* **por** to get enthusiastic *o* excited about.

entusiasmo [entu'sjasmo] *nm* enthusiasm; (*excitación*) excitement.

entusiasta [entu'sjasta] *a* enthusiastic // *nm/f* enthusiast.

enumerar [enume'rar] *vt* to enumerate.

enunciación [enunθja'θjon] *nf*, **enunciado** [enun'θjaðo] *nm* enunciation; (*declaración*) declaration, statement.

envainar [enβai'nar] *vt* to sheathe.

envalentonar [enβalento'nar] *vt* to give courage to; **~se** *vr* (*pey: jactarse*) to boast, brag.

envanecer [enβane'θer] *vt* to make conceited; **~se** *vr* to grow conceited.

envasar [enβa'sar] *vt* (*empaquetar*) to pack, wrap; (*enfrascar*) to bottle; (*enlatar*) to can; (*embolsar*) to pocket.

envase [en'βase] *nm* (*en paquete*) packing, wrapping; (*en botella*) bottling; (*en lata*) canning; (*recipiente*) container; (*paquete*) package; (*botella*) bottle; (*lata*) tin (*Brit*), can.

envejecer [enβexe'θer] *vt* to make old, age // *vi*, **~se** *vr* (*volverse viejo*) to grow old; (*parecer viejo*) to age.

envenenar [enβene'nar] *vt* to poison; (*fig*) to embitter.

envergadura [enβerɣa'ðura] *nf* (*fig*) scope, compass.

envés [en'βes] *nm* (*de tela*) back, wrong side.

enviar [en'βjar] *vt* to send.

envidia [en'βiðja] *nf* (*deseo ferviente*) envy; (*celos*) jealousy; **envidiar** *vt* (*desear*) to envy; (*tener celos de*) to be jealous of.

envío [en'βio] *nm* (*acción*) sending; (*de mercancías*) consignment; (*de dinero*) remittance.

enviudar [enβju'ðar] *vi* to be widowed.

envoltura [enβol'tura] *nf* (*cobertura*) cover; (*embalaje*) wrapper, wrapping.

envolver [enβol'βer] *vt* to wrap (up); (*cubrir*) to cover; (*enemigo*) to surround; (*implicar*) to involve, implicate.

envuelto [en'βwelto] *pp de* **envolver**.

enyesar [enje'sar] *vt* (*pared*) to plaster; (*MED*) to put in plaster.

épico, a ['epiko, a] *a* epic // *nf* epic.

epidemia [epi'ðemja] *nf* epidemic.

epilepsia [epi'lepsja] *nf* epilepsy.

epílogo [e'piloxo] *nm* epilogue.

episodio [epi'soðjo] *nm* episode.

epístola |e'pistola| *nf* epistle.

época |'epoka| *nf* period, time; (*HISTORIA*) age, epoch; **hacer ~** to be epoch-making.

equidad |eki'ðað| *nf* equity.

equilibrar |ekili'ßrar| *vt* to balance; **equilibrio** *nm* balance, equilibrium; **equilibrista** *nm/f* (*funámbulo*) tightrope walker; (*acróbata*) acrobat.

equipaje |eki'paxe| *nm* luggage; (*avíos*) equipment, kit; **~ de mano** hand luggage.

equipar |eki'par| *vt* (*proveer*) to equip.

equipararse |ekipa'rarse| *vr*: **~ con** to be on a level with.

equipo |e'kipo| *nm* (*conjunto de cosas*) equipment; (*DEPORTE, grupo*) team; (: *de obreros*) shift.

equis |'ekis| *nf inv* (the letter) X.

equitación |ekita'θjon| *nf* (*acto*) riding; (*arte*) horsemanship.

equitativo, a |ekita'tißo, a| *a* equitable, fair.

equivalente |ekißa'lente| *a, nm* equivalent.

equivaler |ekißa'ler| *vi* to be equivalent *o* equal.

equivocación |ekißoka'θjon| *nf* mistake, error.

equivocado, a |ekißo'kaðo, a| *a* wrong, mistaken.

equivocarse |ekißo'karse| *vr* to be wrong, make a mistake; **~ de camino** to take the wrong road.

equívoco, a |e'kißoko, a| *a* (*dudoso*) suspect; (*ambiguo*) ambiguous // *nm* ambiguity; (*malentendido*) misunderstanding.

era *vb ver* **ser** // |'era| *nf* era, age.

erais *vb ver* **ser**.

éramos *vb ver* **ser**.

eran *vb ver* **ser**.

erario |e'rarjo| *nm* exchequer (*Brit*), treasury.

eras *vb ver* **ser**.

eres *vb ver* **ser**.

erguir |er'xir| *vt* to raise, lift; (*poner derecho*) to straighten; **~se** *vr* to straighten up.

erigir |eri'xir| *vt* to erect, build; **~se** *vr*: **~se en** to set o.s. up as.

erizado, a |eri'θaðo, a| *a* bristly.

erizarse |eri'θarse| *vr* (*pelo: de perro*) to bristle; (: *de persona*) to stand on end.

erizo |e'riθo| *nm* (*ZOOL*) hedgehog; (*tb*: **~ de mar**) sea-urchin.

ermitaño, a |ermi'taɲo, a| *nm/f* hermit.

erosionar |erosjo'nar| *vt* to erode.

erótico, a |e'rotiko, a| *a* erotic; **erotismo** *nm* eroticism.

erradicar |erraði'kar| *vt* to eradicate.

errante |e'rrante| *a* wandering, errant.

errar |e'rrar| *vi* (*vagar*) to wander, roam; (*equivocarse*) to be mistaken // *vt*: **~ el camino** to take the wrong road; **~ el tiro** to miss.

erróneo, a |e'rroneo, a| *a* (*equivocado*) wrong, mistaken; (*falso*) false, untrue.

error |e'rror| *nm* error, mistake; (*INFORM*) bug; **~ de imprenta** misprint.

eructar |eruk'tar| *vt* to belch, burp.

erudito, a |eru'ðito, a| *a* erudite, learned.

erupción |erup'θjon| *nf* eruption; (*MED*) rash.

es *vb ver* **ser**.

esa, esas *a demostrativo ver* **ese**.

ésa, ésas *pron ver* **ése**.

esbelto, a |es'ßelto, a| *a* slim, slender.

esbozo |es'ßoθo| *nm* sketch, outline.

escabeche |eska'ßetʃe| *nm* brine; (*de aceitunas etc*) pickle; **en ~** pickled.

escabroso, a |eska'ßroso, a| *a* (*accidentado*) rough, uneven; (*fig*) tough, difficult; (: *atrevido*) risqué.

escabullirse |eskaßu'ʎirse| *vr* to slip away, to clear out.

escafandra |eska'fandra| *nf* (*buzo*) diving suit; (**~ espacial**) space suit.

escala |es'kala| *nf* (*proporción, MUS*) scale; (*de mano*) ladder; (*AVIAT*) stopover; **hacer ~ en** to stop *o* call in at.

escalafón |eskala'fon| *nm* (*escala de salarios*) salary scale, wage scale.

escalar |eska'lar| *vt* to climb, scale.

escalera |eska'lera| *nf* stairs *pl*, staircase; (*escala*) ladder; (*NAIPES*) run; **~ mecánica** escalator; **~ de caracol** spiral staircase.

escalfar |eskal'far| *vt* (*huevos*) to poach.

escalinata |eskali'nata| *nf* staircase.

escalofrío |eskalo'frio| *nm* (*MED*) chill; **~s** *nmpl* (*fig*) shivers; **escalofriante** *a* chilling.

escalón |eska'lon| *nm* step, stair; (*de escalera*) rung.

escalope |eska'lope| *nm* (*CULIN*) escalope.

escama |es'kama| *nf* (*de pez, serpiente*) scale; (*de jabón*) flake; (*fig*) resentment.

escamotear |eskamote'ar| *vt* (*fam*: *robar*) to lift, swipe; (*hacer desaparecer*) to make disappear.

escampar |eskam'par| *vb impersonal* to stop raining.

escandalizar |eskandali'θar| *vt* to scandalize, shock; **~se** *vr* to be shocked; (*ofenderse*) to be offended.

escándalo |es'kandalo| *nm* scandal; (*alboroto, tumulto*) row, uproar; **escandaloso, a** *a* scandalous, shocking.

escandinavo, a |eskandi'naßo, a| *a*, *nm/f* Scandinavian.

escaño |es'kaɲo| *nm* bench; (*POL*) seat.

escapar |eska'par| *vi* (*gen*) to escape, run away; (*DEPORTE*) to break away; **~se** *vr* to escape, get away; (*agua, gas*) to leak (out).

escaparate |eskapa'rate| *nm* shop window.

escape [es'kape] *nm* (*de agua, gas*) leak; (*de motor*) exhaust; (*de persona*) escape.

escarabajo [eskara'βaxo] *nm* beetle.

escaramuza [eskara'muθa] *nf* skirmish; (*fig*) brush.

escarbar [eskar'βar] *vt* (*gallina*) to scratch; (*fig*) to inquire into, investigate.

escarcha [es'kartʃa] *nf* frost.

escarlata [eskar'lata] *a inv* scarlet; **escarlatina** *nf* scarlet fever.

escarmentar [eskarmen'tar] *vt* to punish severely // *vi* to learn one's lesson.

escarmiento *etc. vb ver* escarmentar // [eskar'mjento] *nm* (*ejemplo*) lesson; (*castigo*) punishment.

escarnio [es'karnjo] *nm* mockery; (*injuria*) insult.

escarola [eska'rola] *nf* endive.

escarpado, a [eskar'paðo, a] *a* (*pendiente*) sheer, steep; (*rocas*) craggy.

escasear [eskase'ar] *vi* to be scarce.

escasez [eska'seθ] *nf* (*falta*) shortage, scarcity; (*pobreza*) poverty.

escaso, a [es'kaso, a] *a* (*poco*) scarce; (*raro*) rare; (*ralo*) thin, sparse; (*limitado*) limited.

escatimar [eskati'mar] *vt* (*limitar*) to skimp (on), be sparing with.

escena [es'θena] *nf* scene.

escenario [esθe'narjo] *nm* (*TEATRO*) stage; (*CINE*) set; (*fig*) scene; **escenografía** *nf* set design.

escepticismo [esθepti'θismo] *nm* scepticism; **escéptico, a** *a* sceptical // *nm/f* sceptic.

esclarecer [esklare'θer] *vt* (*iluminar*) to light up, illuminate; (*misterio, problema*) to shed light on.

esclavitud [esklaβi'tuð] *nf* slavery.

esclavizar [esklaβi'θar] *vt* to enslave.

esclavo, a [es'klaβo, a] *nm/f* slave.

esclusa [es'klusa] *nf* (*de canal*) lock; (*compuerta*) floodgate.

escoba [es'koβa] *nf* broom.

escocer [esko'θer] *vi* to burn, sting; ~**se** *vr* to chafe, get chafed.

escocés, esa [esko'θes, esa] *a* Scottish // *nm/f* Scotsman/woman, Scot.

Escocia [es'koθja] *nf* Scotland.

escoger [esko'xer] *vt* to choose, pick, select; **escogido, a** *a* chosen, selected; (*calidad*) choice, select.

escolar [esko'lar] *a* school *cpd* // *nm/f* schoolboy/girl, pupil.

escolta [es'kolta] *nf* escort; **escoltar** *vt* to escort.

escombros [es'kombros] *nmpl* (*basura*) rubbish *sg*; (*restos*) debris *sg*.

esconder [eskon'der] *vt* to hide, conceal; ~**se** *vr* to hide; **escondite** *nm* hiding place; (*juego*) hide-and-seek; **escondrijo** *nm* hiding place, hideout.

escopeta [esko'peta] *nf* shotgun.

escoria [es'korja] *nf* (*de alto horno*) slag; (*fig*) scum, dregs *pl*.

Escorpio [es'korpjo] *nm* Scorpio.

escorpión [eskor'pjon] *nm* scorpion.

escotado, a [esko'taðo, a] *a* low-cut.

escote [es'kote] *nm* (*de vestido*) low neck; **pagar a ~** to share the expenses.

escotilla [esko'tiʎa] *nf* (*NAUT*) hatch(way).

escozor [esko'θor] *nm* (*dolor*) sting(ing).

escribano, a [eskri'βano, a], **escribiente** [eskri'βjente] *nm/f* clerk.

escribir [eskri'βir] *vt, vi* to write; ~ a **máquina** to type; **¿cómo se escribe?** how do you spell it?

escrito, a [es'krito, a] *pp de* escribir // *nm* (*documento*) document; (*manuscrito*) text, manuscript; **por ~** in writing.

escritor, a [eskri'tor, a] *nm/f* writer.

escritorio [eskri'torjo] *nm* desk; (*oficina*) office.

escritura [eskri'tura] *nf* (*acción*) writing; (*caligrafía*) (hand)writing; (*JUR*: *documento*) deed.

escrúpulo [es'krupulo] *nm* scruple; (*minuciosidad*) scrupulousness; **escrupuloso, a** *a* scrupulous.

escrutar [eskru'tar] *vt* to scrutinize, examine; (*votos*) to count.

escrutinio [eskru'tinjo] *nm* (*examen atento*) scrutiny; (*POL*: *recuento de votos*) count(ing).

escuadra [es'kwaðra] *nf* (*MIL etc*) squad; (*NAUT*) squadron; (*de coches etc*) fleet; **escuadrilla** *nf* (*de aviones*) squadron; (*AM*: *de obreros*) gang.

escuadrón [eskwa'ðron] *nm* squadron.

escuálido, a [es'kwaliðo, a] *a* skinny, scraggy; (*sucio*) squalid.

escuchar [esku'tʃar] *vt* to listen to // *vi* to listen.

escudilla [esku'ðiʎa] *nf* bowl, basin.

escudo [es'kuðo] *nm* shield.

escudriñar [eskuðri'ɲar] *vt* (*examinar*) to investigate, scrutinize; (*mirar de lejos*) to scan.

escuela [es'kwela] *nf* school; ~ **de artes y oficios** (*Esp*) ≈ technical college; ~ **normal** teacher training college.

escueto, a [es'kweto, a] *a* plain; (*estilo*) simple.

escuincle [es'kwinkle] *nm/f* (*AM fam*) kid.

esculpir [eskul'pir] *vt* to sculpt; (*grabar*) to engrave; (*tallar*) to carve; **escultor, a** *nm/f* sculptor/tress; **escultura** *nf* sculpture.

escupidera [eskupi'ðera] *nf* spittoon.

escupir [esku'pir] *vt, vi* to spit (out).

escurreplatos [eskurre'platos] *nm inv* plate rack.

escurridizo, a [eskurri'ðiθo, a] *a* slippery.

escurrir [esku'rrir] *vt* (*ropa*) to wring

out; (*verduras, platos*) to drain // *vi* (*los líquidos*) to drip; ~se *vr* (*secarse*) to drain; (*resbalarse*) to slip, slide; (*escaparse*) to slip away.

ese, esa, esos, esas ['ese, 'esa, 'esos, 'esas] *a demostrativo* (*sg*) that; (*pl*) those.

ése, ésa, ésos, ésas ['ese, 'esa, 'esos, 'esas] *pron* (*sg*) that (one); (*pl*) those (ones); ~... éste... the former... the latter...; no me vengas con ésas don't give me any more of that nonsense.

esencia [e'senθja] *nf* essence; **esencial** *a* essential.

esfera [es'fera] *nf* sphere; (*de reloj*) face; **esférico, a** *a* spherical.

esforzado, a [esfor'θaðo, a] *a* (*enérgico*) energetic, vigorous.

esforzarse [esfor'θarse] *vr* to exert o.s., make an effort.

esfuerzo *etc vb ver* **esforzar** // [es'fwerθo] *nm* effort.

esfumarse [esfu'marse] *vr* (*apoyo, esperanzas*) to fade away.

esgrima [es'vrima] *nf* fencing.

esguince [es'vinθe] *nm* (MED) sprain.

eslabón [esla'ßon] *nm* link.

esmaltar [esmal'tar] *vt* to enamel; **esmalte** *nm* enamel; **esmalte de uñas** nail varnish *o* polish.

esmerado, a [esme'raðo, a] *a* careful, neat.

esmeralda [esme'ralda] *nf* emerald.

esmerarse [esme'rarse] *vr* (*aplicarse*) to take great pains, exercise great care; (*afanarse*) to work hard.

esmero [es'mero] *nm* (great) care.

esnob [es'nob] *a inv* (*persona*) snobbish; (*coche etc*) posh // (*pl* ~s) *nm/f* snob; **~ismo** *nm* snobbery.

eso ['eso] *pron* that, that thing *o* matter; ~ de su coche that business about his car; ~ de ir al cine all that about going to the cinema; a ~ de las cinco at about five o'clock; en ~ thereupon, at that point; ~ es that's it; ¡~ sí que es vida! now that is really living!; por ~ te lo dije that's why I told you; y ~ que llovía in spite of the fact it was raining.

esos ['esos] *a demostrativo ver* **ese.**

ésos ['esos] *pron ver* **ése.**

espabilar [espaßi'lar] *vt*, **espabilarse** *vr* = **despabilar.**

espacial [espa'θjal] *a* (*del espacio*) space *cpd*.

espaciar [espa'θjar] *vt* to space (out).

espacio [es'paθjo] *nm* space; (MUS) interval; (RADIO, TV) programme (*Brit*), program (US); el ~ space; **~so, a** *a* spacious, roomy.

espada [es'paða] *nf* sword; ~s *nfpl* (NAIPES) spades.

espaguetis [espa'vetis] *nmpl* spaghetti *sg.*

espalda [es'palda] *nf* (*gen*) back; ~s *nfpl* (*hombros*) shoulders; a ~s de uno behind sb's back; **tenderse de ~s** to lie (down) on one's back; volver la ~ a alguien to cold-shoulder sb.

espaldilla [espal'ðiʎa] *nf* shoulder blade.

espantadizo, a [espanta'ðiθo, a] *a* timid, easily frightened.

espantajo [espan'taxo] *nm*, **espantapájaros** [espanta'paxaros] *nm inv* scarecrow.

espantar [espan'tar] *vt* (*asustar*) to frighten, scare; (*ahuyentar*) to frighten off; (*asombrar*) to horrify, appal; ~se *vr* to get frightened *o* scared; to be appalled.

espanto [es'panto] *nm* (*susto*) fright; (*terror*) terror; (*asombro*) astonishment; **~so, a** *a* frightening; terrifying; astonishing.

España [es'paɲa] *nf* Spain; **español, a** *a* Spanish // *nm/f* Spaniard // *nm* (LING) Spanish.

esparadrapo [espara'ðrapo] *nm* (sticking) plaster (*Brit*), adhesive tape (US).

esparcimiento [esparθi'mjento] *nm* (*dispersión*) spreading; (*derramamiento*) scattering; (*fig*) cheerfulness.

esparcir [espar'θir] *vt* to spread; (*derramar*) to scatter; ~se *vr* to spread (out); to scatter; (*divertirse*) to enjoy o.s.

espárrago [es'parravo] *nm* asparagus.

espasmo [es'pasmo] *nm* spasm.

espátula [es'patula] *nf* spatula.

especia [es'peθja] *nf* spice.

especial [espe'θjal] *a* special; **~idad** *nf* speciality (*Brit*), specialty (US).

especie [es'peθje] *nf* (BIO) species; (*clase*) kind, sort; en ~ in kind.

especificar [espeθifi'kar] *vt* to specify; **específico, a** *a* specific.

espécimen [es'peθimen] (*pl* **especímenes**) *nm* specimen.

espectáculo [espek'takulo] *nm* (*gen*) spectacle; (TEATRO *etc*) show.

espectador, a [espekta'ðor, a] *nm/f* spectator.

espectro [es'pektro] *nm* ghost; (*fig*) spectre.

especular [espeku'lar] *vt*, *vi* to speculate.

espejismo [espe'xismo] *nm* mirage.

espejo [es'pexo] *nm* mirror; (*fig*) model; ~ **retrovisor** rear-view mirror.

espeluznante [espeluθ'nante] *a* horrifying, hair-raising.

espera [es'pera] *nf* (*pausa, intervalo*) wait; (JUR: *plazo*) respite; en ~ de waiting for; (*con expectativa*) expecting.

esperanza [espe'ranθa] *nf* (*confianza*) hope; (*expectativa*) expectation; hay pocas ~s de que venga there is little prospect of his coming; **esperanzar** *vt* to give hope to.

esperar [espe'rar] *vt* (*aguardar*) to wait for; (*tener expectativa de*) to expect;

(*desear*) to hope for // *vi* to wait; to expect; to hope.

esperma [es'perma] *nf* sperm.

espesar [espe'sar] *vt* to thicken; ~**se** *vr* to thicken, get thicker.

espeso, a [es'peso, a] *a* thick; **espesor** *nm* thickness.

espía [es'pia] *nm/f* spy; **espiar** *vt* (*observar*) to spy on // *vi*: **espiar para to** spy for.

espiga [es'piɣa] *nf* (BOT: *de trigo etc*) ear.

espina [es'pina] *nf* thorn; (*de pez*) bone; ~ **dorsal** (ANAT) spine.

espinaca [espi'naka] *nf* spinach.

espinazo [espi'naθo] *nm* spine, backbone.

espinilla [espi'niʎa] *nf* (ANAT: *tibia*) shin(bone); (*grano*) blackhead.

espino [es'pino] *nm* hawthorn.

espinoso, a [espi'noso, a] *a* (*planta*) thorny, prickly; (*fig*) difficult.

espionaje [espjo'naxe] *nm* spying, espionage.

espiral [espi'ral] *a, nf* spiral.

espirar [espi'rar] *vt* to breathe out, exhale.

espiritista [espiri'tista] *a, nm/f* spiritualist.

espíritu [es'piritu] *nm* spirit; **espiritual** *a* spiritual.

espita [es'pita] *nf* tap.

espléndido, a [es'plendiðo, a] *a* (*magnífico*) magnificent, splendid; (*generoso*) generous.

esplendor [esplen'dor] *nm* splendour.

espolear [espole'ar] *vt* to spur on.

espoleta [espo'leta] *nf* (*de bomba*) fuse.

espolvorear [espolßore'ar] *vt* to dust, sprinkle.

esponja [es'ponxa] *nf* sponge; (*fig*) sponger; **esponjoso, a** *a* spongy.

espontaneidad [espontanei'ðað] *nf* spontaneity; **espontáneo, a** *a* spontaneous.

esposa [es'posa] *nf* wife; ~**s** *nfpl* handcuffs; **esposar** *vt* to handcuff.

esposo [es'poso] *nm* husband.

espuela [es'pwela] *nf* spur.

espuma [es'puma] *nf* foam; (*de cerveza*) froth, head; (*de jabón*) lather; **espumoso, a** *a* frothy, foamy; (*vino*) sparkling.

esqueje [es'kexe] *nm* (*de planta*) cutting.

esqueleto [eske'leto] *nm* skeleton.

esquema [es'kema] *nm* (*diagrama*) diagram; (*dibujo*) plan; (*plan*) scheme; (FILOSOFIA) schema.

esquí [es'ki] (*pl* ~**s**) *nm* (*objeto*) ski; (DEPORTE) skiing; ~ **acúatico** waterskiing; **esquiar** *vi* to ski.

esquilar [eski'lar] *vt* to shear.

esquimal [eski'mal] *a, nm/f* Eskimo.

esquina [es'kina] *nf* corner.

esquirol [eski'rol] *nm* blackleg.

esquivar [eski'ßar] *vt* to avoid; (*evadir*) to dodge, elude.

esquivo, a [es'kißo, a] *a* (*tímido*) reserved; (*huraño*) unsociable.

esta ['esta] *a demostrativo ver* **este**.

ésta ['esta] *pron ver* **éste**.

está *vb ver* **estar**.

estabilidad [estaßili'ðað] *nf* stability; **estable** *a* stable.

establecer [estaßle'θer] *vt* to establish; ~**se** *vr* to establish o.s.; (*echar raíces*) to settle (down); **establecimiento** *nm* establishment.

estaca [es'taka] *nf* stake, post; (*de tienda de campaña*) peg.

estacada [esta'kaða] *nf* (*cerca*) fence, fencing; (*palenque*) stockade.

estación [esta'θjon] *nf* station; (*del año*) season; ~ **de autobuses** bus station; ~ **balnearia** seaside resort; ~ **de servicio** service station.

estacionamiento [estaθjona'mjento] *nm* (AUTO) parking; (MIL) stationing.

estacionar [estaθjo'nar] *vt* (AUTO) to park; (MIL) to station; ~**io, a** *a* stationary; (COM: *mercado*) slack.

estadio [es'taðjo] *nm* (*fase*) stage, phase; (DEPORTE) stadium.

estadista [esta'ðista] *nm* (POL) statesman; (ESTADISTICA) statistician.

estadística [esta'ðistika] *nf* (*una* ~) figure, statistic; (*ciencia*) statistics *sg*.

estado [es'taðo] *nm* (POL: *condición*) state; ~ **de cuenta** bank statement; ~ **civil** marital status; ~ **mayor** staff; **estar en** ~ to be pregnant; **E~s Unidos** (EE.UU.) *nmpl* United States (of America) (USA) *sg*.

estadounidense [estaðouni'ðense] *a* United States *cpd*, American // *nm/f* American.

estafa [es'tafa] *nf* swindle, trick; **estafar** *vt* to swindle, defraud.

estafeta [esta'feta] *nf* (*oficina de correos*) post office; ~ **diplomática** diplomatic bag.

estáis *vb ver* **estar**.

estallar [esta'ʎar] *vi* to burst; (*bomba*) to explode, go off; (*epidemia, guerra, rebelión*) to break out; ~ **en llanto** to burst into tears; **estallido** *nm* explosion; (*fig*) outbreak.

estampa [es'tampa] *nf* (*impresión, imprenta*) print, engraving; (*imagen, figura: de persona*) appearance.

estampado, a [estam'paðo, a] *a* printed // *nm* (*impresión: acción*) printing; (: *efecto*) print; (*marca*) stamping.

estampar [estam'par] *vt* (*imprimir*) to print; (*marcar*) to stamp; (*metal*) to engrave; (*poner sello en*) to stamp; (*fig*) to stamp, imprint.

estampida [estam'piða] *nf* stampede.

estampido [estam'piðo] *nm* bang, report.

estampilla |estam'piʎa| *nf* stamp.
están *vb ver* **estar**.
estancado, a |estan'kaðo. a| *a* stagnant.
estancar |estan'kar| *vt* (*aguas*) to hold up, hold back; (*COM*) to monopolize; (*fig*) to block, hold up; **~se** *vr* to stagnate.
estancia |es'tanθja| *nf* (*permanencia*) stay; (*sala*) room; (*AM*) farm, ranch; **estanciero** *nm* (*AM*) farmer, rancher.
estanco, a |es'tanko. a| *a* watertight // *nm* tobacconist's (shop).
estándar |es'tandar| *a, nm* standard; **estandarizar** *vt* to standardize.
estandarte |estan'darte| *nm* banner, standard.
estanque |es'tanke| *nm* (*lago*) pool, pond; (*AGR*) reservoir.
estanquero, a |estan'kero. a| *nm/f* tobacconist.
estante |es'tante| *nm* (*armario*) rack, stand; (*biblioteca*) bookcase; (*anaquel*) shelf; (*AM*) prop; **estantería** *nf* shelving, shelves *pl*.
estaño |es'taɲo| *nm* tin.
estar |es'tar| ♦ *vi* **1** (*posición*) to be; **está en la plaza** it's in the square; **¿está Juan?** is Juan in?; **estamos a 30 km de Junín** we're 30 kms from Junín
2 (+ *adjetivo: estado*) to be; **~ enfermo** to be ill; **está muy elegante** he's looking very smart; **¿cómo estás?** how are you keeping?
3 (+ *gerundio*) to be; **estoy leyendo** I'm reading
4 (*uso pasivo*): **está condenado a muerte** he's been condemned to death; **está envasado en ...** it's packed in ...
5 (*con fechas*): **¿a cuántos estamos?** what's the date today?; **estamos a 5 de mayo** it's the 5th of May
6 (*locuciones*): **¿estamos?** (*¿de acuerdo?*) okay?; (*¿listo?*) ready?; **¡ya está bien!** that's enough!
7: **~ de: ~ de vacaciones/viaje** to be on holiday/away *o* on a trip; **está de camarero** he's working as a waiter
8: **~ para: está para salir** he's about to leave; **no estoy para bromas** I'm not in the mood for jokes
9: **~ por** (*propuesta etc*) to be in favour of; (*persona etc*) to support, side with; **está por limpiar** it still has to be cleaned
10: **~ sin: ~ sin dinero** to have no money; **está sin terminar** it isn't finished yet
♦ *vr*: **~se: se estuvo en la cama toda la tarde** he stayed in bed all afternoon.
estas |'estas| *a ver* **este**.
éstas |'estas| *pron ver* **éste**.
estatal |esta'tal| *a* state *cpd*.
estático, a |es'tatiko. a| *a* static.
estatua |es'tatwa| *nf* statue.
estatura |esta'tura| *nf* stature, height.
estatuto |esta'tuto| *nm* (*JUR*) statute;

(*de ciudad*) bye-law; (*de comité*) rule.
este |'este| *nm* east.
este, esta, estos, estas |'este. 'esta. 'estos. 'estas| *a demostrativo* (*sg*) this; (*pl*) these.
éste, ésta, éstos, éstas |'este. 'esta. 'estos. 'estas| *pron* (*sg*) this (one); (*pl*) these (ones); **ése... ~...** the former... the latter....
esté *etc vb ver* **estar**.
estela |es'tela| *nf* wake, wash; (*fig*) trail.
estén *etc vb ver* **estar**.
estenografía |estenoɣra'fia| *nf* shorthand.
estera |es'tera| *nf* mat(ting).
estéreo |es'tereo| *a inv, nm* stereo; **estereotipo** *nm* stereotype.
estéril |es'teril| *a* sterile, barren; (*fig*) vain, futile.
esterlina |ester'lina| *a*: **libra ~** pound sterling.
estético, a |es'tetiko. a| *a* aesthetic // *nf* aesthetics *sg*.
estiércol |es'tjerkol| *nm* dung, manure.
estigma |es'tixma| *nm* stigma.
estilar |esti'lar| *vi*, **estilarse** *vr* (*estar de moda*) to be in fashion; (*usarse*) to be used.
estilo |es'tilo| *nm* style; (*TEC*) stylus; (*NATACIÓN*) stroke; **algo por el ~** something along those lines.
estima |es'tima| *nf* esteem, respect.
estimación |estima'θjon| *nf* (*evaluación*) estimation; (*aprecio, afecto*) esteem, regard.
estimar |esti'mar| *vt* (*evaluar*) to estimate; (*valorar*) to value; (*apreciar*) to esteem, respect; (*pensar, considerar*) to think, reckon.
estimulante |estimu'lante| *a* stimulating // *nm* stimulant.
estimular |estimu'lar| *vt* to stimulate; (*excitar*) to excite.
estímulo |es'timulo| *nm* stimulus; (*ánimo*) encouragement.
estío |es'tio| *nm* summer.
estipulación |estipula'θjon| *nf* stipulation, condition; **estipular** *vt* to stipulate.
estirado, a |esti'raðo. a| *a* (*tenso*) (stretched *o* drawn) tight; (*fig: persona*) stiff, pompous.
estirar |esti'rar| *vt* to stretch; (*dinero, suma etc*) to stretch out; **~se** *vr* to stretch.
estirón |esti'ron| *nm* pull, tug; (*crecimiento*) spurt, sudden growth; **dar un ~** (*niño*) to shoot up.
estirpe |es'tirpe| *nf* stock, lineage.
estival |esti'ßal| *a* summer *cpd*.
esto |'esto| *pron* this, this thing *o* matter; **~ de la boda** this business about the wedding.
Estocolmo |esto'kolmo| *nm* Stockholm.
estofa |es'tofa| *nf*: **de baja ~** poor-

quality.

estofado |esto'taðo| *nm* (*CULIN*) stew.

estofar |esto'far| *vt* (*CULIN*) to stew.

estómago |es'tomaxo| *nm* stomach; **tener** ~ to be thick-skinned.

estorbar |estor'ßar| *vt* to hinder, obstruct; (*fig*) to bother, disturb // *vi* to be in the way; **estorbo** *nm* (*molestia*) bother, nuisance; (*obstáculo*) hindrance, obstacle.

estornudar |estornu'ðar| *vi* to sneeze.

estos |'estos| *a demostrativo ver* **este**.

éstos |'estos| *pron ver* **éste**.

estoy *vb ver* **estar**.

estrafalario, a |estrafa'larjo, a| *a* odd, eccentric; (*desarreglado*) slovenly, sloppy.

estrago |es'traxo| *nm* ruin, destruction; **hacer ~s en** to wreak havoc among.

estragón |estra'xon| *nm* tarragon.

estrangulador, a |estrangula'ðor, a| *nm/f* strangler // *nm* (*TEC*) throttle; (*AUTO*) choke.

estrangulamiento |estrangula'mjento| *nm* (*AUTO*) bottleneck.

estrangular |estrangu'lar| *vt* (*persona*) to strangle; (*MED*) to strangulate.

estraperlo |estra'perlo| *nm* black market.

estratagema |estrata'xema| *nf* (*MIL*) stratagem; (*astucia*) cunning.

estrategia |estra'texja| *nf* strategy; **estratégico, a** *a* strategic.

estratificar |estratifi'kar| *vt* to stratify.

estrato |es'trato| *nm* stratum, layer.

estrechar |estre'tʃar| *vt* (*reducir*) to narrow; (*COSTURA*) to take in; (*persona*) to hug, embrace; ~**se** *vr* (*reducirse*) to narrow, grow narrow; (*2 personas*) to embrace; ~ **la mano** to shake hands.

estrechez |estre'tʃeθ| *nf* narrowness; (*de ropa*) tightness; (*intimidad*) intimacy; (*COM*) want *o* shortage of money; **estrecheces** *nfpl* financial difficulties.

estrecho, a |es'tretʃo, a| *a* narrow; (*apretado*) tight; (*íntimo*) close, intimate; (*miserable*) mean // *nm* strait; ~ **de miras** narrow-minded.

estrella |es'treʎa| *nf* star.

estrellar |estre'ʎar| *vt* (*hacer añicos*) to smash (to pieces); (*huevos*) to fry; ~**se** *vr* to smash; (*chocarse*) to crash; (*fracasar*) to fail.

estremecer |estreme'θer| *vt* to shake; ~**se** *vr* to shake, tremble; **estremecimiento** *nm* (*temblor*) trembling, shaking.

estrenar |estre'nar| *vt* (*vestido*) to wear for the first time; (*casa*) to move into; (*película, obra de teatro*) to première; ~**se** *vr* (*persona*) to make one's début; **estreno** *nm* (*primer uso*) first use; (*CINE etc*) première.

estreñido, a |estre'ɲiðo, a| *a* con-

stipated.

estreñimiento |estreɲi'mjento| *nm* constipation.

estrépito |es'trepito| *nm* noise, racket; (*fig*) fuss; **estrepitoso, a** *a* noisy; (*fiesta*) rowdy.

estría |es'tria| *nf* groove.

estribar |estri'ßar| *vi*: ~ **en** to rest on, be supported by.

estribillo |estri'ßiʎo| *nm* (*LITERATURA*) refrain; (*MUS*) chorus.

estribo |es'trißo| *nm* (*de jinete*) stirrup; (*de coche, tren*) step; (*de puente*) support; (*GEO*) spur; **perder los ~s** to fly off the handle.

estribor |estri'ßor| *nm* (*NAUT*) starboard.

estricnina |estrik'nina| *nf* strychnine.

estricto, a |es'trikto, a| *a* (*riguroso*) strict; (*severo*) severe.

estropajo |estro'paxo| *nm* scourer.

estropear |estrope'ar| *vt* (*arruinar*) to spoil; (*dañar*) to damage; ~**se** *vr* (*objeto*) to get damaged; (*persona: la piel etc*) to be ruined.

estructura |estruk'tura| *nf* structure.

estruendo |es'trwendo| *nm* (*ruido*) racket, din; (*fig: alboroto*) uproar, turmoil.

estrujar |estru'xar| *vt* (*apretar*) to squeeze; (*aplastar*) to crush; (*fig*) to drain, bleed.

estuario |es'twarjo| *nm* estuary.

estuche |es'tutʃe| *nm* box, case.

estudiante |estu'ðjante| *nm/f* student; **estudiantil** *a* student *cpd*.

estudiar |estu'ðjar| *vt* to study.

estudio |es'tuðjo| *nm* study; (*CINE, ARTE, RADIO*) studio; ~**s** *nmpl* studies; (*erudición*) learning *sg*; ~**so, a** *a* studious.

estufa |es'tufa| *nf* heater, fire.

estupefaciente |estupefa'θjente| *nm* drug, narcotic.

estupefacto, a |estupe'fakto, a| *a* speechless, thunderstruck.

estupendo, a |estu'pendo, a| *a* wonderful, terrific; (*fam*) great; ¡~! that's great!, fantastic!

estupidez |estupi'ðeθ| *nf* (*torpeza*) stupidity; (*acto*) stupid thing (to do).

estúpido, a |es'tupiðo, a| *a* stupid, silly.

estupor |estu'por| *nm* stupor; (*fig*) astonishment, amazement.

estupro |es'tupro| *nm* rape.

estuve *etc vb ver* **estar**.

esvástica |es'ßastika| *nf* swastika.

ETA |'eta| *nf abr* (*Esp*) ETA.

etapa |e'tapa| *nf* (*de viaje*) stage; (*DEPORTE*) leg; (*parada*) stopping place; (*fig*) stage, phase.

etarra |e'tarra| *nm/f* member of ETA.

etc. *abr* (= *etcétera*) etc.

etcétera |et'θetera| *ad* etcetera.

eternidad |eterni'ðað| *nf* eternity; **eterno, a** *a* eternal, everlasting.

ético, a |'etiko, a| *a* ethical // *nf* ethics

pl.

etiqueta [eti'keta] *nf* (*modales*) etiquette; (*rótulo*) label, tag.

Eucaristía [eukaris'tia] *nf* Eucharist.

eufemismo [eufe'mismo] *nm* euphemism.

euforia [eu'forja] *nf* euphoria.

eunuco [eu'nuko] *nm* eunuch.

Europa [eu'ropa] *nf* Europe; **europeo, a** *a, nm/f* European.

éuscaro, a ['euskaro, a] *a* Basque // *nm* (*LING*) Basque.

Euskadi [eus'kaði] *nm* the Basque Country *o* Provinces *pl.*

euskera [eus'kera] *nm* (*LING*) Basque.

evacuación [eßakwa'θjon] *nf* evacuation; **evacuar** *vt* to evacuate.

evadir [eßa'ðir] *vt* to evade, avoid; ~se *vr* to escape.

evaluar [eßa'lwar] *vt* to evaluate.

evangélico, a [eßan'xeliko, a] *a* evangelic(al).

evangelio [eßan'xeljo] *nm* gospel.

evaporar [eßapo'rar] *vt* to evaporate; ~se *vr* to vanish.

evasión [eßa'sjon] *nf* escape, flight; (*fig*) evasion.

evasivo, a [eßa'sißo, a] *a* evasive, non-committal // *nf* (*pretexto*) excuse.

evento [e'ßento] *nm* event.

eventual [eßen'twal] *a* possible, conditional (upon circumstances); (*trabajador*) casual, temporary.

evidencia [eßi'ðenθja] *nf* evidence, proof; **evidenciar** *vt* (*hacer patente*) to make evident; (*probar*) to prove, show; **evidenciarse** *vr* to be evident.

evidente [eßi'ðente] *a* obvious, clear, evident.

evitar [eßi'tar] *vt* (*evadir*) to avoid; (*impedir*) to prevent.

evocar [eßo'kar] *vt* to evoke, call forth.

evolución [eßolu'θjon] *nf* (*desarrollo*) evolution, development; (*cambio*) change; (*MIL*) manoeuvre; **evolucionar** *vi* to evolve; to manoeuvre.

ex [eks] *a* ex-; **el ~ ministro** the former minister, the ex-minister.

exacerbar [eksaθer'ßar] *vt* to irritate, annoy.

exactamente [eksakta'mente] *ad* exactly.

exactitud [eksakti'tuð] *nf* exactness; (*precisión*) accuracy; (*puntualidad*) punctuality; **exacto, a** *a* exact; accurate; punctual; ¡**exacto!** exactly!

exageración [eksaxera'θjon] *nf* exaggeration; **exagerar** *vt, vi* to exaggerate.

exaltado, a [eksal'taðo, a] *a* (*apasionado*) over-excited, worked-up; (*exagerado*) extreme.

exaltar [eksal'tar] *vt* to exalt, glorify; ~se *vr* (*excitarse*) to get excited *o* worked-up.

examen [ek'samen] *nm* examination.

examinar [eksami'nar] *vt* to examine; ~se *vr* to be examined, take an examination.

exasperar [eksaspe'rar] *vt* to exasperate; ~se *vr* to get exasperated, lose patience.

Exca. *abr* = **Excelencia.**

excavadora [ekskaßa'ðora] *nf* excavator.

excavar [ekska'ßar] *vt* to excavate.

excedente [eksθe'ðente] *a, nm* excess, surplus.

exceder [eksθe'ðer] *vt* to exceed, surpass; ~se *vr* (*extralimitarse*) to go too far; (*sobrepasarse*) to excel o.s.

excelencia [eksθe'lenθja] *nf* excellence; **E~** Excellency; **excelente** *a* excellent.

excelso, a [eks'θelso, a] *a* lofty, sublime.

excentricidad [eksθentriθi'ðað] *nf* eccentricity; **excéntrico, a** *a, nm/f* eccentric.

excepción [eksθep'θjon] *nf* exception; **excepcional** *a* exceptional.

excepto [eks'θepto] *ad* excepting, except (for).

exceptuar [eksθep'twar] *vt* to except, exclude.

excesivo, a [eksθe'sißo, a] *a* excessive.

exceso [eks'θeso] *nm* (*gen*) excess; (*COM*) surplus; ~ **de equipaje/peso** excess luggage/weight.

excitación [eksθita'θjon] *nf* (*sensación*) excitement; (*acción*) excitation.

excitado, a [eksθi'taðo, a] *a* excited; (*emociones*) aroused.

excitar [eksθi'tar] *vt* to excite; (*incitar*) to urge; ~se *vr* to get excited.

exclamación [eksklama'θjon] *nf* exclamation; **exclamar** *vi* to exclaim.

excluir [eksklu'ir] *vt* to exclude; (*dejar fuera*) to shut out; (*descartar*) to reject; **exclusión** *nf* exclusion.

exclusiva [eksklu'sißa] *nf* (*PRENSA*) exclusive, scoop; (*COM*) sole right.

exclusivo, a [eksklu'sißo, a] *a* exclusive; **derecho ~** sole *o* exclusive right.

Excmo. *abr* = *excelentísimo.*

excomulgar [ekskomul'yar] *vt* (*REL*) to excommunicate.

excomunión [ekskomu'njon] *nf* excommunication.

excursión [ekskur'sjon] *nf* excursion, outing; **excursionista** *nm/f* (*turista*) sightseer.

excusa [eks'kusa] *nf* excuse; (*disculpa*) apology.

excusar [eksku'sar] *vt* to excuse; (*evitar*) to avoid, prevent; ~se *vr* (*disculparse*) to apologize.

exento, a [ek'sento, a] *a* exempt.

exequias [ek'sekjas] *nfpl* funeral rites.

exhalar [eksa'lar] *vt* to exhale, breathe out; (*olor etc*) to give off; (*suspiro*) to breathe, heave.

exhausto, a [ek'sausto, a] *a* exhausted.

exhibición [eksißi'θjon] *nf* exhibition, display, show.

exhibir [eksi'ßir] *vt* to exhibit, display, show.

exhortación [eksorta'θjon] *nf* exhortation; **exhortar** *vt*: exhortar a to exhort to.

exigencia [eksi'xenθja] *nf* demand, requirement; **exigente** *a* demanding.

exigir [eksi'xir] *vt* (*gen*) to demand, require; ~ el pago to demand payment.

exiliado, a [eksi'ljaðo, a] *a* exiled // *nm/f* exile.

exilio [ek'siljo] *nm* exile.

eximio, a [ek'simjo, a] *a* (*eminente*) distinguished, eminent.

eximir [eksi'mir] *vt* to exempt.

existencia [eksis'tenθja] *nf* existence; ~s *nfpl* stock(s) (*pl*).

existir [eksis'tir] *vi* to exist, be.

éxito ['eksito] *nm* (*resultado*) result, outcome; (*triunfo*) success; (*MUS etc*) hit; tener ~ to be successful.

exonerar [eksone'rar] *vt* to exonerate; ~ de una obligación to free from an obligation.

exorcizar [eksorθi'θar] *vt* to exorcize.

exótico, a [ek'sotiko, a] *a* exotic.

expandir [ekspan'dir] *vt* to expand.

expansión [ekspan'sjon] *nf* expansion.

expatriarse [ekspa'trjarse] *vr* to emigrate; (*POL*) to go into exile.

expectativa [ekspekta'tißa] *nf* (*espera*) expectation; (*perspectiva*) prospect.

expedición [ekspeði'θjon] *nf* (*excursión*) expedition.

expediente [ekspe'ðjente] *nm* expedient; (*JUR: procedimiento*) action, proceedings *pl*; (: *papeles*) dossier, file, record.

expedir [ekspe'ðir] *vt* (*despachar*) to send, forward; (*pasaporte*) to issue.

expedito, a [ekspe'ðito, a] *a* (*libre*) clear, free.

expendedor, a [ekspende'ðor, a] *nm/f* (*vendedor*) dealer; (*aparato*) (vending) machine; ~ de cigarrillos cigarette machine.

expendeduría [ekspendedu'ria] *nf* (*estanco*) tobacconist's (shop).

expensas [eks'pensas] *nfpl*: a ~ de at the expense of.

experiencia [ekspe'rjenθja] *nf* experience.

experimentado, a [eksperimen'taðo, a] *a* experienced.

experimentar [eksperimen'tar] *vt* (*en laboratorio*) to experiment with; (*probar*) to test, try out; (*notar, observar*) to experience; (*deterioro, pérdida*) to suffer; **experimento** *nm* experiment.

experto, a [eks'perto, a] *a* expert, skilled // *nm/f* expert.

expiar [ekspi'ar] *vt* to atone for.

expirar [ekspi'rar] *vi* to expire.

explayarse [ekspla'jarse] *vr* (*en discurso*) to speak at length; ~ con uno to confide in sb.

explicación [eksplika'θjon] *nf* explanation; **explicar** *vt* to explain; **explicarse** *vr* to explain (o.s.).

explícito, a [eks'pliθito, a] *a* explicit.

explique *etc vb ver* **explicar**.

explorador, a [eksplora'ðor, a] *nm/f* (*pionero*) explorer; (*MIL*) scout // *nm* (*MED*) probe; (*TEC*) (radar) scanner.

explorar [eksplo'rar] *vt* to explore; (*MED*) to probe; (*radar*) to scan.

explosión [eksplo'sjon] *nf* explosion; **explosivo, a** *a* explosive.

explotación [eksplota'θjon] *nf* exploitation; (*de planta etc*) running.

explotar [eksplo'tar] *vt* to exploit; to run, operate // *vi* to explode.

exponer [ekspo'ner] *vt* to expose; (*cuadro*) to display; (*vida*) to risk; (*idea*) to explain; ~se *vr*: ~se a (hacer) algo to run the risk of (doing) sth.

exportación [eksporta'θjon] *nf* (*acción*) export; (*mercancías*) exports *pl*; **exportar** *vt* to export.

exposición [eksposi'θjon] *nf* (*gen*) exposure; (*de arte*) show, exhibition; (*explicación*) explanation; (*narración*) account, statement.

expresar [ekspre'sar] *vt* to express; **expresión** *nf* expression.

expreso, a *pp de* **expresar** // [eks'preso, a] *a* (*explícito*) express; (*claro*) specific, clear; (*tren*) fast // *nm*: mandar ~ to send by express (delivery).

express [eks'pres] *ad* (*AM*): enviar algo ~ to send sth special delivery.

exprimidor [eksprimi'ðor] *nm* squeezer.

exprimir [ekspri'mir] *vt* (*fruta*) to squeeze; (*zumo*) to squeeze out.

expropiar [ekspro'pjar] *vt* to expropriate.

expuesto, a [eks'pwesto, a] *a* exposed; (*cuadro etc*) on show, on display.

expulsar [ekspul'sar] *vt* (*echar*) to eject, throw out; (*alumno*) to expel; (*despedir*) to sack, fire; (*DEPORTE*) to send off; **expulsión** *nf* expulsion; sending-off.

exquisito, a [ekski'sito, a] *a* exquisite; (*comida*) delicious.

éxtasis ['ekstasis] *nm* ecstasy.

extender [eksten'der] *vt* to extend; (*los brazos*) to stretch out, hold out; (*mapa, tela*) to spread (out), open (out); (*mantequilla*) to spread; (*certificado*) to issue; (*cheque, recibo*) to make out; (*documento*) to draw up; ~se *vr* (*gen*) to extend; (*persona: en el suelo*) to stretch out; (*epidemia*) to spread; **extendido, a** *a* (*abierto*) spread out, open; (*brazos*) outstretched; (*prevaleciente*) widespread.

extensión [eksten'sjon] *nf* (*de terreno, mar*) expanse, stretch; (*de tiempo*) length, duration; (*TEL*) extension; en toda la ~ de la palabra in every sense of the word.

extenso, a [eks'tenso, a] *a* extensive.
extenuar [ekste'nwar] *vt* (*debilitar*) to weaken.
exterior [ekste'rjor] *a* (*de fuera*) external; (*afuera*) outside, exterior; (*apariencia*) outward; (*deuda, relaciones*) foreign // *nm* (*gen*) exterior, outside; (*aspecto*) outward appearance; (*DEPORTE*) wing(er); (*países extranjeros*) abroad; **en el ~** abroad; **al ~** outwardly, on the surface.
exterminar [ekstermi'nar] *vt* to exterminate; **exterminio** *nm* extermination.
externo, a [eks'terno, a] *a* (*exterior*) external, outside; (*superficial*) outward // *nm/f* day pupil.
extinguir [ekstiŋ'gir] *vt* (*fuego*) to extinguish, put out; (*raza, población*) to wipe out; **~se** *vr* (*fuego*) to go out; (*BIO*) to die out, become extinct.
extinto, a [eks'tinto, a] *a* extinct.
extintor [ekstin'tor] *nm* (fire) extinguisher.
extra ['ekstra] *a inv* (*tiempo*) extra; (*chocolate, vino*) good-quality // *nm/f* extra // *nm* extra; (*bono*) bonus.
extracción [ekstrak'θjon] *nf* extraction; (*en lotería*) draw.
extracto [eks'trakto] *nm* extract.
extraer [ekstra'er] *vt* to extract, take out.
extralimitarse [ekstralimi'tarse] *vr* to go too far.
extranjero, a [ekstran'xero, a] *a* foreign // *nm/f* foreigner // *nm* foreign countries *pl*; **en el ~** abroad.
extrañar [ekstra'ɲar] *vt* (*sorprender*) to find strange o odd; (*echar de menos*) to miss; **~se** *vr* (*sorprenderse*) to be amazed, be surprised; (*distanciarse*) to become estranged, grow apart.
extrañeza [ekstra'ɲeθa] *nf* (*rareza*) strangeness, oddness; (*asombro*) amazement, surprise.
extraño, a [eks'traɲo, a] *a* (*extranjero*) foreign; (*raro, sorprendente*) strange, odd.
extraordinario, a [ekstraorði'narjo, a] *a* extraordinary; (*edición, número*) special // *nm* (*de periódico*) special edition; **horas extraordinarias** overtime *sg*.
extrarradio [ekstra'rraðjo] *nm* poor suburban area.
extravagancia [ekstraβa'ɣanθja] *nf* oddness; outlandishness; **extravagante** *a* (*excéntrico*) eccentric; (*estrafalario*) outlandish.
extraviado, a [ekstra'βjaðo, a] *a* lost, missing.
extraviar [ekstra'βjar] *vt* (*persona: desorientar*) to mislead, misdirect; (*perder*) to lose, misplace; **~se** *vr* to lose one's way, get lost; **extravío** *nm* loss; (*fig*) deviation.
extremar [ekstre'mar] *vt* to carry to

extremes; **~se** *vr* to do one's utmost, make every effort.
extremaunción [ekstremaun'θjon] *nf* extreme unction.
extremidad [ekstremi'ðað] *nf* (*punta*) extremity; (*fila*) edge; **~es** *nfpl* (*ANAT*) extremities.
extremo, a [eks'tremo, a] *a* extreme; (*último*) last // *nm* end; (*límite, grado sumo*) extreme; **en último ~** as a last resort.
extrovertido, a [ekstroβer'tiðo, a] *a*, *nm/f* extrovert.
exuberancia [eksuβe'ranθja] *nf* exuberance; **exuberante** *a* exuberant; (*fig*) luxuriant, lush.
eyacular [ejaku'lar] *vt*, *vi* to ejaculate.

F

f.a.b. *abr* (= *franco a bordo*) f.o.b.
fábrica ['faβrika] *nf* factory; **marca de ~** trademark; **precio de ~** factory price.
fabricación [faβrika'θjon] *nf* (*manufactura*) manufacture; (*producción*) production; **de ~ casera** home-made; **~ en serie** mass production.
fabricante [faβri'kante] *nm/f* manufacturer.
fabricar [faβri'kar] *vt* (*manufacturar*) to manufacture, make; (*construir*) to build; (*cuento*) to fabricate, devise.
fábula ['faβula] *nf* (*cuento*) fable; (*chisme*) rumour; (*mentira*) fib.
facción [fak'θjon] *nf* (*POL*) faction; **facciones** *nfpl* (*del rostro*) features.
fácil ['faθil] *a* (*simple*) easy; (*probable*) likely.
facilidad [faθili'ðað] *nf* (*capacidad*) ease; (*sencillez*) simplicity; (*de palabra*) fluency; **~es** *nfpl* facilities.
facilitar [faθili'tar] *vt* (*hacer fácil*) to make easy; (*proporcionar*) to provide.
fácilmente ['faθilmente] *ad* easily.
facsímil [fak'simil] *nm* facsimile, fax.
factible [fak'tiβle] *a* feasible.
factor [fak'tor] *nm* factor.
factura [fak'tura] *nf* (*cuenta*) bill; (*hechura*) manufacture; **facturar** *vt* (*COM*) to invoice, charge for; (*equipaje*) to register (*Brit*), check (*US*).
facultad [fakul'tað] *nf* (*aptitud, ESCOL etc*) faculty; (*poder*) power.
facha ['fatʃa] *nf* (*fam: aspecto*) look; (: *cara*) face.
fachada [fa'tʃaða] *nf* (*ARQ*) façade, front.
faena [fa'ena] *nf* (*trabajo*) work; (*quehacer*) task, job.
fagot [fa'ɣot] (*pl* **~es**) [fa'ɣot] *nm* (*MUS*) bassoon.
faisán [fai'san] *nm* pheasant.
faja ['faxa] *nf* (*para la cintura*) sash; (*de mujer*) corset; (*de tierra*) strip.
fajo ['faxo] *nm* (*de papeles*) bundle; (*de*

billetes) wad.

Falango [fa'laɴxe] *nf* (*POL*) Falange.

falda ['falda] *nf* (*prenda de vestir*) skirt.

falo ['falo] *nm* phallus.

falsedad [false'ðað] *nf* falseness; (*hipocresía*) hypocrisy; (*mentira*) falsehood.

falsificar [falsifi'kar] *vt* (*firma etc*) to forge; (*voto etc*) to rig; (*moneda*) to counterfeit.

falso, a ['falso, a] *a* false; (*erróneo*) mistaken; (*documento, moneda etc*) fake; **en ~** falsely.

falta ['falta] *nf* (*defecto*) fault, flaw; (*privación*) lack, want; (*ausencia*) absence; (*carencia*) shortage; (*equivocación*) mistake; (*DEPORTE*) foul; **echar en ~** to miss; **hacer ~** hacer algo to be necessary to do sth; **me hace falta una pluma** I need a pen.

faltar [fal'tar] *vi* (*escasear*) to be lacking, be wanting; (*ausentarse*) to be absent, be missing; **faltan 2 horas para llegar** there are 2 hours to go till arrival; **~ al respeto a uno** to be disrespectful to sb; **¡no faltaba más!** that's the last straw!

falto, a ['falto, a] *a* (*desposeído*) deficient, lacking; (*necesitado*) poor, wretched.

falla ['faʎa] *nf* (*defecto*) fault, flaw.

fallar [fa'ʎar] *vt* (*JUR*) to pronounce sentence on // *vi* (*memoria*) to fail; (*motor*) to miss.

fallecer [faʎe'θer] *vi* to pass away, die; **fallecimiento** *nm* decease, demise.

fallido, a [fa'ʎiðo] *a* (*gen*) frustrated, unsuccessful.

fallo ['faʎo] *nm* (*JUR*) verdict, ruling; (*fracaso*) failure.

fama ['fama] *nf* (*renombre*) fame; (*reputación*) reputation.

famélico, a [fa'meliko, a] *a* starving.

familia [fa'milja] *nf* family.

familiar [fami'ljar] *a* (*relativo a la familia*) family *cpd*; (*conocido, informal*) familiar // *nm* relative, relation; **~idad** *nf* (*gen*) familiarity; (*informalidad*) homeliness; **~izarse** *vr*: **~izarse con** to familiarize o.s. with.

famoso, a [fa'moso, a] *a* (*renombrado*) famous.

fanático, a [fa'natiko, a] *a* fanatical // *nm/f* fanatic; (*CINE, DEPORTE*) fan; **fanatismo** *nm* fanaticism.

fanfarrón, ona [fanfa'rron, ona] *a* boastful; (*pey*) showy.

fango ['fango] *nm* mud; **~so, a** *a* muddy.

fantasía [fanta'sia] *nf* fantasy, imagination; **joyas de ~** imitation jewellery *sg*.

fantasma [fan'tasma] *nm* (*espectro*) ghost, apparition; (*presumido*) show-off.

fantástico, a [fan'tastiko, a] *a* (*irreal, fam*) fantastic.

farmacéutico, a [farma'θeutiko, a] *a* pharmaceutical // *nm/f* chemist (*Brit*), pharmacist.

farmacia [far'maθja] *nf* chemist's (shop) (*Brit*), pharmacy; **~ de turno** duty chemist.

fármaco ['farmako] *nm* drug.

faro ['faro] *nm* (*NAUT: torre*) lighthouse; (*AUTO*) headlamp; (*foco*) floodlight; **~s antiniebla** fog lamps; **~s delanteros/ traseros** headlights/rear lights.

farol [fa'rol] *nm* lantern, lamp.

farola [fa'rola] *nf* street lamp (*Brit*) o light (*US*).

farsa ['farsa] *nf* (*gen*) farce.

farsante [far'sante] *nm/f* fraud, fake.

fascículo [fas'θikulo] *nm* (*de revista*) part, instalment.

fascinar [fasθi'nar] *vt* (*gen*) to fascinate.

fascismo [fas'θismo] *nm* fascism; **fascista** *a, nm/f* fascist.

fase ['fase] *nf* phase.

fastidiar [fasti'ðjar] *vt* (*disgustar*) to annoy, bother; (*estropear*) to spoil; **~se** *vr* (*disgustarse*) to get annoyed o cross; **¡que se fastidie!** (*fam*) he'll just have to put up with it!

fastidio [fas'tiðjo] *nm* (*disgusto*) annoyance; **~so, a** *a* (*molesto*) annoying.

fatal [fa'tal] *a* (*gen*) fatal; (*desgraciado*) ill-fated; (*fam: malo, pésimo*) awful; **~idad** *nf* (*destino*) fate; (*mala suerte*) misfortune.

fatiga [fa'tiɣa] *nf* (*cansancio*) fatigue, weariness.

fatigar [fati'ɣar] *vt* to tire, weary; **~se** *vr* to get tired.

fatigoso, a [fati'ɣoso, a] *a* (*cansador*) tiring.

fatuo, a ['fatwo, a] *a* (*vano*) fatuous; (*presuntuoso*) conceited.

fauces ['fauθes] *nfpl* jaws, mouth *sg*.

favor [fa'ßor] *nm* favour; **estar a ~ de** to be in favour of; **haga el ~ de...** would you be so good as to..., kindly...; **por ~** please; **~able** *a* favourable.

favorecer [faßore'θer] *vt* to favour; (*vestido etc*) to become, flatter; **este peinado le favorece** this hairstyle suits him.

favorito, a [faßo'rito, a] *a, nm/f* favourite.

faz [faθ] *nf* face; **la ~ de la tierra** the face of the earth.

fe [fe] *nf* (*REL*) faith; (*confianza*) belief; (*documento*) certificate; **prestar ~ a** to believe, credit; **actuar con buena/mala ~** to act in good/bad faith; **dar ~ de** to bear witness to.

fealdad [feal'dað] *nf* ugliness.

febrero [fe'ßrero] *nm* February.

fecundar [fekun'dar] *vt* (*generar*) to fertilize, make fertile; **fecundo, a** *a* (*fértil*) fertile; (*fig*) prolific; (*productivo*) productive.

fecha |'fetʃa| *nf* date; ~ de caducidad, ~ límite de venta (*de producto alimenticio*) sell-by date; en ~ próxima soon; hasta la ~ to date, so far; poner ~ to date; **fechar** *vt* to date.

federación |federa'θjon| *nf* federation.

federal |feðe'ral| *a* federal.

felicidad |feliθi'ðað| *nf* (*satisfacción, contento*) happiness; ~es *nfpl* best wishes, congratulations; **~es** *nfpl* best wishes, congratulations!

felicitación |feliθita'θjon| *nf*: ¡felicitaciones! congratulations!

felicitar |feliθi'tar| *vt* to congratulate.

feligrés, esa |feli'ɣres, esa| *nm/f* parishioner.

feliz |fe'liθ| *a* (*contento*) happy; (*afortunado*) lucky.

felpudo |fel'puðo| *nm* doormat.

femenino, a |feme'nino, a| *a, nm* feminine.

feminista |femi'nista| *a, nm/f* feminist.

fenómeno |fe'nomeno| *nm* phenomenon; (*fig*) freak, accident // *a* great // *excl* great!, marvellous!

feo, a |'feo, a| *a* (*gen*) ugly; (*desagradable*) bad, nasty.

féretro |'feretro| *nm* (*ataúd*) coffin; (*sarcófago*) bier.

feria |'ferja| *nf* (*gen*) fair; (*descanso*) holiday, rest day; (*AM: mercado*) village market; (: *cambio*) loose *o* small change.

fermentar |fermen'tar| *vi* to ferment.

ferocidad |feroθi'ðað| *nf* fierceness, ferocity.

feroz |fe'roθ| *a* (*cruel*) cruel; (*salvaje*) fierce.

férreo, a |'ferreo, a| *a* iron.

ferretería |ferrete'ria| *nf* (*tienda*) ironmonger's (shop) (*Brit*), hardware store.

ferrocarril |ferroka'rril| *nm* railway.

ferroviario, a |ferro'ßjarjo, a| *a* rail *cpd*.

fértil |'fertil| *a* (*productivo*) fertile; (*rico*) rich; **fertilidad** *nf* (*gen*) fertility; (*productividad*) fruitfulness.

fertilizar |fertili'θar| *vt* to fertilize.

fervor |fer'ßor| *nm* fervour; **~oso, a** *a* fervent.

festejar |feste'xar| *vt* (*agasajar*) to wine and dine; (*galantear*) to court; (*celebrar*) to celebrate; **festejo** *nm* (*diversión*) entertainment; (*galanteo*) courtship; (*fiesta*) celebration.

festividad |festißi'ðað| *nf* festivity.

festivo, a |fes'tißo, a| *a* (*de fiesta*) festive; (*fig*) witty; (*CINE, LITERATURA*) humorous; día ~ holiday.

fétido, a |'fetiðo, a| *a* (*hediondo*) foul-smelling.

feto |'feto| *nm* foetus.

fiable |'fjaßle| *a* (*persona*) trustworthy; (*máquina*) reliable.

fiador, a |fia'ðor, a| *nm/f* (*JUR*) surety, guarantor; (*COM*) backer; salir ~ por alguien to stand bail for sb.

fiambre |'fjambre| *nm* cold meat.

fianza |'fjanθa| *nf* surety; (*JUR*): libertad bajo ~ release on bail.

fiar |fi'ar| *vt* (*salir garante de*) to guarantee; (*vender a crédito*) to sell on credit; (*secreto*) to confide (*a* to) // *vi* to trust; **~se** *vr* to trust (in), rely on; **~se de uno** to rely on sb.

fibra |'fißra| *nf* fibre; ~ óptica optical fibre.

ficción |fik'θjon| *nf* fiction.

ficticio, a |fik'tiθjo, a| *a* (*imaginario*) fictitious; (*falso*) fabricated.

ficha |'fitʃa| *nf* (*TEL*) token; (*en juegos*) counter, marker; (*tarjeta*) (index) card; **fichar** *vt* (*archivar*) to file, index; (*DEPORTE*) to sign; estar fichado to have a record; **fichero** *nm* box file; (*INFORM*) file.

fidelidad |fiðeli'ðað| *nf* (*lealtad*) fidelity, loyalty; alta ~ high fidelity, hi-fi.

fideos |fi'ðeos| *nmpl* noodles.

fiebre |'fjeßre| *nf* (*MED*) fever; (*fig*) fever, excitement; ~ amarilla/del heno yellow/hay fever; ~ palúdica malaria; tener ~ to have a temperature.

fiel |fjel| *a* (*leal*) faithful, loyal; (*fiable*) reliable; (*exacto*) accurate, faithful // *nm*: los ~es the faithful.

fieltro |'fjeltro| *nm* felt.

fiero, a |'fjero, a| *a* (*cruel*) cruel; (*feroz*) fierce; (*duro*) harsh // *nf* (*animal feroz*) wild animal *o* beast; (*fig*) dragon // *nm/f* (*fig*) fiend.

fiesta |'fjesta| *nf* party; (*de pueblo*) festival; (*vacaciones, tb*): ~s holiday *sg*; (*REL*): ~ de guardar day of obligation.

figura |fi'ɣura| *nf* (*gen*) figure; (*forma, imagen*) shape, form; (*NAIPES*) face card.

figurar |fiɣu'rar| *vt* (*representar*) to represent; (*fingir*) to figure // *vi* to figure; **~se** *vr* (*imaginarse*) to imagine; (*suponer*) to suppose.

fijador |fixa'ðor| *nm* (*FOTO etc*) fixative; (*de pelo*) gel.

fijar |fi'xar| *vt* (*gen*) to fix; (*estampilla*) to affix, stick (on); (*fig*) to settle (on), decide; **~se** *vr*: ~se en to notice.

fijo, a |'fixo, a| *a* (*gen*) fixed; (*firme*) firm; (*permanente*) permanent // *ad*: mirar ~ to stare.

fila |'fila| *nf* row; (*MIL*) rank; (*cadena*) line; ponerse en ~ to line up, get into line.

filántropo, a |fi'lantropo, a| *nm/f* philanthropist.

filatelia |fila'telja| *nf* philately, stamp collecting.

filete |fi'lete| *nm* (*carne*) fillet steak; (*pescado*) fillet.

filial |fi'ljal| *a* filial // *nf* subsidiary.

Filipinas |fili'pinas| *nfpl*: las ~ the Philippines; **filipino, a** *a, nm/f*

Philippine.

filmar |fil'mar| *vt* to film, shoot.

filo |'filo| *nm* (*gen*) edge; sacar ~ a to sharpen; **al ~ del mediodía** at about midday; **de doble ~** double-edged.

filón |fi'lon| *nm* (*MINERIA*) vein, lode; (*fig*) goldmine.

filosofía |filoso'fia| *nf* philosophy; **filósofo, a** *nm/f* philosopher.

filtrar |fil'trar| *vt*, *vi* to filter, strain; ~**se** *vr* to filter; (*fig*: *dinero*) to dwindle; **filtro** *nm* (*TEC*, *utensilio*) filter.

fin |fin| *nm* end; (*objetivo*) aim, purpose; **al ~ y al cabo** when all's said and done; **a ~ de** in order to; **por ~** finally; **en ~** in short; **~ de semana** weekend.

final |fi'nal| *a* final // *nm* end, conclusion // *nf* final; ~**idad** *nf* (*propósito*) purpose, intention; ~**ista** *nm/f* finalist; ~**izar** *vt* to end, finish; (*INFORM*) to log out *o* off // *vi* to end, come to an end.

financiar |finan'θjar| *vt* to finance; **financiero, a** *a* financial // *nm/f* financier.

finca |'finka| *nf* country estate; (*AM*) farm.

fingir |fin'xir| *vt* (*simular*) to simulate, feign; (*pretextar*) to sham, fake // *vi* (*aparentar*) to pretend; ~**se** *vr* to pretend to be.

finlandés, esa |finlan'des, esa| *a* Finnish // *nm/f* Finn // *nm* (*LING*) Finnish.

Finlandia |fin'landja| *nf* Finland.

fino, a |'fino, a| *a* fine; (*delgado*) slender; (*de buenas maneras*) polite, refined; (*jerez*) fino, dry.

firma |'firma| *nf* signature; (*COM*) firm, company; **firmar** *vt* to sign.

firme |'firme| *a* firm; (*estable*) stable; (*sólido*) solid; (*constante*) steady; (*decidido*) resolute // *nm* road (surface); ~**mente** *ad* firmly; ~**za** *nf* firmness; (*constancia*) steadiness; (*solidez*) solidity.

fiscal |fis'kal| *a* fiscal // *nm/f* public prosecutor; **año** ~ tax *o* fiscal year.

fisco |'fisko| *nm* (*hacienda*) treasury, exchequer (*Brit*).

fisgar |fis'xar| *vt* to pry into.

físico, a |'fisiko, a| *a* physical // *nm* physique // *nm/f* physicist // *nf* physics *sg*.

flaco, a |'flako, a| *a* (*muy delgado*) skinny, thin; (*débil*) weak, feeble.

flagrante |fla'vrante| *a* flagrant.

flamante |fla'mante| *a* (*fam*) brilliant; (: *nuevo*) brand-new.

flamenco, a |fla'menko, a| *a* (*de Flandes*) Flemish; (*baile*, *música*) flamenco // *nm* (*baile*, *música*) flamenco.

flan |flan| *nm* creme caramel.

flaqueza |fla'keθa| *nf* (*delgadez*) thinness, leanness; (*fig*) weakness.

flash |flaʃ| (*pl* ~**s** *o* ~**es**) *nm* (*FOTO*) flash.

flauta |'flauta| *nf* (*MUS*) flute.

fleco |'fleko| *nm* fringe.

flecha |'fletʃa| *nf* arrow.

flema |'flema| *nm* phlegm.

flequillo |fle'kiʎo| *nm* (*pelo*) fringe.

flete |'flete| *nm* (*carga*) freight; (*alquiler*) charter; (*precio*) freightage.

flexible |flek'sißle| *a* flexible.

flipper |'fliper| *nm* pinball (machine).

flojera |flo'xera| *nf* (*AM fam*): me da ~ I can't be bothered.

flojo, a |'floxo, a| *a* (*gen*) loose; (*sin fuerzas*) limp; (*débil*) weak.

flor |flor| *nf* flower; (*piropo*) compliment; **a ~ de** on the surface of; ~**ecer** *vi* (*BOT*) to flower, bloom; (*fig*) to flourish; ~**eciente** *a* (*BOT*) in flower, flowering; (*fig*) thriving; ~**ero** *nm* vase; ~**ista** *nm/f* florist.

flota |'flota| *nf* fleet.

flotador |flota'ðor| *nm* (*gen*) float; (*para nadar*) rubber ring.

flotar |flo'tar| *vi* (*gen*) to float; **flote** *nm*: **a flote** afloat; **salir a flote** (*fig*) to get back on one's feet.

fluctuar |fluk'twar| *vi* (*oscilar*) to fluctuate.

fluidez |flui'ðeθ| *nf* fluidity; (*fig*) fluency.

flúido, a |'fluiðo, a| *a*, *nm* fluid.

fluir |flu'ir| *vi* to flow.

flujo |'fluxo| *nm* flow; ~ **y reflujo** ebb and flow; ~ **de sangre** (*MED*) loss of blood; ~**grama** *nm* flowchart.

foca |'foka| *nf* seal.

foco |'foko| *nm* focus; (*ELEC*) floodlight; (*AM*) (light) bulb.

fogón |fo'von| *nm* (*de cocina*) ring, burner.

fogoso, a |fo'voso, a| *a* spirited.

follaje |fo'ʎaxe| *nm* foliage.

folleto |fo'ʎeto| *nm* pamphlet.

follón |fo'ʎon| *nm* (*fam*: *lío*) mess; (: *conmoción*) fuss; **armar un ~** to kick up a row.

fomentar |fomen'tar| *vt* (*MED*) to foment; **fomento** *nm* (*promoción*) promotion.

fonda |'fonda| *nf* inn.

fondo |'fondo| *nm* (*de mar*) bottom; (*de coche*, *sala*) back; (*ARTE etc*) background; (*reserva*) fund; ~**s** *nmpl* (*COM*) funds, resources; **una investigación a ~** a thorough investigation; **en el ~** at bottom, deep down.

fono |'fono| *nm* (*AM*) telephone number.

fontanería |fontane'ria| *nf* plumbing; **fontanero, a** *nm/f* plumber.

forastero, a |foras'tero, a| *nm/f* stranger.

forcejear |forθexe'ar| *vi* (*luchar*) to struggle.

forjar |for'xar| *vt* to forge.

forma |'forma| *nf* (*figura*) form, shape; (*molde*) mould, pattern; (*MED*) fitness; (*método*) way, means; **las ~s** the conventions; **estar en** ~ to be fit.

formación |forma'θjon| nf (gen) formation; (educación) education; ~ profesional vocational training.

formal |for'mal| a (gen) formal; (fig: persona) serious; (: de fiar) reliable; ~**idad** nf formality; seriousness; ~**izar** vt (JUR) to formalize; (situación) to put in order, regularize; ~**izarse** vr (situación) to be put in order, be regularized.

formar |for'mar| vt (componer) to form, shape; (constituir) to make up, constitute; (ESCOL) to train, educate; ~**se** vr (ESCOL) to be trained, educated; (cobrar forma) to form, take form; (desarrollarse) to develop.

formatear |formate'ar| vt to format.

formidable |formi'ðaßle| a (temible) formidable; (asombroso) tremendous.

formulario |formu'larjo| nm form.

fornido, a |for'niðo, a| a well-built.

foro |'foro| nm (gen) forum; (JUR) court.

forrar |fo'rrar| vt (abrigo) to line; (libro) to cover; **forro** nm (de cuaderno) cover; (COSTURA) lining; (de sillón) upholstery.

fortalecer |fortale'θer| vt to strengthen.

fortaleza |forta'leθa| nf (MIL) fortress, stronghold; (fuerza) strength; (determinación) resolution.

fortuito, a |for'twito, a| a accidental.

fortuna |for'tuna| nf (suerte) fortune, (good) luck; (riqueza) fortune, wealth.

forzar |for'θar| vt (puerta) to force (open); (compeler) to compel.

forzoso, a |for'θoso, a| a necessary.

fosa |'fosa| nf (sepultura) grave; (en tierra) pit; (MED) cavity.

fósforo |'fosforo| nm (QUIMICA) phosphorus; (AM) match.

foso |'foso| nm ditch; (TEATRO) pit; (AUTO): ~ de reconocimiento inspection pit.

foto |'foto| nf photo, snap(shot); **sacar una** ~ to take a photo o picture.

fotocopia |foto'kopja| nf photocopy; **fotocopiadora** nf photocopier; **fotocopiar** vt to photocopy.

fotografía |fotoɣra'fia| nf (ARTE) photography; (una ~) photograph; **fotografiar** vt to photograph.

fotógrafo, a |fo'toɣrafo, a| nm/f photographer.

fracaso |fra'kaso| nm (desgracia, revés) failure; **fracasar** vi (gen) to fail.

fracción |frak'θjon| nf fraction; (POL) faction; **fraccionamiento** nm (AM) housing estate.

fractura |frak'tura| nf fracture, break.

fragancia |fra'ɣanθja| nf (olor) fragrance, perfume.

frágil |'fraxil| a (débil) fragile; (COM) breakable.

fragmento |fraɣ'mento| nm (pedazo) fragment.

fragua |'fraɣwa| nf forge; **fraguar** vt to

forge; (fig) to concoct // vi to harden.

fraile |'fraile| nm (REL) friar; (: monje) monk.

frambuesa |fram'bwesa| nf raspberry.

francés, esa |fran'θes, esa| a French // nm/f Frenchman/woman // nm (LING) French.

Francia |'franθja| nf France.

franco, a |'franko, a| a (cándido) frank, open; (COM: exento) free // nm (moneda) franc.

francotirador, a |frankotira'ðor, a| nm/f sniper.

franela |fra'nela| nf flannel.

franja |'franxa| nf fringe.

franquear |franke'ar| vt (camino) to clear; (carta, paquete postal) to frank, stamp; (obstáculo) to overcome.

franqueo |fran'keo| nm postage.

franqueza |fran'keθa| nf (candor) frankness.

frasco |'frasko| nm bottle, flask; ~ **al vacío** (vacuum) flask.

frase |'frase| nf sentence; ~ **hecha** set phrase; (pey) stock phrase.

fraude |'frauðe| nm (cualidad) dishonesty; (acto) fraud; **fraudulento, a** a fraudulent.

frazada |fra'saða| nf (AM) blanket.

frecuencia |fre'kwenθja| nf frequency; **con** ~ frequently, often.

fregadero |freɣa'ðero| nm (kitchen) sink.

fregar |fre'ɣar| vt (frotar) to scrub; (platos) to wash (up); (AM) to annoy.

fregona |fre'ɣona| nf (utensilio) mop; (pey: sirvienta) skivvy.

freír |fre'ir| vt to fry.

frenar |fre'nar| vt to brake; (fig) to check.

frenesí |frene'si| nm frenzy; **frenético, a** a frantic.

freno |'freno| nm (TEC, AUTO) brake; (de cabalgadura) bit; (fig) check.

frente |'frente| nm (ARQ, POL) front; (de objeto) front part // nf forehead, brow; ~ **a** in front of; (en situación opuesta de) opposite; **al** ~ **de** (fig) at the head of; **chocar de** ~ to crash head-on; **hacer** ~ **a** to face up to.

fresa |'fresa| nf (Esp) strawberry.

fresco, a |'fresko, a| a (nuevo) fresh; (frío) cool; (descarado) cheeky // nm (aire) fresh air; (ARTE) fresco; (AM: jugo) fruit drink // nm/f (fam): **ser un** ~ to have a nerve; **tomar el** ~ to get some fresh air; **frescura** nf freshness; (descaro) cheek, nerve; (calma) calmness.

frialdad |frial'dað| nf (gen) coldness; (indiferencia) indifference.

fricción |frik'θjon| nf (gen) friction; (acto) rub(bing); (MED) massage.

frigidez |frixi'ðeθ| nf frigidity.

frigorífico |friɣo'rifiko| nm refrigerator.

frijol |fri'xol| *nm* kidney bean.

frío, a *etc vb ver* **freír** // |'trio. a| *a* cold; (*indiferente*) indifferent // *nm* cold; indifference; **tener ~** to be cold.

frito, a |'frito. a| *a* fried; **me trae ~ ese hombre** I'm sick and tired of that man.

frívolo, a |'friβolo. a| *a* frivolous.

frontera |fron'tera| *nf* frontier; **fronterizo, a** *a* frontier *cpd*; (*contiguo*) bordering.

frontón |fron'ton| *nm* (*DEPORTE*: *cancha*) pelota court; (: *juego*) pelota.

frotar |fro'tar| *vt* to rub; **~se** *vr*: **~se las manos** to rub one's hands.

fructífero, a |fruk'tifero. a|~a fruitful.

frugal |fru'val| *a* frugal.

fruncir |frun'θir| *vt* to pucker; (*COSTURA*) to pleat; **~ el ceño** to knit one's brow.

frustrar |frus'trar| *vt* to frustrate.

fruta |'fruta| *nf* fruit; **frutería** *nf* fruit shop; **frutero, a** *a* fruit *cpd* // *nm/f* fruiterer // *nm* fruit bowl.

frutilla |fru'tiʎa| *nf* (*AM*) strawberry.

fue *vb ver* **ser, ir**.

fuego |'fweɣo| *nm* (*gen*) fire; **a ~ lento** on a low flame o gas; **¿tienes ~?** have you (got) a light?

fuente |'fwente| *nf* fountain; (*manantial*, *fig*) spring; (*origen*) source; (*plato*) large dish.

fuera *etc vb ver* **ser, ir** // |'fwera| *ad* out(side); (*en otra parte*) away; (*excepto, salvo*) except, save // *prep*: **~ de** outside; (*fig*) besides; **~ de sí** beside o.s.

fuerte |'fwerte| *a* strong; (*golpe*) hard; (*ruido*) loud; (*comida*) rich; (*lluvia*) heavy; (*dolor*) intense // *ad* strongly; hard; loud(ly).

fuerza *etc vb ver* **forzar** // |'fwerθa| *nf* (*fortaleza*) strength; (*TEC*, *ELEC*) power; (*coacción*) force; (*MIL*: *tb*: **~s**) forces *pl*; **a ~ de** by dint of; **cobrar ~s** to recover one's strength; **tener ~s para** to have the strength to; **a la ~** forcibly, by force; **por ~** of necessity.

fuga |'fuɣa| *nf* (*huida*) flight, escape; (*de gas etc*) leak.

fugarse |fu'ɣarse| *vr* to flee, escape.

fugaz |fu'ɣaθ| *a* fleeting.

fugitivo, a |fuxi'tiβo. a| *a*, *nm/f* fugitive.

fui *vb ver* **ser, ir**.

fulano, a |fu'lano. a| *nm/f* so-and-so, what's-his-name/what's-her-name.

fulgor |ful'ɣor| *nm* brilliance.

fumador, a |fuma'ðor. a| *nm/f* smoker.

fumar |fu'mar| *vt*, *vi* to smoke; **~se** *vr* (*disipar*) to squander; **~ en pipa** to smoke a pipe.

funambulista |funambu'lista| *nm/f* tight-rope walker.

función |fun'θjon| *nf* function; (*de puesto*) duties *pl*; (*espectáculo*) show; **entrar en funciones** to take up one's duties.

funcionar |funθjo'nar| *vi* (*gen*) to function; (*máquina*) to work; **'no funciona'** 'out of order'.

funcionario, a |funθjo'narjo. a| *nm/f* official; (*público*) civil servant.

funda |'funda| *nf* (*gen*) cover; (*de almohada*) pillowcase.

fundación |funda'θjon| *nf* foundation.

fundamental |fundamen'tal| *a* fundamental, basic.

fundamentar |fundamen'tar| *vt* (*poner base*) to lay the foundations of; (*establecer*) to found; (*fig*) to base; **fundamento** *nm* (*base*) foundation.

fundar |fun'dar| *vt* to found; **~se** *vr*: **~se en** to be founded on.

fundición |fundi'θjon| *nf* fusing; (*fábrica*) foundry.

fundir |fun'dir| *vt* (*gen*) to fuse; (*metal*) to smelt, melt down; (*nieve etc*) to melt; (*COM*) to merge; (*estatua*) to cast; **~se** *vr* (*colores etc*) to merge, blend; (*unirse*) to fuse together; (*ELEC*: *fusible*, *lámpara etc*) to fuse, blow; (*nieve etc*) to melt.

fúnebre |'funeβre| *a* funeral *cpd*, funereal.

funeral |fune'ral| *nm* funeral.

furgón |fur'ɣon| *nm* wagon; **furgoneta** *nf* (*AUTO*, *COM*) (transit) van (*Brit*), pick-up (truck) (*US*).

furia |'furja| *nf* (*ira*) fury; (*violencia*) violence; **furibundo, a** *a* furious; **furioso, a** *a* (*iracundo*) furious; (*violento*) violent; **furor** *nm* (*cólera*) rage.

furúnculo |fu'runkulo| *nm* boil.

fusible |fu'siβle| *nm* fuse.

fusil |fu'sil| *nm* rifle; **~ar** *vt* to shoot.

fusión |fu'sjon| *nf* (*gen*) melting; (*unión*) fusion; (*COM*) merger.

fusta |'fusta| *nf* (*látigo*) riding crop.

fútbol |'futβol| *nm* football; **futbolista** *nm* footballer.

fútil |'futil| *a* trifling; **futilidad** *nf* triviality.

futuro, a |fu'turo. a| *a*, *nm* future.

G

gabán |ga'βan| *nm* overcoat.

gabardina |gaβar'ðina| *nf* raincoat, gabardine.

gabinete |gaβi'nete| *nm* (*POL*) cabinet; (*estudio*) study; (*de abogados etc*) office.

gaceta |ga'θeta| *nf* gazette.

gachas |'gatʃas| *nfpl* porridge *sg*.

gafar |ga'far| *vt* to jinx.

gafas |'gafas| *nfpl* glasses; **~ de sol** sunglasses.

gafe |'gafe| *nm* jinx.

gaita |'gaita| *nf* bagpipes *pl*.

gajes |'gaxes| *nmpl*: **los ~ del oficio** occupational hazards.

gajo ['gaxo] nm (de naranja) segment.

gala ['gala] nf (traje de etiqueta) full dress; (fig: lo mejor) cream, flower; ~s nfpl finery sg; estar de ~ to be in one's best clothes; hacer ~ de to display, show off.

galán [ga'lan] nm lover; (Don Juan) ladies' man; (TEATRO): primer ~ leading man.

galante [ga'lante] a gallant; **galantear** vt (hacer la corte a) to court, woo; **galantería** nf (caballerosidad) gallantry; (cumplido) politeness; (comentario) compliment.

galápago [ga'lapaxo] nm (ZOOL) turtle.

galaxia [ga'laksja] nf galaxy.

galera [ga'lera] nf (nave) galley; (carro) wagon; (IMPRENTA) galley.

galería [gale'ria] nf (gen) gallery; (balcón) veranda(h); (pasillo) corridor.

Gales ['gales] nm (tb: País de ~) Wales; **galés, esa** a Welsh // nm/f Welshman/woman // nm (LING) Welsh.

galgo, a ['galvo, a] nm/f greyhound.

galimatías [galima'tias] nmpl (lenguaje) gibberish sg, nonsense sg.

galón [ga'lon] nm (MIL) stripe; (COSTURA) braid; (medida) gallon.

galopar [galo'par] vi to gallop.

gallardía [gaʎar'ðia] nf (galantería) dash; (valor) bravery; (elegancia) elegance.

gallego, a [ga'ʎevo, a] a, nm/f Galician.

galleta [ga'ʎeta] nf biscuit (Brit), cookie (US).

gallina [ga'ʎina] nf hen // nm/f (fam: cobarde) chicken.

gallo ['gaʎo] nm cock, rooster.

gama ['gama] nf (fig) range.

gamba ['gamba] nf prawn (Brit), shrimp (US).

gamberro, a [gam'berro, a] nm/f hooligan, lout.

gamuza [ga'muθa] nf chamois.

gana ['gana] nf (deseo) desire, wish; (apetito) appetite; (voluntad) will; (añoranza) longing; de buena ~ willingly; de mala ~ reluctantly; me da ~s de I feel like, I want to; no me da la ~ I don't feel like it; tener ~s de to feel like.

ganadería [ganaðe'ria] nf (ganado) livestock; (ganado vacuno) cattle pl; (cría, comercio) cattle raising.

ganado [ga'naðo] nm livestock; ~ lanar sheep pl; ~ mayor cattle pl; ~ porcino pigs pl.

ganador, a [gana'ðor, a] a winning // nm/f winner.

ganancia [ga'nanθja] nf (lo ganado) gain; (aumento) increase; (beneficio) profit; ~s nfpl (ingresos) earnings; (beneficios) profit sg, winnings.

ganar [ga'nar] vt (obtener) to get, obtain; (sacar ventaja) to gain; (salario etc) to earn; (DEPORTE, premio) to win; (de-rrotar a) to beat; (alcanzar) to reach // vi (DEPORTE) to win; ~se vr: ~se la vida to earn one's living.

gancho ['gantʃo] nm (gen) hook; (colgador) hanger.

gandul, a [gan'dul, a] a, nm/f good-for-nothing, layabout.

ganga ['ganga] nf (cosa buena y barata) bargain; (buena situación) cushy job.

gangrena [gan'grena] nf gangrene.

gansada [gan'saða] nf (fam) stupid thing to do.

ganso, a ['ganso, a] nm/f (ZOOL) goose; (fam) idiot.

ganzúa [gan'θua] nf skeleton key.

garabatear [garaβate'ar] vi, vt (al escribir) to scribble, scrawl.

garabato [gara'βato] nm (escritura) scrawl, scribble.

garaje [ga'raxe] nm garage.

garante [ga'rante] a responsible // nm/f guarantor.

garantía [garan'tia] nf guarantee.

garantizar [garanti'θar] vt (hacerse responsable de) to vouch for; (asegurar) to guarantee.

garbanzo [gar'βanθo] nm chickpea (Brit), garbanzo (US).

garbo ['garβo] nm grace, elegance.

garfio ['garfjo] nm grappling iron.

garganta [gar'vanta] nf (ANAT) throat; (de botella) neck; **gargantilla** nf necklace.

gárgaras ['garvaras] nfpl: hacer ~ to gargle.

garita [ga'rita] nf cabin, hut; (MIL) sentry box.

garito [ga'rito] nm (lugar) gambling house o den.

garra ['garra] nf (de gato, TEC) claw; (de ave) talon; (fam) hand, paw.

garrafa [ga'rrafa] nf carafe, decanter.

garrapata [garra'pata] nf tick.

garrapatear [garrapate'ar] vi, vt = **garabatear**.

garrote [ga'rrote] nm (palo) stick; (porra) cudgel; (suplicio) garrotte.

garúa [ga'rua] nf (AM) drizzle.

garza ['garθa] nf heron.

gas [gas] nm gas.

gasa ['gasa] nf gauze.

gaseoso, a [gase'oso, a] a gassy, fizzy // nf lemonade, pop (Brit).

gasfitero [gasfi'tero] nm (AM) plumber.

gasoil [ga'soil], **gasóleo** [ga'soleo] nm diesel (oil).

gasolina [gaso'lina] nf petrol, gas(oline) (US); **gasolinera** nf petrol (Brit) o gas (US) station.

gastado, a [gas'taðo, a] a (rendido) spent; (raído) worn out; (usado: frase etc) trite.

gastar [gas'tar] vt (dinero, tiempo) to spend; (fuerzas) to use up; (desperdiciar) to waste; (llevar) to wear; ~se *vr* to wear out; (*estropearse*) to waste; ~ bromas to crack jokes; ¿qué número gastas? what size (shoe) do you take?

gasto ['gasto] *nm* (*desembolso*) expenditure, spending; (*consumo, uso*) use; ~s *nmpl* (*desembolsos*) expenses; (*cargos*) charges, costs.

gatear [gate'ar] *vi* (*andar a gatas*) to go on all fours.

gatillo [ga'tiʎo] *nm* (*de arma de fuego*) trigger; (*de dentista*) forceps.

gato, a ['gato, a] *nm/f* cat // *nm* (*TEC*) jack; andar a gatas to go on all fours.

gaveta [ga'ßeta] *nf* drawer.

gaviota [ga'ßjota] *nf* seagull.

gay [ge] *a inv, nm* gay, homosexual.

gazapo [ga'θapo] *nm* young rabbit.

gazpacho [gaθ'patʃo] *nm* gazpacho.

gelatina [xela'tina] *nf* jelly; (*polvos etc*) gelatine.

gema ['xema] *nf* gem.

gemelo, a [xe'melo, a] *a, nm/f* twin; ~s *nmpl* (*de camisa*) cufflinks; ~s de campo field glasses, binoculars.

Géminis ['xeminis] *nm* Gemini.

gemido [xe'miðo] *nm* (*quejido*) moan, groan; (*aullido*) howl.

gemir [xe'mir] *vi* (*quejarse*) to moan, groan; (*aullar*) to howl.

generación [xenera'θjon] *nf* generation.

general [xene'ral] *a* general // *nm* general; por lo o en ~ in general; G~itat *nf* Catalan parliament; ~izar *vt* to generalize; ~izarse *vr* to become generalized, spread; ~mente *ad* generally.

generar [xene'rar] *vt* to generate.

género ['xenero] *nm* (*clase*) kind, sort; (*tipo*) type; (*BIO*) genus; (*LING*) gender; (*COM*) material; ~ humano human race.

generosidad [xenerosi'ðað] *nf* generosity; **generoso, a** *a* generous.

genial [xe'njal] *a* inspired; (*idea*) brilliant; (*afable*) genial.

genio ['xenjo] *nm* (*carácter*) nature, disposition; (*humor*) temper; (*facultad creadora*) genius; de mal ~ bad-tempered.

genitales [xeni'tales] *nmpl* genitals.

gente ['xente] *nf* (*personas*) people *pl*; (*raza*) race; (*nación*) nation; (*parientes*) relatives *pl*.

gentil [xen'til] *a* (*elegante*) graceful; (*encantador*) charming; ~eza *nf* grace; charm; (*cortesía*) courtesy.

gentío [xen'tio] *nm* crowd, throng.

genuino, a [xe'nwino, a] *a* genuine.

geografía [xeoɣra'fia] *nf* geography.

geología [xeolo'xia] *nf* geology.

geometría [xeome'tria] *nf* geometry.

gerencia [xe'renθja] *nf* management; **gerente** *nm/f* (*supervisor*) manager; (*jefe*) director.

geriatría [xeria'tria] *nf* (*MED*) geriatrics *sg.*

germen ['xermen] *nm* germ.

germinar [xermi'nar] *vi* to germinate.

gesticulación [xestikula'θjon] *nf* gesticulation; (*mueca*) grimace.

gestión [xes'tjon] *nf* management; (*diligencia, acción*) negotiation; **gestionar** *vt* (*lograr*) to try to arrange; (*llevar*) to manage.

gesto ['xesto] *nm* (*mueca*) grimace; (*ademán*) gesture.

Gibraltar [xißral'tar] *nm* Gibraltar; **gibraltareño, a** *a, nm/f* Gibraltarian.

gigante [xi'ɣante] *a, nm/f* giant.

gilipollas [xili'poʎas] (*col*) *a inv* daft // *nm/f inv* wally.

gimnasia [xim'nasja] *nf* gymnastics *pl*; **gimnasio** *nm* gymnasium; **gimnasta** *nm/f* gymnast.

gimotear [ximote'ar] *vi* to whine, whimper.

ginebra [xi'neßra] *nf* gin.

ginecólogo, a [xine'koloɣo, a] *nm/f* gynaecologist.

gira ['xira] *nf* tour, trip.

girar [xi'rar] *vt* (*dar la vuelta*) to turn (around); (: *rápidamente*) to spin; (*COM: giro postal*) to draw; (*comerciar: letra de cambio*) to issue // *vi* to turn (round); (*rápido*) to spin; (*COM*) to draw.

girasol [xira'sol] *nm* sunflower.

giratorio, a [xira'torjo, a] *a* (*gen*) revolving; (*puente*) swing.

giro ['xiro] *nm* (*movimiento*) turn, revolution; (*LING*) expression; (*COM*) draft; ~ bancario/postal bank giro/postal order.

gis [xis] *nm* (*AM*) chalk.

gitano, a [xi'tano, a] *a, nm/f* gypsy.

glacial [gla'θjal] *a* icy, freezing.

glaciar [gla'θjar] *nm* glacier.

glándula ['glandula] *nf* gland.

globo ['gloßo] *nm* (*esfera*) globe, sphere; (*aerostato, juguete*) balloon.

glóbulo ['gloßulo] *nm* globule; (*ANAT*) corpuscle.

gloria ['glorja] *nf* glory.

glorieta [glo'rjeta] *nf* (*de jardín*) bower, arbour; (*plazoleta*) roundabout (*Brit*), traffic circle (*US*).

glorificar [glorifi'kar] *vt* (*enaltecer*) to glorify, praise.

glorioso, a [glo'rjoso, a] *a* glorious.

glosa ['glosa] *nf* comment; **glosar** *vt* (*comentar*) to comment on.

glosario [glo'sarjo] *nm* glossary.

glotón, ona [glo'ton, ona] *a* gluttonous, greedy // *nm/f* glutton.

gobernación [goßerna'θjon] *nf* government, governing; G~ (*AM ADMIN*) Ministry of the Interior; **gobernador, a** *a* governing // *nm/f* governor; **gobernante** *a* governing.

gobernar [goßer'nar] *vt* (*dirigir*) to guide, direct; (*POL*) to rule, govern // *vi* to govern; (*NAUT*) to steer.

gobierno *etc vb ver* **gobernar** // [go'βjerno] *nm* (*POL*) government; (*dirección*) guidance, direction; (*NAUT*) steering.

goce *etc vb ver* **gozar** // ['goθe] *nm* enjoyment.

gol [gol] *nm* goal.

golf [golf] *nm* golf.

golfo, a ['golfo, a] *nm* (*GEO*) gulf // *nm/f* (*fam: niño*) urchin; (*gamberro*) lout // *nf* (*fam: mujer*) slut, whore.

golondrina [golon'drina] *nf* swallow.

golosina [golo'sina] *nf* titbit; (*dulce*) sweet; **goloso, a** *a* sweet-toothed.

golpe ['golpe] *nm* blow; (*de puño*) punch; (*de mano*) smack; (*de remo*) stroke; (*fig: choque*) clash; **no dar ~** to be bone idle; **de un ~** with one blow; **de ~ suddenly**; **~ (de estado)** coup (d'état); **golpear** *vt, vi* to strike, knock; (*asestar*) to beat; (*de puño*) to punch; (*golpetear*) to tap.

goma ['goma] *nf* (*caucho*) rubber; (*elástico*) elastic; (*una ~*) elastic band; **~ espuma** foam rubber; **~ de pegar** gum, glue.

gordo, a ['gorðo, a] *a* (*gen*) fat; (*persona*) plump; (*fam*) enormous; **el (premio) ~** (*en lotería*) first prize; **gordura** *nf* fat; (*corpulencia*) fatness, stoutness.

gorila [go'rila] *nm* gorilla.

gorjear [gorxe'ar] *vi* to twitter, chirp.

gorra ['gorra] *nf* cap; (*de niño*) bonnet; (*militar*) bearskin; **entrar de ~** (*fam*) to gatecrash; **ir de ~** to sponge.

gorrión [go'rrjon] *nm* sparrow.

gorro ['gorro] *nm* (*gen*) cap; (*de niño, mujer*) bonnet.

gorrón, ona [go'rron, ona] *nm/f* scrounger.

gota ['gota] *nf* (*gen*) drop; (*de sudor*) bead; (*MED*) gout; **gotear** *vi* to drip; (*lloviznar*) to drizzle; **gotera** *nf* leak.

gozar [go'θar] *vi* to enjoy o.s.; **~ de** (*disfrutar*) to enjoy; (*poseer*) to possess.

gozne ['goθne] *nm* hinge.

gozo ['goθo] *nm* (*alegría*) joy; (*placer*) pleasure.

gr. *abr* (= *gramo, gramos*) g.

grabación [graβa'θjon] *nf* recording.

grabado [gra'βaðo] *nm* print, engraving.

grabadora [graβa'ðora] *nf* tape-recorder.

grabar [gra'βar] *vt* to engrave; (*discos, cintas*) to record.

gracia ['graðja] *nf* (*encanto*) grace, gracefulness; (*humor*) humour, wit; **¡(muchas) ~s!** thanks (very much)!; **~s a** thanks to; **tener ~** (*chiste etc*) to be funny; **no me hace ~** I am not keen; **gracioso, a** *a* (*divertido*) funny, amusing; (*cómico*) comical // *nm/f* (*TEATRO*) comic character.

grada ['graða] *nf* (*de escalera*) step; (*de anfiteatro*) tier, row; **~s** *nfpl* (*DEPORTE:*

de estadio) terraces.

gradación [graða'θjon] *nf* gradation.

gradería [graðe'ria] *nf* (*gradas*) (flight of) steps *pl*; (*de anfiteatro*) tiers *pl*, rows *pl*; (*DEPORTE: de estadio*) terraces *pl*; **~ cubierta** covered stand.

grado ['graðo] *nm* degree; (*de aceite, vino*) grade; (*grada*) step; (*MIL*) rank; **de buen ~** willingly.

graduación [graðwa'θjon] *nf* (*del alcohol*) proof, strength; (*ESCOL*) graduation; (*MIL*) rank.

gradual [gra'ðwal] *a* gradual.

graduar [gra'ðwar] *vt* (*gen*) to graduate; (*MIL*) to commission; **~se** *vr* to graduate; **~se la vista** to have one's eyes tested.

gráfico, a ['grafiko, a] *a* graphic // *nm* diagram // *nf* graph; **~s** *nmpl* (*INFORM*) graphics.

grajo ['graxo] *nm* rook.

Gral *abr* (= *General*) Gen.

gramática [gra'matika] *nf* grammar.

gramo ['gramo] *nm* gramme (*Brit*), gram (*US*).

gran [gran] *a ver* **grande**.

grana ['grana] *nf* (*BOT*) seedling; (*color, tela*) scarlet.

granada [gra'naða] *nf* pomegranate; (*MIL*) grenade.

Gran Bretaña [-bre'taɲa] *nf* Great Britain.

grande ['grande] (*antes de nmsg:* **gran**) *a* (*de tamaño*) big, large; (*alto*) tall; (*distinguido*) great; (*impresionante*) grand // *nm* grandee; **grandeza** *nf* greatness.

grandioso, a [gran'djoso, a] *a* magnificent, grand.

granel [gra'nel]: **a ~** *ad* (*COM*) in bulk.

granero [gra'nero] *nm* granary, barn.

granito [gra'nito] *nm* (*AGR*) small grain; (*roca*) granite.

granizado [grani'θaðo] *nm* iced drink.

granizar [grani'θar] *vi* to hail; **granizo** *nm* hail.

granja ['granxa] *nf* (*gen*) farm; **granjero, a** *nm/f* farmer.

grano ['grano] *nm* grain; (*semilla*) seed; (*baya*) berry; (*MED*) pimple, spot; **~s** *nmpl* cereals.

granuja [gra'nuxa] *nm/f* rogue; (*golfillo*) urchin.

grapa ['grapa] *nf* staple; (*TEC*) clamp.

grasa ['grasa] *nf* (*gen*) grease; (*de cocina*) fat, lard; (*sebo*) suet; (*mugre*) filth; **grasiento, a** *a* greasy; (*de aceite*) oily.

gratificación [gratifika'θjon] *nf* (*propina*) tip; (*bono*) bonus; (*recompensa*) reward; **gratificar** *vt* to tip; to reward.

gratis ['gratis] *ad* free.

gratitud [grati'tuð] *nf* gratitude.

grato, a ['grato, a] *a* (*agradable*) pleasant, agreeable; (*bienvenido*) welcome.

gratuito, a [gra'twito, a] a (gratis) free; (sin razón) gratuitous.

gravamen [gra'βamen] nm (carga) burden; (impuesto) tax.

gravar [gra'βar] vt to burden; (COM) to tax.

grave ['graβe] a heavy; (serio) grave, serious; ~**dad** nf gravity.

gravilla [gra'βiʎa] nf gravel.

gravitar [graβi'tar] vi to gravitate; ~ sobre to rest on.

gravoso, a [gra'βoso, a] a (pesado) burdensome; (costoso) costly.

graznar [graθ'nar] vi (cuervo) to squawk; (pato) to quack; (hablar ronco) to croak.

Grecia ['greθja] nf Greece.

gremio ['gremjo] nm (asociación) trade, industry.

greña ['greɲa] nf (cabellos) shock of hair; (maraña) tangle.

gresca ['greska] nf uproar.

griego, a ['grjevo, a] a, nm/f Greek.

grieta ['grjeta] nf crack.

grifo ['grifo] nm tap; (AM AUTO) petrol (Brit) o gas (US) station.

grilletes [gri'ʎetes] nmpl fetters.

grillo ['griʎo] nm (ZOOL) cricket; (BOT) shoot.

gripe ['gripe] nf flu, influenza.

gris [gris] a (color) grey.

gritar [gri'tar] vt, vi to shout, yell; **grito** nm shout, yell; (de horror) scream.

grosella [gro'seʎa] nf (red)currant; ~ negra blackcurrant.

grosería [grose'ria] nf (actitud) rudeness; (comentario) vulgar comment; **grosero, a** a (poco cortés) rude, bad-mannered; (ordinario) vulgar, crude.

grosor [gro'sor] nm thickness.

grúa ['grua] nf (TEC) crane; (de petróleo) derrick.

grueso, a ['grweso, a] a thick; (persona) stout // nm bulk; el ~ de the bulk of.

grulla ['gruʎa] nf crane.

grumo ['grumo] nm clot, lump.

gruñido [gru'ɲiðo] nm grunt; (fig) grumble; **gruñir** vi (animal) to growl; (fam) to grumble.

grupa ['grupa] nf (ZOOL) rump.

grupo ['grupo] nm group; (TEC) unit, set.

gruta ['gruta] nf grotto.

guadaña [gwa'ðaɲa] nf scythe.

guagua ['gwa'ɣwa] nf (AM: niño) baby; (: bus) bus.

guante ['gwante] nm glove.

guapo, a ['gwapo, a] a good-looking, attractive; (hombre) handsome; (elegante) smart.

guarda ['gwarða] nm/f (persona) guard, keeper // nf (acto) guarding; (custodia) custody; ~**bosques** nm inv gamekeeper; ~**costas** nm inv coastguard vessel; ~**dor, a** a protective // nm/f guardian, protector; ~**espaldas** nm/f inv bodyguard; ~**meta** nm/f goalkeeper; ~**polvo** nm dust cover; (prenda de vestir) overalls pl; **guardar** vt (gen) to keep; (vigilar) to guard, watch over; (dinero: ahorrar) to save; ~ cama to stay in bed; **guardarse** vr (preservarse) to protect o.s.; (evitar) to avoid; **guardarropa** nm (armario) wardrobe; (en establecimiento público) cloakroom.

guardería [gwarðe'ria] nf nursery.

guardia ['gwarðja] nf (MIL) guard; (cuidado) care, custody // nm/f guard; (policía) policeman/woman; estar de ~ to be on guard; montar ~ to mount guard; **G~ Civil** Civil Guard; **G~ Nacional** National Guard.

guardián, ana [gwar'ðjan, ana] nm/f (gen) guardian, keeper.

guardilla [gwar'ðiʎa] nf attic.

guarecer [gware'θer] vt (proteger) to protect; (abrigar) to shelter; ~**se** vr to take refuge.

guarida [gwa'riða] nf (de animal) den, lair; (refugio) refuge.

guarnecer [gwarne'θer] vt (equipar) to provide; (adornar) to adorn; (TEC) to reinforce; **guarnición** nf (de vestimenta) trimming; (de piedra) mount; (CULIN) garnish; (arneses) harness; (MIL) garrison.

guarro, a ['gwarro, a] nm/f pig.

guasa ['gwasa] nf joke; **guasón, ona** a witty; (bromista) joking // nm/f wit; joker.

Guatemala [gwate'mala] nf Guatemala.

gubernativo, a [guβerna'tiβo, a] a governmental.

guerra ['gerra] nf war; (pelea) struggle; ~ civil civil war; ~ fría cold war; dar ~ to annoy; **guerrear** vi to wage war; **guerrero, a** a fighting; (carácter) warlike // nm/f warrior.

guerrilla [ge'rriʎa] nf guerrilla warfare; (tropas) guerrilla band o group.

guía etc vb ver **guiar** // ['gia] nm/f (persona) guide // nf (libro) guidebook; ~ de ferrocarriles railway timetable; ~ telefónica telephone directory.

guiar [gi'ar] vt to guide, direct; (AUTO) to steer; ~**se** vr: ~**se por** to be guided by.

guijarro [gi'xarro] nm pebble.

guinda ['ginda] nf morello cherry.

guindilla [gin'diʎa] nf chilli pepper.

guiñapo [gi'ɲapo] nm (harapo) rag; (persona) reprobate, rogue.

guiñar [gi'ɲar] vt to wink.

guión [gi'on] nm (LING) hyphen, dash; (CINE) script; **guionista** nm/f scriptwriter.

guirnalda [gir'nalda] nf garland.

guisa ['gisa] nf: a ~ de as, like.

guisado [gi'saðo] nm stew.

guisante [gi'sante] nm pea.

guisar [gi'sar] *vt, vi* to cook; **guiso** *nm* cooked dish.

guitarra [gi'tarra] *nf* guitar.

gula ['gula] *nf* gluttony, greed.

gusano [gu'sano] *nm* maggot; (*lombriz*) earthworm.

gustar [gus'tar] *vt* to taste, sample // *vi* to please, be pleasing; ~ **de algo** to like *o* enjoy sth; **me gustan las uvas** I like grapes; **le gusta nadar** she likes *o* enjoys swimming.

gusto ['gusto] *nm* (*sentido, sabor*) taste; (*placer*) pleasure; **tiene** *a* ~ **menta** it tastes of mint; **tener buen** ~ to have good taste; **sentirse a** ~ to feel at ease; **mucho** ~ (**en conocerle**) pleased to meet you; **el** ~ **es mío** the pleasure is mine; **con** ~ willingly, gladly; **~so, a** *a* (*sabroso*) tasty; (*agradable*) pleasant.

gutural [gutu'ral] *a* guttural.

H

ha *vb ver* **haber**.

haba ['aβa] *nf* bean.

Habana [a'βana] *nf*: **la** ~ Havana.

habano [a'βano] *nm* Havana cigar.

habéis *vb ver* **haber**.

haber [a'βer] ♦ *vb auxiliar* **1** (*tiempos compuestos*) to have; **he/había comido** I have/had eaten; **antes/después de** ~**lo visto** before seeing/after seeing *o* having seen it

2: **¡lo dicho antes!** you should have said so before!

3: ~ **de**: **he de hacerlo** I have to do it; **ha de llegar mañana** it should arrive tomorrow

♦ *vb impersonal* **1** (*existencia: sg*) there is; (*: pl*) there are; **hay un hermano/dos hermanos** there is one brother/there are two brothers; **¿cuánto hay de aquí a Sucre?** how far is it from here to Sucre?

2 (*obligación*): **hay que hacer algo** something must be done; **hay que apuntarlo para acordarse** you have to write it down to remember

3: **¡hay que ver!** well I never!

4: **¡no hay de** *o* **por** (*AM*) **qué!** don't mention it!, not at all!

5: **¿qué hay?** (*¿qué pasa?*) what's up?, what's the matter?; (*¿qué tal?*) how's it going?

♦ *vr*: **habérselas con** uno to have it out with sb

♦ *vt*: **he aquí unas sugerencias** here are some suggestions; **no hay cintas blancas pero sí las hay rojas** there aren't any white ribbons but there are some red ones

♦ *nm* (*en cuenta*) credit side; **~es** *nmpl* assets; **¿cuánto tengo en el** ~? how much do I have in my account?; **tiene varias novelas en su** ~ he has several

novels to his credit.

habichuela [aβi'tʃwela] *nf* kidney bean.

hábil ['aβil] *a* (*listo*) clever, smart; (*capaz*) fit, capable; (*experto*) expert; **día** ~ working day; **habilidad** *nf* (*gen*) skill, ability; (*inteligencia*) cleverness.

habilitar [aβili'tar] *vt* (*capacitar*) to enable; (*dar instrumentos*) to equip; (*financiar*) to finance.

hábilmente [aβil'mente] *ad* skilfully, expertly.

habitación [aβita'θjon] *nf* (*cuarto*) room; (*casa*) dwelling, abode; (*BIO: morada*) habitat; ~ **sencilla** *o* **individual** single room; ~ **doble** *o* **de matrimonio** double room.

habitante [aβi'tante] *nm/f* inhabitant.

habitar [aβi'tar] *vt* (*residir en*) to inhabit; (*ocupar*) to occupy // *vi* to live.

hábito ['aβito] *nm* habit.

habituar [aβi'twar] *vt* to accustom; **~se** *vr*: **~se a** to get used to.

habla ['aβla] *nf* (*capacidad de hablar*) speech; (*idioma*) language; (*dialecto*) dialect; **perder el** ~ to become speechless; **de** ~ **francesa** French-speaking; **estar al** ~ to be in contact; (*TEL*) to be on the line; **¡González al** ~! (*TEL*) González speaking!

hablador, a [aβla'ðor, a] *a* talkative // *nm/f* chatterbox.

habladuría [aβlaðu'ria] *nf* rumour; **~s** *nfpl* gossip *sg*.

hablante [a'βlante] *a* speaking // *nm/f* speaker.

hablar [a'βlar] *vt* to speak, talk // *vi* to speak; **~se** *vr* to speak to each other; ~ **con** to speak to; ~ **de** to speak of *o* about; '**se habla inglés**' 'English spoken here'.

habré *etc vb ver* **haber**.

hacedor, a [aθe'ðor, a] *nm/f* maker.

hacendado [asen'daðo] *nm* (*AM*) large landowner.

hacendoso, a [aθen'doso, a] *a* industrious.

hacer [a'θer] ♦ *vt* **1** (*fabricar, producir*) to make; (*construir*) to build; ~ **una película/un ruido** to make a film/noise; **el guisado lo hice yo** I made *o* cooked the stew

2 (*ejecutar: trabajo etc*) to do; ~ **la colada** to do the washing; ~ **la comida** to do the cooking; **¿qué haces?** what are you doing?; ~ **el malo** *o* **el papel del malo** (*TEATRO*) to play the villain

3 (*estudios, algunos deportes*) to do; ~ **español/económicas** to do *o* study Spanish/Economics; ~ **yoga/gimnasia** to do yoga/go to gym

4 (*transformar, incidir en*): **esto lo hará más difícil** this will make it more difficult; **salir te hará sentir mejor** going out will make you feel better

5 (*cálculo*): **2 y 2 hacen 4** 2 and 2 make

4; **éste hace 100** this one makes 100
6 (+ *subjun*): **esto hará que ganemos**
this will make us win; **harás que no
quiera venir** you'll stop him wanting to
come
7 (*como sustituto de vb*) to do; **él bebió
y yo hice lo mismo** he drank and I did
likewise
8: no hace más que criticar all he does
is criticize
♦ *vb semi-auxiliar*: ~ + *infinitivo* **1** (*directo*): **les hice venir** I made o had them
come; ~ **trabajar a los demás** to get
others to work
2 (*por intermedio de otros*): ~ **reparar
algo** to get sth repaired
♦ *vi* **1: haz como que no lo sabes** act as
if you don't know
2 (*ser apropiado*): **si os hace** if it's
alright with you
3: ~ **de:** ~ **de madre para uno** to be like
a mother to sb; (*TEATRO*): ~ **de Otelo** to
play Othello
♦ *vb impersonal* **1: hace calor/frío** it's
hot/cold; *ver tb* **bueno, sol, tiempo**
2 (*tiempo*): **hace 3 años** 3 years ago;
hace un mes que voy/no voy I've been
going/I haven't been for a month
3: **¿cómo has hecho para llegar tan
rápido?** how did you manage to get here
so quickly?
♦ *vr* **1** (*volverse*) to become; **se hicieron
amigos** they became friends
2 (*acostumbrarse*): ~**se a** to get used to
3: se hace con huevos y leche it's made
out of eggs and milk; **eso no se hace**
that's not done
4 (*obtener*): ~**se de** o **con algo** to get
hold of sth
5 (*fingirse*): ~**se el sueco** to turn a deaf
ear.
hacia [ˈaθja] *prep* (*en dirección de*)
towards; (*cerca de*) near; (*actitud*)
towards; ~ **arriba/abajo** up(wards)/
down(wards); ~ **mediodía** about noon.
hacienda [aˈθjenda] *nf* (*propiedad*)
property; (*finca*) farm; (*AM*) ranch; ~
pública public finance; (**Ministerio de**)
H~ Exchequer (*Brit*), Treasury Department (*US*).
hacha [ˈatʃa] *nf* axe; (*antorcha*) torch.
hada [ˈaða] *nf* fairy.
hago *etc vb ver* **hacer.**
Haití [aiˈti] *nm* Haiti.
halagar [alaˈɣar] *vt* (*lisonjear*) to flatter.
halago [aˈlaɣo] *nm* (*adulación*) flattery;
halagüeño, a *a* flattering.
halcón [alˈkon] *nm* falcon, hawk.
hálito [ˈalito] *nm* breath.
halterofilia [alteroˈfilja] *nf* weightlifting.
hallar [aˈʎar] *vt* (*gen*) to find; (*descubrir*)
to discover; (*toparse con*) to run into;
~**se** *vr* to be (situated); **hallazgo** *nm*
discovery; (*cosa*) find.
hamaca [aˈmaka] *nf* hammock.

hambre [ˈambre] *nf* hunger; (*carencia*)
famine; (*fig*) longing; **tener** ~ **to be
hungry; hambriento, a** *a* hungry,
starving.
hamburguesa [amburˈɣesa] *nf*
hamburger.
hampón [amˈpon] *nm* thug.
han *vb ver* **haber.**
haragán, ana [araˈɣan, ana] *a, nm/f*
good-for-nothing.
harapiento, a [araˈpjento, a] *a* tattered,
in rags; **harapo** *nm* rag.
haré *etc vb ver* **hacer.**
harina [aˈrina] *nf* flour.
hartar [arˈtar] *vt* to satiate, glut; (*fig*) to
tire, sicken; ~**se** *vr* (*de comida*) to fill
o.s., gorge o.s.; (*cansarse*) to get fed up
(*de* with); **hartazgo** *nm* surfeit, glut;
harto, a *a* (*lleno*) full; (*cansado*) fed up
// *ad* (*bastante*) enough; (*muy*) very;
estar harto de to be fed up with;
hartura *nf* (*exceso*) surfeit;
(*abundancia*) abundance; (*satisfacción*)
satisfaction.
has *vb ver* **haber.**
hasta [ˈasta] *ad* even // *prep* (*alcanzando
a*) as far as, up to, down to; (*de tiempo*)
a tal hora) till, until; (*antes de*) before //
conj: ~ **que** until; ~ **luego/el sábado** see
you soon/on Saturday.
hastiar [asˈtjar] *vt* (*gen*) to weary;
(*aburrir*) to bore; ~**se** *vr*: ~**se de** to get
fed up with; **hastío** *nm* weariness; bore-
dom.
hatillo [aˈtiʎo] *nm* belongings *pl*, kit;
(*montón*) bundle, heap.
hay *vb ver* **haber.**
Haya [ˈaja] *nf*: **la** ~ The Hague.
haya *etc vb ver* **haber** // [ˈaja] *nf* beech
tree.
haz *vb ver* **hacer** // [aθ] *nm* bundle,
bunch; (*rayo: de luz*) beam.
hazaña [aˈθaɲa] *nf* feat, exploit.
hazmerreír [aθmerreˈir] *nm inv* laughing
stock.
he *vb ver* **haber.**
hebilla [eˈβiʎa] *nf* buckle, clasp.
hebra [ˈeβra] *nf* thread; (*BOT: fibra*)
fibre, grain.
hebreo, a [eˈβreo, a] *a, nm/f* Hebrew //
nm (*LING*) Hebrew.
hectárea [ekˈtarea] *nf* hectare.
hechizar [etʃiˈθar] *vt* to cast a spell on,
bewitch.
hechizo [eˈtʃiθo] *nm* witchcraft, magic;
(*acto de magía*) spell, charm.
hecho, a *pp de* **hacer** // [ˈetʃo, a] *a*
complete; (*maduro*) mature; (*COSTURA*)
ready-to-wear // *nm* deed, act; (*dato*)
fact; (*cuestión*) matter; (*suceso*) event //
excl agreed!, done!; **¡bien** ~! well
done!; **de** ~ in fact, as a matter of fact.
hechura [eˈtʃura] *nf* making, creation;
(*producto*) product; (*forma*) form,
shape; (*de persona*) build; (*TEC*)

craftsmanship.

heder [e'ðer] *vi* to stink, smell; (*fig*) to be unbearable.

hediondo, a [e'ðjondo, a] *a* stinking.

hedor [e'ðor] *nm* stench.

heladera [ela'ðera] *nf* (*AM*: *refrigerador*) refrigerator.

helado, a [e'laðo, a] *a* frozen; (*glacial*) icy; (*fig*) chilly, cold // *nm* ice cream // *nf* frost.

helar [e'lar] *vt* to freeze, ice (up); (*dejar atónito*) to amaze; (*desalentar*) to discourage // *vi*, ~**se** *vr* to freeze.

helecho [e'letʃo] *nm* fern.

hélice [ˈeliθe] *nf* spiral; (*TEC*) propeller.

helicóptero [eli'koptero] *nm* helicopter.

hembra [ˈembra] *nf* (*BOT*, *ZOOL*) female; (*mujer*) woman; (*TEC*) nut.

hemorroides [emo'rroiðes] *nfpl* haemorrhoids, piles.

hemos *vb ver* **haber**.

hendidura [endi'ðura] *nf* crack, split; (*GEO*) fissure.

heno [ˈeno] *nm* hay.

herbicida [erβi'θiða] *nm* weedkiller.

heredad [ere'ðað] *nf* landed property; (*granja*) farm.

heredar [ere'ðar] *vt* to inherit; **heredero, a** *nm/f* heir/heiress.

hereje [e'rexe] *nm/f* heretic.

herencia [e'renθja] *nf* inheritance.

herido, a [e'riðo, a] *a* injured, wounded // *nm/f* casualty // *nf* wound, injury.

herir [e'rir] *vt* to wound, injure; (*fig*) to offend.

hermanastro, a [erma'nastro, a] *nm/f* stepbrother/sister.

hermandad [erman'dað] *nf* brotherhood.

hermano, a [er'mano, a] *nm/f* brother/sister; ~ **gemelo** twin brother; ~ **político** brother-in-law; **hermana política** sister-in-law.

hermético, a [er'metiko, a] *a* hermetic; (*fig*) watertight.

hermoso, a [er'moso, a] *a* beautiful, lovely; (*estupendo*) splendid; (*guapo*) handsome; **hermosura** *nf* beauty.

héroe [ˈeroe] *nm* hero.

heroína [ero'ina] *nf* (*mujer*) heroine; (*droga*) heroin.

heroísmo [ero'ismo] *nm* heroism.

herradura [erra'ðura] *nf* horseshoe.

herramienta [erra'mjenta] *nf* tool.

herrería [erre'ria] *nf* smithy; (*TEC*) forge; **herrero** *nm* blacksmith.

herrumbre [e'rrumbre] *nf* rust.

hervidero [erβi'ðero] *nm* (*fig*) swarm; (*POL etc*) hotbed.

hervir [er'βir] *vi* to boil; (*burbujear*) to bubble; (*fig*): ~ **de** to teem with; ~ **a fuego lento** to simmer; **hervor** *nm* boiling; (*fig*) ardour, fervour.

heterosexual [eterosek'swal] *a* heterosexual.

hice *etc vb ver* **hacer**.

hidratante [iðra'tante] *a*: **crema** ~ moisturizing cream, moisturizer.

hidráulico, a [i'ðrauliko, a] *a* hydraulic // *nf* hydraulics *sg*.

hidro... [iðro] *pref* hydro..., water-...; ~**eléctrico, a** *a* hydroelectric; ~**fobia** *nf* hydrophobia, rabies; **hidrógeno** *nm* hydrogen.

hiedra [ˈjeðra] *nf* ivy.

hiel [jel] *nf* gall, bile; (*fig*) bitterness.

hiela *etc vb ver* **helar**.

hielo [ˈjelo] *nm* (*gen*) ice; (*escarcha*) frost; (*fig*) coldness, reserve.

hiena [ˈjena] *nf* hyena.

hierba [ˈjerβa] *nf* (*pasto*) grass; (*CULIN*, *MED*: *planta*) herb; **mala** ~ weed; (*fig*) evil influence; ~**buena** *nf* mint.

hierro [ˈjerro] *nm* (*metal*) iron; (*objeto*) iron object.

hígado [ˈiɣaðo] *nm* liver.

higiene [i'xjene] *nf* hygiene; **higiénico, a** *a* hygienic.

higo [ˈiɣo] *nm* fig; **higuera** *nf* fig tree.

hijastro, a [i'xastro, a] *nm/f* stepson/daughter.

hijo, a [ˈixo, a] *nm/f* son/daughter, child; ~**s** *nmpl* children, sons and daughters; ~ **de papá/mamá** daddy's/mummy's boy; ~ **de puta** (*fam!*) bastard (!), son of a bitch (!).

hilar [i'lar] *vt* to spin; ~ **fino** to split hairs.

hilera [i'lera] *nf* row, file.

hilo [ˈilo] *nm* thread; (*BOT*) fibre; (*metal*) wire; (*de agua*) trickle, thin stream; (*de luz*) beam, ray.

hilvanar [ilβa'nar] *vt* (*COSTURA*) to tack (*Brit*), baste (*US*); (*fig*) to do hurriedly.

himno [ˈimno] *nm* hymn; ~ **nacional** national anthem.

hincapié [inka'pje] *nm*: **hacer** ~ **en** to emphasize.

hincar [in'kar] *vt* to drive (in), thrust (in); ~**se** *vr*: ~**se de rodillas** to kneel down.

hincha [ˈintʃa] *nm/f* (*fam*) fan.

hinchado, a [in'tʃaðo, a] *a* (*gen*) swollen; (*persona*) pompous.

hinchar [in'tʃar] *vt* (*gen*) to swell; (*inflar*) to blow up, inflate; (*fig*) to exaggerate; ~**se** *vr* (*inflarse*) to swell up; (*fam*: *llenarse*) to stuff o.s.; **hinchazón** *nf* (*MED*) swelling; (*altivez*) arrogance.

hinojo [i'noxo] *nm* fennel.

hipermercado [ipermer'kaðo] *nm* hypermarket, superstore.

hipnotismo [ipno'tismo] *nm* hypnotism; **hipnotizar** *vt* to hypnotize.

hipo [ˈipo] *nm* hiccups *pl*.

hipocresía [ipokre'sia] *nf* hypocrisy; **hipócrita** *a* hypocritical // *nm/f* hypocrite.

hipódromo [i'poðromo] *nm* racetrack.

hipopótamo [ipo'potamo] *nm* hippopotamus.

hipoteca [ipo'teka] *nf* mortgage.

hipótesis [i'potesis] *nf inv* hypothesis.

hiriente [i'rjente] *a* offensive, wounding.

hispánico, a [is'paniko, a] *a* Hispanic.

hispano, a [is'pano, a] *a* Hispanic, Spanish, Hispano- // *nm/f* Spaniard; **H~américa** *nf* Spanish *o* Latin America; **~americano, a** *a, nm/f* Spanish *o* Latin American.

histeria [is'terja] *nf* hysteria.

historia [is'torja] *nf* history; *(cuento)* story, tale; **~s** *nfpl (chismes)* gossip *sg*; **dejarse de ~s** to come to the point; **pasar a la ~** to go down in history; **~dor, a** *nm/f* historian; **historiar** *vt* to chronicle, write the history of; **histórico, a** *a* historical; *(fig)* historic.

historieta [isto'rjeta] *nf* tale, anecdote; *(dibujos)* comic strip.

hito ['ito] *nm (fig)* landmark; *(objetivo)* goal, target.

hizo *vb ver* **hacer.**

Hnos *abr* (= **Hermanos**) Bros.

hocico [o'θiko] *nm* snout; *(fig)* grimace.

hockey ['xoki] *nm* hockey; **~ sobre hielo** ice hockey.

hogar [o'ɣar] *nm* fireplace, hearth; *(casa)* home; *(vida familiar)* home life; **~eño, a** *a* home; *(persona)* home-loving.

hoguera [o'ɣera] *nf (gen)* bonfire.

hoja ['oxa] *nf (gen)* leaf; *(de flor)* petal; *(de papel)* sheet; *(página)* page; **~ de afeitar** razor blade.

hojalata [oxa'lata] *nf* tin(plate).

hojaldre [o'xaldre] *nm (CULIN)* puff pastry.

hojear [oxe'ar] *vt* to leaf through, turn the pages of.

hola ['ola] *excl* hello!

Holanda [o'landa] *nf* Holland; **holandés, esa** *a* Dutch // *nm/f* Dutchman/woman // *nm (LING)* Dutch.

holgado, a [ol'ɣaðo, a] *a* loose, baggy; *(rico)* well-to-do.

holgar [ol'ɣar] *vi (descansar)* to rest; *(sobrar)* to be superfluous; **huelga decir que** it goes without saying that.

holgazán, ana [olɣa'θan, ana] *a* idle, lazy // *nm/f* loafer.

holgura [ol'ɣura] *nf* looseness, bagginess; *(TEC)* play, free movement; *(vida)* comfortable living, luxury.

hollín [o'ʎin] *nm* soot.

hombre ['ombre] *nm (gen)* man; *(raza humana)*: **el ~** man(kind); *(uno)* man // *excl*: ¡**sí ~!** *(claro)* of course!; *(para énfasis)* man, old boy; **~ de negocios** businessman; **~-rana** frogman; **~ de pro** honest man.

hombrera [om'brera] *nf* shoulder strap.

hombro ['ombro] *nm* shoulder.

hombruno, a [om'bruno, a] *a* mannish.

homenaje [ome'naxe] *nm (gen)* homage; *(tributo)* tribute.

homicida [omi'θiða] *a* homicidal // *nm/f* murderer; **homicidio** *nm* murder, homicide.

homosexual [omosek'swal] *a, nm/f* homosexual.

hondo, a ['ondo, a] *a* deep; **lo ~** the depth(s) *(pl)*, the bottom; **~nada** *nf* hollow, depression; *(cañón)* ravine; *(GEO)* lowland; **hondura** *nf* depth, profundity.

Honduras [on'duras] *nf* Honduras.

hondureño, a [ondu'reno, a] *a, nm/f* Honduran.

honestidad [onesti'ðað] *nf* purity, chastity; *(decencia)* decency; **honesto, a** *a* chaste; decent, honest; *(justo)* just.

hongo ['ongo] *nm (BOT: gen)* fungus; *(: comestible)* mushroom; *(: venenoso)* toadstool.

honor [o'nor] *nm (gen)* honour; *(gloria)* glory; **en ~ a la verdad** to be fair; **~able** *a* honourable.

honorario, a [ono'rarjo, a] *a* honorary; **~s** *nmpl* fees.

honra ['onra] *nf (gen)* honour; *(renombre)* good name; **~dez** *nf* honesty; *(de persona)* integrity; **~do, a** *a* honest, upright.

honrar [on'rar] *vt* to honour; **~se** *vr*: **~se con algo/de hacer algo** to be honoured by sth/to do sth.

honroso, a [on'roso, a] *a (honrado)* honourable; *(respetado)* respectable.

hora ['ora] *nf (una ~)* hour; *(tiempo)* time; ¿**qué ~ es?** what time is it?; ¿**a qué ~?** at what time?; **media ~** half an hour; **a la ~ de recreo** at playtime; **a primera ~** first thing (in the morning); **a última ~** at the last moment; **a altas ~s** in the small hours; ¡**una buena ~!** about time, too!; **dar la ~** to strike the hour; **~s de oficina/de trabajo** office/working hours; **~s de visita** visiting times; **~s extras** *o* **extraordinarias** overtime *sg*; **~s punta** rush hours.

horadar [ora'ðar] *vt* to drill, bore.

horario, a [o'rarjo, a] *a* hourly, hour *cpd* // *nm* timetable; **~ comercial** business hours *pl*.

horca ['orka] *nf* gallows *sg*.

horcajadas [orka'xaðas]: **a ~** *ad* astride.

horchata [or'tʃata] *nf* cold drink made from tiger nuts and water, tiger nut milk.

horda ['orða] *nf* horde.

horizontal [oriθon'tal] *a* horizontal.

horizonte [ori'θonte] *nm* horizon.

horma ['orma] *nf* mould.

hormiga [or'miɣa] *nf* ant; **~s** *nfpl (MED)* pins and needles.

hormigón [ormi'ɣon] *nm* concrete; **~ armado/pretensado** reinforced/prestressed concrete.

hormigueo [ormi'ɣeo] *nm (comezón)* itch; *(fig)* uneasiness.

hormona [or'mona] *nf* hormone.
hornada [or'naða] *nf* batch (of loaves *etc*).
hornillo [or'niʎo] *nm* (*cocina*) portable stove.
horno ['orno] *nm* (*CULIN*) oven; (*TEC*) furnace; **alto ~** blast furnace.
horóscopo [o'roskopo] *nm* horoscope.
horquilla [or'kiʎa] *nf* hairpin; (*AGR*) pitchfork.
horrendo, a [o'rrendo, a] *a* horrendous, frightful.
horrible [o'rriβle] *a* horrible, dreadful.
horripilante [orripi'lante] *a* hair-raising, horrifying.
horror [o'rror] *nm* horror, dread; (*atrocidad*) atrocity; **¡qué ~!** (*fam*) oh, my God!; **~izar** *vt* to horrify, frighten; **~izarse** *vr* to be horrified; **~oso, a** *a* horrifying, ghastly.
hortaliza [orta'liθa] *nf* vegetable.
hortelano, a [orte'lano, a] *nm/f* (market) gardener.
hosco, a ['osko, a] *a* dark; (*persona*) sullen, gloomy.
hospedar [ospe'ðar] *vt* to put up; **~se** *vr* to stay, lodge.
hospital [ospi'tal] *nm* hospital.
hospitalario, a [ospita'larjo, a] *a* (*acogedor*) hospitable; **hospitalidad** *nf* hospitality.
hostal [os'tal] *nm* small hotel.
hostelería [ostele'ria] *nf* hotel business *o* trade.
hostelero, a [oste'lero, a] *nm/f* innkeeper, landlord/lady.
hostia ['ostja] *nf* (*REL*) host, consecrated wafer; (*fam: golpe*) whack, punch // *excl*: **¡~(s)!** (*fam!*) damn!
hostigar [osti'var] *vt* to whip; (*fig*) to harass, pester.
hostil [os'til] *a* hostile; **~idad** *nf* hostility.
hotel [o'tel] *nm* hotel; **~ero, a** *a* hotel *cpd* // *nm/f* hotelier.
hoy [oi] *ad* (*este día*) today; (*la actualidad*) now(adays) // *nm* present time; **~ (en) día** now(adays).
hoyo ['ojo] *nm* hole, pit; **hoyuelo** *nm* dimple.
hoz [oθ] *nf* sickle.
hube *etc vb ver* **haber**.
hucha ['utʃa] *nf* money box.
hueco, a ['weko, a] *a* (*vacío*) hollow, empty; (*resonante*) booming // *nm* hollow, cavity.
huelga *etc vb ver* **holgar** // ['welva] *nf* strike; **declararse en ~** to go on strike, come out on strike; **~ de hambre** hunger strike.
huelgo *etc vb ver* **holgar**.
huelguista [wel'vista] *nm/f* striker.
huelo *etc vb ver* **oler**.
huella ['weʎa] *nf* (*acto de pisar, pisada*) tread(ing); (*marca del paso*) footprint,

footstep; (: *de animal, máquina*) track; **~ digital** fingerprint.
huérfano, a ['werfano, a] *a* orphan(ed) // *nm/f* orphan.
huerta ['werta] *nf* market garden; (*en Murcia y Valencia*) irrigated region.
huerto ['werto] *nm* kitchen garden; (*de árboles frutales*) orchard.
hueso ['weso] *nm* (*ANAT*) bone; (*de fruta*) stone.
huésped, a ['wespeð, a] *nm/f* (*invitado*) guest; (*habitante*) resident; (*anfitrión*) host(ess).
huesudo, a [we'suðo, a] *a* bony, big-boned.
huevera [we'βera] *nf* eggcup.
huevo ['weβo] *nm* egg; **~ duro/ escalfado/frito** (*Esp*) *o* **estrellado** (*AM*)/ **pasado por agua** hard-boiled/poached/ fried/soft-boiled egg; **~s revueltos** scrambled eggs.
huida [u'iða] *nf* escape, flight.
huidizo, a [ui'ðiθo, a] *a* (*tímido*) shy; (*pasajero*) fleeting.
huir [u'ir] *vi* (*escapar*) to flee, escape; (*evadir*) to avoid; **~se** *vr* (*escaparse*) to escape.
hule ['ule] *nm* (*encerado*) oilskin.
humanidad [umani'ðað] *nf* (*género humano*) man(kind); (*cualidad*) humanity.
humano, a [u'mano, a] *a* (*gen*) human; (*humanitario*) humane // *nm* human; **ser ~** human being.
humareda [uma'reða] *nf* cloud of smoke.
humedad [ume'ðað] *nf* (*del clima*) humidity; (*de pared etc*) dampness; **a prueba de ~** damp-proof; **humedecer** *vt* to moisten, wet; **humedecerse** *vr* to get wet.
húmedo, a ['umeðo, a] *a* (*mojado*) damp, wet; (*tiempo etc*) humid.
humildad [umil'dað] *nf* humility, humbleness; **humilde** *a* humble, modest.
humillación [umiʎa'θjon] *nf* humiliation; **humillante** *a* humiliating.
humillar [umi'ʎar] *vt* to humiliate; **~se** *vr* to humble o.s., grovel.
humo ['umo] *nm* (*de fuego*) smoke; (*gas nocivo*) fumes *pl*; (*vapor*) steam, vapour; **~s** *nmpl* (*fig*) conceit *sg*.
humor [u'mor] *nm* (*disposición*) mood, temper; (*lo que divierte*) humour; **de buen/mal ~** in a good/bad mood; **~ismo** *nm* humour; **~ista** *nm/f* comic; **~ístico, a** *a* funny, humorous.
hundimiento [undi'mjento] *nm* (*gen*) sinking; (*colapso*) collapse.
hundir [un'dir] *vt* to sink; (*edificio, plan*) to ruin, destroy; **~se** *vr* to sink, collapse.
húngaro, a ['ungaro, a] *a*, *nm/f* Hungarian.
Hungría [un'gria] *nf* Hungary.
huracán [ura'kan] *nm* hurricane.

huraño, a |u'raɲo, a| a shy; (antisocial) unsociable.

hurgar |ur'var| vt to poke, jab; (remover) to stir (up); ~se vr: ~se (las narices) to pick one's nose.

hurón, ona |u'ron, ona| nm (ZOOL) ferret.

hurtadillas |urta'ðiʎas|: a ~ ad stealthily, on the sly.

hurtar |ur'tar| vt to steal; **hurto** nm theft, stealing.

husmear |usme'ar| vt (oler) to sniff out, scent; (fam) to pry into // vi to smell bad.

huyo etc vb ver **huir.**

I

iba etc vb ver **ir.**

ibérico, a |i'βeriko, a| a Iberian.

iberoamericano, a |iβeroameri'kano, a| a, nm/f Latin American.

íbice |'iβiθe| nm ibex.

Ibiza |i'βiθa| nf Ibiza.

iceberg |iθe'βer| nm iceberg.

ícono |'ikono| nm ikon, icon.

iconoclasta |ikono'klasta| a iconoclastic // nm/f iconoclast.

ictericia |ikte'riθja| nf jaundice.

ida |'iða| nf going, departure; ~ y vuelta round trip, return.

idea |i'ðea| nf idea; **no tengo la menor ~** I haven't a clue.

ideal |iðe'al| a, nm ideal; **~ista** nm/f idealist; **~izar** vt to idealize.

idear |iðe'ar| vt to think up; (aparato) to invent; (viaje) to plan.

ídem |'iðem| pron ditto.

idéntico, a |i'ðentiko, a| a identical.

identidad |iðenti'ðað| nf identity.

identificación |iðentifika'θjon| nf identification.

identificar |iðentifi'kar| vt to identify; **~se** vr: **~se con** to identify with.

ideología |iðeolo'xia| nf ideology.

idioma |i'ðjoma| nm (gen) language.

idiota |i'ðjota| a idiotic // nm/f idiot; **idiotez** nf idiocy.

ídolo |'iðolo| nm (tb: fig) idol.

idóneo, a |i'ðoneo, a| a suitable.

iglesia |i'xlesja| nf church.

ignominia |ixno'minja| nf ignominy.

ignorancia |ixno'ranθja| nf ignorance; **ignorante** a ignorant, uninformed // nm/f ignoramus.

ignorar |ixno'rar| vt not to know, be ignorant of; (no hacer caso a) to ignore.

igual |i'ɣwal| a (gen) equal; (similar) like, similar; (mismo) (the) same; (constante) constant; (temperatura) even // nm/f equal; ~ **que** like, the same as; **me da o es ~** I don't care; **son ~es** they're the same; **al ~ que** prep, conj like, just like.

igualada |ixwa'laða| nf equaliser.

igualar |ixwa'lar| vt (gen) to equalize, make equal; (allanar, nivelar) to level (off), even (out); ~se vr (platos de balanza) to balance out.

igualdad |ixwal'dað| nf equality; (similaridad) sameness; (uniformidad) uniformity.

igualmente |ixwal'mente| ad equally; (también) also, likewise // excl the same to you!

ikurriña |iku'rriɲa| nf Basque flag.

ilegal |ile'xal| a illegal.

ilegítimo, a |ile'xitimo, a| a illegitimate.

ileso, a |i'leso, a| a unhurt.

ilícito, a |i'liðito| a illicit.

ilimitado, a |ilimi'taðo, a| a unlimited

ilógico, a |i'loxiko, a| a illogical.

iluminación |ilumina'θjon| nf illumination; (alumbrado) lighting.

iluminar |ilumi'nar| vt to illuminate, light (up); (fig) to enlighten.

ilusión |ilu'sjon| nf illusion; (quimera) delusion; (esperanza) hope; **hacerse ilusiones** to build up one's hopes; **ilusionado, a** a excited.

ilusionista |ilusjo'nista| nm/f conjurer.

iluso, a |i'luso, a| a easily deceived // nm/f dreamer.

ilusorio, a |ilu'sorjo, a| a (de ilusión) illusory, deceptive; (esperanza) vain.

ilustración |ilustra'θjon| nf illustration; (saber) learning, erudition; **la I~** the Enlightenment; **ilustrado, a** a illustrated; learned.

ilustrar |ilus'trar| vt to illustrate; (instruir) to instruct; (explicar) to explain, make clear; **~se** vr to acquire knowledge.

ilustre |i'lustre| a famous, illustrious.

imagen |i'maxen| nf (gen) image; (dibujo) picture.

imaginación |imaxina'θjon| nf imagination.

imaginar |imaxi'nar| vt (gen) to imagine; (idear) to think up; (suponer) to suppose; **~se** vr to imagine; **~io, a** a imaginary; **imaginativo, a** a imaginative.

imán |i'man| nm magnet.

imbécil |im'beθil| nm/f imbecile, idiot.

imbuir |imbu'ir| vt to imbue.

imitación |imita'θjon| nf imitation.

imitar |imi'tar| vt to imitate; (parodiar, remedar) to mimic, ape.

impaciencia |impa'θjenθja| nf impatience; **impaciente** a impatient; (nervioso) anxious.

impacto |im'pakto| nm impact.

impar |im'par| a odd.

imparcial |impar'θjal| a impartial, fair; **~idad** nf impartiality, fairness.

impartir |impar'tir| vt to impart, give.

impasible |impa'siβle| a impassive.

impávido, a |im'paβiðo, a| a fearless,

intrepid.

impecable [impe'kaβle] a impeccable.

impedimento [impeði'mento] nm impediment, obstacle.

impedir [impe'ðir] vt (obstruir) to impede, obstruct; (estorbar) to prevent.

impeler [impe'ler] vt to drive, propel; (fig) to impel.

impenetrable [impene'traβle] a impenetrable; (fig) incomprehensible.

imperar [impe'rar] vi (reinar) to rule, reign; (fig) to prevail, reign; (precio) to be current.

imperativo, a [impera'tiβo, a] a (persona) imperious; (urgente, LING) imperative.

imperceptible [imperθep'tiβle] a imperceptible.

imperdible [imper'ðiβle] nm safety pin.

imperdonable [imperðo'naβle] a unforgivable, inexcusable.

imperfección [imperfek'θjon] nf imperfection.

imperfecto, a [imper'fekto, a] a imperfect.

imperial [impe'rjal] a imperial; ~**ismo** nm imperialism.

imperio [im'perjo] nm empire; (autoridad) rule, authority; (fig) pride, haughtiness; ~**so, a** a imperious; (urgente) urgent; (imperativo) imperative.

impermeable [imperme'aβle] a (a prueba de agua) waterproof // nm raincoat.

impersonal [imperso'nal] a impersonal.

impertérrito, a [imper'territo, a] a undaunted.

impertinencia [imperti'nenθja] nf impertinence; **impertinente** a impertinent.

imperturbable [impertur'βaβle] a imperturbable.

ímpetu ['impetu] nm (impulso) impetus, impulse; (impetuosidad) impetuosity; (violencia) violence.

impetuoso, a [impe'twoso, a] a impetuous; (río) rushing; (acto) hasty.

impío, a [im'pio, a] a impious, ungodly.

implacable [impla'kaβle] a implacable.

implicar [impli'kar] vt to implicate, involve; (entrañar) to imply.

implícito, a [im'pliθito, a] a (tácito) implicit; (sobreentendido) implied.

implorar [implo'rar] vt to beg, implore.

imponente [impo'nente] a (impresionante) impressive, imposing; (solemne) grand.

imponer [impo'ner] vt (gen) to impose; (exigir) to exact, command; ~**se** vr to assert o.s.; (prevalecer) to prevail; **imponible** a (COM) taxable.

impopular [impopu'lar] a unpopular.

importación [importa'θjon] nf (acto) importing; (mercancías) imports pl.

importancia [impor'tanθja] nf importance; (valor) value, significance; (extensión) size, magnitude; **importante** a important; valuable, significant.

importar [impor'tar] vt (del extranjero) to import; (valer) to amount to, be worth // vi to be important, matter; **me importa un rábano** I don't give a damn; **no importa** it doesn't matter; ¿**le importa que fume?** do you mind if I smoke?

importe [im'porte] nm (total) amount; (valor) value.

importunar [importu'nar] vt to bother, pester.

imposibilidad [imposiβili'ðað] nf impossibility; **imposibilitar** vt to make impossible, prevent.

imposible [impo'siβle] a (gen) impossible; (insoportable) unbearable, intolerable.

imposición [imposi'θjon] nf imposition; (COM: impuesto) tax; (: inversión) deposit.

impostor, a [impos'tor, a] nm/f impostor.

impotencia [impo'tenθja] nf impotence; **impotente** a impotent, powerless.

impracticable [imprakti'kaβle] a (irrealizable) impracticable; (intransitable) impassable.

imprecar [impre'kar] vi to curse.

impreciso, a [impre'θiso, a] a imprecise, vague.

impregnar [impreɣ'nar] vt to impregnate; ~**se** vr to become impregnated.

imprenta [im'prenta] nf (acto) printing; (aparato) press; (casa) printer's; (letra) print.

imprescindible [impresθin'diβle] a essential, vital.

impresión [impre'sjon] nf (gen) impression; (IMPRENTA) printing; (edición) edition; (FOTO) print; (marca) imprint; ~ **digital** fingerprint.

impresionable [impresjo'naβle] a (sensible) impressionable.

impresionante [impresjo'nante] a impressive; (tremendo) tremendous; (maravilloso) great, marvellous.

impresionar [impresjo'nar] vt (conmover) to move; (afectar) to impress, strike; (película fotográfica) to expose; ~**se** vr to be impressed; (conmoverse) to be moved.

impreso, a [im'preso, a] pp de **imprimir** // [im'preso, a] a printed ~**s** nmpl; printed matter; **impresora** nf printer.

imprevisto, a [impre'βisto, a] a (gen) unforeseen; (inesperado) unexpected ~**s** nmpl; (gastos) unforeseen expenses.

imprimir [impri'mir] vt to imprint, impress, stamp; (textos) to print; (IN-

FORM) to output, print out.

improbable [impro'βaβle] *a* improbable; (*inverosímil*) unlikely.

improcedente [improθe'ðente] *a* inappropriate.

improductivo, a [improðuk'tiβo, a] *a* unproductive.

improperio [impro'perjo] *nm* insult.

impropiedad [impropje'ðað] *nf* impropriety (of language).

impropio, a [im'propjo, a] *a* improper.

improvisación [improβisa'θjon] *nf* improvisation; **improvisado, a** *a* improvised.

improvisar [improβi'sar] *vt* to improvise.

improviso, a [impro'βiso, a] *a*: **de ~** unexpectedly, suddenly.

imprudencia [impru'ðenθja] *nf* imprudence; (*indiscreción*) indiscretion; (*descuido*) carelessness; **imprudente** *a* imprudent; indiscreet; (*irreflexivo*) unwise.

impúdico, a [im'puðiko, a] *a* shameless; (*lujurioso*) lecherous.

impudor [impu'ðor] *nm* shamelessness; (*lujuria*) lechery.

impuesto, a [im'pwesto, a] *a* imposed // *nm* tax; **~ sobre el valor añadido (IVA)** value added tax (VAT).

impugnar [impuɣ'nar] *vt* to oppose, contest; (*refutar*) to refute, impugn.

impulsar [impul'sar] *vt* = **impeler**.

impulso [im'pulso] *nm* impulse; (*fuerza, empuje*) thrust, drive; (*fig: sentimiento*) urge, impulse.

impune [im'pune] *a* unpunished; **impunidad** *nf* impunity.

impureza [impu're0a] *nf* impurity; (*fig*) lewdness; **impuro, a** *a* impure; lewd.

imputar [impu'tar] *vt* (*atribuir*) to attribute to; (*cargar*) to impute to.

inacabable [inaka'βaβle] *a* (*infinito*) endless; (*interminable*) interminable.

inaccesible [inakθe'siβle] *a* inaccessible.

inacción [inak'θjon] *nf* (*gen*) inaction; (*desocupación*) inactivity.

inaceptable [inaθep'taβle] *a* unacceptable.

inactividad [inaktiβi'ðað] *nf* inactivity; (*COM*) dullness; **inactivo, a** *a* inactive.

inadaptación [inaðapta'θjon] *nf* maladjustment.

inadecuado, a [inaðe'kwaðo, a] *a* (*insuficiente*) inadequate; (*inapto*) unsuitable.

inadmisible [inaðmi'siβle] *a* inadmissible.

inadvertido, a [inaðβer'tiðo, a] *a* (*no visto*) unnoticed.

inagotable [inaɣo'taβle] *a* inexhaustible.

inaguantable [inaɣwan'taβle] *a* unbearable.

inalterable [inalte'raβle] *a* immutable, unchangeable.

inanición [inani'θjon] *nf* starvation.

inanimado, a [inani'maðo, a] *a* inanimate.

inapto, a [in'apto] *a* unsuited.

inaudito, a [inau'ðito, a] *a* unheard-of.

inauguración [inauɣura'θjon] *nf* inauguration; (*de exposición*) opening; **inaugurar** *vt* to inaugurate; to open.

I.N.B. *abr* (*Esp = Instituto Nacional de Bachillerato*) ≈ comprehensive school (*Brit*), ≈ high school (*US*).

inca ['inka] *nm/f* Inca; **~ico, a** *a* Inca *cpd*.

incalculable [inkalku'laβle] *a* incalculable.

incandescente [inkandes'θente] *a* incandescent.

incansable [inkan'saβle] *a* tireless, untiring.

incapacidad [inkapaθi'ðað] *nf* incapacity; (*incompetencia*) incompetence; **~ física/mental** physical/mental disability.

incapacitar [inkapaθi'tar] *vt* (*inhabilitar*) to incapacitate, render unfit; (*descalificar*) to disqualify.

incapaz [inka'paθ] *a* incapable.

incautación [inkauta'θjon] *nf* confiscation.

incautarse [inkau'tarse] *vr*: **~ de** to seize, confiscate.

incauto, a [in'kauto, a] *a* (*imprudente*) incautious, unwary.

incendiar [inθen'djar] *vt* to set fire to; (*fig*) to inflame; **~se** *vr* to catch fire; **~io, a** *a* incendiary.

incendio [in'θendjo] *nm* fire.

incentivo [inθen'tiβo] *nm* incentive.

incertidumbre [inθerti'ðumβre] *nf* (*inseguridad*) uncertainty; (*duda*) doubt.

incesante [inθe'sante] *a* incessant.

incesto [in'θesto] *nm* incest.

incidencia [inθi'ðenθja] *nf* (*MAT*) incidence.

incidente [inθi'ðente] *nm* incident.

incidir [inθi'ðir] *vi* (*influir*) to influence; (*afectar*) to affect; **~ en un error** to fall into error.

incienso [in'θjenso] *nm* incense.

incierto, a [in'θjerto, a] *a* uncertain.

incineración [inθinera'θjon] *nf* incineration; (*de cadáveres*) cremation.

incinerar [inθine'rar] *vt* to burn; (*cadáveres*) to cremate.

incipiente [inθi'pjente] *a* incipient.

incisión [inθi'sjon] *nf* incision.

incisivo, a [inθi'siβo, a] *a* sharp, cutting; (*fig*) incisive.

incitar [inθi'tar] *vt* to incite, rouse.

incivil [inθi'βil] *a* rude, uncivil.

inclemencia [inkle'menθja] *nf* (*severidad*) harshness, severity; (*del tiempo*) inclemency.

inclinación [inklina'θjon] *nf* (*gen*) inclination; (*de tierras*) slope, incline; (*de cabeza*) nod, bow; (*fig*) leaning, bent.

inclinar [inkli'nar] *vt* to incline; (*cabeza*) to nod, bow; (*tierras*) to slope; ~se *vr* to bow; (*encorvarse*) to stoop; ~se a to take after, resemble; ~se ante to bow down to; me **inclino a pensar que** I'm inclined to think that.

incluir [inklu'ir] *vt* to include; (*incorporar*) to incorporate; (*meter*) to enclose.

inclusive [inklu'siße] *ad* inclusive // *prep* including.

incluso, a [in'kluso, a] *a* included // *ad* inclusively; (*hasta*) even.

incógnito [in'koɣnito] *nm*: de ~ incognito.

incoherente [inkoe'rente] *a* incoherent.

incoloro, a [inko'loro, a] *a* colourless.

incólume [in'kolume] *a* (*gen*) safe; (*indemne*) unhurt, unharmed.

incomodar [inkomo'ðar] *vt* to inconvenience; (*molestar*) to bother, trouble; (*fastidiar*) to annoy; ~se *vr* to put o.s. out; (*fastidiarse*) to get annoyed.

incomodidad [inkomoði'ðað] *nf* inconvenience; (*fastidio*, *enojo*) annoyance; (*de vivienda*) discomfort.

incómodo, a [in'komoðo, a] *a* (*inconfortable*) uncomfortable; (*molesto*) annoying; (*inconveniente*) inconvenient.

incomparable [inkompa'raßle] *a* incomparable.

incompatible [inkompa'tißle] *a* incompatible.

incompetencia [inkompe'tenθja] *nf* incompetence; **incompetente** *a* incompetent.

incompleto, a [inkom'pleto, a] *a* incomplete, unfinished.

incomprensible [inkompren'sißle] *a* incomprehensible.

incomunicado, a [inkomuni'kaðo, a] *a* (*aislado*) cut off, isolated; (*confinado*) in solitary confinement.

inconcebible [inkonθe'ßißle] *a* inconceivable.

inconcluso, a [inkon'kluso, a] *a* (*inacabado*) unfinished.

incondicional [inkondiθjo'nal] *a* unconditional; (*apoyo*) wholehearted; (*partidario*) staunch.

inconexo, a [inko'nekso, a] *a* (*gen*) unconnected; (*desunido*) disconnected.

inconfundible [inkonfun'dißle] *a* unmistakable.

incongruente [inkon'grwente] *a* incongruous.

inconmensurable [inkonmensu'raßle] *a* immeasurable, vast.

inconsciencia [inkons'θjenθja] *nf* unconsciousness; (*fig*) thoughtlessness; **inconsciente** *a* unconscious; thoughtless.

inconsecuente [inkonse'kwente] *a* inconsistent.

inconsiderado, a [inkonsiðe'raðo, a] *a* inconsiderate.

inconsistente [inkonsis'tente] *a* weak; (*tela*) flimsy.

inconstancia [inkon'stanθja] *nf* (*veleidad*) inconstancy; (*inestabilidad*) unsteadiness; **inconstante** *a* inconstant.

incontable [inkon'taßle] *a* countless, innumerable.

incontestable [inkontes'taßle] *a* unanswerable; (*innegable*) undeniable.

incontinencia [inkonti'nenθja] *nf* incontinence.

inconveniencia [inkonße'njenθja] *nf* unsuitability, inappropriateness; (*descortesía*) impoliteness; **inconveniente** *a* unsuitable; impolite // *nm* obstacle; (*desventaja*) disadvantage; el inconveniente es que... the trouble is that...

incorporación [inkorpora'θjon] *nf* incorporation.

incorporar [inkorpo'rar] *vt* to incorporate; ~se *vr* to sit/stand up.

incorrección [inkorrek'θjon] *nf* (*gen*) correctness, inaccuracy; (*descortesía*) bad-mannered behaviour; **incorrecto, a** *a* (*gen*) incorrect, wrong; (*comportamiento*) bad-mannered.

incorregible [inkorre'xißle] *a* incorrigible.

incredulidad [inkreðuli'ðað] *nf* incredulity; (*escepticismo*) scepticism; **incrédulo, a** *a* incredulous, unbelieving; sceptical.

increíble [inkre'ißle] *a* incredible.

incremento [inkre'mento] *nm* increment; (*aumento*) rise, increase.

increpar [inkre'par] *vt* to reprimand.

incruento, a [in'krwento, a] *a* bloodless.

incrustar [inkrus'tar] *vt* to incrust; (*piedras: en joya*) to inlay.

incubar [inku'ßar] *vt* to incubate; (*fig*) to hatch.

inculcar [inkul'kar] *vt* to inculcate.

inculpar [inkul'par] *vt* (*acusar*) to accuse; (*achacar, atribuir*) to charge, blame.

inculto, a [in'kulto, a] *a* (*persona*) uneducated; (*grosero*) uncouth // *nm/f* ignoramus.

incumplimiento [inkumpli'mjento] *nm* non-fulfilment; ~ de contrato breach of contract.

incurrir [inku'rrir] *vi*: ~ en to incur; (*crimen*) to commit; ~ en un error to fall into error.

indagación [indaɣa'θjon] *nf* investigation; (*búsqueda*) search; (*JUR*) inquest.

indagar [inda'ɣar] *vt* to investigate; to search; (*averiguar*) to ascertain.

indecente [inde'θente] *a* indecent, improper; (*lascivo*) obscene.

indecible [inde'θißle] *a* unspeakable; (*indescriptible*) indescribable.

indeciso, a [inde'θiso, a] *a* (*por decidir*)

undecided; (*vacilante*) hesitant.

indefenso, a [inde'fenɛo, a] *a* defence less.

indefinido, a [indefi'niðo, a] *a* indefinite; (*vago*) vague, undefined.

indeleble [inde'leßle] *a* indelible.

indemne [in'demne] *a* (*objeto*) undamaged; (*persona*) unharmed, unhurt.

indemnizar [indemni'θar] *vt* to indemnify; (*compensar*) to compensate.

independencia [indepen'denθja] *nf* independence.

independiente [indepen'djente] *a* (*libre*) independent; (*autónomo*) self-sufficient.

indeterminado, a [indetermi'naðo, a] *a* indefinite; (*desconocido*) indeterminate.

India ['indja] *nf*: **la ~** India.

indicación [indika'θjon] *nf* indication; (*señal*) sign; (*sugerencia*) suggestion, hint.

indicador [indika'ðor] *nm* indicator; (*TEC*) gauge, meter.

indicar [indi'kar] *vt* (*mostrar*) to indicate, show; (*termómetro etc*) to read, register; (*señalar*) to point to.

índice ['indiθe] *nm* index; (*catálogo*) catalogue; (*ANAT*) index finger, forefinger.

indicio [in'diθjo] *nm* indication, sign; (*pista*) clue.

indiferencia [indife'renθja] *nf* indifference; (*apatía*) apathy; **indiferente** *a* indifferent.

indígena [in'dixena] *a* indigenous, native // *nm/f* native.

indigencia [indi'xenθja] *nf* poverty, need.

indigestión [indixes'tjon] *nf* indigestion.

indigesto, a [indi'xesto, a] *a* undigested; (*indigestible*) indigestible; (*fig*) turgid.

indignación [indixna'θjon] *nf* indignation.

indignar [indix'nar] *vt* to anger, make indignant; **~se** *vr*: **~se por** to get indignant about.

indigno, a [in'dixno, a] *a* (*despreciable*) low, contemptible; (*inmerecido*) unworthy.

indio, a ['indjo, a] *a, nm/f* Indian.

indirecta [indi'rekta] *nf* insinuation, innuendo; (*sugerencia*) hint.

indirecto, a [indi'rekto, a] *a* indirect.

indiscreción [indiskre'θjon] *nf* (*imprudencia*) indiscretion; (*irreflexión*) tactlessness; (*acto*) gaffe, faux pas.

indiscreto, a [indis'kreto, a] *a* indiscreet.

indiscutible [indisku'tißle] *a* indisputable, unquestionable.

indispensable [indispen'saßle] *a* indispensable, essential.

indisponer [indispo'ner] *vt* to spoil, upset; (*salud*) to make ill; **~se** *vr* to fall ill; **~se con uno** to fall out with sb.

indisposición [indisposi'θjon] *nf* indisposition.

indistinto, a [indis'tinto, a] *a* indistinct; (*vago*) vague.

individual [indiβi'ðwal] *a* individual; (*habitación*) single // *nm* (*DEPORTE*) singles *sg*.

individuo, a [indi'βiðwo, a] *a* individual // *nm* individual.

índole ['indole] *nf* (*naturaleza*) nature; (*clase*) sort, kind.

indolencia [indo'lenθja] *nf* indolence, laziness.

indómito, a [in'domito, a] *a* indomitable.

inducir [indu'θir] *vt* to induce; (*inferir*) to infer; (*persuadir*) to persuade.

indudable [indu'ðaßle] *a* undoubted; (*incuestionable*) unquestionable.

indulgencia [indul'xenθja] *nf* indulgence.

indultar [indul'tar] *vt* (*perdonar*) to pardon, reprieve; (*librar de pago*) to exempt; **indulto** *nm* pardon; exemption.

industria [in'dustrja] *nf* industry; (*habilidad*) skill; **industrial** *a* industrial // *nm* industrialist.

inédito, a [in'eðito, a] *a* (*libro*) unpublished; (*fig*) new.

inefable [ine'faßle] *a* ineffable, indescribable.

ineficaz [inefi'kaθ] *a* (*inútil*) ineffective; (*ineficiente*) inefficient.

ineludible [inelu'ðißle] *a* inescapable, unavoidable.

ineptitud [inepti'tuð] *nf* ineptitude, incompetence; **inepto, a** *a* inept, incompetent.

inequívoco, a [ine'kißoko, a] *a* unequivocal; (*inconfundible*) unmistakable.

inercia [in'erθja] *nf* inertia; (*pasividad*) passivity.

inerme [in'erme] *a* (*sin armas*) unarmed; (*indefenso*) defenceless.

inerte [in'erte] *a* inert; (*inmóvil*) motionless.

inesperado, a [inespe'raðo, a] *a* unexpected, unforeseen.

inestable [ines'taßle] *a* unstable.

inevitable [ineßi'taßle] *a* inevitable.

inexactitud [ineksakti'tuð] *nf* inaccuracy; **inexacto, a** *a* inaccurate; (*falso*) untrue.

inexperto, a [inek'sperto, a] *a* (*novato*) inexperienced.

infalible [infa'lißle] *a* infallible; (*plan*) foolproof.

infame [in'fame] *a* infamous; (*horrible*) dreadful; **infamia** *nf* infamy; (*deshonra*) disgrace.

infancia [in'fanθja] *nf* infancy, childhood.

infante [in'fante] *nm* (*hijo del rey*) infante, prince; (*MIL*) infantryman.

infantería [infante'ria] *nf* infantry.

infantil [infan'til] *a* (*pueril, aniñado*) infantile; (*cándido*) childlike; (*literatura, ropa etc*) children's.

infarto [in'farto] *nm* (*tb: ~ de**

miocardio) heart attack.

infatigable [infati'ɤaβle] a tireless, untiring.

infección [infek'θjon] nf infection; **infeccioso, a** a infectious.

infectar [infek'tar] vt to infect; ~se vr to become infected.

infeliz [infe'liθ] a unhappy, wretched // nm/f wretch.

inferior [infe'rjor] a inferior; (situación) lower // nm/f inferior, subordinate.

inferir [infe'rir] vt (deducir) to infer, deduce; (causar) to cause.

infestar [infes'tar] vt (apestar) to infest; (fig) to harass.

infidelidad [infiðeli'ðað] nf (gen) infidelity, unfaithfulness.

infiel [in'fjel] a unfaithful, disloyal; (erróneo) inaccurate // nm/f infidel, unbeliever.

infierno [in'fjerno] nm hell.

ínfimo, a ['infimo, a] a (más bajo) lowest; (despreciable) vile, mean.

infinidad [infini'ðað] nf infinity; (abundancia) great quantity.

infinito, a [infi'nito, a] a, nm infinite.

inflación [infla'θjon] nf (hinchazón) swelling; (monetaria) inflation; (fig) conceit; **inflacionario, a** a inflationary.

inflamar [infla'mar] vt to set on fire; (MED) to inflame; ~se vr to catch fire; (fig) to become inflamed.

inflar [in'flar] vt (hinchar) to inflate, blow up; (fig) to exaggerate; ~se vr to swell (up); (fig) to get conceited.

inflexible [inflek'siβle] a inflexible; (fig) unbending.

infligir [infli'xir] vt to inflict.

influencia [influ'enθja] nf influence; **influenciar** vt to influence.

influir [influ'ir] vt to influence.

influjo [in'fluxo] nm influence.

influya etc vb ver **influir**.

influyente [influ'jente] a influential.

información [informa'θjon] nf information; (noticias) news sg; (JUR) inquiry; I~ (oficina) Information Office; (mostrador) Information Desk; (TEL) Directory Enquiries.

informal [infor'mal] a (gen) informal.

informante [infor'mante] nm/f informant.

informar [infor'mar] vt (gen) to inform; (revelar) to reveal, make known // vi (JUR) to plead; (denunciar) to inform; (dar cuenta de) to report on; ~se vr to find out; ~se de to inquire into.

informática [infor'matika] nf computer science, information technology.

informe [in'forme] a shapeless // nm report.

infortunio [infor'tunjo] nm misfortune.

infracción [infrak'θjon] nf infraction, infringement.

infranqueable [infranke'aβle] a impass-

able; (fig) insurmountable.

infringir [infrin'xir] vt to infringe, contravene.

infructuoso, a [infruk'twoso, a] a fruitless, unsuccessful.

infundado, a [infun'daðo, a] a groundless, unfounded.

infundir [infun'dir] vt to infuse, instil.

infusión [infu'sjon] nf infusion; ~ de manzanilla camomile tea.

ingeniar [inxe'njar] vt to think up, devise; ~se vr: ~se para to manage to.

ingeniería [inxenje'ria] nf engineering; **ingeniero, a** nm/f engineer; ingeniero de caminos/de sonido civil engineer/ sound engineer.

ingenio [in'xenjo] nm (talento) talent; (agudeza) wit; (habilidad) ingenuity, inventiveness; (TEC): ~ azucarero sugar refinery.

ingenioso, a [inxe'njoso, a] a ingenious, clever; (divertido) witty.

ingenuidad [inxenwi'ðað] nf ingenuousness; (sencillez) simplicity; **ingenuo, a** a ingenuous.

ingerir [inxe'rir] vt to ingest; (tragar) to swallow; (consumir) to consume.

Inglaterra [ingla'terra] nf England.

ingle ['ingle] nf groin.

inglés, esa [in'gles, esa] a English // nm/f Englishman/woman // nm (LING) English.

ingratitud [ingrati'tuð] nf ingratitude; **ingrato, a** a (gen) ungrateful.

ingrediente [ingre'ðjente] nm ingredient.

ingresar [ingre'sar] vt (dinero) to deposit // vi to come in; ~ en un club to join a club; ~ en el hospital to go into hospital.

ingreso [in'greso] nm (entrada) entry; (: en hospital etc) admission; ~s nmpl (dinero) income sg; (: COM) takings pl.

inhabitable [inaβi'taβle] a uninhabitable.

inhalar [ina'lar] vt to inhale.

inherente [ine'rente] a inherent.

inhibir [ini'βir] vt to inhibit; (REL) to restrain.

inhumano, a [inu'mano, a] a inhuman.

INI ['ini] nm abr (Esp = Instituto Nacional de Industria) ≈ NEB (Brit).

inicial [ini'θjal] a, nf initial.

iniciar [ini'θjar] vt (persona) to initiate; (empezar) to begin, commence; (conversación) to start up.

iniciativa [iniθja'tiβa] nf initiative; la ~ privada private enterprise.

inicuo, a [in'ikwo, a] a iniquitous.

ininterrumpido, a [ininterrum'piðo, a] a uninterrupted.

injerencia [inxe'renθja] nf interference.

injertar [inxer'tar] vt to graft; **injerto** nm graft.

injuria [in'xurja] nf (agravio, ofensa) offence; (insulto) insult; **injuriar** vt to insult; **injurioso, a** a offensive; insulting.

injusticia [inxus'tiθja] *nf* injustice.

injusto, a [in'xusto, a] *a* unjust, unfair.

inmadurez [inmaðu'reθ] *nf* immaturity.

inmediaciones [inmeðja'θjones] *nfpl* neighbourhood *sg*, environs.

inmediato, a [inme'ðjato, a] *a* immediate; (*contiguo*) adjoining; (*rápido*) prompt; (*próximo*) neighbouring, next; de ~ immediately.

inmejorable [inmexo'raßle] *a* unsurpassable; (*precio*) unbeatable.

inmenso, a [in'menso, a] *a* immense, huge.

inmerecido, a [inmere'θiðo, a] *a* undeserved.

inmigración [inmiɣra'θjon] *nf* immigration.

inmiscuirse [inmisku'irse] *vr* to interfere, meddle.

inmobiliario, a [inmoßi'ljarjo, a] *a* realestate *cpd*, property *cpd* // *nf* estate agency.

inmolar [inmo'lar] *vt* to immolate, sacrifice.

inmoral [inmo'ral] *a* immoral.

inmortal [inmor'tal] *a* immortal; ~**izar** *vt* to immortalize.

inmóvil [in'moßil] *a* immobile.

inmueble [in'mweßle] *a*: bienes ~s real estate, landed property // *nm* property.

inmundicia [inmun'diθja] *nf* filth; **inmundo, a** *a* filthy.

inmunidad [inmuni'ðað] *nf* immunity.

inmutarse [inmu'tarse] *vr* to turn pale; no se inmutó he didn't turn a hair.

innato, a [in'nato, a] *a* innate.

innecesario, a [inneθe'sarjo, a] *a* unnecessary.

innoble [in'noßle] *a* ignoble.

innovación [innoßa'θjon] *nf* innovation.

innovar [inno'ßar] *vt* to introduce.

inocencia [ino'θenθja] *nf* innocence.

inocentada [inoθen'taða] *nf* practical joke.

inocente [ino'θente] *a* (*ingenuo*) naive, innocent; (*inculpable*) innocent; (*sin malicia*) harmless // *nm/f* simpleton.

inodoro [ino'ðoro] *nm* toilet, lavatory (*Brit*).

inofensivo, a [inofen'sißo, a] *a* inoffensive, harmless.

inolvidable [inolßi'ðaßle] *a* unforgettable.

inoperante [inope'rante] *a* ineffective.

inopinado, a [inopi'naðo, a] *a* unexpected.

inoportuno, a [inopor'tuno, a] *a* untimely; (*molesto*) inconvenient.

inoxidable [inoksi'ðaßle] *a*: acero ~ stainless steel.

inquebrantable [inkeßran'taßle] *a* unbreakable.

inquietar [inkje'tar] *vt* to worry, trouble; ~**se** *vr* to worry, get upset; **inquieto, a** *a* anxious, worried; **inquietud** *nf* anxiety, worry.

inquilino, a [inki'lino, a] *nm/f* tenant.

inquirir [inki'rir] *vt* to enquire into, investigate.

insaciable [insa'θjaßle] *a* insatiable.

insalubre [insa'lußre] *a* unhealthy.

inscribir [inskri'ßir] *vt* to inscribe; (*lista*) to list; (*censo*) to register; ~**se** *vr* to register; (*ESCOL etc*) to enrol.

inscripción [inskrip'θjon] *nf* inscription; (*ESCOL etc*) enrolment; (*censo*) registration.

insecticida [insekti'θiða] *nm* insecticide.

insecto [in'sekto] *nm* insect.

inseguridad [inseɣuri'ðað] *nf* insecurity.

inseguro, a [inse'ɣuro, a] *a* insecure; (*inconstante*) unsteady; (*incierto*) uncertain.

insensato, a [insen'sato, a] *a* foolish, stupid.

insensibilidad [insensißili'ðað] *nf* (*gen*) insensitivity; (*dureza de corazón*) callousness.

insensible [insen'sißle] *a* (*gen*) insensitive; (*movimiento*) imperceptible; (*sin sentido*) numb.

insertar [inser'tar] *vt* to insert.

inservible [inser'ßißle] *a* useless.

insidioso, a [insi'ðjoso, a] *a* insidious.

insignia [in'siɣnja] *nf* (*señal distintiva*) badge; (*estandarte*) flag.

insignificante [insiɣnifi'kante] *a* insignificant.

insinuar [insi'nwar] *vt* to insinuate, imply; ~**se** *vr*: ~**se con uno** to ingratiate o.s. with sb.

insípido, a [in'sipiðo, a] *a* insipid.

insistencia [insis'tenθja] *nf* insistence.

insistir [insis'tir] *vi* to insist; ~ **en algo** to insist on sth; (*enfatizar*) to stress sth.

insolación [insola'θjon] *nf* (*MED*) sunstroke.

insolencia [inso'lenθja] *nf* insolence; **insolente** *a* insolent.

insólito, a [in'solito, a] *a* unusual.

insoluble [inso'lußle] *a* insoluble.

insolvencia [insol'ßenθja] *nf* insolvency.

insomnio [in'somnjo] *nm* insomnia.

insondable [inson'daßle] *a* bottomless; (*fig*) impenetrable.

insonorizado, a [insonori'θaðo, a] *a* (*cuarto etc*) soundproof.

insoportable [insopor'taßle] *a* unbearable.

insospechado, a [insospe'tʃaðo, a] *a* (*inesperado*) unexpected.

inspección [inspek'θjon] *nf* inspection, check; **inspeccionar** *vt* (*examinar*) to inspect, examine; (*controlar*) to check.

inspector, a [inspek'tor, a] *nm/f* inspector.

inspiración [inspira'θjon] *nf* inspiration.

inspirar [inspi'rar] *vt* to inspire; (*MED*) to inhale; ~**se** *vr*: ~**se en** to be inspired by.

instalación [instala'θjon] *nf* (*equipo*)

fittings *pl*, equipment; ~ eléctrica wiring.

instalar [insta'lar] *vt* (*establecer*) to instal; (*erguir*) to set up, erect; ~se *vr* to establish o.s.; (*en una vivienda*) to move into.

instancia [ins'tanθja] *nf* (*JUR*) petition; (*ruego*) request; **en última ~** as a last resort.

instantáneo, a [instan'taneo, a] *a* instantaneous // *nf* snap(shot); **café ~** instant coffee.

instante [ins'tante] *nm* instant, moment.

instar [ins'tar] *vt* to press, urge.

instigar [insti'ɣar] *vt* to instigate.

instinto [ins'tinto] *nm* instinct; **por ~** instinctively.

institución [institu'θjon] *nf* institution, establishment.

instituir [institu'ir] *vt* to establish; (*fundar*) to found; **instituto** *nm* (*gen*) institute; **Instituto Nacional de Enseñanza** (*Esp*) ≈ comprehensive (*Brit*) o high (*US*) school.

institutriz [institu'triθ] *nf* governess.

instrucción [instruk'θjon] *nf* instruction.

instructivo, a [instruk'tiβo, a] *a* instructive.

instruir [instru'ir] *vt* (*gen*) to instruct; (*enseñar*) to teach, educate.

instrumento [instru'mento] *nm* (*gen*) instrument; (*herramienta*) tool, implement.

insubordinarse [insuβorði'narse] *vr* to rebel.

insuficiencia [insufi'θjenθja] *nf* (*carencia*) lack; (*inadecuación*) inadequacy; **insuficiente** *a* (*gen*) insufficient; (*ESCOL: calificación*) unsatisfactory.

insufrible [insu'friβle] *a* insufferable.

insular [insu'lar] *a* insular.

insultar [insul'tar] *vt* to insult; **insulto** *nm* insult.

insuperable [insupe'raβle] *a* (*excelente*) unsurpassable; (*arduo*) insurmountable.

insurgente [insur'xente] *a*, *nm/f* insurgent.

insurrección [insurrek'θjon] *nf* insurrection, rebellion.

intacto, a [in'takto, a] *a* intact.

intachable [inta'tʃaβle] *a* irreproachable.

integral [inte'ɣral] *a* integral; (*completo*) complete; **pan ~** wholemeal (*Brit*) o wholewheat (*US*) bread.

integrar [inte'ɣrar] *vt* to make up, compose; (*MAT, fig*) to integrate.

integridad [inteɣri'ðað] *nf* wholeness; (*carácter*) integrity; **íntegro, a** *a* whole, entire; (*honrado*) honest.

intelectual [intelek'twal] *a*, *nm/f* intellectual.

inteligencia [inteli'xenθja] *nf* intelligence; (*ingenio*) ability; **inteligente** *a* intelligent.

inteligible [inteli'xiβle] *a* intelligible.

intemperie [intem'perje] *nf*: **a la ~** out in the open, exposed to the elements.

intempestivo, a [intempes'tiβo, a] *a* untimely.

intención [inten'θjon] *nf* (*gen*) intention, purpose; **con segundas intenciones** maliciously; **con ~** deliberately.

intencionado, a [intenθjo'naðo, a] *a* deliberate; **bien/mal ~** well-meaning/ill-disposed, hostile.

intensidad [intensi'ðað] *nf* (*gen*) intensity; (*ELEC, TEC*) strength; **llover con ~** to rain hard.

intenso, a [in'tenso, a] *a* intense; (*sentimiento*) profound, deep.

intentar [inten'tar] *vt* (*tratar*) to try, attempt; **intento** *nm* (*intención*) intention, purpose; (*tentativa*) attempt.

intercalar [interka'lar] *vt* to insert.

intercambio [inter'kambjo] *nm* exchange, swap.

interceder [interθe'ðer] *vi* to intercede.

interceptar [interθep'tar] *vt* to intercept.

intercesión [interθe'sjon] *nf* intercession.

interés [inte'res] *nm* (*gen*) interest; (*parte*) share, part; (*pey*) self-interest; **intereses creados** vested interests.

interesado, a [intere'saðo, a] *a* interested; (*prejuiciado*) prejudiced; (*pey*) mercenary, self-seeking.

interesante [intere'sante] *a* interesting.

interesar [intere'sar] *vt*, *vi* to interest, be of interest to; ~se *vr*: ~se en o por to take an interest in.

interface [inter'faθe], **interfase** [-'fase] *nm* (*INFORM*) interface.

interferir [interfe'rir] *vt* to interfere with; (*TEL*) to jam // *vi* to interfere.

interfono [inter'fono] *nm* intercom.

interino, a [inte'rino, a] *a* temporary // *nm/f* temporary holder of a post; (*MED*) locum; (*ESCOL*) supply teacher.

interior [inte'rjor] *a* inner, inside; (*COM*) domestic, internal // *nm* interior, inside; (*fig*) soul, mind; **Ministerio del I~** ≈ Home Office (*Brit*), ≈ Department of the Interior (*US*).

interjección [interxek'θjon] *nf* interjection.

interlocutor, a [interloku'tor, a] *nm/f* speaker.

intermediario, a [interme'ðjarjo, a] *nm/f* intermediary.

intermedio, a [inter'meðjo, a] *a* intermediate // *nm* interval.

interminable [intermi'naβle] *a* endless.

intermitente [intermi'tente] *a* intermittent // *nm* (*AUTO*) indicator.

internacional [internaθjo'nal] *a* international.

internado [inter'naðo] *nm* boarding school.

internar [inter'nar] *vt* to intern; (*en un manicomio*) to commit; ~se *vr* (*pene-

trar) to penetrate.

interno, a [in'tɛrno, a] *a* internal, interior; (POL *etc)* domestic // *nm/f (alumno)* boarder.

interponer [interpo'ner] *vt* to interpose, put in; ~**se** *vr* to intervene.

interpretación [interpreta'θjon] *nf* interpretation.

interpretar [interpre'tar] *vt* to interpret; (TEATRO, MUS) to perform, play; **intérprete** *nm/f* (LING) interpreter, translator; (MUS, TEATRO) performer, artist(e).

interrogación [interroxa'θjon] *nf* interrogation; (LING: *tb:* **signo de** ~) question mark.

interrogar [interro'var] *vt* to interrogate, question.

interrumpir [interrum'pir] *vt* to interrupt.

interrupción [interrup'θjon] *nf* interruption.

interruptor [interrup'tor] *nm* (ELEC) switch.

intersección [intersek'θjon] *nf* intersection.

interurbano, a [interur'ßano, a] *a:* **llamada interurbana** long-distance call.

intervalo [inter'ßalo] *nm* interval; *(descanso)* break; **a** ~**s** at intervals, every now and then.

intervenir [interße'nir] *vt (controlar)* to control, supervise; (MED) to operate on // *vi (participar)* to take part, participate; *(mediar)* to intervene.

interventor, a [interßen'tor, a] *nm/f* inspector; (COM) auditor.

interviú [inter'ßju] *nf* interview.

intestino [intes'tino] *nm* intestine.

intimar [inti'mar] *vi* to become friendly.

intimidad [intimi'ðað] *nf* intimacy; *(familiaridad)* familiarity; *(vida privada)* private life; (JUR) privacy.

íntimo, a ['intimo, a] *a* intimate.

intolerable [intole'raßle] *a* intolerable, unbearable.

intranquilizarse [intrankili'θarse] *vr* to get worried *o* anxious; **intranquilo, a** *a* worried.

intransigente [intransi'xente] *a* intransigent.

intransitable [intransi'taßle] *a* impassable.

intrepidez [intrepi'ðeθ] *nf* courage, bravery; **intrépido, a** *a* intrepid.

intriga [in'triva] *nf* intrigue; *(plan)* plot; **intrigar** *vt, vi* to intrigue.

intrincado, a [intrin'kaðo, a] *a* intricate.

intrínseco, a [in'trinseko, a] *a* intrinsic.

introducción [introðuk'θjon] *nf* introduction.

introducir [introðu'θir] *vt (gen)* to introduce; *(moneda etc)* to insert; (INFORM) to input, enter.

intromisión [intromi'sjon] *nf* interference, meddling.

introvertido, a [introßer'tiðo, a] *a, nm/f* introvert.

intruso, a [in'truso, a] *a* intrusive // *nm/f* intruder.

intuición [intwi'θjon] *nf* intuition.

inundación [inunda'θjon] *nf* flood(ing); **inundar** *vt* to flood; *(fig)* to swamp, inundate.

inusitado, a [inusi'taðo, a] *a* unusual, rare.

inútil [in'util] *a* useless; *(esfuerzo)* vain, fruitless; **inutilidad** *nf* uselessness.

inutilizar [inutili'θar] *vt* to make *o* render useless; ~**se** *vr* to become useless.

invadir [inßa'ðir] *vt* to invade.

inválido, a [in'ßaliðo, a] *a* invalid // *nm/f* invalid.

invariable [inßa'rjaßle] *a* invariable.

invasión [inßa'sjon] *nf* invasion.

invasor, a [inßa'sor, a] *a* invading // *nm/f* invader.

invención [inßen'θjon] *nf* invention.

inventar [inßen'tar] *vt* to invent.

inventario [inßen'tarjo] *nm* inventory.

inventiva [inßen'tißa] *nf* inventiveness.

inventor, a [inßen'tor, a] *nm/f* inventor.

invernadero [inßerna'ðero] *nm* greenhouse.

inverosímil [inßero'simil] *a* implausible.

inversión [inßer'sjon] *nf* (COM) investment.

inverso, a [in'ßerso, a] *a* inverse, opposite; **en el orden** ~ in reverse order; **a la inversa** inversely, the other way round.

inversor, a [inßer'sor, a] *nm/f* (COM) investor.

invertir [inßer'tir] *vt* (COM) to invest; *(volcar)* to turn upside down; *(tiempo etc)* to spend.

investigación [inßestiva'θjon] *nf* investigation; *(ESCOL)* research; ~ **de mercado** market research.

investigar [inßesti'var] *vt* to investigate; *(ESCOL)* to do research into.

invicto, a [in'ßikto, a] *a* unconquered.

invierno [in'ßjerno] *nm* winter.

invisible [inßi'sißle] *a* invisible.

invitado, a [inßi'taðo, a] *nm/f* guest.

invitar [inßi'tar] *vt* to invite; *(incitar)* to entice; *(pagar)* to buy, pay for.

invocar [inßo'kar] *vt* to invoke, call on.

inyección [injek'θjon] *nf* injection.

inyectar [injek'tar] *vt* to inject.

ir [ir] ♦ *vi* **1** to go; *(a pie)* to walk; *(viajar)* to travel; ~ **caminando** to walk; **fui en tren** *o* travelled by train; **¡(ahora) voy!** (I'm just) coming!

2: ~ **(a) por:** ~ **(a) por el médico** to fetch the doctor

3 *(progresar: persona, cosa)* to go; **el trabajo va muy bien** work is going very well; **¿cómo te va?** how are things going?; **me va muy bien** I'm getting on

very well; **le fue fatal** it went awfully
badly for him
4 (funcionar): **el coche no va muy bien**
the car isn't running very well
5: te va estupendamente ese color that
colour suits you fantastically well
6 (locuciones): **¿vino? - ¡que va!** did he
come? - of course not!; **vamos, no llores**
come on, don't cry; **¡vaya coche!** what a
car!, that's some car!
**7: no vaya a ser: tienes que correr, no
vaya a ser que pierdas el tren** you'll
have to run so as not to miss the train
8 (+ pp): **iba vestido muy bien** he was
very well dressed
9: no me etc **va ni me viene** I etc don't
care
♦ vb auxiliar **1: ~ a: voy/iba a hacerlo
hoy** I am/was going to do it today
2 (+ gerundio): **iba anocheciendo** it was
getting dark; **todo se me iba aclarando**
everything was gradually becoming
clearer to me
3 (+ pp = pasivo): **van vendidos 300
ejemplares** 300 copies have been sold so
far
♦ ~**se** vr **1: ¿por dónde se va al
zoológico?** which is the way to the zoo?
2 (marcharse) to leave; **ya se habrán
ido** they must already have left o gone.
ira ['ira] nf anger, rage.
iracundo, a [ira'kundo, a] a irascible.
Irak [i'rak] nm = **Iraq**.
Irán [i'ran] nm Iran; **iraní** a, nm/f Ira-
nian.
Iraq [i'rak], **Irak** nm Iraq; **iraquí** [ira'ki]
a, nm/f Iraqui.
iris ['iris] nm (arco ~) rainbow; (ANAT)
iris.
Irlanda [ir'landa] nf Ireland; **irlandés,
esa** a Irish // nm/f Irishman/woman; **los
irlandeses** the Irish.
ironía [iro'nia] nf irony; **irónico, a** a
ironic(al).
irreal [irre'al] a unreal.
irrecuperable a [irrekupe'raßle]
irrecoverable, irretrievable.
irreflexión [irreflek'sjon] nf thoughtlessness.
irregular [irreɣu'lar] a (gen) irregular;
(situación) abnormal.
irremediable [irreme'ðjaßle] a irremediable; (vicio) incurable.
irresoluto, a [irreso'luto, a] a irresolute,
hesitant.
irrespetuoso, a [irrespe'twoso, a] a disrespectful.
irresponsable [irrespon'saßle] a
irresponsible.
irrigar [irri'ɣar] vt to irrigate.
irrisorio, a [irri'sorjo, a] a derisory,
ridiculous.
irritar [irri'tar] vt to irritate, annoy.
irrupción [irrup'θjon] nf irruption; (invasión) invasion.

isla ['isla] nf island.
islandés, esa [islan'des, esa] a Icelandic
// nm/f Icelander.
Islandia [is'landja] nf Iceland.
isleño, a [is'leɲo, a] a island cpd // nm/f
islander.
Israel [isra'el] nm Israel; **israelí** a, nm/f
Israeli.
istmo ['istmo] nm isthmus.
Italia [i'talja] nf Italy; **italiano, a** a, nm/f
Italian.
itinerario [itine'rarjo] nm itinerary,
route.
IVA ['ißa] nm abr ver **impuesto**.
izar [i'θar] vt to hoist.
izdo, a abr (= izquierdo, a) l.
izquierda [iθ'kjerda] nf left; (POL) left
(wing); **a la ~** (estar) on the left;
(torcer etc) (to the) left.
izquierdista [iθkjer'ðista] nm/f left-
winger, leftist.
izquierdo, a [iθ'kjerðo, a] a left.

J

jabalí [xaßa'li] nm wild boar.
jabalina [xaßa'lina] nf javelin.
jabón [xa'ßon] nm soap; **jabonar** vt to
soap.
jaca ['xaka] nf pony.
jacinto [xa'θinto] nm hyacinth.
jactarse [xak'tarse] vr to boast, brag.
jadear [xaðe'ar] vi to pant, gasp for
breath; **jadeo** nm panting, gasping.
jaguar [xa'ɣwar] nm jaguar.
jalbegue [xal'ßeɣe] nm (pintura) whitewash.
jalea [xa'lea] nf jelly.
jaleo [xa'leo] nm racket, uproar; **armar
un ~** to kick up a racket.
jalón [xa'lon] nm (AM) tug.
Jamaica [xa'maika] nf Jamaica.
jamás [xa'mas] ad never; (sin negación)
ever.
jamón [xa'mon] nm ham; **~ dulce, ~ de
York** cooked ham; **~ serrano** cured ham.
Japón [xa'pon] nm: **el ~** Japan;
japonés, esa a, nm/f Japanese.
jaque ['xake] nm: **~ mate** checkmate.
jaqueca [xa'keka] nf (very bad) head-
ache, migraine.
jarabe [xa'raße] nm syrup.
jarcia ['xarθja] nf (NAUT) ropes pl,
rigging.
jardín [xar'ðin] nm garden; **~ de (la)
infancia** (Esp) o **de niños** (AM) nursery
(school); **jardinería** nf gardening;
jardinero, a nm/f gardener.
jarra ['xarra] nf jar; (jarro) jug.
jarro ['xarro] nm jug.
jaula ['xaula] nf cage.
jauría [xau'ria] nf pack of hounds.
J. C. abr (= Jesucristo) J.C.
jefa ['xefa] nf woman head o boss.

jefatura [xefa'tura] *nf*: ~ de policía police headquarters *sg*.

jefe ['xefe] *nm/f* (*gen*) chief, head; (*patrón*) boss; ~ de camareros head waiter; ~ de cocina chef; ~ de estación stationmaster; ~ de estado head of state; ~ supremo commander-in-chief; ser el ~ (*fig*) to be the boss.

jengibre [xen'xiβre] *nm* ginger.

jeque ['xeke] *nm* sheik.

jerarquía [xerar'kia] *nf* (*orden*) hierarchy; (*rango*) rank; **jerárquico, a** *a* hierarchic(al).

jerez [xe're0] *nm* sherry.

jerga ['xerva] *nf* (*tela*) coarse cloth; (*lenguaje*) jargon.

jerigonza [xeri'von0a] *nf* (*jerga*) jargon, slang; (*galimatías*) nonsense, gibberish.

jeringa [xe'ringa] *nf* syringe; (*AM*) annoyance, bother; ~ de engrase grease gun; **jeringar** *vt* (*AM*) to annoy, bother.

jeroglífico [xero'ylifiko] *nm* hieroglyphic.

jersé, jersey [xer'sei] (*pl* **jerseys**) *nm* jersey, pullover, jumper.

Jerusalén [xerusa'len] *n* Jerusalem.

Jesucristo [xesu'kristo] *nm* Jesus Christ.

jesuita [xe'swita] *a, nm* Jesuit.

Jesús [xe'sus] *nm* Jesus; ¡~! good heavens!; (*al estornudar*) bless you!

jet ['jet] (*pl* ~**s**) *nm* jet (plane).

jícara ['xikara] *nf* small cup.

jinete, a [xi'nete, a] *nm/f* horseman/woman, rider.

jipijapa [xipi'xapa] *nm* (*AM*) straw hat.

jirafa [xi'rafa] *nf* giraffe.

jirón [xi'ron] *nm* rag, shred.

jocoso, a [xo'koso, a] *a* humorous, jocular.

jofaina [xo'faina] *nf* washbasin.

jornada [xor'naδa] *nf* (*viaje de un día*) day's journey; (*camino o viaje entero*) journey; (*día de trabajo*) working day.

jornal [xor'nal] *nm* (day's) wage; ~**ero** *nm* (day) labourer.

joroba [xo'roβa] *nf* hump, hunched back; ~**do, a** *a* hunchbacked // *nm/f* hunchback.

jota ['xota] *nf* (the letter) J; (*danza*) Aragonese dance; (*fam*) jot, iota; **no saber ni** ~ to have no idea.

joven ['xoβen] (*pl* **jóvenes**) *a* young // *nm* young man, youth // *nf* young woman, girl.

jovial [xo'βial] *a* cheerful, jolly; ~**idad** *nf* cheerfulness, jolliness.

joya ['xoja] *nf* jewel, gem; (*fig: persona*) gem; **joyería** *nf* (*joyas*) jewellery; (*tienda*) jeweller's (shop); **joyero** *nm* (*persona*) jeweller; (*caja*) jewel case.

juanete [xwa'nete] *nm* (*del pie*) bunion.

jubilación [xuβila'0jon] *nf* (*retiro*) retirement.

jubilado, a [xuβi'laδo, a] *a* retired // *nm/f* pensioner (*Brit*), senior citizen.

jubilar [xuβi'lar] *vt* to pension off, retire;

(*fam*) to discard; ~**se** *vr* to retire.

jubileo [xuβi'leo] *nm* jubilee.

júbilo ['xuβilo] *nm* joy, rejoicing; **jubiloso, a** *a* jubilant.

judía [xu'δia] *nf* Jewess; (*CULIN*) bean; ~ verde French bean.

judicial [xuδi'0jal] *a* judicial.

judío, a [xu'δio, a] *a* Jewish // *nm/f* Jew(ess).

judo ['juδo] *nm* judo.

juego *etc vb ver* **jugar** // ['xwevo] *nm* (*gen*) play; (*pasatiempo, partido*) game; (*en casino*) gambling; (*conjunto*) set; **fuera de** ~ (*DEPORTE: persona*) offside; (: *pelota*) out of play; **J~s Olímpicos** Olympic Games.

juerga ['xwerva] *nf* binge; (*fiesta*) party; **ir de** ~ to go out on a binge.

jueves ['xweβes] *nm inv* Thursday.

juez [xwe0] *nm/f* judge; ~ de línea linesman; ~ de salida starter.

jugada [xu'vaδa] *nf* play; **buena** ~ good move/shot/stroke *etc*.

jugador, a [xuva'δor, a] *nm/f* player; (*en casino*) gambler.

jugar [xu'var] *vt, vi* to play; (*en casino*) to gamble; (*apostar*) to bet; ~ al fútbol to play football; ~**se** *vr* to gamble (away).

juglar [xu'vlar] *nm* minstrel.

jugo ['xuvo] *nm* (*BOT*) juice; (*fig*) essence, substance; ~ de fruta (*AM*) fruit juice; ~**so, a** *a* juicy; (*fig*) substantial, important.

juguete [xu'vete] *nm* toy; ~**ar** *vi* to play; ~**ría** *nf* toyshop.

juguetón, ona [xuve'ton, ona] *a* playful.

juicio ['xwi0jo] *nm* judgement; (*razón*) sanity, reason; (*opinión*) opinion; **estar fuera de** ~ to be out of one's mind; ~**so, a** *a* wise, sensible.

julio ['xuljo] *nm* July.

junco ['xunko] *nm* rush, reed.

jungla ['xungla] *nf* jungle.

junio ['xunjo] *nm* June.

junta ['xunta] *nf ver* **junto**.

juntar [xun'tar] *vt* to join, unite; (*maquinaria*) to assemble, put together; (*dinero*) to collect; ~**se** *vr* to join, meet; (*reunirse: personas*) to meet, assemble; (*arrimarse*) to approach, draw closer; ~**se con uno** to join sb.

junto, a ['xunto, a] *a* joined; (*unido*) united; (*anexo*) near, close; (*contiguo, próximo*) next, adjacent // *ad*: **todo** ~ all at once // *nf* (*asamblea*) meeting, assembly; (*comité, consejo*) board, council, committee; (*articulación*) joint; ~ a near (to), next to; ~**s** together.

jurado [xu'raδo] *nm* (*JUR: individuo*) juror; (: *grupo*) jury; (*de concurso: grupo*) panel (of judges); (: *individuo*) member of a panel.

juramento [xura'mento] *nm* oath; (*maldición*) oath, curse; **prestar** ~ to take the oath; **tomar** ~ **a** to swear in, administer the oath to.

jurar [xu'rar] *vt, vi* to swear; ~ **en falso** to commit perjury; **jurárselas a uno to have it in for sb.**

jurídico, a [xu'riðiko, a] *a* legal.

jurisdicción [xurisðik'θjon] *nf* (*poder, autoridad*) jurisdiction; (*territorio*) district.

jurisprudencia [xurispru'ðenθja] *nf* jurisprudence.

jurista [xu'rista] *nm/f* jurist.

justamente [xusta'mente] *ad* justly, fairly; (*precisamente*) just, exactly.

justicia [xus'tiθja] *nf* justice; (*equidad*) fairness, justice; **justiciero, a** *a* just, righteous.

justificación [xustifika'θjon] *nf* justification; **justificar** *vt* to justify.

justo, a ['xusto, a] *a* (*equitativo*) just, fair, right; (*preciso*) exact, correct; (*ajustado*) tight // *ad* (*precisamente*) exactly, precisely; (*AM: apenas a tiempo*) just in time.

juvenil [xuße'nil] *a* youthful.

juventud [xußen'tuð] *nf* (*adolescencia*) youth; (*jóvenes*) young people *pl*.

juzgado [xuθ'ɣaðo] *nm* tribunal; (*JUR*) court.

juzgar [xuθ'ɣar] *vt* to judge; **a** ~ **por...** to judge by..., judging by... .

K

kg *abr* (= *kilogramo*) kg.

kilo ['kilo] *nm* kilo // *pref:* ~**gramo** *nm* kilogramme; ~**metraje** *nm* distance in kilometres, ≈ mileage; **kilómetro** *nm* kilometre; ~**vatio** *nm* kilowatt.

kiosco ['kjosko] *nm* = **quiosco.**

km *abr* (= *kilómetro*) km.

kv *abr* (= *kilovatio*) kw.

L

l *abr* (= *litro*) l.

la [la] *artículo definido* the // *pron* her; (*Ud.*) you; (*cosa*) it // *nm* (*MUS*) la; ~ **del sombrero rojo** the girl in the red hat; *tb ver* **el.**

laberinto [laße'rinto] *nm* labyrinth.

labia ['laßja] *nf* fluency; (*pey*) glib tongue.

labial [la'βjal] *a* labial.

labio ['laβjo] *nm* lip.

labor [la'βor] *nf* labour; (*AGR*) farm work; (*tarea*) job, task; (*COSTURA*) needlework; ~**able** *a* (*AGR*) workable; **día** ~**able** working day; ~**ar** *vi* to work.

laboratorio [laßora'torjo] *nm* laboratory.

laborioso, a [laßo'rjoso, a] *a* (*persona*) hard-working; (*trabajo*) tough.

laborista [laßo'rista] *a:* **Partido L**~ La-

bour Party.

labrado, a [la'βraðo, a] *a* worked; (*madera*) carved; (*metal*) wrought // *nm* (*AGR*) cultivated field.

labrador, a [laßra'ðor, a] *a* farming *cpd* // *nm/f* farmer.

labranza [la'βranθa] *nf* (*AGR*) cultivation.

labrar [la'βrar] *vt* (*gen*) to work; (*madera etc*) to carve; (*fig*) to cause, bring about.

labriego, a [la'βrjeɣo, a] *nm/f* peasant.

laca ['laka] *nf* lacquer.

lacayo [la'kajo] *nm* lackey.

lacerar [laθe'rar] *vt* to lacerate.

lacio, a ['laθjo, a] *a* (*pelo*) lank, straight.

lacónico, a [la'koniko, a] *a* laconic.

lacrar [la'krar] *vt* (*cerrar*) to seal (with sealing wax); **lacre** *nm* sealing wax.

lacrimoso, a [lakri'moso, a] *a* tearful.

lactar [lak'tar] *vt, vi* to suckle.

lácteo, a ['lakteo, a] *a:* **productos** ~**s** dairy products.

ladear [laðe'ar] *vt* to tip, tilt // *vi* to tilt; ~**se** *vr* to lean.

ladera [la'ðera] *nf* slope.

ladino, a [la'ðino, a] *a* cunning.

lado ['laðo] *nm* (*gen*) side; (*fig*) protection; (*MIL*) flank; **al** ~ **de** beside; **poner de** ~ to put on its side; **poner a un** ~ to put aside; **por todos** ~**s** on all sides, all round (*Brit*).

ladrar [la'ðrar] *vi* to bark; **ladrido** *nm* bark, barking.

ladrillo [la'ðriʎo] *nm* (*gen*) brick; (*azulejo*) tile.

ladrón, ona [la'ðron, ona] *nm/f* thief.

lagar [la'ɣar] *nm* (*wine/oil*) press.

lagartija [laɣar'tixa] *nf* (small) lizard.

lagarto [la'ɣarto] *nm* (*ZOOL*) lizard.

lago ['laɣo] *nm* lake.

lágrima ['laɣrima] *nf* tear.

laguna [la'ɣuna] *nf* (*lago*) lagoon; (*hueco*) gap.

laico, a ['laiko, a] *a* lay.

lamentable [lamen'taßle] *a* lamentable, regrettable; (*miserable*) pitiful.

lamentar [lamen'tar] *vt* (*sentir*) to regret; (*deplorar*) to lament; **lo lamento mucho** I'm very sorry; ~**se** *vr* to lament; **lamento** *nm* lament.

lamer [la'mer] *vt* to lick.

lámina ['lamina] *nf* (*plancha delgada*) sheet; (*para estampar, estampa*) plate; **laminar** *vt* (*en libro*) to laminate.

lámpara ['lampara] *nf* lamp; ~ **de alcohol/gas** spirit/gas lamp; ~ **de pie** standard lamp.

lamparón [lampa'ron] *nm* grease spot.

lampiño [lam'piɲo] *a* clean-shaven.

lana ['lana] *nf* wool.

lance *vt ver* **lanzar** // ['lanθe] *nm* (*golpe*) stroke; (*suceso*) event, incident.

lancha ['lantʃa] *nf* launch; ~ **de pesca** fishing boat; ~ **salvavidas/torpedera** lifeboat/torpedo boat.

lanero, a [la'nero, a] *a* woollen.

langosta [lan'gosta] *nf* (*insecto*) locust; (*crustáceo*) lobster; (*fig*) plague; **langostino** *nm* king prawn (*Brit*), crayfish (*US*).

languidecer [langiðe'θer] *vi* to languish; **languidez** *nf* languor; **lánguido, a** *a* (*gen*) languid; (*sin energía*) listless.

lanilla [la'niʎa] *nf* nap.

lanudo, a [la'nuðo, a] *a* woolly.

lanza ['lanθa] *nf* (*arma*) lance, spear.

lanzadera [lanθa'ðera] *nf* shuttle.

lanzamiento [lanθa'mjento] *nm* (*gen*) throwing; (*NAUT, COM*) launch, launching; ~ **de peso** putting the shot.

lanzar [lan'θar] *vt* (*gen*) to throw; (*DEPORTE: pelota*) to bowl; (*NAUT, COM*) to launch; (*JUR*) to evict; ~**se** *vr* to throw o.s.

lapa ['lapa] *nf* limpet.

lapicero [lapi'θero] *nm* propelling (*Brit*) *o* mechanical (*US*) pencil; (*AM: bolígrafo*) Biro ®.

lápida ['lapiða] *nf* stone; ~ **mortuoria** headstone; ~ **conmemorativa** memorial stone; **lapidar** *vt* to stone; **lapidario, a** *a, nm* lapidary.

lápiz ['lapiθ] *nm* pencil; ~ **de color** coloured pencil; ~ **de labios** lipstick.

lapón, ona [la'pon, ona] *nm/f* Laplander, Lapp.

Laponia [la'ponja] *nf* Lapland.

lapso ['lapso] *nm* (*de tiempo*) interval; (*error*) error.

lapsus ['lapsus] *nm inv* error, mistake.

largar [lar'var] *vt* (*soltar*) to release; (*aflojar*) to loosen; (*lanzar*) to launch; (*fam*) to let fly; (*velas*) to unfurl; (*AM*) to throw; ~**se** *vr* (*fam*) to beat it; ~**se a** (*AM*) to start to.

largo, a ['larvo, a] *a* (*longitud*) long; (*tiempo*) lengthy; (*fig*) generous // *nm* length; (*MUS*) largo // *ad* widely; **dos años** ~**s** two long years; **tiene 9 metros de** ~ it is 9 metres long; **a lo** ~ **de** along; (*tiempo*) all through, throughout.

laringe [la'rinxe] *nf* larynx; **laringitis** *nf* laryngitis.

larva ['larßa] *nf* larva.

las [las] *artículo definido* the // *pron* them; ~ **que cantan** the ones/women/girls who sing; *tb ver* **el**.

lascivo, a [las'θißo, a] *a* lewd.

láser ['laser] *nm* laser.

lástima ['lastima] *nf* (*pena*) pity; **dar** ~ to be pitiful; **es una** ~ **que** it's a pity that; **¡qué** ~**!** what a pity!; **ella está hecha una** ~ she looks pitiful.

lastimar [lasti'mar] *vt* (*herir*) to wound; (*ofender*) to offend; ~**se** *vr* to hurt o.s.; **lastimero, a** *a* pitiful, pathetic.

lastre ['lastre] *nm* (*TEC, NAUT*) ballast; (*fig*) dead weight.

lata ['lata] *nf* (*metal*) tin; (*caja*) tin (*Brit*), can; (*fam*) nuisance; **en** ~ tinned

(*Brit*), canned; **dar (la)** ~ to be a nuisance.

latente [la'tente] *a* latent.

lateral [late'ral] *a* side *cpd*, lateral // *nm* (*TEATRO*) wings.

latido [la'tiðo] *nm* (*del corazón*) beat.

latifundio [lati'fundjo] *nm* large estate; **latifundista** *nm/f* owner of a large estate.

latigazo [lati'vaθo] *nm* (*golpe*) lash; (*sonido*) crack.

látigo ['latixo] *nm* whip.

latín [la'tin] *nm* Latin.

latino, a [la'tino, a] *a* Latin; ~**americano, a** *a, nm/f* Latin-American.

latir [la'tir] *vi* (*corazón, pulso*) to beat.

latitud [lati'tuð] *nf* (*GEO*) latitude.

latón [la'ton] *nm* brass.

latoso, a [la'toso, a] *a* (*molesto*) annoying; (*aburrido*) boring.

laúd [la'uð] *nm* lute.

laureado, a [laure'aðo, a] *a* honoured // *nm* laureate.

laurel [lau'rel] *nm* (*BOT*) laurel; (*CULIN*) bay.

lava ['laßa] *nf* lava.

lavabo [la'ßaßo] *nm* (*jofaina*) washbasin; (*tb*: ~**s**) toilet.

lavadero [laßa'ðero] *nm* laundry.

lavado [la'ßaðo] *nm* washing; (*de ropa*) laundry; (*ARTE*) wash; ~ **de cerebro** brainwashing; ~ **en seco** dry-cleaning.

lavadora [laßa'ðora] *nf* washing machine.

lavanda [la'ßanda] *nf* lavender.

lavandería [laßande'ria] *nf* laundry; ~ **automática** launderette.

lavaplatos [laßa'platos] *nm inv* dishwasher.

lavar [la'ßar] *vt* to wash; (*borrar*) to wipe away; ~**se** *vr* to wash o.s.; ~**se las manos** to wash one's hands; ~ **y marcar** (*pelo*) to shampoo and set; ~ **en seco** to dry-clean.

lavavajillas [laßaßa'xiʎas] *nm inv* dishwasher.

laxante [lak'sante] *nm* laxative.

lazada [la'θaða] *nf* bow.

lazarillo [laθa'riʎo] *nm*: **perro** ~ guide dog.

lazo ['laθo] *nm* knot; (*lazada*) bow; (*para animales*) lasso; (*trampa*) snare; (*vínculo*) tie.

le [le] *pron* (*directo*) him; (: *usted*) you; (*indirecto*) to him; (: *usted*) to you.

leal [le'al] *a* loyal; ~**tad** *nf* loyalty.

lebrel [le'ßrel] *nm* greyhound.

lección [lek'θjon] *nf* lesson.

lector, a [lek'tor, a] *nm/f* reader.

lectura [lek'tura] *nf* reading.

leche ['letʃe] *nf* milk; **tener mala** ~ (*fam!*) to be nasty; ~ **condensada/en polvo** condensed/powdered milk; ~ **desnatada** skimmed milk; ~**ra** *nf* (*vendedora*) milkmaid; (*recipiente*) milk churn; (*AM*) cow; ~**ría** *nf* dairy; ~**ro,**

a *a* dairy.

lecho ['letʃo] *nm* (*cama, de río*) bed; (*GEO*) layer.

lechón [le'tʃon] *nm* sucking (*Brit*) o suckling (*US*) pig.

lechoso, a [le'tʃoso, a] *a* milky.

lechuga [le'tʃuɣa] *nf* lettuce.

lechuza [le'tʃuθa] *nf* owl.

leer [le'er] *vt* to read.

legado [le'ɣaðo] *nm* (*don*) bequest; (*herencia*) legacy; (*enviado*) legate.

legajo [le'ɣaxo] *nm* file.

legal [le'ɣal] *a* (*gen*) legal; (*persona*) trustworthy; **~idad** *nf* legality; **~izar** *vt* to legalize; (*documento*) to authenticate.

legaña [le'ɣaɲa] *nf* sleep (*in eyes*).

legar [le'ɣar] *vt* to bequeath, leave.

legendario, a [lexen'darjo, a] *a* legendary.

legión [le'xjon] *nf* legion; **legionario, a** *a* legionary // *nm* legionnaire.

legislación [lexisla'θjon] *nf* legislation; **legislar** *vt* to legislate.

legitimar [lexiti'mar] *vt* to legitimize; **legítimo, a** *a* (*genuino*) authentic; (*legal*) legitimate.

lego, a ['leɣo, a] *a* (*REL*) secular; (*ignorante*) ignorant // *nm* layman.

legua ['leɣwa] *nf* league.

legumbres [le'ɣumbres] *nfpl* pulses.

leído, a [le'iðo, a] *a* well-read.

lejanía [lexa'nia] *nf* distance; **lejano, a** *a* far-off; (*en el tiempo*) distant; (*fig*) remote.

lejía [le'xia] *nf* bleach.

lejos ['lexos] *ad* far, far away; **a lo ~** in the distance; **de** o **desde ~** from afar; **~ de** *prep* far from.

lelo, a ['lelo, a] *a* silly // *nm/f* idiot.

lema ['lema] *nm* motto; (*POL*) slogan.

lencería [lenθe'ria] *nf* linen, drapery.

lengua ['lengwa] *nf* tongue; (*LING*) language; **morderse la ~** to hold one's tongue.

lenguado [len'gwaðo] *nm* sole.

lenguaje [len'gwaxe] *nm* language.

lengüeta [len'gweta] *nf* (*ANAT*) epiglottis; (*zapatos, MUS*) tongue.

lente ['lente] *nf* lens; (*lupa*) magnifying glass; **~s** *nfpl* glasses; **~s de contacto** contact lenses.

lenteja [len'texa] *nf* lentil; **lentejuela** *nf* sequin.

lentilla [len'tiʎa] *nf* contact lens.

lentitud [lenti'tuð] *nf* slowness; **con ~** slowly.

lento, a ['lento, a] *a* slow.

leña ['leɲa] *nf* firewood; **~dor, a** *nm/f* woodcutter.

leño ['leɲo] *nm* (*trozo de árbol*) log; (*madera*) timber; (*fig*) blockhead.

Leo ['leo] *nm* Leo.

león [le'on] *nm* lion; **~ marino** sea lion; **leonino, a** *a* leonine.

leopardo [leo'parðo] *nm* leopard.

leotardos [leo'tarðos] *nmpl* tights.

lepra ['lepra] *nf* leprosy; **leproso, a** *nm/f* leper.

lerdo, a ['lerðo, a] *a* (*lento*) slow; (*patoso*) clumsy.

les [les] *pron* (*directo*) them; (: *ustedes*) you; (*indirecto*) to them; (: *ustedes*) to you.

lesbiana [les'βjana] *a, nf* lesbian.

lesión [le'sjon] *nf* wound, lesion; (*DEPORTE*) injury; **lesionado, a** *a* injured // *nm/f* injured person.

letal [le'tal] *a* lethal.

letanía [leta'nia] *nf* litany.

letargo [le'tarɣo] *nm* lethargy.

letra ['letra] *nf* letter; (*escritura*) handwriting; (*MUS*) lyrics *pl*; **~ de cambio** bill of exchange; **~ de imprenta** print; **~do, a** *a* learned; (*fam*) pedantic // *nm* lawyer; **letrero** *nm* (*cartel*) sign; (*etiqueta*) label.

letrina [le'trina] *nf* latrine.

leucemia [leu'θemja] *nf* leukaemia.

levadizo [leβa'ðiθo] *a*: **puente ~** drawbridge.

levadura [leβa'ðura] *nf* (*para el pan*) yeast; (*de la cerveza*) brewer's yeast.

levantamiento [leβanta'mjento] *nm* raising, lifting; (*rebelión*) revolt, rising; **~ de pesos** weight-lifting.

levantar [leβan'tar] *vt* (*gen*) to raise; (*del suelo*) to pick up; (*hacia arriba*) to lift (up); (*plan*) to make, draw up; (*mesa*) to clear away; (*campamento*) to strike; (*fig*) to cheer up, hearten; **~se** *vr* to get up; (*enderezarse*) to straighten up; (*rebelarse*) to rebel; **~ el ánimo** to cheer up.

levante [le'βante] *nm* east coast; **el L~** *region of Spain extending from Castellón to Murcia*.

levar [le'βar] *vt* to weigh anchor.

leve ['leβe] *a* light; (*fig*) trivial; **~dad** *nf* lightness.

levita [le'βita] *nf* frock coat.

léxico ['leksiko] *nm* (*vocabulario*) vocabulary.

ley [lei] *nf* (*gen*) law; (*metal*) standard.

leyenda [le'jenda] *nf* legend.

leyó *etc vb ver* **leer**.

liar [li'ar] *vt* to tie (up); (*unir*) to bind; (*envolver*) to wrap (up); (*enredar*) to confuse; (*cigarrillo*) to roll; **~se** *vr* (*fam*) to get involved; **~se a palos** to get involved in a fight.

Líbano ['liβano] *nm*: **el ~** the Lebanon.

libar [li'βar] *vt* to suck.

libelo [li'βelo] *nm* satire, lampoon; (*JUR*) petition.

libélula [li'βelula] *nf* dragonfly.

liberación [liβera'θjon] *nf* liberation; (*de la cárcel*) release.

liberal [liβe'ral] *a, nm/f* liberal; **~idad** *nf* liberality, generosity.

liberar [liβe'rar] *vt* to liberate.

libertad [liβer'taδ] *nf* liberty, freedom; ~ de culto/de prensa/de comercio freedom of worship/of the press/of trade; ~ condicional probation; ~ bajo palabra parole; ~ bajo fianza bail.

libertar [liβer'tar] *vt* (*preso*) to set free; (*de una obligación*) to release; (*eximir*) to exempt.

libertino, a [liβer'tino, a] *a* permissive // *nm/f* permissive person.

libra ['liβra] *nf* pound; L~ (*ASTROLOGIA*) Libra; ~ esterlina pound sterling.

librador, a [liβra'δor, a] *nm/f* drawer.

libramiento [liβra'mjento] *nm* rescue; (*COM*) delivery.

libranza [li'βranθa] *nf* (*COM*) draft; (*letra de cambio*) bill of exchange.

librar [li'βrar] *vt* (*de peligro*) to save; (*batalla*) to wage, fight; (*de impuestos*) to exempt; (*cheque*) to make out; (*JUR*) to exempt; ~se *vr*: ~se de to escape from, free o.s. from.

libre ['liβre] *a* free; (*lugar*) unoccupied; (*asiento*) vacant; (*de deudas*) free of debts; ~ de impuestos free of tax; tiro ~ free kick; los 100 metros ~ the 100 metres free-style (race); al aire ~ in the open air.

librería [liβre'ria] *nf* (*tienda*) bookshop; **librero, a** *nm/f* bookseller.

libreta [li'βreta] *nf* notebook; ~ de ahorros savings book.

libro ['liβro] *nm* book; ~ de bolsillo paperback; ~ de caja cashbook; ~ de cheques chequebook (*Brit*), checkbook (*US*); ~ de texto textbook.

Lic. *abr* = **licenciado, a.**

licencia [li'θenθja] *nf* (*gen*) licence; (*permiso*) permission; ~ por enfermedad/con goce de sueldo sick leave/paid leave; ~ de caza game licence; ~do, a *a* licensed // *nm/f* graduate; **licenciar** *vt* (*empleado*) to dismiss; (*permitir*) to permit, allow; (*soldado*) to discharge; (*estudiante*) to confer a degree upon; **licenciarse** *vr*: licenciarse en letras to graduate in arts.

licencioso, a [liθen'θjoso, a] *a* licentious.

liceo [li'θeo] *nm* (high) school.

licitar [liθi'tar] *vt* to bid for; (*AM*) to sell by auction.

lícito, a ['liθito, a] *a* (*legal*) lawful; (*justo*) fair, just; (*permisible*) permissible.

licor [li'kor] *nm* spirits *pl* (*Brit*), liquor (*US*); (*de frutas etc*) liqueur.

licuadora [likwa'δora] *nf* blender.

licuar [li'kwar] *vt* to liquidize.

lid [liδ] *nf* combat; (*fig*) controversy.

líder [li'δer] *nm/f* leader; **liderato, liderazgo** *nm* leadership.

lidia ['liδja] *nf* bullfighting; (*una ~*) bullfight; toros de ~ fighting bulls; **lidiar** *vt, vi* to fight.

liebre ['ljeβre] *nf* hare.

lienzo ['ljenθo] *nm* linen; (*ARTE*) canvas; (*ARQ*) wall.

liga ['liɣa] *nf* (*de medias*) garter, suspender; (*AM*: *gomita*) rubber band; (*confederación*) league.

ligadura [liɣa'δura] *nf* bond, tie; (*MED, MUS*) ligature.

ligamento [liɣa'mento] *nm* (*ANAT*) ligament; (*atadura*) tie; (*unión*) bond.

ligar [li'ɣar] *vt* (*atar*) to tie; (*unir*) to join; (*MED*) to bind up; (*MUS*) to slur // *vi* to mix, blend; (*fam*) to pick up; ~se *vr* to commit o.s.

ligereza [lixe'reθa] *nf* lightness; (*rapidez*) swiftness; (*agilidad*) agility; (*superficialidad*) flippancy.

ligero, a [li'xero, a] *a* (*de peso*) light; (*tela*) thin; (*rápido*) swift, quick; (*ágil*) agile, nimble; (*de importancia*) slight; (*de carácter*) flippant, superficial // *ad*: a la ligera superficially.

liguero [li'ɣero] *nm* suspender (*Brit*) o garter (*US*) belt.

lija ['lixa] *nf* (*ZOOL*) dogfish; (*papel de*) ~ sandpaper.

lila ['lila] *nf* lilac.

lima ['lima] *nf* file; (*BOT*) lime; ~ de uñas nailfile; L~ *n* (*GEO*) Lima; **limar** *vt* to file.

limitación [limita'θjon] *nf* limitation, limit; ~ de velocidad speed limit.

limitar [limi'tar] *vt* to limit; (*reducir*) to reduce, cut down // *vi*: ~ con to border on; ~se *vr*: ~se a to limit o.s. to.

límite ['limite] *nm* (*gen*) limit; (*fin*) end; (*frontera*) border; ~ de velocidad speed limit.

limítrofe [li'mitrofe] *a* bordering, neighbouring.

limón [li'mon] *nm* lemon // *a*: amarillo ~ lemon-yellow; **limonada** *nf* lemonade; **limonero** *nm* lemon tree.

limosna [li'mosna] *nf* alms *pl*; vivir de ~ to live on charity.

limpiabotas [limpja'βotas] *nm/f inv* bootblack (*Brit*), shoeshine boy/girl.

limpiaparabrisas [limpjapara'βrisas] *nm inv* windscreen (*Brit*) o windshield (*US*) wiper.

limpiar [lim'pjar] *vt* to clean; (*con trapo*) to wipe; (*quitar*) to wipe away; (*zapatos*) to shine, polish; (*fig*) to clean up.

limpieza [lim'pjeθa] *nf* (*estado*) cleanliness; (*acto*) cleaning; (: *de las calles*) cleansing; (: *de zapatos*) polishing; (*habilidad*) skill; (*fig*: *POLICIA*) clean-up; (*pureza*) purity; (*MIL*): **operación de** ~ mopping-up operation; ~ en seco dry cleaning.

limpio, a ['limpjo, a] *a* clean; (*moralmente*) pure; (*COM*) clear, net; (*fam*) honest // *ad*: jugar ~ to play fair // *nm*: pasar a (*Esp*) o en (*AM*) ~ to make a fair copy.

linaje [li'naxe] *nm* lineage, family.

linaza [li'naθa] *nf* linseed.

lince ['linθe] *nm* lynx.

linchar [lin'tʃar] *vt* to lynch.

lindar [lin'dar] *vi* to adjoin; ~ **con** to border on; **linde** *nm o f* boundary; **lindero, a** *a* adjoining // *nm* boundary.

lindo, a ['lindo, a] *a* pretty, lovely // *ad*: **nos divertimos de lo** ~ we had a marvellous time; **canta muy** ~ (*AM*) he sings beautifully.

línea ['linea] *nf* line; **en** ~ (*INFORM*) on line; ~ **aérea** airline; ~ **de meta** goal line; (*de carrera*) finishing line; ~ **recta** straight line.

lingote [lin'gote] *nm* ingot.

lingüista [lin'gwista] *nm/f* linguist; **lingüística** *nf* linguistics *sg*.

linimento [lini'mento] *nm* liniment.

lino ['lino] *nm* linen; (*BOT*) flax.

linóleo [li'noleo] *nm* lino, linoleum.

linterna [lin'terna] *nf* lantern, lamp; ~ **eléctrica** *o* **a pilas** torch (*Brit*), flashlight (*US*).

lío ['lio] *nm* bundle; (*fam*) fuss; (*desorden*) muddle, mess; **armar un** ~ to make a fuss.

liquen ['liken] *nm* lichen.

liquidación [likiða'θjon] *nf* liquidation; **venta de** ~ clearance sale.

liquidar [liki'ðar] *vt* (*mercancías*) to liquidate; (*deudas*) to pay off; (*empresa*) to wind up.

líquido, a ['likiðo, a] *a* liquid; (*ganancia*) net // *nm* liquid; ~ **imponible** net taxable income.

lira ['lira] *nf* (*MUS*) lyre; (*moneda*) lira.

lírico, a ['liriko, a] *a* lyrical.

lirio ['lirjo] *nm* (*BOT*) iris.

lirón [li'ron] *nm* (*ZOOL*) dormouse; (*fig*) sleepyhead.

Lisboa [lis'βoa] *n* Lisbon.

lisiado, a [li'sjaðo, a] *a* injured // *nm/f* cripple.

lisiar [li'sjar] *vt* to maim; ~**se** *vr* to injure o.s.

liso, a ['liso, a] *a* (*terreno*) flat; (*cabello*) straight; (*superficie*) even; (*tela*) plain.

lisonja [li'sonxa] *nf* flattery; **lisonjear** *vt* to flatter; (*fig*) to please; **lisonjero, a** *a* flattering; (*agradable*) gratifying, pleasing // *nm/f* flatterer.

lista ['lista] *nf* list; (*de alumnos*) school register; (*de libros*) catalogue; (*de platos*) menu; (*de precios*) price list; **pasar** ~ to call the roll; ~ **de correos** poste restante; ~ **de espera** waiting list; **tela a** ~**s** striped material.

listado, a [lis'taðo, a] *a* striped.

listo, a ['listo, a] *a* (*perspicaz*) smart, clever; (*preparado*) ready.

listón [lis'ton] *nm* (*tela*) ribbon; (*de madera, metal*) strip.

litera [li'tera] *nf* (*en barco, tren*) berth;

(*en dormitorio*) bunk, bunk bed.

literal [lite'ral] *a* literal.

literario, a [lite'rarjo, a] *a* literary.

literato, a [lite'rato, a] *a* literary // *nm/f* writer.

literatura [litera'tura] *nf* literature.

litigar [liti'ɣar] *vt* to fight // *vi* (*JUR*) to go to law; (*fig*) to dispute, argue.

litigio [li'tixjo] *nm* (*JUR*) lawsuit; (*fig*): **en** ~ **con** in dispute with.

litografía [litoɣra'fia] *nf* lithography; (*una* ~) lithograph.

litoral [lito'ral] *a* coastal // *nm* coast, seaboard.

litro ['litro] *nm* litre.

liviano, a [li'βjano, a] *a* (*persona*) fickle; (*cosa, objeto*) trivial.

lívido, a ['liβiðo, a] *a* livid.

ll... *ver bajo la letra* LL, *después de* L.

lo [lo] *artículo definido neutro*; ~ **bello** the beautiful, what is beautiful; **that which is beautiful** // *pron* (*persona*) him; (*cosa*) it; *tb ver* **el**.

loa ['loa] *nf* praise; **loable** *a* praiseworthy; **loar** *vt* to praise.

lobato [lo'βato] *nm* (*ZOOL*) wolf cub.

lobo ['loβo] *nm* wolf; ~ **de mar** (*fig*) sea dog; ~ **marino** seal.

lóbrego, a ['loβreɣo, a] *a* dark; (*fig*) gloomy.

lóbulo ['loβulo] *nm* lobe.

local [lo'kal] *a* local // *nm* place, site; (*oficinas*) premises *pl*; ~**idad** *nf* (*barrio*) locality; (*lugar*) location; (*TEATRO*) seat, ticket; (*lugar*) location; **~izar** *vt* (*ubicar*) to locate, find; (*restringir*) to localize; (*situar*) to place.

loción [lo'θjon] *nf* lotion.

loco, a ['loko, a] *a* mad // *nm/f* lunatic, mad person.

locomoción [lokomo'θjon] *nf* locomotion.

locomotora [lokomo'tora] *nf* engine, locomotive.

locuaz [lo'kwaθ] *a* loquacious.

locución [loku'θjon] *nf* expression.

locura [lo'kura] *nf* madness; (*acto*) crazy act.

locutor, a [loku'tor, a] *nm/f* (*RADIO*) announcer; (*comentarista*) commentator; (*TV*) newsreader.

locutorio [loku'torjo] *nm* (*en telefónica*) telephone booth.

lodo ['lodo] *nm* mud.

lógico, a ['loxiko, a] *a* logical // *nf* logic.

logística [lo'xistika] *nf* logistics *pl*.

lograr [lo'ɣrar] *vt* to achieve; (*obtener*) to get, obtain; ~ **hacer** to manage to do; ~ **que uno venga** to manage to get sb to come.

logro ['loɣro] *nm* achievement, success.

loma ['loma] *nf* hillock (*Brit*), small hill.

lombriz [lom'briθ] *nf* worm.

lomo ['lomo] *nm* (*de animal*) back; (*CULIN: de cerdo*) pork loin; (: *de vaca*) rib steak; (*de libro*) spine.

lona ['lona] *nf* canvas.

loncha ['lontʃa] *nf* = **lonja**.

lonche ['lontʃe] *nm* (*AM*) lunch; **~ría** *nf* (*AM*) snack bar, diner (*US*).

Londres ['londres] *n* London.

longaniza [longa'niθa] *nf* pork sausage.

longitud [lonxi'tuð] *nf* length; (*GEO*) longitude; **tener 3 metros de ~** to be 3 metres long; **~ de onda** wavelength.

lonja ['lonxa] *nf* slice; (*de tocino*) rasher; **~ de pescado** fish market.

loro ['loro] *nm* parrot.

los [los] *artículo definido* the // *pron* them; (*ustedes*) you; **mis libros y ~ de** Ud my books and yours; *tb ver* **el**.

losa ['losa] *nf* stone; **~ sepulcral** gravestone.

lote ['lote] *nm* portion; (*COM*) lot.

lotería [lote'ria] *nf* lottery; (*juego*) lotto.

loza ['loθa] *nf* crockery.

lozanía [loθa'nia] *nf* (*lujo*) luxuriance; **lozano, a** *a* luxuriant; (*animado*) lively.

lubricante [luβri'kante] *nm* lubricant.

lubricar [luβri'kar] *vt* to lubricate.

lucero [lu'θero] *nm* bright star; (*fig*) brilliance.

lucidez [luθi'ðeθ] *nf* lucidity; **lúcido, a** *a* lucid.

luciérnaga [lu'θjernaxa] *nf* glow-worm.

lucimiento [luθi'mjento] *nm* (*brillo*) brilliance; (*éxito*) success.

lucir [lu'θir] *vt* to illuminate, light (up); (*ostentar*) to show off // *vi* (*brillar*) to shine; **~se** *vr* (*irónico*) to make a fool of o.s.

lucro ['lukro] *nm* profit, gain.

lucha ['lutʃa] *nf* fight, struggle; **~ de clases** class struggle; **~ libre** wrestling; **luchar** *vi* to fight.

luego ['lweɣo] *ad* (*después*) next; (*más tarde*) later, afterwards; **desde ~** of course.

lugar [lu'ɣar] *nm* place; (*sitio*) spot; **en ~ de** instead of; **hacer ~** to make room; **fuera de ~** out of place; **tener ~** to take place; **~ común** commonplace.

lugareño, a [luɣa'reɲo, a] *a* village *cpd* // *nm/f* villager.

lugarteniente [luɣarte'njente] *nm* deputy.

lúgubre ['luɣuβre] *a* mournful.

lujo ['luxo] *nm* luxury; (*fig*) profusion, abundance; **~so, a** *a* luxurious.

lujuria [lu'xurja] *nf* lust.

lumbre ['lumbre] *nf* (*gen*) light.

lumbrera [lum'brera] *nf* luminary.

luminoso, a [lumi'noso, a] *a* luminous, shining.

luna ['luna] *nf* moon; (*de un espejo*) glass; (*de gafas*) lens; (*fig*) crescent; **~ llena/nueva** full/new moon; **estar en la ~** to have one's head in the clouds; **~ de miel** honeymoon.

lunar [lu'nar] *a* lunar // *nm* (*ANAT*) mole;

tela a **~es** spotted material.

lunes ['lunes] *nm inv* Monday.

lupa ['lupa] *nf* magnifying glass.

lustrar [lus'trar] *vt* (*mueble*) to polish; (*zapatos*) to shine; **lustre** *nm* polish; (*fig*) lustre; **dar lustre a** to polish; **lustroso, a** *a* shining.

luterano, a [lute'rano, a] *a* Lutheran.

luto ['luto] *nm* mourning; (*congoja*) grief, sorrow; **llevar el** *o* **vestirse de ~** to be in mourning.

Luxemburgo [luksem'burɣo] *nm* Luxembourg.

luz [luθ] (*pl* **luces**) *nf* light, **dar a ~ un** niño to give birth to a child; **sacar a la ~** to bring to light; (*ELEC*): **dar** *o* **encender** (*Esp*) *o* **prender** (*AM*)/**apagar la ~** to switch the light on/off; **a todas luces** by any reckoning; **hacer la ~ sobre** to shed light on; **tener pocas luces** to be dim *o* stupid; **~ roja/verde** red/green light; (*AUTO*): **~ de freno** brake light; **luces de tráfico** traffic lights; **traje de luces** bullfighter's costume.

LL

llaga ['ʎaɣa] *nf* wound.

llama ['ʎama] *nf* flame; (*ZOOL*) llama.

llamada [ʎa'maða] *nf* call; **~ al orden** call to order; **~ a pie de página** reference note.

llamamiento [ʎama'mjento] *nm* call.

llamar [ʎa'mar] *vt* to call; (*atención*) to attract // *vi* (*por teléfono*) to telephone; (*a la puerta*) to knock/ring; (*por señas*) to beckon; (*MIL*) to call up; **~se** *vr* to be called, be named; **¿cómo se llama usted?** what's your name?

llamarada [ʎama'raða] *nf* (*llamas*) blaze; (*rubor*) flush; (*fig*) flare-up.

llamativo, a [ʎama'tiβo, a] *a* showy; (*color*) loud.

llamear [ʎame'ar] *vi* to blaze.

llano, a ['ʎano, a] *a* (*superficie*) flat; (*persona*) straightforward; (*estilo*) clear // *nm* plain, flat ground.

llanta ['ʎanta] *nf* (wheel) rim; (*AM*): **~** (**de goma**) tyre; (: **cámara**) inner (tube).

llanto ['ʎanto] *nm* weeping.

llanura [ʎa'nura] *nf* plain.

llave ['ʎaβe] *nf* key; (*del agua*) tap; (*MECÁNICA*) spanner; (*de la luz*) switch; (*MUS*) key; **~ inglesa** monkey wrench; **~ maestra** master key; **~ de contacto** (*AUTO*) ignition key; **~ de paso** stopcock; **echar ~ a** to lock up; **~ro** *nm* keyring; **llavín** *nm* latchkey.

llegada [ʎe'ɣaða] *nf* arrival.

llegar [ʎe'ɣar] *vi* to arrive; (*alcanzar*) to reach; (*bastar*) to be enough; **~se** *vr*: **~se a** to approach; **~ a** to manage to, succeed in; **~ a saber** to find out; **~ a**

ser to become; ~ a las manos de to come into the hands of.

llenar [ʎe'nar] *vt* to fill; *(espacio)* to cover; *(formulario)* to fill in *o* up; *(fig)* to heap.

lleno, a ['ʎeno, a] *a* full, filled; *(repleto)* full up // *nm (abundancia)* abundance; *(TEATRO)* full house; **dar de ~ contra un muro** to hit a wall head-on.

llevadero, a [ʎeβa'ðero, a] *a* bearable, tolerable.

llevar [ʎe'βar] *vt* to take; *(ropa)* to wear; *(cargar)* to carry; *(quitar)* to take away; *(conducir a alguien)* to drive; *(transportar)* to transport; *(traer: dinero)* to carry; *(conducir)* to lead; *(MAT)* to carry; **~se** *vr* to carry off, take away; **llevamos dos días aquí** we have been here for two days; **él me lleva 2 años** he's 2 years older than me; *(COM)*: **~ los libros** to keep the books; **~se bien** to get on well (together).

llorar [ʎo'rar] *vt, vi* to cry, weep; **~ de risa** to cry with laughter.

lloriquear [ʎorike'ar] *vi* to snivel, whimper.

lloro ['ʎoro] *nm* crying, weeping; **llorón, ona** *a* tearful // *nm/f* cry-baby; **~so, a** *a (gen)* weeping, tearful; *(triste)* sad, sorrowful.

llover [ʎo'βer] *vi* to rain.

llovizna [ʎo'βiθna] *nf* drizzle; **lloviznar** *vi* to drizzle.

llueve *etc vb ver* **llover**.

lluvia ['ʎuβja] *nf* rain; **~ radioactiva** radioactive fallout; **lluvioso, a** *a* rainy.

M

m *abr* (= *metro*) m; (= *minuto*) m.

macarrones [maka'rrones] *nmpl* macaroni *sg*.

macedonia [maθe'ðonja] *nf*: **~ de frutas** fruit salad.

macerar [maθe'rar] *vt* to macerate.

maceta [ma'θeta] *nf (de flores)* pot of flowers; *(para plantas)* flowerpot.

macizo, a [ma'θiθo, a] *a (grande)* massive; *(fuerte, sólido)* solid // *nm* mass, chunk.

mácula ['makula] *nf* stain, blemish.

machacar [matʃa'kar] *vt* to crush, pound // *vi (insistir)* to go on, keep on.

machete [ma'tʃete] *nm (AM)* machete, (large) knife.

machista [ma'tʃista] *a, nm* sexist.

macho ['matʃo] *a* male; *(fig)* virile // *nm* male; *(fig)* he-man.

machucar [matʃu'kar] *vt* to pound.

madeja [ma'ðexa] *nf (de lana)* skein, hank; *(de pelo)* mass, mop.

madera [ma'ðera] *nf* wood; *(fig)* nature, character; **una ~** a piece of wood.

madero [ma'ðero] *nm* beam; *(fig)* ship.

madrastra [ma'ðrastra] *nf* stepmother.

madre ['maðre] *a* mother *cpd*; *(AM)* tremendous // *nf* mother; *(de vino etc)* dregs *pl*; **~ política/soltera** mother-in-law/unmarried mother.

madreperla [maðre'perla] *nf* mother-of-pearl.

madreselva [maðre'selβa] *nf* honeysuckle.

Madrid [ma'ðrið] *n* Madrid.

madriguera [maðri'ɣera] *nf* burrow.

madrileño, a [maðri'leɲo, a] *a* of *o* from Madrid // *nm/f* native of Madrid.

madrina [ma'ðrina] *nf* godmother; *(ARQ)* prop, shore; *(TEC)* brace; **~ de boda** bridesmaid.

madrugada [maðru'ɣaða] *nf* early morning; *(alba)* dawn, daybreak.

madrugador, a [maðruɣa'ðor, a] *a* early-rising.

madrugar [maðru'ɣar] *vi* to get up early; *(fig)* to get ahead.

madurar [maðu'rar] *vt, vi (fruta)* to ripen; *(fig)* to mature; **madurez** *nf* ripeness; maturity; **maduro, a** *a* ripe; mature.

maestra [ma'estra] *nf ver* **maestro**.

maestría [maes'tria] *nf* mastery; *(habilidad)* skill, expertise.

maestro, a [ma'estro, a] *a* masterly; *(perito)* skilled, expert; *(principal)* main; *(educado)* trained // *nm/f* master/mistress; *(profesor)* teacher // *nm (autoridad)* authority; *(MUS)* maestro; *(AM)* skilled workman; **~ albañil** master mason.

magia ['maxja] *nf* magic; **mágico, a** *a* magic(al) // *nm/f* magician.

magisterio [maxis'terjo] *nm (enseñanza)* teaching; *(profesión)* teaching profession; *(maestros)* teachers *pl*.

magistrado [maxis'traðo] *nm* magistrate.

magistral [maxis'tral] *a* magisterial; *(fig)* masterly.

magnánimo, a [maɣ'nanimo, a] *a* magnanimous.

magnate [maɣ'nate] *nm* magnate, tycoon.

magnético, a [maɣ'netiko, a] *a* magnetic; **magnetizar** *vt* to magnetize.

magnetofón, [maɣneto'fon] **magnetófono** [maɣne'tofono] *nm* tape recorder; **magnetofónico, a** *a*: **cinta magnetofónica** recording tape.

magnífico, a [maɣ'nifiko, a] *a* splendid, magnificent.

magnitud [maɣni'tuð] *nf* magnitude.

mago, a ['maɣo, a] *nm/f* magician; **los Reyes M~s** the Magi, the Three Wise Men.

magro, a ['maɣro, a] *a (persona)* thin, lean; *(carne)* lean.

maguey [ma'ɣei] *nm* agave.

magullar [maɣu'ʎar] *vt (amoratar)* to

bruise: (dañar) to damage; (fam; golpear) to bash, beat.

mahometano, a [maome'tano, a] a Mohammedan.

mahonesa [mao'nesa] nf = **mayonesa**.

maíz [ma'iθ] nm maize (Brit), corn (US); sweet corn.

majadero, a [maxa'ðero, a] a silly, stupid.

majestad [maxes'tað] nf majesty; **majestuoso, a** a majestic.

majo, a ['maxo, a] a nice; (guapo) attractive, good-looking; (elegante) smart.

mal [mal] ad badly; (equivocadamente) wrongly; (con dificultad) with difficulty // a = **malo** // nm evil; (desgracia) misfortune; (daño) harm, damage; (MED) illness; ¡menos ~! just as well!; ~ que bien rightly or wrongly.

malabarismo [malaβa'rismo] nm juggling; **malabarista** nm/f juggler.

malaconsejado, a [malakonse'xaðo, a] a ill-advised.

malaria [ma'larja] nf malaria.

malcriado, a [mal'krjaðo, a] a (consentido) spoiled.

maldad [mal'dað] nf evil, wickedness.

maldecir [malde'θir] vt to curse // vi: ~ de to speak ill of.

maldición [maldi'θjon] nf curse.

maldito, a [mal'dito, a] a (condenado) damned; (perverso) wicked; ¡~ sea! damn it!

maleante [male'ante] a wicked // nm/f malefactor.

malecón [male'kon] nm pier, jetty.

maledicencia [maleði'θenθja] nf slander, scandal.

maleducado, a [maleðu'kaðo, a] a bad-mannered, rude.

maleficio [male'fiθjo] nm curse, spell.

malestar [males'tar] nm (gen) discomfort; (fig: inquietud) uneasiness; (POL) unrest.

maleta [ma'leta] nf case, suitcase; (AUTO) boot (Brit), trunk (US); **maletera** nf (AM AUTO); **maletero** nm (AUTO) boot (Brit), trunk (US); **maletín** nm small case, bag.

malévolo, a [ma'leβolo, a] a malicious, spiteful.

maleza [ma'leθa] nf (hierbas malas) weeds pl; (arbustos) thicket.

malgastar [malɣas'tar] vt (tiempo, dinero) to waste; (salud) to ruin.

malhechor, a [male'tʃor, a] nm/f malefactor; (criminal) criminal.

malhumorado, a [malumo'raðo, a] a bad-tempered, cross.

malicia [ma'liθja] nf (maldad) wickedness; (astucia) slyness, guile; (mala intención) malice, spite; (carácter travieso) mischievousness; **malicioso, a** a wicked, evil; sly, crafty; malicious,

spiteful; mischievous.

maligno, a [ma'liɣno, a] a evil; (malévolo) malicious; (MED) malignant.

malo, a ['malo, a] a bad; (falso) false // nm/f villain // nf spell of bad luck; **estar** ~ to be ill; **estar de malas** (de mal humor) to be in a bad mood.

malograr [malo'ɣrar] vt to spoil; (plan) to upset; (ocasión) to waste; ~se vr (plan etc) to fail, come to grief; (persona) to die before one's time.

malparado, a [malpa'raðo, a] a: **salir** ~ to come off badly.

malparir [malpa'rir] vi to have a miscarriage.

malsano, a [mal'sano, a] a unhealthy.

Malta ['malta] nf Malta.

malteada [malte'aða] nf (AM) milk shake.

maltratar [maltra'tar] vt to ill-treat, mistreat.

maltrecho, a [mal'tretʃo, a] a battered, damaged.

malvado, a [mal'βaðo, a] a evil, villainous.

malvavisco [malβa'βisko] nm marshmallow.

malversar [malβer'sar] vt to embezzle, misappropriate.

Malvinas [mal'βinas]: **Islas** ~ nfpl Falkland Islands.

malla ['maʎa] nf mesh; (de baño) swimsuit; (de ballet, gimnasia) leotard; ~s nfpl tights; ~ **de alambre** wire mesh.

Mallorca [ma'ʎorka] nf Majorca.

mama ['mama] nf (de animal) teat; (de mujer) breast.

mamá [ma'ma] (pl ~s) nf (fam) mum, mummy.

mamar [ma'mar] vt (pecho) to suck; (fig) to absorb, assimilate // vi to suck.

mamarracho [mama'rratʃo] nm sight, mess.

mamífero [ma'mifero] nm mammal.

mampara [mam'para] nf (entre habitaciones) partition; (biombo) screen.

mampostería [mamposte'ria] nf masonry.

mamut [ma'mut] (pl ~s) nm mammoth.

manada [ma'naða] nf (ZOOL) herd; (: de leones) pride; (: de lobos) pack.

Managua [ma'naɣwa] n Managua.

manantial [manan'tjal] nm spring; (fuente) fountain; (fig) source.

manar [ma'nar] vt to run with, flow with // vi to run, flow; (abundar) to abound.

mancilla [man'θiʎa] nf stain, blemish.

manco, a ['manko, a] a (de un brazo) one-armed; (de una mano) one-handed; (fig) defective, faulty.

mancomunar [mankomu'nar] vt to unite, bring together; (recursos) to pool; (JUR) to make jointly responsible; **mancomunidad** nf union, association; (comunidad) community; (JUR) joint responsibility.

mancha ['mantʃa] *nf* stain, mark; (*ZOOL*) patch; (*boceto*) sketch, outline; **manchar** *vt* (*gen*) to stain, mark; (*ensuciar*) to soil, dirty.

manchego, a [man'tʃeɣo, a] *a* of o from La Mancha.

mandado [man'daðo] *nm* (*orden*) order; (*comisión*) commission, errand.

mandamiento [manda'mjento] *nm* (*orden*) order, command; (*REL*) commandment; ~ **judicial** warrant.

mandar [man'dar] *vt* (*ordenar*) to order; (*dirigir*) to lead, command; (*enviar*) to send; (*pedir*) to order, ask for // *vi* to be in charge; (*pey*) to be bossy; ¿**mande**? pardon?, excuse me?; ~ **hacer un traje** to have a suit made.

mandarín [manda'rin] *nm* mandarin.

mandarina [manda'rina] *nf* (*fruta*) tangerine, mandarin (orange).

mandatario, a [manda'tarjo, a] *nm/f* (*representante*) agent; (*AM: líder*) leader.

mandato [man'dato] *nm* (*orden*) order; (*INFORM*) command; (*POL: período*) term of office; (*: territorio*) mandate; ~ **judicial** (*search*) warrant.

mandíbula [man'diβula] *nf* jaw.

mandil [man'dil] *nm* (*delantal*) apron.

mando ['mando] *nm* (*MIL*) command; (*de país*) rule; (*el primer lugar*) lead; (*POL*) term of office; (*TEC*) control; ~ **a la izquierda** left-hand drive.

mandolina [mando'lina] *nf* mandolin(e).

mandón, ona [man'don, ona] *a* bossy, domineering.

manejable [mane'xaβle] *a* manageable.

manejar [mane'xar] *vt* to manage; (*máquina*) to work, operate; (*caballo etc*) to handle; (*casa*) to run, manage; (*AM: AUTO*) to drive; ~**se** *vr* (*comportarse*) to act, behave; (*arreglárselas*) to manage; **manejo** *nm* management; handling; running; driving; (*facilidad de trato*) ease, confidence; **manejos** *nmpl* intrigues.

manera [ma'nera] *nf* way, manner, fashion; ~**s** *nfpl* (*modales*) manners; **su** ~ **de ser** the way he is; (*aire*) his manner; **de ninguna** ~ no way, by no means; **de otra** ~ otherwise; **de todas** ~**s** at any rate; **no hay** ~ **de persuadirle** there's no way of convincing him.

manga ['manga] *nf* (*de camisa*) sleeve; (*de riego*) hose.

mangana [man'gana] *nf* lasso.

mango ['mango] *nm* handle; (*BOT*) mango.

mangonear [mangone'ar] *vi* (*meterse*) to meddle, interfere; (*ser mandón*) to boss people about.

manguera [man'gera] *nf* (*de riego*) hose; (*tubo*) pipe.

maní [ma'ni] *nm* (*AM*) peanut.

manía [ma'nia] *nf* (*MED*) mania; (*fig:*

moda) rage, craze; (*disgusto*) dislike; (*malicia*) spite; **maníaco, a** *a* maniac(al) // *nm/f* maniac.

maniatar [manja'tar] *vt* to tie the hands of.

maniático, a [ma'njatiko, a] *a* maniac(al) // *nm/f* maniac.

manicomio [mani'komjo] *nm* mental hospital (*Brit*), insane asylum (*US*).

manicura [mani'kura] *nf* manicure.

manifestación [manifesta'θjon] *nf* (*declaración*) statement, declaration; (*de emoción*) show, display; (*POL: desfile*) demonstration; (*: concentración*) mass meeting.

manifestar [manifes'tar] *vt* to show, manifest; (*declarar*) to state, declare; **manifiesto, a** *a* clear, manifest // *nm* manifesto.

manija [ma'nixa] *nf* handle.

maniobra [ma'njoβra] *nf* manœuvring; (*manejo*) handling; (*fig*) manœuvre; (*estratagema*) stratagem; ~**s** *nfpl* manœuvres; **maniobrar** *vt* to manœuvre; (*manejar*) to handle.

manipulación [manipula'θjon] *nf* manipulation; **manipular** *vt* to manipulate; (*manejar*) to handle.

maniquí [mani'ki] *nm* dummy // *nm/f* model.

manirroto, a [mani'rroto, a] *a* lavish, extravagant // *nm/f* spendthrift.

manivela [mani'βela] *nf* crank.

manjar [man'xar] *nm* (*tasty*) dish.

mano ['mano] *nf* hand; (*ZOOL*) foot, paw; (*de pintura*) coat; (*serie*) lot, series; **a** ~ by hand; **a** ~ **derecha/izquierda** on the right(-hand side)/left(-hand side); **de primera** ~ (at) first hand; **de segunda** ~ (at) second hand; **robo a** ~ **armada** armed robbery; ~ **de obra** labour, manpower; **estrechar la** ~ **a uno** to shake sb's hand.

manojo [ma'noxo] *nm* handful, bunch; ~ **de llaves** bunch of keys.

manopla [ma'nopla] *nf* (*guante*) glove; (*paño*) face cloth.

manoseado, a [manose'aðo, a] *a* well-worn; **manosear** *vt* (*tocar*) to handle, touch; (*desordenar*) to mess up, rumple; (*insistir en*) to overwork; (*AM*) to caress, fondle.

manotazo [mano'taθo] *nm* slap, smack.

mansalva [man'salβa]: **a** ~ *ad* indiscriminately.

mansedumbre [manse'ðumbre] *nf* gentleness, meekness.

mansión [man'sjon] *nf* mansion.

manso, a ['manso, a] *a* gentle, mild; (*animal*) tame.

manta ['manta] *nf* blanket; (*AM: poncho*) poncho.

manteca [man'teka] *nf* fat; ~ **de cacahuete/cacao** peanut/cocoa butter; ~ **de cerdo** lard.

mantecado [mante'kaðo] *nm* (*AM*) ice cream

mantel [man'tel] *nm* tablecloth.

mantendré *etc vb ver* **mantener.**

mantener [mante'ner] *vt* to support, maintain; (*alimentar*) to sustain; (*conservar*) to keep; (*TEC*) to maintain, service; ~**se** *vr* (*seguir de pie*) to be still standing; (*no ceder*) to hold one's ground; (*subsistir*) to sustain o.s., keep going; **mantenimiento** *nm* maintenance; sustenance; (*sustento*) support.

mantequilla [mante'kiʎa] *nf* butter.

mantilla [man'tiʎa] *nf* mantilla; ~**s** *nfpl* baby clothes.

manto ['manto] *nm* (*capa*) cloak; (*de ceremonia*) robe, gown.

mantón [man'ton] *nm* shawl.

mantuve, mantuviera *etc vb ver* **mantener.**

manual [ma'nwal] *a* manual // *nm* manual, handbook.

manufactura [manufak'tura] *nf* manufacture; (*fábrica*) factory.

manuscrito, a [manus'krito, a] *a* handwritten // *nm* manuscript.

manutención [manuten'θjon] *nf* maintenance; (*sustento*) support.

manzana [man'θana] *nf* apple; (*ARQ*) block (of houses).

manzanilla [manθa'niʎa] *nf* (*planta*) camomile; (*infusión*) camomile tea; (*vino de jerez*) manzanilla sherry.

manzano [man'θano] *nm* apple tree.

maña ['maɲa] *nf* (*gen*) skill, dexterity; (*pey*) guile; (*costumbre*) habit; (*destreza*) trick, knack.

mañana [ma'ɲana] *ad* tomorrow // *nm* future // *nf* morning; **de o por la** ~ in the morning; **¡hasta** ~**!** see you tomorrow!; ~ **por la** ~ tomorrow morning; **mañanero, a** *a* early-rising.

mañoso, a [ma'ɲoso, a] *a* (*hábil*) skilful; (*astuto*) smart, clever.

mapa ['mapa] *nm* map.

maqueta [ma'keta] *nf* (scale) model.

maquillaje [maki'ʎaxe] *nm* make-up; (*acto*) making up.

maquillar [maki'ʎar] *vt* to make up; ~**se** *vr* to put on (some) make-up.

máquina ['makina] *nf* machine; (*de tren*) locomotive, engine; (*FOTO*) camera; (*fig*) machinery; (: *proyecto*) plan, project; **escrito a** ~ typewritten; ~ **de escribir** typewriter; ~ **de coser/lavar** sewing/washing machine.

maquinación [makina'θjon] *nf* machination, plot.

maquinal [maki'nal] *a* (*fig*) mechanical, automatic.

maquinaria [maki'narja] *nf* (*máquinas*) machinery; (*mecanismo*) mechanism, works *pl*.

maquinilla [maki'niʎa] *nf*: ~ **de afeitar** razor.

maquinista [maki'nista] *nm/f* (*de tren*) engine driver; (*TEC*) operator; (*NAUT*) engineer.

mar [mar] *nm o f* sea; ~ **adentro** *o* **afuera** out at sea; **en alta** ~ on the high seas; **la** ~ **de** (*fam*) lots of; **el M**~ **Negro/Báltico** the Black/Baltic Sea.

maraña [ma'raɲa] *nf* (*maleza*) thicket; (*confusión*) tangle.

maravilla [mara'βiʎa] *nf* marvel, wonder; (*BOT*) marigold; **maravillar** *vt* to astonish, amaze; **maravillarse** *vr* to be astonished, be amazed; **maravilloso, a** *a* wonderful, marvellous.

marca ['marka] *nf* (*gen*) mark; (*sello*) stamp; (*COM*) make, brand; **de** ~ excellent, outstanding; ~ **de fábrica** trademark; ~ **registrada** registered trademark.

marcado, a [mar'kaðo, a] *a* marked, strong.

marcador [marka'ðor] *nm* (*DEPORTE*) scoreboard; (: *persona*) scorer.

marcar [mar'kar] *vt* (*gen*) to mark; (*número de teléfono*) to dial; (*gol*) to score; (*números*) to record, keep a tally of; (*pelo*) to set // *vi* (*DEPORTE*) to score; (*TEL*) to dial.

marcial [mar'θjal] *a* martial, military.

marciano, a [mar'θjano, a] *a* Martian.

marco ['marko] *nm* frame; (*DEPORTE*) goal-posts *pl*; (*moneda*) mark; (*fig*) framework; ~ **de chimenea** mantelpiece.

marcha ['martʃa] *nf* march; (*TEC*) running, working; (*AUTO*) gear; (*velocidad*) speed; (*fig*) progress; (*dirección*) course; **poner en** ~ to put into gear; (*fig*) to set in motion, get going; **dar** ~ **atrás** to reverse, put into reverse; **estar en** ~ to be under way, be in motion.

marchar [mar'tʃar] *vi* (*ir*) to go; (*funcionar*) to work, go; ~**se** *vr* to go (away), leave.

marchitar [martʃi'tar] *vt* to wither, dry up; ~**se** *vr* (*BOT*) to wither; (*fig*) to fade away; **marchito, a** *a* withered, faded; (*fig*) in decline.

marea [ma'rea] *nf* tide; (*llovizna*) drizzle.

marear [mare'ar] *vt* (*fig*) to annoy, upset; (*MED*): ~ **a uno** to make sb feel sick; ~**se** *vr* (*tener náuseas*) to feel sick; (*desvanecerse*) to feel faint; (*aturdirse*) to feel dizzy; (*fam: emborracharse*) to get tipsy.

maremoto [mare'moto] *nm* tidal wave.

mareo [ma'reo] *nm* (*náusea*) sick feeling; (*aturdimiento*) dizziness; (*fam*: *lata*) nuisance.

marfil [mar'fil] *nm* ivory.

margarina [marɣa'rina] *nf* margarine.

margarita [marɣa'rita] *nf* (*BOT*) daisy; (*rueda*) ~ daisywheel.

margen ['marxen] *nm* (*borde*) edge, border; (*fig*) margin, space // *nf* (*de río* *etc*) bank; **dar ~ para** to give an opportunity for; **mantenerse al ~** to keep out (of things).

marica [ma'rika] *nm* (*fam*) sissy.

maricón [mari'kon] *nm* (*fam*) queer.

marido [ma'riðo] *nm* husband.

mariguana [mari'ɣwana], **mariuana** [mari'wana] *nf* marijuana, cannabis.

marimacho [mari'matʃo] *nm* (*fam*) mannish woman.

marina [ma'rina] *nf* navy; **~ mercante** merchant navy.

marinero, a [mari'nero, a] *a* sea *cpd*; (*barco*) seaworthy // *nm* sailor, seaman.

marino, a [ma'rino, a] *a* sea *cpd*, marine // *nm* sailor.

marioneta [marjo'neta] *nf* puppet.

mariposa [mari'posa] *nf* butterfly.

mariquita [mari'kita] *nf* ladybird (*Brit*), ladybug (*US*).

mariscos [ma'riskos] *nmpl* shellfish *inv*, seafood(s).

marisma [ma'risma] *nf* marsh, swamp.

marítimo, a [ma'ritimo, a] *a* sea *cpd*, maritime.

marmita [mar'mita] *nf* pot.

mármol ['marmol] *nm* marble.

marqués, esa [mar'kes, esa] *nm/f* marquis/marchioness.

marrón [ma'rron] *a* brown.

marroquí [marro'ki] *a, nm/f* Moroccan // *nm* Morocco (leather).

Marruecos [ma'rrwekos] *nm* Morocco.

martes ['martes] *nm inv* Tuesday.

martillar [marti'ʎar] *vt* to hammer.

martillo [mar'tiʎo] *nm* hammer; **~ neumático** pneumatic drill (*Brit*), jackhammer.

mártir ['martir] *nm/f* martyr; **martirio** *nm* martyrdom; (*fig*) torture, torment.

marxismo [mark'sismo] *nm* Marxism; **marxista** *a, nm/f* Marxist.

marzo [mar'θo] *nm* March.

mas [mas] *conj* but.

más [mas] ♦ *a, ad* **1**: **~ (que, de)** (*comparativo*) more (than), ...+er (than); **~ grande/inteligente** bigger/more intelligent; **trabaja ~ (que yo)** he works more (than me); *ver tb* **cada**
2 (*superlativo*): **el ~** the most, ...+est; **el ~ grande/inteligente (de)** the biggest/most intelligent (in)
3 (*negativo*): **no tengo ~ dinero** I haven't got any more money; **no viene ~ por aquí** he doesn't come round here any more
4 (*adicional*): **no le veo ~ solución que** ... I see no other solution than to ...; **¿quién ~?** anybody else?
5 (+ *a*: *valor intensivo*): **¡qué perro ~ sucio!** what a filthy dog!; **¡es ~ tonto!** he's so stupid!
6 (*locuciones*): **~ o menos** more or less; **los ~** most people; **es ~** furthermore; **~ bien** rather; **¡qué ~ da!** what does it

matter!; *ver tb* **no**
7: **por ~:** **por ~ que te esfuerces** no matter how hard you try; **por ~ que quisiera** ... much as I should like to ...
8: **de ~:** **veo que aquí estoy de ~** I can see I'm not needed here; **tenemos uno de ~** we've got one extra
♦ *prep*: **2 ~ 2 son 4** 2 and 0 plus 2 are 4
♦ *nm*: **este trabajo tiene sus ~ y sus menos** this job's got its good points and its bad points.

masa ['masa] *nf* (*mezcla*) dough; (*volumen*) volume, mass; (*FISICA*) mass; **en ~ en masse**; **las ~s** (*POL*) the masses.

masacre [ma'sakre] *nf* massacre.

masaje [ma'saxe] *nm* massage.

mascar [mas'kar] *vt* to chew; (*fig*) to mumble, mutter.

máscara ['maskara] *nf* (*gen*) mask // *nm/f* masked person; **mascarada** *nf* masquerade; **mascarilla** *nf* (*de belleza*, *MED*) mask.

masculino, a [masku'lino, a] *a* masculine; (*BIO*) male.

mascullar [masku'ʎar] *vt* to mumble, mutter.

masilla [ma'siʎa] *nf* putty.

masivo, a [ma'sißo, a] *a* (*en masa*) mass, en masse.

masón [ma'son] *nm* (free)mason.

masoquista [maso'kista] *nm/f* masochist.

masticar [masti'kar] *vt* to chew; (*fig*) to ponder.

mástil ['mastil] *nm* (*de navío*) mast; (*de guitarra*) neck.

mastín [mas'tin] *nm* mastiff.

masturbación [masturßa'θjon] *nf* masturbation; **masturbarse** *vr* to masturbate.

mata ['mata] *nf* (*arbusto*) bush, shrub; (*de hierba*) tuft.

matadero [mata'ðero] *nm* slaughter-house, abattoir.

matador, a [mata'ðor, a] *a* killing // *nm/f* killer // *nm* (*TAUR*) matador, bullfighter.

matamoscas [mata'moskas] *nm inv* (*palo*) fly swat.

matanza [ma'tanθa] *nf* (*de personas*) slaughter, killing; (*de animales*) slaughter(ing).

matar [ma'tar] *vt, vi* to kill; **~se** *vr* (*suicidarse*) to kill o.s., commit suicide; (*morir*) to be 0 get killed; **~ el hambre** to stave off hunger.

matasellos [mata'seʎos] *nm inv* post-mark.

mate ['mate] *a* (*sin brillo: color*) dull, matt // *nm* (*en ajedrez*) (check)mate; (*AM: hierba*) maté; (: *vasija*) gourd.

matemáticas [mate'matikas] *nfpl* mathematics; **matemático, a** *a* mathematical // *nm/f* mathematician.

materia [ma'terja] *nf* (*gen*) matter; (*TEC*) material; (*ESCOL*) subject; **en ~ de** on the subject of; **~ prima** raw material; **material** a material; (dolor) physical // nm material; (TEC) equipment; **materialismo** nm materialism; **materialista** a materialist(ic); **materialmente** ad materially; (fig) absolutely.

maternal [mater'nal] a motherly, maternal.

maternidad [materni'ðað] nf motherhood, maternity; **materno, a** a maternal; (lengua) mother cpd.

matinal [mati'nal] a morning cpd.

matiz [ma'tiθ] nm shade; ~ar vt (dar tonos de) to tinge, tint; (variar) to vary; (ARTE) to blend.

matón [ma'ton] nm bully.

matorral [mato'rral] nm thicket.

matraca [ma'traka] nf rattle.

matrícula [ma'trikula] nf (registro) register; (AUTO) registration number; (: placa) number plate; **matricular** vt to register, enrol.

matrimonial [matrimo'njal] a matrimonial.

matrimonio [matri'monjo] nm (pareja) (married) couple; (unión) marriage.

matriz [ma'triθ] nf (ANAT) womb; (TEC) mould; casa ~ (COM) head office.

matrona [ma'trona] nf (persona de edad) matron.

maullar [mau'ʎar] vi to mew, miaow.

mausoleo [mauso'leo] nm mausoleum.

maxilar [maksi'lar] nm jaw(bone).

máxima ['maksima] ver **máximo**.

máxime ['maksime] ad especially.

máximo, a ['maksimo, a] a maximum; (más alto) highest; (más grande) greatest // nm maximum // nf maxim.

mayo ['majo] nm May.

mayonesa [majo'nesa] nf mayonnaise.

mayor [ma'jor] a main, chief; (adulto) adult; (de edad avanzada) elderly; (MUS) major; (comparativo: de tamaño) bigger; (: de edad) older; (superlativo: de tamaño) biggest; (: de edad) oldest // nm chief, boss; (adulto) adult; **al por ~** wholesale; **~ de edad** adult; **~es** nmpl (antepasados) ancestors.

mayoral [majo'ral] nm foreman.

mayordomo [major'ðomo] nm butler.

mayoría [majo'ria] nf majority, greater part.

mayorista [majo'rista] nm/f wholesaler.

mayúsculo, a [ma'juskulo, a] a (fig) big, tremendous // nf capital (letter).

mazapán [maθa'pan] nm marzipan.

mazo ['maθo] nm (martillo) mallet; (de flores) bunch; (DEPORTE) bat.

me [me] pron (directo) me; (indirecto) (to) me; (reflexivo) (to) myself; ¡dámelo! give it to me!

mear [me'ar] vi (fam) to pee, piss.

mecánico, a [me'kaniko, a] a mechanical // nm/f mechanic // nf (estudio) mechanics sg; (mecanismo) mechanism.

mecanismo [meka'nismo] nm mechanism, (marcha) gear.

mecanografía [mekanoɣra'fia] nf typewriting; **mecanógrafo, a** nm/f typist.

mecate [me'kate] nm (AM) rope.

mecedora [meθe'ðora] nf rocking chair.

mecer [me'θer] vt (cuna) to rock; ~se vr to rock; (ramo) to sway.

mecha ['metʃa] nf (de vela) wick; (de bomba) fuse.

mechero [me'tʃero] nm (cigarette) lighter.

mechón [me'tʃon] nm (gen) tuft; (manojo) bundle; (de pelo) lock.

medalla [me'ðaʎa] nf medal.

media ['meðja] nf ver **medio**.

mediado, a [me'ðjaðo, a] a half-full; (trabajo) half-complete; a ~s de in the middle of, halfway through.

mediano, a [me'ðjano, a] a (regular) medium, average; (mediocre) mediocre.

medianoche [meðja'notʃe] nf midnight.

mediante [me'ðjante] ad by (means of), through.

mediar [me'ðjar] vi (interceder) to mediate, intervene.

medicación [meðika'θjon] nf medication, treatment.

medicamento [meðika'mento] nm medicine, drug.

medicina [meði'θina] nf medicine.

medición [meði'θjon] nf measurement.

médico, a ['meðiko, a] a medical // nm/f doctor.

medida [me'ðiða] nf measure; (medición) measurement; (prudencia) moderation, prudence; en cierta/gran ~ up to a point/to a great extent; un traje a la ~ made-to-measure suit; ~ de cuello collar size; a ~ de in proportion to; (de acuerdo con) in keeping with; a ~ que (conforme) as.

medio, a ['meðjo, a] a half (a); (punto) mid, middle; (promedio) average // ad half // nm (centro) middle, centre; (promedio) average; (método) means, way; (ambiente) environment // nf (Esp: prenda de vestir) stocking; (AM: prenda de vestir) sock; (promedio) average; ~s nmpl means, resources; ~ litro half a litre; las tres y media half past three; M~ Oriente Middle East; a ~ terminar half finished; pagar a medias to share the cost.

mediocre [me'ðjokre] a middling, average; (pey) mediocre.

mediodía [meðjo'ðia] nm midday, noon.

medir [me'ðir] vt, vi (gen) to measure.

meditar [meði'tar] vt to ponder, think over, meditate (on); (planear) to think out.

mediterráneo, a [meðite'rraneo, a] a Mediterranean // nm: el M~ the Mediterranean.

médula ['meðula] nf (ANAT) marrow; ~

espinal spinal cord.

medusa [me'ðusa] *nf* (*Esp*) jellyfish.

megáfono [me'vafono] *nm* megaphone.

megalómano, a [meɣa'lomano, a] *nm/f* megalomaniac.

mejicano, a [mexi'kano, a] *a*, *nm/f* Mexican.

Méjico ['mexiko] *nm* Mexico.

mejilla [me'xiʎa] *nf* cheek.

mejillón [mexi'ʎon] *nm* mussel.

mejor [me'xor] *a*, *ad* (*comparativo*) better; (*superlativo*) best; **a lo ~** probably; (*quizá*) maybe; **~ dicho** rather; **tanto ~** so much the better.

mejora [me'xora] *nf* improvement; **mejorar** *vt* to improve, make better // *vi*, **mejorarse** *vr* to improve, get better.

melancólico, a [melan'koliko, a] *a* (*triste*) sad, melancholy; (*soñador*) dreamy.

melena [me'lena] *nf* (*de persona*) long hair; (*ZOOL*) mane.

melocotón [meloko'ton] *nm* (*Esp*) peach.

melodía [melo'ðia] *nf* melody, tune.

melodrama [melo'ðrama] *nm* melodrama; **melodramático, a** *a* melodramatic.

melón [me'lon] *nm* melon.

meloso, a [me'loso, a] *a* honeyed, sweet.

mellizo, a [me'ʎiθo, a] *a*, *nm/f* twin; **~s** *nmpl* (*AM*) cufflinks.

membrete [mem'brete] *nm* letterhead.

membrillo [mem'briʎo] *nm* quince; **carne de ~** quince jelly.

memorable [memo'raßle] *a* memorable.

memorándum [memo'randum] (*pl* **~s**) *nm* (*libro*) notebook; (*comunicación*) memorandum.

memoria [me'morja] *nf* (*gen*) memory; **~s** *nfpl* (*de autor*) memoirs; **~ intermedia** (*INFORM*) buffer; **memorizar** *vt* to memorize.

menaje [me'naxe] *nm*: **~ de cocina** kitchenware.

mencionar [menθjo'nar] *vt* to mention.

mendigar [mendi'ɣar] *vt* to beg (for).

mendigo, a [men'diɣo, a] *nm/f* beggar.

mendrugo [men'druɣo] *nm* crust.

menear [mene'ar] *vt* to move; (*fig*) to handle; **~se** *vr* to shake; (*balancearse*) to sway; (*moverse*) to move; (*fig*) to get a move on.

menester [menes'ter] *nm* (*necesidad*) necessity; **~es** *nmpl* (*deberes*) duties; **es ~ it** is necessary.

menestra [me'nestra] *nf*: **~ de verduras** vegetable stew.

menguante [men'gwante] *a* decreasing, diminishing; **menguar** *vt* to lessen, diminish; (*fig*) to discredit // *vi* to diminish, decrease; (*fig*) to decline.

menopausia [meno'pausja] *nf* menopause.

menor [me'nor] *a* (*más pequeño*: *comparativo*) smaller; (: *superlativo*) smallest; (*más joven*: *comparativo*) younger; (: *superlativo*) youngest; (*MUS*) minor // *nm/f* (*joven*) young person, juvenile; **no tengo la ~ idea** I haven't the faintest idea; **al por ~** retail; **~ de edad** person under age.

Menorca [me'norka] *nf* Minorca.

menoría [meno'ria] *nf*: **a ~** (*AM*) retail.

menos [menos] ♦ *a* 1: **~** (*comparativo*: *cantidad*) less (than); (: *número*) fewer (than); **con ~ entusiasmo** with less enthusiasm; **~ gente** fewer people; *ver tb* **cada**

2 (*superlativo*): **es el que ~ culpa tiene** he is the least to blame

♦ *ad* 1 (*comparativo*): **~** (*que, de*) less (than); **me gusta ~ que el otro** I like it less than the other one

2 (*superlativo*): **es la ~ lista** (*de su clase*) she's the least bright in her class; **de todas ellas es la que ~ me agrada** out of all of them she's the one I like least; **(por) lo ~** at (the very) least

3 (*locuciones*): **no quiero verle y ~ visitarle** I don't want to see him let alone visit him; **tenemos 7 de ~** we're seven short

♦ *prep* except; (*cifras*) minus; **todos ~ él** everyone except (for) him; **5 ~ 2** 5 minus 2

♦ *conj*: **a ~ que**: **a ~ que venga mañana** unless he comes tomorrow.

menoscabar [menoska'ßar] *vt* (*estropear*) to damage, harm; (*fig*) to discredit.

menospreciar [menospre'θjar] *vt* to underrate, undervalue; (*despreciar*) to scorn, despise.

mensaje [men'saxe] *nm* message; **~ro, a** *nm/f* messenger.

menstruación [menstrua'θjon] *nf* menstruation.

menstruar [mens'trwar] *vi* to menstruate.

mensual [men'swal] *a* monthly; **1000 ptas ~es** 1000 ptas a month; **~idad** *nf* (*salario*) monthly salary; (*COM*) monthly payment, monthly instalment.

menta ['menta] *nf* mint.

mental [men'tal] *a* mental; **~idad** *nf* mentality.

mentar [men'tar] *vt* to mention, name.

mente ['mente] *nf* mind.

mentecato, a [mente'kato, a] *a* silly, stupid // *nm/f* fool, idiot.

mentir [men'tir] *vi* to lie.

mentira [men'tira] *nf* (*una ~*) lie; (*acto*) lying; (*invención*) fiction; **parece ~ que...** it seems incredible that..., I can't believe that....

mentiroso, a [menti'roso, a] *a* lying // *nm/f* liar.

menú [me'nu] (*pl* **~s**) *nm* menu; (*AM*) set meal.

menudo, a [me'nuðo, a] *a (pequeño)* small, tiny; *(sin importancia)* petty, insignificant; ¡~ negocio! *(fam)* some deal!; a ~ often, frequently.

meñique [me'nike] *nm* little finger.

meollo [me'oʎo] *nm (fig)* core.

mercadería [merkaðe'ria] *nf* commodity; ~s *nfpl* goods, merchandise *sg*.

mercado [mer'kaðo] *nm* market; **M~ Común** Common Market.

mercancía [merkan'θia] *nf* commodity; ~s *nfpl* goods, merchandise *sg*.

mercantil [merkan'til] *a* mercantile, commercial.

mercenario, a [merθe'narjo, a] *a, nm* mercenary.

mercería [merθe'ria] *nf* haberdashery *(Brit)*, notions *(US)*; *(tienda)* haberdasher's *(Brit)*, notions store *(US)*; *(AM)* drapery.

mercurio [mer'kurjo] *nm* mercury.

merecer [mere'θer] *vt* to deserve, merit // *vi* to be deserving, be worthy; **merece la pena** it's worthwhile; **merecido, a** *a* (well) deserved; **llevar su merecido** to get one's deserts.

merendar [meren'dar] *vt* to have for tea // *vi* to have tea; *(en el campo)* to have a picnic.

merengue [me'renge] *nm* meringue.

meridiano [meri'ðjano] *nm (GEO)* meridian.

merienda [me'rjenda] *nf* (light) tea, afternoon snack; *(de campo)* picnic.

mérito ['merito] *nm* merit; *(valor)* worth, value.

merluza [mer'luθa] *nf* hake.

merma ['merma] *nf* decrease; *(pérdida)* wastage; **mermar** *vt* to reduce, lessen // *vi* to decrease, dwindle.

mermelada [merme'laða] *nf* jam.

mero, a ['mero, a] *a* mere; *(AM: fam)* very.

mes [mes] *nm* month; *(salario)* month's pay.

mesa ['mesa] *nf* table; *(de trabajo)* desk; *(GEO)* plateau; *(ARQ)* landing; ~ **directiva** board; ~ **redonda** *(reunión)* round table; **poner/quitar la** ~ to lay/ clear the table; **mesero, a** *nm/f (AM)* waiter/waitress.

meseta [me'seta] *nf (GEO)* meseta, tableland; *(ARQ)* landing.

mesilla [me'siʎa], **mesita** [me'sita] *nf*: ~ **(de noche)** bedside table.

mesón [me'son] *nm* inn.

mestizo, a [mes'tiθo, a] *a* half-caste, of mixed race; *(ZOOL)* crossbred // *nm/f* half-caste.

mesura [me'sura] *nf (moderación)* moderation, restraint; *(cortesía)* courtesy.

meta ['meta] *nf* goal; *(de carrera)* finish.

metáfora [me'tafora] *nf* metaphor.

metal [me'tal] *nm (materia)* metal;

(MUS) brass; **metálico, a** *a* metallic; *(de metal)* metal // *nm (dinero contante)* cash.

metalurgia [meta'lurxja] *nf* metallurgy.

meteoro [mete'oro] *nm* meteor.

meter [me'ter] *vt (colocar)* to put, place; *(introducir)* to put in, insert; *(involucrar)* to involve; *(causar)* to make, cause; ~**se** *vr*: ~**se en** to go into, enter; *(fig)* to interfere in, meddle in; ~**se a** to start; ~**se a escritor** to become a writer; ~**se con uno** to provoke sb, pick a quarrel with sb.

meticuloso, a [metiku'loso, a] *a* meticulous, thorough.

metódico, a [me'toðiko, a] *a* methodical.

metodismo [meto'ðismo] *nm* Methodism.

método ['metoðo] *nm* method.

metralleta [metra'ʎeta] *nf* sub-machine-gun.

métrico, a ['metriko, a] *a* metric.

metro ['metro] *nm* metre; *(tren)* underground *(Brit)*, subway *(US)*.

México ['mexiko] *nm* Mexico; **Ciudad de** ~ Mexico City.

mezcla ['meθkla] *nf* mixture; **mezclar** *vt* to mix (up); **mezclarse** *vr* to mix, mingle; **mezclarse en** to get mixed up in, get involved in.

mezquino, a [meθ'kino, a] *a (cicatero)* mean.

mezquita [meθ'kita] *nf* mosque.

mg. *abr* (= miligramo) mg.

mi [mi] *adjetivo posesivo* my // *nm (MUS)* E.

mí [mi] *pron* me; myself.

miaja ['mjaxa] *nf* crumb.

micro ['mikro] *nm (AM)* minibus.

microbio [mi'kroßjo] *nm* microbe.

microbús [mikro'ßus] *nm* minibus.

micrófono [mi'krofono] *nm* microphone.

microordenador [mikro(o)rðena'ðor] *nm* microcomputer.

microscopio [mikro'skopjo] *nm* microscope.

miedo ['mjeðo] *nm* fear; *(nerviosismo)* apprehension, nervousness; **tener** ~ to be afraid; **de** ~ wonderful, marvellous; **hace un frío de** ~ *(fam)* it's terribly cold; ~**so, a** *a* fearful, timid.

miel [mjel] *nf* honey.

miembro ['mjembro] *nm* limb; *(socio)* member; ~ **viril** penis.

mientras ['mjentras] *conj* while; *(duración)* as long as // *ad* meanwhile; ~ **tanto** meanwhile; ~ **más tiene, más quiere** the more he has, the more he wants.

miércoles ['mjerkoles] *nm inv* Wednesday.

mierda ['mjerða] *nf (fam!)* shit (!).

miga ['miɣa] *nf* crumb; *(fig: meollo)* essence; **hacer buenas** ~**s** *(fam)* to get

on well.
migración [mixra'θjon] *nf* migration.
mil [mil] *num* thousand; **dos ~ libras** two
thousand pounds.
milagro [mi'laɣro] *nm* miracle; **~so, a**
a miraculous.
mili ['mili] *nf*: **hacer la ~** (*fam*) to do
one's military service.
milicia [mi'liθja] *nf* militia; (*servicio
militar*) military service.
milímetro [mi'limetro] *nm* millimetre.
militante [mili'tante] *a* militant.
militar [mili'tar] *a* (*del ejército*) military
// *nm/f* soldier // *vi* to serve in the army;
(*fig*) to be a member of a party.
milla ['miʎa] *nf* mile.
millar [mi'ʎar] *nm* thousand.
millón [mi'ʎon] *num* million; **millonario,
a** *nm/f* millionaire.
mimar [mi'mar] *vt* (*gen*) to spoil,
pamper.
mimbre ['mimbre] *nm* wicker.
mímica ['mimika] *nf* (*para comunicarse*)
sign language; (*imitación*) mimicry.
mimo ['mimo] *nm* (*caricia*) caress; (*de
niño*) spoiling; (*TEATRO*) mime; (:
actor) mime artist.
mina ['mina] *nf* mine; **minar** *vt* to mine;
(*fig*) to undermine.
mineral [mine'ral] *a* mineral // *nm* (*GEO*)
mineral; (*mena*) ore.
minero, a [mi'nero, a] *a* a mining *cpd* //
nm/f miner.
miniatura [minja'tura] *a inv, nf* miniature.
minifalda [mini'falda] *nf* miniskirt.
mínimo, a ['minimo, a] *a, nm* minimum.
minino, a [mi'nino, a] *nm/f* (*fam*) puss,
pussy.
ministerio [minis'terjo] *nm* Ministry;
M~ de Hacienda/del Exterior Treasury
(*Brit*), Treasury Department (*US*)/For-
eign Office (*Brit*), State Department
(*US*).
ministro, a [mi'nistro, a] *nm/f* minister.
minoría [mino'ria] *nf* minority.
minucioso, a [minu'θjoso, a] *a* thorough,
meticulous; (*prolijo*) very detailed.
minúsculo, a [mi'nuskulo, a] *a* tiny,
minute // *nf* small letter.
minusválido, a [minus'ßalido, a] *a*
(*physically*) handicapped; *nm/f* (*physically*) handicapped person.
minuta [mi'nuta] *nf* (*de comida*) menu.
minutero [minu'tero] *nm* minute hand.
minuto [mi'nuto] *nm* minute.
mío, a ['mio, a] *pron*: **el ~** mine; **un
amigo ~** a friend of mine; **lo ~** what is
mine.
miope [mi'ope] *a* short-sighted.
mira ['mira] *nf* (*de arma*) sight(s) (*pl*);
(*fig*) aim, intention.
mirada [mi'rada] *nf* look, glance; (*expresión*) look, expression; **clavar la ~ en** to
stare at; **echar una ~ a** to glance at.

mirado, a [mi'rado, a] *a* (*sensato*) sensible; (*considerado*) considerate; **bien/
mal ~** well/not well thought of; **bien ~**
ad all things considered.
mirador [mira'ðor] *nm* viewpoint, vantage point.
mirar [mi'rar] *vt* to look at; (*observar*) to
watch; (*considerar*) to consider, think
over; (*vigilar, cuidar*) to watch, look
after // *vi* to look; (*ARQ*) to face; **~se** *vr*
(*dos personas*) to look at each other; **~
bien/mal** to think highly of/have a poor
opinion of; **~se al espejo** to look at o.s.
in the mirror.
mirilla [mi'riʎa] *nf* (*agujero*) spyhole,
peephole.
mirlo ['mirlo] *nm* blackbird.
misa ['misa] *nf* mass.
miserable [mise'raßle] *a* (*avaro*) mean,
stingy; (*nimio*) miserable, paltry;
(*lugar*) squalid; (*fam*) vile, despicable //
nm/f (*perverso*) rotter (*Brit*).
miseria [mi'serja] *nf* misery; (*pobreza*)
poverty; (*tacañería*) meanness, stingi-
ness; (*condiciones*) squalor; **una ~** a
pittance.
misericordia [miseri'korðja] *nf* (*compasión*) compassion, pity; (*piedad*) mercy.
misil [mi'sil] *nm* missile.
misión [mi'sjon] *nf* mission; **misionero,
a** *nm/f* missionary.
mismo, a ['mismo, a] *a* (*semejante*)
same; (*después de pronombre*) -self;
(*para énfasis*) very; **el ~ traje** the same
suit; **en ese ~ momento** at that very
moment; **vino el ~ Ministro** the minister
himself came; **yo ~ lo vi** I saw it
myself; **lo ~** the same (thing); **da lo ~**
it's all the same; **quedamos en las
mismas** we're no further forward // *ad*:
aquí/hoy ~ right here/this very day;
ahora ~ right now // *conj*: **lo ~ que** just
like, just as; **por lo ~** for the same
reason.
misterio [mis'terjo] *nm* (*gen*) mystery;
(*lo secreto*) secrecy; **~so, a** *a* a mysterious.
mitad [mi'tad] *nf* (*medio*) half; (*centro*)
middle; **a ~ de precio** (at) half-price; **en
o a ~ del camino** halfway along the
road; **cortar por la ~** to cut through the
middle.
mitigar [miti'ɣar] *vt* to mitigate; (*dolor*)
to ease; (*sed*) to quench.
mitin ['mitin] *nm* (*pl* **mítines**) meeting.
mito ['mito] *nm* myth.
mixto, a ['miksto, a] *a* mixed.
ml. *abr* (= *mililitro*) ml.
mm. *abr* (= *milímetro*) mm.
mobiliario [moßi'ljarjo] *nm* furniture.
moción [mo'θjon] *nf* motion.
mocos ['mokos] *nmpl* mucus *sg*; (*fam*)
snot *sg*.
mochila [mo'tʃila] *nf* rucksack (*Brit*),
back-pack.

moda ['moða] *nf* fashion; (*estilo*) style; de *o* a la ~ in fashion, fashionable; pasado de ~ out of fashion.

modales [mo'ðales] *nmpl* manners.

modalidad [moðali'ðað] *nf* kind, variety.

modelar [moðe'lar] *vt* to model.

modelo [mo'ðelo] *a inv, nm/f* model.

moderado, a [moðe'raðo, a] *a* moderate.

moderar [moðe'rar] *vt* to moderate; (*violencia*) to restrain, control; (*velocidad*) to reduce; ~se *vr* to restrain o.s., control o.s.

modernizar [moðerni'θar] *vt* to modernize.

moderno, a [mo'ðerno, a] *a* modern; (*actual*) present-day.

modestia [mo'ðestja] *nf* modesty; **modesto, a** *a* modest.

módico, a ['moðiko, a] *a* moderate, reasonable.

modificar [moðifi'kar] *vt* to modify.

modista [mo'ðista] *nm/f* dressmaker.

modo ['moðo] *nm* (*manera, forma*) way, manner; (*MUS*) mode; ~s *nmpl* manners; de ningún ~ in no way; de todos ~s at any rate; ~ de empleo directions *pl* (for use).

modorra [mo'ðorra] *nf* drowsiness.

modular [moðu'lar] *vt* to modulate.

mofa ['mofa] *nf*: hacer ~ de to mock; **mofarse** *vr*: mofarse de to mock, scoff at.

moho ['moo] *nm* (*BOT*) mould, mildew; (*en metal*) rust; ~so, a *a* mouldy; rusty.

mojar [mo'xar] *vt* to wet; (*humedecer*) to damp(en), moisten; (*calar*) to soak; ~se *vr* to get wet.

mojón [mo'xon] *nm* (*en un camino*) boundary stone.

molde ['molde] *nm* mould; (*COSTURA*) pattern; (*fig*) model; ~ar *vt* to mould.

mole ['mole] *nf* mass, bulk; (*edificio*) pile.

moler [mo'ler] *vt* to grind, crush; (*cansar*) to tire out, exhaust.

molestar [moles'tar] *vt* to bother; (*fastidiar*) to annoy; (*incomodar*) to inconvenience, put out // *vi* to be a nuisance; ~se *vr* to bother; (*incomodarse*) to go to trouble; (*ofenderse*) to take offence.

molestia [mo'lestja] *nf* bother, trouble; (*incomodidad*) inconvenience; (*MED*) discomfort; es una ~ it's a nuisance; **molesto, a** *a* (*que fastidia*) annoying; (*incómodo*) inconvenient; (*inquieto*) uncomfortable, ill at ease; (*enfadado*) annoyed.

molinillo [moli'niʎo] *nm*: ~ de carne/café mincer/coffee grinder.

molino [mo'lino] *nm* (*edificio*) mill; (*máquina*) grinder.

momentáneo, a [momen'taneo, a] *a* momentary.

momento [mo'mento] *nm* (*gen*) moment; (*TEC*) momentum; de ~ at the moment, for the moment.

momia ['momja] *nf* mummy.

monarca [mo'narka] *nm/f* monarch, ruler; **monarquía** *nf* monarchy; **monárquico, a** *nm/f* royalist, monarchist.

monasterio [monas'terjo] *nm* monastery.

mondadientes [monda'ðjentes] *nm inv* toothpick.

mondar [mon'dar] *vt* (*limpiar*) to clean; (*pelar*) to peel; ~se *vr*: ~se de risa (*fam*) to split one's sides laughing.

moneda [mo'neða] *nf* (*tipo de dinero*) currency, money; (*pieza*) coin; una ~ de 5 pesetas a 5 peseta piece; **monedero** *nm* purse; **monetario, a** *a* monetary, financial.

monja ['monxa] *nf* nun.

monje ['monxe] *nm* monk.

mono, a ['mono, a] *a* (*bonito*) lovely, pretty; (*gracioso*) nice, charming // *nm/f* monkey, ape // *nm* dungarees *pl*; (*overoles*) overalls *pl*.

monopolio [mono'poljo] *nm* monopoly; **monopolizar** *vt* to monopolize.

monotonía [monoto'nia] *nf* (*sonido*) monotone; (*fig*) monotony.

monótono, a [mo'notono, a] *a* monotonous.

monstruo ['monstrwo] *nm* monster // *a inv* fantastic; ~so, a *a* monstrous.

monta ['monta] *nf* total, sum; de poca ~ unimportant, of little account.

montaje [mon'taxe] *nm* assembly; (*TEATRO*) décor; (*CINE*) montage.

montaña [mon'taɲa] *nf* (*monte*) mountain; (*sierra*) mountains *pl*, mountainous area; (*AM: selva*) forest; ~ rusa roller coaster; **montañés, esa** *a* mountain *cpd* // *nm/f* highlander.

montar [mon'tar] *vt* (*subir a*) to mount, get on; (*TEC*) to assemble, put together; (*negocio*) to set up; (*arma*) to cock; (*colocar*) to lift on to; (*CULIN*) to beat // *vi* to mount, get on; (*sobresalir*) to overlap; ~ en cólera to get angry; ~ a caballo to ride, go horseriding.

montaraz [monta'raθ] *a* mountain *cpd*, highland *cpd*; (*salvaje*) wild, untamed; (*pey*) uncivilized.

monte ['monte] *nm* (*montaña*) mountain; (*bosque*) woodland; (*área sin cultivar*) wild area, wild country; M~ de Piedad pawnshop.

Montevideo [monteßi'ðeo] *n* Montevideo.

monto ['monto] *nm* total, amount.

montón [mon'ton] *nm* heap, pile; (*fig*): un ~ de heaps of, lots of.

monumento [monu'mento] *nm* monument.

monzón [mon'θon] *nm* monsoon.

moño |'moɲo| nm bun.

mora |'mora| nf blackberry.

morado, a |mo'raðo. a| a purple, violet // nm bruise // nf (casa) dwelling, abode.

moral |mo'ral| a moral // nf (ética) ethics pl; (moralidad) morals pl, morality; (ánimo) morale.

moraleja |mora'lexa| nf moral.

moralizar |morali'θar| vt to moralize.

morboso, a |mor'ßoso. a| a morbid.

morcilla |mor'θiʎa| nf blood sausage, ≈ black pudding (Brit).

mordaz |mor'ðaθ| a (crítica) biting, scathing.

mordaza |mor'ðaθa| nf (para la boca) gag; (TEC) clamp.

morder |mor'ðer| vt to bite; (mordisquear) to nibble; (fig: consumir) to eat away, eat into; **mordisco** nm bite.

moreno, a |mo'reno, a| a (color) (dark) brown; (de tez) dark; (de pelo ~) dark-haired; (negro) black.

moretón |more'ton| nm (fam) bruise.

morfina |mor'fina| nf morphine.

moribundo, a |mori'ßundo. a| a dying.

morir |mo'rir| vi to die; (fuego) to die down; (luz) to go out; ~se vr to die; (fig) to be dying; **fue muerto en un accidente** he was killed in an accident; ~se por algo to be dying for sth.

moro, a |'moro. a| a Moorish // nm/f Moor.

moroso, a |mo'roso. a| nm/f (COM) bad debtor, defaulter.

morral |mo'rral| nm haversack.

morro |'morro| nm (ZOOL) snout, nose; (AUTO, AVIAT) nose.

morsa |'morsa| nf walrus.

mortaja |mor'taxa| nf shroud.

mortal |mor'tal| a mortal; (golpe) deadly; ~**idad, mortandad** nf mortality.

mortero |mor'tero| nm mortar.

mortífero, a |mor'tifero. a| a deadly, lethal.

mortificar |mortifi'kar| vt to mortify.

mosca |'moska| nf fly.

Moscú |mos'ku| n Moscow.

mosquearse |moske'arse| vr (fam: enojarse) to get cross; (: ofenderse) to take offence.

mosquitero |moski'tero| nm mosquito net.

mosquito |mos'kito| nm mosquito.

mostaza |mos'taθa| nf mustard.

mostrador |mostra'ðor| nm (de tienda) counter; (de café) bar.

mostrar |mos'trar| vt to show; (exhibir) to display, exhibit; (explicar) to explain; ~se vr: ~se amable to be kind; to prove to be kind; **no se muestra muy inteligente** he doesn't seem (to be) very intelligent.

mota |'mota| nf speck, tiny piece; (en diseño) dot.

mote |'mote| nm (apodo) nickname.

motín |mo'tin| nm (del pueblo) revolt, rising; (del ejército) mutiny.

motivar |moti'ßar| vt (causar) to cause, motivate; (explicar) to explain, justify; **motivo** nm motive, reason.

moto |'moto| (fam), **motocicleta** |motoθi'kleta| nf motorbike (Brit), motorcycle.

motor |mo'tor| nm motor, engine; ~ **a chorro** o **de reacción/de explosión** jet engine/internal combustion engine.

motora |mo'tora| nf, **motorbote** |motor'ßote| nm motorboat.

motosierra |moto'sjerra| nf mechanical saw.

movedizo, a |moße'ðiθo. a| a (inseguro) unsteady; (fig) unsettled, changeable; (persona) fickle.

mover |mo'ßer| vt to move; (cabeza) to shake; (accionar) to drive; (fig) to cause, provoke; ~se vr to move; (fig) to get a move on.

móvil |'moßil| a mobile; (pieza de máquina) moving; (mueble) movable // nm motive; **movilidad** nf mobility; **movilizar** vt to mobilize.

movimiento |moßi'mjento| nm movement; (TEC) motion; (actividad) activity.

mozo, a |'moθo. a| a (joven) young // nm/f (joven) youth, young man/girl; (camarero) waiter; (camarera) waitress.

muchacho, a |mu'tʃatʃo. a| nm/f (niño) boy/girl; (criado) servant; (criada) maid.

muchedumbre |mutʃe'ðumbre| nf crowd.

mucho, a |'mutʃo. a| ♦ a 1 (cantidad) a lot of, much; (número) lots of, a lot of, many; ~ **dinero** a lot of money; **hace** ~ **calor** it's very hot; **muchas amigas** lots o a lot of friends

2 (sg: grande): **ésta es mucha casa para él** this house is much too big for him

♦ pron: **tengo** ~ **que hacer** I've got a lot to do; ~**s dicen que ...** a lot of people say that ...; ver tb **tener**

♦ ad 1: **me gusta** ~ I like it a lot; **lo siento** ~ I'm very sorry; **come** ~ he eats a lot; **¿te vas a quedar** ~? are you going to be staying long?

2 (respuesta) very; **¿estás cansado?** - **¡**~**!** are you tired? - very!

3 (locuciones): **como** ~ at (the) most; **con** ~: **el mejor con** ~ by far the best; **ni** ~ **menos**: **no es rico ni** ~ **menos** he's far from being rich

4: **por** ~ **que**: **por** ~ **que le creas** no matter how o however much you believe her.

muda |'muða| nf change of clothes.

mudanza |mu'ðanθa| nf (cambio) change; (de casa) move.

mudar [mu'ðar] *vt* to change; (*ZOOL*) to shed // *vi* to change; ~se *vr* (*la ropa*) to change; ~se de casa to move house.

mudo, a ['muðo, a] *a* dumb; (*callado*, *CINE*) silent.

mueble ['mweβle] *nm* piece of furniture; ~s *nmpl* furniture *sg*.

mueca ['mweka] *nf* face, grimace; hacer ~s a to make faces at.

muela ['mwela] *nf* (*diente*) tooth; (: *de atrás*) molar.

muelle ['mweʎe] *nm* spring; (*NAUT*) wharf; (*malecón*) pier.

muero *etc vb ver* **morir**.

muerte ['mwerte] *nf* death; (*homicidio*) murder; **dar** ~ a to kill.

muerto, a *pp de* **morir** // ['mwerto, a] *a* dead; (*color*) dull // *nm/f* dead man/ woman; (*difunto*) deceased; (*cadáver*) corpse; **estar** ~ **de cansancio** to be dead tired.

muestra ['mwestra] *nf* (*señal*) indication, sign; (*demostración*) demonstration; (*prueba*) proof; (*estadística*) sample; (*modelo*) model, pattern; (*testimonio*) token.

muestreo [mwes'treo] *nm* sample, sampling.

muestro *etc vb ver* **mostrar**.

muevo *etc vb ver* **mover**.

mugir [mu'xir] *vi* (*vaca*) to moo.

mugre ['muɣre] *nf* dirt, filth; **mugriento, a** *a* dirty, filthy.

mujer [mu'xer] *nf* woman; (*esposa*) wife; ~**iego** *nm* womanizer.

mula ['mula] *nf* mule.

mulato, a [mu'lato, a] *a, nm/f* mulatto.

muleta [mu'leta] *nf* (*para andar*) crutch; (*TAUR*) stick with red cape attached.

multa ['multa] *nf* fine; **multar** *vt* to fine.

multicopista [multiko'pista] *nm* duplicator.

múltiple ['multiple] *a* multiple; (*pl*) many, numerous.

multiplicar [multipli'kar] *vt* (*MAT*) to multiply; (*fig*) to increase; ~se *vr* (*BIO*) to multiply; (*fig*) to be everywhere at once.

multitud [multi'tuð] *nf* (*muchedumbre*) crowd; ~ **de** lots of.

mullido, a [mu'ʎiðo, a] *a* (*cama*) soft; (*hierba*) soft, springy.

mundano, a [mun'dano, a] *a* worldly; (*de moda*) fashionable.

mundial [mun'djal] *a* world-wide, universal; (*guerra, récord*) world *cpd*.

mundo ['mundo] *nm* world; **todo el** ~ everybody; **tener** ~ to be experienced, know one's way around.

munición [muni'θjon] *nf* (*MIL*: *provisiones*) stores *pl*, supplies *pl*; (: *balas*) ammunition.

municipio [muni'θipjo] *nm* (*ayuntamiento*) town council, corporation; (*territorio administrativo*) town, municipality.

muñeca [mu'ɲeka] *nf* (*ANAT*) wrist; (*juguete*) doll.

muñeco [mu'ɲeko] *nm* (*figura*) figure; (*marioneta*) puppet; (*fig*) puppet, pawn.

mural [mu'ral] *a* mural, wall *cpd* // *nm* mural.

muralla [mu'raʎa] *nf* (city) wall(s) (*pl*).

murciélago [mur'θjelaɣo] *nm* bat.

murmullo [mur'muʎo] *nm* murmur(ing); (*cuchicheo*) whispering; (*de arroyo*) murmur, rippling.

murmuración [murmura'θjon] *nf* gossip; **murmurar** *vi* to murmur, whisper; (*criticar*) to criticize; (*cotillear*) to gossip.

muro ['muro] *nm* wall.

muscular [musku'lar] *a* muscular.

músculo ['muskulo] *nm* muscle.

museo [mu'seo] *nm* museum.

musgo ['musɣo] *nm* moss.

músico, a ['musiko, a] *a* musical // *nm/f* musician // *nf* music.

musitar [musi'tar] *vt, vi* to mutter, mumble.

muslo ['muslo] *nm* thigh.

mustio, a ['mustjo, a] *a* (*persona*) depressed, gloomy; (*planta*) faded, withered.

musulmán, ana [musul'man, ana] *nm/f* Moslem.

mutación [muta'θjon] *nf* (*BIO*) mutation; (: *cambio*) (sudden) change.

mutilar [muti'lar] *vt* to mutilate; (*a una persona*) to maim.

mutuamente [mutwa'mente] *ad* mutually.

mutuo, a ['mutwo, a] *a* mutual.

muy [mwi] *ad* very; (*demasiado*) too; **M~ Señor mío** Dear Sir; ~ **de noche** very late at night; **eso es** ~ **de él** that's just like him.

N

N *abr* (= **norte**) N.

n/ *abr* = **nuestro, a**.

nabo ['naβo] *nm* turnip.

nácar ['nakar] *nm* mother-of-pearl.

nacer [na'θer] *vi* to be born; (*de huevo*) to hatch; (*vegetal*) to sprout; (*río*) to rise; **nací en Barcelona** I was born in Barcelona; **nació una sospecha en su mente** a suspicion formed in her mind; **nacido, a** *a* born; **recién nacido** newborn; **naciente** *a* new, emerging; (*sol*) rising; **nacimiento** *nm* birth; (*fig*) birth, origin; (*de Navidad*) Nativity; (*linaje*) descent, family; (*de río*) source.

nación [na'θjon] *nf* nation; **nacional** *a* national; **nacionalismo** *nm* nationalism; **nacionalista** *nm/f* nationalist; **nacionalizar** *vt* to nationalize; **nacionalizarse** *vr* (*persona*) to become naturalized.

nada ['naða] *pron* nothing // *ad* not at all, in no way; **no decir** ~ to say nothing, not to say anything; **de** ~ don't mention it.

nadador, a [naða'ðor, a] *nm/f* swimmer.

nadar [na'ðar] *vi* to swim.

nadie ['naðje] *pron* nobody, no-one; ~ habló nobody spoke; **no había** ~ there was nobody there, there wasn't anybody there.

nado ['naðo]: **a** ~ *ad*: **pasar a** ~ to swim across.

nafta ['nafta] *nf (AM)* petrol *(Brit)*, gas *(US)*.

naipe ['naipe] *nm* (playing) card; ~s *nmpl* cards.

nalgas ['nalɣas] *nfpl* buttocks.

nana ['nana] *nf* lullaby.

naranja [na'ranxa] *a inv, nf* orange; **media** ~ *(fam)* better half; **naranjada** *nf* orangeade; **naranjo** *nm* orange tree.

narciso [nar'θiso] *nm* narcissus.

narcótico, a [nar'kotiko, a] *a, nm* narcotic; **narcotizar** *vt* to drug.

nardo ['narðo] *nm* lily.

narigón, ona [nari'ɣon, ona] **narigudo, a** [nari'ɣuðo, a] *a* big-nosed.

nariz [na'riθ] *nf* nose; **narices** *nfpl* nostrils; **delante de las narices de uno** under one's (very) nose.

narración [narra'θjon] *nf* narration; **narrador, a** *nm/f* narrator.

narrar [na'rrar] *vt* to narrate, recount; **narrativa** *nf* narrative, story.

nata ['nata] *nf* cream.

natación [nata'θjon] *nf* swimming.

natal [na'tal] *a*: **ciudad** ~ home town; ~**icio** *nm* birthday; ~**idad** *nf* birth rate.

natillas [na'tiʎas] *nfpl* custard *sg*.

natividad [natißi'ðað] *nf* nativity.

nativo, a [na'tiβo, a] *a, nm/f* native.

nato, a ['nato, a] *a* born; **un músico** ~ a born musician.

natural [natu'ral] *a* natural; *(fruta etc)* fresh // *nm/f* native // *nm (disposición)* nature.

naturaleza [natura'leθa] *nf* nature; *(género)* nature, kind; ~ **muerta** still life.

naturalidad [naturali'ðað] *nf* naturalness.

naturalización [naturaliθa'θjon] *nf* naturalization.

naturalizarse [naturali'θarse] *vr* to become naturalized; *(aclimatarse)* to become acclimatized.

naturalmente [natural'mente] *ad (de modo natural)* in a natural way; ¡~! of course!

naufragar [naufra'ɣar] *vi* to sink; **naufragio** *nm* shipwreck; **náufrago, a** *nm/f* castaway, shipwrecked person.

nauseabundo, a [nausea'ßundo, a] *a* nauseating, sickening.

náuseas ['nauseas] *nfpl* nausea; **me da** ~ it makes me feel sick.

náutico, a ['nautiko, a] *a* nautical.

navaja [na'ßaxa] *nf (cortaplumas)* clasp knife *(Brit)*, penknife; *(de. barbero, peluquero)* razor.

Navarra [na'ßarra] *n* Navarre.

nave ['naße] *nf (barco)* ship, vessel; *(ARQ)* nave; ~ **espacial** spaceship.

navegación [naßeɣa'θjon] *nf* navigation; *(viaje)* sea journey; ~ **aérea** air traffic; ~ **costera** coastal shipping; **navegante** *nm/f* navigator; **navegar** *vi (barco)* to sail; *(avión)* to fly // *vt* to sail; to fly; *(dirigir el rumbo)* to navigate.

navidad [naßi'ðað] *nf* Christmas; ~**es** *nfpl* Christmas time; **navideño, a** *a* Christmas *cpd*.

navío [na'ßio] *nm* ship.

nazca *etc vb ver* **nacer**.

nazi ['naθi] *a, nm/f* Nazi.

NE *abr (= nor(d)este)* NE.

neblina [ne'ßlina] *nf* mist.

nebuloso, a [neßu'loso, a] *a* foggy; *(calinoso)* misty; *(indefinido)* nebulous, vague // *nf* nebula.

necedad [neθe'ðað] *nf* foolishness; *(una* ~*)* foolish act.

necesario, a [neθe'sarjo, a] *a* necessary.

neceser [neθe'ser] *nm* toilet bag; *(bolsa grande)* holdall.

necesidad [neθesi'ðað] *nf* need; *(lo inevitable)* necessity; *(miseria)* poverty, need; **en caso de** ~ in case of need *o* emergency; **hacer sus** ~**es** to relieve o.s.

necesitado, a [neθesi'taðo, a] *a* needy, poor; ~ **de** in need of.

necesitar [neθesi'tar] *vt* to need, require // *vi*: ~ **de** to have need of.

necio, a ['neθjo, a] *a* foolish.

necrología [nekrolo'xia] *nf* obituary.

necrópolis [ne'kropolis] *nf inv* cemetery.

nectarina [nekta'rina] *nf* nectarine.

nefasto, a [ne'fasto, a] *a* ill-fated, unlucky.

negación [neɣa'θjon] *nf* negation; *(rechazo)* refusal, denial.

negar [ne'ɣar] *vt (renegar, rechazar)* to refuse; *(prohibir)* to refuse, deny; *(desmentir)* to deny; ~**se** *vr*: ~**se a** to refuse to.

negativo, a [neɣa'tiβo, a] *a, nm* negative // *nf (gen)* negative; *(rechazo)* refusal, denial.

negligencia [neɣli'xenθja] *nf* negligence; **negligente** *a* negligent.

negociable [neɣo'θjaßle] *a (COM)* negotiable.

negociado [neɣo'θjaðo] *nm* department, section.

negociante [neɣo'θjante] *nm/f* businessman/woman.

negociar [neɣo'θjar] *vt, vi* to negotiate; ~ **en** to deal in, trade in.

negocio [ne'ɣoθjo] *nm (COM)* business; *(asunto)* affair, business; *(operación comercial)* deal, transaction; *(AM)* firm; *(lugar)* place of business; **los** ~**s** business *sa*; hacer ~ to do business.

negro, a ['neɣro, a] *a* black; (*suerte*) awful // *nm* black // *nm/f* Negro/Negress, Black // *nf* (*MUS*) crotchet; **negrura** *nf* blackness.

nene, a ['nene, a] *nm/f* baby, small child.

nenúfar [ne'nufar] *nm* water lily.

neologismo [neolo'xismo] *nm* neologism.

neoyorquino, a [neojor'kino, a] *a* (of) New York.

nepotismo [nepo'tismo] *nm* nepotism.

nervio ['nerßjo] *nm* (*ANAT*) nerve; (: *tendón*) tendon; (*fig*) vigour; **nerviosismo** *nm* nervousness, nerves *pl*; ~**so, a, nervudo, a** *a* nervous.

neto, a ['neto, a] *a* clear; (*limpio*) clean; (*COM*) net.

neumático, a [neu'matiko, a] *a* pneumatic // *nm* (*Esp*) tyre (*Brit*), tire (*US*); ~ **de recambio** spare tyre.

neurastenia [neuras'tenja] *nf* (*MED*) neurasthenia; (*fig*) excitability.

neurólogo, a [neu'roloɣo, a] *nm/f* neurologist.

neutral [neu'tral] *a* neutral; ~**izar** *vt* to neutralize; (*contrarrestar*) to counteract.

neutro, a ['neutro, a] *a* (*BIO*) neuter; (*LING*) neuter.

neutrón [neu'tron] *nm* neutron.

nevada [ne'ßaða] *nf* snowstorm; (*caída de nieve*) snowfall.

nevar [ne'ßar] *vi* to snow.

nevera [ne'ßera] *nf* (*Esp*) refrigerator (*Brit*), icebox (*US*).

nevería [neße'ria] *nf* (*AM*) ice-cream parlour.

nevisca [ne'ßiska] *nf* flurry of snow.

nexo ['nekso] *nm* link, connection.

ni [ni] *conj* nor, neither; (*tb*: ~ **siquiera**) not ... even; ~ **que** not even if; ~ **blanco** ~ **negro** neither white nor black.

Nicaragua [nika'raɣwa] *nf* Nicaragua; **nicaragüense** *a, nm/f* Nicaraguan.

nicotina [niko'tina] *nf* nicotine.

nicho ['nitʃo] *nm* niche.

nido ['niðo] *nm* nest; (*fig*) hiding place.

niebla ['njeßla] *nf* fog; (*neblina*) mist.

niego *etc vb ver* **negar**.

nieto, a ['njeto, a] *nm/f* grandson/daughter; ~**s** *nmpl* grandchildren.

nieve *etc vb ver* **nevar** // ['njeße] *nf* snow; (*AM*) icecream.

nigromancia [niɣro'manθja] *nf* necromancy, black magic.

Nilo ['nilo] *nm*: el ~ the Nile.

nimiedad [nimje'ðað] *nf* small-mindedness; (*trivialidad*) triviality.

nimio, a ['nimjo, a] *a* trivial, insignificant.

ninfa ['ninfa] *nf* nymph.

ninfómana [nin'fomana] *nf* nymphomaniac.

ninguno, a [nin'guno, a], **ningún** [nin'gun] *a* no // *pron* (*nadie*) nobody; (*ni uno*) none, not one; (*ni uno ni otro*) neither; **de ninguna manera** by no means, not at all.

niña ['niɲa] *nf ver* **niño**.

niñera [ni'ɲera] *nf* nursemaid, nanny; **niñería** *nf* childish act.

niñez [ni'ɲeθ] *nf* childhood; (*infancia*) infancy.

niño, a ['niɲo, a] *a* (*joven*) young; (*inmaduro*) immature // *nm* (*chico*) boy, child // *nf* (*chica*) girl, child; (*ANAT*) pupil.

nipón, ona [ni'pon, ona] *a, nm/f* Japanese.

níquel ['nikel] *nm* nickel; **niquelar** *vt* (*TEC*) to nickel-plate.

níspero ['nispero] *nm* medlar.

nitidez [niti'ðeθ] *nf* (*claridad*) clarity; (: *de atmósfera*) brightness; (: *de imagen*) sharpness; **nítido, a** *a* clear; sharp.

nitrato [ni'trato] *nm* nitrate.

nitrógeno [ni'troxeno] *nm* nitrogen.

nitroglicerina [nitroɣliθe'rina] *nf* nitroglycerine.

nivel [ni'ßel] *nm* (*GEO*) level; (*norma*) level, standard; (*altura*) height; ~ **de aceite** oil level; ~ **de aire** spirit level; ~ **de vida** standard of living; ~**ar** *vt* to level out; (*fig*) to even up; (*COM*) to balance.

NN. UU. *nfpl abr* (= Naciones Unidas) U.N. 3g.

NO *abr* (= noroeste) NW.

no [no] *ad* no; not; (*con verbo*) not // *excl* no!; ~ **tengo nada** I don't have anything, I have nothing; ~ **es el mío** it's not mine; **ahora** ~ not now; **¿~ lo sabes?** don't you know?; ~ **mucho** not much; ~ **bien termine, lo entregaré** as soon as I finish I'll hand it over; **¡a que** ~ **lo sabes!** I bet you don't know!; **¡cómo** ~! of course!; **los países** ~ **alineados** the non-aligned countries; **la** ~ **intervención** non-intervention.

noble ['noßle] *a, nm/f* noble; ~**za** *nf* nobility.

noción [no'θjon] *nf* notion.

nocivo, a [no'θißo, a] *a* harmful.

noctámbulo, a [nok'tambulo, a] *nm/f* sleepwalker.

nocturno, a [nok'turno, a] *a* (*de la noche*) nocturnal, night *cpd*; (*de la tarde*) evening *cpd* // *nm* nocturne.

noche ['notʃe] *nf* night, night-time; (*la tarde*) evening; (*fig*) darkness; **de** ~, **por la** ~ at night.

nochebuena [notʃe'ßwena] *nf* Christmas Eve.

nochevieja [notʃe'ßjexa] *nf* New Year's Eve.

nodriza [no'ðriθa] *nf* wet nurse; **buque** *o* **nave** ~ supply ship.

nogal [no'ɣal] *nm* walnut tree.

nómada ['nomaða] *a* nomadic // *nm/f*

nomad.

nombramiento [nombra'mjento] *nm* naming; (*a un empleo*) appointment.

nombrar [nom'brar] *vt* (*designar*) to name; (*mencionar*) to mention; (*dar puesto a*) to appoint.

nombre ['nombre] *nm* name; (*sustantivo*) noun; (*fama*) renown; ~ y apellidos name in full; ~ común/propio common/proper noun; ~ de pila/de soltera Christian/maiden name.

nomenclatura [nomenkla'tura] *nf* nomenclature.

nomeolvides [nomeol'βiðes] *nm inv* forget-me-not.

nómina ['nomina] *nf* (*lista*) list; (*COM*) payroll.

nominal [nomi'nal] *a* nominal.

nominar [nomi'nar] *vt* to nominate.

nominativo, a [nomina'tiβo, a] *a* (*COM*): cheque ~ a X cheque made out to X.

non [non] *a* odd, uneven // *nm* odd number.

nono, a ['nono, a] *a* ninth.

nordeste [nor'ðeste] *a* north-east, north-eastern, north-easterly // *nm* north-east.

nórdico, a ['norðiko, a] *a* (*del norte*) northern, northerly; (*escandinavo*) Nordic.

noreste [no'reste] *a, nm* = **nordeste**.

noria ['norja] *nf* (*AGR*) waterwheel; (*de carnaval*) big (*Brit*) o Ferris (*US*) wheel.

normal [nor'mal] *a* (*corriente*) normal; (*habitual*) usual, natural; (*gasolina*) ~ two-star petrol; ~idad *nf* normality; restablecer la ~idad to restore order; ~izar *vt* (*reglamentar*) to normalize; (*TEC*) to standardize; ~izarse *vr* to return to normal.

normando, a [nor'mando, a] *a, nm/f* Norman.

noroeste [noro'este] *a* north-west, north-western, north-westerly // *nm* north-west.

norte ['norte] *a* north, northern, northerly // *nm* north; (*fig*) guide.

norteamericano, a [norteameri'kano, a] *a, nm/f* (North) American.

Noruega [no'rweta] *nf* Norway.

noruego, a [no'rweto, a] *a, nm/f* Norwegian.

nos [nos] *pron* (*directo*) us; (*indirecto*) us; to us; for us; from us; (*reflexivo*) (to) ourselves; (*recíproco*) (to) each other; ~ levantamos a las 7 we get up at 7.

nosotros, as [no'sotros, as] *pron* (*sujeto*) we; (*después de prep*) us.

nostalgia [nos'talxja] *nf* nostalgia.

nota ['nota] *nf* note; (*ESCOL*) mark.

notable [no'taβle] *a* notable; (*ESCOL*) outstanding // *nm/f* notable.

notar [no'tar] *vt* to notice, note; ~se *vr* to be obvious; se nota que ... one observes

that ....

notarial [nota'rjal] *a*: acta ~ affidavit.

notario [no'tarjo] *nm* notary.

noticia [no'tiθja] *nf* (*información*) piece of news; las ~s the news *sg*; tener ~s de alguien to hear from sb.

noticiario [noti'θjarjo] *nm* (*CINE*) newsreel; (*TV*) news bulletin.

noticiero [noti'θjero] *nm* (*AM*) news bulletin.

notificación [notifika'θjon] *nf* notification; **notificar** *vt* to notify, inform.

notoriedad [notorje'ðað] *nf* fame, renown; **notorio, a** *a* (*público*) wellknown; (*evidente*) obvious.

novato, a [no'βato, a] *a* inexperienced // *nm/f* beginner, novice.

novecientos, as [noβe'θjentos, as] *a, num* nine hundred.

novedad [noβe'ðað] *nf* (*calidad de nuevo*) newness; (*noticia*) piece of news; (*cambio*) change, (new) development.

novedoso, a [noβe'ðoso, a] *a* novel.

novel [no'βel] *a* new; (*inexperto*) inexperienced // *nm/f* beginner.

novela [no'βela] *nf* novel.

novelero, a [noβe'lero, a] *a* highly imaginative.

novelesco, a [noβe'lesko, a] *a* fictional; (*romántico*) romantic; (*fantástico*) fantastic.

noveno, a [no'βeno, a] *a* ninth.

noventa [no'βenta] *num* ninety.

novia ['noβja] *nf ver* **novio**.

noviazgo [no'βjaθo] *nm* engagement.

novicio, a [no'βiθjo, a] *nm/f* novice.

noviembre [no'βjembre] *nm* November.

novilla [no'βiʎa] *nf* heifer; **~da** *nf* (*TAUR*) bullfight with young bulls; **novillero** *nm* novice bullfighter; **novillo** *nm* young bull, bullock; **hacer novillos** (*fam*) to play truant.

novio, a ['noβjo, a] *nm/f* boyfriend/girlfriend; (*prometido*) fiancé/fiancée; (*recién casado*) bridegroom/bride; los ~s the newly-weds.

N. S. *abr = Nuestro Señor.*

nubarrón [nuβa'rron] *nm* storm cloud.

nube ['nuβe] *nf* cloud.

nublado, a [nu'βlaðo, a] *a* cloudy // *nm* storm cloud; **nublar** *vt* (*oscurecer*) to darken; (*confundir*) to cloud; **nublarse** *vr* to grow dark.

nuca ['nuka] *nf* nape of the neck.

nuclear [nukle'ar] *a* nuclear.

núcleo ['nukleo] *nm* (*centro*) core; (*FISICA*) nucleus.

nudillo [nu'ðiʎo] *nm* knuckle.

nudo ['nuðo] *nm* knot; (*unión*) bond; (*de problema*) crux; **~so, a** *a* knotty.

nuera ['nwera] *nf* daughter-in-law.

nuestro, a ['nwestro, a] *adjetivo posesivo* our // *pron* ours; ~ padre our father; un amigo ~ a friend of ours; es el ~ it's ours.

nueva |'nweβa| af, nf ver **nuevo**.

nuevamente |nweßa'mente| ad (otra vez) again; (de nuevo) anew.

nueve |'nweβe| num nine.

nuevo, a |'nweβo, a| a (gen) new // nf piece of news; de ~ again; **Nueva York** n New York; **Nueva Zelandia** nf New Zealand.

nuez |nweθ| nf (fruto) nut; (del nogal) walnut; (de **Adán** Adam's apple; ~ moscada nutmeg.

nulidad |nuli'ðað| nf (incapacidad) incompetence; (abolición) nullity.

nulo, a |'nulo, a| a (inepto, torpe) useless; (inválido) (null and) void; (DEPORTE) drawn, tied.

núm. abr (= número) no.

numeración |numera'θjon| nf (cifras) numbers pl; (arábiga, romana etc) numerals pl.

numeral |nume'ral| nm numeral.

numerar |nume'rar| vt to number.

numérico, a |nu'meriko, a| a numerical.

número |'numero| nm (gen) number; (tamaño: de zapato) size; (ejemplar: de diario) number, issue; sin ~ numberless, unnumbered; ~ de matrícula/de teléfono registration/telephone number; ~ atrasado back number.

numeroso, a |nume'roso, a| a numerous.

nunca |'nunka| ad (jamás) never; ~ lo pensé I never thought it; **no viene** ~ he never comes; ~ más never again.

nuncio |'nunθjo| nm (REL) nuncio.

nupcias |'nupθjas| nfpl wedding sg, nuptials.

nutria |'nutrja| nf otter.

nutrición |nutri'θjon| nf nutrition.

nutrido, a |nu'triðo, a| a (alimentado) nourished; (fig: grande) large; (abundante) abundant.

nutrir |nu'trir| vt (alimentar) to nourish; (dar de comer) to feed; (fig) to strengthen; **nutritivo, a** a nourishing, nutritious.

nylon |ni'lon| nm nylon.

Ñ

ñato, a |'ɲato, a| a (AM) snub-nosed.

ñoñería |ɲoɲe'ria|, **ñoñez** |ɲo'ɲeθ| nf insipidness.

ñoño, a |'ɲoɲo, a| a (AM: tonto) silly, stupid; (soso) insipid; (persona) spineless.

O

o |o| conj or.

O abr (= oeste) W.

o/ abr (= orden) o.

oasis |o'asis| nm inv oasis.

obcecar |oßθe'kar| vt to blind.

obedecer |oßeðe'θer| vt to obey; **obediencia** nf obedience; **obediente** a obedient.

obertura |oßer'tura| nf overture.

obesidad |oßesi'ðað| nf obesity; **obeso, a** a obese.

obispo |o'ßispo| nm bishop.

objeción |oßxe'θjon| nf objection.

objetar |oßxe'tar| vt, vi to object.

objetivo, a |oßxe'tißo, a| a, nm objective.

objeto |oß'xeto| nm (cosa) object; (fin) aim.

objetor, a |oßxe'tor, a| nm/f objector.

oblicuo, a |o'ßlikwo, a| a oblique; (mirada) sidelong.

obligación |oßlixa'θjon| nf obligation; (COM) bond.

obligar |oßli'var| vt to force; ~se vr to bind o.s.; **obligatorio, a** a compulsory, obligatory.

oboe |o'ßoe| nm oboe.

obra |'oßra| nf work; (hechura) piece of work; (ARQ) construction, building; (TEATRO) play; ~ **maestra** masterpiece; o~s **públicas** public works; **por** ~ **de** thanks to (the efforts of); **obrar** vt to work; (tener efecto) to have an effect on // vi to act, behave; (tener efecto) to have an effect; **la carta obra en su poder** the letter is in his/her possession.

obrero, a |o'ßrero, a| a (clase) working; (movimiento) labour cpd; **clase obrera** working class // nm/f (gen) worker; (sin oficio) labourer.

obscenidad |oßsθeni'ðað| nf obscenity; **obsceno, a** a obscene.

obscu... = oscu...

obsequiar |oßse'kjar| vt (ofrecer) to present with; (agasajar) to make a fuss of, lavish attention on; **obsequio** nm (regalo) gift; (cortesía) courtesy, attention; **obsequioso, a** a attentive.

observación |oßserßa'θjon| nf observation; (reflexión) remark.

observador, a |oßserßa'ðor, a| nm/f observer.

observancia |oßser'ßanθja| nf observance.

observar |oßser'ßar| vt to observe; (anotar) to notice; ~se vr to keep to, observe.

obsesión |oßse'sjon| nf obsession; **obsesionar** vt to obsess.

obstaculizar |oßstakuli'θar| vt (dificultar) to hinder, hamper.

obstáculo |oß'stakulo| nm (gen) obstacle; (impedimento) hindrance, drawback.

obstante |oß'stante|: **no** ~ ad nevertheless // prep in spite of.

obstetricia |oßste'triθja| nf obstetrics sg; **obstétrico, a** a obstetric // nm/f obstetrician.

obstinado, a |oßsti'naðo, a| a (gen)
obstinate, stubborn.

obstinarse |oßsti'narse| vr to be
obstinate; ~ **en** to persist in.

obstrucción |oßstruk'θjon| nf obstruction; **obstruir** vt to obstruct.

obtener |oßte'ner| vt (conseguir) to
obtain; (ganar) to gain.

obturador |oßtura'ðor| nm (FOTO)
shutter.

obtuso, a |oß'tuso, a| a (filo) blunt;
(MAT, fig) obtuse.

obviar |oß'ßjar| vt to obviate, remove.

obvio, a |'oßßjo, a| a obvious.

ocasión |oka'sjon| nf (oportunidad)
opportunity, chance; (momento) occasion, time; (causa) cause; **de ~** secondhand; **ocasionar** vt to cause.

ocaso |o'kaso| nm (fig) decline.

occidente |okθi'ðente| nm west.

océano |o'θeano| nm ocean; **el ~ Índico**
the Indian Ocean.

OCDE nf abr (= Organización de
Cooperación y Desarrollo Económico)
OECD.

ocio |'oθjo| nm (tiempo) leisure; (pey)
idleness; ~**sidad** nf idleness; ~**so, a** a
(inactivo) idle; (inútil) useless.

octanaje |okta'naxe| nm: **de alto ~** high
octane; **octano** nm octane.

octavilla |okta'viʎa| nf leaflet, pamphlet.

octavo, a |ok'taßo, a| a eighth.

octogenario, a |oktoxe'narjo, a| a
octogenarian.

octubre |ok'tußre| nm October.

ocular |oku'lar| a ocular, eye cpd; **testigo
~** eyewitness.

oculista |oku'lista| nm/f oculist.

ocultar |okul'tar| vt (esconder) to hide;
(callar) to conceal; **oculto, a** a hidden;
(fig) secret.

ocupación |okupa'θjon| nf occupation.

ocupado, a |oku'paðo, a| a (persona)
busy; (plaza) occupied, taken; (teléfono)
engaged; **ocupar** vt (gen) to occupy;
ocuparse vr: **ocuparse de** o **en** (gen)
to concern o.s. with; (cuidar) to look
after.

ocurrencia |oku'rrenθja| nf (suceso) incident, event; (idea) bright idea.

ocurrir |oku'rrir| vi to happen; ~**se** vr: **se
me ocurrió que...** it occurred to me
that... .

ochenta |o'tʃenta| num eighty.

ocho |'otʃo| num eight; ~ **días** a week.

odiar |o'ðjar| vt to hate; **odio** nm (gen)
hate, hatred; (disgusto) dislike; **odioso,
a** a (gen) hateful; (malo) nasty.

odontólogo, a |oðon'toloxo, a| nm/f
dentist, dental surgeon.

OEA nf abr (= Organización de Estados
Americanos) OAS.

oeste |o'este| nm west; **una película del
~** a western.

ofender |ofen'der| vt (agraviar) to

offend; (insultar) to insult; ~**se** vr to
take offence; **ofensa** nf offence;
ofensivo, a a (insultante) insulting;
(MIL) offensive // a offensive.

oferta |o'ferta| nf offer; (propuesta)
proposal; **la ~ y la demanda** supply and
demand; **artículos en ~** goods on offer.

oficial |ofi'θjal| a official // nm official;
(MIL) officer.

oficina |ofi'θina| nf office; ~ **de correos**
post office; ~ **de turismo** tourist office;
oficinista nm/f clerk.

oficio |o'fiθjo| nm (profesión) profession;
(puesto) post; (REL) service; **ser del ~**
to be an old hand; **tener mucho ~** to
have a lot of experience; ~ **de difuntos**
funeral service; **de ~** officially.

oficioso, a |ofi'θjoso, a| a (pey) officious; (no oficial) unofficial, informal.

ofimática |ofi'matika| nf office automation.

ofrecer |ofre'θer| vt (dar) to offer;
(proponer) to propose; ~**se** vr (persona)
to offer o.s., volunteer; (situación) to
present itself; **¿qué se le ofrece?, ¿se le
ofrece algo?** what can I do for you?, can
I get you anything?

ofrecimiento |ofreθi'mjento| nm offer,
offering.

ofrendar |ofren'dar| vt to offer, contribute.

oftalmólogo, a |oftal'moloxo, a| nm/f
ophthalmologist.

ofuscación |ofuska'θjon| nf,
ofuscamiento |ofuska'mjento| nm (fig)
bewilderment.

ofuscar |ofus'kar| vt (confundir) to
bewilder; (enceguecer) to dazzle, blind.

oída |o'iða| nf: **de ~s** by hearsay.

oído |o'iðo| nm (ANAT) ear; (sentido)
hearing.

oigo etc vb ver **oír.**

oír |o'ir| vt (gen) to hear; (atender a) to
listen to; **¡oiga!** listen!; ~ **misa** to attend
mass.

OIT nf abr (= Organización
Internacional del Trabajo) ILO.

ojal |o'xal| nm buttonhole.

ojalá |oxa'la| excl if only (it were so)!,
some hope! // conj if only...!, would
that...!; ~ **que venga hoy** I hope he
comes today.

ojeada |oxe'aða| nf glance.

ojera |o'xera| nf: **tener ~s** to have bags
under one's eyes.

ojeriza |oxe'riθa| nf ill-will.

ojeroso, a |oxe'roso, a| a haggard.

ojete |o'xete| nm eye(let).

ojo |'oxo| nm eye; (de puente) span; (de
cerradura) keyhole // excl careful!;
tener ~ para to have an eye for; ~ **de
buey** porthole.

ola |'ola| nf wave.

olé |o'le| excl bravo!, olé!

oleada |ole'aða| nf big wave, swell; (fig)

wave
oleaje [ole'axe] *nm* swell.
óleo ['oleo] *nm* oil; **oleoducto** *nm* (oil) pipeline.
oler [o'ler] *vt* (*gen*) to smell; (*inquirir*) to pry into; (*fig: sospechar*) to sniff out // *vi* to smell; ~ a to smell of.
olfatear [olfate'ar] *vt* to smell; (*fig: sospechar*) to sniff out; (*inquirir*) to pry into; **olfato** *nm* sense of smell.
oligarquía [olivar'kia] *nf* oligarchy.
olimpíada [olim'piaða] *nf*: las O~s the Olympics.
oliva [o'lißa] *nf* (*aceituna*) olive; aceite de ~ olive oil; **olivo** *nm* olive tree.
olmo ['olmo] *nm* elm (tree).
olor [o'lor] *nm* smell; **~oso, a** *a* scented.
olvidadizo, a [olßiða'ðiθo, a] *a* (*desmemoriado*) forgetful; (*distraído*) absent-minded.
olvidar [olßi'ðar] *vt* to forget; (*omitir*) to omit; ~se *vr* (*fig*) to forget o.s.; se me olvidó I forgot.
olvido [ol'ßiðo] *nm* oblivion; (*despiste*) forgetfulness.
olla ['oʎa] *nf* pan; (*comida*) stew; ~ a presión o exprés pressure cooker; ~ podrida *type of Spanish stew*.
ombligo [om'blivo] *nm* navel.
ominoso [omi'noso, a] *a* ominous.
omisión [omi'sjon] *nf* (*abstención*) omission; (*descuido*) neglect.
omiso, a [o'miso, a] *a*: hacer caso ~ de to ignore, pass over.
omitir [omi'tir] *vt* to omit.
omnipotente [omnipo'tente] *a* omnipotent.
omnívoro, a [om'nißoro, a] *a* omnivorous.
omóplato [o'moplato] *nm* shoulder blade.
OMS *nf abr* (= Organización Mundial de la Salud) WHO.
once ['onθe] *num* eleven; ~s *nmpl* (*AM*) tea break.
onda ['onda] *nf* wave; ~ corta/larga/media short/long/medium wave; **ondear** *vt, vi* to wave; (*tener ondas*) to be wavy; (*agua*) to ripple; **ondearse** *vr* to swing, sway.
ondulación [ondula'θjon] *nf* undulation; **ondulado, a** *a* wavy // *nm* wave; **ondulante** *a* undulating.
ondular [ondu'lar] *vt* (*el pelo*) to wave // *vi*, ~se *vr* to undulate.
oneroso, a [one'roso, a] *a* onerous.
ONU ['onu] *nf abr* (= Organización de las Naciones Unidas) UNO.
opaco, a [o'pako, a] *a* opaque; (*fig*) dull.
ópalo ['opalo] *nm* opal.
opción [op'θjon] *nf* (*gen*) option; (*derecho*) right, option.
OPEP ['opep] *nf abr* (= Organización de Países Exportadores de Petróleo) OPEC.

ópera ['opera] *nf* opera; ~ bufa o cómica comic opera.
operación [opera'θjon] *nf* (*gen*) operation; (*COM*) transaction, deal.
operador, a [opera'ðor, a] *nm/f* operator; (*CINE: proyección*) projectionist; (: *rodaje*) cameraman.
operante [ope'rante] *a* operating.
operar [ope'rar] *vt* (*producir*) to produce, bring about; (*MED*) to operate on // *vi* (*COM*) to operate, deal; ~se *vr* to occur; (*MED*) to have an operation.
opereta [ope'reta] *nf* operetta.
opinar [opi'nar] *vt* (*estimar*) to think // *vi* (*enjuiciar*) to give one's opinion; **opinión** *nf* (*creencia*) belief; (*criterio*) opinion.
opio ['opjo] *nm* opium.
oponente [opo'nente] *nm/f* opponent.
oponer [opo'ner] *vt* (*resistencia*) to put up, offer; (*negativa*) to raise; ~se *vr* (*objetar*) to object; (*estar frente a frente*) to be opposed; (*dos personas*) to oppose each other; ~ A a B to set A against B; me opongo a pensar que... I refuse to believe o think that... .
oportunidad [oportuni'ðað] *nf* (*ocasión*) opportunity; (*posibilidad*) chance.
oportunismo [oportu'nismo] *nm* opportunism; **oportunista** *nm/f* opportunist.
oportuno, a [opor'tuno, a] *a* (*en su tiempo*) opportune, timely; (*respuesta*) suitable; en el momento ~ at the right moment.
oposición [oposi'θjon] *nf* opposition; **oposiciones** *nfpl* public examinations.
opositor, a [oposi'tor, a] *nm/f* (*adversario*) opponent; (*candidato*) candidate.
opresión [opre'sjon] *nf* oppression; **opresivo, a** *a* oppressive; **opresor, a** *nm/f* oppressor.
oprimir [opri'mir] *vt* to squeeze; (*fig*) to oppress.
oprobio [o'proßjo] *nm* (*infamia*) ignominy; (*descrédito*) shame.
optar [op'tar] *vi* (*elegir*) to choose; ~ a o por to opt for; **optativo, a** *a* optional.
óptico, a ['optiko, a] *a* optic(al) // *nm/f* optician.
optimismo [opti'mismo] *nm* optimism; **optimista** *nm/f* optimist.
óptimo, a ['optimo, a] *a* (*el mejor*) very best.
opuesto, a [o'pwesto, a] *a* (*contrario*) opposite; (*antagónico*) opposing.
opulencia [opu'lenθja] *nf* opulence; **opulento, a** *a* opulent.
oración [ora'θjon] *nf* (*discurso*) speech; (*REL*) prayer; (*LING*) sentence.
oráculo [o'rakulo] *nm* oracle.
orador, a [ora'ðor, a] *nm/f* (*conferenciante*) speaker, orator.
oral [o'ral] *a* oral.
orangután [orangu'tan] *nm* orang-utan.

orar [o'rar] *vi* (*REL*) to pray.
oratoria [ora'torja] *nf* oratory.
órbita ['orβita] *nf* orbit.
orden ['orðen] *nm* (*gen*) order // *nf* (*gen*) order; (*INFORM*) command; **~ del día** agenda; **de primer ~** first-rate; **en ~ de** prioridad in order of priority.
ordenado, a [orðe'naðo, a] *a* (*metódico*) methodical; (*arreglado*) orderly.
ordenador [orðena'ðor] *nm* computer; **~ central** mainframe computer.
ordenanza [orðe'nanθa] *nf* ordinance.
ordenar [orðe'nar] *vt* (*mandar*) to order; (*poner orden*) to put in order, arrange; **~se** *vr* (*REL*) to be ordained.
ordeñar [orðe'ɲar] *vt* to milk.
ordinario, a [orði'narjo, a] *a* (*común*) ordinary, usual; (*vulgar*) vulgar, common.
orégano [o'reɣano] *nm* oregano.
oreja [o'rexa] *nf* ear; (*MECÁNICA*) lug, flange.
orfanato [orfa'nato] *nm* orphanage.
orfandad [orfan'dað] *nf* orphanhood.
orfebrería [orfeβre'ria] *nf* gold/silver work.
orgánico, a [or'ɣaniko, a] *a* organic.
organigrama [orɣani'ɣrama] *nm* flow chart.
organismo [orɣa'nismo] *nm* (*BIO*) organism; (*POL*) organization.
organista [orɣa'nista] *nm/f* organist.
organización [orɣaniθa'θjon] *nf* organization; **organizar** *vt* to organize.
órgano ['orɣano] *nm* organ.
orgasmo [or'ɣasmo] *nm* orgasm.
orgía [or'xia] *nf* orgy.
orgullo [or'ɣuʎo] *nm* (*altanería*) pride; (*autorespeto*) self-respect; **orgulloso, a** *a* (*gen*) proud; (*altanero*) haughty.
orientación [orjenta'θjon] *nf* (*posición*) position; (*dirección*) direction.
orientar [orjen'tar] *vt* (*situar*) to orientate; (*señalar*) to point; (*dirigir*) to direct; (*guiar*) to guide; **~se** *vr* to get one's bearings; (*decidirse*) to decide on a course of action.
oriente [o'rjente] *nm* east; **Cercano/Medio/Lejano O~** Near/Middle/Far East.
origen [o'rixen] *nm* origin; (*nacimiento*) lineage, birth.
original [orixi'nal] *a* (*nuevo*) original; (*extraño*) odd, strange; **~idad** *nf* originality.
originar [orixi'nar] *vt* to start, cause; **~se** *vr* to originate; **~io, a** *a* (*nativo*) native; (*primordial*) original.
orilla [o'riʎa] *nf* (*borde*) border; (*de río*) bank; (*de bosque, tela*) edge; (*de mar*) shore.
orín [o'rin] *nm* rust.
orina [o'rina] *nf* urine; **orinal** *nm* (chamber) pot; **orinar** *vi* to urinate; **orinarse** *vr* to wet o.s.; **orines** *nmpl* urine *sg*.

oriundo, a [o'rjundo, a] *a*: **~ de** native of.
ornamento [orna'mento] *nm* ornament.
ornar [or'nar] *vt* to adorn.
ornitología [ornitolo'xia] *nf* ornithology, bird-watching.
oro ['oro] *nm* gold; **~s** *nmpl* (*NAIPES*) hearts.
oropel [oro'pel] *nm* tinsel.
orquesta [or'kesta] *nf* orchestra; **~ de cámara/sinfónica** chamber/symphony orchestra.
orquídea [or'kiðea] *nf* orchid.
ortiga [or'tiɣa] *nf* nettle.
ortodoxo, a [orto'ðokso, a] *a* orthodox.
ortografía [ortoɣra'fia] *nf* spelling.
ortopedia [orto'peðja] *nf* orthopaedics *sg*.
oruga [o'ruɣa] *nf* caterpillar.
orzuelo [or'θwelo] *nm* (*MED*) stye.
os [os] *pron* (*gen*) you; (*a vosotros*) to you.
osa ['osa] *nf* (she-)bear; **O~ Mayor/Menor** Great/Little Bear.
osadía [osa'ðia] *nf* daring.
osar [o'sar] *vi* to dare.
oscilación [osθila'θjon] *nf* (*movimiento*) oscillation; (*fluctuación*) fluctuation; (*vacilación*) hesitation; (*columpio*) swinging, movement to and fro.
oscilar [osθi'lar] *vi* to oscillate; to fluctuate; to hesitate.
oscurecer [oskure'θer] *vt* to darken // *vi* to grow dark; **~se** *vr* to grow o get dark.
oscuridad [oskuri'ðað] *nf* obscurity; (*tinieblas*) darkness.
oscuro, a [os'kuro, a] *a* dark; (*fig*) obscure; **a oscuras** in the dark.
óseo, a ['oseo, a] *a* bony.
oso ['oso] *nm* bear; **~ de peluche** teddy bear; **~ hormiguero** anteater.
ostensible [osten'siβle] *a* obvious.
ostentación [ostenta'θjon] *nf* (*gen*) ostentation; (*acto*) display.
ostentar [osten'tar] *vt* (*gen*) to show; (*pey*) to flaunt, show off; (*poseer*) to have, possess; **ostentoso, a** *a* ostentatious, showy.
ostra ['ostra] *nf* oyster.
OTAN ['otan] *nf abr* (= *Organización del Tratado del Atlántico Norte*) NATO.
otear [ote'ar] *vt* to observe; (*fig*) to look into.
otitis [o'titis] *nf* earache.
otoñal [oto'ɲal] *a* autumnal.
otoño [o'toɲo] *nm* autumn.
otorgamiento [otorɣa'mjento] *nm* conferring, granting; (*JUR*) execution.
otorgar [otor'ɣar] *vt* (*conceder*) to concede; (*dar*) to grant.
otorrino, a [oto'rrino, a], **otorrinolaringólogo, a** [otorrinolarin'ɣoloɣo, a] *nm/f* ear, nose and throat specialist.
otro, a ['otro, a] ♦ *a* **1** (*distinto: sg*)

another; (: *pl*) other; **con** ~s **amigos** with other *o* different friends
2 (*adicional*): **tráigame** ~ **café** (**más**), **por favor can** I have another coffee please; ~s **10 días más** another ten days
♦ *pron* **1: el** ~ the other one; (**los**) ~s (the) others; **de** ~ somebody else's; **que lo haga** ~ let somebody else do it
2 (*recíproco*): **se odian** (**la**) **una a** (**la**) **otra** they hate one another *o* each other
3: ~ **tanto: comer** ~ **tanto** to eat the same *o* as much again; **recibió una decena de telegramas y otras tantas llamadas** he got about ten telegrams and as many calls.
ovación [oβa'θjon] *nf* ovation.
oval [o'βal], **ovalado, a** [oβa'laðo, a] *a* oval; **óvalo** *nm* oval.
oveja [o'βexa] *nf* sheep.
overol [oβe'rol] *nm* (*AM*) overalls *pl*.
ovillo [o'βiʎo] *nm* (*de lana*) ball of wool; **hacerse un** ~ to curl up.
OVNI ['oβni] *nm abr* (= *objeto volante no identificado*) UFO.
ovulación [oβula'θjon] *nf* ovulation; **óvulo** *nm* ovum.
oxidación [oksiða'θjon] *nf* rusting.
oxidar [oksi'ðar] *vt* to rust; ~**se** *vr* to go rusty.
óxido ['oksiðo] *nm* oxide.
oxigenado, a [oksixe'naðo, a] *a* (*QUIMICA*) oxygenated; (*pelo*) bleached.
oxígeno [ok'sixeno] *nm* oxygen.
oyente [o'jente] *nm/f* listener, hearer.
oyes, oyó *etc vb ver* **oír**.

P

P *abr* (= *padre*) Fr.
pabellón [paβe'ʎon] *nm* bell tent; (*ARQ*) pavilion; (*de hospital etc*) block, section; (*bandera*) flag.
pábilo ['paβilo] *nm* wick.
pacer [pa'θer] *vi* to graze.
paciencia [pa'θjenθja] *nf* patience.
paciente [pa'θjente] *a*, *nm/f* patient.
pacificación [paθifika'θjon] *nf* pacification.
pacificar [paθifi'kar] *vt* to pacify; (*tranquilizar*) to calm.
pacífico, a [pa'θifiko, a] *a* (*persona*) peaceable; (*existencia*) peaceful; **el** (*océano*) **P**~ the Pacific (Ocean).
pacifismo [paθi'fismo] *nm* pacifism; **pacifista** *nm/f* pacifist.
pacotilla [pako'tiʎa] *nf*: **de** ~ (*actor, escritor*) third-rate; (*mueble etc*) cheap.
pactar [pak'tar] *vt* to agree to *o* on // *vi* to come to an agreement.
pacto ['pakto] *nm* (*tratado*) pact; (*acuerdo*) agreement.
padecer [paðe'θer] *vt* (*sufrir*) to suffer; (*soportar*) to endure, put up with; (*engaño, error*) to be a victim of;

padecimiento *nm* suffering.
padrastro [pa'ðrastro] *nm* stepfather.
padre ['paðre] *nm* father // *a* (*fam*): **un éxito** ~ a tremendous success; ~s *nmpl* parents.
padrino [pa'ðrino] *nm* (*REL*) godfather; (*tb*: ~ **de boda**) best man; (*fig*) sponsor, patron; ~s *nmpl* godparents.
padrón [pa'ðron] *nm* (*censo*) census, roll; (*de socios*) register.
paella [pa'eʎa] *nf* paella, dish of rice with meat, shellfish etc.
pág(s). *abr* (= *página(s)*) p(p).
paga ['paxa] *nf* (*pago*) payment; (*sueldo*) pay, wages *pl*.
pagadero, a [paxa'ðero, a] *a* payable; ~ **a plazos** payable in instalments.
pagano, a [pa'xano, a] *a*, *nm/f* pagan, heathen.
pagar [pa'xar] *vt* to pay; (*las compras, crimen*) to pay for; (*fig: favor*) to repay // *vi* to pay; ~ **al contado/a plazos** to pay (in) cash/in instalments.
pagaré [paxa're] *nm* I.O.U.
página ['paxina] *nf* page.
pago ['paxo] *nm* (*dinero*) payment; (*fig*) return; **estar** ~ to be even *o* quits; ~ **anticipado/a cuenta/contra reembolso/en especie** advance payment/payment on account/cash on delivery/payment in kind.
pague *etc vb ver* **pagar**.
país [pa'is] *nm* (*gen*) country; (*región*) land; **los P**~**es Bajos** the Low Countries; **el P**~ **Vasco** the Basque Country.
paisaje [pai'saxe] *nm* countryside, scenery.
paisano, a [pai'sano, a] *a* of the same country // *nm/f* (*compatriota*) fellow countryman/woman; **vestir de** ~ (*soldado*) to be in civvies; (*guardia*) to be in plain clothes.
paja ['paxa] *nf* straw; (*fig*) rubbish (*Brit*), trash (*US*).
pájara ['paxara] *nf* hen (bird).
pajarita [paxa'rita] *nf* (*corbata*) bow tie.
pájaro ['paxaro] *nm* bird; ~ **carpintero** woodpecker.
pajita [pa'xita] *nf* (drinking) straw.
pala ['pala] *nf* spade, shovel; (*raqueta etc*) bat; (: *de tenis*) racquet; (*CULIN*) slice; ~ **matamoscas** fly swat.
palabra [pa'laβra] *nf* word; (*facultad*) (power of) speech; (*derecho de hablar*) right to speak; **tomar la** ~ (*en mitin*) to take the floor.
palabrota [pala'brota] *nf* swearword.
palacio [pa'laθjo] *nm* palace; (*mansión*) mansion, large house; ~ **de justicia** courthouse; ~ **municipal** town/city hall.
paladar [pala'ðar] *nm* palate; **paladear** *vt* to taste.
palanca [pa'lanka] *nf* lever; (*fig*) pull, influence.
palangana [palan'gana] *nf* washbasin.

palco ['palko] *nm* box.
Palestina [pales'tina] *nf* Palestine;
palestino, a *nm/f* Palestinian.
paleta [pa'leta] *nf* (*de pintor*) palette;
(*de albañil*) trowel; (*de ping-pong*) bat;
(*AM*) ice lolly.
paliar [pa'ljar] *vt* (*mitigar*) to mitigate,
alleviate; **paliativo** *nm* palliative.
palidecer [paliðe'θer] *vi* to turn pale;
palidez *nf* paleness; **pálido, a** *a* pale.
palillo [pa'liʎo] *nm* small stick; (*mondadientes*) toothpick.
paliza [pa'liθa] *nf* beating, thrashing.
palma ['palma] *nf* (*ANAT*) palm; (*árbol*)
palm tree; **batir** *o* **dar** ~**s** to clap,
applaud; ~**da** *nf* slap; ~**s** *nfpl* clapping
sg, applause *sg*.
palmear [palme'ar] *vi* to clap.
palmo ['palmo] *nm* (*medida*) span; (*fig*)
small amount; ~ **a** ~ inch by inch.
palmotear [palmote'ar] *vi* to clap,
applaud; **palmoteo** *nm* clapping,
applause.
palo ['palo] *nm* stick; (*poste*) post, pole;
(*mango*) handle, shaft; (*golpe*) blow,
hit; (*de golf*) club; (*de béisbol*) bat;
(*NAUT*) mast; (*NAIPES*) suit.
paloma [pa'loma] *nf* dove, pigeon.
palomilla [palo'miʎa] *nf* moth; (*TEC:
tuerca*) wing nut; (: *hierro*) angle iron.
palomitas [palo'mitas] *nfpl* popcorn *sg*.
palpar [pal'par] *vt* to touch, feel.
palpitación [palpita'θjon] *nf* palpitation.
palpitante [palpi'tante] *a* palpitating;
(*fig*) burning.
palpitar [palpi'tar] *vi* to palpitate; (*latir*)
to beat.
palta ['palta] *nf* (*AM*) avocado (pear).
palúdico, a [pa'luðiko, a] *a* marshy.
paludismo [palu'ðismo] *nm* malaria.
pampa ['pampa] *nf* (*AM*) pampa(s),
prairie.
pan [pan] *nm* bread; (*una barra*) loaf; ~
integral wholemeal (*Brit*) *o* wholewheat
(*US*) bread; ~ **rallado** breadcrumbs *pl*.
pana ['pana] *nf* corduroy.
panadería [panaðe'ria] *nf* baker's
(shop); **panadero, a** *nm/f* baker.
Panamá [pana'ma] *nm* Panama;
panameño, a *a* Panamanian.
pancarta [pan'karta] *nf* placard, banner.
panda ['panda] *nm* (*ZOOL*) panda.
pandereta [pande'reta] *nf* tambourine.
pandilla [pan'diʎa] *nf* set, group; (*de
criminales*) gang; (*pey: camarilla*)
clique.
panecillo [pane'θiʎo] *nm* (bread) roll.
panel [pa'nel] *nm* panel.
panfleto [pan'fleto] *nm* pamphlet.
pánico ['paniko] *nm* panic.
panorama [pano'rama] *nm* panorama;
(*vista*) view.
pantalón [panta'lon] *nm*, **pantalones**
[panta'lones] *nmpl* trousers.
pantalla [pan'taʎa] *nf* (*de cine*) screen;

(*de lámpara*) lampshade.
pantano [pan'tano] *nm* (*ciénaga*) marsh,
swamp; (*depósito: de agua*) reservoir;
(*fig*) jam, difficulty.
panteón [pante'on] *nm:* ~ **familiar**
family tomb.
pantera [pan'tera] *nf* panther.
pantomima [panto'mima] *nf* pantomime.
pantorrilla [panto'rriʎa] *nf* calf (of the
leg).
pantufla [pan'tufla] *nf* slipper.
panza ['panθa] *nf* belly, paunch;
panzón, ona, panzudo, a *a* fat,
potbellied.
pañal [pa'ɲal] *nm* nappy (*Brit*), diaper
(*US*); ~**es** *nmpl* (*fig*) early stages, infancy *sg*.
pañería [paɲe'ria] *nf* drapery.
paño ['paɲo] *nm* (*tela*) cloth; (*pedazo de
tela*) (piece of) cloth; (*trapo*) duster,
rag; ~ **higiénico** sanitary towel; ~**s**
menores underclothes.
pañuelo [pa'ɲwelo] *nm* handkerchief,
hanky (*fam*); (*para la cabeza*)
(head)scarf.
papa ['papa] *nf* (*AM*) potato // *nm:* **el P~**
the Pope.
papá [pa'pa] (*pl* ~**s**) *nm* (*fam*) dad(dy),
pa (*US*).
papagayo [papa'ɣajo] *nm* parrot.
papanatas [papa'natas] *nm inv* (*fam*)
simpleton.
paparrucha [papa'rrutʃa] *nf* piece of nonsense.
papaya [pa'paja] *nf* papaya.
papel [pa'pel] *nm* paper; (*hoja de* ~)
sheet of paper; (*TEATRO, fig*) role; ~ **de
calco/carbón/de cartas** tracing paper/
carbon paper/stationery; ~ **de envolver/
pintado** wrapping paper/wallpaper; ~ **de
aluminio/higiénico** aluminium (*Brit*) *o*
aluminum (*US*) foil/toilet paper; ~ **de
lija** sandpaper; ~ **moneda** paper money;
~ **secante** blotting paper.
papeleo [pape'leo] *nm* red tape.
papelera [pape'lera] *nf* wastepaper
basket; (*escritorio*) desk.
papelería [papele'ria] *nf* stationer's
(shop).
papeleta [pape'leta] *nf* (*pedazo de papel*)
slip of paper; (*POL*) ballot paper;
(*ESCOL*) report.
paperas [pa'peras] *nfpl* mumps.
papilla [pa'piʎa] *nf* (*para niños*) baby
food.
paquete [pa'kete] *nm* (*de cigarrillos etc*)
packet; (*CORREOS etc*) parcel; (*AM*)
package tour; (: *fam*) nuisance, bore.
par [par] *a* (*igual*) like, equal; (*MAT*)
even // *nm* equal; (*de guantes*) pair; (*de
veces*) couple; (*POL*) peer; (*GOLF, COM*)
par; **abrir de** ~ **en** ~ to open wide.
para ['para] *prep* for; **no es** ~ **comer** it's
not for eating; **decir** ~ **sí** to say to o.s.;
¿~ **qué lo quieres?** what do you want it

for?; **se casaron ~ separarse** otra vez they married only to separate again; **lo tendré ~ mañana** I'll have it (for) tomorrow; **ir ~ casa** to go home, head for home; **~ profesor es muy estúpido** he's very stupid for a teacher; **¿quién es usted ~ gritar así?** who are you to shout like that?; **tengo bastante ~ vivir** I have enough to live on.

parabién |para'βjen| nm congratulations pl.

parábola |pa'raβola| nf parable; (MAT) parabola.

parabrisas |para'βrisas| nm inv windscreen (Brit), windshield (US).

paracaídas |paraka'iðas| nm inv parachute; **paracaidista** nm/f parachutist; (MIL) paratrooper.

parachoques |para'tʃokes| nm inv (AUTO) bumper; (MECÁNICA etc) shock absorber.

parada |pa'raða| nf stop; (acto) stopping; (de industria) shutdown, stoppage; (lugar) stopping place; **~ de autobús** bus stop.

paradero |para'ðero| nm stopping-place; (situación) whereabouts.

parado, a |pa'raðo, a| a (persona) motionless, standing still; (fábrica) closed, at a standstill; (coche) stopped; (AM) standing (up); (sin empleo) unemployed, idle.

paradoja |para'ðoxa| nf paradox.

parador |para'ðor| nm parador, state-owned hotel.

paráfrasis |pa'rafrasis| nf inv paraphrase.

paraguas |pa'raɣwas| nm inv umbrella.

Paraguay |para'ɣwai| nm: **el ~** Paraguay; **paraguayo, a** a, nm/f Paraguayan.

paraíso |para'iso| nm paradise, heaven.

paraje |pa'raxe| nm place, spot.

paralelo, a |para'lelo, a| a parallel.

parálisis |pa'ralisis| nf inv paralysis; **paralítico, a** a, nm/f paralytic.

paralizar |parali'θar| vt to paralyse; **~se** vr to become paralysed; (fig) to come to a standstill.

paramilitar |paramili'tar| a paramilitary.

páramo |'paramo| nm bleak plateau.

parangón |paran'gon| nm: **sin ~** incomparable.

paranoico, a |para'noiko, a| nm/f paranoiac.

parapléjico, a |para'plexiko, a| a, nm/f paraplegic.

parar |pa'rar| vt to stop; (golpe) to ward off // vi to stop; **~se** vr to stop; (AM) to stand up; **ha parado de llover** it has stopped raining; **van a ~ en la comisaría** they're going to end up in the police station; **~se en** to pay attention to.

parásito, a |pa'rasito, a| nm/f parasite.

parasol |para'sol| nm parasol, sunshade.

parcela |par'θela| nf plot, piece of ground.

parcial |par'θjal| a (pago) part-; (eclipse) partial; (JUR) prejudiced, biased; (POL) partisan; **~idad** nf (prejuicio) prejudice, bias.

parco, a |'parko, a| a (moderado) moderate.

parche |'partʃe| nm (gen) patch.

parear |pare'ar| vt (juntar, hacer par) to match, put together; (BIO) to mate, pair.

parecer |pare'θer| nm (opinión) opinion, view; (aspecto) looks pl // vi (tener apariencia) to seem, look, (asemejarse) to look o seem like; (aparecer, llegar) to appear; **~se** vr to look alike, resemble each other; **~se a** to look like, resemble; **según** o **a lo que parece** evidently, apparently; **me parece que** I think (that), it seems to me that.

parecido, a |pare'θiðo, a| a similar // similarity, likeness, resemblance; **bien ~** good-looking, nice-looking.

pared |pa'reð| nf wall.

parejo, a |pa'rexo, a| a (igual) equal; (liso) smooth, even // nf (par) pair; (dos personas) couple; (otro: de un par) other one (of a pair); (persona) partner.

parentela |paren'tela| nf relations pl.

parentesco |paren'tesko| nm relationship.

paréntesis |pa'rentesis| nm inv parenthesis; (digresión) digression; (en escrito) bracket.

parezco etc vb ver **parecer**.

pariente |pa'rjente, a| nm/f relative, relation.

parir |pa'rir| vt to give birth to // vi (mujer) to give birth, have a baby.

París |pa'ris| n Paris.

parking |'parkin| nm car park (Brit), parking lot (US).

parlamentar |parlamen'tar| vi (negociar) to parley.

parlamentario, a |parlamen'tarjo, a| a parliamentary // nm/f member of parliament.

parlamento |parla'mento| nm (POL) parliament.

parlanchín, ina |parlan'tʃin, ina| a indiscreet // nm/f chatterbox.

paro |'paro| nm (huelga) stoppage (of work), strike; (desempleo) unemployment; **subsidio de ~** unemployment benefit; **hay ~ en la industria** work in the industry is at a standstill.

parodia |pa'roðja| nf parody; **parodiar** vt to parody.

parpadear |parpaðe'ar| vi (ojos) to blink; (luz) to flicker.

párpado |'parpaðo| nm eyelid.

parque |'parke| nm (lugar verde) park; **~ de atracciones/infantil/zoológico** fairground/playground/zoo.

parquímetro |par'kimetro| nm parking

meter.

parra ['parra] *nf* (grape)vine.

párrafo ['parrafo] *nm* paragraph; **echar un ~** (*fam*) to have a chat.

parranda [pa'rranda] *nf* (*fam*) spree, binge.

parrilla [pa'rriʎa] *nf* (*CULIN*) grill; (*de coche*) grille; (**carne a la**) ~ barbecue; **~da** *nf* barbecue.

párroco ['parroko] *nm* parish priest.

parroquia [pa'rrokja] *nf* parish; (*iglesia*) parish church; (*COM*) clientele, customers *pl*; **~no, a** *nm/f* parishioner; client, customer.

parte ['parte] *nm* message; (*informe*) report // *nf* part; (*lado, cara*) side; (*de reparto*) share; (*JUR*) party; **en alguna ~ de Europa** somewhere in Europe; **en/por todas ~s** everywhere; **en gran ~** to a large extent; **la mayor ~ de los españoles** most Spaniards; **de un tiempo a esta ~** for some time past; **de ~ de alguien** on sb's behalf; **¿de ~ de quién?** (*TEL*) who is speaking?; **por ~ de** on the part of; **yo pór mi ~** I for my part; **por otra ~** on the other hand; **dar ~** to inform; **tomar ~** to take part.

partera [par'tera] *nf* midwife.

partición [parti'θjon] *nf* division, sharing-out; (*POL*) partition.

participación [partiθipa'θjon] *nf* (*acto*) participation, taking part; (*parte, COM*) share; (*de lotería*) shared prize; (*aviso*) notice, notification.

participante [partiθi'pante] *nm/f* participant.

participar [partiθi'par] *vt* to notify, inform // *vi* to take part, participate.

partícipe [par'tiθipe] *nm/f* participant.

particular [partiku'lar] *a* (*especial*) particular, special; (*individual, personal*) private, personal // *nm* (*punto, asunto*) particular, point; (*individuo*) individual; **tiene coche ~** he has a car of his own; **~izar** *vt* to distinguish; (*especificar*) to specify; (*detallar*) to give details about.

partida [par'tiða] *nf* (*salida*) departure; (*COM*) entry, item; (*juego*) game; (*grupo de personas*) band, group; **mala ~** dirty trick; **~ de nacimiento/matrimonio/defunción** birth/marriage/death certificate.

partidario, a [parti'ðarjo, a] *a* partisan // *nm/f* supporter, follower.

partido [par'tiðo] *nm* (*POL*) party; (*DEPORTE: encuentro*) game, match; (: *equipo*) team; (*apoyo*) support; **sacar ~ de** to profit o benefit from; **tomar ~** to take sides.

partir [par'tir] *vt* (*dividir*) to split, divide; (*compartir, distribuir*) to share (out), distribute; (*romper*) to break open, split open; (*rebanada*) to cut (off) // *vi* (*ponerse en camino*) to set off o out;

(*comenzar*) to start (off o out); **~se** *vr* to crack o split o break (in two *etc*); **a ~ de** (starting) from.

parto ['parto] *nm* birth; (*fig*) product, creation; **estar de ~** to be in labour.

parvulario [parβu'larjo] *nm* nursery school, kindergarten.

pasa ['pasa] *nf* raisin; **~ de Corinto/de Esmirna** currant/sultana.

pasada [pa'saða] *af*, *nf ver* **pasado**.

pasadizo [pasa'ðiθo] *nm* (*pasillo*) passage, corridor; (*callejuela*) alley.

pasado, a [pa'saðo, a] *a* past; (*malo: comida, fruta*) bad; (*muy cocido*) overdone; (*anticuado*) out of date // *nm* past // *nf* passing, passage; **~ mañana** the day after tomorrow; **el mes ~** last month; **de pasada** in passing, incidentally; **una mala pasada** a dirty trick.

pasador [pasa'ðor] *nm* (*gen*) bolt; (*de pelo*) hair slide; (*horquilla*) grip.

pasaje [pa'saxe] *nm* passage; (*pago de viaje*) fare; (*los pasajeros*) passengers *pl*; (*pasillo*) passageway.

pasajero, a [pasa'xero, a] *a* passing // *nm/f* passenger.

pasamanos [pasa'manos] *nm inv* (hand)rail; (*de escalera*) banisters *pl*.

pasamontañas [pasamon'taɲas] *nm inv* balaclava helmet.

pasaporte [pasa'porte] *nm* passport.

pasar [pa'sar] *vt* to pass; (*tiempo*) to spend; (*desgracias*) to suffer, endure; (*noticia*) to give, pass on; (*río*) to cross; (*barrera*) to pass through; (*falta*) to overlook, tolerate; (*contrincante*) to surpass, do better than; (*coche*) to overtake; (*CINE*) to show; (*enfermedad*) to give, infect with // *vi* (*gen*) to pass; (*terminarse*) to be over; (*ocurrir*) to happen; **~se** *vr* (*flores*) to fade; (*comida*) to go bad o off; (*fig*) to overdo it, go too far; **~ de** to go beyond, exceed; **~ por** (*AM*) to fetch; **~lo bien/mal** to have a good/bad time; **¡pase!** come in!; **~se al enemigo** to go over to the enemy; **se me pasó** I forgot; **no se le pasa nada** he misses nothing; **pase lo que pase** come what may.

pasarela [pasa'rela] *nf* footbridge; (*en barco*) gangway.

pasatiempo [pasa'tjempo] *nm* pastime, hobby.

Pascua ['paskwa] *nf*: **~ (de Resurrección)** Easter; **~ de Navidad** Christmas; **~s** *nfpl* Christmas (time); **¡felices ~s!** Merry Christmas!

pase ['pase] *nm* pass; (*CINE*) performance, showing.

pasear [pase'ar] *vt* to take for a walk; (*exhibir*) to parade, show off // *vi*, **~se** *vr* to walk, go for a walk; **~ en coche** to go for a drive; **paseo** *nm* (*avenida*) avenue; (*distancia corta*) walk, stroll; **dar un o ir de paseo** to go for a walk.

pasillo |pa'siʎo| *nm* passage, corridor.

pasión |pa'sjon| *nf* passion.

pasivo, a |pu'sißo, a| *a* passive, (*inactivo*) inactive // *nm* (*COM*) liabilities *pl*, debts *pl*; (*LING*) passive.

pasmar |pas'mar| *vt* (*asombrar*) to amaze, astonish; **pasmo** *nm* amazement, astonishment; (*resfriado*) chill; (*fig*) wonder, marvel; **pasmoso, a** *a* amazing, astonishing.

paso, a |'paso, a| *a* dried // *nm* step; (*modo de andar*) walk; (*huella*) footprint; (*rapidez*) speed, pace, rate; (*camino accesible*) way through, passage; (*cruce*) crossing; (*pasaje*) passing, passage; (*GEO*) pass; (*estrecho*) strait; ~ **de peatones** pedestrian crossing; **a ese** ~ (*fig*) at that rate; **salir al** ~ **de** *o* **a** to waylay; **estar de** ~ to be passing through; ~ **elevado** flyover; **prohibido el** ~ no entry; **ceda el** ~ give way.

pasota |pa'sota| *a, nm/f* (*fam*) ≈ dropout; **ser un** (**tipo**) ~ to be a bit of a dropout; (*ser indiferente*) not to care about anything.

pasta |'pasta| *nf* paste; (*CULIN: masa*) dough; (: *de bizcochos etc*) pastry; (*fam*) dough; ~**s** *nfpl* (*bizcochos*) pastries, small cakes; (*fideos, espaguetis etc*) pasta; ~ **de dientes** *o* **dentífrica** toothpaste.

pastar |pas'tar| *vt, vi* to graze.

pastel |pas'tel| *nm* (*dulce*) cake; ~ **de carne** meat pie; (*ARTE*) pastel; ~**ería** *nf* cake shop.

pasteurizado, a |pasteuri'θaðo, a| *a* pasteurized.

pastilla |pas'tiʎa| *nf* (*de jabón, chocolate*) bar; (*píldora*) tablet, pill.

pasto |'pasto| *nm* (*hierba*) grass; (*lugar*) pasture, field.

pastor, a |pas'tor, a| *nm/f* shepherd/ess // *nm* (*REL*) clergyman, pastor.

pata |'pata| *nf* (*pierna*) leg; (*pie*) foot; (*de muebles*) leg; ~**s arriba** upside down; **meter la** ~ to put one's foot in it; (*TEC*): ~ **de cabra** crowbar; **tener buena/mala** ~ to be lucky/unlucky; ~**da** *nf* kick; (*en el suelo*) stamp.

patalear |patale'ar| *vi* (*en el suelo*) to stamp one's feet.

patata |pa'tata| *nf* potato; ~**s fritas** *o* **a la española** chips, French fries; ~**s fritas** (*de bolsa*) crisps.

paté |pa'te| *nm* pâté.

patear |pate'ar| *vt* (*pisar*) to stamp on, trample (on); (*pegar con el pie*) to kick // *vi* to stamp (with rage), stamp one's feet.

patente |pa'tente| *a* obvious, evident; (*COM*) patent // *nf* patent.

paternal |pater'nal| *a* fatherly, paternal; **paterno, a** *a* paternal.

patético, a |pa'tetiko, a| *a* pathetic,

moving.

patillas |pa'tiʎas| *nfpl* sideburns.

patín |pa'tin| *nm* skate; (*de trineo*) runner; **patinaje** *nm* skating; **patinar** *vi* to skate; (*resbalarse*) to skid, slip; (*fam*) to slip up, blunder.

patio |'patjo| *nm* (*de casa*) patio, courtyard; ~ **de recreo** playground.

pato |'pato| *nm* duck; **pagar el** ~ (*fam*) to take the blame, carry the can.

patológico, a |pato'loxiko, a| *a* pathological.

patoso, a |pa'toso, a| *a* (*fam*) clumsy.

patraña |pa'traɲa| *nf* story, fib.

patria |'patrja| *nf* native land, mother country.

patrimonio |patri'monjo| *nm* inheritance; (*fig*) heritage.

patriota |pa'trjota| *nm/f* patriot; **patriotismo** *nm* patriotism.

patrocinar |patroθi'nar| *vt* to sponsor; (*apoyar*) to back, support; **patrocinio** *nm* sponsorship; backing, support.

patrón, ona |pa'tron, ona| *nm/f* (*jefe*) boss, chief, master/mistress; (*propietario*) landlord/lady; (*REL*) patron saint // *nm* (*TEC, COSTURA*) pattern.

patronal |patro'nal| *a*: **la clase** ~ management.

patronato |patro'nato| *nm* sponsorship; (*acto*) patronage; (*fundación benéfica*) trust, foundation.

patrulla |pa'truʎa| *nf* patrol.

pausa |'pausa| *nf* pause, break.

pausado, a |pau'saðo, a| *a* slow, deliberate.

pauta |'pauta| *nf* line, guide line.

pavimento |paßi'mento| *nm* (*con losas*) pavement, paving.

pavo |'paßo| *nm* turkey; ~ **real** peacock.

pavor |pa'ßor| *nm* dread, terror.

payaso, a |pa'jaso, a| *nm/f* clown.

payo, a |'pajo| *nm/f* (*para gitanos*) nongipsy.

paz |paθ| *nf* peace; (*tranquilidad*) peacefulness, tranquillity; **hacer las paces** to make peace; (*fig*) to make up; **La P**~ *n* (*GEO*) La Paz.

PC *abr* = *Partido Comunista*.

P.D. *abr* (= *posdata*) PS, ps.

peaje |pe'axe| *nm* toll.

peatón |pea'ton| *nm* pedestrian.

peca |'peka| *nf* freckle.

pecado |pe'kaðo| *nm* sin; **pecador, a** *a* sinful // *nm/f* sinner.

pecaminoso, a |pekami'noso, a| *a* sinful.

pecar |pe'kar| *vi* (*REL*) to sin; (*fig*): **peca de generoso** he is generous to a fault.

peculiar |peku'ljar| *a* special, peculiar; (*característico*) typical, characteristic; ~**idad** *nf* peculiarity; special feature, characteristic.

pecho |'petʃo| *nm* (*ANAT*) chest; (*de mujer*) breast(s) (*pl*), bosom; (*fig*: *co-*

razón) heart, breast; (: *valor*) courage, spirit; **dar el ~ a** to breast-feed; **tomar algo a ~** to take sth to heart.

pechuga [pe'tʃuɣa] *nf* breast.

pedal [pe'ðal] *nm* pedal; **~ear** *vi* to pedal.

pédalo ['peðalo] *nm* pedal boat.

pedante [pe'ðante] *a* pedantic // *nm/f* pedant; **~ría** *nf* pedantry.

pedazo [pe'ðaθo] *nm* piece, bit; **hacerse ~s** (*romperse*) to smash, shatter.

pedernal [peðer'nal] *nm* flint.

pediatra [pe'ðjatra] *nm/f* paediatrician.

pedicuro, a [peði'kuro, a] *nm/f* chiropodist.

pedido [pe'ðiðo] *nm* (*COM*: *mandado*) order; (*petición*) request.

pedir [pe'ðir] *vt* to ask for, request; (*comida*, *COM*: *mandar*) to order; (*exigir*: *precio*) to ask; (*necesitar*) to need, demand, require // *vi* to ask; **me pidió que cerrara la puerta** he asked me to shut the door; **¿cuánto piden por el coche?** how much are they asking for the car?

pegadizo, a [peɣa'ðiθo, a] *a* (*MUS*) catchy.

pegajoso, a [peɣa'xoso, a] *a* sticky, adhesive.

pegamento [peɣa'mento] *nm* gum, glue.

pegar [pe'ɣar] *vt* (*papel*, *sellos*) to stick (on); (*cartel*) to stick up; (*coser*) to sew (on); (*unir*: *partes*) to join, fix together; (*MED*) to give, infect with; (*dar*: *golpe*) to give, deal // *vi* (*adherirse*) to stick, adhere; (*ir juntos*: *colores*) to match, go together; (*golpear*) to hit; (*quemar*: *el sol*) to strike hot, burn (*fig*); **~se** *vr* (*gen*) to stick; (*dos personas*) to hit each other, fight; (*fam*): **~ un grito** to let out a yell; **~ un salto** to jump (with fright); **~ en** to touch; **~se un tiro** to shoot o.s.

pegatina [peɣa'tina] *nf* sticker.

peinado [pei'naðo] *nm* (*en peluquería*) hairdo; (*estilo*) hair style.

peinar [pei'nar] *vt* to comb; (*hacer estilo*) to style; **~se** *vr* to comb one's hair.

peine ['peine] *nm* comb; **~ta** *nf* ornamental comb.

p.ej. *abr* (= *por ejemplo*) eg.

Pekín [pe'kin] *n* Pekin(g).

pelado, a [pe'laðo, a] *a* (*fruta, patata etc*) peeled; (*cabeza*) shorn; (*campo, fig*) bare; (*fam*: *sin dinero*) broke.

pelaje [pe'laxe] *nm* (*ZOOL*) fur, coat; (*fig*) appearance.

pelambre [pe'lambre] *nm* (*pelo largo*) long hair, mop.

pelar [pe'lar] *vt* (*fruta, patatas etc*) to peel; (*cortar el pelo a*) to cut the hair of; (*quitar la piel: animal*) to skin; **~se** *vr* (*la piel*) to peel off; **voy a ~me** I'm going to get my hair cut.

peldaño [pel'daɲo] *nm* step.

pelea [pe'lea] *nf* (*lucha*) fight; (*discusión*) quarrel, row.

peleado, a [pele'aðo, a] *a*: **estar ~ (con uno)** to have fallen out (with sb).

pelear [pele'ar] *vi* to fight; **~se** *vr* to fight; (*reñirse*) to fall out, quarrel.

peletería [pelete'ria] *nf* furrier's, fur shop.

pelícano [pe'likano] *nm* pelican.

película [pe'likula] *nf* film; (*cobertura ligera*) thin covering; (*FOTO*: *rollo*) roll *o* reel of film.

peligro [pe'liɣro] *nm* danger; (*riesgo*) risk; **correr ~ de** to run the risk of; **~so, a** *a* dangerous; risky.

pelirrojo, a [peli'rroxo, a] *a* red-haired, red-headed // *nm/f* redhead.

pelma ['pelma] *nm/f*, **pelmazo** [pel'maθo] *nm* (*fam*) pain (in the neck).

pelo ['pelo] *nm* (*cabellos*) hair; (*de barba, bigote*) whisker; (*de animal: pellejo*) hair, fur, coat; **al ~** just right; **venir al ~** to be exactly what one needs; **un hombre de ~ en pecho** a brave man; **por los ~s** by the skin of one's teeth; **no tener ~s en la lengua** to be outspoken, not mince words; **tomar el ~ a uno** to pull sb's leg.

pelón, ona [pe'lon, ona] *a* hairless, bald.

pelota [pe'lota] *nf* ball; (*fam*: *cabeza*) nut; **en ~** stark naked; **hacer la ~** (*a uno*) (*fam*) to creep (to sb); **~ vasca** pelota.

pelotari [pelo'tari] *nm* pelota player.

pelotón [pelo'ton] *nm* (*MIL*) squad, detachment.

peluca [pe'luka] *nf* wig.

peluche [pe'lutʃe] *nm*: **oso/muñeco de ~** teddy bear/soft toy.

peludo, a [pe'luðo, a] *a* hairy, shaggy.

peluquería [peluke'ria] *nf* hairdresser's; (*para hombres*) barber's (shop); **peluquero, a** *nm/f* hairdresser; barber.

pelusa [pe'lusa] *nf* (*BOT*) down; (*COSTURA*) fluff.

pellejo [pe'ʎexo] *nm* (*de animal*) skin, hide.

pellizcar [peʎiθ'kar] *vt* to pinch, nip.

pena ['pena] *nf* (*congoja*) grief, sadness; (*remordimiento*) regret; (*dificultad*) trouble; (*dolor*) pain; (*JUR*) sentence; **merecer** *o* **valer la ~** to be worthwhile; **a duras ~s** with great difficulty; **~ de muerte** death penalty; **~ pecuniaria** fine; **¡qué ~!** what a shame!

penal [pe'nal] *a* penal // *nm* (*cárcel*) prison.

penalidad [penali'ðað] *nf* (*problema, dificultad*) trouble, hardship; (*JUR*) penalty, punishment.

penalti, penalty [pe'nalti] (*pl* **penaltis, penálty(e)s, penalties**) *nm* penalty (kick).

penar [pe'nar] *vt* to penalize; (*castigar*) to punish // *vi* to suffer.

pendiente |pen'djente| *a* pending, unsettled // *nm* earring // *nf* hill, slope.

pene |'pene| *nm* penis.

penetración |penetra'θjon| *nf* (*acto*) penetration; (*agudeza*) sharpness, insight.

penetrante |pene'trante| *a* (*herida*) deep; (*persona, arma*) sharp; (*sonido*) penetrating, piercing; (*mirada*) searching; (*viento, ironía*) biting.

penetrar |pene'trar| *vt* to penetrate, pierce; (*entender*) to grasp // *vi* to penetrate, go in; (*entrar*) to enter, go in; (*líquido*) to soak in; (*fig*) to pierce.

penicilina |peniθi'lina| *nf* penicillin.

península |pe'ninsula| *nf* peninsula; **peninsular** *a* peninsular.

penique |pe'nike| *nm* penny.

penitencia |peni'tenθja| *nf* (*remordimiento*) penitence; (*castigo*) penance; **~ría** *nf* prison, penitentiary.

penoso, a |pe'noso, a| *a* (*difícil*) arduous, difficult.

pensador, a |pensa'ðor, a| *nm/f* thinker.

pensamiento |pensa'mjento| *nm* thought; (*mente*) mind; (*idea*) idea.

pensar |pen'sar| *vt* to think; (*considerar*) to think over, think out; (*proponerse*) to intend, plan; (*imaginarse*) to think up, invent // *vi* to think; **~ en** to aim at, aspire to; **pensativo, a** *a* thoughtful, pensive.

pensión |pen'sjon| *nf* (*casa*) boarding *o* guest house; (*dinero*) pension; (*cama y comida*) board and lodging; **~ completa** full board; **pensionista** *nm/f* (*jubilado*) (old-age) pensioner; (*huésped*) lodger.

penúltimo, a |pe'nultimo, a| *a* penultimate, last but one.

penumbra |pe'numbra| *nf* half-light.

penuria |pe'nurja| *nf* shortage, want.

peña |'pena| *nf* (*roca*) rock; (*cuesta*) cliff, crag; (*grupo*) group, circle; (*AM: club*) folk club.

peñasco |pe'nasko| *nm* large rock, boulder.

peñón |pe'non| *nm* wall of rock; **el P~** the Rock (of Gibraltar).

peón |pe'on| *nm* labourer; (*AM*) farm labourer, farmhand; (*AJEDREZ*) pawn.

peonza |pe'onθa| *nf* spinning top.

peor |pe'or| *a* (*comparativo*) worse; (*superlativo*) worst // *ad* worse; worst; **de mal en ~** from bad to worse.

pepinillo |pepi'niʎo| *nm* gherkin.

pepino |pe'pino| *nm* cucumber; **(no) me importa un ~** I don't care one bit.

pepita |pe'pita| *nf* (*BOT*) pip; (*MINERÍA*) nugget.

pequeñez |peke'neθ| *nf* smallness, littleness; (*trivialidad*) trifle, triviality.

pequeño, a |pe'keno, a| *a* small, little.

pera |'pera| *nf* pear; **peral** *nm* pear tree.

percance |per'kanθe| *nm* setback, misfortune.

percatarse |perka'tarse| *vr*: **~ de** to notice, take note of.

percepción |perθep'θjon| *nf* (*vista*) perception; (*idea*) notion, idea.

perceptible |perθep'tiβle| *a* perceptible, noticeable; (*COM*) payable, receivable.

percibir |perθi'βir| *vt* to perceive, notice; (*COM*) to earn, get.

percusión |perku'sjon| *nf* percussion.

percha |'pertʃa| *nf* (*ganchos*) coat hooks *pl*; (*colgador*) coat hanger; (*de ave*) perch.

perdedor, a |perðe'ðor, a| *a* losing // *nm/f* loser.

perder |per'ðer| *vt* to lose; (*tiempo, palabras*) to waste; (*oportunidad*) to lose, miss; (*tren*) to miss // *vi* to lose; **~se** *vr* (*extraviarse*) to get lost; (*desaparecer*) to disappear, be lost to view; (*arruinarse*) to be ruined; **echar a ~** (*comida*) to spoil, ruin; (*oportunidad*) to waste.

perdición |perði'θjon| *nf* perdition, ruin.

pérdida |'perðiða| *nf* loss; (*de tiempo*) waste; **~s** *nfpl* (*COM*) losses.

perdido, a |per'ðiðo, a| *a* lost.

perdiz |per'ðiθ| *nf* partridge.

perdón |per'ðon| *nm* (*disculpa*) pardon, forgiveness; (*clemencia*) mercy; **¡~!** sorry!, I beg your pardon!; **perdonar** *vt* to pardon, forgive; (*la vida*) to spare; (*excusar*) to exempt, excuse; **¡perdone (usted)!** sorry!, I beg your pardon!

perdurable |perðu'raβle| *a* lasting; (*eterno*) everlasting.

perdurar |perðu'rar| *vi* (*resistir*) to last, endure; (*seguir existiendo*) to stand, still exist.

perecedero, a |pereθe'ðero, a| *a* (*COM etc*) perishable.

perecer |pere'θer| *vi* (*morir*) to perish, die; (*objeto*) to shatter.

peregrinación |pereɣrina'θjon| *nf* (*REL*) pilgrimage.

peregrino, a |pere'ɣrino, a| *a* (*idea*) strange, absurd // *nm/f* pilgrim.

perejil |pere'xil| *nm* parsley.

perenne |pe'renne| *a* everlasting, perennial.

perentorio, a |peren'torjo, a| *a* (*urgente*) urgent, peremptory; (*fijo*) set, fixed.

pereza |pe'reθa| *nf* laziness, idleness; **perezoso, a** *a* lazy, idle.

perfección |perfek'θjon| *nf* perfection; **perfeccionar** *vt* to perfect; (*mejorar*) to improve; (*acabar*) to complete, finish.

perfectamente |perfekta'mente| *ad* perfectly.

perfecto, a |per'fekto, a| *a* perfect; (*terminado*) complete, finished.

perfidia |per'fiðja| *nf* perfidy, treachery.

perfil |per'fil| *nm* profile; (*contorno*) silhouette, outline; (*ARQ*) (cross) section; **~es** *nmpl* features; (*fig*) social graces; **~ado, a** a (*bien formado*) well-shaped; (*largo: cara*) long; **~ar** vt (*trazar*) to outline; (*fig*) to shape, give character to.

perforación [perfora'θjon] nf perforation; (*con taladro*) drilling; **perforadora** nf punch.

perforar [perfo'rar] vt to perforate; (*agujero*) to drill, bore; (*papel*) to punch a hole in // vi to drill, bore.

perfume [per'fume] nm perfume, scent.

pericia [pe'riθja] nf skill, expertise.

periferia [peri'ferja] nf periphery; (*de ciudad*) outskirts pl.

periférico [peri'feriko] nm (*AM*) ring road (*Brit*), beltway (*US*).

perímetro [pe'rimetro] nm perimeter.

periódico, a [pe'rjoðiko, a] a periodic(al) // nm newspaper.

periodismo [perjo'ðismo] nm journalism; **periodista** nm/f journalist.

periodo [pe'rjoðo], **período** [pe'rioðo] nm period.

periquito [peri'kito] nm budgerigar, budgie.

perito, a [pe'rito, a] a (*experto*) expert; (*diestro*) skilled, skilful // nm/f expert; skilled worker; (*técnico*) technician.

perjudicar [perxuði'kar] vt (*gen*) to damage, harm; **perjudicial** a damaging, harmful; (*en detrimento*) detrimental; **perjuicio** nm damage, harm.

perjurar [perxu'rar] vi to commit perjury.

perla ['perla] nf pearl; **me viene de ~** it suits me fine.

permanecer [permane'θer] vi (*quedarse*) to stay, remain; (*seguir*) to continue to be.

permanencia [perma'nenθja] nf permanence; (*estancia*) stay.

permanente [perma'nente] a permanent, constant // nf perm.

permisible [permi'sißle] a permissible, allowable.

permiso [per'miso] nm permission; (*licencia*) permit, licence; **con ~** excuse me; **estar de ~** (*MIL*) to be on leave; **~ de conducir** driving licence (*Brit*), driver's license (*US*).

permitir [permi'tir] vt to permit, allow.

pernera [per'nera] nf trouser leg.

pernicioso, a [perni'θjoso, a] a (*maligno, MED*) pernicious; (*persona*) wicked.

pernio ['pernjo] nm hinge.

perno ['perno] nm bolt.

pero ['pero] conj but; (*aún*) yet // nm (*defecto*) flaw, defect; (*reparo*) objection.

perol [pe'rol] nm, **perola** [pe'rola] nf (large metal) pan.

perpendicular [perpendiku'lar] a perpendicular.

perpetrar [perpe'trar] vt to perpetrate.

perpetuar [perpe'twar] vt to perpetuate;

perpetuo, a a perpetual.

perplejo, a [per'plexo, a] a perplexed, bewildered.

perra ['perra] nf (*ZOOL*) bitch; (*fam: dinero*) money; **estar sin una ~** to be flat broke.

perrera [pe'rrera] nf kennel.

perro ['perro] nm dog.

persa ['persa] a, nm/f Persian.

persecución [perseku'θjon] nf pursuit, chase; (*REL, POL*) persecution.

perseguir [perse'vir] vt to pursue, hunt; (*cortejar*) to chase after; (*molestar*) to pester, annoy; (*REL, POL*) to persecute.

perseverante [perseße'rante] a persevering, persistent.

perseverar [perseße'rar] vi to persevere, persist; **~ en** to persevere in, persist with.

persiana [per'sjana] nf (Venetian) blind.

persignarse [persiv'narse] vr to cross o.s.

persistente [persis'tente] a persistent.

persistir [persis'tir] vi to persist.

persona [per'sona] nf person; **~ mayor** elderly person; **10 ~s** 10 people.

personaje [perso'naxe] nm important person, celebrity; (*TEATRO etc*) character.

personal [perso'nal] a (*particular*) personal; (*para una persona*) single, for one person // nm personnel, staff; **~idad** nf personality.

personarse [perso'narse] vr to appear in person.

personificar [personifi'kar] vt to personify.

perspectiva [perspek'tißa] nf perspective; (*vista, panorama*) view, panorama; (*posibilidad futura*) outlook, prospect.

perspicacia [perspi'kaθja] nf (*fig*) discernment, perspicacity.

perspicaz [perspi'kaθ] a shrewd.

persuadir [perswa'ðir] vt (*gen*) to persuade; (*convencer*) to convince; **~se** vr to become convinced; **persuasión** nf persuasion; **persuasivo, a** a persuasive; convincing.

pertenecer [pertene'θer] vi to belong; (*fig*) to concern; **pertenencia** nf ownership; **pertenencias** nfpl possessions, property sg; **perteneciente** a: **perteneciente a** belonging to.

pertenezca etc vb ver **pertenecer**.

pértiga ['pertiva] nf: **salto de ~** pole vault.

pertinaz [perti'naθ] a (*persistente*) persistent; (*terco*) obstinate.

pertinente [perti'nente] a relevant, pertinent; (*apropiado*) appropriate; **~ a** concerning, relevant to.

perturbación [perturßa'θjon] nf (*POL*) disturbance; (*MED*) upset, disturbance.

perturbado, a [pertur'ßaðo, a] a mentally unbalanced.

perturbador, a [perturßa'ðor, a] *a* perturbing, disturbing; (*subversivo*) subversive.

perturbar [pertur'ßar] *vt* (*el orden*) to disturb; (*MED*) to upset, disturb; (*mentalmente*) to perturb.

Perú [pe'ru] *nm*: el ~ Peru; **peruano, a** *a, nm/f* Peruvian.

perversión [perßer'sjon] *nf* perversion; **perverso, a** *a* perverse; (*depravado*) depraved.

pervertido, a [perßer'tiðo, a] *a* perverted // *nm/f* pervert.

pervertir [perßer'tir] *vt* to pervert, corrupt.

pesa ['pesa] *nf* weight; (*DEPORTE*) shot.

pesadez [pesa'ðeθ] *nf* (*peso*) heaviness; (*lentitud*) slowness; (*aburrimiento*) tediousness.

pesadilla [pesa'ðiʎa] *nf* nightmare, bad dream.

pesado, a [pe'saðo, a] *a* heavy; (*lento*) slow; (*difícil, duro*) tough, hard; (*aburrido*) boring, tedious; (*tiempo*) sultry.

pesadumbre [pesa'ðumbre] *nf* grief, sorrow.

pésame ['pesame] *nm* expression of condolence, message of sympathy; **dar el ~** to express one's condolences.

pesar [pe'sar] *vt* to weigh // *vi* to weigh; (*ser pesado*) to weigh a lot, be heavy; (*fig: opinión*) to carry weight; **no pesa mucho** it doesn't weigh much // *nm* (*arrepentimiento*) regret; (*pena*) grief, sorrow; **a ~ de** o **pese a (que)** in spite of, despite.

pesario [pe'sarjo] *nm* pessary.

pesca ['peska] *nf* (*acto*) fishing; (*lo pescado*) catch; **ir de ~** to go fishing.

pescadería [peskaðe'ria] *nf* fish shop, fishmonger's (*Brit*).

pescado [pes'kaðo] *nm* fish.

pescador, a [peska'ðor, a] *nm/f* fisherman/woman.

pescar [pes'kar] *vt* (*tomar*) to catch; (*intentar tomar*) to fish for; (*conseguir: trabajo*) to manage to get // *vi* to fish, go fishing.

pescuezo [pes'kweθo] *nm* (*ZOOL*) neck.

pesebre [pe'seßre] *nm* manger.

peseta [pe'seta] *nf* peseta.

pesimista [pesi'mista] *a* pessimistic // *nm/f* pessimist.

pésimo, a ['pesimo, a] *a* awful, dreadful.

peso ['peso] *nm* weight; (*balanza*) scales *pl*; (*moneda*) peso; ~ **bruto/neto** gross/net weight; **vender a ~** to sell by weight.

pesquero, a [pes'kero, a] *a* fishing *cpd*.

pesquisa [pes'kisa] *nf* inquiry, investigation.

pestaña [pes'taɲa] *nf* (*ANAT*) eyelash; (*borde*) rim; **pestañear** *vi* to blink.

peste ['peste] *nf* plague; (*mal olor*) stink, stench.

pesticida [pesti'θiða] *nm* pesticide.

pestilencia [pesti'lenθja] *nf* (*mal olor*) stink, stench.

pestillo [pes'tiʎo] *nm* (*cerrojo*) bolt; (*picaporte*) doorhandle.

petaca [pe'taka] *nf* (*AM*) suitcase.

pétalo ['petalo] *nm* petal.

petardo [pe'tardo] *nm* firework, firecracker.

petición [peti'θjon] *nf* (*pedido*) request, plea; (*memorial*) petition; (*JUR*) plea.

petrificar [petrifi'kar] *vt* to petrify.

petróleo [pe'troleo] *nm* oil, petroleum; **petrolero, a** *a* petroleum *cpd* // *nm* (*COM: persona*) oil man; (*buque*) (oil) tanker.

peyorativo, a [pejora'tißo, a] *a* pejorative.

pez [peθ] *nm* fish.

pezón [pe'θon] *nm* teat, nipple.

pezuña [pe'θuɲa] *nf* hoof.

piadoso, a [pja'ðoso, a] *a* (*devoto*) pious, devout; (*misericordioso*) kind, merciful.

pianista [pja'nista] *nm/f* pianist.

piano ['pjano] *nm* piano.

piar [pjar] *vi* to cheep.

pibe, a ['piße, a] *nm/f* (*AM*) boy/girl.

picadero [pika'ðero] *nm* riding school.

picadillo [pika'ðiʎo] *nm* mince, minced meat.

picado, a [pi'kaðo, a] *a* pricked, punctured; (*CULIN*) minced, chopped; (*mar*) choppy; (*diente*) bad; (*tabaco*) cut; (*enfadado*) cross.

picador [pika'ðor] *nm* (*TAUR*) picador; (*minero*) faceworker.

picadura [pika'ðura] *nf* (*pinchazo*) puncture; (*de abeja*) sting; (*de mosquito*) bite; (*tabaco picado*) cut tobacco.

picante [pi'kante] *a* hot; (*comentario*) racy, spicy.

picaporte [pika'porte] *nm* (*manija*) doorhandle; (*pestillo*) latch.

picar [pi'kar] *vt* (*agujerear, perforar*) to prick, puncture; (*abeja*) to sting; (*mosquito, serpiente*) to bite; (*CULIN*) to mince, chop; (*incitar*) to incite, goad; (*dañar, irritar*) to annoy, bother; (*quemar: lengua*) to burn, sting // *vi* (*pez*) to bite, take the bait; (*sol*) to burn, scorch; (*abeja, MED*) to sting; (*mosquito*) to bite; ~**se** *vr* (*agriarse*) to turn sour, go off; (*ofenderse*) to take offence.

picardía [pikar'ðia] *nf* villainy; (*astucia*) slyness, craftiness; (*una ~*) dirty trick; (*palabra*) rude/bad word o expression.

pícaro, a ['pikaro, a] *a* (*malicioso*) villainous; (*travieso*) mischievous // *nm* (*astuto*) crafty sort; (*sinvergüenza*) rascal, scoundrel.

pico ['piko] *nm* (*de ave*) beak; (*punta*)

sharp point; (*TEC*) pick, pickaxe; (*GEO*) peak, summit; **y ~** and a bit.

picotear [pikote'ar] *vt* to peck // *vi* to nibble, pick.

picudo, a [pi'kuðo, a] *a* pointed, with a point.

pichón [pi'tʃon] *nm* young pigeon.

pido, pidió *etc vb ver* **pedir**.

pie [pje] (*pl* ~**s**) *nm* foot; (*fig*: *motivo*) motive, basis; (: *fundamento*) foothold; **ir a ~** to go on foot, walk; **estar de ~** to be standing (up); **ponerse de ~** to stand up; **de ~s a cabeza** from top to bottom; **al ~ de la letra** (*citar*) literally, verbatim; (*copiar*) exactly, word for word; **en ~ de guerra** on a war footing; **dar ~ a** to give cause for; **hacer ~** (*en el agua*) to touch (the) bottom.

piedad [pje'ðað] *nf* (*lástima*) pity, compassion; (*clemencia*) mercy; (*devoción*) piety, devotion.

piedra ['pjeðra] *nf* stone; (*roca*) rock; (*de mechero*) flint; (*METEOROLOGIA*) hailstone.

piel [pjel] *nf* (*ANAT*) skin; (*ZOOL*) skin, hide, fur; (*cuero*) leather; (*BOT*) skin, peel.

pienso *etc vb ver* **pensar**.

pierdo *etc vb ver* **perder**.

pierna ['pjerna] *nf* leg.

pieza ['pjeθa] *nf* piece; (*habitación*) room; **~ de recambio** *o* **repuesto** spare (part).

pigmeo, a [piɣ'meo, a] *a, nm/f* pigmy.

pijama [pi'xama] *nm* pyjamas *pl*.

pila ['pila] *nf* (*ELEC*) battery; (*montón*) heap, pile; (*lavabo*) sink.

píldora ['pildora] *nf* pill; **la ~** (*anticonceptiva*) the (contraceptive) pill.

pileta [pi'leta] *nf* basin, bowl; (*AM*) swimming pool.

piloto [pi'loto] *nm* pilot; (*de aparato*) (pilot) light; (*AUTO*: *luz*) tail *o* rear light; (: *conductor*) driver.

pillaje [pi'ʎaxe] *nm* pillage, plunder.

pillar [pi'ʎar] *vt* (*saquear*) to pillage, plunder; (*fam*: *coger*) to catch; (: *agarrar*) to grasp, seize; (: *entender*) to grasp, catch on to; **~se** *vr*: **~se un dedo con la puerta** to catch one's finger in the door.

pillo, a ['piʎo, a] *a* villainous; (*astuto*) sly, crafty // *nm/f* rascal, rogue, scoundrel.

pimentón [pimen'ton] *nm* paprika.

pimienta [pi'mjenta] *nf* pepper.

pimiento [pi'mjento] *nm* pepper, pimiento.

pinacoteca [pinako'teka] *nf* art gallery.

pinar [pi'nar] *nm* pine forest (*Brit*), pine grove (*US*).

pincel [pin'θel] *nm* paintbrush.

pinchar [pin'tʃar] *vt* (*perforar*) to prick, pierce; (*neumático*) to puncture; (*fig*) to prod.

pinchazo [pin'tʃaθo] *nm* (*perforación*) prick; (*de neumático*) puncture; (*fig*) prod.

pinchito [pin'tʃito] *nm* shish kebab.

pincho ['pintʃo] *nm* savoury (snack); **~ moruno** shish kebab; **~ de tortilla** small slice of omelette.

ping-pong ['pin'pon] *nm* table tennis.

pingüino [pin'gwino] *nm* penguin.

pino ['pino] *nm* pine (tree).

pinta ['pinta] *nf* spot; (*de líquidos*) spot, drop; (*aspecto*) appearance, look(s) (*pl*); **~do, a** *a* spotted; (*de muchos colores*) colourful.

pintar [pin'tar] *vt* to paint // *vi* to paint; (*fam*) to count, be important; **~se** *vr* to put on make-up.

pintor, a [pin'tor, a] *nm/f* painter.

pintoresco, a [pinto'resko, a] *a* picturesque.

pintura [pin'tura] *nf* painting; **~ a la acuarela** watercolour; **~ al óleo** oil painting.

pinza ['pinθa] *nf* (*ZOOL*) claw; (*para colgar ropa*) clothes peg; (*TEC*) pincers *pl*; **~s** *nfpl* (*para depilar etc*) tweezers *pl*.

piña ['piɲa] *nf* (*fruto del pino*) pine cone; (*fruta*) pineapple; (*fig*) group.

piñon [pi'ɲon] *nm* (*fruto*) pine nut; (*TEC*) pinion.

pío, a ['pio, a] *a* (*devoto*) pious, devout; (*misericordioso*) merciful.

piojo ['pjoxo] *nm* louse.

pionero, a [pjo'nero, a] *a* pioneering // *nm/f* pioneer.

pipa ['pipa] *nf* pipe; (*BOT*) (edible) sunflower seed.

pipí [pi'pi] *nm* (*fam*): **hacer ~** to have a wee(-wee) (*Brit*), have to go (wee-wee) (*US*).

pique ['pike] *nm* (*resentimiento*) pique, resentment; (*rivalidad*) rivalry, competition; **irse a ~** to sink; (*esperanza, familia*) to be ruined.

piqueta [pi'keta] *nf* pick(axe).

piquete [pi'kete] *nm* (*agujerito*) small hole; (*MIL*) squad, party; (*de obreros*) picket.

piragua [pi'raɣwa] *nf* canoe; **piragüismo** *nm* canoeing.

pirámide [pi'ramiðe] *nf* pyramid.

pirata [pi'rata] *a, nm* pirate.

Pirineo(s) [piri'neo(s)] *nm* (*pl*) Pyrenees *pl*.

piropo [pi'ropo] *nm* compliment, (piece of) flattery.

pirueta [pi'rweta] *nf* pirouette.

pisada [pi'saða] *nf* (*paso*) footstep; (*huella*) footprint.

pisar [pi'sar] *vt* (*caminar sobre*) to walk on, tread on; (*apretar con el pie*) to press; (*fig*) to trample on, walk all over // *vi* to tread, step, walk.

piscina [pis'θina] *nf* swimming pool.

Piscis ['pisθis] nm Pisces

piso ['piso] nm (suelo, planta) floor; (apartamento) flat (Brit), apartment; **primer** ~ (Esp) first floor; (AM) ground floor.

pisotear [pisote'ar] vt to trample (on o underfoot).

pista ['pista] nf track, trail; (indicio) clue; ~ **de aterrizaje** runway; ~ **de baile** dance floor; ~ **de tenis** tennis court; ~ **de hielo** ice rink.

pistola [pis'tola] nf pistol; (TEC) spray-gun; **pistolero, a** nm/f gunman/woman, **gangster** // nf holster.

pistón [pis'ton] nm (TEC) piston; (MUS) key.

pitar [pi'tar] vt (silbato) to blow; (re-chiflar) to whistle at, boo // vi to whistle; (AUTO) to sound o toot one's horn; (AM) to smoke.

pitillo [pi'tiʎo] nm cigarette.

pito ['pito] nm whistle; (de coche) horn.

pitón [pi'ton] nm (ZOOL) python.

pitonisa [pito'nisa] nf fortune-teller.

pitorreo [pito'rreo] nm joke; **estar de** ~ to be joking.

pizarra [pi'θarra] nf (piedra) slate; (en-cerado) blackboard.

pizca ['piθka] nf pinch, spot; (fig) spot, speck; **ni** ~ **not a bit.**

placa ['plaka] nf plate; (distintivo) badge, insignia; ~ **de matrícula** number plate.

placentero, a [plaθen'tero, a] a pleasant, agreeable.

placer [pla'θer] nm pleasure // vt to please.

plácido, a ['plaθiðo, a] a placid.

plaga ['plaɣa] nf pest; (MED) plague; (abundancia) abundance; **plagar** vt to infest, plague; (llenar) to fill.

plagio ['plaxjo] nm plagiarism.

plan [plan] nm (esquema, proyecto) plan; (idea, intento) idea, intention; **tener** ~ (fam) to have a date; **tener un** ~ (fam) to have an affair; **en** ~ **económico** (fam) on the cheap; **vamos en** ~ **de turismo** we're going as tourists; **si te pones en ese** ~... if that's your attitude... .

plana ['plana] nf ver **plano.**

plancha ['plantʃa] nf (para planchar) iron; (rótulo) plate, sheet; (NAUT) gangway; **a la** ~ grilled; ~**do** nm ironing; **planchar** vt, vi to iron.

planeador [planea'ðor] nm glider.

planear [plane'ar] vt to plan // vi to glide.

planeta [pla'neta] nm planet.

planicie [pla'niθje] nf plain.

planificación [planifika'θjon] nf planning; ~ **familiar** family planning.

plano, a ['plano, a] a flat, level, even // nm (MAT, TEC, AVIAT) plane; (FOTO) shot; (ARQ) plan; (GEO) map; (de ciudad) map, street plan // nf sheet (of paper), page; (TEC) trowel; **primer** ~

close-up; **caer de** ~ to fall flat; **en primera plana** on the front page; **plana mayor** staff.

planta ['planta] nf (BOT, TEC) plant; (ANAT) sole of the foot, foot; (piso) floor; (AM: personal) staff; ~ **baja** ground floor.

plantación [planta'θjon] nf (AGR) plantation; (acto) planting.

plantar [plan'tar] vt (BOT) to plant; (levantar) to erect, set up; ~**se** vr to stand firm; ~ **a uno en la calle** to throw sb out; **dejar plantado a uno** (fam) to stand sb up.

plantear [plante'ar] vt (problema) to pose; (dificultad) to raise.

plantilla [plan'tiʎa] nf (de zapato) insole; (personal) personnel; **ser de** ~ to be on the staff.

plantón [plan'ton] nm (MIL) guard, sentry; (fam) long wait; **dar (un)** ~ **a uno** to stand sb up.

plañir [pla'ɲir] vi to mourn.

plasmar [plas'mar] vt (dar forma) to mould, shape; (representar) to represent // vi: ~ **en** to take the form of.

Plasticina ® [plasti'θina] nf Plasticine ®.

plástico, a ['plastiko, a] a plastic // nm plastic // nf (art of) sculpture, modelling.

Plastilina ® [plasti'lina] nf (AM) Plasticine ®.

plata ['plata] nf (metal) silver; (cosas hechas de) ~ silverware; (AM) cash, dough; **hablar en** ~ to speak bluntly o frankly.

plataforma [plata'forma] nf platform; ~ **de lanzamiento/perforación** launch(ing) pad/drilling rig.

plátano ['platano] nm (fruta) banana; (árbol) banana tree.

platea [pla'tea] nf (TEATRO) pit.

plateado, a [plate'aðo, a] a silver; (TEC) silver-plated.

plática ['platika] nf talk, chat; **platicar** vi to talk, chat.

platillo [pla'tiʎo] nm saucer; ~**s** nmpl cymbals; ~ **volador** o **volante** flying saucer.

platino [pla'tino] nm platinum; ~**s** nmpl (AUTO) contact points.

plato ['plato] nm plate, dish; (parte de comida) course; (comida) dish; **primer** ~ first course.

playa ['plaja] nf beach; (costa) seaside; ~ **de estacionamiento** (AM) car park.

playera [pla'jera] nf (AM: camiseta) T-shirt; ~**s** nfpl (slip-on) canvas shoes.

plaza ['plaθa] nf square; (mercado) market(place); (sitio) room, space; (en vehículo) seat, place; (colocación) post, job; ~ **de toros** bullring.

plazo ['plaθo] nm (lapso de tiempo) time, period; (fecha de vencimiento) expiry date; (pago parcial) instalment; **a corto/largo** ~ short-/long-term; **comprar**

a ~s to buy on hire purchase, pay for in instalments.

plazoleta [plaθo'leta], **plazuela** [pla'θwela] *nf* small square.

pleamar [plea'mar] *nf* high tide.

plebe ['pleβe] *nf*: la ~ the common people *pl*, the masses *pl*; (*pey*) the plebs *pl*; ~**yo, a** *a* plebeian; (*pey*) coarse, common.

plebiscito [pleβis'θito] *nm* plebiscite.

plegable [ple'xaβle] *a* pliable; (*silla*) folding.

plegar [ple'xar] *vt* (*doblar*) to fold, bend; (*COSTURA*) to pleat; ~**se** *vr* to yield, submit.

pleito ['pleito] *nm* (*JUR*) lawsuit, case; (*fig*) dispute, feud.

plenilunio [pleni'lunjo] *nm* full moon.

plenitud [pleni'tuð] *nf* plenitude, fullness; (*abundancia*) abundance.

pleno, a ['pleno, a] *a* full; (*completo*) complete // *nm* plenum; **en ~ día** in broad daylight; **en ~ verano** at the height of summer; **en plena cara** full in the face.

pleuresía [pleure'sia] *nf* pleurisy.

Plexiglás ® [pleksi'ɣlas] *nm* acrylic glass, Plexiglas (*US*).

pliego *etc vb ver* **plegar** // ['pljeɣo] *nm* (*hoja*) sheet (of paper); (*carta*) sealed letter/document; ~ **de condiciones** details *pl*, specifications *pl*.

pliegue *etc vb ver* **plegar** // ['pljeɣe] *nm* fold, crease; (*de vestido*) pleat.

plisado [pli'saðo] *nm* pleating.

plomero [plo'mero] *nm* (*AM*) plumber.

plomo ['plomo] *nm* (*metal*) lead; (*ELEC*) fuse.

pluma ['pluma] *nf* feather; (*para escribir*) pen.

plumero [plu'mero] *nm* (*quitapolvos*) feather duster.

plumón [plu'mon] *nm* (*AM: fino*) felt-tip pen; (: *ancho*) marker.

plural [plu'ral] *a* plural; ~**idad** *nf* plurality; **una ~idad de votos** a majority of votes.

plus [plus] *nm* bonus; ~**valía** *nf* (*COM*) appreciation.

plutocracia [pluto'kraθja] *nf* plutocracy.

población [poβla'θjon] *nf* population; (*pueblo, ciudad*) town, city.

poblado, a [po'βlaðo, a] *a* inhabited // *nm* (*aldea*) village; (*pueblo*) (small) town; **densamente ~** densely populated.

poblador, a [poβla'ðor, a] *nm/f* settler, colonist.

poblar [po'βlar] *vt* (*colonizar*) to colonize; (*fundar*) to found; (*habitar*) to inhabit.

pobre ['poβre] *a* poor // *nm/f* poor person; **¡~!** poor thing!; ~**za** *nf* poverty.

pocilga [po'θilɣa] *nf* pigsty.

pocillo [po'siʎo] *nm* (*AM*) coffee cup.

poción [po'θjon], **pócima** ['poθima] *nf* potion.

poco, a ['poko, a] ♦ *a* (*sg*) little, not much; ~ **tiempo** little *o* not much time; **de ~ interés** of little interest, not very interesting; **poca cosa** not much

2 (*pl*) few, not many; **unos ~s** a few, some; ~**s niños comen lo que les conviene** few children eat what they should

♦ *ad* **1** little, not much; **cuesta ~** it doesn't cost much

2 (+ *a*: = *negativo, antónimo*): ~ **amable/inteligente** not very nice/ intelligent

3: **por ~ me caigo** I almost fell

4: **a ~: a ~ de haberse casado** shortly after getting married

5: ~ **a ~** little by little

♦ *nm* a little, a bit; **un ~ triste/de dinero** a little sad/money.

podar [po'ðar] *vt* to prune.

poder [po'ðer] ♦ *vi* **1** (*capacidad*) can, be able to; **no puedo hacerlo** I can't do it, I'm unable to do it

2 (*permiso*) can, may, be allowed to; **¿se puede?** may I (*o* we)?; **puedes irte ahora** you may go now; **no se puede fumar en este hospital** smoking is not allowed in this hospital

3 (*posibilidad*) may, might, could; **puede llegar mañana** he may *o* might arrive tomorrow; **pudiste haberte hecho daño** you might *o* could have hurt yourself; **¡podías habérmelo dicho antes!** you might have told me before!

4: **puede ser: puede ser** perhaps; **puede ser que lo sepa Tomás** Tomás may *o* might know

5: **¡no puedo más!** I've had enough!; **no pude menos que dejarlo** I couldn't help but leave it; **es tonto a más no ~** he's as stupid as they come

6: ~ **con: no puedo con este crío** this kid's too much for me

♦ *nm* power; ~ **adquisitivo** purchasing power; **detentar** *o* **ocupar** *o* **estar en el ~** to be in power.

podrido, a [po'ðriðo, a] *a* rotten, bad; (*fig*) rotten, corrupt.

podrir [po'ðrir] = **pudrir**.

poema [po'ema] *nm* poem.

poesía [poe'sia] *nf* poetry.

poeta [po'eta] *nm* poet; **poético, a** *a* poetic(al).

poetisa [poe'tisa] *nf* (woman) poet.

póker ['poker] *nm* poker.

polaco, a [po'lako, a] *a* Polish // *nm/f* Pole.

polar [po'lar] *a* polar; ~**idad** *nf* polarity; ~**izarse** *vr* to polarize.

polea [po'lea] *nf* pulley.

polémica [po'lemika] *nf* polemics *sg*; (*una ~*) controversy, polemic.

polen ['polen] *nm* pollen.

policía [poli'θia] *nm/f* policeman/woman // *nf* police; **~co, a** *a* police *cpd*: **novela policíaca** detective story; **policial** *a* police *cpd*.

polideportivo [poliðepor'tiβo] *nm* sports centre *o* complex.

polietileno [polieti'leno] *nm* polythene (*Brit*), polyethylene (*US*).

poligamia [poli'xamja] *nf* polygamy.

polilla [po'liʎa] *nf* moth.

polio ['poljo] *nf* polio.

politécnico [poli'tekniko] *nm* polytechnic.

politico, a [po'litiko, a] *a* political; (*discreto*) tactful; (*de familia*) -in-law // *nm/f* politician // *nf* politics *sg*; (*económica, agraria etc*) policy; **padre ~** father-in-law; **politicastro** *nm* (*pey*) politician, politico.

póliza ['poliθa] *nf* certificate, voucher; (*impuesto*) tax stamp; **~ de seguros** insurance policy.

polizón [poli'θon] *nm* (*en barco etc*) stowaway.

polo ['polo] *nm* (*GEO, ELEC*) pole; (*helado*) ice lolly; (*DEPORTE*) polo; (*suéter*) polo-neck; **~ Norte/Sur** North/South Pole.

Polonia [po'lonja] *nf* Poland.

poltrona [pol'trona] *nf* easy chair.

polución [polu'θjon] *nf* pollution.

polvera [pol'βera] *nf* powder compact.

polvo ['polβo] *nm* dust; (*QUIMICA, CULIN, MED*) powder; **~s** *nmpl* powder *sg*; **~ de talco** talcum powder; **estar hecho ~** (*fam*) to be worn out *o* exhausted.

pólvora ['polβora] *nf* gunpowder; (*fuegos artificiales*) fireworks *pl*.

polvoriento, a [polβo'rjento, a] *a* (*superficie*) dusty; (*sustancia*) powdery.

pollera [po'ʎera] *nf* (*AM*) skirt.

pollería [poʎe'ria] *nf* poulterer's (shop).

pollo ['poʎo] *nm* chicken.

pomada [po'maða] *nf* (*MED*) cream, ointment.

pomelo [po'melo] *nm* grapefruit.

pómez ['pomeθ] *nf*: **piedra ~** pumice stone.

pompa ['pompa] *nf* (*burbuja*) bubble; (*bomba*) pump; (*esplendor*) pomp, splendour; **pomposo, a** *a* splendid, magnificent; (*pey*) pompous.

pómulo ['pomulo] *nm* cheekbone.

pon [pon] *vb ver* **poner**.

ponche ['pontʃe] *nm* punch.

poncho ['pontʃo] *nm* (*AM*) poncho.

ponderar [ponde'rar] *vt* (*considerar*) to weigh up, consider; (*elogiar*) to praise highly, speak in praise of.

pondré *etc vb ver* **poner**.

poner [po'ner] ♦ *vt* **1** (*colocar*) to put; (*telegrama*) to send; (*obra de teatro*) to put on; (*película*) to show; **ponlo más fuerte** turn it up; **¿qué ponen en el Excelsior?** what's on at the Excelsior?

2 (*tienda*) to open; (*instalar*: *gas etc*) to put in; (*radio, TV*) to switch *o* turn on

3 (*suponer*): **pongamos que ...** let's suppose that

4 (*contribuir*): **el gobierno ha puesto otro millón** the government has contributed another million

5 (*TELEC*): **póngame con el Sr. López** can you put me through to Mr. López

6: **~ de**: **le han puesto de director general** they've appointed him general manager

7 (+ *a*) to make; **me estás poniendo nerviosa** you're making me nervous

8 (*dar nombre*): **al hijo le pusieron Diego** they called their son Diego

♦ *vi* (*gallina*) to lay

♦ **~se** *vr* **1** (*colocarse*): **se puso a mi lado** he came and stood beside me; **tú ponte en esa silla** you go and sit on that chair

2 (*vestido, cosméticos*) to put on; **¿por qué no te pones el vestido nuevo?** why don't you put on *o* wear your new dress?

3: (+ *a*) to turn; to get, become; **se puso muy serio** he got very serious; **después de lavarla la tela se puso azul** after washing it the material turned blue

4: **~se a**: **se puso a llorar** he started to cry; **tienes que ~te a estudiar** you must get down to studying

5: **~se a bien con uno** to make it up with sb; **~se a mal con uno** to get on the wrong side of sb.

pongo *etc vb ver* **poner.**

poniente [po'njente] *nm* (*occidente*) west; (*viento*) west wind.

pontificado [pontifi'kaðo] *nm* papacy, pontificate; **pontifice** *nm* pope, pontiff.

pontón [pon'ton] *nm* pontoon.

ponzoña [pon'θoɲa] *nf* poison, venom.

popa ['popa] *nf* stern.

popular [popu'lar] *a* popular; (*cultura*) of the people, folk *cpd*; **~idad** *nf* popularity; **~izarse** *vr* to become popular.

por [por] ♦ *prep* **1** (*objetivo*) for; **luchar ~ la patria** to fight for one's country

2 (+ *infinitivo*): **~ no llegar tarde** so as not to arrive late; **~ citar unos ejemplos** to give a few examples

3 (*causa*) out of, because of; **~ escasez de fondos** through *o* for lack of funds

4 (*tiempo*): **~ la mañana/noche** in the morning/at night; **se queda ~ una semana** she's staying (for) a week

5 (*lugar*): **pasar ~ Madrid** to pass through Madrid; **ir a Guayaquil ~ Quito** to go to Guayaquil via Quito; **caminar ~ la calle** to walk along the street; *ver tb* **todo**

6 (*cambio, precio*): **te doy uno nuevo ~ el que tienes** I'll give you a new one (in return) for the one you've got

7 (*valor distributivo*): **550 pesetas ~**

hora/cabeza 550 pesetas an *o* per hour/a *o* per head
8 (*modo, medio*) by; ~ **correo/avión** by post/air; **día** ~ **día** day by day; **entrar** ~ **la entrada principal** to go in through the main entrance
9: 10 ~ 10 son 100 10 by 10 is 100
10 (*en lugar de*): **vino él** ~ **su jefe he** came instead of his boss
11: ~ **mí que revienten** as far as I'm concerned they can drop dead.

porcelana [porθe'lana] *nf* porcelain; (*china*) china.

porcentaje [porθen'taxe] *nm* percentage.

porción [por'θjon] *nf* (*parte*) portion, share; (*cantidad*) quantity, amount.

pordiosero, a [porðjo'sero, a] *nm/f* beggar.

porfía [por'fia] *nf* persistence; (*terquedad*) obstinacy.

porfiado, a [por'fjaðo, a] *a* persistent; obstinate.

porfiar [por'fjar] *vi* to persist, insist; (*disputar*) to argue stubbornly.

pormenor [porme'nor] *nm* detail, particular.

pornografía [pornoɣra'fia] *nf* pornography.

poro ['poro] *nm* pore; ~**so, a** *a* porous.

porque ['porke] *conj* (*a causa de*) because; (*ya que*) since; (*con el fin de*) so that, in order that.

porqué [por'ke] *nm* reason, cause.

porquería [porke'ria] *nf* (*suciedad*) filth, dirt; (*acción*) dirty trick; (*objeto*) small thing, trifle; (*fig*) rubbish.

porra ['porra] *nf* (*arma*) stick, club.

porrón [po'rron] *nm* glass wine jar with a long spout.

portada [por'taða] *nf* (*de revista*) cover.

portador, a [porta'ðor, a] *nm/f* carrier, bearer; (*COM*) bearer, payee.

portaequipajes [portaeki'paxes] *nm inv* (*AUTO: maletero*) boot; (: . *baca*) luggage rack.

portal [por'tal] *nm* (*entrada*) vestibule, hall; (*portada*) porch, doorway; (*puerta de entrada*) main door; (*DEPORTE*) goal.

portaligas [porta'liɣas] *nm inv* suspender belt.

portamaletas [portama'letas] *nm inv* (*AUTO: maletero*) boot; (: *baca*) roof rack.

portamonedas [portamo'neðas] *nm inv* purse.

portarse [por'tarse] *vr* to behave, conduct o.s.

portátil [por'tatil] *a* portable.

porta(a)viones [porta'(a)ßjones] *nm inv* aircraft carrier.

portavoz [porta'ßoθ] *nm/f* (*persona*) spokesman/woman.

portazo [por'taθo] *nm*: **dar un** ~ to slam the door.

porte ['porte] *nm* (*COM*) transport; (*pre-*

cio) transport charges *pl*.

portento [por'tento] *nm* marvel, wonder; ~**so, a** *a* marvellous, extraordinary.

porteño, a [por'teɲo, a] *a* of *o* from Buenos Aires.

portería [porte'ria] *nf* (*oficina*) porter's office; (*gol*) goal.

portero, a [por'tero, a] *nm/f* porter; (*conserje*) caretaker; (*ujier*) doorman; (*DEPORTE*) goalkeeper.

pórtico ['portiko] *nm* (*patio*) portico, porch; (*fig*) gateway; (*arcada*) arcade.

portilla [por'tiʎa] *nf*, **portillo** [por'tiʎo] *nm* (*cancela*) gate.

portorriqueño, a [portorri'keɲo, a] *a* Puerto Rican.

Portugal [portu'ɣal] *nm* Portugal; **portugués, esa** *a*, *nm/f* Portuguese // *nm* (*LING*) Portuguese.

porvenir [porße'nir] *nm* future.

pos [pos] *prep*: **en** ~ **de** after, in pursuit of.

posada [po'saða] *nf* (*refugio*) shelter, lodging; (*mesón*) guest house; **dar** ~ **a** to give shelter to, take in.

posaderas [posa'ðeras] *nfpl* backside *sg*, buttocks.

posar [po'sar] *vt* (*en el suelo*) to lay down, put down; (*la mano*) to place, put gently // *vi* to sit, pose; ~**se** *vr* to settle; (*pájaro*) to perch; (*avión*) to land, come down.

posdata [pos'ðata] *nf* postscript.

pose ['pose] *nf* pose.

poseedor, a [pose'ðor, a] *nm/f* owner, possessor; (*de récord, puesto*) holder.

poseer [pose'er] *vt* to possess, own; (*ventaja*) to enjoy; (*récord, puesto*) to hold; **poseído, a** *a* possessed.

posesión [pose'sjon] *nf* possession; **posesionarse** *vr*: **posesionarse de** to take possession of, take over.

posesivo, a [pose'sißo, a] *a* possessive.

posibilidad [posißili'ðað] *nf* possibility; (*oportunidad*) chance; **posibilitar** *vt* to make possible; (*hacer realizable*) to make feasible.

posible [po'sißle] *a* possible; (*realizable*) feasible; **de ser** ~ if possible; **en lo** ~ as far as possible.

posición [posi'θjon] *nf* position; (*rango social*) status.

positivo, a [posi'tißo, a] *a* positive // *nf* (*FOTO*) print.

poso ['poso] *nm* sediment; (*heces*) dregs *pl*.

posponer [pospo'ner] *vt* to put behind/below; (*aplazar*) to postpone.

posta ['posta] *nf*: **a** ~ *ad* deliberately, on purpose.

postal [pos'tal] *a* postal // *nf* postcard.

poste ['poste] *nm* (*de telégrafos etc*) post, pole; (*columna*) pillar.

póster ['poster] (*pl* **pósteres, pósters**) *nm* poster.

postergar |poster'ɣar| vt to postpone, delay.

posteridad |posteri'ðað| nf posterity.

posterior |poste'rjor| a back, rear; (siguiente) following, subsequent; (más tarde) later; ~**idad** nf: con ~**idad** later, subsequently.

postizo, a |pos'tiθo, a| a false, artificial // nm hairpiece.

postor, a |pos'tor, a| nm/f bidder.

postrado, a |pos'traðo, a| a prostrate.

postre |'postre| nm sweet, dessert.

postrero, a |pos'trero, a| a (delante de nmsg: **postrer**) (último) last; (que viene detrás) rear.

postulado |postu'laðo| nm postulate.

póstumo, a |'postumo, a| a posthumous.

postura |pos'tura| nf (del cuerpo) posture, position; (fig) attitude, position.

potable |po'taßle| a drinkable; **agua** ~ drinking water.

potaje |po'taxe| nm thick vegetable soup.

pote |'pote| nm pot, jar.

potencia |po'tenθja| nf power.

potencial |poten'θjal| a, nm potential.

potenciar |po'tenθjar| vt to boost.

potente |po'tente| a powerful.

potro, a |'potro, a| nm/f (ZOOL) colt/filly // nm (de gimnasia) vaulting horse.

pozo |'poθo| nm well; (de río) deep pool; (de mina) shaft.

P.P. abr (= porte pagado) CP.

p.p. abr (= por poder) p.p.

práctica |'praktika| nf ver **práctico**.

practicable |prakti'kaßle| a practicable; (camino) passable.

practicante |prakti'kante| nm/f (MED: ayudante de doctor) medical assistant; (: enfermero) male nurse; (quien practica algo) practitioner // a practising.

practicar |prakti'kar| vt to practise; (DEPORTE) to go in for (Brit) o out for (US), play; (realizar) to carry out, perform.

práctico, a |'praktiko, a| a (práctical); (instruido: persona) skilled, expert // nf practice; (método) method; (arte, capacidad) skill; **en la práctica** in practice.

practique etc vb ver **practicar**.

pradera |pra'ðera| nf meadow; (US etc) prairie.

prado |'praðo| nm (campo) meadow, field; (pastizal) pasture.

Praga |'praɣa| n Prague.

pragmático, a |praɣ'matiko, a| a pragmatic.

preámbulo |pre'ambulo| nm preamble, introduction.

precario, a |pre'karjo, a| a precarious.

precaución |prekau'θjon| nf (medida preventiva) preventive measure, precaution; (prudencia) caution, wariness.

precaver |preka'ßer| vt to guard against;

(impedir) to forestall; ~**se** vr: ~**se de** o **contra algo** to (be on one's) guard against sth; **precavido, a** a cautious, wary.

precedencia |preθe'ðenθja| nf precedence; (prioridad) priority; (preeminencia) greater importance, superiority; **precedente** a preceding; (anterior) former // nm precedent.

preceder |preθe'ðer| vt, vi to precede, go before, come before.

precepto |pre'θepto| nm precept.

preciado, a |pre'θjaðo, a| a (estimado) esteemed, valuable.

preciar |pre'θjar| vt to esteem, value; ~**se** vr to boast; ~**se de** to pride o.s. on, boast of being.

precinto |pre'θinto| nm (tb: ~ **de garantía**) seal.

precio |'preθjo| nm price; (costo) cost; (valor) value, worth; (de viaje) fare; ~ **al contado/de coste/de oportunidad** cash/cost/bargain price; ~ **al detalle** o **al por menor** retail price; ~ **tope** top price.

preciosidad |preθjosi'ðað| nf (valor) (high) value, (great) worth; (encanto) charm; (cosa bonita) beautiful thing; **es una** ~ it's lovely, it's really beautiful.

precioso, a |pre'θjoso, a| a precious; (de mucho valor) valuable; (fam) lovely, beautiful.

precipicio |preθi'piθjo| nm cliff, precipice; (fig) abyss.

precipitación |preθipita'θjon| nf haste; (lluvia) rainfall.

precipitado, a |preθipi'taðo, a| a (conducta) hasty, rash; (salida) hasty, sudden.

precipitar |preθipi'tar| vt (arrojar) to hurl down, throw; (apresurar) to hasten; (acelerar) to speed up, accelerate; ~**se** vr to throw o.s.; (apresurarse) to rush; (actuar sin pensar) to act rashly.

precisamente |preθisa'mente| ad precisely; (exactamente) precisely, exactly.

precisar |preθi'sar| vt (necesitar) to need, require; (fijar) to determine exactly, fix; (especificar) to specify.

precisión |preθi'sjon| nf (exactitud) precision.

preciso, a |pre'θiso, a| a (exacto) precise; (necesario) necessary, essential.

preconcebido, a |prekonθe'ßiðo, a| a preconceived.

precoz |pre'koθ| a (persona) precocious; (calvicie etc) premature.

precursor, a |prekur'sor, a| nm/f predecessor, forerunner.

predecir |preðe'θir| vt to predict, forecast.

predestinado, a |preðesti'naðo, a| a predestined.

predeterminar |preðetermi'nar| vt to predetermine.

prédica |'preðika| nf sermon.

predicador, a [preðika'ðor, a] *nm/f* preacher.

predicar [preði'kar] *vt, vi* to preach.

predicción [preðik'θjon] *nf* prediction.

predilecto, a [preði'lekto, a] *a* favourite.

predisponer [preðispo'ner] *vt* to predispose; *(pey)* to prejudice; **predisposición** *nf* inclination; prejudice, bias.

predominante [preðomi'nante] *a* predominant.

predominar [preðomi'nar] *vt* to dominate // *vi* to predominate; *(prevalecer)* to prevail; **predominio** *nm* predominance; prevalence.

preescolar [pre(e)sko'lar] *a* preschool.

prefabricado, a [prefaβri'kaðo, a] *a* prefabricated.

prefacio [pre'faθjo] *nm* preface.

preferencia [prefe'renθja] *nf* preference; **de** ~ preferably, for preference.

preferible [prefe'riβle] *a* preferable.

preferir [prefe'rir] *vt* to prefer.

prefiero *etc vb ver* **preferir.**

prefigurar [prefiɣu'rar] *vt* to foreshadow, prefigure.

pregonar [preɣo'nar] *vt* to proclaim, announce.

pregunta [pre'ɣunta] *nf* question; **hacer una** ~ to ask *o* put (forth *(US)*) a question.

preguntar [preɣun'tar] *vt* to ask; *(cuestionar)* to question // *vi* to ask; ~**se** *vr* to wonder; ~ **por alguien** to ask for sb.

preguntón, ona [preɣun'ton, ona] *a* inquisitive.

prehistórico, a [preis'toriko, a] *a* prehistoric.

prejuicio [pre'xwiθjo] *nm* *(acto)* prejudgement; *(idea preconcebida)* preconception; *(parcialidad)* prejudice, bias.

preliminar [prelimi'nar] *a* preliminary.

preludio [pre'luðjo] *nm* prelude.

prematuro, a [prema'turo, a] *a* premature.

premeditación [premeðita'θjon] *nf* premeditation.

premeditar [premeði'tar] *vt* to premeditate.

premiar [pre'mjar] *vt* to reward; *(en un concurso)* to give a prize to.

premio ['premjo] *nm* reward; prize; *(COM)* premium.

premonición [premoni'θjon] *nf* premonition.

premura [pre'mura] *nf* *(aprieto)* pressure; *(prisa)* haste, urgency.

prenatal [prena'tal] *a* antenatal, prenatal.

prenda ['prenda] *nf* *(ropa)* garment, article of clothing; *(garantía)* pledge; ~**s** *nfpl* talents, gifts.

prendar [pren'dar] *vt* to captivate, en-

chant; ~**se de uno** to fall in love with sb.

prendedor [prende'ðor] *nm* brooch.

prender [pren'der] *vt* *(captar)* to catch, capture; *(detener)* to arrest; *(COSTURA)* to pin, attach; *(sujetar)* to fasten // *vi* to catch; *(arraigar)* to take root; ~**se** *vr* *(encenderse)* to catch fire.

prendido, a [pren'diðo, a] *a* *(AM: luz etc)* on.

prensa ['prensa] *nf* press; **la P**~ the press; **prensar** *vt* to press.

preñado, a [pre'ɲaðo, a] *a* *(ZOOL)* pregnant; ~ **de** pregnant with, full of; **preñez** *nf* pregnancy.

preocupación [preokupa'θjon] *nf* worry, concern; *(ansiedad)* anxiety.

preocupado, a [preoku'paðo, a] *a* worried, concerned; *(ansioso)* anxious.

preocupar [preoku'par] *vt* to worry; ~**se** *vr* to worry; ~**se de algo** *(hacerse cargo)* to take care of sth.

preparación [prepara'θjon] *nf* *(acto)* preparation; *(estado)* readiness; *(entrenamiento)* training.

preparado, a [prepa'raðo, a] *a* *(dispuesto)* prepared; *(CULIN)* ready (to serve) // *nm* preparation.

preparador, a [prepara'ðor, a] *nm/f* trainer.

preparar [prepa'rar] *vt* *(disponer)* to prepare, get ready; *(TEC: tratar)* to prepare, process; *(entrenar)* to teach, train; ~**se** *vr*: ~**se a** *o* **para** to prepare to *o* for, get ready to *o* for; **preparativo, a** *a* preparatory, preliminary; **preparativos** *nmpl* preparations; **preparatorio, a** *a* preparatory // *nf* *(AM)* sixth-form college *(Brit)*, senior high school *(US)*.

prerrogativa [prerroɣa'tiβa] *nf* prerogative, privilege.

presa ['presa] *nf* *(cosa apresada)* catch; *(víctima)* victim; *(de animal)* prey; *(de agua)* dam.

presagiar [presa'xjar] *vt* to presage, forebode.

presbítero [pres'βitero] *nm* priest.

prescindir [presθin'dir] *vi*: ~ **de** *(privarse de)* to do without, go without; *(descartar)* to dispense with.

prescribir [preskri'βir] *vt* to prescribe; **prescripción** *nf* prescription.

presencia [pre'senθja] *nf* presence; **presencial** *a*: **testigo presencial** eyewitness; **presenciar** *vt* to be present at; *(asistir a)* to attend; *(ver)* to see, witness.

presentación [presenta'θjon] *nf* presentation; *(introducción)* introduction.

presentador, a [presenta'ðor, a] *nm/f* presenter, compère.

presentar [presen'tar] *vt* to present; *(ofrecer)* to offer; *(mostrar)* to show, display; *(a una persona)* to introduce; ~**se** *vr* *(llegar inesperadamente)* to appear, turn up; *(ofrecerse como candidato)* to run, stand; *(aparecer)* to show, appear; (*solicitar empleo*) to apply.

presente |pre'sente| *a* present // *nm* present; **hacer** ~ to state, declare; **tener** ~ to remember, bear in mind.

presentimiento [presenti'mjento] *nm* premonition, presentiment.

presentir [presen'tir] *vt* to have a premonition of.

preservación [preserßa'θjon] *nf* protection, preservation.

preservar [preser'ßar] *vt* to protect, preserve; **preservativo** *nm* sheath, condom.

presidencia [presi'ðɛnθja] *nf* presidency; (*de comité*) chairmanship.

presidente [presi'ðente] *nm/f* president; (*de comité*) chairman/woman.

presidiario [presi'ðjarjo] *nm* convict.

presidio [pre'sidjo] *nm* prison, penitentiary.

presidir [presi'ðir] *vt* (*dirigir*) to preside at, preside over; (: *comité*) to take the chair at; (*dominar*) to dominate, rule // *vi* to preside; to take the chair.

presión [pre'sjon] *nf* pressure; **presionar** *vt* to press; (*fig*) to press, put pressure on // *vi*: **presionar para** to press for.

preso, a ['preso, a] *nm/f* prisoner; **tomar** *o* **llevar** ~ **a uno** to arrest sb, take sb prisoner.

prestado, a [pres'taðo, a] *a* on loan; **pedir** ~ to borrow.

prestamista [presta'mista] *nm/f* money-lender.

préstamo ['prestamo] *nm* loan; ~ **hipotecario** mortgage.

prestar [pres'tar] *vt* to lend, loan; (*atención*) to pay; (*ayuda*) to give.

presteza [pres'teθa] *nf* speed, promptness.

prestigio [pres'tixjo] *nm* prestige; ~**so, a** *a* (*honorable*) prestigious; (*famoso, renombrado*) renowned, famous.

presto, a ['presto, a] *a* (*rápido*) quick, prompt; (*dispuesto*) ready // *ad* at once, right away.

presumir [presu'mir] *vt* to presume // *vi* (*tener aires*) to be conceited; **según cabe** ~ as may be presumed, presumably; **presunción** *nf* presumption; **presunto, a** *a* (*supuesto*) supposed, presumed; (*así llamado*) so-called; **presuntuoso, a** *a* conceited, presumptuous.

presuponer [presupo'ner] *vt* to presuppose.

presupuesto *pp de* **presuponer** // [presu'pwesto] *nm* (FINANZAS) budget; (*estimación: de costo*) estimate.

presuroso, a [presu'roso, a] *a* (*rápido*) quick, speedy; (*que tiene prisa*) hasty.

pretencioso, a [preten'θjoso, a] *a* pretentious.

pretender [preten'der] *vt* (*intentar*) to

try to, seek to; (*reivindicar*) to claim; (*buscar*) to seek, try for; (*cortejar*) to woo, court; ~ **que** to expect that; **pretendiente** *nm/f* (*candidato*) candidate, applicant; (*amante*) suitor; **pretensión** *nf* (*aspiración*) aspiration; (*reivindicación*) claim; (*orgullo*) pretension.

pretexto [pre'teksto] *nm* pretext; (*excusa*) excuse.

prevalecer [preßale'θer] *vi* to prevail.

prevención [preßen'θjon] *nf* (*preparación*) preparation; (*estado*) preparedness, readiness; (*el evitar*) prevention; (*previsión*) foresight, forethought; (*precaución*) precaution.

prevenido, a [preße'niðo, a] *a* prepared, ready; (*cauteloso*) cautious.

prevenir [preße'nir] *vt* (*impedir*) to prevent; (*prever*) to foresee, anticipate; (*predisponer*) to prejudice, bias; (*avisar*) to warn; (*preparar*) to prepare, get ready; ~**se** *vr* to get ready, prepare; ~**se contra** to take precautions against; **preventivo, a** *a* preventive, precautionary.

prever [pre'ßer] *vt* to foresee.

previo, a ['preßjo, a] *a* (*anterior*) previous; (*preliminar*) preliminary // *prep*: ~ **acuerdo de los otros** subject to the agreement of the others.

previsión [preßi'sjon] *nf* (*perspicacia*) foresight; (*predicción*) forecast.

prima ['prima] *nf ver* **primo**.

primacía [prima'θia] *nf* primacy.

primario, a [pri'marjo, a] *a* primary.

primavera [prima'ßera] *nf* spring(time).

primero, a [pri'mero, a] *a* (*delante de nmsg*: **primer**) first; (*principal*) prime // *ad* first; (*más bien*) sooner, rather // *nf* (AUTO) first gear; (FERRO: *tb*: **primera clase**) first class; **de primera** (*fam*) first-class, first-rate; **primera plana** front page.

primitivo, a [primi'tißo, a] *a* primitive; (*original*) original.

primo, a ['primo, a] *a* prime // *nm/f* cousin; (*fam*) fool, idiot // *nf* (COM) bonus; ~ **de seguro** insurance premium; ~ **hermano** first cousin; **materias primas** raw materials.

primogénito, a [primo'xenito, a] *a* first-born.

primordial [primor'ðjal] *a* basic, fundamental.

primoroso, a [primo'roso, a] *a* exquisite, delicate.

princesa [prin'θesa] *nf* princess.

principal [prinθi'pal] *a* principal, main // *nm* (*jefe*) chief, principal.

príncipe ['prinθipe] *nm* prince.

principiante [prinθi'pjante] *nm/f* beginner.

principiar [prinθi'pjar] *vt* to begin.

principio [prin'θipjo] *nm* (*comienzo*) beginning, start; (*origen*) origin;

(*primera etapa*) rudiment, basic idea; (*moral*) principle; a ~s de at the beginning of.

pringoso, a [prin'γoso, a] *a* (*grasiento*) greasy; (*pegajoso*) sticky.

pringue ['pringe] *nm* (*grasa*) grease, fat, dripping.

prioridad [priori'ðað] *nf* priority.

prisa ['prisa] *nf* (*apresuramiento*) hurry, haste; (*rapidez*) speed; (*urgencia*) (sense of) urgency; a o de ~ quickly; correr ~ to be urgent; darse ~ to hurry up; estar de o tener ~ to be in a hurry.

prisión [pri'sjon] *nf* (*cárcel*) prison; (*período de cárcel*) imprisonment; **prisionero, a** *nm/f* prisoner.

prismáticos [pris'matikos] *nmpl* binoculars.

privación [priβa'θjon] *nf* deprivation; (*falta*) want, privation.

privado, a [pri'βaðo, a] *a* private.

privar [pri'βar] *vt* to deprive; **privativo, a** *a* exclusive.

privilegiado, a [priβile'xjaðo, a] *a* privileged; (*memoria*) very good.

privilegiar [priβile'xjar] *vt* to grant a privilege to; (*favorecer*) to favour.

privilegio [priβi'lexjo] *nm* privilege; (*concesión*) concession.

pro [pro] *nm o f* profit, advantage // *prep*: asociación ~ ciegos association for the blind // *pref*: ~ soviético/americano pro-Soviet/American; en ~ de on behalf of, for; los ~s y los contras the pros and cons.

proa ['proa] *nf* bow, prow; de ~ bow *cpd*, fore.

probabilidad [proβaβili'ðað] *nf* probability, likelihood; (*oportunidad*, *posibilidad*) chance, prospect; **probable** *a* probable, likely.

probador [proβa'ðor] *nm* (*en tienda*) fitting room.

probar [pro'βar] *vt* (*demostrar*) to prove; (*someter a prueba*) to test, try out; (*ropa*) to try on; (*comida*) to taste // *vi* to try; ~se un traje to try on a suit.

probeta [pro'βeta] *nf* test tube.

problema [pro'βlema] *nm* problem.

procedente [proθe'ðente] *a* (*razonable*) reasonable; (*conforme a derecho*) proper, fitting; ~ de coming from, originating in.

proceder [proθe'ðer] *vi* (*avanzar*) to proceed; (*actuar*) to act; (*ser correcto*) to be right (and proper), be fitting; ~ de to come from, originate in // *nm* (*comportamiento*) behaviour, conduct; **procedimiento** *nm* procedure; (*proceso*) process; (*método*) means *pl*, method.

procesado, a [proθe'saðo, a] *nm/f* accused.

procesador [proθesa'ðor] *nm*: ~ de textos word processor.

procesar [proθe'sar] *vt* to try, put on trial.

procesión [proθe'sjon] *nf* procession.

proceso [pro'θeso] *nm* process; (*JUR*) trial; (*lapso*) course (of time).

proclamar [prokla'mar] *vt* to proclaim.

procreación [prokrea'θjon] *nf* procreation.

procrear [prokre'ar] *vt, vi* to procreate.

procurador, a [prokura'ðor, a] *nm/f* attorney.

procurar [proku'rar] *vt* (*intentar*) to try, endeavour; (*conseguir*) to get, obtain; (*asegurar*) to secure; (*producir*) to produce.

prodigio [pro'ðixjo] *nm* prodigy; (*milagro*) wonder, marvel; **~so, a** *a* prodigious, marvellous.

pródigo, a ['proðiγo, a] *a*: **hijo ~** prodigal son.

producción [proðuk'θjon] *nf* (*gen*) production; (*producto*) product; ~ **en serie** mass production.

producir [proðu'θir] *vt* to produce; (*causar*) to cause, bring about; **~se** *vr* (*cambio*) to come about; (*accidente*) to take place; (*problema etc*) to arise; (*hacerse*) to be produced, be made; (*estallar*) to break out.

productividad [proðuktiβi'ðað] *nf* productivity; **productivo, a** *a* productive; (*provechoso*) profitable.

producto [pro'ðukto] *nm* product; (*producción*) production.

productor, a [proðuk'tor, a] *a* productive, producing // *nm/f* producer.

proeza [pro'eθa] *nf* exploit, feat.

profanar [profa'nar] *vt* to desecrate, profane; **profano, a** *a* profane // *nm/f* layman/woman.

profecía [profe'θia] *nf* prophecy.

proferir [profe'rir] *vt* (*palabra*, *sonido*) to utter; (*injuria*) to hurl, let fly.

profesar [profe'sar] *vt* (*practicar*) to practise.

profesión [profe'sjon] *nf* profession; **profesional** *a* professional.

profesor, a [profe'sor, a] *nm/f* teacher; **~ado** *nm* teaching profession.

profeta [pro'feta] *nm/f* prophet; **profetizar** *vt, vi* to prophesy.

prófugo, a ['profuγo, a] *nm/f* fugitive; (*MIL: desertor*) deserter.

profundidad [profundi'ðað] *nf* depth; **profundizar** *vt* (*fig*) to go deeply into; **profundo, a** *a* deep; (*misterio*, *pensador*) profound.

profusión [profu'sjon] *nf* (*abundancia*) profusion; (*prodigalidad*) extravagance.

progenitor [proxeni'tor] *nm* ancestor; **~es** *nmpl* (*padres*) parents.

programa [pro'γrama] *nm* programme (*Brit*), program (*US*); **~ción** *nf* programming; **~dor, a** *nm/f* programmer; **programar** *vt* to program.

progresar |proɣre'sar| *vi* to progress, make progress; **progresista** *a, nm/f* progressive; **progresivo, a** *a* progressive; (*gradual*) gradual; (*continuo*) continuous; **progreso** *nm* progress.

prohibición |proißi'θjon| *nf* prohibition, ban.

prohibir |proi'ßir| *vt* to prohibit, ban, forbid; **se prohíbe fumar, prohibido fumar** no smoking.

prójimo, a |'proximo. a| *nm/f* fellow man; (*vecino*) neighbour.

proletariado |proleta'rjaðo| *nm* proletariat.

proletario, a |prole'tarjo. a| *a, nm/f* proletarian.

proliferación |prolifera'θjon| *nf* proliferation.

proliferar |prolife'rar| *vi* to proliferate; **prolífico, a** *a* prolific.

prolijo, a |pro'lixo. a| *a* long-winded, tedious.

prólogo |'proloɣo| *nm* prologue.

prolongación |prolonga'θjon| *nf* extension; **prolongado, a** *a* (*largo*) long; (*alargado*) lengthy.

prolongar |prolon'xar| *vt* to extend; (*reunión etc*) to prolong; (*calle, tubo*) to extend.

promedio |pro'meðjo| *nm* average; (*de distancia*) middle, mid-point.

promesa |pro'mesa| *nf* promise.

prometer |prome'ter| *vt* to promise // *vi* to show promise; **se** *vr* (*novios*) to get engaged; **prometido, a** *a* promised; engaged // *nm/f* fiancé/fiancée.

prominente |promi'nente| *a* prominent.

promiscuo, a |pro'miskwo. a| *a* promiscuous.

promoción |promo'θjon| *nf* promotion.

promotor |promo'tor| *nm* promoter; (*instigador*) instigator.

promover |promo'ßer| *vt* to promote; (*causar*) to cause; (*instigar*) to instigate, stir up.

promulgar |promul'xar| *vt* to promulgate; (*fig*) to proclaim.

pronombre |pro'nombre| *nm* pronoun.

pronosticar |pronosti'kar| *vt* to predict, foretell, forecast; **pronóstico** *nm* prediction, forecast; **pronóstico del tiempo** weather forecast.

pronto, a |'pronto. a| *a* (*rápido*) prompt, quick; (*preparado*) ready // *ad* quickly, promptly; (*en seguida*) at once, right away; (*dentro de poco*) soon; (*temprano*) early // *nm:* **tener ~s de enojo** to be quick-tempered; **al ~** at first; **de ~** suddenly; **por lo ~** meanwhile, for the present.

pronunciación |pronunθja'θjon| *nf* pronunciation.

pronunciar |pronun'θjar| *vt* to pronounce; (*discurso*) to make, deliver; **se** *vr* to revolt, rebel; (*declararse*) to declare o.s.

propagación |propaɣa'θjon| *nf* propagation.

propaganda |propa'ɣanda| *nf* (*política*) propaganda; (*comercial*) advertising.

propagar |propa'ɣar| *vt* to propagate.

propensión |propen'sjon| *nf* inclination, propensity; **propenso, a** *a* inclined to; **ser propenso a** to be inclined to, have a tendency to.

propiamente |propja'mente| *ad* properly; (*realmente*) really, exactly.

propicio, a |pro'piθjo. a| *a* favourable, propitious.

propiedad |propje'ðað| *nf* property; (*posesión*) possession, ownership; **~ particular** private property.

propietario, a |propje'tarjo. a| *nm/f* owner, proprietor.

propina |pro'pina| *nf* tip.

propio, a |'propjo. a| *a* own, of one's own; (*característico*) characteristic, typical; (*debido*) proper; (*mismo*) self-same, very; **el ~ ministro** the minister himself; **¿tienes casa propia?** have you a house of your own?

proponer |propo'ner| *vt* to propose, put forward; (*problema*) to pose; **se** *vr* to propose, intend.

proporción |propor'θjon| *nf* proportion; (*MAT*) ratio; **proporciones** *nfpl* dimensions; (*fig*) size *sg;* **proporcionado, a** *a* proportionate; (*regular*) medium, middling; (*justo*) just right; **proporcionar** *vt* (*dar*) to give, supply, provide.

proposición |proposi'θjon| *nf* proposition; (*propuesta*) proposal.

propósito |pro'posito| *nm* purpose; (*intento*) aim, intention // *ad:* **a ~** by the way, incidentally; (*a posta*) on purpose, deliberately; **a ~ de** about, with regard to.

propuesta *vb ver* **proponer** // |pro'pwesta| *nf* proposal.

propulsar |propul'sar| *vt* to drive, propel; (*fig*) to promote, encourage; **propulsión** *nf* propulsion; **propulsión a chorro** *o* **por reacción** jet propulsion.

prórroga |'prorroɣa| *nf* extension; (*JUR*) stay; (*COM*) deferment; (*DEPORTE*) extra time; **prorrogar** *vt* (*periodo*) to extend; (*decisión*) to defer, postpone.

prorrumpir |prorrum'pir| *vi* to burst forth, break out.

prosa |'prosa| *nf* prose.

proscripción |proscrip'θjon| *nf* prohibition, ban; (*destierro*) banishment; (*de un partido*) proscription.

proscrito, a |pro'skrito. a| *a* (*prohibido, desterrado*) banned.

prosecución |prosecu'θjon| *nf* continuation.

proseguir |prose'ɣir| *vt* to continue, carry on // *vi* to continue, go on.

prospección |prospek'θjon| *nf* exploration; (del oro) prospecting.

prospecto [pros'pekto] nm prospectus.

prosperar [prospe'rar] vi to prosper, thrive, flourish; **prosperidad** nf prosperity; (éxito) success; **próspero, a** a prosperous, flourishing; (que tiene éxito) successful.

prostíbulo [pros'tiβulo] nm brothel (Brit), house of prostitution (US).

prostitución [prostitu'θjon] nf prostitution.

prostituir [prosti'twir] vt to prostitute; ~**se** vr to prostitute o.s., become a prostitute.

prostituta [prosti'tuta] nf prostitute.

protagonista [protaɣo'nista] nm/f protagonist.

protagonizar [protaɣoni'θar] vt to take the chief rôle in.

protección [protek'θjon] nf protection.

protector, a [protek'tor, a] a protective, protecting // nm/f protector.

proteger [prote'xer] vt to protect; **protegido, a** nm/f protégé/protégée.

proteína [prote'ina] nf protein.

protesta [pro'testa] nf protest; (declaración) protestation.

protestante [protes'tante] a Protestant.

protestar [protes'tar] vt to protest, declare; (fe) to protest // vi to protest.

protocolo [proto'kolo] nm protocol.

prototipo [proto'tipo] nm prototype.

prov. abr (= provincia) prov.

provecho [pro'βetʃo] nm advantage, benefit; (FINANZAS) profit; ¡buen ~! bon appétit!; en ~ de to the benefit of; sacar ~ de to benefit from, profit by.

proveer [proβe'er] vt to provide, supply // vi: ~ a to provide for.

provenir [proβe'nir] vi: ~ de to come from, stem from.

proverbio [pro'βerβjo] nm proverb.

providencia [proβi'ðenθja] nf providence; (previsión) foresight.

provincia [pro'βinθja] nf province; ~**no, a** a provincial; (del campo) country cpd.

provisión [proβi'sjon] nf provision; (abastecimiento) provision, supply; (medida) measure, step.

provisional [proβisjo'nal] a provisional.

provocación [proβoka'θjon] nf provocation.

provocar [proβo'kar] vt to provoke; (alentar) to tempt, invite; (causar) to bring about, lead to; (promover) to promote; (estimular) to rouse, stimulate; ¿te provoca un café? (AM) would you like a coffee?; **provocativo, a** a provocative.

próximamente [proksima'mente] ad shortly, soon.

proximidad [proksimi'ðað] nf closeness, proximity; **próximo, a** a near, close; (vecino) neighbouring; (siguiente) next.

proyectar [projek'tar] vt (objeto) to hurl,

throw; (luz) to cast, shed; (CINE) to screen, show; (planear) to plan.

proyectil [projek'til] nm projectile, missile.

proyecto [pro'jekto] nm plan; (estimación de costo) detailed estimate.

proyector [projek'tor] nm (CINE) projector.

prudencia [pru'ðenθja] nf (sabiduría) wisdom; (cuidado) care; **prudente** a sensible, wise; (conductor) careful.

prueba etc vb ver **probar** // ['prweβa] nf proof; (ensayo) test, trial; (degustación) tasting, sampling; (de ropa) fitting; a ~ on trial; a ~ de proof against; a ~ de agua/fuego waterproof/fireproof; someter a ~ to put to the test.

prurito [pru'rito] nm itch; (de bebé) nappy (Brit) o diaper (US) rash.

psico... [siko] pref psycho...; ~**análisis** nm inv psychoanalysis; ~**logía** nf psychology; ~**lógico, a** a psychological; **psicólogo, a** nm/f psychologist; **psicópata** nm/f psychopath; ~**sis** nf inv psychosis.

psiquiatra [si'kjatra] nm/f psychiatrist; **psiquiátrico, a** a psychiatric.

psíquico, a ['sikiko, a] a psychic(al).

PSOE [pe'soe] nm abr = Partido Socialista Obrero Español.

pta(s) abr = **peseta(s)**.

pts abr = **pesetas**.

púa ['pua] nf sharp point; (BOT, ZOOL) prickle, spine; (para guitarra) plectrum (Brit), pick (US); **alambre de ~** barbed wire.

pubertad [puβer'tað] nf puberty.

publicación [puβlika'θjon] nf publication.

publicar [puβli'kar] vt (editar) to publish; (hacer público) to publicize; (divulgar) to make public, divulge.

publicidad [puβliθi'ðað] nf publicity; (COM: propaganda) advertising; **publicitario, a** a publicity cpd; advertising cpd.

público, a ['puβliko, a] a public // nm public; (TEATRO etc) audience.

puchero [pu'tʃero] nm (CULIN: guiso) stew; (: olla) cooking pot; **hacer ~s** to pout.

pude etc vb ver **poder**.

púdico, a ['puðiko, a] a modest.

pudiente [pu'ðjente] a (rico) wealthy, well-to-do.

pudiera etc vb ver **poder**.

pudor [pu'ðor] nm modesty.

pudrir [pu'ðrir] vt to rot; (fam) to upset, annoy; ~**se** vr to rot, decay.

pueblo ['pweβlo] nm people; (nación) nation; (aldea) village.

puedo etc vb ver **poder**.

puente ['pwente] nm bridge; ~ **aéreo** shuttle service; ~ **colgante** suspension bridge; **hacer ~** (fam) to take an extra day off work between 2 public holidays;

to take a long weekend.

puerco, a ['pwerko, a] *nm/f* pig/sow // *a* (*sucio*) dirty, filthy; (*obsceno*) disgusting; ~ **de mar** porpoise; ~ **marino** dolphin.

pueril [pwe'ril] *a* childish.

puerro ['pwerro] *nm* leek.

puerta ['pwerta] *nf* door; (*de jardín*) gate; (*portal*) doorway; (*fig*) gateway; (*portería*) goal; **a la ~** at the door; **a ~ cerrada** behind closed doors; ~ **giratoria** revolving door.

puertaventana [pwertaβen'tana] *nf* shutter.

puerto ['pwerto] *nm* port; (*paso*) pass; (*fig*) haven, refuge.

Puerto Rico [pwerto'riko] *nm* Puerto Rico; **puertorriqueño, a** *a, nm/f* Puerto Rican.

pues [pwes] *ad* (*entonces*) then; (*bueno*) well, well then; (*así que*) so // *conj* (*ya que*) since; ¡~! (*sí*) yes!, certainly!

puesto, a ['pwesto, a] *pp de* **poner** // *a* dressed // *nm* (*lugar, posición*) place; (*trabajo*) post, job; (*COM*) stall // *conj:* ~ **que** since, as // *nf* (*apuesta*) bet, stake; **puesta en marcha** starting; **puesta del sol** sunset.

púgil ['puxil] *nm* boxer.

pugna ['puxna] *nf* battle, conflict; ~**cidad** *nf* pugnacity, aggressiveness; **pugnar** *vi* (*luchar*) to struggle, fight; (*pelear*) to fight.

pujar [pu'xar] *vi* (*en subasta*) to bid; (*esforzarse*) to struggle, strain.

pulcro, a ['pulkro, a] *a* neat, tidy; (*bello*) exquisite.

pulga ['pulxa] *nf* flea.

pulgada [pul'xaða] *nf* inch.

pulgar [pul'xar] *nm* thumb.

pulir [pu'lir], **pulimentar** [pulimen'tar] *vt* to polish; (*alisar*) to smooth; (*fig*) to polish up, touch up.

pulmón [pul'mon] *nm* lung; **pulmonía** *nf* pneumonia.

pulpa ['pulpa] *nf* pulp; (*de fruta*) flesh, soft part.

pulpería [pulpe'ria] *nf* (*AM: tienda*) small grocery store.

púlpito ['pulpito] *nm* pulpit.

pulpo ['pulpo] *nm* octopus.

pulsación [pulsa'θjon] *nf* beat, pulsation; (*ANAT*) throb(bing).

pulsador [pulsa'ðor] *nm* button, push button.

pulsar [pul'sar] *vt* (*tecla*) to touch, tap; (*MUS*) to play; (*botón*) to press, push // *vi* to pulsate; (*latir*) to beat, throb; (*MED*): ~ **a uno** to take sb's pulse.

pulsera [pul'sera] *nf* bracelet.

pulso ['pulso] *nm* (*ANAT*) pulse; (: *muñeca*) wrist; (*fuerza*) strength; (*firmeza*) steadiness, steady hand; (*tacto*) tact, good sense.

pulverizador [pulβeriθa'ðor] *nm* spray, spray gun.

pulverizar [pulβeri'θar] *vt* to pulverize; (*líquido*) to spray.

pulla ['puʎa] *nf* cutting remark; (*expresión grosera*) obscene remark.

puna ['puna] *nf* (*AM MED*) mountain sickness.

pungir [pun'xir] *vt* to puncture, pierce; (*fig*) to cause suffering to.

punición [puni'θjon] *nf* punishment; **punitivo, a** *a* punitive.

punta ['punta] *nf* point, tip; (*extremidad*) end; (*fig*) touch, trace; **horas** ~**s** peak hours, rush hours; **sacar** ~ **a** to sharpen; **estar de** ~ to be edgy.

puntada [pun'taða] *nf* (*COSTURA*) stitch.

puntal [pun'tal] *nm* prop, support.

puntapié [punta'pje] *nm* kick.

puntear [punte'ar] *vt* to tick, mark.

puntería [punte'ria] *nf* (*de arma*) aim, aiming; (*destreza*) marksmanship.

puntero, a [pun'tero, a] *a* leading // *nm* (*palo*) pointer.

puntiagudo, a [puntja'xuðo, a] *a* sharp, pointed.

puntilla [pun'tiʎa] *nf* (*encaje*) lace edging *o* trim; (**andar**) **de** ~**s** (to walk) on tiptoe.

punto ['punto] *nm* (*gen*) point; (*señal diminuta*) spot, dot; (*COSTURA, MED*) stitch; (*lugar*) spot, place; (*momento*) point, moment; **a** ~ ready; **estar a** ~ **de** to be on the point of *o* about to; **en** ~ on the dot; ~ **muerto** dead centre; (*AUTO*) neutral (gear); ~ **final** full stop (*Brit*), period (*US*); ~ **y coma** semicolon; ~ **de interrogación** question mark; **hacer** ~ (*tejer*) to knit.

puntuación [puntwa'θjon] *nf* punctuation; (*puntos: en examen*) mark(s) (*pl*); (: *DEPORTE*) score.

puntual [pun'twal] *a* (*a tiempo*) punctual; (*exacto*) exact, accurate; (*seguro*) reliable; ~**idad** *nf* punctuality; exactness, accuracy; reliability; ~**izar** *vt* to fix, specify.

punzante [pun'θante] *a* (*dolor*) shooting, sharp; (*herramienta*) sharp; **punzar** *vt* to prick, pierce // *vi* to shoot, stab.

puñado [pu'ɲaðo] *nm* handful.

puñal [pu'ɲal] *nm* dagger; ~**ada** *nf* stab.

puñetazo [puɲe'taθo] *nm* punch.

puño ['puɲo] *nm* (*ANAT*) fist; (*cantidad*) fistful, handful; (*COSTURA*) cuff; (*de herramienta*) handle.

pupila [pu'pila] *nf* pupil.

pupitre [pu'pitre] *nm* desk.

puré [pu're] *nm* puree; (*sopa*) (thick) soup; ~ **de patatas** mashed potatoes.

pureza [pu'reθa] *nf* purity.

purga ['purxa] *nf* purge; **purgante** *a, nm* purgative; **purgar** *vt* to purge.

purgatorio [purxa'torjo] *nm* purgatory.

purificar [purifi'kar] *vt* to purify; (*refinar*) to refine.

puritano, a [puri'tano, a] *a (actitud)* puritanical; *(iglesia, tradición)* puritan // *nm/f* puritan.

puro, a ['puro, a] *a* pure; *(cielo)* clear; *(verdad)* simple, plain // *ad:* **de ~ cansado** out of sheer tiredness // *nm* cigar.

púrpura ['purpura] *nf* purple; **purpúreo, a** *a* purple.

pus [pus] *nm* pus.

puse, pusiera *etc vb ver* **poner.**

pústula ['pustula] *nf* pimple, sore.

puta ['puta] *nf* whore, prostitute.

putrefacción [putrefak'θjon] *nf* rotting, putrefaction.

pútrido, a ['putriðo, a] *a* rotten.

PVP *abr* (*Esp:* = *precio venta al público*) RRP.

Q

q.e.p.d. *abr* (= *que en paz descanse*) R.I.P.

que [ke] ♦ *conj* **1** *(con oración subordinada: muchas veces no se traduce)* that; **dijo ~ vendría** he said (that) he would come; **espero ~ lo encuentres** I hope (that) you find it; *ver tb* **el**

2 *(en oración independiente):* **¡~ entre!** send him in; **¡que se mejore tu padre!** I hope your father gets better

3 *(enfático):* **¿me quieres? - ¡~ sí!** do you love me? - of course!

4 *(consecutivo: muchas veces no se traduce)* that; **es tan grande ~ no lo puedo levantar** it's so big (that) I can't lift it

5 *(comparaciones)* than; **yo ~ tú/él** if I were you/him; *ver tb* **más, menos, mismo**

6 *(valor disyuntivo):* **~ le guste o no** whether he likes it or not; **~ venga o ~ no venga** whether he comes or not

7 *(porque):* **no puedo, ~ tengo ~ quedarme en casa** I can't, I've got to stay in

♦ *pron* **1** *(cosa)* that, which; (+ *prep*) which; **el sombrero ~ te compraste** the hat (that *o* which) you bought; **la cama en ~ dormí** the bed (that *o* which) I slept in

2 *(persona: suj)* that, who; (: *objeto*) that, whom; **el amigo ~ me acompañó al museo** the friend that *o* who went to the museum with me; **la chica que invité** the girl (that *o* whom) I invited

qué [ke] *a* what?, which? // *pron* what?; **¡~ divertido!** how funny!; **¿~ edad tienes?** how old are you?; **¿de ~ me hablas?** what are you saying to me?; **¿~ tal?** how are you?, how are things?; **¿~ hay (de nuevo)?** what's new?

quebrada [ke'βraða] *nf ver* **quebrado.**

quebradizo, a [keβra'ðiθo, a] *a* fragile;

(persona) frail.

quebrado, a [ke'βraðo, a] *a (roto)* broken // *nm/f* bankrupt // *nm (MAT)* fraction // *nf* ravine.

quebradura [keβra'ðura] *nf (fisura)* fissure; *(GEO)* gorge; *(MED)* rupture.

quebrantar [keβran'tar] *vt (infringir)* to violate, transgress; **~se** *vr (persona)* to fail in health.

quebranto [ke'βranto] *nm* damage, harm; *(decaimiento)* exhaustion; *(dolor)* grief, pain.

quebrar [ke'βrar] *vt* to break, smash // *vi* to go bankrupt; **~se** *vr* to break, get broken; *(MED)* to be ruptured.

quedar [ke'ðar] *vi* to stay, remain; *(encontrarse: sitio)* to be; *(restar)* to remain, be left; **~se** *vr* to remain, stay (behind); **~se (con) algo** to keep sth; **~ en** *(acordar)* to agree on/to; **~ en nada** to come to nothing; **~ por hacer** to be still to be done; **~ ciego/mudo** to be left blind/dumb; **no te queda bien ese vestido** that dress doesn't suit you; **eso queda muy lejos** that's a long way (away); **quedamos a las seis** we agreed to meet at six.

quedo, a ['keðo, a] *a* still // *ad* softly, gently.

quehacer [kea'θer] *nm* task, job; **~es** *(domésticos)* *nmpl* household chores.

queja ['kexa] *nf* complaint; **quejarse** *vr (enfermo)* to moan, groan; *(protestar)* to complain; **quejarse de que** to complain (about the fact) that; **quejido** *nm* moan; **quejoso, a** *a* complaining.

quemado, a [ke'maðo, a] *a* burnt.

quemadura [kema'ðura] *nf* burn, scald.

quemar [ke'mar] *vt* to burn; *(fig: malgastar)* to burn up, squander // *vi* to be burning hot; **~se** *vr (consumirse)* to burn (up); *(del sol)* to get sunburnt.

quemarropa [kema'rropa]: **a ~** *ad* point-blank.

quemazón [kema'θon] *nf* burn; *(calor)* intense heat; *(sensación)* itch.

quepo *etc vb ver* **caber.**

querella [ke're ʎa] *nf (JUR)* charge; *(disputa)* dispute.

querer [ke'rer] *vt* **1** *(desear)* to want; **quiero más dinero** I want more money; **quisiera o querría un té** I'd like a tea; **sin ~** unintentionally; **quiero ayudar/que vayas** I want to help/you to go

2 *(preguntas: para pedir algo):* **¿quiere abrir la ventana?** could you open the window?; **¿quieres echarme una mano?** can you give me a hand?

3 *(amar)* to love; *(tener cariño a)* to be fond of; **quiere mucho a sus hijos** he's very fond of his children

4 *(requerir):* **esta planta quiere más luz** this plant needs more light

5: le pedí que me dejara ir pero no quiso I asked him to let me go but he refused.

querido, a [ke'riðo, a] *a* dear // *nm/f* darling; (*amante*) lover.

quesería [kese'ria] *nf* dairy; (*fábrica*) cheese factory.

queso ['keso] *nm* cheese; ~ **crema** cream cheese.

quicio ['kiθjo] *nm* hinge; **sacar a uno de** ~ to get on sb's nerves.

quiebra ['kjeβra] *nf* break, split; (*COM*) bankruptcy; (*ECON*) slump.

quiebro ['kjeβro] *nm* (*del cuerpo*) swerve.

quien [kjen] *pron* who; **hay ~ piensa que** there are those who think that; **no hay ~ lo haga** no-one will do it.

quién [kjen] *pron* who, whom; ¿~ **es?** who's there?

quienquiera [kjen'kjera] (*pl* **quienesquiera**) *pron* whoever.

quiero *etc vb ver* **querer**.

quieto, a ['kjeto, a] *a* still; (*carácter*) placid; **quietud** *nf* stillness.

quijada [ki'xaða] *nf* jaw, jawbone.

quilate [ki'late] *nm* carat.

quilla ['kiʎa] *nf* keel.

quimera [ki'mera] *nf* chimera; **quimérico, a** *a* fantastic.

químico, a ['kimiko, a] *a* chemical // *nm/f* chemist // *nf* chemistry.

quincalla [kin'kaʎa] *nf* hardware, ironmongery (*Brit*).

quince ['kinθe] *num* fifteen; ~ **días** a fortnight; **~añero, a** *nm/f* teenager; **~na** *nf* fortnight; (*pago*) fortnightly pay; **~nal** *a* fortnightly.

quiniela [ki'njela] *nf* football pools *pl*; **~s** *nfpl* pools coupon *sg*.

quinientos, as [ki'njentos, as] *a, num* five hundred.

quinina [ki'nina] *nf* quinine.

quinqui ['kinki] *nm* delinquent.

quinto, a ['kinto, a] *a* fifth // *nf* country house; (*MIL*) call-up, draft.

quiosco ['kjosko] *nm* (*de música*) bandstand; (*de periódicos*) news stand.

quirúrgico, a [ki'rurxiko, a] *a* surgical.

quise, quisiera *etc vb ver* **querer**.

quisquilloso, a [kiski'ʎoso, a] *a* (*susceptible*) touchy; (*meticuloso*) pernickety.

quiste ['kiste] *nm* cyst.

quitaesmalte [kitaes'malte] *nm* nailpolish remover.

quitamanchas [kita'mantʃas] *nm inv* stain remover.

quitanieves [kita'njeβes] *nm inv* snowplough (*Brit*), snowplow (*US*).

quitar [ki'tar] *vt* to remove, take away; (*ropa*) to take off; (*dolor*) to relieve; **¡quita de ahí!** get away!; **~se** *vr* to withdraw; (*ropa*) to take off; **se quitó el sombrero** he took off his hat.

quitasol [kita'sol] *nm* sunshade (*Brit*), parasol.

quite ['kite] *nm* (*esgrima*) parry; (*evasión*) dodge.

Quito ['kito] *n* Quito.

quizá(s) [ki'θa(s)] *ad* perhaps, maybe.

R

rábano ['raβano] *nm* radish; **me importa un** ~ I don't give a damn.

rabia ['raβja] *nf* (*MED*) rabies *sg*; (*fig: ira*) fury, rage; **rabiar** *vi* to have rabies; to rage, be furious; **rabiar por algo** to long for sth.

rabieta [ra'βjeta] *nf* tantrum, fit of temper.

rabino [ra'βino] *nm* rabbi.

rabioso, a [ra'βjoso, a] *a* rabid; (*fig*) furious.

rabo ['raβo] *nm* tail.

racial [ra'θjal] *a* racial, race *cpd*.

racimo [ra'θimo] *nm* bunch.

raciocinio [raθjo'θinjo] *nm* reason.

ración [ra'θjon] *nf* portion; **raciones** *nfpl* rations.

racional [raθjo'nal] *a* (*razonable*) reasonable; (*lógico*) rational; **~izar** *vt* to rationalize.

racionar [raθjo'nar] *vt* to ration (out).

racismo [ra'θismo] *nm* racialism, racism; **racista** *a, nm/f* racist.

racha ['ratʃa] *nf* gust of wind: **buena/mala** ~ (*fig*) spell of good/bad luck.

radar [ra'ðar] *nm* radar.

radiactivo, a [raðiak'tiβo, a] *a* = **radioactivo**.

radiador [raðja'ðor] *nm* radiator.

radiante [ra'ðjante] *a* radiant.

radical [raði'kal] *a, nm/f* radical.

radicar [raði'kar] *vi* to take root; ~ **en** to lie *o* consist in; **~se** *vr* to establish o.s., put down (one's) roots.

radio ['raðjo] *nf* radio; (*aparato*) radio (set) // *nm* (*MAT*) radius; (*QUIMICA*) radium; **~activo, a** *a* radioactive; **~difusión** *nf* broadcasting; **~emisora** *nf* transmitter, radio station; **~escucha** **radioyente** *nm/f* listener; **~grafía** *nf* X-ray; **~grafiar** *vt* to X-ray; **~terapia** *nf* radiotherapy.

raer [ra'er] *vt* to scrape (off).

ráfaga ['rafaxa] *nf* gust; (*de luz*) flash; (*de tiros*) burst.

raído, a [ra'iðo, a] *a* (*ropa*) threadbare.

raigambre [rai'vambre] *nf* (*BOT*) roots *pl*; (*fig*) tradition.

raíz [ra'iθ] *nf* root; ~ **cuadrada** square root; **a** ~ **de** as a result of.

raja ['raxa] *nf* (*de melón etc*) slice; (*grieta*) crack; **rajar** *vt* to split; (*fam*) to slash; **rajarse** *vr* to split, crack; **rajarse de** to back out of.

rajatabla [raxa'taβla]: **a** ~ *ad* (*estrictamente*) strictly, to the letter.

ralo, a ['ralo, a] *a* thin, sparse.

rallado, a |ra'ʎaðo. a| *a* grated; **rallador** *nm* grater.

rallar |ra'ʎar| *vt* to grate.

RAM |ram| *nf · abr* (= *memoria de acceso aleatorio*) RAM.

rama |'rama| *nf* branch; **~je** *nm* branches *pl*, foliage; **ramal** *nm* (*de cuerda*) strand; (*FERRO*) branch line (*Brit*); (*AUTO*) branch (road) (*Brit*).

rambla |'rambla| *nf* (*avenida*) avenue.

ramera |ra'mera| *nf* whore.

ramificación |ramifika'θjon| *nf* ramification.

ramificarse |ramifi'karse| *vr* to branch out.

ramillete |rami'ʎete| *nm* bouquet.

ramo |'ramo| *nm* branch; (*sección*) department, section.

ramplón, ona |ram'plon. ona| *a* uncouth, coarse.

rana |'rana| *nf* frog; salto de ~ leapfrog.

rancio, a |'ranθjo. a| *a* (*comestibles*) rancid; (*vino*) aged, mellow; (*fig*) ancient.

ranchero |ran'tʃero| *nm* (*AM*) rancher; smallholder.

rancho |'rantʃo| *nm* grub (*fam*); (*AM*: *grande*) ranch; (: *pequeño*) small farm.

rango |'rango| *nm* rank, standing.

ranura |ra'nura| *nf* groove; (*de teléfono etc*) slot.

rapar |ra'par| *vt* to shave; (*los cabellos*) to crop.

rapaz |ra'paθ| *a* (*ZOOL*) predatory // *nm/f* (*f*: **rapaza**) young boy/girl.

rape |'rape| *nm* quick shave; (*pez*) angler (fish); al ~ cropped.

rapé |ra'pe| *nm* snuff.

rapidez |rapi'ðeθ| *nf* speed, rapidity; **rápido, a** *a* fast, quick // *ad* quickly // *nm* (*FERRO*) express; **rápidos** *nmpl* rapids.

rapiña |ra'piɲa| *nm* robbery; ave de ~ bird of prey.

raptar |rap'tar| *vt* to kidnap; **rapto** *nm* kidnapping; (*impulso*) sudden impulse; (*éxtasis*) ecstasy, rapture.

raqueta |ra'keta| *nf* racquet.

raquítico, a |ra'kitiko. a| *a* stunted; (*fig*) poor, inadequate; **raquitismo** *nm* rickets *sg*.

rareza |ra'reθa| *nf* rarity; (*fig*) eccentricity.

raro, a |'raro. a| *a* (*poco común*) rare; (*extraño*) odd, strange; (*excepcional*) remarkable.

ras |ras| *nm*: a ~ de level with; a ~ de tierra at ground level.

rasar |ra'sar| *vt* (*igualar*) to level.

rascacielos |raska'θjelos| *nm inv* skyscraper.

rascar |ras'kar| *vt* (*con las uñas etc*) to scratch; (*raspar*) to scrape; **~se** *vr* to scratch (o.s.).

rasgar |ras'xar| *vt* to tear, rip (up).

rasgo |'rasxo| *nm* (*con pluma*) stroke; **~s** *nmpl* features, characteristics; a grandes ~s in outline, broadly.

rasguñar |rasxu'ɲar| *vt* to scratch; **rasguño** *nm* scratch.

raso, a |'raso. a| *a* (*liso*) flat, level; (*a baja altura*) very low // *nm* satin; cielo ~ clear sky.

raspadura |raspa'ðura| *nf* (*acto*) scrape, scraping; (*marca*) scratch; **~s** *nfpl* scrapings.

raspar |ras'par| *vt* to scrape; (*arañar*) to scratch; (*limar*) to file.

rastra |'rastra| *nf* (*AGR*) rake; a ~s by dragging; (*fig*) unwillingly.

rastreador |rastrea'ðor| *nm* tracker; ~ de minas minesweeper.

rastrear |rastre'ar| *vt* (*seguir*) to track.

rastrero, a |ras'trero. a| *a* (*BOT, ZOOL*) creeping; (*fig*) despicable, mean.

rastrillar |rastri'ʎar| *vt* to rake; **rastrillo** *nm* rake.

rastro |'rastro| *nm* (*AGR*) rake; (*pista*) track, trail; (*vestigio*) trace; el R~ the Madrid fleamarket.

rastrojo |ras'troxo| *nm* stubble.

rasurador |rasura'ðor| *nm*, **rasuradora** |rasura'ðora| *nf* (*AM*) electric shaver.

rasurarse |rasu'rarse| *vr* to shave.

rata |'rata| *nf* rat.

ratear |rate'ar| *vt* (*robar*) to steal.

ratería |rate'ria| *nf* petty theft.

ratero, a |ra'tero. a| *a* light-fingered // *nm/f* (*carterista*) pickpocket; (*AM*: *de casas*) burglar.

ratificar |ratifi'kar| *vt* to ratify.

rato |'rato| *nm* while, short time; a ~s from time to time; hay para ~ there's still a long way to go; al poco ~ soon afterwards; pasar el ~ to kill time; pasar un buen/mal ~ to have a good/ rough time.

ratón |ra'ton| *nm* mouse; **ratonera** *nf* mousetrap.

raudal |rau'ðal| *nm* torrent; a ~es in abundance.

raya |'raja| *nf* line; (*marca*) scratch; (*en tela*) stripe; (*de pelo*) parting; (*límite*) boundary; (*pez*) ray; (*puntuación*) hyphen; a ~s striped; pasarse de la ~ to go too far; tener a ~ to keep in check; **rayar** *vt* to line; to scratch; (*subrayar*) to underline // *vi*: rayar en *o* con to border on.

rayo |'rajo| *nm* (*del sol*) ray, beam; (*de luz*) shaft; (*en una tormenta*) (flash of) lightning; ~s X X-rays.

rayón |ra'jon| *nm* rayon.

raza |'raθa| *nf* race; ~ humana human race.

razón |ra'θon| *nf* reason; (*justicia*) right, justice; (*razonamiento*) reasoning; (*motivo*) reason, motive; (*MAT*) ratio; a ~ de 10 cada día at the rate of 10 a day;

'~: 'inquiries to ...'; **en ~ de** with regard to; **dar ~ a uno** to agree that sb is right; **tener ~ to** be right; **~ directa/inversa** direct/inverse proportion; **~ de ser** raison d'être; **razonable** *a* reasonable; *(justo, moderado)* fair; **razonamiento** *nm (juicio)* judgement; *(argumento)* reasoning; **razonar** *vt* to reason, argue // *vi* to reason, argue.

reacción [reak'θjon] *nf* reaction; **avión a ~ jet** plane; **~ en cadena** chain reaction; **reaccionar** *vi* to react; **reaccionario, a** *a* reactionary.

reacio, a [re'aθjo, a] *a* stubborn.

reactor [reak'tor] *nm* reactor.

readaptación [reaðapta'θjon] *nf:* **~ profesional** industrial retraining.

reajuste [rea'xuste] *nm* readjustment.

real [re'al] *a* real; *(del rey, fig)* royal.

realce [re'alθe] *nm (TEC)* embossing; *(lustre, fig)* splendour; *(ARTE)* highlight; **poner de ~** to emphasize.

realidad [reali'ðað] *nf* reality, fact; *(verdad)* truth.

realista [rea'lista] *nm/f* realist.

realización [realiθa'θjon] *nf* fulfilment; *(COM)* selling up *(Brit)*, conversion into money *(US)*.

realizador, a [realiθa'ðor, a] *nm/f (TV etc)* producer.

realizar [reali'θar] *vt (objetivo)* to achieve; *(plan)* to carry out; *(viaje)* to make, undertake; *(COM)* to sell up *(Brit)*, convert into money *(US)*; **~se** *vr* to come about, come true.

realmente [real'mente] *ad* really, actually.

realquilar [realki'lar] *vt (subarrendar)* to sublet.

realzar [real'θar] *vt (TEC)* to raise; *(embellecer)* to enhance; *(acentuar)* to highlight.

reanimar [reani'mar] *vt* to revive; *(alentar)* to encourage; **~se** *vr* to revive.

reanudar [reanu'ðar] *vt (renovar)* to renew; *(historia, viaje)* to resume.

reaparición [reapari'θjon] *nf* reappearance.

rearme [re'arme] *nm* rearmament.

rebaja [re'βaxa] *nf (COM)* reduction; *(menoscabo)* lessening; **~s** *nfpl (COM)* sale; **rebajar** *vt (bajar)* to lower; *(reducir)* to reduce; *(disminuir)* to lessen; *(humillar)* to humble.

rebanada [reβa'naða] *nf* slice.

rebaño [re'βaɲo] *nm* herd; *(de ovejas)* flock.

rebasar [reβa'sar] *vt (tb: ~ de)* to exceed.

rebatir [reβa'tir] *vt* to refute.

rebeca [re'βeka] *nf* cardigan.

rebelarse [reβe'larse] *vr* to rebel, revolt.

rebelde [re'βelde] *a* rebellious; *(niño)* unruly // *nm/f* rebel; **rebeldía** *nf* rebelliousness; *(desobediencia)* disobedience.

rebelión [reβe'ljon] *nf* rebellion.

reblandecer [reβlande'θer] *vt* to soften.

rebosante [reβo'sante] *a* overflowing.

rebosar [reβo'sar] *vi (líquido, recipiente)* to overflow; *(abundar)* to abound, be plentiful.

rebotar [reβo'tar] *vt* to bounce; *(rechazar)* to repel // *vi (pelota)* to bounce; *(bala)* to ricochet; **rebote** *nm* rebound; **de rebote** on the rebound.

rebozado, a [reβo'θaðo, a] *a* fried in batter o breadcrumbs.

rebozar [reβo'θar] *vt* to wrap up; *(CULIN)* to fry in batter o breadcrumbs.

rebuscado, a [reβus'kaðo, a] *a (amanerado)* affected; *(palabra)* recherché; *(idea)* far-fetched.

rebuznar [reβuθ'nar] *vi* to bray.

recabar [reka'βar] *vt (obtener)* to manage to get.

recado [re'kaðo] *nm* message; **tomar un ~** *(TEL)* to take a message.

recaer [reka'er] *vi* to relapse; **~ en** to fall to o on; *(criminal etc)* to fall back into, relapse into; **recaída** *nf* relapse.

recalcar [rekal'kar] *vt (fig)* to stress, emphasize.

recalcitrante [rekalθi'trante] *a* recalcitrant.

recalentar [rekalen'tar] *vt (volver a calentar)* to reheat; *(calentar demasiado)* to overheat.

recámara [re'kamara] *nf (AM)* bedroom.

recambio [re'kambjo] *nm* spare; *(de pluma)* refill.

recapacitar [rekapaθi'tar] *vi* to reflect.

recargado, a [rekar'xaðo, a] *a* overloaded.

recargar [rekar'xar] *vt* to overload; *(batería)* to recharge; **recargo** *nm* surcharge; *(aumento)* increase.

recatado, a [reka'taðo, a] *a (modesto)* modest, demure; *(prudente)* cautious.

recato [re'kato] *nm (modestia)* modesty, demureness; *(cautela)* caution.

recaudación [rekauða'θjon] *nf (acción)* collection; *(cantidad)* takings *pl*; *(en deporte)* gate; **recaudador, a** *nm/f* tax collector.

recelar [reθe'lar] *vt:* **~ que** *(sospechar)* to suspect that; *(temer)* to fear that // *vi:* **~ de** to distrust; **recelo** *nm* distrust, suspicion; **receloso, a** *a* distrustful, suspicious.

recepción [reθep'θjon] *nf* reception; **recepcionista** *nm/f* receptionist.

receptáculo [reθep'takulo] *nm* receptacle.

receptivo, a [reθep'tiβo, a] *a* receptive.

receptor, a [reθep'tor, a] *nm/f* recipient // *nm (TEL)* receiver.

recesión [reθe'sjon] *nf (COM)* recession.

receta [re'θeta] *nf (CULIN)* recipe; *(MED)* prescription.

recibidor, a [reθiβi'ðor, a] *nm* entrance

hall.

recibimiento [reθiβi'mjento] *nm* reception, welcome.

recibir [reθi'βir] *vt* to receive; (*dar la bienvenida*) to welcome // *vi* to entertain; ~se *vr*: ~se de (*AM*) to qualify as; **recibo** *nm* receipt.

recién [re'θjen] *ad* recently, newly; los ~ casados the newly-weds; el ~ llegado the newcomer; el ~ nacido the newborn child.

reciente [re'θjente] *a* recent; (*fresco*) fresh; ~mente *ad* recently.

recinto [re'θinto] *nm* enclosure; (*área*) area, place.

recio, a ['reθjo, a] *a* strong, tough; (*voz*) loud // *ad* hard; loud(ly).

recipiente [reθi'pjente] *nm* receptacle.

reciprocidad [reθiproθi'ðað] *nf* reciprocity; **recíproco, a** *a* reciprocal.

recital [reθi'tal] *nm* (*MUS*) recital; (*LITERATURA*) reading.

recitar [reθi'tar] *vt* to recite.

reclamación [reklama'θjon] *nf* claim, demand; (*queja*) complaint.

reclamar [rekla'mar] *vt* to claim, demand // *vi*: ~ contra to complain about; ~ a uno en justicia to take sb to court; **reclamo** *nm* (*anuncio*) advertisement; (*tentación*) attraction.

reclinar [rekli'nar] *vt* to recline, lean; ~se *vr* to lean back.

recluir [reklu'ir] *vt* to intern, confine.

reclusión [reklu'sjon] *nf* (*prisión*) prison; (*refugio*) seclusion; ~ perpetua life imprisonment.

recluta [re'kluta] *nm/f* recruit // *nf* recruitment.

reclutamiento [rekluta'mjento] *nm* recruitment.

recobrar [reko'βrar] *vt* (*salud*) to recover; (*rescatar*) to get back; ~se *vr* to recover.

recodo [re'koðo] *nm* (*de río, camino*) bend.

recoger [reko'xer] *vt* to collect; (*AGR*) to harvest; (*levantar*) to pick up; (*juntar*) to gather; (*pasar a buscar*) to come for, get; (*dar asilo*) to give shelter to; (*faldas*) to gather up; (*pelo*) to put up; ~se *vr* (*retirarse*) to retire; **recogido, a** *a* (*lugar*) quiet, secluded; (*pequeño*) small // *nf* (*CORREOS*) collection; (*AGR*) harvest.

recolección [rekolek'θjon] *nf* (*AGR*) harvesting; (*colecta*) collection.

recomendación [rekomenda'θjon] *nf* (*sugerencia*) suggestion, recommendation; (*referencia*) reference.

recomendar [rekomen'dar] *vt* to suggest, recommend; (*confiar*) to entrust.

recompensa [rekom'pensa] *nf* reward, recompense; **recompensar** *vt* to reward, recompense.

recomponer [rekompo'ner] *vt* to mend.

reconciliación [rekonθilja'θjon] *nf* reconciliation.

reconciliar [rekonθi'ljar] *vt* to reconcile; ~se *vr* to become reconciled.

recóndito, a [re'kondito, a] *a* (*lugar*) hidden, secret.

reconfortar [rekonfor'tar] *vt* to comfort.

reconocer [rekono'θer] *vt* to recognize; (*registrar*) to search; (*MED*) to examine; **reconocido, a** *a* recognized; (*agradecido*) grateful; **reconocimiento** *nm* recognition; search; examination; gratitude; (*confesión*) admission.

reconquista [rekon'kista] *nf* reconquest; la R~ the Reconquest (of Spain).

reconstituyente [rekonstitu'jente] *nm* tonic.

reconstruir [rekonstru'ir] *vt* to reconstruct.

reconversión [rekonβer'sjon] *nf*: ~ industrial industrial rationalization.

recopilación [rekopila'θjon] *nf* (*resumen*) summary; (*compilación*) compilation; **recopilar** *vt* to compile.

récord ['rekorð] *a inv, nm* record.

recordar [rekor'ðar] *vt* (*acordarse de*) to remember; (*acordar a otro*) to remind // *vi* to remember.

recorrer [reko'rrer] *vt* (*país*) to cross, travel through; (*distancia*) to cover; (*registrar*) to search; (*repasar*) to look over; **recorrido** *nm* run, journey; tren de largo recorrido main-line train.

recortado, a [rekor'taðo, a] *a* uneven, irregular.

recortar [rekor'tar] *vt* to cut out; **recorte** *nm* (*acción, de prensa*) cutting; (*de telas, chapas*) trimming.

recostado, a [rekos'taðo, a] *a* leaning; estar ~ to be lying down.

recostar [rekos'tar] *vt* to lean; ~se *vr* to lie down.

recoveco [reko'βeko] *nm* (*de camino, río etc*) bend; (*en casa*) cubbyhole.

recreación [rekrea'θjon] *nf* recreation.

recrear [rekre'ar] *vt* (*entretener*) to entertain; (*volver a crear*) to recreate; **recreativo, a** *a* recreational; **recreo** *nm* recreation; (*ESCOL*) break, playtime.

recriminar [rekrimi'nar] *vt* to reproach // *vi* to recriminate; ~se *vr* to reproach each other.

recrudecer [rekruðe'θer] *vt, vi*, **recrudecerse** *vr* to worsen.

recrudecimiento [rekruðeθi'mjento] *nm* upsurge.

recta ['rekta] *nf ver* **recto**.

rectángulo, a [rek'tangulo, a] *a* rectangular // *nm* rectangle.

rectificar [rektifi'kar] *vt* to rectify; (*volverse recto*) to straighten // *vi* to correct o.s.

rectitud [rekti'tuð] *nf* straightness; (*fig*) rectitude.

recto, a ['rekto, a] *a* straight; (*persona*)

honest, upright // nm rectum // nf straight line.
rector, a [rek'tor, a] a governing.
recua ['rekwa] nf mule train.
recuadro [re'kwaðro] nm box; (TIPO-GRAFIA) inset.
recuento [re'kwento] nm inventory; **hacer el ~ de** to count o reckon up.
recuerdo [re'kwerðo] nm souvenir; ~s nmpl memories; ¡~s a tu madre! give my regards to your mother!
recular [reku'lar] vi to back down.
recuperable [rekupe'raßle] a recoverable.
recuperación [rekupera'θjon] nf recovery.
recuperar [rekupe'rar] vt to recover; (tiempo) to make up; ~se vr to recuperate.
recurrir [reku'rrir] vi (JUR) to appeal; ~ a to resort to; (persona) to turn to; **recurso** nm resort; (medios) means pl, resources pl; (JUR) appeal.
recusar [reku'sar] vt to reject, refuse.
rechazar [retʃa'θar] vt to repel, drive back; (idea) to reject; (oferta) to turn down.
rechazo [re'tʃaθo] nm (de fusil) recoil; (rebote) rebound; (negación) rebuff.
rechifla [re'tʃifla] nf hissing, booing; (fig) derision.
rechiflar [retʃi'flar] vt to hiss, boo.
rechinar [retʃi'nar] vi to creak; (dientes) to grind.
rechistar [retʃis'tar] vi: sin ~ without a murmur.
rechoncho, a [re'tʃontʃo, a] a (fam) thickset (Brit), heavy-set (US).
red [reð] nf net, mesh; (FERRO etc) network; (trampa) trap.
redacción [reðak'θjon] nf (acción) editing; (personal) editorial staff; (ESCOL) essay, composition.
redactar [reðak'tar] vt to draw up, draft; (periódico) to edit.
redactor, a [reðak'tor, a] nm/f editor.
redada [re'ðaða] nf: ~ policial police raid, round-up.
rededor [reðe'ðor] nm: al o en ~ around, round about.
redención [reðen'θjon] nf redemption; **redentor, a** a redeeming.
redescubrir [reðesku'ßrir] vt to rediscover.
redicho, a [re'ðitʃo, a] a affected.
redil [re'ðil] nm sheepfold.
redimir [reði'mir] vt to redeem.
rédito ['reðito] nm interest, yield.
redoblar [reðo'ßlar] vt to redouble // vi (tambor) to play a roll on the drums.
redomado, a [reðo'maðo, a] a (astuto) sly, crafty; (perfecto) utter.
redonda [re'ðonda] nf ver **redondo**.
redondear [reðonde'ar] vt to round, round off.

redondel [reðon'del] nm (círculo) circle; (TAUR) bullring, arena; (AUTO) roundabout.
redondo, a [re'ðondo, a] a (circular) round; (completo) complete // nf: **a la redonda** around, round about.
reducción [reðuk'θjon] nf reduction.
reducido, a [reðu'θiðo, a] a reduced; (limitado) limited; (pequeño) small.
reducir [reðu'θir] vt to reduce; to limit; ~se vr to diminish.
redundancia [reðun'danθja] nf redundancy.
reembolsar [re(e)mbol'sar] vt (persona) to reimburse; (dinero) to repay, pay back; (depósito) to refund; **reembolso** nm reimbursement; refund.
reemplazar [re(e)mpla'θar] vt to replace; **reemplazo** nm replacement; de reemplazo (MIL) reserve.
referencia [refe'renθja] nf reference; con ~ a with reference to.
referéndum [refe'rendum] (pl ~s) nm referendum.
referente [refe'rente] a: ~ a concerning, relating to.
referir [refe'rir] vt (contar) to tell, recount; (relacionar) to refer, relate; ~se vr: ~se a to refer to.
refilón [refi'lon]: de ~ ad obliquely.
refinado, a [refi'naðo, a] a refined.
refinamiento [refina'mjento] nm refinement.
refinar [refi'nar] vt to refine; **refinería** nf refinery.
reflejar [refle'xar] vt to reflect; **reflejo, a** a reflected; (movimiento) reflex // nm reflection; (ANAT) reflex.
reflexión [reflek'sjon] nf reflection; **reflexionar** vt to reflect on // vi to reflect; (detenerse) to pause (to think).
reflexivo, a [reflek'sißo, a] a thoughtful; (LING) reflexive.
reflujo [re'fluxo] nm ebb.
reforma [re'forma] nf reform; (ARQ etc) repair; ~ agraria agrarian reform.
reformar [refor'mar] vt to reform; (modificar) to change, alter; (ARQ) to repair; ~se vr to mend one's ways.
reformatorio [reforma'torjo] nm reformatory.
reforzar [refor'θar] vt to strengthen; (ARQ) to reinforce; (fig) to encourage.
refractario, a [refrak'tarjo, a] a (TEC) heat-resistant.
refrán [re'fran] nm proverb, saying.
refregar [refre'xar] vt to scrub.
refrenar [refre'nar] vt to check, restrain.
refrendar [refren'dar] vt (firma) to endorse, countersign; (ley) to approve.
refrescante [refres'kante] a refreshing, cooling.
refrescar [refres'kar] vt to refresh // vi to cool down; ~se vr to get cooler; (tomar aire fresco) to go out for a breath of

fresh air; (*beber*) to have a drink.

refresco [re'fresko] *nm* soft drink, cool drink; '~s' 'refreshments'.

refriega [re'frjeɣa] *nf* scuffle, brawl.

refrigeración [refrixera'θjon] *nf* refrigeration; (*de sala*) air-conditioning.

refrigerador [refrixera'ðor] *nm*, **refrigeradora** [-a] *nf* (*AM*) refrigerator (*Brit*), icebox (*US*).

refrigerar [refrixe'rar] *vt* to refrigerate; (*sala*) to air-condition.

refuerzo [re'fwerθo] *nm* reinforcement; (*TEC*) support.

refugiado, a [refu'xjaðo, a] *nm/f* refugee.

refugiarse [refu'xjarse] *vr* to take refuge, shelter.

refugio [re'fuxjo] *nm* refuge; (*protección*) shelter.

refulgir [reful'xir] *vi* to shine, be dazzling.

refunfuñar [refunfu'ɲar] *vi* to grunt, growl; (*quejarse*) to grumble.

refutar [refu'tar] *vt* to refute.

regadera [reɣa'ðera] *nf* watering can.

regadío [reɣa'ðio] *nm* irrigated land.

regalado, a [reɣa'laðo, a] *a* comfortable, luxurious; (*gratis*) free, for nothing.

regalar [reɣa'lar] *vt* (*dar*) to give (as a present); (*entregar*) to give away; (*mimar*) to pamper, make a fuss of.

regalía [reɣa'lia] *nf* privilege, prerogative; (*COM*) bonus; (*de autor*) royalty.

regaliz [reɣa'liθ] *nm* liquorice.

regalo [re'ɣalo] *nm* (*obsequio*) gift, present; (*gusto*) pleasure; (*comodidad*) comfort.

regalón, ona [reɣa'lon, ona] *a* spoiled, pampered.

regañadientes [reɣaɲa'ðjentes]: a ~ *ad* reluctantly.

regañar [reɣa'ɲar] *vt* to scold // *vi* to grumble; **regaño** *nm* scolding, telling-off; (*queja*) grumble; **regañón, ona** *a* nagging.

regar [re'ɣar] *vt* to water, irrigate; (*fig*) to scatter, sprinkle.

regatear [reɣate'ar] *vt* (*COM*) to bargain over; (*escatimar*) to be mean with // *vi* to bargain, haggle; (*DEPORTE*) to dribble; **regateo** *nm* bargaining; dribbling; (*del cuerpo*) swerve, dodge.

regazo [re'ɣaθo] *nm* lap.

regeneración [rexenera'θjon] *nf* regeneration.

regenerar [rexene'rar] *vt* to regenerate.

regentar [rexen'tar] *vt* to direct, manage; **regente** *nm* (*COM*) manager; (*POL*) regent.

régimen ['reximen] (*pl* **regímenes**) *nm* regime; (*MED*) diet.

regimiento [rexi'mjento] *nm* regiment.

regio, a ['rexjo, a] *a* royal, regal; (*fig: suntuoso*) splendid; (*AM fam*) great, terrific.

región [re'xjon] *nf* region; **regionalista**

nm/f regionalist.

regir [re'xir] *vt* to govern, rule; (*dirigir*) to manage, run // *vi* to apply, be in force.

registrador [rexistra'ðor] *nm* registrar, recorder.

registrar [rexis'trar] *vt* (*buscar*) to search; (: *en cajón*) to look through; (*inspeccionar*) to inspect; (*anotar*) to register, record; (*INFORM*) to log; ~**se** *vr* to register; (*ocurrir*) to happen.

registro [re'xistro] *nm* (*acto*) registration; (*MUS, libro*) register; (*inspección*) inspection, search; ~ **civil** registry office.

regla ['reɣla] *nf* (*ley*) rule, regulation; (*de medir*) ruler, rule; (*MED: período*) period.

reglamentación [reɣlamenta'θjon] *nf* (*acto*) regulation; (*lista*) rules *pl*.

reglamentar [reɣlamen'tar] *vt* to regulate; **reglamentario, a** *a* statutory; **reglamento** *nm* rules *pl*, regulations *pl*.

reglar [re'ɣlar] *vt* (*acciones*) to regulate.

regocijarse [reɣoθi'xarse] *vr* (*pasarlo bien*) to have a good time; (*alegrarse*) to rejoice; **regocijo** *nm* joy, happiness.

regodearse [reɣoðe'arse] *vr* to be glad, be delighted; **regodeo** *nm* delight.

regresar [reɣre'sar] *vi* to come back, go back, return; **regresivo, a** *a* backward; (*fig*) regressive; **regreso** *nm* return.

reguero [re'ɣero] *nm* (*de sangre etc*) trickle; (*de humo*) trail.

regulador [reɣula'ðor] *nm* regulator; (*de radio etc*) knob, control.

regular [reɣu'lar] *a* regular; (*normal*) normal, usual; (*común*) ordinary; (*organizado*) regular, orderly; (*mediano*) average; (*fam*) not bad, so-so // *ad* so-so, alright // *vt* (*controlar*) to control, regulate; (*TEC*) to adjust; **por lo** ~ as a rule; ~**idad** *nf* regularity; ~**izar** *vt* to regularize.

regusto [re'ɣusto] *nm* aftertaste.

rehabilitación [reaßilita'θjon] *nf* rehabilitation; (*ARQ*) restoration.

rehabilitar [reaßili'tar] *vt* to rehabilitate; (*ARQ*) to restore; (*reintegrar*) to reinstate.

rehacer [rea'θer] *vt* (*reparar*) to mend, repair; (*volver a hacer*) to redo, repeat; ~**se** *vr* (*MED*) to recover.

rehén [re'en] *nm* hostage.

rehuir [reu'ir] *vt* to avoid, shun.

rehusar [reu'sar] *vt, vi* to refuse.

reina ['reina] *nf* queen; ~**do** *nm* reign.

reinante [rei'nante] *a* (*fig*) prevailing.

reinar [rei'nar] *vi* to reign.

reincidir [reinθi'ðir] *vi* to relapse.

reincorporarse [reinkorpo'rarse] *vr*: ~ **a** to rejoin.

reino ['reino] *nm* kingdom; **el R**~ **Unido** the United Kingdom.

reintegrar [reinte'ɣrar] *vt* (*reconstituir*) to reconstruct; (*persona*) to reinstate;

(*dinero*) to refund, pay back; ~se ur:
~se a to return to.

reír [re'ir] *vi*, **reírse** *vr* to laugh; ~se de
to laugh at.

reiterar [reite'rar] *vt* to reiterate.

reivindicación [reißindika'θjon] *nf* (*demanda*) claim, demand; (*justificación*)
vindication.

reivindicar [reißindi'kar] *vt* to claim.

reja ['rexa] *nf* (*de ventana*) grille, bars
pl; (*en la calle*) grating.

rejilla [re'xiʎa] *nf* grating, grille;
(*muebles*) wickerwork; (*de ventilación*)
vent; (*de coche etc*) luggage rack.

rejoneador [rexonea'ðor] *nm* mounted
bullfighter.

rejuvenecer [rexuße̞ne'θer] *vt*, *vi* to rejuvenate.

relación [rela'θjon] *nf* relation, relationship; (*MAT*) ratio; (*narración*) report;
relaciones públicas public relations; con
~ a, en ~ con in relation to; **relacionar**
vt to relate, connect; **relacionarse** *vr* to
be connected, be linked.

relajación [relaxa'θjon] *nf* relaxation.

relajado, a [rela'xaðo, a] *a* (*disoluto*)
loose; (*cómodo*) relaxed; (*MED*) ruptured.

relajar [rela'xar] *vt*, **relajarse** *vr* to relax.

relamerse [rela'merse] *vr* to lick one's
lips.

relamido, a [rela'miðo, a] *a* (*pulcro*)
overdressed; (*afectado*) affected.

relámpago [re'lampaɣo] *nm* flash of
lightning; **visita/huelga** ~ lightning visit/
strike; **relampaguear** *vi* to flash.

relatar [rela'tar] *vt* to tell, relate.

relativo, a [rela'tiβo, a] *a* relative; **en lo**
~ a concerning.

relato [re'lato] *nm* (*narración*) story,
tale.

relax [re'la(k)s] *nm*: **hacer** ~ to relax.

relegar [rele'ɣar] *vt* to relegate.

relevante [rele'ßante] *a* eminent, outstanding.

relevar [rele'ßar] *vt* (*sustituir*) to relieve;
~se *vr* to relay; ~ a **uno de un cargo** to
relieve sb of his post.

relevo [re'leßo] *nm* relief; **carrera de** ~s
relay race.

relieve [re'ljeße] *nm* (*ARTE*, *TEC*) relief;
(*fig*) prominence, importance; **bajo** ~
bas-relief.

religión [reli'xjon] *nf* religion; **religioso,**
a *a* religious // *nm/f* monk/nun.

relinchar [relin'tʃar] *vi* to neigh; **relincho** *nm* neigh; (*acto*) neighing.

reliquia [re'likja] *nf* relic; ~ **de familia**
heirloom.

reloj [re'lo(x)] *nm* clock; ~ (**de pulsera**)
wristwatch; ~ **despertador** alarm
(clock); **poner el** ~ to set one's watch (o
the clock); ~**ero, a** *nm/f* clockmaker;
watchmaker.

reluciente [relu'θjente] *a* brilliant, shin-

ing.

relucir [relu'θir] *vi* to shine; (*fig*) to
excel.

relumbrar [relum'brar] *vi* to dazzle, shine
brilliantly.

rellano [re'ʎano] *nm* (*ARQ*) landing.

rellenar [reʎe'nar] *vt* (*llenar*) to fill up;
(*CULIN*) to stuff; (*COSTURA*) to pad; **relleno, a** *a* full up; stuffed // *nm* stuffing;
(*de tapicería*) padding.

remachar [rema'tʃar] *vt* to rivet; (*fig*) to
hammer home, drive home; **remache**
nm rivet.

remanente [rema'nente] *nm* remainder;
(*COM*) balance; (*de producto*) surplus.

remangar [reman'gar] *vt* to roll up.

remanso [re'manso] *nm* pool.

remar [re'mar] *vi* to row.

rematado, a [rema'taðo, a] *a* complete,
utter.

rematar [rema'tar] *vt* to finish off; (*COM*)
to sell off cheap // *vi* to end, finish off;
(*DEPORTE*) to shoot.

remate [re'mate] *nm* end, finish; (*punta*)
tip; (*DEPORTE*) shot; (*ARQ*) top; (*COM*)
auction sale; **de** o **para** ~ to crown it all
(*Brit*), to top it off.

remedar [reme'ðar] *vt* to imitate.

remediar [reme'ðjar] *vt* to remedy; (*subsanar*) to make good, repair; (*evitar*) to
avoid.

remedio [re'meðjo] *nm* remedy; (*alivio*)
relief, help; (*JUR*) recourse, remedy;
poner ~ a to correct, stop; **no tener más**
~ to have no alternative; ¡**qué** ~! there's
no choice!; **sin** ~ hopeless.

remedo [re'meðo] *nm* imitation; (*pey*)
parody.

remendar [remen'dar] *vt* to repair; (*con
parche*) to patch.

remesa [re'mesa] *nf* remittance; (*COM*)
shipment.

remiendo [re'mjendo] *nm* mend; (*con
parche*) patch; (*cosido*) darn.

remilgado, a [remil'ɣaðo, a] *a* prim;
(*afectado*) affected.

remilgo [re'milɣo] *nm* primness; (*afectación*) affectation.

reminiscencia [reminis'θenθja] *nf* remi-
niscence.

remiso, a [re'miso, a] *a* slack, slow.

remitir [remi'tir] *vt* to remit, send // *vi* to
slacken; (*en carta*) **remite: X** sender:
X; **remitente** *nm/f* sender.

remo ['remo] *nm* (*de barco*) oar;
(*DEPORTE*) rowing.

remojar [remo'xar] *vt* to steep, soak;
(*galleta etc*) to dip, dunk.

remojo [re'moxo] *nm*: **dejar la ropa en** ~
to leave clothes to soak.

remolacha [remo'latʃa] *nf* beet, beetroot.

remolcador [remolka'ðor] *nm* (*NAUT*)
tug; (*AUTO*) breakdown lorry.

remolcar [remol'kar] *vt* to tow.

remolino [remo'lino] *nm* eddy; (*de*

agua) whirlpool; (*de viento*) whirlwind; (*de gente*) crowd.

remolque |re'molke| *nm* tow, towing; (*cuerda*) towrope; **llevar a ~** to tow.

remontar |remon'tar| *vt* to mend; **~se** *vr* to soar; **~se a** (*COM*) to amount to; **~ el vuelo** to soar.

remorder |remor'ðer| *vt* to distress, disturb; **~le la conciencia a uno** to have a guilty conscience; **remordimiento** *nm* remorse.

remoto, a |re'moto, a| *a* remote.

remover |remo'ßer| *vt* to stir; (*tierra*) to turn over; (*objetos*) to move round.

remozar |remo'θar| *vt* (*ARQ*) to refurbish.

remuneración |remunera'θjon| *nf* remuneration.

remunerar |remune'rar| *vt* to remunerate; (*premiar*) to reward.

renacer |rena'θer| *vi* to be reborn; (*fig*) to revive; **renacimiento** *nm* rebirth; **el Renacimiento** the Renaissance.

renacuajo |rena'kwaxo| *nm* (*ZOOL*) tadpole.

renal |re'nal| *a* renal, kidney *cpd*.

rencilla |ren'θiʎa| *nf* quarrel.

rencor |ren'kor| *nm* rancour, bitterness; **~oso, a** *a* spiteful.

rendición |rendi'θjon| *nf* surrender.

rendido, a |ren'diðo, a| *a* (*sumiso*) submissive; (*cansado*) worn-out, exhausted.

rendija |ren'dixa| *nf* (*hendedura*) crack, cleft.

rendimiento |rendi'mjento| *nm* (*producción*) output; (*TEC, COM*) efficiency.

rendir |ren'dir| *vt* (*vencer*) to defeat; (*producir*) to produce; (*dar beneficio*) to yield; (*agotar*) to exhaust // *vi* to pay; **~se** *vr* (*someterse*) to surrender; (*cansarse*) to wear o.s. out; **~ homenaje** *o* **culto a** to pay homage to.

renegado, a |rene'xaðo, a| *a, nm/f* renegade.

renegar |rene'xar| *vi* (*renunciar*) to renounce; (*blasfemar*) to blaspheme; (*quejarse*) to complain.

RENFE |'renfe| *nf abr* (= *Red Nacional de los Ferrocarriles Españoles*) ≈ BR (*Brit*).

renglón |ren'glon| *nm* (*línea*) line; (*COM*) item, article; **a ~ seguido** immediately after.

renombrado, a |renom'braðo, a| *a* renowned.

renombre |re'nombre| *nm* renown.

renovación |renoßa'θjon| *nf* (*de contrato*) renewal; (*ARQ*) renovation.

renovar |reno'ßar| *vt* to renew; (*ARQ*) to renovate.

renta |'renta| *nf* (*ingresos*) income; (*beneficio*) profit; (*alquiler*) rent; **~ vitalicia** annuity; **rentable** *a* profitable; **rentar** *vt* to produce, yield.

rentista |ren'tista| *nm/f* (*accionista*)

stockholder.

renuencia |re'nwenθja| *nf* reluctance.

renuncia |re'nunθja| *nf* resignation.

renunciar |renun'θjar| *vt* to renounce // *vi* to resign; **~ a hacer algo** to give up doing sth.

reñido, a |re'ɲiðo, a| *a* (*batalla*) bitter, hard-fought; **estar ~ con uno** to be on bad terms with sb.

reñir |re'ɲir| *vt* (*regañar*) to scold // *vi* (*estar peleado*) to quarrel, fall out; (*combatir*) to fight.

reo |'reo| *nm/f* culprit, offender; **~ de muerte** prisoner condemned to death.

reojo |re'oxo|: **de ~** *ad* out of the corner of one's eye.

reparación |repara'θjon| *nf* (*acto*) mending, repairing; (*TEC*) repair; (*fig*) amends, reparation.

reparar |repa'rar| *vt* to repair; (*fig*) to make amends for; (*observar*) to observe // *vi*: **~ en** (*darse cuenta de*) to notice; (*prestar atención a*) to pay attention to.

reparo |re'paro| *nm* (*advertencia*) observation; (*duda*) doubt; (*dificultad*) difficulty; **poner ~s (a)** to raise objections (to).

repartición |reparti'θjon| *nf* distribution; (*división*) division; **repartidor, a** *nm/f* distributor.

repartir |repar'tir| *vt* to distribute, share out; (*CORREOS*) to deliver; **reparto** *nm* distribution; delivery; (*TEATRO, CINE*) cast; (*AM: urbanización*) housing estate (*Brit*), real estate development (*US*).

repasar |repa'sar| *vt* (*ESCOL*) to revise; (*MECÁNICA*) to check, overhaul; (*COSTURA*) to mend; **repaso** *nm* revision; overhaul, checkup; mending.

repatriar |repa'trjar| *vt* to repatriate.

repecho |re'petʃo| *nm* steep incline.

repelente |repe'lente| *a* repellent, repulsive.

repeler |repe'ler| *vt* to repel.

repensar |repen'sar| *vt* to reconsider.

repente |re'pente| *nm*: **de ~** suddenly; **~ de ira** fit of anger.

repentino, a |repen'tino, a| *a* sudden.

repercusión |reperku'sjon| *nf* repercussion.

repercutir |reperku'tir| *vi* (*objeto*) to rebound; (*sonido*) to echo; **~ en** (*fig*) to have repercussions on.

repertorio |reper'torjo| *nm* list; (*TEATRO*) repertoire.

repetición |repeti'θjon| *nf* repetition.

repetir |repe'tir| *vt* to repeat; (*plato*) to have a second helping of // *vi* to repeat; (*sabor*) to come back; **~se** *vr* (*volver sobre un tema*) to repeat o.s.

repicar |repi'kar| *vt* (*campanas*) to ring.

repique |re'pike| *nm* pealing, ringing; **~teo** *nm* pealing; (*de tambor*) drumming.

repisa |re'pisa| *nf* ledge, shelf; (*de*

ventana) windowsill; ~ **de chimenea** mantelpiece.

repito *etc vb ver* **repetir.**

replegarse [reple'varse] *vr* to fall back, retreat.

repleto, a [re'pleto, a] *a* replete, full up.

réplica ['replika] *nf* answer; (*ARTE*) replica.

replicar [repli'kar] *vi* to answer; (*objetar*) to argue, answer back.

repliegue [re'pljeve] *nm* (*MIL*) withdrawal.

repoblación [repoβla'θjon] *nf* repopulation; (*de río*) restocking; ~ forestal reafforestation.

repoblar [repo'βlar] *vt* to repopulate; (*con árboles*) to reafforest.

repollo [re'poʎo] *nm* cabbage.

reponer [repo'ner] *vt* to replace, put back; (*TEATRO*) to revive; ~**se** *vr* to recover; ~ **que** to reply that.

reportaje [repor'taxe] *nm* report, article.

reportero, a [repor'tero, a] *nm/f* reporter.

reposacabezas [reposaka'βeθas] *nm inv* headrest.

reposado, a [repo'saðo, a] *a* (*descansado*) restful; (*tranquilo*) calm.

reposar [repo'sar] *vi* to rest, repose.

reposición [reposi'θjon] *nf* replacement; (*CINE*) remake.

reposo [re'poso] *nm* rest.

repostar [repos'tar] *vt* to replenish; (*AUTO*) to fill up (with petrol (*Brit*) o gasoline (*US*)).

repostería [reposte'ria] *nf* confectioner's (shop); **repostero, a** *nm/f* confectioner.

reprender [repren'der] *vt* to reprimand.

represa [re'presa] *nf* dam; (*lago artificial*) lake, pool.

represalia [repre'salja] *nf* reprisal.

representación [representa'θjon] *nf* representation; (*TEATRO*) performance; **representante** *nm/f* representative; performer.

representar [represen'tar] *vt* to represent; (*TEATRO*) to perform; (*edad*) to look; ~**se** *vr* to imagine; **representativo, a** *a* representative.

represión [repre'sjon] *nf* repression.

reprimenda [repri'menda] *nf* reprimand, rebuke.

reprimir [repri'mir] *vt* to repress.

reprobar [repro'βar] *vt* to censure, reprove.

réprobo, a ['reproβo, a] *nm/f* reprobate.

reprochar [repro'tʃar] *vt* to reproach; **reproche** *nm* reproach.

reproducción [reproðuk'θjon] *nf* reproduction.

reproducir [reproðu'θir] *vt* to reproduce; ~**se** *vr* to breed; (*situación*) to recur.

reproductor, a [reproðuc'tor, a] *a* reproductive.

reptil [rep'til] *nm* reptile.

república [re'puβlika] *nf* republic; **republicano, a** *a, nm/f* republican.

repudiar [repu'ðjar] *vt* to repudiate; (*fe*) to renounce; **repudio** *nm* repudiation.

repuesto [re'pwesto] *nm* (*pieza de recambio*) spare (part); (*abastecimiento*) supply; **rueda de** ~ spare wheel.

repugnancia [repuγ'nanθja] *nf* repugnance; **repugnante** *a* repugnant, repulsive.

repugnar [repuγ'nar] *vt* to disgust.

repujar [repu'xar] *vt* to emboss.

repulsa [re'pulsa] *nf* rebuff.

repulsión [repul'sjon] *nf* repulsion, aversion; **repulsivo, a** *a* repulsive.

reputación [reputa'θjon] *nf* reputation.

reputar [repu'tar] *vt* to consider, deem.

requemado, a [reke'maðo, a] *a* (*quemado*) scorched; (*bronceado*) tanned.

requerimiento [rekeri'mjento] *nm* request; (*JUR*) summons.

requerir [reke'rir] *vt* (*pedir*) to ask, request; (*exigir*) to require; (*llamar*) to send for, summon.

requesón [reke'son] *nm* cottage cheese.

requete... [rekete] *pref* extremely.

réquiem ['rekjem] (*pl* ~**s**) *nm* requiem.

requisa [re'kisa] *nf* (*inspección*) survey, inspection; (*MIL*) requisition.

requisito [reki'sito] *nm* requirement, requisite.

res [res] *nf* beast, animal.

resabido, a [resa'βiðo, a] *a*: **tener algo sabido y** ~ to know sth perfectly well.

resabio [re'saβjo] *nm* (*maña*) vice, bad habit; (*dejo*) (unpleasant) aftertaste.

resaca [re'saka] *nf* (*en el mar*) undertow, undercurrent; (*fig*) backlash; (*fam*) hangover.

resalado, a [resa'laðo, a] *a* (*fam*) lively.

resaltar [resal'tar] *vi* to project, stick out; (*fig*) to stand out.

resarcir [resar'θir] *vt* to compensate; ~**se** *vr* to make up for.

resbaladizo, a [resβala'ðiθo, a] *a* slippery.

resbalar [resβa'lar] *vi*, **resbalarse** *vr* to slip, slide; (*fig*) to slip (up); **resbalón** *nm* (*acción*) slip.

rescatar [reska'tar] *vt* (*salvar*) to save, rescue; (*objeto*) to get back, recover; (*cautivos*) to ransom.

rescate [res'kate] *nm* rescue; (*objeto*) recovery; **pagar un** ~ to pay a ransom.

rescindir [resθin'dir] *vt* to rescind.

rescisión [resθi'sjon] *nf* cancellation.

rescoldo [res'koldo] *nm* embers *pl*.

resecar [rese'kar] *vt* to dry thoroughly; (*MED*) to cut out, remove; ~**se** *vr* to dry up.

reseco, a [re'seko, a] *a* very dry; (*fig*) skinny.

resentido, a [resen'tiðo, a] *a* resentful.

resentimiento [resenti'mjento] *nm* resentiment, bitterness.

resentirse [resen'tirse] vr (debilitarse: persona) to suffer; ~ de (consecuencias) to feel the effects of; ~ de (o por) algo to resent sth, be bitter about sth.

reseña [re'seɲa] nf (cuenta) account; (informe) report; (LITERATURA) review.

reseñar [rese'ɲar] vt to describe; (LITERATURA) to review.

reserva [re'serßa] nf reserve; (reservación) reservation; a ~ de que ... unless ...; con toda ~ in strictest confidence.

resérvado, a [reser'Baðo, a] a reserved; (retraído) cold, distant // nm private room.

reservar [reser'Bar] vt (guardar) to keep; (habitación, entrada) to reserve; ~se vr to save o.s.; (callar) to keep to o.s.

resfriado [resfri'aðo] nm cold; **resfriarse** vr to cool; (MED) to catch (a) cold.

resguardar [resɣwar'ðar] vt to protect, shield; ~se vr: ~se de to guard against; **resguardo** nm defence; (vale) voucher; (recibo) receipt, slip.

residencia [resi'ðenθja] nf residence; ~l nf (urbanización) housing estate.

residente [resi'ðente] a, nm/f resident.

residir [resi'ðir] vi to reside, live; ~ en to reside in, lie in.

residuo [re'siðwo] nm residue.

resignación [resiɣna'θjon] nf resignation; **resignarse** vr: **resignarse** a o con to resign o.s. to, be resigned to.

resina [re'sina] nf resin.

resistencia [resis'tenθja] nf (dureza) endurance, strength; (oposición, ELEC) resistance; **resistente** a strong, hardy; resistant.

resistir [resis'tir] vt (soportar) to bear; (oponerse a) to resist, oppose; (aguantar) to put up with // vi to resist; (aguantar) to last, endure; ~se vr: ~se a to refuse to, resist.

resma ['resma] nf ream.

resol [re'sol] nm glare of the sun.

resolución [resolu'θjon] nf resolution; (decisión) decision; **resoluto, a** a resolute.

resolver [resol'ßer] vt to resolve; (solucionar) to solve, resolve; (decidir) to decide, settle; ~se vr to make up one's mind.

resollar [reso'ʎar] vi to breathe noisily, wheeze.

resonancia [reso'nanθja] nf (del sonido) resonance; (repercusión) repercussion; **resonante** a resonant, resounding; (fig) tremendous.

resonar [reso'nar] vi to ring, echo.

resoplar [reso'plar] vi to snort; **resoplido** nm heavy breathing.

resorte [re'sorte] nm spring; (fig) lever.

respaldar [respal'dar] vt to back (up), support; ~se vr to lean back; ~se con o en (fig) to take one's stand on; **respaldo**

nm (de sillón) back; (fig) support, backing.

respectivo, a [respek'tißo, a] a respective; en lo ~ a with regard to.

respecto [res'pekto] nm: al ~ on this matter; con ~ a, ~ de with regard to, in relation to.

respetable [respe'taßle] a respectable.

respetar [respe'tar] vt to respect; **respeto** nm respect; (acatamiento) deference; **respetos** nmpl respects; **respetuoso, a** a respectful.

respingar [respin'gar] vi to shy; **respingo** nm start, jump.

respiración [respira'θjon] nf breathing; (MED) respiration; (ventilación) ventilation.

respirar [respi'rar] vi to breathe; **respiratorio, a** a respiratory; **respiro** nm breathing; (fig: descanso) respite.

resplandecer [resplande'θer] vi to shine; **resplandeciente** a resplendent, shining; **resplandor** nm brilliance, brightness; (de luz, fuego) blaze.

responder [respon'der] vt to answer // vi to answer; (fig) to respond; (pey) to answer back; ~ de o por to answer for; **respondón, ona** a cheeky.

responsabilidad, [responsaßili'ðað] nf responsibility.

responsabilizarse [responsaßili'θarse] vr to make o.s. responsible, take charge.

responsable [respon'saßle] a responsible.

respuesta [res'pwesta] nf answer, reply.

resquebrajar [reskeßra'xar] vt, **resquebrajarse** vr to crack, split.

resquemor [reske'mor] nm resentment.

resquicio [res'kiθjo] nm chink; (hendedura) crack.

restablecer [restaßle'θer] vt to re-establish, restore; ~se vr to recover.

restallar [resta'ʎar] vi to crack.

restante [res'tante] a remaining; lo ~ the remainder.

restar [res'tar] vt (MAT) to subtract; (fig) to take away // vi to remain, be left.

restauración [restaura'θjon] nf restoration.

restaurante [restau'rante] nm restaurant.

restaurar [restau'rar] vt to restore.

restitución [restitu'θjon] nf return, restitution.

restituir [restitu'ir] vt (devolver) to return, give back; (rehabilitar) to restore.

resto ['resto] nm (residuo) rest, remainder; (apuesta) stake; ~s nmpl remains.

restregar [restre'ɣar] vt to scrub, rub.

restricción [restrik'θjon] nf restriction.

restrictivo, a [restrik'tißo, a] a restrictive.

restringir [restrin'xir] vt to restrict, limit.

resucitar [resuθi'tar] vt, vi to resuscitate,

revive.

resuelto, a pp de **resolver** // [re'swelto, a] a resolute, determined.

resuello [re'sweʎo] nm (aliento) breath; **estar sin ~ to** be breathless.

resultado [resul'taðo] nm result; (conclusión) outcome; **resultante** a resulting, resultant.

resultar [resul'tar] vi (ser) to be; (llegar a ser) to turn out to be; (salir bien) to turn out well; (COM) to amount to; **~ de** to stem from; **me resulta difícil hacerlo** it's difficult for me to do it.

resumen [re'sumen] (pl **resúmenes**) nm summary, résumé; **en ~** in short.

resumir [resu'mir] vt to sum up; (cortar) to abridge, cut down; (condensar) to summarize.

resurgir [resur'xir] vi (reaparecer) to reappear.

resurrección [resurre(k)'θjon] nf resurrection.

retablo [re'taβlo] nm altarpiece.

retaguardia [reta'ɣwarðja] nf rearguard.

retahíla [reta'ila] nf series, string.

retal [re'tal] nm remnant.

retar [re'tar] vt to challenge; (desafiar) to defy, dare.

retardar [retar'ðar] vt (demorar) to delay; (hacer más lento) to slow down; (retener) to hold back; **retardo** nm delay.

retazo [re'taθo] nm snippet (Brit), fragment.

rete... [rete] pref very, extremely.

retener [rete'ner] vt (intereses) to withhold.

retina [re'tina] nf retina.

retintín [retin'tin] nm jangle, jingle.

retirada [reti'raða] nf (MIL, refugio) retreat; (de dinero) withdrawal; (de embajador) recall; **retirado, a** a (lugar) remote; (vida) quiet; (jubilado) retired.

retirar [reti'rar] vt to withdraw; (quitar) to remove; (jubilar) to retire, pension off; **~se** vr to retreat, withdraw; to retire; (acostarse) to retire, go to bed; **retiro** nm retreat; retirement; (pago) pension.

reto ['reto] nm dare, challenge.

retocar [reto'kar] vt (fotografía) to touch up, retouch.

retoño [re'toɲo] nm sprout, shoot; (fig) offspring, child.

retoque [re'toke] nm retouching.

retorcer [retor'θer] vt to twist; (manos, lavado) to wring; **~se** vr to become twisted; (mover el cuerpo) to writhe.

retorcimiento [retorθi'mjento] nm twist, twisting.

retórica [re'torika] nf rhetoric; (pey) affectedness.

retornar [retor'nar] vt to return, give back // vi to return, go/come back;

retorno nm return.

retortijón [retorti'xon] nm twist, twisting.

retozar [reto'θar] vi (juguetear) to frolic, romp; (saltar) to gambol; **retozón, ona** a playful.

retracción [retrak'θjon] nf retraction.

retractarse [retrak'tarse] vr to retract; **me retracto** I take that back.

retraerse [retra'erse] vr to retreat, withdraw; **retraído, a** a shy, retiring; **retraimiento** nm retirement; (timidez) shyness.

rotransmisión [rctransmi'sjon] nf repeat (broadcast).

retransmitir [retransmi'tir] vt (mensaje) to relay; (TV etc) to repeat, retransmit; (: en vivo) to broadcast live.

retrasado, a [retra'saðo, a] a late; (MED) mentally retarded; (país etc) backward, underdeveloped.

retrasar [retra'sar] vt (demorar) to postpone, put off; (retardar) to slow down // vi, **~se** vr (atrasarse) to be late; (reloj) to be slow; (producción) to fall (away); (quedarse atrás) to lag behind.

retraso [re'traso] nm (demora) delay; (lentitud) slowness; (tardanza) lateness; (atraso) backwardness; **~s** nmpl arrears; **llegar con ~** to arrive late; **~ mental** mental deficiency.

retratar [retra'tar] vt (ARTE) to paint the portrait of; (fotografiar) to photograph; (fig) to depict, describe; **~se** vr to have one's portrait painted; to have one's photograph taken; **retrato** nm portrait; (fig) likeness; **retrato-robot** nm identikit picture.

retreta [re'treta] nf retreat.

retrete [re'trete] nm toilet.

retribución [retriβu'θjon] nf (recompensa) reward; (pago) pay, payment.

retribuir [retri'βwir] vt (recompensar) to reward; (pagar) to pay.

retro... [retro] pref retro... .

retroactivo, a [retroak'tiβo, a] a retroactive, retrospective.

retroceder [retroθe'ðer] vi (echarse atrás) to move back(wards); (fig) to back down.

retroceso [retro'θeso] nm backward movement; (MED) relapse; (fig) backing down.

retrógrado, a [re'troɣraðo, a] a retrograde, retrogressive; (POL) reactionary.

retropropulsión [retropropul'sjon] nf jet propulsion.

retrospectivo, a [retrospek'tiβo, a] a retrospective.

retrovisor [retroβi'sor] nm rear-view mirror.

retumbar [retum'bar] vi to echo, resound.

reuma ['reuma], **reumatismo** [reuma-

'tismo] *nm* rheumatism.

reunificar [reunifi'kar] *vt* to reunify.

reunión [reu'njon] *nf* (*asamblea*) meeting; (*fiesta*) party.

reunir [reu'nir] *vt* (*juntar*) to reunite, join (together); (*recoger*) to gather (together); (*personas*) to get together; (*cualidades*) to combine; ~**se** *vr* (*personas: en asamblea*) to meet, gather.

revalidar [reβali'ðar] *vt* (*ratificar*) to confirm, ratify.

revalorar [reβalo'rar], **revalorizar** [reβalori'θar] *vt* to revalue, reassess.

revancha [re'βantʃa] *nf* revenge.

revelación [reβela'θjon] *nf* revelation.

revelado [reβe'laðo] *nm* developing.

revelar [reβe'lar] *vt* to reveal; (*FOTO*) to develop.

reventar [reβen'tar] *vt* to burst, explode.

reventón [reβen'ton] *nm* (*AUTO*) blowout (*Brit*), flat (*US*).

reverberación [reβerβera'θjon] *nf* reverberation.

reverberar [reβerβe'rar] *vi* to reverberate.

reverencia [reβe'renθja] *nf* reverence; **reverenciar** *vt* to revere.

reverendo, a [reβe'rendo, a] *a* reverend.

reverente [reβe'rente] *a* reverent.

reverso [re'βerso] *nm* back, other side; (*de moneda*) reverse.

revertir [reβer'tir] *vi* to revert.

revés [re'βes] *nm* back, wrong side; (*fig*) reverse, setback; (*DEPORTE*) backhand; **al ~** the wrong way round; (*de arriba abajo*) upside down; (*ropa*) inside out; **volver algo al ~** to turn sth round; (*ropa*) to turn sth inside out.

revestir [reβes'tir] *vt* (*poner*) to put on; (*cubrir*) to cover, coat; ~ **con** *o* **de** to invest with.

revisar [reβi'sar] *vt* (*examinar*) to check; (*texto etc*) to revise; **revisión** *nf* revision.

revisor, a [reβi'sor, a] *nm/f* inspector; (*FERRO*) ticket collector.

revista [re'βista] *nf* magazine, review; (*TEATRO*) revue; (*inspección*) inspection; **pasar ~ a** to review, inspect.

revivir [reβi'βir] *vi* to revive.

revocación [reβoka'θjon] *nf* repeal.

revocar [reβo'kar] *vt* to revoke.

revolcarse [reβol'karse] *vr* to roll about.

revolotear [reβolote'ar] *vi* to flutter.

revoltijo [reβol'tixo] *nm* mess, jumble.

revoltoso, a [reβol'toso, a] *a* (*travieso*) naughty, unruly.

revolución [reβolu'θjon] *nf* revolution; **revolucionar** *vt* to revolutionize; **revolucionario, a** *a, nm/f* revolutionary.

revolver [reβol'βer] *vt* (*desordenar*) to disturb, mess up; (*mover*) to move about; (*POL*) to stir up // *vi*: ~ **en** to go through, rummage (about) in; ~**se** *vr* (*volver contra*) to turn on *o* against.

revólver [re'βolβer] *nm* revolver.

revuelo [re'βwelo] *nm* fluttering; (*fig*) commotion.

revuelto, a *pp de* **revolver** // [re'βwelto, a] *a* (*mezclado*) mixed-up, in disorder // *nf* (*motín*) revolt; (*agitación*) commotion.

revulsivo [reβul'siβo] *nm* enema.

rey [rei] *nm* king; **Día de R~es** Epiphany.

reyerta [re'jerta] *nf* quarrel, brawl.

rezagado, a [reθa'yaðo, a] *nm/f* straggler.

rezagar [reθa'yar] *vt* (*dejar atrás*) to leave behind; (*retrasar*) to delay, postpone.

rezar [re'θar] *vi* to pray; ~ **con** (*fam*) to concern, have to do with; **rezo** *nm* prayer.

rezongar [reθon'gar] *vi* to grumble.

rezumar [reθu'mar] *vt* to ooze.

ría ['ria] *nf* estuary.

riada [ri'aða] *nf* flood.

ribera [ri'βera] *nf* (*de río*) bank; (: *área*) riverside.

ribete [ri'βete] *nm* (*de vestido*) border; (*fig*) addition; ~**ar** *vt* to edge, border.

ricino [ri'θino] *nm*: **aceite de ~** castor oil.

rico, a ['riko, a] *a* rich; (*adinerado*) wealthy, rich; (*lujoso*) luxurious; (*comida*) delicious; (*niño*) lovely, cute // *nm/f* rich person.

rictus ['riktus] *nm* (*mueca*) sneer, grin.

ridiculez [riðiku'leθ] *nf* absurdity.

ridiculizar [riðikuli'θar] *vt* to ridicule.

ridículo, a [ri'ðikulo, a] *a* ridiculous; **hacer el ~** to make a fool of o.s.; **poner a uno en ~** to make a fool of sb.

riego ['rjeyo] *nm* (*aspersión*) watering; (*irrigación*) irrigation.

riel [rjel] *nm* rail.

rienda ['rjenda] *nf* rein; **dar ~ suelta a** to give free rein to.

riesgo ['rjesyo] *nm* risk; **correr el ~ de** to run the risk of.

rifa ['rifa] *nf* (*lotería*) raffle; **rifar** *vt* to raffle.

rifle ['rifle] *nm* rifle.

rigidez [rixi'ðeθ] *nf* rigidity, stiffness; (*fig*) strictness; **rígido, a** *a* rigid, stiff; strict, inflexible.

rigor [ri'yor] *nm* strictness, rigour; (*inclemencia*) harshness; **de ~** de rigueur, essential; **riguroso, a** *a* rigorous; harsh; (*severo*) severe.

rimar [ri'mar] *vi* to rhyme.

rimbombante [rimbom'bante] *a* (*fig*) pompous.

rímel, rímmel ['rimel] *nm* mascara.

rincón [rin'kon] *nm* corner (*inside*).

rinoceronte [rinoθe'ronte] *nm* rhinoceros.

riña ['riɲa] *nf* (*disputa*) argument; (*pelea*) brawl.

riñón [ri'ɲon] *nm* kidney; **tener riñones**

to have guts.

río etc vb ver **reír** // ['rio] nm river; (fig) torrent, stream; ~ **abajo/arriba** downstream/upstream; ~ **de la Plata** River Plate.

rioja [ri'oxa] nm (vino) rioja (wine).

rioplatense [riopla'tense] a of o from the River Plate region.

riqueza [ri'keθa] nf wealth, riches pl; (cualidad) richness.

risa ['risa] nf laughter; (una ~) laugh; ¡qué ~! what a laugh!

risco ['risko] nm crag, cliff.

risible [rl'sIßle] a ludicrous, laughable.

risotada [riso'taða] nf guffaw, loud laugh.

ristra ['ristra] nf string.

risueño, a [ri'sweɲo, a] a (sonriente) smiling; (contento) cheerful.

ritmo ['ritmo] nm rhythm; a ~ **lento** slowly; **trabajar a ~ lento** to go slow.

rito ['rito] nm rite.

ritual [ri'twal] a, nm ritual.

rival [ri'ßal] a, nm/f rival; **~idad** nf rivalry; **~izar** vi: **~izar con** to rival, vie with.

rizado, a [ri'θaðo, a] a curly // nm curls pl.

rizar [ri'θar] vt to curl; **~se** vr (pelo) to curl; (agua) to ripple; **rizo** nm curl; ripple.

RNE nf abr = **Radio Nacional de España.**

robar [ro'ßar] vt to rob; (objeto) to steal; (casa etc) to break into; (NAIPES) to draw.

roble ['roßle] nm oak; **~do**, **~dal** nm oakwood.

robo ['roßo] nm robbery, theft.

robot [ro'ßot] nm robot; ~ **(de cocina)** food processor.

robustecer [roßuste'θer] vt to strengthen.

robusto, a [ro'ßusto, a] a robust, strong.

roca ['roka] nf rock.

rocalla [ro'kaʎa] nf pebbles pl.

roce ['roθe] nm (caricia) brush; (TEC) friction; (en la piel) graze; **tener ~ con** to be in close contact with.

rociar [ro'θjar] vt to spray.

rocín [ro'θin] nm nag, hack.

rocío [ro'θio] nm dew.

rocoso, a [ro'koso, a] a rocky.

rodado, a [ro'ðaðo, a] a (con ruedas) wheeled // nf rut.

rodaja [ro'ðaxa] nf (raja) slice.

rodaje [ro'ðaxe] nm (CINE) shooting, filming; (AUTO): **en ~** running in.

rodar [ro'ðar] vt (vehículo) to wheel (along); (escalera) to roll down; (viajar por) to travel (over) // vi to roll; (coche) to go, run; (CINE) to shoot, film.

rodear [roðe'ar] vt to surround // vi to go round; **~se** vr: **~se de amigos** to surround o.s. with friends.

rodeo [ro'ðeo] nm (ruta indirecta) detour; (evasión) evasion; (AM) rodeo; **hablar sin ~s** to come to the point, speak plainly.

rodilla [ro'ðiʎa] nf knee; **de ~s** kneeling; **ponerse de ~s** to kneel (down).

rodillo [ro'ðiʎo] nm roller; (CULIN) rolling-pin.

rododendro [roðo'ðendro] nm rhododendron.

roedor, a [roe'ðor, a] a gnawing // nm rodent.

roer [ro'er] vt (masticar) to gnaw; (corroer, fig) to corrode.

rogar [ro'ʁar] vt, vi (pedir) to ask for; (suplicar) to beg, plead; **se ruega no fumar** please do not smoke.

rojizo, a [ro'xiθo, a] a reddish.

rojo, a [ro'xo, a] a, nm red; **al ~ vivo** red-hot.

rol [rol] nm list, roll; (AM: papel) role.

rollizo, a [ro'ʎiθo, a] a (objeto) cylindrical; (persona) plump.

rollo ['roʎo] nm roll; (de cuerda) coil; (madera) log; (fam) bore; ¡qué ~! what a carry-on!

ROM [rom] nf abr (= memoria de sólo lectura) ROM.

Roma ['roma] n Rome.

romance [ro'manθe] nm (idioma castellano) Romance language; (LITERATURA) ballad; **hablar en ~** to speak plainly.

romanticismo [romanti'θismo] nm romanticism.

romántico, a [ro'mantiko, a] a romantic.

romería [rome'ria] nf (REL) pilgrimage; (excursión) trip, outing.

romero, a [ro'mero, a] a nm/f pilgrim // nm rosemary.

romo, a ['romo, a] a blunt; (fig) dull.

rompecabezas [rompeka'ßeθas] nm inv riddle, puzzle; (juego) jigsaw (puzzle).

rompehuelgas [rompe'welʁas] nm inv strikebreaker, blackleg.

rompeolas [rompe'olas] nm inv breakwater.

romper [rom'per] vt to break; (hacer pedazos) to smash; (papel, tela etc) to tear, rip // vi (olas) to break; (sol, diente) to break through; ~ **un contrato** to break a contract; ~ **a** to start (suddenly) to; ~ **a llorar** to burst into tears; ~ **con uno** to fall out with sb.

rompimiento [rompi'mjento] nm (acto) breaking; (fig) break; (quiebra) crack.

ron [ron] nm rum.

roncar [ron'kar] vi to snore.

ronco, a ['ronko, a] a (afónico) hoarse; (áspero) raucous.

roncha ['rontʃa] nf weal; (contusión) bruise.

ronda ['ronda] nf (gen) round; (patrulla) patrol; **rondar** vt to patrol // vi to pa-

trol; (fig) to prowl round.
ronquido [ron'kiðo] nm snore, snoring.
ronronear [ronrone'ar] vi to purr; **ronroneo** nm purr.
roña ['roɲa] nf (VETERINARIA) mange; (mugre) dirt, grime; (óxido) rust.
roñoso, a [ro'ɲoso, a] a (mugriento) filthy; (tacaño) mean.
ropa ['ropa] nf clothes pl, clothing; ~ blanca linen; ~ de cama bed linen; ~ interior underwear; ~ para lavar washing; **~je** nm gown, robes pl; **~vejero, a** nm/f second-hand clothes dealer.
ropero [ro'pero] nm linen cupboard; (guardarropa) wardrobe.
rosa ['rosa] a inv pink // nf rose; (ANAT) red birthmark; ~ de los vientos the compass.
rosado, a [ro'saðo, a] a pink // nm rosé.
rosal [ro'sal] nm rosebush.
rosario [ro'sarjo] nm (REL) rosary; **rezar el ~** to say the rosary.
rosca ['roska] nf (de tornillo) thread; (de humo) coil, spiral; (pan, postre) ring-shaped roll/pastry.
rosetón [rose'ton] nm rosette; (ARQ) rose window.
rosquilla [ros'kiʎa] nf doughnut-shaped fritter.
rostro ['rostro] nm (cara) face.
rotación [rota'θjon] nf rotation; ~ de cultivos crop rotation.
rotativo, a [rota'tiβo, a] a rotary.
roto, a pp de **romper** // ['roto, a] a broken.
rótula ['rotula] nf kneecap; (TEC) ball-and-socket joint.
rotulador [rotula'ðor] nm felt-tip pen.
rotular [rotu'lar] vt (carta, documento) to head, entitle; (objeto) to label; **rótulo** nm heading, title; label; (letrero) sign.
rotundo, a [ro'tundo, a] a round; (enfático) emphatic.
rotura [ro'tura] nf (rompimiento) breaking; (MED) fracture.
roturar [rotu'rar] vt to plough.
rozadura [roθa'ðura] nf abrasion, graze.
rozar [ro'θar] vt (frotar) to rub; (arañar) to scratch; (tocar ligeramente) to shave, touch lightly; **~se** vr to rub (together); **~se con** (fam) to rub shoulders with.
r.p.m. abr (= revoluciones por minuto) rpm.
rte. abr (= remite, remitente) sender.
RTVE nf abr = Radiotelevisión Española.
rubí [ru'βi] nm ruby; (de reloj) jewel.
rubicundo, a [ruβi'kundo, a] a ruddy.
rubio, a ['ruβjo, a] a fair-haired, blond(e) // nm/f blond/blonde; **tabaco ~** Virginia tobacco.
rubor [ru'βor] nm (sonrojo) blush; (timidez) bashfulness; **~izarse** vr to blush; **~oso, a** a blushing.
rúbrica ['ruβrika] nf (título) title, head-

ing; (de la firma) flourish; **rubricar** vt (firmar) to sign with a flourish; (concluir) to sign and seal.
rudeza [ru'ðeθa] nf (tosquedad) coarseness; (sencillez) simplicity.
rudimento [ruði'mento] nm rudiment.
rudo, a ['ruðo, a] a (sin pulir) unpolished; (grosero) coarse; (violento) violent; (sencillo) simple.
rueda ['rweða] nf wheel; (círculo) ring, circle; (rodaja) slice, round; ~ delantera/trasera/de repuesto front/back/spare wheel; ~ de prensa press conference.
ruedo ['rweðo] nm (contorno) edge, border; (de vestido) hem; (círculo) circle; (TAUR) arena, bullring.
ruego etc vb ver **rogar** // ['rweɣo] nm request.
rufián [ru'fjan] nm scoundrel.
rugby ['ruɣβi] nm rugby.
rugido [ru'xiðo] nm roar.
rugir [ru'xir] vi to roar.
rugoso, a [ru'ɣoso, a] a (arrugado) wrinkled; (áspero) rough; (desigual) ridged.
ruibarbo [rui'βarβo] nm rhubarb.
ruido ['rwiðo] nm noise; (sonido) sound; (alboroto) racket, row; (escándalo) commotion, rumpus; **~so, a** a noisy, loud; (fig) sensational.
ruin [rwin] a contemptible, mean.
ruina ['rwina] nf ruin; (colapso) collapse; (de persona) ruin, downfall.
ruindad [rwin'dað] nf lowness, meanness; (acto) low o mean act.
ruinoso, a [rwi'noso, a] a ruinous; (destartalado) dilapidated, tumbledown; (COM) disastrous.
ruiseñor [rwise'ɲor] nm nightingale.
rula ['rula], **ruleta** [ru'leta] nf roulette.
rulo ['rulo] nm (para el pelo) curler.
rulota [ru'lota] nf caravan (Brit), trailer (US).
Rumania [ru'manja] nf Rumania.
rumba ['rumba] nf rumba.
rumbo ['rumbo] nm (ruta) route, direction; (ángulo de dirección) course, bearing; (fig) course of events: **ir con ~ a** to be heading for.
rumboso, a [rum'boso, a] a (generoso) generous.
rumiante [ru'mjante] nm ruminant.
rumiar [ru'mjar] vt to chew; (fig) to chew over // vi to chew the cud.
rumor [ru'mor] nm (ruido sordo) low sound; (murmuración) murmur, buzz; **rumorearse** vr: **se rumorea que** it is rumoured that.
runrún [run'run] nm (voces) murmur, sound of voices; (fig) rumour.
rupestre [ru'pestre] a rock cpd.
ruptura [rup'tura] nf rupture.
rural [ru'ral] a rural.
Rusia ['rusja] nf Russia; **ruso, a** a, nm/f

Russian.

rústico, a ['rustiko, a] *a* rustic; (*ordinario*) coarse, uncouth // *nm/f* yokel // *nf*: **libro en rústica** paperback.

ruta ['ruta] *nf* route.

rutina [ru'tina] *nf* routine; **~rio, a** *a* routine.

S

S *abr* (= *santo, a*) St; (= *sur*) S.

s. *abr* (= *siglo*) C.; (= *siguiente*) foll.

S.A. *abr* (= *Sociedad Anónima*) Ltd (*Brit*), Inc (*US*).

sábado ['saβaðo] *nm* Saturday.

sábana ['saβana] *nf* sheet.

sabandija [saβan'dixa] *nf* bug, insect.

sabañón [saβa'ɲon] *nm* chilblain.

sabelotodo [saβelo'toðo] *nm/f inv* know-all.

saber [sa'βer] *vt* to know; (*llegar a conocer*) to find out, learn; (*tener capacidad de*) to know how to // *vi*: **~ a** to taste of, taste like // *nm* knowledge, learning; **a ~** namely; *¿sabes conducir/nadar?* can you drive/swim?; *¿sabes francés?* do you speak French?; **~ de memoria** to know by heart; **hacer ~ algo a uno** to inform sb of sth, let sb know sth.

sabiduría [saβiðu'ria] *nf* (*conocimientos*) wisdom; (*instrucción*) learning.

sabiendas [sa'βjendas]: **a ~** *ad* knowingly.

sabio, a ['saβjo,a] *a* (*docto*) learned; (*prudente*) wise, sensible.

sabor [sa'βor] *nm* taste, flavour; **~ear** *vt* to taste, savour; (*fig*) to relish.

sabotaje [saβo'taxe] *nm* sabotage.

saboteador, a [saβotea'ðor, a] *nm/f* saboteur.

sabotear [saβote'ar] *vt* to sabotage.

sabré *etc vb ver* **saber.**

sabroso, a [sa'βroso, a] *a* tasty; (*fig: fam*) racy, salty.

sacacorchos [saka'kortʃos] *nm inv* corkscrew.

sacapuntas [saka'puntas] *nm inv* pencil sharpener.

sacar [sa'kar] *vt* to take out; (*fig: extraer*) to get (out); (*quitar*) to remove, get out; (*hacer salir*) to bring out; (*conclusión*) to draw; (*novela etc*) to publish, bring out; (*ropa*) to take off; (*obra*) to make; (*premio*) to receive; (*entradas*) to get; (*TENIS*) to serve; **~ adelante** (*niño*) to bring up; (*negocio*) to carry on, go on with; **~ a uno a bailar** to get sb up to dance; **~ una foto** to take a photo; **~ la lengua** to stick out one's tongue; **~ buenas/malas notas** to get good/bad marks.

sacarina [saka'rina] *nf* saccharin(e).

sacerdote [saθer'ðote] *nm* priest.

saco ['sako] *nm* bag; (*grande*) sack; (*su*

contenido) bagful; (*AM*) jacket; **~ de dormir** sleeping bag.

sacramento [sakra'mento] *nm* sacrament.

sacrificar [sakrifi'kar] *vt* to sacrifice; **sacrificio** *nm* sacrifice.

sacrilegio [sakri'lexjo] *nm* sacrilege; **sacrílego, a** *a* sacrilegious.

sacristía [sakris'tia] *nf* sacristy.

sacro, a ['sakro, a] *a* sacred.

sacudida [saku'ðiða] *nf* (*agitación*) shake, shaking; (*sacudimiento*) jolt, bump; **~ eléctrica** electric shock.

sacudir [saku'ðir] *vt* to shake; (*golpear*) to hit.

sádico, a ['saðiko, a] *a* sadistic // *nm/f* sadist; **sadismo** *nm* sadism.

saeta [sa'eta] *nf* (*flecha*) arrow.

sagacidad [sayaθi'ðað] *nf* shrewdness, cleverness; **sagaz** *a* shrewd, clever.

sagitario [saxi'tarjo] *nm* Sagittarius.

sagrado, a [sa'yraðo, a] *a* sacred, holy.

Sáhara ['saara] *nm*: **el ~** the Sahara (desert).

sal *vb ver* **salir** // [sal] *nf* salt.

sala ['sala] *nf* (*cuarto grande*) large room; (~ *de estar*) living room; (*TEATRO*) house, auditorium; (*de hospital*) ward; **~ de apelación** court; **~ de espera** waiting room; **~ de estar** living room; **~ de fiestas** dance hall.

salado, a [sa'laðo, a] *a* salty; (*fig*) witty, amusing; **agua salada** salt water.

salar [sa'lar] *vt* to salt, add salt to.

salarial [sala'rjal] *a* (*aumento, revisión*) wage *cpd*, salary *cpd*.

salario [sa'larjo] *nm* wage, pay.

salchicha [sal'tʃitʃa] *nf* (*pork*) sausage; **salchichón** *nm* (*salami-type*) sausage.

saldar [sal'dar] *vt* to pay; (*vender*) to sell off; (*fig*) to settle, resolve; **saldo** *nm* (*pago*) settlement; (*de una cuenta*) balance; (*lo restante*) remnant(s) (*pl*), remainder; **~s** *nmpl* (*en tienda*) sale.

saldré *etc vb ver* **salir.**

salero [sa'lero] *nm* salt cellar.

salgo *etc vb ver* **salir.**

salida [sa'liða] *nf* (*puerta etc*) exit, way out; (*acto*) leaving, going out; (*de tren,* *AVIAT*) departure; (*TEC*) output, production; (*fig*) way out; (*COM*) opening; (*GEO, válvula*) outlet; (*de gas*) leak; **calle sin ~** cul-de-sac; **~ de incendios** fire escape.

saliente [sa'ljente] *a* (*ARQ*) projecting; (*sol*) rising; (*fig*) outstanding.

salir [sa'lir] ♦ *vi* **1** (*partir*: *tb*: **~ de**) to leave; **Juan ha salido** Juan is out; **salió de la cocina** he came out of the kitchen

2 (*aparecer*) to appear; (*disco, libro*) to come out; **anoche salió en la tele** she appeared *o* was on TV last night; **salió en todos los periódicos** it was in all the papers

3 (*resultar*): **la muchacha nos salió muy**

trabajadora the girl turned out to be a very hard worker; **la comida te ha salido exquisita** the food was delicious; sale muy caro it's very expensive

4: ~le a uno algo: **la entrevista que hice me salió bien/mal** the interview I did went o turned out well/badly

5: ~ **adelante**: no sé como haré para ~ adelante I don't know how I'll get by ♦ ~se *vr* (*líquido*) to spill; (*animal*) to escape.

saliva [sa'liβa] *nf* saliva.

salmo ['salmo] *nm* psalm.

salmón [sal'mon] *nm* salmon.

salmuera [sal'mwera] *nf* pickle, brine.

salón [sa'lon] *nm* (*de casa*) living room, lounge; (*muebles*) lounge suite; ~ **de belleza** beauty parlour; ~ **de baile** dance hall.

salpicadero [salpika'ðero] *nm* (*AUTO*) dashboard.

salpicar [salpi'kar] *vt* (*rociar*) to sprinkle, spatter; (*esparcir*) to scatter.

salsa ['salsa] *nf* sauce; (*con carne asada*) gravy; (*fig*) spice.

saltado, a [sal'taðo, a] *a* (*botón etc*) missing; (*ojos*) bulging.

saltamontes [salta'montes] *nm inv* grasshopper.

saltar [sal'tar] *vt* to jump (over), leap (over); (*dejar de lado*) to skip, miss out // *vi* to jump, leap; (*pelota*) to bounce; (*al aire*) to fly up; (*quebrarse*) to break; (*al agua*) to dive; (*fig*) to explode, blow up.

saltear [salte'ar] *vt* (*robar*) to rob (in a holdup); (*asaltar*) to assault, attack; (*CULIN*) to sauté.

saltimbanqui [saltim'banki] *nm/f* acrobat.

salto ['salto] *nm* jump, leap; (*al agua*) dive; ~ **de agua** waterfall; ~ **de altura** high jump.

saltón, ona [sal'ton, ona] *a* (*ojos*) bulging, popping; (*dientes*) protruding.

salubre [sa'luβre] *a* healthy, salubrious.

salud [sa'luð] *nf* health; **¡(a su) ~!** cheers!, good health!; ~**able** *a* (*de buena ~*) healthy; (*provechoso*) good, beneficial.

saludar [salu'ðar] *vt* to greet; (*MIL*) to salute; **saludo** *nm* greeting; **saludos** (*en carta*) best wishes, regards.

salva ['salβa] *nf*: ~ **de aplausos** ovation.

salvación [salβa'θjon] *nf* salvation; (*rescate*) rescue.

salvado [sal'βaðo] *nm* bran.

Salvador [salβa'ðor]: **El** ~ El Salvador; **San** ~ San Salvador; **s~eño, a** *a, nm/f* Salvadorian.

salvaguardar [salβaɣwar'ðar] *vt* to safeguard.

salvaje [sal'βaxe] *a* wild; (*tribu*) savage; **salvajismo** *nm* savagery.

salvar [sal'βar] *vt* (*rescatar*) to save,

rescue; (*resolver*) to overcome, resolve; (*cubrir distancias*) to cover, travel; (*hacer excepción*) to except, exclude; (*un barco*) to salvage.

salvavidas [salβa'βiðas] *a inv*: **bote/chaleco/cinturón** ~ lifeboat/life jacket/life belt.

salvia ['salβja] *nf* sage.

salvo, a ['salβo, a] *a* safe // *ad* except (for), save; **a** ~ out of danger; ~ **que** unless; ~**conducto** *nm* safe-conduct.

san [san] *a* saint; ~ **Juan** St. John.

sanar [sa'nar] *vt* (*herida*) to heal; (*persona*) to cure // *vi* (*persona*) to get well, recover; (*herida*) to heal.

sanatorio [sana'torjo] *nm* sanatorium.

sanción [san'θjon] *nf* sanction; **sancionar** *vt* to sanction.

sandalia [san'dalja] *nf* sandal.

sandía [san'dia] *nf* watermelon.

sandwich ['sandwitʃ] (*pl* ~**s**, ~**es**) *nm* sandwich.

saneamiento [sanea'mjento] *nm* sanitation.

sanear [sane'ar] *vt* (*terreno*) to drain.

sangrar [san'grar] *vt, vi* to bleed; **sangre** *nf* blood.

sangría [san'gria] *nf* sangria, *sweetened drink of red wine with fruit*.

sangriento, a [san'grjento, a] *a* bloody.

sanguijuela [sangi'xwela] *nf* (*ZOOL, fig*) leech.

sanguinario, a [sangi'narjo, a] *a* bloodthirsty.

sanguíneo, a [san'gineo, a] *a* blood *cpd*.

sanidad [sani'ðað] *nf* sanitation; (*calidad de sano*) health, healthiness; ~ **pública** public health.

sanitario, a [sani'tarjo, a] *a* sanitary; (*de la salud*) health; ~**s** *nmpl* toilets (*Brit*), washroom (*US*).

sano, a ['sano, a] *a* healthy; (*sin daños*) sound; (*comida*) wholesome; (*entero*) whole, intact; ~ **y salvo** safe and sound.

Santiago [san'tjaɣo] *nm*: ~ **(de Chile)** Santiago.

santiamén [santja'men] *nm*: **en un** ~ in no time at all.

santidad [santi'ðað] *nf* holiness, sanctity; **santificar** *vt* to sanctify, make holy.

santiguarse [santi'ɣwarse] *vr* to make the sign of the cross.

santo, a ['santo, a] *a* holy; (*fig*) wonderful, miraculous // *nm/f* saint // *nm* saint's day; ~ **y seña** password.

santuario [san'twarjo] *nm* sanctuary, shrine.

saña ['saɲa] *nf* rage, fury.

sapo ['sapo] *nm* toad.

saque ['sake] *nm* (*TENIS*) service, serve; (*FÚTBOL*) throw-in; ~ **de esquina** corner (kick).

saquear [sake'ar] *vt* (*MIL*) to sack; (*robar*) to loot, plunder; (*fig*) to ransack; **saqueo** *nm* sacking; looting, plundering; ransacking.

sarampión [saram'pjon] *nm* measles *sg*.

sarcasmo [sar'kasmo] *nm* sarcasm; **sarcástico, a** *a* sarcastic.

sardina [sar'ðina] *nf* sardine.

sardónico, a [sar'ðoniko, a] *a* sardonic; (*irónico*) ironical, sarcastic.

sargento [sar'xento] *nm* sergeant.

sarna ['sarna] *nf* itch; (*MED*) scabies.

sarpullido [sarpu'ʎiðo] *nm* (*MED*) rash.

sartén [sar'ten] *nf* frying pan.

sastre ['sastre] *nm* tailor; ~**ría** *nf* (*arte*) tailoring; (*tienda*) tailor's (shop).

Satanás [cata'nac] *nm* Satan.

satélite [sa'telite] *nm* satellite.

sátira ['satira] *nf* satire.

satisfacción [satisfak'θjon] *nf* satisfaction.

satisfacer [satisfa'θer] *vt* to satisfy; (*gastos*) to meet; (*pérdida*) to make good; ~**se** *vr* to satisfy o.s., be satisfied; (*vengarse*) to take revenge; **satisfecho, a** *a* satisfied; (*contento*) content(ed), happy; (*tb*: ~ **de sí mismo**) self-satisfied, smug.

saturar [satu'rar] *vt* to saturate.

sauce ['sauθe] *nm* willow; ~ **llorón** weeping willow.

sauna ['sauna] *nf* sauna.

savia ['saβja] *nf* sap.

saxofón [sakso'fon] *nm* saxophone.

sazonado, a [saθo'naðo, a] *a* (*fruta*) ripe; (*CULIN*) flavoured, seasoned.

sazonar [saθo'nar] *vt* to ripen; (*CULIN*) to flavour, season.

scotch [es'kotʃ] *nm* ® adhesive *o* sticky tape.

se [se] *pron* **1** (*reflexivo: sg: m*) himself; (: *f*) herself; (: *pl*) themselves; (: *cosa*) itself; (: *de Vd*) yourself; (: *de Vds*) yourselves; ~ **está preparando** she's preparing herself; *para usos léxicos del pronombre ver el vb en cuestión, p.ej.* arrepentirse

2 (*con complemento indirecto*) to him; to her; to them; to it; to you; a usted ~ **lo dije ayer** I told you yesterday; ~ **compró un sombrero** he bought himself a hat; ~ **rompió la pierna** he broke his leg

3 (*uso recíproco*) each other, one another; ~ **miraron** (**el uno al otro**) they looked at each other *o* one another

4 (*en oraciones pasivas*): **se han vendido muchos libros** a lot of books have been sold

5 (*impersonal*): ~ **dice que ...** people say that, it is said that; **allí** ~ **come muy bien** the food there is very good, you can eat very well there.

SE *abr* (= sudeste) SE.

sé *vb ver* **saber, ser.**

sea *etc vb ver* **ser.**

sebo ['seβo] *nm* fat, grease.

secador [seka'ðor] *nm*: ~ **de pelo** hairdryer.

secadora [seka'ðora] *nf* (*ELEC*) tumble dryer.

secar [se'kar] *vt* to dry; ~**se** *vr* to dry (off); (*río, planta*) to dry up.

sección [sek'θjon] *nf* section.

seco, a ['seko, a] *a* dry; (*carácter*) cold; (*respuesta*) sharp, curt; **habrá pan a secas** there will be just bread; **decir algo a secas** to say sth curtly; **parar en** ~ to stop dead.

secretaría [sekreta'ria] *nf* secretariat.

secretario, a [sekre'tarjo, a] *nm/f* secretary.

secreto, a [ce'kreto, a] *a* secret; (*persona*) secretive // *nm* secret; (*calidad*) secrecy.

secta ['sekta] *nf* sect; ~**rio, a** *a* sectarian.

sector [sek'tor] *nm* sector.

secuela [se'kwela] *nf* consequence.

secuencia [se'kwenθja] *nf* sequence.

secuestrar [sekwes'trar] *vt* to kidnap; (*bienes*) to seize, confiscate; **secuestro** *nm* kidnapping; seizure, confiscation.

secular [seku'lar] *a* secular.

secundar [sekun'dar] *vt* to second, support.

secundario, a [sekun'darjo, a] *a* secondary.

sed [seð] *nf* thirst; **tener** ~ to be thirsty.

seda ['seða] *nf* silk.

sedal [se'ðal] *nm* fishing line.

sedante [se'ðante] *nm* sedative.

sede ['seðe] *nf* (*de gobierno*) seat; (*de compañía*) headquarters *pl*; **Santa S**~ Holy See.

sediento, a [se'ðjento, a] *a* thirsty.

sedimentar [seðimen'tar] *vt* to deposit; ~**se** *vr* to settle; **sedimento** *nm* sediment.

sedoso, a [se'ðoso, a] *a* silky, silken.

seducción [seðuk'θjon] *nf* seduction.

seducir [seðu'θir] *vt* to seduce; (*sobornar*) to bribe; (*cautivar*) to charm, fascinate; (*atraer*) to attract; **seductor, a** *a* seductive; charming, fascinating; attractive; (*engañoso*) deceptive, misleading // *nm/f* seducer.

segadora-trilladora [seɣa'ðora triʎa-'ðora] *nf* combine harvester.

seglar [se'ɣlar] *a* secular, lay.

segregación [seɣreɣa'θjon] *nf* segregation. ~ **racial** racial segregation.

segregar [seɣre'ɣar] *vt* to segregate, separate.

seguido, a [se'ɣiðo, a] *a* (*continuo*) continuous, unbroken; (*recto*) straight; ~**s** consecutive, successive // *ad* (*directo*) straight (on); (*después*) after; (*AM*: *a menudo*) often // *nf*: **en seguida** at once, right away; **5 días** ~**s** 5 days running, 5 days in a row.

seguimiento [seɣi'mjento] *nm* chase, pursuit; (*continuación*) continuation.

seguir [se'ɣir] *vt* to follow; (*venir*

después) to follow on, come after; (*proseguir*) to continue; (*perseguir*) to chase, pursue // *vi* (*gen*) to follow; (*continuar*) to continue, carry o go on; ~se *vr* to follow; **sigo sin comprender** I still don't understand; **sigue lloviendo** it's still raining.

según [se'ɣun] *prep* according to // *ad* according to circumstances; ~ **esté el tiempo** depending on the weather; **está ~ lo dejaste** it is just as you left it.

segundo, a [se'ɣundo, a] *a* second // *nm* (*gen, medida de tiempo*) second // *nf* second meaning; **segunda** (**clase**) second class; **segunda** (**marcha**) (*AUTO*) second (gear); **de segunda mano** second hand.

seguramente [seɣura'mente] *ad* surely; (*con certeza*) for sure, with certainty.

seguridad [seɣuri'ðað] *nf* safety; (*del estado, de casa etc*) security; (*certidumbre*) certainty; (*confianza*) confidence; (*estabilidad*) stability; ~ **social** social security.

seguro, a [se'ɣuro, a] *a* (*cierto*) sure, certain; (*fiel*) trustworthy; (*libre del peligro*) safe; (*bien defendido, firme*) secure // *ad* for sure, certainly // *nm* (*COM*) insurance; ~ **contra terceros/a todo riesgo** third party/comprehensive insurance; ~**s sociales** social security *sg*.

seis [seis] *num* six.

seísmo [se'ismo] *nm* tremor, earthquake.

selección [selek'θjon] *nf* selection; **seleccionar** *vt* to pick, choose, select.

selectividad [selektiβi'ðað] *nf* (*Esp*) university entrance examination.

selecto, a [se'lekto, a] *a* select, choice; (*escogido*) selected.

selva ['selβa] *nf* (*bosque*) forest, woods *pl*; (*jungla*) jungle.

sellar [se'ʎar] *vt* (*documento oficial*) to seal; (*pasaporte, visado*) to stamp.

sello ['seʎo] *nm* stamp; (*precinto*) seal.

semáforo [se'maforo] *nm* (*AUTO*) traffic lights *pl*; (*FERRO*) signal.

semana [se'mana] *nf* week; **entre ~** during the week; **S~ Santa** Holy Week; **semanal** *a* weekly.

semblante [sem'blante] *nm* face; (*fig*) look.

sembrar [sem'brar] *vt* to sow; (*objetos*) to sprinkle, scatter about; (*noticias etc*) to spread.

semejante [seme'xante] *a* (*parecido*) similar; ~**s** alike, similar // *nm* fellow man, fellow creature; **nunca hizo cosa ~** he never did any such thing; **semejanza** *nf* similarity, resemblance.

semejar [seme'xar] *vi* to seem like, resemble; ~**se** *vr* to look alike, be similar.

semen ['semen] *nm* semen; ~**tal** *nm* stud.

semestral [semes'tral] *a* half-yearly, bi-annual.

semicírculo [semi'θirkulo] *nm* semi-circle.

semiconsciente [semikons'θjente] *a* semiconscious.

semifinal [semifi'nal] *nf* semifinal.

semilla [se'miʎa] *nf* seed.

seminario [semi'narjo] *nm* (*REL*) seminary; (*ESCOL*) seminar.

sémola ['semola] *nf* semolina.

sempiterno, a [sempi'terno, a] *a* everlasting.

Sena ['sena] *nm*: **el ~** the (river) Seine.

senado [se'naðo] *nm* senate; **senador, a** *nm/f* senator.

sencillez [senθi'ʎeθ] *nf* simplicity; (*de persona*) naturalness; **sencillo, a** *a* simple; natural, unaffected.

senda ['senda] *nf*, **sendero** [sen'dero] *nm* path, track.

sendos, as ['sendos, as] *apl*: **les dio ~ golpes** he hit both of them.

senil [se'nil] *a* senile.

seno ['seno] *nm* (*ANAT*) bosom, bust; (*fig*) bosom; ~**s** breasts.

sensación [sensa'θjon] *nf* sensation; (*sentido*) sense; (*sentimiento*) feeling; **sensacional** *a* sensational.

sensato, a [sen'sato, a] *a* sensible.

sensible [sen'sible] *a* sensitive; (*apreciable*) perceptible, appreciable; (*pérdida*) considerable; ~**ro, a** *a* sentimental.

sensitivo, a [sensi'tiβo, a], **sensorial** [senso'rjal] *a* sense.

sensual [sen'swal] *a* sensual.

sentado, a [sen'taðo, a] *a* (*establecido*) settled; (*carácter*) sensible; **estar ~** to sit, be sitting (down) // *nf* sitting; (*protesta*) sit-in; **dar por ~** to take for granted, assume.

sentar [sen'tar] *vt* to sit, seat; (*fig*) to establish // *vi* (*vestido*) to suit; (*alimento*): ~ **bien/mal a** to agree/disagree with; ~**se** *vr* (*persona*) to sit, sit down; (*el tiempo*) to settle (down); (*los depósitos*) to settle.

sentencia [sen'tenθja] *nf* (*máxima*) maxim, saying; (*JUR*) sentence; **sentenciar** *vt* to sentence.

sentido, a [sen'tiðo, a] *a* (*pérdida*) regrettable; (*carácter*) sensitive // *nm* sense; (*sentimiento*) feeling; (*significado*) sense, meaning; (*dirección*) direction; **mi más ~ pésame** my deepest sympathy; ~ **del humor** sense of humour; ~ **único** one-way (street); **tener ~** to make sense.

sentimental [sentimen'tal] *a* sentimental; **vida ~** love life.

sentimiento [senti'mjento] *nm* (*emoción*) feeling, emotion; (*sentido*) sense; (*pesar*) regret, sorrow.

sentir [sen'tir] *vt* to feel; (*percibir*) to perceive, sense; (*lamentar*) to regret, be sorry for // *vi* (*tener la sensación*) to feel; (*lamentarse*) to feel sorry // *nm* opinion, judgement; ~**se bien/mal** to feel well/ill; **lo siento** I'm sorry.

seña ['seɲa] *nf* sign; (*MIL*) password; **~s** *nfpl* address *sg*; **~s personales** personal description *sg*.

señal [se'ɲal] *nf* sign; (*síntoma*) symptom; (*FERRO, TELEC*) signal; (*marca*) mark; (*COM*) deposit; **en ~ de** as a token of, as a sign of; **~ar** *vt* to mark; (*indicar*) to point out, indicate; (*fijar*) to fix, settle.

señor [se'ɲor] *nm* (*hombre*) man; (*caballero*) gentleman; (*dueño*) owner, master; (*trato: antes de nombre propio*) Mr; (: *hablando directamente*) sir; **muy ~ mío** Dear Sir; **el ~ alcalde/presidente** the mayor/president.

señora [se'ɲora] *nf* (*dama*) lady; (*trato: antes de nombre propio*) Mrs; (: *hablando directamente*) madam; (*esposa*) wife; **Nuestra S~** Our Lady.

señorita [seɲo'rita] *nf* (*con nombre y/o apellido*) Miss; (*mujer joven*) young lady.

señorito [seɲo'rito] *nm* young gentleman; (*pey*) rich kid.

señuelo [se'ɲwelo] *nm* decoy.

sepa *etc vb ver* **saber**.

separación [separa'θjon] *nf* separation; (*división*) division; (*distancia*) gap, distance.

separar [sepa'rar] *vt* to separate; (*dividir*) to divide; **~se** *vr* (*parte*) to come away; (*partes*) to come apart; (*persona*) to leave, go away; (*matrimonio*) to separate; **separatismo** *nm* separatism.

sepia ['sepja] *nf* cuttlefish.

septiembre [sep'tjembre] *nm* September.

séptimo, a ['septimo, a] *a, nm* seventh.

sepultar [sepul'tar] *vt* to bury; **sepultura** *nf* (*acto*) burial; (*tumba*) grave, tomb; **sepulturero, a** *nm/f* gravedigger.

sequedad [seke'ðað] *nf* dryness; (*fig*) brusqueness, curtness.

sequía [se'kia] *nf* drought.

séquito ['sekito] *nm* (*de rey etc*) retinue; (*POL*) followers *pl*.

ser [ser] **♦** *vi* **1** (*descripción*) to be; **es médica/muy alta** she's a doctor/very tall; **la familia es de Cuzco** his (*o her etc*) family is from Cuzco; **soy Anna** (*TELEC*) Anna speaking *o* here

2 (*propiedad*): **es de Joaquín** it's Joaquín's, it belongs to Joaquín

3 (*horas, fechas, números*): **es la una** it's one o'clock; **son las seis y media** it's half-past six; **es el 1 de junio** it's the first of June; **somos/son seis** there are six of us/them

4 (*en oraciones pasivas*): **ha sido descubierto ya** it's already been discovered

5: **es de esperar que ...** it is to be hoped *o* I *etc* hope that ...

6 (*locuciones con subjun*): **o sea** that is

to say; **sea él sea su hermana** either him or his sister

7: **a no ~ por él** ... but for him ...

8: **a no ~ que: a no ~ que tenga uno ya** unless he's got one already

♦ *nm* being; **~ humano** human being.

serenarse [sere'narse] *vr* to calm down.

sereno, a [se'reno, a] *a* (*persona*) calm, unruffled; (*el tiempo*) fine, settled; (*ambiente*) calm, peaceful // *nm* night watchman.

serial [ser'jal] *nm* serial.

serie ['serje] *nf* series; (*cadena*) sequence, succession; **fuera de ~** out of order; (*fig*) special, out of the ordinary; **fabricación en ~** mass production.

seriedad [serje'ðað] *nf* seriousness; (*formalidad*) reliability; (*de crisis*) gravity, seriousness; **serio, a** *a* serious; reliable, dependable; grave, serious; **en serio** *ad* seriously.

sermón [ser'mon] *nm* (*REL*) sermon.

serpentear [serpente'ar] *vi* to wriggle; (*camino, río*) to wind, snake.

serpentina [serpen'tina] *nf* streamer.

serpiente [ser'pjente] *nf* snake; **~ boa** boa constrictor; **~ de cascabel** rattlesnake.

serranía [serra'nia] *nf* mountainous area.

serrano, a [se'rrano] *a* highland *cpd*, hill *cpd* // *nm/f* highlander.

serrar [se'rrar] *vt* = **aserrar**.

serrín [se'rrin] *nm* = **aserrín**.

serrucho [se'rrutʃo] *nm* saw.

servicio [ser'βiθjo] *nm* service; **~s** *nmpl* toilet(s); **~ incluido** service charge included; **~ militar** military service.

servidor, a [serβi'ðor, a] *nm/f* servant.

servidumbre [serβi'ðumbre] *nf* (*sujeción*) servitude; (*criados*) servants *pl*, staff.

servil [ser'βil] *a* servile.

servilleta [serβi'ʎeta] *nf* serviette, napkin.

servir [ser'βir] *vt* to serve // *vi* to serve; (*tener utilidad*) to be of use, be useful; **~se** *vr* to serve *o* help o.s.; **~se de algo** to make use of sth, use sth; **sírvase pasar** please come in.

sesenta [se'senta] *num* sixty.

sesgo ['sesɤo] *nm* slant; (*fig*) slant, twist.

sesión [se'sjon] *nf* (*POL*) session, sitting; (*CINE*) showing.

seso ['seso] *nm* brain; **sesudo, a** *a* sensible, wise.

seta ['seta] *nf* mushroom; **~ venenosa** toadstool.

setecientos, as [sete'θjentos, as] *a, num* seven hundred.

setenta [se'tenta] *num* seventy.

seudo... [seuðo] *pref* pseudo... .

seudónimo [seu'ðonimo] *nm* pseudonym.

severidad [seβeri'ðað] *nf* severity;

severo, a *a* severe.

Sevilla [se'βiʎa] *n* Seville; **sevillano, a** *a* of *o* from Seville // *nm/f* native *o* inhabitant of Seville.

sexo ['sekso] *nm* sex.

sexto, a ['seksto, a] *a, nm* sixth.

sexual [sek'swal] *a* sexual; **vida ~ sex** life.

si [si] *conj* if; **me pregunto ~...** I wonder if *o* whether... .

sí [si] *ad* yes // *nm* consent // *pron* (*uso impersonal*) oneself; (*sg: m*) himself; (: *f*) herself; (: *de cosa*) itself; (*de usted*) yourself; (*pl*) themselves; (*de ustedes*) yourselves; (*recíproco*) each other; **él no quiere pero yo ~** he doesn't want to but I do; **ella ~ vendrá** she will certainly come, she is sure to come; **claro que ~** of course; **creo que ~** I think so.

siamés, esa [sja'mes, esa] *a, nm/f* Siamese.

SIDA ['siða] *nm abr* (= *Síndrome de Inmuno-deficiencia Adquirida*) AIDS.

siderúrgico, a [siðe'rurxico, a] *a* iron and steel *cpd* // *nf*: **la siderúrgica** the iron and steel industry.

sidra ['siðra] *nf* cider.

siembra ['sjembra] *nf* sowing.

siempre ['sjempre] *ad* always; (*todo el tiempo*) all the time; **~ que** *conj* (*cada vez*) whenever; (*dado que*) provided that; **como ~** as usual; **para ~** for ever.

sien [sjen] *nf* temple.

siento *etc vb ver* **sentar, sentir.**

sierra ['sjerra] *nf* (*TEC*) saw; (*cadena de montañas*) mountain range.

siervo, a ['sjerβo, a] *nm/f* slave.

siesta ['sjesta] *nf* siesta, nap; **echar la ~** to have an afternoon nap *o* a siesta.

siete ['sjete] *num* seven.

sífilis ['sifilis] *nf* syphilis.

sifón [si'fon] *nm* syphon; **whisky con ~** whisky and soda.

sigla ['siɣla] *nf* abbreviation; acronym.

siglo ['siɣlo] *nm* century; (*fig*) age.

significación [siɣnifika'θjon] *nf* significance.

significado [siɣnifi'kaðo] *nm* significance; (*de palabra etc*) meaning.

significar [siɣnifi'kar] *vt* to mean, signify; (*notificar*) to make known, express; **significativo, a** *a* significant.

signo ['siɣno] *nm* sign; **~ de admiración** *o* **exclamación** exclamation mark; **~ de interrogación** question mark.

sigo *etc vb ver* **seguir.**

siguiente [si'ɣjente] *a* next, following.

siguió *etc vb ver* **seguir.**

sílaba ['silaβa] *nf* syllable.

silbar [sil'βar] *vt, vi* to whistle; **silbato** *nm* whistle; **silbido** *nm* whistle, whistling.

silenciador [silenθja'ðor] *nm* silencer.

silenciar [silen'θjar] *vt* (*persona*) to silence; (*escándalo*) to hush up; **silencio**

nm silence, quiet; **silencioso, a** *a* silent, quiet.

silicio [si'liθjo] *nm* silicon.

silueta [si'lweta] *nf* silhouette; (*de edificio*) outline; (*figura*) figure.

silvestre [sil'βestre] *a* (*BOT*) wild; (*fig*) rustic, rural.

silla ['siʎa] *nf* (*asiento*) chair; (*tb*: **~ de montar**) saddle; **~ de ruedas** wheelchair.

sillón [si'ʎon] *nm* armchair, easy chair.

simbólico, a [sim'boliko, a] *a* symbolic(al).

simbolizar [simboli'θar] *vt* to symbolize.

símbolo ['simbolo] *nm* symbol.

simetría [sime'tria] *nf* symmetry.

simiente [si'mjente] *nf* seed.

similar [simi'lar] *a* similar.

simio ['simjo] *nm* ape.

simpatía [simpa'tia] *nf* liking; (*afecto*) affection; (*amabilidad*) kindness; (*solidaridad*) mutual support, solidarity; **simpático, a** *a* nice, pleasant; kind.

simpatizante [simpati'θante] *nm/f* sympathizer.

simpatizar [simpati'θar] *vi*: **~ con** to get on well with.

simple ['simple] *a* simple; (*elemental*) simple, easy; (*mero*) mere; (*puro*) pure, sheer // *nm/f* simpleton; **~za** *nf* simpleness; (*necedad*) silly thing; **simplicidad** *nf* simplicity; **simplificar** *vt* to simplify.

simular [simu'lar] *vt* to simulate.

simultáneo, a [simul'taneo, a] *a* simultaneous.

sin [sin] *prep* without; **la ropa está ~ lavar** the clothes are unwashed; **~ que** *conj* without; **~ embargo** however, still.

sinagoga [sina'ɣoɣa] *nf* synagogue.

sinceridad [sinθeri'ðað] *nf* sincerity; **sincero, a** *a* sincere.

sincronizar [sinkroni'θar] *vt* to synchronize.

sindical [sindi'kal] *a* union *cpd*, trade-union *cpd*; **~ista** *a, nm/f* trade-unionist.

sindicato [sindi'kato] *nm* (*de trabajadores*) trade(s) union; (*de negociantes*) syndicate.

sinfín [sin'fin] *nm*: **un ~ de** a great many, no end of.

sinfonía [sinfo'nia] *nf* symphony.

singular [singu'lar] *a* singular; (*fig*) outstanding, exceptional; (*pey*) peculiar, odd; **~idad** *nf* singularity, peculiarity; **~izar** *vt* to single out; **~izarse** *vr* to distinguish o.s., stand out.

siniestro, a [si'njestro, a] *a* left; (*fig*) sinister // *nm* (*accidente*) accident.

sinnúmero [sin'numero] *nm* = **sinfín.**

sino ['sino] *nm* fate, destiny // *conj* (*pero*) but; (*salvo*) except, save.

sinónimo, a [si'nonimo, a] *a* synonymous // *nm* synonym.

síntesis ['sintesis] *nf* synthesis; **sintético, a** *a* synthetic.

sintetizar [sinteti'θar] *vt* to synthesize.

sintió *vb ver* **sentir.**

síntoma ['sintoma] *nm* symptom.

sinvergüenza [simber'xwenθa] *nm/f* rogue, scoundrel; ¡es un ~! he's got a nerve!

sionismo [sjo'nismo] *nm* Zionism.

siquiera [si'kjera] *conj* even if, even though // *ad* at least; ni ~ not even.

sirena [si'rena] *nf* siren.

Siria ['sirja] *nf* Syria; **sirio, a** *a, nm/f* Syrian.

sirviente, a [sir'ßjente, a] *nm/f* servant.

sirvo *etc vb ver* **servir.**

sisear [sise'ar] *vt, vi* to hiss.

sismógrafo [sis'moɣrato] *nm* seismograph.

sistema [sis'tema] *nm* system; (*método*) method; **sistemático, a** *a* systematic.

sitiar [si'tjar] *vt* to besiege, lay seige to.

sitio ['sitjo] *nm* (*lugar*) place; (*espacio*) room, space; (*MIL*) siege.

situación [sitwa'θjon] *nf* situation, position; (*estatus*) position, standing.

situado, a [situ'aðo] *a* situated, placed.

situar [si'twar] *vt* to place, put; (*edificio*) to locate, situate.

slip [slip] *nm* pants *pl*, briefs *pl*.

smoking ['smokin, es'mokin] (*pl* ~s) *nm* dinner jacket (*Brit*), tuxedo (*US*).

snob [es'nob] = **esnob.**

so [so] *prep* under.

SO *abr* (= *suroeste*) SW.

sobaco [so'ßako] *nm* armpit.

soberanía [soßera'nia] *nf* sovereignty; **soberano, a** *a* sovereign; (*fig*) supreme // *nm/f* sovereign.

soberbio, a [so'ßerßjo, a] *a* (*orgulloso*) proud; (*altivo*) haughty, arrogant; (*fig*) magnificent, superb // *nf* pride; haughtiness, arrogance; magnificence.

sobornar [soßor'nar] *vt* to bribe; **soborno** *nm* bribe.

sobra ['soßra] *nf* excess, surplus; ~s *nfpl* left-overs, scraps; de ~ surplus, extra; tengo de ~ I've more than enough; ~do, a *a* (*más que suficiente*) more than enough; (*superfluo*) excessive // *ad* too, exceedingly; **sobrante** *a* remaining, extra // *nm* surplus, remainder.

sobrar [so'ßrar] *vt* to exceed, surpass // *vi* (*tener de más*) to be more than enough; (*quedar*) to remain, be left (over).

sobrasada [soßra'saða] *nf* pork sausage spread.

sobre ['soßre] *prep* (*gen*) on; (*encima*) on (top of); (*por encima de, arriba de*) over, above; (*más que*) more than; (*además*) in addition to, besides; (*alrededor de, tratando de*) about // *nm* envelope; ~ **todo** above all.

sobrecama [soßre'kama] *nf* bedspread.

sobrecargar [soßrekar'xar] *vt* (*camión*) to overload; (*COM*) to surcharge.

sobredosis [soßre'ðosis] *nf inv* overdose.

sobreentender [soßre(e)nten'der] *vt* (*adivinar*) to deduce, infer; ~se *vr*: se sobreentiende que ... it is implied that ....

sobrehumano, a [soßreu'mano, a] *a* superhuman.

sobrellevar [soßreʎe'ßar] *vt* (*fig*) to bear, endure.

sobrenatural [soßrenatu'ral] *a* supernatural.

sobrepasar [soßrepa'sar] *vt* to exceed, surpass.

sobreponer [soßrepo'ner] *vt* (*poner encima*) to put on top; (*añadir*) to add; ~se *vr*: ~se a to win through, pull through.

sobresaliente [soßresa'ljente] *a* projecting; (*fig*) outstanding, excellent.

sobresalir [soßresa'lir] *vi* to project, jut out; (*fig*) to stand out, excel.

sobresaltar [soßresal'tar] *vt* (*asustar*) to scare, frighten; (*sobrecoger*) to startle; **sobresalto** *nm* (*movimiento*) start; (*susto*) scare; (*turbación*) sudden shock.

sobretodo [soßre'toðo] *nm* overcoat.

sobrevenir [soßreße'nir] *vi* (*ocurrir*) to happen (unexpectedly); (*resultar*) to follow, ensue.

sobreviviente [soßreßi'ßjente] *a* surviving // *nm/f* survivor.

sobrevivir [soßreßi'ßir] *vi* to survive.

sobrevolar [soßreßo'lar] *vt* to fly over.

sobriedad [soßrje'ðað] *nf* sobriety, soberness; (*moderación*) moderation, restraint.

sobrino, a [so'ßrino, a] *nm/f* nephew/niece.

sobrio, a ['soßrjo, a] *a* (*moderado*) moderate, restrained.

socarrón, ona [soka'rron, ona] *a* (*sarcástico*) sarcastic, ironic(al).

socavón [soka'ßon] *nm* (*hoyo*) hole.

sociable [so'θjaßle] *a* (*persona*) sociable, friendly; (*animal*) social.

social [so'θjal] *a* social; (*COM*) company *cpd*.

socialdemócrata [soθjalde'mokrata] *nm/f* social democrat.

socialista [soθja'lista] *a, nm/f* socialist.

socializar [soθjali'θar] *vt* to socialize.

sociedad [soθje'ðað] *nf* society; (*COM*) company; ~ **anónima** limited company; ~ **de consumo** consumer society.

socio, a ['soθjo, a] *nm/f* (*miembro*) member; (*COM*) partner.

sociología [soθjolo'xia] *nf* sociology; **sociólogo, a** *nm/f* sociologist.

socorrer [soko'rrer] *vt* to help; **socorrista** *nm/f* first aider; (*en piscina, playa*) lifeguard; **socorro** *nm* (*ayuda*) help, aid; (*MIL*) relief; ¡socorro! help!

soda ['soða] *nf* (*sosa*) soda; (*bebida*) soda (water).

sofá [so'fa] (*pl* ~s) *nm* sofa, settee; ~**cama** *nm* studio couch, sofa bed.

sofisticación [sofistika'θjon] *nf* sophistication.

sofocar [sofo'kar] *vt* to suffocate; (*apagar*) to smother, put out; ~**se** *vr* to suffocate; (*fig*) to blush, feel embarrassed; **sofoco** *nm* suffocation; embarrassment.

soga ['soɣa] *nf* rope.

sois *vb ver* **ser**.

soja ['soxa] *nf* soya.

sojuzgar [soxuθ'ɣar] *vt* to subdue, rule despotically.

sol [sol] *nm* sun; (*luz*) sunshine, sunlight; **hace** *o* **hay** ~ it is sunny.

solamente [sola'mente] *ad* only, just.

solapa [so'lapa] *nf* (*de chaqueta*) lapel; (*de libro*) jacket.

solar [so'lar] *a* solar, sun *cpd*.

solaz [so'laθ] *nm* recreation, relaxation; ~**ar** *vt* (*divertir*) to amuse.

soldada [sol'daða] *nf* pay.

soldado [sol'daðo] *nm* soldier; ~ **raso** private.

soldador [solda'ðor] *nm* soldering iron; (*persona*) welder.

soldar [sol'dar] *vt* to solder, weld; (*unir*) to join, unite.

soleado, a [sole'aðo, a] *a* sunny.

soledad [sole'ðað] *nf* solitude; (*estado infeliz*) loneliness.

solemne [so'lemne] *a* solemn; **solemnidad** *nf* solemnity.

soler [so'ler] *vi* to be in the habit of, be accustomed to; **suele salir a las ocho** she usually goes out at 8 o'clock.

solfeo [sol'feo] *nm* solfa.

solicitar [soliθi'tar] *vt* (*permiso*) to ask for, seek; (*puesto*) to apply for; (*votos*) to canvass for; (*atención*) to attract; (*persona*) to pursue, chase after.

solícito, a [so'liθito, a] *a* (*diligente*) diligent; (*cuidadoso*) careful; **solicitud** *nf* (*calidad*) great care; (*petición*) request; (*a un puesto*) application.

solidaridad [soliðari'ðað] *nf* solidarity; **solidario, a** *a* (*participación*) joint, common; (*compromiso*) mutually binding.

solidez [soli'ðeθ] *nf* solidity; **sólido, a** *a* solid.

soliloquio [soli'lokjo] *nm* soliloquy.

solista [so'lista] *nm/f* soloist.

solitario, a [soli'tarjo, a] *a* (*persona*) lonely, solitary; (*lugar*) lonely, desolate // *nm/f* (*reclusa*) recluse; (*en la sociedad*) loner // *nm* solitaire.

solo, a ['solo, a] *a* (*único*) single, sole; (*sin compañía*) alone; (*solitario*) lonely; **hay una sola dificultad** there is just one difficulty; **a solas** alone, by o.s.

sólo ['solo] *ad* only, just.

solomillo [solo'miʎo] *nm* sirloin.

soltar [sol'tar] *vt* (*dejar ir*) to let go of; (*desprender*) to unfasten, loosen; (*librar*) to release, set free; (*risa etc*) to let out.

soltero, a [sol'tero, a] *a* single, unmarried // *nm/f* bachelor/single woman; **solterón, ona** *nm/f* old bachelor/spinster.

soltura [sol'tura] *nf* looseness, slackness; (*de los miembros*) agility, ease of movement; (*en el hablar*) fluency, ease.

soluble [so'luβle] *a* (*QUÍMICA*) soluble; (*problema*) solvable; ~ **en agua** soluble in water.

solución [solu'θjon] *nf* solution; **solucionar** *vt* (*problema*) to solve; (*asunto*) to settle, resolve.

solventar [solβen'tar] *vt* (*pagar*) to settle, pay; (*resolver*) to resolve.

sollozar [soʎo'θar] *vi* to sob; **sollozo** *nm* sob.

sombra ['sombra] *nf* shadow; (*como protección*) shade; ~**s** *nfpl* darkness *sg*, shadows; **tener buena/mala** ~ to be lucky/unlucky.

sombrero [som'brero] *nm* hat.

sombrilla [som'briʎa] *nf* parasol, sunshade.

sombrío, a [som'brio, a] *a* (*oscuro*) dark; (*fig*) sombre, sad; (*persona*) gloomy.

somero, a [so'mero, a] *a* superficial.

someter [some'ter] *vt* (*país*) to conquer; (*persona*) to subject to one's will; (*informe*) to present, submit; ~**se** *vr* to give in, yield, submit; ~ **a** to subject to.

somnífero [som'nifero] *nm* sleeping pill.

somos *vb ver* **ser**.

son *vb ver* **ser** // [son] *nm* sound; **en** ~ **de broma** as a joke.

sonajero [sona'xero] *nm* (baby's) rattle.

sonambulismo [sonambu'lismo] *nm* sleepwalking; **sonámbulo, a** *nm/f* sleepwalker.

sonar [so'nar] *vt* to ring // *vi* to sound; (*hacer ruido*) to make a noise; (*pronunciarse*) to be sounded, be pronounced; (*ser conocido*) to sound familiar; (*campana*) to ring; (*reloj*) to strike, chime; ~**se** *vr*: ~**se (las narices)** to blow one's nose; **me suena ese nombre** that name rings a bell.

sonda ['sonda] *nf* (*NAUT*) sounding; (*TEC*) bore, drill; (*MED*) probe.

sondear [sonde'ar] *vt* to sound; to bore (into), drill; to probe, sound; (*fig*) to sound out; **sondeo** *nm* sounding; boring, drilling; (*fig*) poll, enquiry.

sónico, a ['soniko, a] *a* sonic, sound *cpd*.

sonido [so'niðo] *nm* sound.

sonoro, a [so'noro, a] *a* sonorous; (*resonante*) loud, resonant.

sonreír [sonre'ir] *vi*, **sonreírse** *vr* to smile; **sonriente** *a* smiling; **sonrisa** *nf* smile.

sonrojo [son'roxo] *nm* blush.

soñador, a [soɲa'ðor, a] *a, nm/f* dreamer.

soñar [so'ɲar] *vt*, *vi* to dream; ~ **con** to dream about *o* of.

soñoliento, a [soɲo'ljento, a] *a* sleepy, drowsy.

sopa ['sopa] *nf* soup; **sopera** *nf* soup tureen.

soplar [so'plar] *vt* (*polvo*) to blow away, blow off; (*inflar*) to blow up; (*vela*) to blow out // *vi* to blow; **soplo** *nm* blow, puff; (*de viento*) puff, gust.

soporífero [sopo'rifero] *nm* sleeping pill.

soportable [sopor'taβle] *a* bearable.

soportar [sopor'tar] *vt* to bear, carry; (*fig*) to bear, put up with; **soporte** *nm* support; (*fig*) pillar, support.

soprano [so'prano] *nf* soprano.

sorber [sor'βer] *vt* (*chupar*) to sip; (*inhalar*) to inhale; (*tragar*) to swallow (up); (*absorber*) to soak up, absorb.

sorbete [sor'βete] *nm* iced fruit drink.

sorbo ['sorβo] *nm* (*trago: grande*) gulp, swallow; (: *pequeño*) sip.

sordera [sor'ðera] *nf* deafness.

sórdido, a ['sorðiðo, a] *a* dirty, squalid.

sordo, a ['sorðo, a] *a* (*persona*) deaf // *nm/f* deaf person; **~mudo, a** *a* deaf and dumb.

soroche [so'rotʃe] *nm* (*AM*) mountain sickness.

sorprendente [sorpren'dente] *a* surprising.

sorprender [sorpren'der] *vt* to surprise; **sorpresa** *nf* surprise.

sortear [sorte'ar] *vt* to draw lots for; (*rifar*) to raffle; (*dificultad*) to avoid; **sorteo** *nm* (*en lotería*) draw; (*rifa*) raffle.

sortija [sor'tixa] *nf* ring; (*rizo*) ringlet, curl.

sosegado, a [sose'ɣaðo, a] *a* quiet, calm.

sosegar [sose'ɣar] *vt* to quieten, calm; (*el ánimo*) to reassure // *vi* to rest; **sosiego** *nm* quiet(ness), calm(ness).

soslayo [sos'lajo]: de ~ *ad* obliquely, sideways.

soso, a ['soso, a] *a* (*CULIN*) tasteless; (*fig*) dull, uninteresting.

sospecha [sos'petʃa] *nf* suspicion; **sospechar** *vt* to suspect; **sospechoso, a** *a* suspicious; (*testimonio, opinión*) suspect // *nm/f* suspect.

sostén [sos'ten] *nm* (*apoyo*) support; (*sujetador*) bra; (*alimentación*) sustenance, food.

sostener [soste'ner] *vt* to support; (*mantener*) to keep up, maintain; (*alimentar*) to sustain, keep going; **~se** *vr* to support o.s.; (*seguir*) to continue, remain; **sostenido, a** *a* continuous, sustained; (*prolongado*) prolonged.

sótano ['sotano] *nm* basement.

soviético, a [so'βjetiko, a] *a* Soviet; los **~s** the Soviets.

soy *vb ver* **ser**.

Sr. *abr* (= *Señor*) Mr.

Sra. *abr* (= *Señora*) Mrs.

S.R.C. *abr* (= *se ruega contestación*) R.S.V.P.

Sres. *abr* (= *Señores*) Messrs.

Srta. *abr* (= *Señorita*) Miss.

Sta. *abr* (= *Santa*) St.

status ['status, e'status] *nm inv* status.

Sto. *abr* (= *Santo*) St.

su [su] *pron* (*de él*) his; (*de ella*) her; (*de una cosa*) its; (*de ellos, ellas*) their; (*de usted, ustedes*) your.

suave ['swaβe] *a* gentle; (*superficie*) smooth; (*trabajo*) easy; (*música, voz*) soft, sweet; **suavidad** *nf* gentleness, smoothness; softness, sweetness; **suavizar** *vt* to soften; (*quitar la aspereza*) to smooth (out).

subalimentado, a [suβalimen'taðo, a] *a* undernourished.

subasta [su'βasta] *nf* auction; **subastar** *vt* to auction (off).

subcampeón, ona [suβkampe'on, ona] *nm/f* runner-up.

subconsciente [suβkon'sθjente] *a, nm* subconscious.

subdesarrollado, a [suβðesarro'ʎaðo, a] *a* underdeveloped.

subdesarrollo [suβðesa'rroʎo] *nm* underdevelopment.

subdirector, a [suβðirek'tor, a] *nm/f* assistant director.

súbdito, a ['suβðito, a] *nm/f* subject.

subdividir [suβðiβi'ðir] *vt* to subdivide.

subestimar [suβesti'mar] *vt* to underestimate, underrate.

subido, a [su'βiðo, a] *a* (*color*) bright, strong; (*precio*) high // *nf* (*de montaña etc*) ascent, climb; (*de precio*) rise, increase; (*pendiente*) slope, hill.

subir [su'βir] *vt* (*objeto*) to raise, lift up; (*cuesta, calle*) to go up; (*colina, montaña*) to climb; (*precio*) to raise, put up // *vi* to go up, come up; (*a un coche*) to get in; (*a un autobús, tren o avión*) to get on, board; (*precio*) to rise, go up; (*río, marea*) to rise; **~se** *vr* to get up, climb.

súbito, a ['suβito, a] *a* (*repentino*) sudden; (*imprevisto*) unexpected.

subjetivo, a [suβxe'tiβo, a] *a* subjective.

sublevación [suβleβa'θjon] *nf* revolt, rising.

sublevar [suβle'βar] *vt* to rouse to revolt; **~se** *vr* to revolt, rise.

sublime [su'βlime] *a* sublime.

submarino, a [suβma'rino, a] *a* underwater // *nm* submarine.

subnormal [suβnor'mal] *a* subnormal // *nm/f* subnormal person.

subordinado, a [suβorði'naðo, a] *a, nm/f* subordinate.

subrayar [suβra'jar] *vt* to underline.

subrepticio, a [suβrep'tiθjo, a] *a* surreptitious.

subsanar [suβsa'nar] *vt* (*reparar*) to make good; (*perdonar*) to excuse; (*so-*

breponerse a) to overcome.
subscribir [sußskri'ßir] *vt* = **suscribir**.
subsidiario, a [sußsi'ðjarjo, a] *a* subsidiary.
subsidio [suß'siðjo] *nm (ayuda)* aid, financial help; *(subvención)* subsidy, grant; *(de enfermedad, paro etc)* benefit, allowance.
subsistencia [sußsis'tenθja] *nf* subsistence.
subsistir [sußsis'tir] *vi* to subsist; *(vivir)* to live; *(sobrevivir)* to survive, endure.
subterráneo, a [sußte'rraneo, a] *a* underground, subterranean // *nm* underpass, underground passage.
suburbano, a [sußur'ßano, a] *a* suburban.
suburbio [su'ßurßjo] *nm (barrio)* slum quarter; *(afueras)* suburbs *pl*.
subvencionar [sußßenθjo'nar] *vt* to subsidize.
subversión [sußßer'sjon] *nf* subversion; **subversivo, a** *a* subversive.
subyugar [sußju'var] *vt (país)* to subjugate, subdue; *(enemigo)* to overpower; *(voluntad)* to dominate.
succión [suk'θjon] *nf* suction.
sucedáneo, a [suθe'ðaneo, a] *a* substitute // *nm* substitute (food).
suceder [suθe'ðer] *vt, vi* to happen; *(seguir)* to succeed, follow; **lo que sucede es que...** the fact is that...; **sucesión** *nf* succession; *(serie)* sequence, series.
sucesivamente [suθesißa'mente] *ad:* **y así ~** and so on.
sucesivo, a [suθe'sißo, a] *a* successive, following; **en lo ~** in future, from now on.
suceso [su'θeso] *nm (hecho)* event, happening; *(incidente)* incident.
suciedad [suθje'ðað] *nf (estado)* dirtiness; *(mugre)* dirt, filth.
sucinto, a [su'θinto, a] *a (conciso)* succinct, concise.
sucio, a [su'θjo, a] *a* dirty.
Sucre ['sukre] *n* Sucre.
suculento, a [suku'lento, a] *a* succulent.
sucumbir [sukum'bir] *vi* to succumb.
sucursal [sukur'sal] *nf* branch (office).
Sudáfrica [suð'afrika] *nf* South Africa.
Sudamérica [suða'merika] *nf* South America; **sudamericano, a** *a, nm/f* South American.
sudar [su'ðar] *vt, vi* to sweat.
sudeste [su'ðeste] *nm* south-east.
sudoeste [suðo'este] *nm* south-west.
sudor [su'ðor] *nm* sweat; **~oso, a** *a* sweaty, sweating.
Suecia ['sweθja] *nf* Sweden; **sueco, a** *a* Swedish // *nm/f* Swede.
suegro, a ['swevro, a] *nm/f* father-/mother-in-law.
suela ['swela] *nf* sole.
sueldo ['sweldo] *nm* pay, wage(s) *(pl)*.

suele *etc vb ver* **soler**.
suelo ['swelo] *nm (tierra)* ground; *(de casa)* floor.
suelto, a ['swelto, a] *a* loose; *(libre)* free; *(separado)* detached; *(ágil)* quick, agile; *(corriente)* fluent, flowing // *nm (loose)* change, small change.
sueño *etc vb ver* **soñar** // ['sweɲo] *nm* sleep; *(somnolencia)* sleepiness, drowsiness; *(lo soñado, fig)* dream; **tener ~ to** be sleepy.
suero ['swero] *nm (MED)* serum; *(de leche)* whey.
suerte ['swerte] *nf (fortuna)* luck; *(azar)* chance; *(destino)* fate, destiny; *(condición)* lot; *(género)* sort, kind; **tener ~ to** be lucky; **de otra ~** otherwise, if not; **de ~ que** so that, in such a way that.
suéter ['sweter] *nm* sweater.
suficiente [sufi'θjente] *a* enough, sufficient // *nm (ESCOL)* pass.
sufragio [su'fraxjo] *nm (voto)* vote; *(derecho de voto)* suffrage.
sufrido, a [su'friðo, a] *a (persona)* tough; *(paciente)* long-suffering, patient.
sufrimiento [sufri'mjento] *nm (dolor)* suffering.
sufrir [su'frir] *vt (padecer)* to suffer; *(soportar)* to bear, put up with; *(apoyar)* to hold up, support // *vi* to suffer.
sugerencia [suxe'renθja] *nf* suggestion.
sugerir [suxe'rir] *vt* to suggest; *(sutilmente)* to hint.
sugestión [suxes'tjon] *nf* suggestion; *(sutil)* hint; **sugestionar** *vt* to influence.
sugestivo, a [suxes'tißo, a] *a* stimulating; *(fascinante)* fascinating.
suicida [sui'θiða] *a* suicidal // *nm/f* suicidal person; *(muerto)* suicide, person who has committed suicide; **suicidarse** *vr* to commit suicide, kill o.s.; **suicidio** *nm* suicide.
Suiza ['swiθa] *nf* Switzerland; **suizo, a** *a, nm/f* Swiss.
sujeción [suxe'θjon] *nf* subjection.
sujetador [suxeta'ðor] *nm* fastener, clip; *(sostén)* bra.
sujetar [suxe'tar] *vt (fijar)* to fasten; *(detener)* to hold down; *(fig)* to subject, subjugate; **~se** *vr* to subject o.s.; **sujeto, a** *a* fastened, secure // *nm* subject; *(individuo)* individual; **sujeto a** subject to.
suma ['suma] *nf (cantidad)* total, sum; *(de dinero)* sum; *(acto)* adding (up), addition; **en ~** in short.
sumamente [suma'mente] *ad* extremely, exceedingly.
sumar [su'mar] *vt* to add (up); *(reunir)* to collect, gather // *vi* to add up.
sumario, a [su'marjo, a] *a* brief, concise // *nm* summary.
sumergir [sumer'xir] *vt* to submerge; *(hundir)* to sink; *(bañar)* to immerse,

dip.

sumidero [sumi'ðero] *nm* drain, sewer; (*TEC*) sump.

suministrar [sumini'strar] *vt* to supply, provide; **suministro** *nm* supply; (*acto*) supplying, providing.

sumir [su'mir] *vt* to sink, submerge; (*fig*) to plunge.

sumisión [sumi'sjon] *nf* (*acto*) submission; (*calidad*) submissiveness, docility; **sumiso, a** *a* submissive, docile.

sumo, a ['sumo, a] *a* great, extreme; (*mayor*) highest, supreme.

suntuoso, a [sun'twoso, a] *a* sumptuous, magnificent.

supe *etc vb ver* **saber**.

super... [super] *pref* super..., over...; ~**bueno** great, fantastic.

súper ['super] *nm* (*gasolina*) three-star (petrol).

superar [supe'rar] *vt* (*sobreponerse a*) to overcome; (*rebasar*) to surpass, do better than; (*pasar*) to go beyond; ~**se** *vr* to excel o.s.

superávit [supe'raßit] *nm inv* surplus.

superficial [superfi'θjal] *a* superficial; (*medida*) surface *cpd*, of the surface.

superficie [super'fiθje] *nf* surface; (*área*) area.

superfluo, a [su'perflwo, a] *a* superfluous.

superintendente [superinten'dente] *nm/f* supervisor, superintendent.

superior [supe'rjor] *a* (*piso, clase*) upper; (*temperatura, número, nivel*) higher; (*mejor: calidad, producto*) superior, better // *nm/f* superior; ~**idad** *nf* superiority.

supermercado [supermer'kaðo] *nm* supermarket.

supersónico, a [super'soniko, a] *a* supersonic.

superstición [supersti'θjon] *nf* superstition; **supersticioso, a** *a* superstitious.

supervisor, a [superßi'sor, a] *nm/f* supervisor.

supervivencia [superßi'ßenθja] *nf* survival.

superviviente [superßi'ßjente] *a* surviving.

supiera *etc vb ver* **saber**.

suplantar [suplan'tar] *vt* (*persona*) to supplant.

suplementario, a [suplemen'tarjo, a] *a* supplementary; **suplemento** *nm* supplement.

suplente [su'plente] *a, nm/f* substitute.

supletorio, a [suple'torjo, a] *a* supplementary // *nm* supplement; **mesa supletoria** spare table.

súplica ['suplika] *nf* request; (*JUR*) petition.

suplicar [supli'kar] *vt* (*cosa*) to beg (for), plead for; (*persona*) to beg, plead with.

suplicio [su'pliθjo] *nm* torture.

suplir [su'plir] *vt* (*compensar*) to make good, make up for; (*reemplazar*) to replace, substitute // *vi*: ~ **a** to take the place of, substitute for.

supo *etc vb ver* **saber**.

suponer [supo'ner] *vt* to suppose // *vi* to have authority; **suposición** *nf* supposition.

supremacía [suprema'θia] *nf* supremacy.

supremo, a [su'premo, a] *a* supreme.

supresión [supre'sjon] *nf* suppression; (*de derecho*) abolition; (*de dificultad*) removal; (*de palabra etc*) deletion; (*de restricción*) cancellation, lifting.

suprimir [supri'mir] *vt* to suppress; (*derecho, costumbre*) to abolish; (*dificultad*) to remove; (*palabra etc*) to delete; (*restricción*) to cancel, lift.

supuesto, a *pp de* **suponer** // [su'pwesto, a] *a* (*hipotético*) supposed; (*falso*) false // *nm* assumption, hypothesis; ~ **que** *conj* since; **por** ~ of course.

sur [sur] *nm* south.

surcar [sur'kar] *vt* to plough; (*superficie*) to cut, score; **surco** *nm* (*en metal, disco*) groove; (*AGR*) furrow.

surgir [sur'xir] *vi* to arise, emerge; (*dificultad*) to come up, crop up.

surtido, a [sur'tiðo, a] *a* mixed, assorted // *nm* (*selección*) selection, assortment; (*abastecimiento*) supply, stock.

surtir [sur'tir] *vt* to supply, provide // *vi* to spout, spurt.

susceptible [susθep'tißle] *a* susceptible; (*sensible*) sensitive; ~ **de** capable of.

suscitar [susθi'tar] *vt* to cause, provoke; (*interés, sospechas*) to arouse.

suscribir [suskri'ßir] *vt* (*firmar*) to sign; (*respaldar*) to subscribe to, endorse; ~**se** *vr* to subscribe; **suscripción** *nf* subscription.

susodicho, a [suso'ðitʃo, a] *a* above-mentioned.

suspender [suspen'der] *vt* (*objeto*) to hang (up), suspend; (*trabajo*) to stop, suspend; (*ESCOL*) to fail; **suspensión** *nf* suspension; (*fig*) stoppage, suspension.

suspenso, a [sus'penso, a] *a* hanging, suspended; (*ESCOL*) failed // *nm*: **quedar** **o estar en** ~ to be pending.

suspicacia [suspi'kaθja] *nf* suspicion, mistrust; **suspicaz** *a* suspicious, distrustful.

suspirar [suspi'rar] *vi* to sigh; **suspiro** *nm* sigh.

sustancia [sus'tanθja] *nf* substance.

sustentar [susten'tar] *vt* (*alimentar*) to sustain, nourish; (*objeto*) to hold up, support; (*idea, teoría*) to maintain, uphold; (*fig*) to sustain, keep going; **sustento** *nm* support; (*alimento*) sustenance, food.

sustituir [sustitu'ir] *vt* to substitute, replace; **sustituto, a** *nm/f* substitute, replacement.

susto ['susto] nm fright, scare.

sustraer [sustra'er] vt to remove, take away; (MAT) to subtract.

susurrar [susu'rrar] vi to whisper; **susurro** nm whisper.

sutil [su'til] a (aroma, diferencia) subtle; (tenue) thin; (inteligencia, persona) sharp; **~eza** nf subtlety; thinness.

suyo, a ['sujo, a] a (con artículo o después del verbo ser: de él) his; (: de ella) hers; (: de ellos, ellas) theirs; (: de Ud, Uds) yours; un amigo ~ a friend of his (o hers o theirs o yours).

T

taba ['taβa] nf (ANAT) anklebone; (juego) jacks sg.

tabacalero, a [taβaka'lero, a] nm/f (vendedor) tobacconist // nf: T~ Spanish state tobacco monopoly.

tabaco [ta'βako] nm tobacco; (fam) cigarettes pl: **tabaquería** nf tobacconist's (Brit), cigar store (US).

taberna [ta'βerna] nf bar, pub (Brit); **tabernero, a** nm/f (encargado) publican; (camarero) barman/maid.

tabique [ta'βike] nm partition (wall).

tabla ['taβla] nf (de madera) plank; (estante) shelf; (de vestido) pleat; (ARTE) panel; **~s** nfpl: estar o quedar en ~s to draw; **~do** nm (plataforma) platform; (TEATRO) stage.

tablero [ta'βlero] nm (de madera) plank, board; (de ajedrez, damas) board; (AUTO) dashboard; ~ de anuncios notice (Brit) o bulletin (US) board.

tableta [ta'βleta] nf (MED) tablet; (de chocolate) bar.

tablilla [ta'βliλa] nf small board; (MED) splint.

tablón [ta'βlon] nm (de suelo) plank; (de techo) beam; ~ de anuncios notice board (Brit), bulletin board (US).

tabú [ta'βu] nm taboo.

tabular [taβu'lar] vt to tabulate.

taburete [taβu'rete] nm stool.

tacaño, a [ta'kaɲo, a] a (avaro) mean.

tácito, a ['taθito, a] a tacit.

taciturno, a [taθi'turno, a] a (callado) silent; (malhumorado) sullen.

taco ['tako] nm (BILLAR) cue; (libro de billetes) book; (AM: de zapato) heel; (tarugo) peg; (palabrota) swear word.

tacón [ta'kon] nm heel; de ~ alto high-heeled; **taconeo** nm (heel) stamping.

táctico, a ['taktiko, a] a tactical // nf tactics pl.

tacto ['takto] nm touch; (fig) tact.

tacha ['tatʃa] nf flaw; (TEC) stud; **tachar** vt (borrar) to cross out; **tachar de** to accuse of.

tafetán [tafe'tan] nm taffeta.

tafilete [tafi'lete] nm morocco leather.

tahona [ta'ona] nf (panadería) bakery.

tahúr, a [ta'ur, a] nm/f gambler; (pey) cheat.

taimado, a [tai'maðo, a] a (astuto) sly.

taita ['taita] nm (fam) dad, daddy.

tajada [ta'xaða] nf slice.

tajante [ta'xante] a sharp.

tajar [ta'xar] vt to cut; **tajo** nm (corte) cut; (GEO) cleft.

tal [tal] a such; ~ vez perhaps // pron (persona) someone, such a one; (cosa) something, such a thing; ~ como such as; ~ para cual tit for tat; (dos iguales) two of a kind // ad: ~ como (igual) just as; ~ cual (como es) just as it is; ¿qué ~? how are things?; ¿qué ~ te gusta? how do you like it? // conj: con ~ de que provided that.

taladrar [tala'ðrar] vt to drill; **taladro** nm drill; (hoyo) drill hole.

talante [ta'lante] nm (humor) mood; (voluntad) will, willingness.

talar [ta'lar] vt to fell, cut down; (devastar) to devastate.

talco ['talko] nm (polvos) talcum powder.

talego [ta'leɣo] nm, **talega** [ta'leɣa] nf sack.

talento [ta'lento] nm talent; (capacidad) ability.

TALGO ['talɣo] nm abr (Esp = tren articulado ligero Goicoechea-Oriol) ≈ HST (Brit).

talismán [talis'man] nm talisman.

talón [ta'lon] nm (ANAT) heel; (COM) counterfoil; (cheque) cheque (Brit), check (US).

talonario [talo'narjo] nm (de cheques) chequebook (Brit), checkbook (US); (de billetes) book of tickets; (de recibos) receipt book.

talla ['taλa] nf (estatura, fig, MED) height, stature; (palo) measuring rod; (ARTE) carving; (medida) size.

tallado, a [ta'λaðo, a] a carved // nm carving.

tallar [ta'λar] vt (madera) to carve; (metal etc) to engrave; (medir) to measure.

tallarines [taλa'rines] nmpl noodles.

talle ['taλe] nm (ANAT) waist; (fig) appearance.

taller [ta'λer] nm (TEC) workshop; (de artista) studio.

tallo ['taλo] nm (de planta) stem; (de hierba) blade; (brote) shoot.

tamaño, a [ta'maɲo, a] a (tan grande) such a big; (tan pequeño) such a small // nm size; de ~ natural full-size.

tamarindo [tama'rindo] nm tamarind.

tambalearse [tambale'arse] vr (persona) to stagger; (vehículo) to sway.

también [tam'bjen] ad (igualmente) also, too, as well; (además) besides.

tambor [tam'bor] nm drum; (ANAT) eardrum; ~ del freno brake drum.

tamiz [ta'miθ] nm sieve; **~ar** vt to sieve.

tampoco [tam'poko] ad nor, neither; yo ~ lo compré I didn't buy it either.

tampón [tam'pon] nm tampon.

tan [tan] ad so; ~ es así que ... so much so that ...

tanda ['tanda] nf (gen) series; (turno) shift.

tangente [tan'xente] nf tangent.

Tánger ['tanxer] n Tangier(s).

tangible [tan'xiβle] a tangible.

tanque ['tanke] nm (cisterna, MIL) tank; (AUTO) tanker.

tantear [tante'ar] vt (calcular) to reckon (up); (medir) to take the measure of; (probar) to test, try out; (tomar la medida: persona) to take the measurements of; (situación) to weigh up; (persona: opinión) to sound out // vi (DEPORTE) to score; **tanteo** nm (cálculo) (rough) calculation; (prueba) test, trial; (DEPORTE) scoring.

tanto, a ['tanto, a] a (cantidad) so much, as much; ~s so many, as many; 20 y ~s 20-odd // ad (cantidad) so much, as much; (tiempo) so long, as long; ~ tú como yo both you and I; ~ como eso it's not as bad as that; ~ más ... cuanto que it's all the more ... because; ~ mejor/peor so much the better/the worse; ~ si viene como si va whether he comes or whether he goes; ~ es así que so much so that; por o por lo ~ therefore; me he vuelto ronco de o con ~ hablar I have become hoarse with so much talking // conj: en ~ que while; hasta ~ (que) until such time as // nm (suma) certain amount; (proporción) so much; (punto) point; (gol) goal; un ~ perezoso somewhat lazy // pron: cada uno paga ~ each one pays so much; a ~s de agosto on such and such a day in August.

tapa ['tapa] nf (de caja, olla) lid; (de botella) top; (de libro) cover; (comida) snack.

tapadera [tapa'ðera] nf lid, cover.

tapar [ta'par] vt (cubrir) to cover; (envolver) to wrap o cover up; (la vista) to obstruct; (persona, falta) to conceal; (AM) to fill; ~se vr to wrap o.s. up.

taparrabo [tapa'rraβo] nm loincloth.

tapete [ta'pete] nm table cover.

tapia ['tapja] nf (garden) wall; **tapiar** vt to wall in.

tapicería [tapiθe'ria] nf tapestry; (para muebles) upholstery; (tienda) upholsterer's (shop).

tapiz [ta'piθ] nm (alfombra) carpet; (tela tejida) tapestry; **~ar** vt (muebles) to upholster.

tapón [ta'pon] nm (corcho) stopper; (TEC) plug; ~ de rosca screw-top.

taquigrafía [takivra'fia] nf shorthand; **taquígrafo, a** nm/f shorthand writer,

stenographer.

taquilla [ta'kiʎa] nf (donde se compra) booking office; (suma recogida) takings pl; **taquillero, a** a: función taquillera box office success // nm/f ticket clerk.

tara ['tara] nf (defecto) defect; (COM) tare.

tarántula [ta'rantula] nf tarantula.

tararear [tarare'ar] vi to hum.

tardanza [tar'ðanθa] nf (demora) delay.

tardar [tar'ðar] vi (tomar tiempo) to take a long time; (llegar tarde) to be late; (demorar) to delay; ¿tarda mucho el tren? does the train take (very) long?; a más ~ at the latest; no tardes en venir come soon.

tarde ['tarðe] ad late // nf (de día) afternoon; (al anochecer) evening; de ~ en ~ from time to time; ¡buenas ~s! good afternoon!; a o por la ~ in the afternoon; in the evening.

tardío, a [tar'ðio, a] a (retrasado) late; (lento) slow (to arrive).

tardo, a ['tarðo, a] a (lento) slow; (torpe) dull.

tarea [ta'rea] nf task; (ESCOL) homework.

tarifa [ta'rifa] nf (lista de precios) price list; (precio) tariff.

tarima [ta'rima] nf (plataforma) platform.

tarjeta [tar'xeta] nf card; ~ postal/de crédito/de Navidad postcard/credit card/ Christmas card.

tarro ['tarro] nm jar, pot.

tarta ['tarta] nf (pastel) cake; (torta) tart.

tartamudear [tartamuðe'ar] vi to stammer; **tartamudo, a** a stammering // nm/f stammerer.

tártaro, a ['tartaro, a] a: salsa tártara tartare sauce.

tasa ['tasa] nf (precio) (fixed) price, rate; (valoración) valuation; (medida, norma) measure, standard; ~ de cambio/interés exchange/interest rate; **~dor, a** nm/f valuer.

tasar [ta'sar] vt (arreglar el precio) to fix a price for; (valorar) to value, assess.

tasca ['taska] nf (fam) pub.

tatarabuelo, a [tatara'βwelo, a] nm/f great-great-grandfather/mother.

tatuaje [ta'twaxe] nm (dibujo) tattoo; (acto) tattooing.

tatuar [ta'twar] vt to tattoo.

taurino, a [tau'rino, a] a bullfighting cpd.

Tauro ['tauro] nm Taurus.

tauromaquia [tauro'makja] nf tauromachy, (art of) bullfighting.

taxi ['taksi] nm taxi.

taxista [tak'sista] nm/f taxi driver.

taza ['taθa] nf cup; (de retrete) bowl; ~ para café coffee cup; **tazón** nm (~ grande) mug, large cup; (de fuente) basin.

te |te| *pron* (*complemento de objeto*) you; (*complemento indirècto*) (to) you; (*reflexivo*) (to) yourself; ¿~ **duele mucho el brazo?** does your arm hurt a lot?; ~ **equivocas** you're wrong; ¡**cálma**~! calm down!

té |te| *nm* tea.

tea |'tea| *nf* torch.

teatral |tea'tral| *a* theatre *cpd*; (*fig*) theatrical.

teatro |te'atro| *nm* theatre; (*LITERATURA*) plays *pl*, drama.

tebeo |te'βeo| *nm* comic.

tecla |'tekla| *nf* key; ~**do** *nm* keyboard; **teclear** *vi* to strum; (*fig*) to drum; **tecleo** *nm* (*MUS*: *sonido*) strumming; (*fig*) drumming.

técnico, a |'tekniko, a| *a* technical // *nm/f* technician; (*experto*) expert // *nf* (*procedimientos*) technique; (*arte, oficio*) craft.

tecnócrata |tek'nokrata| *nm/f* technocrat.

tecnología |teknolo'xia| *nf* technology; **tecnológico, a** *a* technological.

techo |'tetʃo| *nm* (*externo*) roof; (*interno*) ceiling; ~ **corredizo** sunroof.

tedio |'teðjo| *nm* boredom, tedium; ~**so, a** *a* boring, tedious.

teja |'texa| *nf* (*azulejo*) tile; (*BOT*) lime (tree); ~**do** *nm* (tiled) roof.

tejanos |te'xanos| *nmpl* jeans.

tejemaneje |texema'nexe| *nm* (*lío*) fuss; (*intriga*) intrigue.

tejer |te'xer| *vt* to weave; (*hacer punto*) to knit; (*fig*) to fabricate; **tejido** *nm* (*tela*) material, fabric; (*telaraña*) web; (*ANAT*) tissue.

tel *abr* (= *teléfono*) tel.

tela |'tela| *nf* (*tejido*) material; (*telaraña*) web; (*en líquido*) skin; **telar** *nm* (*máquina*) loom; **telares** *nmpl* textile mill *sg*.

telaraña |tela'raɲa| *nf* cobweb.

tele |'tele| *nf* (*fam*) telly (*Brit*), tube (*US*).

tele... |tele| *pref* tele...; ~**comunicación** *nf* telecommunication; ~**control** *nm* remote control; ~**diario** *nm* television news; ~**difusión** *nf* (television) broadcast; ~**dirigido, a** *a* remote-controlled.

teléf *abr* (= *teléfono*) tel.

telefax |tele'faks| *nm inv* fax; (*aparato*) fax (machine).

teleférico |tele'feriko| *nm* (*tren*) cablerailway; (*de esquí*) ski-lift.

telefonear |telefone'ar| *vi* to telephone.

telefónicamente |tele'fonikamente| *ad* by (tele)phone.

telefónico, a |tele'foniko, a| *a* telephone *cpd*.

telefonista |telefo'nista| *nm/f* telephonist.

teléfono |te'lefono| *nm* (tele)phone; **estar hablando al ~** to be on the phone; **llamar a uno por ~** to ring *o* phone sb up.

telegrafía |televra'fia| *nf* telegraphy.

telégrafo |te'levrafo| *nm* telegraph.

telegrama |tele'vrama| *nm* telegram.

tele: ~**impresor** *nm* teleprinter (*Brit*), teletype (*US*); ~**objetivo** *nm* telephoto lens; ~**pático, a** *a* telepathic; ~**scópico, a** *a* telescopic; ~**scopio** *nm* telescope; ~**silla** *nm* chairlift; ~**spectador, a** *nm/f* viewer; ~**squí** *nm* ski-lift; ~**tipo** *nm* teletype.

televidente |teleβi'ðente| *nm/f* viewer.

televisar |teleβi'sar| *vt* to televise.

televisión |teleβi'sjon| *nf* television; ~ **en colores** colour television.

televisor |teleβi'sor| *nm* television set.

télex |'teleks| *nm inv* telex.

telón |te'lon| *nm* curtain; ~ **de acero** (*POL*) iron curtain; ~ **de fondo** backcloth, background.

tema |'tema| *nm* (*asunto*) subject, topic; (*MUS*) theme // *nf* (*obsesión*) obsession; **temático, a** *a* thematic.

temblar |tem'blar| *vi* to shake, tremble; (*de frío*) to shiver; **tembleque** *nm* shaking; **temblón, ona** *a* shaking; **temblor** *nm* trembling; (*de tierra*) earthquake; **tembloroso, a** *a* trembling.

temer |te'mer| *vt* to fear // *vi* to be afraid; **temo que llegue tarde** I am afraid he may be late.

temerario, a |teme'rarjo, a| *a* (*descuidado*) reckless; (*irreflexivo*) hasty; **temeridad** *nf* (*imprudencia*) rashness; (*audacia*) boldness.

temeroso, a |teme'roso, a| *a* (*miedoso*) fearful; (*que inspira temor*) frightful.

temible |te'miβle| *a* fearsome.

temor |te'mor| *nm* (*miedo*) fear; (*duda*) suspicion.

témpano |'tempano| *nm*: ~ **de hielo** ice-floe.

temperamento |tempera'mento| *nm* temperament.

temperatura |tempera'tura| *nf* temperature.

tempestad |tempes'tað| *nf* storm; **tempestuoso, a** *a* stormy.

templado, a |tem'plaðo, a| *a* (*moderado*) moderate; (: *en el comer*) frugal; (: *en el beber*) abstemious; (*agua*) lukewarm; (*clima*) mild; (*MUS*) welltuned; **templanza** *nf* moderation; abstemiousness; mildness.

templar |tem'plar| *vt* (*moderar*) to moderate; (*furia*) to restrain; (*calor*) to reduce; (*afinar*) to tune (up); (*acero*) to temper; (*tuerca*) to tighten up; **temple** *nm* (*ajuste*) tempering; (*afinación*) tuning; (*clima*) temperature; (*pintura*) tempera.

templete |tem'plete| *nm* bandstand.

templo |'templo| *nm* (*iglesia*) church; (*pagano etc*) temple.

temporada [tempo'raða] *nf* time, period; (*estación*) season.

temporal [tempo'ral] *a* (*no permanente*) temporary; (*REL*) temporal // *nm* storm.

tempranero, a [tempra'nero, a] *a* (*BOT*) early; (*persona*) early-rising.

temprano, a [tem'prano, a] *a* early; (*demasiado pronto*) too soon, too early.

ten *vb ver* **tener.**

tenaces [te'naθes] *apl ver* **tenaz.**

tenacidad [tenaθi'ðað] *nf* tenacity; (*dureza*) toughness; (*terquedad*) stubbornness.

tenacillas [tena'θiʎas] *nfpl* tongs; (*para el pelo*) curling tongs (*Brit*) o iron (*US*); (*MED*) forceps.

tenaz [te'naθ] *a* (*material*) tough; (*persona*) tenacious; (*creencia, resistencia*) stubborn.

tenaza(s) [te'naθa(s)] *nf(pl)* (*MED*) forceps; (*TEC*) pliers; (*ZOOL*) pincers.

tendedero [tende'ðero] *nm* (*para ropa*) drying place; (*cuerda*) clothes line.

tendencia [ten'denθja] *nf* tendency; (*proceso*) trend; **tener ~ a** to tend to, have a tendency to; **tendencioso, a** *a* tendentious.

tender [ten'der] *vt* (*extender*) to spread out; (*colgar*) to hang out; (*vía férrea, cable*) to lay; (*estirar*) to stretch // *vi:* **~ a** to tend to, have a tendency towards; **~se** *vr* to lie down; **~ la cama/la mesa** (*AM*) to make the bed/lay (*Brit*) o set (*US*) the table.

tenderete [tende'rete] *nm* (*puesto*) stall; (*exposición*) display of goods.

tendero, a [ten'dero, a] *nm/f* shopkeeper.

tendido, a [ten'diðo, a] *a* (*acostado*) lying down, flat; (*colgado*) hanging // *nm* (*TAUR*) front rows of seats; **a galope ~** flat out.

tendón [ten'don] *nm* tendon.

tendré *etc vb ver* **tener.**

tenebroso, a [tene'βroso, a] *a* (*oscuro*) dark; (*fig*) gloomy; (*complot*) sinister.

tenedor [tene'ðor] *nm* (*CULIN*) fork; (*poseedor*) holder; **~ de libros** bookkeeper.

teneduría [teneðu'ria] *nf* keeping; **~ de libros** book-keeping.

tenencia [te'nenθja] *nf* (*de casa*) tenancy; (*de oficio*) tenure; (*de propiedad*) possession.

tener [te'ner] ♦ *vt* **1** (*poseer, gen*) to have; (*en la mano*) to hold; *¿tienes un boli?* have you got a pen?; **va a ~ un niño** she's going to have a baby; **¡ten** (*o tenga*)!, **¡aquí tienes** (*o tiene*)! here you are!

2 (*edad, medidas*) to be; **tiene 7 años** she's 7 (years old); **tiene 15 cm. de largo** it's 15 cms long; *ver* **calor, hambre** *etc*

3 (*considerar*): **lo tengo por brillante** I consider him to be brilliant; **~ en mucho a uno** to think very highly of sb

4 (+ *pp*: = *pretérito*): **tengo terminada ya la mitad del trabajo** I've done half the work already

5: **~ que hacer algo** to have to do sth; **tengo que acabar este trabajo hoy** I have to finish this job today

6: *¿qué tienes, estás enfermo?* what's the matter with you, are you ill?

♦ **~se** *vr* **1**: **~se en pie** to stand up

2: **~se por:** to think o.s.; **se tiene por muy listo** he thinks himself very clever.

tengo *etc vb ver* **tener.**

tenia ['tenja] *nf* tapeworm.

teniente [te'njente] *nm* (*rango*) lieutenant; (*ayudante*) deputy.

tenis ['tenis] *nm* tennis; **~ de mesa** table tennis; **~ta** *nm/f* tennis player.

tenor [te'nor] *nm* (*sentido*) meaning; (*MUS*) tenor; **a ~ de** on the lines of.

tensar [ten'sar] *vt* to tauten; (*arco*) to draw.

tensión [ten'sjon] *nf* tension; (*TEC*) stress; (*MED*): **~ arterial** blood pressure; **tener la ~ alta** to have high blood pressure.

tenso, a ['tenso, a] *a* tense.

tentación [tenta'θjon] *nf* temptation.

tentáculo [ten'takulo] *nm* tentacle.

tentador, a [tenta'ðor, a] *a* tempting // *nm/f* tempter/temptress.

tentar [ten'tar] *vt* (*tocar*) to touch, feel; (*seducir*) to tempt; (*atraer*) to attract; **tentativa** *nf* attempt; **tentativa de asesinato** attempted murder.

tentempié [tentem'pje] *nm* (*fam*) snack.

tenue ['tenwe] *a* (*delgado*) thin, slender; (*neblina*) light; (*lazo, vínculo*) slight.

teñir [te'nir] *vt* to dye; (*fig*) to tinge; **~se** *vr* to dye; **~se el pelo** to dye one's hair.

teología [teolo'xia] *nf* theology.

teorema [teo'rema] *nm* theorem.

teoría [teo'ria] *nf* theory; **en ~** in theory; **teóricamente** *ad* theoretically; **teórico, a** *a* theoretic(al) // *nm/f* theoretician, theorist; **teorizar** *vi* to theorize.

terapéutico, a [tera'peutiko, a] *a* therapeutic.

terapia [te'rapja] *nf* therapy.

tercer [ter'θer] *a ver* **tercero.**

tercermundista [terθermun'dista] *a* Third World *cpd.*

tercer(o), a [ter'θer(o), a] *a* third // *nm* (*JUR*) third party.

terceto [ter'θeto] *nm* trio.

terciado, a [ter'θjaðo, a] *a* slanting.

terciar [ter'θjar] *vt* (*llevar*) to wear (across the shoulder) // *vi* (*participar*) to take part; (*hacer de árbitro*) to mediate; **~se** *vr* to come up; **~io, a** *a* tertiary.

tercio ['terθjo] *nm* third.

terciopelo [terθjo'pelo] *nm* velvet.

terco, a ['terko, a] *a* obstinate.

tergiversar [terxiβer'sar] *vt* to distort.

termal [ter'mal] *a* thermal.

termas ['termas] *nf/pl* hot springs.
terminación [termina'θjon] *nf* (*final*) end; (*conclusión*) conclusion, ending.
terminal [termi'nal] *a, nm, nf* terminal.
terminante [termi'nante] *a* (*final*) final, definitive; (*tajante*) categorical.
terminar [termi'nar] *vt* (*completar*) to complete, finish; (*concluir*) to end // *vi* (*llegar a su fin*) to end; (*parar*) to stop; (*acabar*) to finish; **~se** *vr* to come to an end; **~ por hacer algo** to end up (by) doing sth.
término ['termino] *nm* end, conclusion; (*parada*) terminus; (*límite*) boundary; **~ medio** average; (*fig*) middle way; **en último ~** (*a fin de cuentas*) in the last analysis; (*como último recurso*) as a last resort; **en ~s de** in terms of.
terminología [terminolo'xia] *nf* terminology.
termodinámico, a [termoði'namiko, a] *a* thermodynamic.
termómetro [ter'mometro] *nm* thermometer.
termonuclear [termonukle'ar] *a* thermonuclear.
termo(s) ® ['termo(s)] *nm* Thermos ® (flask).
termostato [termo'stato] *nm* thermostat.
ternero, a [ter'nero, a] *nm/f* (*animal*) calf // *nf* (*carne*) veal.
terno ['terno] *nm* (*AM*) three-piece suit.
ternura [ter'nura] *nf* (*trato*) tenderness; (*palabra*) endearment; (*cariño*) fondness.
terquedad [terke'ðað] *nf* obstinacy; (*dureza*) harshness.
terrado [te'rraðo] *nm* terrace.
terraplén [terra'plen] *nm* (*AGR*) terrace; (*cuesta*) slope.
terrateniente [terrate'njente] *nm/f* landowner.
terraza [te'rraθa] *nf* (*balcón*) balcony; (*techo*) (flat) roof; (*AGR*) terrace.
terremoto [terre'moto] *nm* earthquake.
terrenal [terre'nal] *a* earthly.
terreno [te'rreno] *nm* (*tierra*) land; (*parcela*) plot; (*suelo*) soil; (*fig*) field; **un ~ a piece of land.
terrestre [te'rrestre] *a* terrestrial; (*ruta*) land *cpd*.
terrible [te'rriβle] *a* terrible, awful.
territorio [terri'torjo] *nm* territory.
terrón [te'rron] *nm* (*de azúcar*) lump; (*de tierra*) clod, lump.
terror [te'rror] *nm* terror; **~ífico, a** *a* terrifying; **~ista** *a, nm/f* terrorist.
terroso, a [te'rroso, a] *a* earthy.
terruño [te'rruɲo] *nm* (*parcela*) plot; (*fig*) native soil.
terso, a ['terso, a] *a* (*liso*) smooth; (*pulido*) polished; **tersura** *nf* smoothness.
tertulia [ter'tulja] *nf* (*reunión informal*) social gathering; (*grupo*) group, circle.

tesis ['tesis] *nf inv* thesis.
tesón [te'son] *nm* (*firmeza*) firmness; (*tenacidad*) tenacity.
tesorero, a [teso'réro, a] *nm/f* treasurer.
tesoro [te'soro] *nm* treasure; (*COM, POL*) treasury.
testaferro [testa'ferro] *nm* figurehead.
testamentaría [testamenta'ria] *nf* execution of a will.
testamentario, a [testamen'tarjo, a] *a* testamentary // *nm/f* executor/executrix.
testamento [testa'mento] *nm* will.
testar [tes'tar] *vi* to make a will.
testarudo, a [testa'ruðo, a] *a* stubborn.
testículo [tes'tikulo] *nm* testicle.
testificar [testifi'kar] *vt* to testify; (*fig*) to attest // *vi* to give evidence.
testigo [tes'tivo] *nm/f* witness; **~ de cargo/descargo** witness for the prosecution/defence; **~ ocular** eye witness.
testimoniar [testimo'njar] *vt* to testify to; (*fig*) to show; **testimonio** *nm* testimony.
teta ['teta] *nf* (*de biberón*) teat; (*ANAT: pezón*) nipple; (: *fam*) breast.
tétanos ['tetanos] *nm* tetanus.
tetera [te'tera] *nf* teapot.
tetilla [te'tiʎa] *nf* (*ANAT*) nipple; (*de biberón*) teat.
tétrico, a ['tetriko, a] *a* gloomy, dismal.
textil [teks'til] *a* textile; **~es** *nmpl* textiles.
texto ['teksto] *nm* text; **textual** *a* textual.
textura [teks'tura] *nf* (*de tejido*) texture.
tez [teθ] *nf* (*cutis*) complexion; (*color*) colouring.
ti [ti] *pron* you; (*reflexivo*) yourself.
tía ['tia] *nf* (*pariente*) aunt; (*fam*) chick, bird.
tibieza [ti'βjeθa] *nf* (*temperatura*) tepidness; (*fig*) coolness; **tibio, a** *a* lukewarm.
tiburón [tiβu'ron] *nm* shark.
tic [tik] *nm* (*ruido*) click; (*de reloj*) tick; (*MED*): **~ nervioso** nervous tic.
tictac [tik'tak] *nm* (*de reloj*) tick tock.
tiempo ['tjempo] *nm* time; (*época, período*) age, period; (*METEOROLOGIA*) weather; (*LING*) tense; (*DEPORTE*) half; **a ~** in time; **a un o al mismo ~** at the same time; **al poco ~** very soon (after); **se quedó poco ~** he didn't stay very long; **hace poco ~** not long ago; **mucho ~** a long time; **de ~ en ~** from time to time; **hace buen/mal ~** the weather is fine/bad; **estar a ~** to be in time; **hace ~** some time ago; **hacer ~** to while away the time; **motor de 2 ~s** two-stroke engine; **primer ~** first half.
tienda ['tjenda] *nf* shop, store; **~ (de campaña)** tent.
tienes *etc vb ver* **tener**.
tienta *etc vb ver* **tentar** // ['tjenta] *nf*:

andar a ~s to grope one's way along.

tiento *vb ver* **tentar** // ['tjento] *nm* (*tacto*) touch; (*precaución*) wariness.

tierno, a ['tjerno, a] *a* (*blando*) tender; (*fresco*) fresh; (*amable*) sweet.

tierra ['tjerra] *nf* earth; (*suelo*) soil; (*mundo*) earth, world; (*país*) country, land; ~ **adentro** inland.

tieso, a ['tjeso, a] *a* (*rígido*) rigid; (*duro*) stiff; (*fam: orgulloso*) conceited.

tiesto ['tjesto] *nm* flowerpot.

tifoidea [tifoi'ðea] *nf* typhoid.

tifón [ti'fon] *nm* typhoon.

tifus ['tifus] *nm* typhus.

tigre ['tiyre] *nm* tiger

tijera [ti'xera] *nf* scissors *pl*; (*ZOOL*) claw; ~s *nfpl* scissors; (*para plantas*) shears.

tijereta [tixe'reta] *nf* earwig.

tijeretear [tixerete'ar] *vt* to snip.

tildar [til'dar] *vt*: ~ **de** to brand as.

tilde ['tilde] *nf* (*TIPOGRAFIA*) tilde.

tilín [ti'lin] *nm* tinkle.

tilo ['tilo] *nm* lime tree.

timar [ti'mar] *vt* (*robar*) to steal; (*estafar*) to swindle.

timbal [tim'bal] *nm* small drum.

timbrar [tim'brar] *vt* to stamp.

timbre ['timbre] *nm* (*sello*) stamp; (*campanilla*) bell; (*tono*) timbre; (*COM*) stamp duty.

timidez [timi'ðeθ] *nf* shyness; **tímido, a** *a* shy.

timo ['timo] *nm* swindle.

timón [ti'mon] *nm* helm, rudder; **timonel** *nm* helmsman.

tímpano ['timpano] *nm* (*ANAT*) eardrum; (*MUS*) small drum.

tina ['tina] *nf* tub; (*baño*) bath(tub); **tinaja** *nf* large jar.

tinglado [tin'glaðo] *nm* (*cobertizo*) shed; (*fig: truco*) trick; (*intriga*) intrigue.

tinieblas [ti'njeβlas] *nfpl* darkness *sg*; (*sombras*) shadows.

tino ['tino] *nm* (*habilidad*) skill; (*juicio*) insight.

tinta ['tinta] *nf* ink; (*TEC*) dye; (*ARTE*) colour.

tinte ['tinte] *nm* (*acto*) dyeing.

tintero [tin'tero] *nm* inkwell.

tintinear [tintine'ar] *vt* to tinkle.

tinto, a ['tinto, a] *a* (*teñido*) dyed // *nm* red wine.

tintorería [tintore'ria] *nf* dry cleaner's.

tintura [tin'tura] *nf* (*acto*) dyeing; (*QUIMICA*) dye; (*farmacéutico*) tincture.

tío ['tio] *nm* (*pariente*) uncle; (*fam: individuo*) bloke (*Brit*), guy.

tiovivo [tio'βiβo] *nm* merry-go-round.

típico, a ['tipiko, a] *a* typical.

tiple ['tiple] *nm* soprano (voice) // *nf* soprano.

tipo ['tipo] *nm* (*clase*) type, kind; (*norma*) norm; (*patrón*) pattern; (*hombre*) fellow; (*ANAT: de hombre*)

build; (: *de mujer*) figure; (*IMPRENTA*) type; ~ **bancario/de descuento/de interés/de cambio** bank/discount/interest/exchange rate.

tipografía [tipoγra'fia] *nf* (*tipo*) printing *cpd*; (*lugar*) printing press; **tipográfico, a** *a* printing *cpd*; **tipógrafo, a** *nm/f* printer.

tiquet ['tiket] (*pl* ~s) *nm* ticket; (*en tienda*) cash slip.

tiquismiquis [tikis'mikis] *nm inv* fussy person // *nmpl* (*querellas*) squabbling *sg*; (*escrúpulos*) silly scruples.

tira ['tira] *nf* strip; (*fig*) abundance; ~ **y afloja** give and take.

tirabuzón [tiraβu'θon] *nm* (*rizo*) curl.

tirachinas [tira'tʃinas] *nm inv* catapult.

tiradero [tira'ðero] *nm* rubbish dump.

tirado, a [ti'raðo, a] *a* (*barato*) dirt-cheap; (*fam: fácil*) very easy // *nf* (*acto*) cast, throw; (*distancia*) distance; (*serie*) series; (*TIPOGRAFIA*) printing, edition; **de una tirada** at one go.

tirador [tira'ðor] *nm* (*mango*) handle.

tiranía [tira'nia] *nf* tyranny; **tirano, a** *a* tyrannical // *nm/f* tyrant.

tirante [ti'rante] *a* (*cuerda etc*) tight, taut; (*relaciones*) strained // *nm* (*ARQ*) brace; (*TEC*) stay; (*correa*) shoulder strap; ~s *nmpl* braces (*Brit*), suspenders (*US*); **tirantez** *nf* tightness; (*fig*) tension.

tirar [ti'rar] *vt* to throw; (*dejar caer*) to drop; (*volcar*) to upset; (*derribar*) to knock down *o* over; (*jalar*) to pull; (*desechar*) to throw out *o* away; (*disipar*) to squander; (*imprimir*) to print; (*dar: golpe*) to deal // *vi* (*disparar*) to shoot; (*jalar*) to pull; (*fig*) to draw; (*fam: andar*) to go; (*tender a, buscar realizar*) to tend to; (*DEPORTE*) to shoot; ~**se** *vr* to throw o.s.; (*fig*) to cheapen o.s.; ~ **abajo** to bring down, destroy; **tira más a su padre** he takes more after his father; **ir tirando** to manage; **a todo** ~ at the most.

tirita [ti'rita] *nf* (sticking) plaster (*Brit*), bandaid (*US*).

tiritar [tiri'tar] *vi* to shiver.

tiro ['tiro] *nm* (*lanzamiento*) throw; (*disparo*) shot; (*disparar*) shooting; (*DEPORTE*) shot; (*GOLF, TENIS*) drive; (*alcance*) range; (*golpe*) blow; (*engaño*) hoax; ~ **al blanco** target practice; **caballo de** ~ cart-horse; **andar de** ~s **largos** to be all dressed up; **al** ~ (*AM*) at once.

tirón [ti'ron] *nm* (*sacudida*) pull, tug; **de un** ~ in one go, all at once.

tiroteo [tiro'teo] *nm* exchange of shots, shooting.

tísico, a ['tisiko, a] *a* consumptive.

tisis ['tisis] *nf inv* consumption, tuberculosis.

títere ['titere] *nm* puppet.

titilar [titi'lar] *vi* (*luz, estrella*) to

titiritero — 196 — topo

titiritero, a [titiri'tero, a] *nm/f* puppeteer.

titubeante [tituße'ante] *a* (*inestable*) shaky, tottering; (*farfullante*) stammering; (*dudoso*) hesitant.

titubear [tituße'ar] *vi* to stagger; to stammer; (*fig*) to hesitate; **titubeo** *nm* staggering; stammering; hesitation.

titulado, a [titu'laðo, a] *a* (*libro*) entitled; (*persona*) titled.

titular [titu'lar] *a* titular // *nm/f* occupant // *nm* headline // *vt* to title; ~se *vr* to be entitled; **título** *nm* title; (*de diario*) headline; (*certificado*) professional qualification; (*universitario*) (university) degree; (*fig*) right; **a título de** in the capacity of.

tiza ['tiθa] *nf* chalk.

tiznar [tiθ'nar] *vt* to blacken; (*fig*) to tarnish.

tizón [ti'θon], **tizo** ['tiθo] *nm* brand; (*fig*) stain.

toalla [to'aʎa] *nf* towel.

tobillo [to'ßiʎo] *nm* ankle.

tobogán [toßo'yan] *nm* toboggan; (*montaña rusa*) roller-coaster; (*resbaladilla*) chute, slide.

toca ['toka] *nf* headdress.

tocadiscos [toka'ðiskos] *nm inv* record player.

tocado, a [to'kaðo, a] *a* (*fam*) touched // *nm* headdress.

tocador [toka'ðor] *nm* (*mueble*) dressing table; (*cuarto*) boudoir; (*fam*) ladies' toilet (*Brit*) o room (*US*).

tocante [to'kante]: ~ a *prep* with regard to.

tocar [to'kar] *vt* to touch; (*MUS*) to play; (*topar con*) to run into, strike; (*referirse a*) to allude to; (*padecer*) to suffer // *vi* (*a la puerta*) to knock (on o at the door); (*ser de turno*) to fall to, be the turn of; (*ser hora*) to be due; (*barco, avión*) to call at; (*atañer*) to concern; ~se *vr* (*cubrirse la cabeza*) to cover one's head; (*tener contacto*) to touch (each other); **por lo que a mí me toca** as far as I am concerned.

tocayo, a [to'kajo, a] *nm/f* namesake.

tocino [to'θino] *nm* bacon.

todavía [toða'ßia] *ad* (*aun*) even; (*aún*) still, yet; ~ **más** yet more; ~ **no** not yet.

todo, a [to'ðo, a] ♦ *a* **1** (*con artículo sg*) all; **toda la carne** all the meat; **toda la noche** all night, the whole night; ~ **el libro** the whole book; **toda una botella** a whole bottle; ~ **lo contrario** quite the opposite; **está toda sucia** she's all dirty; **por ~ el país** throughout the whole country

2 (*con artículo pl*) all; every; ~**s los libros** all the books; **todas las noches** every night; ~**s los que quieran salir** all those who want to leave

♦ *pron* **1** everything, all; ~**s** everyone,

everybody; **lo sabemos** ~ we know everything; ~**s querían más tiempo** everybody o everyone wanted more time; **nos marchamos** ~**s** all of us left

2: **con** ~: **con** ~ **él me sigue gustando** even so I still like him

♦ *ad* all; **vaya** ~ ~ **seguido** keep straight on o ahead

♦ *nm*: **como un** ~ as a whole; **del** ~: **no me agrada del** ~ I don't entirely like it.

todopoderoso, a [toðopoðe'roso, a] *a* all powerful; (*REL*) almighty.

toga ['toya] *nf* toga; (*ESCOL*) gown.

Tokio ['tokjo] *n* Tokyo.

toldo ['toldo] *nm* (*para el sol*) sunshade (*Brit*), parasol; (*tienda*) marquee.

tole ['tole] *nm* (*fam*) commotion.

tolerancia [tole'ranθja] *nf* tolerance.

tolerar [tole'rar] *vt* to tolerate; (*resistir*) to endure.

toma ['toma] *nf* (*acto*) taking; (*MED*) dose; ~ (*de corriente*) socket.

tomar [to'mar] *vt* to take; (*aspecto*) to take on; (*beber*) to drink // *vi* to take; (*AM*) to drink; ~se *vr* to take; ~se **por** to consider o.s. to be; ~ **a bien/a mal** to take well/badly; ~ **en serio** to take seriously; ~ **el pelo a alguien** to pull sb's leg; ~**la con uno** to pick a quarrel with sb.

tomate [to'mate] *nm* tomato; ~**ra** *nf* tomato plant.

tomavistas [toma'ßistas] *nm inv* movie camera.

tomillo [to'miʎo] *nm* thyme.

tomo ['tomo] *nm* (*libro*) volume.

ton [ton] *abr* = **tonelada** // *nm*: **sin** ~ **ni son** son without rhyme or reason.

tonada [to'naða] *nf* tune.

tonalidad [tonali'ðað] *nf* tone.

tonel [to'nel] *nm* barrel.

tonelada [tone'laða] *nf* ton; **tonelaje** *nm* tonnage.

tonelero [tone'lero] *nm* cooper.

tónico, a ['toniko, a] *a* tonic // *nm* (*MED*) tonic // *nf* (*MUS*) tonic; (*fig*) keynote.

tonificar [tonifi'kar] *vt* to tone up.

tono ['tono] *nm* tone; **fuera de** ~ inappropriate; **darse** ~ to put on airs.

tontería [tonte'ria] *nf* (*estupidez*) foolishness; (*cosa*) stupid thing; (*acto*) foolish act; ~**s** *nfpl* rubbish *sg*, nonsense *sg*.

tonto, a ['tonto, a] *a* stupid, silly // *nm/f* fool; (*payaso*) clown.

topacio [to'paθjo] *nm* topaz.

topar [to'par] *vt* (*tropezar*) to bump into; (*encontrar*) to find, come across; (*ZOOL*) to butt // *vi*: ~ **contra** o **en** to run into; ~ **con** to run up against.

tope ['tope] *a* maximum // *nm* (*fin*) end; (*límite*) limit; (*FERRO*) buffer; (*AUTO*) bumper; **al** ~ end to end.

tópico, a ['topiko, a] *a* topical // *nm* platitude.

topo ['topo] *nm* (*ZOOL*) mole; (*fig*)

blunderer.

topografía [topoɣra'fia] *nf* topography;
topógrafo, a *nm/f* topographer.

toque *etc vb ver* **tocar** // ['toke] *nm*
touch; (*MUS*) beat; (*de campana*) peal;
(*fig*) crux; **dar un ~ a** to test; **~ de
queda** curfew.

toquetear [tokete'ar] *vt* to handle.

toquilla [to'kiʎa] *nf* (*pañuelo*) headscarf;
(*chal*) shawl.

tórax ['toraks] *nm* thorax.

torbellino [torbe'ʎino] *nm* whirlwind;
(*fig*) whirl.

torcedura [torθe'ðura] *nf* twist; (*MED*)
sprain.

torcer [tor'θer] *vt* to twist; (*la esquina*)
to turn; (*MED*) to sprain // *vi* (*desviar*)
to turn off; **~se** *vr* (*ladearse*) to bend;
(*desviarse*) to go astray; (*fracasar*) to
go wrong; **torcido, a** *a* twisted; (*fig*)
crooked // *nm* curl.

tordo, a ['torðo, a] *a* dappled // *nm*
thrush.

torear [tore'ar] *vt* (*fig: evadir*) to avoid;
(*jugar con*) to tease // *vi* to fight bulls;
toreo *nm* bullfighting; **torero, a** *nm/f*
bullfighter.

tormenta [tor'menta] *nf* storm; (*fig: confusión*) turmoil.

tormento [tor'mento] *nm* torture; (*fig*)
anguish.

tornar [tor'nar] *vt* (*devolver*) to return,
give back; (*transformar*) to transform //
vi to go back; **~se** *vr* (*ponerse*) to
become.

tornasolado, a [tornaso'laðo, a] *a*
(*brillante*) iridescent; (*reluciente*)
shimmering.

torneo [tor'neo] *nm* tournament.

tornillo [tor'niʎo] *nm* screw.

torniquete [torni'kete] *nm* (*puerta*) turnstile; (*MED*) tourniquet.

torno [tor'no] *nm* (*TEC*) winch; (*tambor*)
drum; **en ~ (a)** round, about.

toro ['toro] *nm* bull; (*fam*) he-man; **los
~s** bullfighting.

toronja [to'ronxa] *nf* grapefruit.

torpe ['torpe] *a* (*poco hábil*) clumsy,
awkward; (*necio*) dim; (*lento*) slow.

torpedo [tor'peðo] *nm* torpedo.

torpeza [tor'peθa] *nf* (*falta de agilidad*)
clumsiness; (*lentitud*) slowness; (*error*)
mistake.

torre ['torre] *nf* tower; (*de petróleo*)
derrick.

torrefacto, a [torre'facto, a] *a* roasted.

torrente [to'rrente] *nm* torrent.

tórrido, a ['torriðo, a] *a* torrid.

torrija [to'rrixa] *nf* French toast.

torsión [tor'sjon] *nf* twisting.

torso ['torso] *nm* torso.

torta ['torta] *nf* cake; (*fam*) slap.

tortícolis [tor'tikolis] *nm inv* stiff neck.

tortilla [tor'tiʎa] *nf* omelette; (*AM*)
maize pancake; **~ francesa/española**

plain/potato omelette.

tórtola ['tortola] *nf* turtledove.

tortuga [tor'tuɣa] *nf* tortoise.

tortuoso, a [tor'twoso, a] *a* winding.

tortura [tor'tura] *nf* torture; **torturar** *vt*
to torture.

tos [tos] *nf* cough; **~ ferina** whooping
cough.

tosco, a ['tosko, a] *a* coarse.

toser [to'ser] *vi* to cough.

tostado, a [tos'taðo, a] *a* toasted; (*por
el sol*) dark brown; (*piel*) tanned.

tostador [tosta'ðor] *nm* toaster.

tostar [tos'tar] *vt* to toast; (*café*) to
roast; (*persona*) to tan; **~se** *vr* to get
brown.

total [to'tal] *a* total // *ad* in short; (*al fin
y al cabo*) when all is said and done //
nm total; **~ que** to cut (*Brit*) o make
(*US*) a long story short.

totalidad [totali'ðað] *nf* whole.

totalitario, a [totali'tarjo, a] *a* totalitarian.

tóxico, a ['toksiko, a] *a* toxic // *nm*
poison; **toxicómano, a** *nm/f* drug
addict.

tozudo, a [to'θuðo, a] *a* obstinate.

traba ['traβa] *nf* bond, tie; (*cadena*)
shackle.

trabajador, a [traβaxa'ðor, a] *a* hard-
working // *nm/f* worker.

trabajar [traβa'xar] *vt* to work; (*AGR*) to
till; (*empeñarse en*) to work at;
(*empujar: persona*) to push; (*convencer*) to persuade // *vi* to work;
(*esforzarse*) to strive; **trabajo** *nm*
work; (*tarea*) task; (*POL*) labour; (*fig*)
effort; **tomarse el trabajo de** to take the
trouble to; **trabajo por turno/a destajo**
shift work/ piecework; **trabajoso, a** *a*
hard.

trabalenguas [traβa'lengwas] *nm inv*
tongue twister.

trabar [tra'βar] *vt* (*juntar*) to join, unite;
(*atar*) to tie down, fetter; (*agarrar*) to
seize; (*amistad*) to strike up; **~se** *vr* to
become entangled; **trabársele a uno la
lengua** to be tongue-tied.

tracción [trak'θjon] *nf* traction; **~
delantera/trasera** front-wheel/rear-wheel
drive.

tractor [trak'tor] *nm* tractor.

tradición [traði'θjon] *nf* tradition;
tradicional *a* traditional.

traducción [traðuk'θjon] *nf* translation.

traducir [traðu'θir] *vt* to translate;
traductor, a *nm/f* translator.

traer [tra'er] *vt* to bring; (*llevar*) to
carry; (*ropa*) to wear; (*incluir*) to
carry; (*fig*) to cause; **~se** *vr*: **~se algo**
to be up to sth.

traficar [trafi'kar] *vi* to trade.

tráfico ['trafiko] *nm* (*COM*) trade;
(*AUTO*) traffic.

tragaluz [traɣa'luθ] *nm* skylight.

tragaperras [traɣa'perras] *nm o f inv* slot machine.

tragar [tra'ɣar] *vt* to swallow; (*devorar*) to devour, bolt down; ~se *vr* to swallow.

tragedia [tra'xeðja] *nf* tragedy; **trágico, a** *a* tragic.

trago ['traɣo] *nm* (*líquido*) drink; (*bocado*) gulp; (*fam: de bebida*) swig; (*desgracia*) blow.

traición [trai'θjon] *nf* treachery; (*JUR*) treason; (*una* ~) act of treachery; **traicionar** *vt* to betray.

traicionero, a [traiθjo'nero, a] *a* treacherous.

traidor, a [trai'ðor, a] *a* treacherous // *nm/f* traitor.

traigo *etc vb ver* **traer**.

traje *vb ver* **traer** // ['traxe] *nm* (*de hombre*) suit; (*de mujer*) dress; (*vestido típico*) costume; ~ **de baño** swimsuit; ~ **de luces** bullfighter's costume.

trajera *etc vb ver* **traer**.

trajín [tra'xin] *nm* haulage; (*fam: movimiento*) bustle; **trajinar** *vt* (*llevar*) to carry, transport // *vi* (*moverse*) to bustle about; (*viajar*) to travel around.

trama ['trama] *nf* (*intriga*) plot; (*de tejido*) weft (*Brit*), woof (*US*); **tramar** *vt* to plot; (*TEC*) to weave.

tramitar [trami'tar] *vt* (*asunto*) to transact; (*negociar*) to negotiate; (*manejar*) to handle.

trámite ['tramite] *nm* (*paso*) step; (*JUR*) transaction; ~**s** *nmpl* (*burocracia*) procedure *sg*; (*JUR*) proceedings.

tramo ['tramo] *nm* (*de tierra*) plot; (*de escalera*) flight; (*de vía*) section.

tramoya [tra'moja] *nf* (*TEATRO*) piece of stage machinery; (*fig*) scheme; **tramoyista** *nm/f* scene shifter; (*fig*) trickster.

trampa ['trampa] *nf* trap; (*en el suelo*) trapdoor; (*engaño*) trick; (*fam*) fiddle; **trampear** *vt, vi* to cheat.

trampolín [trampo'lin] *nm* trampoline; (*de piscina etc*) diving board.

tramposo, a [tram'poso, a] *a* crooked, cheating // *nm/f* crook, cheat.

tranca ['tranka] *nf* (*palo*) stick; (*de puerta, ventana*) bar; **trancar** *vt* to bar.

trance ['tranθe] *nm* (*momento difícil*) difficult moment o juncture; (*estado hipnotizado*) trance.

tranco ['tranko] *nm* stride.

tranquilidad [trankili'ðað] *nf* (*calma*) calmness, stillness; (*paz*) peacefulness.

tranquilizar [trankili'θar] *vt* (*calmar*) to calm (down); (*asegurar*) to reassure; ~**se** *vr* to calm down; **tranquilo, a** *a* (*calmado*) calm; (*apacible*) peaceful; (*mar*) calm; (*mente*) untroubled.

transacción [transak'θjon] *nf* transaction.

transbordador [transβorða'ðor] *nm* ferry.

transbordar [transβor'ðar] *vt* to transfer; **transbordo** *nm* transfer; **hacer transbordo** to change (trains).

transcurrir [transku'rrir] *vi* (*tiempo*) to pass; (*hecho*) to turn out.

transcurso [trans'kurso] *nm*: ~ **del tiempo** lapse (of time).

transeúnte [transe'unte] *a* transient // *nm/f* passer-by.

transferencia [transfe'renθja] *nf* transference; (*COM*) transfer.

transferir [transfe'rir] *vt* to transfer.

transformador [transforma'ðor] *nm* (*ELEC*) transformer.

transformar [transfor'mar] *vt* to transform; (*convertir*) to convert.

tránsfuga ['transfuɣa] *nm/f* (*MIL*) deserter; (*POL*) turncoat.

transfusión [transfu'sjon] *nf* transfusion.

transición [transi'θjon] *nf* transition.

transido, a [tran'siðo, a] *a* overcome.

transigir [transi'xir] *vi* to compromise, make concessions.

transistor [transis'tor] *nm* transistor.

transitar [transi'tar] *vi* to go (from place to place); **tránsito** *nm* transit; (*AUTO*) traffic; **transitorio, a** *a* transitory.

transmisión [transmi'sjon] *nf* (*TEC*) transmission; (*transferencia*) transfer; ~ **en directo/exterior** live/outside broadcast.

transmitir [transmi'tir] *vt* to transmit; (*RADIO, TV*) to broadcast.

transparencia [transpa'renθja] *nf* transparency; (*claridad*) clearness, clarity; (*foto*) slide.

transparentar [transparen'tar] *vt* to reveal // *vi* to be transparent; **transparente** *a* transparent; (*claro*) clear; (*ligero*) diaphanous.

transpirar [transpi'rar] *vi* to perspire; (*fig*) to transpire.

transponer [transpo'ner] *vt* to transpose; (*cambiar de sitio*) to change the place of.

transportar [transpor'tar] *vt* to transport; (*llevar*) to carry; **transporte** *nm* transport; (*COM*) haulage.

transversal [transβer'sal] *a* transverse, cross.

tranvía [tram'bia] *nm* tram.

trapecio [tra'peθjo] *nm* trapeze; **trapecista** *nm/f* trapeze artist.

trapero, a [tra'pero, a] *nm/f* ragman.

trapicheo [trapi'tʃeo] *nm* (*fam*) scheme, fiddle.

trapo ['trapo] *nm* (*tela*) rag; (*de cocina*) cloth.

tráquea ['trakea] *nf* windpipe.

traqueteo [trake'teo] *nm* (*golpeteo*) rattling.

tras [tras] *prep* (*detrás*) behind; (*después*) after; ~ **de** besides.

trascendencia [trasθen'denθja] *nf* (*importancia*) importance; (*FILOSOFIA*) transcendence.

trascendental [trasθenden'tal] a important; (FILOSOFIA) transcendental.

trascender [trasθen'der] vi (noticias) to come out; (suceso) to have a wide effect.

trasegar [trase'γar] vt (moverse) to move about; (vino) to decant.

trasero, a [tra'sero, a] a back, rear // nm (ANAT) bottom.

trasfondo [tras'fondo] nm background.

trasgredir [trasγre'ðir] vt to contravene.

trashumante [trasu'mante] a (animales) migrating.

trasladar [trasla'ðar] vt to move; (persona) to transfer; (postergar) to postpone; (copiar) to copy; ~se vr (mudarse) to move; **traslado** nm move; (mudanza) move, removal.

traslucir [traslu'θir] vt to show; ~se vr to be translucent; (fig) to be revealed.

trasluz [tras'luθ] nm reflected light; al ~ against o up to the light.

trasnochar [trasno'tʃar] vi (acostarse tarde) to stay up late; (no dormir) to have a sleepless night.

traspasar [traspa'sar] vt (bala etc) to pierce, go through; (propiedad) to sell, transfer; (calle) to cross over; (límites) to go beyond; (ley) to break; **traspaso** nm (venta) transfer, sale.

traspié [tras'pje] nm (tropezón) trip; (fig) blunder.

trasplantar [trasplan'tar] vt to transplant.

traste ['traste] nm (MUS) fret; dar al ~ con algo to ruin sth.

trastienda [tras'tjenda] nf backshop.

trasto ['trasto] nm (pey: cosa) piece of junk; (: persona) dead loss.

trastornado, a [trastor'naðo, a] a (loco) mad, crazy.

trastornar [trastor'nar] vt to overturn, upset; (fig: ideas) to confuse; (: nervios) to shatter; (: persona) to drive crazy; ~se vr (volverse loco) to go mad o crazy; **trastorno** nm (acto) overturning; (confusión) confusion.

tratable [tra'taβle] a friendly.

tratado [tra'taðo] nm (POL) treaty; (COM) agreement.

tratamiento [trata'mjento] nm treatment.

tratar [tra'tar] vt (ocuparse de) to treat; (manejar, TEC) to handle; (MED) to treat; (dirigirse a: persona) to address // vi: ~ de (hablar sobre) to deal with, be about; (intentar) to try to; ~ con (COM) to trade in; (negociar) to negotiate with; (tener contactos) to have dealings with; ~se vr to treat each other; ¿de qué se trata? what's it about?; **trato** nm dealings pl; (relaciones) relationship; (comportamiento) manner; (COM) agreement; (título) (form of) address.

trauma ['trauma] nm trauma.

través [tra'βes] nm (fig) reverse; al ~ ad across, crossways; a ~ de prep across; (sobre) over; (por) through.

travesaño [traβe'saɲo] nm (ARQ) crossbeam; (DEPORTE) crossbar.

travesía [traβe'sia] nf (calle) crossstreet; (NAUT) crossing.

travesura [traβe'sura] nf (broma) prank; (ingenio) wit; **travieso, a** a (niño) naughty // nf (ARQ) crossbeam.

trayecto [tra'jekto] nm (ruta) road, way; (viaje) journey; (tramo) stretch; (curso) course; ~ria nf trajectory; (fig) path.

traza ['traθa] nf (aspecto) looks pl; (señal) sign; ~do, a a: bien ~do shapely, well-formed // nm (ARQ) plan, design; (fig) outline.

trazar [tra'θar] vt (ARQ) to plan; (ARTE) to sketch; (fig) to trace; (plan) to follow; **trazo** nm (línea) line; (bosquejo) sketch.

trébol ['treβol] nm (BOT) clover.

trece ['treθe] num thirteen.

trecho ['tretʃo] nm (distancia) distance; (de tiempo) while; (fam) piece; de ~ en ~ at intervals.

tregua ['treγwa] nf (MIL) truce; (fig) lull.

treinta ['treinta] num thirty.

tremendo, a [tre'mendo, a] a (terrible) terrible; (imponente: cosa) imposing; (fam: fabuloso) tremendous.

trémulo, a ['tremulo, a] a quivering.

tren [tren] nm train; ~ de aterrizaje undercarriage.

trenza ['trenθa] nf (de pelo) plait (Brit), braid (US); **trenzar** vt (pelo) to plait; trenzarse vr (AM) to become involved with.

trepadora [trepa'ðora] nf (BOT) climber.

trepar [tre'par] vt, vi to climb.

trepidar [trepi'ðar] vi to shake, vibrate.

tres [tres] num three.

tresillo [tre'siʎo] nm three-piece suite; (MUS) triplet.

treta ['treta] nf (COM etc) gimmick; (fig) trick.

triángulo ['trjangulo] nm triangle.

tribu ['triβu] nf tribe.

tribuna [tri'βuna] nf (plataforma) platform; (DEPORTE) (grand)stand; (fig) public speaking.

tribunal [triβu'nal] nm (JUR) court; (comisión, fig) tribunal.

tributar [triβu'tar] vt (gen) to pay; **tributo** nm (COM) tax.

tricotar [triko'tar] vi to knit.

trigal [tri'γal] nm wheat field.

trigo ['triγo] nm wheat.

trigueño, a [tri'γeɲo, a] a (pelo) corncoloured; (piel) olive-skinned.

trillado, a [tri'ʎaðo, a] a threshed; (fig) trite, hackneyed; **trilladora** nf threshing machine.

trillar [tri'ʎar] vt (AGR) to thresh.
trimestral [trimes'tral] a quarterly; (ESCOL) termly.
trimestre [tri'mestre] nm (ESCOL) term.
trinar [tri'nar] vi (pájaros) to sing; (rabiar) to fume, be angry.
trincar [trin'kar] vt (atar) to tie up; (inmovilizar) to pinion.
trinchar [trin'tʃar] vt to carve.
trinchera [trin'tʃera] nf (fosa) trench.
trineo [tri'neo] nm sledge.
trinidad [trini'ðað] nf trio; (REL): la T~ the Trinity.
trino ['trino] nm trill.
tripa ['tripa] nf (ANAT) intestine; (fam: tb: ~s) insides pl.
triple ['triple] a triple.
triplicado, a [tripli'kaðo, a] a: por ~ in triplicate.
tripulación [tripula'θjon] nf crew.
tripulante [tripu'lante] nm/f crewman/woman.
tripular [tripu'lar] vt (barco) to man; (AUTO) to drive.
triquiñuela [triki'nwela] nf trick.
tris [tris] nm inv crack; **en un ~** in an instant.
triste ['triste] a (afligido) sad; (sombrío) melancholy, gloomy; (lamentable) sorry, miserable; **~za** nf (aflicción) sadness; (melancolía) melancholy.
triturar [tritu'rar] vt (moler) to grind; (mascar) to chew.
triunfar [trjun'far] vi (tener éxito) to triumph; (ganar) to win; **triunfo** nm triumph.
trivial [tri'βjal] a trivial; **~izar** vt to minimize, play down.
triza ['triθa] nf: **hacer ~s** to smash to bits; (papel) to tear to shreds.
trizar [tri'θar] vt to smash to bits; (papel) to tear to shreds.
trocar [tro'kar] vt to exchange.
trocha ['trotʃa] nf short cut.
troche ['trotʃe]: a ~ **y moche** ad helter-skelter, pell-mell.
trofeo [tro'feo] nm (premio) trophy; (éxito) success.
tromba ['tromba] nf whirlwind.
trombón [trom'bon] nm trombone.
trombosis [trom'bosis] nf inv thrombosis.
trompa ['trompa] nf horn; (trompo) humming top; (hocico) snout; (fam): **cogerse una ~** to get tight.
trompeta [trom'peta] nf trumpet; (clarín) bugle.
trompo ['trompo] nm spinning top.
trompón [trom'pon] nm bump.
tronar [tro'nar] vt (AM) to shoot // vi to thunder; (fig) to rage.
tronco ['tronko] nm (de árbol, ANAT) trunk.
tronchar [tron'tʃar] vt (árbol) to chop down; (fig: vida) to cut short; (: espe-

ranza) to shatter; (persona) to tire out; **~se** vr to fall down.
tronera [tro'nera] nf (MIL) loophole; (ARQ) small window.
trono ['trono] nm throne.
tropa ['tropa] nf (MIL) troop; (soldados) soldiers pl.
tropel [tro'pel] nm (muchedumbre) crowd.
tropelía [trope'lia] nm outrage.
tropezar [trope'θar] vi to trip, stumble; (fig) to slip up; **~ con** to run into; (topar con) to bump into; **tropezón** nm trip; (fig) blunder.
tropical [tropi'kal] a tropical.
trópico ['tropiko] nm tropic.
tropiezo vb ver **tropezar** // [tro'pjeθo] nm (error) slip, blunder; (desgracia) misfortune; (obstáculo) snag.
trotamundos [trota'mundos] nm inv globetrotter.
trotar [tro'tar] vi to trot; **trote** nm trot; (fam) travelling; **de mucho trote** hard-wearing.
trozo ['troθo] nm bit, piece.
truco ['truko] nm (habilidad) knack; (engaño) trick.
trucha ['trutʃa] nf trout.
trueno ['trweno] nm thunder; (estampido) bang.
trueque etc vb ver **trocar** // ['trweke] nm exchange; (COM) barter.
trufa ['trufa] nf (BOT) truffle.
truhán, ana [tru'an, ana] nm/f rogue.
truncar [trun'kar] vt (cortar) to truncate; (fig: la vida etc) to cut short; (: el desarrollo) to stunt.
tu [tu] a your.
tú [tu] pron you.
tubérculo [tu'βerkulo] nm (BOT) tuber.
tuberculosis [tußerku'losis] nf inv tuberculosis.
tubería [tuße'ria] nf pipes pl; (conducto) pipeline.
tubo ['tußo] nm tube, pipe; **~ de ensayo** test tube; **~ de escape** exhaust (pipe).
tuerca ['twerka] nf nut.
tuerto, a ['twerto, a] a blind in one eye // nm/f one-eyed person.
tuerza etc vb ver **torcer**.
tuétano ['twetano] nm marrow; (BOT) pith.
tufo ['tufo] nm vapour; (fig: pey) stench.
tugurio [tu'vurio] nm slum.
tul [tul] nm tulle.
tulipán [tuli'pan] nm tulip.
tullido, a [tu'ʎiðo, a] a crippled.
tumba ['tumba] nf (sepultura) tomb.
tumbar [tum'bar] vt to knock down; **~se** vr (echarse) to lie down; (extenderse) to stretch out.
tumbo ['tumbo] nm (caída) fall; (de vehículo) jolt.
tumbona [tum'bona] nf (butaca) easy chair; (de playa) deckchair (Brit),

beach chair (US).

tumido, a |tu'miðo, a| a swollen.

tumor |tu'mor| nm tumour.

tumulto |tu'multo| nm turmoil.

tuna |'tuna| nf ver **tuno**.

tunante |tu'nante| nm/f rascal.

tunda |'tunda| nf (golpeo) beating.

túnel |'tunel| nm tunnel.

Túnez |'tuneθ| nm Tunisia; (ciudad) Tunis.

tuno, a |'tuno, a| nm/f (fam) rogue // nm member of student music group // nf (BOT) prickly pear; (MUS) student music group.

tuntún |tun'tun|: **al ~** ad thoughtlessly.

tupido, a |tu'piðo, a| a (denso) dense; (tela) close-woven; (fig) dim.

turba |'turßa| nf crowd.

turbación |turßa'θjon| nf (molestia) disturbance; (preocupación) worry; **turbado, a** a (molesto) disturbed; (preocupado) worried.

turbar |tur'ßar| vt (molestar) to disturb; (incomodar) to upset; **~se** vr to be disturbed.

turbina |tur'ßina| nf turbine.

turbio, a |'turßjo, a| a cloudy; (tema etc) confused // ad indistinctly.

turbulencia |turßu'lenθja| nf turbulence; (fig) restlessness; **turbulento, a** a turbulent; (fig: intranquilo) restless; (: ruidoso) noisy.

turco, a |'turko, a| a Turkish // nm/f Turk.

turismo |tu'rismo| nm tourism; (coche) saloon car; **turista** nm/f tourist; **turístico, a** a tourist cpd.

turnar |tur'nar| vi, **turnarse** vr to take (it in) turns; **turno** nm (INDUSTRIA) shift; (oportunidad, orden de prioridad) opportunity; (juegos etc) turn.

turquesa |tur'kesa| nf turquoise.

Turquía |tur'kia| nf Turkey.

turrón |tu'rron| nm (dulce) nougat.

tutear |tute'ar| vt to address as familiar 'tú'; **~se** vr to be on familiar terms.

tutela |tu'tela| nf (legal) guardianship; (instrucción) guidance; **tutelar** a tutelary // vt to protect.

tutor, a |tu'tor, a| nm/f (legal) guardian; (ESCOL) tutor.

tuve, tuviera etc vb ver **tener**.

tuyo, a |'tujo, a| a yours, of yours // pron yours; **los ~s** (fam) your relations, your family.

TV |'te'ße| nf abr (= televisión) TV.

TVE nf abr = Televisión Española.

U

u |u| conj or.

ubicar |uβi'kar| vt to place, situate; (: fig) to install in a post; (AM: encontrar) to find; **~se** vr to lie, be located.

ubre |'uβre| nf udder.

UCD nf abr = Unión del Centro Democrático.

Ud(s) abr = **usted(es)**.

ufanarse |ufa'narse| vr to boast; **~ de** to pride o.s. on; **ufano, a** a (arrogante) arrogant; (presumido) conceited.

UGT nf abr = Unión General de Trabajadores.

ujier |u'xjer| nm usher; (portero) doorkeeper.

úlcera |'ulθera| nf ulcer.

ulcerar |ulθe'rar| vt to make sore; **~se** vr to ulcerate.

ulterior |ulte'rjor| a (más allá) farther, further; (subsecuente, siguiente) subsequent.

últimamente |'ultimamente| ad (recientemente) lately, recently.

ultimar |ulti'mar| vt to finish; (finalizar) to finalize; (AM: rematar) to finish off.

último, a |'ultimo, a| a last; (más reciente) latest, most recent; (más bajo) bottom; (más alto) top; (fig) final, extreme; **en las últimas** on one's last legs; **por ~** finally.

ultra |'ultra| a ultra // nm/f extreme right-winger.

ultrajar |ultra'xar| vt (escandalizar) to outrage; (insultar) to insult, abuse; **ultraje** nm outrage; insult.

ultramar |ultra'mar| nm: **de o en ~** abroad, overseas.

ultramarinos |ultrama'rinos| nmpl groceries; **tienda de ~** grocer's (shop).

ultranza |ul'tranθa|: **a ~** ad (a todo trance) at all costs; (completo) outright.

ultrasónico, a |ultra'soniko, a| a ultrasonic.

ultratumba |ultra'tumba| nf: **la vida de ~** the next life.

ulular |ulu'lar| vi to howl; (búho) to hoot.

umbral |um'bral| nm (gen) threshold.

umbroso, a |um'broso, a|, **umbrío, a** |um'brio, a| a shady.

un, una |un, 'una| ♦ artículo definido a; (antes de vocal) an; **una mujer/naranja** a woman/an orange

♦ a: **unos** (o **unas**): **hay unos regalos para ti** there are some presents for you; **hay unas cervezas en la nevera** there are some beers in the fridge.

unánime |u'nanime| a unanimous; **unanimidad** nf unanimity.

unción |un'θjon| nf anointing; **extrema~** extreme unction.

undécimo, a |un'deθimo, a| a eleventh.

ungir |un'xir| vt to rub with ointment; (REL) to anoint.

ungüento |un'gwento| nm ointment; (fig) salve, balm.

únicamente |'unikamente| ad solely, only.

único, a |'uniko, a| a only, sole; (sin par) unique.

unidad |uni'ðað| *nf* unity; (*COM. TEC etc*) unit.

unido, a |u'niðo. a| *a* joined, linked; (*fig*) united.

unificar |unifi'kar| *vt* to unite, unify.

uniformar |unifor'mar| *vt* to make uniform, level up; (*persona*) to put into uniform.

uniforme |uni'forme| *a* uniform, equal; (*superficie*) even // *nm* uniform; **uniformidad** *nf* uniformity; (*llaneza*) levelness, evenness.

unilateral |unilate'ral| *a* unilateral.

unión |u'njon| *nf* union; (*acto*) uniting, joining; (*calidad*) unity; (*TEC*) joint; (*fig*) closeness, togetherness; **la U~ Soviética** the Soviet Union.

unir |u'nir| *vt* (*juntar*) to join, unite; (*atar*) to tie, fasten; (*combinar*) to combine; **~se** *vr* to join together, unite; (*empresas*) to merge.

unísono |u'nisono| *nm*: **al ~** in unison.

universal |unißer'sal| *a* universal; (*mundial*) world *cpd*.

universidad |unißersi'ðað| *nf* university.

universitario, a |unißersi'tarjo. a| *a* university *cpd* // *nm/f* (*profesor*) lecturer; (*estudiante*) (university) student; (*graduado*) graduate.

universo |uni'ßerso| *nm* universe.

uno, a |'uno. a| ♦ *a* one; **es todo ~** it's all one and the same; **~s pocos** a few; **~s cien** about a hundred
♦ *pron* **1** one; **quiero ~ solo** I only want one; **~ de ellos** one of them
2 (*alguien*) somebody, someone; **conozco a ~ que se te parece** I know somebody *o* someone who looks like you; **~ mismo** oneself; **~s querían quedarse** some (people) wanted to stay
3: (**los**) **~s ... (los) otros ...** some ... others; each other, one another; **una y otra son muy agradables** they're both very nice
♦ *nf* one; **es la una** it's one o'clock
♦ *nm* (number) one.

untar |un'tar| *vt* to rub; (*engrasar*) to grease, oil; (*fig*) to bribe.

uña |'uɲa| *nf* (*ANAT*) nail; (*garra*) claw; (*casco*) hoof; (*arrancaclavos*) claw.

uranio |u'ranjo| *nm* uranium.

urbanidad |urßani'ðað| *nf* courtesy, politeness.

urbanismo |urßa'nismo| *nm* town planning.

urbanización |urßaniθa'θjon| *nf* (*barrio, colonia*) housing estate.

urbano, a |ur'ßano. a| *a* (*de ciudad*) urban; (*cortés*) courteous, polite.

urbe |'urße| *nf* large city.

urdimbre |ur'ðimbre| *nf* (*de tejido*) warp; (*intriga*) intrigue.

urdir |ur'ðir| *vt* to warp; (*fig*) to plot, contrive.

urgencia |ur'xenθja| *nf* urgency; (*prisa*)

haste, rush; (*emergencia*) emergency; **servicios de ~** emergency services; **urgente** *a* urgent.

urgir |ur'xir| *vi* to be urgent; **me urge** I'm in a hurry for it.

urinario, a |uri'narjo. a| *a* urinary // *nm* urinal.

urna |'urna| *nf* urn; (*POL*) ballot box.

urraca |u'rraka| *nf* magpie.

URSS *nf*: **la ~** the USSR.

Uruguay |uru'ɣwai| *nm*: **el ~** Uruguay; **uruguayo, a** *a, nm/f* Uruguayan.

usado, a |u'saðo. a| *a* used; (*ropa etc*) worn.

usanza |u'sanθa| *nf* custom, usage.

usar |u'sar| *vt* to use; (*ropa*) to wear; (*tener costumbre*) to be in the habit of; **~se** *vr* to be used; **uso** *nm* use; wear; (*costumbre*) usage, custom; (*moda*) fashion; **al uso** in keeping with custom; **al uso de** in the style of.

usted |us'teð| *pron* (*sg*) you *sg*; (*pl*) **~es** you *pl*.

usual |u'swal| *a* usual.

usuario, a |usu'arjo. a| *nm/f* user.

usufructo |usu'frukto| *nm* use.

usura |u'sura| *nf* usury; **usurero, a** *nm/f* usurer.

usurpar |usur'par| *vt* to usurp.

utensilio |uten'siljo| *nm* tool; (*CULIN*) utensil.

útero |'utero| *nm* uterus, womb.

útil |'util| *a* useful // *nm* tool; **utilidad** *nf* usefulness; (*COM*) profit; **utilizar** *vt* to use, utilize.

utopía |uto'pia| *nf* Utopia; **utópico, a** *a* Utopian.

uva |'ußa| *nf* grape.

V

v *abr* = (*voltio*) v.

va *vb ver* **ir**.

vaca |'baka| *nf* (*animal*) cow; **carne de ~** beef.

vacaciones |baka'θjones| *nfpl* holidays.

vacante |ba'kante| *a* vacant, empty // *nf* vacancy.

vaciar |ba'θjar| *vt* to empty out; (*ahuecar*) to hollow out; (*moldear*) to cast // *vi* (*río*) to flow (*en* into); **~se** *vr* to empty.

vaciedad |baθje'ðað| *nf* emptiness.

vacilación |baθila'θjon| *nf* hesitation.

vacilante |baθi'lante| *a* unsteady; (*habla*) faltering; (*fig*) hesitant.

vacilar |baθi'lar| *vi* to be unsteady; (*al hablar*) to falter; (*fig*) to hesitate, waver; (*memoria*) to fail.

vacío, a |ba'θio. a| *a* empty; (*puesto*) vacant; (*desocupado*) idle; (*vano*) vain // *nm* emptiness; (*FISICA*) vacuum; (*un ~*) (empty) space.

vacuna [ba'kuna] *nf* vaccine; **vacunar** *vt* to vaccinate.

vacuno, a [ba'kuno, a] *a* cow *cpd*; ganado ~ cattle.

vacuo, a ['bakwo, a] *a* empty.

vadear [baðe'ar] *vt* (*río*) to ford; **vado** *nm* ford.

vagabundo, a [baɣa'ßundo, a] *a* wandering; (*pey*) vagrant // *nm* tramp.

vagamente [baɣa'mente] *ad* vaguely.

vagancia [ba'ɣanθja] *nf* vagrancy.

vagar [ba'ɣar] *vi* to wander; (*no hacer nada*) to idle.

vagina [ba'xina] *nf* vagina.

vago, a ['baɣo, a] *a* vague; (*perezoso*) lazy; (*ambulante*) wandering // *nm/f* (*vagabundo*) tramp; (*flojo*) lazybones *sg*, idler.

vagón [ba'ɣon] *nm* (*FERRO*: *de pasajeros*) carriage; (: *de mercancías*) wagon.

vaguedad [baɣe'ðað] *nf* vagueness.

vaho ['bao] *nm* (*vapor*) vapour, steam; (*respiración*) breath.

vaina ['baina] *nf* sheath.

vainilla [bai'niʎa] *nf* vanilla.

vainita [bai'nita] *nf* (*AM*) green *o* French bean.

vais *vb ver* **ir.**

vaivén [bai'ßen] *nm* to-and-fro movement; (*de tránsito*) coming and going; vaivenes *nmpl* (*fig*) ups and downs.

vajilla [ba'xiʎa] *nf* crockery, dishes *pl*; lavar la ~ to do the washing-up (*Brit*), wash the dishes (*US*).

valdré *etc vb ver* **valer.**

vale ['bale] *nm* voucher; (*recibo*) receipt; (*pagaré*) IOU.

valedero, a [bale'ðero, a] *a* valid.

valenciano, a [balen'θjano, a] *a* Valencian.

valentía [balen'tia] *nf* courage, bravery; (*acción*) heroic deed; **valentón, ona** *a* blustering.

valer [ba'ler] *vi* to be worth; (*costar*) to cost; (*ser útil*) to be useful; (*ser válido*) to be valid; ~se *vr* to defend o.s.; ~se de to make use of, take advantage of; ~ la pena to be worthwhile; ¿vale? (*Esp*) OK?

valeroso, a [bale'roso, a] *a* brave, valiant.

valgo *etc vb ver* **valer.**

valía [ba'lia] *nf* worth, value.

validar [bali'ðar] *vt* to validate; **validez** *nf* validity; **válido, a** *a* valid.

valiente [ba'ljente] *a* brave, valiant // *nm* hero.

valija [ba'lixa] *nf* suitcase; ~ diplomática diplomatic bag.

valioso, a [ba'ljoso, a] *a* valuable; (*rico*) wealthy.

valor [ba'lor] *nm* value, worth; (*precio*) price; (*valentía*) valour, courage; (*importancia*) importance; ~es *nmpl*

(*COM*) securities; ~**ación** *nf* valuation; ~**ar** *vt* to value.

vals [bals] *nm inv* waltz.

válvula ['balßula] *nf* valve.

valla ['baʎa] *nf* fence; (*DEPORTE*) hurdle; (*fig*) barrier; **vallar** *vt* to fence in.

valle ['baʎe] *nm* valley.

vamos *vb ver* **ir.**

vampiro, resa [bam'piro, 'resa] *nm/f* vampire.

van *vb ver* **ir.**

vanagloriarse [banaɣlo'rjarse] *vr* to boast.

vándalo, a ['bandalo, a] *nm/f* vandal; **vandalismo** *nm* vandalism.

vanguardia [ban'gwardja] *nf* vanguard; (*ARTE etc*) avant-garde.

vanidad [bani'ðað] *nf* vanity; **vanidoso, a** *a* vain, conceited.

vano, a ['bano, a] *a* (*irreal*) unreal, vain; (*inútil*) useless; (*persona*) vain, conceited; (*frívolo*) frivolous.

vapor [ba'por] *nm* vapour; (*vaho*) steam; al ~ (*CULIN*) steamed; ~**izador** *nm* atomizer; ~**izar** *vt* to vaporize; ~**oso, a** *a* vaporous.

vaquero, a [ba'kero, a] *a* cattle *cpd* // *nm* cowboy; ~s *nmpl* jeans.

vara ['bara] *nf* stick; (*TEC*) rod; ~ mágica magic wand.

variable [ba'rjaßle] *a, nf* variable.

variación [barja'θjon] *nf* variation.

variar [ba'rjar] *vt* to vary; (*modificar*) to modify; (*cambiar de posición*) to switch around // *vi* to vary.

varices [ba'riθes] *nfpl* varicose veins.

variedad [barje'ðað] *nf* variety.

varilla [ba'riʎa] *nf* stick; (*BOT*) twig; (*TEC*) rod; (*de rueda*) spoke.

vario, a ['barjo, a] *a* varied; ~s various, several.

varón [ba'ron] *nm* male, man; **varonil** *a* manly, virile.

Varsovia [bar'soßja] *n* Warsaw.

vas *vb ver* **ir.**

vasco, a ['basko, a] *a, nm/f* Basque.

vascongado, a [baskon'gaðo, a], **vascuence** [bas'kwenθe] *a* Basque; **las Vascongadas** the Basque Country.

vaselina [base'lina] *nf* Vaseline ®.

vasija [ba'sixa] *nf* container, vessel.

vaso ['baso] *nm* glass, tumbler; (*ANAT*) vessel.

vástago ['bastaɣo] *nm* (*BOT*) shoot; (*TEC*) rod; (*fig*) offspring.

vasto, a ['basto, a] *a* vast, huge.

Vaticano [bati'kano] *nm*: el ~ the Vatican.

vaticinio [bati'θinjo] *nm* prophecy.

vatio ['batjo] *nm* (*ELEC*) watt.

vaya *etc vb ver* **ir.**

Vd(s) *abr* = **usted(es).**

ve *vb ver* **ir, ver.**

vecindad [beθin'dað] *nf*, **vecindario** [beθin'darjo] *nm* neighbourhood;

(*habitantes*) residents *pl*.
vecino, a [be'θino, a] *a* neighbouring // *nm/f* neighbour; (*residente*) resident.
veda ['beða] *nf* prohibition.
vedado [be'ðaðo] *nm* preserve.
vedar [be'ðar] *vt* (*prohibir*) to ban, prohibit; (*impedir*) to stop, prevent.
vegetación [bexeta'θjon] *nf* vegetation.
vegetariano, a [bexeta'rjano, a] *a, nm/f* vegetarian.
vegetal [bexe'tal] *a, nm* vegetable.
vehemencia [be(e)'menθja] *nf* (*insistencia*) vehemence; (*pasión*) passion; (*fervor*) fervour; (*violencia*) violence; **vehemente** *a* vehement; passionate; fervent.
vehículo [be'ikulo] *nm* vehicle; (*MED*) carrier.
veía *etc vb ver* **ver**.
veinte ['beinte] *num* twenty.
vejación [bexa'θjon] *nf* vexation; (*humillación*) humiliation.
vejar [be'xar] *vt* (*irritar*) to annoy, vex; (*humillar*) to humiliate.
vejez [be'xeθ] *nf* old age.
vejiga [be'xiya] *nf* (*ANAT*) bladder.
vela ['bela] *nf* (*de cera*) candle; (*NAUT*) sail; (*insomnio*) sleeplessness; (*vigilia*) vigil; (*MIL*) sentry duty; **estar a dos ~s** (*fam*) to be skint.
velado, a [be'laðo, a] *a* veiled; (*sonido*) muffled; (*FOTO*) blurred // *nf* soirée.
velador [bela'ðor] *nm* (*mesa*) pedestal table; (*AM*) lampshade.
velar [be'lar] *vt* (*vigilar*) to keep watch over // *vi* to stay awake; **~ por** to watch over, look after.
veleidad [belei'ðað] *nf* (*ligereza*) fickleness; (*capricho*) whim.
velero [be'lero] *nm* (*NAUT*) sailing ship; (*AVIAT*) glider.
veleta [be'leta] *nf* weather vane.
veliz [be'lis] *nm* (*AM*) suitcase.
velo ['belo] *nm* veil.
velocidad [beloθi'ðað] *nf* speed; (*TEC, AUTO*) gear.
velocímetro [belo'θimetro] *nm* speedometer.
veloz [be'loθ] *a* fast.
vello ['beʎo] *nm* down, fuzz; **vellón** *nm* fleece; **~so, a** *a* fuzzy; **velludo, a** *a* shaggy.
ven *vb ver* **venir**.
vena ['bena] *nf* vein.
venado [be'naðo] *nm* deer.
vencedor, a [benθe'ðor, a] *a* victorious // *nm/f* victor, winner.
vencer [ben'θer] *vt* (*dominar*) to defeat, beat; (*derrotar*) to vanquish; (*superar, controlar*) to overcome, master // *vi* (*triunfar*) to win (through), triumph; (*plazo*) to expire; **vencido, a** *a* (*derrotado*) defeated, beaten; (*COM*) due // *ad*: **pagar vencido** to pay in arrears; **vencimiento** *nm* (*COM*) maturity.

venda ['benda] *nf* bandage; **~je** *nm* bandage, dressing; **vendar** *vt* to bandage; **vendar los ojos** to blindfold.
vendaval [benda'ßal] *nm* (*viento*) gale.
vendedor, a [bende'ðor, a] *nm/f* seller.
vender [ben'der] *vt* to sell; **~ al contado/al por mayor/al por menor** to sell for cash/wholesale/retail.
vendimia [ben'dimja] *nf* grape harvest.
vendré *etc vb ver* **venir**.
veneno [be'neno] *nm* poison; (*de serpiente*) venom; **~so, a** *a* poisonous; venomous.
venerable [bene'raßle] *a* venerable; **venerar** *vt* (*respetar*) to revere; (*adorar*) to worship.
venéreo, a [be'nereo, a] *a*: **enfermedad venérea** venereal disease.
venezolano, a [beneθo'lano, a] *a* Venezuelan.
Venezuela [bene'θwela] *nf* Venezuela.
venganza [ben'ganθa] *nf* vengeance, revenge; **vengar** *vt* to avenge; **vengarse** *vr* to take revenge; **vengativo, a** *a* (*persona*) vindictive.
vengo *etc vb ver* **venir**.
venia ['benja] *nf* (*perdón*) pardon; (*permiso*) consent.
venial [be'njal] *a* venial.
venida [be'niða] *nf* (*llegada*) arrival; (*regreso*) return.
venidero, a [beni'ðero, a] *a* coming, future.
venir [be'nir] *vi* to come; (*llegar*) to arrive; (*ocurrir*) to happen; (*fig*): **~ de** to stem from; **~ bien/mal** to be suitable/unsuitable; **el año que viene** next year; **~se abajo** to collapse.
venta ['benta] *nf* (*COM*) sale; **~ a plazos** hire purchase; **~ al contado/al por mayor/al por menor** *o* **al detalle** cash sale/ wholesale/retail; **~ con derecho a retorno** sale or return; **'en ~'** 'for sale'.
ventaja [ben'taxa] *nf* advantage; **ventajoso, a** *a* advantageous.
ventana [ben'tana] *nf* window; **~ de guillotina/salediza** sash/bay window; **ventanilla** *nf* (*de taquilla*) window (*of booking office etc*).
ventilación [bentila'θjon] *nf* ventilation; (*corriente*) draught; **ventilar** *vt* to ventilate; (*para secar*) to put out to dry; (*fig*) to air, discuss.
ventisca [ben'tiska] *nf*, **ventisquero** [bentis'kero] *nm* blizzard; (*nieve amontonada*) snowdrift.
ventoso, a [ben'toso, a] *a* windy.
ventrílocuo, a [ben'trilokwo, a] *nm/f* ventriloquist.
ventura [ben'tura] *nf* (*felicidad*) happiness; (*buena suerte*) luck; (*destino*) fortune; **a la (buena) ~** at random; **venturoso, a** *a* happy; (*afortunado*) lucky, fortunate.
veo *etc vb ver* **ver**.

ver [ber] *vt* to see; *(mirar)* to look at, watch; *(entender)* to understand; *(investigar)* to look into; // *vi* to see; to understand; ~**se** *vr* *(encontrarse)* to meet; *(dejarse* ~*)* to be seen; *(hallarse: en un apuro)* to find o.s., be // *nm* looks *pl*, appearance; a ~ let's see; **dejarse** ~ to become apparent; **no tener nada que** ~ con to have nothing to do with; **a mi modo de** ~ as I see it.

vera ['bera] *nf* edge, verge; *(de río)* bank.

veracidad [beraθi'ðað] *nf* truthfulness.

veranear [berane'ar] *vi* to spend the summer; **veraneo** *nm* summer holiday; **veraniego** *a* a summer *cpd*.

verano [be'rano] *nm* summer.

veras ['beras] *nfpl* truth *sg*; **de** ~ really, truly.

veraz [be'raθ] *a* truthful.

verbal [ber'βal] *a* verbal.

verbena [ber'βena] *nf* *(fiesta)* fair; *(baile)* open-air dance.

verbo ['berβo] *nm* verb; ~**so, a** *a* verbose.

verdad [ber'ðað] *nf* truth; *(fiabilidad)* reliability; **de** ~ a real, proper; **a decir** ~ to tell the truth; ~**ero, a** *a* *(veraz)* true, truthful; *(fiable)* reliable; *(fig)* real.

verde ['berðe] *a* green; *(chiste)* blue, dirty // *nm* green; **viejo** ~ dirty old man; ~**ar,** ~**cer** *vi* to turn green; **verdor** *nm* *(lo* ~*)* greenness; *(BOT)* verdure.

verdugo [ber'ðuɣo] *nm* executioner.

verdulero, a [berðu'lero, a] *nm/f* greengrocer.

verduras [ber'ðuras] *nfpl* *(CULIN)* greens.

vereda [be'reða] *nf* path; *(AM)* pavement *(Brit)*, sidewalk *(US)*.

veredicto [bere'ðikto] *nm* verdict.

vergonzoso, a [berɣon'θoso, a] *a* shameful; *(tímido)* timid, bashful.

vergüenza [ber'ɣweɲθa] *nf* shame, sense of shame; *(timidez)* bashfulness; *(pudor)* modesty; **me da** ~ I'm ashamed.

verídico, a [be'riðiko, a] *a* true, truthful.

verificar [berifi'kar] *vt* to check; *(corroborar)* to verify; *(llevar a cabo)* to carry out; ~**se** *vr* to occur, happen.

verja ['berxa] *nf* grating.

vermut [ber'mut] *(pl* ~**s)** *nm* vermouth.

verosímil [bero'simil] *a* likely, probable; *(relato)* credible.

verruga [be'rruɣa] *nf* wart.

versado, a [ber'saðo, a] *a:* ~ **en** versed in.

versátil [ber'satil] *a* versatile.

versión [ber'sjon] *nf* version.

verso ['berso] *nm* verse; **un** ~ a line of poetry.

vértebra ['berteβra] *nf* vertebra.

verter [ber'ter] *vt* *(líquido: adrede)* to empty, pour (out); *(: sin querer)* to spill; *(basura)* to dump // *vi* to flow.

vertical [berti'kal] *a* vertical.

vértice ['bertiθe] *nm* vertex, apex.

vertiente [ber'tjente] *nf* slope; *(fig)* aspect.

vertiginoso, a [bertixi'noso, a] *a* giddy, dizzy.

vértigo ['bertiɣo] *nm* vertigo; *(mareo)* dizziness.

vesícula [be'sikula] *nf* blister.

vespertino, a [besper'tino, a] *a* evening *cpd*.

vestíbulo [bes'tiβulo] *nm* hall; *(de teatro)* foyer.

vestido [bes'tiðo] *pp de* vestir; ~ **de azul/marinero** dressed in blue/as a sailor // *nm* *(ropa)* clothes *pl*, clothing; *(de mujer)* dress, frock.

vestigio [bes'tixjo] *nm* *(huella)* trace; ~**s** *nmpl* remains.

vestimenta [besti'menta] *nf* clothing.

vestir [bes'tir] *vt* *(poner: ropa)* to put on; *(llevar: ropa)* to wear; *(proveer de ropa a)* to clothe; *(suj: sastre)* to make clothes for // *vi* to dress; *(verse bien)* to look good; ~**se** *vr* to get dressed, dress o.s.

vestuario [bes'twarjo] *nm* clothes *pl*, wardrobe; *(TEATRO: cuarto)* dressing room; *(DEPORTE)* changing room.

veta ['beta] *nf* *(vena)* vein, seam; *(en carne)* streak; *(de madera)* grain.

vetar [be'tar] *vt* to veto.

veterano, a [bete'rano, a] *a, nm* veteran.

veterinario, a [beteri'narjo, a] *nm/f* vet(erinary surgeon) // *nf* veterinary science.

veto ['beto] *nm* veto.

vetusto, a [be'tusto, a] *a* ancient.

vez [beθ] *nf* time; *(turno)* turn; **a la** ~ **que** at the same time as; **a su** ~ in its turn; **otra** ~ again; **una** ~ once; **de una** ~ in one go; **de una** ~ **para siempre** once and for all; **en** ~ **de** instead of; **a** *o* **algunas veces** sometimes; **una y otra** ~ repeatedly; **de** ~ **en cuando** from time to time; **7 veces 9** 7 times 9; **hacer las veces de** to stand in for; **tal** ~ perhaps.

vía ['bia] *nf* track, route; *(FERRO)* line; *(fig)* way; *(ANAT)* passage, tube // *prep* via, by way of; **por** ~ **judicial** by legal means; **por** ~ **oficial** through official channels; **en** ~**s de** in the process of; ~ **aérea** airway; **V**~ **Láctea** Milky Way.

viaducto [bja'ðukto] *nm* viaduct.

viajante [bja'xante] *nm* commercial traveller.

viajar [bja'xar] *vi* to travel; **viaje** *nm* journey; *(gira)* tour; *(NAUT)* voyage; **estar de viaje** to be on a journey; **viaje de ida y vuelta** round trip; **viaje de novios** honeymoon; **viajero, a** *a* travelling; *(ZOOL)* migratory // *nm/f* *(quien viaja)* traveller; *(pasajero)* passenger.

vial [bjal] a road cpd, traffic cpd.

víbora ['biβora] nf viper; (AM) poisonous snake.

vibración [biβra'θjon] nf vibration; **vibrador** nm vibrator; **vibrante** a vibrant.

vibrar [bi'βrar] vt, vi to vibrate.

vicario [bi'karjo] nm curate.

vicegerente [biθexe'rente] nm assistant manager.

vicepresidente [biθepresi'ðente] nm/f vice-president.

viceversa [biθe'ßersa] ad vice versa.

viciado, a [bi'θjaðo, a] a (corrompido) corrupt; (contaminado) foul, contaminated; **viciar** vt (pervertir) to pervert; (JUR) to nullify; (estropear) to spoil; **viciarse** vr to become corrupted.

vicio ['biθjo] nm vice; (mala costumbre) bad habit; **~so, a** a (muy malo) vicious; (corrompido) depraved // nm/f depraved person.

vicisitud [biθisi'tuð] nf vicissitude.

víctima ['biktima] nf victim.

victoria [bik'torja] nf victory; **victorioso, a** a victorious.

vicuña [bi'kuɲa] nf vicuna.

vid [bið] nf vine.

vida ['biða] nf (gen) life; (duración) lifetime; **de por ~** for life; **en la/mi ~** never; **estar con ~** to be still alive; **ganarse la ~** to earn one's living.

vídeo ['biðeo] nm video // a inv: **película ~** video film.

vidriero, a [bi'ðrjero, a] nm/f glazier // nf (ventana) stained-glass window; (AM: de tienda) shop window; (puerta) glass door.

vidrio ['biðrjo] nm glass; **~so, a** a glassy.

vieira ['bjeira] nf scallop.

viejo, a ['bjexo, a] a old // nm/f old man/ woman; **hacerse ~** to get old.

Viena ['bjena] n Vienna.

vienes etc vb ver **venir**.

vienés, esa [bje'nes, esa] a Viennese.

viento ['bjento] nm wind; **hacer ~** to be windy.

vientre ['bjentre] nm belly; (matriz) womb.

viernes ['bjernes] nm inv Friday; **V~ Santo** Good Friday.

Vietnam [bjet'nam] nm: **el ~** Vietnam; **vietnamita** a Vietnamese.

viga ['biɣa] nf beam, rafter; (de metal) girder.

vigencia [bi'xenθja] nf validity; **estar en ~** to be in force; **vigente** a valid, in force; (imperante) prevailing.

vigésimo, a [bi'xesimo, a] a twentieth.

vigía [bi'xia] nm look-out // nf (atalaya) watchtower; (acción) watching.

vigilancia [bixi'lanθja] nf: **tener a uno bajo ~** to keep watch on sb.

vigilar [bixi'lar] vt to watch over // vi (gen) to be vigilant; (hacer guardia) to keep watch; **~ por** to take care of.

vigilia [vi'xilja] nf wakefulness, being awake; (REL) fast.

vigor [bi'vor] nm vigour, vitality; **en ~** in force; **entrar/poner en ~** to take/put into effect; **~oso, a** a vigorous.

vil [bil] a vile, low; **~eza** nf vileness; (acto) base deed.

vilipendiar [bilipen'djar] vt to vilify, revile.

vilo ['bilo]: **en ~** ad in the air, suspended; (fig) on tenterhooks, in suspense.

villa ['biʎa] nf (casa) villa; (pueblo) small town; (municipalidad) municipality; **~ miseria** (AM) shantytown.

villancico [biʎan'θiko] nm (Christmas) carol.

villorio [bi'ʎorjo] nm (AM) shantytown.

vinagre [bi'naɣre] nm vinegar; **~ras** nfpl cruet sg.

vinagreta [bina'ɣreta] nf vinaigrette, French dressing.

vinculación [binkula'θjon] nf (lazo) link, bond; (acción) linking.

vincular [binku'lar] vt to link, bind; **vínculo** nm link, bond.

vine etc vb ver **venir**.

vinicultura [binikul'tura] nf wine growing.

viniera etc vb ver **venir**.

vino vb ver **venir** // ['bino] nm wine; **~ blanco/tinto** white/red wine.

viña ['biɲa] nf, **viñedo** [bi'ɲeðo] nm vineyard.

viola ['bjola] nf viola.

violación [bjola'θjon] nf violation; (estupro): **~ (sexual)** rape.

violar [bjo'lar] vt to violate; (cometer estupro) to rape.

violencia [bjo'lenθja] nf (fuerza) violence, force; (embarazo) embarrassment; (acto injusto) unjust act; **violentar** vt to force; (casa) to break into; (agredir) to assault; (violar) to violate; **violento, a** a violent; (furioso) furious; (situación) embarrassing; (acto) forced, unnatural.

violeta [bjo'leta] nf violet.

violín [bjo'lin] nm violin.

violón [bjo'lon] nm double bass.

viraje [bi'raxe] nm turn; (de vehículo) swerve; (de carretera) bend; (fig) change of direction; **virar** vi to change direction.

virgen ['birxen] a, nf virgin.

Virgo ['birvo] nm Virgo.

viril [bi'ril] a virile; **~idad** nf virility.

virtualmente [birtwal'mente] ad virtually.

virtud [bir'tuð] nf virtue; **en ~ de** by virtue of; **virtuoso, a** a virtuous // nm/f virtuoso.

viruela [bi'rwela] *nf* smallpox; **~s** *nfpl* pockmarks.

virulento, a [biru'lento, a] *a* virulent.

virus ['birus] *nm inv* virus.

visa ['bisa] *nf* (*AM*), **visado** [bi'saðo] *nm* visa.

viscoso, a [bis'koso, a] *a* viscous.

visera [bi'sera] *nf* visor.

visibilidad [bisiβili'ðað] *nf* visibility; **visible** *a* visible; (*fig*) obvious.

visillos [bi'siʎos] *nmpl* lace curtains.

visión [bi'sjon] *nf* (*ANAT*) vision, (eye)sight; (*fantasía*) vision, fantasy; **visionario, a** *a* (*que prevé*) visionary; (*alucinado*) deluded // *nm/f* visionary.

visita [bi'sita] *nf* call, visit; (*persona*) visitor; **hacer una ~** to pay a visit.

visitar [bisi'tar] *vt* to visit, call on.

vislumbrar [bislum'brar] *vt* to glimpse, catch a glimpse of; **vislumbre** *nf* glimpse; (*centelleo*) gleam; (*idea vaga*) glimmer.

viso ['biso] *nm* (*del metal*) glint, gleam; (*de tela*) sheen; (*aspecto*) appearance.

visón [bi'son] *nm* mink.

visor [bi'sor] *nm* (*FOTO*) viewfinder.

víspera ['bispera] *nf*: **la ~ de ...** the day before ....

vista, a [bista] *nf* sight, vision; (*capacidad de ver*) (eye)sight; (*mirada*) look(s) (*pl*) // *nm* customs officer; **a primera ~** at first glance; **hacer la ~ gorda** to turn a blind eye; **volver la ~** to look back; **está a la ~ que** it's obvious that; **en ~ de** in view of; **en ~ de que** in view of the fact that; **¡hasta la ~!** so long!, see you!; **con ~s a** with a view to; **~zo** *nm* glance; **dar** *o* **echar un ~zo a** to glance at.

visto, a *pp de* **ver** // *vb ver tb* **vestir** // ['bisto, a]. *a* seen; (*considerado*) considered // *nm*: **~ bueno** approval; **'~ bueno'** 'approved'; **por lo ~** evidently; **está ~ que** it's clear that; **está bien/mal ~** it's acceptable/unacceptable; **~ que** *conj* since, considering that.

vistoso, a [bis'toso, a] *a* colourful.

vital [bi'tal] *a* life *cpd*, living *cpd*; (*fig*) vital; (*persona*) lively, vivacious; **~icio, a** *a* for life.

vitamina [bita'mina] *nf* vitamin.

viticultor, a [bitikul'tor, a] *nm/f* wine grower; **viticultura** *nf* wine growing.

vitorear [bitore'ar] *vt* to cheer, acclaim.

vítreo, a ['bitreo, a] *a* vitreous.

vitrina [bi'trina] *nf* show case; (*AM*) shop window.

vituperio [bitu'perjo] *nm* (*condena*) condemnation; (*censura*) censure; (*insulto*) insult.

viudo, a ['bjuðo, a] *nm/f* widower/widow; **viudez** *nf* widowhood.

vivacidad [biβaθi'ðað] *nf* (*vigor*) vigour; (*vida*) liveliness.

vivaracho, a [biβa'ratʃo, a] *a* jaunty, lively; (*ojos*) bright, twinkling.

vivaz [bi'βaθ] *a* lively.

víveres ['biβeres] *nmpl* provisions.

vivero [bi'βero] *nm* (*para plantas*) nursery; (*para peces*) fish farm; (*fig*) hotbed.

viveza [bi'βeθa] *nf* liveliness; (*agudeza: mental*) sharpness.

vivienda [bi'βjenda] *nf* housing; (*una ~*) house; (*piso*) flat (*Brit*), apartment (*US*).

viviente [bi'βjente] *a* living.

vivir [bi'βir] *vt*, *vi* to live // *nm* life, living.

vivo, a ['biβo, a] *a* living, alive; (*fig*: *descripción*) vivid; (*persona*: *astuto*) smart, clever; **en ~** (*transmisión etc*) live.

vocablo [bo'kaβlo] *nm* (*palabra*) word; (*término*) term.

vocabulario [bokaβu'larjo] *nm* vocabulary.

vocación [boka'θjon] *nf* vocation; **vocacional** *nf* (*AM*) ≈ technical college.

vocal [bo'kal] *a* vocal // *nf* vowel; **~izar** *vt* to vocalize.

vocear [boθe'ar] *vt* (*para vender*) to cry; (*aclamar*) to acclaim; (*fig*) to proclaim // *vi* to yell; **vocerío** *nm*, **vocería** *nf* shouting.

vocero [bo'θero] *nm/f* spokesman/woman.

voces ['boθes] *nfpl ver* **voz**.

vociferar [boθife'rar] *vt* to shout // *vi* to yell.

vodka ['boðka] *nm o f* vodka.

vol *abr* = **volumen**.

volador, a [bola'ðor, a] *a* flying.

volandas [bo'landas]: **en ~** *ad* in the air; (*fig*) swiftly.

volante [bo'lante] *a* flying // *nm* (*de coche*) steering wheel; (*de reloj*) balance.

volar [bo'lar] *vt* (*edificio*) to blow up // *vi* to fly.

volátil [bo'latil] *a* volatile.

volcán [bol'kan] *nm* volcano; **~ico, a** *a* volcanic.

volcar [bol'kar] *vt* to upset, overturn; (*tumbar, derribar*) to knock over; (*vaciar*) to empty out // *vi* to overturn; **~se** *vr* to tip over.

voleibol [bolei'βol] *nm* volleyball.

volqué, volquemos *etc vb ver* **volcar**.

volquete [bol'kete] *nm* (*carro*) tipcart; (*AUTO*) dumper.

voltaje [bol'taxe] *nm* voltage.

voltear [bolte'ar] *vt* to turn over; (*volcar*) to turn upside down.

voltereta [bolte'reta] *nf* somersault.

voltio ['boltjo] *nm* volt.

voluble [bo'luβle] *a* fickle.

volumen [bo'lumen] (*pl* **volúmenes**) *nm* volume; **voluminoso, a** *a* voluminous; (*enorme*) massive.

voluntad [bolun'tað] *nf* will; (*resolución*) willpower; (*deseo*) desire, wish.

voluntario, a |bolun'tarjo, a| *a* voluntary // *nm/f* volunteer.

voluntarioso, a |bolunta'rjoso, a| *a* headstrong.

voluptuoso, a |bolup'twoso, a| *a* voluptuous.

volver |bol'ßer| *vt* (*gen*) to turn; (*dar vuelta a*) to turn (over); (*voltear*) to turn round, turn upside down; (*poner al revés*) to turn inside out; (*devolver*) to return // *vi* to return, go back, come back; **~se** *vr* to turn round; **~ la espalda** to turn one's back; **~ triste** *etc* a uno to make sb sad *etc*; **~ a hacer** to do again; **~ en sí** to come to; **~se insoportable/ muy caro** to get o become unbearable/ very expensive; **~se loco** to go mad.

vomitar |bomi'tar| *vt, vi* to vomit; **vómito** *nm* (*acto*) vomiting; (*resultado*) vomit.

voraz |bo'raθ| *a* voracious.

vórtice |'bortiθe| *nm* whirlpool; (*de aire*) whirlwind.

vos |bos| *pron* (*AM*) you.

vosotros, as |bo'sotros, as| *pron* you; (*reflexivo*): **entre/para ~** among/for yourselves.

votación |bota'θjon| *nf* (*acto*) voting; (*voto*) vote.

votar |bo'tar| *vi* to vote.

voto |'boto| *nm* vote; (*promesa*) vow; **~s** (*good*) wishes.

voy *vb ver* **ir**.

voz |boθ| *nf* voice; (*grito*) shout; (*chisme*) rumour; (*LING*) word; **dar voces** to shout, yell; **a media ~** in a low voice; **a ~ en cuello** o **en grito** at the top of one's voice; **de viva ~** verbally; **en ~ alta** aloud; **~ de mando** command.

vuelco *vb ver* **volcar** // |'bwelko| *nm* spill, overturning.

vuelo *vb ver* **volar** // |'bwelo| *nm* flight; (*encaje*) lace, frill; **coger al ~** to catch in flight; **~ charter/regular** charter/ regular flight.

vuelque *etc vb ver* **volcar**.

vuelta |'bwelta| *nf* (*gen*) turn; (*curva*) bend, curve; (*regreso*) return; (*revolución*) revolution; (*circuito*) lap; (*de papel, tela*) reverse; (*cambio*) change; **a la ~** on one's return; **a ~ de correo** by return of post; **dar ~s** (*suj: cabeza*) to spin; **dar ~s a una idea** to turn over an idea (in one's head); **estar de ~** to be back; **dar una ~** to go for a walk; (*en coche*) to go for a drive.

vuelto *pp de* **volver**.

vuelvo *etc vb ver* **volver**.

vuestro, a |'bwestro, a| *a* your; **un amigo ~** a friend of yours // *pron*: **el ~/la vuestra, los ~s/las vuestras** yours.

vulgar |bul'ɣar| *a* (*ordinario*) vulgar; (*común*) common; **~idad** *nf* commonness; (*acto*) vulgarity; (*expresión*) coarse expression; **~idades** *nfpl*

banalities; **~izar** *vt* to popularize.

vulgo |'bulɣo| *nm* common people.

vulnerable |bulne'raßle| *a* vulnerable.

W

wáter |'bater| *nm* toilet.

whisky |'wiski| *nm* whisky, whiskey.

X

xenofobia |kseno'foßja| *nf* xenophobia.

xilófono |ksi'lofono| *nm* xylophone.

Y

y |i| *conj* and.

ya |ja| *ad* (*gen*) already; (*ahora*) now; (*en seguida*) at once; (*pronto*) soon // *excl* all right! // *conj* (*ahora que*) now that; **~ lo sé** I know; **~ que** since.

yacer |ja'θer| *vi* to lie.

yacimiento |jaθi'mjento| *nm* deposit.

yanqui |'janki| *a, nm/f* Yankee.

yate |'jate| *nm* yacht.

yazco *etc vb ver* **yacer**.

yedra |'jeðra| *nf* ivy.

yegua |'jewa| *nf* mare.

yema |'jema| *nf* (*del huevo*) yoke; (*BOT*) leaf bud; (*fig*) best part; **~ del dedo** fingertip.

yergo *etc vb ver* **erguir**.

yermo, a |'jermo, a| *a* (*despoblado*) uninhabited; (*estéril, fig*) barren // *nm* wasteland.

yerno |'jerno| *nm* son-in-law.

yerro *etc vb ver* **errar**.

yerto, a |'jerto, a| *a* stiff.

yesca |'jeska| *nf* tinder.

yeso |'jeso| *nm* (*GEO*) gypsum; (*ARQ*) plaster.

yodo |'joðo| *nm* iodine.

yogur |jo'ɣur| *nm* yoghurt.

yugo |'juɣo| *nm* yoke.

Yugoslavia |juɣos'laßja| *nf* Yugoslavia.

yugular |juɣu'lar| *a* jugular.

yunque |'junke| *nm* anvil.

yunta |'junta| *nf* yoke; **yuntero** *nm* ploughman.

yute |'jute| *nm* jute.

yuxtaponer |jukstapo'ner| *vt* to juxtapose; **yuxtaposición** *nf* juxtaposition.

Z

zafar |θa'far| *vt* (*soltar*) to untie; (*superficie*) to clear; **~se** *vr* (*escaparse*) to escape; (*TEC*) to slip off.

zafio, a |'θafjo, a| *a* coarse.

zafiro |θa'firo| *nm* sapphire.
zaga |'θaɣa| *nf*: a la ~ behind, in the rear.
zagal, a |θa'ɣal, a| *nm/f* boy/girl, lad/lass (*Brit*).
zaguán |θa'ɣwan| *nm* hallway.
zaherir |θae'rir| *vt* (*criticar*) to criticize.
zahorí |θao'ri| *nm* clairvoyant.
zaino, a |'θaino, a| *a* (*color de caballo*) chestnut.
zalamería |θalame'ria| *nf* flattery; **zalamero, a** *a* flattering; (*relamido*) suave.
zamarra |θa'marra| *nf* (*piel*) sheepskin; (*chaqueta*) sheepskin jacket.
zambullirse |θambu'ʎirse| *vr* to dive; (*ocultarse*) to hide o.s.
zampar |θam'par| *vt* to gobble down // *vi* to gobble (up).
zanahoria |θana'orja| *nf* carrot.
zancada |θan'kaða| *nf* stride.
zancadilla |θanka'ðiʎa| *nf* trip; (*fig*) stratagem.
zanco |'θanko| *nm* stilt.
zancudo, a |θan'kuðo, a| *a* long-legged // *nm* (*AM*) mosquito.
zángano |'θangano| *nm* drone.
zanja |'θanxa| *nf* ditch; **zanjar** *vt* (*superar*) to surmount; (*resolver*) to resolve.
zapata |θa'pata| *nf* half-boot; (*MECANICA*) shoe.
zapatear |θapate'ar| *vi* to tap with one's feet.
zapatería |θapate'ria| *nf* (*oficio*) shoemaking; (*tienda*) shoe shop; (*fábrica*) shoe factory; **zapatero, a** *nm/f* shoemaker.
zapatilla |θapa'tiʎa| *nf* slipper.
zapato |θa'pato| *nm* shoe.

zar |θar| *nm* tsar, czar.
zarandear |θarande'ar| *vt* (*fam*) to shake vigorously.
zarpa |'θarpa| *nf* (*garra*) claw.
zarpar |θar'par| *vi* to weigh anchor.
zarza |'θarθa| *nf* (*BOT*) bramble; **zarzal** *nm* (*matorral*) bramble patch.
zarzamora |θarθa'mora| *nf* blackberry.
zarzuela |θarθ'wela| *nf* Spanish light opera.
zigzag |θiɣ'θaɣ| *a* zigzag; **zigzaguear** *vi* to zigzag.
zinc |θink| *nm* zinc.
zócalo |'θokalo| *nm* (*ARQ*) plinth, base.
zona |'θona| *nf* zone; ~ fronteriza border area.
zoo |'θoo| *nm* zoo.
zoología |θoolo'xia| *nf* zoology; **zoológico, a** *a* zoological // *nm* zoo; **zoólogo, a** *nm/f* zoologist.
zopenco, a |θo'penko, a| *nm/f* fool.
zopilote |θopi'lote| *nm* (*AM*) buzzard.
zoquete |θo'kete| *nm* (*madera*) block; (*fam*) blockhead.
zorro, a |'θorro, a| *a* crafty // *nm/f* fox/vixen.
zozobra |θo'θoβra| *nf* (*fig*) anxiety; **zozobrar** *vi* (*hundirse*) to capsize; (*fig*) to fail.
zueco |'θweko| *nm* clog.
zumbar |θum'bar| *vt* (*golpear*) to hit // *vi* to buzz; **zumbido** *nm* buzzing.
zumo |'θumo| *nm* juice.
zurcir |θur'θir| *vt* (*coser*) to darn.
zurdo, a |'θurðo, a| *a* (*mano*) left; (*persona*) left-handed.
zurrar |θu'rrar| *vt* (*fam*) to wallop.
zurrón |θu'rron| *nm* pouch.
zutano, a |θu'tano, a| *nm/f* so-and-so.

ENGLISH-SPANISH
INGLÉS-ESPAÑOL

A

A |eɪ| *n* (*MUS*) la *m*; (*AUT*): ~ **road** ≈ carretera nacional.

a *indefinite article* (*before vowel or silent h*: **an**) |ə, æn| **1** un(a); ~ **book** un libro; **an apple** una manzana; **she's** ~ **doctor** (ella) es médica
2 (*instead of the number 'one'*) un(a); ~ **year ago** hace un año; ~ **hundred/thousand** *etc* **pounds** cien/mil *etc* libras
3 (*in expressing ratios, prices etc*): **3** ~ **day/week** 3 al día/a la semana; **10 km an hour** 10 km por hora; **£5** ~ **person** £5 por persona; **30p** ~ **kilo** 30p el kilo.

A.A. *n abbr* (*Brit*: = *Automobile Association*) ≈ RACE *m* (*Sp*); (= *Alcoholics Anonymous*) Alcohólicos Anónimos.

A.A.A. *n abbr* (*US*: = *American Automobile Association*) ≈ RACE *m* (*Sp*).

aback |ə'bæk| *ad*: **to be taken** ~ quedar desconcertado.

abandon |ə'bændən| *vt* abandonar; (*renounce*) renunciar a // *n* abandono; (*wild behaviour*): **with** ~ sin reparos.

abashed |ə'bæʃt| *a* avergonzado.

abate |ə'beɪt| *vi* (*noise, pain*) aplacarse; (*storm*) amainar // *vt* reducir.

abattoir |'æbətwɑ:*| *n* (*Brit*) matadero.

abbey |'æbɪ| *n* abadía.

abbot |'æbət| *n* abad *m*.

abbreviate |ə'bri:vɪeɪt| *vt* abreviar; **abbreviation** |-'eɪʃən| *n* (*short form*) abreviatura; (*act*) abreviación *f*.

abdicate |'æbdɪkeɪt| *vt, vi* abdicar; **abdication** |-'keɪʃən| *n* abdicación *f*.

abdomen |'æbdəmən| *n* abdomen *m*.

abduct |æb'dʌkt| *vt* raptar, secuestrar.

aberration |æbə'reɪʃən| *n* aberración *f*.

abet |ə'bɛt| *vt see* **aid**.

abeyance |ə'beɪəns| *n*: **in** ~ (*law*) en desuso; (*matter*) en suspenso.

abhor |əb'hɔ:*| *vt* aborrecer, abominar (de).

abide |ə'baɪd| *vt*: **I can't** ~ **it/him** no lo/le puedo ver; **to** ~ **by** *vt fus* atenerse a.

ability |ə'bɪlɪtɪ| *n* habilidad *f*, capacidad *f*; (*talent*) talento.

abject |'æbdʒɛkt| *a* (*poverty*) miserable; (*apology*) rastrero.

ablaze |ə'bleɪz| *a* en llamas, ardiendo.

able |'eɪbl| *a* capaz; (*skilled*) hábil; **to be** ~ **to do sth** poder hacer algo; ~**-bodied** *a* sano; **ably** *ad* hábilmente.

abnormal |æb'nɔ:məl| *a* anormal.

aboard |ə'bɔ:d| *ad* a bordo // *prep* a bordo de.

abode |ə'bəud| *n*: **of no fixed** ~ sin domi-

cilio fijo.

abolish |ə'bɔlɪʃ| *vt* suprimir, abolir; **abolition** |æbəu'lɪʃən| *n* supresión *f*, abolición *f*.

abominable |ə'bɔmɪnəbl| *a* abominable.

aborigine |æbə'rɪdʒɪnɪ| *n* aborigen *m/f*.

abort |ə'bɔ:t| *vt* abortar; ~**ion** |ə'bɔ:ʃən| *n* aborto (provocado); **to have an** ~**ion** abortarse, hacerse abortar; ~**ive** *a* malogrado.

abound |ə'baund| *vi*: **to** ~ (**in** *or* **with**) abundar (de *or* en).

about |ə'baut| ♦ *ad* **1** (*approximately*) más o menos, aproximadamente; ~ **a hundred/thousand** *etc* unos(unas) cien/mil *etc*; **it takes** ~ **10 hours** se tarda unas *or* más o menos 10 horas; **at** ~ **2 o'clock** sobre las dos; **I've just** ~ **finished** casi he terminado
2 (*referring to place*) por todas partes; **to leave things lying** ~ dejar las cosas (tiradas) por ahí; **to run** ~ correr por todas partes; **to walk** ~ pasearse, ir y venir
3: **to be** ~ **to do sth** estar a punto de hacer algo
♦ *prep* **1** (*relating to*) de, sobre, acerca de; **a book** ~ **London** un libro sobre *or* acerca de Londres; **what is it** ~? ¿de qué se trata?, ¿qué pasa?; **we talked** ~ **it** hablamos de eso *or* ello; **what** *or* **how** ~ **doing this?** ¿qué tal si hacemos esto?
2 (*referring to place*) por; **to walk** ~ **the town** caminar por la ciudad.

above |ə'bʌv| *ad* encima, por encima, arriba // *prep* encima de; **mentioned** ~ susodicho; ~ **all** sobre todo; ~ **board** *a* legítimo.

abrasive |ə'breɪzɪv| *a* abrasivo.

abreast |ə'brɛst| *ad* de frente; **to keep** ~ **of** mantenerse al corriente de.

abridge |ə'brɪdʒ| *vt* (*book*) abreviar.

abroad |ə'brɔ:d| *ad* (*to be*) en el extranjero; (*to go*) al extranjero.

abrupt |ə'brʌpt| *a* (*sudden*) brusco; (*gruff*) áspero.

abruptly |ə'brʌptlɪ| *ad* (*leave*) repentinamente; (*speak*) bruscamente.

abscess |'æbsɪs| *n* absceso.

abscond |əb'skɔnd| *vi* fugarse.

absence |'æbsəns| *n* ausencia.

absent |'æbsənt| *a* ausente; ~**ee** |-'ti:| *n* ausente *m/f*; ~**eeism** |-'ti:ɪzəm| *n* absentismo; ~**-minded** *a* distraído.

absolute |'æbsəlu:t| *a* absoluto; ~**ly** |-'lu:tlɪ| *ad* totalmente.

absolve |ab'zɔlv| *vt*: to ~ **sb (from)** absolver a alguien (de).

absorb |ab'zɔːb| *vt* absorber; **to be ~ed in a book** estar absorto en un libro; **~ent cotton** *n* (*US*) algodón *m* hidrófilo; **~ing** *a* absorbente.

absorption |ab'zɔːpʃən| *n* absorción *f*.

abstain |ab'steɪn| *vi*: to ~ **(from)** abstenerse (de).

abstemious |ab'stiːmɪəs| *a* abstemio.

abstention |ab'stɛnʃən| *n* abstención *f*.

abstinence |'æbstɪnəns| *n* abstinencia.

abstract |'æbstrækt| *a* abstracto.

abstruse |æb'struːs| *a* oscuro.

absurd |ab'sɔːd| *a* absurdo.

abundance |ə'bʌndəns| *n* abundancia.

abuse |ə'bjuːs| *n* (*insults*) improperios *mpl*, injurias *fpl*; (*misuse*) abuso // *vt* |ə'bjuːz| (*ill-treat*) maltratar; (*take advantage of*) abusar de; **abusive** *a* ofensivo.

abysmal |ə'bɪzməl| *a* pésimo; (*ignorance*) supino.

abyss |ə'bɪs| *n* abismo.

AC *abbr* (= *alternating current*) corriente *f* alterna.

academic |ækə'dɛmɪk| *a* académico, universitario; (*pej: issue*) puramente teórico // *n* estudioso/a; profesor(a) *m/f* universitario/a.

academy |ə'kædəmɪ| *n* (*learned body*) academia; (*school*) instituto, colegio; ~ **of music** conservatorio.

accelerate |æk'sɛləreɪt| *vt* acelerar // *vi* acelerarse; **accelerator** *n* (*Brit*) acelerador *m*.

accent |'æksɛnt| *n* acento.

accept |ək'sɛpt| *vt* aceptar; (*approve*) aprobar; (*concede*) admitir; **~able** *a* aceptable; admisible; **~ance** *n* aceptación *f*; aprobación *f*.

access |'æksɛs| *n* acceso; **to have ~ to** tener libre acceso a; **~ible** |-'sɛsəbl| *a* accesible.

accessory |æk'sɛsərɪ| *n* accesorio; **toilet accessories** *mpl* de tocador.

accident |'æksɪdənt| *n* accidente *m*; (*chance*) casualidad *f*; **by ~** (*unintentionally*) sin querer; (*by coincidence*) por casualidad; **~al** |-'dɛntl| *a* accidental, fortuito; **~ally** |-'dɛntəlɪ| *ad* sin querer; por casualidad; **~-prone** *a* propenso a los accidentes.

acclaim |ə'kleɪm| *vt* aclamar, aplaudir // *n* aclamación *f*, aplausos *mpl*.

acclimatize |ə'klaɪmətaɪz|, (*US*) **acclimate** |ə'klaɪmət| *vt*: **to become ~d** aclimatarse.

accolade |'ækəleɪd| *n* (*prize*) premio; (*praise*) alabanzas *fpl*.

accommodate |ə'kɔmədeɪt| *vt* alojar, hospedar; (*oblige, help*) complacer; **accommodating** *a* servicial, complaciente.

accommodation *n*, (*US*) **accommoda-** **tions** *npl* |əkɔmə'deɪʃən(z)| alojamiento.

accompany |ə'kʌmpənɪ| *vt* acompañar.

accomplice |ə'kʌmplɪs| *n* cómplice *m/f*.

accomplish |ə'kʌmplɪʃ| *vt* (*finish*) acabar; (*aim*) realizar; (*task*) llevar a cabo; **~ed** *a* experto, hábil; **~ment** *n* (*skill*) talento; (*feat*) hazaña; (*realization*) realización *f*.

accord |ə'kɔːd| *n* acuerdo // *vt* conceder; **of his own ~** espontáneamente; **~ance** *n*: **in ~ance with** de acuerdo con; **~ing to** *prep* según; (*in accordance with*) conforme a; **~ingly** *ad* (*thus*) por consiguiente.

accordion |ə'kɔːdɪən| *n* acordeón *m*.

accost |ə'kɔst| *vt* abordar, dirigirse a.

account |ə'kaunt| *n* (*COMM*) cuenta, factura; (*report*) informe *m*; **~s** *npl* (*COMM*) cuentas *fpl*; **of little ~** de poca importancia; **on ~** a cuenta; **on no ~** bajo ningún concepto; **on ~ of** a causa de, por motivo de; **to take into ~**, **take ~ of** tener en cuenta; **to ~ for** *vt fus* (*explain*) explicar; **~able** *a* responsable.

accountancy |ə'kauntənsɪ| *n* contabilidad *f*.

accountant |ə'kauntənt| *n* contable *m/f*, contador(a) *m/f*.

account number *n* (*at bank etc*) número de cuenta.

accredited |ə'krɛdɪtɪd| *a* (*agent etc*) autorizado.

accrue |ə'kruː| *vi*: **~d interest** interés *m* acumulado.

accumulate |ə'kjuːmjuleɪt| *vt* acumular // *vi* acumularse.

accuracy |'ækjurəsɪ| *n* exactitud *f*, precisión *f*.

accurate |'ækjurɪt| *a* (*number*) exacto; (*answer*) acertado; (*shot*) certero; **~ly** *ad* (*count, shoot, answer*) con precisión.

accusation |ækju'zeɪʃən| *n* acusación *f*.

accuse |ə'kjuːz| *vt* acusar; (*blame*) echar la culpa a; **~d** *n* acusado/a.

accustom |ə'kʌstəm| *vt* acostumbrar; **~ed** *a*: **~ed to** acostumbrado a.

ace |eɪs| *n* as *m*.

acetate |'æsɪteɪt| *n* acetato.

ache |eɪk| *n* dolor *m* // *vi* doler; **my head ~s** me duele la cabeza.

achieve |ə'tʃiːv| *vt* (*reach*) alcanzar; (*realize*) realizar; (*victory, success*) lograr, conseguir; **~ment** *n* (*completion*) realización *f*; (*success*) éxito.

acid |'æsɪd| *a* ácido; (*bitter*) agrio // *n* ácido; **~ rain** *n* lluvia ácida.

acknowledge |ək'nɔlɪdʒ| *vt* (*letter: also*: ~ **receipt of**) acusar recibo de; (*fact*) reconocer; **~ment** *n* acuse *m* de recibo; reconocimiento.

acne |'æknɪ| *n* acné *m*.

acorn |'eɪkɔːn| *n* bellota.

acoustic |ə'kuːstɪk| *a* acústico; **~s** *n, npl* acústica *sg*.

acquaint |ə'kweɪnt| *vt*: to ~ **sb with sth**

(*inform*) poner a uno al corriente de algo; **to be ~ed with** (*person*) conocer; (*fact*) estar al corriente de; **~ance** *n* conocimiento; (*person*) conocido/a.

acquiesce [ækwɪˈɛs] *vi*: **to ~ (in)** consentir (en), conformarse (con).

acquire [əˈkwaɪə*] *vt* adquirir; **acquisition** [ækwɪˈzɪʃən] *n* adquisición *f*; **acquisitive** [əˈkwɪzɪtɪv] *a* codicioso.

acquit [əˈkwɪt] *vt* absolver, exculpar; **to ~ o.s. well** salir con éxito; **~tal** *n* absolución *f*, exculpación *f*.

acre [ˈeɪkə*] *n* acre *m*.

acrid [ˈækrɪd] *a* acre.

acrimonious [ækrɪˈməʊnɪəs] *a* (*remark*) mordaz; (*argument*) reñido.

acrobat [ˈækrəbæt] *n* acróbata *m/f*.

acronym [ˈækrənɪm] *n* siglas *fpl*.

across [əˈkrɒs] *prep* (*on the other side of*) al otro lado de, del otro lado de; (*crosswise*) a través de // **ad** de un lado a otro, de una parte a otra; a través, al través; **to run/swim ~** atravesar corriendo/nadando; **~ from** enfrente de.

acrylic [əˈkrɪlɪk] *a* acrílico.

act [ækt] *n* acto, acción *f*; (*THEATRE*) acto; (*in music hall etc*) número; (*LAW*) decreto, ley *f* // *vi* (*behave*) comportarse; (*THEATRE*) actuar; (*pretend*) fingir; (*take action*) obrar // *vt* (*part*) hacer el papel de; **to ~ as** actuar *or* hacer de; **~ing** *a* suplente // *n*: **to do some ~ing** hacer algo de teatro.

action [ˈækʃən] *n* acción *f*, acto; (*MIL*) acción *f*, batalla; (*LAW*) proceso, demanda; **out of ~** (*person*) fuera de combate; (*thing*) descompuesto; **to take ~** tomar medidas; **~ replay** *n* (*TV*) repetición *f*.

activate [ˈæktɪveɪt] *vt* activar.

active [ˈæktɪv] *a* activo, enérgico; (*volcano*) en actividad; **~ly** *ad* (*participate*) activamente; (*discourage, dislike*) enérgicamente; **activist** *n* activista *m/f*; **activity** [-ˈtɪvɪtɪ] *n* actividad *f*.

actor [ˈæktə*] *n* actor *m*.

actress [ˈæktrɪs] *n* actriz *f*.

actual [ˈæktjʊəl] *a* verdadero, real; **~ly** *ad* realmente, en realidad.

acumen [ˈækjʊmən] *n* perspicacia.

acute [əˈkjuːt] *a* agudo.

ad [æd] *n abbr* = **advertisement**.

A.D. *ad abbr* (= *Anno Domini*) A.C.

adamant [ˈædəmənt] *a* firme, inflexible.

adapt [əˈdæpt] *vt* adaptar // *vi*: **to ~ (to)** adaptarse (a), ajustarse (a); **~able** *a* (*device*) adaptable; (*person*) que se adapta; **~er** *or* **~or** *n* (*ELEC*) adaptador *m*.

add [æd] *vt* añadir, agregar; (*figures: also*: **~ up**) sumar // *vi*: **to ~ to** (*increase*) aumentar, acrecentar; **it doesn't ~ up** (*fig*) no tiene sentido.

adder [ˈædə*] *n* víbora.

addict [ˈædɪkt] *n* (*to drugs etc*) adicto/a; (*enthusiast*) entusiasta *m/f*; **~ed**

[əˈdɪktɪd] *a*: **to be ~ed to** ser adicto a; ser aficionado de; **~ion** [əˈdɪkʃən] *n* (*dependence*) hábito morboso; (*enthusiasm*) afición *f*; **~ive** [əˈdɪktɪv] *a* que causa adicción.

addition [əˈdɪʃən] *n* (*adding up*) adición *f*; (*thing added*) añadidura, añadido; **in ~** además, por añadidura; **in ~ to** además de; **~al** *a* adicional.

additive [ˈædɪtɪv] *n* aditivo.

address [əˈdrɛs] *n* dirección *f*, señas *fpl*; (*speech*) discurso // *vt* (*letter*) dirigir; (*speak to*) dirigirse a, dirigir la palabra a.

adenoids [ˈædənɔɪdz] *npl* vegetaciones *fpl* adenoideas.

adept [ˈædɛpt] *a*: **~ at** experto *or* hábil en.

adequate [ˈædɪkwɪt] *a* (*apt*) adecuado; (*enough*) suficiente.

adhere [ədˈhɪə*] *vi*: **to ~ to** pegarse a; (*fig: abide by*) observar.

adhesive [ədˈhiːzɪv] *a*, *n* adhesivo; **~ tape** *n* (*Brit*) cinta adhesiva; (*US: MED*) esparadrapo.

adjacent [əˈdʒeɪsənt] *a*: **~ to** contiguo a, inmediato a.

adjective [ˈædʒɛktɪv] *n* adjetivo.

adjoining [əˈdʒɔɪnɪŋ] *a* contiguo, vecino.

adjourn [əˈdʒɜːn] *vt* aplazar // *vi* suspenderse.

adjudicate [əˈdʒuːdɪkeɪt] *vi* sentenciar.

adjust [əˈdʒʌst] *vt* (*change*) modificar; (*machine*) ajustar // *vi*: **to ~ (to)** adaptarse (a); **~able** *a* ajustable; **~ment** *n* modificación *f*; ajuste *m*.

adjutant [ˈædʒətənt] *n* ayudante *m*.

ad-lib [ædˈlɪb] *vt*, *vi* improvisar; **ad lib** *ad* a voluntad, a discreción.

administer [ədˈmɪnɪstə*] *vt* proporcionar; (*justice*) administrar; **administration** [-ˈtreɪʃən] *n* administración *f*; (*government*) gobierno; **administrative** [-trətɪv] *a* administrativo.

admiral [ˈædmərəl] *n* almirante *m*; **A~ty** *n* (*Brit*) Ministerio de Marina, Almirantazgo.

admiration [ædməˈreɪʃən] *n* admiración *f*.

admire [ədˈmaɪə*] *vt* admirar; **~r** *n* admirador(a) *m/f*; (*suitor*) pretendiente *m*.

admission [ədˈmɪʃən] *n* (*exhibition, nightclub*) entrada; (*enrolment*) ingreso; (*confession*) confesión *f*.

admit [ədˈmɪt] *vt* dejar entrar, dar entrada a; (*permit*) admitir; (*acknowledge*) reconocer; **to ~ to** *vt fus* confesarse culpable de; **~tance** *n* entrada; **~tedly** *ad* de acuerdo que.

admonish [ədˈmɒnɪʃ] *vt* amonestar.

ad nauseam [ædˈnɔːsɪæm] *ad* hasta el cansancio.

ado [əˈduː] *n*: **without (any) more ~** sin más (ni más).

adolescence [ædəʊˈlɛsns] *n* adolescencia.

adolescent |ædəʊ'lɛsnt| *a*, *n* adolescente *m/f*.

adopt |ə'dɒpt| *vt* adoptar; ~**ed**, ~**ive** *a* adoptivo; ~**ion** |ə'dɒpʃən| *n* adopción *f*.

adore |ə'dɔː*| *vt* adorar.

adorn |ə'dɔːn| *vt* adornar.

Adriatic |eɪdrɪ'ætɪk| *n*: the ~ (Sea) el (Mar) Adriático.

adrift |ə'drɪft| *ad* a la deriva.

adult |'ædʌlt| *n* adulto/a.

adultery |ə'dʌltərɪ| *n* adulterio.

advance |əd'vɑːns| *n* adelanto, progreso; (*money*) anticipo, préstamo; (*MIL*) avance *m* // *vt* avanzar, adelantar; (*money*) anticipar // *vi* avanzar, adelantarse; in ~ por adelantado; ~**d** *a* avanzado; (*SCOL: studies*) adelantado; ~**ment** *n* progreso; (*in rank*) ascenso.

advantage |əd'vɑːntɪdʒ| *n* (*also TENNIS*) ventaja; to take ~ of aprovecharse de; ~**ous** |ædvən'teɪdʒəs| *a* ventajoso, provechoso.

advent |'ædvənt| *n* advenimiento; A~ Adviento.

adventure |əd'vɛntʃə*| *n* aventura; **adventurous** -tʃərəs| *a* aventurero.

adverb |'ædvɜːb| *n* adverbio.

adversary |'ædvəsərɪ| *n* adversario/a, contrario/a.

adverse |'ædvəːs| *a* adverso, contrario; ~ to adverso a.

adversity |əd'vəːsɪtɪ| *n* infortunio.

advert |'ædvəːt| *n* *abbr* (*Brit*) = **advertisement**.

advertise |'ædvətaɪz| *vi* hacer propaganda; (*in newspaper etc*) poner un anuncio; to ~ for (*staff*) buscar por medio de anuncios // *vt* anunciar; (*publicise*) dar publicidad a; ~**ment** |əd'vəːtɪsmənt| *n* (*COMM*) anuncio; ~**r** *n* anunciante *m/f*; **advertising** *n* publicidad *f*, propaganda; anuncios *mpl*.

advice |əd'vaɪs| *n* consejo, consejos *mpl*; (*notification*) aviso; a piece of ~ un consejo; to take legal ~ consultar con un abogado.

advisable |əd'vaɪzəbl| *a* aconsejable, conveniente.

advise |əd'vaɪz| *vt* aconsejar; (*inform*): to ~ sb of sth informar a uno de algo; to ~ sb against sth/doing sth desaconsejar algo a uno/aconsejar a uno que no haga algo; ~**dly** |əd'vaɪzɪdlɪ| *ad* (*deliberately*) deliberadamente; ~**r** *n* consejero/a; (*business adviser*) asesor(a) *m/f*; **advisory** *a* consultivo.

advocate |'ædvəkeɪt| *vt* (*argue for*) abogar por; (*give support to*) ser partidario de // *n* |-kɪt| abogado/a.

Aegean |iː'dʒiːən| *n*: the ~ (Sea) el Mar Egeo.

aerial |'ɛərɪəl| *n* antena // *a* aéreo.

aerobics |ɛə'rəʊbɪks| *n* aerobic *m*.

aerodrome |'ɛərədrəʊm| *n* (*Brit*) aeródromo.

aeroplane |'ɛərəpleɪn| *n* (*Brit*) avión *m*.

aerosol |'ɛərəsɒl| *n* aerosol *m*.

aesthetic |iːs'θetɪk| *a* estético.

afar |ə'fɑː*| *ad*: from ~ desde lejos.

affair |ə'fɛə*| *n* asunto; (*also:* love ~) relación *f* amorosa.

affect |ə'fɛkt| *vt* afectar, influir en; (*move*) conmover; ~**ed** *a* afectado.

affection |ə'fɛkʃən| *n* afecto, cariño; ~**ate** *a* afectuoso, cariñoso.

affirmation |æfə'meɪʃən| *n* afirmación *f*.

affix |ə'fɪks| *vt* (*signature*) estampar; (*stamp*) pegar.

afflict |ə'flɪkt| *vt* afligir.

affluence |'æfluəns| *n* opulencia, riqueza.

affluent |'æfluənt| *a* acaudalado.

afford |ə'fɔːd| *vt* (*provide*) dar, proporcionar; can we ~ it/to buy it? ¿tenemos bastante dinero para comprarlo?

affront |ə'frʌnt| *n* afrenta, ofensa.

Afghanistan |æf'gænɪstæn| *n* Afganistán *m*.

afield |ə'fiːld| *ad*: far ~ muy lejos.

afloat |ə'fləʊt| *ad* (*floating*) a flote; (*at sea*) en el mar.

afoot |ə'fʊt| *ad*: there is something ~ algo se está tramando.

afraid |ə'freɪd| *a*: to be ~ of (*person*) tener miedo a; (*thing*) tener miedo de; to be ~ to tener miedo de, temer; I am ~ that me temo que.

afresh |ə'frɛʃ| *ad* de nuevo, otra vez.

Africa |'æfrɪkə| *n* África; ~**n** *a*, *n* africano/a *m/f*.

aft |ɑːft| *ad* (*to be*) en popa; (*to go*) a popa.

after |'ɑːftə*| *prep* (*time*) después de; (*place, order*) detrás de, tras // *ad* después // *conj* después (de) que; what/who are you ~? ¿qué/a quién busca usted?; ~ having done/he left después de haber hecho/después de que se marchó; to ask ~ sb preguntar por alguien; ~ all después de todo, al fin y al cabo; ~ you! ¡pase usted!; ~-**effects** *npl* consecuencias *fpl*, efectos *mpl*; ~-**life** *n* vida eterna; ~**math** *n* consecuencias *fpl*, resultados *mpl*; ~**noon** *n* tarde *f*; ~**s** *n* (*col: dessert*) postre *m*; ~-**sales service** *n* (*Brit: for car, washing machine etc*) servicio de asistencia pos-venta; ~-**shave (lotion)** *n* aftershave *m*; ~**thought** *n* ocurrencia (tardía); ~**wards** *ad* después, más tarde.

again |ə'gɛn| *ad* otra vez, de nuevo; to do sth ~ volver a hacer algo; ~ and ~ una y otra vez.

against |ə'gɛnst| *prep* (*opposed*) en contra de; (*close to*) contra, junto a.

age |eɪdʒ| *n* edad *f*; (*old* ~) vejez *f*; (*period*) época // *vi* envejecer(se) // *vt* envejecer; she is 20 years of ~ tiene 20 años; to come of ~ llegar a la mayoría de edad; it's been ~s since I saw you hace siglos que no te veo; ~**d** *a*: ~**d** 10 de 10 años de edad; the ~d ['eɪdʒɪd] npl los ancianos; ~ **group** n: to be in the same ~ group tener la misma edad; ~ **limit** n edad f mínima/máxima.

agency ['eɪdʒənsɪ] n agencia; **through** or by the ~ of por medio de.

agenda [ə'dʒendə] n orden m del día.

agent ['eɪdʒənt] n (gen) agente m/f; (representative) representante m/f, delegado/a.

aggravate ['ægrəveɪt] vt agravar; (annoy) irritar.

aggregate ['ægrɪgeɪt] n (whole) conjunto; (collection) agregado.

aggressive [ə'gresɪv] a agresivo; (vigorous) enérgico.

aggrieved [ə'griːvd] a ofendido, agraviado.

aghast [ə'gɑːst] a horrorizado.

agile ['ædʒaɪl] a ágil.

agitate ['ædʒɪteɪt] vt (shake) agitar; (trouble) inquietar; to ~ for hacer campaña pro or en favor de; **agitator** n agitador(a) m/f.

ago [ə'gəu] ad: 2 days ~ hace 2 días; not long ~ hace poco; how long ~? ¿hace cuánto tiempo?

agog [ə'gɔg] a (anxious) ansiado; (excited) emocionado.

agonizing ['ægənaɪzɪŋ] a (pain) atroz; (suspense) angustioso.

agony ['ægənɪ] n (pain) dolor m agudo; (distress) angustia; to be in ~ retorcerse de dolor.

agree [ə'griː] vt (price) acordar, quedar en // vi (statements etc) coincidir, concordar; to ~ (with) (person) estar de acuerdo (con), ponerse de acuerdo (con); to ~ to do aceptar hacer; to ~ to sth consentir en algo; to ~ that (admit) estar de acuerdo en que; **garlic doesn't** ~ **with me** el ajo no me sienta bien; ~**able** a agradable; (person) simpático; (willing) de acuerdo, conforme; ~**d** a (time, place) convenido; ~**ment** n acuerdo; (COMM) contrato; in ~ment de acuerdo, conforme.

agricultural [ægrɪ'kʌltʃərəl] a agrícola.

agriculture ['ægrɪkʌltʃə*] n agricultura.

aground [ə'graund] ad: to run ~ encallar, embarrancar.

ahead [ə'hed] ad delante; ~ of delante de; (fig: schedule etc) antes de; ~ of time antes de la hora; to be ~ of sb (fig) llevar la ventaja a alguien; go right or straight ~ siga adelante; they were (right) ~ of us iban (justo) delante de nosotros.

aid [eɪd] n ayuda, auxilio // vt ayudar, auxiliar; in ~ of a beneficio de; to ~ and abet (LAW) ser cómplice de.

aide [eɪd] n (POL) ayudante m/f.

AIDS [eɪdz] n abbr (= acquired immune deficiency syndrome) SIDA m.

ailing ['eɪlɪŋ] a (person, economy) enfermizo.

ailment ['eɪlmənt] n enfermedad f, achaque m.

aim [eɪm] vt (gun, camera) apuntar; (missile, remark) dirigir; (blow) asestar // vi (also: take ~) apuntar // n puntería; (objective) propósito, meta; to ~ at (objective) aspirar a, pretender; to ~ to do tener la intención de hacer; ~**less** a sin propósito, sin objeto; ~**lessly** ad a la ventura, a la deriva.

ain't [eɪnt] (col) = **am not; aren't; isn't.**

air [ɛə*] n aire m; (appearance) aspecto // vt ventilar; (grievances, ideas) airear // cpd aéreo; to throw sth into the ~ (ball etc) lanzar algo al aire; by ~ (travel) en avión; to be on the ~ (RADIO, TV) estar en antena; ~ **bed** n (Brit) colchón m neumático; ~**borne** a (in the air) en el aire; (MIL) aerotransportado; ~-**conditioned** a climatizado; ~ **conditioning** n aire acondicionado; ~**craft** n, pl inv avión m; ~**craft carrier** n porta(a)viones m inv; ~ **field** n campo de aviación; ~ **force** n fuerzas fpl aéreas, aviación f; ~ **freshener** n ambientador m; ~**gun** n escopeta de aire comprimido; ~ **hostess** (Brit) n azafata; ~ **letter** n (Brit) carta aérea; ~**lift** n parte m aéreo; ~**line** n línea aérea; ~**liner** n avión m de pasajeros; ~**lock** n (in pipe) esclusa de aire; ~**mail** n: by ~mail por avión; ~ **mattress** n colchón m neumático; ~**plane** n (US) avión m; ~**port** n aeropuerto; ~ **raid** n ataque m aéreo; ~**sick** a: to be ~sick marearse (en avión); ~**strip** n pista de aterrizaje; ~ **terminal** n terminal f; ~**tight** a hermético; ~ **traffic controller** n controlador(a) m/f aéreo/a; ~**y** a (room) bien ventilado; (manners) ligero.

aisle [aɪl] n (of church) nave f; (of theatre) pasillo.

ajar [ə'dʒɑː*] a entreabierto.

akin [ə'kɪn] a: ~ to parecido a.

alacrity [ə'lækrɪtɪ] n: with ~ con presteza.

alarm [ə'lɑːm] n alarma; (anxiety) inquietud f // vt asustar, inquietar; ~ (**clock**) n despertador m.

alas [ə'læs] ad desgraciadamente.

albeit [ɔːl'biːɪt] conj aunque.

album ['ælbəm] n álbum m; (L.P.) elepé m.

alcohol ['ælkəhɔl] n alcohol m; ~**ic** [-'hɔlɪk] a, n alcohólico/a m/f.

alcove ['ælkəuv] n nicho, hueco.

alderman ['ɔːldəmən] n concejal m.

ale [eɪl] n cerveza.

alert [ə'ləːt] a alerta; (sharp) despierto, despabilado // n alerta m, alarma // vt poner sobre aviso; to be on the ~ estar alerta or sobre aviso.

algebra ['ældʒɪbrə] n álgebra.

Algeria [æl'dʒɪərɪə] n Argelia; **~n** a, n argelino/a m/f.

alias ['eɪlɪəs] ad alias, conocido por // n alias m.

alibi ['ælɪbaɪ] n coartada.

alien ['eɪlɪən] n (foreigner) extranjero/a // a: ~ to ajeno a; **~ate** vt enajenar, alejar.

alight [ə'laɪt] a ardiendo // vi apearse, bajar.

align [ə'laɪn] vt alinear.

alike [ə'laɪk] a semejantes, iguales // ad igualmente, del mismo modo; **to look ~** parecerse.

alimony ['ælɪmənɪ] n (LAW) manutención f.

alive [ə'laɪv] a (gen) vivo; (lively) activo.

all [ɔːl] ♦ a (singular) todo/a; (plural) todos/as; ~ **day** todo el día; ~ **night** toda la noche; ~ **men** todos los hombres; ~ **five** came vinieron los cinco; ~ **the books** todos los libros; ~ **his life** toda su vida
♦ pron 1 todo; I ate it ~, I ate ~ of it me lo comí todo; ~ of us went fuimos todos; ~ **the boys** went fueron todos los chicos; is that ~? ¿eso es todo?, ¿algo más?; (in shop) ¿algo más?, ¿alguna cosa más?
2 (in phrases): above ~ sobre todo; por encima de todo; after ~ después de todo; at ~: not at ~ (in answer to question) en absoluto; (in answer to thanks) ¡de nada!, ¡no hay de qué!; I'm not at ~ tired no estoy nada cansado/a; anything at ~ will do cualquier cosa viene bien; ~ in ~ a fin de cuentas
♦ ad: ~ **alone** completamente solo/a; it's not as hard as ~ that no es tan difícil como la pintas; **the more/the better** tanto más/mejor; ~ **but** casi; the score is 2 ~ están empatados a 2.

allay [ə'leɪ] vt (fears) aquietar; (pain) aliviar.

all clear n (after attack etc) fin m de la alerta; (fig) luz f verde.

allegation [ælɪ'geɪʃən] n alegato.

allege [ə'ledʒ] vt pretender; **~dly** [ə'ledʒɪdlɪ] ad supuestamente, según se afirma.

allegiance [ə'liːdʒəns] n lealtad f.

allergy ['ælədʒɪ] n alergia.

alleviate [ə'liːvɪeɪt] vt aliviar.

alley ['ælɪ] n (street) callejuela; (in garden) paseo.

alliance [ə'laɪəns] n alianza.

allied ['ælaɪd] a aliado.

alligator ['ælɪgeɪtə*] n caimán m.

all-in ['ɔːlɪn] a (Brit) (also ad: charge) todo incluido; ~ **wrestling** n lucha libre.

all-night ['ɔːl'naɪt] a (café, shop) abierto toda la noche.

allocate ['æləkeɪt] vt (share out) repartir; (devote) asignar; **allocation** [-'keɪʃən] n (of money) cuota; (distribu-

tion) reparto.

allot [ə'lɔt] vt asignar; **~ment** n ración f; (garden) parcela.

all-out ['ɔːlaut] a (effort etc) supremo; **all out** ad con todas las fuerzas.

allow [ə'lau] vt (permit) permitir, dejar; (a claim) admitir; (sum to spend etc, time estimated) dar, conceder; (concede): to ~ **that** reconocer que; to ~ **sb to do** permitir a alguien hacer; he is **~ed** to ... se le permite ...; **to ~ for** vt fus tener en cuenta; **~ance** n concesión f; (payment) subvención f, pensión f; (discount) descuento, rebaja; **to make ~ances for** disculpar a; tener en cuenta.

alloy ['ælɔɪ] n (mix) mezcla.

all: ~ **right** ad (feel, work) bien; (as answer) ¡conforme!, ¡está bien!; ~-**round** a completo; (view) amplio; ~-**time** a (record) de todos los tiempos.

allude [ə'luːd] vi: to ~ to aludir a.

alluring [ə'ljuərɪŋ] a seductor(a), atractivo.

allusion [ə'luːʒən] n referencia, alusión f.

ally ['ælaɪ] n aliado/a.

almighty [ɔːl'maɪtɪ] a todopoderoso.

almond ['ɑːmənd] n almendra.

almost ['ɔːlməust] ad casi.

alms [ɑːmz] npl limosna sg.

aloft [ə'lɔft] ad arriba.

alone [ə'ləun] a solo // ad sólo, solamente; **to leave sb ~** dejar a uno en paz; **to leave sth ~** no tocar algo, dejar algo sin tocar; **let ~** ... sin hablar de ...

along [ə'lɔŋ] prep a lo largo de, por // ad: is he coming ~ with us? ¿viene con nosotros?; he was limping ~ iba cojeando; ~ **with** junto con; all ~ (all the time) desde el principio; **~side** prep al lado de // ad (NAUT) de costado.

aloof [ə'luːf] a reservado // ad: to stand ~ mantenerse apartado.

aloud [ə'laud] ad en voz alta.

alphabet ['ælfəbet] n alfabeto; **~ical** [-'betɪkəl] a alfabético.

alpine ['ælpaɪn] a alpino, alpestre.

Alps [ælps] npl: the ~ los Alpes.

already [ɔːl'redɪ] ad ya.

alright ['ɔːl'raɪt] ad (Brit) = **all right**.

Alsatian [æl'seɪʃən] n (Brit: dog) pastor m alemán.

also ['ɔːlsəu] ad también, además.

altar ['ɔltə*] n altar m.

alter ['ɔltə*] vt cambiar, modificar.

alternate [ɔl'təːnɪt] a alterno // vi ['ɔltəːneɪt]: to ~ **(with)** alternar (con); **on ~ days** un día sí y otro no; **alternating** [-'neɪtɪŋ] a (current) alterno.

alternative [ɔl'təːnətɪv] a alternativo // n alternativa; **~ly** ad: **~ly one could...** por otra parte se podría... .

alternator ['ɔltəːneɪtə*] n (AUT) alternador m.

although [ɔːl'ðəu] conj aunque; (given that) si bien.

altitude [ˈæltɪtjuːd] n altitud f, altura.

alto [ˈæltəu] n (female) contralto f; (male) alto.

altogether [ɔːltəˈgɛðə*] ad completamente, del todo; (on the whole, in all) en total, en conjunto.

aluminium [æljuˈmɪnɪəm], (US) **aluminum** [əˈluːmɪnəm] n aluminio.

always [ˈɔːlweɪz] ad siempre.

am [æm] vb see **be**.

a.m. ad abbr (= ante meridiem) de la mañana.

amalgamate [əˈmælgəmeɪt] vi amalgamarse // vt amalgamar, unir.

amass [əˈmæs] vt amontonar, acumular.

amateur [ˈæmətə*] n aficionado/a, amateur m/f; **~ish** a (pej) torpe, inexperto.

amaze [əˈmeɪz] vt asombrar, pasmar; to be **~d** (at) quedar pasmado (de); **~ment** n asombro, sorpresa; **amazing** a extraordinario, pasmoso.

Amazon [ˈæməzən] n (GEO) Amazonas m.

ambassador [æmˈbæsədə*] n embajador(a) m/f.

amber [ˈæmbə*] n ámbar m; at ~ (Brit AUT) en el amarillo.

ambiguity [æmbɪˈgjuɪtɪ] n ambigüedad f; (of meaning) doble sentido; **ambiguous** [-ˈbɪgjuəs] a ambiguo.

ambition [æmˈbɪʃən] n ambición f; **ambitious** [-ʃəs] a ambicioso.

amble [ˈæmbl] vi (gen: ~ along) deambular, andar sin prisa.

ambulance [ˈæmbjuləns] n ambulancia; **~man/woman** n (Brit) ambulanciero/a.

ambush [ˈæmbuʃ] n emboscada // vt tender una emboscada a.

amenable [əˈmiːnəbl] a: ~ to (advice etc) sensible a.

amend [əˈmɛnd] vt (law, text) enmendar; to make **~s** enmendarlo; (apologize) dar cumplida satisfacción; **~ment** n enmienda.

amenities [əˈmiːnɪtɪz] npl comodidades fpl.

America [əˈmɛrɪkə] n (North ~) América del norte; (USA) Estados mpl Unidos; **~n** a, n norteamericano/a m/f.

amiable [ˈeɪmɪəbl] a (kind) amable, simpático.

amicable [ˈæmɪkəbl] a amistoso, amigable.

amid(st) [əˈmɪd(st)] prep entre, en medio de.

amiss [əˈmɪs] ad: to take sth ~ tomar algo a mal; there's something ~ pasa algo.

ammonia [əˈməunɪə] n amoníaco.

ammunition [æmjuˈnɪʃən] n municiones fpl.

amnesia [æmˈniːzɪə] n amnesia.

amnesty [ˈæmnɪstɪ] n amnistía.

amok [əˈmɔk] ad: to run ~ enloquecerse, desbocarse.

among(st) [əˈmʌŋ(st)] prep entre, en medio de.

amoral [æˈmɔrəl] a amoral.

amorous [ˈæmərəs] a cariñoso.

amorphous [əˈmɔːfəs] a amorfo.

amount [əˈmaunt] n (gen) cantidad f; (of bill etc) suma, importe m // vi: to ~ to (total) sumar; (be same as) equivaler a, significar.

amp(ère) [ˈæmp(ɛə*)] n amperio.

amphibian [æmˈfɪbɪən] n anfibio; **amphibious** [-bɪəs] a anfibio.

amphitheatre [ˈæmfɪθɪətə*] n anfiteatro.

ample [ˈæmpl] a (spacious) amplio; (abundant) abundante; (enough) bastante, suficiente.

amplifier [ˈæmplɪfaɪə*] n amplificador m.

amputate [ˈæmpjuteɪt] vt amputar.

amuck [əˈmʌk] ad = **amok**.

amuse [əˈmjuːz] vt divertir; (distract) distraer, entretener; **~ment** n diversión f; (pastime) pasatiempo; (laughter) risa; **~ment arcade** n mini-casino.

an [æn, ən, n] indefinite article see **a**.

anaemia [əˈniːmɪə] n (Brit) anemia; **anaemic** [-mɪk] a anémico; (fig) soso, insípido.

anaesthetic [ænɪsˈθɛtɪk] n (Brit) anestesia; **anaesthetist** [æˈniːsθɪtɪst] n anestesista m/f.

analog(ue) [ˈænələg] a (computer, watch) analógico.

analogy [əˈnælədʒɪ] n análogo.

analyse [ˈænəlaɪz] vt (Brit) analizar; **analysis** [əˈnæləsɪs], pl **-ses** [-siːz] n análisis m inv; **analyst** [-lɪst] n (political ~, psycho~) analista m/f; **analytic(al)** [-ˈlɪtɪk(əl)] a analítico.

analyze [ˈænəlaɪz] vt (US) = **analyse**.

anarchist [ˈænəkɪst] a, n anarquista m/f.

anarchy [ˈænəkɪ] n anarquía; (fam) desorden m.

anathema [əˈnæθɪmə] n: that is ~ to him eso es pecado para él.

anatomy [əˈnætəmɪ] n anatomía.

ancestor [ˈænsɪstə*] n antepasado.

anchor [ˈæŋkə*] n ancla, áncora // vi (also: to drop ~) anclar // vt (fig) sujetar, afianzar; to weigh ~ levar anclas; **~age** n ancladero.

anchovy [ˈæntʃəvɪ] n anchoa.

ancient [ˈeɪnʃənt] a antiguo.

ancillary [ænˈsɪlərɪ] a (worker, staff) auxiliar.

and [ænd] conj y; (before i-, hi- + consonant) e; men ~ women hombres y mujeres; father ~ son padre e hijo; trees ~ grass árboles y hierba; ~ so on etcétera, y así sucesivamente; try ~ come procura venir; he talked ~ talked habló sin parar; better ~ better cada vez mejor.

Andalusia [ændəˈluːzɪə] n Andalucía.

Andes [ˈændiːz] npl: the ~ los Andes.

anemia etc [əˈniːmɪə] n (US) = **anae-**

mia *etc*.

anesthetic *etc* |æns'θetɪk| *n* (*US*) = **anaesthetic** *etc*.

anew |ə'nju:| *ad* de nuevo, otra vez.

angel |'eɪndʒəl| *n* ángel *m*.

anger |'æŋgə*| *n* cólera // *vt* enojar, enfurecer.

angina |æn'dʒaɪnə| *n* angina (del pecho).

angle |'æŋgl| *n* ángulo; **from their ~** desde su punto de vista.

angler |'æŋglə*| *n* pescador(a) *m/f* (de caña).

Anglican |'æŋglɪkən| *a*, *n* anglicano/a *m/f*.

angling |'æŋglɪŋ| *n* pesca con caña.

Anglo... |æŋgləu| *pref* anglo... .

angrily |'æŋgrɪlɪ| *ad* enojado, enfadado.

angry |'æŋgrɪ| *a* enfadado, enojado; **to be ~ with sb/at sth** estar enfadado con alguien/por algo; **to get ~** enfadarse, enojarse.

anguish |'æŋgwɪʃ| *n* (*physical*) tormentos *mpl*; (*mental*) angustia.

angular |'æŋgjulə*| *a* (*shape*) angular; (*features*) anguloso.

animal |'ænɪməl| *n* animal *m*, bestia // *a* animal.

animate |'ænɪmeɪt| *vt* (*enliven*) animar; (*encourage*) estimular, alentar // *a* |'ænɪmɪt| vivo; **~d** a vivo.

animosity |ænɪ'mɔsɪtɪ| *n* animosidad *f*, rencor *m*.

aniseed |'ænɪsi:d| *n* anís *m*.

ankle |'æŋkl| *n* tobillo *m*; **~ sock** *n* calcetín *m*.

annex |'æneks| *n* (*also: Brit*: **annexe**) (*building*) edificio anexo // *vt* |æ'neks| (*territory*) anexar.

annihilate |ə'naɪəleɪt| *vt* aniquilar.

anniversary |ænɪ'və:sərɪ| *n* aniversario.

announce |ə'nauns| *vt* (*gen*) anunciar; (*inform*) comunicar; **~ment** *n* (*gen*) anuncio; (*declaration*) declaración *f*; **~r** *n* (*RADIO, TV*) locutor(a) *m/f*.

annoy |ə'nɔɪ| *vt* molestar, fastidiar; **don't get ~ed!** ¡no se enfade!; **~ance** *n* enojo; (*thing*) molestia; **~ing** *a* molesto, fastidioso; (*person*) pesado.

annual |'ænjuəl| *a* anual // *n* (*BOT*) anual *m*; (*book*) anuario; **~ly** *ad* anualmente, cada año.

annul |ə'nʌl| *vt* anular; (*law*) revocar; **~ment** *n* anulación *f*.

annum |'ænəm| *n see* **per**.

anomaly |ə'nɔmǝlɪ| *n* anomalía.

anonymity |ænə'nɪmɪtɪ| *n* anonimato.

anonymous |ə'nɔnɪməs| *a* anónimo.

anorak |'ænəræk| *n* anorak *m*.

anorexia |ænə'reksɪə| *n* (*MED*) anorexia.

another |ə'nʌðə*| *a*: **~ book** (*one more*) otro libro; (*a different one*) un libro distinto // *pron* otro; *see also* **one**.

answer |'ɑ:nsə*| *n* contestación *f*, respuesta; (*to problem*) solución *f* // *vi* contestar, responder // *vt* (*reply to*) contestar a, responder a; (*problem*) resolver; **to ~ the phone** contestar el teléfono; **in ~ to your letter** contestando *or* en contestación a su carta; **to ~ the door** acudir a la puerta; **to ~ back** *vi* replicar, ser respondón/ona; **to ~ for** *vt fus* responder de *or* por; **to ~ to** *vt fus* (*description*) corresponder a; **~able** *a*: **~able to sb for sth** responsable ante uno de algo; **~ing machine** *n* contestador *m* automático.

ant |ænt| *n* hormiga.

antagonism |æn'tægənɪzm| *n* hostilidad *f*.

antagonize |æn'tægənaɪz| *vt* provocar.

Antarctic |ænt'ɑ:ktɪk| *n*: **the ~** el Antártico.

antelope |'æntɪləup| *n* antílope *m*.

antenatal |'æntɪ'neɪtl| *a* antenatal, prenatal; **~ clinic** *n* clínica prenatal.

antenna |æn'tenə|, *pl* **~e** |-ni:| *n* antena.

anthem |'ænθəm| *n*: **national ~** himno nacional.

anthology |æn'θɔlədʒɪ| *n* antología.

anthropology |ænθrə'pɔlədʒɪ| *n* antropología.

anti-aircraft |æntɪ'ɛəkrɑ:ft| *a* antiaéreo.

antibiotic |æntɪbaɪ'ɔtɪk| *a*, *n* antibiótico.

antibody |'æntɪbɔdɪ| *n* anticuerpo.

anticipate |æn'tɪsɪpeɪt| *vt* (*foresee*) prever; (*expect*) esperar, contar con; (*forestall*) anticiparse a, adelantarse a; **anticipation** |-'peɪʃən| *n* previsión *f*; esperanza; anticipación *f*.

anticlimax |æntɪ'klaɪmæks| *n* decepción *f*.

anticlockwise |æntɪ'klɔkwaɪz| *ad* en dirección contraria a la de las agujas del reloj.

antics |'æntɪks| *npl* payasadas *fpl*; (*of child*) travesuras *fpl*.

anticyclone |æntɪ'saɪkləun| *n* anticiclón *m*.

antidote |'æntɪdəut| *n* antídoto.

antifreeze |'æntɪfri:z| *n* anticongelante *m*.

antihistamine |æntɪ'hɪstəmi:n| *n* antihistamínico.

antipathy |æn'tɪpəθɪ| *n* (*between people*) antipatía; (*to person, thing*) aversión *f*.

antiquated |'æntɪkweɪtɪd| *a* anticuado.

antique |æn'ti:k| *n* antigüedad *f* // *a* antiguo; **~ dealer** *n* anticuario/a; **~ shop** *n* tienda de antigüedades.

antiquity |æn'tɪkwɪtɪ| *n* antigüedad *f*.

anti-semitism |æntɪ'semɪtɪzm| *n* antisemitismo.

antiseptic |æntɪ'septɪk| *a*, *n* antiséptico.

antisocial |æntɪ'səuʃəl| *a* antisocial.

antlers |'æntləz| *npl* cuernas *fpl*.

anus |'eɪnəs| *n* ano.

anvil |'ænvɪl| *n* yunque *m*.

anxiety |æg'zaɪətɪ| *n* (*worry*) inquietud *f*; (*eagerness*) ansia, anhelo.

anxious |'æŋkʃəs| *a* (*worried*) inquieto; (*keen*) deseoso.

any [ˈɛni] ♦ *a* **1** (*in questions etc*) algún/ alguna; **have you ~ butter/children?** ¿tienes mantequilla/hijos?; **if there are ~ tickets left** si quedan billetes, si queda algún billete **2** (*with negative*): **I haven't ~ money/ books** no tengo dinero/libros **3** (*no matter which*) cualquier; **~ excuse will do** valdrá *or* servirá cualquier excusa; **choose ~ book you like** escoge el libro que quieras; **~ teacher you ask will tell you** cualquier profesor al que preguntes te lo dirá **4** (*in phrases*): **in ~ case** de todas formas, en cualquier caso; **~ day now** cualquier día (de estos); **at ~ moment** en cualquier momento, de un momento a otro; **at ~ rate** en todo caso; **~ time: come (at) ~ time** venga cuando quieras; **he might come (at) ~ time** podría llegar de un momento a otro ♦ *pron* **1** (*in questions etc*): **have you got ~?** ¿tienes alguno(s)/a(s)?; **can ~ of you sing?** ¿sabéis/saben cantar alguno de vosotros/ustedes? **2** (*with negative*): **I haven't ~ (of them)** no tengo ninguno **3** (*no matter which one(s)*): **take ~ of those books (you like)** toma cualquier libro que quieras de ésos ♦ *ad* **1** (*in questions etc*): **do you want ~ more soup/sandwiches?** ¿quieres más sopa/bocadillos?; **are you feeling ~ better?** ¿te sientes algo mejor? **2** (*with negative*): **I can't hear him ~ more** ya no le oigo; **don't wait ~ longer** no esperes más.

anybody [ˈɛnibɔdɪ] *pron* cualquiera; (*in interrogative sentences*) alguien; (*in negative sentences*) **I don't see ~** no veo a nadie; **if ~ should phone...** si llama alguien....

anyhow [ˈɛnihau] *ad* (*at any rate*) de todos modos, de todas formas; (*haphazard*): **do it ~ you like** hazlo como quieras; **she leaves things just ~** deja las cosas como quiera *or* de cualquier modo; **I shall go ~** de todos modos iré.

anyone [ˈɛniwʌn] *pron* = **anybody**.

anything [ˈɛniθiŋ] *pron* (*in questions etc*) algo, alguna cosa; (*with negative*) nada; **can you see ~?** ¿ves algo?; **if ~ happens to me...** si algo me ocurre...; (*no matter what*): **you can say ~** you like puedes decir lo que quieras; **~ will do** vale todo *or* cualquier cosa; **he'll eat ~** come de todo *or* lo que sea.

anyway [ˈɛniwei] *ad* (*at any rate*) de todos modos, de todas formas; **I shall go ~** iré de todos modos; (*besides*): **~, I couldn't come even if I wanted to** además, no podría venir aunque quisiera; **why are you phoning, ~?** ¿entonces, por qué llamas?, ¿por qué llamas, pues?

anywhere [ˈɛniwɛə*] *ad* (*in questions etc*): **can you see him ~?** ¿le ves por algún lado?; **are you going ~?** ¿vas a algún sitio?; (*with negative*): **I can't see him ~** no le veo por ninguna parte; (*no matter where*): **~ in the world** en cualquier parte (del mundo); **put the books down ~** posa los libros donde quieras.

apart [əˈpɑːt] *ad* aparte, separadamente; **10 miles ~** separados por 10 millas; **to take ~** desmontar; **~ from** *prep* aparte de.

apartheid [əˈpɑːteit] *n* apartheid *m*.

apartment [əˈpɑːtmənt] *n* (*US*) piso, departamento (*LAm*), apartamento; (*room*) cuarto; **~ house** *n* (*US*) casa de apartamentos.

apathetic [æpəˈθɛtik] *a* apático, indiferente.

apathy [ˈæpəθi] *n* apatía, indiferencia.

ape [eip] *n* mono // *vt* remedar.

aperitif [əˈpɛritif] *n* aperitivo.

aperture [ˈæpətʃuə*] *n* rendija, resquicio; (*PHOT*) abertura.

apex [ˈeipɛks] *n* ápice *m*; (*fig*) cumbre *f*.

apiece [əˈpiːs] *ad* cada uno.

aplomb [əˈplɔm] *n* aplomo.

apologetic [əpɔləˈdʒɛtik] *a* (*look, remark*) de disculpa.

apologize [əˈpɔlədʒaiz] *vi*: **to ~ (for sth to sb)** disculparse (con alguien de algo).

apology [əˈpɔlədʒi] *n* disculpa, excusa.

apostle [əˈpɔsl] *n* apóstol *m/f*.

apostrophe [əˈpɔstrəfi] *n* apóstrofe *m*.

appal [əˈpɔːl] *vt* horrorizar, espantar; **~ling** a espantoso; (*awful*) pésimo.

apparatus [æpəˈreitəs] *n* aparato; (*in gymnasium*) aparatos *mpl*.

apparel [əˈpærəl] *n* (*US*) ropa.

apparent [əˈpærənt] *a* aparente; **~ly** *ad* por lo visto, al parecer.

appeal [əˈpiːl] *vi* (*LAW*) apelar // *n* (*LAW*) apelación *f*; (*request*) llamamiento; (*plea*) súplica; (*charm*) atractivo, encanto; **to ~ for** suplicar, reclamar; **to ~ to** (*subj: person*) rogar a, suplicar a; (*subj: thing*) atraer, interesar; **it doesn't ~ to me** no me atrae, no me llama la atención; **~ing** *a* (*nice*) atractivo; (*touching*) conmovedor(a), emocionante.

appear [əˈpiə*] *vi* aparecer, presentarse; (*LAW*) comparecer; (*publication*) salir (a luz), publicarse; (*seem*) parecer; **it would ~ that** parecería que; **~ance** *n* aparición *f*; (*look, aspect*) apariencia, aspecto.

appease [əˈpiːz] *vt* (*pacify*) apaciguar; (*satisfy*) satisfacer.

appendicitis [əpɛndiˈsaitis] *n* apendicitis *f*.

appendix [əˈpɛndiks], *pl* **-dices** [-disiːz] *n* apéndice *m*.

appetite [ˈæpitait] *n* apetito; (*fig*) deseo, anhelo.

appetizer [ˈæpitaizə*] *n* (*drink*) aperitivo; (*food*) tapas *fpl* (*Sp*).

applaud [ə'plɔːd] *vt*, *vi* aplaudir.

applause [ə'plɔːz] *n* aplausos *mpl*.

apple ['æpl] *n* manzana; ~ **tree** *n* manzano.

appliance [ə'plaɪəns] *n* aparato.

applicant ['æplɪkənt] *n* candidato/a; solicitante *m/f*.

application [æplɪ'keɪʃən] *n* aplicación *f*; (*for a job, a grant etc*) solicitud *f*, petición *f*; ~ **form** *n* solicitud *f*.

applied [ə'plaɪd] *a* aplicado.

apply [ə'plaɪ] *vt*: to ~ (to) aplicar (a); (*fig*) emplear (para) // *vi*: to ~ to (*ask*) dirigirse a; (*be suitable for*) ser aplicable a; (*be relevant to*) tener que ver con; to ~ **for** (*permit, grant, job*) solicitar; to ~ **the brakes** aplicar los frenos; to ~ **o.s. to** aplicarse a, dedicarse a.

appoint [ə'pɔɪnt] *vt* (*to post*) nombrar; (*date, place*) fijar, señalar; ~**ment** *n* (*engagement*) cita; (*date*) compromiso; (*act*) nombramiento; (*post*) puesto.

appraisal [ə'preɪzl] *n* apreciación *f*.

appreciable [ə'priːʃəbl] *a* sensible.

appreciate [ə'priːʃɪeɪt] *vt* (*like*) apreciar, tener en mucho; (*be grateful for*) agradecer; (*be aware of*) comprender // *vi* (*COMM*) aumentar(se) en valor; **appreciation** [-'eɪʃən] *n* aprecio; reconocimiento, agradecimiento; aumento en valor.

appreciative [ə'priːʃɪətɪv] *a* apreciativo, agradecido.

apprehend [æprɪ'hend] *vt* percibir; (*arrest*) detener.

apprehension [æprɪ'henʃən] *n* (*fear*) aprensión *f*; **apprehensive** [-'hensɪv] *a* aprensivo.

apprentice [ə'prentɪs] *n* aprendiz/a *m/f*; ~**ship** *n* aprendizaje *m*.

approach [ə'prəʊtʃ] *vi* acercarse // *vt* acercarse a; (*be approximate*) aproximarse a; (*ask, apply to*) dirigirse a // *n* acercamiento; aproximación *f*; (*access*) acceso; (*proposal*) proposición *f*; ~**able** *a* (*person*) abordable; (*place*) accesible.

appropriate [ə'prəʊprɪɪt] *a* apropiado, conveniente // *vt* [-rɪeɪt] (*take*) apropiarse de; (*allot*): to ~ **sth for** destinar algo a.

approval [ə'pruːvəl] *n* aprobación *f*, visto bueno; on ~ (*COMM*) a prueba.

approve [ə'pruːv] *vt* aprobar; **to** ~ **of** *vt fus* aprobar; ~**d school** *n* (*Brit*) correccional *m*.

approximate [ə'prɔksɪmɪt] *a* aproximado; ~**ly** *ad* aproximadamente, más o menos.

apricot ['eɪprɪkɔt] *n* albaricoque *m* (*Sp*), damasco (*LAm*).

April ['eɪprəl] *n* abril *m*; ~ **Fool's Day** *n* (*1 April*) ≈ día *m* de los Inocentes (*28 December*).

apron ['eɪprən] *n* delantal *m*.

apt [æpt] *a* (*to the point*) acertado, opor-

tuno; (*appropriate*) apropiado; (*likely*): ~ **to do** propenso a hacer.

aqualung ['ækwəlʌŋ] *n* escafandra autónoma.

aquarium [ə'kwɛərɪəm] *n* acuario.

Aquarius [ə'kwɛərɪəs] *n* Acuario.

aquatic [ə'kwætɪk] *a* acuático.

aqueduct ['ækwɪdʌkt] *n* acueducto.

Arab ['ærəb] *n* árabe *m/f*.

Arabian [ə'reɪbɪən] *a* árabe.

Arabic ['ærəbɪk] *a* (*language, manuscripts*) árabe // *n* árabe *m*; ~ **numerals** numeración *f* arábiga.

arable ['ærəbl] *a* cultivable.

Aragon ['ærəgən] *n* Aragón *m*.

arbitrary ['ɑːbɪtrərɪ] *a* arbitrario.

arbitration [ɑːbɪ'treɪʃən] *n* arbitraje *m*.

arcade [ɑː'keɪd] *n* (*ARCH*) arcada; (*round a square*) soportales *mpl*; (*shopping* ~) galería, pasaje *m*.

arch [ɑːtʃ] *n* arco; (*vault*) bóveda; (*of foot*) arco del pie // *vt* arquear.

archaeologist [ɑːkɪ'ɔlədʒɪst] *n* arqueólogo/a.

archaeology [ɑːkɪ'ɔlədʒɪ] *n* arqueología.

archaic [ɑː'keɪɪk] *a* arcaico.

archbishop [ɑːtʃ'bɪʃəp] *n* arzobispo.

arch-enemy ['ɑːtʃ'enəmɪ] *n* enemigo jurado.

archeology *etc* [ɑːkɪ'ɔlədʒɪ] (*US*) = **archaeology** *etc.*

archer ['ɑːtʃə*] *n* arquero; ~**y** *n* tiro al arco.

archipelago [ɑːkɪ'pelɪɡəʊ] *n* archipiélago.

architect ['ɑːkɪtekt] *n* arquitecto/a; ~**ural** [-'tektʃərəl] *a* arquitectónico; ~**ure** *n* arquitectura.

archives ['ɑːkaɪvz] *npl* archivo *sg*.

archway ['ɑːtʃweɪ] *n* arco, arcada.

Arctic ['ɑːktɪk] *a* ártico // *n*: **the** ~ el Ártico.

ardent ['ɑːdənt] *a* (*desire*) ardiente; (*supporter, lover*) apasionado.

arduous ['ɑːdjuəs] *a* (*gen*) arduo; (*journey*) penoso.

are [ɑː*] *vb see* **be**.

area ['ɛərɪə] *n* área; (*MATH etc*) superficie *f*, extensión *f*; (*zone*) región *f*, zona; ~ **code** *n* (*US TEL*) prefijo.

arena [ə'riːnə] *n* arena; (*of circus*) pista; (*for bullfight*) plaza, ruedo.

aren't [ɑːnt] = **are not**.

Argentina [ɑːdʒən'tiːnə] *n* Argentina; **Argentinian** [-'tɪnɪən] *a*, *n* argentino/a *m/f*.

arguably ['ɑːgjuəblɪ] *ad* posiblemente.

argue ['ɑːgjuː] *vi* (*quarrel*) discutir, pelearse; (*reason*) razonar, argumentar; to ~ **that** sostener que.

argument ['ɑːgjumənt] *n* (*reasons*) argumento; (*quarrel*) discusión *f*, pelea; (*debate*) debate *m*, disputa; ~**ative** [-'mentətɪv] *a* discutidor(a).

aria ['ɑːrɪə] *n* (*MUS*) aria.

Aries |'ɛəriz| *n* Aries *m*.

arise |ə'raiz|, *pt* **arose**, *pp* **arisen** |ə'rizn| *vi* (*rise up*) levantarse, alzarse; (*emerge*) surgir, presentarse; **to ~ from** derivar de.

aristocrat |'ærɪstəkræt| *n* aristócrata *m/f*.

arithmetic |ə'riθmətik| *n* aritmética.

ark |ɑːk| *n*: Noah's A~ el Arca *f* de Noé.

arm |ɑːm| *n* (*ANAT*) brazo // *vt* armar; **~s** *npl* (*weapons*) armas *fpl*; (*HERALDRY*) escudo *sg*; **~ in ~** cogidos del brazo; **~s race** *n* carrera de armamentos.

armaments |'ɑːməmənts| *npl* (*weapons*) armamentos *mpl*.

armchair |'ɑːmtʃɛə*| *n* sillón *m*.

armed |ɑːmd| *a* armado; **~ robbery** *n* robo a mano armada.

armour, (*US*) **armor** |'ɑːmə*| *n* armadura; **~ed car** *n* coche *m or* carro (*LAm*) blindado; **~y** *n* arsenal *m*.

armpit |'ɑːmpit| *n* sobaco, axila.

armrest |'ɑːmrest| *n* apoyabrazos *m inv*.

army |'ɑːmi| *n* ejército.

aroma |ə'rəumə| *n* aroma *m*, fragancia.

arose |ə'rauz| *pt of* **arise**.

around |ə'raund| *ad* alrededor; (*in the area*) a la redonda // *prep* alrededor de.

arouse |ə'rauz| *vt* despertar.

arrange |ə'reindʒ| *vt* arreglar, ordenar; (*programme*) organizar; **to ~ to do sth** quedar en hacer algo; **~ment** *n* arreglo; (*agreement*) acuerdo; **~ments** *npl* (*preparations*) preparativos *mpl*.

array |ə'rei| *n*: **~ of** (*things*) serie *f* de; (*people*) conjunto de.

arrears |ə'riəz| *npl* atrasos *mpl*; **to be in ~ with one's rent** estar retrasado en el pago del alquiler.

arrest |ə'rest| *vt* detener; (*sb's attention*) llamar // *n* detención *f*; **under ~** detenido.

arrival |ə'raivəl| *n* llegada; **new ~** recién llegado/a.

arrive |ə'raiv| *vi* llegar.

arrogant |'ærəgənt| *a* arrogante.

arrow |'ærəu| *n* flecha.

arse |ɑːs| *n* (*Brit col!*) culo, trasero.

arsenal |'ɑːsinl| *n* arsenal *m*.

arsenic |'ɑːsnik| *n* arsénico.

arson |'ɑːsn| *n* incendio premeditado.

art |ɑːt| *n* arte *m*; (*skill*) destreza; (*technique*) técnica; A~s *npl* (*SCOL*) Letras *fpl*.

artery |'ɑːtəri| *n* arteria.

artful |'ɑːtful| *a* (*cunning: person, trick*) mañoso.

art gallery *n* pinacoteca; (*saleroom*) galería de arte.

arthritis |ɑː'θraitis| *n* artritis *f*.

artichoke |'ɑːtitʃəuk| *n* alcachofa; Jerusalem ~ aguaturma.

article |'ɑːtikl| *n* artículo, (*in newspaper*) artículo; (*Brit LAW: training*): **~s** *npl* contrato *sg* de aprendizaje; **~ of clothing** prenda de vestir.

articulate |ɑː'tikjulit| *a* (*speech*) claro; (*person*) que se expresa bien // *vi* |·leit| articular; **~d lorry** *n* (*Brit*) trailer *m*.

artificial |ɑːti'fiʃəl| *a* artificial; (*teeth etc*) postizo.

artillery |ɑː'tiləri| *n* artillería.

artisan |'ɑːtizæn| *n* artesano.

artist |'ɑːtist| *n* artista *m/f*; (*MUS*) intérprete *m/f*; **~ic** |ɑː'tistik| *a* artístico; **~ry** *n* arte *m*, habilidad *f* (artística).

artless |'ɑːtlis| *a* (*innocent*) natural, sencillo; (*clumsy*) torpe.

art school *n* escuela de bellas artes.

as |æz| *conj* **1** (*referring to time*) cuando, mientras; a medida que; **~ the years went by** con el paso de los años; **he came in ~** I was leaving entró cuando me marchaba; **~ from tomorrow** desde *or* a partir de mañana
2 (*in comparisons*): **~ big ~** tan grande como; **twice ~ big ~** el doble de grande que; **~ much money/many books ~** tanto dinero/tantos libros como; **~ soon ~** en cuanto
3 (*since, because*) como, ya que; **he left early ~** he had to be home by 10 se fue temprano como tenía que estar en casa a las 10
4 (*referring to manner, way*): **do ~ you** wish haz lo que quieras; **~** she said como dijo; **he gave it to me ~** a present me lo dio de regalo
5 (*in the capacity of*): **he works ~** a barman trabaja de barman; **~ chairman** of the company, he... como presidente de la compañía, ...
6 (*concerning*): **~ for** *or* **to that** por *or* en lo que respecta a eso
7: **~ if** *or* **though** como si: **he looked ~ if** he was ill parecía como si estuviera enfermo, tenía aspecto de enfermo
see also **long, such, well.**

a.s.a.p. *abbr* (= *as soon as possible*) cuanto antes.

asbestos |æz'bestəs| *n* asbesto, amianto.

ascend |ə'send| *vt* subir; **~ancy** *n* ascendiente *m*, dominio.

ascent |ə'sent| *n* subida; (*of plane*) ascenso.

ascertain |æsə'tein| *vt* averiguar.

ascribe |ə'skraib| *vt*: **to ~ sth to** atribuir algo a.

ash |æʃ| *n* ceniza; (*tree*) fresno; **~can** *n* (*US*) cubo *or* bote *m* (*LAm*) de la basura.

ashamed |ə'feimd| *a* avergonzado, apenado (*LAm*); **to be ~ of** avergonzarse de.

ashen |'æʃn| *a* pálido.

ashore |ə'ʃɔː*| *ad* en tierra.

ashtray |'æʃtrei| *n* cenicero.

Ash Wednesday *n* miércoles *m* de Cenizas.

Asia |'eiʃə| *n* Asia; **~n, ~tic** |eisi'ætik|

a, n asiático/a *m/f.*

aside [ə'saɪd] *ad* a un lado.

ask [ɑːsk] *vt* (*question*) preguntar; (*demand*) pedir; (*invite*) invitar; **to ~ sb sth/to do sth** preguntar algo a alguien/ pedir a alguien que haga algo; **to ~ sb about sth** preguntar algo a alguien; **to ~ (sb) a question** hacer una pregunta (a alguien); **to ~ sb out to dinner** invitar a cenar a uno; **to ~ after** *vt fus* preguntar por; **to ~ for** *vt fus* pedir.

askance [ə'skɑːns] *ad*: **to look ~ at sb** mirar con recelo a uno.

askew [ə'skjuː] *ad* sesgado, ladeado.

asking price *n* precio inicial.

asleep [ə'sliːp] *a* dormido; **to fall ~** dormirse, quedarse dormido.

asparagus [əs'pærəgəs] *n* espárragos *mpl.*

aspect ['æspekt] *n* aspecto, apariencia; (*direction in which a building etc faces*) orientación *f.*

aspersions [əs'pəːʃənz] *npl*: **to cast ~ on** difamar a, calumniar a.

asphyxiation [æsfɪksɪ'eɪʃən] *n* asfixia.

aspirations [æspə'reɪʃənz] *npl* anhelo *sg*, deseo *sg*; (*ambition*) ambición *fsg.*

aspire [əs'paɪə*] *vi*: **to ~ to** aspirar a, ambicionar.

aspirin ['æsprɪn] *n* aspirina.

ass [æs] *n* asno, burro; (*col*) imbécil *m/f*; (*US col!*) culo, trasero.

assailant [ə'seɪlənt] *n* asaltador(a) *m/f*, agresor(a) *m/f.*

assassin [ə'sæsɪn] *n* asesino/a; **~ate** *vt* asesinar; **~ation** [-'neɪʃən] *n* asesinato.

assault [ə'sɔːlt] *n* (*gen: attack*) asalto // *vt* asaltar, atacar; (*sexually*) violar.

assemble [ə'sɛmbl] *vt* reunir, juntar; (*TECH*) montar // *vi* reunirse, juntarse.

assembly [ə'sɛmblɪ] *n* (*meeting*) reunión *f*, asamblea; (*construction*) montaje *m*; **~ line** *n* cadena de montaje.

assent [ə'sɛnt] *n* asentimiento, aprobación *f* // *vi* consentir, asentir.

assert [ə'səːt] *vt* afirmar; (*insist on*) hacer valer.

assess [ə'sɛs] *vt* valorar, calcular; (*tax, damages*) fijar; (*property etc: for tax*) gravar; **~ment** *n* valoración *f*; gravamen *m*; **~or** *n* asesor(a) *m/f*; (*of tax*) tasador(a) *m/f.*

asset ['æsɛt] *n* posesión *f*; (*quality*) ventaja; **~s** *npl* (*funds*) activo *sg*, fondos *mpl.*

assign [ə'saɪn] *vt* (*date*) fijar; (*task*) asignar; (*resources*) destinar; (*property*) traspasar; **~ment** *n* asignación *f*; (*task*) tarea.

assist [ə'sɪst] *vt* ayudar; **~ance** *n* ayuda, auxilio; **~ant** *n* ayudante *m/f*; (*Brit: also:* **shop ~ant**) dependiente/a *m/f.*

associate [ə'səʊʃɪɪt] *a* asociado // *n* socio/a, colega *m/f*; (*in crime*) cómplice *m/f*; (*member*) miembro // *vb* [-ʃɪeɪt] *vt*

asociar; (*ideas*) relacionar // *vi*: **to ~ with sb** tratar con alguien.

association [əsəʊsɪ'eɪʃən] *n* asociación *f*; (*COMM*) sociedad *f.*

assorted [ə'sɔːtɪd] *a* surtido, variado.

assortment [ə'sɔːtmənt] *n* surtido.

assume [ə'sjuːm] *vt* (*suppose*) suponer; (*responsibilities etc*) asumir; (*attitude, name*) adoptar, tomar; **~d name** *n* nombre *m* falso.

assumption [ə'sʌmpʃən] *n* (*supposition*) suposición *f*, presunción *f*; (*act*) asunción *f.*

assurance [ə'ʃʊərəns] *n* garantía, promesa; (*confidence*) confianza, aplomo; (*insurance*) seguro.

assure [ə'ʃʊə*] *vt* asegurar.

astern [ə'stəːn] *ad* a popa.

asthma ['æsmə] *n* asma.

astonish [ə'stɒnɪʃ] *vt* asombrar, pasmar; **~ment** *n* asombro, sorpresa.

astound [ə'staʊnd] *vt* asombrar, pasmar.

astray [ə'streɪ] *ad*: **to go ~** extraviarse; **to lead ~** llevar por mal camino.

astride [ə'straɪd] *prep* a caballo *or* horcajadas sobre.

astrology [æs'trɒlədʒɪ] *n* astrología.

astronaut ['æstrənɔːt] *n* astronauta *m/f.*

astronomical [æstrə'nɒmɪkəl] *a* astronómico.

astronomy [æs'trɒnəmɪ] *n* astronomía.

astute [əs'tjuːt] *a* astuto.

asylum [ə'saɪləm] *n* (*refuge*) asilo; (*hospital*) manicomio.

at [æt] *prep* **1** (*referring to position*) en; (*direction*) a; **~ the top** en lo alto; **~ home/school** en casa/la escuela; **to look ~ sth/sb** mirar algo/a uno

2 (*referring to time*): **~ 4 o'clock** a las 4; **~ night** por la noche; **~ Christmas** en Navidad; **~ times** a veces

3 (*referring to rates, speed etc*): **~ £1 a kilo** a una libra el kilo; **two ~ a time** de dos en dos; **~ 50 km/h** a 50 km/h

4 (*referring to manner*): **~ a stroke** de un golpe; **~ peace** en paz

5 (*referring to activity*): **to be ~ work** estar trabajando; (*in the office etc*) estar en el trabajo; **to play ~ cowboys** jugar a los vaqueros; **to be good ~ sth** ser bueno en algo

6 (*referring to cause*): **shocked/ surprised/annoyed ~ sth** asombrado/ sorprendido/fastidiado por algo; **I went ~ his suggestion** fui a instancias suyas.

ate [eɪt] *pt of* **eat.**

atheist ['eɪθɪɪst] *n* ateo/a.

Athens ['æθɪnz] *n* Atenas *f.*

athlete ['æθliːt] *n* atleta *m/f.*

athletic [æθ'lɛtɪk] *a* atlético; **~s** *n* atletismo.

Atlantic [ət'læntɪk] *a* atlántico // *n*: **the ~ (Ocean)** el (Océano) Atlántico.

atlas ['ætləs] *n* atlas *m.*

atmosphere ['ætməsfɪə*] *n* atmósfera;

(*fig*) ambiente *m*.

atom ['ætəm] *n* átomo; **~ic** [ə'tɔmɪk] *a* atómico; **~(ic) bomb** *n* bomba atómica; **~izer** ['ætəmaɪzə*] *n* atomizador *m*.

atone [ə'təun] *vi*: to ~ for expiar.

atrocious [ə'trəuʃəs] *a* atroz.

attach [ə'tætʃ] *vt* sujetar; (*stick*) pegar; (*document*, *letter*) adjuntar; to be ~ed to sb/sth (*to like*) tener cariño a alguien/algo.

attaché [ə'tæʃeɪ] *n* agregado/a; ~ **case** *n* (*Brit*) maletín *m*.

attachment [ə'tætʃmənt] *n* (*tool*) accesorio; (*love*): ~ (to) apego (a).

attack [ə'tæk] *vt* (*MIL*) atacar; (*criminal*) agredir, asaltar; (*task etc*) emprender // *n* ataque *m*, asalto; (*on sb's life*) atentado; heart ~ infarto (de miocardio); **~er** *n* agresor(a) *m/f*, asaltante *m/f*.

attain [ə'teɪn] *vt* (*also*: ~ to) alcanzar; (*achieve*) lograr, conseguir; **~ments** *npl* (*skill*) talento *sg*.

attempt [ə'tɛmpt] *n* tentativa, intento; (*attack*) atentado // *vt* intentar; **~ed** *a*: ~ed burglary tentativa *or* intento de robo.

attend [ə'tɛnd] *vt* asistir a; (*patient*) atender; to ~ to *vt fus* (*needs*, *affairs etc*) ocuparse de; (*speech etc*) prestar atención a; (*customer*) atender a; **~ance** *n* asistencia, presencia; (*people present*) concurrencia; **~ant** *n* sirviente/a *m/f*, mozo/a; (*THEATRE*) acomodador(a) *m/f* // *a* concomitante.

attention [ə'tɛnʃən] *n* atención *f* // excl (*MIL*) ¡firme(s)!; for the ~ of... (*ADMIN*) atención... .

attentive [ə'tɛntɪv] *a* atento; (*polite*) cortés.

attest [ə'tɛst] *vi*: to ~ to dar fe de.

attic ['ætɪk] *n* desván *m*.

attitude ['ætɪtjuːd] *n* (*gen*) actitud *f*; (*disposition*) disposición *f*.

attorney [ə'tɔːnɪ] *n* (*lawyer*) abogado/a; (*having proxy*) apoderado; **A~** **General** *n* (*Brit*) ≈ Presidente *m* del Consejo del Poder Judicial (*Sp*); (*US*) ≈ ministro de justicia.

attract [ə'trækt] *vt* atraer; (*attention*) llamar; **~ion** [ə'trækʃən] *n* (*gen*) encanto; (*amusements*) diversiones *fpl*; (*PHYSICS*) atracción *f*; (*fig*: *towards sth*) atractivo; **~ive** *a* atractivo; (*interesting*) atrayente; (*pretty*) guapo, mono.

attribute ['ætrɪbjuːt] *n* atributo // *vt* [ə'trɪbjuːt]: to ~ sth to atribuir algo a; (*accuse*) achacar algo a.

attrition [ə'trɪʃən] *n*: war of ~ guerra de agotamiento.

aubergine ['əubəʒiːn] *n* (*Brit*) berenjena.

auburn ['ɔːbən] *a* color castaño rojizo.

auction ['ɔːkʃən] *n* (*also*: sale by ~) subasta // *vt* subastar; **~eer** [-'nɪə*] *n* subastador(a) *m/f*.

audacity [ɔː'dæsɪtɪ] *n* audacia, atrevimiento; (*pej*) descaro.

audience ['ɔːdɪəns] *n* auditorio; (*gathering*) público; (*interview*) audiencia.

audio-typist [ɔːdɪəu'taɪpɪst] *n* mecanógrafo/a de dictáfono.

audio-visual [ɔːdɪəu'vɪzjuəl] *a* audiovisual; ~ **aid** *n* ayuda audiovisual.

audit ['ɔːdɪt] *vt* revisar, intervenir.

audition [ɔː'dɪʃən] *n* audición *f*.

auditor ['ɔːdɪtə*] *n* interventor(a) *m/f*, censor(a) *m/f* de cuentas.

augment [ɔːg'mɛnt] *vt* aumentar // *vi* aumentarse.

augur ['ɔːgə*] *vi*: it ~s well es de buen agüero.

August ['ɔːgəst] *n* agosto.

aunt [uːnt] *n* tía; **~ie**, **~y** *n* diminutive of aunt.

au pair ['əu'pɛə*] *n* (*also*: ~ girl) au pair *f*.

aura ['ɔːrə] *n* aura; (*atmosphere*) ambiente *m*.

auspices ['ɔːspɪsɪz] *npl*: under the ~ of bajo los auspicios de.

auspicious [ɔːs'pɪʃəs] *a* propicio, de buen augurio.

austerity [ə'stɛrətɪ] *n* austeridad *f*.

Australia [ɔs'treɪlɪə] *n* Australia; **~n** *a*, *n* australiano/a *m/f*.

Austria ['ɔstrɪə] *n* Austria; **~n** *a*, *n* austríaco/a *m/f*.

authentic [ɔː'θɛntɪk] *a* auténtico.

author ['ɔːθə] *n* autor(a) *m/f*.

authoritarian [ɔːθɔrɪ'tɛərɪən] *a* autoritario.

authoritative [ɔː'θɔrɪtətɪv] *a* autorizado; (*manner*) autoritario.

authority [ɔː'θɔrɪtɪ] *n* autoridad *f*; the authorities *npl* las autoridades.

authorize ['ɔːθəraɪz] *vt* autorizar.

auto ['ɔːtəu] *n* (*US*) coche *m*, carro (*LAm*), automóvil *m*.

autobiography [ɔːtəbaɪ'ɔgrəfɪ] *n* autobiografía.

autograph ['ɔːtəgrɑːf] *n* autógrafo // *vt* firmar; (*photo etc*) dedicar.

automated ['ɔːtəmeɪtɪd] *a* automatizado.

automatic [ɔːtə'mætɪk] *a* automático // *n* (*gun*) pistola automática; **~ally** *ad* automáticamente.

automation [ɔːtə'meɪʃən] *n* reconversión *f*.

automaton [ɔː'tɔmətən], *pl* **-mata** [-tə] *n* autómata *m/f*.

automobile ['ɔːtəməbiːl] *n* (*US*) coche *m*, carro (*LAm*), automóvil *m*.

autonomy [ɔː'tɔnəmɪ] *n* autonomía.

autopsy ['ɔːtɔpsɪ] *n* autopsia.

autumn ['ɔːtəm] *n* otoño.

auxiliary [ɔːg'zɪlɪərɪ] *a* auxiliar.

Av. *abbr* = **avenue**.

avail [ə'veɪl] *vt*: to ~ o.s. of aprovechar(se) de, valerse de // *n*: to no ~ en vano, sin resultado.

available |ə'veɪləbl| a disponible.

avalanche |'ævəlɑːnʃ| n alud m, avalancha.

avant-garde |'ævāŋ'gɑːd| a de vanguardia.

Ave. abbr = **avenue**.

avenge |ə'vendʒ| vt vengar.

avenue |'ævənjuː| n avenida; (fig) camino.

average |'ævərɪdʒ| n promedio, término medio // a (mean) medio, de término medio; (ordinary) regular, corriente // vt calcular el promedio de, prorratear; **on ~** por regla general; **to ~ out** vi: **to ~ out at** salir en un promedio de.

averse |ə'vɜːs| a: **to be ~ to** sth/doing sentir aversión or antipatía por algo/por hacer.

avert |ə'vɜːt| vt prevenir; (blow) desviar; (one's eyes) apartar.

aviary |'eɪvɪərɪ| n pajarera, avería.

avid |'ævɪd| a ávido, ansioso.

avocado |ævə'kɑːdəu| n (also: Brit: ~ pear) aguacate m, palta (LAm).

avoid |ə'vɔɪd| vt evitar, eludir.

avuncular |ə'vʌŋkjulə*| a paternal.

await |ə'weɪt| vt esperar, aguardar.

awake |ə'weɪk| a despierto // vb (pt awoke, pp awoken or awaked) vt despertar // vi despertarse; **to be ~** estar despierto; **~ning** n el despertar.

award |ə'wɔːd| n (prize) premio; (medal) condecoración f; (LAW) fallo, sentencia; (act) concesión f // vt (prize) otorgar, conceder; (LAW: damages) adjudicar.

aware |ə'wɛə*| a consciente; (awake) despierto; (informed) enterado; **to become ~ of** darse cuenta de, enterarse de; **~ness** n conciencia, conocimiento.

awash |ə'wɔʃ| a inundado.

away |ə'weɪ| ad (gen) fuera; (far ~) lejos; **two kilometres ~** a dos kilómetros de distancia; **two hours ~ by car** a dos horas en coche; **the holiday was two weeks ~** faltaba dos semanas para las vacaciones; **~ from** lejos de, fuera de; **he's ~ for a week** estará ausente una semana; **to work/pedal ~** seguir trabajando/pedaleando; **to fade ~** desvanecerse; (sound) apagarse; **~ game** n (SPORT) partido de fuera.

awe |ɔː| n pavor m, respeto, temor m reverencial; **~-inspiring**, **~some** a imponente, pasmoso.

awful |'ɔːful| a terrible, pasmoso; **~ly** ad (very) terriblemente.

awhile |ə'waɪl| ad (durante) un rato, algún tiempo.

awkward |'ɔːkwəd| a (clumsy) desmañado, torpe; (shape) incómodo; (problem) difícil; (embarrassing) delicado.

awning |'ɔːnɪŋ| n (of shop) toldo; (of window etc) marquesina.

awoke |ə'wəuk|, **awoken** |-kən| pt, pp of

awake.

awry |ə'raɪ| ad: **to be ~** estar descolocado or atravesado; **to go ~** salir mal, fracasar.

axe, (US) **ax** |æks| n hacha // vt (employee) despedir; (project etc) cortar; (jobs) reducir.

axis |'æksɪs|, pl **axes** |-siːz| n eje m.

axle |'æksl| n eje m, árbol m.

ay(e) |aɪ| excl (yes) sí; **the ayes** npl los que votan a favor.

B

B |biː| n (MUS) si m.

B.A. abbr = **Bachelor of Arts**.

babble |'bæbl| n barbullar.

baby |'beɪbɪ| n bebé m/f; **~ carriage** n (US) cochecito; **~-sit** vi hacer de canguro; **~-sitter** n canguro/a.

bachelor |'bætʃələ*| n soltero; **B~ of Arts/Science (B.A./B.Sc.)** licenciado/a en Filosofía y Letras/Ciencias.

back |bæk| n (of person) espalda; (of animal) lomo; (of hand) dorso; (as opposed to front) parte f de atrás; (of room, car, etc) fondo; (of chair) respaldo; (of page) reverso; (FOOTBALL) defensa m // vt (candidate: also: ~ up) respaldar, apoyar; (horse: at races) apostar a; (car) dar marcha atrás a or con // vi (car etc) dar marcha atrás // a (in compounds) de atrás; **~ seats/wheels** (AUT) asientos mpl/ruedas fpl de atrás; **~ payments** pagos mpl con efecto retroactivo; **~ rent** renta atrasada // ad (not forward) (hacia) atrás; (returned): **he's ~** está de vuelta, ha vuelto; **he ran ~** volvió corriendo; (restitution): **throw the ball ~** devuelve la pelota; **can I have it ~?** ¿me lo devuelve?; (again): **he called ~** llamó de nuevo; **to ~ down** vi echarse atrás; **to ~ out** vi (of promise) volverse atrás; **to ~ up** vt (support: person) apoyar, respaldar; (: theory) defender; (car) dar marcha atrás a; (COMPUT) hacer una copia preventiva or de reserva; **~bencher** n (Brit) miembro del parlamento sin portafolio; **~bone** n columna vertebral; **~-cloth** n telón m de fondo; **~date** vt (letter) poner fecha atrasada a; **~drop** n = **~cloth**; **~fire** vi (AUT) petardear; (plans) fallar, salir mal; **~ground** n fondo; (of events) antecedentes mpl; (basic knowledge) bases fpl; (experience) conocimientos mpl, educación f; **family ~ground** origen m, antecedentes mpl; **~hand** n (TENNIS: also: **~hand stroke**) revés m; **~handed** a (fig) ambiguo; **~hander** n (Brit: bribe) soborno; **~ing** n (fig) apoyo, respaldo; **~lash** n reacción f, resaca; **~log** n: **~log of work** atrasos mpl; **~ num-**

ber *n* (*of magazine etc*) número atrasado; **~pack** *n* mochila; **~ pay** *n* pago atrasado; **~side** *n* (*col*) trasero, culo; **~stage** *ad* entre bastidores; **~stroke** *n* braza de espaldas; **~up** *a* (*train, plane*) suplementario; (*COMPUT*: *disk, file*) de reserva // *n* (*support*) apoyo; (*also:* **~up file**) copia preventiva *or* de reserva; **~up lights** *npl* (*US*) luces *fpl* de marcha atrás; **~ward** *a* (*movement*) hacia atrás; (*person, country*) atrasado; (*shy*) tímido; **~wards** *ad* (*move, go*) hacia atrás; (*read a list*) al revés; (*fall*) de espaldas; **~water** *n* (*fig*) lugar *m* atrasado *or* apartado; **~yard** *n* traspatio.

bacon [ˈbeɪkən] *n* tocino, beicon *m*.

bad [bæd] *a* malo; (*serious*) grave; (*meat, food*) podrido, pasado; **his ~ leg** su pierna lisiada; **to go ~** pasarse.

bade [bæd, beɪd] *pt of* **bid**.

badge [bædʒ] *n* insignia; (*metal ~*) chapa, placa.

badger [ˈbædʒə*] *n* tejón *m*.

badly [ˈbædlɪ] *ad* (*work, dress etc*) mal; **~ wounded** gravemente herido; **he needs it ~** le hace gran falta; **to be ~ off** (*for money*) andar mal de dinero.

badminton [ˈbædmɪntən] *n* bádminton *m*.

bad-tempered [ˈbædˈtempəd] *a* de mal genio *or* carácter; (*temporary*) de mal humor.

baffle [ˈbæfl] *vt* desconcertar, confundir.

bag [bæg] *n* bolsa, saco; (*handbag*) bolso; (*satchel*) mochila; (*case*) maleta; (*of hunter*) caza // *vt* (*col: take*) coger (*Sp*), agarrar (*LAm*), pescar; **~s** *n* (*col: lots of*) un montón de; **~gage** *n* equipaje *m*; **~gy** *a* (*clothing*) amplio; **~pipes** *npl* gaita *sg*.

Bahamas [bəˈhɑːməz] *npl:* **the ~** las Islas Bahama.

bail [beɪl] *n* fianza // *vt* (*prisoner: gen:* **grant ~ to**) poner en libertad bajo fianza; (*boat: also:* **~ out**) achicar; **on ~** (*prisoner*) bajo fianza; **to ~ sb out** obtener la libertad de uno bajo fianza; **bail bond** *n* fianza; *see also* **bale**.

bailiff [ˈbeɪlɪf] *n* alguacil *m*.

bait [beɪt] *n* cebo // *vt* cebar.

bake [beɪk] *vt* cocer (al horno) // *vi* (*cook*) cocerse; (*be hot*) hacer un calor terrible; **~d beans** *npl* judías *fpl* en salsa de tomate; **~r** *n* panadero; **~ry** *n* (*for bread*) panadería; (*for cakes*) pastelería; **baking** *n* (*act*) amasar *m*; (*batch*) hornada; **baking powder** *n* levadura (en polvo).

balance [ˈbæləns] *n* equilibrio; (*COMM: sum*) balance *m*; (*remainder*) resto; (*scales*) balanza // *vt* equilibrar; (*budget*) nivelar; (*account*) saldar; (*compensate*) contrapesar; **~ of trade/payments** balanza de comercio/pagos; **~d** *a* (*personality, diet*) equilibrado; **~ sheet** *n*

balance *m*.

balcony [ˈbælkənɪ] *n* (*open*) balcón *m*; (*closed*) galería.

bald [bɔːld] *a* calvo; (*tyre*) liso.

bale [beɪl] *n* (*AGR*) paca, fardo; **to ~ out** *vi* (*of a plane*) lanzarse en paracaídas.

Balearics [bælɪˈærɪks] *npl:* **the ~** las Baleares.

baleful [ˈbeɪlful] *a* (*look*) triste; (*sinister*) funesto, siniestro.

ball [bɔːl] *n* (*sphere*) bola; (*football*) balón *m*; (*for tennis, golf etc*) pelota; (*dance*) baile *m*.

ballad [ˈbæləd] *n* balada, romance *m*.

ballast [ˈbæləst] *n* lastre *m*.

ball bearings *npl* cojinetes *mpl* de bolas.

ballerina [bæləˈriːnə] *n* bailarina.

ballet [ˈbæleɪ] *n* ballet *m*; **~ dancer** *n* bailarín/ina *m/f*.

ballistic [bəˈlɪstɪk] *a* balístico.

balloon [bəˈluːn] *n* globo.

ballot [ˈbælət] *n* votación *f*.

ball-point (pen) [ˈbɔːlpɔɪnt-] *n* bolígrafo.

ballroom [ˈbɔːlrum] *n* salón *m* de baile.

balm [bɑːm] *n* (*also fig*) bálsamo.

Baltic [ˈbɔːltɪk] *a* báltico // *n:* **the ~ (Sea)** el (Mar) Báltico.

balustrade [bæləstreɪd] *n* barandilla.

bamboo [bæmˈbuː] *n* bambú *m*.

ban [bæn] *n* prohibición *f*, proscripción *f* // *vt* prohibir, proscribir.

banal [bəˈnɑːl] *a* banal, vulgar.

banana [bəˈnɑːnə] *n* plátano, banana (*LAm*).

band [bænd] *n* (*group*) banda; (*gang*) pandilla; (*strip*) faja, tira; (*: circular*) anillo; (*at a dance*) orquesta; (*MIL*) banda; **to ~ together** *vi* juntarse, asociarse.

bandage [ˈbændɪdʒ] *n* venda, vendaje *m* // *vt* vendar.

bandaid [ˈbændeɪd] *n* ® (*US*) tirita.

bandit [ˈbændɪt] *n* bandido.

bandstand [ˈbændstænd] *n* quiosco.

bandwagon [ˈbændwægən] *n:* **to jump on the ~** (*fig*) subirse al carro.

bandy [ˈbændɪ] *vt* (*jokes, insults*) cambiar.

bandy-legged [ˈbændɪˈlɛgd] *a* estevado.

bang [bæŋ] *n* estallido; (*of door*) portazo; (*blow*) golpe *m* // *vt* hacer estallar; (*door*) cerrar de golpe // *vi* estallar.

bangle [ˈbæŋgl] *n* ajorca.

bangs [bæŋz] *npl* (*US*) flequillo *sg*.

banish [ˈbænɪʃ] *vt* desterrar.

banister(s) [ˈbænɪstə(z)] *n(pl)* pasamanos *m inv*.

bank [bæŋk] *n* (*COMM*) banco; (*of river, lake*) ribera, orilla; (*of earth*) terraplén *m* // *vi* (*AVIAT*) ladearse; **to ~ on** *vt fus* contar con; **~ account** *n* cuenta de banco; **~ card** *n* tarjeta bancaria; **~er** *n* banquero; **~er's card** *n* (*Brit*) = **~**

card; **B~ holiday** n (Brit) día m festivo; **~ing** n banca; **~note** n billete m de banco; **~ rate** n tipo de interés bancario.

bankrupt |'bæŋkrʌpt| a quebrado, insolvente; **to go ~** hacer bancarrota; **to be ~** estar en quiebra; **~cy** n quiebra, bancarrota.

bank statement n balance m or detalle m de cuenta.

banner |'bænə*| n bandera; (in demonstration) pancarta.

banns |bænz| npl amonestaciones fpl.

banquet |'bæŋkwɪt| n banquete m.

baptism |'bæptɪzəm| n bautismo.

baptize |bæp'taɪz| vt bautizar.

bar |ba:*| n barra; (on door) tranca; (of window, cage) reja; (of soap) pastilla; (fig: hindrance) obstáculo; (prohibition) proscripción f; (pub) bar m; (counter: in pub) mostrador m; (MUS) barra // it (road) obstruir; (window, door) atrancar; (person) excluir; (activity) prohibir; **behind ~s** entre rejas; **the B~** (LAW: profession) la abogacía; (: people) el cuerpo de abogados; **~ none** sin excepción.

barbaric |ba:'bærɪk| a bárbaro.

barbarous |'ba:bərəs| a bárbaro.

barbecue |'ba:bɪkju:| n barbacoa.

barbed wire |'ba:bd-| n alambre m de púas.

barber |'ba:bə*| n peluquero, barbero.

bar code n código de barras.

bare |beə*| a desnudo; (head) descubierto // vt desnudar; **~back** ad sin silla; **~faced** a descarado; **~foot** a, ad descalzo; **~ly** ad apenas.

bargain |'ba:gɪn| n pacto, negocio; (good buy) ganga // vi negociar; (haggle) regatear; **into the ~** además, por añadidura; **to ~ for** vt fus: he got more than he **~ed for** le resultó peor de lo que esperaba.

barge |ba:dʒ| n barcaza; **to ~ in** vi irrumpir; (conversation) entrometerse; **to ~ into** vt fus dar contra.

bark |ba:k| n (of tree) corteza; (of dog) ladrido // vi ladrar.

barley |'ba:lɪ| n cebada; **~ sugar** n azúcar m cande.

barmaid |'ba:meɪd| n camarera.

barman |'ba:mən| n camarero, barman m.

barn |ba:n| n granero.

barometer |bə'rɒmɪtə*| n barómetro.

baron |'bærən| n barón m; **~ess** n baronesa.

barracks |'bærəks| npl cuartel m.

barrage |'bæra:ʒ| n (MIL) descarga, bombardeo; (dam) presa; (fig: of criticism etc) lluvia, aluvión m.

barrel |'bærəl| n tonel m, barril m; (of gun) cañón m.

barren |'bærən| a estéril.

barricade |bærɪ'keɪd| n barricada // vt cerrar con barricadas.

barrier |'bærɪə*| n barrera.

barring |'ba:rɪŋ| prep excepto, salvo.

barrister |'bærɪstə*| n (Brit) abogado/a.

barrow |'bærəu| n (cart) carretilla (de mano).

bartender |'ba:tɛndə*| n (US) camarero, barman m.

barter |'ba:tə*| vt: **to ~ sth for sth** trocar algo por algo.

base |beɪs| n base f // vt: **to ~ sth on** basar or fundar algo en // a bajo, infame.

baseball |'beɪsbɔ:l| n béisbol m.

basement |'beɪsmənt| n sótano.

bases |'beɪsi:z| npl of **basis**; |'beɪsɪz| npl of **base**.

bash |bæʃ| vt (col) golpear.

bashful |'bæʃful| a tímido, vergonzoso.

basic |'beɪsɪk| a básico; **~ally** ad fundamentalmente, en el fondo.

basil |'bæzl| n albahaca.

basin |'beɪsn| n (vessel) cuenco, tazón m; (GEO) cuenca; (also: wash~) palangana, jofaina.

basis |'beɪsɪs|, pl **bases** |'beɪsi:z| n base f.

bask |ba:sk| vi: **to ~ in the sun** tomar el sol.

basket |'ba:skɪt| n cesta, cesto; (with handle) canasta; **~ball** n baloncesto.

Basque |bæsk| a, n vasco/a m/f; **~ Country** n Euskadi m, País m Vasco.

bass |beɪs| n (MUS) contrabajo.

bassoon |bə'su:n| n fagot m.

bastard |'ba:stəd| n bastardo; (col!) hijo de puta (!).

bastion |'bæstɪən| n baluarte m.

bat |bæt| n (ZOOL) murciélago; (for ball games) palo; (for cricket, baseball) bate m; (Brit: for table tennis) pala; **he didn't ~ an eyelid** ni pestañeó.

batch |bætʃ| n (of bread) hornada; (of goods) lote m.

bated |'beɪtɪd| a: **with ~ breath** sin respirar.

bath |ba:θ, pl ba:ðz| n (action) baño; (~tub) baño, bañera, tina (LAm); (see also baths) piscina // vt bañar; **to have a ~** bañarse, tomar un baño; **~chair** n silla de ruedas.

bathe |beɪð| vi bañarse // vt bañar; **~r** n bañista m/f.

bathing |'beɪðɪŋ| n el bañarse; **~ cap** n gorro de baño; **~ costume**, (US) **~ suit** n traje m de baño; **~ trunks** npl bañador m.

bath: **~ robe** n (man's) batín m; (woman's) bata; **~room** n (cuarto de) baño.

baths |ba:ðz| npl piscina sg.

baton |'bætən| n (MUS) batuta.

battalion |bə'tælɪən| n batallón m.

batter |'bætə*| vt apalear, azotar // n batido; **~ed** a (hat, pan) estropeado.

battery |'bætərɪ| n batería; (of torch)

pila.

battle ['bætl] n batalla; (fig) lucha // vi luchar; ~**field** n campo de batalla; ~**ship** n acorazado.

bawdy ['bɔːdɪ] a indecente; (joke) verde.

bawl [bɔːl] vi chillar, gritar.

bay [beɪ] n (GEO) bahía; (BOT) laurel m // vi aullar; B~ of Biscay ≈ mar Cantábrico; to hold sb at ~ mantener a alguien a raya.

bay window n ventana salediza.

bazaar [bə'zɑː*] n bazar m.

b. & b., **B. & B.** abbr (= bed and breakfast) cama y desayuno.

BBC n abbr (= British Broadcasting Corporation) cadena de radio y televisión estatal británica.

B.C. ad abbr (= before Christ) a. de C.

be [biː], pl was, were, pp been ♦ auxiliary vb 1 (with present participle: forming continuous tenses): what are you doing? ¿qué estás haciendo?, ¿qué haces?; they're coming tomorrow vienen mañana; I've been waiting for you for hours llevo horas esperándote

2 (with pp: forming passives) ser (but often replaced by active or reflective constructions); to ~ murdered ser asesinado; the box had been opened habían abierto la caja; the thief was nowhere to ~ seen no se veía al ladrón por ninguna parte

3 (in tag questions): it was fun, wasn't it? fue divertido, ¿no? or ¿verdad?; he's good-looking, isn't he? es guapo, ¿no te parece?; she's back again, is she? entonces, ¿ha vuelto?

4 (+to + infinitive): the house is to ~ sold (necessity) hay que vender la casa; (future) van a vender la casa; he's not to open it no tiene que abrirlo

♦ vb + complement 1 (with noun or numeral complement, but see also 3, 4, 5 and impersonal vb below) ser; he's a doctor es médico; 2 and 2 are 4 2 y 2 son 4

2 (with adjective complement: expressing permanent or inherent quality) ser; (: expressing state seen as temporary or reversible) estar; I'm English soy inglés/esa; she's tall/pretty es alta/bonita; he's young es joven; ~ careful/quiet/good ten cuidado/cállate/pórtate bien; I'm tired estoy cansado/a; it's dirty está sucio/a

3 (of health) estar; how are you? ¿cómo estás?; he's very ill está muy enfermo; I'm better now ya estoy mejor

4 (of age) tener; how old are you? ¿cuántos años tienes?; I'm sixteen (years old) tengo dieciséis años

5 (cost) costar; ser; how much was the meal? ¿cuánto fue or costó la comida?; that'll ~ £5.75, please son £5.75, por favor; this shirt is £17.00 esta camisa cuesta £17.00

♦ vi 1 (exist, occur etc) existir, haber; the best singer that ever was el mejor cantante que existió jamás; is there a God? ¿hay un Dios?, ¿existe Dios?; ~ that as it may sea como sea; so ~ it así sea

2 (referring to place) estar; I won't ~ here tomorrow no estaré aquí mañana

3 (referring to movement): where have you been? ¿dónde has estado?

♦ impersonal vb 1 (referring to time): it's 5 o'clock son las 5; it's the 28th of April estamos a 28 de abril

2 (referring to distance): it's 10 km to the village el pueblo está a 10 km

3 (referring to the weather): it's too hot/cold hace demasiado calor/frío; it's windy today hace viento hoy

4 (emphatic): it's me soy yo; it was Maria who paid the bill fue María la que pagó la cuenta.

beach [biːtʃ] n playa // vt varar.

beacon ['biːkən] n (lighthouse) faro; (marker) guía.

bead [biːd] n cuenta, abalorio; (of sweat) gota.

beak [biːk] n pico.

beaker ['biːkə*] n jarra.

beam [biːm] n (ARCH) viga, travesaño; (of light) rayo, haz m de luz // vi brillar; (smile) sonreír.

bean [biːn] n judía; runner/broad ~ habichuela/haba; coffee ~ grano de café; ~**sprouts** npl brotes mpl de soja.

bear [bɛə*] n oso // vb (pt bore, pp borne) vt (weight etc) llevar; (cost) pagar; (responsibility) tener; (endure) soportar, aguantar; (stand up to) resistir a; (children) parir // vi: to ~ right/left torcer a la derecha/izquierda; to ~ out vt (suspicions) corroborar, confirmar; (person) llevar; to ~ up vi (person: remain cheerful) animarse.

beard [bɪəd] n barba.

bearer ['bɛərə*] n (of news, cheque) portador(a) m/f.

bearing ['bɛərɪŋ] n porte m, comportamiento; (connection) relación f; (ball) ~s npl cojinetes mpl a bolas; to take a ~ marcarse; to find one's ~s orientarse.

beast [biːst] n bestia; (col) bruto, salvaje m; ~**ly** a bestial; (awful) horrible.

beat [biːt] n (of heart) latido; (MUS) ritmo, compás m; (of policeman) ronda // vb (pt beat, pp beaten) vt (hit) golpear; (eggs) batir; (defeat) vencer, derrotar; (better) sobrepasar; (drum) tocar; (rhythm) marcar // vi (heart) latir; off the ~en track aislado; to ~ it largarse; to ~ off vt rechazar; to ~ up vt (col: person) dar una paliza a; ~**ing** n golpeo.

beautiful ['bjuːtɪful] a hermoso, bello; ~**ly** ad maravillosamente.

beauty |'bjuːtɪ| n belleza, hermosura; (person) belleza; ~ **salon** n salón m de belleza; ~ **spot** n lunar m postizo; (Brit TOURISM) lugar m pintoresco.

beaver |'biːvə*| n castor m.

became |bɪ'keɪm| pt of **become**.

because |bɪ'kɔz| conj porque; ~ **of** prep debido a, a causa de.

beck |bek| n: to be at the ~ and call of estar a disposición de.

beckon |'bekən| vt (also: ~ to) llamar con señas.

become |bɪ'kʌm| (irg: like come) vt (suit) favorecer, sentar bien a // vi (+ noun) hacerse, llegar a ser; (+ adj) ponerse, volverse; to ~ fat engordarse.

becoming |bɪ'kʌmɪŋ| a (behaviour) decoroso; (clothes) favorecedor(a).

bed |bed| n cama; (of flowers) macizo; (of coal, clay) capa; to go to ~ acostarse; ~ **and breakfast (b.&b.)** n (place) pensión f; (terms) cama y desayuno; ~**clothes** npl ropa sg de cama; ~**ding** n ropa de cama.

bedlam |'bedləm| n confusión f.

bedraggled |bɪ'drægld| a mojado; desastrado.

bed: ~**ridden** a postrado (en cama); ~**room** n dormitorio, alcoba; ~**side** n: at sb's ~**side** a la cabecera de alguien; ~**sit(ter)** n (Brit) estudio, suite m (LAm); ~**spread** n sobrecama m, colcha; ~**time** n hora de acostarse.

bee |biː| n abeja.

beech |biːtʃ| n haya.

beef |biːf| n carne f de vaca; **roast** ~ rosbif m; ~**burger** n hamburguesa; ~**eater** n alabardero de la Torre de Londres.

bee: ~**hive** n colmena; ~**line** n: to make a ~line for ir derecho a.

been |biːn| pp of **be**.

beer |bɪə*| n cerveza.

beet |biːt| n (US) remolacha.

beetle |'biːtl| n escarabajo.

beetroot |'biːtruːt| n (Brit) remolacha.

before |bɪ'fɔː*| prep (of time) antes de; (of space) delante de // conj antes (de) que // ad (time) antes, anteriormente; (space) delante, adelante; ~ **going** antes de marcharse; ~ she goes antes de que se vaya; the week ~ la semana anterior; I've never seen it ~ no lo he visto nunca; ~**hand** ad de antemano, con anticipación.

beg |beg| vi pedir limosna // vt pedir, rogar; (entreat) suplicar.

began |bɪ'gæn| pt of **begin**.

beggar |'begə*| n mendigo/a.

begin |bɪ'gɪn|, pt **began**, pp **begun** vt, vi empezar, comenzar; to ~ **doing** or to do sth empezar a hacer algo; ~**ner** n principiante m/f; ~**ning** n principio, comienzo.

begun |bɪ'gʌn| pp of **begin**.

behalf |bɪ'hɑːf| n: on ~ of en nombre de, por.

behave |bɪ'heɪv| vi (person) portarse, comportarse; (thing) funcionar; (well: also: ~ o.s.) portarse bien; **behaviour**, (US) **behavior** n comportamiento, conducta.

behead |bɪ'hed| vt decapitar.

beheld |bɪ'held| pt, pp of **behold**.

behind |bɪ'haɪnd| prep detrás de // ad detrás, por detrás, atrás // n trasero; to be ~ (schedule) ir retrasado; ~ the scenes (fig) entre bastidores.

behold |bɪ'həuld| vt (irg: like **hold**) contemplar.

beige |beɪʒ| a color beige.

being |'biːɪŋ| n ser m; to come into ~ nacer, aparecer.

belated |bɪ'leɪtɪd| a atrasado, tardío.

belch |beltʃ| vi eructar // vt (also: ~ out: smoke etc) arrojar.

belfry |'belfrɪ| n campanario.

Belgian |'beldʒən| a, n belga m/f.

Belgium |'beldʒəm| n Bélgica.

belie |bɪ'laɪ| vt desmentir, contradecir.

belief |bɪ'liːf| n (opinion) opinión f; (trust, faith) fe f; (acceptance as true) creencia.

believe |bɪ'liːv| vt, vi creer; to ~ in creer en; ~**r** n (in idea, activity) partidario/a; (REL) creyente m/f, fiel m/f.

belittle |bɪ'lɪtl| vt minimizar, despreciar.

bell |bel| n campana; (small) campanilla; (on door) timbre m; (animal's) cencerro; (on toy etc) cascabel m.

belligerent |bɪ'lɪdʒərənt| a (at war) beligerante; (fig) agresivo.

bellow |'beləu| vi bramar; (person) rugir.

bellows |'beləuz| npl fuelle msg.

belly |'belɪ| n barriga, panza.

belong |bɪ'lɔŋ| vi: to ~ to pertenecer a; (club etc) ser socio de; this book ~s here este libro va aquí; ~**ings** npl pertenencias fpl.

beloved |bɪ'lʌvɪd| a, n querido/a m/f, amado/a m/f.

below |bɪ'ləu| prep bajo, debajo de // ad abajo, (por) debajo; see ~ véase más abajo.

belt |belt| n cinturón m; (TECH) correa, cinta // vt (thrash) golpear con correa; ~**way** n (US AUT) carretera de circunvalación.

bemused |bɪ'mjuːzd| a aturdido.

bench |bentʃ| n banco; the B~ (LAW) tribunal m; (people) judicatura.

bend |bend| vb (pt, pp **bent**) vt doblar, inclinar; (leg, arm) torcer // vi inclinarse; (road) curvarse // n (Brit: in road, river) recodo; (in pipe) codo; to ~ **down** vi inclinarse, doblarse; to ~ **over** vi inclinarse.

beneath |bɪ'niːθ| prep bajo, debajo de; (unworthy of) indigno de // ad abajo, (por) debajo.

benefactor ['bɛnɪfæktə*] *n* bienhechor *m*.

beneficial [bɛnɪ'fɪʃəl] *a* beneficioso.

benefit ['bɛnɪfɪt] *n* beneficio, provecho; (*allowance of money*) subsidio // *vt* beneficiar // *vi*: he'll ~ from it le sacará provecho.

benevolent [bɪ'nɛvələnt] *a* benévolo.

benign [bɪ'naɪn] *a* (*person*, MED) benigno; (*smile*) afable.

bent [bɛnt] *pt, pp* of bend // *n* inclinación *f* // *a*: to be ~ on estar empeñado en.

bequeath [bɪ'kwiːð] *vt* legar.

bequest [bɪ'kwɛst] *n* legado.

bereaved [bɪ'riːvd] *npl*: the ~ los afligidos *mpl*.

beret ['bɛreɪ] *n* boina.

Berlin [bəː'lɪn] *n* Berlín *m*.

berm [bəːm] *n* (*US AUT*) arcén *m*.

Bermuda [bəː'mjuːdə] *n* las Bermudas *fpl*.

berry ['bɛrɪ] *n* baya.

berserk [bə'səːk] *a*: to go ~ perder los estribos.

berth [bəːθ] *n* (*bed*) litera; (*cabin*) camarote *m*; (*for ship*) amarradero // *vi* atracar, amarrar.

beseech [bɪ'siːtʃ], *pt, pp* **besought** [-'sɔːt] *vt* suplicar.

beset [bɪ'sɛt], *pt, pp* beset *vt* (*person*) acosar.

beside [bɪ'saɪd] *prep* junto a, al lado de; to be ~ o.s. with anger estar fuera de sí; that's ~ the point eso no tiene nada que ver.

besides [bɪ'saɪdz] *ad* además // *prep* (*as well as*) además de; (*except*) excepto.

besiege [bɪ'siːdʒ] *vt* (*town*) sitiar; (*fig*) asediar.

besought [bɪ'sɔːt] *pt, pp* of **beseech**.

best [bɛst] *a* (el/la) mejor // *ad* (lo) mejor; the ~ part of (*quantity*) la mayor parte de; at ~ en el mejor de los casos; to make the ~ of sth sacar el mejor partido de algo; to do one's ~ hacer todo lo posible; to the ~ of my knowledge que yo sepa; to the ~ of my ability como mejor puedo; ~ man *n* padrino de boda.

bestow [bɪ'stəʊ] *vt* otorgar; (*honour, praise*) dispensar.

bestseller ['bɛst'sɛlə*] *n* éxito de librería, bestseller *m*.

bet [bɛt] *n* apuesta // *vt, vi* (*pt, pp* bet or betted) apostar (on a).

betray [bɪ'treɪ] *vt* traicionar; (*inform on*) delatar; ~al *n* traición *f*.

better ['bɛtə*] *a* mejor // *ad* mejor // *vt* mejorar; (*record etc*) superar // *n*: to get the ~ of sb quedar por encima de alguien; you had ~ do it más vale que lo hagas; he thought ~ of it cambió de parecer; to get ~ mejorar(se); (*MED*) reponerse; ~ off *a* más acomodado.

betting ['bɛtɪŋ] *n* juego, el apostar; ~ shop *n* (*Brit*) agencia de apuestas.

between [bɪ'twiːn] *prep* entre // *ad* (*time*) mientras tanto; (*place*) en medio.

beverage ['bɛvərɪdʒ] *n* bebida.

bevy ['bɛvɪ] *n*: a ~ of una bandada de.

beware [bɪ'wɛə*] *vi*: to ~ (of) tener cuidado (con) // *excl* ¡cuidado!

bewildered [bɪ'wɪldəd] *a* aturdido, perplejo.

bewitching [bɪ'wɪtʃɪŋ] *a* hechicero, encantador(a).

beyond [bɪ'jɔnd] *prep* más allá de; (*exceeding*) además de, fuera de; (*above*) superior a // *ad* más allá, más lejos; ~ doubt fuera de toda duda; ~ repair irreparable.

bias ['baɪəs] *n* (*prejudice*) prejuicio, pasión *f*; (*preference*) predisposición *f*; ~(s)ed *a* parcial.

bib [bɪb] *n* babero.

Bible ['baɪbl] *n* Biblia.

bicarbonate of soda [baɪ'kɑːbənɪt-] *n* bicarbonato de soda.

bicker ['bɪkə*] *vi* reñir.

bicycle ['baɪsɪkl] *n* bicicleta.

bid [bɪd] *n* (*at auction*) oferta, postura; (*attempt*) tentativa, conato // *vi* (*pt, pp* bid) hacer una oferta // *vt* (*pt* bade [bæd], *pp* bidden ['bɪdn]) mandar, ordenar; to ~ sb good day dar a uno los buenos días; ~der *n*: the highest ~der el mejor postor; ~ding *n* (*at auction*) ofertas *fpl*; (*order*) orden *f*, mandato.

bide [baɪd] *vt*: to ~ one's time esperar el momento adecuado.

bifocals [baɪ'fəʊklz] *npl* gafas *fpl* or anteojos *mpl* (*LAm*) bifocales.

big [bɪg] *a* grande.

bigamy ['bɪgəmɪ] *n* bigamia.

big dipper [-'dɪpə*] *n* montaña rusa.

bigheaded ['bɪg'hɛdɪd] *a* engreído.

bigot ['bɪgət] *n* fanático/a, intolerante *m/f*; ~ed *a* fanático, intolerante; ~ry *n* fanatismo, intolerancia.

big top *n* (*circus*) circo; (*main tent*) tienda principal.

bike [baɪk] *n* bici *f*.

bikini [bɪ'kiːnɪ] *n* bikini *m*.

bile [baɪl] *n* bilis *f*.

bilingual [baɪ'lɪŋgwəl] *a* bilingüe.

bill [bɪl] *n* (*account*) cuenta; (*invoice*) factura; (*POL*) proyecto de ley; (*US*: banknote) billete *m*; (*of bird*) pico; 'post no ~s' 'prohibido fijar carteles'; ~board *n* (*US*) cartelera.

billet ['bɪlɪt] *n* alojamiento.

billfold ['bɪlfəʊld] *n* (*US*) cartera.

billiards ['bɪljədz] *n* billar *m*.

billion ['bɪljən] *n* (*Brit*) billón *m* (*millón de millones*); (*US*) mil millones.

billy ['bɪlɪ] *n* (*US*) porra.

bin [bɪn] *n* (*gen*) cubo *or* bote *m* (*LAm*) de la basura; **litter** ~ *n* (*Brit*) papelera.

bind [baɪnd], *pt, pp* **bound** *vt* atar, liar; (*wound*) vendar; (*book*) encuadernar; (*oblige*) obligar; ~ing *a* (*contract*) obligatorio.

binge [bɪndʒ] n borrachera, juerga.
bingo ['bɪŋɡəu] n bingo m.
binoculars [bɪ'nɔkjuləz] npl prismáticos mpl.
bio... [baɪə'] pref: **~chemistry** n bioquímica; **~graphy** [baɪ'ɔɡrəfɪ] n biografía; **~logical** a biológico; **~logy** [baɪ'ɔlədʒɪ] n biología.
birch [bəːtʃ] n abedul m; (cane) vara.
bird [bəːd] n ave f, pájaro; (Brit col: girl) chica; **~'s eye view** n vista de pájaro; **~ watcher** n ornitólogo/a.
Biro ['baɪrəu] n ® bolígrafo.
birth [bəːθ] n nacimiento; (MED) parto; to give ~ to parir, dar a luz; **~ certificate** n partida de nacimiento; **~ control** n control m de natalidad; (methods) métodos mpl anticonceptivos; **~day** n cumpleaños m inv; **~ rate** n (tasa de) natalidad f.
biscuit ['bɪskɪt] n (Brit) galleta, bizcocho (LAm).
bisect [baɪ'sɛkt] vt bisecar.
bishop ['bɪʃəp] n obispo.
bit [bɪt] pt of **bite** // n trozo, pedazo, pedacito; (COMPUT) bit m, bitio; (for horse) freno, bocado; a ~ of un poco de; a ~ mad un poco loco; **~ by ~** poco a poco.
bitch [bɪtʃ] n (dog) perra; (col!) zorra (!).
bite [baɪt] (pt bit, pp bitten) vt, vi morder; (insect etc) picar // n mordedura; (insect ~) picadura; (mouthful) bocado; to ~ one's nails comerse las uñas; let's have a ~ (to eat) comamos algo.
biting ['baɪtɪŋ] a (wind) que traspasa los huesos; (criticism) mordaz.
bitten ['bɪtn] pp of **bite**.
bitter ['bɪtə*] a amargo; (wind, criticism) cortante, penetrante; (battle) encarnizado // n (Brit: beer) cerveza típica británica a base de lúpulos; **~ness** n amargura; (anger) rencor m.
bizarre [bɪ'zɑː*] a raro, estrafalario.
blab [blæb] vi chismear, soplar.
black [blæk] a (colour) negro; (dark) oscuro // n (colour) color m negro; (person): B~ negro/a // vt (shoes) lustrar; (Brit: INDUSTRY) boicotear; to give sb a ~ eye ponerle a uno el ojo morado; ~ and blue amoratado; to be in the ~ (bank account) estar en números negros; **~berry** n zarzamora; **~bird** n mirlo; **~board** n pizarra; ~ **coffee** n café m solo; **~currant** n grosella negra; **~en** vt ennegrecer; (fig) denigrar; **~head** n espinilla; ~ **ice** n hielo invisible en la carretera; **~jack** n (US) veintiuna; **~leg** n (Brit) esquirol m, rompehuelgas m inv; **~list** n lista negra; **~mail** n chantaje m // vt chantajear; ~ **market** n mercado negro; **~out** n apagón m; (fainting) desmayo, pérdida de conocimiento; **the B~ Sea** n el Mar Negro; ~ **sheep** n oveja negra; **~smith** n

herrero; ~ **spot** n (AUT) lugar m peligroso.
bladder ['blædə*] n vejiga.
blade [bleɪd] n hoja; (cutting edge) filo; a ~ of grass una brizna de hierba.
blame [bleɪm] n culpa // vt: to ~ sb for sth echar a uno la culpa de algo; to be ~ tener la culpa de; **~less** a (person) inocente.
bland [blænd] a suave; (taste) soso.
blank [blæŋk] a en blanco; (shot) sin bala; (look) sin expresión // n blanco, espacio en blanco; cartucho sin bala or de fogueo; ~ **cheque** n cheque m en blanco.
blanket ['blæŋkɪt] n manta, cobija (LAm).
blare [blɛə*] vi resonar.
blasé ['blɑːzeɪ] a hastiado.
blasphemy ['blæsfɪmɪ] n blasfemia.
blast [blɑːst] n (of wind) ráfaga, soplo; (of whistle) toque m; (of explosive) carga explosiva; (force) choque m // vt (blow up) volar; (blow open) abrir con carga explosiva; **~-off** n (SPACE) lanzamiento.
blatant ['bleɪtənt] a descarado.
blaze [bleɪz] n (fire) fuego; (flames) llamarada; (fig) arranque m // vi (fire) arder en llamas; (fig) brillar // vt: to ~ a trail (fig) abrir (un) camino.
blazer ['bleɪzə*] n chaqueta de uniforme de colegial o de socio de club.
bleach [bliːtʃ] n (also: household ~) lejía // vt (linen) blanquear; **~ed** a (hair) teñido de rubio; (clothes) decolorado; **~ers** npl (US SPORT) gradas fpl al sol.
bleak [bliːk] a (countryside) desierto; (prospect) poco prometedor(a).
bleary-eyed ['blɪərɪ'aɪd] a: to be ~ tener ojos de cansado.
bleat [bliːt] vi balar.
bleed [bliːd], pt, pp bled [blɛd] vt, vi sangrar.
bleeper ['bliːpə*] n (of doctor etc) busca m.
blemish ['blɛmɪʃ] n mancha, tacha.
blend [blɛnd] n mezcla // vt mezclar // vi (colours etc) combinarse, mezclarse.
bless [blɛs], pt, pp blessed or blest [blɛst] vt bendecir; **~ing** n bendición f; (advantage) beneficio, ventaja.
blew [bluː] pt of **blow**.
blight [blaɪt] vt (hopes etc) frustrar, arruinar.
blimey ['blaɪmɪ] excl (Brit col) ¡caray!
blind [blaɪnd] a ciego // n (for window) persiana // vt cegar; (dazzle) deslumbrar; ~ **alley** n callejón m sin salida; ~ **corner** n (Brit) esquina escondida; **~ers** npl (US) anteojeras fpl; **~fold** n venda // a, ad con los ojos vendados // vt vendar los ojos a; **~ly** ad a ciegas, ciegamente; **~ness** n ceguera; ~ **spot** n mácula.

blink |blɪŋk| vi parpadear, pestañear; (light) oscilar; ~ers npl (esp Brit) anteojeras fpl.

bliss |blɪs| n felicidad f.

blister |'blɪstə*| n (on skin) ampolla // vi (paint) ampollarse.

blithely |'blaɪðlɪ| ad alegremente.

blitz |blɪts| n bombardeo aéreo.

blizzard |'blɪzəd| n ventisca.

bloated |'bləʊtɪd| a hinchado.

blob |blɔb| n (drop) gota; (stain, spot) mancha.

bloc |blɔk| n (POL.) bloque m.

block |blɔk| n bloque m, (in pipes) obstáculo; (of buildings) manzana, cuadra (LAm) // vt (gen) obstruir, cerrar; (progress) estorbar; ~ade |-'keɪd| n bloqueo // vt bloquear; ~age n estorbo, obstrucción f; ~buster n (book) bestseller m; (film) éxito de público; ~ of flats n (Brit) bloque m de pisos; ~ letters npl letras fpl de molde.

bloke |bləʊk| n (Brit col) tipo, tío.

blond(e) |blɔnd| a, n rubio/a m/f.

blood |blʌd| n sangre f; ~ donor n donador(a) m/f de sangre; ~ group n grupo sanguíneo; ~hound n sabueso; ~ poisoning n envenenamiento de la sangre; ~ pressure n presión f sanguínea; ~shed n derramamiento de sangre; ~shot a inyectado en sangre; ~stream n corriente f sanguínea; ~ test n análisis m inv de sangre; ~thirsty a sanguinario; ~ transfusion n transfusión f de sangre; ~y a sangriento; (Brit col!): this ~y... este condenado o puñetero... (!) // ad: ~y strong/good (Brit col!) terriblemente fuerte/bueno; ~y-minded a (Brit col): to be ~y-minded ser un malasangre.

bloom |bluːm| n floración f; in ~ en flor // vi florecer; ~ing a (col): this ~ing... este condenado... .

blossom |'blɔsəm| n flor f // vi (also fig) florecer; (person) realizarse.

blot |blɔt| n borrón m // vt (dry) secar; (stain) manchar; to ~ out vt (view) tapar; (memories) borrar.

blotchy |'blɔtʃɪ| a (complexion) lleno de manchas.

blotting paper |'blɔtɪŋ-| n papel m secante.

blouse |blauz| n blusa.

blow |bləʊ| n golpe m // vb (pt blew |bluː|, pp blown |bləʊn|) vi soplar; (fuse) fundirse // vt (glass) soplar; (fuse) quemar; (instrument) tocar; to ~ one's nose sonarse; to ~ away vt llevarse, arrancar; to ~ down vt derribar; to ~ off vt arrebatar; to ~ out vi apagarse; to ~ over vi amainar; to ~ up vi estallar // vt volar; (tyre) inflar; (PHOT) ampliar; **blow-dry** n moldeado (con secador); ~lamp n (Brit) soplete m, lámpara de soldar; ~-out n (of tyre) pincha-

zo; ~torch n = ~lamp.

blubber |'blʌbə*| n grasa de ballena // vi (pej) lloriquear.

blue |bluː| a azul; ~ film/joke film/chiste verde; out of the ~ (fig)completamente inesperado; to have the ~s estar decaído; ~bell n campanilla, campánula azul; ~bottle n moscarda, mosca azul; ~ jeans npl bluejean m inv, vaqueros mpl; ~print n (fig) anteproyecto.

bluff |blʌf| vi hacer un bluff, farolear // n bluff m, farol m; to call sb's ~ coger a uno en un renuncio.

blunder |'blʌndə*| n patinazo, metedura de pata // vi cometer un error, meter la pata.

blunt |blʌnt| a embotado, desafilado; (person) franco, directo // vt embotar, desafilar.

blur |blə:*| n aspecto borroso // vt (vision) enturbiar; (memory) empañar.

blurb |blə:b| n comentario de sobrecubierta.

blurt |blə:t| vt: to ~ out (say) descolgarse con, dejar escapar.

blush |blʌʃ| vi ruborizarse, ponerse colorado // n rubor m.

blustering |'blʌstərɪŋ| a (person) fanfarrón/ona.

blustery |'blʌstərɪ| a (weather) tempestuoso, tormentoso.

boar |bɔ:*| n verraco, cerdo.

board |bɔ:d| n tabla, tablero; (on wall) tablón m; (for chess etc) tablero; (committee) junta, consejo; (in firm) mesa or junta directiva; (NAUT, AVIAT): on ~ a bordo // vt (ship) embarcarse en; (train) subir a; full ~ (Brit) pensión completa; half ~ (Brit) media pensión; to go by the ~ (fig) ser abandonado or olvidado; to ~ up vt (door) tapiar; ~ and lodging n casa y comida; ~er n huésped(a) m/f; (SCOL) interno/a; ~ing card n (Brit) tarjeta de embarque; ~ing house n casa de huéspedes; ~ing pass n (US) = ~ing card; ~ing school n internado; ~ room n sala de juntas.

boast |bəʊst| vi: to ~ (about or of) alardear (de) // vt ostentar // n alarde m, baladronada.

boat |bəʊt| n barco, buque m; (small) barca, bote m; ~er n (hat) canotié m; ~swain |'bəʊsn| n contramaestre m.

bob |bɔb| vi (boat, cork on water: also: ~ up and down) menearse, balancearse // n (Brit col) = shilling; to ~ up vi (re)aparecer de repente.

bobby |'bɔbɪ| n (Brit col) poli m.

bobsleigh |'bɔbsleɪ| n bob m.

bode |bəʊd| vi: to ~ well/ill (for) ser prometedor/poco prometedor (para).

bodily |'bɔdɪlɪ| a corpóreo, corporal // ad (move: person) en peso; (: building) de una pieza.

body ['bɔdɪ] *n* cuerpo; (*corpse*) cadáver *m*; (*of car*) caja, carrocería; (*fig*: *organization*) organismo; (*fig*: *quantity*) masa; **~building** *n* culturismo; **~guard** *n* guardaespaldas *m inv*; **~work** *n* carrocería.

bog [bɔg] *n* pantano, ciénaga // *vt*: **to get ~ged down** (*fig*) empantanarse, atascarse.

boggle ['bɔgl] *vi*: **the mind ~s!** ¡no puedo creerlo!

bogus ['bəugəs] *a* falso, fraudulento; (*person*) fingido.

boil [bɔɪl] *vt* cocer; (*eggs*) pasar por agua // *vi* hervir // *n* (*MED*) furúnculo, divieso; **to come to the** (*Brit*) **or a** (*US*) **~** comenzar a hervir; **to ~ down to** (*fig*) reducirse a; **to ~ over** *vi* rebosar; (*anger etc*) llegar al colmo; **~ed egg** *n* huevo cocido (*Sp*) *or* pasado (*LAm*); **~ed potatoes** *npl* patatas *fpl or* papas *fpl* (*LAm*) hervidas; **~er** *n* caldera; **~er suit** *n* (*Brit*) mono; **~ing point** *n* punto de ebullición.

boisterous ['bɔɪstərəs] *a* (*noisy*) bullicioso; (*excitable*) exuberante; (*crowd*) tumultuoso.

bold [bəuld] *a* (*brave*) valiente, audaz; (*pej*) descarado; (*outline*) grueso; (*colour*) llamativo.

Bolivia [bə'lɪvɪə] *n* Bolivia; **~n** *a*, *n* boliviano/a *m/f*.

bollard ['bɔləd] *n* (*Brit AUT*) poste *m*.

bolster ['bəulstə*] *n* travesero, cabezal *m;* **to ~ up** *vt* reforzar.

bolt [bəult] *n* (*lock*) cerrojo; (*with nut*) perno, tornillo // *ad*: **~ upright** rígido, erguido // *vt* (*door*) echar el cerrojo a; (*food*) engullir // *vi* fugarse; (*horse*) desbocarse.

bomb [bɔm] *n* bomba // *vt* bombardear; **~ard** [-'baːd] *vt* bombardear; (*fig*) asediar; **~ardment** [-'baːdmənt] *n* bombardeo.

bombastic [bɔm'bæstɪk] *a* rimbombante; (*person*) farolero.

bomb: **~ disposal** *n* desmontaje *m* de explosivos; **~er** *n* (*AVIAT*) bombardero; **~shell** *n* obús *m*, granada; (*fig*) bomba.

bona fide ['bəunə'faɪdɪ] *a* genuino, auténtico.

bond [bɔnd] *n* (*binding promise*) fianza; (*FINANCE*) bono; (*link*) vínculo, lazo; (*COMM*): **in ~** en depósito bajo fianza.

bondage ['bɔndɪdʒ] *n* esclavitud *f*.

bone [bəun] *n* hueso; (*of fish*) espina // *vt* deshuesar; quitar las espinas a; **~-dry** *a* completamente seco; **~ idle** *a* gandul.

bonfire ['bɔnfaɪə*] *n* hoguera, fogata.

bonnet ['bɔnɪt] *n* gorra; (*Brit: of car*) capó *m*.

bonus ['bəunəs] *n* sobrepaga, prima.

bony ['bəunɪ] *a* (*arm, face, MED: tissue*) huesudo; (*meat*) lleno de huesos; (*fish*) lleno de espinas.

boo [buː] *vt* abuchear, rechiflar.

booby trap ['buːbɪ-] *n* trampa explosiva.

book [buk] *n* (*notebook*) libreta; (*of stamps etc*) librito; (*COMM*): **~s** cuentas *fpl*, contabilidad *f* // *vt* (*ticket, seat, room*) reservar; (*driver*) fichar; **~case** *n* librería, estante *m* para libros; **~ing office** *n* (*Brit RAIL*) despacho de billetes *or* boletos (*LAm*); (*THEATRE*) taquilla, boletería (*LAm*); **~-keeping** *n* contabilidad *f;* **~let** *n* folleto; **~maker** *n* corredor *m* de apuestas; **~seller** *n* librero; **~shop**, **~ store** *n* librería.

boom [buːm] *n* (*noise*) trueno, estampido; (*in prices etc*) alza rápida; (*ECON*) boom *m*, auge *m* // *vi* (*cannon*) hacer gran estruendo, retumbar; (*ECON*) estar en alza.

boon [buːn] *n* favor *m*, beneficio.

boost [buːst] *n* estímulo, empuje *m* // *vt* estimular, empujar; **~er** *n* (*MED*) reinyección *f*.

boot [buːt] *n* bota; (*Brit: of car*) maleta, maletero // *vt* dar un puntapié a; (*COMPUT*) arrancar; **to ~** (*in addition*) además, por añadidura.

booth [buːð] *n* (*at fair*) barraca; (*telephone ~, voting ~*) cabina.

booty ['buːtɪ] *n* botín *m*.

booze [buːz] *n* (*col*) bebida, trago // *vi* emborracharse.

border ['bɔːdə*] *n* borde *m*, margen *m*; (*of a country*) frontera // *a* fronterizo; **the B~s** *región fronteriza entre Escocia e Inglaterra;* **to ~ on** *vt fus* lindar con; (*fig*) rayar en; **~line** *n* (*fig*) frontera.

bore [bɔː*] *pt of* **bear** // *vt* (*hole*) hacer un agujero en; (*well*) perforar; (*person*) aburrir // *n* (*person*) pelmazo, pesado; (*of gun*) calibre *m*; **~d** *a* aburrido; **~dom** *n* aburrimiento.

boring ['bɔːrɪŋ] *a* aburrido.

born [bɔːn] *a*: **to be ~** nacer; **I was ~ in 1960** nací en 1960.

borne [bɔːn] *pp of* **bear**.

borough ['bʌrə] *n* municipio.

borrow ['bɔrəu] *vt*: **to ~ sth (from sb)** tomar algo prestado (a alguien).

bosom ['buzəm] *n* pecho; (*fig*) seno.

boss [bɔs] *n* jefe/a *m/f*; (*employer*) patrón/ona *m/f*; (*political etc*) cacique *m* // *vt* (*also*: **~ about** *or* **around**) mangonear; **~y** *a* mandón/ona.

bosun ['bəusn] *n* contramaestre *m*.

botany ['bɔtənɪ] *n* botánica.

botch [bɔtʃ] *vt* (*also*: **~ up**) arruinar, estropear.

both [bəuθ] *a*, *pron* ambos/as, los/las dos; **~ of us went**, **we ~ went** fuimos los dos, ambos fuimos // *ad*: **~ A and B** tanto A como B.

bother ['bɔðə*] *vt* (*worry*) preocupar; (*disturb*) molestar, fastidiar // *vi* (*gen*: **~ o.s.**) molestarse // *n*: **what a ~!** ¡qué lata!; **to** ~ **doing** tomarse la molestia de hacer.

bottle |'bɔtl] *n* botella; (*small*) frasco; (*baby's*) biberón *m* // *vt* embotellar; **to** ~ **up** *vt* suprimir; ~**neck** *n* embotellamiento; ~**-opener** *n* abrebotellas *m inv*.

bottom |'bɔtəm] *n* (*of box, sea*) fondo; (*buttocks*) trasero, culo; (*of page*) pie *m*; (*of list*) final *m* // *a* (*lowest*) más bajo; (*last*) último; ~**less** *a* sin fondo, insondable.

bough [bau] *n* rama.

bought [bɔːt] *pt, pp of* **buy.**

boulder |'bəuldə*] *n* canto rodado.

bounce [bauns] *vi* (*ball*) (re)botar; (*cheque*) ser rechazado // *vt* hacer (re)botar // *n* (*rebound*) (re)bote *m*; ~**r** *n* (*col*) matón/ona *m/f*.

bound [baund] *pt, pp of* **bind** // *n* (*leap*) salto; (*gen pl: limit*) límite *m* // *vi* (*leap*) saltar // *a*: ~ **by** rodeado de; **to be** ~ **to do sth** (*obliged*) tener el deber de hacer algo; **he's** ~ **to come** es seguro que vendrá; **out of** ~**s** prohibido el paso; ~ **for** con destino a.

boundary |'baundrɪ] *n* límite *m*.

boundless |'baundlɪs] *a* ilimitado.

bouquet |'bukeɪ] *n* (*of flowers*) ramo; (*of wine*) aroma *m*.

bourgeois |'buəʒwa] *a, n* burgués/esa *m/f*.

bout [baut] *n* (*of malaria etc*) ataque *m*; (*BOXING etc*) combate *m*, encuentro.

bow [bəu] *n* (*knot*) lazo; (*weapon, MUS*) arco // *n* [bau] (*of the head*) reverencia; (*NAUT: also*: ~**s**) proa // *vi* [bau] inclinarse, hacer una reverencia; (*yield*): **to** ~ **to** *or* **before** ceder ante, someterse a.

bowels [bauəlz] *npl* intestinos *mpl*, vientre *m*.

bowl [bəul] *n* tazón *m*, cuenco; (*for washing*) palangana, jofaina; (*ball*) bola // *vi* (*CRICKET*) arrojar la pelota; ~**s** *n* juego de las bochas, bolos *mpl*.

bow-legged |'bəu'lɛgɪd] *a* estevado.

bowler |'bəulə*] *n* (*CRICKET*) lanzador *m* (de la pelota); (*Brit: also*: ~ **hat**) hongo, bombín *m*.

bowling |'bəulɪŋ] *n* (*game*) bochas *fpl*, bolos *mpl*; ~ **alley** *n* bolera; ~ **green** *n* pista para bochas.

bow tie |'bəu-] *n* corbata de lazo, pajarita.

box [bɔks] *n* (*also*: **cardboard** ~) caja, cajón *m*; (*for jewels*) estuche *m*; (*for money*) cofre *m*; (*THEATRE*) palco // *vt* encajonar // *vi* (*SPORT*) boxear; ~**er** *n* (*person*) boxeador *m*; (*dog*) boxer *m*; ~**ing** *n* (*SPORT*) boxeo; **B**~**ing Day** *n* (*Brit*) día de San Esteban, 26 de diciembre; ~**ing gloves** *npl* guantes *mpl* de boxeo; ~**ing ring** *n* ring *m*, cuadrilátero; ~ **office** *n* taquilla, boletería (*LAm*); ~**room** *n* trastero.

boy [bɔɪ] *n* (*young*) niño; (*older*) mucha-

cho.

boycott |'bɔɪkɔt] *n* boicot *m* // *vt* boicotear.

boyfriend |'bɔɪfrɛnd] *n* novio.

boyish |'bɔɪʃ] *a* muchachil.

B.R. *abbr* = **British Rail.**

bra [braː] *n* sostén *m*, sujetador *m*.

brace [breɪs] *n* refuerzo, abrazadera; (*Brit: also*: ~**s**: **on teeth**) corrector *m*; (*tool*) berbiquí *m* // *vt* asegurar, reforzar; ~**s** *npl* (*Brit*) tirantes *mpl*; **to** ~ **o.s.** (**for**) (*fig*) prepararse (para).

bracelet |'breɪslɪt] *n* pulsera, brazalete *m*.

bracing |'breɪsɪŋ] *a* vigorizante, tónico.

bracken |'brækən] *n* helecho.

bracket |'brækɪt] *n* (*TECH*) soporte *m*, puntal *m*; (*group*) clase *f*, categoría; (*also*: **brace** ~) soporte *m*, abrazadera; (*also*: **round** ~) paréntesis *m inv*; (*gen*: **square** ~) corchete *m* // *vt* (*group*) agrupar.

brag [bræg] *vi* jactarse.

braid [breɪd] *n* (*trimming*) galón *m*; (*of hair*) trenza.

brain [breɪn] *n* cerebro; ~**s** *npl* sesos *mpl*; **she's got** ~**s** es muy lista; ~**child** *n* parto del ingenio; ~**wash** *vt* lavar el cerebro; ~**wave** *n* idea luminosa; ~**y** *a* muy inteligente.

braise [breɪz] *vt* cocer a fuego lento.

brake [breɪk] *n* (*on vehicle*) freno // *vt, vi* frenar; ~ **fluid** *n* líquido de frenos; ~ **light** *n* luz *f* de frenado.

bramble |'bræmbl] *n* zarza.

bran [bræn] *n* salvado.

branch [braːntʃ] *n* rama; (*fig*) ramo; (*COMM*) sucursal *f* // *vi* (*also*: ~ **out**) ramificarse; (: (*fig*) extenderse.

brand [brænd] *n* marca; (*iron*) hierro de marcar // *vt* (*cattle*) marcar con hierro candente.

brandish |'brændɪʃ] *vt* blandir.

brand-new |'brænd'njuː] *a* flamante, completamente nuevo.

brandy |'brændɪ] *n* coñac *m*, brandy *m*.

brash [bræʃ] *a* (*rough*) tosco; (*cheeky*) descarado.

brass [braːs] *n* latón *m*; **the** ~ (*MUS*) los cobres; ~ **band** *n* banda de metal.

brassière |'bræsɪə*] *n* sostén *m*, sujetador *m*.

brat [bræt] *n* (*pej*) mocoso/a.

bravado [brə'vaːdəu] *n* fanfarronería.

brave [breɪv] *a* valiente, valeroso // *n* guerrero indio // *vt* (*challenge*) desafiar; (*resist*) aguantar; ~**ry** *n* valor *m*, valentía.

brawl [brɔːl] *n* pendencia, reyerta // *vi* pelearse.

brawn [brɔːn] *n* fuerza muscular; (*meat*) carne *f* en gelatina.

bray [breɪ] *n* rebuzno // *vi* rebuznar.

brazen |'breɪzn] *a* descarado, cínico // *vt*: **to** ~ **it out** echarle cara.

brazier |'breɪzɪə*| n brasero.

Brazil |brə'zɪl| n (el) Brasil; ~**ian** a, n brasileño/a m/f.

breach |briːtʃ| vt abrir brecha en // n (gap) brecha; (breaking): ~ of confidence abuso de confianza; ~ of contract infracción f de contrato; ~ of the peace perturbación f del órden público.

bread |brɛd| n pan m; ~ **and butter** n pan con mantequilla; (fig) pan (de cada día) // a común y corriente; ~**bin**, (US) ~**box** n panera; ~**crumbs** npl migajas fpl; (CULIN) pan molido; ~**line** n: on the ~**line** en la miseria.

breadth |brɛtθ| n anchura; (fig) amplitud f.

breadwinner |'brɛdwɪnə*| n sostén m de la familia.

break |breɪk| vb (pt broke, pp broken) vt (gen) romper; (promise) faltar a; (fall) amortiguar; (journey) interrumpir; (law) violar, infringir; (record) batir; (news) comunicar // vi romperse, quebrarse; (storm) estallar; (weather) cambiar // n (gap) abertura; (crack) grieta; (fracture) fractura; (in relations) ruptura; (rest) descanso; (time) intérvalo; (: at school) (período de recreo; (chance) oportunidad f; to ~ **down** vt (figures, data) analizar, descomponer; (undermine) acabar con // vi estropearse; (MED) sufrir un colapso; (AUT) averiarse; (person) romper a llorar; to ~ **even** vi cubrir los gastos; to ~ **free** or **loose** vi escaparse; to ~ **in** vt (horse etc) domar // vi (burglar) forzar una entrada; to ~ **into** vt fus (house) forzar; to ~ **off** vi (speaker) pararse, detenerse; (branch) partir; to ~ **open** vt (door etc) abrir por la fuerza, forzar; to ~ **out** vi estallar; to ~ out in spots salir a uno granos; to ~ **up** vi (partnership) disolverse; (friends) romper // vt (rocks etc) partir; (crowd) disolver; ~**age** n rotura; (AUT) avería; (in communications) interrupción f; (MED: also: nervous ~**down**) colapso, crisis f nerviosa; ~**down van** n (Brit) (camión m) grúa; ~**er** n rompiente m.

breakfast |'brɛkfəst| n desayuno.

break: ~-**in** n robo con allanamiento de morada; ~**ing and entering** n (LAW) violación f de domicilio, allanamiento de morada; ~**through** n (fig) avance m; ~**water** n rompeolas m inv.

breast |brɛst| n (of woman) pecho, seno; (chest) pecho; (of bird) pechuga; to ~-**feed** vt, vi (irg: like feed) amamantar, criar a los pechos; ~-**stroke** n braza de pecho.

breath |brɛθ| n aliento, respiración f; out of ~ sin aliento, sofocado.

Breathalyser |'brɛθəlaɪzə*| n ® (Brit) alcoholímetro m; ~ **test** n prueba de alcoholemia.

breathe |briːð| vt, vi respirar; (noisily) resollar; **to ~ in** vt, vi aspirar; **to ~ out** vt, vi espirar; ~**r** n respiro; **breathing** n respiración f.

breath: ~**less** a sin aliento, jadeante; ~**taking** a imponente, pasmoso.

breed |briːd| vb (pt, pp bred |brɛd|) vt criar // vi reproducirse, procrear // n raza, casta; ~**er** n (person) criador(a) m/f; ~**ing** n (of person) educación f.

breeze |briːz| n brisa.

breezy |'briːzɪ| a de mucho viento, ventoso; (person) despreocupado.

brevity |'brɛvɪtɪ| n brevedad f.

brew |bruː| vt (tea) hacer; (beer) elaborar; (plot) tramar // vi hacerse; elaborarse; tramarse; (storm) amenazar; ~**er** n cervecero; ~**ery** n fábrica de cerveza, cervecería.

bribe |braɪb| n soborno // vt sobornar, cohechar; ~**ry** n soborno, cohecho.

bric-a-brac |'brɪkəbræk| n inv baratijas fpl.

brick |brɪk| n ladrillo; ~**layer** n albañil m; ~**works** n ladrillar m.

bridal |'braɪdl| a nupcial.

bride |braɪd| n novia; ~**groom** n novio; ~**smaid** n dama de honor.

bridge |brɪdʒ| n puente m; (NAUT) puente m de mando; (of nose) caballete m; (CARDS) bridge m // vt (river) tender un puente sobre.

bridle |'braɪdl| n brida, freno // vt poner la brida a; (fig) reprimir, refrenar; ~ **path** n camino de herradura.

brief |briːf| a breve, corto // n (LAW) escrito // vt (inform) informar; (instruct) dar instrucciones a; ~**s** npl (for men) calzoncillos mpl; (for women) bragas fpl; ~**case** n cartera, portafolio (LAm); ~**ing** n (PRESS) informe m; ~**ly** ad (smile, glance) fugazmente; (explain, say) en pocas palabras.

brigadier |brɪgə'dɪə*| n general m de brigada.

bright |braɪt| a claro; (room) luminoso; (day) de sol; (person: clever) listo, inteligente; (: lively) alegre; (colour) vivo; ~**en** (also: ~**en up**) vt (room) hacer más alegre // vi (weather) despejarse; (person) animarse, alegrarse.

brilliance |'brɪljəns| n brillo, brillantez f.

brilliant |'brɪljənt| a brillante.

brim |brɪm| n borde m; (of hat) ala.

brine |braɪn| n (CULIN) salmuera.

bring |brɪŋ|, pt, pp brought vt (thing) traer; (person) conducir; **to ~ about** vt ocasionar, producir; **to ~ back** vt volver a traer; (return) devolver; **to ~ down** vt bajar; (price) rebajar; **to ~ forward** vt adelantar; **to ~ off** vt (task, plan) lograr, conseguir; **to ~ out** vt (object) sacar; **to ~ round** vt (unconscious person) hacer volver en sí;

(*convince*) convencer; **to ~ up** *vt* (*person*) educar, criar; (*carry up*) subir; (*question*) sacar a colación; (*food: vomit*) devolver, vomitar.

brink [brɪŋk] *n* borde *m*.

brisk [brɪsk] *a* enérgico, vigoroso; (*speedy*) rápido; (*trade*) activo.

brisket ['brɪskɪt] *n* carne *f* de vaca para asar.

bristle ['brɪsl] *n* cerda // *vi* erizarse.

Britain ['brɪtən] *n* (*also*: Great ~) Gran Bretaña.

British ['brɪtɪʃ] *a* británico; **the ~** *npl* los británicos; **the ~ Isles** *npl* las Islas Británicas; **~ Rail (B.R.)** *n* ≈ RENFE *f* (*Sp*).

Briton ['brɪtən] *n* británico/a.

brittle ['brɪtl] *a* quebradizo, frágil.

broach [brəʊtʃ] *vt* (*subject*) abordar.

broad [brɔːd] *a* ancho, amplio; (*accent*) cerrado; **in ~ daylight** en pleno día; **~cast** *n* emisión *f* // *vb* (*pt, pp* **~cast**) *vt* (*RADIO*) emitir; (*TV*) transmitir // *vi* emitir; transmitir; **~casting** *n* radiodifusión *f*, difusión *f*; **~en** *vt* ensanchar // *vi* ensancharse; **~ly** *ad* en general; **~minded** *a* tolerante, liberal.

broccoli ['brɔkəlɪ] *n* brécol *m*.

brochure ['brəʊʃjuə*] *n* folleto.

broil [brɔɪl] *vt* (*US*) asar a la parrilla.

broke [brəʊk] *pt of* **break** // *a* (*col*) pelado, sin blanca.

broken ['brəʊkən] *pp of* **break** // *a*: **~ leg** pierna rota; **in ~ English** en un inglés imperfecto; **~-hearted** *a* con el corazón partido.

broker ['brəʊkə*] *n* agente *m/f*, bolsista *m/f*.

brolly ['brɔlɪ] *n* (*Brit col*) paraguas *m inv*.

bronchitis [brɔŋ'kaɪtɪs] *n* bronquitis *f*.

bronze [brɔnz] *n* bronce *m*.

brooch [brəʊtʃ] *n* prendedor *m*.

brood [bruːd] *n* camada, cría; (*children*) progenie *f* // *vi* (*hen*) empollar; **to ~ over** sth dejarse obsesionar por algo.

brook [bruk] *n* arroyo.

broom [brum] *n* escoba; (*BOT*) retama; **~stick** *n* palo de escoba.

Bros. *abbr* (= *Brothers*) Hnos.

broth [brɔθ] *n* caldo.

brothel ['brɔθl] *n* burdel *m*.

brother ['brʌðə*] *n* hermano; **~-in-law** *n* cuñado.

brought [brɔːt] *pt, pp of* **bring**.

brow [brau] *n* (*forehead*) frente *m*; (*of hill*) cumbre *f*.

brown [braun] *a* moreno; (*hair*) castaño; (*tanned*) bronceado // *n* (*colour*) color *m* moreno o pardo // *vt* (*tan*) broncear; (*CULIN*) dorar; **~ bread** *n* pan moreno.

brownie ['braunɪ] *n* niña exploradora.

brown paper *n* papel *m* de estraza.

brown sugar *n* azúcar *m* terciado.

browse [brauz] *vi* (*among books*) hojear libros.

bruise [bruːz] *n* cardenal *m*, moretón *m* (*LAm*) // *vt* magullar.

brunch [brʌnʃ] *n* desayuno-almuerzo.

brunette [bruː'nɛt] *n* morena.

brunt [brʌnt] *n*: **to bear the ~ of** llevar el peso de.

brush [brʌʃ] *n* cepillo; (*large*) escoba; (*for painting, shaving etc*) brocha; (*artist's*) pincel *m*; (*BOT*) maleza; (*with police etc*) roce *m* // *vt* cepillar; (*gen: past, ~ against*) rozar al pasar; **to ~ aside** *vt* rechazar, no hacer caso a; **to ~ up** *vt* (*knowledge*) repasar, refrescar; **~wood** *n* (*bushes*) maleza; (*sticks*) leña.

brusque [bruːsk] *a* brusco, áspero.

Brussels ['brʌslz] *n* Bruselas; **~ sprout** *n* col de Bruselas.

brutal ['bruːtl] *a* brutal.

brute [bruːt] *n* bruto; (*person*) bestia // *a*: **by ~ force** a fuerza bruta.

B.Sc. *abbr* = **Bachelor of Science.**

bubble ['bʌbl] *n* burbuja; (*in paint*) ampolla // *vi* burbujear, borbotar; **~ bath** *n* espuma para el baño; **~ gum** *n* chicle *m* de globo.

buck [bʌk] *n* macho; (*US col*) dólar *m* // *vi* corcovear; **to pass the ~** (**to sb**) echar (a uno) el muerto; **to ~ up** *vi* (*cheer up*) animarse, cobrar ánimo.

bucket ['bʌkɪt] *n* cubo, balde *m*.

buckle ['bʌkl] *n* hebilla // *vt* abrochar con hebilla // *vi* combarse.

bud [bʌd] *n* brote *m*, yema; (*of flower*) capullo // *vi* brotar, echar brotes.

Buddhism ['budɪzm] *n* Budismo.

budding ['bʌdɪŋ] *a* en ciernes, en embrión.

buddy ['bʌdɪ] *n* (*US*) compañero, compinche *m*.

budge [bʌdʒ] *vt* mover; (*fig*) hacer ceder // *vi* moverse.

budgerigar ['bʌdʒərɪgɑː*] *n* periquito.

budget ['bʌdʒɪt] *n* presupuesto // *vi*: **to ~ for** sth presupuestar algo.

budgie ['bʌdʒɪ] *n* = **budgerigar.**

buff [bʌf] *a* (*colour*) color de ante // *n* (*enthusiast*) entusiasta *m/f*.

buffalo ['bʌfələu], *pl* **~** *or* **~es** *n* (*Brit*) búfalo; (*US: bison*) bisonte *m*.

buffer ['bʌfə*] *n* amortiguador *m*; (*COMPUT*) memoria intermedia.

buffet ['bufeɪ] *n* (*Brit: bar*) bar *m*, cafetería; (*food*) buffet *m* // *vt* ['bʌfɪt] (*strike*) abofetear; (*wind etc*) golpear; **~ car** *n* (*Brit RAIL*) coche-comedor *m*.

bug [bʌg] *n* (*insect*) chinche *m*; (: *gen*) bicho, sabandija; (*germ*) microbio, bacilo; (*spy device*) micrófono oculto // *vt* (*fam*) fastidiar; (*room*) poner micrófono oculto en.

bugle ['bjuːgl] *n* corneta, clarín *m*.

build [bɪld] *n* (*of person*) talle *m*, tipo // *vt* (*pt, pp* **built**) construir, edificar; **to**

~ **up** vt (MED) fortalecer; (stocks) acumular; ~**er** n constructor(a) m/f; (contractor) contratista m/f; ~**ing** n (act of) construcción f; (habitation, offices) edificio; ~**ing society** n (Brit) sociedad f inmobiliaria, cooperativa de construcciones.

built [bɪlt] pt, pp of **build** // a: ~**-in** (cupboard) empotrado; (device) interior, incorporado; ~**-up** (area) urbanizado.

bulb [bʌlb] n (BOT) bulbo; (ELEC) bombilla, foco (LAm).

Bulgaria [bʌl'gɛərɪə] n Bulgaria; ~**n** a, n búlgaro/a m/f.

bulge [bʌldʒ] n bombeo, pandeo // vi bombearse, pandearse; (pocket etc) hacer bulto.

bulk [bʌlk] n (mass) bulto, volumen m; (major part) grueso; **in** ~ (COMM) a granel; **the** ~ **of** la mayor parte de; ~**head** n mamparo; ~**y** a voluminoso, abultado.

bull [bul] n toro; ~**dog** n dogo.

bulldozer ['buldəʊzə*] n aplanadora, motoniveladora.

bullet ['bulɪt] n bala.

bulletin ['bulɪtɪn] n anuncio, parte m; ~ **board** n (US) tablón m de anuncios.

bullet: ~**proof** a a prueba de balas; ~ **wound** n balazo.

bullfight ['bulfaɪt] n corrida de toros; ~**er** n torero; ~**ing** n los toros mpl, el toreo; (art of ~ing) tauromaquia.

bullion ['buljən] n oro o plata en barras.

bullock ['bulək] n novillo.

bullring ['bulrɪŋ] n plaza de toros.

bull's-eye ['bulzaɪ] n centro del blanco.

bully ['bulɪ] n valentón m, matón m // vt intimidar, tiranizar.

bum [bʌm] n (Brit: col: backside) culo; (tramp) vagabundo.

bumblebee ['bʌmblbiː] n abejorro.

bump [bʌmp] n (blow) tope m, choque m; (jolt) sacudida; (on road etc) bache m; (on head) chichón m // vt (strike) chocar contra, topetar // vi dar sacudidas; **to** ~ **into** vt fus chocar contra, tropezar con; (person) topar con; ~**er** n (Brit) parachoques m inv // a: ~**er crop/harvest** cosecha abundante; ~**er cars** npl coches mpl de choque.

bumptious ['bʌmpʃəs] a engreído, presuntuoso.

bumpy ['bʌmpɪ] a (road) lleno de baches; (journey) zarandeado.

bun [bʌn] n (Brit: cake) pastel m; (US: bread) bollo; (of hair) moño.

bunch [bʌntʃ] n (of flowers) ramo; (of keys) manojo; (of bananas) piña; (of people) grupo; (pej) pandilla.

bundle ['bʌndl] n (gen) bulto, fardo; (of sticks) haz m; (of papers) legajo // vt (also: ~ up) atar, envolver; **to** ~ **sth/sb into** meter algo/a alguien precipitadamente en.

bungalow ['bʌŋgələu] n bungalow m, chalé m.

bungle ['bʌŋgl] vt chapucear.

bunion ['bʌnjən] n juanete m.

bunk [bʌŋk] n litera; ~ **beds** npl literas fpl.

bunker ['bʌŋkə*] n (coal store) carbonera; (MIL) refugio; (GOLF) bunker m.

bunny ['bʌnɪ] n (also: ~ **rabbit**) conejito.

bunting ['bʌntɪŋ] n empavesada, banderas fpl.

buoy [bɔɪ] n boya; **to** ~ **up** vt mantener a flote; (fig) animar; ~**ancy** n (of ship) capacidad f para flotar; ~**ant** a (carefree) boyante, optimista.

burden ['bɜːdn] n carga // vt cargar.

bureau [bjuə'rəu], pl ~**x** [-z] n (Brit: writing desk) escritorio, buró m; (US: chest of drawers) cómoda; (office) oficina, agencia.

bureaucracy [bjuə'rɔkrəsɪ] n burocracia; **bureaucrat** ['bjuərəkræt] n burócrata m/f.

burglar ['bɜːglə*] n ladrón/ona m/f; ~ **alarm** n alarma de ladrones; ~**y** n robo con allanamiento, robo de una casa.

burial ['berɪəl] n entierro.

burly ['bɜːlɪ] a fornido, membrudo.

Burma ['bɜːmə] n Birmania.

burn [bɜːn] vb (pt, pp **burned** or **burnt**) vt quemar; (house) incendiar // vi quemarse, arder; incendiarse; (sting) escocer // n quemadura; **to** ~ **down** vt incendiar; ~**er** n (gas) quemador m; ~**ing** a ardiente.

burrow ['bʌrəu] n madriguera // vt hacer una madriguera.

bursar ['bɜːsə*] n tesorero; (Brit: student) becario/a; ~**y** n (Brit) beca.

burst [bɜːst] (pt, pp **burst**) vt (balloon, pipe) reventar; (banks etc) romper // vi reventarse; romperse; (tyre) pincharse; (bomb) estallar // n (explosion) estallido; (also: ~ **pipe**) reventón m; **a** ~ **of energy** una explosión f de energía; **to** ~ **into flames** estallar en llamas; **to** ~ **out laughing** soltar la carcajada; **to** ~ **into tears** deshacerse en lágrimas; **to be** ~**ing with** reventar por or de; **to** ~ **into** vt fus (room etc) irrumpir en; **to** ~ **open** vi abrirse de golpe.

bury ['berɪ] vt enterrar; (body) enterrar, sepultar.

bus [bʌs] n autobús m.

bush [buʃ] n arbusto; (scrub land) monte m; **to beat about the** ~ andar(se) con rodeos; ~**y** a (thick) espeso, poblado.

busily ['bɪzɪlɪ] ad afanosamente.

business ['bɪznɪs] n (matter) asunto; (trading) comercio, negocios mpl; (firm) empresa, casa; (occupation) oficio; (affair) asunto; **to be away on** ~ estar en viaje de negocios; **it's my** ~ **to...** me toca or corresponde...; **it's none of my** ~ yo no tengo nada que ver; **he means** ~

habla en serio; ~**like** a (company) serio; (person) eficiente; ~**man** n hombre
m de negocios; ~**trip** n viaje m de negocios; ~**woman** n mujer f de negocios.
busker ['bʌskə*] n (Brit) músico/a ambulante.
bus-stop ['bʌsstɔp] n parada de autobús.
bust [bʌst] n (ANAT) pecho // a (col: broken) roto, estropeado; **to go ~** quebrarse.
bustle ['bʌsl] n bullicio, movimiento // vi
menearse, apresurarse; **bustling** a
(town) animado, bullicioso.
busy ['bɪzɪ] a ocupado, atareado; (shop,
street) concurrido, animado // vr: **to ~
o.s.** with ocuparse en; ~**body** n
entrometido/a; ~ **signal** n (US TEL) señal f de comunicando.
but [bʌt] ♦ conj 1 pero; he's not very
bright, ~ he's hard-working no es muy
inteligente, pero es trabajador
2 (in direct contradiction) sino; he's not
English ~ French no es inglés sino francés; he didn't sing ~ he shouted no cantó
sino que gritó
3 (showing disagreement, surprise etc):
~ that's far too expensive! ¡pero eso es
carísimo!; ~ it does work! ¡(pero) sí
que funciona!
♦ prep (apart from, except) menos, salvo; we've had nothing ~ trouble no hemos tenido más que problemas; no-one
~ him can do it nadie más que él puede
hacerlo; who ~ a lunatic would do such
a thing? ¡sólo un loco haría una cosa
así!; ~ for you/your help si no fuera por
ti/tu ayuda; anything ~ that cualquier
cosa menos eso
♦ ad (just, only): she's ~ a child no es
más que una niña; had I ~ known si lo
hubiera sabido; I can ~ try al menos lo
puedo intentar; it's all ~ finished está
casi acabado.
butcher ['butʃə*] n carnicero // vt hacer
una carnicería con; (cattle etc for meat)
matar; ~**'s (shop)** n carnicería.
butler ['bʌtlə*] n mayordomo.
butt [bʌt] n (cask) tonel m; (for rain)
tina; (thick end) cabo, extremo; (of
gun) culata; (of cigarette) colilla; (Brit
fig: target) blanco // vt dar cabezadas
contra, topetar; **to ~ in** vi (interrupt)
interrumpir.
butter ['bʌtə*] n mantequilla // vt untar
con mantequilla; ~**cup** n ranúnculo.
butterfly ['bʌtəflaɪ] n mariposa; (SWIM-
MING: also: ~ **stroke**) braza de mariposa.
buttocks ['bʌtəks] npl nalgas fpl.
button ['bʌtn] n botón m // vt (also: ~
up) abotonar, abrochar // vi abrocharse.
buttress ['bʌtrɪs] n contrafuerte m; (fig)
apoyo, sostén m.
buxom ['bʌksəm] a (woman) frescacho-
na.

buy [baɪ] vt (pt, pp bought) comprar // n
compra; **to ~ sb sth/sth from sb** com-
prarle algo a alguien; **to ~ sb a drink** invitar a alguien a tomar algo; ~**er** n
comprador(a) m/f.
buzz [bʌz] n zumbido; (col: phone call)
llamada (por teléfono) // vi zumbar.
buzzer ['bʌzə*] n timbre m.
buzz word n palabra que está de moda.
by [baɪ] ♦ prep 1 (referring to cause,
agent) por; de; killed ~ lightning muerto por un relámpago; a painting ~ Picasso un cuadro de Picasso
2 (referring to method, manner,
means): ~ bus/car/train en autobús/
coche/tren; to pay ~ cheque pagar con
un cheque; ~ moonlight/candlelight a la
luz de la luna/una vela; ~ saving hard,
he ... ahorrando, ...
3 (via, through) por; we came ~ Dover
vinimos por Dover
4 (close to, past): the house ~ the river
la casa junto al río; she rushed ~ me pasó a mi lado como una exhalación; I go
~ the post office every day paso por delante de Correos todos los días
5 (time: not later than) para; (: during): ~ daylight de día; ~ 4 o'clock para
las cuatro; ~ this time tomorrow para
mañana a esta hora; ~ the time I got
here it was too late cuando llegué ya era
demasiado tarde
6 (amount): ~ the kilo/metre por kilo/
metro; paid ~ the hour pagado/a por
hora
7 (MATH, measure): to divide/multiply
~ 3 dividir/multiplicar por 3; a room 3
metres ~ 4 una habitación de 3 metros
por 4; it's broader ~ a metre es un metro más ancho
8 (according to) según, de acuerdo con;
it's 3 o'clock ~ my watch según mi reloj,
son las tres; it's all right ~ me por mí,
está bien
9: (all) ~ oneself etc todo solo/a; he did
it (all) ~ himself lo hizo él solo; he was
standing (all) ~ himself in a corner estaba de pie solo en un rincón
10: ~ the way a propósito, por cierto;
this wasn't my idea ~ the way pues, no
fue idea mía
♦ ad 1 see go, pass etc
2: ~ and ~ finalmente; they'll come
back ~ and ~ acabarán volviendo; ~
and large en líneas generales, en general.
bye(-bye) ['baɪ('baɪ)] excl adiós, hasta
luego.
by(e)-law ['baɪlɔ:] n ordenanza municipal.
by-election ['baɪɪlekʃən] n (Brit) elección f parcial.
bygone ['baɪgɔn] a pasado, del pasado //
n: let ~s be ~s lo pasado, pasado está.
bypass ['baɪpɑ:s] n carretera de circun-

valación; (*MED*) (operación *f* de) by-pass *m* // *vt* evitar.

by-product |'baɪprɔdʌkt| *n* subproducto, derivado.

bystander |'baɪstændə*| *n* espectador(a) *m/f*.

byte |baɪt| *n* (*COMPUT*) byte *m*, octeto.

byword |'baɪwə:d| *n*: **to be a ~ for** ser conocidísimo por.

by-your-leave |'baɪjɔ:'li:v| *n*: **without so much as a ~** sin decir nada, sin dar ningún tipo de explicación.

C

C |si:| *n* (*MUS*) do *m*.

C. *abbr* = **centigrade**.

C.A. *abbr* = **chartered accountant**.

cab |kæb| *n* taxi *m*; (*of truck*) cabina.

cabbage |'kæbɪdʒ| *n* col *f*, berza.

cabin |'kæbɪn| *n* cabaña; (*on ship*) camarote *m*.

cabinet |'kæbɪnɪt| *n* (*POL*) consejo de ministros; (*furniture*) armario; (*also*: **display ~**) vitrina; **~-maker** *n* ebanista *m*.

cable |'keɪbl| *n* cable *m* // *vt* cablegrafiar; **~-car** *n* teleférico; **~ television** *n* televisión *f* por cable.

cache |kæʃ| *n* (*of weapons, drugs etc*) alijo.

cackle |'kækl| *vi* cacarear.

cactus |'kæktəs|, *pl* **cacti** |-taɪ| *n* cacto.

cadet |kə'dɛt| *n* (*MIL*) cadete *m*.

cadge |kædʒ| *vt* gorronear.

Caesarean |si:'zɛərɪən| *a*: **~ (section)** cesárea.

café |'kæfeɪ| *n* café *m*.

cafeteria |kæfɪ'tɪərɪə| *n* café *m*.

caffein(e) |'kæfi:n| *n* cafeína.

cage |keɪdʒ| *n* jaula // *vt* enjaular.

cagey |'keɪdʒɪ| *a* (*col*) cauteloso, reservado.

cagoule |kə'gu:l| *n* chubasquero.

Cairo |'kaɪərəu| *n* el Cairo.

cajole |kə'dʒəul| *vt* engatusar.

cake |keɪk| *n* pastel *m*; (*of soap*) pastilla; **~d** *a*: **~d with** cubierto de.

calculate |'kælkjuleɪt| *vt* calcular; **calculating** *a* (*scheming*) calculador(a); **calculation** |-'leɪʃən| *n* cálculo, cómputo; **calculator** *n* calculadora.

calendar |'kæləndə*| *n* calendario; **~ month/year** *n* mes *m*/año civil.

calf |ka:f|, *pl* **calves** *n* (*of cow*) ternero, becerro; (*of other animals*) cría; (*also*: **~skin**) piel *f* de becerro; (*ANAT*) pantorrilla.

calibre, (*US*) **caliber** |'kælɪbə*| *n* calibre *m*.

call |kɔ:l| *vt* (*gen*) llamar // *vi* (*shout*) llamar; (*TEL*) llamar (por teléfono), telefonear (*esp LAm*); (*visit*: *also*: **~ in, ~ round**) hacer una visita // *n* (*shout, TEL*) llamada; (*of bird*) canto; (*appeal*) lla-

mamiento; **to be ~ed** (*person, object*) llamarse; **on ~** (*nurse, doctor etc*) de guardia; **to ~ back** *vi* (*return*) volver; (*TEL*) volver a llamar; **to ~ for** *vt fus* (*demand*) pedir, exigir; (*fetch*) venir por, pasar por (*LAm*); **to ~ off** *vt* suspender; (*cancel*) cancelar; **to ~ on** *vt fus* (*visit*) visitar; (*turn to*) acudir a; **to ~ out** *vi* gritar, dar voces; **to ~ up** *vt* (*MIL*) llamar al servicio militar; **~box** *n* (*Brit*) cabina telefónica; **~er** *n* visita *f*; (*TEL*) usuario/a; **~ girl** *n* prostituta; **~-in** *n* (*US*) (programa *m*) coloquio (por teléfono); **~ing** *n* vocación *f*, profesión *f*; **~ing card** *n* (*US*) tarjeta de visita *or* comercial.

callous |'kæləs| *a* insensible, cruel.

calm |ka:m| *a* tranquilo; (*sea*) liso, en calma // *n* calma, tranquilidad *f* // *vt* calmar, tranquilizar; **to ~ down** *vi* calmarse, tranquilizarse // *vt* calmar, tranquilizar.

Calor gas |'kælə*-| *n* ® butano.

calorie |'kælərɪ| *n* caloría.

calve |ka:v| *vi* parir.

calves |ka:vz| *pl of* **calf**.

camber |'kæmbə*| *n* (*of road*) combadura, comba.

Cambodia |kæm'bəudjə| *n* Camboya.

came |keɪm| *pt of* **come**.

camel |'kæməl| *n* camello.

cameo |'kæmɪəu| *n* camafeo.

camera |'kæmərə| *n* máquina fotográfica; (*CINEMA, TV*) cámara; **in ~** en secreto; **~man** *n* cámara *m*.

camouflage |'kæməfla:ʒ| *n* camuflaje *m* // *vt* camuflar.

camp |kæmp| *n* campo, campamento // *vi* acampar // *a* afectado, afeminado.

campaign |kæm'peɪn| *n* (*MIL, POL etc*) campaña // *vi* hacer campaña.

camp: **~bed** *n* (*Brit*) cama de campaña; **~er** *n* campista *m/f*; (*vehicle*) caravana; **~ing** *n* camping *m*; **to go ~ing** hacer camping; **~site** *n* camping *m*.

campus |'kæmpəs| *n* ciudad *f* universitaria.

can |kæn| ♦ *n, vt see next headword* ♦ *auxiliary vb* (*negative* **cannot, can't**; *conditional and pt* **could**) **1** (*be able to*) poder; **you ~ do it if you try** puedes hacerlo si lo intentas; **I ~'t see you** no te veo

2 (*know how to*) saber; **I ~ swim/play tennis/drive** sé nadar/jugar al tenis/conducir; **~ you speak French?** ¿hablas *or* sabes hablar francés?

3 (*may*) poder; **~ I use your phone?** ¿me dejas *or* puedo usar tu teléfono?

4 (*expressing disbelief, puzzlement etc*): **it ~'t be true!** ¡no puede ser (verdad)!; **what CAN he want?** ¿qué querrá?

5 (*expressing possibility, suggestion etc*): **he could be in the library** podría estar en la biblioteca; **she could have**

been delayed pudo haberse retrasado.

can [kæn] *auxiliary vb see previous headword* // *n* (*of oil, water*) bidón *m*; (*tin*) lata, bote *m* // *vt* enlatar; (*preserve*) conservar en lata.

Canada ['kænədə] *n* el Canadá; **Canadian** [kə'neɪdɪən] *a, n* canadiense *m/f*.

canal [kə'næl] *n* canal *m*.

canary [kə'nɛərɪ] *n* canario; **C~ Islands** *npl* las (Islas) Canarias.

cancel ['kænsəl] *vt* cancelar; (*train*) suprimir; (*appointment*) anular; (*cross out*) tachar, borrar; **~lation** [-'leɪʃən] *n* cancelación *f*; supresión *f*.

cancer ['kænsə*] *n* cáncer *m*; **C~** (*ASTRO*) Cáncer *m*.

candid ['kændɪd] *a* franco, abierto.

candidate ['kændɪdeɪt] *n* candidato/a.

candle ['kændl] *n* vela; (*in church*) cirio; **by ~ light** a la luz de una vela; **~stick** *n* (*also*: **~ holder**) (*single*) candelero; (*low*) palmatoria; (*bigger, ornate*) candelabro.

candour, (*US*) **candor** ['kændə*] *n* franqueza.

candy ['kændɪ] *n* azúcar *m* cande; (*US*) caramelo; **~-floss** *n* (*Brit*) algodón *m* (azucarado).

cane [keɪn] *n* (*BOT*) caña; (*stick*) vara, palmeta // *vt* (*Brit SCOL*) castigar (con palmeta).

canister ['kænɪstə*] *n* bote *m*, lata.

cannabis ['kænəbɪs] *n* marijuana.

canned [kænd] *a* en lata, de lata.

cannibal ['kænɪbəl] *n* caníbal *m/f*.

cannon ['kænən], *pl* **~** *or* **~s** *n* cañón *m*.

cannot ['kænɔt] = **can not.**

canny ['kænɪ] *a* astuto.

canoe [kə'nuː] *n* canoa; (*SPORT*) piragua.

canon ['kænən] *n* (*clergyman*) canónigo; (*standard*) canon *m*.

can opener ['kænəupnə*] *n* abrelatas *m inv*.

canopy ['kænəpɪ] *n* dosel *m*; toldo.

can't [kænt] = **can not.**

cantankerous [kæn'tæŋkərəs] *a* arisco, malhumorado.

canteen [kæn'tiːn] *n* (*eating place*) cantina; (*Brit: of cutlery*) juego.

canter ['kæntə*] *n* medio galope // *vi* ir a medio galope.

canvas ['kænvəs] *n* (*material*) lona; (*painting*) lienzo; (*NAUT*) velas *fpl*.

canvass ['kænvəs] *vt* (*POL*) solicitar votos de; (*COMM*) sondear.

canyon ['kænjən] *n* cañón *m*.

cap [kæp] *n* (*hat*) gorra; (*of pen*) capuchón *m*; (*of bottle*) tapa, cápsula // *vt* (*outdo*) superar; (*bottle etc*) tapar; (*tooth*) poner una corona a.

capability [keɪpə'bɪlɪtɪ] *n* capacidad *f*.

capable ['keɪpəbl] *a* capaz.

capacity [kə'pæsɪtɪ] *n* capacidad *f*; (*position*) calidad *f*.

cape [keɪp] *n* capa; (*GEO*) cabo.

capital ['kæpɪtl] *n* (*also:* **~ city**) capital *f*; (*money*) capital *m*; (*also:* **~ letter**) mayúscula; **~ gains tax** *n* impuesto sobre las ganancias de capital; **~ism** *n* capitalismo; **~ist** *a, n* capitalista *m/f*; **to ~ize on** *vt fus* aprovechar; **~ punishment** *n* pena de muerte.

capitulate [kə'pɪtjuleɪt] *vi* capitular, rendirse.

Capricorn ['kæprɪkɔːn] *n* Capricornio.

capsize [kæp'saɪz] *vt* volcar, hacer zozobrar // *vi* volcarse, zozobrar.

capsule ['kæpsjuːl] *n* cápsula.

captain ['kæptɪn] *n* capitán *m*.

caption ['kæpʃən] *n* (*heading*) título; (*to picture*) leyenda.

captive ['kæptɪv] *a, n* cautivo/a *m/f*; **captivity** ['tɪvɪtɪ] *n* cautiverio.

capture ['kæptʃə*] *vt* prender, apresar; (*place*) tomar; (*attention*) captar, llamar // *n* apresamiento; toma; (*data ~*) formulación *f* de datos.

car [kɑː*] *n* coche *m*, carro (*LAm*), automóvil *m*; (*US RAIL*) vagón *m*.

carafe [kə'ræf] *n* garrafa.

caramel ['kærəməl] *n* caramelo.

carat ['kærət] *n* quilate *m*.

caravan ['kærəvæn] *n* (*Brit*) caravana, ruló *f*; (*of camels*) caravana; **~ site** *n* (*Brit*) camping *m* para caravanas.

carbohydrates [kɑːbəu'haɪdreɪts] *npl* hidratos *mpl* de carbono; (*food*) fécula *sg*.

carbon ['kɑːbən] *n* carbono; **~ copy** *n* copia al carbón; **~ paper** *n* papel *m* carbón.

carburettor, (*US*) **carburetor** [kɑːbju'retə*] *n* carburador *m*.

card [kɑːd] *n* (*playing ~*) carta, naipe *m*; (*visiting ~, post~ etc*) tarjeta; **~board** *n* cartón *m*, cartulina; **~ game** *n* juego de naipes.

cardiac ['kɑːdɪæk] *a* cardíaco.

cardigan ['kɑːdɪgən] *n* rebeca.

cardinal ['kɑːdɪnl] *a* cardinal // *n* cardenal *m*.

card index *n* fichero.

care [kɛə*] *n* cuidado; (*worry*) inquietud *f*; (*charge*) cargo, custodia // *vi*: **to ~ about** preocuparse por; **~ of** en casa de, al cuidado de; **in sb's ~** a cargo de uno; **to take ~ to** cuidarse de, tener cuidado de; **to take ~ of** cuidar; **I don't ~** no me importa; **I couldn't ~ less** eso me trae sin cuidado; **to ~ for** *vt fus* cuidar a; (*like*) querer.

career [kə'rɪə*] *n* carrera // *vi* (*also:* **~ along**) correr a toda velocidad.

carefree ['kɛəfriː] *a* despreocupado.

careful ['kɛəful] *a* cuidadoso; (*cautious*) cauteloso; **(be) ~!** ¡tenga cuidado!; **~ly** *ad* con cuidado, cuidadosamente.

careless ['kɛəlɪs] *a* descuidado; (*heedless*) poco atento; **~ness** *n* descuido, falta de atención.

caress [kə'rɛs] *n* caricia // *vt* acariciar.

caretaker ['kɛəteɪkə*] n portero, conserje m/f.

car-ferry ['ka:fɛrɪ] n transbordador m para coches.

cargo ['ka:gəu], pl ~es n cargamento, carga.

car hire n alquiler m de automóviles.

Caribbean [kærɪ'bi:ən] n: the ~ (Sea) el (Mar) Caribe.

caring ['kɛərɪŋ] a humanitario.

carnal ['ka:nl] a carnal.

carnation [ka:'neɪʃən] n clavel m.

carnival ['ka:nɪvəl] n carnaval m; (US) parque m de atracciones.

carnivorous [ka:'nɪvrəs] a carnívoro.

carol ['kærəl] n: (Christmas) ~ villancico.

carp [ka:p] n (fish) carpa; **to ~ at** or **about** vt fus quejarse de.

car park n (Brit) aparcamiento, parking m.

carpenter ['ka:pɪntə*] n carpintero/a.

carpentry ['ka:pɪntrɪ] n carpintería.

carpet ['ka:pɪt] n alfombra // vt alfombrar; ~ **slippers** npl zapatillas fpl; ~ **sweeper** n escoba mecánica.

carriage ['kærɪdʒ] n coche m; (Brit RAIL) vagón m; (for goods) transporte m; (: cost) porte m, flete m; (of typewriter) carro; (bearing) porte m; ~ **return** n (on typewriter etc) retorno del carro; ~**way** n (Brit: part of road) calzada.

carrier ['kærɪə*] n trajinista m/f; (company) empresa de transportes; ~ **bag** n (Brit) bolsa de papel or plástico.

carrot ['kærət] n zanahoria.

carry ['kærɪ] vt (subj: person) llevar; (transport) transportar; (a motion, bill) aprobar; (involve: responsibilities etc) entrañar, implicar // vi (sound) oírse; **to get carried away** (fig) entusiasmarse; **to ~ on** vi (continue) seguir (adelante), continuar; (fam: complain) quejarse, protestar // vt proseguir, continuar; **to ~ out** vt (orders) cumplir; (investigation) llevar a cabo, realizar; ~ **cot** n (Brit) cuna portátil; ~**-on** n (col: fuss) lío.

cart [ka:t] n carro, carreta // vt llevar (en carro).

carton ['ka:tən] n (box) caja (de cartón); (of yogurt) pote m.

cartoon [ka:'tu:n] n (PRESS) caricatura; (comic strip) tira cómica; (film) dibujos mpl animados; ~**ist** n dibujante m/f de historietas.

cartridge ['ka:trɪdʒ] n cartucho.

carve [ka:v] vt (meat) trinchar; (wood, stone) cincelar, esculpir; (on tree) grabar; **to ~ up** vt dividir, repartir; **carving** n (in wood etc) escultura, (obra de) talla; **carving knife** n trinchante m.

car wash n lavado de coches.

case [keɪs] n (container) caja; (MED) caso; (for jewels etc) estuche m; (LAW) causa, proceso; (Brit: also: suit~) maleta; **in ~ of** en caso de, por si; **in any ~** en todo caso; **just in ~** por si acaso; **to make a good ~** tener buenos argumentos.

cash [kæʃ] n dinero en efectivo, dinero contante // vt cobrar, hacer efectivo; **to pay (in) ~** pagar al contado; ~ **on delivery** cóbrese al entregar; ~**book** n libro de caja; ~ **card** n tarjeta f dinero; ~**desk** n (Brit) caja; ~ **dispenser** n cajero automático.

cashew [kæ'ʃu:] n (also: ~ nut) anacardo.

cashier [kæ'ʃɪə*] n cajero/a.

cashmere ['kæʃmɪə*] n casimir m, cachemira.

cash register n caja.

casing ['keɪsɪŋ] n revestimiento.

casino [kə'si:nəu] n casino.

cask [ka:sk] n tonel m, barril m.

casket ['ka:skɪt] n cofre m, estuche m; (US: coffin) ataúd m.

casserole ['kæsərəul] n (food, pot) cazuela.

cassette [kæ'sɛt] n cassette m; ~ **player/recorder** n tocacassettes m inv.

cast [ka:st] vb (pt, pp cast) vt (throw) echar, arrojar, lanzar; (skin) mudar, perder; (metal) fundir; (THEATRE): **to ~ sb as Othello** dar a alguien el papel de Otelo // vi (FISHING) lanzar // n (THEATRE) reparto; (mould) forma, molde m; (also: plaster ~) vaciado; **to ~ one's vote** votar; **to ~ off** vi (NAUT) desamarrar.

castanets [kæstə'nɛts] npl castañuelas fpl.

castaway ['ka:stəwəɪ] n náufrago/a.

caste [ka:st] n casta.

caster sugar [ka:stə*-] n (Brit) azúcar m extrafino.

Castile [kæs'ti:l] n Castilla.

casting vote ['ka:stɪŋ-] n (Brit) voto decisivo.

cast iron n hierro fundido.

castle ['ka:sl] n castillo; (CHESS) torre f.

castor ['ka:stə*] n (wheel) ruedecilla; ~ **oil** n aceite m de ricino.

castrate [kæs'treɪt] vt castrar.

casual ['kæʒjul] a (by chance) fortuito; (irregular: work etc) eventual, temporero; (unconcerned) despreocupado; (informal: clothes) de sport; ~**ly** ad de manera despreocupada.

casualty ['kæʒjultɪ] n víctima, herido; (dead) muerto; (MIL) baja.

cat [kæt] n gato.

Catalan ['kætəlæn] a, n catalán/ana m/f.

catalogue, (US) **catalog** ['kætələg] n catálogo // vt catalogar.

Catalonia [kætə'ləunɪə] n Cataluña.

catalyst ['kætəlɪst] n catalizador m.

catapult ['kætəpʌlt] n tirador m.

catarrh [kə'tɑː:*] n catarro.

catastrophe [kə'tæstrəfɪ] n catástrofe f.

catch [kætʃ] vb (pt, pp **caught**) vt coger (Sp), agarrar (LAm); (arrest) detener; (grasp) asir; (breath) suspender; (person: by surprise) sorprender; (attract: attention) ganar; (MED) contagiarse de, coger; (also: ~ up) alcanzar // vi (fire) encenderse; (in branches etc) enredarse // n (fish etc) pesca; (act of catching) cogida; (trick) trampa; (of lock) pestillo, cerradura; to ~ fire encenderse; to ~ sight of divisar; to ~ on vi (understand) caer en la cuenta; (grow popular) hacerse popular; to ~ up vi (fig) ponerse al día.

catching ['kætʃɪŋ] a (MED) contagioso.

catchment area ['kætʃmənt-] n (Brit) zona de captación.

catchphrase ['kætʃfreɪz] n lema m, eslogan m.

catchy ['kætʃɪ] a (tune) pegadizo.

categorize ['kætɪgəraɪz] vt clasificar.

category ['kætɪgərɪ] n categoría, clase f.

cater ['keɪtə*] vi: to ~ for (Brit) abastecer a; (needs) atender a; (consumers) proveer a; ~er n abastecedor(a) m/f, proveedor(a) m/f; ~ing n (trade) (ramo de la) alimentación f.

caterpillar ['kætəpɪlə*] n oruga, gusano; ~ track n rodado de oruga.

cathedral [kə'θiːdrəl] n catedral f.

catholic ['kæθəlɪk] a católico; **C~** a, n (REL) católico/a m/f.

cat's-eye ['kætsaɪ] n (Brit AUT) catafoto.

cattle ['kætl] npl ganado sg.

catty ['kætɪ] a malicioso, rencoroso.

caucus ['kɔːkəs] n (POL: local committee) comité m local; (: US: to elect candidates) comité m electoral.

caught ['kæˈ] pt, pp of **catch**.

cauliflower ['kɔlɪflauə*] n coliflor f.

cause [kɔːz] n causa, motivo, razón f // vt causar; (provoke) provocar.

caustic ['kɔːstɪk] a cáustico; (fig) mordaz.

caution ['kɔːʃən] n cautela, prudencia; (warning) advertencia, amonestación f // vt amonestar.

cautious ['kɔːʃəs] a cauteloso, prudente, precavido; ~ly ad con cautela.

cavalier [kævə'lɪə*] a arrogante, desdeñoso.

cavalry ['kævəlrɪ] n caballería.

cave [keɪv] n cueva, caverna; to ~ in vi (roof etc) derrumbarse, hundirse; ~man/woman n cavernícola m/f, troglodita m/f.

cavern ['kævən] n caverna.

caviar(e) ['kævɪɑː:*] n caviar m.

cavity ['kævɪtɪ] n hueco, cavidad f.

cavort [kə'vɔːt] vi dar cabrioladas.

CB n abbr (= Citizen's Band (Radio)) banda ciudadana.

CBI n abbr (= Confederation of British Industry) ≈ C.E.O.E. f (Sp).

cc abbr = **cubic centimetres**; = **carbon copy**.

cease [siːs] vt cesar; ~**fire** n alto m el fuego; ~**less** a incesante; ~**lessly** ad sin cesar.

cedar ['siːdə*] n cedro.

ceiling ['siːlɪŋ] n techo; (fig) límite m.

celebrate ['sɛlɪbreɪt] vt celebrar; (have a party) festejar // vi divertirse; ~d a célebre; **celebration** [-'breɪʃən] n fiesta, celebración f.

celery ['sɛlərɪ] n apio.

celibacy ['sɛlɪbəsɪ] n celibato.

cell [sɛl] n celda; (BIOL) célula; (ELEC) elemento.

cellar ['sɛlə*] n sótano; (for wine) bodega.

'cello ['tʃɛləu] n violoncelo.

cellophane ['sɛləfeɪn] n celofán m.

Celt [kɛlt, sɛlt] a, n celta m/f; ~**ic** a celta.

cement [sə'mɛnt] n cemento // vt cementar; (fig) cimentar, fortalecer; ~ **mixer** n hormigonera.

cemetery ['sɛmɪtrɪ] n cementerio.

censor ['sɛnsə*] n censor m // vt (cut) censurar; ~**ship** n censura.

censure ['sɛnʃə*] vt censurar.

census ['sɛnsəs] n censo.

cent [sɛnt] n (US: coin) centavo, céntimo; see also **per**.

centenary [sɛn'tiːnərɪ] n centenario.

center ['sɛntə*] n (US) = **centre**.

centi... [sɛntɪ] pref: ~**grade** a centígrado; ~**litre**, (US) ~**liter** n centilitro; ~**metre**, (US) ~**meter** n centímetro.

centipede ['sɛntɪpiːd] n ciempiés m inv.

central ['sɛntrəl] a central; (of house etc) céntrico; **C~ America** n Centroamérica; ~ **heating** n calefacción f central; ~**ize** vt centralizar.

centre ['sɛntə*] n centro // vt centrar; ~-**forward** n (SPORT) delantero centro; ~-**half** n (SPORT) medio centro.

century ['sɛntjurɪ] n siglo; **20th** ~ siglo veinte.

ceramic [sɪ'ræmɪk] a cerámico; ~**s** n cerámica.

cereal ['siːrɪəl] n cereal m.

cerebral ['sɛrɪbrəl] a cerebral; intelectual.

ceremony ['sɛrɪmənɪ] n ceremonia; to stand on ~ hacer ceremonias, estar de cumplido.

certain ['sɜːtən] a seguro; (correct) cierto; (person) seguro; (a particular) cierto; for ~ a ciencia cierta; ~**ly** ad desde luego, por supuesto; ~**ty** n certeza, certidumbre f, seguridad f.

certificate [sə'tɪfɪkɪt] n certificado.

certified ['sɜːtɪfaɪd] a: ~ **mail** n (US) correo certificado; ~ **public accountant (C.P.A)** n (US) contable m/f diplomado/a.

certify ['sɜːtɪfaɪ] vt certificar.

cervical ['sɜːvɪkl] a (of cervix: smear, cancer) cervical.

cervix ['sɜːvɪks] n cerviz f.

cessation [sə'seɪʃən] n cese m, suspensión f.

cesspit ['sɛspɪt] n pozo negro.

cf. abbr (= compare) cfr.

ch. abbr (= chapter) cap.

chafe [tʃeɪf] vt (rub) rozar; (irritate) irritar.

chaffinch ['tʃæfɪntʃ] n pinzón m (vulgar).

chagrin ['ʃæɡrɪn] n (annoyance) disgusto; (disappointment) desazón f.

chain [tʃeɪn] n cadena // vt (also: ~ up) encadenar; **to ~-smoke** vi fumar un cigarrillo tras otro; ~ **reaction** n reacción f en cadena; ~ **store** n tienda de una cadena, ≈ gran almacén.

chair [tʃɛə*] n silla; (armchair) sillón m; (of university) cátedra // vt (meeting) presidir; ~**lift** n telesilla; ~**man** n presidente m.

chalet ['ʃæleɪ] n chalet m.

chalk [tʃɔːk] n (GEO) creta; (for writing) tiza, gis m (LAm).

challenge ['tʃælɪndʒ] n desafío, reto // vt desafiar, retar; (statement, right) poner en duda; **to ~ sb to do sth** retar a uno a que haga algo; **challenging** a desafiante; (tone) de desafío.

chamber ['tʃeɪmbə*] n cámara, sala; ~ **of commerce** cámara de comercio; ~**maid** n camarera; ~ **music** n música de cámara.

champagne [ʃæm'peɪn] n champaña m, champán m.

champion ['tʃæmpɪən] n campeón/ona m/f; ~**ship** n campeonato.

chance [tʃɑːns] n (coincidence) casualidad f; (luck) suerte f; (fate) azar m; (opportunity) ocasión f, oportunidad f; (likelihood) posibilidad f; (risk) riesgo // vt arriesgar, probar // a fortuito, casual; **to ~ it** arriesgarse, intentarlo; **to take a ~** arriesgarse; **by ~** por casualidad.

chancellor ['tʃɑːnsələ*] n canciller m; **C~ of the Exchequer** n (Brit) Ministro de Hacienda.

chandelier [ʃændə'lɪə*] n araña (de luces).

change [tʃeɪndʒ] vt cambiar; (replace) reemplazar; (gear) cambiar de; (clothes, house) mudarse de; (exchange) trocar; (transform) transformar // vi cambiar(se); (trains) hacer transbordo; (be transformed): **to ~ into** transformarse en // n cambio; (alteration) modificación f, transformación f; (coins) suelto, sencillo; (money returned) vuelta; **to ~ one's mind** cambiar de opinión or idea; **for a ~** para variar; ~**able** a (weather) cambiable; ~ **machine** n máquina de cambio; ~**over** n (to new system) cambio.

changing ['tʃeɪndʒɪŋ] a cambiante; ~

room n (Brit) vestuario.

channel ['tʃænl] n (TV) canal m; (of river) cauce m; (of sea) estrecho; (groove, fig: medium) conducto, medio // vt (river etc) encauzar; **the (English) C~** el Canal (de la Mancha); **the C~ Islands** las Islas Normandas.

chant [tʃɑːnt] n canto // vt cantar.

chaos ['keɪɔs] n caos m.

chap [tʃæp] n (Brit col: man) tío, tipo.

chapel ['tʃæpəl] n capilla.

chaperone ['ʃæpərəʊn] n carabina.

chaplain ['tʃæplɪn] n capellán m.

chapped [tʃæpt] a agrietado.

chapter ['tʃæptə*] n capítulo.

char [tʃɑː*] vt (burn) carbonizar, chamuscar // n (Brit) = **charlady**.

character ['kærɪktə*] n carácter m, naturaleza, índole f; (in novel, film) personaje m; (role) papel m; ~**istic** [-'rɪstɪk] a característico // n característica; ~**ize** vt caracterizar.

charcoal ['tʃɑːkəʊl] n carbón m vegetal; (ART) carboncillo.

charge [tʃɑːdʒ] n carga; (LAW) cargo, acusación f; (cost) precio, coste m; (responsibility) cargo; (task) encargo // vt (LAW) acusar (with de); (gun, battery, MIL: enemy) cargar; (price) pedir; (customer) cobrar; (sb with task) encargar // vi precipitarse; (make pay) cobrar; ~**s** npl: **bank** ~**s** comisiones fpl bancarias; **free of** ~ gratis; **to reverse the** ~**s** (Brit TEL) revertir el cobro; **to take** ~ of hacerse cargo de, encargarse de; **to be in** ~ **of** estar encargado de; **how much do you** ~? ¿cuánto cobra usted?; **to** ~ **an expense (up) to sb's account** cargar algo a cuenta de alguien; ~ **card** n tarjeta de cuenta.

charitable ['tʃærɪtəbl] a caritativo.

charity ['tʃærɪtɪ] n (gen) caridad f; (organization) sociedad f benéfica.

charlady ['tʃɑːleɪdɪ] n (Brit) mujer f de la limpieza.

charlatan ['ʃɑːlətən] n farsante m/f.

charm [tʃɑːm] n encanto, atractivo // vt encantar; ~**ing** a encantador(a).

chart [tʃɑːt] n (table) cuadro; (graph) gráfica; (map) carta de navegación // vt (course) trazar.

charter ['tʃɑːtə*] vt (plane) alquilar; (ship) fletar // n (document) carta; ~**ed accountant** n (Brit) contable m/f diplomado/a; ~ **flight** n vuelo chárter.

charwoman ['tʃɑːwumən] n = **charlady**.

chase [tʃeɪs] vt (pursue) perseguir; (hunt) cazar // n persecución f; caza; **to** ~ **after** correr tras.

chasm ['kæzəm] n abismo.

chassis ['ʃæsɪ] n chasis m.

chat [tʃæt] vi (also: **have a** ~) charlar // n charla; ~ **show** n (Brit) (programa m) magazine m.

chatter ['tʃætə*] vi (person) charlar; (teeth) castañetear // n (of birds) parloteo; (of people) charla, cháchara; ~**box** n parlanchín/ina m/f.

chatty ['tʃætɪ] a (style) familiar; (person) hablador(a).

chauffeur ['ʃəufə*] n chófer m.

chauvinist ['ʃəuvɪnɪst] n (male ~) machista m; (nationalist) chovinista m/f.

cheap [tʃiːp] a barato; (joke) de mal gusto; (poor quality) de mala calidad // ad barato; ~**en** vt rebajar el precio, abaratar; ~**er** a más barato; ~**ly** ad barato, a bajo precio.

cheat [tʃiːt] vi hacer trampa // vt estafar, timar // n trampa; estafa; (person) tramposo/a.

check [tʃɛk] vt (examine) controlar; (facts) comprobar; (count) contar; (halt) parar, detener; (restrain) refrenar, restringir // n (inspection) control m, inspección f; (curb) freno; (bill) nota, cuenta; (US) = **cheque**; (pattern: gen pl) cuadro // a (also ~ed: pattern, cloth) a cuadros; **to** ~ **in** vi (in hotel, airport) registrarse // vt (luggage) facturar; **to** ~ **out** vi (of hotel) desocupar su cuarto; **to** ~ **up** vi: **to** ~ **up on sth** comprobar algo; **to** ~ **up on sb** investigar a alguien; ~**ered** a (US) = **chequered**; ~**ers** n (US) juego de damas; ~**in (desk)** n mesa de facturación; ~**ing account** n (US) cuenta corriente; ~**mate** n jaque m mate; ~**out** n caja; ~**point** n (punto de) control m; ~**room** n (US) consigna; ~**up** n (MED) reconocimiento general; (of machine) repaso.

cheek [tʃiːk] n mejilla; (impudence) descaro; ~**bone** n pómulo; ~**y** a fresco, descarado.

cheep [tʃiːp] vi piar.

cheer [tʃɪə*] vt vitorear, aplaudir; (gladden) alegrar, animar // vi aplaudir, dar vivas // n viva m; ~**s** npl aplausos mpl; ~**s!** ¡salud!; **to** ~ **up** vi animarse // vt alegrar, animar; ~**ful** a alegre.

cheerio [tʃɪərɪ'əu] excl (Brit) ¡hasta luego!

cheese [tʃiːz] n queso; ~**board** n plato de quesos.

cheetah ['tʃiːtə] n leopardo cazador.

chef [ʃɛf] n jefe/a m/f de cocina.

chemical ['kɛmɪkəl] a químico // n producto químico.

chemist ['kɛmɪst] n (Brit: pharmacist) farmacéutico/a; (scientist) químico/a; ~**ry** n química; ~**'s (shop)** n (Brit) farmacia.

cheque [tʃɛk] n (Brit) cheque m; ~**book** n libro de cheques, chequera (LAm); ~ **card** n tarjeta de cheque.

chequered ['tʃɛkəd] a (fig) accidentado.

cherish ['tʃɛrɪʃ] vt (love) querer, apreciar; (protect) cuidar; (hope etc) abrigar.

cherry ['tʃɛrɪ] n cereza.

chess [tʃɛs] n ajedrez m; ~**board** n tablero (de ajedrez); ~**man** n pieza, trebejo.

chest [tʃɛst] n (ANAT) pecho; (box) cofre m, cajón m; ~ **of drawers** n cómoda.

chestnut ['tʃɛsnʌt] n castaña; ~ **(tree)** n castaño.

chew [tʃuː] vt mascar, masticar; ~**ing gum** n chicle m.

chic [ʃiːk] a elegante.

chick [tʃɪk] n pollito, polluelo; (US col) chica.

chicken ['tʃɪkɪn] n gallina, pollo; (food) pollo; **to** ~ **out** vi (col) rajarse; ~**pox** n varicela.

chicory ['tʃɪkərɪ] n (for coffee) achicoria; (salad) escarola.

chief [tʃiːf] n jefe/a m/f // a principal; ~ **executive** n director(a) m/f general; ~**ly** ad principalmente.

chiffon ['ʃɪfɔn] n gasa.

chilblain ['tʃɪlbleɪn] n sabañón m.

child [tʃaɪld], pl ~**ren** ['tʃɪldrən] n niño/a; (offspring) hijo/a; ~**birth** n parto; ~**hood** n niñez f, infancia; ~**ish** a pueril, aniñado; ~**like** a de niño; ~ **minder** n (Brit) niñera.

Chile ['tʃɪlɪ] n Chile m; ~**an** a, n chileno/a m/f.

chill [tʃɪl] n frío; (MED) resfriado // a frío // vt enfriar; (CULIN) congelar.

chilli ['tʃɪlɪ] n (Brit) chile m, ají m (LAm).

chilly ['tʃɪlɪ] a frío.

chime [tʃaɪm] n repique m, campanada // vi repicar, sonar.

chimney ['tʃɪmnɪ] n chimenea; ~**sweep** n deshollinador m.

chimpanzee [tʃɪmpæn'ziː] n chimpancé m.

chin [tʃɪn] n mentón m, barbilla.

china ['tʃaɪnə] n porcelana; (crockery) loza.

China ['tʃaɪnə] n China; **Chinese** [tʃaɪ'niːz] a chino // n, pl inv chino/a; (LING) chino.

chink [tʃɪŋk] n (opening) grieta, hendedura; (noise) tintineo.

chip [tʃɪp] n (gen pl: CULIN: Brit) patata or papa (LAm) frita; (: US: also: **potato** ~) patata or papa frita; (of wood) astilla; (of glass, stone) lasca; (at poker) ficha; (COMPUT) chip m // vt (cup, plate) desconchar; **to** ~ **in** vi interrumpir; (contribute) compartir los gastos.

chiropodist [kɪ'rɔpədɪst] n (Brit) pedicuro/a.

chirp [tʃəːp] vi gorjear, piar.

chisel ['tʃɪzl] n (for wood) formón m; (for stone) cincel m.

chit [tʃɪt] n nota.

chitchat ['tʃɪttʃæt] n chismes mpl, habladurías fpl.

chivalry [ʃɪvəlrɪ] n caballerosidad f.

chives [tʃaɪvz] *npl* cebollinos *mpl*.
chlorine ['klɔːriːn] *n* cloro.
chock [tʃɔk]: **~-a-block**, **~-full** *a* atestado.
chocolate ['tʃɔklɪt] *n* chocolate *m*.
choice [tʃɔɪs] *n* elección *f* // *a* escogido.
choir ['kwaɪə*] *n* coro; **~boy** *n* corista *m*.
choke [tʃəuk] *vi* sofocarse; (*on food*) atragantarse // *vt* ahogar, sofocar; (*block*) obstruir // *n* (*AUT*) estárter *m*.
choose [tʃuːz], *pt* **chose**, *pp* **chosen** *vt* escoger, elegir; (*team*) seleccionar.
choosy ['tʃuːzɪ] *a* remilgado.
chop [tʃɔp] *vt* (*wood*) cortar, tajar; (*CULIN: also*: **~ up**) picar // *n* golpe *m* cortante; (*CULIN*) chuleta; **~s** *npl* (*jaws*) boca *sg*, labios *mpl*.
chopper ['tʃɔpə*] *n* (*helicopter*) helicóptero.
choppy ['tʃɔpɪ] *a* (*sea*) picado, agitado.
chopsticks ['tʃɔpstɪks] *npl* palillos *mpl*.
chord [kɔːd] *n* (*MUS*) acorde *m*.
chore [tʃɔː*] *n* faena, tarea; (*routine task*) trabajo rutinario.
chortle ['tʃɔːtl] *vi* reír entre dientes.
chorus ['kɔːrəs] *n* coro; (*repeated part of song*) estribillo.
chose [tʃəuz] *pt of* choose.
chosen ['tʃəuzn] *pp of* choose.
Christ [kraɪst] *n* Cristo.
christen ['krɪsn] *vt* bautizar.
Christian ['krɪstɪən] *a, n* cristiano/a *m/f*; **~ity** [-'ænɪtɪ] *n* cristianismo; **~ name** *n* nombre *m* de pila.
Christmas ['krɪsməs] *n* Navidad *f*; Merry **~!** ¡Felices Pascuas!; **~ card** *n* crismas *m inv*, tarjeta de Navidad; **~ Day** *n* día *m* de Navidad; **~ Eve** *n* Nochebuena; **~ tree** *n* árbol *m* de Navidad.
chrome [krəum] *n* = **chromium plating**.
chromium ['krəumɪəm] *n* cromo; **~ plating** *n* cromado.
chronic ['krɔnɪk] *a* crónico.
chronicle ['krɔnɪkl] *n* crónica.
chronological [krɔnə'lɔdʒɪkəl] *a* cronológico.
chrysanthemum [krɪ'sænθəməm] *n* crisantemo.
chubby ['tʃʌbɪ] *a* rechoncho.
chuck [tʃʌk] *vt* lanzar, arrojar; **to ~ out** *vt* echar (fuera), tirar; **to ~ (up)** *vt* (*Brit*) abandonar.
chuckle ['tʃʌkl] *vi* reírse entre dientes.
chug [tʃʌg] *vi* resoplar.
chum [tʃʌm] *n* compañero/a.
chunk [tʃʌŋk] *n* pedazo, trozo.
church [tʃɜːtʃ] *n* iglesia; **~yard** *n* campo santo.
churlish ['tʃɜːlɪʃ] *a* grosero.
churn [tʃɜːn] *n* (*for butter*) mantequera; (*for milk*) lechera; **to ~ out** *vt* producir en serie.
chute [ʃuːt] *n* (*also*: **rubbish ~**) vertede-

ro; (*Brit: children's slide*) tobogán *m*.
chutney ['tʃʌtnɪ] *n* salsa picante.
CIA *n abbr* (*US*: = *Central Intelligence Agency*) CIA *f*.
CID *n abbr* (*Brit*: = *Criminal Investigation Department*) ≈ B.I.C. *f* (*Sp*).
cider ['saɪdə*] *n* sidra.
cigar [sɪ'gɑː*] *n* puro.
cigarette [sɪgə'rɛt] *n* cigarrillo, cigarro (*LAm*); pitillo; **~ case** *n* pitillera; **~ end** *n* colilla; **~ holder** *n* boquilla.
Cinderella [sɪndə'rɛlə] *n* Cenicienta.
cine ['sɪnɪ]: **~-camera** *n* (*Brit*) cámara cinematográfica; **~-film** *n* (*Brit*) película de cine.
cinema ['sɪnəmə] *n* cine *m*.
cinnamon ['sɪnəmən] *n* canela.
cipher ['saɪfə*] *n* cifra.
circle ['sɜːkl] *n* círculo; (*in theatre*) anfiteatro // *vi* dar vueltas // *vt* (*surround*) rodear, cercar; (*move round*) dar la vuelta a.
circuit ['sɜːkɪt] *n* circuito; (*track*) pista; (*lap*) vuelta; **~ous** [sɜː'kjuɪtəs] *a* indirecto.
circular ['sɜːkjulə*] *a* circular // *n* circular *f*.
circulate ['sɜːkjuleɪt] *vi* circular // *vt* poner en circulación; **circulation** [-'leɪʃən] *n* circulación *f*; (*of newspaper*) tirada.
circumcise ['sɜːkəmsaɪz] *vt* circuncidar.
circumstances ['sɜːkəmstənsɪz] *npl* circunstancias *fpl*; (*financial condition*) situación *f* económica.
circumvent ['sɜːkəmvɛnt] *vt* burlar.
circus ['sɜːkəs] *n* circo.
cistern ['sɪstən] *n* tanque *m*, depósito; (*in toilet*) cisterna.
citizen ['sɪtɪzn] *n* (*POL*) ciudadano/a; (*of city*) vecino/a, habitante *m/f*; **~ship** *n* ciudadanía.
citrus fruits ['sɪtrəs-] *npl* agrios *mpl*.
city ['sɪtɪ] *n* ciudad *f*; **the C~** centro financiero de Londres.
civic ['sɪvɪk] *a* cívico, municipal; **~ centre** *n* (*Brit*) centro público.
civil ['sɪvɪl] *a* civil; (*polite*) atento, cortés; (*well-bred*) educado; **~ defence** *n* protección *f* civil; **~ engineer** *n* ingeniero civil; **~ian** [sɪ'vɪlɪən] *a* civil (*no militar*) // *n* civil *m/f*, paisano/a; **~ian clothing** *n* ropa de paisano.
civilization [sɪvɪlaɪ'zeɪʃən] *n* civilización *f*.
civilized ['sɪvɪlaɪzd] *a* civilizado.
civil: **~ law** *n* derecho civil; **~ servant** *n* funcionario/a del Estado; **C~ Service** *n* administración *f* pública; **~ war** *n* guerra civil.
clad [klæd] *a*: **~ (in)** vestido (de).
claim [kleɪm] *vt* exigir, reclamar; (*rights etc*) reivindicar; (*assert*) pretender // *vi* (*for insurance*) reclamar // *n* reclamación *f*; (*LAW*) demanda; (*pretension*) pretensión *f*; **~ant** *n* (*ADMIN, LAW*) de-

mandante *m/f*.

clairvoyant [klɛɔ'vɔɪɔnt] *n* clarividento *m/f*.

clam [klæm] *n* almeja.

clamber ['klæmbə*] *vi* trepar.

clammy ['klæmɪ] *a* (*cold*) frío y húmedo; (*sticky*) pegajoso.

clamour ['klæmə*] *vi*: to ~ for clamar por, pedir a voces.

clamp [klæmp] *n* abrazadera, grapa // *vt* afianzar (con abrazadera); **to ~ down on** *vt fus* (*subj: government, police*) reforzar la lucha contra.

clang [klæŋ] *n* estruendo // *vi* sonar, hacer estruendo.

clap [klæp] *vi* aplaudir; **~ping** *n* aplausos *mpl*.

claret ['klærɔt] *n* clarete *m*.

clarify ['klærɪfaɪ] *vt* aclarar.

clarinet [klærɪ'nɛt] *n* clarinete *m*.

clarity ['klærɪtɪ] *n* claridad *f*.

clash [klæʃ] *n* estruendo; (*fig*) choque *m* // *vi* (*battle*) chocar; (*disagree*) estar en desacuerdo.

clasp [klɑːsp] *n* broche *m*; ' (*on jewels*) cierre *m* // *vt* abrochar; (*hand*) apretar; (*embrace*) abrazar.

class [klɑːs] *n* (*gen*) clase *f* // *a* clasista, de clase // *vt* clasificar.

classic ['klæsɪk] *a*, *n* clásico; **~al** *a* clásico.

classified ['klæsɪfaɪd] *a* (*information*) reservado; **~ advertisement** *n* anuncio por palabras.

classify ['klæsɪfaɪ] *vt* clasificar.

classmate ['klɑːsmeɪt] *n* compañero/a de clase.

classroom ['klɑːsrum] *n* aula.

clatter ['klætə*] *n* ruido, estruendo; (*of hooves*) trápala // *vi* hacer ruido *or* estruendo.

clause [klɔːz] *n* cláusula; (*LING*) oración *f*.

claw [klɔː] *n* (*of cat*) uña; (*of bird of prey*) garra; (*of lobster*) pinza; (*TECH*) garfio; **to ~ at** *vt fus* arañar; (*tear*) desgarrar.

clay [kleɪ] *n* arcilla.

clean [kliːn] *a* limpio; (*clear*) neto, bien definido // *vt* limpiar; **to ~ out** *vt* limpiar; **to ~ up** *vt* limpiar, asear; **~er** *n* (*person*) asistenta; **~ing** *n* limpieza; **~liness** ['klɛnlɪnɪs] *n* limpieza.

cleanse [klɛnz] *vt* limpiar; **~r** *n* detergente *m*; (*for face*) crema limpiadora; **cleansing department** *n* (*Brit*) departamento de limpieza.

clear [klɪə*] *a* claro; (*road, way*) libre // *vt* (*space*) despejar, limpiar; (*LAW: suspect*) absolver; (*obstacle*) salvar, saltar por encima de; (*debt*) liquidar; (*cheque*) pasar por un banco // *vi* (*fog etc*) despejarse // *ad*: ~ of a distancia de; **to ~ the table** recoger *or* levantar la mesa; **to ~ up** *vt* limpiar; (*mystery*) aclarar, resol-

ver; **~ance** *n* (*removal*) despeje *m*; (*pormiooion*) acreditación *f*, **~-cut** *a* bien definido, nítido; **~ing** *n* (*in wood*) claro; **~ing bank** *n* (*Brit*) cámara de compensación; **~ly** *ad* claramente; **~way** *n* (*Brit*) carretera donde no se puede aparcar.

cleaver ['kliːvə] *n* cuchilla (de carnicero).

clef [klɛf] *n* (*MUS*) clave *f*.

cleft [klɛft] *n* (*in rock*) grieta, hendedura.

clench [klɛntʃ] *vt* apretar, cerrar.

clergy ['klɔːdʒɪ] *n* clero; **~man** *n* clérigo.

clerical ['klɛrɪkəl] *a* de oficina; (*REL*) clerical.

clerk [klɑːk, (*US*) klɔːrk] *n* oficinista *m/f*; (*US*) dependiente/a *m/f*, vendedor(a) *m/f*.

clever ['klɛvə*] *a* (*mentally*) inteligente, listo; (*skilful*) hábil; (*device, arrangement*) ingenioso.

click [klɪk] *vt* (*tongue*) chasquear; (*heels*) taconear.

client ['klaɪənt] *n* cliente *m/f*.

cliff [klɪf] *n* acantilado.

climate ['klaɪmɪt] *n* clima *m*.

climax ['klaɪmæks] *n* colmo, punto culminante; (*sexual*) clímax *m*.

climb [klaɪm] *vi* subir, trepar // *vt* (*stairs*) subir; (*tree*) trepar a; (*mountain*) escalar // *n* subida; **~-down** *n* vuelta atrás; **~er** *n* alpinista *m/f*, andinista *m/f* (*LAm*); **~ing** *n* alpinismo, andinismo (*LAm*).

clinch [klɪntʃ] *vt* (*deal*) cerrar; (*argument*) remachar.

cling [klɪŋ], *pt*, *pp* **clung** [klʌŋ] *vi*: to ~ to agarrarse a; (*clothes*) pegarse a.

clinic ['klɪnɪk] *n* clínica.

clink [klɪŋk] *vi* tintinar.

clip [klɪp] *n* (*for hair*) horquilla; (*also*: paper ~) sujetapapeles *m inv*, clip *m*; (*clamp*) grapa // *vt* (*cut*) cortar; (*hedge*) podar; (*also*: ~ **together**) unir; **~pers** *npl* (*for gardening*) tijeras *fpl*; (*for hair*) maquinilla *sg*; (*for nails*) cortañas *m inv*; **~ping** *n* (*newspaper*) recorte *m*.

clique [kliːk] *n* camarilla.

cloak [kləuk] *n* capa, manto // *vt* (*fig*) encubrir, disimular; **~room** *n* guardarropa; (*Brit: WC*) lavabo, aseos *mpl*, baño (*LAm*).

clock [klɔk] *n* reloj *m*; (*in taxi*) taxímetro; **to ~ in** *or* **on** *vi* fichar, picar; **to ~ off** *or* **out** *vi* fichar *or* picar la salida; **~wise** *ad* en el sentido de las agujas del reloj; **~work** *n* aparato de relojería // *a* (*toy*) de cuerda.

clog [klɔg] *n* zueco, chanclo // *vt* atascar // *vi* atascarse.

cloister ['klɔɪstə*] *n* claustro.

close *a*, *ad and derivatives* [kləus] *a* cercano, próximo; (*near*): ~ **(to)** cerca (de); (*print, weave*) tupido, compacto;

(*friend*) íntimo; (*connection*) estrecho; (*examination*) detallado, minucioso; (*weather*) bochornoso; (*atmosphere*) sofocante; (*room*) mal ventilado; **to have a ~ shave** (*fig*) escaparse por un pelo // *ad* cerca; **~ by**, **~ at hand** *a*, *ad* muy cerca; **~ to** *prep* cerca de // *vb and derivatives* [kləuz] *vt* (*shut*) cerrar; (*end*) concluir, terminar // *vi* (*shop etc*) cerrarse; (*end*) concluirse, terminarse // *n* (*end*) fin *m*, final *m*, conclusión *f*; **to ~ down** *vi* cerrarse definitivamente; **~d** *a* (*shop etc*) cerrado; **~d shop** *n* taller *m* gremial; **~-knit** *a* (*fig*) muy unido; **~ly** *ad* (*study*) con detalle; (*listen*) con atención; (*watch*) de cerca.

closet ['klɔzıt] *n* (*cupboard*) armario.

close-up ['kləusʌp] *n* primer plano.

closure ['kləuʒə*] *n* cierre *m*.

clot [klɔt] *n* (*gen: blood* **~**) embolia; (*fam: idiot*) imbécil *m/f* // *vi* (*blood*) coagularse.

cloth [klɔθ] *n* (*material*) tela, paño; (*rag*) trapo.

clothe [kləuð] *vt* vestir; (*fig*) revestir; **~s** *npl* ropa *sg*; **~s brush** *n* cepillo (para la ropa); **~s line** *n* cuerda (para tender la ropa); **~s peg**, (*US*) **~s pin** *n* pinza.

clothing ['klauðıŋ] *n* = **clothes**.

cloud [klaud] *n* nube *f*; (*storm* **~**) nubarrón *m*; **~y** *a* nublado, nubloso; (*liquid*) turbio.

clout [klaut] *vt* dar un tortazo a.

clove [kləuv] *n* clavo; **~ of garlic** diente *m* de ajo.

clover ['kləuvə*] *n* trébol *m*.

clown [klaun] *n* payaso // *vi* (*also:* **~ about**, **~ around**) hacer el payaso.

cloying ['klɔıŋ] *a* (*taste*) empalagoso.

club [klʌb] *n* (*society*) club *m*; (*weapon*) porra, cachiporra; (*also: golf* **~**) palo // *vt* aporrear // *vi*: **to ~ together** (*join forces*) unir fuerzas; **~s** *npl* (*CARDS*) tréboles *mpl*; **~ car** *n* (*US RAIL*) coche *m* sálon; **~house** *n* local social, sobre todo en clubs deportivos.

cluck [klʌk] *vi* cloquear.

clue [klu:] *n* pista; (*in crosswords*) indicación *f*; **I haven't a ~** no tengo ni idea.

clump [klʌmp] *n* (*of trees*) grupo.

clumsy ['klʌmzı] *a* (*person*) torpe, desmañado; (*tool*) difícil de manejar.

clung [klʌŋ] *pt, pp of* **cling**.

cluster ['klʌstə*] *n* grupo; (*BOT*) racimo // *vi* agruparse, apiñarse.

clutch [klʌtʃ] *n* (*AUT*) embrague *m*; (*pedal*) pedal *m* de embrague; **to fall into sb's ~es** caer en las garras de alguien // *vt* asir; agarrar.

clutter ['klʌtə*] *vt* atestar.

cm *abbr* (= *centimetre*) cm.

CND *n abbr* (= *Campaign for Nuclear Disarmament*) plataforma pro desarme nuclear.

Co. *abbr* = **county**; = **company**.

c/o *abbr* (= *care of*) c/a, a/c.

coach [kəutʃ] *n* (*bus*) autocar *m* (*Sp*), autobús *m*; (*horse-drawn*) coche *m*; (*of train*) vagón *m*, coche *m*; (*SPORT*) entrenador(a) *m/f*, instructor(a) *m/f* // *vt* (*SPORT*) entrenar; (*student*) preparar, enseñar; **~ trip** *n* excursión *f* en autocar.

coal [kəul] *n* carbón *m*; **~ face** *n* frente *m* de carbón; **~field** *n* yacimiento de carbón.

coalition [kəuə'lıʃən] *n* coalición *f*.

coal man, **coal merchant** *n* carbonero.

coalmine ['kəulmaın] *n* mina de carbón.

coarse [kɔ:s] *a* basto, burdo; (*vulgar*) grosero, ordinario.

coast [kəust] *n* costa, litoral *m* // *vi* (*AUT*) ir en punto muerto; **~al** *a* costero, costanero; **~guard** *n* guardacostas *m inv*; **~line** *n* litoral *m*.

coat [kəut] *n* (*jacket*) chaqueta; (*overcoat*) abrigo; (*of animal*) pelo, lana; (*of paint*) mano *f*, capa // *vt* cubrir, revestir; **~ of arms** *n* escudo de armas; **~ hanger** *n* percha, gancho (*LAm*); **~ing** *n* capa, baño.

coax [kəuks] *vt* engatusar.

cob [kɔb] *n see* **corn**.

cobbler ['kɔblə*] *n* zapatero (remendón).

cobbles ['kɔblz], **cobblestones** ['kɔblstəunz] *npl* adoquines *mpl*.

cobweb ['kɔbweb] *n* telaraña.

cocaine [kə'keın] *n* cocaína.

cock [kɔk] *n* (*rooster*) gallo; (*male bird*) macho // *vt* (*gun*) amartillar; **~erel** *n* gallito; **~-eyed** *a* (*fig: crooked*) torcido; (: *idea*) disparatado.

cockle ['kɔkl] *n* berberecho.

cockney ['kɔknı] *n* habitante *m/f* de ciertos barrios de Londres.

cockpit ['kɔkpıt] *n* (*in aircraft*) cabina.

cockroach ['kɔkrəutʃ] *n* cucaracha.

cocktail ['kɔkteıl] *n* coctel *m*, cóctel *m*; **~ cabinet** *n* mueble-bar *m*; **~ party** *n* coctel *m*, cóctel *m*.

cocoa ['kəukəu] *n* cacao; (*drink*) chocolate *m*.

coconut ['kəukənʌt] *n* coco.

cod [kɔd] *n* bacalao.

C.O.D. *abbr* (= *cash on delivery*) C.A.E.

code [kəud] *n* código; (*cipher*) clave *f*.

cod-liver oil ['kɔdlıvə*-] *n* aceite *m* de hígado de bacalao.

coercion [kəu'ə:ʃən] *n* coacción *f*.

coffee ['kɔfı] *n* café *m*; **~ bar** *n* (*Brit*) cafetería; **~ break** *n* descanso (para tomar café); **~pot** *n* cafetera; **~ table** *n* mesita (para servir el café).

coffin ['kɔfın] *n* ataúd *m*.

cog [kɔg] *n* diente *m*.

cogent ['kəudʒənt] *a* convincente.

cognac ['kɔnjæk] *n* coñac *m*.

coil [kɔıl] *n* rollo; (*rope*) adujada;

(*ELEC*) bobina, carrete *m*; (*contraceptive*) espiral *f* // *vt* enrollar.

coin [kɔɪn] *n* moneda // *vt* (*word*) inventar, idear; **~age** *n* moneda; **~box** *n* (*Brit*) cabina telefónica.

coincide [kəʊɪn'saɪd] *vi* coincidir; (*agree*) estar de acuerdo; **~nce** [kəʊ'ɪnsɪdəns] *n* casualidad *f*.

coke [kəʊk] *n* (*coal*) coque *m*.

Coke ® [kəʊk] *n* Coca Cola ®.

colander ['kɔləndə*] *n* colador *m*, escurridor *m*.

cold [kəʊld] *a* frío // *n* frío; (*MED*) resfriado; it's ~ hace frío; to be ~ tener frío; to catch ~ resfriarse, acatarrarse; in ~ blood a sangre fría; ~ sore *n* herpes *m* labial.

coleslaw ['kəʊlslɔ:] *n* especie de ensalada de col.

colic ['kɔlɪk] *n* cólico.

collapse [kə'læps] *vi* (*gen*) hundirse, derrumbarse; (*MED*) sufrir un colapso // *n* (*gen*) hundimiento; (*MED*) colapso; **collapsible** *a* plegable.

collar ['kɔlə*] *n* (*of coat, shirt*) cuello; **~bone** *n* clavícula.

collateral [kɔ'lætərəl] *n* garantía colateral.

colleague ['kɔli:g] *n* colega *m/f*.

collect [kə'lɛkt] *vt* reunir; (*as a hobby*) coleccionar; (*Brit: call and pick up*) recoger; (*wages*) cobrar; (*debts*) recaudar; (*donations, subscriptions*) colectar // *vi* reunirse; coleccionar; to call ~ (*US TEL*) llamar a cobro revertido; **~ion** [kə'lɛkʃən] *n* colección *f*; (*of post*) recogida.

collector [kə'lɛktə*] *n* coleccionista *m/f*; (*of taxes etc*) recaudador(a) *m/f*.

college ['kɔlɪdʒ] *n* colegio.

collide [kə'laɪd] *vi* chocar.

collie ['kɔlɪ] *n* perro pastor.

colliery ['kɔlɪərɪ] *n* (*Brit*) mina de carbón.

collision [kə'lɪʒən] *n* choque *m*.

colloquial [kə'ləʊkwɪəl] *a* familiar, coloquial.

collusion [kə'lu:ʒən] *n* confabulación *f*, connivencia.

cologne [kə'ləʊn] *n* = eau de cologne.

Colombia [kə'lɔmbɪə] *n* Colombia; **Colombian** *a*, *n* colombiano/a.

colon ['kəʊlən] *n* (*sign*) dos puntos; (*MED*) colón *m*.

colonel ['kɔ:nl] *n* coronel *m*.

colonial [kə'ləʊnɪəl] *a* colonial.

colony ['kɔlənɪ] *n* colonia.

colour, (*US*) **color** ['kʌlə*] *n* color *m* // *vt* color(e)ar (al pastel); (*dye*) teñir // *vi* (*blush*) sonrojarse; **~s** *npl* (*of party, club*) colores *mpl*; ~ **bar** *n* segregación *f* racial; **~-blind** *a* daltoniano; **~ed** *a* de color; (*photo*) en color; ~ **film** *n* película en color; **~ful** *a* lleno de color; (*person*)

excéntrico; **~ing** *n* colorido; **~less** *a* incoloro, sin color; ~ **scheme** *n* combinación *f* de colores; ~ **television** *n* televisión *f* en color.

colt [kəʊlt] *n* potro.

column ['kɔləm] *n* columna; **~ist** ['kɔləmnɪst] *n* columnista *m/f*.

coma ['kəʊmə] *n* coma *m*.

comb [kəʊm] *n* peine *m*; (*ornamental*) peineta // *vt* (*hair*) peinar; (*area*) registrar a fondo.

combat ['kɔmbæt] *n* combate *m* // *vt* combatir.

combination [kɔmbɪ'neɪʃən] *n* (*gen*) combinación *f*.

combine [kəm'baɪn] *vt* combinar; (*qualities*) reunir // *vi* combinarse // *n* ['kɔmbaɪn] (*ECON*) cartel *m*; ~ **(harvester)** *n* cosechadora.

come [kʌm], *pt* **came**, *pp* **come** *vi* venir; to ~ **undone** desatarse; to ~ **loose** aflojarse; to ~ **about** *vi* suceder, ocurrir; to ~ **across** *vt fus* (*person*) topar con; (*thing*) dar con; to ~ **away** *vi* marcharse; desprenderse; to ~ **back** *vi* volver; to ~ **by** *vt fus* (*acquire*) conseguir; to ~ **down** *vi* bajar; (*buildings*) ser derribado; derrumbarse; to ~ **forward** *vi* presentarse; to ~ **from** *vt fus* ser de; to ~ **in** *vi* entrar; (*train*) llegar; (*fashion*) ponerse de moda; to ~ **in for** *vt fus* (*criticism etc*) merecer; to ~ **into** *vt fus* (*money*) heredar; to ~ **off** *vi* (*button*) soltarse, desprenderse; (*succeed*) salir bien; to ~ **on** *vi* (*pupil, work, project*) desarrollarse; (*lights*) encenderse; ~ **on!** ¡vamos!; to ~ **out** *vi* salir; (*book*) aparecer; (*be revealed*) salir a luz; (*strike*) declararse en huelga; to ~ **out for/against** declararse por/contra; to ~ **round** *vi* (*after faint, operation*) volver en sí; to ~ **to** *vi* volver en sí; (*total*) sumar; to ~ **up** *vi* subir; (*sun*) salir; (*problem*) surgir; to ~ **up against** *vt fus* (*resistance, difficulties*) tropezar con; to ~ **up with** *vt fus* (*idea*) sugerir, proponer; to ~ **upon** *vt fus* dar *or* topar con; **~back** *n*: to make a **~back** (*THEATRE*) volver a las tablas.

comedian [kə'mi:dɪən] *n* cómico; **comedienne** [-'ɛn] *n* cómica.

comedown ['kʌmdaʊn] *n* revés *m*, bajón *m*.

comedy ['kɔmɪdɪ] *n* comedia.

comet ['kɔmɪt] *n* cometa *m*.

comeuppance [kʌm'ʌpəns] *n*: to get one's ~ llevar su merecido.

comfort ['kʌmfət] *n* comodidad *f*, confort *m*; (*well-being*) bienestar *m*; (*solace*) consuelo; (*relief*) alivio // *vt* consolar; **~able** *a* cómodo; **~ably** *ad* (*sit*) cómodamente; (*live*) holgadamente; **~er** *n* (*US: pacifier*) chupete *m*; (: *bed cover*) colcha; ~ **station** *n* (*US*) servicios *mpl*.

comic ['kɔmɪk] *a* (*also*: **~al**) cómico // *n*

(*for children*) tebeo; (*for adults*) comic *m*; ~ **strip** *n* tira cómica.

coming ['kʌmɪŋ] *n* venida, llegada // *a* que viene; ~(s) **and going**(s) *n*(*pl*) ir y venir *m*, ajetreo.

comma ['kɔmə] *n* coma.

command [kə'mɑːnd] *n* orden *f*, mandato; (*MIL*: *authority*) mando; (*mastery*) dominio // *vt* (*troops*) mandar; (*give orders to*) mandar, ordenar; (*be able to get*) disponer de; (*deserve*) merecer; ~**eer** [kɔmən'dɪə*] *vt* requisar; ~**er** *n* (*MIL*) comandante *m/f*, jefe/a *m/f*; ~**ment** *n* (*REL*) mandamiento.

commando [kə'mɑːndəu] *n* comando.

commemorate [kə'memərert] *vt* conmemorar.

commence [kə'mens] *vt*, *vi* comenzar, empezar.

commend [kə'mend] *vt* (*praise*) elogiar, alabar; (*recommend*) recomendar; (*entrust*) encomendar.

commensurate [kə'menfərɪt] *a*: ~ **with** en proporción a, que corresponde a.

comment ['kɔment] *n* comentario // *vi*: to ~ **on** hacer comentarios sobre; ~**ary** ['kɔməntərɪ] *n* comentario; ~**ator** ['kɔməntertə*] *n* comentarista *m/f*.

commerce ['kɔmɔːs] *n* comercio.

commercial [kə'mɔːʃəl] *a* comercial // *n* (*TV*: *also*: ~ **break**) anuncio.

commiserate [kə'mɪzərert] *vi*: to ~ **with** compadecerse de, condolerse de.

commission [kə'mɪʃən] *n* (*committee*, *fee*) comisión *f*; (*act*) perpetración *f* // *vt* (*MIL*) nombrar; (*work of art*) encargar; **out of** ~ fuera de servicio; ~**aire** [kəmɪʃə'neə*] *n* (*Brit*) portero; ~**er** *n* comisario; (*POLICE*) comisario *m* de policía.

commit [kə'mɪt] *vt* (*act*) cometer; (*to sb's care*) entregar; to ~ **o.s.** (**to do**) comprometerse (a hacer); to ~ **suicide** suicidarse; ~**ment** *n* compromiso.

committee [kə'mɪtɪ] *n* comité *m*.

commodity [kə'mɔdɪtɪ] *n* mercancía.

common ['kɔmən] *a* (*gen*) común; (*pej*) ordinario // *n* campo común; **the C~s** *npl* (*Brit*) (la Cámara de) los Comunes *mpl*; **in** ~ en común; ~**er** *n* plebeyo; ~ **law** *n* ley *f* consuetudinaria; ~**ly** *ad* comúnmente; **C~ Market** *n* Mercado Común; ~**place** *a* de lo más común; ~**room** *n* sala común; ~ **sense** *n* sentido común; **the C~wealth** *n* la Mancomunidad (Británica).

commotion [kə'məuʃən] *n* tumulto, confusión *f*.

commune ['kɔmjuːn] *n* (*group*) comuna // *vi* [kə'mjuːn]: to ~ **with** comulgar or conversar con.

communicate [kə'mjuːnɪkert] *vt* comunicar // *vi*: to ~ (**with**) comunicarse (con).

communication [kəmjuːnɪ'keɪʃən] *n* comunicación *f*; ~ **cord** *n* (*Brit*) timbre

m de alarma.

communion [kə'mjuːnɪən] *n* (*also*: **Holy C~**) comunión *f*.

communiqué [kə'mjuːnɪkeɪ] *n* comunicado, parte *m*.

communism ['kɔmjunɪzəm] *n* comunismo; **communist** *a*, *n* comunista *m/f*.

community [kə'mjuːnɪtɪ] *n* comunidad *f*; (*large group*) colectividad *f*; (*local*) vecindario; ~ **centre** *n* centro social; ~ **chest** *n* (*US*) arca comunitaria, fondo común.

commutation ticket [kɔmju'teɪʃən-] *n* (*US*) billete *m* de abono.

commute [kə'mjuːt] *vi* viajar a diario de la casa al trabajo // *vt* conmutar; ~**r** *n* persona (que ... *see vi*).

compact [kəm'pækt] *a* compacto // *n* ['kɔmpækt] (*pact*) pacto; (*also*: **powder** ~) polvera; ~ **disc** *n* compact disc *m*.

companion [kəm'pænɪən] *n* compañero/a; ~**ship** *n* compañerismo.

company ['kʌmpənɪ] *n* (*gen*) compañía; (*COMM*) sociedad *f*, compañía; **to keep sb** ~ acompañar a uno; ~ **secretary** *n* (*Brit*) secretario/a de compañía.

comparative [kəm'pærətɪv] *a* relativo; ~**ly** *ad* (*relatively*) relativamente.

compare [kəm'peə*] *vt* comparar; (*set side by side*) cotejar // *vi*: to ~ (**with**) compararse (con); **comparison** [-'pærɪsn] *n* comparación *f*; cotejo.

compartment [kəm'pɑːtmənt] *n* (*also*: *RAIL*) departamento.

compass ['kʌmpəs] *n* brújula; ~**es** *npl* compás *msg*.

compassion [kəm'pæʃən] *n* compasión *f*; ~**ate** *a* compasivo.

compatible [kəm'pætɪbl] *a* compatible.

compel [kəm'pel] *vt* obligar; ~**ling** *a* (*fig*: *argument*) convincente.

compensate ['kɔmpənseɪt] *vt* compensar // *vi*: to ~ **for** compensar; **compensation** [-'seɪʃən] *n* (*for loss*) indemnización *f*.

compère ['kɔmpeə*] *n* presentador *m*.

compete [kəm'piːt] *vi* (*take part*) tomar parte, concurrir; (*vie with*) competir, hacer competencia.

competence ['kɔmpɪtəns] *n* capacidad *f*, aptitud *f*.

competent ['kɔmpɪtənt] *a* competente, capaz.

competition [kɔmpɪ'tɪʃən] *n* (*contest*) concurso; (*ECON*, *rivalry*) competencia.

competitive [kəm'petɪtɪv] *a* (*ECON*, *SPORT*) competitivo; (*spirit*) competidor(a), de competencia.

competitor [kəm'petɪtə*] *n* (*rival*) competidor(a) *m/f*; (*participant*) concursante *m/f*.

compile [kəm'paɪl] *vt* recopilar.

complacency [kəm'pleɪsnsɪ] *n* autosatisfacción *f*.

complacent [kəm'pleɪsənt] a autocomplaciente.

complain [kəm'pleɪn] vi (gen) quejarse; (COMM) reclamar; ~t n (gen) queja; reclamación f; (LAW) demanda; (MED) enfermedad f.

complement ['kɒmplɪmənt] n complemento; (especially of ship's crew) dotación f // [-ment] vt (enhance) complementar; ~ary [kɒmplɪ'mentərɪ] a complementario.

complete [kəm'pli:t] a (full) completo; (finished) acabado // vt (fulfil) completar; (finish) acabar; (a form) llenar; ~ly ad completamente; **completion** [-'pli:ʃən] n terminación f.

complex ['kɒmpleks] a, n complejo.

complexion [kəm'plekʃən] n (of face) tez f, cutis m; (fig) aspecto.

compliance [kəm'plaɪəns] n (submission) sumisión f; (agreement) conformidad f; **in** ~ **with** de acuerdo con.

complicate ['kɒmplɪkeɪt] vt complicar; ~d a complicado; **complication** [-'keɪʃən] n complicación f.

complicity [kəm'plɪsɪtɪ] n complicidad f.

compliment n ['kɒmplɪmənt] (formal) cumplido; (flirtation) piropo // vt felicitar; ~s npl saludos mpl; **to pay sb a** ~ (formal) hacer cumplidos a alguien; (flirt) piropear o echar piropos a alguien; ~ary [-'mentərɪ] a lisonjero; (free) de favor.

comply [kəm'plaɪ] vi: **to** ~ **with** cumplir con.

component [kəm'pəunənt] a componente // n (TECH) pieza.

compose [kəm'pəuz] vt componer; **to** ~ **o.s.** tranquilizarse; ~d a sosegado; ~r n (MUS) compositor(a) m/f.

composite ['kɒmpəzɪt] a compuesto.

composition [kɒmpə'zɪʃən] n composición f.

compost ['kɒmpɒst] n abono.

composure [kəm'pəuʒə*] n serenidad f, calma.

compound ['kɒmpaund] n (CHEM) compuesto; (LING) palabra compuesta; (enclosure) recinto // a (gen) compuesto; (fracture) complicado.

comprehend [kɒmprɪ'hend] vt comprender; **comprehension** [-'henʃən] n comprensión f.

comprehensive [kɒmprɪ'hensɪv] a (broad) extenso; (general) de conjunto; (INSURANCE) contra todo riesgo; ~ **(school)** n centro estatal de enseñanza secundaria; ≈ Instituto Nacional de Bachillerato (Sp).

compress [kəm'pres] vt comprimir // n ['kɒmpres] (MED) compresa.

comprise [kəm'praɪz] vt (also: **be** ~**d of**) comprender, constar de.

compromise ['kɒmprəmaɪz] n (agreement) arreglo // vt comprometer // vi

transigir.

compulsion [kəm'pʌlʃən] n obligación f.

compulsive [kəm'pʌlsɪv] a compulsivo.

compulsory [kəm'pʌlsərɪ] a obligatorio.

computer [kəm'pju:tə*] n ordenador m, computador m, computadora; ~**ize** vt (data) computerizar; (system) informatizar; ~ **programmer** n programador(a) m/f; ~ **programming** n programación f; ~ **science** n informática.

computing [kəm'pju:tɪŋ] n (activity) informática.

comrade ['kɒmrɪd] n compañero/a; ~**ship** n camaradería, compañerismo.

con [kɒn] vt estafar // n estafa.

conceal [kən'si:l] vt ocultar; (thoughts etc) disimular.

conceit [kən'si:t] n presunción f; ~**ed** a presumido.

conceivable [kən'si:vəbl] a concebible.

conceive [kən'si:v] vt, vi concebir.

concentrate ['kɒnsəntreɪt] vi concentrarse // vt concentrar.

concentration [kɒnsən'treɪʃən] n concentración f; ~ **camp** n campo de concentración.

concept ['kɒnsept] n concepto.

conception [kən'sepʃən] n (idea) concepto, idea; (BIOL) concepción f.

concern [kən'sə:n] n (matter) asunto; (COMM) empresa; (anxiety) preocupación f // vt tener que ver con; **to be** ~**ed** (about) interesarse (por), preocuparse (por); ~**ing** prep sobre, acerca de.

concert ['kɒnsət] n concierto; ~**ed** [kən'sə:təd] a (efforts etc) concertado; ~ **hall** n sala de conciertos.

concertina [kɒnsə'ti:nə] n concertina.

concerto [kən'tʃə:təu] n concierto.

concession [kən'seʃən] n concesión f, **tax** ~ privilegio fiscal.

concise [kən'saɪs] a conciso.

conclude [kən'klu:d] vt (finish) concluir; (treaty etc) firmar; (agreement) llegar a; (decide) llegar a la conclusión de; **conclusion** [-'klu:ʒən] n conclusión f; **conclusive** [-'klu:sɪv] a decisivo, concluyente.

concoct [kən'kɒkt] vt (gen) confeccionar; (plot) tramar; ~**ion** [-'kɒkʃən] n confección f.

concourse ['kɒnkɔ:s] n (hall) vestíbulo.

concrete ['kɒnkri:t] n hormigón m // a concreto.

concur [kən'kə:*] vi estar de acuerdo, asentir.

concurrently [kən'kʌrntlɪ] ad al mismo tiempo.

concussion [kən'kʌʃən] n conmoción f cerebral.

condemn [kən'dem] vt condenar; ~**ation** [kɒndem'neɪʃən] n (gen) condena; (blame) censura.

condense [kən'dens] vi condensarse // vt condensar, abreviar; ~**d milk** n leche f

condensada.
condescending [kɔndɪ'sɛndɪŋ] a condes-
cendiente.
condition [kən'dɪʃən] n condición f // vt
condicionar; on ~ that a condición (de)
que; ~al a condicional; ~er n (for
hair) acondicionador m.
condolences [kən'dəulənsɪz] npl pésame
msg.
condom ['kɔndəm] n condón m.
condominium [kɔndə'mɪnɪəm] n (US)
condominio.
condone [kən'dəun] vt condonar.
conducive [kən'djuːsɪv] a: ~ to condu-
cente a.
conduct ['kɔndʌkt] n conducta, comportamiento // vt [kən'dʌkt] (lead) conducir; (manage) llevar, dirigir; (MUS) dirigir // vi (MUS) llevar la batuta; to ~ o.s.
comportarse; ~ed tour n (Brit) visita
acompañada; ~or n (of orchestra) director m; (US: on train) revisor(a) m/f;
(on bus) cobrador m; (ELEC) conductor
m; ~ress n (on bus) cobradora.
cone [kəun] n cono; (pine ~) piña; (for
ice-cream) barquillo.
confectioner [kən'fekʃənə*] n (of cakes)
pastelero; (of sweets) confitero/a; ~'s
(shop) n pastelería; confitería; ~y n
pasteles mpl; dulces mpl.
confer [kən'fəː*] vt: to ~ sth on otorgar
algo a // vi conferenciar.
conference ['kɔnfərns] n (meeting) reunión f; (convention) congreso.
confess [kən'fes] vt confesar // vi confesarse; ~ion [-'feʃən] n confesión f;
~ional [-'feʃənl] n confesionario.
confetti [kən'feti] n confeti m.
confide [kən'faɪd] vi: to ~ in confiar en.
confidence ['kɔnfɪdns] n (gen, also: self
~) confianza; (secret) confidencia; in ~
(speak, write) en confianza; ~ trick n
timo; **confident** a seguro de sí mismo;
confidential [kɔnfɪ'denʃəl] a confidencial; (secretary) de confianza.
confine [kən'faɪn] vt (limit) limitar;
(shut up) encerrar; ~s ['kɔnfaɪnz] npl
confines mpl; ~d a (space) reducido;
~ment n (prison) prisión f; (MED) parto.
confirm [kən'fəːm] vt confirmar; ~ation
[kɔnfə'meɪʃən] n confirmación f; ~ed a
empedernido.
confiscate ['kɔnfɪskeɪt] vt confiscar.
conflict ['kɔnflɪkt] n conflicto // vi
[kən'flɪkt] (opinions) chocar; ~ing a
contradictorio.
conform [kən'fɔːm] vi conformarse; to ~
to ajustarse a.
confound [kən'faund] vt confundir.
confront [kən'frʌnt] vt (problems) hacer
frente a; (enemy, danger) enfrentarse
con; ~ation [kɔnfrən'teɪʃən] n enfrentamiento.
confuse [kən'fjuːz] vt (perplex) aturdir,

desconcertar; (mix up) confundir; ~d a
confuso; (person) perplejo; **confusing** a
confuso; **confusion** [-'fjuːʒən] n confusión f.
congeal [kən'dʒiːl] vi (blood) coagularse.
congenial [kən'dʒiːnɪəl] a agradable.
congenital [kən'dʒenɪtl] a congénito.
congested [kən'dʒestɪd] a (gen) atestado.
congestion [kən'dʒestʃən] n congestión
f.
conglomerate [kən'glɔmərət] n (COMM,
GEO) conglomerado.
conglomeration [kənglɔmə'reɪʃən] n
conglomeración f.
congratulate [kən'grætjuleɪt] vt: to ~ sb
(on) felicitar a uno (por); **congratulations** [-'leɪʃənz] npl felicidades fpl.
congregate ['kɔngrɪgeɪt] vi congregarse;
congregation [-'geɪʃən] n (in church)
fieles mpl.
congress ['kɔngres] n congreso; ~man
n (US) miembro del Congreso.
conifer ['kɔnɪfə*] n conífera.
conjecture [kən'dʒektʃə*] n conjetura.
conjugal ['kɔndʒugl] a conyugal.
conjugate ['kɔndʒugeɪt] vt conjugar.
conjunction [kən'dʒʌŋkʃən] n conjunción
f.
conjunctivitis [kɔndʒʌŋktɪ'vaɪtɪs] n con-
juntivitis f.
conjure ['kʌndʒə*] vi hacer juegos de
manos; to ~ up vt (ghost, spirit) hacer
aparecer; (memories) evocar; ~r n ilu-
sionista m/f.
conk out [kɔŋk-] vi (col) descomponerse.
con man ['kɔn-] n timador m.
connect [kə'nekt] vt juntar, unir; (ELEC)
conectar; (fig) relacionar, asociar // vi:
to ~ with (train) enlazar con; to be ~ed
with (associated) estar relacionado con;
(related) estar emparentado con; ~ion
[-ʃən] n juntura, unión f; (ELEC) conexión f; (RAIL) enlace m; (TEL) comunicación f; (fig) relación f.
connive [kə'naɪv] vi: to ~ at hacer la
vista gorda a.
connoisseur [kɔnɪ'sə*] n experto/a,
entendido/a.
conquer ['kɔŋkə*] vt (territory) conquistar; (enemy, feelings) vencer; ~or n
conquistador m.
conquest ['kɔŋkwest] n conquista.
cons [kɔnz] npl see **convenience, pro.**
conscience ['kɔnʃəns] n conciencia.
conscientious [kɔnʃɪ'enʃəs] a concienzudo; (objection) de conciencia.
conscious ['kɔnʃəs] a consciente; ~ness
n conciencia; (MED) conocimiento.
conscript ['kɔnskrɪpt] n recluta m; ~ion
[kən'skrɪpʃən] n servicio militar (obligatorio).
consecrate ['kɔnsɪkreɪt] vt consagrar.
consensus [kən'sensəs] n consenso.

consent [kən'sɛnt] *n* consentimiento // *vi*: to ~ (to) consentir (en).

consequence ['kɔnsɪkwəns] *n* consecuencia.

consequently ['kɔnsɪkwəntlɪ] *ad* por consiguiente.

conservation [kɔnsə'veɪʃən] *n* conservación *f*.

conservative [kən'sə:vətɪv] *a* conservador(a); (*cautious*) cauteloso; **C~** *a*, *n* (*Brit POL*) conservador(a) *m/f*.

conservatory [kən'sə:vətrɪ] *n* (*greenhouse*) invernadero.

conserve [kən'sə:v] *vt* conservar // *n* conserva.

consider [kən'sɪdə*] *vt* considerar; (*take into account*) tomar en cuenta; (*study*) estudiar, examinar; to ~ doing sth pensar en (la posibilidad de) hacer algo; **~able** *a* considerable; **~ably** *ad* notablemente.

considerate [kən'sɪdərɪt] *a* considerado; **consideration** [-'reɪʃən] *n* consideración *f*; (*reward*) retribución *f*.

considering [kən'sɪdərɪŋ] *prep* teniendo en cuenta.

consign [kən'saɪn] *vt* consignar; **~ment** *n* envío.

consist [kən'sɪst] *vi*: to ~ of consistir en.

consistency [kən'sɪstənsɪ] *n* (*of person etc*) consecuencia; (*thickness*) consistencia.

consistent [kən'sɪstənt] *a* (*person, argument*) consecuente; (*results*) constante.

consolation [kɔnsə'leɪʃən] *n* consuelo.

console [kən'səul] *vt* consolar // *n* ['kɔnsəul] consola.

consonant ['kɔnsənənt] *n* consonante *f*.

consortium [kən'sɔ:tɪəm] *n* consorcio.

conspicuous [kən'spɪkjuəs] *a* (*visible*) visible; (*garish etc*) llamativo; (*outstanding*) notable.

conspiracy [kən'spɪrəsɪ] *n* conjura, complot *m*.

conspire [kən'spaɪə*] *vi* conspirar.

constable ['kʌnstəbl] *n* (*Brit*) policía *m/f*; chief ~ ≈ jefe *m* de policía.

constabulary [kən'stæbjulərɪ] *n* ≈ policía.

constant ['kɔnstənt] *a* (*gen*) constante; (*loyal*) leal, fiel; **~ly** *ad* constantemente.

consternation [kɔnstə'neɪʃən] *n* consternación *f*.

constipated ['kɔnstɪpeɪtəd] *a* estreñido.

constipation [kɔnstɪ'peɪʃən] *n* estreñimiento.

constituency [kən'stɪtjuənsɪ] *n* (*POL*) distrito electoral; **constituent** [-ənt] *n* (*POL*) elector(a) *m/f*; (*part*) componente *m*.

constitute ['kɔnstɪtju:t] *vt* constituir.

constitution [kɔnstɪ'tju:ʃən] *n* constitución *f*; **~al** *a* constitucional.

constrain [kən'streɪn] *vt* obligar; **~ed** *a*: to feel ~ed to ... sentirse en la necesidad

de ....

constraint [kən'streɪnt] *n* (*force*) fuerza; (*limit*) restricción *f*; (*restraint*) reserva.

construct [kən'strʌkt] *vt* construir; **~ion** [-ʃən] *n* construcción *f*; **~ive** *a* constructivo.

construe [kən'stru:] *vt* interpretar.

consul ['kɔnsl] *n* cónsul *m/f*; **~ate** ['kɔnsjulɪt] *n* consulado.

consult [kən'sʌlt] *vt*, *vi* consultar; **~ant** *n* (*Brit MED*) especialista *m/f*; (*other specialist*) asesor(a) *m/f*; **~ation** [kɔnsəl'teɪʃən] *n* consulta; **~ing room** *n* (*Brit*) consultorio.

consume [kən'sju:m] *vt* (*eat*) comerse; (*drink*) beberse; (*fire etc, COMM*) consumir; **~r** *n* consumidor(a) *m/f*; **~r goods** *npl* bienes *mpl* de consumo; **~rism** *n* consumismo; **~r society** *n* sociedad *f* de consumo.

consummate ['kɔnsʌmeɪt] *vt* consumar.

consumption [kən'sʌmpʃən] *n* consumo; (*MED*) tisis *f*.

cont. *abbr* = (*continued*) sigue.

contact ['kɔntækt] *n* contacto; (*person*) enchufe *m* // *vt* ponerse en contacto con; ~ **lenses** *npl* lentes *fpl* de contacto.

contagious [kən'teɪdʒəs] *a* contagioso.

contain [kən'teɪn] *vt* contener; to ~ o.s. contenerse; **~er** *n* recipiente *m*; (*for shipping etc*) contenedor *m*.

contaminate [kən'tæmɪneɪt] *vt* contaminar; **contamination** [-'neɪʃən] *n* contaminación *f*.

cont'd *abbr* = (*continued*) sigue.

contemplate ['kɔntəmpleɪt] *vt* (*gen*) contemplar; (*reflect upon*) considerar; (*intend*) pensar.

contemporary [kən'tɛmpərərɪ] *a*, *n* contemporáneo/a *m/f*.

contempt [kən'tɛmpt] *n* desprecio; ~ of court (*LAW*) desacato (a los tribunales); **~ible** *a* despreciable; **~uous** *a* desdeñoso.

contend [kən'tɛnd] *vt* (*argue*) afirmar // *vi* (*struggle*) luchar; **~er** *n* (*SPORT*) contendiente *m/f*.

content [kən'tɛnt] *a* (*happy*) contento; (*satisfied*) satisfecho // *vt* contentar; satisfacer // *n* ['kɔntɛnt] contenido; (*table of*) **~s** índice *m* de materias; **~ed** *a* contento; satisfecho.

contention [kən'tɛnʃən] *n* discusión *f*; (*belief*) argumento.

contentment [kən'tɛntmənt] *n* contento.

contest ['kɔntɛst] *n* contienda; (*competition*) concurso // *vt* [kən'tɛst] (*dispute*) impugnar; (*POL*) presentarse como candidato/a en; **~ant** [kən'tɛstənt] *n* concursante *m/f*; (*in fight*) contendiente *m/f*.

continent ['kɔntɪnənt] *n* continente *m*; the C~ (*Brit*) el continente europeo; **~al** [-'nɛntl] *a* continental; **~al quilt** *n* (*Brit*) edredón *m*.

contingency [kən'tɪndʒənsɪ] *n* contingencia.

contingent [kən'tındʒənt] (*group*) grupo.

continual [kən'tınjuəl] *a* continuo; **~ly** *ad* constantemente.

continuation [kəntınju'eıʃən] *n* prolongación *f*; (*after interruption*) reanudación *f*.

continue [kən'tınju:] *vi*, *vt* seguir, continuar.

continuous [kən'tınjuəs] *a* continuo; ~ **stationery** *n* papel *m* continuo.

contort [kən'tɔ:t] *vt* retorcer; **~ion** [-'tɔ:ʃən] *n* (*movement*) contorsión *f*.

contour ['kɒntuə*] *n* contorno; (*also:* ~ **line**) curva de nivel.

contraband ['kɒntrəbænd] *n* contrabando.

contraception [kɒntrə'sɛpʃən] *n* contracepción *f*.

contraceptive [kɒntrə'sɛptıv] *a*, *n* anticonceptivo.

contract ['kɒntrækt] *n* contrato // (*vb*: [kən'trækt]) *vi* (*COMM*): **to ~ to do sth** comprometerse por contrato a hacer algo; (*become smaller*) contraerse, encogerse // *vt* contraer; **~ion** [kən'trækʃən] *n* contracción *f*; **~or** *n* contratista *m/f*.

contradict [kɒntrə'dıkt] *vt* (*declare to be wrong*) desmentir; (*be contrary to*) contradecir; **~ion** [-ʃən] *n* contradicción *f*; **~ory** *a* (*statements*) contradictorio.

contraption [kən'træpʃən] *n* (*pej*) artilugio *m*.

contrary ['kɒntrərı] *a* (*opposite, different*) contrario; [kən'trɛərı] (*perverse*) terco // *n*: **on the ~** al contrario; **unless you hear to the ~** a no ser que le digan lo contrario.

contrast ['kɒntrɑ:st] *n* contraste *m* // *vt* [kən'trɑ:st] comparar; **~ing** *a* (*opinion*) opuesto; (*colour*) que hace contraste.

contravene [kɒntrə'vi:n] *vt* infringir.

contribute [kən'trıbju:t] *vi* contribuir // *vt*: **to ~ to** (*gen*) contribuir a; (*newspaper*) escribir para; **contribution** [kɒntrı'bju:ʃən] *n* (*money*) contribución *f*; (*to debate*) intervención *f*; (*to journal*) colaboración *f*; **contributor** *n* (*to newspaper*) colaborador(a) *m/f*.

contrive [kən'traıv] *vt* (*invent*) idear // *vi*: **to ~ to do** lograr hacer.

control [kən'trəul] *vt* controlar; (*traffic etc*) dirigir; (*machinery*) manejar; (*temper*) dominar // *n* (*command*) control *m*; (*of car*) conducción *f*; (*check*) freno; **~s** *npl* mando *sg*; **everything is under ~** todo está bajo control; **to be in ~ of** tener el mando de; **the car went out of ~** se perdió el control del coche; **~ panel** *n* tablero de instrumentos; **~ room** *n* sala de mando; **~ tower** *n* (*AVIAT*) torre *f* de control.

controversial [kɒntrə'və:ʃl] *a* polémico.

controversy ['kɒntrəvə:sı] *n* polémica.

conurbation [kɒnə:'beıʃən] *n* urbaniza-

ción *f*.

convalesce [kɒnvə'lɛs] *vi* convalecer; **convalescence** *n* convalecencia; **convalescent** *a*, *n* convaleciente *m/f*.

convene [kən'vi:n] *vt* convocar // *vi* reunirse.

convenience [kən'vi:nıəns] *n* (*comfort*) comodidad *f*; (*advantage*) ventaja; **at your ~** cuando le sea conveniente; **all modern ~s**, (*Brit*) **all mod cons** todo confort.

convenient [kən'vi:nıənt] *a* (*useful*) útil; (*place, time*) conveniente.

convent ['kɒnvənt] *n* convento.

convention [kən'venʃən] *n* convención *f*; (*meeting*) asamblea; **~al** *a* convencional.

conversant [kən'və:snt] *a*: **to be ~ with** estar al tanto de.

conversation [kɒnvə'seıʃən] *n* conversación *f*; **~al** *a* (*familiar*) familiar; (*talkative*) locuaz.

converse ['kɒnvə:s] *n* inversa // *vi* [kən'və:s] conversar; **~ly** [-'və:slı] *ad* a la inversa.

conversion [kən'və:ʃən] *n* conversión *f*.

convert [kən'və:t] *vt* (*REL, COMM*) convertir; (*alter*) transformar // *n* ['kɒnvə:t] converso/a *m*; **~ible** *a* convertible // *n* descapotable *m*.

convex ['kɒn'vɛks] *a* convexo.

convey [kən'veı] *vt* llevar; (*thanks*) comunicar; (*idea*) expresar; **~or belt** *n* cinta transportadora.

convict [kən'vıkt] *vt* (*gen*) condenar; (*find guilty*) declarar culpable a // *n* ['kɒnvıkt] presidiario/a; **~ion** [-ʃən] *n* condena; (*belief*) creencia, convicción *f*.

convince [kən'vıns] *vt* convencer; **~d** *a*: **~d of/that** convencido de/de que; **convincing** *a* convincente.

convoluted ['kɒnvəlu:tıd] *a* (*argument etc*) enrevesado.

convoy ['kɒnvɔı] *n* convoy *m*.

convulse [kən'vʌls] *vt* convulsionar; **to be ~d with laughter** dislocarse de risa; **convulsion** [-'vʌlʃən] *n* convulsión *f*.

coo [ku:] *vi* arrullar.

cook [kuk] *vt* cocinar; (*stew etc*) guisar; (*meal*) preparar // *vi* cocer; (*person*) cocinar // *n* cocinero/a; **~ book** *n* libro de cocina; **~er** *n* cocina; **~ery** *n* (*dishes*) cocina; (*art*) arte *m* culinario; **~ery book** *n* (*Brit*) = **book**; **~ie** *n* (*US*) galleta; **~ing** *n* cocina.

cool [ku:l] *a* fresco; (*not hot*) tibio; (*not afraid*) tranquilo; (*unfriendly*) frío // *vt* enfriar // *vi* enfriarse; **~ness** *n* frescura; tranquilidad *f*; (*hostility*) frialdad *f*; (*indifference*) falta de entusiasmo.

coop [ku:p] *n* gallinero // *vt*: **to ~ up** (*fig*) encerrar.

cooperate [kəu'ɔpəreıt] *vi* cooperar, colaborar; **cooperation** [-'reıʃən] *n* cooperación *f*, colaboración *f*; **cooperative**

[-rətɪv] a cooperativo // n cooperativa.
coordinate [kəʊˈɔːdɪneɪt] vt coordinar // n [kəʊˈɔːdɪnət] (MATH) coordenada; ~s npl (clothes) coordinados mpl; **coordination** [-ˈneɪʃən] n coordinación f.
co-ownership [kəʊˈəʊnəʃɪp] n copropiedad f.
cop [kɔp] n (col) poli m, tira m (LAm).
cope [kəʊp] vi: to ~ with poder con; (problem) hacer frente a.
copious [ˈkəʊpɪəs] a copioso, abundante.
copper [ˈkɔpə*] n (metal) cobre m; (col: policeman) poli m; ~s npl perras fpl, centavos mpl (LAm).
coppice [ˈkɔpɪs], **copse** [kɔps] n bosquecillo.
copulate [ˈkɔpjuleɪt] vi copularse.
copy [ˈkɔpɪ] n copia; (of book etc) ejemplar m; (of writing) original m // vt copiar; ~**right** n derechos mpl de autor.
coral [ˈkɔrəl] n coral m; ~ **reef** n arrecife m (de coral).
cord [kɔːd] n cuerda; (ELEC) cable m; (fabric) pana.
cordial [ˈkɔːdɪəl] a afectuoso // n cordial m.
cordon [ˈkɔːdn] n cordón m; **to** ~ **off** vt acordonar.
corduroy [ˈkɔːdərɔɪ] n pana.
core [kɔː*] n (gen) centro, núcleo; (of fruit) corazón m // vt quitar el corazón de.
coriander [kɔrɪˈændə*] n culantro.
cork [kɔːk] n corcho; (tree) alcornoque m; ~**screw** n sacacorchos m inv.
corn [kɔːn] n (Brit: wheat) trigo; (US: maize) maíz m; (on foot) callo; ~ **on the cob** (CULIN) maíz en la mazorca, choclo (LAm).
cornea [ˈkɔːnɪə] n córnea.
corned beef [ˈkɔːnd-] n carne f acecinada.
corner [ˈkɔːnə*] n ángulo; (outside) esquina; (inside) rincón m; (in road) curva; (FOOTBALL) córner m // vt (trap) arrinconar; (COMM) acaparar // vi (in car) tomar las curvas; ~**stone** n piedra angular.
cornet [ˈkɔːnɪt] n (MUS) corneta; (Brit: of ice-cream) barquillo.
cornflakes [ˈkɔːnfleɪks] npl copos mpl de maíz, cornflakes mpl.
cornflour [ˈkɔːnflaʊə*] n (Brit) harina de maíz.
cornstarch [ˈkɔːnstɑːtʃ] n (US) = **cornflour**.
Cornwall [ˈkɔːnwəl] n Cornualles m.
corny [ˈkɔːnɪ] a (col) gastado.
corollary [kəˈrɔlərɪ] n corolario.
coronary [ˈkɔrənərɪ] n: ~ (**thrombosis**) infarto.
coronation [kɔrəˈneɪʃən] n coronación f.
coroner [ˈkɔrənə*] n juez m (de instrucción).
coronet [ˈkɔrənɪt] n corona.

corporal [ˈkɔːpərl] n cabo // a: ~ **punishment** castigo corporal.
corporate [ˈkɔːpərɪt] a corporativo.
corporation [kɔːpəˈreɪʃən] n (of town) ayuntamiento; (COMM) corporación f.
corps [kɔː*], pl **corps** [kɔːz] n cuerpo.
corpse [kɔːps] n cadáver m.
corpuscle [ˈkɔːpʌsl] n corpúsculo.
corral [kəˈrɑːl] n corral m.
correct [kəˈrekt] a (accurate) justo, exacto; (proper) correcto // vt corregir; (exam) calificar; ~**ion** [-ʃən] n rectificación f; (erasure) tachadura.
correlation [kɔrɪˈleɪʃən] n correlación f.
correspond [kɔrɪsˈpɔnd] vi (write) escribirse; (be equal to) corresponder; ~**ence** n correspondencia; ~**ence course** n curso por correspondencia; ~**ent** n corresponsal m/f.
corridor [ˈkɔrɪdɔː*] n pasillo.
corroborate [kəˈrɔbəreɪt] vt corroborar.
corrode [kəˈrəʊd] vt corroer // vi corroerse; **corrosion** [-ˈrəʊʒən] n corrosión f.
corrugated [ˈkɔrəgeɪtɪd] a ondulado; ~ **iron** n chapa ondulada.
corrupt [kəˈrʌpt] a corrompido; (person) corrupto // vt corromper; (bribe) sobornar; ~**ion** [-ʃən] n corrupción f.
corset [ˈkɔːsɪt] n faja.
Corsica [ˈkɔːsɪkə] n Córcega.
cortège [kɔːˈteɪʒ] n cortejo, desfile m.
cosh [kɔʃ] n (Brit) cachiporra.
cosmetic [kɔzˈmetɪk] n cosmético.
cosmic [ˈkɔzmɪk] a cósmico.
cosmonaut [ˈkɔzmənɔːt] n cosmonauta m/f.
cosmopolitan [kɔzməˈpɔlɪtn] a cosmopolita.
cosset [ˈkɔsɪt] vt mimar.
cost [kɔst] n (gen) coste m, costo; (price) precio; ~s npl costas fpl // vb (pt, pp cost) vi costar, valer // vt preparar el presupuesto de; **how much does it** ~? ¿cuánto cuesta?; **at all** ~s cueste lo que cueste.
co-star [ˈkəʊstɑː*] n colega m/f de reparto.
Costa Rican [ˈkɔstəˈriːkən] a, n costarriqueño/a m/f.
cost-effective [kɔstɪˈfektɪv] a rentable.
costly [ˈkɔstlɪ] a (expensive) costoso.
cost-of-living [kɔstəvˈlɪvɪŋ] a: ~ **allowance** n plus m de carestía de vida; ~ **index** n índice m del costo de vida.
cost price n (Brit) precio de coste.
costume [ˈkɔstjuːm] n traje m; (Brit: also: **swimming** ~) traje de baño; ~ **jewellery** n bisutería.
cosy, (US) **cozy** [ˈkəʊzɪ] a cómodo; (atmosphere) acogedor(a).
cot [kɔt] n (Brit: child's) cuna.
cottage [ˈkɔtɪdʒ] n casita de campo; (rustic) barraca; ~ **cheese** n requesón m; ~ **industry** n industria casera; ~ **pie** n pastel m de carne cubierta de

puré de patatas.

cotton ['kɔtn] *n* algodón *m*; (*thread*) hilo; **to ~ on to** *vt fus* (*col*) caer en la cuenta de; **~ candy** *n* (*US*) algodón *m* (azucarado); **~ wool** *n* (*Brit*) algodón *m* (hidrófilo).

couch [kautʃ] *n* sofá *m*.

couchette [ku:'ʃet] *n* litera.

cough [kɔf] *vi* toser // *n* tos *f*; **~ drop** *n* pastilla para la tos.

could [kud] *pt of* can; **~n't** = **could not.**

council ['kaunsl] *n* consejo; **city** *or* **town ~** consejo municipal; **~ estate** *n* (*Brit*) urbanización *f* de viviendas municipales de alquiler; **~ house** *n* (*Brit*) vivienda municipal de alquiler; **~lor** *n* concejal(a) *m/f*.

counsel ['kaunsl] *n* (*advice*) consejo; (*lawyer*) abogado/a // *vt* aconsejar; **~lor** *n* consejero/a; **~or** *n* (*US*) abogado/a.

count [kaunt] *vt* (*gen*) contar; (*include*) incluir // *vi* contar // *n* cuenta; (*of votes*) escrutinio; (*nobleman*) conde *m*; (*sum*) total *m*, suma; **to ~ on** *vt fus* contar con; **that doesn't ~!** ¡eso no vale!; **~down** *n* cuenta atrás.

countenance ['kauntinəns] *n* semblante *m*, rostro // *vt* (*tolerate*) aprobar, tolerar.

counter ['kauntə*] *n* (*in shop*) mostrador *m*; (*in games*) ficha // *vt* contrarrestar.

counterfeit ['kauntəfɪt] *n* falsificación *f*, simulación *f* // *vt* falsificar // *a* falso, falsificado.

counterfoil ['kauntəfɔil] *n* (*Brit*) talón *m*.

countermand ['kauntəmɑ:nd] *vt* revocar, cancelar.

counterpart ['kauntəpɑ:t] *n* (*of person*) homólogo/a.

counter-productive [kauntəprə'dʌktɪv] *a* contraproducente.

countersign ['kauntəsain] *vt* refrendar.

countess ['kauntis] *n* condesa.

countless ['kauntlis] *a* innumerable.

country ['kʌntri] *n* país *m*; (*native land*) patria; (*as opposed to town*) campo; (*region*) región *f*, tierra; **~ dancing** *n* (*Brit*) baile *m* regional; **~ house** *n* casa de campo; **~man** *n* (*national*) compatriota *m*; (*rural*) campesino, paisano; **~side** *n* campo.

county ['kaunti] *n* condado.

coup [ku:], *pl* **~s** [-z] *n* (*also*: **~ d'état**) golpe *m* (de estado).

coupé ['ku:pei] *n* cupé *m*.

couple ['kʌpl] *n* (*of things*) par *m*; (*of people*) pareja; (*married ~*) matrimonio // *vt* (*ideas, names*) unir, juntar; (*machinery*) acoplar; **a ~ of** un par de.

coupling ['kʌpliŋ] *n* (*RAIL*) enganche *m*.

coupon ['ku:pɔn] *n* cupón *m*; (*pools ~*) boleto de quiniela.

courage ['kʌridʒ] *n* valor *m*, valentía;

~ous [kə'reidʒəs] *a* valiente.

courgette [kuə'ʒet] *n* (*Brit*) calabacín *m*, calabacita.

courier ['kuriə*] *n* mensajero/a; (*diplomatic*) correo; (*for tourists*) guía *m/f* (de turismo).

course [kɔ:s] *n* (*direction*) dirección *f*; (*of river*, SCOL) curso; (*of ship*) rumbo; (*fig*) proceder *m*; (*GOLF*) campo; (*part of meal*) plato; **of ~** *ad* desde luego, naturalmente; **of ~!** ¡claro!

court [kɔ:t] *n* (*royal*) corte *f*; (*LAW*) tribunal *m*, juzgado; (*TENNIS*) pista, cancha // *vt* (*woman*) cortejar a; (*danger etc*) buscar; **to take to ~** demandar.

courteous ['kə:tiəs] *a* cortés.

courtesan [kɔ:ti'zæn] *n* cortesana.

courtesy ['kə:təsi] *n* cortesía *f*; **by ~ of** por cortesía de.

court-house ['kɔ:thaus] *n* (*US*) palacio de justicia.

courtier ['kɔ:tiə*] *n* cortesano.

court-martial ['kɔ:t'mɑ:ʃəl], *pl* **courts-martial** *n* consejo de guerra // *vt* someter a consejo de guerra.

courtroom ['kɔ:trum] *n* sala de justicia.

courtyard ['kɔ:tjɑ:d] *n* patio.

cousin ['kʌzn] *n* primo/a; **first ~** primo/a carnal.

cove [kəuv] *n* cala, ensenada.

covenant ['kʌvənənt] *n* convenio.

cover ['kʌvə*] *vt* cubrir; (*with lid*) tapar; (*chairs etc*) revestir; (*distance*) recorrer; (*include*) abarcar; (*protect*) abrigar; (*journalist*) investigar; (*issues*) tratar // *n* cubierta; (*lid*) tapa; (*for chair etc*) funda; (*for bed*) cobertor *m*; (*envelope*) sobre *m*; (*for book*) forro; (*of magazine*) portada; (*shelter*) abrigo; (*insurance*) cobertura; **to take ~** (*shelter*) protegerse, resguardarse; **under ~** (*indoors*) bajo techo; **under ~ of darkness** al amparo de la oscuridad; **under separate ~** (*COMM*) por separado; **to ~ up for sb** encubrir a uno; **~age** *n* alcance *m*; **~alls** *npl* (*US*) mono *sg*; **~ charge** *n* precio del cubierto; **~ing** *n* cubierta, envoltura; **~ing letter**, (*US*) **~ letter** *n* carta de explicación; **~ note** *n* (*INSURANCE*) póliza provisional.

covert ['kəuvət] *a* secreto, encubierto.

cover-up ['kʌvərʌp] *n* encubrimiento.

covet ['kʌvit] *vt* codiciar.

cow [kau] *n* vaca // *vt* intimidar.

coward ['kauəd] *n* cobarde *m/f*; **~ice** [-is] *n* cobardía; **~ly** *a* cobarde.

cowboy ['kaubɔi] *n* vaquero.

cower ['kauə*] *vi* encogerse (de miedo).

coxswain ['kɔksn] *n* (*abbr*: cox) timonel *m/f*.

coy [kɔi] *a* tímido.

cozy ['kəuzi] *a* (*US*) = **cosy.**

CPA *n abbr* (*US*) = **certified public accountant.**

crab [kræb] *n* cangrejo; **~ apple** *n* manzana silvestre.

crack [kræk] *n* grieta; (*noise*) crujido; (:
of whip) chasquido; (*joke*) chiste *m*; **to
have a ~** at intentar // *vt* agrietar, romper; (*nut*) cascar; (*safe*) forzar; (*whip
etc*) chasquear; (*knuckles*) crujir;
(*joke*) contar // *a* (*athlete*) de primera
clase; **to ~ down on** *vt fus* reprimen-
dar fuertemente; **to ~ up** *vi* (*MED*) sufrir una crisis nerviosa; **~er** *n* (*biscuit*)
crácker *m*; (*Christmas cracker*) petardo
sorpresa.

crackle ['krækl] *vi* crepitar.

cradle ['kreidl] *n* cuna.

craft [krɑːft] *n* (*skill*) arte *m*; (*trade*) oficio; (*cunning*) astucia; (*boat*) barco.

craftsman ['krɑːftsmən] *n* artesano;
~ship *n* artesanía.

crafty ['krɑːftɪ] *a* astuto.

crag [kræg] *n* peñasco.

cram [kræm] *vt* (*fill*): **to ~ sth with** llenar
algo (a reventar) de; (*put*): **to ~ sth into**
meter algo a la fuerza en // *vi* (*for
exams*) empollar; **~med** *a* atestado.

cramp [kræmp] *n* (*MED*) calambre *m*;
(*TECH*) grapa // *vt* (*limit*) poner trabas
a; **~ed** *a* apretado, estrecho.

crampon ['kræmpən] *n* crampón *m*.

cranberry ['krænbərɪ] *n* arándano agrio.

crane [krein] *n* (*TECH*) grúa; (*bird*) grulla.

crank [kræŋk] *n* manivela; (*person*) chiflado; **~shaft** *n* cigüeñal *m*.

cranny ['krænɪ] *n see* **nook**.

crash [kræʃ] *n* (*noise*) estrépito; (*of cars
etc*) choque *m*; (*of plane*) accidente *m*
de aviación; (*COMM*) quiebra // *vt*
(*plane*) estrellar // *vi* (*plane*) estrellarse;
(*two cars*) chocar; (*fall noisily*) caer con
estrépito; **~ course** *n* curso acelerado;
~ helmet *n* casco (protector); **~ landing** *n* aterrizaje *m* forzado.

crass [kræs] *a* grosero, maleducado.

crate [kreit] *n* cajón *m* de embalaje.

crater ['kreitə*] *n* cráter *m*.

cravat(e) [krə'væt] *n* pañuelo.

crave [kreiv] *vt*, *vi*: **to ~ (for)** ansiar,
anhelar; **craving** *n* (*of pregnant woman*) antojo.

crawl [krɔːl] *vi* (*drag o.s.*) arrastrarse;
(*child*) andar a gatas, gatear; (*vehicle*)
avanzar (lentamente) // *n* (*SWIMMING*)
crol *m*.

crayfish ['kreifiʃ] *n*, *pl inv* (*freshwater*)
cangrejo de río; (*saltwater*) cigala.

crayon ['kreiən] *n* lápiz *m* de color.

craze [kreiz] *n* manía; (*fashion*) moda.

crazy ['kreizi] *a* (*person*) loco; (*idea*) disparatado; **~ paving** *n* pavimento de
baldosas irregulares.

creak [kriːk] *vi* crujir; (*hinge etc*) chirriar, rechinar.

cream [kriːm] *n* (*of milk*) nata, crema;
(*lotion*) crema; (*fig*) flor *f* y nata // *a*
(*colour*) color crema; **~ cake** *n* pastel

m de nata; **~ cheese** *n* queso crema;
~y *a* cremoso.

crease [kriːs] *n* (*fold*) pliegue *m*; (*in
trousers*) raya; (*wrinkle*) arruga // *vt*
(*fold*) doblar, plegar; (*wrinkle*) arrugar
// *vi* (*wrinkle up*) arrugarse.

create [kriː'eit] *vt* crear; **creation** [-ʃən]
n creación *f*; **creative** *a* creador(a);
creator *n* creador(a) *m/f*.

creature ['kriːtʃə*] *n* (*animal*) animal *m*,
bicho; (*living thing*) criatura.

crèche, creche [kreʃ] *n* (*Brit*) guardería
(infantil).

credence ['kriːdəns] *n*; **to lend** *or* **give ~**
to creer en, dar crédito a.

credentials [krɪ'denʃlz] *npl* credenciales
fpl.

credible ['krɛdɪbl] *a* creíble.

credit ['krɛdɪt] *n* (*gen*) crédito; (*merit*)
honor *m*, mérito // *vt* (*COMM*) abonar;
(*believe*) creer, prestar fe a // *a* crediti-
cio; **~s** *npl* (*CINEMA*) fichas *fpl* técnicas;
to be in ~ (*person*) tener saldo a favor;
to ~ sb with (*fig*) reconocer a uno el mérito de; **~ card** *n* tarjeta de crédito;
~or *n* acreedor(a) *m/f*.

creed [kriːd] *n* credo.

creek [kriːk] *n* cala, ensenada; (*US*) riachuelo.

creep [kriːp], *pt*, *pp* **crept** *vi* (*animal*)
deslizarse; (*gen*) arrastrarse; (*plant*)
trepar; **~er** *n* enredadera; **~y** *a* (*frightening*) horripilante.

cremate [krɪ'meit] *vt* incinerar.

crematorium [krɛmə'tɔːrɪəm], *pl* **-ria**
[-rɪə] *n* crematorio.

crêpe [kreip] *n* (*fabric*) crespón *m*;
(*also: ~ rubber*) crepé *m*; **~ bandage**
n (*Brit*) venda de crepé.

crept [krɛpt] *pt*, *pp* of **creep**.

crescent ['krɛsnt] *n* media luna; (*street*)
calle *f* (*en forma de semicírculo*).

cress [krɛs] *n* berro.

crest [krɛst] *n* (*of bird*) cresta; (*of hill*)
cima, cumbre *f*; (*of helmet*) cimera; (*of
coat of arms*) blasón *m*; **~fallen** *a* ali-
caído.

crevasse [krɪ'væs] *n* grieta.

crevice ['krɛvɪs] *n* grieta, hendedura.

crew [kruː] *n* (*of ship etc*) tripulación *f*;
(*gang*) banda; (*MIL*) dotación *f*; **~-cut**
n corte *m* al rape; **~-neck** *n* cuello plano.

crib [krɪb] *n* pesebre *m* // *vt* (*col*) plagiar.

crick [krɪk] *n* (*in neck*) torticolis *m*.

cricket ['krɪkɪt] *n* (*insect*) grillo; (*game*)
críquet *m*.

crime [kraim] *n* crimen *m*; (*less serious*)
delito; **criminal** ['krɪmɪnl] *n* criminal *m/
f*, delincuente *m/f* // *a* criminal; (*law*) penal.

crimson ['krɪmzn] *a* carmesí.

cringe [krɪndʒ] *vi* agacharse, encogerse.

crinkle ['krɪŋkl] *vt* arrugar.

cripple ['krɪpl] *n* lisiado/a, cojo/a // *vt* li-

siar, mutilar.
crisis ['kraısıs], *pl* **-ses** [-si:z] *n* crisis *f*
inv.
crisp [krısp] *a* fresco; (*cooked*) tostado;
(*manner*) seco; **~s** *npl* (*Brit*) patatas
fpl or papas *fpl* fritas.
criss-cross ['krıskrɒs] *a* entrelazado.
criterion [kraı'tıərıən], *pl* **-ria** [-rıə] *n* criterio.
critic ['krıtık] *n* (*paper*) crítico/a; **~al** *a*
(*gen*) crítico; (*illness*) grave; **~ally** *ad*
(*speak etc*) en tono crítico; (*ill*) gravemente; **~ism** ['krıtısızm] *n* crítica; **~ize**
['krıtısaız] *vt* criticar.
croak [krəuk] *vi* (*frog*) croar; (*raven*)
graznar.
crochet ['krəuʃeı] *n* ganchillo.
crockery ['krɒkərı] *n* loza, vajilla.
crocodile ['krɒkədaıl] *n* cocodrilo.
crocus ['krəukəs] *n* azafrán *m*.
croft [krɒft] *n* (*Brit*) granja pequeña.
crony ['krəunı] *n* compinche *m/f*.
crook [kruk] *n* (*fam*) ladrón/ona *m/f*; (*of
shepherd*) cayado; (*of arm*) pliegue *m*;
~ed ['krukıd] *a* torcido; (*path*) tortuoso;
(*fam*) sucio.
crop [krɒp] *n* (*produce*) cultivo; (*amount
produced*) cosecha; (*riding ~*) látigo de
montar // *vt* cortar, recortar; **to ~ up**
vi surgir, presentarse.
croquette [krə'kɛt] *n* croqueta.
cross [krɒs] *n* cruz *f* // *vt* (*street etc*) cruzar, atravesar // *a* de mal humor, enoja-
do; **to ~ o.s.** santiguarse; **to ~ out** *vt*
tachar; **to ~ over** *vi* cruzar; **~bar** *n*
travesaño; **~country (race)** *n* carrera a
campo traviesa, cross *m*; **to ~-
examine** *vt* interrogar; **~-eyed** *a* bizco; **~fire** *n* fuego cruzado; **~ing** *n*
(*road*) cruce *m*; (*rail*) paso a nivel; (*sea
passage*) travesía; (*also:* **pedestrian
~ing**) paso para peatones; **~ing guard**
n (*US*) persona encargada de ayudar a
los niños a cruzar la calle; **~ purposes**
npl: **to be at ~ purposes** malentenderse
uno a otro; **~-reference** *n* contrarrefe-
rencia; **~roads** *n* cruce *m*, encrucijada;
~ section *n* corte *m* transversal; (*of
population*) muestra (representativa);
~walk *n* (*US*) paso de peatones;
~wind *n* viento de costado; **~word** *n*
crucigrama *m*.
crotch [krɒtʃ] *n* (*of garment*) entrepierna.
crotchet ['krɒtʃıt] *n* (*Brit MUS*) negra.
crotchety ['krɒtʃıtı] *a* (*person*) arisco.
crouch [krautʃ] *vi* agacharse, acurrucarse.
crow [krəu] *n* (*bird*) cuervo; (*of cock*)
canto, cacareo // *vi* (*cock*) cantar; (*fig*)
jactarse.
crowbar ['krəuba:*] *n* palanca.
crowd [kraud] *n* muchedumbre *f*;
(*SPORT*) público; (*common herd*) vulgo //
vt (*gather*) amontonar; (*fill*) llenar // *vi*

(*gather*) reunirse; (*pile up*) amontonarse; **~ed** *a* (*full*) atestado; (*well-
attended*) concurrido.
crown [kraun] *n* corona; (*of head*) coronilla; (*of hat*) copa; (*of hill*) cumbre *f* //
vt coronar; **~ jewels** *npl* joyas *fpl* rea-
les; **~ prince** *n* príncipe *m* heredero.
crow's feet *npl* patas *fpl* de gallo.
crucial ['kru:ʃl] *a* decisivo.
crucifix ['kru:sıfıks] *n* crucifijo; **~ion**
[-'fıkʃən] *n* crucifixión *f*.
crucify ['kru:sıfaı] *vt* crucificar.
crude [kru:d] *a* (*materials*) bruto; (*fig:
basic*) tosco; (: *vulgar*) ordinario; **~
(oil)** *n* petróleo crudo.
cruel ['kruəl] *a* cruel; **~ty** *n* crueldad *f*.
cruet ['kru:ıt] *n* angarillas *fpl*.
cruise [kru:z] *n* crucero // *vi* (*ship*) hacer
un crucero; (*car*) mantener la veloci-
dad; **~r** *n* crucero.
crumb [krʌm] *n* miga, migaja.
crumble ['krʌmbl] *vt* desmenuzar // *vi*
(*gen*) desmenuzarse; (*building*) desmoronarse; **crumbly** *a* desmenuzable.
crumpet ['krʌmpıt] *n* ≈ bollo para tostar.
crumple ['krʌmpl] *vt* (*paper*) estrujar;
(*material*) arrugar.
crunch [krʌntʃ] *vt* (*with teeth*) ronzar;
(*underfoot*) hacer crujir // *n* (*fig*) crisis
f; **~y** *a* crujiente.
crusade [kru:'seıd] *n* cruzada.
crush [krʌʃ] *n* (*crowd*) aglomeración *f* //
vt (*gen*) aplastar; (*paper*) estrujar;
(*cloth*) arrugar; (*fruit*) exprimir.
crust [krʌst] *n* corteza.
crutch [krʌtʃ] *n* muleta.
crux [krʌks] *n* lo esencial.
cry [kraı] *vi* llorar; (*shout: also:* **~ out**)
gritar // *n* grito; **to ~ off** *vi* echarse
atrás.
cryptic ['krıptık] *a* enigmático, secreto.
crystal ['krıstl] *n* cristal *m*; **~-clear** *a*
claro como el agua; **~lize** *vt* cristalizar
// *vi* cristalizarse.
cub [kʌb] *n* cachorro; (*also:* **~ scout**) niño explorador.
Cuba ['kju:bə] *n* Cuba; **~n** *a, n* cubano/a
m/f.
cubbyhole ['kʌbıhəul] *n* chiribitil *m*.
cube [kju:b] *n* cubo; (*of sugar*) terrón *m*
// *vt* (*MATH*) cubicar; **~ root** *n* raíz *f*
cúbica; **cubic** *a* cúbico.
cubicle ['kju:bıkl] *n* (*at pool*) caseta; (*for
bed*) cubículo.
cuckoo ['kuku:] *n* cuco; **~ clock** *n* cucú
m.
cucumber ['kju:kʌmbə*] *n* pepino.
cuddle ['kʌdl] *vt* abrazar // *vi* abrazarse.
cue [kju:] *n* (*snooker ~*) taco; (*THEATRE
etc*) entrada.
cuff [kʌf] *n* (*Brit: of shirt, coat etc*) puño; (*US: of trousers*) vuelta; (*blow*) bofetada; **off the ~** *ad* improvisado;
~links *npl* gemelos *mpl*.

cuisine [kwɪ'ziːn] n cocina.
cul-de-sac ['kʌldəsæk] n callejón m sin salida.
cull [kʌl] vt (select) entresacar.
culminate ['kʌlmɪneɪt] vi: to ~ in terminar en; **culmination** [-'neɪʃən] n culminación f, colmo.
culottes [kuː'lɒts] npl falda fsg pantalón.
culprit ['kʌlprɪt] n culpable m/f, delincuente m/f.
cult [kʌlt] n culto.
cultivate ['kʌltɪveɪt] vt (also fig) cultivar; ~d a culto; **cultivation** [-'veɪʃən] n cultivo; (fig) cultura.
cultural ['kʌltʃərəl] a cultural.
culture ['kʌltʃə*] n (also fig) cultura; ~d a culto.
cumbersome ['kʌmbəsəm] a de mucho bulto, voluminoso.
cunning ['kʌnɪŋ] n astucia // a astuto.
cup [kʌp] n taza; (prize, event) copa.
cupboard ['kʌbəd] n armario; (kitchen) alacena.
cup-tie ['kʌptaɪ] n (Brit) partido de copa.
curate ['kjuərɪt] n cura m.
curator [kjuə'reɪtə*] n conservador(a) m/f.
curb [kəːb] vt refrenar // n freno; (US) bordillo.
curdle ['kəːdl] vi cuajarse.
cure [kjuə*] vt curar // n cura, curación f.
curfew ['kəːfjuː] n toque m de queda.
curio ['kjuərɪəu] n curiosidad f.
curiosity [kjuərɪ'ɒsɪtɪ] n curiosidad f.
curious ['kjuərɪəs] a curioso.
curl [kəːl] n rizo // vt (hair) rizar; (paper) arrollar; (lip) fruncir // vi rizarse; arrollarse; **to ~ up** vi arrollarse; (person) hacerse un ovillo; **~er** n bigudí m; **~y** a rizado.
currant ['kʌrnt] n pasa.
currency ['kʌrnsɪ] n moneda; **to gain ~** (fig) difundirse.
current ['kʌrnt] n corriente f // a corriente, actual; ~ **account** n (Brit) cuenta corriente; ~ **affairs** npl actualidades fpl; ~**ly** ad actualmente.
curriculum [kə'rɪkjuləm], pl ~**s** or **curricula** [-lə] n plan m de estudios; ~ **vitae (CV)** n currículum m.
curry ['kʌrɪ] n curry m // vt: **to ~ favour with** buscar favores con; ~ **powder** n curry m en polvo.
curse [kəːs] vi echar pestes // vt maldecir // n maldición f; (swearword) palabrota.
cursor ['kəːsə*] n (COMPUT) cursor m.
cursory ['kəːsərɪ] a rápido, superficial.
curt [kəːt] a corto, seco.
curtail [kəː'teɪl] vt (cut short) acortar; (restrict) restringir.
curtain ['kəːtn] n cortina; (THEATRE) telón m.
curts(e)y ['kəːtsɪ] n reverencia // vi hacer una reverencia.
curve [kəːv] n curva // vi encorvarse, tor-

cerse; (road) hacer curva.
cushion ['kuʃən] n cojín m; (SNOOKER) banda // vt (shock) amortiguar.
custard ['kʌstəd] n (for pouring) natillas fpl.
custodian [kʌs'təudɪən] n custodio m/f.
custody ['kʌstədɪ] n custodia; **to take into ~** detener.
custom ['kʌstəm] n costumbre f; (COMM) clientela; ~**ary** a acostumbrado.
customer ['kʌstəmə*] n cliente m/f.
customized ['kʌstəmaɪzd] a (car etc) hecho a encargo.
custom-made ['kʌstəm'meɪd] a hecho a la medida.
customs ['kʌstəmz] npl aduana sg; ~ **duty** n derechos mpl de aduana; ~ **officer** n aduanero/a.
cut [kʌt] vb (pt, pp cut) vt cortar; (price) rebajar; (record) grabar; (reduce) reducir // vi cortar; (intersect) cruzarse // n corte m; (in skin) cortadura; (with sword) tajo; (of knife) cuchillada; (in salary etc) rebaja; (slice of meat) tajada; **to ~ a tooth** echar un diente; **to ~ down** vt (tree) derribar; (reduce) reducir; **to ~ off** vt cortar; (fig) aislar; (troops) cercar; **to ~ out** vt (shape) recortar; (delete) suprimir; **to ~ up** vt cortar (en pedazos); ~**back** n reducción f.
cute [kjuːt] a lindo; (shrewd) listo.
cuticle ['kjuːtɪkl] n cutícula.
cutlery ['kʌtlərɪ] n cubiertos mpl.
cutlet ['kʌtlɪt] n chuleta.
cut: ~**out** n (cardboard ~) recortable m; ~**price**, (US) ~**rate** a a precio reducido; ~**throat** n asesino/a // a feroz.
cutting ['kʌtɪŋ] a (gen) cortante; (remark) mordaz // n (Brit: from newspaper) recorte m; (: RAIL) desmonte m.
CV n abbr = **curriculum vitae**.
cwt abbr = **hundredweight(s)**.
cyanide ['saɪənaɪd] n cianuro.
cycle ['saɪkl] n ciclo; (bicycle) bicicleta // vi ir en bicicleta; **cycling** n ciclismo; **cyclist** n ciclista m/f.
cyclone ['saɪkləun] n ciclón m.
cygnet ['sɪgnɪt] n pollo de cisne.
cylinder ['sɪlɪndə*] n cilindro; ~**head gasket** n junta de culata.
cymbals ['sɪmblz] npl platillos mpl.
cynic ['sɪnɪk] n cínico/a; ~**al** a cínico; ~**ism** ['sɪnɪsɪzəm] n cinismo.
cypress ['saɪprɪs] n ciprés m.
Cypriot ['sɪprɪət] a, n chipriota m/f.
Cyprus ['saɪprəs] n Chipre f.
cyst [sɪst] n quiste m; ~**itis** n cistitis f.
czar [zɑː*] n zar m.
Czech [tʃɛk] a, n checo/a m/f.
Czechoslovakia [tʃɛkəslə'vækɪə] n Checoslovaquia; ~**n** a, n checo/a m/f.

D

D [diː] n (MUS) re m.

dab [dæb] vt (eyes, wound) tocar (ligeramente); (paint, cream) mojar ligeramente // n (light stroke) toque m; (small amount) pizca.

dabble ['dæbl] vi: to ~ in ser algo aficionado a.

Dacron ['deɪkrɔn] n ® (US) terylene m.

dad [dæd], **daddy** ['dædɪ] n papá m; **daddy-long-legs** n típula.

daffodil ['dæfədɪl] n narciso.

daft [dɑːft] a chiflado.

dagger ['dægə*] n puñal m, daga.

daily ['deɪlɪ] a diario, cotidiano // n (paper) diario; (domestic help) asistenta // ad todos los días, cada día.

dainty ['deɪntɪ] a delicado; (tasteful) elegante; primoroso.

dairy ['dɛərɪ] n (shop) lechería; (on farm) vaquería // a (cow etc) lechero; ~ **farm** n granja; ~ **produce** n productos mpl lácteos.

dais ['deɪɪs] n estrado.

daisy ['deɪzɪ] n margarita; ~ **wheel** n margarita.

dale [deɪl] n valle m.

dam [dæm] n presa // vt represar.

damage ['dæmɪdʒ] n daño; (fig) perjuicio; (to machine) avería // vt dañar; perjudicar; averiar; ~s npl (LAW) daños mpl y perjuicios.

damn [dæm] vt condenar; (curse) maldecir // n (col): I don't give a ~ me importa un pito // a (col: also: ~ed) maldito; ~ (it)! ¡maldito sea!; ~ing a (evidence) irrecusable.

damp [dæmp] a húmedo, mojado // n humedad f // vt (also: ~en) (cloth, rag) mojar; (fig) desalentar; ~ness n humedad f.

damson ['dæmzən] n ciruela damascena.

dance [dɑːns] n baile m // vi bailar; ~ **hall** n salón m de baile; ~**r** n bailador(a) m/f; (professional) bailarín/ina m/f; **dancing** n baile m.

dandelion ['dændɪlaɪən] n diente m de león.

dandruff ['dændrəf] n caspa.

Dane [deɪn] n danés/esa m/f.

danger ['deɪndʒə*] n peligro; (risk) riesgo; ~! (on sign) ¡peligro de muerte!; to be in ~ of correr riesgo de; ~**ous** a peligroso; ~**ously** ad peligrosamente.

dangle ['dæŋgl] vt colgar // vi pender, estar colgado.

Danish ['deɪnɪʃ] a danés/esa // n (LING) danés m.

dapper ['dæpə*] a pulcro, apuesto.

dare [dɛə*] vt: to ~ sb to do desafiar a uno a hacer // vi: to ~ (to) do sth atreverse a hacer algo; I ~ say (I suppose) puede ser, a lo mejor; ~**devil** n temerario/a, atrevido/a; **daring** a atrevido, osado // n atrevimiento, osadía.

dark [dɑːk] a oscuro; (hair, complexion) moreno; (fig: cheerless) triste, sombrío // n (gen) oscuridad f; (night) tinieblas fpl; in the ~ about (fig) en ignorancia de; after ~ después del anochecer; ~**en** vt oscurecer; (colour) hacer más oscuro // vi oscurecerse; (cloud over) anublarse; ~ **glasses** npl gafas fpl negras; ~**ness** n (in room) oscuridad f; (night) tinieblas fpl; ~**room** n cuarto oscuro.

darling ['dɑːlɪŋ] a, n querido/a m/f.

darn [dɑːn] vt zurcir.

dart [dɑːt] n dardo; (in sewing) sisa // vi precipitarse; **to** ~ **away/along** vi salir/marchar disparado; ~**board** n diana; ~**s** n dardos mpl.

dash [dæʃ] n (small quantity: of liquid) gota, chorrito; (: of solid) pizca; (sign) guión m; (: long) raya // vt (break) romper, estrellar; (hopes) defraudar // vi precipitarse, ir de prisa; **to** ~ **away** or **off** vi marcharse apresuradamente.

dashboard ['dæʃbɔːd] n (AUT) tablero de instrumentos.

dashing ['dæʃɪŋ] a gallardo.

data ['deɪtə] npl datos mpl; ~**base** n base f de datos; ~ **processing** n proceso de datos.

date [deɪt] n (day) fecha; (with friend) cita; (fruit) dátil m // vt fechar; ~ **of birth** fecha de nacimiento; to ~ ad hasta la fecha; **out of** ~ pasado de moda; **up to** ~ moderno; ~**d** a anticuado.

daub [dɔːb] vt embadurnar.

daughter ['dɔːtə*] n hija; ~-**in-law** n nuera, hija política.

daunting ['dɔːntɪŋ] a desalentador(a).

dawdle ['dɔːdl] vi (waste time) perder el tiempo; (go slowly) andar muy despacio.

dawn [dɔːn] n alba, amanecer m // vi (day) amanecer; (fig): it ~ed on him that... cayó en la cuenta de que... .

day [deɪ] n día m; (working ~) jornada; the ~ before el día anterior; the ~ after tomorrow pasado mañana; the ~ before yesterday anteayer; the ~ after, the following ~ el día siguiente; by ~ de día; ~**break** n amanecer m; ~**dream** vi soñar despierto; ~**light** n luz f (del día); ~**light saving time** n (US) hora de verano; ~ **return** n (Brit) billete m de ida y vuelta (en un día); ~**time** n día m; ~-**to**-~ a cotidiano.

daze [deɪz] vt (stun) aturdir // n: **in a** ~ aturdido.

dazzle ['dæzl] vt deslumbrar; **dazzling** a deslumbrante.

DC abbr (= direct current) corriente f continua.

deacon ['diːkən] n diácono.

dead [dɛd] a muerto; (limb) dormido; (telephone) cortado; (battery) agotado //

ad totalmente; **to shoot sb** ~ matar a uno a tiros; ~ **tired** muerto (de cansancio); **to stop** ~ parar en seco; **the** ~ *npl* los muertos; **to be a** ~ **loss** (*col: person*) ser un inútil; (: *thing*) ser una birria; ~**en** *vt* (*blow, sound*) amortiguar; (*make numb*) calmar, aliviar; ~ **end** *n* callejón *m* sin salida; ~ **heat** *n* (*SPORT*) empate *m*; ~**line** *n* fecha *or* hora tope; ~**lock** *n* punto muerto; ~**ly** *a* mortal, fatal; ~**pan** *a* sin expresión.

deaf [def] *a* sordo; ~**en** *vt* ensordecer; ~**-mute** *n* sordomudo/a; ~**ness** *n* sordera.

deal [di:l] *n* (*agreement*) pacto, convenio; (*business*) negocio, transacción *f*; (*CARDS*) reparto // *vt* (*pt, pp* dealt [delt]) (*gen*) dar; **a great** ~ (**of**) bastante, mucho; **to** ~ **in** *vt fus* tratar en, comerciar en; **to** ~ **with** *vt fus* (*people*) tratar con; (*problem*) ocuparse de; (*subject*) tratar de; ~**er** *n* comerciante *m/f*; (*CARDS*) mano *f*; ~**ings** *npl* (*COMM*) transacciones *fpl*; (*relations*) relaciones *fpl*.

dean [di:n] *n* (*REL*) deán *m*; (*SCOL*) decano/a.

dear [dɪə*] *a* querido; (*expensive*) caro // *n*: **my** ~ mi querido/a; ~ **me**! ¡Dios mío!; **D**~ **Sir/Madam** (*in letter*) Muy Señor Mío, Estimado Señor/Estimada Señora; **D**~ **Mr/Mrs X** Estimado/a Señor(a) X; ~**ly** *ad* (*love*) mucho; (*pay*) caro.

death [deθ] *n* muerte *f*; ~ **certificate** *n* partida de defunción; ~ **duties** *npl* (*Brit*) derechos *mpl* de sucesión; ~**ly** *a* mortal; (*silence*) profundo; ~ **penalty** *n* pena de muerte; ~ **rate** *n* mortalidad *f*.

debacle [deɪ'bɑ:kl] *n* desastre *m*.

debar [dɪ'bɑ:*] *vt*: **to** ~ **sb from doing** prohibir a uno hacer.

debase [dɪ'beɪs] *vt* degradar.

debatable [dɪ'beɪtəbl] *a* discutible.

debate [dɪ'beɪt] *n* debate *m* // *vt* discutir.

debauchery [dɪ'bɔːtʃərɪ] *n* libertinaje *m*.

debilitating [dɪ'bɪlɪteɪtɪŋ] *a* (*illness etc*) debilitante.

debit ['debɪt] *n* debe *m* // *vt*: **to** ~ **a sum to sb** *or* **to sb's account** cargar una suma en cuenta a alguien.

debris ['debri:] *n* escombros *mpl*.

debt [det] *n* deuda; **to be in** ~ tener deudas; ~**or** *n* deudor(a) *m/f*.

debunk [di:'bʌŋk] *vt* desprestigiar, desacreditar.

début ['deɪbju:] *n* presentación *f*.

decade ['dekeɪd] *n* decenio.

decadence ['dekədəns] *n* decadencia.

decaffeinated [dɪ'kæfɪneɪtɪd] *a* descafeinado.

decanter [dɪ'kæntə*] *n* garrafa.

decay [dɪ'keɪ] *n* (*fig*) decadencia; (*of building*) desmoronamiento; (*rotting*) pudrición *f*; (*of tooth*) caries *f inv* // *vi*

(*rot*) pudrirse; (*fig*) decaer.

deceased [dɪ'si:st] *a* difunto.

deceit [dɪ'si:t] *n* engaño; ~**ful** *a* engañoso.

deceive [dɪ'si:v] *vt* engañar.

December [dɪ'sembə*] *n* diciembre *m*.

decent ['di:sənt] *a* (*proper*) decente; (*person*) amable, bueno.

deception [dɪ'sepʃən] *n* engaño.

deceptive [dɪ'septɪv] *a* engañoso.

decibel ['desɪbel] *n* decibel(io) *m*.

decide [dɪ'saɪd] *vt* (*person*) decidir; (*question, argument*) resolver // *vi*: **to** ~ **to do/that** decidir hacer/que; **to** ~ **on sth** decidir por algo; ~**d** *a* (*resolute*) decidido; (*clear, definite*) indudable; ~**dly** [-dɪdlɪ] *ad* decididamente.

deciduous [dɪ'sɪdjuəs] *a* de hoja caduca.

decimal ['desɪməl] *a* decimal // *n* decimal *f*; ~ **point** *n* coma decimal.

decimate ['desɪmeɪt] *vt* diezmar.

decipher [dɪ'saɪfə*] *vt* descifrar.

decision [dɪ'sɪʒən] *n* decisión *f*.

deck [dek] *n* (*NAUT*) cubierta; (*of bus*) piso; (*of cards*) baraja; ~**chair** *n* tumbona.

declaration [deklə'reɪʃən] *n* declaración *f*.

declare [dɪ'kleə*] *vt* (*gen*) declarar.

decline [dɪ'klaɪn] *n* decaimiento, decadencia; (*lessening*) disminución *f* // *vt* rehusar // *vi* decaer; disminuir.

declutch ['di:'klʌtʃ] *vi* desembragar.

decode [di:'kəud] *vt* descifrar.

decompose [di:kəm'pəuz] *vi* descomponerse.

décor ['deɪkɔ:*] *n* decoración *f*; (*THEATRE*) decorado.

decorate ['dekəreɪt] *vt* (*adorn*): **to** ~ (**with**) adornar (de), decorar (de); (*paint*) pintar; (*paper*) empapelar; **decoration** [-'reɪʃən] *n* adorno; (*act*) decoración *f*; (*medal*) condecoración *f*; **decorative** ['dekərətɪv] *a* decorativo; **decorator** *n* (*workman*) pintor *m* decorador.

decorum [dɪ'kɔ:rəm] *n* decoro.

decoy ['di:kɔɪ] *n* señuelo.

decrease ['di:kri:s] *n* disminución *f* // (*vb*: [di:'kri:s]) *vt* disminuir, reducir // *vi* reducirse.

decree [dɪ'kri:] *n* decreto; ~ **nisi** *n* sentencia provisional de divorcio.

dedicate ['dedɪkeɪt] *vt* dedicar; **dedication** [-'keɪʃən] *n* (*devotion*) dedicación *f*; (*in book*) dedicatoria.

deduce [dɪ'dju:s] *vt* deducir.

deduct [dɪ'dʌkt] *vt* restar; (*from wage etc*) descontar; ~**ion** [dɪ'dʌkʃən] *n* (*amount deducted*) descuento; (*conclusion*) deducción *f*, conclusión *f*.

deed [di:d] *n* hecho, acto; (*feat*) hazaña; (*LAW*) escritura.

deem [di:m] *vt* juzgar.

deep [di:p] *a* profundo; (*voice*) bajo;

(*breath*) profundo, a pleno pulmón // *ad*: **the spectators stood 20 ~** los espectadores se formaron de 20 en fondo; **to be 4 metres ~** tener 4 metros de profundo; **~en** *vt* ahondar, profundizar // *vi* (*darkness*) intensificarse; **~-freeze** *n* congeladora; **~-fry** *vt* freír en aceite abundante; **~ly** *ad* (*breathe*) a pleno pulmón; (*interested, moved, grateful*) profundamente, hondamente; **~-sea diving** *n* buceo de altura; **~-seated** *a* (*beliefs*) (profundamente) arraigado.

deer [dɪə*] *n, pl inv* ciervo.

deface [dɪ'feɪs] *vt* desfigurar, mutilar.

defamation [dɛfə'meɪʃən] *n* difamación *f*.

default [dɪ'fɔːlt] *vi* faltar al pago; (*SPORT*) dejar de presentarse // *n* (*COMPUT*) defecto; **by ~** (*LAW*) en rebeldía; (*SPORT*) por incomparecencia; **~er** *n* (*in debt*) moroso/a.

defeat [dɪ'fiːt] *n* derrota // *vt* derrotar, vencer; (*fig: efforts*) frustrar; **~ist** *a, n* derrotista *m/f*.

defect [di'fɛkt] *n* defecto // *vi* [dɪ'fɛkt]: **to ~ to the enemy** pasarse al enemigo; **~ive** [dɪ'fɛktɪv] *a* (*gen*) defectuoso; (*person*) anormal.

defence [dɪ'fɛns] *n* defensa; **~less** *a* indefenso.

defend [dɪ'fɛnd] *vt* defender; **~ant** *n* acusado/a; (*in civil case*) demandado/a; **~er** *n* defensor(a) *m/f*.

defense [dɪ'fɛns] *n* (*US*) = **defence**.

defensive [dɪ'fɛnsɪv] *a* defensivo; **on the ~** a la defensiva.

defer [dɪ'fə:*] *vt* (*postpone*) aplazar; **to ~** diferir a; **~ence** ['dɛfərəns] *n* deferencia, respeto.

defiance [dɪ'faɪəns] *n* desafío; **in ~ of** en contra de.

defiant [dɪ'faɪənt] *a* (*insolent*) insolente; (*challenging*) retador(a).

deficiency [dɪ'fɪʃənsɪ] *n* (*lack*) falta; (*defect*) defecto.

deficient [dɪ'fɪʃənt] *a* (*lacking*) insuficiente; (*incomplete*) incompleto; (*defective*) defectuoso; (*mentally*) anormal; **~ in** deficiente en.

deficit ['dɛfɪsɪt] *n* déficit *m*.

defile [dɪ'faɪl] *vt* manchar; (*violate*) violar.

define [dɪ'faɪn] *vt* definir.

definite ['dɛfɪnɪt] *a* (*fixed*) determinado; (*clear, obvious*) claro; **he was ~ about it** no dejó lugar a dudas (sobre ello); **~ly** *ad*: **he's ~ly mad** no cabe duda de que está loco.

definition [dɛfɪ'nɪʃən] *n* definición *f*.

deflate [di:'fleɪt] *vt* (*gen*) desinflar; (*person*) quitar los humos a.

deflect [dɪ'flɛkt] *vt* desviar.

defraud [dɪ'frɔːd] *vt* estafar; **to ~ sb of** sth estafar algo a uno.

defray [dɪ'freɪ] *vt*: **to ~ sb's expenses** reembolsar(le) a uno los gastos.

defrost [di:'frɔst] *vt* (*food*) deshelar; (*fridge*) descongelar; **~er** *n* (*US: demister*) eliminador *m* de vaho.

deft [dɛft] *a* diestro, hábil.

defunct [dɪ'fʌŋkt] *a* difunto.

defuse [di:'fjuːz] *vt* desarmar; (*situation*) calmar.

defy [dɪ'faɪ] *vt* (*resist*) oponerse a; (*challenge*) desafiar; (*order*) contravenir.

degenerate [dɪ'dʒɛnəreɪt] *vi* degenerar // *a* [dɪ'dʒɛnərət] degenerado.

degree [dɪ'griː] *n* grado; (*SCOL*) título; **to have a ~ in maths** tener una licenciatura en matemáticas; **by ~s** (*gradually*) poco a poco, por etapas; **to some ~** hasta cierto punto.

dehydrated [di:haɪ'dreɪtɪd] *a* deshidratado; (*milk*) en polvo.

deign [deɪn] *vi*: **to ~ to do** dignarse hacer.

deity ['di:ɪtɪ] *n* deidad *f*, divinidad *f*.

dejected [dɪ'dʒɛktɪd] *a* abatido, desanimado.

delay [dɪ'leɪ] *vt* demorar, aplazar; (*person*) entretener; (*train*) retrasar // *vi* tardar // *n* demora, retraso; **without ~** en seguida, sin tardar.

delectable [dɪ'lɛktəbl] *a* (*person*) encantador(a); (*food*) delicioso.

delegate ['dɛlɪgɪt] *n* delegado/a // *vt* ['dɛlɪgeɪt] delegar.

delete [dɪ'liːt] *vt* suprimir, tachar.

deliberate [dɪ'lɪbərɪt] *a* (*intentional*) intencionado; (*slow*) pausado, lento // *vi* [dɪ'lɪbəreɪt] deliberar; **~ly** *ad* (*on purpose*) a propósito; (*slowly*) pausadamente.

delicacy ['dɛlɪkəsɪ] *n* delicadeza; (*choice food*) golosina.

delicate ['dɛlɪkɪt] *a* (*gen*) delicado; (*fragile*) frágil.

delicatessen [dɛlɪkə'tɛsn] *n* ultramarinos *mpl* finos.

delicious [dɪ'lɪʃəs] *a* delicioso, rico.

delight [dɪ'laɪt] *n* (*feeling*) placer *m*, deleite *m*; (*object*) encanto, delicia // *vt* encantar, deleitar; **to take ~ in** deleitarse en; **~ed** *a*: **~ed** (**at** *or* **with/to do**) encantado (con/de hacer); **~ful** *a* encantador(a), delicioso.

delinquent [dɪ'lɪŋkwənt] *a, n* delincuente *m/f*.

delirious [dɪ'lɪrɪəs] *a*: **to be ~** delirar, desvariar.

deliver [dɪ'lɪvə*] *vt* (*distribute*) repartir; (*hand over*) entregar; (*message*) comunicar; (*speech*) pronunciar; (*blow*) lanzar, dar; (*MED*) asistir al parto de; **~y** *n* reparto; entrega; (*of speaker*) modo de expresarse; (*MED*) parto, alumbramiento; **to take ~y of** recibir.

delude [dɪ'luːd] *vt* engañar.

deluge ['dɛljuːdʒ] *n* diluvio // *vt* inundar.

delusion [dɪ'luːʒən] *n* ilusión *f*, engaño.

de luxe [dəˈlʌks] a de lujo.

delve [dɛlv] vi: to ~ into hurgar en.

demand [dɪˈmɑːnd] vt (gen) exigir; (rights) reclamar // n (gen) exigencia; (claim) reclamación f; (ECON) demanda; **to be in ~** ser muy solicitado; **on ~** a solicitud; **~ing** a (boss) exigente; (work) absorbente.

demean [dɪˈmiːn] vt: to ~ o.s. rebajarse.

demeanour, (US) **demeanor** [dɪˈmiːnə*] n porte m, conducta.

demented [dɪˈmɛntɪd] a demente.

demise [dɪˈmaɪz] n (death) fallecimiento.

demister [diːˈmɪstə*] n (AUT) eliminador m de vaho.

demo [ˈdɛməu] n abbr (col: = demonstration) manifestación f.

democracy [dɪˈmɔkrəsɪ] n democracia; **democrat** [ˈdɛməkræt] n demócrata m/f; **democratic** [dɛməˈkrætɪk] a democrático.

demolish [dɪˈmɔlɪʃ] vt derribar, demoler; **demolition** [dɛməˈlɪʃən] n derribo, demolición f.

demon [ˈdiːmən] n (evil spirit) demonio.

demonstrate [ˈdɛmənstreɪt] vt demostrar // vi manifestarse; **demonstration** [-ˈstreɪʃən] n (POL) manifestación f; (proof) prueba, demostración f; **demonstrator** n (POL) manifestante m/f.

demoralize [dɪˈmɔrəlaɪz] vt desmoralizar.

demote [dɪˈməut] vt degradar.

demure [dɪˈmjuə*] a recatado.

den [dɛn] n (of animal) guarida; (study) estudio.

denatured alcohol [diːˈneɪtʃəd-] n (US) alcohol m desnaturalizado.

denial [dɪˈnaɪəl] n (refusal) negativa; (of report etc) negación f.

denim [ˈdɛnɪm] n tela vaquera; **~s** npl vaqueros mpl.

Denmark [ˈdɛnmɑːk] n Dinamarca.

denomination [dɪnɔmɪˈneɪʃən] n valor m; (REL) confesión f.

denote [dɪˈnəut] vt indicar, significar.

denounce [dɪˈnauns] vt denunciar.

dense [dɛns] a (thick) espeso; (: foliage etc) tupido; (stupid) torpe; **~ly** ad: **~ly populated** con una alta densidad de población.

density [ˈdɛnsɪtɪ] n densidad f; **double~ disk** n (COMPUT) disco de doble densidad.

dent [dɛnt] n abolladura // vt (also: **make a ~ in**) abollar.

dental [ˈdɛntl] a dental; **~ surgeon** n odontólogo/a.

dentist [ˈdɛntɪst] n dentista m/f; **~ry** n odontología.

dentures [ˈdɛntʃəz] npl dentadura sg (postiza).

denunciation [dɪnʌnsɪˈeɪʃən] n denuncia, denunciación f.

deny [dɪˈnaɪ] vt negar; (charge) recha-

zar; (report) desmentir.

deodorant [diːˈəudərənt] n desodorante m.

depart [dɪˈpɑːt] vi irse, marcharse; (train) salir; **to ~ from** (fig: differ from) apartarse de.

department [dɪˈpɑːtmənt] n (COMM) sección f; (SCOL) departamento; (POL) ministerio; **~ store** n gran almacén m.

departure [dɪˈpɑːtʃə*] n partida, ida; (of train) salida; **a new ~** un nuevo rumbo; **~ lounge** n (at airport) sala de embarque.

depend [dɪˈpɛnd] vi: **to ~ on** depender de; (rely on) contar con; **it ~s** depende, según; **~ing on the result** según el resultado; **~able** a (person) formal, serio; **~ant** n dependiente m/f; **~ence** n dependencia; **~ent** a: **to be ~ent on** depender de // n = **~ant**.

depict [dɪˈpɪkt] vt (in picture) pintar; (describe) representar.

depleted [dɪˈpliːtɪd] a reducido.

deplorable [dɪˈplɔːrəbl] a deplorable.

deplore [dɪˈplɔː*] vt deplorar.

deploy [dɪˈplɔɪ] vt desplegar.

depopulation [ˈdiːpɔpjuˈleɪʃən] n despoblación f.

deport [dɪˈpɔːt] vt deportar.

deportment [dɪˈpɔːtmənt] n comportamiento.

depose [dɪˈpəuz] vt deponer.

deposit [dɪˈpɔzɪt] n depósito; (CHEM) sedimento; (of ore, oil) yacimiento // vt (gen) depositar; **~ account** n (Brit) cuenta de ahorros; **~or** n depositante m/f.

depot [ˈdɛpəu] n (storehouse) depósito; (for vehicles) parque m.

depreciate [dɪˈpriːʃɪeɪt] vi depreciarse, perder valor; **depreciation** [-ˈeɪʃən] n depreciación f.

depress [dɪˈprɛs] vt deprimir; (press down) apretar; **~ed** a deprimido; **~ing** a deprimente; **~ion** [dɪˈprɛʃən] n depresión f.

deprivation [dɛprɪˈveɪʃən] n privación f; (loss) pérdida.

deprive [dɪˈpraɪv] vt: **to ~ sb of** privar a uno de; **~d** a necesitado.

depth [dɛpθ] n profundidad f; **in the ~s of** en lo más hondo de.

deputation [dɛpjuˈteɪʃən] n delegación f.

deputize [ˈdɛpjutaɪz] vi: **to ~ for sb** suplir a uno.

deputy [ˈdɛpjutɪ] a: **~ head** subdirector(a) m/f // n sustituto/a, suplente m/f; (POL) diputado/a; (agent) representante m/f.

derail [dɪˈreɪl] vt: **to be ~ed** descarrilarse; **~ment** n descarrilamiento.

deranged [dɪˈreɪndʒd] a trastornado.

derby [ˈdəːbɪ] n (US) hongo.

derelict [ˈdɛrɪlɪkt] a abandonado.

deride [dɪˈraɪd] vt ridiculizar, mofarse

de.
derisive [dɪ'raɪsɪv] a burlón/ona.
derisory [dɪ'raɪzərɪ] a (sum) irrisorio.
derivative [dɪ'rɪvətɪv] n derivado // a (work) poco original.
derive [dɪ'raɪv] vt derivar // vi: to ~ from derivarse de.
derogatory [dɪ'rɒgətərɪ] a despectivo.
derrick ['derɪk] n torre f de perforación.
derv [dɜːv] n (Brit) gasoil m.
descend [dɪ'send] vt, vi descender, bajar; to ~ from descender de; ~ant n descendiente m/f.
descent [dɪ'sent] n descenso; (origin) descendencia.
describe [dɪs'kraɪb] vt describir; **description** [-'krɪpʃən] n descripción f; (sort) clase f, género.
desecrate ['desɪkreɪt] vt profanar.
desert ['dezət] n desierto // (vb: [dɪ'zɜːt]) vt abandonar, desamparar // vi (MIL) desertar; ~s [dɪ'zɜːts] npl: to get one's just ~s llevar su merecido; ~er [dɪ'zɜːtə*] n desertor(a) m/f; ~ion [dɪ'zɜːʃən] n deserción f; ~ island n isla desierta.
deserve [dɪ'zɜːv] vt merecer, ser digno de; **deserving** a (person) digno; (action, cause) meritorio.
design [dɪ'zaɪn] n (sketch) bosquejo; (layout, shape) diseño; (pattern) dibujo // vt (gen) diseñar; to have ~s on sb tener la(s) mira(s) puesta(s) en uno.
designate ['dezɪgneɪt] vt (appoint) nombrar; (destine) designar // a ['dezɪgnɪt] designado.
designer [dɪ'zaɪnə*] n diseñador(a) m/f; (fashion ~) modisto/a.
desirable [dɪ'zaɪərəbl] a (proper) deseable; (attractive) atractivo.
desire [dɪ'zaɪə*] n deseo // vt desear.
desk [desk] n (in office) escritorio; (for pupil) pupitre m; (in hotel, at airport) recepción f; (Brit: in shop, restaurant) caja.
desolate ['desəlɪt] a (place) desierto; (person) afligido; **desolation** [-'leɪʃən] n (of place) desolación f; (of person) aflicción f.
despair [dɪs'peə*] n desesperación f // vi: to ~ of desesperarse de.
despatch [dɪs'pætʃ] n, vt = **dispatch**.
desperate ['despərɪt] a desesperado; (fugitive) peligroso; ~ly ad desesperadamente; (very) terriblemente, gravemente.
desperation [despə'reɪʃən] n desesperación f; in ~ desesperado.
despicable [dɪs'pɪkəbl] a vil, despreciable.
despise [dɪs'paɪz] vt despreciar.
despite [dɪs'paɪt] prep a pesar de, pese a.
despondent [dɪs'pɒndənt] a deprimido, abatido.

dessert [dɪ'zɜːt] n postre m; ~spoon n cuchara (de postre).
destination [destɪ'neɪʃən] n destino.
destine ['destɪn] vt destinar.
destiny ['destɪnɪ] n destino.
destitute ['destɪtjuːt] a desamparado, indigente.
destroy [dɪs'trɔɪ] vt destruir; (finish) acabar con; ~er n (NAUT) destructor m.
destruction [dɪs'trʌkʃən] n destrucción f; (fig) ruina.
destructive [dɪs'trʌktɪv] a destructivo, destructor(a).
detach [dɪ'tætʃ] vt separar; (unstick) despegar; ~able a separable; (TECH) desmontable; ~ed a (attitude) objetivo, imparcial; ~ed house n ≈ chalé m, chalet m; ~ment n separación f; (MIL) destacamento; (fig) objetividad f, imparcialidad f.
detail ['diːteɪl] n detalle m // vt detallar; (MIL) destacar; in ~ detalladamente; ~ed a detallado.
detain [dɪ'teɪn] vt retener; (in captivity) detener.
detect [dɪ'tekt] vt (gen) descubrir; (MED, POLICE) identificar; (MIL, RADAR, TECH) detectar; ~ion [dɪ'tekʃən] n descubrimiento; identificación f; ~ive m/f en detective m/f; ~ive story n novela policíaca; ~or n detector m.
détente [deɪ'taːnt] n distensión f.
detention [dɪ'tenʃən] n detención f, arresto.
deter [dɪ'tɜː*] vt (dissuade) disuadir; (prevent) impedir; to ~ sb from doing sth disuadir a uno de que haga algo.
detergent [dɪ'tɜːdʒənt] n detergente m.
deteriorate [dɪ'tɪərɪəreɪt] vi deteriorarse; **deterioration** [-'reɪʃən] n deterioro.
determination [dɪtɜːmɪ'neɪʃən] n resolución f.
determine [dɪ'tɜːmɪn] vt determinar; ~d a: ~d to do resuelto a hacer.
deterrent [dɪ'terənt] n fuerza de disuasión.
detest [dɪ'test] vt aborrecer.
detonate ['detəneɪt] vi estallar // vt hacer detonar.
detour ['diːtuə*] n (gen, US AUT: diversion) desviación f // vt (US AUT) desviar.
detract [dɪ'trækt] vt: to ~ from quitar mérito a, desvirtuar.
detriment ['detrɪmənt] n: to the ~ of en perjuicio de; ~al [detrɪ'mentl] a: ~al (to) perjudicial (a).
devaluation [dɪvælju'eɪʃən] n devaluación f.
devastating ['devəsteɪtɪŋ] a devastador(a); (fig) arrollador(a).
develop [dɪ'veləp] vt desarrollar; (PHOT) revelar; (disease) coger; (habit) adquirir // vi desarrollarse; (advance) progresar; ~ing country país m en (vías

de) desarrollo; **~ment** n desarrollo; (*advance*) progreso; (*of affair, case*) desenvolvimiento; (*of land*) urbanización f.

deviate ['diːvɪeɪt] vi: to ~ (**from**) desviarse (de); **deviation** [-'eɪʃən] n desviación f.

device [dɪ'vaɪs] n (*scheme*) estratagema, recurso; (*apparatus*) aparato, mecanismo.

devil ['dɛvl] n diablo, demonio; **~ish** a diabólico.

devious ['diːvɪəs] a intricado, enrevesado; (*person*) taimado.

devise [dɪ'vaɪz] vt idear, inventar.

devoid [dɪ'vɔɪd] a: ~ **of** desprovisto de.

devolution [diːvə'luːʃən] n (*POL*) descentralización f.

devote [dɪ'vəut] vt: to ~ **sth** to dedicar algo a; **~d** a (*loyal*) leal, fiel; **the book is ~d** to politics el libro trata de la política; **~e** [dɛvəu'tiː] n devoto/a.

devotion [dɪ'vəuʃən] n dedicación f; (*REL*) devoción f.

devour [dɪ'vauə*] vt devorar.

devout [dɪ'vaut] a devoto.

dew [djuː] n rocío.

dexterity [dɛks'tɛrɪtɪ] n destreza.

diabetes [daɪə'biːtiːz] n diabetes f; **diabetic** [-'bɛtɪk] a, n diabético/a m/f.

diabolical [daɪə'bɔlɪkəl] a (col: *weather*, *behaviour*) pésimo.

diagnose [daɪəg'nəuz] vt diagnosticar; **diagnosis** [-'nəusɪs], pl **-ses** [-'nəusiːz] n diagnóstico.

diagonal [daɪ'ægənl] a, n diagonal f.

diagram ['daɪəgræm] n diagrama m, esquema m.

dial ['daɪəl] n esfera, cuadrante m, cara (*LAm*); (*of phone*) disco // vt (*number*) marcar; ~ **code** n (*US*) prefijo; ~ **tone** n (*US*) señal f or tono de marcar.

dialect ['daɪəlɛkt] n dialecto.

dialling ['daɪəlɪŋ]: ~ **code** n (*Brit*) prefijo; ~ **tone** n (*Brit*) señal f or tono de marcar.

dialogue ['daɪəlɔg] n diálogo.

diameter [daɪ'æmɪtə*] n diámetro.

diamond ['daɪəmənd] n diamante m; ~**s** npl (*CARDS*) diamantes mpl.

diaper ['daɪəpə*] n (*US*) pañal m.

diaphragm ['daɪəfræm] n diafragma m.

diarrhoea, (*US*) **diarrhea** [daɪə'riːə] n diarrea.

diary ['daɪərɪ] n (*daily account*) diario; (*book*) agenda.

dice [daɪs] n, pl inv dados mpl // vt (*CULIN*) cortar en cuadritos.

dichotomy [daɪ'kɔtəmɪ] n dicotomía.

Dictaphone ['dɪktəfəun] n ® dictáfono ®.

dictate [dɪk'teɪt] vt dictar; ~**s** ['dɪkteɪts] npl dictados mpl; **dictation** [-'teɪʃən] n dictado.

dictator [dɪk'teɪtə*] n dictador m; ~**ship**

n dictadura.

dictionary ['dɪkʃənrɪ] n diccionario.

did [dɪd] pt of **do**.

didn't ['dɪdənt] = **did not**.

die [daɪ] vi morir; **to be dying for sth/to do sth** morirse por algo/de ganas de hacer algo; **to ~ away** vi (*sound, light*) perderse; **to ~ down** vi (*gen*) apagarse; (*wind*) amainar; **to ~ out** vi desaparecer, extinguirse.

diehard ['daɪhaːd] n reaccionario/a.

diesel ['diːzəl]: ~ **engine** n motor m Diesel; ~ (**oil**) n gasoil m.

diet ['daɪət] n dieta; (*restricted food*) régimen m // vi (*also*: **be on a ~**) estar a dieta, hacer régimen.

differ ['dɪfə*] vi (*be different*) ser distinto, diferenciarse; (*disagree*) discrepar; **~ence** n diferencia; (*quarrel*) desacuerdo; **~ent** a diferente, distinto; **~entiate** [-'rɛnʃɪeɪt] vt distinguir // vi diferenciarse; **to ~entiate between** distinguir entre; **~ently** ad de otro modo, en forma distinta.

difficult ['dɪfɪkəlt] a difícil; ~**y** n dificultad f.

diffident ['dɪfɪdənt] a tímido.

diffuse [dɪ'fjuːs] a difuso // vt [dɪ'fjuːz] difundir.

dig [dɪg] vt (pt, pp **dug**) (*hole*) cavar; (*ground*) remover // n (*prod*) empujón m; (*archaeological*) excavación f; (*remark*) indirecta; **to ~ one's nails into** clavar las uñas en; **to ~ in** vi atrincherarse; **to ~ into** vt fus (*savings*) consumir; **to ~ out** vt (*hole*) excavar; (*fig*) sacar; **to ~ up** vt desenterrar; (*plant*) desarraigar.

digest [daɪ'dʒɛst] vt (*food*) digerir; (*facts*) asimilar // n ['daɪdʒɛst] resumen m; ~**ion** [dɪ'dʒɛstʃən] n digestión f.

digit ['dɪdʒɪt] n (*number*) dígito; (*finger*) dedo; ~**al** a digital.

dignified ['dɪgnɪfaɪd] a grave, solemne; (*action*) decoroso.

dignity ['dɪgnɪtɪ] n dignidad f.

digress [daɪ'grɛs] vi: **to ~ from** apartarse de.

digs [dɪgz] npl (*Brit: col*) pensión fsg, alojamiento sg.

dike [daɪk] n = **dyke**.

dilapidated [dɪ'læpɪdeɪtɪd] a desmoronado, ruinoso.

dilemma [daɪ'lɛmə] n dilema m.

diligent ['dɪlɪdʒənt] a diligente.

dilute [daɪ'luːt] vt diluir.

dim [dɪm] a (*light*) débil; (*sight*) turbio; (*outline*) indistinto; (*stupid*) lerdo; (*room*) oscuro // vt (*light*) bajar.

dime [daɪm] n (*US*) moneda de diez centavos.

dimension [dɪ'mɛnʃən] n dimensión f.

diminish [dɪ'mɪnɪʃ] vt, vi disminuir.

diminutive [dɪ'mɪnjutɪv] a diminuto // n (*LING*) diminutivo.

dimly ['dɪmlɪ] ad débilmente; (not clearly) indistintamente.

dimmer ['dɪmə*] n (US AUT) interruptor m.

dimple ['dɪmpl] n hoyuelo.

din [dɪn] n estruendo, estrépito.

dine [daɪn] vi cenar; ~r n (person) comensal m/f; (Brit RAIL) = **dining car**; (US) restaurante m económico.

dinghy ['dɪŋgɪ] n bote m; (also: rubber ~) lancha (neumática).

dingy ['dɪndʒɪ] a (room) sombrío; (dirty) sucio; (dull) deslucido.

dining ['daɪnɪŋ]: ~ **car** n (Brit RAIL) coche-comedor m; ~ **room** n comedor m.

dinner ['dɪnə*] n (evening meal) cena; (lunch) comida; (public) cena, banquete m; ~'s ready! ¡la cena está servida!; ~ **jacket** n smoking m; ~ **party** n cena; ~ **time** n hora de cenar or comer.

dinosaur ['daɪnəsɔ:*] n dinosaurio.

dint [dɪnt] n: by ~ of a fuerza de.

diocese ['daɪəsɪs] n diócesis f inv.

dip [dɪp] n (slope) pendiente m; (in sea) baño // vt (in water) mojar; (ladle etc) meter; (Brit AUT): to ~ one's lights poner luces de cruce // vi inclinarse hacia abajo.

diphthong ['dɪfθɔŋ] n diptongo.

diploma [dɪ'pləumə] n diploma m.

diplomacy [dɪ'pləuməsɪ] n diplomacia.

diplomat ['dɪpləmæt] n diplomático/a; ~**ic** [dɪplə'mætɪk] a diplomático.

dipstick ['dɪpstɪk] n (AUT) varilla de nivel (del aceite).

dipswitch ['dɪpswɪtʃ] n (Brit AUT) interruptor m.

dire [daɪə*] a calamitoso.

direct [daɪ'rɛkt] a (gen) directo // vt dirigir; can you ~ me to...? ¿puede indicarme dónde está...?

direction [dɪ'rɛkʃən] n dirección f; sense of ~ sentido de la dirección; ~s npl (advice) órdenes fpl, instrucciones fpl; ~s for use modo de empleo.

directly [dɪ'rɛktlɪ] ad (in straight line) directamente; (at once) en seguida.

director [dɪ'rɛktə*] n director(a) m/f.

directory [dɪ'rɛktərɪ] n (TEL) guía (telefónica).

dirt [dɜ:t] n suciedad f; ~-**cheap** a baratísimo; ~**y** a sucio; (joke) verde, colorado (LAm) // vt ensuciar; (stain) manchar; ~**y trick** n juego sucio.

disability [dɪsə'bɪlɪtɪ] n incapacidad f.

disabled [dɪs'eɪbld] a minusválido.

disadvantage [dɪsəd'vɑ:ntɪdʒ] n desventaja, inconveniente m.

disaffection [dɪsə'fɛkʃən] n desafecto.

disagree [dɪsə'gri:] vi (differ) discrepar; to ~ (with) no estar de acuerdo (con); ~**able** a desagradable; ~**ment** n (gen) desacuerdo; (quarrel) riña.

disallow ['dɪsə'lau] vt (goal) anular;

(claim) rechazar.

disappear [dɪsə'pɪə*] vi desaparecer; ~**ance** n desaparición f.

disappoint [dɪsə'pɔɪnt] vt decepcionar; (hopes) defraudar; ~**ed** a decepcionado; ~**ing** a decepcionante; ~**ment** n decepción f.

disapproval [dɪsə'pru:vəl] n desaprobación f.

disapprove [dɪsə'pru:v] vi: to ~ of desaprobar.

disarm [dɪs'ɑ:m] vt desarmar; ~**ament** n desarme m.

disarray [dɪsə'reɪ] n: in ~ (army, organization) desorganizado; (hair, clothes) desarreglado.

disaster [dɪ'zɑ:stə*] n desastre m.

disband [dɪs'bænd] vt disolver // vi desbandarse.

disbelief [dɪsbə'li:f] n incredulidad f.

disc [dɪsk] n disco; (COMPUT) = **disk**.

discard [dɪs'kɑ:d] vt (old things) tirar; (fig) descartar.

discern [dɪ'sɜ:n] vt percibir, discernir; (understand) comprender; ~**ing** a perspicaz.

discharge [dɪs'tʃɑ:dʒ] vt (task, duty) cumplir; (ship etc) descargar; (patient) dar de alta; (employee) despedir; (soldier) licenciar; (defendant) poner en libertad // n ['dɪstʃɑ:dʒ] (ELEC) descarga; (dismissal) despedida; (of duty) desempeño; (of debt) pago, descargo.

disciple [dɪ'saɪpl] n discípulo.

discipline ['dɪsɪplɪn] n disciplina // vt disciplinar.

disc jockey n pinchadiscos m/f inv.

disclaim [dɪs'kleɪm] vt negar.

disclose [dɪs'kləuz] vt revelar; disclosure [-'kləuʒə*] n revelación f.

disco ['dɪskəu] n abbr = **discothèque**.

discoloured, (US) **discolored** [dɪs'kʌləd] a descolorado.

discomfort [dɪs'kʌmfət] n incomodidad f; (unease) inquietud f; (physical) malestar m.

disconcert [dɪskən'sɜ:t] vt desconcertar.

disconnect [dɪskə'nɛkt] vt (gen) separar; (ELEC etc) desconectar; (supply) cortar (el suministro) a.

discontent [dɪskən'tɛnt] n descontento; ~**ed** a descontento.

discontinue [dɪskən'tɪnju:] vt interrumpir; (payments) suspender.

discord ['dɪskɔ:d] n discordia; (MUS) disonancia; ~**ant** [dɪs'kɔ:dənt] a disonante.

discothèque ['dɪskəutɛk] n discoteca.

discount ['dɪskaunt] n descuento // vt [dɪs'kaunt] descontar.

discourage [dɪs'kʌrɪdʒ] vt desalentar; (oppose) oponerse a; **discouraging** a desalentador(a).

discover [dɪs'kʌvə*] vt descubrir; ~**y** n descubrimiento.

discredit [dɪs'krɛdɪt] vt desacreditar.

discreet [dɪ'skriːt] *a* (*tactful*) discreto; (*careful*) circunspecto, prudente.

discrepancy [dɪ'skrepənsɪ] *n* diferencia.

discretion [dɪ'skreʃən] *n* (*tact*) discreción *f*; (*care*) prudencia, circunspección *f*.

discriminate [dɪ'skrɪmɪneɪt] *vi*: to ~ between distinguir entre; to ~ against discriminar contra; **discriminating** *a* entendido; **discrimination** [-'neɪʃən] *n* (*discernment*) perspicacia; (*bias*) discriminación *f*.

discuss [dɪ'skʌs] *vt* (*gen*) discutir; (*a theme*) tratar; ~**ion** [dɪ'skʌʃən] *n* discusión *f*.

disdain [dɪs'deɪn] *n* desdén *m* // *vt* desdeñar.

disease [dɪ'ziːz] *n* enfermedad *f*.

disembark [dɪsɪm'bɑːk] *vt*, *vi* desembarcar.

disenchanted [dɪsɪn'tʃɑːntɪd] *a*: ~ (**with**) desilusionado (con).

disengage [dɪsɪn'geɪdʒ] *vt* soltar; to ~ the clutch (*AUT*) desembragar.

disentangle [dɪsɪn'tæŋgl] *vt* desenredar.

disfigure [dɪs'fɪgə*] *vt* desfigurar.

disgrace [dɪs'greɪs] *n* ignominia; (*shame*) vergüenza, escándalo // *vt* deshonrar; ~**ful** *a* vergonzoso; (*behaviour*) escandaloso.

disgruntled [dɪs'grʌntld] *a* disgustado, descontento.

disguise [dɪs'gaɪz] *n* disfraz *m* // *vt* disfrazar; in ~ disfrazado.

disgust [dɪs'gʌst] *n* repugnancia // *vt* repugnar, dar asco a; ~**ing** *a* repugnante, asqueroso.

dish [dɪʃ] *n* (*gen*) plato; to do *or* wash the ~es fregar los platos; to ~ up *vt* servir; to ~ out *vt* repartir; ~**cloth** *n* paño de cocina, bayeta.

dishearten [dɪs'hɑːtn] *vt* desalentar.

dishevelled [dɪ'ʃevəld] *a* (*hair*) despeinado; (*clothes, appearance*) desarreglado.

dishonest [dɪs'ɔnɪst] *a* (*person*) poco honrado, tramposo; (*means*) fraudulento; ~**y** *n* falta de honradez.

dishonour, (*US*) **dishonor** [dɪs'ɔnə*] *n* deshonra; ~**able** *a* deshonroso.

dishtowel ['dɪʃtauəl] *n* (*US*) trapo de fregar.

dishwasher ['dɪʃwɔʃə*] *n* lavaplatos *m inv*; (*person*) friegaplatos *m/f inv*.

disillusion [dɪsɪ'luːʒən] *vt* desilusionar.

disincentive [dɪsɪn'sentɪv] *n* desincentivo.

disinfect [dɪsɪn'fekt] *vt* desinfectar; ~**ant** *n* desinfectante *m*.

disintegrate [dɪs'ɪntɪgreɪt] *vi* disgregarse, desintegrarse.

disinterested [dɪs'ɪntrəstɪd] *a* desinteresado.

disjointed [dɪs'dʒɔɪntɪd] *a* inconexo.

disk [dɪsk] *n* (*esp US*) = **disc**; (*COMPUT*)

disco, disquete *m*; **single-/double-sided** ~ disco de una cara/dos caras; ~ **drive** *n* disc drive *m*; ~**ette** *n* (*US*) = **disk**.

dislike [dɪs'laɪk] *n* antipatía, aversión *f* // *vt* tener antipatía a.

dislocate ['dɪsləkeɪt] *vt* dislocar.

dislodge [dɪs'lɔdʒ] *vt* sacar; (*enemy*) desalojar.

disloyal [dɪs'lɔɪəl] *a* desleal.

dismal ['dɪzml] *a* (*gloomy*) deprimente, triste.

dismantle [dɪs'mæntl] *vt* desmontar, desarmar.

dismay [dɪs'meɪ] *n* consternación *f*.

dismiss [dɪs'mɪs] *vt* (*worker*) despedir; (*official*) destituir; (*idea, LAW*) rechazar; (*possibility*) descartar // *vi* (*MIL*) romper filas; ~**al** *n* despedida; destitución *f*.

dismount [dɪs'maunt] *vi* apearse.

disobedience [dɪsə'biːdɪəns] *n* desobediencia.

disobedient [dɪsə'biːdɪənt] *a* desobediente.

disobey [dɪsə'beɪ] *vt* desobedecer.

disorder [dɪs'ɔːdə*] *n* desorden *m*; (*rioting*) disturbio; (*MED*) trastorno; (*disease*) enfermedad *f*; ~**ly** *a* (*untidy*) desordenado; (*meeting*) alborotado; (*conduct*) escandaloso.

disorientated [dɪs'ɔːrɪenteɪtəd] *a* desorientado.

disown [dɪs'əun] *vt* desconocer.

disparaging [dɪs'pærɪdʒɪŋ] *a* despreciativo.

disparity [dɪs'pærɪtɪ] *n* disparidad *f*.

dispassionate [dɪs'pæʃənɪt] *a* (*unbiased*) imparcial; (*unemotional*) desapasionado.

dispatch [dɪs'pætʃ] *vt* enviar // *n* (*sending*) envío; (*PRESS*) informe *m*; (*MIL*) parte *m*.

dispel [dɪs'pel] *vt* disipar, dispersar.

dispensary [dɪs'pensərɪ] *n* dispensario, farmacia.

dispense [dɪs'pens] *vt* dispensar, repartir; to ~ **with** *vt fus* prescindir de; ~**r** *n* (*container*) distribuidor *m* automático; **dispensing chemist** *n* (*Brit*) farmacia.

dispersal [dɪs'pəːsl] *n* dispersión *f*.

disperse [dɪs'pəːs] *vt* dispersar // *vi* dispersarse.

dispirited [dɪ'spɪrɪtɪd] *a* desanimado, desalentado.

displace [dɪs'pleɪs] *vt* (*person*) desplazar; (*replace*) reemplazar; ~**d person** *n* (*POL*) desplazado/a.

display [dɪs'pleɪ] *n* (*exhibition*) exposición *f*; (*COMPUT*) visualización *f*; (*MIL*) exhibición *f*; (*of feeling*) manifestación *f*; (*pej*) aparato, pompa // *vt* exponer; manifestar; (*ostentatiously*) lucir.

displease [dɪs'pliːz] *vt* (*offend*) ofender; (*annoy*) fastidiar; ~**d** *a*: ~**d with** disgustado con; **displeasure** [-'pleʒə*] *n* disgusto.

disposable [dɪs'pəuzəbl] *a* (*not reusable*) desechable; (*income*) disponible; ~ **nappy** *n* pañal *m* desechable.

disposal [dɪs'pəuzl] *n* (*sale*) venta; (*of house*) traspaso; (*arrangement*) colocación *f*; (*of rubbish*) destrucción *f*; at one's ~ a su disposición.

dispose [dɪs'pəuz] *vt* disponer; **to ~ of** *vt* (*time, money*) disponer de; (*unwanted goods*) deshacerse de; (*throw away*) tirar; ~**d** *a*: ~**d to do** dispuesto a hacer; **disposition** [-'zɪʃən] *n* disposición *f*.

disproportionate [dɪsprə'pɔːʃənət] *a* desproporcionado.

disprove [dɪs'pruːv] *vt* refutar.

dispute [dɪs'pjuːt] *n* disputa; (*verbal*) discusión *f*; (*also*: **industrial ~**) conflicto (laboral) // *vt* (*argue*) disputar; (*question*) cuestionar.

disqualify [dɪs'kwɔlɪfaɪ] *vt* (*SPORT*) desclasificar; **to ~ sb for sth/from doing sth** incapacitar a alguien para algo/hacer algo.

disquiet [dɪs'kwaɪət] *n* preocupación *f*, inquietud *f*.

disregard [dɪsrɪ'gɑːd] *vt* desatender; (*ignore*) no hacer caso de.

disrepair [dɪsrɪ'pɛə*] *n*: **to fall into ~** desmoronarse.

disreputable [dɪs'rɛpjutəbl] *a* (*person*) de mala fama; (*behaviour*) vergonzoso.

disrespectful [dɪsrɪ'spɛktful] *a* irrespetuoso.

disrupt [dɪs'rʌpt] *vt* (*plans*) desbaratar, trastornar; (*conversation*) interrumpir; ~**ion** [-'rʌpʃən] *n* trastorno; desbaratamiento; interrupción *f*.

dissatisfaction [dɪssætɪs'fækʃən] *n* disgusto, descontento.

dissect [dɪ'sɛkt] *vt* disecar.

disseminate [dɪ'sɛmɪneɪt] *vt* divulgar, difundir.

dissent [dɪ'sɛnt] *n* disensión *f*.

dissertation [dɪsə'teɪʃən] *n* tesina.

disservice [dɪs'səːvɪs] *n*: **to do sb a ~** perjudicar a alguien.

dissident ['dɪsɪdnt] *a, n* disidente *m/f*.

dissimilar [dɪ'sɪmɪlə*] *a* distinto.

dissipate ['dɪsɪpeɪt] *vt* disipar; (*waste*) desperdiciar.

dissociate [dɪ'səuʃɪeɪt] *vt* disociar.

dissolute ['dɪsəluːt] *a* disoluto.

dissolution [dɪsə'luːʃən] *n* (*of organization, marriage, POL*) disolución *f*.

dissolve [dɪ'zɔlv] *vt* disolver // *vi* disolverse.

dissuade [dɪ'sweɪd] *vt*: **to ~ sb (from)** disuadir a uno (de).

distance ['dɪstns] *n* distancia; **in the ~** a lo lejos.

distant ['dɪstnt] *a* lejano; (*manner*) reservado, frío.

distaste [dɪs'teɪst] *n* repugnancia; ~**ful** *a* repugnante, desagradable.

distended [dɪ'stɛndɪd] *a* (*stomach*) hinchado.

distil [dɪs'tɪl] *vt* destilar; ~**lery** *n* destilería.

distinct [dɪs'tɪŋkt] *a* (*different*) distinto; (*clear*) claro; (*unmistakeable*) inequívoco; **as ~ from** a diferencia de; ~**ion** [dɪs'tɪŋkʃən] *n* distinción *f*; (*in exam*) sobresaliente *m*; ~**ive** *a* distintivo.

distinguish [dɪs'tɪŋgwɪʃ] *vt* distinguir; ~**ed** *a* (*eminent*) distinguido; ~**ing** *a* (*feature*) distintivo.

distort [dɪs'tɔːt] *vt* torcer, retorcer; ~**ion** [dɪs'tɔːʃən] *n* deformación *f*; (*of sound*) distorsión *f*.

distract [dɪs'trækt] *vt* distraer; ~**ed** *a* distraído; ~**ion** [dɪs'trækʃən] *n* distracción *f*; (*confusion*) aturdimiento.

distraught [dɪs'trɔːt] *a* turbado, enloquecido.

distress [dɪs'trɛs] *n* (*anguish*) angustia; (*pain*) dolor *m* // *vt* afligir; (*pain*) doler; ~**ing** *a* angustioso; doloroso; ~ **signal** *n* señal *f* de socorro.

distribute [dɪs'trɪbjuːt] *vt* (*gen*) distribuir; (*share out*) repartir; **distribution** [-'bjuːʃən] *n* distribución *f*; **distributor** *n* (*AUT*) distribuidor *m*; (*COMM*) distribuidora.

district ['dɪstrɪkt] *n* (*of country*) zona, región *f*; (*of town*) barrio; (*ADMIN*) distrito; ~ **attorney** *n* (*US*) fiscal *m/f*; ~ **nurse** *n* (*Brit*) enfermera que atiende a pacientes a domicilio.

distrust [dɪs'trʌst] *n* desconfianza // *vt* desconfiar de.

disturb [dɪs'təːb] *vt* (*person: bother, interrupt*) molestar; (*meeting*) interrumpir; ~**ance** *n* (*political etc*) disturbio; (*violence*) alboroto; ~**ed** *a* (*worried, upset*) preocupado, angustiado; **emotionally** ~**ed** trastornado; ~**ing** *a* inquietante, perturbador(a).

disuse [dɪs'juːs] *n*: **to fall into ~** caer en desuso.

disused [dɪs'juːzd] *a* abandonado.

ditch [dɪtʃ] *n* zanja; (*irrigation ~*) acequia // *vt* (*col*) deshacerse de.

dither ['dɪðə*] *vi* vacilar.

ditto ['dɪtəu] *ad* ídem, lo mismo.

dive [daɪv] *n* (*from board*) salto; (*underwater*) buceo; (*of submarine*) sumersión *f*; (*AVIAT*) picada // *vi* saltar; bucear; sumergirse; picar; ~**r** *n* (*SPORT*) saltador(a) *m/f*; (*underwater*) buzo.

diverge [daɪ'vəːdʒ] *vi* divergir.

diverse [daɪ'vəːs] *a* diversos/as, varios/as.

diversion [daɪ'vəːʃən] *n* (*Brit AUT*) desviación *f*; (*distraction, MIL*) diversión *f*.

divert [daɪ'vəːt] *vt* (*turn aside*) desviar.

divide [dɪ'vaɪd] *vt* dividir; (*separate*) separar // *vi* dividirse; (*road*) bifurcarse; ~**d highway** *n* (*US*) carretera de doble calzada.

dividend ['dɪvɪdend] *n* dividendo; (*fig*)

beneficio.

divine [dɪ'vaɪn] a divino.

diving ['daɪvɪŋ] n (SPORT) salto; (underwater) buceo; ~ **board** n trampolín m.

divinity [dɪ'vɪnɪtɪ] n divinidad f; (SCOL) teología.

division [dɪ'vɪʒən] n división f; (sharing out) repartimiento.

divorce [dɪ'vɔːs] n divorcio // vt divorciarse de; ~d a divorciado; ~e [-'siː] n divorciado/a.

divulge [daɪ'vʌldʒ] vt divulgar, revelar.

D.I.Y. a, n abbr (Brit) = do-it-yourself.

dizziness ['dɪzɪnɪs] n vértigo.

dizzy ['dɪzɪ] a (person) mareado; (height) vertiginoso; to feel ~ marearse.

DJ n abbr = disc jockey.

do [duː] ♦ n (col: party etc): we're having a little ~ on Saturday damos una fiestecita el sábado; it was rather a grand ~ fue un acontecimiento a lo grande
♦ auxiliary vb (pt did, pp done) 1 (in negative constructions) not translated: I don't understand no entiendo
2 (to form questions) not translated: didn't you know? ¿no lo sabías?; what ~ you think? ¿qué opinas?
3 (for emphasis, in polite expressions): people ~ make mistakes sometimes sí que se cometen errores a veces; she does seem rather late a mí también me parece que se ha retrasado; ~ sit down/help yourself siéntate/sírvete por favor; ~ take care! ten cuidado, te pido
4 (used to avoid repeating vb): she sings better than I ~ canta mejor que yo; ~ you agree? — yes, I ~/no, I don't ¿estás de acuerdo? — sí (lo estoy)/no (lo estoy); she lives in Glasgow — so ~ I vive en Glasgow — yo también; he didn't like it and neither did we no le gustó y a nosotros tampoco; who made this mess? — I did ¿quién hizo esta chapuza? — yo; he asked me to help him and I did me pidió qué le ayudara y lo hice
5 (in question tags): you like him, don't you? te gusta, ¿verdad? or ¿no?; I don't know him, ~ I? creo que no le conozco
♦ vt 1 (gen, carry out, perform etc): what are you ~ing tonight? ¿qué haces esta noche?; what can I ~ for you? ¿en qué puedo servirle?; to ~ the washing-up/cooking fregar los platos/cocinar; to ~ one's teeth/hair/nails lavarse los dientes/arreglarse el pelo/arreglarse las uñas
2 (AUT etc): the car was ~ing 100 el coche iba a 100; we've done 200 km already ya hemos hecho 200 km; he can ~ 100 in that car puede dar los 100 en ese coche
♦ vi 1 (act, behave) hacer; ~ as I ~ haz como yo

2 (get on, fare): he's ~ing well/badly at school va bien/mal en la escuela; the firm is ~ing well la empresa anda or va bien; how ~ you ~? mucho gusto; (less formal) ¿qué tal?
3 (suit): will it ~? ¿sirve?, ¿está or va bien?
4 (be sufficient) bastar; will £10 ~? ¿será bastante con £10?; that'll ~ así está bien; that'll ~! (in annoyance) ¡ya está bien!, ¡basta ya!; to make ~ (with) arreglárselas (con)

to ~ away with vt fus (kill, disease) eliminar; (abolish: law etc) abolir; (withdraw) retirar

to ~ up vt (laces) atar; (zip, dress, shirt) abrochar; (renovate: room, house) renovar

to ~ with vt fus (need): I could ~ with a drink/some help no me vendría mal un trago/un poco de ayuda; (be connected): tener que ver con; what has it got to ~ with you? ¿qué tiene que ver contigo?

to do without vi pasar sin; if you're late for tea then you'll ~ without si llegas tarde para la merienda pasarás sin él ♦ vt fus pasar sin; I can ~ without a car puedo pasar sin coche

dock [dɔk] n (NAUT) muelle m; (LAW) banquillo (de los acusados); ~s npl muelles mpl, puerto sg // vi (enter ~) atracar el muelle; ~er n trabajador m portuario, estibador m; ~yard n astillero.

doctor ['dɔktə*] n médico/a; (Ph.D. etc) doctor(a) m/f // vt (fig) arreglar, falsificar; (drink etc) adulterar; D~ of Philosophy (Ph.D.) n Doctor en Filosofía y Letras.

doctrine ['dɔktrɪn] n doctrina.

document ['dɔkjumənt] n documento; ~ary [-'mentərɪ] a documental // n documental m.

dodge [dɔdʒ] n (of body) regate m; (fig) truco // vt (gen) evadir; (blow) esquivar.

dodgems ['dɔdʒəmz] npl (Brit) coches mpl de choque.

doe [dəʊ] n (deer) cierva, gama; (rabbit) coneja.

does [dʌz] vb see do; ~n't = ~ not.

dog [dɔg] n perro // vt seguir los pasos de; ~ collar n collar m de perro; (fig) cuello de cura; ~-eared a sobado.

dogged ['dɔgɪd] a tenaz, obstinado.

dogsbody ['dɔgzbɔdɪ] n (Brit) burro de carga.

doings ['duːɪŋz] npl (events) sucesos mpl; (acts) hechos mpl.

do-it-yourself [duːɪtjɔː'self] n bricolaje m.

doldrums ['dɔldrəmz] npl: to be in the ~ (person) estar abatido; (business) estar encalmado.

dole [dəʊl] n (Brit: payment) subsidio de paro; on the ~ parado; to ~ out vt repartir.

doleful ['dəulful] a triste, lúgubre.

doll [dɔl] n muñeca; to ~ o.s. up ataviarse.

dollar ['dɔlə*] n dólar m.

dolphin ['dɔlfɪn] n delfín m.

domain [də'meɪn] n (fig) campo, competencia; (land) dominios mpl.

dome [dəum] n (ARCH) cúpula; (shape) bóveda.

domestic [də'mestɪk] a (animal, duty) doméstico; (flight, policy) nacional; ~ated a domesticado; (home-loving) casero, hogareño.

dominant ['dɔmɪnənt] a dominante.

dominate ['dɔmɪneɪt] vt dominar.

domineering [dɔmɪ'nɪərɪŋ] a dominante.

dominion [də'mɪnɪən] n dominio.

domino ['dɔmɪnəu], pl ~es n ficha de dominó; ~es n (game) dominó.

don [dɔn] n (Brit) profesor(a) m/f universitario/a.

donate [də'neɪt] vt donar; **donation** [də'neɪʃən] n donativo.

done [dʌn] pp of **do**.

donkey ['dɔŋkɪ] n burro.

donor ['dəunə*] n donante m/f.

don't [dəunt] = **do not**.

doodle ['du:dl] vi hacer dibujitos or garabatos.

doom [du:m] n (fate) suerte f; (death) muerte f // vt: to be ~ed to failure ser condenado al fracaso; ~sday n día m del juicio final.

door [dɔ:*] n puerta; (entry) entrada; ~bell n timbre m; ~ handle n tirador m; (of car) manija; ~man n (in hotel) portero; ~mat n felpudo, estera; ~step n peldaño; ~way n entrada, puerta.

dope [dəup] n (col: person) imbécil m/f // vt (horse etc) drogar.

dopey ['dəupɪ] a atontado.

dormant ['dɔ:mənt] a inactivo; (latent) latente.

dormitory ['dɔ:mɪtrɪ] n (Brit) dormitorio; (US) colegio mayor.

dormouse ['dɔ:maus], pl **-mice** [-maɪs] n lirón m.

DOS n abbr (= disk operating system) DOS m.

dosage ['dəusɪdʒ] n dosis f inv.

dose [dəus] n dósis f inv.

doss house ['dɔss-] n (Brit) pensión f de mala muerte.

dossier ['dɔsɪeɪ] n expediente m.

dot [dɔt] n punto; ~ted with salpicado de; on the ~ en punto.

dote [dəut]: to ~ on vt fus adorar, idolatrar.

dot matrix printer n impresora matricial (or de matriz) de puntos.

double ['dʌbl] a doble // ad (twice): to cost ~ costar el doble // n (gen) doble m // vt doblar; (efforts) redoblar // vi doblarse; on the ~, (Brit) at the ~ corriendo; ~s n (TENNIS) juego de dobles; ~

bass n contrabajo; ~ **bed** n cama matrimonial; ~ **bend** n (Brit) doble curva; ~-**breasted** a cruzado; ~**cross** vt (trick) engañar; (betray) traicionar; ~**decker** n autobús m de dos pisos; ~ **glazing** n (Brit) doble acristalamiento; ~ **room** n cuarto para dos; **doubly** ad doblemente.

doubt [daut] n duda // vt dudar; (suspect) dudar de; to ~ that dudar que; there is no ~ that no cabe duda de que; ~**ful** a dudoso; (person): to be ~**ful** about sth tener dudas sobre algo; ~**less** ad sin duda.

dough [dəu] n masa, pasta; ~**nut** n buñuelo.

douse [daus] vt (drench) mojar; (extinguish) apagar.

dove [dʌv] n paloma.

dovetail ['dʌvteɪl] vi (fig) encajar.

dowdy ['daudɪ] a (person) mal vestido; (clothes) pasado de moda.

down [daun] n (fluff) pelusa; (feathers) plumón m, flojel m // ad (~wards) abajo, hacia abajo; (on the ground) por/en tierra // prep abajo // vt (col: drink) beberse; ~ with X! ¡abajo X!; ~ under (Australia etc) Australia, Nueva Zelanda; ~-**and-out** n vagabundo/a; ~-**at-heel** a venido a menos; (appearance) desaliñado; ~**cast** a abatido; ~**fall** n caída, ruina; ~-**hearted** a desanimado; ~**hill** ad: to go ~**hill** ir cuesta abajo; ~ **payment** n entrada, pago al contado; ~**pour** n aguacero; ~**right** a (nonsense, lie) manifiesto; (refusal) terminante; ~**stairs** ad (below) (en la casa de) abajo; (~wards) escaleras abajo; ~**stream** ad aguas or río abajo; ~-**to-earth** a práctico; ~**town** ad en el centro de la ciudad; ~**ward** a, ad [-wəd], ~**wards** [-wədz] ad hacia abajo.

dowry ['daurɪ] n dote f.

doz. abbr = **dozen**.

doze [dəuz] vi dormitar; to ~ off vi quedarse medio dormido.

dozen ['dʌzn] n docena; a ~ books una docena de libros; ~s of cantidad de.

Dr. abbr = **doctor; drive**.

drab [dræb] a gris, monótono.

draft [drɑ:ft] n (first copy) borrador m; (COMM) giro; (US: call-up) quinta // vt (write roughly) hacer un borrador de; see also **draught**.

draftsman ['drɑ:ftsmən] n (US) = **draughtsman**.

drag [dræg] vt arrastrar; (river) dragar, rastrear // vi arrastrarse por el suelo // n (col) lata; (women's clothing): in ~ vestido de travesti; to ~ on vi ser interminable.

dragon ['drægən] n dragón m.

dragonfly ['drægənflaɪ] n libélula.

drain [dreɪn] n desaguadero; (in street) sumidero // vt (land, marshes) desaguar;

(*MED*) drenar; (*reservoir*) desecar; (*fig*) agotar // *vi* escurrirse; **to be a ~ on** agotar; **~age** *n* (*act*) desagüe *m*; (*MED*, *AGR*) drenaje *m*; (*sewage*) alcantarillado; **~ing board**, (*US*) **~board** *n* escurridera, escurridor *m*; **~pipe** *n* tubo de desagüe.

dram [dræm] *n* (*drink*) traguito, copita.

drama ['drɑːmə] *n* (*art*) teatro; (*play*) drama *m*; **~tic** [drə'mætɪk] *a* dramático; **~tist** ['dræmətɪst] *n* dramaturgo/a; **~tize** ['dræmətaɪz] *vt* (*events*) dramatizar; (*adapt: for TV, cinema*) adaptar a la televisión/al cine.

drank [dræŋk] *pt of* **drink**.

drape [dreɪp] *vt* cubrir; **~s** *npl* (*US*) cortinas *fpl*; **~r** *n* (*Brit*) pañero/a.

drastic ['dræstɪk] *a* (*measure, reduction*) severo; (*change*) radical.

draught, (*US*) **draft** [drɑːft] *n* (*of air*) corriente *f* de aire; (*drink*) trago; (*NAUT*) calado; **~s** *n* (*Brit*) juego de damas; **on ~** (*beer*) de barril; **~board** (*Brit*) *n* tablero de damas.

draughtsman ['drɑːftsmən] *n* delineante *m*.

draw [drɔː] *vb* (*pt* **drew**, *pp* **drawn**) *vt* (*pull*) tirar; (*take out*) sacar; (*attract*) atraer; (*picture*) dibujar; (*money*) retirar // *vi* (*SPORT*) empatar // *n* (*SPORT*) empate *m*; (*lottery*) sorteo; (*attraction*) atracción *f*; **to ~ near** *vi* acercarse; **to ~ out** *vi* (*lengthen*) alargarse; **to ~ up** *vi* (*stop*) pararse // *vt* (*document*) redactar; **~back** *n* inconveniente *m*, desventaja; **~bridge** *n* puente *m* levadizo.

drawer [drɔː*] *n* cajón *m*; (*of cheque*) librador(a) *m/f*.

drawing ['drɔːɪŋ] *n* dibujo; **~ board** *n* tablero (de dibujante); **~ pin** *n* (*Brit*) chinche *m*; **~ room** *n* salón *m*.

drawl [drɔːl] *n* habla lenta y cansina.

drawn [drɔːn] *pp of* **draw**.

dread [drɛd] *n* pavor *m*, terror *m* // *vt* temer, tener miedo *or* pavor a; **~ful** *a* espantoso.

dream [driːm] *n* sueño // *vt*, *vi* (*pt*, *pp* **dreamed** *or* **dreamt** [drɛmt]) soñar; **~er** *n* soñador(a) *m/f*; **~y** *a* (*distracted*) soñador(a), distraído.

dreary ['drɪərɪ] *a* monótono.

dredge [drɛdʒ] *vt* dragar.

dregs [drɛgz] *npl* heces *fpl*.

drench [drɛntʃ] *vt* empapar.

dress [drɛs] *n* vestido; (*clothing*) ropa // *vt* vestir; (*wound*) vendar; (*CULIN*) aliñar // *vi* vestirse; **to ~ up** *vi* vestirse de etiqueta; (*in fancy dress*) disfrazarse; **~ circle** *n* (*Brit*) principal *m*; **~er** *n* (*furniture*) aparador *m*; (: *US*) cómoda con espejo; (*THEAT*) camarero/a; **~ing** *n* (*MED*) vendaje *m*; (*CULIN*) aliño; **~ing gown** *n* (*Brit*) bata; **~ing room** *n* (*THEATRE*) camarín *m*; (*SPORT*) vestidor *m*; **~ing table** *n* tocador *m*;

~maker *n* modista, costurera; **~ rehearsal** *n* ensayo general; **~ shirt** *n* camisa de frac; **~y** *a* (*col*) elegante.

drew [druː] *pt of* **draw**.

dribble ['drɪbl] *vi* gotear, caer gota a gota; (*baby*) babear // *vt* (*ball*) regatear.

dried [draɪd] *a* (*gen*) seco; (*fruit*) paso; (*milk*) en polvo.

drier ['draɪə*] *n* = **dryer**.

drift [drɪft] *n* (*of current etc*) velocidad *f*; (*of sand*) montón *m*; (*of snow*) ventisquero; (*meaning*) significado // *vi* (*boat*) ir a la deriva; (*sand, snow*) amontonarse; **~wood** *n* madera de deriva.

drill [drɪl] *n* taladro; (*bit*) broca; (*of dentist*) fresa; (*for mining etc*) perforadora, barrena; (*MIL*) instrucción *f* // *vt* perforar, taladrar // *vi* (*for oil*) perforar.

drink [drɪŋk] *n* bebida // *vt*, *vi* (*pt* **drank**, *pp* **drunk**) beber; **to have a ~** tomar algo; tomar una copa *or* un trago; **a ~ of water** un trago de agua; **~er** *n* bebedor(a) *m/f*; **~ing water** *n* agua potable.

drip [drɪp] *n* (*act*) goteo; (*one ~*) gota; (*MED*) gota a gota *m* // *vi* gotear, caer gota a gota; **~-dry** *a* (*shirt*) de lava y pon; **~ping** *n* (*animal fat*) pringue *m*.

drive [draɪv] *n* paseo (en coche); (*journey*) viaje *m* (en coche); (*also:* **~way**) entrada; (*energy*) energía, vigor *m*; (*PSYCH*) impulso; (*SPORT*) ataque *m*; (*COMPUT: also:* **disk ~**) drive *m* // *vb* (*pt* **drove**, *pp* **driven**) *vt* (*car*) conducir, manejar (*LAm*); (*nail*) clavar; (*push*) empujar; (*TECH: motor*) impulsar // *vi* (*AUT: at controls*) conducir; (: *travel*) pasearse en coche; **left-/right-hand ~** conducción *f* a la izquierda/derecha; **to ~ sb mad** volverle loco a uno.

drivel ['drɪvl] *n* (*col*) tonterías *fpl*.

driven ['drɪvn] *pp of* **drive**.

driver ['draɪvə*] *n* conductor(a) *m/f*, chofer *m* (*LAm*); (*of taxi, bus*) chofer; **~'s license** *n* (*US*) carnet *m* de conducir.

driveway ['draɪvweɪ] *n* entrada.

driving ['draɪvɪŋ] *n* el conducir, el manejar (*LAm*); **~ instructor** *n* instructor(a) *m/f* de conducción *or* manejo (*LAm*); **~ lesson** *n* clase *f* de conducción *or* manejo (*LAm*); **~ licence** *n* (*Brit*) permiso de conducir; **~ mirror** *n* retrovisor *m*; **~ school** *n* autoescuela; **~ test** *n* examen *m* de conducción *or* manejo (*LAm*).

drizzle ['drɪzl] *n* llovizna // *vi* lloviznar.

droll [drəʊl] *a* gracioso.

drone [drəʊn] *n* (*noise*) zumbido.

drool [druːl] *vi* babear; **to ~ over sth** extasiarse ante algo.

droop [druːp] *vi* (*fig*) decaer, desanimarse.

drop [drɒp] *n* (*of water*) gota; (*lessening*) baja // *vt* (*allow to fall*) dejar caer; (*voice, eyes, price*) bajar; (*set down from car*) dejar; (*price, temperature*) bajar; (*wind*) amainar; ~s npl (*MED*) gotas fpl; **to ~ off** vi (*sleep*) dormirse // vt (*passenger*) bajar; **to ~ out** vi (*withdraw*) retirarse; **~-out** n marginado/a; **~per** n cuentagotas m inv; **~pings** npl excremento sg.

drought [draut] n sequía.

drove [drəuv] pt of **drive**.

drown [draun] vt ahogar // vi ahogarse.

drowsy ['drauzɪ] a soñoliento; **to be ~** tener sueño.

drudgery ['drʌdʒərɪ] n trabajo monótono.

drug [drʌg] n medicamento; (*narcotic*) droga // vt drogar; **~ addict** n drogadicto/a; **~gist** n (*US*) farmacéutico; **~store** n (*US*) farmacia.

drum [drʌm] n tambor m; (*large*) bombo; (*for oil, petrol*) bidón m; **~s** npl batería sg // vi tocar el tambor; (*with fingers*) tamborilear; **~mer** n tambor m.

drunk [drʌŋk] pp of **drink** // a borracho // n (*also*: **~ard**) borracho/a; **~en** a borracho.

dry [draɪ] a seco; (*day*) sin lluvia; (*climate*) árido, seco // vt secar; (*tears*) enjugarse // vi secarse; **to ~ up** vi agotarse; (*in speech*) atascarse; **~-cleaner's** n tintorería; **~-cleaning** n lavado en seco; **~er** n (*for hair*) secador m; (*for clothes*) secadora; **~ goods store** n (*US*) mercería; **~ness** n sequedad f; **~rot** n putrefacción f fungoide.

dual ['djuəl] a doble; **~ carriageway** n (*Brit*) carretera de doble calzada; **~-control** a de doble mando; **~-nationality** n doble nacionalidad f; **~-purpose** a de doble uso.

dubbed [dʌbd] a (*CINEMA*) doblado.

dubious ['djuːbɪəs] a indeciso; (*reputation, company*) sospechoso.

duchess ['dʌtʃɪs] n duquesa.

duck [dʌk] n pato // vi agacharse; **~ling** n patito.

duct [dʌkt] n conducto, canal m.

dud [dʌd] n (*shell*) obús m que no estalla; (*object, tool*): **it's a ~** es una filfa // a: **~ cheque** (*Brit*) cheque m sin fondos.

due [djuː] a (*proper*) debido; (*fitting*) conveniente, oportuno // ad: **~ north** derecho al norte; **~s** npl (*for club, union*) cuota sg; (*in harbour*) derechos mpl; **in ~ course** a su debido tiempo; **~ to** debido a; **to be ~ to do** deberse a; **the train is ~ to arrive at 8.00** el tren debe llegar a las ocho.

duet [djuː'ɛt] n dúo.

duffel ['dʌfəl] a: **~ bag** n bolsa de lona; **~ coat** n comando, abrigo de tres cuartos.

dug [dʌg] pt, pp of **dig**.

duke [djuːk] n duque m.

dull [dʌl] a (*light*) apagado; (*stupid*) torpe; (*boring*) pesado; (*sound, pain*) sordo; (*weather, day*) gris // vt (*pain, grief*)

aliviar; (*mind, senses*) entorpecer.

duly ['djuːlɪ] ad debidamente; (*on time*) a su debido tiempo.

dumb [dʌm] a mudo; (*stupid*) estúpido; **~founded** [dʌm'faundɪd] a pasmado.

dummy ['dʌmɪ] n (*tailor's model*) maniquí m; (*Brit: for baby*) chupete m // a falso, postizo.

dump [dʌmp] n (*heap*) montón m de basura; (*place*) basurero, vaciadero; (*col*) casucha; (*MIL*) depósito // vt (*put down*) dejar; (*get rid of*) deshacerse de; **~ing** n (*ECON*) dumping m; (*of rubbish*): 'no **~ing**' 'prohibido verter basura'.

dumpling ['dʌmplɪŋ] n bola de masa hervida.

dumpy ['dʌmpɪ] a regordete/a.

dunce [dʌns] n zopenco.

dung [dʌŋ] n estiércol m.

dungarees [dʌŋgə'riːz] npl mono sg.

dungeon ['dʌndʒən] n calabozo.

duo ['djuːəu] n (*gen, MUS*) dúo.

dupe [djuːp] n (*victim*) víctima // vt engañar.

duplex ['djuːplɛks] n dúplex m.

duplicate ['djuːplɪkət] n duplicado // vt ['djuːplɪkeɪt] duplicar; (*on machine*) multicopiar; **in ~** por duplicado.

durable ['djuərəbl] a duradero.

duration [djuə'reɪʃən] n duración f.

duress [djuə'rɛs] n: **under ~** por compulsión.

during ['djuərɪŋ] prep durante.

dusk [dʌsk] n crepúsculo, anochecer m.

dust [dʌst] n polvo // vt (*furniture*) desempolvorar; (*cake etc*): **to ~ with** espolvorear de; **~bin** n (*Brit*) cubo de la basura, balde m (*LAm*); **~er** n paño, trapo; (*feather ~er*) plumero; **~ jacket** n sobrecubierta; **~man** n (*Brit*) basurero; **~y** a polvoriento.

Dutch [dʌtʃ] a holandés/esa // n (*LING*) holandés m; **the ~** npl los holandeses; **to go ~** pagar cada uno lo suyo; **~man/ woman** n holandés/esa m/f.

dutiful ['djuːtɪful] a obediente, sumiso.

duty ['djuːtɪ] n deber m; (*tax*) derechos mpl de aduana; **on ~** de servicio; (*at night etc*) de guardia; **off ~** libre (de servicio); **~-free** a libre de derechos de aduana.

duvet ['duːveɪ] n (*Brit*) edredón m.

dwarf [dwɔːf], pl **dwarves** [dwɔːvz] n enano/a // vt empequeñecer.

dwell [dwɛl], pt, pp **dwelt** [dwɛlt] vi morar; **to ~ on** vt fus explayarse en; **~ing** n vivienda.

dwindle ['dwɪndl] vi menguar, disminuir.

dye [daɪ] n tinte m // vt teñir.

dying ['daɪɪŋ] a moribundo, agonizante; (*moments*) final; (*words*) último.

dyke [daɪk] n (*Brit*) dique m.

dynamic [daɪ'næmɪk] a dinámico.

dynamite ['daɪnəmaɪt] n dinamita.

dynamo ['daɪnəməu] n dinamo f.

dynasty ['dɪnəstɪ] n dinastía.

E

E |iː| n (MUS) mi m.

each |iːtʃ| a cada inv // pron cada uno; ~ other el uno al otro; they hate ~ other se odian (entre ellos or mutuamente); they have 2 books ~ tienen 2 libros por persona.

eager ['iːgə*] a (gen) impaciente; (hopeful) ilusionado; (keen) entusiasmado; to be ~ to do sth tener muchas ganas de hacer algo, impacientarse por hacer algo; to be ~ for tener muchas ganasde; (news) esperar ansiosamente.

eagle ['iːgl] n águila.

ear |ɪə*| n oreja; (sense of hearing) oído; (of corn) espiga; ~ache n dolor m de oídos; ~drum n tímpano.

earl |əːl| n conde m.

early ['əːlɪ] ad (gen) temprano; (before time) con tiempo, con anticipación // a (gen) temprano; (reply) pronto; to have an ~ night acostarse temprano; in the ~ or ~ in the spring/19th century a principios de primavera/del siglo diecinueve; ~ retirement n jubilación f anticipada.

earmark ['ɪəmaːk] vt: to ~ (for) reservar (para), destinar (a).

earn |əːn| vt (gen) ganar; (salary) percibir; (interest) devengar; (praise) merecerse.

earnest ['əːnɪst] a serio, formal; in ~ ad en serio.

earnings ['əːnɪŋz] npl (personal) sueldo sg, ingresos mpl; (company) ganancias fpl.

ear: ~phones npl auriculares mpl; ~ring n pendiente m, arete m; ~shot n: within ~shot al alcance del oído.

earth |əːθ| n (gen) tierra; (Brit: ELEC) cable m de toma de tierra // vt (Brit: ELEC) conectar a tierra; ~enware n loza (de barro); ~quake n terremoto; ~y a (fig: uncomplicated) sencillo; (: sensual) sensual.

earwig ['ɪəwɪg] n tijereta.

ease |iːz| n facilidad f; (comfort) comodidad f // vt (task) facilitar; (pain) aliviar; (loosen) soltar; (help pass): to ~ sth in/out meter/sacar algo con cuidado; at ~! (MIL) ¡descansen!; to ~ off or up vi (work, business) aflojar; (person) relajarse.

easel ['iːzl] n caballete m.

easily ['iːzɪlɪ] ad fácilmente; it is ~ the best es con mucho el/la mejor.

east |iːst| n este m, oriente m // a del este, oriental // ad al este, hacia el este; the E~ el Oriente.

Easter ['iːstə*] n Pascua (de Resurrección); ~ egg n huevo de Pascua.

easterly ['iːstəlɪ] a (to the east) al este;

(from the east) del este.

eastern ['iːstən] a del este, oriental.

East Germany n Alemania Oriental.

eastward(s) ['iːstwəd(z)] ad hacia el este.

easy ['iːzɪ] a fácil; (problem) sencillo; (comfortable) holgado, cómodo; (relaxed) natural, llano // ad: to take it or things ~ (not worry) tomarlo con calma; (go slowly) ir despacio; (rest) descansar; ~ chair n sillón m; ~-going a acomodadizo.

eat |iːt|, pt ate, pp eaten ['iːtn] vt comer; to ~ into, to ~ away at vt fus corroer; (wear away) desgastar.

eau de Cologne [əudəkə'ləun] n (agua de) Colonia.

eaves |iːvz| npl alero sg.

eavesdrop ['iːvzdrɔp] vi: to ~ (on a conversation) escuchar (una conversación) a escondidas.

ebb |ɛb| n reflujo // vt bajar; (fig: also: ~ away) decaer; ~ tide n marea menguante.

ebony ['ɛbənɪ] n ébano.

eccentric |ɪk'sɛntrɪk| a, n excéntrico/a.

echo ['ɛkəu], pl ~es n eco m // vt (sound) repetir // vi resonar, hacer eco.

eclipse |ɪ'klɪps| n eclipse m.

ecology |ɪ'kɔlədʒɪ| n ecología.

economic |iːkə'nɔmɪk| a económico; (business etc) rentable; ~al a económico; ~s n economía.

economize |ɪ'kɔnəmaɪz| vi economizar, ahorrar.

economy |ɪ'kɔnəmɪ| n economía.

ecstasy ['ɛkstəsɪ] n éxtasis m inv; **ecstatic** [-'tætɪk] a extático.

Ecuador ['ɛkwədɔːr] n Ecuador m; E~ian a, n ecuatoriano/a m/f.

eczema ['ɛksɪmə] n eczema m.

edge |ɛdʒ| n (of knife etc) filo; (of object) borde m; (of lake etc) orilla // vt (SEWING) ribetear; on ~ (fig) = edgy; to ~ away from alejarse poco a poco de; ~ways ad: he couldn't get a word in ~ways no pudo meter ni baza; edging n (SEWING) ribete m; (of path) borde m.

edgy ['ɛdʒɪ] a nervioso, inquieto.

edible ['ɛdɪbl] a comestible.

edict ['iːdɪkt] n edicto.

edifice ['ɛdɪfɪs] n edificio.

Edinburgh ['ɛdɪnbərə] n Edimburgo.

edit ['ɛdɪt] vt (be editor of) dirigir; (rewrite) redactar; (cut) cortar; ~ion |ɪ'dɪʃən| n (gen) edición f; (number printed) tirada; ~or n (of newspaper) director(a) m/f; (of book) redactor(a) m/f; ~orial [-'tɔːrɪəl] a editorial // n editorial m.

educate ['ɛdjukeɪt] vt (gen) educar; (instruct) instruir.

education |ɛdju'keɪʃən| n educación f; (schooling) enseñanza; (SCOL) pedagogía; ~al a (policy etc) educacional;

(*teaching*) docente.

EEC *n abbr* (= *European Economic Community*) CEE *f*.

eel [i:l] *n* anguila.

eerie ['ɪərɪ] *a* (*sound, experience*) espeluznante.

effect [ɪ'fɛkt] *n* efecto // *vt* efectuar, llevar a cabo; ~s *npl* efectos *mpl*; to take ~ (*law*) entrar en vigor *or* vigencia; (*drug*) surtir efecto; in ~ en realidad; ~ive *a* (*gen*) eficaz; (*real*) efectivo; to become ~ive (*law*) entrar en vigor; ~ively *ad* eficazmente; efectivamente; ~iveness *n* eficacia.

effeminate [ɪ'fɛmɪnɪt] *a* afeminado.

efficiency [ɪ'fɪʃənsɪ] *n* (*gen*) eficiencia; (*of machine*) rendimiento.

efficient [ɪ'fɪʃənt] *a* eficaz; (*person*) eficiente.

effigy ['ɛfɪdʒɪ] *n* efigie *f*.

effort ['ɛfət] *n* esfuerzo; ~less *a* sin ningún esfuerzo.

effrontery [ɪ'frʌntərɪ] *n* descaro.

effusive [ɪ'fju:sɪv] *a* efusivo.

e.g. *ad abbr* (= *exempli gratia*) p. ej.

egg [ɛg] *n* huevo; **hard-boiled/soft-boiled/poached** ~ huevo duro/pasado por agua/escalfado; **scrambled** ~s huevos revueltos; to ~ on *vt* incitar; ~cup *n* huevera; ~ **plant** *n* (*esp US*) berenjena; ~shell *n* cáscara de huevo.

ego ['i:gəu] *n* ego; ~tism *n* egoísmo; ~tist *n* egoísta *m/f*.

Egypt ['i:dʒɪpt] *n* Egipto; ~ian [ɪ'dʒɪpʃən] *a, n* egipcio/a *m/f*.

eiderdown ['aɪdədaun] *n* edredón *m*.

eight [eɪt] *num* ocho; ~een *num* diez y ocho, dieciocho; ~h *a, n* octavo; ~y *num* ochenta.

Eire ['ɛərə] *n* Eire *m*.

either ['aɪðə*] *a* cualquier de los dos; (*both, each*) cada; on ~ side en ambos lados // *pron*: ~ (*of them*) cualquiera (de los dos); I don't like ~ no me gusta ninguno de los dos // *ad* tampoco; no, I don't ~ no, yo tampoco // *conj*: ~ yes or no o sí o no.

eject [ɪ'dʒɛkt] *vt* echar; (*tenant*) desahuciar; ~or seat *n* asiento proyectable.

eke [i:k]: to ~ out *vt* (*money*) hacer que alcance; (*add to*) suplir las deficiencias de.

elaborate [ɪ'læbərɪt] *a* (*design*) elaborado; (*pattern*) intrincado // *vb* [ɪ'læbəreɪt] *vt* elaborar // *vi* explicarse con muchos detalles.

elapse [ɪ'læps] *vi* transcurrir.

elastic [ɪ'læstɪk] *a, n* elástico; ~ **band** *n* (*Brit*) gomita.

elated [ɪ'leɪtɪd] *a*: to be ~ regocijarse; **elation** [ɪ'leɪʃən] *n* regocijo.

elbow ['ɛlbəu] *n* codo.

elder ['ɛldə*] *a* mayor // *n* (*tree*) saúco; (*person*) mayor; (*of tribe*) anciano; ~ly

a de edad, mayor // *npl*: the ~ly los mayores.

eldest ['ɛldɪst] *a, n* el/la mayor.

elect [ɪ'lɛkt] *vt* elegir; to ~ to do optar por hacer // *a*: the president ~ el presidente electo; ~ion [ɪ'lɛkʃən] *n* elección *f*; ~ioneering [ɪlɛkʃə'nɪərɪŋ] *n* campaña electoral; ~or *n* elector(a) *m/f*; ~oral *a* electoral; ~orate *n* electorado.

electric [ɪ'lɛktrɪk] *a* eléctrico; ~al *a* eléctrico; ~ **blanket** *n* manta eléctrica; ~ **cooker** *n* cocina eléctrica; ~ **fire** *n* estufa eléctrica.

electrician [ɪlɛk'trɪʃən] *n* electricista *m/f*.

electricity [ɪlɛk'trɪsɪtɪ] *n* electricidad *f*.

electrify [ɪ'lɛktrɪfaɪ] *vt* (*RAIL*) electrificar; (*fig: audience*) electrizar.

electron [ɪ'lɛktrɔn] *n* electrón *m*.

electronic [ɪlɛk'trɔnɪk] *a* electrónico; ~s *n* electrónica.

elegant [ɛlɪgənt] *a* elegante.

element ['ɛlɪmənt] *n* (*gen*) elemento; (*of heater, kettle etc*) resistencia; ~ary [-'mɛntərɪ] *a* elemental; (*primitive*) rudimentario; (*school, education*) primario.

elephant ['ɛlɪfənt] *n* elefante *m*.

elevate ['ɛlɪveɪt] *vt* (*gen*) elevar; (*in rank*) ascender.

elevation [ɛlɪ'veɪʃən] *n* elevación *f*; (*height*) altura.

elevator ['ɛlɪveɪtə*] *n* (*US*) ascensor *m*.

eleven [ɪ'lɛvn] *num* once; ~ses *npl* (*Brit*) café de las once; ~th *a* undécimo.

elicit [ɪ'lɪsɪt] *vt*: to ~ (from) sacar (de).

eligible ['ɛlɪdʒəbl] *a* elegible; to be ~ for sth llenar los requisitos para algo.

eliminate [ɪ'lɪmɪneɪt] *vt* eliminar; (*strike out*) suprimir; (*suspect*) descartar.

elm [ɛlm] *n* olmo.

elongated ['i:lɔŋgeɪtɪd] *a* alargado, estirado.

elope [ɪ'ləup] *vi* fugarse (para casarse); ~ment *n* fuga.

eloquent ['ɛləkwənt] *a* elocuente.

else [ɛls] *ad*: something ~ otra cosa; somewhere ~ en otra parte; everywhere ~ en todas partes menos aquí; where ~? ¿dónde más?, ¿en qué otra parte?; there was little ~ to do apenas quedaba otra cosa que hacer; nobody ~ spoke no habló nadie más; ~where *ad* (*be*) en otra parte; (*go*) a otra parte.

elucidate [ɪ'lu:sɪdeɪt] *vt* aclarar.

elude [ɪ'lu:d] *vt* eludir; (*blow, pursuer*) esquivar.

elusive [ɪ'lu:sɪv] *a* esquivo; (*answer*) difícil de encontrar.

emaciated [ɪ'meɪsɪeɪtɪd] *a* demacrado.

emanate ['ɛməneɪt] *vi*: to ~ from (*idea*) surgir de; (*light, smell*) proceder de.

emancipate [ɪ'mænsɪpeɪt] *vt* emancipar.

embankment [ɪm'bæŋkmənt] *n* terraplén *m*; (*riverside*) dique *m*.

embargo [ɪm'bɑ:gəu], *pl* ~es *n* prohibición *f*.

embark [ɪm'bɑːk] *vi* embarcarse // *vt* embarcar; **to ~ on** (*fig*) emprender, lanzarse a; **~ation** [ɛmbɑː'keɪʃən] *n* (*people*) embarco; (*goods*) embarque *m*.

embarrass [ɪm'bærəs] *vt* avergonzar; (*financially etc*) poner en un aprieto; **~ed** *a* azorado; **~ing** *a* (*situation*) violento; (*question*) embarazoso; **~ment** *n* desconcierto, azoramiento; (*financial*) apuros *mpl*.

embassy ['ɛmbəsɪ] *n* embajada.

embed [ɪm'bɛd] *vt* (*jewel*) empotrar; (*teeth etc*) clavar.

embellish [ɪm'bɛlɪʃ] *vt* embellecer; (*fig*) adornar.

embers ['ɛmbəz] *npl* rescoldo *sg*, ascua *sg*.

embezzle [ɪm'bɛzl] *vt* desfalcar, malversar.

embitter [ɪm'bɪtə*] *vt* (*person*) amargar; (*relationship*) envenenar; **~ed** *a* resentido, amargado.

embody [ɪm'bɔdɪ] *vt* (*spirit*) encarnar; (*ideas*) expresar.

embossed [ɪm'bɔst] *a* realzado.

embrace [ɪm'breɪs] *vt* abrazar, dar un abrazo a; (*include*) abarcar; (*adopt: idea*) adherirse a // *vi* abrazarse // *n* abrazo.

embroider [ɪm'brɔɪdə*] *vt* bordar; (*fig: story*) adornar, embellecer; **~y** *n* bordado.

embryo ['ɛmbrɪəu] *n* (*also fig*) embrión *m*.

emerald ['ɛmərəld] *n* esmeralda.

emerge [ɪ'mɜːdʒ] *vi* (*gen*) salir; (*arise*) surgir; **~nce** *n* salida; surgimiento.

emergency [ɪ'mɜːdʒənsɪ] *n* (*event*) emergencia; (*crisis*) crisis *f inv*; **in an ~** en caso de urgencia; **state of ~** estado de emergencia; **~ cord** *n* (*US*) timbre *m* de alarma; **~ exit** *n* salida de emergencia; **~ landing** *n* aterrizaje *m* forzoso; **~ meeting** *n* reunión *f* extraordinaria; **the ~ services** *npl* (*fire, police, ambulance*) los servicios *mpl* de urgencia *or* emergencia.

emery board ['ɛmərɪ-] *n* lima de uñas.

emigrant ['ɛmɪgrənt] *n* emigrante *m/f*.

emigrate ['ɛmɪgreɪt] *vi* emigrarse.

emit [ɪ'mɪt] *vt* emitir; (*smoke*) arrojar; (*smell*) despedir; (*sound*) producir.

emotion [ɪ'məuʃən] *n* emoción *f*; **~al** *a* (*person*) sentimental; (*scene*) conmovedor(a), emocionante; **~ally** *ad* con emoción.

emotive [ɪ'məutɪv] *a* emotivo.

emperor ['ɛmpərə*] *n* emperador *m*.

emphasis ['ɛmfəsɪs] *pl* **-ses** [-siːz] *n* énfasis *m inv*.

emphasize ['ɛmfəsaɪz] *vt* (*word, point*) subrayar, recalcar; (*feature*) hacer resaltar.

emphatic [ɛm'fætɪk] *a* (*reply*) categóri-

co; (*person*) insistente; **~ally** *ad* con énfasis.

empire ['ɛmpaɪə*] *n* imperio.

employ [ɪm'plɔɪ] *vt* emplear; **~ee** [-'iː] *n* empleado/a; **~er** *n* patrón/ona *m/f*; empresario; **~ment** *n* (*gen*) empleo; (*work*) trabajo; **~ment agency** *n* agencia de colocaciones.

empower [ɪm'pauə*] *vt*: **to ~ sb to do** sth autorizar a uno para hacer algo.

empress ['ɛmprɪs] *n* emperatriz *f*.

emptiness ['ɛmptɪnɪs] *n* (*gen*) vacío; (*of life etc*) vaciedad *f*.

empty ['ɛmptɪ] *a* vacío; (*place*) desierto; (*house*) desocupado; (*threat*) vano // *n* (*bottle*) envase *m* // *vt* vaciar; (*place*) dejar vacío // *vi* vaciarse; (*house*) quedar desocupado; (*place*) quedar desierto; **~-handed** *a* con las manos vacías.

emulate ['ɛmjuleɪt] *vt* emular.

emulsion [ɪ'mʌlʃən] *n* emulsión *f*.

enable [ɪ'neɪbl] *vt*: **to ~ sb to do** sth (*allow*) permitir a uno hacer algo; (*prepare*) capacitar a uno para hacer algo.

enact [ɪn'ækt] *vt* (*law*) promulgar; (*play*) representar; (*role*) hacer.

enamel [ɪ'næməl] *n* esmalte *m*.

enamoured [ɪ'næməd] *a*: **to be ~ of** (*person*) estar enamorado de; (*activity etc*) tener gran afición a; (*idea*) aferrarse a.

encased [ɪn'keɪst] *a*: **~ in** (*covered*) revestido de.

enchant [ɪn'tʃɑːnt] *vt* encantar; **~ing** *a* encantador(a).

encircle [ɪn'sɜːkl] *vt* rodear.

encl. *abbr* (= *enclosed*) adj.

enclose [ɪn'kləuz] *vt* (*land*) cercar; (*with letter etc*) adjuntar; (*in receptacle*): **to ~ (with)** encerrar (con); **please find ~d** le mandamos adjunto.

enclosure [ɪn'kləuʒə*] *n* cercado, recinto; (*COMM*) adjunto.

encompass [ɪn'kʌmpəs] *vt* abarcar.

encore [ɔŋ'kɔː*] *excl* ¡otra!, ¡bis! // *n* bis *m*.

encounter [ɪn'kauntə*] *n* encuentro // *vt* encontrar, encontrarse con; (*difficulty*) tropezar con.

encourage [ɪn'kʌrɪdʒ] *vt* alentar, animar; (*growth*) estimular; **~ment** *n* estímulo; (*of industry*) fomento.

encroach [ɪn'krəutʃ] *vi*: **to ~ (up)on** (*gen*) invadir; (*time*) adueñarse de.

encrusted [ɪn'krʌstəd] *a*: **~ with** incrustado de.

encumber [ɪn'kʌmbə*] *vt*: **to be ~ed with** (*carry*) estar cargado de; (*debts*) estar gravado de.

encyclop(a)edia [ɛnsaɪkləu'piːdɪə] *n* enciclopedia.

end [ɛnd] *n* (*gen, also aim*) fin *m*; (*of table*) extremo; (*of street*) final *m*; (*SPORT*) lado // *vt* terminar, acabar; (*also*: **bring to an ~, put an ~ to**) aca-

bar con // *vi* terminar, acabar; **in the ~
al fin; on ~** (*object*) de punta, de cabeza; **to stand on ~** (*hair*) erizarse; **for
hours on ~** hora tras hora; **to ~ up** *vi*:
to ~ up in terminar en; (*place*) ir a parar en.

endanger [in'deindʒə*] *vt* poner en peligro.

endearing [in'diəriŋ] *a* simpático, atractivo.

endeavour, (*US*) **endeavor** [in'devə*] *n*
esfuerzo; (*attempt*) tentativa // *vi*: **to ~
to do** esforzarse por hacer; (*try*) procurar hacer.

ending ['endiŋ] *n* fin *m*, conclusión *f*; (*of
book*) desenlace *m*; (*LING*) terminación
f.

endive ['endaiv] *n* endibia, escarola.

endless ['endlis] *a* interminable, inacabable.

endorse [in'dɔːs] *vt* (*cheque*) endosar;
(*approve*) aprobar; **~ment** *n* (*on driving licence*) nota de inhabilitación.

endow [in'dau] *vt* (*provide with money*)
dotar (*with* de); (*found*) fundar; **to be
~ed with** (*fig*) estar dotado de.

endurance [in'djuərəns] *n* resistencia.

endure [in'djuə*] *vt* (*bear*) aguantar, soportar; (*resist*) resistir // *vi* (*last*) durar;
(*resist*) resistir.

enemy ['enəmi] *a, n* enemigo/a *m/f*.

energetic [enə'dʒetik] *a* enérgico.

energy ['enədʒi] *n* energía.

enforce [in'fɔːs] *vt* (*LAW*) hacer cumplir;
~d *a* forzoso, forzado.

engage [in'geidʒ] *vt* (*attention*) llamar;
(*in conversation*) abordar; (*worker*) contratar; (*clutch*) embragar // *vi* (*TECH*)
engranar, to ~ in dedicarse a, ocuparse
en; **~d** *a* (*Brit*: *busy, in use*) ocupado;
(*betrothed*) prometido; **to get ~d** prometerse; **he is ~d in research** se dedica a
la investigación; **~d tone** *n* (*Brit TEL*)
señal *f* de comunicando; **~ment** *n* (*appointment*) compromiso, cita; (*battle*)
combate *m*; (*to marry*) compromiso;
(*period*) noviazgo; **~ment ring** *n* alianza, anillo de prometida.

engaging [in'geidʒiŋ] *a* atractivo, simpático.

engender [in'dʒendə*] *vt* engendrar.

engine ['endʒin] *n* (*AUT*) motor *m*;
(*RAIL*) locomotora; **~ driver** *n* maquinista *m/f*.

engineer [endʒi'niə*] *n* ingeniero; (*US
RAIL*) maquinista *m*; **~ing** *n* ingeniería.

England ['iŋglənd] *n* Inglaterra.

English ['iŋgliʃ] *a* inglés/esa // *n* (*LING*)
inglés *m*; **the ~** *npl* los ingleses *mpl*;
the ~ Channel *n* (el Canal de) la Mancha; **~man/woman** *n* inglés/esa *m/f*.

engraving [in'greiviŋ] *n* grabado.

engrossed [in'grəust] *a*: **~ in** absorto en.

engulf [in'gʌlf] *vt* sumergir, hundir.

enhance [in'hɑːns] *vt* (*gen*) aumentar;
(*beauty*) realzar.

enjoy [in'dʒɔi] *vt* (*health, fortune*) disfrutar de, gozar de; (*food*) comer con
gusto; **I enjoy dancing** me gusta bailar;
to ~ o.s. divertirse; **~able** *a* (*pleasant*)
agradable; (*amusing*) divertido; **~ment**
n (*use*) disfrute *m*; (*joy*) placer *m*.

enlarge [in'lɑːdʒ] *vt* aumentar; (*broaden*) extender; (*PHOT*) ampliar // *vi*: **to
~ on** (*subject*) tratar con más detalles.

enlighten [in'laitn] *vt* (*inform*) informar,
~ed *a* iluminado, (*tolerant*) comprensivo; **the E~ment** *n* (*HISTORY*) ≈ la Ilustración, el Siglo de las Luces.

enlist [in'list] *vt* alistar; (*support*) conseguir // *vi* alistarse.

enmity ['enmiti] *n* enemistad *f*.

enormous [i'nɔːməs] *a* enorme.

enough [i'nʌf] *a*: **~ time/books** bastante
tiempo/bastantes libros // *n*: **have you got
~?** ¿tiene usted bastante? // *ad*: **big ~**
bastante grande; **he has not worked ~**
no ha trabajado bastante; **~!** ¡basta
ya!; **that's ~,** thanks con eso basta, gracias; **I've had ~ of him** estoy harto de
él; **...which, funnily ~...** ...lo que, por extraño que parezca... .

enquire [in'kwaiə*] *vt, vi* = **inquire.**

enrage [in'reidʒ] *vt* enfurecer.

enrich [in'ritʃ] *vt* enriquecer.

enrol [in'rəul] *vt* (*members*) inscribir;
(*SCOL*) matricular // *vi* inscribirse; matricularse; **~ment** *n* inscripción *f*; matriculación *f*.

en route [ɔn'ruːt] *ad* durante el viaje.

ensign ['ensain] *n* (*flag*) bandera;
(*NAUT*) alférez *m*.

enslave [in'sleiv] *vt* esclavizar.

ensue [in'sjuː] *vi* seguirse; (*result*) resultar.

ensure [in'ʃuə*] *vt* asegurar.

entail [in'teil] *vt* suponer.

entangle [in'tæŋgl] *vt* enredar, enmarañar.

enter ['entə*] *vt* (*room*) entrar en;
(*club*) hacerse socio de; (*army*) alistarse en; (*sb for a competition*) inscribir;
(*write down*) anotar, apuntar; (*COMPUT*)
meter // *vi* entrar; **to ~ for** *vt fus* presentarse para; **to ~ into** *vt fus* (*relations*) establecer; (*plans*) formar parte
de; (*debate*) tomar parte en; (*agreement*) llegar a, firmar; **to ~ (up)on** *vt
fus* (*career*) emprender.

enterprise ['entəpraiz] *n* empresa; (*spirit*) iniciativa; **free ~** la libre empresa;
private ~ la iniciativa privada; **enterprising** *a* emprendedor(a).

entertain [entə'tein] *vt* (*amuse*) divertir;
(*receive*: *guest*) recibir (en casa);
(*idea*) abrigar; **~er** *n* artista *m/f*; **~ing**
a divertido, entretenido; **~ment** *n*
(*amusement*) diversión *f*; (*show*) espectáculo; (*party*) fiesta.

enthralled [in'θrɔːld] *a* encantado.

enthusiasm [ɪn'θuːzɪæzəm] n entusiasmo.

enthusiast [ɪn'θuːzɪæst] n entusiasta m/f; **~ic** [-'æstɪk] a entusiasta; **to be ~ic about** entusiasmarse por.

entice [ɪn'taɪs] vt tentar; (seduce) seducir.

entire [ɪn'taɪə*] a entero; **~ly** ad totalmente; **~ty** [ɪn'taɪərətɪ] n: **in its ~ty** en su totalidad.

entitle [ɪn'taɪtl] vt: **to ~ sb to sth** dar a uno derecho a algo; **~d** a (book) que se titula; **to be ~d to do** tener derecho a hacer.

entourage [ɔntu'rɑːʒ] n séquito.

entrails ['entreɪlz] npl entrañas fpl; (US) asadura sg, menudos mpl.

entrance ['entrəns] n entrada // vt [ɪn'trɑːns] encantar, hechizar; **to gain ~ to** (university etc) ingresar en; **~ examination** n examen m de ingreso; **~ fee** n cuota; **~ ramp** n (US AUT) rampa de acceso.

entrant ['entrənt] n (race, competition) participante m/f; (examination) candidato/a.

entreat [en'triːt] vt rogar, suplicar.

entrenched [en'trentʃd] a: **~ interests** intereses mpl creados.

entrepreneur [ɔntrəprə'nɔː] n empresario.

entrust [ɪn'trʌst] vt: **to ~ sth to sb** confiar algo a uno.

entry ['entrɪ] n entrada; (permission to enter) acceso; (in register) apunte m; (in account) partida; **no ~** prohibido el paso; (AUT) dirección prohibida; **~ phone** n portero automático.

enunciate [ɪ'nʌnsɪeɪt] vt pronunciar; (principle etc) enunciar.

envelop [ɪn'veləp] vt envolver.

envelope ['envələup] n sobre m.

envious ['envɪəs] a envidioso; (look) de envidia.

environment [ɪn'vaɪərnmənt] n medio ambiente; **~al** [-'mentl] a ambiental.

envisage [ɪn'vɪzɪdʒ] vt (foresee) prever; (imagine) concebir.

envoy ['envɔɪ] n enviado.

envy ['envɪ] n envidia // vt tener envidia a; **to ~ sb sth** envidiar algo a uno.

epic ['epɪk] n épica // a épico.

epidemic [epɪ'demɪk] n epidemia.

epilepsy ['epɪlepsɪ] n epilepsia.

episode ['epɪsəud] n episodio.

epistle [ɪ'pɪsl] n epístola.

epitome [ɪ'pɪtəmɪ] n epítome m; **epitomize** vt epitomar, resumir.

equable ['ekwəbl] a (climate) templado; (character) tranquilo, afable.

equal ['iːkwl] a (gen) igual; (treatment) equitativo // n igual m/f // vt ser igual a; (fig) igualar; **to be ~ to** (task) estar a la altura de; **~ity** [iː'kwɔlɪtɪ] n igualdad f; **~ize** vt, vi igualar; (SPORT) empatar; **~izer** n igualada; **~ly** ad igualmente; (share etc) a partes iguales.

equanimity [ekwə'nɪmɪtɪ] n ecuanimidad f.

equate [ɪ'kweɪt] vt: **to ~ sth with** equiparar algo con; **equation** [ɪ'kweɪzən] n (MATH) ecuación f.

equator [ɪ'kweɪtə*] n ecuador m; **~ial** [ekwə'tɔːrɪəl] a ecuatorial.

equilibrium [iːkwɪ'lɪbrɪəm] n equilibrio.

equip [ɪ'kwɪp] vt (gen) equipar; (person) proveer; **to be well ~ped** estar bien equipado; **~ment** n equipo; (tools) avíos mpl.

equitable ['ekwɪtəbl] a equitativo.

equities ['ekwɪtɪz] npl (Brit COMM) derechos mpl sobre or en el activo.

equivalent [ɪ'kwɪvəlnt] a: **~ (to)** equivalente (a) // n equivalente m.

equivocal [ɪ'kwɪvəkl] a equívoco.

era ['ɪərə] n era, época.

eradicate [ɪ'rædɪkeɪt] vt erradicar, extirpar.

erase [ɪ'reɪz] vt borrar; **~r** n goma de borrar.

erect [ɪ'rekt] a erguido // vt erigir, levantar; (assemble) montar.

erection [ɪ'rekʃən] n construcción f; (assembly) montaje m; (structure) edificio; (MED) erección f.

ermine ['əːmɪn] n armiño.

erode [ɪ'rəud] vt (GEO) erosionar; (metal) corroer, desgastar.

erotic [ɪ'rɔtɪk] a erótico.

err [əː*] vi equivocarse; (REL) pecar.

errand ['ernd] n recado, mandado (LAm); **~ boy** n recadero.

erratic [ɪ'rætɪk] a variable; (results etc) desigual, poco uniforme.

erroneous [ɪ'rəunɪəs] a erróneo.

error ['erə*] n error m, equivocación f.

erupt [ɪ'rʌpt] vi entrar en erupción; (MED) hacer erupción; (fig) estallar; **~ion** [ɪ'rʌpʃən] n erupción f.

escalate ['eskəleɪt] vi extenderse, intensificarse.

escalation [eskə'leɪʃən] n escalamiento, intensificación f.

escalator ['eskəleɪtə*] n escalera móvil.

escapade [eskə'peɪd] n travesura.

escape [ɪ'skeɪp] n (gen) fuga; (from duties) escapatoria; (from chase) evasión f // vi (gen) escaparse; (flee) huir, evadirse; (leak) fugarse // vt evitar, eludir; (consequences) escapar a; **to ~ from** (place) escaparse de; (person) escaparse a; **escapism** n escapismo.

escort ['eskɔːt] n acompañante m/f; (MIL) escolta; (NAUT) convoy m // vt [ɪ'skɔːt] acompañar; (MIL, NAUT) escoltar.

Eskimo ['eskɪməu] n esquimal m/f.

especially [ɪ'speʃlɪ] ad (gen) especialmente; (above all) sobre todo; (particularly) en particular.

espionage ['ɛspɪənɑːʒ] *n* espionaje *m*.

esplanade [ɛspləˈneɪd] *n* (*by sea*) paseo marítimo.

espouse [ɪˈspauz] *vt* adherirse a.

Esquire [ɪˈskwaɪə] *n* (*abbr* Esq.): J. Brown, ~ Sr. D. J. Brown.

essay ['ɛseɪ] *n* (*SCOL*) ensayo.

essence ['ɛsns] *n* esencia.

essential [ɪˈsɛnʃl] *a* (*necessary*) imprescindible; (*basic*) esencial; **~s** *npl* lo esencial *sg*; **~ly** *ad* esencialmente.

establish [ɪˈstæblɪʃ] *vt* establecer; (*identity*) verificar; (*prove*) demostrar; (*relations*) entablar; **~ment** *n* establecimiento; the **E~ment** la clase dirigente.

estate [ɪˈsteɪt] *n* (*land*) finca, hacienda; (*property*) propiedad *f*; (*inheritance*) herencia; (*POL*) estado; ~ **agent** *n* (*Brit*) agente *m/f* inmobiliario/a; ~ **car** *n* (*Brit*) furgoneta.

esteem [ɪˈstiːm] *n*: to hold sb in high ~ estimar en mucho a uno // *vt* estimar.

esthetic [ɪsˈθɛtɪk] *a* (*US*) = **aesthetic**.

estimate ['ɛstɪmət] *n* estimación *f*, apreciación *f*; (*assessment*) tasa, cálculo; (*COMM*) presupuesto // *vt* [-meit] estimar, tasar, calcular; **estimation** [-ˈmeɪʃən] *n* opinión *f*, juicio; (*esteem*) aprecio.

estranged [ɪˈstreɪndʒd] *a* separado.

estuary ['ɛstjuərɪ] *n* estuario, ría.

etc *abbr* (= *et cetera*) etc.

etching ['ɛtʃɪŋ] *n* aguafuerte *m o f*.

eternal [ɪˈtəːnl] *a* eterno.

eternity [ɪˈtəːnɪtɪ] *n* eternidad *f*.

ethical ['ɛθɪkl] *a* ético; (*honest*) honrado.

ethics ['ɛθɪks] *n* ética // *npl* moralidad *fsg*.

Ethiopia [iːθɪˈəupɪə] *n* Etiopia.

ethnic ['ɛθnɪk] *a* étnico.

ethos ['iːθɔs] *n* genio, carácter *m*.

etiquette ['ɛtɪkɛt] *n* etiqueta.

Eurocheque ['juərəutʃɛk] *n* Eurocheque *m*.

Europe ['juərəp] *n* Europa; **~an** [-ˈpiːən] *a*, *n* europeo/a *m/f*.

evacuate [ɪˈvækjueɪt] *vt* desocupar; **evacuation** [-ˈeɪʃən] *n* evacuación *f*.

evade [ɪˈveɪd] *vt* evadir, eludir.

evaluate [ɪˈvæljueɪt] *vt* evaluar; (*value*) tasar; (*evidence*) interpretar.

evangelist [ɪˈvændʒəlɪst] *n* (*biblical*) evangelista *m*; (*preacher*) evangelizador(a) *m/f*.

evaporate [ɪˈvæpəreɪt] *vi* evaporarse; (*fig*) desvanecerse // *vt* evaporar; **~d milk** *n* leche *f* evaporada.

evasion [ɪˈveɪʒən] *n* evasiva, evasión *f*.

eve [iːv] *n*: on the ~ of en vísperas de.

even ['iːvn] *a* (*level*) llano; (*smooth*) liso; (*speed, temperature*) uniforme; (*number*) par; (*SPORT*) igual(es) // *ad* hasta, incluso; ~ **if**, ~ **though** aunque + *subjun*; ~ more aun más; ~ so aun así; **not** ~ ni siquiera; ~ **he** was there hasta él estuvo allí; ~ **on Sundays** incluso los domingos; **to get** ~ **with sb** ajustar cuentas con uno; **to** ~ **out** *vi* nivelarse.

evening ['iːvnɪŋ] *n* tarde *f*; (*dusk*) atardecer *m*; (*night*) noche *f*; **in the** ~ por la tarde; ~ **class** *n* clase *f* nocturna; ~ **dress** *n* (*man's*) traje *m* de etiqueta; (*woman's*) traje *m* de noche.

event [ɪˈvɛnt] *n* suceso, acontecimiento; (*SPORT*) prueba; **in the** ~ **of** en caso de; **~ful** *a* accidentado; (*game etc*) lleno de emoción.

eventual [ɪˈvɛntʃuəl] *a* final; **~ity** [-ˈælɪtɪ] *n* eventualidad *f*; **~ly** *ad* (*finally*) finalmente.

ever ['ɛvə*] *ad* nunca, jamás; (*at all times*) siempre; **the best** ~ lo nunca visto; **have you** ~ **seen it?** ¿lo ha visto usted alguna vez?; **better than** ~ mejor que nunca; ~ **since** *ad* desde entonces // *conj* después de que; **~green** *n* árbol *m* de hoja perenne; **~lasting** *a* eterno, perpetuo.

every ['ɛvrɪ] *a* 1 (*each*) cada; ~ **one of them** (*persons*) todos ellos/as; (*objects*) cada uno de ellos/as; ~ **shop in the town was closed** todas las tiendas de la ciudad estaban cerradas

2 (*all possible*) todo/a; I gave you ~ assistance te di toda la ayuda posible; I have ~ confidence in him tiene toda mi confianza; we wish you ~ success te deseamos toda suerte de éxitos

3 (*showing recurrence*) todo/a; ~ **day/week** todos las días/todas las semanas; ~ **other car** had been broken into habían entrado en uno de cada dos coches; **she visits me** ~ **other/third day** me visita cada dos/tres días; ~ **now and then** de vez en cuando.

everybody ['ɛvrɪbɔdɪ] *pron* = **everyone**.

everyone ['ɛvrɪwʌn] *pron* todos/as, todo el mundo; ~ **knows that** todo el mundo lo sabe; ~ **has his own view** cada uno piensa de una manera.

everything ['ɛvrɪθɪŋ] *pron* todo; **~'s ready** está todo listo; ~ **you say is true** todo lo que dices es cierto; **this shop sells** ~ esta tienda vende de todo.

everywhere ['ɛvrɪwɛə*] *ad*: I've been looking for you ~ te he estado buscando por todas partes; ~ **you go you meet...** en todas partes encuentras....

evict [ɪˈvɪkt] *vt* desahuciar; **~ion** [ɪˈvɪkʃən] *n* desahucio.

evidence ['ɛvɪdəns] *n* (*proof*) prueba; (*of witness*) testimonio; (*facts*) datos *mpl*, hechos *mpl*; **to give** ~ prestar declaración, dar testimonio.

evident ['ɛvɪdənt] *a* evidente, manifiesto; **~ly** *ad*: it is **~ly difficult** por lo visto es difícil.

evil ['iːvl] *a* malo; (*influence*) funesto; (*smell*) horrible // *n* mal *m*, maldad *f*.

evocative [ɪˈvɔkətɪv] *a* sugestivo, evocador(a).

evoke [ɪ'vəuk] vt evocar.

evolution [iːvə'luːʃən] n evolución f, desarrollo.

evolve [ɪ'vɔlv] vt desarrollar // vi evolucionar, desarrollarse.

ewe [juː] n oveja.

ex- [ɛks] pref ex.

exacerbate [ɛk'sæsəbeɪt] vt (pain, disease) exacerbar; (fig) empeorar.

exact [ɪg'zækt] a exacto // vt: to ~ sth (from) exigir algo (de); ~ing a exigente; (conditions) arduo; ~ly ad exactamente.

exaggerate [ɪg'zædʒəreɪt] vt, vi exagerar; **exaggeration** [-'reɪʃən] n exageración f.

exalted [ɪg'zɔːltɪd] a (position) exaltado; (elated) excitado.

exam [ɪg'zæm] n abbr (SCOL) = **examination**.

examination [ɪgzæmɪ'neɪʃən] n (gen) examen m; (LAW) interrogación f; (inquiry) investigación f.

examine [ɪg'zæmɪn] vt (gen) examinar; (inspect) inspeccionar, escudriñar; (SCOL, LAW: person) interrogar; (at customs: luggage) registrar; ~r n inspector(a) m/f.

example [ɪg'zɑːmpl] n ejemplo; **for** ~ por ejemplo.

exasperate [ɪg'zɑːspəreɪt] vt exasperar, irritar; **exasperation** [-ʃən] n exasperación f, irritación f.

excavate [ˈɛkskəveɪt] vt excavar.

exceed [ɪk'siːd] vt exceder; (number) pasar de; (speed limit) sobrepasar; (limits) rebasar; (powers) excederse en; (hopes) superar; ~**ingly** ad sumamente, sobremanera.

excel [ɪk'sɛl] vi sobresalir.

excellent [ˈɛksələnt] a excelente.

except [ɪk'sɛpt] prep (also: ~ **for**, ~**ing**) excepto, salvo // vt exceptuar, excluir; ~ **if/when** excepto si/cuando; ~ **that** salvo que; ~**ion** [ɪk'sɛpʃən] n excepción f; **to take** ~**ion to** ofenderse por; ~**ional** [ɪk'sɛpʃənl] a excepcional.

excerpt [ˈɛksɜːpt] n extracto.

excess [ɪk'sɛs] n exceso; ~ **baggage** n exceso de equipaje; ~ **fare** n suplemento; ~**ive** a excesivo.

exchange [ɪks'tʃeɪndʒ] n cambio; (of goods) canje m; (of ideas) intercambio; (also: **telephone** ~) central f (telefónica) // vt: **to** ~ (**for**) cambiar (por); ~ **rate** n tipo de cambio.

exchequer [ɪks'tʃɛkə*] n: **the** ~ (Brit) la Hacienda del Fisco.

excise [ˈɛksaɪz] n impuestos mpl sobre el comercio exterior.

excite [ɪk'saɪt] vt (stimulate) estimular; (anger) provocar; (move) entusiasmar; ~**d** a: **to get** ~**d** emocionarse; ~**ment** n emoción f; **exciting** a emocionante.

exclaim [ɪk'skleɪm] vi exclamar; **exclamation** [ɛksklə'meɪʃən] n exclamación f; **exclamation mark** n punto de admiración.

exclude [ɪk'skluːd] vt excluir; (except) exceptuar.

exclusive [ɪk'skluːsɪv] a exclusivo; (club, district) selecto; ~ **of tax** excluyendo impuestos; ~**ly** ad únicamente.

excommunicate [ɛkskə'mjuːnɪkeɪt] vt excomulgar.

excruciating [ɪk'skruːʃɪeɪtɪŋ] a (pain) agudísimo, atroz.

excursion [ɪk'skəːʃən] n excursión f.

excusable [ɪk'skjuːzəbl] a perdonable.

excuse [ɪk'skjuːs] n disculpa, excusa; (evasion) pretexto // vt [ɪk'skjuːz] disculpar, perdonar; **to** ~ **sb from doing sth** dispensar a uno de hacer algo; ~ **me!** ¡perdón!; **if you will** ~ **me** con su permiso.

ex-directory [ˈɛksdɪ'rɛktərɪ] a (Brit) que no consta en la guía.

execute [ˈɛksɪkjuːt] vt (plan) realizar; (order) cumplir; (person) ajusticiar, ejecutar; **execution** [-'kjuːʃən] n realización f; cumplimiento; ejecución f; **executioner** [-'kjuːʃənə*] n verdugo.

executive [ɪg'zɛkjutɪv] n (COMM) ejecutivo; (POL) poder m ejecutivo // a ejecutivo.

executor [ɪg'zɛkjutə*] n albacea m, testamentario.

exemplify [ɪg'zɛmplɪfaɪ] vt ejemplificar.

exempt [ɪg'zɛmpt] a: ~ **from** exento de // vt: **to** ~ **sb from** eximir a uno de; ~**ion** [-ʃən] n exención f; (immunity) inmunidad f.

exercise [ˈɛksəsaɪz] n ejercicio // vt ejercer; (right) valerse de; (dog) llevar de paseo // vi hacer ejercicio(s); ~ **book** n cuaderno.

exert [ɪg'zəːt] vt ejercer; **to** ~ **o.s.** esforzarse; ~**ion** [-ʃən] n esfuerzo.

exhale [ɛks'heɪl] vt despedir // vi exhalar.

exhaust [ɪg'zɔːst] n (pipe) escape m; (fumes) gases mpl de escape // vt agotar; ~**ed** a agotado; ~**ion** [ɪg'zɔːstʃən] n agotamiento; **nervous** ~**ion** postración f nerviosa; ~**ive** a exhaustivo.

exhibit [ɪg'zɪbɪt] n (ART) obra expuesta; (LAW) objeto expuesto // vt (show: emotions) manifestar; (:courage, skill) demostrar; (paintings) exponer; ~**ion** [ɛksɪ'bɪʃən] n exposición f.

exhilarating [ɪg'zɪləreɪtɪŋ] a estimulante, tónico.

exile [ˈɛksaɪl] n exilio; (person) exiliado/a // vt desterrar, exiliar.

exist [ɪg'zɪst] vi existir; ~**ence** n existencia; ~**ing** a existente, actual.

exit [ˈɛksɪt] n salida // vi (THEATRE) hacer mutis; (COMPUT) salir (al sistema); ~ **ramp** n (US AUT) vía de acceso.

exodus [ˈɛksədəs] n éxodo.

exonerate [ɪgˈzɔnəreɪt] vt: **to ~ from** exculpar de.

exotic [ɪgˈzɔtɪk] a exótico.

expand [ɪkˈspænd] vt ampliar; (number) aumentar // vi (trade etc) expandirse; (gas, metal) dilatarse.

expanse [ɪkˈspæns] n extensión f.

expansion [ɪkˈspænʃən] n ampliación f; aumento; (of trade) expansión f.

expect [ɪkˈspɛkt] vt (gen) esperar; (count on) contar con; (suppose) suponer // vi: **to be ~ing** estar encinta; **~ancy** n (anticipation) esperanza; **life ~ancy** esperanza de vida; **~ant mother** n mujer f encinta; **~ation** [ɛkspɛkˈteɪʃən] n esperanza, expectativa.

expedience [ɪkˈspiːdɪəns], **expediency** [ɪkˈspiːdɪənsɪ] n conveniencia.

expedient [ɪkˈspiːdɪənt] a conveniente, oportuno // n recurso, expediente m.

expedition [ɛkspəˈdɪʃən] n expedición f.

expel [ɪkˈspɛl] vt arrojar; (SCOL) expulsar.

expend [ɪkˈspɛnd] vt gastar; (use up) consumir; **~able** a prescindible; **~iture** n gastos mpl, desembolso.

expense [ɪkˈspɛns] n gasto, gastos mpl; (high cost) costa; **~s** npl (COMM) gastos mpl; **at the ~ of** a costa de; **~ account** n cuenta de gastos.

expensive [ɪkˈspɛnsɪv] a caro, costoso.

experience [ɪkˈspɪərɪəns] n experiencia // vt experimentar; (suffer) sufrir; **~d** a experimentado.

experiment [ɪkˈspɛrɪmənt] n experimento // vi hacer experimentos; **~al** [-ˈmɛntl] a experimental.

expert [ˈɛkspəːt] a experto, perito // n experto/a, perito/a; (specialist) especialista m/f; **~ise** [-ˈtiːz] n pericia.

expire [ɪkˈspaɪə*] vi (gen) caducar, vencerse; **expiry** n vencimiento.

explain [ɪkˈspleɪn] vt explicar; (mystery) aclarar; **explanation** [ɛkspləˈneɪʃən] n explicación f; aclaración f; **explanatory** [ɪkˈsplænətrɪ] a explicativo; aclaratorio.

explicit [ɪkˈsplɪsɪt] a explícito.

explode [ɪkˈspləud] vi estallar, explotar; (with anger) reventar // vt volar, explotar.

exploit [ˈɛksplɔɪt] n hazaña // vt [ɪkˈsplɔɪt] explotar; **~ation** [-ˈteɪʃən] n explotación f.

exploratory [ɪkˈsplɔrətrɪ] a (fig: talks) exploratorio, preliminar.

explore [ɪkˈsplɔː*] vt explorar; (fig) examinar, sondear; **~r** n explorador(a) m/f.

explosion [ɪkˈspləuʒən] n explosión f.

explosive [ɪksˈpləusɪv] a, n explosivo.

exponent [ɪkˈspəunənt] n partidario/a, intérprete m/f.

export [ɛkˈspɔːt] vt exportar // n [ˈɛkspɔːt] exportación f // cpd de exportación; **~er** n exportador m.

expose [ɪkˈspəuz] vt exponer; (unmask) desenmascarar; **~d** a expuesto.

exposure [ɪkˈspəuʒə*] n exposición f; (PHOT: speed) velocidad f de obturación (: shot) fotografía; **to die from ~** (MED) morir de frío; **~ meter** n fotómetro.

expound [ɪkˈspaund] vt exponer.

express [ɪkˈsprɛs] a (definite) expreso, explícito; (Brit: letter etc) urgente // n (train) rápido // ad (send) por correo extraordinario // vt expresar; **~ion** [ɪkˈsprɛʃən] n expresión f; **~ly** ad expresamente; **~way** n (US: urban motorway) autopista.

exquisite [ɛkˈskwɪzɪt] a exquisito.

extend [ɪkˈstɛnd] vt (visit, street) prolongar; (building) ensanchar; (thanks, friendship etc) extender // vi (land) extenderse.

extension [ɪkˈstɛnʃən] n extensión f; (building) ampliación f; (TEL: line) línea derivada; (: telephone) extensión f; (of deadline) prórroga.

extensive [ɪkˈstɛnsɪv] a (gen) extenso; (damage) importante; (knowledge) amplio; **~ly** ad: **he's travelled ~ly** ha viajado por muchos países.

extent [ɪkˈstɛnt] n (breadth) extensión f; (scope) alcance m; **to some ~** hasta cierto punto; **to the ~ of...** hasta el punto de...; **to such an ~ that...** hasta tal punto que...; **to what ~?** ¿hasta qué punto?

extenuating [ɪkˈstɛnjueɪtɪŋ] a: **~ circumstances** circunstancias fpl atenuantes.

exterior [ɛkˈstɪərɪə*] a exterior, externo // n exterior m.

exterminate [ɪkˈstəːmɪneɪt] vt exterminar; **extermination** [-ˈneɪʃən] n exterminación f.

external [ɛkˈstəːnl] a externo, exterior; **~ly** ad por fuera.

extinct [ɪkˈstɪŋkt] a (volcano) extinguido; (race) extinto.

extinguish [ɪkˈstɪŋgwɪʃ] vt extinguir, apagar; **~er** n extintor m.

extort [ɪkˈstɔːt] vt: **to ~ sth from sb** sacar algo de uno a la fuerza; **~ion** [ɪkˈstɔːʃən] n exacción f; **~ionate** [ɪkˈstɔːʃnət] a excesivo, exorbitante.

extra [ˈɛkstrə] a adicional // ad (in addition) de más // n (addition) extra m, suplemento; (THEATRE) extra m/f, comparsa m/f; (newspaper) edición f extraordinaria.

extra... [ˈɛkstrə] pref extra... .

extract [ɪkˈstrækt] vt sacar; (tooth) extraer; (confession) arrancar, obtener // n [ˈɛkstrækt] extracto.

extracurricular [ɛkstrəkəˈrɪkjulə*] a extraescolar, extra-académico.

extradite [ˈɛkstrədaɪt] vt extraditar.

extramarital [ɛkstrəˈmærɪtl] a extramatrimonial.

extramural [ɛkstrəˈmjuərl] a extraescolar.

extraordinary [ɪkˈstrɔːdnrɪ] a extraordinario; (*odd*) raro.

extravagance |ɪk'strævəgəns| *n* prodigalidad *f*; derroche *m*; (*thing bought*) extravagancia.

extravagant |ɪk'strævəgənt| *a* (*lavish*) pródigo; (*wasteful*) derrochador(a); (*price*) exorbitante.

extreme |ɪk'striːm| *a* extremo; (*poverty etc*) extremado; (*case*) excepcional // *n* extremo, extremidad *f*; **~ly** *ad* sumamente, extremadamente; **extremist** *a*, *n* extremista *m/f*.

extremity |ɪk'strɛmətɪ| *n* extremidad *f*, punta; (*need*) apuro, necesidad *f*.

extricate ['ekstrɪkeɪt] *vt*: to ~ o.s. from librarse de.

extrovert ['ɛkstrəvɜːt] *a*, *n* extrovertido/a.

exuberant |ɪg'zjuːbərnt| *a* (*person*) eufórico; (*style*) exuberante.

exude |ɪg'zjuːd| *vt* rezumar, sudar.

exult |ɪg'zʌlt| *vi* regocijarse.

eye |aɪ| *n* ojo // *vt* mirar de soslayo, ojear; to keep an ~ on vigilar; **~ball** *n* globo del ojo; **~bath** *n* ojera; **~brow** *n* ceja; **~brow pencil** *n* lápiz *m* de cejas; **~drops** *npl* gotas *fpl* para los ojos; **~lash** *n* pestaña; **~lid** *n* párpado; **~liner** *n* lápiz *m* de ojos; **~-opener** *n* revelación *f*, gran sorpresa; **~shadow** *n* sombreador *m* de ojos; **~sight** *n* vista; **~sore** *n* monstruosidad *f*; ~ **witness** *n* testigo *m/f* presencial.

F

F |ɛf| *n* (*MUS*) fa *m*.
F. *abbr* = **Fahrenheit**.
fable ['feɪbl] *n* fábula.
fabric ['fæbrɪk] *n* tejido, tela.
fabrication [fæbrɪ'keɪʃən] *n* invención *f*.
fabulous ['fæbjuləs] *a* fabuloso.
façade [fə'sɑːd] *n* fachada.
face [feɪs] *n* (*ANAT*) cara, rostro; (*of clock*) esfera, cara (*LAm*); (*side, surface*) superficie *f* // *vt* (*subj: person*) encararse con; (: *building*) dar a; ~ **down** (*person, card*) boca abajo; to lose ~ desprestigiarse; to make *or* pull a ~ hacer muecas; in the ~ of (*difficulties etc*) ante; on the ~ of it a primera vista; ~ to ~ cara a cara; to ~ up to *vt fus* hacer frente a, arrostrar; ~ **cloth** *n* (*Brit*) manopla; ~ **cream** *n* crema (de belleza); ~ **lift** *n* estirado facial; ~ **powder** *n* polvos *mpl*; **~-saving** *a* para salvar las apariencias.
facetious [fə'siːʃəs] *a* chistoso.
face value *n* (*of stamp*) valor *m* nominal; to take sth at ~ (*fig*) tomar algo en sentido literal.
facile ['fæsaɪl] *a* superficial.
facilities [fə'sɪlɪtɪz] *npl* facilidades *fpl*; **credit** ~ facilidades de crédito.

facing ['feɪsɪŋ] *prep* frente a // *a* de enfrente.
facsimile |fæk'sɪmɪlɪ| *n* (*document*) facsímil(e) *m*; (*machine*) telefax *m*.
fact [fækt] *n* hecho; in ~ en realidad.
factor ['fæktə*] *n* factor *m*.
factory ['fæktərɪ] *n* fábrica.
factual ['fæktjuəl] *a* basado en los hechos.
faculty ['fækəltɪ] *n* facultad *f*; (*US: teaching staff*) personal *m* docente.
fad [fæd] *n* novedad *f*, moda.
fade [feɪd] *vi* desteñirse; (*sound, hope*) desvanecerse; (*light*) apagarse; (*flower*) marchitarse.
fag [fæg] *n* (*Brit: col: cigarette*) pitillo (*Sp*), cigarro; (*US: pej: homosexual*) maricón *m*.
fail [feɪl] *vt* (*candidate*) suspender; (*exam*) no aprobar (*Sp*), reprobar (*LAm*); (*subj: memory etc*) fallar a // *vi* suspender; (*be unsuccessful*) fracasar; (*strength, engine*) fallar; to ~ to do sth (*neglect*) dejar de hacer algo; (*be unable*) no poder hacer algo; without ~ sin falta; **~ing** *n* falta, defecto // *prep* a falta de; **~ure** ['feɪljə*] *n* fracaso; (*person*) fracasado/a; (*mechanical etc*) fallo.
faint [feɪnt] *a* débil; (*recollection*) vago; (*mark*) apenas visible // *n* desmayo // *vi* desmayarse; to feel ~ estar mareado, marearse.
fair [fɛə*] *a* justo; (*hair, person*) rubio; (*weather*) bueno; (*good enough*) regular; (*sizeable*) considerable // *ad* (*play*) limpio // *n* feria; (*Brit: funfair*) parque *m* de atracciones; **~ly** *ad* (*justly*) con justicia; (*equally*) equitativamente; (*quite*) bastante; **~ness** *n* justicia; (*impartiality*) imparcialidad *f*; ~ **play** *n* juego limpio.
fairy ['fɛərɪ] *n* hada; ~ **tale** *n* cuento de hadas.
faith [feɪθ] *n* fe *f*; (*trust*) confianza; (*sect*) religión *f*; **~ful** *a* fiel; **~fully** *ad* fielmente; yours **~fully** (*Brit: in letters*) le saluda atentamente.
fake [feɪk] *n* (*painting etc*) falsificación *f*; (*person*) impostor(a) *m/f* // *a* falso // *vt* fingir; (*painting etc*) falsificar.
falcon ['fɔːlkən] *n* halcón *m*.
fall [fɔːl] *n* caída; (*US*) otoño // *vi* (*pt* fell, *pp* fallen) [*fɔːlən*] caer(se); (*price*) bajar; **~s** *npl* (*waterfall*) cascada *sg*, salto *sg* de agua; to ~ flat *vi* (*on one's face*) caerse (boca abajo); (*joke, story*) no hacer gracia; to ~ back *vi* retroceder; to ~ back on *vt fus* (*remedy etc*) recurrir a; to ~ behind *vi* quedarse atrás; to ~ down *vi* (*person*) caerse; (*building, hopes*) derrumbarse; to ~ for *vt fus* (*trick*) dejarse engañar por; (*person*) enamorarse de; to ~ in *vi* (*roof*) hundirse; (*MIL*) alinearse; to ~ off *vi* caerse; (*diminish*) disminuir; to ~ out *vi* (*friends etc*) reñir; (*MIL*) romper filas;

to ~ **through** vi (plan, project) fracasar.

fallacy ['fæləsɪ] n error m.

fallen ['fɔːlən] pp of **fall**.

fallout ['fɔːlaut] n lluvia radioactiva; ~ **shelter** n refugio antiatómico.

fallow ['fæləu] a en barbecho.

false [fɔːls] a (gen) falso; (hair, teeth etc) postizo; (disloyal) desleal, traidor(a); **under ~ pretences** con engaños; ~ **alarm** n falsa alarma; ~ **teeth** npl (Brit) dentadura sg postiza.

falter ['fɔːltə*] vi vacilar.

fame [feɪm] n fama.

familiar [fə'mɪlɪə*] a familiar; (well-known) conocido; (tone) de confianza; **to be ~ with** (subject) estar enterado de; ~**ity** [fəmɪlɪˈærɪtɪ] n familiaridad f.

family ['fæmɪlɪ] n familia; ~ **business** n negocio familiar; ~ **doctor** n médico/a de cabecera.

famine ['fæmɪn] n hambruna.

famished ['fæmɪʃt] a hambriento.

famous ['feɪməs] a famoso, célebre; ~**ly** ad (get on) estupendamente.

fan [fæn] n abanico; (ELEC) ventilador m; (person) aficionado/a // vt abanicar; (fire, quarrel) atizar; **to ~ out** vi desparramarse.

fanatic [fə'nætɪk] n fanático/a.

fan belt n correa de ventilador.

fanciful ['fænsɪful] a (gen) fantástico; (imaginary) fantasioso.

fancy ['fænsɪ] n (whim) capricho, antojo; (imagination) imaginación f // a (luxury) de lujo; (price) exorbitado // vt (feel like, want) tener ganas de; (imagine) imaginarse; **to take a ~ to sb** tomar cariño a uno; **he fancies her** le gusta (ella) mucho; ~ **dress** n disfraz m; ~-**dress ball** n baile m de disfraces.

fanfare ['fænfeə*] n fanfarria (de trompeta).

fang [fæŋ] n colmillo.

fantastic [fæn'tæstɪk] a fantástico.

fantasy ['fæntəzɪ] n fantasía.

far [fɑː*] a (distant) lejano // ad lejos; ~ **away**, ~ **off** (a lo) lejos; ~ **better** mucho mejor; ~ **from** lejos de; **by** ~ con mucho; **go as** ~ **as the farm** vaya hasta la granja; **as** ~ **as I know** que yo sepa; **how** ~? ¿hasta dónde?; (fig) ¿hasta qué punto?; ~**away** a remoto.

farce [fɑːs] n farsa; **farcical** a absurdo.

fare [feə*] n (on trains, buses) precio (del billete); (in taxi: cost) tarifa; (: passenger) pasajero/a; (food) comida; **half/full ~** medio pasaje/pasaje m completo.

Far East n: the ~ el Extremo Oriente.

farewell [feə'wɛl] excl, n adiós m.

farm [fɑːm] n granja, finca (LAm), estancia (LAm) // vt cultivar; ~**er** n granjero, estanciero (LAm); ~**hand** n peón m; ~**house** n granja, casa de hacienda

(LAm); ~**ing** n (gen) agricultura; (tilling) cultivo; ~**land** n tierra de cultivo; ~ **worker** n = ~**hand**; ~**yard** n corral m.

far-reaching [fɑːˈriːtʃɪŋ] a (reform, effect) de gran alcance.

fart [fɑːt] (col!) n pedo(!) // vi tirarse un pedo(!)

farther ['fɑːðə*] ad más lejos, más allá // a más lejano.

farthest ['fɑːðɪst] superlative of **far**.

fascinate ['fæsɪneɪt] vt fascinar; **fascinating** a fascinante; **fascination** [-'neɪʃən] n fascinación f.

fascism ['fæʃɪzəm] n fascismo.

fashion ['fæʃən] n moda; (manner) manera // vt formar; **in ~** a la moda; **out of ~** pasado de moda; ~**able** a de moda; ~ **show** n desfile m de modelos.

fast [fɑːst] a rápido; (dye, colour) sólido; (clock): **to be ~** estar adelantado // ad rápidamente, de prisa; (stuck, held) firmemente // n ayuno // vi ayunar; ~ **asleep** profundamente dormido.

fasten ['fɑːsn] vt asegurar, sujetar; (coat, belt) abrochar // vi cerrarse; ~**er**, ~**ing** n cierre m; (of door etc) cerrojo.

fast food n comida rápida, platos mpl preparados.

fastidious [fæs'tɪdɪəs] a (fussy) delicado; (demanding) exigente.

fat [fæt] a gordo; (meat) con mucha grasa; (greasy) grasiento // n grasa; (on person) carnes fpl; (lard) manteca.

fatal ['feɪtl] a (mistake) fatal; (injury) mortal; (consequence) funesto; ~**ism** n fatalismo; ~**ity** [fəˈtælɪtɪ] n (road death etc) víctima f; ~**ly** ad: ~**ly injured** herido a muerte.

fate [feɪt] n destino; ~**ful** a fatídico.

father ['fɑːðə*] n padre m; ~-**in-law** n suegro; ~**ly** a paternal.

fathom ['fæðəm] n braza // vt (mystery) desentrañar; (understand) lograr comprender.

fatigue [fə'tiːg] n fatiga, cansancio.

fatten ['fætn] vt, vi engordar.

fatty ['fætɪ] a (food) graso // n (fam) gordito/a, gordinflón/ona m/f.

fatuous ['fætjuəs] a fatuo, necio.

faucet ['fɔːsɪt] n (US) grifo, llave f (LAm).

fault [fɔːlt] n (blame) culpa; (defect: in character) defecto; (in manufacture) desperfecto; (GEO) falla // vt criticar; **it's my ~** es culpa mía; **to find ~ with** criticar, poner peros a; **at ~** culpable; ~**less** a (action) intachable; (person) sin defectos; ~**y** a defectuoso.

fauna ['fɔːnə] n fauna.

faux pas ['fəu'pɑː] n plancha.

favour, (US) **favor** ['feɪvə*] n favor m; (approval) aprobación f // vt (proposition) estar a favor de, aprobar; (person etc) favorecer; (assist) ser propicio a;

to ask a ~ of pedir un favor a; **to do sb a** ~ hacer un favor a uno; **to find** ~ **with** caer en gracia de; **in** ~ **of** a favor de; ~**able** *a* favorable; ~**ite** [-rɪt] *a*, *n* favorito, preferido; ~**itism** *n* favoritismo.

fawn [fɔːn] *n* cervato // *a* (*also*: ~**coloured**) color de cervato, leonado // *vi*: **to** ~ **(up)on** adular.

fax [fæks] *n* (*document*) facsímil(e) *m*; (*machine*) telefax *m* // *vt* mandar por telefax.

FBI *n abbr* (*US*: = *Federal Bureau of Investigation*) ≈ BIC *f* (*Sp*).

fear [fɪə*] *n* miedo, temor *m* // *vt* temer; **for** ~ **of** por temor a; ~**ful** *a* temeroso, miedoso; (*awful*) terrible.

feasible ['fiːzəbl] *a* factible.

feast [fiːst] *n* banquete *m*; (*REL*: *also*: ~ **day**) fiesta // *vi* banquetear.

feat [fiːt] *n* hazaña.

feather ['fɛðə*] *n* pluma.

feature ['fiːtʃə*] *n* (*gen*) característica; (*ANAT*) rasgo; (*article*) artículo de fondo // *vt* (*subj*: *film*) presentar // *vi* figurar; ~**s** *npl* (*of face*) facciones *fpl*; ~ **film** *n* largometraje *m*.

February ['fɛbruəri] *n* febrero.

fed [fɛd] *pt*, *pp of* **feed**.

federal ['fɛdərəl] *a* federal.

fed-up [fɛd'ʌp] *a*: **to be** ~ **(with)** estar harto (de).

fee [fiː] *n* (*professional*) derechos *mpl*, honorarios *mpl*; (*of school*) matrícula; (*of club*) cuota.

feeble ['fiːbl] *a* débil.

feed [fiːd] *n* (*gen*, *of baby*) comida; (*of animal*) pienso; (*on printer*) dispositivo de alimentación // *vt* (*pt*, *pp* **fed**) (*gen*) alimentar; (*Brit*: *baby*: *breastfeed*) dar el pecho a; (*animal*) dar de comer a; (*data*, *information*): **to** ~ **into** meter en; **to** ~ **on** *vt fus* alimentarse de; ~**back** *n* reacción *f*, feedback *m*; ~**ing bottle** *n* (*Brit*) biberón *m*.

feel [fiːl] *n* (*sensation*) sensación *f*; (*sense of touch*) tacto // *vt* (*pt*, *pp* **felt**) tocar; (*cold*, *pain etc*) sentir; (*think*, *believe*) creer; **to** ~ **hungry/cold** tener hambre/frío; **to** ~ **lonely/better** sentirse solo/mejor; **I don't** ~ **well** no me siento bien; **it** ~**s soft** es suave al tacto; **to** ~ **like** (*want*) tener ganas de; **to** ~ **about** *or* **around** *vi* tantear; ~**er** *n* (*of insect*) antena; **to put out** ~**ers** (*fig*) sondear; ~**ing** *n* (*physical*) sensación *f*; (*foreboding*) presentimiento; (*emotion*) sentimiento.

feet [fiːt] *pl of* **foot**.

feign [feɪn] *vt* fingir.

fell [fɛl] *pt of* **fall** // *vt* (*tree*) talar.

fellow ['fɛləu] *n* tipo, tío (*Sp*); (*of learned society*) socio/a // *cpd*: ~ **students** compañeros/as *m/fpl* de curso, condiscípulos/as *m/fpl*; ~ **citizen** *n* conciudadano/a; ~ **countryman** *n* com-

patriota *m*; ~ **men** *npl* semejantes *mpl*; ~**ship** *n* compañerismo; (*grant*) beca; ~ **student** *n* compañero/a de curso.

felony ['fɛlənɪ] *n* crimen *m*.

felt [fɛlt] *pt*, *pp of* **feel** // *n* fieltro; ~**-tip pen** *n* rotulador *m*.

female ['fiːmeɪl] *n* (*woman*) mujer *f*; (*ZOOL*) hembra // *a* femenino.

feminine ['fɛmɪnɪn] *a* femenino.

feminist ['fɛmɪnɪst] *n* feminista.

fence [fɛns] *n* valla, cerca // *vt* (*also*: ~ **in**) cercar // *vi* (*SPORT*) hacer esgrima; **fencing** *n* esgrima.

fend [fɛnd] *vi*: **to** ~ **for o.s.** valerse por sí mismo; **to** ~ **off** *vt* (*attack*) rechazar.

fender ['fɛndə*] *n* guardafuego, (*US*: *AUT*) parachoques *m inv*; (: *RAIL*) trompa.

ferment [fə'mɛnt] *vi* fermentar // *n* ['fəːmɛnt] (*fig*) agitación *f*.

fern [fəːn] *n* helecho.

ferocious [fə'rəuʃəs] *a* feroz; **ferocity** [-'rɒsɪtɪ] *n* ferocidad *f*.

ferret ['fɛrɪt] *n* hurón *m* // *vt*: **to** ~ **out** desentrañar.

ferry ['fɛrɪ] *n* (*small*) barca (de pasaje), balsa; (*large*: *also*: ~**boat**) transbordador *m* (*Sp*), embarcadero (*LAm*) // *vt* transportar.

fertile ['fəːtaɪl] *a* fértil; (*BIOL*) fecundo; **fertility** [fə'tɪlɪtɪ] *n* fertilidad *f*; fecundidad *f*; **fertilize** ['fəːtɪlaɪz] *vt* (*BIOL*) fecundar; (*AGR*) abonar; **fertilizer** *n* abono.

fervent ['fəːvənt] *a* (*admirer*) entusiasta; (*hope*) ferviente.

fervour ['fəːvə*] *n* fervor *m*, ardor *m*.

fester ['fɛstə*] *vi* ulcerarse.

festival ['fɛstɪvəl] *n* (*REL*) fiesta; (*ART*, *MUS*) festival *m*.

festive ['fɛstɪv] *a* festivo; **the** ~ **season** (*Brit*: *Christmas*) las Navidades.

festivities [fɛs'tɪvɪtɪz] *npl* fiestas *fpl*.

festoon [fɛs'tuːn] *vt*: **to** ~ **with** engalanar de.

fetch [fɛtʃ] *vt* ir a buscar; (*sell for*) venderse por.

fetching ['fɛtʃɪŋ] *a* atractivo.

fête [feɪt] *n* fiesta.

fetus ['fiːtəs] *n* (*US*) = **foetus**.

feud [fjuːd] *n* (*hostility*) enemistad *f*; (*quarrel*) disputa.

feudal ['fjuːdl] *a* feudal.

fever ['fiːvə*] *n* fiebre *f*; ~**ish** *a* febril.

few [fjuː] *a* (*not many*) pocos; (*some*) algunos, unos; **a** ~ *a* unos pocos // *pron* algunos, unos; ~**er** *a* menos; ~**est** *a* los/las menos.

fiancé [fɪ'ãːŋseɪ] *n* novio, prometido; ~**e** *n* novia, prometida.

fib [fɪb] *n* mentirilla // *vi* decir mentirillas.

fibre, (*US*) **fiber** ['faɪbə*] *n* fibra; ~**glass** *n* fibra de vidrio.

fickle ['fɪkl] *a* inconstante.

fiction ['fɪkʃən] *n* (*gen*) ficción *f*; **~al** *a* novelesco; **fictitious** [fɪk'tɪʃəs] *a* ficticio.

fiddle ['fɪdl] *n* (*MUS*) violín *m*; (*cheating*) trampa // *vt* (*Brit: accounts*) falsificar; **to ~ with** *vt fus* jugar con.

fidelity [fɪ'dɛlɪtɪ] *n* fidelidad *f*.

fidget ['fɪdʒɪt] *vi* inquietarse.

field [fiːld] *n* campo; (*fig*) campo, esfera; (*SPORT*) campo, cancha (*LAm*); (*competitors*) competidores *mpl*; **~ marshal** *n* mariscal *m*; **~work** *n* trabajo de campo.

fiend [fiːnd] *n* demonio; **~ish** *a* diabólico.

fierce [fɪəs] *a* feroz; (*wind, attack*) violento; (*heat*) intenso; (*fighting, enemy*) encarnizado.

fiery ['faɪərɪ] *a* (*burning*) ardiente; (*temperament*) apasionado.

fifteen [fɪf'tiːn] *num* quince.

fifth [fɪfθ] *a, n* quinto.

fifty ['fɪftɪ] *num* cincuenta; **~-~** *a*: **a ~-~ chance** el cincuenta por ciento de posibilidades // *ad* a medias, mitad por mitad.

fig [fɪg] *n* higo.

fight [faɪt] *n* (*gen*) pelea; (*MIL*) combate *m*; (*struggle*) lucha // (*vb: pt, pp* **fought**) *vt* luchar contra; (*cancer, alcoholism*) combatir // *vi* pelear, luchar; **~er** *n* combatiente *m/f*; (*fig*) luchador(a) *m/f*; (*plane*) caza *m*; **~ing** *n* combate *m*.

figment ['fɪgmənt] *n*: **a ~ of the imagination** una quimera.

figurative ['fɪgjʊrətɪv] *a* (*meaning*) figurado.

figure ['fɪgə*] *n* (*DRAWING, GEOM*) figura, dibujo; (*number, cipher*) cifra; (*body, outline*) talle *m*, tipo // *vt* (*esp US*) imaginar // *vi* (*appear*) figurar; (*US: make sense*) ser lógico; **to ~ out** *vt* (*understand*) comprender; **~head** *n* (*fig*) testaferro; **~ of speech** *n* figura retórica.

filch [fɪltʃ] *vt* (*col: steal*) hurtar, robar.

file [faɪl] *n* (*tool*) lima; (*dossier*) expediente *m*; (*folder*) carpeta; (*COMPUT*) fichero; (*row*) fila // *vt* limar; (*papers*) clasificar; (*LAW: claim*) presentar; (*store*) archivar; **to ~ in/out** *vi* entrar/salir en fila; **to ~ past** *vt fus* desfilar ante; **filing** *n*: **to do the filing** llevar los archivos; **filing cabinet** *n* fichero, archivo.

fill [fɪl] *vt* llenar // *n*: **to eat one's ~** llenarse; **to ~ in** *vt* rellenar; **to ~ up** *vt* llenar (hasta el borde) // *vi* (*AUT*) poner gasolina.

fillet ['fɪlɪt] *n* filete *m*; **~ steak** *n* filete *m* de ternera.

filling ['fɪlɪŋ] *n* (*CULIN*) relleno; (*for tooth*) empaste *m*; **~ station** *n* estación *f* de servicio.

film [fɪlm] *n* película // *vt* (*scene*) filmar // *vi* rodar (una película); **~ star** *n* astro,

estrella de cine; **~strip** *n* tira de película.

filter ['fɪltə*] *n* filtro // *vt* filtrar; **~ lane** *n* (*Brit*) carril *m* de selección; **~-tipped** *a* con filtro.

filth [fɪlθ] *n* suciedad *f*; **~y** *a* sucio; (*language*) obsceno.

fin [fɪn] *n* (*gen*) aleta.

final ['faɪnl] *a* (*last*) final, último; (*definitive*) definitivo, terminante // *n* (*Brit: SPORT*) final *f*; **~s** *npl* (*SCOL*) examen *m* de fin de curso; (*US: SPORT*) final *f*.

finale [fɪ'nɑːlɪ] *n* final *m*.

final: **~ist** *n* (*SPORT*) finalista *m/f*; **~ize** *vt* concluir, completar; **~ly** *ad* (*lastly*) por último, finalmente; (*eventually*) por fin.

finance [faɪ'næns] *n* (*money*) fondos *mpl*; **~s** *npl* finanzas *fpl* // *vt* financiar; **financial** [-'nænʃəl] *a* financiero; **financier** *n* financiero/a.

find [faɪnd] *vt* (*pt, pp* **found**) (*gen*) encontrar, hallar; (*come upon*) descubrir // *n* hallazgo; descubrimiento; **to ~ sb guilty** (*LAW*) declarar culpable a uno; **to ~ out** *vt* averiguar; (*truth, secret*) descubrir; **to ~ out about** enterarse de; **~ings** *npl* (*LAW*) veredicto *sg*, fallo *sg*; (*of report*) recomendaciones *fpl*.

fine [faɪn] *a* (*delicate*) fino; (*beautiful*) hermoso // *ad* (*well*) bien // *n* (*LAW*) multa // *vt* (*LAW*) multar; **the weather is ~** hace buen tiempo; **~ arts** *npl* bellas artes *fpl*.

finery ['faɪnərɪ] *n* adornos *mpl*.

finesse [fɪ'nɛs] *n* sutileza.

finger ['fɪŋgə*] *n* dedo // *vt* (*touch*) manosear; (*MUS*) puntear; **little/index ~** (*dedo*) meñique *m*/índice *m*; **~nail** *n* uña; **~print** *n* huella dactilar; **~tip** *n* yema del dedo.

finicky ['fɪnɪkɪ] *a* (*fussy*) delicado.

finish ['fɪnɪʃ] *n* (*end*) fin *m*; (*SPORT*) meta; (*polish etc*) acabado // *vt, vi* terminar; **to ~ doing sth** acabar de hacer algo; **to ~ third** llegar el tercero; **to ~ off** *vt* acabar, terminar; (*kill*) acabar con; **to ~ up** *vt* acabar, terminar // *vi* ir a parar, terminar; **~ing line** *n* línea de llegada *or* meta; **~ing school** *n* academia para señoritas.

finite ['faɪnaɪt] *a* finito; (*verb*) conjugado.

Finland ['fɪnlənd] *n* Finlandia.

Finn [fɪn] *n* finlandés/esa *m/f*; **~ish** *a* finlandés/esa // *n* (*LING*) finlandés *m*.

fir [fə:*] *n* abeto.

fire ['faɪə*] *n* (*gen*) fuego; (*accidental*) incendio // *vt* (*gun*) disparar; (*set fire to*) incendiar; (*excite*) exaltar; (*interest*) despertar; (*dismiss*) despedir // *vi* encenderse; **on ~** ardiendo, en llamas; **~ alarm** *n* alarma de incendios; **~arm** *n* arma de fuego; **~ brigade**, (*US*) **~ department** *n* (*cuerpo de*) bomberos *mpl*; **~ engine** *n* coche *m* de bomberos;

~ **escape** n escalera de incendios; ~ **extinguisher** n extintor m (de fuego); ~**man** n bombero; ~**place** n chimenea; ~**side** n: by the ~ al lado de la chimenea; ~ **station** n parque m de bomberos; ~**wood** n leña; ~**works** npl fuegos mpl artificiales.

firing ['faɪərɪŋ] n (MIL) disparos mpl, tiroteo; ~ **squad** n pelotón m de ejecución.

firm [fəːm] a firme // n firma, empresa; ~**ly** ad firmemente; ~**ness** n firmeza.

first [fəːst] a primero // ad (before others) primero/a; (when listing reasons etc) en primer lugar, primeramente // n (person: in race) primero/a; (AUT) primera; at ~ al principio; ~ of all ante todo; ~ **aid** n primera ayuda, primeros auxilios mpl; ~-**aid kit** n botiquín m; ~-**class** a de primera clase; ~-**hand** a de primera mano; F~ **Lady** n (esp US) primera dama; ~**ly** ad en primer lugar; ~ **name** n nombre m de pila; ~-**rate** a de primera clase.

fish [fɪʃ] n, pl inv pez m; (food) pescado // vt, vi pescar; to go ~**ing** ir de pesca; ~**erman** n pescador m; ~ **farm** n criadero de peces; ~ **fingers** npl (Brit) croquetas fpl de pescado; ~**ing boat** n barca de pesca; ~**ing line** n sedal m; ~**ing rod** n caña (de pescar); ~**ing tackle** n aparejo (de pescar); ~ **market** n mercado de pescado; ~**monger** n (Brit) pescadero; ~**monger's (shop)** n (Brit) pescadería; ~ **sticks** npl (US) = ~ **fingers**; ~**seller** n (US) = **fishmonger**; ~**y** a (fig) sospechoso; ~**store** n (US) = **fishmonger's**.

fist [fɪst] n puño.

fit [fɪt] a (MED. SPORT) en (buena) forma; (proper) adecuado, apropiado // vt (subj: clothes) sentar bien a; (try on: clothes) probar; (facts) cuadrar or corresponder con; (accommodate) ajustar, adaptar // vi (clothes) entallar; (in space, gap) caber; (facts) coincidir // n (MED) ataque m; ~ to apto para; ~ for apropiado para; a ~ of anger/pride un arranque de cólera/orgullo; **this dress is a good ~** este vestido me sienta bien; **by ~s and starts** a rachas; **to ~ in** vi (gen) encajarse; (fig: person) llevarse bien (con todos); **to ~ out** (Brit: also: ~ **up**) vt equipar; ~**ful** a espasmódico, intermitente; ~**ment** n módulo adosable; ~**ness** n (MED) salud f; (of remark) conveniencia; ~**ted carpet** n moqueta; ~**ted kitchen** n cocina amueblada; ~**ter** n ajustador m; ~**ting** a apropiado // n (of dress) prueba; ~**ting room** n probador m; ~**tings** npl instalaciones fpl.

five [faɪv] num cinco; ~**r** n (col: Brit) billete m de cinco libras; (: US) billete m de cinco dólares.

fix [fɪks] vt (secure) fijar, asegurar; (mend) arreglar // n: **to be in a** ~ estar en un aprieto; **to** ~ **up** vt (meeting) arreglar; **to** ~ **sb up with sth** proveer a uno de algo; ~**ation** [fɪk'seɪʃən] n obsesión f; ~**ed** [fɪkst] a (prices etc) fijo; ~**ture** ['fɪkstʃə*] n (SPORT) encuentro; ~**tures** npl instalaciones fpl fijas.

fizz [fɪz] vi hacer efervescencia.

fizzle out ['fɪzl]: vi apagarse.

fizzy ['fɪzɪ] a (drink) gaseoso.

flabbergasted ['flæbəgɑːstɪd] a pasmado.

flabby ['flæbɪ] a flojo (de carnes); (skin) fofo.

flag [flæg] n bandera; (stone) losa // vi decaer; **to** ~ **sb down** hacer señas a uno para que se pare; ~**pole** n asta de bandera; ~ **stop** n (US) parada a petición.

flair [fleə*] n aptitud f especial.

flak [flæk] n (MIL) fuego antiaéreo; (col: criticism) lluvia de críticas.

flake [fleɪk] n (of rust, paint) escama; (of snow, soap powder) copo // vi (also: ~ off) (paint) desconcharse; (skin) descamarse.

flamboyant [flæm'bɔɪənt] a (dress) vistoso; (person) extravagante.

flame [fleɪm] n llama.

flamingo [flə'mɪŋgəu] n flamenco.

flammable ['flæməbl] a inflamable.

flan [flæn] n (Brit) tarta.

flank [flæŋk] n flanco; (of person) costado // vt flanquear.

flannel ['flænl] n (Brit: also: face ~) manopla; (fabric) franela; ~s npl pantalones mpl de franela.

flap [flæp] n (of pocket) solapa; (of envelope) solapa; (of table) hoja (plegadiza); (wing movement) aletazo // vt (wings) aletear // vi (sail, flag) ondear.

flare [fleə*] n llamarada; (MIL) bengala; (in skirt etc) vuelo; **to** ~ **up** vi encenderse; (fig: person) encolerizarse; (: revolt) estallar.

flash [flæʃ] n relámpago; (also: news ~) noticias fpl de última hora; (PHOT) flash m // vt (light, headlights) encender y apagar; (torch) encender // vi brillar; **in a** ~ en un instante; **he** ~**ed by** or **past** pasó como un rayo; ~**bulb** n bombilla fusible; ~ **cube** n cubo de flash; ~**light** n linterna.

flashy ['flæʃɪ] a (pej) ostentoso.

flask [flɑːsk] n frasco; (also: vacuum ~) termo(s) m.

flat [flæt] a llano; (smooth) liso; (tyre) desinflado; (beer) muerto; (MUS) desafinado // n (Brit: apartment) piso (Sp); departamento (LAm), apartamento; (AUT) pinchazo; (MUS) bemol m; **to work** ~ **out** trabajar a toda mecha; ~**ly** ad terminantemente, de plano; ~**ten** vt (also: ~**ten out**) allanar; (smooth out) alisar.

flatter ['flætə*] *vt* adular, halagar; ~ing *a* halagüeño; ~y *n* adulación *f*.
flaunt [flɔːnt] *vt* ostentar, lucir.
flavour, (*US*) **flavor** ['fleɪvə*] *n* sabor *m*, gusto // *vt* sazonar, condimentar; ~ed *a*: **strawberry** ~ed con sabor a fresa; ~ing *n* (*in product*) aromatizante *m*.
flaw [flɔː] *n* defecto.
flax [flæks] *n* lino; ~en *a* rubio.
flea [fliː] *n* pulga.
fleck [flɛk] *n* (*mark*) mota; (*pattern*) punto.
flee [fliː], *pt, pp* **fled** [flɛd] *vt* huir de, abandonar // *vi* huir, fugarse.
fleece [fliːs] *n* vellón *m*; (*wool*) lana // *vt* (*col*) pelar.
fleet [fliːt] *n* flota; (*of lorries etc*) escuadra.
fleeting ['fliːtɪŋ] *a* fugaz.
Flemish ['flɛmɪʃ] *a* flamenco.
flesh [flɛʃ] *n* carne *f*; (*of fruit*) pulpa; **of ~ and blood** de carne y hueso; ~ **wound** *n* herida superficial.
flew [fluː] *pt of* **fly**.
flex [flɛks] *n* cordón *m* // *vt* (*muscles*) tensar; ~**ibility** [-'bɪlɪtɪ] *n* flexibilidad *f*; ~**ible** *a* flexible.
flick [flɪk] *n* golpecito; (*with finger*) capirotazo // *vt* dar un golpecito a; **to ~ through** *vt fus* hojear.
flicker ['flɪkə*] *vi* (*light*) parpadear; (*flame*) vacilar // *n* parpadeo.
flier ['flaɪə*] *n* aviador(a) *m/f*.
flight [flaɪt] *n* vuelo; (*escape*) huida, fuga; (*also*: ~ **of steps**) tramo (de escaleras); **to take** ~ huir, darse a la fuga; **to put to** ~ ahuyentar; ~ **attendant** *n* (*US*) (*male*) camarero, (*female*) azafata; ~ **deck** *n* (*AVIAT*) cabina de mandos.
flimsy ['flɪmzɪ] *a* (*thin*) muy ligero; (*excuse*) flojo.
flinch [flɪntʃ] *vi* encogerse.
fling [flɪŋ], *pt, pp* **flung** *vt* arrojar.
flint [flɪnt] *n* pedernal *m*; (*in lighter*) piedra.
flip [flɪp] *vt* dar la vuelta a; (*coin*) echar a cara o cruz.
flippant ['flɪpənt] *a* poco serio.
flipper ['flɪpə*] *n* aleta.
flirt [flɜːt] *vi* coquetear, flirtear // *n* coqueta *f*; ~**ation** [-'teɪʃən] *n* coqueteo, flirteo.
flit [flɪt] *vi* revolotear.
float [fləut] *n* flotador *m*; (*in procession*) carroza; (*money*) reserva // *vi* flotar; (*swimmer*) hacer la plancha // *vt* (*gen*) hacer flotar; (*company*) lanzar.
flock [flɔk] *n* (*of sheep*) rebaño; (*of birds*) bandada; (*of people*) multitud *f*.
flog [flɔg] *vt* azotar; (*col*) vender.
flood [flʌd] *n* inundación *f*; (*of words, tears etc*) torrente *m* // *vt* inundar; ~**ing** *n* inundación *f*; ~**light** *n* foco.
floor [flɔː*] *n* suelo; (*storey*) piso; (*of sea*) fondo; (*dance* ~) pista // *vt* (*fig*) de-

jar sin respuesta; **ground** ~, (*US*) **first** ~ planta baja; **first** ~, (*US*) **second** ~ primer piso; ~**board** *n* tabla; ~ **lamp** *n* (*US*) lámpara de pie; ~ **show** *n* cabaret *m*.
flop [flɔp] *n* fracaso.
floppy ['flɔpɪ] *a* flojo // *n* (*COMPUT*: *also* ~ **disk**) floppy *m*.
flora ['flɔːrə] *n* flora.
florist ['flɔrɪst] *n* florista *m/f*; ~'s (**shop**) *n* florería.
flounce [flauns] *n* volante *m*; **to ~ out** *vi* salir enfadado.
flounder ['flaundə*] *vi* tropezar // *n* (*ZOOL*) platija.
flour ['flauə*] *n* harina.
flourish ['flʌrɪʃ] *vi* florecer // *n* ademán *m*, movimiento (ostentoso); ~**ing** *a* floreciente.
flout [flaut] *vt* burlarse de.
flow [fləu] *n* (*movement*) flujo; (*direction*) curso; (*tide*) corriente *f* // *vi* (*river, traffic, blood*) fluir; ~ **chart** *n* organigrama *m*.
flower ['flauə*] *n* flor *f* // *vi* florecer; ~**bed** *n* macizo; ~**pot** *n* tiesto; ~**y** *a* florido.
flown [fləun] *pp of* **fly**.
flu [fluː] *n* gripe *f*.
fluctuate ['flʌktjueɪt] *vi* fluctuar.
fluent ['fluːənt] *a* (*speech*) elocuente; **he speaks ~ French, he's ~ in French** domina el francés; ~**ly** *ad* con fluidez.
fluff [flʌf] *n* pelusa; ; ~**y** *a* velloso.
fluid ['fluːɪd] *a, n* fluido, líquido.
fluke [fluːk] *n* (*col*) chiripa.
flung [flʌŋ] *pt, pp of* **fling**.
fluoride ['fluərˈaɪd] *n* fluoruro.
flurry ['flʌrɪ] *n* (*of snow*) temporal *m*; (*haste*) agitación *f*; ~ **of activity** frenesí *m* de actividad.
flush [flʌʃ] *n* (*on face*) rubor *m*; (*fig: of youth, beauty*) resplandor *m* // *vt* limpiar con agua // *vi* ruborizarse // *a*: ~ **with** a ras de; **to ~ the toilet** hacer funcionar el WC; **to ~ out** *vt* (*game, birds*) levantar; (*fig*) desalojar; ~**ed** *a* ruborizado.
flustered ['flʌstəd] *a* aturdido.
flute [fluːt] *n* flauta.
flutter ['flʌtə*] *n* (*of wings*) revoloteo, aleteo // *vi* revolotear.
flux [flʌks] *n*: **to be in a state of** ~ estar continuamente cambiando.
fly [flaɪ] *n* (*insect*) mosca; (*on trousers: also*: **flies**) bragueta // *vb* (*pt* **flew**, *pp* **flown**) *vt* (*plane*) pilot(e)ar; (*cargo*) transportar (en avión); (*distances*) recorrer (en avión) // *vi* volar; (*passengers*) ir en avión; (*escape*) evadirse; (*flag*) ondear; **to ~ away** *or* **off** *vi* (*bird, insect*) emprender el vuelo; ~**ing** *n* (*activity*) (el) volar // *a*: ~**ing visit** visita relámpago; **with** ~**ing colours** con lucimiento; ~**ing saucer** *n* platillo volan-

te; ~**ing start** *n*: **to get off to a** ~**ing
start** empezar con buen pie; ~**over** *n*
(*Brit*: *bridge*) paso a desnivel *or* superior; ~**past** *n* desfile *m* aéreo; ~**sheet** *n*
(*for tent*) doble techo.

foal [fəul] *n* potro.

foam [fəum] *n* espuma // *vi* echar espuma; ~ **rubber** *n* espuma de caucho.

fob [fɔb] *vt*: **to ~ sb off with sth** despachar a uno con algo.

focus ['fəukəs], *pl* ~**es** *n* foco // *vt* (*field
glasses etc*) enfocar // *vi*: **to ~ on** enfocar a; (*issue etc*) centrarse en; **in/out of**
~ enfocado/desenfocado.

fodder ['fɔdə*] *n* pienso.

foe [fəu] *n* enemigo.

foetus ['fiːtəs] *n* feto.

fog [fɔg] *n* niebla; ~**gy** *a*: **it's** ~**gy** hay
niebla, está brumoso; ~ **lamp**, (*US*) ~
light *n* (*AUT*) faro de niebla.

foil [fɔil] *vt* frustrar // *n* hoja; (*kitchen* ~)
papel *m* (de) aluminio; (*FENCING*) flore-
te *m*.

fold [fəuld] *n* (*bend, crease*) pliegue *m*;
(*AGR*) redil *m* // *vt* doblar; **to ~ up** *vi*
plegarse, doblarse; (*business*) quebrar //
vt (*map etc*) plegar; ~**er** *n* (*for papers*)
carpeta; (*brochure*) folleto; ~**ing** *a*
(*chair, bed*) plegable.

foliage ['fəulɪdʒ] *n* follaje *m*.

folk [fəuk] *npl* gente *f* // *a* popular, folkló-
rico; ~**s** *npl* familia, parientes *mpl*;
~**lore** ['fəuklɔ:*] *n* folklore *m*; ~ **song**
n canción *f* popular *or* folklórica.

follow ['fɔləu] *vt* seguir // *vi* seguir; (*result*) resultar; **he** ~**ed suit** hizo lo mismo; **to ~ up** *vt* (*letter, offer*) responder
a; (*case*) investigar; ~**er** *n* seguidor/a)
m/f; (*POL*) partidario/a; ~**ing** *a* siguiente // *n* afición *f*, partidarios *mpl*.

folly ['fɔlɪ] *n* locura.

fond [fɔnd] *a* (*loving*) cariñoso; **to be ~
of** tener cariño a.

fondle ['fɔndl] *vt* acariciar.

fondness ['fɔndnɪs] *n* (*for things*) gusto;
(*for people*) cariño.

font [fɔnt] *n* pila bautismal.

food [fuːd] *n* comida; ~ **mixer** *n* batido-
ra; ~ **poisoning** *n* botulismo; ~ **processor** *n* robot *m* de cocina; ~**stuffs**
npl comestibles *mpl*.

fool [fuːl] *n* tonto/a; '(*CULIN*) puré *m* de
frutas con nata // *vt* engañar // *vi* (*gen*:
~ **around**) bromear; (*waste time*) perder el tiempo; ~**hardy** *a* temerario;
~**ish** *a* tonto; (*careless*) imprudente;
~**proof** *a* (*plan etc*) infalible.

foot [fut], *pl* **feet** *n* pie *m*; (*measure*) pie
m (= 304 *mm*); (*of animal*) pata // *vt*
(*bill*) pagar; **on a ~** pie; ~**age** *n* (*CINE-
MA*) imágenes *fpl*; ~**ball** *n* balón *m*;
(*game*: *Brit*) fútbol *m*; (: *US*) fútbol *m*
americano; ~**ball player** *n* (*Brit*: *also*:
~**er**) *n* futbolista *m*; (*US*) jugador *m* de
fútbol americano; ~**brake** *n* freno de

pie; ~**bridge** *n* puente *m* para peatones; ~**hills** *npl* estribaciones *fpl*; ~**hold**
n pie *m* firme; ~**ing** *n* (*fig*) posición *f*;
to lose one's ~**ing** perder el pie; **on an
equal** ~**ing** en pie de igualdad; ~**lights**
npl candilejas *fpl*; ~**man** *n* lacayo;
~**note** *n* nota de pie; ~**path** *n* sendero;
~**print** *n* huella, pisada; ~**sore** *a* con
los pies doloridos; ~**step** *n* paso;
~**wear** *n* calzado.

for [fɔː] ♦ *prep* **1** (*indicating destination,
intention*) para; **the train ~ London** el
tren con destino a *or* de Londres; **he left
~ Rome** marchó para Roma; **he went ~
the paper** fue por el periódico; **is this ~
me?** ¿es esto para mí?; **it's time ~ lunch**
es la hora de comer

2 (*indicating purpose*) para; **what('s it)
~?** ¿para qué (es)?; **to pray ~ peace** rezar por la paz

3 (*on behalf of, representing*): **the MP ~
Hove** el diputado por Hove; **he works ~
the government/a local firm** trabaja para
el gobierno/en una empresa local; **I'll
ask him ~ you** se lo pediré por ti; **G ~
George** G de George

4 (*because of*) por esta razón; ~ **fear of
being criticized** por temor a ser criticado

5 (*with regard to*) para; **it's cold ~ July**
hace frío para julio; **he has a gift ~ languages** tiene don de lenguas

6 (*in exchange for*) por; **I sold it ~ £5** lo
vendí por £5; **to pay 50 pence ~ a ticket**
pagar 50p por un billete

7 (*in favour of*): **are you ~ or against
us?** ¿estás con nosotros o contra nosotros?; **I'm all ~ it** estoy totalmente a favor; **vote ~ X** vote (a) X

8 (*referring to distance*): **there are
roadworks ~ 5 km** hay obras en 5 km;
we walked ~ miles caminamos kilómetros y kilómetros

9 (*referring to time*): **he was away ~ 2
years** estuvo fuera (durante) dos años; **it
hasn't rained ~ 3 weeks** no ha llovido durante *or* en 3 semanas; **I have known
her ~ years** la conozco desde hace años;
can you do it ~ tomorrow? ¿lo podrás
hacer para mañana?

10 (*with infinitive clauses*): **it is not ~
me to decide** la decisión no es cosa mía;
it would be best ~ you to leave sería mejor que te fueras; **there is still time ~
you to do it** todavía te queda tiempo
para hacerlo; ~ **this to be possible...**
para que esto sea posible...

11 (*in spite of*) a pesar de; ~ **all his
complaints** a pesar de sus quejas

♦ *conj* (*since, as*: *rather formal*) puesto
que.

forage ['fɔrɪdʒ] *n* forraje *m*.

foray ['fɔreɪ] *n* incursión *f*.

forbid [fə'bɪd], *pt* **forbad(e)** [fə'bæd], *pp*
forbidden [fə'bɪdn] *vt* prohibir; **to ~ sb
to do sth** prohibir a uno hacer algo;

~**ding** a (landscape) inhóspito; (severe) severo.

force [fɔːs] n fuerza // vt forzar; **to ~ o.s. to do** hacer un esfuerzo por hacer; **the F~s** npl (Brit) las Fuerzas Armadas; **in ~ en vigor**; ~**d** [fɔːst] a forzado; **to ~-feed** vt (animal, prisoner) alimentar a la fuerza; ~**ful** a enérgico.

forcibly ['fɔːsəblɪ] ad a la fuerza.

ford [fɔːd] n vado // vt vadear.

fore [fɔː*] n: **to the ~** en evidencia.

forearm ['fɔːrɑːm] n antebrazo.

foreboding [fɔː'bəudɪŋ] n presentimiento.

forecast ['fɔːkɑːst] n pronóstico // vt (irg: like cast) pronosticar.

forecourt ['fɔːkɔːt] n (of garage) patio.

forefathers ['fɔːfɑːðəz] npl antepasados mpl.

forefinger ['fɔːfɪŋgə*] n (dedo) índice m.

forefront ['fɔːfrʌnt] n: **in the ~ of** en la vanguardia de.

forego vt = **forgo**.

foregone ['fɔːgɒn] a: **it's a ~ conclusion** es una conclusión evidente.

foreground ['fɔːgraund] n primer plano.

forehead ['fɒrɪd] n frente f.

foreign ['fɒrɪn] a extranjero; (trade) exterior; ~**er** n extranjero/a; ~ **exchange** n divisas fpl; **F~ Office** n (Brit) Ministerio de Asuntos Exteriores; **F~ Secretary** n (Brit) Ministro de Asuntos Exteriores.

foreleg ['fɔːleg] n pata delantera.

foreman ['fɔːmən] n capataz m; (in construction) maestro de obras.

foremost ['fɔːməust] a principal // ad: **first and ~** ante todo.

forensic [fə'rɛnsɪk] a forense.

forerunner ['fɔːrʌnə*] n precursor(a) m/f.

foresee, pt **foresaw**, pp **foreseen** [fɔː'siː, -'sɔː, -siːn] vt prever; ~**able** a previsible.

foreshadow [fɔː'ʃædəu] vt prefigurar, anunciar.

foresight ['fɔːsaɪt] n previsión f.

forest ['fɒrɪst] n bosque m.

forestall [fɔː'stɔːl] vt prevenir.

forestry ['fɒrɪstrɪ] n silvicultura.

foretaste ['fɔːteɪst] n muestra.

foretell, pt, pp **foretold** [fɔː'tɛl:, -'təuld] vt predecir, pronosticar.

forever [fə'rɛvə*] ad para siempre.

foreword ['fɔːwəːd] n prefacio.

forfeit ['fɔːfɪt] n (in game) prenda // vt perder (derecho a).

forgave [fə'geɪv] pt of **forgive**.

forge [fɔːdʒ] n fragua; (smithy) herrería // vt (signature, Brit: money) falsificar; (metal) forjar; **to ~ ahead** vi avanzar constantemente; ~**r** n falsificador(a) m/f; ~**ry** n falsificación f.

forget [fə'gɛt], pt **forgot**, pp **forgotten** vt olvidar // vi olvidarse; ~**ful** a olvida-

dizo; ~**-me-not** n nomeolvides f inv.

forgive [fə'gɪv], pt **forgave**, pp **forgiven** vt perdonar; **to ~ sb for sth** perdonar algo a uno; ~**ness** n perdón m.

forgo [fɔː'gəu], pt **forwent**, pp **forgone** vt (give up) renunciar a; (go without) privarse de.

forgot [fə'gɒt] pt of **forget**.

forgotten [fə'gɒtn] pp of **forget**.

fork [fɔːk] n (for eating) tenedor m; (for gardening) horca; (of roads) bifurcación f // vi (road) bifurcarse; **to ~ out** vt (col: pay) desembolsar; ~**-lift truck** n máquina elevadora.

forlorn [fə'lɔːn] a (person) triste, melancólico; (place) abandonado; (attempt, hope) desesperado.

form [fɔːm] n forma; (Brit SCOL) clase f; (document) formulario // vt formar; **in top ~** en plena forma.

formal ['fɔːməl] a (offer, receipt) por escrito; (person etc) correcto; (occasion, dinner) ceremonioso; (dress) de etiqueta; ~**ity** [-'mælɪtɪ] n ceremonia; ~**ly** ad oficialmente.

format ['fɔːmæt] n formato // vt (COMPUT) formatear.

formation [fɔː'meɪʃən] n formación f.

formative ['fɔːmətɪv] a (years) formativo.

former ['fɔːmə*] a anterior; (earlier) antiguo; (ex) ex; **the ~ ... the latter ...** aquél ... éste ...; ~**ly** ad antiguamente.

formula ['fɔːmjulə] n fórmula.

forsake, pt **forsook**, pp **forsaken** [fə'seɪk, -'suk, -seɪkən] vt (gen) abandonar; (plan) renunciar a.

fort [fɔːt] n fuerte m.

forte ['fɔːtɪ] n fuerte m.

forth [fɔːθ] ad: **back and ~** de acá para allá; **and so ~** y así sucesivamente; ~**coming** a próximo, venidero; (character) comunicativo; ~**right** a franco; ~**with** ad en el acto.

fortify ['fɔːtɪfaɪ] vt fortalecer.

fortitude ['fɔːtɪtjuːd] n fortaleza.

fortnight ['fɔːtnaɪt] n (Brit) quincena; ~**ly** a quincenal // ad quincenalmente.

fortress ['fɔːtrɪs] n fortaleza.

fortunate ['fɔːtʃənɪt] a: **it is ~ that...** (es una) suerte que...; ~**ly** ad afortunadamente.

fortune ['fɔːtʃən] n suerte f; (wealth) fortuna; ~**-teller** n adivino/a.

forty ['fɔːtɪ] num cuarenta.

forum ['fɔːrəm] n foro.

forward ['fɔːwəd] a (movement, position) avanzado; (front) delantero; (not shy) atrevido // n (SPORT) delantero // vt (letter) remitir; (career) promocionar; **to move ~** avanzar; ~**(s)** ad (hacia) adelante.

forwent [fɔː'wɛnt] pt of **forgo**.

fossil ['fɒsl] n fósil m.

foster ['fɒstə*] vt fomentar; ~ **child** n

hijo/a adoptivo/a; ~ **mother** n madre f adoptiva.

fought [fɔ:t] pt, pp of **fight**.

foul [faul] a (gen) sucio, puerco; (weather, smell etc) asqueroso // n (FOOTBALL) falta // vt (dirty) ensuciar; (block) atascar; (football player) cometer una falta contra; ~ **play** n (SPORT) mala jugada; (LAW) muerte f violenta.

found [faund] pt, pp of **find** // vt (establish) fundar; ~**ation** [-'deɪʃən] n (act) fundación f; (basis) base f; (also: ~ation cream) crema base; ~**ations** npl (of building) cimientos mpl.

founder ['faundə*] n fundador(a) m/f // vi hundirse.

foundry ['faundrɪ] n fundición f.

fountain ['fauntɪn] n fuente f; ~ **pen** n (pluma) estilográfica, pluma-fuente f (LAm).

four [fɔ:*] num cuatro; **on all** ~**s** a gatas; ~**-poster (bed)** n cama de dosel; ~**some** ['fɔ:səm] n grupo de cuatro personas; ~**teen** num catorce; ~**th** a cuarto.

fowl [faul] n ave f (de corral).

fox [fɔks] n zorro // vt confundir.

foyer ['fɔɪeɪ] n vestíbulo.

fracas ['frækɑ:] n gresca, riña.

fraction ['frækʃən] n fracción f.

fracture ['fræktʃə*] n fractura.

fragile ['frædʒaɪl] a frágil.

fragment ['frægmənt] n fragmento.

fragrance ['freɪgrəns] n (of flowers) fragancia; (perfume) perfume m.

fragrant ['freɪgrənt] a fragante, oloroso.

frail [freɪl] a frágil; (person) débil.

frame [freɪm] n (TECH) armazón m; (of picture, door etc) marco; (of spectacles: also: ~s) montura // vt encuadrar; (reply) formular; (fam) incriminar; ~ **of mind** n estado de ánimo; ~**work** n marco.

France [frɑ:ns] n Francia.

franchise ['fræntʃaɪz] n (POL) derecho de votar, sufragio; (COMM) licencia, concesión f.

frank [fræŋk] a franco // vt (Brit: letter) franquear; ~**ly** ad francamente; ~**ness** n franqueza.

frantic ['fræntɪk] a frenético.

fraternal [frə'tə:nl] a fraterno.

fraternity [frə'tə:nɪtɪ] n (club) fraternidad f; (US) club m de estudiantes; (guild) cofradía.

fraud [frɔ:d] n fraude m; (person) impostor(a) m/f.

fraught [frɔ:t] a: ~ **with** cargado de.

fray [freɪ] n combate m, lucha // vi deshilacharse; tempers were ~ed el ambiente se ponía tenso.

freak [fri:k] n (person) fenómeno; (event) suceso anormal.

freckle ['frekl] n peca.

free [fri:] a (person: at liberty) libre; (not fixed) suelto; (gratis) gratuito; (unoccupied) desocupado; (liberal) generoso // vt (prisoner etc) poner en libertad; (jammed object) soltar; ~ (of charge), **for** ~ ad gratis; ~**dom** ['fri:dəm] n libertad f; ~**-for-all** n riña general; ~ **gift** n prima; ~**hold** n propiedad f vitalicia; ~ **kick** n tiro libre; ~**lance** a, ad por cuenta propia; ~**ly** ad libremente; generosamente; ~**mason** n francmasón m; ~**post** n porte m pagado; ~**-range** a (hen, eggs) de granja; ~ **trade** n libre comercio; ~**way** n (US) autopista; ~**wheel** vi ir en punto muerto; ~ **will** n libre albedrío m; **of one's own** ~ **will** por su propia voluntad.

freeze [fri:z] vb (pt **froze**, pp **frozen**) vi helarse, congelarse // vt helar; (prices, food, salaries) congelar // n helada; congelación f; ~**-dried** a liofilizado; ~**r** n congelador m (Sp), congeladora (LAm).

freezing ['fri:zɪŋ] a helado; ~ **point** n punto de congelación; **3 degrees below** ~ tres grados bajo cero.

freight [freɪt] n (goods) carga; (money charged) flete m; ~ **train** n (US) tren m de mercancías.

French [frentʃ] a francés/esa // n (LING) francés m; **the** ~ npl los franceses; ~ **bean** n judía verde; ~ **fried (potatoes)**, (US) ~ **fries** npl patatas fpl or papas fpl (LAm) fritas; ~**man/woman** n francés/esa m/f; ~ **window** n puerta-ventana.

frenzy ['frenzɪ] n frenesí m.

frequent ['fri:kwənt] a frecuente // vt [frɪ'kwent] frecuentar; ~**ly** [-əntlɪ] ad frecuentemente, a menudo.

fresh [freʃ] a (gen) fresco; (new) nuevo; (water) dulce; ~**en** vi (wind, air) soplar más recio; **to** ~**en up** vi (person) refrescarse; ~**er** n (Brit SCOL: col) estudiante m/f de primer año; ~**ly** ad (newly) nuevamente; (recently) recientemente; ~**man** n (US) = ~**er**; ~**ness** n frescura ~**water** a (fish) de agua dulce.

fret [fret] vi inquietarse.

friar ['fraɪə*] n fraile m; (before name) fray m.

friction ['frɪkʃən] n fricción f.

Friday ['fraɪdɪ] n viernes m inv.

fridge [frɪdʒ] n (Brit) nevera, frigo, refrigeradora (LAm).

friend [frend] n amigo/a; ~**liness** n simpatía; ~**ly** a simpático; ~**ship** n amistad f.

frieze [fri:z] n friso.

frigate ['frɪgɪt] n fragata.

fright [fraɪt] n susto; **to take** ~ asustarse; ~**en** vt asustar; ~**ened** a asustado; ~**ening** a espantoso; ~**ful** a espantoso, horrible; ~**fully** ad terriblemente.

frigid ['frɪdʒɪd] a (MED) frígido, frío.

frill [frɪl] n volante m.

fringe |frɪndʒ| n (Brit: of hair) flequillo; (edge: of forest etc) borde m, margen m; ~ **benefits** npl ventajas fpl supletorias.

frisk |frɪsk| vt cachear, registrar.

frisky |'frɪskɪ| a juguetón/ona.

fritter |'frɪtə*| n buñuelo; **to ~ away** vt desperdiciar.

frivolous |'frɪvələs| a frívolo.

frizzy |'frɪzɪ| a rizado.

fro |frəu| see **to**.

frock |frɔk| n vestido.

frog |frɔg| n rana; ~**man** n hombre-rana m.

frolic |'frɔlɪk| vi juguetear.

from |frɔm| prep 1 (indicating starting place) de, desde; **where do you come ~?** ¿de dónde eres?; ~ **London to Glasgow** de Londres a Glasgow; **to escape ~** sth/ sb escaparse de algo/alguien 2 (indicating origin etc) de; **a letter/ telephone call ~ my sister** una carta/ llamada de mi hermana; **tell him ~ me that...** dígale de mi parte que... 3 (indicating time): ~ **one o'clock to** or **until** or **till two de(sde)** la una a or hasta las 2; ~ **January (on)** desde enero 4 (indicating distance) de; **the hotel is 1 km from the beach** el hotel está a 1 km de la playa 5 (indicating price, number etc) de; **prices range ~ £10 to £50** los precios van desde £10 a or hasta £50; **the interest rate was increased ~ 9% to 10%** el tipo de interés fue incrementado de un 9% a un 10% 6 (indicating difference) de; **he can't tell red ~ green** no sabe distinguir el rojo del verde; **to be different ~** sb/sth ser diferente a algo/alguien 7 (because of, on the basis of): ~ **what he says** por lo que dice; **weak ~ hunger** debilitado por el hambre.

front |frʌnt| n (foremost part) parte f delantera; (of house) fachada; (promenade: also: **sea** ~) paseo marítimo; (MIL, POL, METEOROLOGY) frente m; (fig: appearances) apariencias fpl // a (wheel, leg) delantero; (row, line) primero; **in ~ (of)** delante (de); ~ **door** n puerta principal; ~**ier** |'frʌntɪə*| n frontera; ~ **page** n primera plana; ~-**room** n (Brit) salón m, sala; ~-**wheel drive** n tracción f delantera.

frost |frɔst| n (gen) helada; (also: **hoar~**) escarcha // vt (US CULIN) escarchar; ~**bite** n congelación f; ~**ed** a (glass) deslustrado; ~**y** a (surface) cubierto de escarcha; (welcome etc) glacial.

froth |frɔθ| n espuma.

frown |fraun| vi fruncir el ceño.

froze |frəuz| pt of **freeze**.

frozen |'frəuzn| pp of **freeze** // a (food) congelado.

fruit |fruːt| n, pl inv fruta; ~**erer** n frutero/a; ~**erer's (shop)** n frutería; ~**ful** a provechoso; ~**ion** |fruː'ɪʃən| n: **to come to ~ion** realizarse; ~ **juice** n zumo or jugo (LAm) de fruta; ~ **machine** n (Brit) máquina f tragaperras; ~ **salad** n macedonia or ensalada (LAm) de frutas.

frustrate |frʌs'treɪt| vt frustrar; ~**d** a frustrado.

fry |fraɪ|, pt, pp **fried** vt freír; **small ~** gente f menuda; ~**ing pan** n sartén f.

ft. abbr = **foot, feet**.

fuddy-duddy |'fʌdɪdʌdɪ| n carroza m/f.

fudge |fʌdʒ| n (CULIN) caramelo blando.

fuel |fjuəl| n (for heating) combustible m; (coal) carbón m; (wood) leña; (for engine) carburante m; ~ **oil** n fuel oil m; ~ **tank** n depósito (de combustible).

fugitive |'fjuːdʒɪtɪv| n fugitivo/a.

fulfil |ful'fɪl| vt (function) cumplir con; (condition) satisfacer; (wish, desire) realizar; ~**ment** n satisfacción f; realización f.

full |ful| a lleno; (fig) pleno; (complete) completo; (information) detallado // ad: ~ **well** perfectamente; **I'm ~ (up)** no puedo más; ~ **employment** pleno empleo; **a ~ two hours** dos horas completas; **at ~ speed** a máxima velocidad; **in ~** (reproduce, quote) íntegramente; ~ **moon** n luna llena; ~-**scale** a (attack, war) en gran escala; (model) de tamaño natural; ~ **stop** n punto; ~-**time** a (work) de tiempo completo // ad: **to work** ~-**time** trabajar a tiempo completo; ~**y** ad completamente; ~-**fledged** a (teacher, barrister) diplomado.

fulsome |'fulsəm| a (pej: praise, gratitude) excesivo, exagerado.

fumble |'fʌmbl| vi: **to ~ for** sth buscar algo con las manos; **to ~ with** sth manejar algo torpemente.

fume |fjuːm| vi humear, echar humo; ~**s** npl humo sg, gases mpl.

fun |fʌn| n (amusement) diversión f; (joy) alegría; **to have ~** divertirse; **for ~** en broma; **to make ~ of** vt fus burlarse de.

function |'fʌŋkʃən| n función f // vi funcionar; ~**al** a funcional.

fund |fʌnd| n fondo; (reserve) reserva; ~**s** npl fondos mpl.

fundamental |fʌndə'mɛntl| a fundamental.

funeral |'fjuːnərəl| n (burial) entierro; (ceremony) funerales mpl; ~ **parlour** n (Brit) funeraria; ~ **service** n misa de difuntos.

funfair |'fʌnfɛə*| n (Brit) parque m de atracciones.

fungus |'fʌŋgəs|, pl -gi |-gaɪ| n hongo.

funnel |'fʌnl| n embudo; (of ship) chimenea.

funny |'fʌnɪ| a gracioso, divertido;

(*strange*) curioso, raro.
fur [fə:*] *n* piel *f*; (*Brit: on tongue etc*)
sarro; ~ **coat** *n* abrigo de pieles.
furious ['fjuərıəs] *a* furioso; (*effort*) violento.
furlong ['fə:lɒŋ] *n* octava parte de una
milla, = 201.17 *m*.
furlough ['fə:ləu] *n* (MIL, US) permiso.
furnace ['fə:nıs] *n* horno.
furnish ['fə:nıʃ] *vt* amueblar; (*supply*)
suministrar; (*information*) facilitar;
~**ings** *npl* muebles *mpl*.
furniture ['fə:nıtʃə*] *n* muebles *mpl*;
piece of ~ mueble *m*.
furrow ['fʌrəu] *n* surco.
furry ['fə:rı] *a* peludo.
further ['fə:ðə*] *a* (*new*) nuevo, adicional; (*place*) más lejano // *ad* más lejos; (*more*) más; (*moreover*) además //
vt promover, adelantar; ~ **education** *n*
educación *f* superior; ~**more**
[fə:ðə'mɔ:*] *ad* además.
furthest ['fə:ðıst] *superlative of* **far**.
fury ['fjuərı] *n* furia.
fuse, (US) **fuze** [fju:z] *n* fusible *m*; (*for
bomb etc*) mecha // *vt* (*metal*) fundir;
(*fig*) fusionar // *vi* fundirse; fusionarse;
(*Brit ELEC*): to ~ **the lights** fundir los
plomos; ~ **box** *n* caja de fusibles.
fuss [fʌs] *n* (*noise*) bulla; (*dispute*) lío;
(*complaining*) protesta; to make a ~ armar un lío or jaleo; ~**y** *a* (*person*) exigente.
futile ['fju:taıl] *a* vano; **futility** [-'tılıtı] *n*
inutilidad *f*.
future ['fju:tʃə*] *a* (*gen*) futuro; (*coming*) venidero // *n* futuro; porvenir; **in** ~
de ahora en adelante.
fuze [fju:z] (US) = **fuse**.
fuzzy ['fʌzı] *a* (PHOT) borroso; (*hair*)
muy rizado.

G

G [dʒi:] *n* (MUS) sol *m*.
g. *abbr* = **gram(s)**.
gabble ['gæbl] *vi* hablar atropelladamen-
te; (*gossip*) cotorrear.
gable ['geıbl] *n* aguilón *m*.
gadget ['gædʒıt] *n* aparato.
Gaelic ['geılık] *a*, *n* (LING) gaélico.
gaffe [gæf] *n* plancha.
gag [gæg] *n* (*on mouth*) mordaza; (*joke*)
chiste *m* // *vt* amordazar.
gaiety ['geıtı] *n* alegría.
gaily ['geılı] *ad* alegremente.
gain [geın] *n* ganancia // *vt* ganar // *vi*
(*watch*) adelantarse; to ~ **by sth** sacar
provecho de algo; to ~ **on sb** ganar terreno a uno; to ~ **3 lbs (in weight)** engordar 3 libras.
gait [geıt] *n* (modo de) andar *m*.
gal. *abbr* = **gallon**.
gala ['gɑ:lə] *n* fiesta.

gale [geıl] *n* (*wind*) vendaval *m*.
gallant ['gælənt] *a* valiente; (*towards ladies*) atento.
gall bladder ['gɔ:l-] *n* vesícula biliar.
gallery ['gælərı] *n* galería; (*also:* **art** ~)
pinacoteca.
galley ['gælı] *n* (*ship's kitchen*) cocina;
(*ship*) galera.
gallon ['gæln] *n* galón *m* (= 8 pints; Brit
= 4,546 litros, US = 3,785 litros).
gallop ['gæləp] *n* galope *m* // *vi* galopar.
gallows ['gæləuz] *n* horca.
gallstone ['gɔ:lstəun] *n* cálculo biliario.
galore [gə'lɔ:*] *ad* en cantidad, en abundancia.
galvanize ['gælvənaız] *vt* (*metal*) galva-
nizar; (*fig*): to ~ **sb into action** animar a
uno para que haga algo.
gambit ['gæmbıt] *n* (*fig*): **opening** ~ estrategia inicial.
gamble ['gæmbl] *n* (*risk*) riesgo; (*bet*)
apuesta // *vt*: to ~ **on** apostar a; (*fig*)
confiar en que // *vi* jugar; (COMM) especular; ~**r** *n* jugador(a) *m/f*; **gambling**
n juego.
game [geım] *n* juego; (*match*) partido;
(*of cards*) partida; (HUNTING) caza // *a*
valiente; (*ready*): to be ~ **for anything**
atreverse a todo; **big** ~ caza mayor;
~**keeper** *n* guardabosques *m inv*.
gammon ['gæmən] *n* tocino or jamón *m*
ahumado.
gamut ['gæmət] *n* gama.
gang [gæŋ] *n* pandilla; (*of workmen*) brigada // *vi*: to ~ **up on sb** conspirar contra uno.
gangster ['gæŋstə*] *n* gángster *m*.
gangway ['gæŋweı] *n* (Brit: *in theatre,
bus etc*) pasillo; (*on ship*) pasarela.
gaol [dʒeıl] *n*, *vt* (Brit) = **jail**.
gap [gæp] *n* vacío, hueco (LAm); (*in
trees, traffic*) claro; (*in time*) intervalo.
gape [geıp] *vi* mirar boquiabierto; **gap-
ing** *a* (*hole*) muy abierto.
garage ['gærɑ:ʒ] *n* garaje *m*.
garbage ['gɑ:bıdʒ] *n* (US) basura; ~
can *n* cubo or bote *m* (LAm) de la basura; ~ **man** *n* basurero.
garbled ['gɑ:bld] *a* (*distorted*) falsificado,
amañado.
garden ['gɑ:dn] *n* jardín *m*; ~**er** *n*
jardinero/a; ~**ing** *n* jardinería.
gargle ['gɑ:gl] *vi* hacer gárgaras, garga-
rear (LAm).
gargoyle ['gɑ:gɔıl] *n* gárgola.
garish ['gɛərıʃ] *a* chillón/ona.
garland ['gɑ:lənd] *n* guirnalda.
garlic ['gɑ:lık] *n* ajo.
garment ['gɑ:mənt] *n* prenda (de vestir).
garnish ['gɑ:nıʃ] *vt* adornar; (CULIN)
aderezar.
garrison ['gærısn] *n* guarnición *f*.
garrulous ['gærjuləs] *a* charlatán/ana.
garter ['gɑ:tə*] *n* (US) liga.
gas [gæs] *n* gas *m*; (US: *gasoline*) gasoli-

na // vt asfixiar con gas; ~ **cooker** n (Brit) cocina de gas; ~ **cylinder** n bombona de gas; ~ **fire** n estufa de gas; ~ **pedal** n (esp US) acelerador m.

gash [gæʃ] n raja; (on face) cuchillada // vt rajar; (with knife) acuchillar.

gasket ['gæskɪt] n (AUT) junta de culata.

gas mask n careta antigás.

gas meter n contador m de gas.

gasoline ['gæsəliːn] n (US) gasolina.

gasp [gɑːsp] n grito sofocado // vi (pant) jadear; to ~ **out** vt (say) decir con voz entrecortada.

gas ring n hornillo de gas.

gas station n (US) gasolinera.

gassy ['gæsɪ] a gaseoso.

gas tap n llave f del gas.

gastric ['gæstrɪk] a gástrico.

gate [geɪt] n puerta; (RAIL) barrera; ~**crash** vt (Brit) colarse en; ~**way** n puerta.

gather ['gæðə*] vt (flowers, fruit) coger (Sp), recoger; (assemble) reunir; (pick up) recoger; (SEWING) fruncir; (understand) entender // vi (assemble) reunirse; to ~ **speed** ganar velocidad; ~**ing** n reunión f, asamblea.

gauche [gəʊʃ] a torpe.

gaudy ['gɔːdɪ] a chillón/ona.

gauge [geɪdʒ] n calibre m; (RAIL) entrevía; (instrument) indicador m // vt medir.

gaunt [gɔːnt] a descarnado.

gauntlet ['gɔːntlɪt] n (fig): to run the ~ of exponerse a; to throw down the ~ arrojar el guante.

gauze [gɔːz] n gasa.

gave [geɪv] pt of **give**.

gay [geɪ] a (person) alegre; (colour) vivo; (homosexual) gay.

gaze [geɪz] n mirada fija // vi: to ~ **at sth** mirar algo fijamente.

gazelle [gə'zɛl] n gacela.

gazetteer [gæzə'tɪə*] n diccionario geográfico.

gazumping [gə'zʌmpɪŋ] n (Brit) la subida del precio de una casa una vez que ya ha sido apalabrado.

GB abbr = **Great Britain**.

GCE n abbr (Brit) = General Certificate of Education.

GCSE n abbr (Brit: = General Certificate of Secondary Education) ≈ Bachillerato Elemental y Superior.

gear [gɪə*] n equipo, herramientas fpl; (TECH) engranaje m; (AUT) velocidad f, marcha // vt (fig: adapt): to ~ **sth to** adaptar or ajustar algo a; **top** or (US) **high/low** ~ cuarta/primera velocidad; **in** ~ en marcha; ~ **box** n caja de cambios; ~ **lever**, (US) ~ **shift** n palanca de cambio; ~ **wheel** n rueda dentada.

geese [giːs] pl of **goose**.

gel [dʒɛl] n gel m.

gelignite ['dʒɛlɪgnaɪt] n gelignita.

gem [dʒɛm] n joya.

Gemini ['dʒɛmɪnaɪ] n Géminis m, Gemelos mpl.

gender ['dʒɛndə*] n género.

gene [dʒiːn] n gen(e) m.

general ['dʒɛnərl] n general m // a general; **in** ~ en general; ~ **delivery** n (US) lista de correos; ~ **election** n elecciones fpl generales; ~**ization** [-aɪ'zeɪʃən] n generalización f; ~**ize** vi generalizar; ~**ly** ad generalmente, en general; ~ **practitioner** (G.P.) n médico general.

generate ['dʒɛnəreɪt] vt (ELEC) generar; (fig) producir.

generation [dʒɛnə'reɪʃən] n generación f.

generator ['dʒɛnəreɪtə*] n generador m.

generosity [dʒɛnə'rɔsɪtɪ] n generosidad f.

generous ['dʒɛnərəs] a generoso; (copious) abundante.

genetics [dʒɪ'nɛtɪks] n genética.

Geneva [dʒɪ'niːvə] n Ginebra.

genial ['dʒiːnɪəl] a afable, simpático.

genitals ['dʒɛnɪtlz] npl (órganos mpl) genitales mpl.

genius ['dʒiːnɪəs] n genio.

gent [dʒɛnt] n abbr = **gentleman**.

genteel [dʒɛn'tiːl] a fino, elegante.

gentle ['dʒɛntl] a (sweet) amable, dulce; (touch etc) ligero, suave.

gentleman ['dʒɛntlmən] n señor m; (well-bred man) caballero.

gentleness ['dʒɛntlnɪs] n dulzura; (of touch) suavidad f.

gently ['dʒɛntlɪ] ad suavemente.

gentry ['dʒɛntrɪ] n alta burguesía.

gents [dʒɛnts] n aseos (de caballeros).

genuine ['dʒɛnjuɪn] a auténtico; (person) sincero.

geography [dʒɪ'ɔgrəfɪ] n geografía.

geology [dʒɪ'ɔlədʒɪ] n geología.

geometric(al) [dʒɪə'mɛtrɪk(l)] a geométrico.

geometry [dʒɪ'ɔmɪtrɪ] n geometría.

geranium [dʒɪ'reɪnjəm] n geranio.

geriatric [dʒɛrɪ'ætrɪk] a, n geriátrico/a m/f.

germ [dʒəːm] n (microbe) microbio, bacteria; (seed, fig) germen m.

German ['dʒəːmən] a alemán/ana // n alemán/ana m/f; (LING) alemán m; ~ **measles** n rubéola; ~ **Shepherd Dog** n pastor m alemán.

Germany ['dʒəːmənɪ] n Alemania.

gesture ['dʒɛstʃə*] n gesto.

get [gɛt], pt, pp **got**, pp **gotten** (US) vi 1 (become, be) ponerse, volverse; to ~ **old/tired** envejecer/cansarse; to ~ **drunk** emborracharse; to ~ **dirty** ensuciarse; to ~ **married** casarse; **when do I** ~ **paid?** ¿cuándo me pagan or se me paga?; **it's** ~**ting late** se está haciendo tarde
2 (go): to ~ **to/from** llegar a/de; to ~ **home** llegar a casa
3 (begin) empezar a; to ~ **to know sb**

(llegar a) conocer a uno; **I'm ~ting to like him** me está empezando a gustar; **let's ~ going** or **started** ¡vamos (a empezar)!

4 (*modal auxiliary vb*): **you've got to do it** tienes que hacerlo

♦ *vt* **1**: **to ~ sth done** (*finish*) terminar algo; (*have done*) mandar hacer algo; **to ~ one's hair cut** cortarse el pelo; **to ~ the car going** or **to go** arrancar el coche; **to ~ sb to do sth** conseguir or hacer que alguien haga algo; **to ~ sth/sb ready** preparar algo/a alguien

2 (*obtain: money, permission, results*) conseguir; (*find: job, flat*) encontrar; (*fetch: person, doctor*) buscar; (*object*) ir a buscar, traer; **to ~ sth for sb** conseguir algo para alguien; **~ me Mr Jones, please** (*TEL*) póngame or comuníqueme (*LAm*) con el Sr. Jones, por favor; **can I ~ you a drink?** ¿te pido algo?

3 (*receive: present, letter*) recibir; (*acquire: reputation*) alcanzar; (: *prize*) ganar; **what did you ~ for your birthday?** ¿qué te regalaron por tu cumpleaños?; **how much did you ~ for the painting?** ¿cuánto sacaste por el cuadro?

4 (*catch*) coger (*Sp*), agarrar (*LAm*); (*hit: target etc*) dar en; **to ~ sb by the arm/throat** coger (*Sp*) or agarrar (*LAm*) a uno por el brazo/cuello; **~ him!** ¡cógelo! (*Sp*), ¡atrápalo! (*LAm*); **the bullet got him in the leg** la bala le dio en una pierna

5 (*take, move*) llevar; **to ~ sth to sb** llevar algo a alguien; **do you think we'll ~ it through the door?** ¿crees que lo podremos meter por la puerta?

6 (*catch, take: plane, bus etc*) coger (*Sp*), tomar (*LAm*); **where do I ~ the train for Birmingham?** ¿dónde se coge (*Sp*) or se toma (*LAm*) el tren para Birmingham?

7 (*understand*) entender; (*hear*) oír; **I've got it!** ¡ya lo tengo!, ¡eureka!; **I don't ~ your meaning** no te entiendo; **I'm sorry, I didn't ~ your name** lo siento, no cogí tu nombre

8 (*have, possess*): **to have got** tener.

geyser ['giːzə*] *n* (*water heater*) calentador *m* de agua; (*GEO*) géiser *m*.

Ghana ['gɑːnə] *n* Ghana.

ghastly ['gɑːstlɪ] *a* horrible.

gherkin ['gəːkɪn] *n* pepinillo.

ghost [gəust] *n* fantasma *m*.

giant ['dʒaɪənt] *n* gigante *m/f* // *a* gigantesco, gigante.

gibberish ['dʒɪbərɪʃ] *n* galimatías *m*.

gibe [dʒaɪb] *n* mofa.

giblets ['dʒɪblɪts] *npl* menudillos *mpl*.

Gibraltar [dʒɪ'brɔːltə*] *n* Gibraltar *m*.

giddiness ['gɪdɪnɪs] *n* vértigo.

giddy ['gɪdɪ] *a* (*height, speed*) vertiginoso; **to be ~** estar mareado/a.

gift [gɪft] *n* regalo; (*offering*) obsequio;

(*ability*) talento; **~ed** *a* dotado; **~ token** or **voucher** *n* vale *m* canjeable por un regalo.

gigantic [dʒaɪ'gæntɪk] *a* gigantesco.

giggle ['gɪgl] *vi* reírse tontamente // *n* risilla.

gill [dʒɪl] *n* (*measure*) = *0.25 pints* (*Brit* = *0.148 l*, *US* = *0.118l*).

gills [gɪlz] *npl* (*of fish*) branquias *fpl*, agallas *fpl*.

gilt [gɪlt] *a, n* dorado; **~-edged** *a* (*COMM*) de máxima garantía.

gimmick ['gɪmɪk] *n* truco.

gin [dʒɪn] *n* (*liquor*) ginebra.

ginger ['dʒɪndʒə*] *n* Jengibre *m*; **~ ale**, **~ beer** *n* (*Brit*) gaseosa de jengibre; **~bread** *n* pan *m* de jengibre; **~-haired** *a* pelirrojo.

gingerly ['dʒɪndʒəlɪ] *ad* con cautela.

gipsy ['dʒɪpsɪ] *n* gitano/a.

giraffe [dʒɪ'rɑːf] *n* jirafa.

girder ['gəːdə*] *n* viga.

girdle ['gəːdl] *n* (*corset*) faja.

girl [gəːl] *n* (*small*) niña; (*young woman*) chica, joven *f*, muchacha; **an English ~** una (chica) inglesa; (*of girl*) amiga; (*of boy*) novia; **~ish** *a* de niña.

giro ['dʒaɪrəu] *n* (*Brit: bank ~*) giro bancario; (*post office ~*) giro postal; (*state benefit*) cheque quincenal del subsidio de desempleo.

girth [gəːθ] *n* circunferencia; (*of saddle*) cincha.

gist [dʒɪst] *n* lo esencial.

give [gɪv], *pt* **gave**, *pp* **given** *vt* dar; (*deliver*) entregar; (*as gift*) regalar // *vi* (*break*) romperse; (*stretch: fabric*) dar de sí; **to ~ sb sth**, **~ sth to sb** dar algo a uno; **to ~ away** *vt* (*give free*) regalar; (*betray*) traicionar; (*disclose*) revelar; **to ~ back** *vt* devolver; **to ~ in** *vi* ceder // *vt* entregar; **to ~ off** *vt* despedir; **to ~ out** *vt* distribuir; **to ~ up** *vi* rendirse, darse por vencido // *vt* renunciar a; **to ~ up smoking** dejar de fumar; **to ~ o.s. up** entregarse; **to ~ way** *vi* ceder; (*Brit AUT*) ceder el paso.

glacier ['glæsɪə*] *n* glaciar *m*.

glad [glæd] *a* contento.

gladly ['glædlɪ] *ad* con mucho gusto.

glamorous ['glæmərəs] *a* encantador(a), atractivo.

glamour ['glæmə*] *n* encanto, atractivo.

glance [glɑːns] *n* ojeada, mirada // *vi*: **to ~ at** echar una ojeada a; **to ~ off** (*bullet*) rebotar; **glancing** *a* (*blow*) oblicuo.

gland [glænd] *n* glándula.

glare [glɛə*] *n* deslumbramiento, brillo // *vi* deslumbrar; **to ~ at** mirar ferozmente a; **glaring** *a* (*mistake*) manifiesto.

glass [glɑːs] *n* vidrio, cristal *m*; (*for drinking*) vaso; (: *with stem*) copa; (*also: looking ~*) espejo; **~es** *npl* gafas *fpl*; **~house** *n* invernadero; **~ware** *n* cristalería; **~y** *a* (*eyes*) vidrioso.

glaze [gleɪz] vt (window) poner cristales a; (pottery) barnizar // n barniz m.

glazier ['gleɪzɪə*] n vidriero/a.

gleam [gliːm] n destello // vi brillar; ~ing a reluciente.

glean [gliːn] vt (information) recoger.

glee [gliː] n alegría, regocijo.

glen [glɛn] n cañada.

glib [glɪb] a de mucha labia.

glide [glaɪd] vi deslizarse; (AVIAT, birds) planear; ~r n (AVIAT) planeador m; **gliding** n (AVIAT) vuelo sin motor.

glimmer ['glɪmə*] n luz f tenue.

glimpse [glɪmps] n vislumbre m // vt vislumbrar, entrever.

glint [glɪnt] vi centellear.

glisten ['glɪsn] vi relucir, brillar.

glitter ['glɪtə*] vi relucir, brillar // n brillo.

gloat [gləʊt] vi: to ~ over (money) recrearse en; (sb's misfortune) saborear.

global ['gləʊbl] a mundial.

globe [gləʊb] n globo, esfera.

gloom [gluːm] n tinieblas fpl, oscuridad f; (sadness) tristeza, melancolía; ~y a (dark) oscuro; (sad) triste; (pessimistic) pesimista.

glorious ['glɔːrɪəs] a glorioso.

glory ['glɔːrɪ] n gloria.

gloss [glɒs] n (shine) brillo; (paint) pintura de aceite; to ~ over vt fus encubrir.

glossary ['glɒsərɪ] n glosario.

glossy ['glɒsɪ] a lustroso.

glove [glʌv] n guante m; ~ compartment n (AUT) guantera.

glow [gləʊ] vi (shine) brillar // n brillo.

glower ['glaʊə*] vi: to ~ at mirar con ceño.

glue [gluː] n goma (de pegar), cemento (LAm) // vt pegar.

glum [glʌm] a (mood) abatido; (person, tone) melancólico.

glut [glʌt] n superabundancia.

glutton ['glʌtn] n glotón/ona m/f; a ~ for punishment masoquista m/f.

gnarled [nɑːld] a nudoso.

gnat [næt] n mosquito.

gnaw [nɔː] vt roer.

gnome [nəʊm] n gnomo.

go [gəʊ] vb (pt went, pp gone) vi ir; (travel) viajar; (depart) irse, marcharse; (work) funcionar, marchar; (be sold) venderse; (time) pasar; (fit, suit): to ~ with hacer juego con; (become) ponerse; (break etc) estropearse, romperse // n (pl: ~es): to have a ~ (at) probar suerte (con); to be on the ~ no parar; whose ~ is it? ¿a quién le toca?; he's going to do it va a hacerlo; to ~ for a walk ir de paseo; to ~ dancing ir a bailar; how did it ~? ¿qué tal salió or resultó?, ¿cómo ha ido?; to ~ round the back pasar por detrás; to ~ about vt (rumour) propagarse // vt fus: how do I ~ about this?

¿cómo me las arreglo para hacer esto?; to ~ ahead vi seguir adelante; to ~ along vi ir // vt fus bordear; to ~ along with (agree) estar de acuerdo con; to ~ away vi irse, marcharse; to ~ back vi volver; to ~ back on vt fus (promise) faltar a; to ~ by vi (years, time) pasar // vt fus guiarse por; to ~ down vi bajar; (ship) hundirse; (sun) ponerse // vt fus bajar por; to ~ for vt fus (fetch) ir por; (like) gustar; (attack) atacar; to ~ in vi entrar; to ~ in for vt fus (competition) presentarse a; to ~ into vt fus entrar en; (investigate) investigar; (embark on) dedicarse a; to ~ off vi irse, marcharse; (food) pasarse; (explode) estallar; (event) realizarse; I'm going off her/the idea ya no me gusta tanto ella/la idea // vt fus dejar de gustar; to ~ on vi (continue) seguir, continuar; (happen) pasar, ocurrir; to ~ on doing sth seguir haciendo algo; to ~ out vi salir; (fire, light) apagarse; to ~ over vi (ship) zozobrar // vt fus (check) revisar; to ~ through vt fus (town etc) atravesar; to ~ up vi subir; to ~ without vt fus pasarse sin.

goad [gəʊd] vt aguijonear.

go-ahead ['gəʊəhɛd] a emprendedor(a) // n luz f verde.

goal [gəʊl] n meta; (score) gol m; ~keeper n portero; ~-post n poste m (de la portería).

goat [gəʊt] n cabra f.

gobble ['gɒbl] vt (also: ~ down, ~ up) engullirse.

go-between ['gəʊbɪtwiːn] n medianero/a, intermediario/a.

goblet ['gɒblɪt] n copa.

god [gɒd] n dios m; G~ n Dios m; ~child n ahijado/a; ~daughter n ahijada; ~dess n diosa; ~father n padrino; ~forsaken a dejado de la mano de Dios; ~mother n madrina; ~send n don m del cielo; ~son n ahijado.

goggles ['gɒglz] npl (AUT) anteojos mpl; (of skindiver) gafas fpl submarinas.

going ['gəʊɪŋ] n (conditions) estado del terreno // a: the ~ rate la tarifa corriente or en vigor.

gold [gəʊld] n oro // a de oro; ~en a (made of ~) de oro; (~ in colour) dorado; ~fish n pez m de colores; ~-plated a chapado en oro; ~smith n orfebre m/f.

golf [gɒlf] n golf m; ~ ball n (for game) pelota de golf; (on typewriter) esfera; ~ club n club m de golf; (stick) palo (de golf); ~ course n campo de golf; ~er n golfista m/f.

gone [gɒn] pp of **go**.

good [gʊd] a bueno; (kind) bueno, amable; (well-behaved) educado // n bien m, provecho; ~s npl bienes mpl; (COMM) mercancías fpl; ~! ¡qué bien!; to be ~

at tener aptitud para; **to be ~ for** servir para; **it's ~ for you** te hace bien; **would you be ~ enough to...?** ¿podría hacerme el favor de...?, ¿sería tan amable de...?; **a ~ deal (of)** mucho; **a ~ many** muchos; **to make ~** reparar; **it's no ~** complaining no vale la pena (de) quejarse; **for ~** para siempre, definitivamente; **~ morning/afternoon** ¡buenos días/buenas tardes!; **~ evening!** ¡buenas noches!; **~ night!** ¡buenas noches!; **~bye!** ¡adiós!; **to say ~bye** despedirse; **G~ Friday** *n* Viernes *m* Santo; **~-looking** *a* guapo; **~-natured** *a* amable, simpático; **~ness** *n (of person)* bondad *f*; **for ~ness sake!** ¡por Dios!; **~ness gracious!** ¡Dios mío!; **~s train** *n (Brit)* tren *m* de mercancías; **~will** *n* buena voluntad *f*.

goose [guːs], *pl* **geese** *n* ganso, oca.

gooseberry ['guzbəri] *n* grosella espinosa.

gooseflesh ['guːsfleʃ] *n*, **goose pimples** *npl* carne *f* de gallina.

gore [gɔː*] *vt* cornear // *n* sangre *f*.

gorge [gɔːdʒ] *n* barranco // *vr:* **to ~ o.s. (on)** atracarse (de).

gorgeous ['gɔːdʒəs] *a* magnífico, maravilloso.

gorilla [gə'rɪlə] *n* gorila *m*.

gorse [gɔːs] *n* aulaga.

gory ['gɔːrɪ] *a* sangriento.

go-slow ['gəu'sləu] *n (Brit)* huelga de manos caídas.

gospel ['gɔspl] *n* evangelio.

gossip ['gɔsɪp] *n (scandal)* chismorreo, chismes *mpl; (chat)* charla; *(scandalmonger)* chismoso/a; *(talker)* hablador(a) *m/f* // *vi* chismear.

got [gɔt] *pt, pp of* **get**; **~ten** *(US) pp of* **get**.

gout [gaut] *n* gota.

govern ['gʌvən] *vt* gobernar.

governess ['gʌvənɪs] *n* institutriz *f*.

government ['gʌvnmənt] *n* gobierno; **~al** [-'mentl] *a* gubernamental.

governor ['gʌvənə*] *n* gobernador(a) *m/f; (of jail)* director(a) *m/f*.

gown [gaun] *n* traje *m; (of teacher; Brit: of judge)* toga.

G.P. *n abbr* = **general practitioner**.

grab [græb] *vt* coger *(Sp)* or agarrar *(LAm)*, arrebatar.

grace [greɪs] *n* gracia // *vt* honrar; **5 days' ~** un plazo de 5 días; **to say ~** bendecir la mesa; **~ful** *a* elegante, gracioso; **gracious** ['greɪʃəs] *a* amable.

grade [greɪd] *n (quality)* clase *f*, calidad *f; (in hierarchy)* grado; *(US SCOL)* curso // *vt* clasificar; **~ crossing** *n (US)* paso a nivel; **~ school** *n (US)* escuela primaria.

gradient ['greɪdɪənt] *n* pendiente *f*.

gradual ['grædjuəl] *a* paulatino; **~ly** *ad* paulatinamente.

graduate ['grædjuɪt] *n* graduado/a,

licenciado/a // *vi* ['grædjueɪt] graduarse, licenciarse; **graduation** [-'eɪʃən] *n* graduación *f*.

graffiti [grə'fiːtɪ] *n* pintadas *fpl*.

graft [grɑːft] *n (AGR, MED)* injerto; *(bribery)* corrupción *f* // *vt* injertar; **hard ~** *(col)* trabajo duro.

grain [greɪn] *n (single particle)* grano; *(corn)* granos *mpl*, cereales *mpl*.

gram [græm] *n (US)* gramo.

grammar ['græmə*] *n* gramática: **~ school** *n (Brit)* ≈ instituto de segunda enseñanza, liceo *(Sp)*.

grammatical [grə'mætɪkl] *a* gramatical.

gramme [græm] *n* = **gram**.

gramophone ['græməfəun] *n (Brit)* tocadiscos *m inv*.

granary ['grænərɪ] *n* granero, troj *f*.

grand [grænd] *a* magnífico, imponente; **~children** *npl* nietos *mpl*; **~dad** *n* yayo, abuelito; **~daughter** *n* nieta; **~eur** ['grændjə*] *n* magnificencia, lo grandioso; **~father** *n* abuelo; **~ma** *n* yaya, abuelita; **~mother** *n* abuela; **~pa** *n* = **~dad**; **~parents** *npl* abuelos *mpl*; **~ piano** *n* piano de cola; **~son** *n* nieto; **~stand** *n (SPORT)* tribuna.

granite ['grænɪt] *n* granito.

granny ['grænɪ] *n* abuelita, yaya.

grant [grɑːnt] *vt (concede)* conceder; *(admit)* reconocer // *n (SCOL)* beca; **to take sth for ~ed** dar algo por sentado.

granulated ['grænjuleɪtɪd] *n:* **~ sugar** *(Brit)* azúcar *m* blanquilla refinado.

granule ['grænjuːl] *n* gránulo.

grape [greɪp] *n* uva.

grapefruit ['greɪpfruːt] *n* pomelo, toronja *(LAm)*.

graph [grɑːf] *n* gráfica; **~ic** *a* gráfico; **~ics** *n* artes *fpl* gráficas // *npl (COMPUT)* gráficos *mpl*.

grapple ['græpl] *vi:* **to ~ with a problem** enfrentar un problema.

grasp [grɑːsp] *vt* agarrar, asir; *(understand)* comprender // *n (grip)* asimiento; *(reach)* alcance *m; (understanding)* comprensión *f*; **~ing** *a* avaro.

grass [grɑːs] *n* hierba; *(lawn)* césped *m;* **~hopper** *n* saltamontes *m inv;* **~land** *n* pradera, pampa *(LAm);* **~roots** *a* popular; **~ snake** *n* culebra.

grate [greɪt] *n* parrilla de chimenea // *vi* chirriar // *vt (CULIN)* rallar.

grateful ['greɪtful] *a* agradecido.

grater ['greɪtə*] *n* rallador *m*.

gratify ['grætɪfaɪ] *vt* complacer; *(whim)* satisfacer; **~ing** *a* grato.

grating ['greɪtɪŋ] *n (iron bars)* rejilla // *a (noise)* áspero.

gratitude ['grætɪtjuːd] *n* agradecimiento.

gratuity [grə'tjuːɪtɪ] *n* gratificación *f*.

grave [greɪv] *n* tumba // *a* serio, grave.

gravel ['grævl] *n* grava.

gravestone ['greɪvstəun] *n* lápida.

graveyard ['greɪvjɑːd] *n* cementerio.

gravity ['græviti] n gravedad f.

gravy ['greivi] n salsa de carne.

gray [grei] a = **grey**.

graze [greiz] vi pacer // vt (touch lightly) rozar; (scrape) raspar // n (MED) abrasión f.

grease [gri:s] n (fat) grasa; (lubricant) lubricante m // vt engrasar; ~**proof** a a prueba de grasa; ~**proof paper** n (Brit) papel m apergaminado; **greasy** a grasiento.

great [greit] a grande; (col) magnífico, estupendo; **G~ Britain** n Gran Bretaña; ~-**grandfather/-grandmother** n bisabuelo/a; ~**ly** ad muy; (with verb) mucho; ~**ness** n grandeza.

Greece [gri:s] n Grecia.

greed [gri:d] n (also: ~**iness**) codicia, avaricia; (for food) gula; ~**y** a avaro; (for food) glotón/ona.

Greek [gri:k] a griego/a // n griego/a; (LING) griego.

green [gri:n] a verde; (inexperienced) novato // n verde m; (stretch of grass) césped m; ~**s** npl verduras fpl; ~ **belt** n zona verde; ~**card** n (AUT) carta verde; ~**ery** n verdura; ~**gage** n claudia; ~**grocer** n (Brit) verdulero/a; ~**house** n invernadero; ~**ish** a verdoso.

Greenland ['gri:nlənd] n Groenlandia.

greet [gri:t] vt saludar; (welcome) dar la bienvenida a; ~**ing** n (gen) saludo; (welcome) bienvenida; ~**ing(s) card** n tarjeta de felicitaciones.

grenade [grə'neid] n granada.

grew [gru:] pt of **grow**.

grey [grei] a gris; ~-**haired** a canoso; ~**hound** n galgo.

grld [grid] n reja, (ELEC) red f.

grief [gri:f] n dolor m, pena.

grievance ['gri:vəns] n motivo de queja, agravio.

grieve [gri:v] vi afligirse, acongojarse // vt dar pena a; **to ~ for** llorar por.

grievous ['gri:vəs] a : ~ **bodily harm** (LAW) daños mpl corporales graves.

grill [gril] n (on cooker) parrilla // vt (Brit) asar a la parrilla; (question) interrogar.

grille [gril] n reja.

grim [grim] a (place) sombrío; (person) ceñudo.

grimace [gri'meis] n mueca // vi hacer muecas.

grimy ['graimi] a mugriento.

grin [grin] n sonrisa abierta // vi sonreír abiertamente.

grind [graind] vt (pt, pp ground) (coffee, pepper etc) moler; (US: meat) picar; (make sharp) afilar // n: **the daily ~** la rutina diaria; **to ~ one's teeth** hacer rechinar los dientes.

grip [grip] n (hold) asimiento; (of hands) apretón m; (handle) asidero; (holdall) maletín m // vt agarrar; **to get to ~s**

with enfrentarse con; ~**ping** a absorbente.

grisly ['grizli] a horripilante, horrible.

gristle ['grisl] n cartílago.

grit [grit] n gravilla; (courage) valor m // vt (road) poner gravilla en; **to ~ one's teeth** apretar los dientes.

groan [grəun] n gemido; quejido // vi gemir; quejarse.

grocer ['grəusə*] n tendero (de ultramarinos); ~**ies** npl comestibles mpl; ~**'s (shop)** n tienda de ultramarinos or de abarrotes (LAm).

groggy ['grɔgi] a atontado.

groin [grɔin] n ingle f.

groom [gru:m] n mozo/a de cuadra; (also: bride~) novio // vt (horse) almohazar.

groove [gru:v] n ranura, surco.

grope [grəup] vi ir a tientas; **to ~ for** vt fus buscar a tientas.

gross [grəus] a grueso; (COMM) bruto; ~**ly** ad (greatly) enormemente.

grotesque [grə'tɛsk] a grotesco.

grotto ['grɔtəu] n gruta.

ground [graund] pt, pp of **grind** // n suelo, tierra; (SPORT) campo, terreno; (reason: gen pl) causa, razón f; (US: also: ~ wire) tierra // vt (plane) conectar con tierra en tierra; (US ELEC) conectar con tierra // vi (ship) varar, encallar; ~**s** npl (of coffee etc) poso sg; (gardens etc) jardines mpl, parque m; **on the ~** en el suelo; **to the ~** al suelo; **to gain/lose ~** ganar/perder terreno; ~ **cloth** n (US) = ~**sheet**; ~**ing** n (in education) conocimientos mpl básicos; ~**less** a infundado; ~**sheet** n (Brit) n tela impermeable; ~ **staff** n personal m de tierra; ~**work** n preparación f.

group [gru:p] n grupo; (musical) conjunto // (vb: also: ~ **together**) vt agrupar // vi agruparse.

grouse [graus] n, pl inv (bird) urogallo // vi (complain) quejarse.

grove [grəuv] n arboleda.

grovel ['grɔvl] vi arrastrarse.

grow [grəu], pt **grew**, pp **grown** vi crecer; (increase) aumentarse; (expand) desarrollarse; (become) volverse; **to ~ rich/weak** enriquecerse/debilitarse // vt cultivar; (hair, beard) dejar crecer; **to ~ up** vi crecer, hacerse hombre/mujer; ~**er** n cultivador(a) m/f, productor(a) m/f; ~**ing** a creciente.

growl [graul] vi gruñir.

grown [grəun] pp of **grow**; ~-**up** n adulto, mayor m/f.

growth [grəuθ] n crecimiento, desarrollo; (what has grown) brote m; (MED) tumor m.

grub [grʌb] n gusano; (col: food) comida.

grubby ['grʌbi] a sucio, mugriento.

grudge [grʌdʒ] n rencor // vt: **to ~ sb sth** dar algo a uno de mala gana; **to bear sb**

a ~ guardar rencor a uno; **he ~s** (giving) the money da el dinero de mala gana.

gruelling ['gruəlɪŋ] a penoso, duro.

gruesome ['gruːsəm] a horrible.

gruff [grʌf] a (voice) ronco; (manner) brusco.

grumble ['grʌmbl] vi refunfuñar, quejarse.

grumpy ['grʌmpɪ] a gruñón/ona.

grunt [grʌnt] vi gruñir // n gruñido.

G-string ['dʒiːstrɪŋ] n taparrabo.

guarantee [gærən'tiː] n garantía // vt garantizar.

guard [gɑːd] n guardia; (one man) guardia m; (Brit RAIL) jefe m de tren // vt guardar; **~ed** a (fig) cauteloso; **~ian** n guardián/ana m/f; (of minor) tutor(a) m/f; **~'s van** n (Brit RAIL) furgón m.

Guatemala [gwætɪ'mɑːlə] n Guatemala; **~n** a, n guatemalteco/a m/f.

guerrilla [gə'rɪlə] n guerrillero/a; **~ warfare** n guerra de guerrillas.

guess [ges] vi adivinar // vt adivinar; (US) suponer // n suposición f, conjetura; **to take** or **have a ~** tratar de adivinar; **~work** n conjeturas fpl.

guest [gest] n invitado/a; (in hotel) huésped(a) m/f; **~-house** n casa de huéspedes, pensión f; **~ room** n cuarto de huéspedes.

guffaw [gʌ'fɔː] n reírse a carcajadas.

guidance ['gaɪdəns] n (gen) dirección f; (advice) consejos mpl.

guide [gaɪd] n (person) guía m/f; (book, fig) guía f // vt guiar; (girl) **~** n exploradora; **~book** n guía; **~ dog** n perro m guía; **~lines** npl (fig) directiva sg.

guild [gɪld] n gremio; **~hall** n (Brit) ayuntamiento.

guile [gaɪl] n astucia.

guillotine ['gɪlətiːn] n guillotina.

guilt [gɪlt] n culpabilidad f; **~y** a culpable.

guinea pig ['gɪnɪ-] n cobayo.

guise [gaɪz] n: in or under the ~ of bajo apariencia de.

guitar [gɪ'tɑː*] n guitarra.

gulf [gʌlf] n golfo; (abyss) abismo.

gull [gʌl] n gaviota.

gullet ['gʌlɪt] n esófago.

gullible ['gʌlɪbl] a crédulo.

gully ['gʌlɪ] n barranco.

gulp [gʌlp] vi tragar saliva // vt (also: ~ down) tragar.

gum [gʌm] n (ANAT) encía; (glue) goma, cemento (LAm); (sweet) caramelo de goma; (also: chewing-~) chicle m // vt pegar con goma; **~boots** npl (Brit) botas fpl de goma.

gun [gʌn] n (small) pistola, revólver m; (shotgun) escopeta; (rifle) fusil m; (cannon) cañón m; **~boat** n cañonero; **~fire** n disparos mpl; **~man** n pistolero; **~ner** n artillero; **~point** n: at

~point a mano armada; **~powder** n pólvora; **~shot** n escopetazo; **~smith** n armero.

gurgle ['gɔːgl] vi gorgotear.

guru ['guːruː] n gurú m.

gush [gʌʃ] vi chorrear; (fig) deshacerse en efusiones.

gusset ['gʌsɪt] n escudete m.

gust [gʌst] n (of wind) ráfaga.

gusto ['gʌstəu] n entusiasmo.

gut [gʌt] n intestino; (MUS etc) cuerda de tripa; **~s** npl (courage) valor m.

gutter ['gʌtə*] n (of roof) canalón m; (in street) arroyo.

guy [gaɪ] n (also: ~rope) cuerda; (col: man) tío (Sp), tipo.

guzzle ['gʌzl] vi tragar // vt engullir.

gym [dʒɪm] n (also: gymnasium) gimnasio; (also: gymnastics) gimnasia; **~nast** n gimnasta m/f; **~ shoes** npl zapatillas fpl deportivas; **~ slip** n (Brit) túnica de colegiala.

gynaecologist, (US) **gynecologist** [gaɪnɪ'kɔlədʒɪst] n ginecólogo/a.

gypsy ['dʒɪpsɪ] n = **gipsy**.

gyrate [dʒaɪ'reɪt] vi girar.

H

haberdashery ['hæbə'dæʃərɪ] n (Brit) mercería; (US: men's clothing) prendas fpl de caballero.

habit ['hæbɪt] n hábito, costumbre f.

habitat ['hæbɪtæt] n habitat m.

habitual [hə'bɪtjuəl] a acostumbrado, habitual; (drinker, liar) empedernido; **~ly** ad por costumbre.

hack [hæk] vt (cut) cortar; (slice) tajar // n corte m; (axe blow) hachazo; (pej: writer) escritor(a) m/f a sueldo.

hackneyed ['hæknɪd] a trillado, gastado.

had [hæd] pt, pp of **have**.

haddock ['hædək], pl **~** or **~s** n especie de merluza.

hadn't ['hædnt] = **had not**.

haemorrhage, (US) **hemorrhage** ['hemərɪdʒ] n hemorragia.

haemorrhoids, (US) **hemorrhoids** ['hemərɔɪdz] npl hemorroides fpl.

haggard ['hægəd] a ojeroso.

haggle ['hægl] vi (argue) discutir; (bargain) regatear.

Hague [heɪg] n: The ~ La Haya.

hail [heɪl] n (weather) granizo // vt saludar; (call) llamar a // vi granizar; **~stone** n (piedra) de granizo.

hair [hɛə*] n (gen) pelo, cabellos mpl; (one ~) pelo, cabello; (head of ~) pelo, cabellera; (on legs etc) vello; **to do one's ~** arreglarse el pelo; **grey ~** canas fpl; **~brush** n cepillo (para el pelo); **~cut** n corte m (de pelo); **~do** n peinado; **~dresser** n peluquero/a; **~dresser's** n peluquería; **~-dryer** n secador m de pelo; ~**grip**, ~**pin** n horquilla; ~**net** n redecilla; ~**piece** n postizo; ~**pin bend**, (US) ~**pin curve** n curva de horquilla; ~**raising** a espeluznante; ~ **remover** n depilatorio; ~ **spray** n laca; ~**style** n peinado; ~**y** a peludo; velludo.

hake [heɪk] n merluza.

half [hɑːf], pl **halves** n mitad f // a medio // ad medio, a medias; ~**-an-hour** media hora; **two and a** ~ dos y media; ~ **a dozen** media docena; ~ **a pound** media libra; **to cut sth in** ~ cortar algo por la mitad; ~ **asleep** medio dormido; ~**back** n (SPORT) medio; ~**breed**, ~**caste** n mestizo/a; ~**hearted** a indiferente, poco entusiasta; ~**hour** n media hora; ~**mast** n: **at** ~**mast** (flag) a media asta; ~**price** a a mitad de precio; ~ **term** n (Brit SCOL) vacaciones de mediados del trimestre; ~**time** n descanso; ~**way** ad a medio camino.

halibut ['hælɪbət] n, pl inv halibut m.

hall [hɔːl] n (for concerts) sala; (entrance way) entrada, vestíbulo; ~ **of residence** n (Brit) colegio mayor.

hallmark ['hɔːlmɑːk] n (mark) contraste m; (fig) sello.

hallo [hə'ləu] excl = **hello.**

Hallowe'en [hæləu'iːn] n víspera de Todos los Santos.

hallucination [həluːsɪ'neɪʃən] n alucinación f.

hallway ['hɔːlweɪ] n vestíbulo.

halo ['heɪləu] n (of saint) aureola.

halt [hɔːlt] n (stop) alto, parada; (RAIL) apeadero // vt parar // vi pararse; (process) interrumpirse.

halve [huːv] vt partir por la mitad.

halves [huːvz] pl of **half.**

ham [hæm] n jamón m (cocido).

hamburger ['hæmbəːgə*] n hamburguesa.

hamlet ['hæmlɪt] n aldea.

hammer ['hæmə*] n martillo // vt (nail) clavar.

hammock ['hæmək] n hamaca.

hamper ['hæmpə*] vt estorbar // n cesto.

hand [hænd] n mano f; (of clock) aguja; (writing) letra; (worker) obrero // vt dar, pasar; **to give sb a** ~ echar una mano a uno, ayudar a uno; **at** ~ a la mano; **in** ~ entre manos; **on** ~ (person, services) a mano, al alcance; **to** ~ (information etc) a mano; **on the one** ~ ..., **on the other** ~ ... por una parte ... por otra (parte) ...; **to** ~ **in** vt entregar; **to** ~ **out** vt distribuir; **to** ~ **over** vt (deliver) entregar; (surrender) ceder; ~**bag** n bolso, cartera (LAm); ~**book** n manual m; ~**brake** n freno de mano; ~**cuffs** npl esposas fpl; ~**ful** n puñado.

handicap ['hændɪkæp] n desventaja, (SPORT) handicap m // vt estorbar; **handicapped** a: **to be mentally/**

physically ~**ped** ser deficiente m/f (mental)/minusválido/a (físico/a).

handicraft ['hændɪkrɑːft] n artesanía.

handiwork ['hændɪwəːk] n manualidad(es) f(pl); (fig) obra.

handkerchief ['hæŋkətʃɪf] n pañuelo.

handle ['hændl] n (of door etc) manija; (of cup etc) asa; (of knife etc) mango; (for winding) manivela // vt (touch) tocar; (deal with) encargarse de; (treat: people) manejar; '~ **with care**' '(manéjese) con cuidado'; **to fly off the** ~ perder los estribos; ~**bar(s)** n(pl) manillar msg.

hand: ~**luggage** n equipaje m de mano; ~**made** ['hændmeɪd] a hecho a mano; ~**out** ['hændaut] n (leaflet) folleto; ~**rail** ['hændreɪl] n pasamanos m inv; ~**shake** ['hændʃeɪk] n apretón m de manos.

handsome ['hænsəm] a guapo.

handwriting ['hændraɪtɪŋ] n letra.

handy ['hændɪ] a (close at hand) a la mano; (tool etc) práctico; (skilful) hábil, diestro; ~**man** n manitas m inv.

hang [hæŋ], pt, pp **hung** vt colgar; (head) bajar; (criminal: pt, pp **hanged**) ahorcar // vi colgar; **to get the** ~ **of sth** (col) lograr dominar algo; **to** ~ **about** vi haraganear; **to** ~ **on** vi (wait) esperar; **to** ~ **up** vi (TEL) colgar.

hanger ['hæŋə*] n percha.

hang-gliding ['hæŋglaɪdɪŋ] n vuelo libre.

hangover ['hæŋəuvə*] n (after drinking) resaca.

hang-up ['hæŋʌp] n complejo.

hanker ['hæŋkə*] vi: **to** ~ **after** añorar.

hankie, **hanky** ['hæŋkɪ] n abbr = **handkerchief.**

haphazard [hæp'hæzəd] a fortuito.

happen ['hæpən] vi suceder, ocurrir; (take place) tener lugar, realizarse; **as it** ~**s** da la casualidad de que; ~**ing** n suceso, acontecimiento.

happily ['hæpɪlɪ] ad (luckily) afortunadamente; (cheerfully) alegremente.

happiness ['hæpɪnɪs] n (contentment) felicidad f; (joy) alegría.

happy ['hæpɪ] a feliz; (cheerful) alegre; **to be** ~ **(with)** estar contento (con); ~ **birthday!** ¡feliz cumpleaños!; ~**go-lucky** a despreocupado.

harangue [hə'ræŋ] vt arengar.

harass ['hærəs] vt acosar, hostigar; ~**ment** n persecución f.

harbour, (US) **harbor** ['hɑːbə*] n puerto // vt dar abrigo a.

hard [hɑːd] a duro; (difficult) difícil; (work) arduo; (person) severo // ad (work) mucho, duro; (think) profundamente; **to look** ~ **at sb/sth** clavar los ojos en uno/algo; **to try** ~ esforzarse; **no** ~ **feelings!** ¡sin rencor(es)!; **to be** ~ **of hearing** ser duro de oído; **to be** ~ **done by** ser tratado injustamente; ~**back** n libro de tapas duras; ~ **cash** n dinero contante; ~ **disk** n (COMPUT) disco duro or rígido; ~**en** vt endurecer; (fig) curtir // vi endurecerse; ~**headed** a poco sentimental, realista; ~ **labour** n trabajos mpl forzados.

hardly ['hɑːdlɪ] ad (scarcely) apenas; that can ~ be true eso difícilmente puede ser cierto; ~ ever casi nunca.

hardship ['hɑːdʃɪp] n (troubles) penas fpl; (financial) apuro.

hard-up [hɑːd'ʌp] a (col) sin un duro (Sp), sin plata (LAm).

hardware ['hɑːdwɛə*] n ferretería; (COMPUT) hardware m; ~ **shop** n ferretería.

hard wearing [hɑːd'wɛərɪŋ] a resistente, duradero.

hard-working [hɑːd'wəːkɪŋ] a trabajador(a).

hardy ['hɑːdɪ] a fuerte; (plant) resistente.

hare [hɛə*] n liebre f; ~**-brained** a casquivano.

haricot (bean) ['hærɪkəu-] n alubia.

harm [hɑːm] n daño, mal m // vt (person) hacer daño a; (health, interests) perjudicar; (thing) dañar; out of ~'s way a salvo; ~**ful** a (gen) dañino; (to reputation) perjudicial; ~**less** a (person) inofensivo; (drugs) inocuo.

harmonize ['hɑːmənaɪz] vt, vi armonizar.

harmony ['hɑːmənɪ] n armonía.

harness ['hɑːnɪs] n arreos mpl // vt enjaezar; (fig) aprovechar.

harp [hɑːp] n arpa // vi: to ~ on (about) machacar (con).

harpoon [hɑː'puːn] n arpón m.

harrowing ['hærəuɪŋ] a angustioso.

harsh [hɑːʃ] a (cruel) duro, cruel; (severe) severo; (words) hosco; (colour) chillón/ona; (contrast) violento.

harvest ['hɑːvɪst] n cosecha; (of grapes) vendimia // vt, vi cosechar; ~**er** n (machine) cosechadora.

has [hæz] vb see **have**.

hash [hæʃ] n (CULIN) picadillo; (fig: mess) lío.

hashish ['hæʃɪʃ] n hachís m, hachich m.

hasn't ['hæznt] = **has not**.

hassle ['hæsl] n pelea.

haste [heɪst] n prisa; ~**n** ['heɪsn] vt acelerar // vi darse prisa; **hastily** ad de prisa; **hasty** a apresurado.

hat [hæt] n sombrero.

hatch [hætʃ] n (NAUT: also: ~**way**) escotilla // vi salir del cascarón // vt incubar; (plot) tramar.

hatchback ['hætʃbæk] n (AUT) tres or cinco puertas m.

hatchet ['hætʃɪt] n hacha.

hate [heɪt] vt odiar, aborrecer // n odio; ~**ful** a odioso; **hatred** ['heɪtrɪd] n odio.

hat trick n: to score a ~ (Brit: SPORT)

marcar tres goles or tantos.

haughty ['hɔːtɪ] a altanero, arrogante.

haul [hɔːl] vt tirar; (by lorry) transportar // n (of fish) redada; (of stolen goods etc) botín m; ~**age** n (Brit) transporte m; (costs) gastos mpl de transporte; ~**ier**, (US) ~**er** n transportista m/f.

haunch [hɔːntʃ] n anca; (of meat) pierna.

haunt [hɔːnt] vt (subj: ghost) aparecer en; (frequent) frecuentar; (obsess) obsesionar // n guarida.

have [hæv], pt, pp **had** ♦ auxiliary vb **1** (gen) haber; to ~ arrived/eaten haber llegado/comido; **having finished** or **when he had finished, he left** cuando terminó, se fue

2 (in tag questions): **you've done it**, ~**n't you?** lo has hecho, ¿verdad? or ¿no?

3 (in short answers and questions): **I** ~**n't** no; **so I** ~ pues, es verdad; **we** ~**n't paid — yes we** ~**!** no hemos pagado — sí que hemos pagado; **I've been there before**, ~ **you?** he estado allí antes, ¿y tú?

♦ modal auxiliary vb (be obliged): to ~ (got) to do sth tener que hacer algo; **you** ~**n't to tell her** no hay que or no debes decírselo

♦ vt **1** (possess): **he has (got) blue eyes/ dark hair** tiene los ojos azules/el pelo negro

2 (referring to meals etc): to ~ **breakfast/lunch/dinner** desayunar/comer/ cenar; **to ~ a drink/a cigarette** tomar algo/fumar un cigarrillo

3 (receive) recibir; (obtain) obtener; **may I** ~ **your address?** ¿puedes darme tu dirección?; **you can** ~ **it for £5** te lo puedes quedar por £5; **I must** ~ **it by tomorrow** lo necesito para mañana; **to ~ a baby** tener un niño or bebé

4 (maintain, allow): **I won't** ~ **it/this nonsense!** ¡no lo permitiré!/¡no permitiré estas tonterías!; **we can't** ~ **that** no podemos permitir eso

5: **to ~ sth done** hacer or mandar hacer algo; **to ~ one's hair cut** cortarse el pelo; **to ~ sb do sth** hacer que alguien haga algo

6 (experience, suffer): **to ~ a cold/flu** tener un resfriado/gripe; **she had her bag stolen/her arm broken** le robaron el bolso/se rompió un brazo; **to ~ an operation** operarse

7 (+ noun): **to ~ a swim/walk/bath/rest** nadar/dar un paseo/darse un baño/ descansar; **let's ~ a look** vamos a ver; **to ~ a meeting/party** celebrar una reunión/una fiesta; **let me ~ a try** déjame intentarlo;

to ~ out vt: **to ~ it out with sb** (settle a problem etc) dejar las cosas en claro con alguien.

haven ['heɪvn] n puerto; (fig) refugio.

haven't ['hævnt] = **have not**.

haversack ['hævəsæk] n mochila.
havoc ['hævək] n estragos mpl.
hawk [hɔːk] n halcón m.
hay [heɪ] n heno; ~ **fever** n fiebre f del heno; ~**stack** n almiar m.
haywire ['heɪwaɪə*] a (col): to go ~ (person) volverse loco; (plan) embrollarse.
hazard ['hæzəd] n riesgo; (danger) peligro // vt aventurar; ~**ous** a peligroso; ~ **warning lights** npl (AUT) señales fpl de emergencia.
haze [heɪz] n neblina.
hazelnut ['heɪzlnʌt] n avellana.
hazy ['heɪzɪ] a brumoso; (idea) vago.
he [hiː] pron él; ~ **who...** él que..., quien... .
head [hed] n cabeza; (leader) jefe/a m/f // vt (list) encabezar; (group) capitanear; ~**s** (or tails) cara (o cruz); ~ **first** de cabeza; ~ **over heels** patas arriba; to ~ **the ball** cabecear (la pelota); to ~ **for** vt fus dirigirse a; ~**ache** n dolor m de cabeza; ~**dress** n tocado; ~**ing** n título; ~**lamp** n (Brit) = ~**light**; ~**land** n promontorio; ~**light** n faro; ~**line** n titular m; ~**long** ad (fall) de cabeza; (rush) precipitadamente; ~**master/ mistress** n director(a) m/f (de escuela); ~ **office** n oficina central, central f; ~**on** a (collision) de frente; ~**phones** npl auriculares mpl; ~**quarters (HQ)** npl sede f central; (MIL) cuartel m general; ~**rest** n reposa-cabezas m inv; ~**room** n (in car) altura interior; (under bridge) (límite m de) altura; ~**scarf** n pañuelo; ~**strong** a testarudo; ~**y** a (experience, period) apasionante; (wine) cabezón.
heal [hiːl] vt curar // vi cicatrizarse.
health [helθ] n salud f; ~ **food** n alimentos mpl orgánicos; **the H~ Service** n (Brit) servicio de salud pública; ≈ Insalud m (Sp); ~**y** a (gen) sano.
heap [hiːp] n montón m // vt amontonar.
hear [hɪə*], pt, pp **heard** [hɜːd] vt oír; (perceive) sentir; (listen to) escuchar; (lecture) asistir a // vi oír; to ~ **about** oír hablar de; to ~ **from sb** tener noticias de uno; ~**ing** n (sense) oído; (LAW) vista; ~**ing aid** n audífono; ~**say** n rumores mpl, hablillas fpl.
hearse [hɜːs] n coche m fúnebre.
heart [hɑːt] n corazón m; ~**s** npl (CARDS) corazones mpl; at ~ en el fondo; by ~ (learn, know) de memoria; ~ **attack** n infarto (de miocardio); ~**beat** n latido (del corazón); ~**breaking** a desgarrador(a); ~**broken** a: she was ~**broken about it** esto le partió el corazón; ~**burn** n acidía; ~ **failure** n fallo cardíaco; ~**felt** a (cordial) cordial; (deeply felt) más sentido.

hearth [hɑːθ] n (gen) hogar m; (fireplace) chimenea.
heartily ['hɑːtɪlɪ] ad sinceramente, cordialmente; (laugh) a carcajadas; (eat) con buen apetito.
heartless ['hɑːtlɪs] a cruel.
hearty ['hɑːtɪ] a cordial.
heat [hiːt] n (gen) calor m; (SPORT: also: qualifying ~) prueba eliminatoria // vt calentar; to ~ **up** vi (gen) calentarse; ~**ed** a caliente; (fig) acalorado; ~**er** n calentador m.
heath [hiːθ] n (Brit) brezal m.
heathen ['hiːðn] a, n pagano/a m/f.
heather ['hɛðə*] n brezo.
heating ['hiːtɪŋ] n calefacción f.
heatstroke ['hiːtstrəuk] n insolación f.
heatwave ['hiːtweɪv] n ola de calor.
heave [hiːv] vt (pull) tirar; (push) empujar con esfuerzo; (lift) levantar (con esfuerzo) // vi (water) subir y bajar // n tirón m; empujón m.
heaven ['hɛvn] n cielo; ~**ly** a celestial.
heavily ['hɛvɪlɪ] ad pesadamente; (drink, smoke) con exceso; (sleep, sigh) profundamente.
heavy ['hɛvɪ] a pesado; (work) duro; (sea, rain, meal) fuerte; (drinker, smoker) gran; ~ **goods vehicle (HGV)** n vehículo pesado; ~**weight** n (SPORT) peso pesado.
Hebrew ['hiːbruː] a, n (LING) hebreo.
Hebrides ['hebrɪdiːz] npl: the ~ las Hébridas.
heckle ['hɛkl] vt interrumpir.
hectic ['hɛktɪk] a agitado.
he'd [hiːd] = he would, he had.
hedge [hedʒ] n seto // vt cercar (con un seto) // vi contestar con evasivas; to ~ **one's bets** (fig) cubrirse.
hedgehog ['hedʒhɔg] n erizo.
heed [hiːd] vt (also: take ~ of) (pay attention) hacer caso de; (bear in mind) tener en cuenta; ~**less** a desatento.
heel [hiːl] n talón m // vt (shoe) poner tacón a.
hefty ['hɛftɪ] a (person) fornido; (piece) grande; (price) gordo.
heifer ['hɛfə*] n novilla, ternera.
height [haɪt] n (of person) talle m; (of building) altura; (high ground) cerro; (altitude) altitud f; ~**en** vt elevar; (fig) aumentar.
heir [ɛə*] n heredero; ~**ess** n heredera; ~**loom** n reliquia de familia.
held [held] pt, pp of **hold**.
helicopter ['hɛlɪkɔptə*] n helicóptero.
helium ['hiːlɪəm] n helio.
hell [hɛl] n infierno; ~! (col) ¡demonios!
he'll [hiːl] = he will, he shall.
hellish ['hɛlɪʃ] a infernal.
hello [hə'ləu] excl ¡hola!; (surprise) ¡caramba!
helm [hɛlm] n (NAUT) timón m.
helmet ['hɛlmɪt] n casco.

help [hɛlp] n ayuda; (charwoman) criada, asistenta // vt ayudar; ~! ¡socorro!; ~ yourself sírvete; he can't ~ it no es culpa suya; ~er n ayudante m/f; ~ful a útil; (person) servicial; ~ing n ración f; ~less a (incapable) incapaz; (defenceless) indefenso.

hem [hɛm] n dobladillo // vt poner or coser el dobladillo; to ~ in vt cercar.

he-man ['hiːmæn] n macho.

hemorrhage ['hɛmərɪdʒ] n (US) = haemorrhage.

hemorrhoids ['hɛmərɔɪdʒ] npl (US) = haemorrhoids.

hen [hɛn] n gallina.

hence [hɛns] ad (therefore) por lo tanto; 2 years ~ de aquí a 2 años; ~forth ad de hoy en adelante.

henchman ['hɛntʃmən] n (pej) secuaz m.

henpecked ['hɛnpɛkt] a: to be ~ ser un calzonazos.

hepatitis [hɛpə'taɪtɪs] n hepatitis f.

her [həː*] pron (direct) la; (indirect) le; (stressed, after prep) ella // a su; see also me, my.

herald ['hɛrəld] n heraldo // vt anunciar.

herb [həːb] n hierba.

herd [həːd] n rebaño.

here [hɪə*] ad aquí; ~! (present) ¡presente!; (offering sth) ¡toma!; ~ is/are aquí está/están; ~ she is aquí está; ~after ad en el futuro // n: the ~after el más allá; ~by ad (in letter) por la presente.

heredity [hɪ'rɛdɪtɪ] n herencia.

heresy ['hɛrəsɪ] n herejía.

heretic ['hɛrətɪk] n hereje m/f.

heritage ['hɛrɪtɪdʒ] n (gen) herencia; (fig) patrimonio.

hermetically [həː'mɛtɪklɪ] ad: ~ sealed cerrado herméticamente.

hermit ['həːmɪt] n ermitaño/a.

hernia ['həːnɪə] n hernia.

hero ['hɪərəu] pl ~es n héroe m; (in book, film) protagonista m; ~ic [hɪ'rəuɪk] a heroico.

heroin ['hɛrəuɪn] n heroína.

heroine ['hɛrəuɪn] n heroína; (in book, film) protagonista.

heron ['hɛrən] n garza.

herring ['hɛrɪŋ] n arenque m.

hers [həːz] pron (el) suyo/(la) suya etc; see also mine.

herself [həː'sɛlf] pron (reflexive) se; (emphatic) ella misma; (after prep) sí (misma); see also oneself.

he's [hiːz] = he is; he has.

hesitant ['hɛzɪtənt] a vacilante.

hesitate ['hɛzɪteɪt] vi vacilar; **hesitation** ['-teɪʃən] n indecisión f.

heterosexual [hɛtərəu'sɛksjuəl] a, n heterosexual m/f.

heyday ['heɪdeɪ] n: the ~ of el apogeo de.

HGV n abbr = **heavy goods vehicle**.

hi [haɪ] excl ¡hola!

hiatus [haɪ'eɪtəs] n laguna; (LING) hiato.

hibernate ['haɪbəneɪt] vi invernar.

hiccough, hiccup ['hɪkʌp] vi hipar; ~s npl hipo sg.

hide [haɪd] n (skin) piel f // vb (pt hid, pp hidden) vt esconder, ocultar // vi: to ~ (from sb) esconderse or ocultarse (de uno); ~-and-seek n escondite m; ~away n escondite m.

hideous ['hɪdɪəs] a horrible.

hiding ['haɪdɪŋ] n (beating) paliza; to be in ~ (concealed) estar escondido; ~ place n escondrijo.

hierarchy ['haɪərɑːkɪ] n jerarquía.

hi-fi ['haɪfaɪ] n estéreo, hifi m // a de alta fidelidad.

high [haɪ] a alto; (speed, number) grande; (price) elevado; (wind) fuerte; (voice) agudo // ad alto, a gran altura; it is 20 m ~ tiene 20 m de altura; ~ in the air en las alturas; ~boy n (US) cómoda alta; ~brow a, n intelectual m/f; ~chair n silla alta; ~er education n educación f or enseñanza superior; ~handed a despótico; ~jack = hijack; ~ jump n (SPORT) salto de altura; the H~lands npl las tierras altas de Escocia; ~light n (fig: of event) punto culminante // vt subrayar; ~ly ad sumamente; ~ly strung a hipertenso; ~ness n altura; Her or His H~ness Su Alteza; ~-pitched a agudo; ~-rise block n torre f de pisos; ~ school n centro de enseñanza secundaria; ≈ Instituto Nacional de Bachillerato (Sp); ~ season n (Brit) temporada alta; ~ street n (Brit) calle f mayor; ~way n carretera; H~way Code n (Brit) código de la circulación.

hijack ['haɪdʒæk] vt secuestrar; ~er n secuestrador(a) m/f.

hike [haɪk] vi (go walking) ir de excursión (de pie) // n caminata; ~r n excursionista m/f.

hilarious [hɪ'lɛərɪəs] a divertidísimo.

hill [hɪl] n colina; (high) montaña; (slope) cuesta; ~side n ladera; ~y a montañoso; (uneven) accidentado.

hilt [hɪlt] n (of sword) empuñadura; to the ~ (fig: support) incondicionalmente.

him [hɪm] pron (direct) le, lo; (indirect) le; (stressed, after prep) él; see also me; ~self pron (reflexive) se; (emphatic) él mismo; (after prep) sí (mismo); see also oneself.

hind [haɪnd] a posterior // n cierva.

hinder ['hɪndə*] vt estorbar, impedir; **hindrance** ['hɪndrəns] n estorbo, obstáculo.

hindsight ['haɪndsaɪt] n: with ~ en retrospectiva.

Hindu ['hɪnduː] n hindú m/f.

hinge [hɪndʒ] n bisagra, gozne m // vi

(fig): to ~ on depender de.

hint [hɪnt] *n* indirecta; *(advice)* consejo // *vt:* to ~ that insinuar que // *vi:* to ~ at hacer alusión a.

hip [hɪp] *n* cadera.

hippopotamus [hɪpə'pɒtəməs], *pl* ~**es** *or* -**mi** [-maɪ] *n* hipopótamo.

hire ['haɪə*] *vt (Brit: car, equipment)* alquilar; *(worker)* contratar // *n* alquiler *m*; **for** ~ se alquila; *(taxi)* libre; ~ **purchase (H.P.)** *n (Brit)* compra a plazos.

his [hɪz] *pron* (el) suyo/(la) suya *etc* // *a* su; *see also* **my, mine.**

Hispanic [hɪs'pænɪk] *a* hispánico.

hiss [hɪs] *vi* silbar.

historian [hɪ'stɔːrɪən] *n* historiador(a) *m/f*.

historic(al) [hɪ'stɒrɪk(l)] *a* histórico.

history ['hɪstərɪ] *n* historia.

hit [hɪt] *vt (pt, pp* **hit)** *(strike)* golpear, pegar; *(reach: target)* alcanzar; *(collide with: car)* chocar contra; *(fig: affect)* afectar // *n* golpe *m*; *(success)* éxito; to ~ **it off with sb** llevarse bien con uno; ~**and-run driver** *n* conductor(a) que atropella y huye.

hitch [hɪtʃ] *vt (fasten)* atar, amarrar; *(also:* ~ **up)** remangar // *n (difficulty)* dificultad *f*; to ~ **a lift** hacer autostop.

hitch-hike ['hɪtʃhaɪk] *vi* hacer autostop; ~**r** *n* autostopista *m/f*.

hi-tech [haɪ'tɛk] *a* de alta tecnología.

hitherto [hɪðə'tuː] *ad* hasta ahora.

hive [haɪv] *n* colmena; **to** ~ **off** *vt* transferir; privatizar.

HMS *abbr* = *His (Her) Majesty's Ship.*

hoard [hɔːd] *n (treasure)* tesoro; *(stockpile)* provisión *f* // *vt* acumular; ~**ing** *n (for posters)* cartelera.

hoarfrost ['hɔːfrɒst] *n* escarcha.

hoarse [hɔːs] *a* ronco.

hoax [həʊks] *n* trampa.

hob [hɒb] *n* quemador *m*.

hobble ['hɒbl] *vi* cojear.

hobby ['hɒbɪ] *n* pasatiempo, afición *f*; ~**-horse** *n (fig)* caballo de batalla.

hobo ['həʊbəʊ] *n (US)* vagabundo.

hockey ['hɒkɪ] *n* hockey *m*.

hoe [həʊ] *n* azadón *m* // *vt* azadonar.

hog [hɒg] *n* cerdo, puerco // *vt (fig)* acaparar; **to go the whole** ~ poner toda la carne en el asador.

hoist [hɔɪst] *n (crane)* grúa // *vt* levantar, alzar.

hold [həʊld] *vt (pt, pp* **held)** tener; *(contain)* contener; *(keep back)* retener; *(believe)* sostener; *(take* ~ *of)* coger *(Sp)*, agarrar *(LAm)*; *(take weight)* soportar; *(meeting)* celebrar // *vi (withstand pressure)* resistir; *(be valid)* valer; *(stick)* pegarse // *n (grasp)* asimiento; *(fig)* dominio; *(WRESTLING)* presa; *(NAUT)* bodega; ~ **the line!** *(TEL)* ¡no cuelgue!; **to** ~ **one's own** *(fig)* defenderse; **to catch** *or*

get (a) ~ **of** agarrarse *or* asirse de; **to** ~ **back** *vt* retener; *(secret)* ocultar; **to** ~ **down** *vt (person)* sujetar; *(job)* mantener; **to** ~ **off** *vt (enemy)* rechazar; **to** ~ **on** *vi* agarrarse bien; *(wait)* esperar; **to** ~ **on to** *vt fus* agarrarse a; *(keep)* guardar; **to** ~ **out** *vt* ofrecer // *vi (resist)* resistir; **to** ~ **up** *vt (raise)* levantar; *(support)* apoyar; *(delay)* retrasar; *(rob)* asaltar; ~**all** *n (Brit)* bolsa; ~**er** *n (of ticket, record)* poseedor(a) *m/f*; *(of office, title etc)* titular *m/f*; ~**ing** *n (share)* interés *m*; ~**up** *n (robbery)* atraco; *(delay)* retraso; *(Brit: in traffic)* embotellamiento.

hole [həʊl] *n* agujero // *vt* agujerear.

holiday ['hɒlɪdɪ] *n* vacaciones *fpl*; *(day off)* (día *m* de) fiesta, día *m* feriado; **on** ~ de vacaciones; ~ **camp** *n* colonia veraniega; ~**-maker** *n (Brit)* turista *m/f*; ~ **resort** *n* centro turístico.

holiness ['həʊlɪnɪs] *n* santidad *f*.

Holland ['hɒlənd] *n* Holanda.

hollow ['hɒləʊ] *a* hueco; *(fig)* vacío; *(eyes)* hundido; *(sound)* sordo // *n (gen)* hueco; *(in ground)* hoyo // *vt:* to ~ **out** ahuecar.

holly ['hɒlɪ] *n* acebo.

holocaust ['hɒləkɔːst] *n* holocausto.

holster ['həʊlstə*] *n* pistolera.

holy ['həʊlɪ] *a (gen)* santo, sagrado; *(water)* bendito; **H**~ **Ghost** *or* **Spirit** *n* Espíritu *m* Santo.

homage ['hɒmɪdʒ] *n* homenaje *m*.

home [həʊm] *n* casa; *(country)* patria; *(institution)* asilo // *a (domestic)* casero, de casa; *(ECON, POL)* nacional // *ad (direction)* a casa; **at** ~ en casa; **to go/ come** ~ ir/volver a casa; **make yourself at** ~ ¡estás en tu casa!; ~ **address** *n* domicilio; ~ **computer** *n* ordenador *m* doméstico; ~**land** *n* tierra natal; ~**less** *a* sin hogar, sin casa; ~**ly** *a (domestic)* casero; *(simple)* sencillo; ~**-made** *a* hecho en casa; **H**~ **Office** *n (Brit)* Ministerio del Interior; ~ **rule** *n* autonomía; **H**~ **Secretary** *n (Brit)* Ministro del Interior; ~**sick** *a:* **to be** ~**sick** tener morriña, sentir nostalgia; ~ **town** *n* ciudad *f* natal; ~**ward** ['həʊmwəd] *a (journey)* hacia casa; ~**work** *n* deberes *mpl*.

homogeneous [hɒmə'dʒiːnɪəs] *a* homogéneo.

homicide ['hɒmɪsaɪd] *n (US)* homicidio.

homosexual [hɒməʊ'sɛksjʊəl] *a, n* homosexual *m/f*.

Honduran [hɒn'djʊərən] *a, n* hondureño/a *m/f*.

Honduras [hɒn'djʊərəs] *n* Honduras *f*.

honest ['ɒnɪst] *a* honrado; *(sincere)* franco, sincero; ~**ly** *ad* honradamente; francamente; ~**y** *n* honradez *f*.

honey ['hʌnɪ] *n* miel *f*; ~**comb** *n* panal *m*; ~**moon** *n* luna de miel; ~**suckle** *n* madreselva.

honk [hɔŋk] vi (AUT) tocar la bocina.
honorary [ˈɔnərərɪ] a (member, president) de honor; ~ **degree** doctorado honoris causa.
honour, (US) **honor** [ˈɔnə*] vt honrar // n honor m, honra; **~able** a honorable; **~s degree** n (SCOL) título de licenciado de categoría superior.
hood [hud] n capucha; (Brit AUT) capota; (US: AUT) capó m.
hoodlum [ˈhuːdləm] n matón m.
hoodwink [ˈhudwɪŋk] vt (Brit) timar.
hoof [huːf], pl **hooves** n pezuña.
hook [huk] n gancho; (on dress) corchete m, broche m; (for fishing) anzuelo // vt enganchar.
hooligan [ˈhuːlɪgən] n gamberro.
hoop [huːp] n aro.
hoot [huːt] vi (Brit AUT) tocar la bocina; (siren) sonar la sirena // n bocinazo, toque m de sirena; to ~ **with laughter** morirse de risa; **~er** n (Brit AUT) bocina; (NAUT) sirena.
hoover ® [ˈhuːvə*] (Brit) n aspiradora // vt pasar la aspiradora por.
hooves [huːvz] pl of **hoof.**
hop [hɔp] vi saltar, brincar; (on one foot) saltar con un pie.
hope [həup] vt, vi esperar // n esperanza; I ~ **so/not** espero que sí/no; **~ful** a (person) optimista; (situation) prometedor(a); **~fully** ad con optimismo, con esperanza; **~less** a desesperado.
hops [hɔps] npl lúpulo sg.
horizon [həˈraɪzn] n horizonte m; **~tal** [hɔrɪˈzɔntl] a horizontal.
hormone [ˈhɔːməun] n hormona.
horn [hɔːn] n cuerno; (MUS: also: French ~) trompa; (AUT) bocina, claxón m (LAm).
hornet [ˈhɔːnɪt] n avispón m.
horny [ˈhɔːnɪ] a (material) córneo; (hands) calloso; (col) cachondo.
horoscope [ˈhɔrəskəup] n horóscopo.
horrendous [hɔˈrendəs] a horrendo.
horrible [ˈhɔrɪbl] a horrible.
horrid [ˈhɔrɪd] a horrible, horroroso.
horrify [ˈhɔrɪfaɪ] vt horrorizar.
horror [ˈhɔrə*] n horror m; ~ **film** n película de horror.
hors d'œuvre [ɔːˈdəːvrə] n entremeses mpl.
horse [hɔːs] n caballo; on **~back** a caballo; ~ **chestnut** n (tree) castaño de Indias; **~man/woman** n jinete/a m/f; **~power (h.p.)** n caballo (de fuerza); **~-racing** n carreras fpl de caballos; **~radish** n rábano picante; **~shoe** n herradura.
hose [həuz] n (also: **~pipe**) manga.
hoslery [ˈhəuzɪərɪ] n calcetería.
hospitable [hɔsˈpɪtəbl] a hospitalario.
hospital [ˈhɔspɪtl] n hospital m.
hospitality [hɔspɪˈtælɪtɪ] n hospitalidad f.
host [həust] n anfitrión m; (of inn etc)

mesonero; (REL) hostia; (large number): a ~ **of** multitud de.
hostage [ˈhɔstɪdʒ] n rehén m.
hostel [ˈhɔstl] n hostal m; **(youth)** ~ n albergue m juvenil.
hostess [ˈhəustɪs] n anfitriona.
hostile [ˈhɔstaɪl] a hostil; **hostility** [-ˈstɪlɪtɪ] n hostilidad f.
hot [hɔt] a caliente; (weather) caluroso, de calor; (as opposed to only warm) muy caliente; (spicy) picante; (fig) ardiente, acalorado; to be ~ (person) tener calor; (object) estar caliente; (weather) hacer calor; **~bed** n (fig) semillero; ~ **dog** n perro caliente.
hotel [həuˈtɛl] n hotel m; **~ier** n hotelero.
hot: **~headed** a exaltado; **~house** n invernadero; ~ **line** n (POL) teléfono rojo; **~ly** ad con pasión, apasionadamente; **~plate** n (on cooker) hornillo; **~-water bottle** n bolsa de agua caliente.
hound [haund] vt acosar // n perro de caza.
hour [ˈauə*] n hora; **~ly** a (de) cada hora // ad cada hora.
house [haus, pl: ˈhauzɪz] n (also: firm) casa; (POL) cámara; (THEATRE) sala // vt [hauz] (person) alojar; on the ~ (fig) la casa invita; ~ **arrest** n arresto domiciliario; **~boat** n casa flotante; **~breaking** n allanamiento de morada; **~coat** n bata; **~hold** n familia; **~keeper** n ama de llaves; **~keeping** n (work) trabajos mpl domésticos; **~keeping (money)** n dinero para gastos domésticos; **~-warming party** n fiesta de estreno de una casa; **~wife** n ama de casa; **~work** n faenas fpl (de la casa).
housing [ˈhauzɪŋ] n (act) alojamiento; (houses) viviendas fpl; ~ **development**, (Brit) ~ **estate** n urbanización f.
hovel [ˈhɔvl] n casucha.
hover [ˈhɔvə*] vi flotar (en el aire); **~craft** n aerodeslizador m.
how [hau] ad (in what way) cómo; ~ **are you?** ¿cómo estás?; ~ **much milk/many people?** ¿cuánta leche/gente?; ~ **much does it cost?** ¿cuánto cuesta?; ~ **long have you been here?** ¿cuánto hace que estás aquí?; ~ **old are you?** ¿cuántos años tienes?; ~ **tall is he?** ¿cuánto es de alto?; ~ **is school?** ¿cómo (te) va (en) la escuela?; ~ **was the film?** ¿qué tal la película?; ~ **lovely/awful!** ¡qué bonito/horror!
howl [haul] n aullido // vi aullar.
H.P. n abbr = **hire purchase.**
h.p. abbr = **horse power.**
HQ n abbr = **headquarters.**
hub [hʌb] n (of wheel) centro.
hubbub [ˈhʌbʌb] n barahúnda, barullo.

hubcap ['hʌbkæp] n tapacubos m inv.

huddle ['hʌdl] vi: to ~ together amontonarse.

hue [hju:] n color m, matiz m; ~ and **cry** n alarma.

huff [hʌf] n: in a ~ enojado.

hug [hʌg] vt abrazar // n abrazo.

huge [hju:dʒ] a enorme.

hulk [hʌlk] n (ship) barco viejo; (person, building etc) mole f.

hull [hʌl] n (of ship) casco.

hullo [hə'ləu] excl = hello.

hum [hʌm] vt tararear, canturrear // vi tararear, canturrear; (insect) zumbar.

human ['hju:mən] a, n humano m/f.

humane [hju:'meɪn] a humano, humanitario.

humanitarian [hju:mænɪ'tɛərɪən] a humanitario.

humanity [hju:'mænɪtɪ] n humanidad f.

humble ['hʌmbl] a humilde // vt humillar.

humbug ['hʌmbʌg] n tonterías fpl; (Brit: sweet) caramelo de menta.

humdrum ['hʌmdrʌm] a (boring) monótono, aburrido; (routine) rutinario.

humid ['hju:mɪd] a húmedo; ~ity [-'mɪdɪtɪ] n humedad f.

humiliate [hju:'mɪlɪeɪt] vt humillar; **humiliation** [-'eɪʃən] n humillación f.

humility [hju:'mɪlɪtɪ] n humildad f.

humorous ['hju:mərəs] a gracioso, divertido.

humour, (US) **humor** ['hju:mə*] n humorismo, sentido del humor; (mood) humor m // vt (person) complacer.

hump [hʌmp] n (in ground) montículo; (camel's) giba.

hunch [hʌntʃ] n (premonition) presentimiento; ~**back** n joroba m/f; ~**ed** a jorobado.

hundred ['hʌndrəd] num ciento; (before n) cien; ~s of centenares de; ~**weight** n (Brit) = 50.8 kg; 112 lb; (US) = 45.3 kg; 100 lb.

hung [hʌŋ] pt, pp of **hang.**

Hungarian [hʌŋ'gɛərɪən] a, n húngaro/a m/f.

Hungary ['hʌŋgərɪ] n Hungría.

hunger ['hʌŋgə*] n hambre f // vi: to ~ for (fig) tener hambre de, anhelar; ~ **strike** n huelga de hambre.

hungry ['hʌŋgrɪ] a hambriento; to be ~ tener hambre.

hunk [hʌŋk] n (of bread etc) trozo, pedazo.

hunt [hʌnt] vt (seek) buscar; (SPORT) cazar // vi cazar // n caza, cacería; ~**er** n cazador(a) m/f; ~**ing** n caza.

hurdle ['hə:dl] n (SPORT) valla; (fig) obstáculo.

hurl [hə:l] vt lanzar, arrojar.

hurrah [hu'rɑ:], **hurray** [hu'reɪ] n ¡viva!, ¡vítor!

hurricane ['hʌrɪkən] n huracán m.

hurried ['hʌrɪd] a (fast) apresurado; (rushed) hecho de prisa; ~**ly** ad con prisa, apresuradamente.

hurry ['hʌrɪ] n prisa // vb (also: ~ up) vi apresurarse, darse prisa // vt (person) dar prisa a; (work) apresurar, hacer de prisa; to be in a ~ tener prisa.

hurt [hə:t], pt, pp hurt vt hacer daño a // vi doler // a lastimado; ~**ful** a (remark etc) dañoso.

hurtle ['hə:tl] vi: to ~ past pasar como un rayo.

husband ['hʌzbənd] n marido.

hush [hʌʃ] n silencio // vt hacer callar; (cover up) encubrir; ~! ¡chitón!, ¡cállate!

husk [hʌsk] n (of wheat) cáscara.

husky ['hʌskɪ] a ronco // n perro esquimal.

hustle ['hʌsl] vt (push) empujar; (hurry) dar prisa a // n bullicio, actividad f febril; ~ **and bustle** n vaivén m.

hut [hʌt] n cabaña; (shed) cobertizo.

hutch [hʌtʃ] n conejera.

hyacinth ['haɪəsɪnθ] n jacinto.

hydrant ['haɪdrənt] n (also: fire ~) boca de incendios.

hydraulic [haɪ'drɔːlɪk] a hidráulico.

hydroelectric [haɪdrəu'lektrɪk] a hidroeléctrico.

hydrofoil ['haɪdrəfɔɪl] n aerodeslizador m.

hydrogen ['haɪdrədʒən] n hidrógeno.

hyena [haɪ'iːnə] n hiena.

hygiene ['haɪdʒiːn] n higiene f; **hygienic** [-'dʒiːnɪk] a higiénico.

hymn [hɪm] n himno.

hype [haɪp] n (col) bombardeo publicitario.

hypermarket ['haɪpəmɑːkɪt] n hipermercado.

hyphen ['haɪfn] n guión m.

hypnotize ['hɪpnətaɪz] vt hipnotizar.

hypochondriac [haɪpəu'kɒndrɪæk] n hipocondríaco/a.

hypocrisy [hɪ'pɒkrɪsɪ] n hipocresía; **hypocrite** ['hɪpəkrɪt] n hipócrita m/f; **hypocritical** [hɪpə'krɪtɪkl] a hipócrita.

hypothesis [haɪ'pɒθɪsɪs], pl -ses [-siːz] n hipótesis f inv.

hysteria [hɪ'stɪərɪə] n histeria; **hysterical** [-'sterɪkl] a histérico; **hysterics** [-'sterɪks] npl histeria sg, histerismo sg.

I

I [aɪ] pron yo.

ice [aɪs] n hielo // vt (cake) alcorzar // vi (also: ~ over, ~ up) helarse; ~ **axe** n piqueta (de alpinista); ~**berg** n iceberg m; ~**box** n (Brit) congelador m; (US) nevera, refrigeradora (LAm); ~ **cream** n helado; ~ **cube** n cubito de hielo; ~ **hockey** n hockey m sobre hielo.

Iceland ['aɪslənd] n Islandia.
ice: ~ **lolly** n (Brit) polo; ~ **rink** n pista de hielo; ~ **skating** n patinaje m sobre hielo.
icicle ['aɪɪkl] n carámbano.
icing ['aɪsɪŋ] n (CULIN) alcorza; (AVIAT etc) formación f de hielo; ~ **sugar** n (Brit) azúcar m glas(eado).
icy ['aɪsɪ] a (road) helado; (fig) glacial.
I'd [aɪd] = **I would; I had.**
idea [aɪ'dɪə] n idea.
ideal [aɪ'dɪəl] n ideal m // a ideal; ~**ist** n idealista m/f.
identical [aɪ'dɛntɪkl] a idéntico.
identification [aɪdɛntɪfɪ'keɪʃən] n identificación f; **means of** ~ documentos mpl personales.
identify [aɪ'dɛntɪfaɪ] vt identificar.
identikit picture [aɪ'dɛntɪkɪt-] n retrato-robot m.
identity [aɪ'dɛntɪtɪ] n identidad f; ~ **card** n carnet m de identidad.
ideology [aɪdɪ'ɔlədʒɪ] n ideología.
idiom ['ɪdɪəm] n modismo; (style of speaking) lenguaje m; ~**atic** [-'mætɪk] a idiomático.
idiosyncrasy [ɪdɪəu'sɪŋkrəsɪ] n idiosincrasia.
idiot ['ɪdɪət] n (gen) idiota m/f; (fool) tonto/a; ~**ic** [-'ɔtɪk] a idiota; tonto.
idle ['aɪdl] a (lazy) holgazán/ana; (unemployed) parado, desocupado; (talk) frívolo // vi (machine) marchar en vacío // vt: **to** ~ **away the time** malgastar el tiempo; ~**ness** n holgazanería; paro, desocupación f.
idol ['aɪdl] n ídolo; ~**ize** vt idolatrar.
idyllic [ɪ'dɪlɪk] a idílico.
i.e. abbr (= that is) esto es.
if [ɪf] conj si; ~ **necessary** si fuera necesario, si hiciese falta; ~ **I were you** yo en tu lugar; ~ **so/not** de ser así/si no; ~ **only I could!** ¡ojalá pudiera!; see also **as, even.**
igloo ['ɪglu:] n iglú m.
ignite [ɪg'naɪt] vt (set fire to) encender // vi encenderse.
ignition [ɪg'nɪʃən] n (AUT) encendido; **to switch on/off the** ~ arrancar/apagar el motor; ~ **key** n (AUT) llave f de contacto.
ignorance ['ɪgnərəns] n ignorancia.
ignorant ['ɪgnərənt] a ignorante; **to be** ~ **of** ignorar.
ignore [ɪg'nɔ:*] vt (person) no hacer caso de; (fact) pasar por alto.
ill [ɪl] a enfermo, malo // n mal m // ad mal; **to take** or **be taken** ~ caer or ponerse enfermo; ~**-advised** a (decision) imprudente; **he was** ~**-advised to go se** equivocaba al ir; ~**-at-ease** a incómodo.
I'll [aɪl] = **I will, I shall.**
illegal [ɪ'li:gl] a ilegal.
illegible [ɪ'lɛdʒɪbl] a ilegible.

illegitimate [ɪlɪ'dʒɪtɪmət] a ilegítimo.
ill-fated [ɪlfeɪtɪd] a malogrado.
ill feeling n rencor m.
illicit [ɪ'lɪsɪt] a ilícito.
illiterate [ɪ'lɪtərət] a analfabeto.
ill-mannered [ɪl'mænəd] a mal educado
illness ['ɪlnɪs] n enfermedad f.
ill-treat [ɪl'tri:t] vt maltratar.
illuminate [ɪ'lu:mɪneɪt] vt (room, street) iluminar, alumbrar; (subject) aclarar; **illumination** [-'neɪʃən] n alumbrado; **illuminations** npl iluminaciones fpl, luces fpl.
illusion [ɪ'lu:ʒən] n ilusión f; **to be under the** ~ **that...** hacerse ilusiones de que ....
illusory [ɪ'lu:sərɪ] a ilusorio.
illustrate ['ɪləstreɪt] vt ilustrar.
illustration [ɪlə'streɪʃən] n (example) ejemplo, ilustración f; (in book) lámina.
illustrious [ɪ'lʌstrɪəs] a ilustre.
ill will n rencor m.
I'm [aɪm] = **I am.**
image ['ɪmɪdʒ] n imagen f; ~**ry** [-ərɪ] n imágenes fpl.
imaginary [ɪ'mædʒɪnərɪ] a imaginario.
imagination [ɪmædʒɪ'neɪʃən] n imaginación f; (inventiveness) inventiva; (illusion) fantasía.
imaginative [ɪ'mædʒɪnətɪv] a imaginativo.
imagine [ɪ'mædʒɪn] vt imaginarse; (delude o.s.) hacerse la ilusión (de que).
imbalance [ɪm'bæləns] n desequilibrio.
imbecile ['ɪmbəsi:l] n imbécil m/f.
imitate ['ɪmɪteɪt] vt imitar; **imitation** [-'teɪʃən] n imitación f; (copy) copia; (pej) remedo.
immaculate [ɪ'mækjulət] a perfectamente limpio; (REL) inmaculado.
immaterial [ɪmə'tɪərɪəl] a incorpóreo; **it is** ~ **whether...** no importa si... .
immature [ɪmə'tjuə*] a (person) inmaduro; (of one's youth) joven.
immediate [ɪ'mi:dɪət] a inmediato; (pressing) urgente, apremiante; ~**ly** ad (at once) en seguida; ~**ly next to** muy junto a.
immense [ɪ'mɛns] a inmenso, enorme.
immerse [ɪ'mɔ:s] vt (submerge) sumergir; **to be** ~**d in** (fig) estar absorto en.
immersion heater [ɪ'mɔ:ʃən-] n (Brit) calentador m de inmersión.
immigrant ['ɪmɪgrənt] n inmigrante m/f.
immigrate ['ɪmɪgreɪt] vi inmigrar; **immigration** [-'greɪʃən] n inmigración f.
imminent ['ɪmɪnənt] a inminente.
immobile [ɪ'məubaɪl] a inmóvil.
immoral [ɪ'mɔrl] a inmoral.
immortal [ɪ'mɔ:tl] a inmortal.
immune [ɪ'mju:n] a: ~ **(to)** inmune (contra); **immunity** n (MED, of diplomat) inmunidad f.
immunize ['ɪmjunaɪz] vt inmunizar.
imp [ɪmp] n diablillo.
impact ['ɪmpækt] n (gen) impacto.

impair |ɪm'pɛə*| vt perjudicar.
impart |ɪm'paːt| vt comunicar.
impartial |ɪm'paːʃl| a imparcial.
impassable |ɪm'paːsəbl| a (barrier) infranqueable; (river, road) intransitable.
impasse |æm'paːs| n: to reach an ~ alcanzar un punto muerto.
impassive |ɪm'pæsɪv| a impasible.
impatience |ɪm'peɪʃəns| n impaciencia.
impatient |ɪm'peɪʃənt| a impaciente; to get or grow ~ impacientarse.
impeccable |ɪm'pɛkəbl| a impecable.
impede |ɪm'piːd| vt estorbar.
impediment |ɪm'pɛdɪmənt| n obstáculo, estorbo; (also: **speech** ~) defecto (del habla).
impending |ɪm'pɛndɪŋ| a inminente.
impenetrable |ɪm'pɛnɪtrəbl| a (gen) impenetrable; (unfathomable) insondable.
imperative |ɪm'pɛrətɪv| a (tone) imperioso; (necessary) imprescindible // n (LING) imperativo.
imperfect |ɪm'pəːfɪkt| a imperfecto; (goods etc) defectuoso; **~ion** |-'fɛkʃən| n (blemish) desperfecto; (fault) defecto.
imperial |ɪm'pɪərɪəl| a imperial; **~ism** n imperialismo.
impersonal |ɪm'pəːsənl| a impersonal.
impersonate |ɪm'pəːsəneɪt| vt hacerse pasar por.
impertinent |ɪm'pəːtɪnənt| a impertinente, insolente.
impervious |ɪm'pəːvɪəs| a impermeable; (fig): ~ to insensible a.
impetuous |ɪm'pɛtjuəs| a impetuoso.
impetus |'ɪmpɪtəs| n ímpetu m; (fig) impulso.
impinge |ɪm'pɪndʒ|: to ~ on vt fus (affect) afectar a.
implacable |ɪm'plækəbl| a implacable.
implement |'ɪmplɪmənt| n instrumento, herramienta // vt |'ɪmplɪmɛnt| hacer efectivo; (carry out) realizar.
implicate |'ɪmplɪkeɪt| vt (compromise) comprometer; (involve) enredar; **implication** |-'keɪʃən| n consecuencia.
implicit |ɪm'plɪsɪt| a (gen) implícito; (complete) absoluto.
implore |ɪm'plɔː*| vt (person) suplicar.
imply |ɪm'plaɪ| vt (involve) suponer; (hint) dar a entender que.
impolite |ɪmpə'laɪt| a mal educado.
import |ɪm'pɔːt| vt importar // n |'ɪmpɔːt| (COMM) importación f; (meaning) significado, sentido.
importance |ɪm'pɔːtəns| n importancia.
important |ɪm'pɔːtənt| a importante; it's not ~ no importa, no tiene importancia.
importer |ɪm'pɔːtə*| n importador(a) m/f.
impose |ɪm'pəuz| vt imponer // vi: to ~ on sb abusar de uno; **imposing** a imponente, impresionante.
imposition |ɪmpə'zɪʃn| n (of tax etc) imposición f; to be an ~ (on person) molestar.

impossible |ɪm'pɔsɪbl| a imposible; (person) insoportable.
impostor |ɪm'pɔstə*| n impostor(a) m/f.
impotent |'ɪmpətənt| a impotente.
impound |ɪm'paund| vt embargar.
impoverished |ɪm'pɔvərɪʃt| a necesitado; (land) agotado.
impracticable |ɪm'præktɪkəbl| a no factible, irrealizable.
impractical |ɪm'præktɪkl| a (person) poco práctico.
imprecise |ɪmprɪ'saɪs| a impreciso.
impregnable |ɪm'prɛgnəbl| a invulnerable; (castle) inexpugnable.
impregnate |'ɪmprɛgneɪt| vt impregnar; (BIOL) fecundar.
impress |ɪm'prɛs| vt impresionar; (mark) estampar // vi hacer buena impresión; to ~ sth on sb hacer entender algo a uno.
impression |ɪm'prɛʃən| n impresión f; (footprint etc) huella; (print run) edición f; to be under the ~ that tener la impresión de que; **~able** a impresionable; **~ist** n impresionista m/f.
impressive |ɪm'prɛsɪv| a impresionante.
imprint |'ɪmprɪnt| n (PUBLISHING) pie m de imprenta; (fig) sello.
imprison |ɪm'prɪzn| vt encarcelar; **~ment** n encarcelamiento; (term of ~) cárcel f.
improbable |ɪm'prɔbəbl| a improbable, inverosímil.
impromptu |ɪm'prɔmptjuː| a improvisado // ad de improviso.
improper |ɪm'prɔpə*| a (incorrect) impropio; (unseemly) indecoroso; (indecent) indecente.
improve |ɪm'pruːv| vt mejorar; (foreign language) perfeccionar // vi mejorarse; (pupils) hacer progresos; **~ment** n mejoramiento; perfección f; progreso.
improvise |'ɪmprəvaɪz| vt, vi improvisar.
imprudent |ɪm'pruːdnt| a imprudente.
impudent |'ɪmpjudnt| a descarado, insolente.
impulse |'ɪmpʌls| n impulso; to act on ~ obrar sin reflexión; **impulsive** |-'pʌlsɪv| a irreflexivo.
impunity |ɪm'pjuːnɪtɪ| n: with ~ impunemente.
impure |ɪm'pjuə*| a (adulterated) adulterado; (morally) impuro; **impurity** n (gen) impureza.
in |ɪn| ♦ prep 1 (indicating place, position, with place names) en; ~ the house/garden en (la) casa/el jardín; ~ here/there aquí/ahí or allí dentro; ~ London/England en Londres/Inglaterra
2 (indicating time) en; ~ spring en (la) primavera; ~ the afternoon por la tarde; at 4 o'clock ~ the afternoon a las 4 de la tarde; I did it ~ 3 hours/days lo hice en 3 horas/días; I'll see you ~ 2

weeks *or* ~ **2 weeks' time** te veré dentro de 2 semanas
3 (*indicating manner etc*) en; ~ **a loud/ soft voice** en voz alta/baja; ~ **pencil/ink** a lápiz/bolígrafo; **the boy ~ the blue shirt** el chico de la camisa azul
4 (*indicating circumstances*): ~ **the sun/shade/rain** al sol/a la sombra/bajo la lluvia; **a change ~ policy** un cambio de política
5 (*indicating mood, state*): ~ **tears** en lágrimas, llorando; ~ **anger/despair** enfadado(a)/desesperado(a); **to live ~ luxury** vivir lujosamente
6 (*with ratios, numbers*): **1 ~ 10 households, 1 household ~ 10** una de cada 10 familias; **20 pence ~ the pound** 20 peniques por libra; **they lined up ~ twos** se alinearon de dos en dos
7 (*referring to people, works*) en; entre; **the disease is common ~ children** la enfermedad es común entre los niños; ~ **(the works of) Dickens** en (las obras de) Dickens
8 (*indicating profession etc*): **to be ~ teaching** estar en la enseñanza
9 (*after superlative*) de; **the best pupil ~ the class** el/la mejor alumno/a de la clase
10 (*with present participle*): ~ **saying this** al decir esto
♦ *ad*: **to be ~** (*person: at home*) estar en casa; (*work*) estar; (*train, ship, plane*) haber llegado; (*in fashion*) estar de moda; **she'll be ~ later today** llegará más tarde hoy; **to ask sb ~** hacer pasar a uno; **to run/limp etc ~** entrar corriendo/cojeando *etc*
♦ *n*: **the ~s and outs** (*of proposal, situation etc*) los detalles
in., ins *abbr* = **inch(es)**.
inability |ɪnəˈbɪlɪtɪ| *n* incapacidad *f*.
inaccessible |ɪnəkˈsɛsɪbl| *a* inaccesible.
inaccurate |ɪnˈækjʊrət| *a* inexacto, incorrecto.
inactivity |ɪnækˈtɪvɪtɪ| *n* inactividad *f*.
inadequate |ɪnˈædɪkwət| *a* (*insufficient*) insuficiente; (*unsuitable*) inadecuado; (*person*) incapaz.
inadvertently |ɪnədˈvɜːtntlɪ| *ad* por descuido.
inadvisable |ɪnədˈvaɪzəbl| *a* poco aconsejable.
inane |ɪˈneɪn| *a* necio, fatuo.
inanimate |ɪnˈænɪmət| *a* inanimado.
inappropriate |ɪnəˈprəʊprɪət| *a* inadecuado.
inarticulate |ɪnɑːˈtɪkjʊlət| *a* (*person*) incapaz de expresarse; (*speech*) mal pronunciado.
inasmuch as |ɪnəzˈmʌtʃæz| *conj* puesto que, ya que.
inaudible |ɪnˈɔːdɪbl| *a* inaudible.
inaugural |ɪˈnɔːgjʊrəl| *a* (*speech*) de apertura.

inaugurate |ɪˈnɔːgjʊreɪt| *vt* inaugurar; **inauguration** |-ˈreɪʃən| *n* ceremonia de apertura.
in-between |ɪnbɪˈtwiːn| *a* intermedio.
inborn |ɪnˈbɔːn| *a* (*feeling*) innato.
inbred |ɪnˈbred| *a* innato; (*family*) engendrado por endogamia.
Inc. *abbr* (*US*) = **incorporated**.
incapable |ɪnˈkeɪpəbl| *a* incapaz.
incapacitate |ɪnkəˈpæsɪteɪt| *vt*: **to ~ sb** incapacitar a uno.
incapacity |ɪnkəˈpæsɪtɪ| *n* (*inability*) incapacidad *f*.
incarcerate |ɪnˈkɑːsəreɪt| *vt* encarcelar
incarnation |ɪnkɑːˈneɪʃən| *n* encarnación *f*.
incendiary |ɪnˈsendɪərɪ| *a* incendiario.
incense |ˈɪnsens| *n* incienso // *vt* |ɪnˈsens| (*anger*) indignar, encolerizar.
incentive |ɪnˈsentɪv| *n* incentivo, estímulo.
incessant |ɪnˈsesnt| *a* incesante, continuo; **~ly** *ad* constantemente.
incest |ˈɪnsest| *n* incesto.
inch |ɪntʃ| *n* pulgada; **to be within an ~ of** estar a dos dedos de; **he didn't give an ~** no dio concesión alguna; **to ~ forward** *vi* avanzar palmo a palmo.
incidence |ˈɪnsɪdns| *n* (*of crime, disease*) incidencia.
incident |ˈɪnsɪdnt| *n* incidente *m*; (*in book*) episodio.
incidental |ɪnsɪˈdentl| *a* circunstancial, accesorio; (*unplanned*) fortuito; ~ **to** relacionado con; ~ **music** ambientación *f* musical; **~ly** |-ˈdentəlɪ| *ad* (*by the way*) a propósito.
incinerator |ɪnˈsɪnəreɪtə*| *n* incinerador *m*.
incipient |ɪnˈsɪpɪənt| *a* incipiente.
incision |ɪnˈsɪʒən| *n* incisión *f*.
incisive |ɪnˈsaɪsɪv| *a* (*mind*) penetrante; (*remark etc*) incisivo.
incite |ɪnˈsaɪt| *vt* provocar.
inclination |ɪnklɪˈneɪʃən| *n* (*tendency*) tendencia, inclinación *f*.
incline |ˈɪnklaɪn| *n* pendiente *m*, cuesta // *vb* |ɪnˈklaɪn| *vt* (*slope*) inclinar; (*head*) poner de lado // *vi* inclinarse; **to be ~d to** (*tend*) ser propenso a; (*be willing*) estar dispuesto a.
include |ɪnˈkluːd| *vt* incluir, comprender; (*in letter*) adjuntar; **including** *prep* incluso, inclusive.
inclusion |ɪnˈkluːʒən| *n* inclusión *f*.
inclusive |ɪnˈkluːsɪv| *a* inclusivo // *ad* inclusive; ~ **of tax** incluidos los impuestos.
incognito |ɪnkɒgˈniːtəʊ| *ad* de incógnito.
incoherent |ɪnkəʊˈhɪərənt| *a* incoherente.
income |ˈɪŋkʌm| *n* (*personal*) ingresos *mpl*; (*from property etc*) renta; (*profit*) rédito; ~ **tax** *n* impuesto sobre la renta; ~ **tax return** *n* declaración *f* de renta.
incoming |ˈɪnkʌmɪŋ| *a*: ~ **flight** vuelo entrante.

incomparable [ɪnˈkɔmpərəbl] *a* incomparable, sin par.

incompatible [ɪnkəmˈpætɪbl] *a* incompatible.

incompetence [ɪnˈkɔmpɪtəns] *n* incompetencia.

incompetent [ɪnˈkɔmpɪtənt] *a* incompetente.

incomplete [ɪnkəmˈpliːt] *a* incompleto; (*unfinished*) sin terminar.

incomprehensible [ɪnkɔmprɪˈhɛnsɪbl] *a* incomprensible.

inconceivable [ɪnkənˈsiːvəbl] *a* inconcebible.

incongruous [ɪnˈkɔŋgruəs] *a* discordante.

inconsiderate [ɪnkənˈsɪdərət] *a* desconsiderado; **how ~ of him!** ¡qué falta de consideración (de su parte)!

inconsistency [ɪnkənˈsɪstənsɪ] *n* inconsecuencia.

inconsistent [ɪnkənˈsɪstnt] *a* inconsecuente; **~ with** (que) no concuerda con.

inconspicuous [ɪnkənˈspɪkjuəs] *a* (*discreet*) discreto; (*person*) que llama poca la atención.

inconvenience [ɪnkənˈviːnjəns] *n* (*gen*) inconvenientes *mpl*; (*trouble*) molestia, incomodidad *f* // *vt* incomodar.

inconvenient [ɪnkənˈviːnjənt] *a* incómodo, poco práctico; (*time, place*) inoportuno.

incorporate [ɪnˈkɔːpəreɪt] *vt* incorporar; (*contain*) comprender; (*add*) agregar; **~d** *a*: **~d company** (*US: abbr* Inc.) ≈ Sociedad *f* Anónima (S.A.).

incorrect [ɪnkəˈrɛkt] *a* incorrecto.

incorrigible [ɪnˈkɔrɪdʒəbl] *a* incorregible.

increase [ˈɪnkriːs] *n* aumento // *vi* [ɪnˈkriːs] aumentarse; (*grow*) crecer; (*price*) subir // *vt* aumentar; **increasing** [ɪnˈkriːsɪŋ] *a* (*number*) creciente, que va en aumento; **increasingly** [ɪnˈkriːsɪŋlɪ] *ad* de más en más, cada vez más.

incredible [ɪnˈkrɛdɪbl] *a* increíble.

incredulous [ɪnˈkrɛdjuləs] *a* incrédulo.

increment [ˈɪnkrɪmənt] *n* aumento, incremento.

incriminate [ɪnˈkrɪmɪneɪt] *vt* incriminar.

incubator [ˈɪnkjubeɪtə*] *n* incubadora.

incumbent [ɪnˈkʌmbənt] *n* titular *m/f* // *a*: **it is ~ on him to...** le incumbe... .

incur [ɪnˈkəː*] *vt* (*expenditure*) incurrir; (*loss*) sufrir.

incurable [ɪnˈkjuərəbl] *a* incurable.

indebted [ɪnˈdɛtɪd] *a*: **to be ~ to sb** estar agradecido a uno.

indecent [ɪnˈdiːsnt] *a* indecente; **~ assault** *n* (*Brit*) atentado contra el pudor; **~ exposure** *n* exhibicionismo.

indecisive [ɪndɪˈsaɪsɪv] *a* indeciso; (*discussion*) no resuelto, inconcluyente.

indeed [ɪnˈdiːd] *ad* efectivamente, en realidad; **yes ~!** ¡claro que sí!

indefinite [ɪnˈdɛfɪnɪt] *a* indefinido; (*un-certain*) incierto; **~ly** *ad* (*wait*) indefinidamente.

indelible [ɪnˈdɛlɪbl] *a* imborrable.

indemnify [ɪnˈdɛmnɪfaɪ] *vt* indemnizar, resarcir.

indemnity [ɪnˈdɛmnɪtɪ] *n* (*insurance*) indemnidad *f*; (*compensation*) indemnización *f*.

independence [ɪndɪˈpɛndns] *n* independencia.

independent [ɪndɪˈpɛndənt] *a* independiente; **to become ~** independizarse.

indestructible [ɪndɪsˈtrʌktəbl] *a* indestructible.

index [ˈɪndɛks] *n* (*pl*: **~es**: *in book*) índice *m*; (: *in library etc*) catálogo; (*pl*: **indices** [ˈɪndɪsiːz]: *ratio, sign*) exponente *m*; **~ card** *n* ficha; **~ finger** *n* índice *m*; **~-linked**, (*US*) **~ed** *a* vinculado al índice del coste de la vida.

India [ˈɪndɪə] *n* la India; **~n** *a*, *n* indio/a *m/f*; **Red ~n** piel roja *m/f*; **the ~n Ocean** *n* el Océano Índico.

indicate [ˈɪndɪkeɪt] *vt* indicar; **indication** [-ˈkeɪʃən] *n* indicio, señal *f*; **indicative** [ɪnˈdɪkətɪv] *a*: **to be indicative of** indicar // *n* (LING) indicativo; **indicator** *n* (*gen*) indicador *m*.

indices [ˈɪndɪsiːz] *pl of* **index**.

indict [ɪnˈdaɪt] *vt* acusar; **~ment** *n* acusación *f*.

indifference [ɪnˈdɪfrəns] *n* indiferencia.

indifferent [ɪnˈdɪfrənt] *a* indiferente; (*poor*) regular.

indigenous [ɪnˈdɪdʒɪnəs] *a* indígena.

indigestion [ɪndɪˈdʒɛstʃən] *n* indigestión *f*.

indignant [ɪnˈdɪgnənt] *a*: **to be ~ about sth** indignarse por algo.

indignity [ɪnˈdɪgnɪtɪ] *n* indignidad *f*.

indigo [ˈɪndɪgəu] *a* de color añil // *n* añil *m*.

indirect [ɪndɪˈrɛkt] *a* indirecto; **~ly** *ad* indirectamente.

indiscreet [ɪndɪˈskriːt] *a* indiscreto, imprudente.

indiscriminate [ɪndɪˈskrɪmɪnət] *a* indiscriminado.

indispensable [ɪndɪˈspɛnsəbl] *a* indispensable, imprescindible.

indisposed [ɪndɪˈspəuzd] *a* (*unwell*) indispuesto.

indisputable [ɪndɪˈspjuːtəbl] *a* incontestable.

individual [ɪndɪˈvɪdjuəl] *n* individuo // *a* individual; (*personal*) personal; (*for/of one only*) particular; **~ist** *n* individualista *m/f*; **~ity** [-ˈælɪtɪ] *n* individualidad *f*; **~ly** *ad* individualmente; particularmente.

indoctrinate [ɪnˈdɔktrɪneɪt] *vt* adoctrinar; **indoctrination** [-ˈneɪʃən] *n* adoctrinamiento.

indolent [ˈɪndələnt] *a* indolente, perezoso.

Indonesia [ɪndəuˈniːzɪə] *n* Indonesia.

indoor ['ɪndɔː*] a (swimming pool) cubierto; (plant) de interior; (sport) bajo cubierta; ~s [ɪn'dɔːz] ad dentro; (at home) en casa.

induce [ɪn'djuːs] vt inducir, persuadir; (bring about) producir; ~ment n (incentive) incentivo, aliciente m.

induction [ɪn'dʌkʃən] n (MED: of birth) inducción f; ~ course n (Brit) curso de inducción.

indulge [ɪn'dʌldʒ] vt (whim) satisfacer; (person) complacer; (child) mimar // vi: to ~ in darse el gusto de; ~nce n vicio; ~nt a indulgente.

industrial [ɪn'dʌstrɪəl] a industrial; ~ action n huelga; ~ estate n (Brit) polígono or zona (LAm) industrial; ~ist n industrial m/f; ~ize vt industrializar; ~ park n (US) = ~ estate.

industrious [ɪn'dʌstrɪəs] a (gen) trabajador(a); (student) aplicado.

industry ['ɪndəstrɪ] n industria; (diligence) aplicación f.

inebriated [ɪ'niːbrɪeɪtɪd] a borracho.

inedible [ɪn'edɪbl] a incomible; (plant etc) no comestible.

ineffective [ɪnɪ'fektɪv], **ineffectual** [ɪnɪ'fektʃuəl] a ineficaz, inútil.

inefficiency [ɪnɪ'fɪʃənsɪ] n ineficacia.

inefficient [ɪnɪ'fɪʃənt] a ineficaz, ineficiente.

inept [ɪ'nept] a incompetente.

inequality [ɪnɪ'kwɔlɪtɪ] n desigualdad f.

inert [ɪ'nɜːt] a inerte, inactivo; (immobile) inmóvil; ~ia [ɪ'nɜːʃə] n inercia; (laziness) pereza.

inescapable [ɪnɪ'skeɪpəbl] a ineludible.

inevitable [ɪn'evɪtəbl] a inevitable; (necessary) forzoso; **inevitably** ad inevitablemente.

inexcusable [ɪnɪks'kjuːzəbl] a imperdonable.

inexhaustible [ɪnɪg'zɔːstɪbl] a inagotable.

inexpensive [ɪnɪk'spensɪv] a económico.

inexperience [ɪnɪk'spɪərɪəns] n falta de experiencia; ~d a inexperto.

inextricably [ɪnɪks'trɪkəblɪ] ad indisolublemente.

infallible [ɪn'fælɪbl] a infalible.

infamous ['ɪnfəməs] a infame.

infancy ['ɪnfənsɪ] n infancia.

infant ['ɪnfənt] n niño/a; ~ile a infantil; (pej) aniñado; ~ school n (Brit) escuela de párvulos.

infantry ['ɪnfəntrɪ] n infantería.

infatuated [ɪn'fætjueɪtɪd] a: ~ with (in love) loco por.

infatuation [ɪnfætju'eɪʃən] n enamoramiento.

infect [ɪn'fekt] vt (wound) infectar; (person) contagiar; (fig: pej) corromper; ~ed with (illness) contagiado de; ~ion [ɪn'fekʃən] n infección f; (fig) contagio; ~ious [ɪn'fekʃəs] a contagioso; (also fig) infeccioso.

infer [ɪn'fɜː*] vt deducir, inferir; ~ence ['ɪnfərəns] n deducción f, inferencia.

inferior [ɪn'fɪərɪə*] a, n inferior m/f; ~ity [-rɪ'ɔrətɪ] n inferioridad f; ~ity complex n complejo de inferioridad.

inferno [ɪn'fɜːnəu] n (fire) hoguera.

infertile [ɪn'fɜːtaɪl] a estéril; (person) infecundo; **infertility** [-'tɪlɪtɪ] n esterilidad f; infecundidad f.

infested [ɪn'festɪd] a: ~ with plagado de.

in-fighting ['ɪnfaɪtɪŋ] n (fig) lucha(s) f(pl) interna(s).

infiltrate ['ɪnfɪltreɪt] vt (troops etc) infiltrar en // vi infiltrarse.

infinite ['ɪnfɪnɪt] a infinito.

infinitive [ɪn'fɪnɪtɪv] n infinitivo.

infinity [ɪn'fɪnɪtɪ] n (also MATH) infinito; (an ~) infinidad f.

infirm [ɪn'fɜːm] a enfermo, débil; ~ary n hospital m; ~ity n debilidad f; (illness) enfermedad f, achaque m.

inflamed [ɪn'fleɪmd] a: to become ~ inflamarse.

inflammable [ɪn'flæməbl] a (Brit) inflamable; (situation etc) explosivo.

inflammation [ɪnflə'meɪʃən] n inflamación f.

inflatable [ɪn'fleɪtəbl] a (ball, boat) inflable.

inflate [ɪn'fleɪt] vt (tyre, balloon) inflar; (fig) hinchar; **inflation** [ɪn'fleɪʃən] n (ECON) inflación f.

inflict [ɪn'flɪkt] vt: to ~ on infligir en; (tax etc) imponer a.

influence ['ɪnfluəns] n influencia // vt influir en, influenciar; under the ~ of alcohol en estado de embriaguez; **influential** [-'enʃl] a influyente.

influenza [ɪnflu'enzə] n gripe f.

influx ['ɪnflʌks] n afluencia.

inform [ɪn'fɔːm] vt: to ~ sb of sth informar a uno sobre or de algo; (warn) avisar a uno de algo; (communicate) comunicar algo a uno // vi: to ~ on sb delatar a uno.

informal [ɪn'fɔːml] a (manner, tone) desenfadado; (dress, interview, occasion) informal; ~ity [-'mælɪtɪ] n desenfado; falta de ceremonia.

informant [ɪn'fɔːmənt] n informante m/f.

information [ɪnfə'meɪʃən] n información f; (news) noticias fpl; (knowledge) conocimientos mpl; (LAW) delación f; a piece of ~ un dato; ~ office n información f.

informative [ɪn'fɔːmətɪv] a informativo.

informer [ɪn'fɔːmə*] n delator(a) m/f; (also: police ~) soplón/ona m/f.

infra-red [ɪnfrə'red] a infrarrojo.

infrastructure ['ɪnfrəstrʌktʃə*] n (of system etc, ECON) infraestructura.

infringe [ɪn'frɪndʒ] vt infringir, violar // vi: to ~ on abusar de; ~ment n infracción f; (of rights) usurpación f; (SPORT)

falta.
infuriating [ɪnˈfjuərɪeɪtɪŋ] a: I find it ~ me saca de quicio.
infusion [ɪnˈfjuːʒən] n (tea etc) infusión f.
ingenious [ɪnˈdʒiːnjəs] a ingenioso; **ingenuity** [-dʒɪˈnjuːɪtɪ] n ingeniosidad f.
ingenuous [ɪnˈdʒɛnjuəs] a ingenuo.
ingot [ˈɪŋgət] n lingote m, barra.
ingrained [ɪnˈgreɪnd] a arraigado.
ingratiate [ɪnˈgreɪʃɪeɪt] vt: to ~ o.s. with congraciarse con.
ingredient [ɪnˈgriːdɪənt] n ingrediente m.
inhabit [ɪnˈhæbɪt] vt vivir en; (occupy) ocupar; ~**ant** n habitante m/f.
inhale [ɪnˈheɪl] vt inhalar // vi (in smoking) tragar.
inherent [ɪnˈhɪərənt] a: ~ in or to inherente a.
inherit [ɪnˈhɛrɪt] vt heredar; ~**ance** n herencia; (fig) patrimonio.
inhibit [ɪnˈhɪbɪt] vt inhibir, impedir; to ~ sb from doing sth impedir a uno hacer algo; ~**ed** a cohibido; ~**ion** [-ˈbɪʃən] n cohibición f.
inhospitable [ɪnhɔsˈpɪtəbl] a (person) inhospitalario; (place) inhóspito.
inhuman [ɪnˈhjuːmən] a inhumano.
iniquity [ɪˈnɪkwɪtɪ] n iniquidad f; (injustice) injusticia.
initial [ɪˈnɪʃl] a inicial; (first) primero // n inicial f // vt firmar con las iniciales; ~**s** npl iniciales fpl; (abbreviation) siglas fpl; ~**ly** ad al principio.
initiate [ɪˈnɪʃɪeɪt] vt (start) iniciar; to ~ proceedings against sb (LAW) entablar proceso contra uno; **initiation** [-ˈeɪʃən] n (into secret etc) iniciación f; (beginning) comienzo.
initiative [ɪˈnɪʃətɪv] n iniciativa.
inject [ɪnˈdʒɛkt] vt inyectar; ~**ion** [ɪnˈdʒɛkʃən] n inyección f.
injunction [ɪnˈdʒʌŋkʃən] n interdicto.
injure [ˈɪndʒə*] vt herir; (hurt) lastimar; (fig: reputation etc) perjudicar; ~**d** a (person, arm) herido; **injury** n herida, lesión f; (wrong) perjuicio, daño; **injury time** n (SPORT) descuento.
injustice [ɪnˈdʒʌstɪs] n injusticia.
ink [ɪŋk] n tinta.
inkling [ˈɪŋklɪŋ] n sospecha; (idea) idea.
inlaid [ˈɪnleɪd] a (wood) taraceado; (tiles) entarimado.
inland [ˈɪnlənd] a interior; (town) del interior // ad [ɪnˈlænd] tierra adentro; ~ **Revenue** n (Brit) departamento de impuestos; ≈ Hacienda (Sp).
in-laws [ˈɪnlɔːz] npl suegros mpl.
inlet [ˈɪnlɛt] n (GEO) ensenada, cala; (TECH) admisión f, entrada.
inmate [ˈɪnmeɪt] n (in prison) preso/a; presidiario/a; (in asylum) internado/a.
inn [ɪn] n posada, mesón m.
innate [ɪˈneɪt] a innato.
inner [ˈɪnə*] a interior, interno; ~ **city** n

barrios deprimidos del centro de una ciudad; ~ **tube** n (of tyre) cámara or llanta (LAm).
innings [ˈɪnɪŋz] n (CRICKET) entrada, turno.
innocence [ˈɪnəsns] n inocencia.
innocent [ˈɪnəsnt] a inocente.
innocuous [ɪˈnɔkjuəs] a inocuo.
innovation [ɪnəʊˈveɪʃən] n novedad f.
innuendo [ɪnjuˈɛndəʊ] pl ~**es** n indirecta.
inoculation [ɪnɔkjuˈleɪʃən] n inoculación f.
inopportune [ɪnˈɔpətjuːn] a inoportuno.
inordinately [ɪˈnɔːdɪnətlɪ] ad desmesuradamente.
in-patient [ˈɪnpeɪʃənt] n paciente m/f interno/a.
input [ˈɪnput] n (ELEC) entrada; (COMPUT) entrada de datos.
inquest [ˈɪnkwɛst] n (coroner's) encuesta judicial.
inquire [ɪnˈkwaɪə*] vi preguntar // vt: to ~ whether preguntar si; to ~ about (person) preguntar por; (fact) informarse de; to ~ into vt fus investigar, indagar; **inquiry** n pregunta; (LAW) investigación f, pesquisa; (commission) comisión f investigadora; **inquiry office** n (Brit) oficina de informaciones.
inquisitive [ɪnˈkwɪzɪtɪv] a (mind) inquisitivo; (person) fisgón/ona.
inroad [ˈɪnrəʊd] n incursión f; (fig) invasión f.
insane [ɪnˈseɪn] a loco; (MED) demente.
insanity [ɪnˈsænɪtɪ] n demencia, locura.
insatiable [ɪnˈseɪʃəbl] a insaciable.
inscribe [ɪnˈskraɪb] vt inscribir; (book etc): to ~ (to sb) dedicar (a uno).
inscription [ɪnˈskrɪpʃən] n (gen) inscripción f; (in book) dedicatoria.
inscrutable [ɪnˈskruːtəbl] a inescrutable, insondable.
insect [ˈɪnsɛkt] n insecto; ~**icide** [ɪnˈsɛktɪsaɪd] n insecticida m.
insecure [ɪnsɪˈkjuə*] a inseguro.
insemination [ɪnsɛmɪˈneɪʃn] n : **artificial** ~ inseminación f artificial.
insensible [ɪnˈsɛnsɪbl] a inconsciente; (unconscious) sin conocimiento.
insensitive [ɪnˈsɛnsɪtɪv] a insensible.
inseparable [ɪnˈsɛprəbl] a inseparable.
insert [ɪnˈsəːt] vt (into sth) introducir; // n [ˈɪnsəːt] encarte m; ~**ion** [ɪnˈsəːʃən] n inserción f.
in-service [ɪnˈsəːvɪs] a (training, course) a cargo de la empresa.
inshore [ɪnˈʃɔː*] a : ~ **fishing** pesca f costera // ad (fish) a lo largo de la costa; (move) hacia la orilla.
inside [ˈɪnsaɪd] n interior m; (lining) forro // a interior, interno; (information) confidencial // ad (within) (por) dentro; (with movement) hacia dentro; (fam: in prison) en la cárcel // prep dentro de;

(*of time*): ~ **10 minutes** en menos de 10 minutos; ~s *npl* (*col*) tripas *fpl*; ~ **forward** *n* (*SPORT*) interior *m*; ~ **lane** *n* (*AUT*: *in Britain*) carril *m* izquierdo; ~ **out** *ad* (*turn*) al revés; (*know*) a fondo.

insidious [ɪnˈsɪdɪəs] *a* insidioso.

insight [ˈɪnsaɪt] *n* perspicacia.

insignia [ɪnˈsɪgnɪə] *npl* insignias *fpl*.

insignificant [ɪnsɪgˈnɪfɪknt] *a* insignificante.

insincere [ɪnsɪnˈsɪə*] *a* poco sincero.

insinuate [ɪnˈsɪnjueɪt] *vt* insinuar.

insipid [ɪnˈsɪpɪd] *a* soso, insulso.

insist [ɪnˈsɪst] *vi* insistir; **to ~ on doing** empeñarse en hacer; **to ~ that** insistir en que; (*claim*) exigir que; **~ence** *n* insistencia; (*stubbornness*) empeño; **~ent** *a* insistente.

insole [ˈɪnsəul] *n* plantilla.

insolent [ˈɪnsələnt] *a* insolente, descarado.

insoluble [ɪnˈsɔljubl] *a* insoluble.

insomnia [ɪnˈsɔmnɪə] *n* insomnio.

inspect [ɪnˈspɛkt] *vt* inspeccionar, examinar; (*troops*) pasar revista a; **~ion** [ɪnˈspɛkʃən] *n* inspección *f*, examen *m*; **~or** *n* inspector(a) *m/f*; (*Brit*: *on buses, trains*) revisor(a) *m/f*.

inspiration [ɪnspəˈreɪʃən] *n* inspiración *f*; **inspire** [ɪnˈspaɪə*] *vt* inspirar.

instability [ɪnstəˈbɪlɪtɪ] *n* inestabilidad *f*.

install [ɪnˈstɔːl] *vt* instalar; **~ation** [ɪnstəˈleɪʃən] *n* instalación *f*.

instalment, (*US*) **installment** [ɪnˈstɔːlmənt] *n* plazo; (*of story*) entrega; (*of TV serial etc*) capítulo; **in ~s** (*pay, receive*) a plazos; ~ **plan** *n* (*US*) compra a plazos.

instance [ˈɪnstəns] *n* ejemplo, caso; **for ~** por ejemplo; **in the first ~** en primer lugar.

instant [ˈɪnstənt] *n* instante *m*, momento // *a* inmediato; (*coffee*) instantáneo.

instantly [ˈɪnstəntlɪ] *ad* en seguida.

instead [ɪnˈstɛd] *ad* en cambio; ~ **of** en lugar de, en vez de.

instep [ˈɪnstɛp] *n* empeine *m*.

instil [ɪnˈstɪl] *vt*: **to ~ into** inculcar a.

instinct [ˈɪnstɪŋkt] *n* instinto; **~ive** [ɪnˈstɪŋktɪv] *a* instintivo.

institute [ˈɪnstɪtjuːt] *n* instituto; (*professional body*) colegio // *vt* (*begin*) iniciar, empezar; (*proceedings*) entablar.

institution [ɪnstɪˈtjuːʃən] *n* institución *f*; (*MED*: *home*) asilo; (: *asylum*) manicomio.

instruct [ɪnˈstrʌkt] *vt*: **to ~ sb in sth** instruir a uno en *or* sobre algo; **to ~ sb to do sth** dar instrucciones a uno de hacer algo; **~ion** [ɪnˈstrʌkʃən] *n* (*teaching*) instrucción *f*; **~ions** *npl* órdenes *fpl*; **~ions** (*for use*) modo *sg* de empleo; **~ive** *a* instructivo; **~or** *n* instructor(a) *m/f*.

instrument [ˈɪnstrəmənt] *n* instrumento; ~ **panel** *n* tablero (de instrumentos);

~**al** [-ˈmɛntl] *a* (*MUS*) instrumental; **to be ~al in** ser (el) artífice de.

insubordinate [ɪnsəˈbɔːdɪnət] *a* insubordinado.

insufferable [ɪnˈsʌfrəbl] *a* insoportable.

insufficient [ɪnsəˈfɪʃənt] *a* insuficiente.

insular [ˈɪnsjulə*] *a* insular, (*person*) estrecho de miras.

insulate [ˈɪnsjuleɪt] *vt* aislar; **insulating tape** *n* cinta aislante; **insulation** [-ˈleɪʃən] *n* aislamiento.

insulin [ˈɪnsjulɪn] *n* insulina.

insult [ˈɪnsʌlt] *n* insulto; (*offence*) ofensa // *vt* [ɪnˈsʌlt] insultar; ofender; **~ing** *a* insultante; ofensivo.

insuperable [ɪnˈsjuːprəbl] *a* insuperable.

insurance [ɪnˈʃuərəns] *n* seguro; **fire/life ~** seguro contra incendios/sobre la vida; ~ **agent** *n* agente *m/f* de seguros; ~ **policy** *n* póliza (de seguros).

insure [ɪnˈʃuə*] *vt* asegurar.

intact [ɪnˈtækt] *a* íntegro; (*untouched*) intacto.

intake [ˈɪnteɪk] *n* (*TECH*) entrada, toma; (: *pipe*) tubo de admisión; (*of food*) ingestión *f*; (*Brit SCOL*): **an ~ of 200 a year** 200 matriculados al año.

integral [ˈɪntɪgrəl] *a* (*whole*) íntegro; (*part*) integrante.

integrate [ˈɪntɪgreɪt] *vt* integrar // *vi* integrarse.

integrity [ɪnˈtɛgrɪtɪ] *n* honradez *f*, rectitud *f*.

intellect [ˈɪntɪlɛkt] *n* intelecto; **~ual** [-ˈlɛktjuəl] *a, n* intelectual *m/f*.

intelligence [ɪnˈtɛlɪdʒəns] *n* inteligencia; **I~ Service** *n* Servicio de Inteligencia.

intelligent [ɪnˈtɛlɪdʒənt] *a* inteligente.

intelligentsia [ɪntɛlɪˈdʒɛntsɪə] *n* intelectualidad *f*.

intelligible [ɪnˈtɛlɪdʒɪbl] *a* inteligible, comprensible.

intend [ɪnˈtɛnd] *vt* (*gift etc*): **to ~ sth for** destinar algo a; **to ~ to do sth** tener intención de *or* pensar hacer algo; **~ed** *a* (*effect*) deseado.

intense [ɪnˈtɛns] *a* (*gen*) intenso; **~ly** *ad* intensamente; (*very*) sumamente.

intensify [ɪnˈtɛnsɪfaɪ] *vt* intensificar; (*increase*) aumentar.

intensity [ɪnˈtɛnsɪtɪ] *n* (*gen*) intensidad *f*.

intensive [ɪnˈtɛnsɪv] *a* intensivo; ~ **care unit** *n* unidad de vigilancia intensiva.

intent [ɪnˈtɛnt] *n* propósito // *a* (*absorbed*) absorto; (*attentive*) atento; **to all ~s and purposes** prácticamente; **to be ~ on doing sth** estar resuelto a hacer algo.

intention [ɪnˈtɛnʃən] *n* intención *f*, propósito; **~al** *a* deliberado; **~ally** *ad* a propósito.

intently [ɪnˈtɛntlɪ] *ad* atentamente.

interact [ɪntərˈækt] *vi* influirse mutuamente; **~ion** [-ˈækʃən] *n* interacción *f*, acción *f* recíproca.

intercede |intə'si:d| *vi*: to ~ (with) interceder (con).

intercept |intə'sɛpt| *vt* interceptar; *(stop)* detener.

interchange |'intətʃeindʒ| *n* intercambio; *(on motorway)* intersección *f* // *vi* |intə'tʃeindʒ| intercambiar; canjear; ~able *a* intercambiable.

intercom |'intəkɒm| *n* interfono.

intercourse |'intəkɔ:s| *n (sexual)* relaciones *fpl* sexuales; *(social)* trato.

interest |'intrist| *n (also COMM)* interés *m* // *vt* interesar; to be ~ed in interesarse por; ~ing *a* interesante; ~ rate *n* tipo *or* tasa de interés.

interface |'intəfeis| *n (COMPUT)* junción *f*.

interfere |intə'fiə*| *vi*: to ~ in *(quarrel, other people's business)* entrometerse en; to ~ with *(hinder)* estorbar; *(damage)* estropear; *(radio)* interferir con.

interference |intə'fiərəns| *n (gen)* intromisión *f*; *(RADIO, TV)* interferencia.

interim |'intərim| *n*: in the ~ en el ínterin // *a* provisional.

interior |in'tiəriə*| *n* interior *m* // *a* interior; ~ designer *n* interiorista *m/f*.

interlock |intə'lɒk| *vi* entrelazarse; *(wheels etc)* endentarse.

interloper |'intələupə*| *n* intruso/a.

interlude |'intəlu:d| *n* intervalo; *(rest)* descanso; *(THEATRE)* intermedio.

intermediary |intə'mi:diəri| *n* intermediario/a.

intermediate |intə'mi:diət| *a* intermedio.

interminable |in'tə:minəbl| *a* inacabable.

intermission |intə'miʃən| *n (THEATRE)* descanso.

intermittent |intə'mitnt| *a* intermitente.

intern |in'tə:n| *vt* internar; *(enclose)* encerrar // *n* |'intə:n| *(US)* interno/a.

internal |in'tə:nl| *a* interno, interior; ~ly *ad* interiormente; 'not to be taken ~ly' 'uso externo'; I~ **Revenue Service** (IRS) *n (US)* departamento de impuestos; ≈ Hacienda *(Sp)*.

international |intə'næʃənl| *a* internacional; ~ *(game)* partido internacional; ~ *(player)* jugador(a) *m/f* internacional.

interplay |'intəplei| *n* interacción *f*.

interpret |in'tə:prit| *vt* interpretar; *(translate)* traducir; *(understand)* entender // *vi* hacer de intérprete; ~ation |-'teiʃən| *n* interpretación *f*; traducción *f*; entendimiento; ~er *n* intérprete *m/f*.

interrelated |intəri'leitid| *a* interrelacionado.

interrogate |in'tɛrəugeit| *vt* interrogar; **interrogation** |-'geiʃən| *n* interrogatorio; **interrogative** |intə'rɒgətiv| *a* interrogativo.

interrupt |intə'rʌpt| *vt, vi* interrumpir; ~ion |-'rʌpʃən| *n* interrupción *f*.

intersect |intə'sɛkt| *vt* cruzar // *vi*

(roads) cruzarse; ~ion |-'sɛkʃən| *n* intersección *f*; *(of roads)* cruce *m*.

intersperse |intə'spə:s| *vt*: to ~ with salpicar de.

intertwine |intə'twain| *vt* entrelazar // *vi* entrelazarse.

interval |'intəvl| *n* intervalo; *(Brit: THEATRE, SPORT)* descanso; at ~s a ratos, de vez en cuando.

intervene |intə'vi:n| *vi* intervenir; *(take part)* participar; *(occur)* sobrevenir; **intervention** |-'venʃən| *n* intervención *f*.

interview |'intəvju:| *n (RADIO, TV etc)* entrevista // *vt* entrevistarse con; ~er *n* entrevistador(a) *m/f*.

intestine |in'tɛstin| *n*: large/small ~ intestino grueso/delgado.

intimacy |'intiməsi| *n* intimidad *f*; *(relations)* relaciones *fpl* íntimas.

intimate |'intimət| *a* íntimo; *(friendship)* estrecho; *(knowledge)* profundo // *vt* |'intimeit| *(announce)* dar a entender.

intimidate |in'timideit| *vt* intimidar, amedrentar.

into |'intu:| *prep (gen)* en; *(towards)* a; *(inside)* hacia el interior de; ~ 3 pieces/ French in 3 pedazos/al francés.

intolerable |in'tɒlərəbl| *a* intolerable, insoportable.

intolerance |in'tɒlərəns| *n* intolerancia.

intolerant |in'tɒlərənt| *a*: ~ of intolerante con *or* para.

intonation |intəu'neiʃən| *n* entonación *f*.

intoxicate |in'tɒksikeit| *vt* embriagar; ~d *a* embriagado; **intoxication** |-'keiʃən| *n* embriaguez *f*.

intractable |in'træktəbl| *a (person)* intratable; *(problem)* espinoso.

intransitive |in'trænsitiv| *a* intransitivo.

intravenous |intrə'vi:nəs| *a* intravenoso.

in-tray |'intrei| *n* bandeja de entrada.

intricate |'intrikət| *a* intrincado; *(plot, problem)* complejo.

intrigue |in'tri:g| *n* intriga // *vt* fascinar // *vi* andar en intrigas; **intriguing** *a* fascinante.

intrinsic |in'trinsik| *a* intrínseco.

introduce |intrə'dju:s| *vt* introducir, meter; to ~ sb (to sb) presentar uno (a otro); to ~ sb to *(pastime, technique)* introducir a uno a; **introduction** |-'dʌkʃən| *n* introducción *f*; *(of person)* presentación *f*; **introductory** |-'dʌktəri| *a* introductorio.

introvert |'intrəvə:t| *a, n* introvertido/a *m/f*.

intrude |in'tru:d| *vi (person)* entrometerse; to ~ on estorbar; ~r *n* intruso/a; **intrusion** |-ʒən| *n* invasión *f*.

intuition |intju:'iʃən| *n* intuición *f*.

inundate |'inʌndeit| *vt*: to ~ with inundar de.

invade |in'veid| *vt* invadir; ~r *n* invasor(a) *m/f*.

invalid |'invəlid| *n* minusválido/a // *a*

[ɪn'vælɪd] (*not valid*) inválido, nulo.
invaluable [ɪn'væljuəbl] *a* inestimable.
invariably [ɪn'vɛərɪəblɪ] *ad* sin excepción.
invasion [ɪn'veɪʒən] *n* invasión *f*.
invent [ɪn'vɛnt] *vt* inventar; **~ion**
[ɪn'vɛnʃən] *n* invento; (*inventiveness*) inventiva; (*lie*) ficción *f*, mentira; **~ive** *a* inventivo; **~iveness** *n* ingenio, inventiva; **~or** *n* inventor(a) *m/f*.
inventory ['ɪnvəntrɪ] *n* inventario.
invert [ɪn'vɜːt] *vt* invertir; **~ed commas** *npl* (*Brit*) comillas *fpl*.
invertebrate [ɪn'vɜːtɪbrət] *n* invertebrado.
invest [ɪn'vɛst] *vt, vi* invertir.
investigate [ɪn'vɛstɪgeɪt] *vt* investigar; (*study*) estudiar, examinar; **investigation** [-'geɪʃən] *n* investigación *f*, pesquisa; examen *m*; **investigator** *n* investigador(a) *m/f*.
investment [ɪn'vɛstmənt] *n* inversión *f*.
investor [ɪn'vɛstə*] *n* inversionista *m/f*.
inveterate [ɪn'vɛtərət] *a* empedernido.
invidious [ɪn'vɪdɪəs] *a* odioso.
invigilate [ɪn'vɪdʒɪleɪt] *vt, vi* (*in exam*) vigilar.
invigorating [ɪn'vɪgəreɪtɪŋ] *a* vigorizante.
invincible [ɪn'vɪnsɪbl] *a* invencible.
invisible [ɪn'vɪzɪbl] *a* invisible; **~ ink** *n* tinta simpática.
invitation [ɪnvɪ'teɪʃən] *n* invitación *f*.
invite [ɪn'vaɪt] *vt* invitar; (*opinions etc*) solicitar, pedir; (*trouble*) buscarse; **inviting** *a* atractivo; (*look*) provocativo; (*food*) apetitoso.
invoice ['ɪnvɔɪs] *n* factura // *vt* facturar.
invoke [ɪn'vəʊk] *vt* invocar; (*aid*) pedir; (*law*) recurrir a.
involuntary [ɪn'vɒləntrɪ] *a* involuntario.
involve [ɪn'vɒlv] *vt* (*entail*) suponer, implicar; **to ~ sb (in)** comprometer a uno (con); **~d** *a* complicado; **~ment** *n* (*gen*) enredo; (*obligation*) compromiso; (*difficulty*) apuro.
inward ['ɪnwəd] *a* (*movement*) interior, interno; (*thought, feeling*) íntimo; **~(s)** *ad* hacia dentro.
I/O *abbr* (*COMPUT* = *input/output*) entrada/salida.
iodine ['aɪəʊdiːn] *n* yodo.
iota [aɪ'əʊtə] *n* (*fig*) jota, ápice *m*.
IOU *n abbr* (= *I owe you*) pagaré *m*.
IQ *n abbr* (= *intelligence quotient*) cociente *m* intelectual.
IRA *n abbr* (= *Irish Republican Army*) IRA m.
Iran [ɪ'rɑːn] *n* Irán *m*; **~ian** [ɪ'reɪnɪən] *a, n* iraní *m/f*.
Iraq [ɪ'rɑːk] *n* Irak; **~i** *a, n* iraquí *m/f*.
irascible [ɪ'ræsɪbl] *a* irascible.
irate [aɪ'reɪt] *a* enojado, airado.
Ireland ['aɪələnd] *n* Irlanda.
iris ['aɪrɪs], *pl* **~es** *n* (*ANAT*) iris *m*; (*BOT*) lirio.

Irish ['aɪrɪʃ] *a* irlandés/esa // *npl*: **the ~** los irlandeses; **~man/woman** *n* irlandés/esa *m/f*; **the ~ Sea** *n* el Mar de Irlanda.
irk [ɜːk] *vt* fastidiar; **~some** *a* fastidioso.
iron ['aɪən] *n* hierro; (*for clothes*) plancha // *a* de hierro // *vt* (*clothes*) planchar; **to ~ out** *vt* (*crease*) quitar; (*fig*) allanar; **the I~ Curtain** *n* el Telón de Acero.
ironic(al) [aɪ'rɒnɪk(l)] *a* irónico.
ironing ['aɪənɪŋ] *n* (*act*) planchado; (*clothes: ironed*) ropa planchada; (: *to be ironed*) ropa por planchar; **~ board** *n* tabla de planchar.
ironmonger ['aɪənmʌŋgə*] *n* (*Brit*) ferretero/a; **~'s (shop)** *n* ferretería, quincallería.
iron ore *n* mineral *m* de hierro.
irony ['aɪrənɪ] *n* ironía.
irrational [ɪ'ræʃənl] *a* irracional.
irreconcilable [ɪrekən'saɪləbl] *a* (*idea*) incompatible; (*enemies*) irreconciliable.
irregular [ɪ'regjulə*] *a* irregular; (*surface*) desigual.
irrelevant [ɪ'reləvənt] *a* fuera de lugar, inoportuno.
irreplaceable [ɪrɪ'pleɪsəbl] *a* irremplazable.
irrepressible [ɪrɪ'presəbl] *a* incontenible.
irresistible [ɪrɪ'zɪstɪbl] *a* irresistible.
irresolute [ɪ'rezəluːt] *a* indeciso.
irrespective [ɪrɪ'spektɪv]: **~ of** *prep* sin tener en cuenta, no importa.
irresponsible [ɪrɪ'spɒnsɪbl] *a* (*act*) irresponsable; (*person*) poco serio.
irrigate ['ɪrɪgeɪt] *vt* regar; **irrigation** [-'geɪʃən] *n* riego.
irritable ['ɪrɪtəbl] *a* (*person: temperament*) de (mal) carácter; (: *mood*) de mal humor.
irritate ['ɪrɪteɪt] *vt* fastidiar; (*MED*) picar; **irritating** *a* fastidioso; **irritation** [-'teɪʃən] *n* fastidio; picazón *f*, picor *m*.
IRS *n abbr* (*US*) = **Internal Revenue Service**.
is [ɪz] *vb see* **be**.
Islam ['ɪzlɑːm] *n* Islam *m*.
island ['aɪlənd] *n* isla; (*also*: **traffic ~**) isleta; **~er** *n* isleño/a.
isle [aɪl] *n* isla.
isn't ['ɪznt] = **is not**.
isolate ['aɪsəleɪt] *vt* aislar; **~d** *a* aislado; **isolation** [-'leɪʃən] *n* aislamiento.
Israel ['ɪzreɪl] *n* Israel *m*; **~i** [ɪz'reɪlɪ] *a, n* israelí *m/f*.
issue ['ɪsjuː] *n* cuestión *f*, asunto; (*outcome*) resultado; (*of banknotes etc*) emisión *f*; (*of newspaper etc*) número; (*offspring*) sucesión *f*, descendencia // *vt* (*rations, equipment*) distribuir, repartir; (*orders*) dar; (*certificate, passport*) expedir; (*decree*) promulgar; (*magazine*) publicar; (*cheques*) extender; (*bank-*

notes, stamps) emitir; **at ~ en cuestión;
to take ~ with sb (over)** estar en desacuerdo con uno (sobre).

isthmus ['ismǝs] *n* istmo.

it [ɪt] *pron* **1** (*specific: subject: not generally translated*) él/ella; (: *direct object*) lo, la; (: *indirect object*) le; (*after
prep*) él/ella; (*abstract concept*) ello;
~'s on the table está en la mesa; **I can't
find ~** no lo (*or* la) encuentro; **give ~ to
me** dámelo (*or* dámela); **I spoke to him
about ~** le hablé del asunto; **what did
you learn from ~?** ¿qué aprendiste de él
(*or* ella)?; **did you go to ~?** (*party, concert etc*) ¿fuiste?
2 (*impersonal*): **~'s raining** llueve, está
lloviendo; **~'s 6 o'clock/the 10th of August** son las 6/es el 10 de agosto; **how far
is ~?** — **~'s 10 miles/2 hours on the train**
¿a qué distancia está? — a 10 millas/2
horas en tren; **who is ~?** — **~'s me**
¿quién es? — soy yo.

Italian [ɪ'tæljǝn] *a* italiano // *n* italiano/a;
(*LING*) italiano.

italic [ɪ'tælɪk] *a* cursivo; **~s** *npl* cursiva
sg.

Italy ['ɪtǝlɪ] *n* Italia.

itch [ɪtʃ] *n* picazón *f*; (*fig*) prurito // *vi*
(*person*) sentir *or* tener comezón; (*part
of body*) picar; **to be ~ing to do sth** rabiar por hacer algo; **~y** *a*: **to be ~y** =
to ~.

it'd ['ɪtd] = **it would, it had.**

item ['aɪtǝm] *n* artículo; (*on agenda*)
asunto (a tratar); (*in programme*) número; (*also:* **news ~**) noticia; **~ize** *vt*
detallar.

itinerant [ɪ'tɪnǝrǝnt] *a* ambulante.

itinerary [aɪ'tɪnǝrǝrɪ] *n* itinerario.

it'll ['ɪtl] = **it will, it shall.**

its [ɪts] *a* su.

it's [ɪts] = **it is, it has.**

itself [ɪt'self] *pron* (*reflexive*) sí mismo/a;
(*emphatic*) él mismo/ella misma.

ITV *n abbr* (*Brit:* = *Independent Television*) *cadena de televisión comercial
independiente del Estado.*

I.U.D. *n abbr* (= *intra-uterine device*)
DIU *m*.

I've [aɪv] = **I have.**

ivory ['aɪvǝrɪ] *n* marfil *m*.

ivy ['aɪvɪ] *n* hiedra.

J

jab [dʒæb] *vt*: **to ~ sth into sth** clavar
algo en algo // *n* (*MED: col*) pinchazo.

jabber ['dʒæbǝ*] *vt, vi* farfullar.

jack [dʒæk] *n* (*AUT*) gato; (*BOWLS*) boliche *m*; (*CARDS*) sota; **to ~ up** *vt* (*AUT*)
levantar con el gato.

jackal ['dʒækɔ:l] *n* (*ZOOL*) chacal *m*.

jackdaw ['dʒækdɔ:] *n* grajo.

jacket ['dʒækɪt] *n* chaqueta, americana,

saco (*LAm*); (*of boiler etc*) camisa; (*of
book*) sobrecubierta.

jack-knife ['dʒæknaɪf] *vi* colear.

jack plug *n* (*ELEC*) enchufe *m* de clavija.

jackpot ['dʒækpɔt] *n* premio gordo.

jaded ['dʒeɪdɪd] *a* (*tired*) cansado; (*fed-
up*) hastiado.

jagged ['dʒægɪd] *a* dentado.

jail [dʒeɪl] *n* cárcel *f* // *vt* encarcelar;
~break *n* fuga *or* evasión *f* (de la cárcel); **~er** *n* carcelero/a.

jam [dʒæm] *n* mermelada; (*also:* **traffic
~**) embotellamiento; (*difficulty*) apuro //
vt (*passage etc*) obstruir; (*mechanism,
drawer etc*) atascar; (*RADIO*) interferir
// *vi* atascarse, trabarse; **to ~ sth into
sth** meter algo a la fuerza en algo.

Jamaica [dʒǝ'meɪkǝ] *n* Jamaica.

jangle ['dʒæŋgl] *vi* sonar (de manera)
discordante.

janitor ['dʒænɪtǝ*] *n* (*caretaker*) portero,
conserje *m*.

January ['dʒænjuǝrɪ] *n* enero.

Japan [dʒǝ'pæn] *n* (el) Japón; **~ese**
[dʒæpǝ'ni:z] *a* japonés/esa // *n, pl inv*
japonés/esa *m/f*; (*LING*) japonés *m*.

jar [dʒɑ:*] *n* (*glass: large*) jarra; (:
small) tarro // *vi* (*sound*) chirriar;
(*colours*) desentonar.

jargon ['dʒɑ:gǝn] *n* jerga.

jasmin(e) ['dʒæzmɪn] *n* jazmín *m*.

jaundice ['dʒɔ:ndɪs] *n* ictericia; **~d** *a*
(*fig: embittered*) amargado; (: *disillusioned*) desilusionado.

jaunt [dʒɔ:nt] *n* excursión *f*; **~y** *a* alegre.

javelin ['dʒævlɪn] *n* jabalina.

jaw [dʒɔ:] *n* mandíbula.

jay [dʒeɪ] *n* (*ZOOL*) arrendajo.

jaywalker ['dʒeɪwɔ:kǝ*] *n* peatón/ona *m/f*
imprudente.

jazz [dʒæz] *n* jazz *m*; **to ~ up** *vt* (*liven
up*) animar, avivar.

jealous ['dʒelǝs] *a* celoso; (*envious*) envidioso; **to be ~** tener celos; tener envidia;
~y *n* celos *mpl*; envidia.

jeans [dʒi:nz] *npl* (pantalones *mpl*) vaqueros *mpl or* tejanos *mpl*.

jeep [dʒi:p] *n* jeep *m*.

jeer [dʒɪǝ*] *vi*: **to ~ (at)** (*boo*) abuchear; (*mock*) mofarse (de).

jelly ['dʒelɪ] *n* jalea, gelatina; **~fish** *n*
medusa.

jeopardize ['dʒepǝdaɪz] *vt* arriesgar, poner en peligro.

jeopardy ['dʒepǝdɪ] *n*: **to be in ~** estar
en peligro.

jerk [dʒǝ:k] *n* (*jolt*) sacudida; (*wrench*)
tirón *m* // *vt* dar una sacudida a; tirar
bruscamente de // *vi* (*vehicle*) traquetear.

jerkin ['dʒǝ:kɪn] *n* chaleco.

jerky ['dʒǝ:kɪ] *a* espasmódico.

jersey ['dʒǝ:zɪ] *n* jersey *m*.

jest [dʒɛst] n broma.
Jesus ['dʒiːzəs] n Jesús m.
jet [dʒɛt] n (of gas, liquid) chorro; (AVIAT) avión m a reacción; **~-black** a negro como el azabache; **~ engine** n motor m a reacción; **~ lag** n desorientación f después de un largo vuelo.
jettison ['dʒɛtɪsn] vt desechar.
jetty ['dʒɛtɪ] n muelle m, embarcadero.
Jew [dʒuː] n judío.
jewel ['dʒuːəl] n joya; (in watch) rubí m; **~ler** n joyero/a; **~ler's (shop)**, (US) **~ry store** n joyería; (US) **~ery**, **~lery** n joyas fpl, alhajas fpl.
Jewess ['dʒuːɪs] n judía.
Jewish ['dʒuːɪʃ] a judío.
jibe [dʒaɪb] n mofa.
jiffy ['dʒɪfɪ] n (col): **in a ~** en un santiamén.
jig [dʒɪg] n jiga.
jigsaw ['dʒɪgsɔː] n (also: **~ puzzle**) rompecabezas m inv.
jilt [dʒɪlt] vt dejar plantado a.
jingle ['dʒɪŋgl] n (advert) musiquilla // vi tintinear.
jinx [dʒɪŋks] n: **there's a ~ on it** está gafado.
jitters ['dʒɪtəz] npl (col): **to get the ~** ponerse nervioso.
job [dʒɔb] n trabajo; (task) tarea; (duty) deber m; (post) empleo; **it's a good ~ that...** menos mal que...; **just the ~!** ¡estupendo!; **~ centre** n (Brit) oficina estatal de colocaciones; **~less** a sin trabajo.
jockey ['dʒɔkɪ] n jockey m/f // vi: **to ~ for position** maniobrar para conseguir una posición.
jocular ['dʒɔkjulə*] a (humorous) gracioso; (merry) alegre.
jog [dʒɔg] vt empujar (ligeramente) // vi (run) hacer footing; **to ~ along** ir tirando; **to ~ sb's memory** refrescar la memoria a uno; **~ging** n footing m.
join [dʒɔɪn] vt (things) juntar, unir; (become member of: club) hacerse socio de; (POL: party) afiliarse a; (meet: people) reunirse con // vi (roads) empalmar; (rivers) confluir // in juntura; **to ~ in** vi tomar parte, participar // vt fus tomar parte o participar en; **to ~ up** vi unirse; (MIL) alistarse.
joiner ['dʒɔɪnə*] n carpintero/a; **~y** n carpintería.
joint [dʒɔɪnt] n (TECH) junta, unión f; (ANAT) articulación f; (Brit CULIN) pieza de carne (para asar); (col: place) garito // a (common) común; (combined) combinado; (committee) mixto; **~ account** (with bank etc) cuenta común; **~ly** ad en común; conjuntamente.
joist [dʒɔɪst] n viga.
joke [dʒəuk] n chiste m; (also: **practical ~**) broma // vi bromear; **to play a ~ on** gastar una broma a; **~r** n chistoso/a,

bromista m/f; (CARDS) comodín m.
jolly ['dʒɔlɪ] a (merry) alegre; (enjoyable) divertido // ad (col) muy, terriblemente.
jolt [dʒəult] n (shake) sacudida; (blow) golpe m; (shock) susto // vt sacudir; asustar.
jostle ['dʒɔsl] vt dar empellones a, codear.
jot [dʒɔt] n: **not one ~** ni jota, ni pizca; **to ~ down** vt apuntar; **~ter** n (Brit) bloc m.
journal ['dʒəːnl] n (paper) periódico; (magazine) revista; (diary) diario; **~ism** n periodismo; **~ist** n periodista m/f, reportero/a.
journey ['dʒəːnɪ] n viaje m; (distance covered) trayecto // vi viajar.
jovial ['dʒəuvɪəl] a risueño.
joy [dʒɔɪ] n alegría; **~ful**, **~ous** a alegre; **~ ride** n (illegal) paseo en coche robado; **~ stick** n (AVIAT) palanca de mando; (COMPUT) palanca de control.
J.P. n abbr = **Justice of the Peace**.
Jr abbr = **junior**.
jubilant ['dʒuːbɪlnt] a jubiloso.
jubilee ['dʒuːbɪliː] n aniversario.
judge [dʒʌdʒ] n juez m/f // vt juzgar; (estimate) considerar; **judg(e)ment** n juicio; (punishment) sentencia, fallo.
judiciary [dʒuː'dɪʃɪərɪ] n poder m judicial.
judicious [dʒuː'dɪʃəs] a juicioso.
judo ['dʒuːdəu] n judo.
jug [dʒʌg] n jarro.
juggernaut ['dʒʌgənɔːt] n (Brit: huge truck) camionazo.
juggle ['dʒʌgl] vi hacer juegos malabares; **~r** n malabarista m/f.
Jugoslav ['juːgəuslɑːv] etc = **Yugoslav** etc.
juice [dʒuːs] n zumo, jugo (esp LAm); **juicy** a jugoso.
jukebox ['dʒuːkbɔks] n tocadiscos m inv tragaperras.
July [dʒuː'laɪ] n julio.
jumble ['dʒʌmbl] n revoltijo // vt (also: **~ up**: mix up) revolver; (: disarrange) mezclar; **~ sale** n (Brit) venta de objetos usados con fines benéficos.
jumbo (jet) ['dʒʌmbəu-] n jumbo.
jump [dʒʌmp] vi saltar, dar saltos; (start) asustarse, sobresaltarse; (increase) aumentar // vt saltar // n salto; aumento; **to ~ the queue** (Brit) colarse.
jumper ['dʒʌmpə*] n (Brit: pullover) suéter m, jersey m; (US: dress) mandil m; **~ cables** npl (US) = **jump leads**.
jump leads npl (Brit) cables mpl puente de batería.
jumpy ['dʒʌmpɪ] a nervioso.
Jun. abbr = **junior**.
junction ['dʒʌŋkʃən] n (Brit: of roads) cruce m; (RAIL) empalme m.

juncture [ˈdʒʌŋktʃəˀ] *n*: at this ~ en este momento, en esta coyuntura.

June [dʒuːn] *n* junio.

jungle [ˈdʒʌŋgl] *n* selva, jungla.

junior [ˈdʒuːnɪəˀ] *a* (*in age*) menor, más joven; (*competition*) juvenil; (*position*) subalterno // *n* menor *m/f*, joven *m/f*; he's ~ to me es menor que yo; ~ **school** *n* (*Brit*) escuela primaria.

junk [dʒʌŋk] *n* (*cheap goods*) baratijas *fpl*; (*lumber*) trastos *mpl* viejos; (*rubbish*) basura; ~ **food** *n* alimentos preparados y envasados de escaso valor nutritivo; ~ **shop** *n* tienda de objetos usados.

Junr *abbr* = **junior**.

jurisdiction [dʒuərɪsˈdɪkʃən] *n* jurisdicción *f*.

juror [ˈdʒuərəˀ] *n* jurado.

jury [ˈdʒuərɪ] *n* jurado.

just [dʒʌst] *a* justo // *ad* (*exactly*) exactamente; (*only*) sólo, solamente; he's ~ done it/left acaba de hacerlo/irse; ~ **right** perfecto; ~ **two o'clock** las dos en punto; she's ~ **as clever as you** (ella) es tan clever como tú; ~ **as well that...** menos mal que...; ~ **as he was leaving** es el momento en que se marchaba; ~ **before/enough** justo antes/lo suficiente; ~ **here** aquí mismo; he ~ **missed** ha fallado por poco; ~ **listen to this** escucha esto un momento.

justice [ˈdʒʌstɪs] *n* justicia; **J~ of the Peace (J.P.)** *n* juez *m* de paz.

justifiable [dʒʌstɪˈfaɪəbl] *a* justificable.

justify [ˈdʒʌstɪfaɪ] *vt* justificar; (*text*) alinear.

justly [ˈdʒʌstlɪ] *ad* (*gen*) justamente; (*with reason*) con razón.

jut [dʒʌt] *vi* (*also*: ~ **out**) sobresalir.

juvenile [ˈdʒuːvənaɪl] *a* juvenil; (*court*) de menores // *n* joven *m/f*, menor *m* de edad.

juxtapose [ˈdʒʌkstəpəuz] *vt* yuxtaponer.

K

K *abbr* (= *one thousand*) mil; (= *kilobyte*) kilobyte *m*, kilocteto.

kaleidoscope [kəˈlaɪdəskəup] *n* calidoscopio.

Kampuchea [kæmpuˈtʃɪə] *n* Kampuchea.

kangaroo [kæŋgəˈruː] *n* canguro.

karate [kəˈrɑːtɪ] *n* karate *m*.

kebab [kəˈbæb] *n* pincho moruno.

keel [kiːl] *n* quilla; **on an even ~** (*fig*) en equilibrio.

keen [kiːn] *a* (*interest, desire*) grande, vivo; (*eye, intelligence*) agudo; (*competition*) intenso; (*edge*) afilado; (*Brit*: *eager*) entusiasta; **to be ~ to do** *or* **on doing sth** tener muchas ganas de hacer algo; **to be ~ on sth/sb** interesarse por algo/uno.

keep [kiːp] *vb* (*pt, pp* **kept**) *vt* (*retain, preserve*) guardar; (*hold back*) quedarse con; (*shop*) ser propietario de; (*feed: family etc*) mantener; (*promise*) cumplir; (*chickens, bees etc*) criar // *vi* (*food*) conservarse; (*remain*) seguir, continuar // *n* (*of castle*) torreón *m*; (*food etc*) comida, subsistencia; (*col*): **for ~s** para siempre; **to ~ doing sth** seguir haciendo algo; **to ~ sb from doing sth** impedir a uno hacer algo; **to ~ sth from happening** impedir que algo ocurra; **to ~ sb happy** tener a uno contento; **to ~ a place tidy** mantener un lugar limpio; **to ~ sth to o.s.** guardar algo para sí mismo; **to ~ sth (back) from sb** ocultar algo a uno; **to ~ time** (*clock*) mantener la hora exacta; **to ~ on** *vi* seguir, continuar; **to ~ out** *vi* (*stay out*) permanecer fuera; '~ **out**' prohibida la entrada; **to ~ up** *vt* mantener, conservar // *vi* no retrasarse; **to ~ up with** (*pace*) ir al paso de; (*level*) mantenerse a la altura de; ~**er** *n* guardián/ana *m/f*; ~**fit** *n* gimnasia (para mantenerse en forma); ~**ing** *n* (*care*) cuidado; **in ~ing with** de acuerdo con; ~**sake** *n* recuerdo.

keg [kɛg] *n* barrilete *m*, barril *m*.

kennel [ˈkɛnl] *n* perrera; ~**s** *npl* perreras *fpl*.

Kenya [ˈkɛnjə] *n* Kenia; ~**n** *a, n* keniano/a *m/f*.

kept [kɛpt] *pt, pp* of **keep**.

kerb [kəːb] *n* (*Brit*) bordillo.

kernel [ˈkəːnl] *n* (*nut*) fruta; (*fig*) meollo.

kerosene [ˈkɛrəsiːn] *n* keroseno.

ketchup [ˈkɛtʃəp] *n* salsa de tomate, catsup *m*.

kettle [ˈkɛtl] *n* hervidor *m*, olla; ~ **drum** *n* (*MUS*) timbal *m*.

key [kiː] *n* (*gen*) llave *f*; (*MUS*) tono; (*of piano, typewriter*) tecla // *vt* (*also*: ~ **in**) teclear; ~**board** *n* teclado; ~**ed up** *a* (*person*) nervioso; ~**hole** *n* ojo (de la cerradura); ~**note** *n* (*MUS*) tónica; ~**ring** *n* llavero.

khaki [ˈkɑːkɪ] *n* caqui.

kick [kɪk] *vt* (*person*) dar una patada a; (*ball*) dar un puntapié a // *vi* (*horse*) dar coces // *n* patada; puntapié *m*; (*of rifle*) culetazo; (*thrill*): he does it for ~**s** lo hace por pura diversión; **to ~ off** *vi* (*SPORT*) hacer el saque inicial.

kid [kɪd] *n* (*col: child*) chiquillo/a; (*animal*) cabrito; (*leather*) cabritilla // *vi* (*col*) bromear.

kidnap [ˈkɪdnæp] *vt* secuestrar; ~**per** *n* secuestrador(a) *m/f*; ~**ping** *n* secuestro.

kidney [ˈkɪdnɪ] *n* riñón *m*.

kill [kɪl] *vt* matar; (*murder*) asesinar; (*fig: story*) suprimir; (: *rumour*) acabar con; **to be ~ed (by a bullet)** ser muerto (por una bala) // *n* matanza; ~**er** *n* asesino/a; ~**ing** *n* (*one*) asesinato; (*several*) matanza; ~**joy** *n* (*Brit*) aguafiestas m/f inv.

kiln |kıln| n horno.

kilo |'ki:ləu| n kilo; **~byte** n (COMPUT) kilobyte m, kilooctecto; **~gram(me)** |'kıləugræm| n kilo, kilogramo; **~metre**, (US) **~meter** |'kıləmi:tə*| n kilómetro; **~watt** |'kıləuwɔt| n kilovatio.

kilt |kılt| n falda escocesa.

kin |kın| n parientes mpl.

kind |kaınd| a (treatment) bueno, cariñoso; (person, act, word) amable, atento // n clase f, especie f; (species) género; in ~ (COMM) en especie; a ~ of una especie de; to be two of a ~ ser tal para cual.

kindergarten |'kındəga:tn| n jardín m de infantes.

kind-hearted |kaınd'ha:tıd| a bondadoso, de buen corazón.

kindle |'kındl| vt encender.

kindly |'kaındlı| a bondadoso; (gentle) cariñoso // ad bondadosamente, amablemente; will you ~... sea usted tan amable de... .

kindness |'kaındnıs| n bondad f, amabilidad f.

kindred |'kındrıd| a: ~ spirits almas fpl gemelas.

kinetic |kı'netık| a cinético.

king |kıŋ| n rey m; **~dom** n reino; **~fisher** n martín m pescador; **~-size** a de tamaño gigante.

kinky |'kıŋkı| a (pej) perverso.

kiosk |'ki:ɔsk| n quiosco; (Brit TEL) cabina.

kipper |'kıpə*| n arenque m ahumado.

kiss |kıs| n beso // vt besar; to ~ (each other) besarse.

kit |kıt| n avíos mpl; (equipment) equipo; (set of tools etc) (caja de) herramientas fpl; (assembly ~) juego de armar.

kitchen |'kıtʃın| n cocina; ~ **sink** n fregadero.

kite |kaıt| n (toy) cometa.

kith |kıθ| n: ~ **and kin** parientes mpl y allegados.

kitten |'kıtn| n gatito/a.

kitty |'kıtı| n (pool of money) fondo común; (CARDS) puesta.

km abbr (= kilometre) km.

knack |næk| n: to have the ~ of doing sth tener el don de hacer algo.

knapsack |'næpsæk| n mochila.

knead |ni:d| vt amasar.

knee |ni:| n rodilla; **~cap** n rótula.

kneel |ni:l|, pt, pp **knelt** vi (also: ~ **down**) arrodillarse.

knell |nel| n toque m de difuntos.

knelt |nelt| pt, pp of **kneel**.

knew |nju:| pt of **know**.

knickers |'nıkəz| npl (Brit) bragas fpl.

knife |naıf|, pl **knives** n cuchillo // vt acuchillar.

knight |naıt| n caballero; (CHESS) caballo; **~hood** n (title): to get a **~hood** re-

cibir el título de Sir.

knit |nıt| vt tejer, tricotar; (brows) fruncir // vi tejer, tricotar; (bones) soldarse; to ~ **together** vt (fig) unir, juntar; **~ting** n labor f de punto; **~ting machine** n máquina de tricotar; **~ting needle**, (US) ~ **pin** n aguja de tejer; **~wear** n prendas fpl de punto.

knives |naıvz| pl of **knife**.

knob |nɔb| n (of door) tirador m; (of stick) puño; a ~ of butter (Brit) un pedazo de mantequilla.

knock |nɔk| vt (strike) golpear; (bump into) chocar contra; (fig: col) criticar // vi (at door etc): to ~ at/on llamar a // n golpe m; (on door) llamada; to ~ **down** vt (pedestrian) atropellar; to ~ **off** vi (col: finish) salir del trabajo // vt (col: steal) birlar; to ~ **out** vt dejar sin sentido; (BOXING) poner fuera de combate, dejar K.O.; to ~ **over** vt (object) tirar; (person) atropellar; **~er** n (on door) aldaba; **~-kneed** a patizambo; **~out** n (BOXING) K.O. m, knockout m.

knot |nɔt| n (gen) nudo // vt anudar; **~ty** a (fig) complicado.

know |nəu|, pt **knew**, pp **known** vt (gen) saber; (person, author, place) conocer; to ~ **how to do** saber como hacer; to ~ **how to swim** saber nadar; to ~ **about** or of sb/sth saber de uno/algo; **~all** sabelotodo m/f; **~-how** n conocimientos mpl; **~ing** a (look) de complicidad; **~ingly** ad (purposely) adrede; (smile, look) con complicidad.

knowledge |'nɔlıdʒ| n (gen) conocimiento; (learning) saber m, conocimientos mpl; **~able** a: **~able about** enterado de.

known |nəun| pp of **know**.

knuckle |'nʌkl| n nudillo.

K.O. n abbr = **knockout**.

Koran |kɔ'ra:n| n Corán m.

Korea |kə'rıə| n Corea.

kosher |'kəuʃə*| a autorizado por la ley judía.

L

l. abbr = **litre**.

lab |læb| n abbr = **laboratory**.

label |'leıbl| n etiqueta; (brand: of record) sello (discográfico) // vt poner etiqueta a.

laboratory |lə'bɔrətərı| n laboratorio.

laborious |lə'bɔ:rıəs| a penoso.

labour, (US) **labor** |'leıbə*| n (task) trabajo; (~ force) mano f de obra; (MED) parto // vi: to ~ (at) trabajar (en) // vt insistir en; **in** ~ (MED) de parto; **L~, the L~ party** (Brit) el partido laborista, los laboristas mpl; **~ed** a (breathing) fatigoso; (style) pesado; **~er** n peón m; (on farm) peón m; (day **~er**) jornalero.

labyrinth ['læbɪrɪnθ] n laberinto.

lace |leɪs| n encaje m; (of shoe etc) cordón m // vt (shoes: also: ~ up) atarse (los zapatos).

lack |læk| n (absence) falta; (scarcity) escasez f // vt faltarle a uno, carecer de; **through** or **for ~ of** por falta de; **to be ~ing** faltar, no haber.

lackadaisical |lækə'deɪzɪkl| a (careless) descuidado; (indifferent) indiferente.

lacquer ['lækə*] n laca.

lad |læd| n muchacho, chico; (in stable etc) mozo.

ladder ['lædə*] n escalera (de mano); (Brit: in tights) carrera // vt (Brit: tights) hacer una carrera en.

laden ['leɪdn] a: ~ (with) cargado (de).

ladle ['leɪdl] n cucharón m.

lady ['leɪdɪ] n señora; (distinguished, noble) dama; **young ~** señorita; **the ladies' (room)** los servicios de señoras; **~bird**, (US) **~bug** n mariquita; **~-in-waiting** n dama de honor; **~like** a fino; **L~ship** n: **your L~ship** su Señoría.

lag |læg| vi (also: ~ **behind**) retrasarse, quedarse atrás // vt (pipes) revestir.

lager ['lɑːgə*] n cerveza (rubia).

lagoon |lə'guːn| n laguna.

laid |leɪd| pt, pp of **lay**; ~ **back** a (col) relajado.

lain |leɪn| pp of **lie**.

lair |leə*| n guarida.

laity ['leɪtɪ] n laicado.

lake |leɪk| n lago.

lamb |læm| n cordero; (meat) carne f de cordero; ~ **chop** n chuleta de cordero; **~swool** n lana de cordero.

lame |leɪm| a cojo; (excuse) poco convincente.

lament |lə'mɛnt| vt lamentarse de.

laminated ['læmɪneɪtɪd] a laminado.

lamp |læmp| n lámpara.

lampoon |læm'puːn| vt satirizar.

lamp: **~post** n (Brit) (poste m de) farol m; **~shade** n pantalla.

lance |lɑːns| n lanza // vt (MED) abrir con lanceta; ~ **corporal** n (Brit) soldado de primera clase.

land |lænd| n tierra; (country) país m; (piece of ~) terreno; (estate) tierras fpl, finca; (AGR) campo // vi (from ship) desembarcar; (AVIAT) aterrizar; (fig: fall) caer, terminar // vt (obtain) conseguir; (passengers, goods) desembarcar; **to ~ up** in/at ir a parar a/en; **~ing** n desembarco; aterrizaje m; (of staircase) rellano; **~ing stage** n (Brit) desembarcadero; **~ing strip** n pista de aterrizaje; **~lady** n (of boarding house) patrona; (owner) dueña; **~lord** n propietario; (of pub etc) patrón m; **~mark** n lugar m conocido; **to be a ~mark** (fig) hacer época; **~owner** n terrateniente m/f.

landscape ['lænskeɪp] n paisaje m.

landslide ['lændslaɪd] n (GEO) corrimiento de tierras; (fig: POL) victoria arrolladora.

lane |leɪn| n (in country) camino; (in town) callejón m; (AUT) carril m; (in race) calle f; (for air or sea traffic) ruta.

language ['læŋgwɪdʒ] n lenguaje m; (national tongue) idioma m, lengua; **bad ~** palabrotas fpl; ~ **laboratory** n laboratorio de idiomas.

languid ['læŋgwɪd] a lánguido.

languish ['læŋgwɪʃ] vi languidecer.

lank |læŋk| a (hair) lacio.

lanky ['læŋkɪ] a larguirucho.

lantern ['læntn] n linterna, farol m.

lap |læp| n (of track) vuelta; (of body): **to sit on sb's ~** sentarse en las rodillas de uno // vt (also: ~ **up**) lamer // vi (waves) chapotear.

lapel |lə'pɛl| n solapa.

Lapland ['læplænd] n Laponia.

lapse |læps| n error m, fallo; (moral) desliz m // vi (expire) caducar; (morally) cometer un desliz; (time) pasar, transcurrir; **to ~ into bad habits** caer en malos hábitos; ~ **of time** lapso, período.

larceny ['lɑːsənɪ] n latrocinio.

lard |lɑːd| n manteca (de cerdo).

larder ['lɑːdə*] n despensa.

large |lɑːdʒ| a grande; **at ~** (free) en libertad; (generally) en general; **~ly** ad en gran parte; **~-scale** a (map) en gran escala; (fig) importante.

largesse |lɑː'ʒɛs| n generosidad f.

lark |lɑːk| n (bird) alondra; (joke) broma; **to ~ about** vi bromear, hacer el tonto.

laryngitis |lærɪn'dʒaɪtɪs| n laringitis f.

larynx ['lærɪŋks| n laringe f.

laser ['leɪzə*] n láser m; ~ **printer** n impresora (por) láser.

lash |læʃ| n latigazo; (punishment) azote m; (also: eyelash) pestaña // vt azotar; (tie) atar; **to ~ out** vi (col: spend) gastar a la loca; **to ~ out at** or **against sb** lanzar invectivas contra uno.

lass |læs| n chica.

lasso |læ'suː| n lazo.

last |lɑːst| a (gen) último; (final) último, final // ad por último // vi (endure) durar; (continue) continuar, seguir; ~ **night** anoche; ~ **week** la semana pasada; **at ~** por fin; **but one** penúltimo; **~-ditch** a (attempt) último, desesperado; **~ing** a duradero; **~ly** ad por último, finalmente; **~-minute** a de última hora.

latch |lætʃ| n picaporte m, pestillo.

late |leɪt| a (not on time) tarde, atrasado; (towards end of period, life) tardío; (hour) avanzado; (dead) fallecido // ad tarde; (behind time, schedule) con retraso; **of ~** últimamente; **in ~ May** hacia fines de mayo; **the ~ Mr X** el difunto Sr X; **~comer** n recién llegado/a; **~ly** ad últimamente.

later ['leɪtə*] *a* (*date etc*) posterior; (*version etc*) más reciente // *ad* más tarde, después.

lateral ['lætərl] *a* lateral.

latest ['leɪtɪst] *a* último; **at the ~** a más tardar.

lathe [leɪð] *n* torno.

lather ['lɑːðə*] *n* espuma (de jabón) // *vt* enjabonar.

Latin ['lætɪn] *n* latín *m* // *a* latino; **~ America** *n* América latina; **~-American** *a* latinoamericano.

latitude ['lætɪtjuːd] *n* latitud *f*.

latter ['lætə*] *a* último; (*of two*) segundo // *n*: **the ~** el último, éste; **~ly** *ad* últimamente.

lattice ['lætɪs] *n* enrejado.

laudable ['lɔːdəbl] *a* loable.

laugh [lɑːf] *n* risa; (*loud*) carcajada // *vi* reír(se); **to ~ at** *vt fus* reírse de; **to ~ off** *vt* tomar algo a risa; **~able** *a* ridículo; **~ing stock** *n*: **the ~ing stock of** el hazmerreír de; **~ter** *n* risa.

launch [lɔːntʃ] *n* (*boat*) lancha; *see also* **~ing** // *vt* (*ship, rocket, plan*) lanzar; **~ing** *n* (*of rocket etc*) lanzamiento; (*inauguration*) estreno; **~(ing) pad** *n* plataforma de lanzamiento.

launder ['lɔːndə*] *vt* lavar.

launderette [lɔːn'drɛt], (*US*) **laundromat** ['lɔːdrəmæt] *n* lavandería (automática).

laundry ['lɔːndrɪ] *n* lavandería; (*clothes*) ropa sucia; **to do the ~** hacer la colada.

laureate ['lɔːrɪət] *a see* **poet**.

lavatory ['lævətərɪ] *n* wáter *m*; **lavatories** *npl* servicios *mpl*, aseos *mpl*, sanitarios *mpl* (*LAm*).

lavender ['lævəndə*] *n* lavanda.

lavish ['lævɪʃ] *a* abundante; (*giving freely*): **~ with** pródigo en // *vt*: **to ~ sth on sb** colmar a uno de algo.

law [lɔː] *n* ley *f*; (*study*) derecho; (*of game*) regla; **~-abiding** *a* respetuoso de la ley; **~ and order** *n* orden *m* público; **~ court** *n* tribunal *m* (de justicia); **~ful** *a* legítimo, lícito; **~fully** *ad* legalmente.

lawn [lɔːn] *n* césped *m*; **~mower** *n* cortacésped *m*; **~ tennis** *n* tenis *m* sobre hierba.

law school *n* facultad *f* de derecho.

lawsuit ['lɔːsuːt] *n* pleito.

lawyer ['lɔːjə*] *n* abogado/a; (*for sales, wills etc*) notario/a.

lax [læks] *a* (*discipline*) relajado; (*person*) negligente al hacer.

laxative ['læksətɪv] *n* laxante *m*.

laxity ['læksɪtɪ] *n* flojedad *f*; (*moral*) relajamiento; (*negligence*) negligencia.

lay [leɪ] *pt of* **lie** // *a* laico; (*not expert*) lego // *vt* (*pt, pp* **laid**) (*place*) colocar; (*eggs, table*) poner; (*trap*) tender; **to ~ aside** *or* **by** *vt* dejar a un lado; **to ~ down** *vt* (*pen etc*) dejar; (*arms*) ren-

dir; (*policy*) asentar; **to ~ down the law** imponer las normas; **to ~ off** *vt* (*workers*) despedir; **to ~ on** *vt* (*water, gas*) instalar; (*meal, facilities*) proveer; **to ~ out** *vt* (*plan*) trazar; (*display*) disponer; (*spend*) gastar; **to ~ up** *vt* (*store*) guardar; (*ship*) desarmar; (*subj: illness*) obligar a guardar cama; **~about** *n* vago/a; **~-by** *n* (*Brit AUT*) área de aparcamiento.

layer ['leɪə*] *n* capa.

layette [leɪ'ɛt] *n* ajuar *m* (de niño).

layman ['leɪmən] *n* lego.

layout ['leɪaut] *n* (*design*) plan *m*, trazado; (*disposition*) disposición *f*, (*PRESS*) composición *f*.

laze [leɪz] *vi* holgazanear.

laziness ['leɪzɪnɪs] *n* pereza.

lazy ['leɪzɪ] *a* perezoso, vago.

lb. *abbr* = **pound** (*weight*).

lead [liːd] *n* (*front position*) delantera; (*distance, time ahead*) ventaja; (*clue*) pista; (*ELEC*) cable *m*; (*for dog*) correa; (*THEATRE*) papel *m* principal; [led] (*metal*) plomo; (*in pencil*) mina // (*vb: pt, pp* led) *vt* conducir; (*life*) llevar; (*be leader of*) dirigir; (*SPORT*) ir en cabeza de // *vi* ir primero; **to be in the ~** (*SPORT*) llevar la delantera; (*fig*) ir a la cabeza; **to ~ astray** llevar por mal camino; **to ~ away** *vt* llevar; **to ~ back** *vt* (*person, route*) llevar de vuelta; **to ~ on** *vt* (*tease*) engañar; **to ~ on to** (*induce*) incitar a; **to ~ to** *vt fus* producir, provocar; **to ~ up to** *vt fus* conducir a.

leaden ['lɛdn] *a* (*sky, sea*) plomizo; (*heavy: footsteps*) pesado.

leader ['liːdə*] *n* jefe/a *m/f*, líder *m*; (*of union etc*) dirigente *m/f*; (*guide*) guía *m/f*; (*of newspaper*) artículo de fondo; **~ship** *n* dirección *f*.

leading ['liːdɪŋ] *a* (*main*) principal; (*outstanding*) destacado; (*first*) primero; (*front*) delantero; **~ lady** *n* (*THEATRE*) primera actriz *f*; **~ light** *n* (*person*) figura principal.

leaf [liːf], *pl* **leaves** *n* hoja // *vi*: **to ~ through** hojear; **to turn over a new ~** reformarse.

leaflet ['liːflɪt] *n* folleto.

league [liːg] *n* sociedad *f*; (*FOOTBALL*) liga; **to be in ~ with** estar de manga con.

leak [liːk] *n* (*of liquid, gas*) escape *m*, fuga; (*in pipe*) agujero; (*in roof*) gotera; (*in security*) filtración *f* // *vi* (*shoes, ship*) hacer agua; (*pipe*) tener (un) escape; (*roof*) gotear; (*also*: **~ out**: *liquid, gas*) escaparse, fugarse; (*fig: news*) divulgarse // *vt* (*gen*) dejar escapar; (*fig: information*) filtrarse.

lean [liːn] *a* (*thin*) flaco; (*meat*) magro // (*vb: pt, pp* leaned *or* leant [lɛnt]) *vt*: **to ~ sth on sth** apoyar algo en algo // *vi* (*slope*) inclinarse; (*rest*): **to ~ against** apoyarse contra; **to ~ on** apoyarse en; (*fig: rely on*) contar con (el apoyo de); **to ~ back/forward** *vi* inclinarse hacia atrás/adelante; **to ~ out** *vi* asomarse; **to ~ over** *vi* inclinarse; **~ing** *n*: **~ing (towards)** inclinación *f* (hacia); **~-to** *n* cobertizo.

leap [liːp] *n* salto // *vi* (*pt, pp* **leaped** *or* **leapt** [lɛpt]) saltar; **~frog** *n* pídola; **~ year** *n* año bisiesto.

learn [ləːn], *pt, pp* **learned** *or* **learnt** *vt* (*gen*) aprender; (*come to know of*) enterarse de // *vi* aprender; **to ~ how to do sth** aprender a hacer algo; **~ed** [ˈləːnɪd] *a* erudito; **~er** *n* principiante *m/f*; (*Brit: also: ~er driver*) aprendiz(a) *m/f*; **~ing** *n* el saber *m*, conocimientos *mpl*.

lease [liːs] *n* arriendo // *vt* arrendar.

leash [liːʃ] *n* correa.

least [liːst] *a* (*slightest*) menor, más pequeño; (*smallest amount of*) mínimo // *ad* menos // *n*: **the ~** lo menos; **the ~ expensive car** el coche menos costoso; **at ~** por lo menos, al menos; **not in the ~** en absoluto.

leather [ˈlɛðə*] *n* cuero.

leave [liːv], *pt, pp* **left** *vt* dejar; (*go away from*) abandonar // *vi* irse; (*train*) salir // *n* permiso; **to be left** quedar, sobrar; **there's some milk left over** sobra *or* queda algo de leche; **on ~** de permiso; **to ~ behind** *vt* (*on purpose*) dejar (atrás); (*accidentally*) olvidar; **to take one's ~ of** despedirse de; **to ~ out** *vt* omitir; **~ of absence** permiso de ausentarse.

leaves [liːvz] *pl of* **leaf**.

Lebanon [ˈlɛbənən] *n*: **the ~** el Líbano.

lecherous [ˈlɛtʃərəs] *a* lascivo.

lecture [ˈlɛktʃə*] *n* conferencia; (*SCOL*) clase *f* // *vi* dar una clase // *vt* (*scold*) sermonear; **to give a ~ on** dar una conferencia sobre; **~r** *n* conferenciante *m/f*; (*Brit: at university*) profesor(a) *m/f*.

led [lɛd] *pt, pp of* **lead**.

ledge [lɛdʒ] *n* (*of window, on wall*) repisa, reborde *m*; (*of mountain*) saliente *m*.

ledger [ˈlɛdʒə*] *n* libro mayor.

lee [liː] *n* sotavento.

leech [liːtʃ] *n* sanguijuela.

leek [liːk] *n* puerro.

leer [lɪə*] *vi*: **to ~ at sb** mirar de manera lasciva a uno.

leeway [ˈliːweɪ] *n* (*fig*): **to have some ~** tener cierta libertad de acción.

left [lɛft] *pt, pp of* **leave** // *a* izquierdo // *n* izquierda // *ad* a la izquierda; **on** *or* **to the ~** a la izquierda; **the L~** (*POL*) la izquierda; **~-handed** *a* zurdo; **the ~-hand side** *n* la izquierda; **~-luggage (office)** *n* (*Brit*) consigna; **~-overs** *npl* sobras *fpl*; **~-wing** *a* (*POL*) de izquierda, izquierdista.

leg [lɛg] *n* pierna; (*of animal*) pata; (*of*

chair) pie *m*; (*CULIN: of meat*) pierna; (*of journey*) etapa; **1st/2nd ~** (*SPORT*) partido de ida/de vuelta.

legacy [ˈlɛgəsɪ] *n* herencia.

legal [ˈliːgl] *a* (*permitted by law*) lícito; (*of law*) legal; (*inquiry etc*) jurídico; **~ holiday** *n* (*US*) fiesta oficial; **~ize** *vt* legalizar; **~ly** *ad* legalmente; **~ tender** *n* moneda de curso legal.

legend [ˈlɛdʒənd] *n* leyenda.

legislation [lɛdʒɪsˈleɪʃən] *n* legislación *f*.

legislature [ˈlɛdʒɪslətʃə*] *n* cuerpo legislativo.

legitimate [lɪˈdʒɪtɪmət] *a* legítimo.

leg-room [ˈlɛgruːm] *n* espacio para las piernas.

leisure [ˈlɛʒə*] *n* ocio, tiempo libre; **at ~** con tranquilidad; **~ centre** *n* centro de recreo; **~ly** *a* sin prisa; lento.

lemon [ˈlɛmən] *n* limón *m*; **~ade** [-ˈneɪd] *n* (*fruit juice*) limonada; (*fizzy*) gaseosa; **~ tea** *n* té *m* con limón.

lend [lɛnd], *pt, pp* **lent** *vt*: **to ~ sth to sb** prestar algo a alguien; **~ing library** *n* biblioteca de préstamo.

length [lɛŋθ] *n* (*size*) largo, longitud *f*; (*section: of road, pipe*) tramo; (: *rope etc*) largo; **at ~** (*at last*) por fin, finalmente; (*lengthily*) largamente; **~en** *vt* alargar // *vi* alargarse; **~ways** *ad* a lo largo; **~y** *a* largo, extenso; (*meeting*) prolongado.

lenient [ˈliːnɪənt] *a* indulgente.

lens [lɛnz] *n* (*of spectacles*) lente *f*; (*of camera*) objetivo.

lent [lɛnt] *pt, pp of* **lend**.

Lent [lɛnt] *n* Cuaresma.

lentil [ˈlɛntɪl] *n* lenteja.

Leo [ˈliːəu] *n* Leo.

leotard [ˈliːətɑːd] *n* leotardo.

leper [ˈlɛpə*] *n* leproso/a.

leprosy [ˈlɛprəsɪ] *n* lepra.

lesbian [ˈlɛzbɪən] *n* lesbiana.

less [lɛs] *a* (*in size, degree etc*) menor; (*in quantity*) menos // *pron, ad* menos; **~ than half** menos de la mitad; **~ than ever** menos que nunca; **~ and ~** cada vez menos; **the ~ he works...** cuanto menos trabaja...

lessen [ˈlɛsn] *vi* disminuir, reducirse // *vt* disminuir, reducir.

lesser [ˈlɛsə*] *a* menor; **to a ~ extent** en menor grado.

lesson [ˈlɛsn] *n* clase *f*; **a maths ~** una clase de matemáticas.

lest [lɛst] *conj*: **~ it happen** para que no pase.

let [lɛt], *pt, pp* **let** *vt* (*allow*) dejar, permitir; (*Brit: lease*) alquilar; **to ~ sb do sth** dejar que uno haga algo; **to ~ sb know sth** comunicar algo a uno; **~'s go** ¡vamos!; **~ him come** que venga; **'to ~'** 'se alquila'; **to ~ down** *vt* (*lower*) bajar; (*dress*) alargar; (*tyre*) desinflar; (*hair*) soltar; (*disappoint*) defraudar; **to**

~ go vi soltar; (fig) dejarse ir // vt soltar; **to ~ in** vt dejar entrar; (visitor etc) hacer pasar; **to ~ off** vt dejar escapar; (firework etc) disparar; (bomb) accionar; **to ~ on** vi (col) divulgar; **to ~ out** vt dejar salir; (dress) ensanchar; **to ~ up** vi amainar, disminuir.

lethal ['li:θl] a (weapon) mortífero; (poison, wound) mortal.

lethargy ['leθədʒɪ] n letargo.

letter ['letə*] n (of alphabet) letra; (correspondence) carta; **~ bomb** n cartabomba; **~box** n (Brit) buzón m; **~ of credit** n carta de crédito; **~ing** n letras fpl.

lettuce ['letɪs] n lechuga.

leukaemia, (US) leukemia [lu:'ki:mɪə] n leucemia.

level ['levl] a (flat) llano; (flattened) nivelado; (uniform) igual // ad a nivel // n nivel m // vt nivelar; allanar; **to be ~ with** estar a nivel de; **'A' ~s** npl (Brit) ≈ Bachillerato Superior, B.U.P.; **'O' ~s** npl (Brit) ≈ bachillerato elemental, octavo de básica; **on the ~** (fig: honest) en serio; **to ~ off** or **out** vi (prices etc) estabilizarse; **~ crossing** n (Brit) paso a nivel; **~-headed** a sensato.

lever ['li:və*] n palanca // vt: **to ~ up** levantar con palanca; **~age** n (fig: influence) influencia.

levy ['levɪ] n impuesto // vt exigir, recaudar.

lewd [lu:d] a lascivo; (joke) obsceno, colorado (LAm).

liability [laɪə'bɪlətɪ] n responsabilidad f; (handicap) desventaja; **liabilities** npl obligaciones fpl; (COMM) pasivo sg.

liable ['laɪəbl] a (subject): **~ to** sujeto a; (responsible): **~ for** responsable de; (likely): **~ to do** propenso a hacer.

liaise [lɪ'eɪz] vi: **to ~ with** enlazar con.

liaison [li:'eɪzɔn] n (coordination) enlace m; (affair) relación f.

liar ['laɪə*] n mentiroso/a.

libel ['laɪbl] n calumnia // vt calumniar.

liberal ['lɪbərl] a (gen) liberal; (generous): **~ with** generoso con.

liberty ['lɪbətɪ] n libertad f; **to be at ~ to do** estar libre para hacer.

Libra ['li:brə] n Libra.

librarian [laɪ'breərɪən] n bibliotecario/a.

library ['laɪbrərɪ] n biblioteca.

libretto [lɪ'bretəu] n libreto.

Libya ['lɪbɪə] n Libia; **~n** a, n libio/a m/f.

lice [laɪs] pl of **louse**.

licence, (US) license ['laɪsns] n licencia; (permit) permiso; (also: **driving ~**, (US) **driver's ~**) carnet m de conducir (Sp), permiso (LAm); (excessive freedom) libertad f; **~ number** n matrícula; **~ plate** n placa (de matrícula).

license ['laɪsns] n (US) = **licence** // vt autorizar, dar permiso a; **~d** a (for alcohol) autorizado para vender bebidas alcohólicas.

licentious [laɪ'senʃəs] a licencioso

lichen ['laɪkən] n liquen m.

lick [lɪk] vt lamer // n lamedura; **a ~ of paint** una mano de pintura.

licorice ['lɪkərɪs] n = **liquorice**.

lid [lɪd] n (of box, case) tapa; (of pan) cobertera.

lido ['laɪdəu] n (Brit) piscina.

lie [laɪ] n mentira // vi mentir; (pt lay, pp lain) (rest) estar echado, estar acostado; (of object: be situated) estar, encontrarse; **to ~ low** (fig) mantenerse a escondidas; **to ~ about** vi (things) estar tirado; (Brit) (people) estar tumbado; **to have a ~-down** (Brit) echarse (una siesta); **to have a ~-in** (Brit) quedarse en la cama.

lieu [lu:]: **in ~ of** prep en lugar de.

lieutenant [lef'tenənt, (US) lu:'tenənt] n (MIL) teniente m.

life [laɪf], pl **lives** n vida; (way of ~) modo de vivir; (of licence etc) vigencia; **~ assurance** n (Brit) seguro de vida; **~belt** n (Brit) cinturón m salvavidas; **~boat** n lancha de socorro; **~guard** n vigilante m/f; **~ insurance** n = **~ assurance**; **~ jacket** n chaleco salvavidas; **~less** a sin vida; (dull) soso; **~like** a natural; **~line** n (fig) cordón m umbilical; **~long** a de toda la vida; **~ preserver** n (US) = **~belt**; **~-saver** n socorrista m/f; **~ sentence** n condena perpetua; **~-sized** a de tamaño natural; **~ span** n vida; **lifestyle** n estilo de vida; **~ support system** n (MED) sistema m de respiración asistida; **~time** n: **in his ~time** durante su vida; **once in a ~time** una vez en la vida.

lift [lɪft] vt levantar; (copy) plagiar // vi (fog) disiparse // n (Brit: elevator) ascensor m; **to give sb a ~** (Brit) llevar a uno en el coche; **~-off** n despegue m.

light [laɪt] n luz f; (flame) lumbre f; (lamp) luz f, lámpara; (daylight) luz f del día; (headlight) faro; (rear ~) luz f trasera; (for cigarette etc): **have you got a ~?** ¿tienes fuego? // vt (pt, pp **lighted** or **lit**) (candle, cigarette, fire) encender (Sp), prender (LAm); (room) alumbrar // a (colour) claro; (not heavy, also fig) ligero; (room) alumbrado; **to come to ~** salir a luz; **to ~ up** vi (smoke) encender un cigarrillo; (face) iluminarse // vt (illuminate) iluminar, alumbrar; **~ bulb** n bombilla, foco (LAm); **~en** vi (grow ~) clarear // vt (give light to) iluminar; (make lighter) aclarar; (make less heavy) aligerar; **~er** n (also: **cigarette ~er**) encendedor m, mechero; **~-headed** a (dizzy) mareado; (excited) exaltado; (by nature) casquivano; **~-hearted** a alegre; **~house** n faro; **~ing** n (act) iluminación f; (system) alumbrado; **~ly** ad ligeramente; (*not seriously*) con poca seriedad; **to get off ~ly** ser castigado con poca severidad; **~ness** *n* claridad *f*; (*in weight*) ligereza.

lightning ['laɪtnɪŋ] *n* relámpago, rayo; **~ conductor,** (*US*) **~ rod** *n* pararrayos *m inv.*

light: ~ pen *n* lápiz *m* óptico; **~weight** *a* (*suit*) ligero // *n* (*BOXING*) peso ligero; **~ year** *n* año luz.

like [laɪk] *vt* gustarle a uno // *prep* como // *a* parecido, semejante // *n:* **the ~** semejante *m/f*; **his ~s and dislikes** sus gustos y aversiones; **I would ~, I'd ~** me gustaría; (*for purchase*) quisiera; **would you ~ a coffee?** ¿te apetece un café?; **I ~ swimming** me gusta nadar; **she ~s apples** le gustan las manzanas; **to be** *or* **look ~ sb/sth** parecerse a alguien/algo; **that's just ~ him** es muy de él, es característico de él; **do it ~ this** hazlo así; **it is nothing ~...** no tiene parecido alguno con...; **~able** *a* simpático, agradable.

likelihood ['laɪklɪhud] *n* probabilidad *f*.

likely ['laɪklɪ] *a* probable; **he's ~ to leave** es probable que se vaya; **not ~!** ¡ni hablar!

likeness ['laɪknɪs] *n* semejanza, parecido.

likewise ['laɪkwaɪz] *ad* igualmente.

liking ['laɪkɪŋ] *n:* **~ (for)** (*person*) cariño (a); (*thing*) afición (a).

lilac ['laɪlək] *n* lila // *a* (*colour*) de color lila.

lily ['lɪlɪ] *n* lirio, azucena; **~ of the valley** *n* lirio de los valles.

limb [lɪm] *n* miembro.

limber ['lɪmbə*]: **to ~ up** *vi* (*fig*) entrenarse; (*SPORT*) desentumecerse.

limbo ['lɪmbəu] *n:* **to be in ~** (*fig*) quedar a la expectativa.

lime [laɪm] *n* (*tree*) limero; (*fruit*) lima; (*GEO*) cal *f.*

limelight ['laɪmlaɪt] *n:* **to be in the ~** (*fig*) ser el centro de atención.

limerick ['lɪmərɪk] *n* quintilla humorística.

limestone ['laɪmstəun] *n* piedra caliza.

limit ['lɪmɪt] *n* límite *m* // *vt* limitar; **~ed** *a* limitado; **to be ~ed to** limitarse a; **~ed (liability) company (Ltd)** *n* (*Brit*) sociedad *f* anónima.

limousine ['lɪməzi:n] *n* limusina.

limp [lɪmp] *n:* **to have a ~** tener cojera // *vi* cojear // *a* flojo.

limpet ['lɪmpɪt] *n* lapa.

line [laɪn] *n* (*gen*) línea; (*straight ~*) raya; (*rope*) cuerda; (*for fishing*) sedal *m*; (*wire*) hilo; (*row, series*) fila, hilera; (*of writing*) renglón *m*; (*on face*) arruga; (*speciality*) rama // *vt* (*SEWING*) forrar (*with* de); **to ~ the streets** ocupar las aceras; **in ~ with** de acuerdo con; **to ~ up** *vi* hacer cola // *vt* alinear, poner en fila.

linear ['lɪnɪə*] *a* lineal.

lined [laɪnd] *a* (*face*) arrugado; (*paper*) rayado.

linen ['lɪnɪn] *n* ropa blanca; (*cloth*) lino.

liner ['laɪnə*] *n* vapor *m* de línea, trans-atlántico.

linesman ['laɪnzmən] *n* (*SPORT*) juez *m* de línea.

line-up ['laɪnʌp] *n* alineación *f.*

linger ['lɪŋgə*] *vi* retrasarse, tardar en marcharse; (*smell, tradition*) persistir.

lingerie ['lænʒəri:] *n* ropa interior (de mujer).

lingo ['lɪŋgəu], *pl* **~es** *n* (*pej*) jerga.

linguist ['lɪŋgwɪst] *n* lingüista *m/f*; **~ic** *a* lingüístico; **~ics** *n* lingüística.

lining ['laɪnɪŋ] *n* forro.

link [lɪŋk] *n* (*of a chain*) eslabón *m*; (*connection*) conexión *f*; (*bond*) vínculo, lazo // *vt* vincular, unir; **~s** *npl* (*GOLF*) campo *sg* de golf; **to ~ up** *vt* acoplar // *vi* unirse; **~-up** *n* (*gen*) unión *f*; (*in space*) acoplamiento.

lino ['laɪnəu], **linoleum** [lɪ'nəuliəm] *n* linóleo.

lion ['laɪən] *n* león *m*; **~ess** *n* leona.

lip [lɪp] *n* labio; (*of jug*) pico; (*of cup etc*) borde *m*; **~read** *vi* leer los labios; **~ salve** *n* crema protectora para labios; **~ service** *n:* **to pay ~ service to** sth prometer algo de palabra; **~stick** *n* lápiz *m* de labios, carmín *m.*

liqueur [lɪ'kjuə*] *n* licor *m.*

liquid ['lɪkwɪd] *a, n* líquido.

liquidize ['lɪkwɪdaɪz] *vt* (*CULIN*) licuar.

liquidizer ['lɪkwɪdaɪzə*] *n* licuadora.

liquor ['lɪkə*] *n* licor *m*, bebidas *fpl* alcohólicas.

liquorice ['lɪkərɪs] *n* regaliz *m.*

liquor store *n* (*US*) bodega, *tienda de vinos y bebidas alcohólicas.*

Lisbon ['lɪzbən] *n* Lisboa.

lisp [lɪsp] *n* ceceo.

list [lɪst] *n* lista; (*of ship*) inclinación *f* // *vt* (*write down*) hacer una lista de; (*enumerate*) catalogar // *vi* (*ship*) inclinarse.

listen ['lɪsn] *vi* escuchar, oír; (*pay attention*) atender; **~er** *n* oyente *m/f.*

listless ['lɪstlɪs] *a* apático, indiferente.

lit [lɪt] *pt, pp* of **light.**

litany ['lɪtənɪ] *n* letanía.

liter ['li:tə*] *n* (*US*) = **litre.**

literacy ['lɪtərəsɪ] *n* capacidad *f* de leer y escribir.

literal ['lɪtərl] *a* literal.

literary ['lɪtərərɪ] *a* literario.

literate ['lɪtərət] *a* que sabe leer y escribir; (*fig*) culto.

literature ['lɪtərɪtʃə*] *n* literatura; (*brochures etc*) folletos *mpl.*

lithe [laɪð] *a* ágil.

litigation [lɪtɪ'geɪʃən] *n* litigio.

litre, (*US*) **liter** ['li:tə*] *n* litro.

litter ['lɪtə*] *n* (*rubbish*) basura; (*paper*) papel *m* tirado; (*young animals*) camada, cría; **~ bin** *n* (*Brit*) papelera; **~ed**

a: ~**ed with** (*scattered*) esparcido con; (*covered with*) lleno de.

little |'lɪtl| *a* (*small*) pequeño; (*not much*) poco; (*often translated by suffix: eg* ~ **house** casita) // *ad* poco; **a** ~ **un** poco (de); ~ **by** ~ poco a poco.

live |lɪv| *vi* vivir // *vt* (*a life*) llevar; (*experience*) vivir // *a* |laɪv| (*animal*) vivo; (*wire*) conectado; (*broadcast*) en directo; (*shell*) cargado; **to** ~ **down** *vt* hacer olvidar; **to** ~ **on** *vt fus* (*food*) vivirse de, alimentarse de; **to** ~ **together** *vi* vivir juntos; **to** ~ **up to** *vt fus* (*fulfil*) cumplir con; (*justify*) justificar.

livelihood |'laɪvlɪhud| *n* sustento.

lively |'laɪvlɪ| *a* (*gen*) vivo; (*talk*) animado; (*pace*) rápido; (*party, tune*) alegre.

liven up |'laɪvn-| *vt* animar.

liver |'lɪvə*| *n* hígado.

livery |'lɪvərɪ| *n* librea.

lives |laɪvz| *pl of* **life**.

livestock |'laɪvstɔk| *n* ganado.

livid |'lɪvɪd| *a* lívido; (*furious*) furioso.

living |'lɪvɪŋ| *a* (*alive*) vivo // *n*: **to earn** *or* **make a** ~ ganarse la vida; ~ **conditions** *npl* condiciones *fpl* de vida; ~ **room** *n* sala (de estar); ~ **wage** *n* sueldo suficiente para vivir.

lizard |'lɪzəd| *n* lagartija.

load |ləud| *n* (*gen*) carga; (*weight*) peso // *vt* (*COMPUT*) cargar; (*also:* ~ **up**): **to** ~ (**with**) cargar (con *or* de); **a** ~ **of**, ~**s of** (*fig*) (gran) cantidad de, montones de; ~**ed** *a* (*dice*) cargado; (*question*) intencionado; (*col: rich*) forrado (de dinero); ~**ing bay** *n* área de carga y descarga.

loaf |ləuf|, *pl* **loaves** *n* (barra de) pan *m* // *vi* (*also:* ~ **about,** ~ **around**) holgazanear.

loan |ləun| *n* préstamo; (*COMM*) empréstito // *vt* prestar; **on** ~ prestado.

loath |ləuθ| *a:* **to be** ~ **to do sth** estar poco dispuesto a hacer algo.

loathe |ləuð| *vt* aborrecer; (*person*) odiar; **loathing** *n* aversión *f*; odio.

loaves |ləuvz| *pl of* **loaf**.

lobby |'lɔbɪ| *n* vestíbulo, sala de espera; (*POL: pressure group*) grupo de presión // *vt* presionar.

lobe |ləub| *n* lóbulo.

lobster |'lɔbstə*| *n* langosta.

local |'ləukl| *a* local // *n* (*pub*) bar *m*; **the** ~**s** los vecinos, los del lugar; ~ **anaesthetic** *n* (*MED*) anestesia local; ~ **authority** *n* municipio, ayuntamiento (*Sp*); ~ **call** (*TEL*) llamada local; ~ **government** *n* gobierno municipal; ~**ity** |-'kælɪtɪ| *n* localidad *f*; ~**ly** |-kəlɪ| *ad* en la vecindad.

locate |ləu'keɪt| *vt* (*find*) localizar; (*situate*) colocar.

location |ləu'keɪʃən| *n* situación *f*; **on** ~ (*CINEMA*) en exteriores.

loch |lɔx| *n* lago.

lock |lɔk| *n* (*of door, box*) cerradura; (*of canal*) esclusa; (*of hair*) mechón *m* // *vt* (*with key*) cerrar con llave; (*immobilize*) inmovilizar // *vi* (*door etc*) cerrarse con llave; (*wheels*) trabarse.

locker |'lɔkə*| *n* casillero; ~**-room** *n* (*US SPORT*) vestuario.

locket |'lɔkɪt| *n* medallón *m*.

lockout |'lɔkaut| *n* paro patronal, lockout *m*.

locksmith |'lɔksmɪθ| *n* cerrajero/a.

lock-up |'lɔkʌp| *n* (*garage*) cochera.

locomotive |ləukə'məutɪv| *n* locomotora.

locum |'ləukəm| *n* (*MED*) (médico/a) interino/a,

locust |'ləukəst| *n* langosta.

lodge |lɔdʒ| *n* casa del guarda; (*porter's*) portería; (*FREEMASONRY*) logia // *vi* (*person*): **to** ~ (**with**) alojarse (en casa de) // *vt* (*complaint*) presentar; ~**r** *n* huésped(a) *m/f*.

lodgings |'lɔdʒɪŋz| *npl* alojamiento *sg*; (*house*) casa *sg* de huéspedes.

loft |lɔft| *n* desván *m*.

lofty |'lɔftɪ| *a* alto; (*haughty*) orgulloso.

log |lɔg| *n* (*of wood*) leño, tronco; (*book*) = **logbook**.

logbook |'lɔgbuk| *n* (*NAUT*) diario de a bordo; (*AVIAT*) libro de vuelo; (*of car*) documentación *f* (del coche).

loggerheads |'lɔgəhedz| *npl*: **at** ~ (**with**) de pique (con).

logic |'lɔdʒɪk| *n* lógica; ~**al** *a* lógico.

logo |'ləugəu| *n* logotipo.

loin |lɔɪn| *n* (*CULIN*) lomo, solomillo; ~**s** *npl* lomos *mpl*.

loiter |'lɔɪtə*| *vi* vagar; (*pej*) merodear.

loll |lɔl| *vi* (*also:* ~ **about**) repantigarse.

lollipop |'lɔlɪpɔp| *n* piruli *m*; (*iced*) polo; ~ **man/lady** *n* (*Brit*) persona encargada de ayudar a los niños a cruzar la calle.

London |'lʌndən| *n* Londres; ~**er** *n* londinense *m/f*.

lone |ləun| *a* solitario.

loneliness |'ləunlɪnɪs| *n* soledad *f*, aislamiento.

lonely |'ləunlɪ| *a* solitario, solo.

long |lɔŋ| *a* largo // *ad* mucho tiempo, largamente // *vi*: **to** ~ **for sth** anhelar algo; **in the** ~ **run** a la larga; **so** *or* **as** ~ **as** mientras, con tal que; **don't be** ~! ¡no tardes!, ¡vuelve pronto!; **how** ~ **is the street?** ¿cuánto tiene la calle de largo?; **how** ~ **is the lesson?** ¿cuánto dura la clase?; **6 metres** ~ que mide 6 metros, de 6 metros de largo; **6 months** ~ que dura 6 meses, de 6 meses de duración; **all night** ~ toda la noche; **he no** ~**er comes** ya no viene; ~ **before** mucho antes; **before** ~ (+ *future*) dentro de poco; (+ *past*) poco tiempo después; **at** ~ **last** al fin, por fin; ~**-distance** *a* (*race*) de larga distancia; (*call*) interurbano; ~**-haired** *a* de pelo largo; ~**hand** *n* escritura sin abreviaturas; ~ing n anhelo, ansia; (nostalgia) nostalgia // a anhelante.

longitude ['lɔŋgɪtjuːd] n longitud f.

long: ~ **jump** n salto de longitud; ~-**lost** a desaparecido hace mucho tiempo; ~-**playing record (L.P.)** n elepé m, disco de larga duración; ~-**range** a de gran alcance; ~-**sighted** a (Brit) présbita; ~-**standing** a de mucho tiempo; ~-**suffering** a sufrido; ~-**term** a a largo plazo; ~ **wave** n onda larga; ~-**winded** a prolijo.

loo [luː] n (Brit: col) wáter m.

look [luk] vi mirar; (seem) parecer; (building etc): to ~ south/on to the sea dar al sur/al mar // n mirada; (glance) vistazo; (appearance) aire m, aspecto; ~s npl físico sg, apariencia sg; to ~ **after** vt fus cuidar; to ~ **at** vt fus mirar; (consider) considerar; to ~ **back** vi mirar hacia atrás; to ~ **down on** vt fus (fig) despreciar, mirar con desprecio; to ~ **for** vt fus buscar; to ~ **forward** to vt fus esperar con ilusión; (in letters): we ~ forward to hearing from you quedamos a la espera de sus gratas noticias; to ~ **into** vt investigar; to ~ **on** vi mirar (como espectador); to ~ **out** vi (beware): to ~ out (for) tener cuidado (de); to ~ **out for** vt fus (seek) buscar; (await) esperar; to ~ **round** vi volver la cabeza; to ~ **to** vt fus ocuparse de; (rely on) contar con; to ~ **up** vi mirar hacia arriba; (improve) mejorar // vt (word) buscar; (friend) visitar; to ~ **up to** vt fus admirar; ~-**out** n (tower etc) puesto de observación; (person) vigía m/f; to be on the ~-out for sth estar al acecho de algo.

loom [luːm] n telar m // vi (threaten) amenazar.

loony ['luːnɪ] n (col) loco/a.

loop [luːp] n lazo; (bend) vuelta, recodo; ~**hole** n escapatoria.

loose [luːs] a (gen) suelto; (not tight) flojo; (wobbly etc) movedizo; (clothes) ancho; (morals, discipline) relajado; to be at a ~ end or (US) at ~ ends no saber qué hacer; ~ **change** n cambio; ~ **chippings** npl (on road) gravilla sg suelta; ~**ly** ad libremente, aproximadamente; ~**n** vt (free) soltar; (untie) desatar; (slacken) aflojar.

loot [luːt] n botín m // vt saquear.

lop [lɔp]: to ~ **off** vt cortar; (branches) podar.

lop-sided ['lɔp'saɪdɪd] a desequilibrado.

lord [lɔːd] n señor m; L~ Smith Lord Smith; the L~ el Señor; the (House of) L~s (Brit) la Cámara de los Lores; ~**ship** n: your L~ship su Señoría.

lore [lɔː*] n tradiciones fpl.

lorry ['lɔrɪ] n (Brit) camión m; ~ **driver** n camionero/a.

lose [luːz], pt, pp **lost** vt perder // vi perder, ser vencido; to ~ (time) (clock) atrasarse; ~**r** n perdedor(a) m/f.

loss [lɔs] n pérdida; heavy ~es (MIL) grandes pérdidas; to be at a ~ no saber qué hacer; to make a ~ sufrir pérdidas.

lost [lɔst] pt, pp of **lose** // a perdido; ~ **property**, (US) ~ **and found** n objetos mpl perdidos.

lot [lɔt] n (at auctions) lote m; (destiny) suerte f; the ~ el todo, todos; a ~ mucho, bastante; a ~ **of**, ~s of mucho(s) (pl); I read a ~ leo bastante; to draw ~s (for sth) echar suertes (para decidir algo).

lotion ['ləuʃən] n loción f.

lottery ['lɔtərɪ] n lotería f.

loud [laud] a (voice, sound) fuerte; (laugh, shout) estrepitoso; (gaudy) chillón/ona // ad (speak etc) en alta voz; ~**hailer** n (Brit) megáfono; ~**ly** ad (noisily) fuerte; (aloud) en alta voz; ~**speaker** n altavoz m.

lounge [laundʒ] n salón m, sala (de estar) // vi reposar, holgazanear; ~ **suit** n (Brit) traje m de calle.

louse [laus], pl **lice** n piojo.

lousy ['lauzɪ] a (fig) vil, asqueroso.

lout [laut] n gamberro/a.

louvre, (US) **louver** ['luːvə*] a (door) de rejilla; (window) de libro.

lovable ['lʌvəbl] a amable, simpático.

love [lʌv] n amor m // vt amar, querer; to ~ to do encantarle a uno hacer; to be in ~ with estar enamorado de; to make ~ hacer el amor; for the ~ of por amor de; '15 ~' (TENNIS) 15 a cero; I ~ **paella** me encanta la paella; ~ **affair** n aventura sentimental; ~ **letter** n carta de amor; ~ **life** n vida sentimental.

lovely ['lʌvlɪ] a (delightful) precioso, encantador(a); (beautiful) hermoso.

lover ['lʌvə*] n amante m/f; (amateur): a ~ of un aficionado/a or un amante de.

loving ['lʌvɪŋ] a amoroso, cariñoso.

low [ləu] a, ad bajo // n (METEOROLOGY) área de baja presión // vi (cow) mugir; to feel ~ sentirse deprimido; to turn (down) ~ bajar; ~-**cut** a (dress) escotado.

lower ['ləuə*] vt bajar; (reduce) reducir // vr: to ~ o.s. to (fig) rebajarse a.

low: ~-**fat** a (milk, yoghurt) desnatado; (diet) bajo en calorías; ~**lands** npl (GEO) tierras fpl bajas; ~**ly** a humilde; ~-**lying** a bajo.

loyal ['lɔɪəl] a leal; ~**ty** n lealtad f.

lozenge ['lɔzɪndʒ] n (MED) pastilla.

L.P. n abbr = **long-playing record**.

L-plates ['ɛlpleɪts] npl (Brit) placas de aprendiz de conductor.

Ltd abbr (= limited company) S.A.

lubricant ['luːbrɪkənt] n lubricante m.

lubricate ['luːbrɪkeɪt] vt lubricar, engrasar.

lucid ['luːsɪd] a lúcido.

luck [lʌk] n suerte f; **bad** ~ mala suerte; **good** ~! ¡que tengas suerte!, ¡suerte!; ~**ily** ad afortunadamente; ~**y** a afortunado.

ludicrous ['lu:dɪkrəs] a absurdo.

lug [lʌg] vt (drag) arrastrar.

luggage ['lʌgɪdʒ] n equipaje m; ~ **rack** n (in train) rejilla, redecilla; (on car) baca, portaequipajes m inv.

lukewarm ['lu:kwɔ:m] a tibio, templado.

lull [lʌl] n tregua // vt (child) acunar; (person, fear) calmar.

lullaby ['lʌləbaɪ] n nana.

lumbago [lʌm'beɪgəu] n lumbago.

lumber ['lʌmbə*] n (junk) trastos mpl viejos; (wood) maderos mpl; ~**jack** n maderero.

luminous ['lu:mɪnəs] a luminoso.

lump [lʌmp] n terrón m; (fragment) trozo; (in sauce) grumo; (in throat) nudo; (swelling) bulto // vt (also: ~ **together**) juntar; ~ **sum** n suma global.

lunacy ['lu:nəsɪ] n locura.

lunar ['lu:nə*] a lunar.

lunatic ['lu:nətɪk] a, n loco/a; ~ **asylum** n manicomio.

lunch [lʌntʃ] n almuerzo, comida // vi almorzar.

luncheon ['lʌntʃən] n almuerzo; ~ **meat** n tipo de fiambre; ~ **voucher** n vale m de comida.

lung [lʌŋ] n pulmón m.

lunge [lʌndʒ] vi (also: ~ **forward**) abalanzarse; **to** ~ **at** arremeter contra.

lurch [lɜ:tʃ] vi dar sacudidas // n sacudida; **to leave sb in the** ~ dejar a uno plantado.

lure [luə*] n (bait) cebo; (decoy) señuelo // vt convencer con engaños.

lurid ['luərɪd] a (colour) chillón/ona; (account) sensacional; (detail) horripilante.

lurk [lɜ:k] vi (hide) esconderse; (wait) estar al acecho.

luscious ['lʌʃəs] a delicioso.

lush [lʌʃ] a exuberante.

lust [lʌst] n lujuria; (greed) codicia; **to** ~ **after** vt fus codiciar.

lustre, (US) **luster** ['lʌstə*] n lustre m, brillo.

lusty ['lʌstɪ] a robusto, fuerte.

Luxembourg ['lʌksəmbə:g] n Luxemburgo.

luxuriant [lʌg'zjuərɪənt] a exuberante.

luxurious [lʌg'zjuərɪəs] a lujoso.

luxury ['lʌkʃərɪ] n lujo // cpd de lujo.

lying ['laɪɪŋ] n mentiras fpl.

lyric ['lɪrɪk] a lírico; ~**s** npl (of song) letra sg; ~**al** a lírico.

M

m. abbr = **metre; mile; million.**

M.A. abbr = **Master of Arts.**

mac [mæk] n (Brit) impermeable m.

macaroni [mækə'rəunɪ] n macarrones mpl.

mace [meɪs] n (weapon, ceremonial) maza; (spice) macis f.

machine [mə'ʃi:n] n máquina // vt (dress etc) coser a máquina; ~ **gun** n ametralladora; ~ **language** n (COMPUT) lenguaje m máquina; ~**ry** n maquinaria; (fig) mecanismo.

mackerel ['mækrl] n, pl inv caballa.

mackintosh ['mækɪntɔʃ] n (Brit) impermeable m.

mad [mæd] a loco; (idea) disparatado; (angry) furioso.

madam ['mædəm] n señora.

madden ['mædn] vt volver loco.

made [meɪd] pt, pp of **make.**

Madeira [mə'dɪərə] n (GEO) Madera; (wine) vino de Madera.

made-to-measure ['meɪdtəmɛʒə*] a (Brit) hecho a la medida.

madly ['mædlɪ] ad locamente.

madman ['mædmən] n loco.

madness ['mædnɪs] n locura.

Madrid [mə'drɪd] n Madrid.

Mafia ['mæfɪə] n Mafia.

magazine [mægə'zi:n] n revista; (MIL: store) almacén m; (of firearm) recámara.

maggot ['mægət] n gusano.

magic ['mædʒɪk] n magia // a mágico; ~**al** a mágico; ~**ian** [mə'dʒɪʃən] n mago/a; (conjurer) prestidigitador(a) m/f.

magistrate ['mædʒɪstreɪt] n juez m/f (municipal).

magnet ['mægnɪt] n imán m; ~**ic** [-'netɪk] a magnético.

magnificent [mæg'nɪfɪsnt] a magnífico.

magnify ['mægnɪfaɪ] vt aumentar; (fig) exagerar; ~**ing glass** n lupa.

magnitude ['mægnɪtjuːd] n magnitud f.

magpie ['mægpaɪ] n urraca.

mahogany [mə'hɔgənɪ] n caoba // cpd de caoba.

maid [meɪd] n criada; **old** ~ (pej) solterona.

maiden ['meɪdn] n doncella // a (aunt etc) solterona; (speech, voyage) inaugural; ~ **name** n nombre m de soltera.

mail [meɪl] n correo; (letters) cartas fpl // vt (post) echar al correo; (send) mandar por correo; ~**box** n (US) buzón m; ~**ing list** n lista de direcciones; ~-**order** n pedido postal; (business) venta por correo.

maim [meɪm] vt mutilar, lisiar.

main [meɪn] a principal, mayor // n (pipe) cañería maestra; (US) red f eléctrica; **the** ~**s** (Brit ELEC) la red eléctrica; **in the** ~ en general; ~**frame** n (COMPUT) ordenador m central; ~**land** n continente m; ~**ly** ad principalmente; ~ **road** n carretera; ~**stay** n (fig) pilar m; ~**stream** n corriente f principal; ~

street n calle f mayor.

maintain [meɪnˈteɪn] vt mantener; (affirm) sostener; **maintenance** [ˈmeɪntənəns] n mantenimiento; (alimony) pensión f alimenticia.

maize [meɪz] n (Brit) maíz m, choclo (LAm).

majestic [məˈdʒɛstɪk] a majestuoso.

majesty [ˈmædʒɪstɪ] n majestad f.

major [ˈmeɪdʒə*] n (MIL) comandante m // a principal; (MUS) mayor.

Majorca [məˈjɔːkə] n Mallorca.

majority [məˈdʒɔrɪtɪ] n mayoría.

make [meɪk] vt (pt, pp made) hacer; (manufacture) hacer, fabricar; (cause to be): to ~ sb sad hacer or poner triste a alguien; (force): to ~ sb do sth obligar a alguien a hacer algo; (equal): 2 and 2 ~ 4 2 y 2 son 4 // n marca; to ~ a fool of sb poner a alguien en ridículo; to ~ a profit/loss obtener ganancias/sufrir pérdidas; to ~ it (arrive) llegar; (achieve sth) tener éxito; what time do you ~ it? ¿qué hora tienes?; to ~ do with contentarse con; **to ~ for** vt fus (place) dirigirse a; **to ~ out** vt (decipher) descifrar; (understand) entender; (see) distinguir; (write: cheque) extender; **to ~ up** vt (invent) inventar; (parcel) hacer // vi reconciliarse; (with cosmetics) maquillarse; **to ~ up for** vt fus compensar; **~-believe** n ficción f, invención f; **~r** n fabricante m/f; **~shift** a improvisado; **~-up** n maquillaje m; **~-up remover** n desmaquillador m.

making [ˈmeɪkɪŋ] n (fig): in the ~ en vías de formación; to have the ~s of (person) tener madera de.

malaise [mæˈleɪz] n malestar m.

malaria [məˈlɛərɪə] n malaria.

Malaya [məˈleɪə] n Malaya, Malaca.

Malaysia [məˈleɪzɪə] n Malasia.

male [meɪl] n (BIOL, ELEC) macho // a (sex, attitude) masculino; (child etc) varón.

malevolent [məˈlɛvələnt] a malévolo.

malfunction [mælˈfʌŋkʃən] n mal funcionamiento.

malice [ˈmælɪs] n (ill will) malicia; (rancour) rencor m; **malicious** [məˈlɪʃəs] a malicioso; rencoroso.

malign [məˈlaɪn] vt difamar, calumniar // a maligno.

malignant [məˈlɪɡnənt] a (MED) maligno.

mall [mɔːl] n (US: also: shopping ~) centro comercial.

malleable [ˈmælɪəbl] a maleable.

mallet [ˈmælɪt] n mazo.

malnutrition [mælnjuːˈtrɪʃən] n desnutrición f.

malpractice [mælˈpræktɪs] n negligencia profesional.

malt [mɔːlt] n malta.

Malta [ˈmɔːltə] n Malta.

maltreat [mælˈtriːt] vt maltratar.

mammal [ˈmæml] n mamífero.

mammoth [ˈmæməθ] n mamut m // a gigantesco.

man [mæn], pl **men** n hombre m; (CHESS) pieza // vt (NAUT) tripular; (MIL) guarnecer; **an old** ~ un viejo; ~ **and wife** marido y mujer.

manage [ˈmænɪdʒ] vi arreglárselas, ir tirando // vt (be in charge of) dirigir; (person etc) manejar; **~able** a manejable; **~ment** n dirección f, administración f; **~r** n director m; (SPORT) entrenador m; **~ress** n directora; (SPORT) entrenadora; **~rial** [-ɔˈdʒɪərɪəl] a directivo; **managing director** n director(a) m/f general.

mandarin [ˈmændərɪn] n (also: ~ orange) mandarina.

mandate [ˈmændeɪt] n mandato.

mandatory [ˈmændətərɪ] a obligatorio.

mane [meɪn] n (of horse) crin f; (of lion) melena.

maneuver [məˈnuːvə*] (US) = **manoeuvre**.

manfully [ˈmænfəlɪ] ad valientemente.

mangle [ˈmæŋɡl] vt mutilar, destrozar // n rodillo.

mango [ˈmæŋɡəu], pl **~es** n mango.

mangy [ˈmeɪndʒɪ] a roñoso; (MED) sarnoso.

manhandle [ˈmænhændl] vt maltratar.

manhood [ˈmænhud] n edad f viril; virilidad f.

man-hour [ˈmænˈauə*] n hora-hombre f.

mania [ˈmeɪnɪə] n manía; **~c** [ˈmeɪnɪæk] n maníaco/a; (fig) maniático.

manic [ˈmænɪk] a (behaviour, activity) frenético; **~-depressive** n maníaco/a depresivo/a.

manicure [ˈmænɪkjuə*] n manicura; ~ **set** n estuche m de manicura.

manifest [ˈmænɪfɛst] vt manifestar, mostrar // a manifiesto.

manifesto [mænɪˈfɛstəu] n manifiesto.

manipulate [məˈnɪpjuleɪt] vt manipular.

mankind [mænˈkaɪnd] n humanidad f, género humano.

manly [ˈmænlɪ] a varonil.

man-made [ˈmænˈmeɪd] a artificial.

manner [ˈmænə*] n manera, modo; (behaviour) conducta, manera de ser; (type) clase f; **~s** npl modales mpl, educación fsg; **bad ~s** mala educación; **~ism** n peculiaridad f de lenguaje (or de comportamiento).

manoeuvre, (US) **maneuver** [məˈnuːvə*] vt, vi maniobrar // n maniobra.

manor [ˈmænə*] n (also: ~ **house**) casa solariega.

manpower [ˈmænpauə*] n mano f de obra.

mansion [ˈmænʃən] n palacio, casa grande.

manslaughter |'mænslɔːtə*| n homicidio no premeditado.

mantelpiece |'mæntlpiːs| n repisa, chimenea.

manual |'mænjuəl| a manual // n manual m.

manufacture |mænju'fæktʃə*| vt fabricar // n fabricación f; ~r n fabricante m/f.

manure |mə'njuə*| n estiércol m, abono.

manuscript |'mænjuskrɪpt| n manuscrito.

many |'menɪ| a muchos/as // pron muchos/as; a great ~ muchísimos, buen número de; ~ a time muchas veces.

map |mæp| n mapa m // vt trazar el mapa de; to ~ out vt proyectar.

maple |'meɪpl| n arce m, maple m (LAm).

mar |maː*| vt estropear.

marathon |'mærəθən| n maratón m.

marauder |mə'rɔːdə*| n merodeador(a) m/f, intruso/a.

marble |'maːbl| n mármol m; (toy) canica.

March |maːtʃ| n marzo.

march |maːtʃ| vi (MIL) marchar; (fig) caminar con resolución // n marcha; (demonstration) manifestación f; ~-past n desfile m.

mare |meə*| n yegua.

margarine |maːdʒə'riːn| n margarina.

margin |'maːdʒɪn| n margen m; ~al a marginal; ~al seat n (POL) escaño electoral difícil de asegurar.

marigold |'mærɪɡəuld| n caléndula.

marijuana |mærɪ'waːnə| n marijuana.

marinate |'mærɪneɪt| vt adobar.

marine |mə'riːn| a marino // n soldado de marina.

marital |'mærɪtl| a matrimonial; ~ status estado civil.

maritime |'mærɪtaɪm| a marítimo.

marjoram |'maːdʒərəm| n mejorana.

mark |maːk| n marca, señal f; (imprint) huella; (stain) mancha; (Brit SCOL) nota; (currency) marco // vt marcar; manchar; (Brit SCOL) calificar, corregir; to ~ time marcar el paso; to ~ out vt trazar; ~ed a marcado, acusado; ~er n (sign) marcador m; (bookmark) registro.

market |'maːkɪt| n mercado // vt (COMM) comercializar; ~ garden n (Brit) huerto; ~ing n márketing m, mercadotecnia; ~place n mercado; ~ research n (COMM) análisis m inv de mercados; ~ value n valor m en el mercado.

marksman |'maːksmən| n tirador m.

marmalade |'maːməleɪd| n mermelada de naranja.

maroon |mə'ruːn| vt (fig): to be ~ed (in or at) quedar bloqueado (en) // a marrón.

marquee |maː'kiː| n entoldado.

marriage |'mærɪdʒ| n (state) matrimonio; (wedding) boda; (act) casamiento; ~ bureau n agencia matrimonial; ~ certificate n partida de casamiento.

married |'mærɪd| a casado; (life, love) conyugal.

marrow |'mærəu| n médula; (vegetable) calabacín m.

marry |'mærɪ| vt casarse con; (subj: father, priest etc) casar // vi (also: get married) casarse.

Mars |maːz| n Marte m.

marsh |maːʃ| n pantano; (salt ~) marisma.

marshal |'maːʃl| n (MIL) mariscal m; (at sports meeting etc) oficial m; (US: of police, fire department) jefe/a // vt (facts) ordenar; (soldiers) formar.

marshy |'maːʃɪ| a pantanoso.

martial |'maːʃl| a marcial; ~ law n ley f marcial.

martyr |'maːtə*| n mártir m/f // vt martirizar; ~dom n martirio.

marvel |'maːvl| n maravilla, prodigio // vi: to ~ (at) maravillarse (de); ~lous, (US) ~ous a maravilloso.

Marxist |'maːksɪst| a, n marxista m/f.

marzipan |'maːzɪpæn| n mazapán m.

mascara |mæs'kaːrə| n rimel m.

masculine |'mæskjulɪn| a masculino.

mash |mæʃ| n (mix) mezcla; (pulp) amasijo; ~ed potatoes npl puré m de patatas or papas (LAm).

mask |maːsk| n máscara // vt enmascarar.

masochist |'mæsəkɪst| n masoquista m/f.

mason |'meɪsn| n (also: stone~) albañil m; (also: free~) masón m; ~ic |mə'sɔnɪk| a masónico; ~ry n masonería; (in building) mampostería.

masquerade |mæskə'reɪd| n baile m de máscaras; (fig) mascarada // vi: to ~ as disfrazarse de, hacerse pasar por.

mass |mæs| n (people) muchedumbre f; (PHYSICS) masa; (REL) misa; (great quantity) montón m // vi reunirse; (MIL) concentrarse; the ~es las masas.

massacre |'mæsəkə*| n masacre f.

massage |'mæsaːʒ| n masaje m // vt dar masaje a.

masseur |mæ'səː*| n masajista m; **masseuse** |-'səːz| n masajista f.

massive |'mæsɪv| a enorme; (support, intervention) masivo.

mass media npl medios mpl de comunicación masiva.

mass-production |'mæsprə'dʌkʃən| n fabricación f en serie.

mast |maːst| n (NAUT) mástil m; (RADIO etc) torre f.

master |'maːstə*| n maestro; (in secondary school) profesor m; (title for boys): M~ X Señorito X // vt dominar; (learn) aprender a fondo; **M~ of Arts/ Science (M.A./M.Sc.)** n licenciatura superior en Letras/Ciencias; ~ **key** n llave *f* maestra; **~ly** *a* magistral; **~mind** *n* inteligencia superior // *vt* dirigir, planear; **~piece** *n* obra maestra; **~y** *n* maestría.

mat [mæt] *n* estera; (*also*: **door~**) felpudo // *a* = **matt**.

match [mætʃ] *n* cerilla, fósforo; (*game*) partido; (*fig*) igual *m/f* // *vt* emparejar; (*go well with*) hacer juego con; (*equal*) igualar // *vi* hacer juego; **to be a good ~** hacer buena pareja; **~box** *n* caja de cerillas; **~ing** *a* que hace juego.

mate [meɪt] *n* (*work~*) colega *m/f*; (*col: friend*) amigo/a; (*animal*) macho *m/* hembra *f*; (*in merchant navy*) segundo de a bordo // *vi* acoplarse, parearse // *vt* acoplar, parear.

material [mə'tɪərɪəl] *n* (*substance*) materia; (*equipment*) material *m*; (*cloth*) tela, tejido // *a* material; (*important*) esencial; **~s** *npl* materiales *mpl*.

maternal [mə'tə:nl] *a* maternal.

maternity [mə'tə:nɪtɪ] *n* maternidad *f*; **~ dress** *n* vestido premamá; **~ hospital** *n* hospital *m* de maternidad.

math [mæθ] *n* (*US*) = **maths**.

mathematical [mæθə'mætɪkl] *a* matemático.

mathematician [mæθəmə'tɪʃən] *n* matemático/a.

mathematics [mæθə'mætɪks], **maths** [mæθs], (*US*) **math** [mæθ] *n* matemáticas *fpl*.

matinée ['mætɪneɪ] *n* función *f* de la tarde.

mating ['meɪtɪŋ] *n* aparejamiento; **~ call** *n* llamada del macho.

matrices ['meɪtrɪsi:z] *pl of* **matrix**.

matrimonial [mætrɪ'məunɪəl] *a* matrimonial.

matrimony ['mætrɪmənɪ] *n* matrimonio.

matrix ['meɪtrɪks], *pl* **matrices** *n* matriz *f*.

matron ['meɪtrən] *n* (*in hospital*) enfermera *f* jefe; (*in school*) ama de llaves; **~ly** *a* de matrona; (*fig: figure*) corpulento.

mat(t) [mæt] *a* mate.

matted ['mætɪd] *a* enmarañado.

matter ['mætə*] *n* cuestión *f*, asunto; (PHYSICS) sustancia, materia; (*content*) contenido; (*MED*: *pus*) pus *m* // *vi* importar; **it doesn't ~** no importa; **what's the ~?** ¿qué pasa?; **no ~ what** pase lo que pase; **as a ~ of course** por rutina; **as a ~ of fact** de hecho; **~-of-fact** *a* prosaico, práctico.

mattress ['mætrɪs] *n* colchón *m*.

mature [mə'tjuə*] *a* maduro // *vi* madurar; **maturity** *n* madurez *f*.

maul [mɔ:l] *vt* magullar.

mauve [məuv] *a* de color malva *or* guinda (*LAm*).

maxim ['mæksɪm] *n* máxima.

maximum ['mæksɪməm] *a* máximo // *n* (*pl* **maxima** ['mæksɪmə]) máximo.

May [meɪ] *n* mayo.

may [meɪ] *vi* (*conditional*: **might**) (*indicating possibility*): **he ~ come** puede que venga; (*be allowed to*): **~ I smoke?** ¿puedo fumar?; (*wishes*): **~ God bless you!** ¡que Dios le bendiga!

maybe ['meɪbi:] *ad* quizá(s).

May Day *n* el primero de Mayo.

mayday ['meɪdeɪ] *n* S.O.S. *m*.

mayhem ['meɪhɛm] *n* caos *m* total.

mayonnaise [meɪə'neɪz] *n* mayonesa.

mayor [mɛə*] *n* alcalde *m*; **~ess** *n* alcaldesa.

maze [meɪz] *n* laberinto.

M.D. *abbr* = **Doctor of Medicine**.

me [mi:] *pron* (*direct*) me; (*stressed, after pronoun*) mí; (*can you hear me?* ¿me oyes?; **he heard ME!** me oyó a mí; **it's ~** soy yo; **give them to ~** dámelos (*or* dámelas); **with/without ~** conmigo/sin mí.

meadow ['mɛdəu] *n* prado, pradera.

meagre, (*US*) **meager** ['mi:gə*] *a* escaso, pobre.

meal [mi:l] *n* comida; (*flour*) harina; **~time** *n* hora de comer.

mean [mi:n] *a* (*with money*) tacaño; (*unkind*) mezquino, malo; (*average*) medio // *vt* (*pt*, *pp* **meant**) (*signify*) querer decir, significar; (*intend*): **to ~ to do sth** pensar *or* pretender hacer algo // *n* medio, término medio; **~s** *npl* medio *sg*, manera *sg*; (*resource*) recursos *mpl*, medios *mpl*; **by ~s of** mediante, por medio de; **by all ~s!** ¡naturalmente!, ¡claro que sí!; **do you ~ it?** ¿lo dices en serio?; **what do you ~?** ¿qué quiere decir?; **to be meant for sb/sth** ser para uno/algo.

meander [mɪ'ændə*] *vi* (*river*) serpentear; (*person*) vagar.

meaning ['mi:nɪŋ] *n* significado, sentido; **~ful** *a* significativo; **~less** *a* sin sentido.

meanness ['mi:nnɪs] *n* (*with money*) tacañería; (*unkindness*) maldad *f*, mezquindad *f*.

meant [mɛnt] *pt*, *pp of* **mean**.

meantime ['mi:ntaɪm], **meanwhile** ['mi:nwaɪl] *ad* (*also*: **in the ~**) mientras tanto.

measles ['mi:zlz] *n* sarampión *m*.

measly ['mi:zlɪ] *a* (*col*) miserable.

measure ['mɛʒə*] *vt* medir; (*for clothes etc*) tomar las medidas a // *vi* medir // *n* medida; (*ruler*) regla; **~ments** *npl* medidas *fpl*.

meat [mi:t] *n* carne *f*; **cold ~** fiambre *m*; **~ball** *n* albóndiga; **~ pie** *n* pastel *m* de carne; **~y** *a* carnoso; (*fig*) sustancioso.

Mecca ['mɛkə] *n* La Meca.

mechanic [mɪ'kænɪk] *n* mecánico/a; **~s** *n* mecánica // *npl* mecanismo *sg*; **~al** *a* mecánico.

mechanism ['mɛkənɪzəm] *n* mecanismo.

medal |'mɛdl| *n* medalla; **~lion** |mɪ'dælɪən| *n* medallón *m*; **~list**, (*US*) **~ist** *n* (*SPORT*) medallero/a.

meddle |'mɛdl| *vi*: to ~ in entrometerse en; to ~ with sth manosear algo.

media |'miːdɪə| *npl* medios *mpl* de comunicación.

mediaeval |mɛdɪ'iːvl| *a* = **medieval.**

median |'miːdɪən| *n* (*US*: *also*: ~ strip) mediana.

mediate |'miːdɪeɪt| *vi* mediar; **mediator** *n* intermediario/a, mediador(a) *m/f*.

Medicaid |'mɛdɪkeɪd| *n* (*US*) *programa de ayuda médica.*

medical |'mɛdɪkl| *a* médico // *n* reconocimiento médico.

Medicare |'mɛdɪkɛə*| *n* (*US*) seguro médico del Estado.

medicated |'mɛdɪkeɪtɪd| *a* medicinal.

medicine |'mɛdsɪn| *n* medicina; (*drug*) medicamento.

medieval |mɛdɪ'iːvl| *a* medieval.

mediocre |miːdɪ'əukə*| *a* mediocre.

meditate |'mɛdɪteɪt| *vi* meditar.

Mediterranean |mɛdɪtə'reɪnɪən| *a* mediterráneo; **the ~ (Sea)** el (Mar) Mediterráneo.

medium |'miːdɪəm| *a* mediano, regular // *n* (*pl* **media:** *means*) medio; (*pl* **mediums:** *person*) médium *m/f*; **happy ~** justo medio; ~ **wave** *n* onda media.

medley |'mɛdlɪ| *n* mezcla; (*MUS*) popurrí *m*.

meek |miːk| *a* manso, sumiso.

meet |miːt|, *pt*, *pp* **met** *vt* encontrar; (*accidentally*) encontrarse con, tropezar con; (*by arrangement*) reunirse con; (*for the first time*) conocer; (*go and fetch*) ir a buscar; (*opponent*) enfrentarse con; (*obligations*) cumplir // *vi* encontrarse; (*in session*) reunirse; (*join: objects*) unirse; (*get to know*) conocerse; **to ~ with** *vt fus* reunirse con; (*difficulty*) tropezar con; **~ing** *n* encuentro; (*arranged*) cita, compromiso (*LAm*); (*session, business ~*) reunión *f*; (*POL*) mitin *m*.

megabyte |'mɛgə'baɪt| *n* (*COMPUT*) megabyte *m*, megaocteto.

megaphone |'mɛgəfəun| *n* megáfono.

melancholy |'mɛlənkəlɪ| *n* melancolía // *a* melancólico.

mellow |'mɛləu| *a* (*wine*) añejo; (*sound, colour*) suave; (*fruit*) maduro // *vi* (*person*) ablandar.

melody |'mɛlədɪ| *n* melodía.

melon |'mɛlən| *n* melón *m*.

melt |mɛlt| *vi* (*metal*) fundirse; (*snow*) derretirse; (*fig*) ablandarse // *vt* (*also*: ~ **down**) fundir; **to ~ away** *vi* desvanecerse; **~down** *n* (*in nuclear reactor*) fusión *f* de un reactor (nuclear); **~ing point** *n* punto de fusión; **~ing pot** *n* (*fig*) crisol *m*.

member |'mɛmbə*| *n* (*gen*) miembro; (*of club*) socio/a; **M~ of Parliament (MP)** (*Brit*) diputado/a; **M~ of the European Parliament (MEP)** (*Brit*) eurodiputado/a; **~ship** *n* (*members*) número de miembros; **to seek ~ship of** pedir el ingreso a; **~ship card** *n* carnet *m* de socio.

memento |mə'mɛntəu| *n* recuerdo.

memo |'mɛməu| *n* apunte *m*, nota.

memoirs |'mɛmwaːz| *npl* memorias *fpl*.

memorandum |mɛmə'rændəm|, *pl* **-da** |-də| *n* apunte *m*, nota; (*POL*) memorándum *m*.

memorial |mɪ'mɔːrɪəl| *n* monumento conmemorativo // *a* conmemorativo.

memorize |'mɛməraɪz| *vt* aprender de memoria.

memory |'mɛmərɪ| *n* memoria; (*recollection*) recuerdo.

men |mɛn| *pl of* **man.**

menace |'mɛnəs| *n* amenaza // *vt* amenazar; **menacing** *a* amenazador(a).

menagerie |mɪ'nædʒərɪ| *n* casa de fieras.

mend |mɛnd| *vt* reparar, arreglar; (*darn*) zurcir // *vi* reponerse // *n* (*gen*) remiendo; (*darn*) zurcido; **to be on the ~** ir mejorando; **~ing** *n* reparación *f*; (*clothes*) ropa por remendar.

menial |'miːnɪəl| *a* doméstico; (*pej*) bajo.

meningitis |mɛnɪn'dʒaɪtɪs| *n* meningitis *f*.

menopause |'mɛnəupɔːz| *n* menopausia.

menstruation |mɛnstru'eɪʃən| *n* menstruación *f*.

mental |'mɛntl| *a* mental; **~ity** |-'tælɪtɪ| *n* mentalidad *f*.

mention |'mɛnʃən| *n* mención *f* // *vt* mencionar; (*speak of*) hablar de; **don't ~ it!** ¡de nada!

mentor |'mɛntɔː*| *n* mentor *m*.

menu |'mɛnjuː| *n* (*set ~*) menú *m*; (*printed*) carta; (*COMPUT*) menú *m*.

MEP *n abbr* = **Member of the European Parliament.**

mercenary |'məːsɪnərɪ| *a*, *n* mercenario.

merchandise |'məːtʃəndaɪz| *n* mercancías *fpl*.

merchant |'məːtʃənt| *n* comerciante *m/f*; ~ **bank** *n* (*Brit*) banco comercial; ~ **navy**, (*US*) ~ **marine** *n* marina mercante.

merciful |'məːsɪful| *a* compasivo.

merciless |'məːsɪlɪs| *a* despiadado.

mercury |'məːkjurɪ| *n* mercurio.

mercy |'məːsɪ| *n* compasión *f*; (*REL*) misericordia; **at the ~ of** a la merced de.

mere |mɪə*| *a* simple, mero; **~ly** *ad* simplemente, sólo.

merge |məːdʒ| *vt* (*join*) unir; (*mix*) mezclar; (*fuse*) fundir // *vi* unirse; (*COMM*) fusionarse; **~r** *n* (*COMM*) fusión *f*.

meringue |mə'ræŋ| *n* merengue *m*.

merit |'mɛrɪt| *n* mérito // *vt* merecer.

mermaid |'məːmeɪd| *n* sirena.

merry |'mɛrɪ| *a* alegre; **M~ Christmas!**

¡Felices Pascuas!; **~-go-round** n tiovivo.

mesh [mɛʃ] n malla; (TECH) engranaje m // vi (gears) engranar.

mesmerize ['mɛzmǝraɪz] vt hipnotizar.

mess [mɛs] n confusión f; (of objects) revoltijo; (tangle) lío; (MIL) comedor m; **to ~ about** or **around** vi (col) perder el tiempo; (pass the time) entretenerse; **to ~ about** or **around with** vt fus (col: play with) divertirse con; (: handle) manosear; **to ~ up** vt (disarrange) desordenar; (spoil) estropear; (dirty) ensuciar.

message ['mɛsɪdʒ] n recado, mensaje m.

messenger ['mɛsɪndʒǝ*] n mensajero/a.

Messrs abbr (on letters: = Messieurs) Sres.

messy ['mɛsɪ] a (dirty) sucio; (untidy) desordenado.

met [mɛt] pt, pp of **meet**.

metabolism [mɛ'tæbǝlɪzǝm] n metabolismo.

metal ['mɛtl] n metal m; **~lic** [-'tælɪk] a metálico; **~lurgy** [-'tælǝdʒɪ] n metalurgia.

metaphor ['mɛtǝfǝ*] n metáfora.

mete [miːt] : **to ~ out** vt fus (punishment) imponer.

meteor ['miːtɪǝ*] n meteoro; **~ite** [-aɪt] n meteorito.

meteorology [miːtɪǝ'rɔlǝdʒɪ] n meteorología.

meter ['miːtǝ*] n (instrument) contador m; (US: unit) = metre // vt (US POST) franquear.

method ['mɛθǝd] n método; **~ical** [mɪ'θɔdɪkl] a metódico.

Methodist ['mɛθǝdɪst] a, n metodista m/f.

meths [mɛθs], **methylated spirit** ['mɛθɪleɪtɪd-] n (Brit) alcohol m metilado or desnaturalizado.

metre, (US) **meter** ['miːtǝ*] n metro.

metric ['mɛtrɪk] a métrico.

metropolis [mɪ'trɔpǝlɪs] n metrópoli f.

metropolitan [mɛtrǝ'pɔlɪtǝn] a metropolitano; the **M~ Police** n (Brit) la policía londinense.

mettle ['mɛtl] n valor m, ánimo.

mew [mjuː] vi (cat) maullar.

mews [mjuːz] n: **~ cottage** (Brit) casa acondicionada en antiguos establos o cocheras.

Mexican ['mɛksɪkǝn] a, n mejicano/a m/f, mexicano/a m/f (LAm).

Mexico ['mɛksɪkǝu] n Méjico, México (LAm); **~ City** n Ciudad f de Méjico or México (LAm).

mezzanine ['mɛtsǝniːn] n entresuelo.

miaow [miː'au] vi maullar.

mice [maɪs] pl of **mouse**.

micro... [maɪkrǝu] pref micro....

microbe ['maɪkrǝub] n microbio.

micro: ~chip n microplaqueta; **~**

(computer) n microordenador m; **~cosm** n microcosmo; **~phone** n micrófono; **~processor** n microprocesador m; **~scope** n microscopio; **~wave** n (also: ~wave oven) horno microondas.

mid [mɪd] a: **in ~ May** a mediados de mayo; **in ~ afternoon** a media tarde; **in ~ air** en el aire; **~day** n mediodía m.

middle ['mɪdl] n medio, centro; (waist) cintura // a de en medio; **in the ~ of the night** en plena noche; **~-aged** a de mediana edad; **the M~ Ages** npl la Edad Media; **~-class** a de clase media; **the ~ class(es)** n(pl) la clase media; **M~ East** n Oriente m Medio; **~man** n intermediario; **~ name** n segundo nombre; **~weight** n (BOXING) peso medio.

middling ['mɪdlɪŋ] a mediano.

midge [mɪdʒ] n mosca.

midget ['mɪdʒɪt] n enano/a.

Midlands ['mɪdlǝndz] npl la región central de Inglaterra.

midnight ['mɪdnaɪt] n medianoche f.

midriff ['mɪdrɪf] n diafragma m.

midst [mɪdst] n: **in the ~ of** en medio de.

midsummer [mɪd'sʌmǝ*] n: **in ~** en pleno verano.

midway [mɪd'weɪ] a, ad: **~ (between)** a medio camino (entre).

midweek [mɪd'wiːk] ad entre semana.

midwife ['mɪdwaɪf], pl **-wives** [-waɪvz] n comadrona, partera; **~ry** [-wɪfǝrɪ] n partería.

midwinter [mɪd'wɪntǝ*] n: **in ~** en pleno invierno.

might [maɪt] vb see **may**: **he ~ be there** podría estar allí, puede que esté allí; **I ~ as well go** más vale que vaya; **you ~ like to try** podría intentar // n fuerza, poder m; **~y** a fuerte, poderoso.

migraine ['miːgreɪn] n jaqueca.

migrant ['maɪgrǝnt] n a (bird) migratorio; (worker) emigrante.

migrate [maɪ'greɪt] vi emigrar.

mike [maɪk] n abbr (= microphone) micro.

mild [maɪld] a (person) apacible; (climate) templado; (slight) ligero; (taste) suave; (illness) leve.

mildew ['mɪldjuː] n moho.

mildly ['maɪldlɪ] ad ligeramente; suavemente; **to put it ~** para no decir más.

mile [maɪl] n milla; **~age** n número de millas, ≈ kilometraje m; **~stone** n mojón m.

milieu ['miːljǝ:] n (medio) ambiente m.

militant ['mɪlɪtnt] a, n militante m/f.

military ['mɪlɪtǝrɪ] a militar.

militia [mɪ'lɪʃǝ] n milicia.

milk [mɪlk] n leche f // vt (cow) ordeñar; (fig) chupar; **~ chocolate** n chocolate m con leche; **~man** n lechero; **~ shake** n batido, malteada (LAm); **~y** a lechoso; **M~y Way** n Vía Láctea.

mill [mɪl] n (windmill etc) molino; (cof-

fee ~) molinillo; (*factory*) fábrica; (*spinning* ~) hilandería // *vt* moler // *vi* (*also:* ~ about) arremolinarse.

millennium [mɪˈlɛnɪəm], *pl* ~s or -ia [-nɪə] *n* milenio, milenario.

miller [ˈmɪlə*] *n* molinero.

millet [ˈmɪlɪt] *n* mijo.

milli... [ˈmɪlɪ] *pref*: ~gram(me) *n* miligramo; ~litre *n*, (US) ~liter *n* mililitro; ~metre, (US) ~meter *n* milímetro.

milliner [ˈmɪlɪnə*] *n* sombrerero/a; ~y *n* sombrerería.

million [ˈmɪljən] *n* millón *m*; a ~ times un millón de veces; ~aire *n* millonario/a.

millstone [ˈmɪlstəun] *n* piedra de molino.

milometer [maɪˈlɒmɪtə*] *n* (*Brit*) ≈ cuentakilómetros *m inv*.

mime [maɪm] *n* mímica; (*actor*) mimo/a // *vt* remedar // *vi* actuar de mimo.

mimic [ˈmɪmɪk] *n* imitador(a) *m/f* // *a* mímico // *vt* remedar, imitar; ~ry *n* imitación *f*.

min. *abbr* = **minute(s); minimum.**

minaret [mɪnəˈrɛt] *n* alminar *m*.

mince [mɪns] *vt* picar // *vi* (*in walking*) andar con pasos menudos // *n* (*Brit CULIN*) carne *f* picada, picadillo; ~meat *n* conserva de fruta picada; ~ pie *n* empanadilla rellena de fruta picada; ~r *n* picadora de carne.

mind [maɪnd] *n* (*gen*) mente *f*; (*contrasted with matter*) espíritu // *vt* (*attend to, look after*) ocuparse de, cuidar; (*be careful of*) tener cuidado con; (*object to*): I don't ~ the noise no me molesta el ruido; it is on my ~ me preocupa; to my ~ en mi opinión; to be out of one's ~ estar fuera de juicio; to bear sth in ~ tomar *or* tener algo en cuenta; to make up one's ~ decidirse; I don't ~ me es igual; ~ you, ... te advierto que ...; never ~! ¡es igual!, ¡no importa!; (*don't worry*) ¡no te preocupes!; '~ the step' 'cuidado con el escalón'; ~er *n* guardaespaldas *m inv*; ~ful *a*: ~ful of consciente de; ~less *a* (*crime*) sin motivo; (*work*) de autómata.

mine [maɪn] *pron* el mío/la mía *etc*; a friend of ~ un(a) amigo/a mío/mía // *a*: this book is ~ este libro es mío // *n* mina // *vt* (*coal*) extraer; (*ship, beach*) minar; ~field *n* campo de minas; **miner** *n* minero/a.

mineral [ˈmɪnərəl] *a* mineral // *n* mineral *m*; ~s *npl* (*Brit*: *soft drinks*) aguas *fpl* minerales, gaseosa *sg*; ~ water *n* agua mineral.

minesweeper [ˈmaɪnswiːpə*] *n* dragaminas *m inv*.

mingle [ˈmɪŋgl] *vi*: to ~ with mezclarse con.

miniature [ˈmɪnətʃə*] *a* (en) miniatura // *n* miniatura.

minibus [ˈmɪnɪbʌs] *n* microbús *m*.

minim [ˈmɪnɪm] *n* (*Brit MUS*) blanca.

minimal [ˈmɪnɪml] *a* mínimo.

minimum [ˈmɪnɪməm] *n*, *pl* **minima** [ˈmɪnɪmə] mínimo // *a* mínimo.

mining [ˈmaɪnɪŋ] *n* explotación *f* minera // *a* minero.

miniskirt [ˈmɪnɪskəːt] *n* minifalda.

minister [ˈmɪnɪstə*] *n* (*Brit POL*) ministro/a (*Sp*), secretario/a (*LAm*); (*REL*) pastor *m* // *vi*: to ~ to atender a; ~ial [-ˈtɪərɪəl] *a* (*Brit POL*) ministerial.

ministry [ˈmɪnɪstrɪ] *n* (*Brit POL*) ministerio (*Sp*), secretaría (*LAm*); (*REL*) sacerdocio.

mink [mɪŋk] *n* visón *m*

minnow [ˈmɪnəu] *n* pececillo (*de agua dulce*).

minor [ˈmaɪnə*] *a* (*unimportant*) secundario; (*MUS*) menor // *n* (*LAW*) menor *m/f* de edad.

Minorca [mɪˈnɔːkə] *n* Menorca.

minority [maɪˈnɔrɪtɪ] *n* minoría.

mint [mɪnt] *n* (*plant*) menta, hierbabuena; (*sweet*) caramelo de menta // *vt* (*coins*) acuñar; the (Royal) M~, (US) the (US) M~ la Casa de la Moneda; in ~ condition en perfecto estado.

minus [ˈmaɪnəs] *n* (*also:* ~ sign) signo de menos // *prep* menos.

minute [ˈmɪnɪt] *n* minuto; (*fig*) momento; ~s *npl* actas *fpl* // *a* [maɪˈnjuːt] diminuto; (*search*) minucioso; at the last ~ a última hora.

miracle [ˈmɪrəkl] *n* milagro; **miraculous** [mɪˈrækjuləs] *a* milagroso.

mirage [ˈmɪrɑːʒ] *n* espejismo.

mire [maɪə*] *n* fango, lodo.

mirror [ˈmɪrə*] *n* espejo; (*in car*) retrovisor *m* // *vt* reflejar.

mirth [məːθ] *n* alegría.

misadventure [mɪsədˈvɛntʃə*] *n* desgracia; death by ~ muerte *f* accidental.

misanthropist [mɪˈzænθrəpɪst] *n* misántropo/a.

misapprehension [ˈmɪsæprɪˈhɛnʃən] *n* equivocación *f*.

misbehave [mɪsbɪˈheɪv] *vi* portarse mal.

miscalculate [mɪsˈkælkjuleɪt] *vt* calcular mal.

miscarriage [ˈmɪskærɪdʒ] *n* (*MED*) aborto; ~ of justice error *m* judicial.

miscellaneous [mɪsɪˈleɪnɪəs] *a* varios/as, diversos/as.

mischief [ˈmɪstʃɪf] *n* (*naughtiness*) travesura; (*harm*) mal *m*, daño; (*maliciousness*) malicia; **mischievous** [-ʃɪvəs] *a* travieso; dañoso; (*playful*) malicioso.

misconception [ˈmɪskənˈsɛpʃən] *n* concepto erróneo; equivocación *f*.

misconduct [mɪsˈkɔndʌkt] *n* mala conducta; **professional** ~ falta profesional.

miscount [mɪsˈkaunt] *vt, vi* contar mal.

misconstrue [mɪskənˈstruː] *vt* interpretar mal.

misdeed [mɪsˈdiːd] *n* delito.

misdemeanour, (*US*) **misdemeanor**
[mɪsdɪ'miːnə*] *n* delito, ofensa.

miser ['maɪzə*] *n* avaro/a.

miserable ['mɪzərəbl] *a* (*unhappy*) triste,
desgraciado; (*wretched*) miserable.

miserly ['maɪzəlɪ] *a* avariento, tacaño.

misery ['mɪzərɪ] *n* (*unhappiness*) tristeza; (*wretchedness*) miseria, desdicha.

misfire [mɪs'faɪə*] *vi* fallar.

misfit ['mɪsfɪt] *n* (*person*) inadaptado/a.

misfortune [mɪs'fɔːtʃən] *n* desgracia.

misgiving(s) [mɪs'gɪvɪŋ(z)] *n(pl)* (*mistrust*) recelo; (*apprehension*) presentimiento.

misguided [mɪs'gaɪdɪd] *a* equivocado.

mishandle [mɪs'hændl] *vt* (*treat roughly*)
maltratar; (*mismanage*) manejar mal.

mishap ['mɪshæp] *n* desgracia, contratiempo.

misinform [mɪsɪn'fɔːm] *vt* informar mal.

misinterpret [mɪsɪn'təːprɪt] *vt* interpretar mal.

misjudge [mɪs'dʒʌdʒ] *vt* juzgar mal.

mislay [mɪs'leɪ] (*irg: like* lay) *vt* extraviar, perder.

mislead [mɪs'liːd] (*irg: like* lead) *vt* llevar a conclusiones erróneas; **~ing** *a* engañoso.

mismanage [mɪs'mænɪdʒ] *vt* administrar
mal.

misnomer [mɪs'nəumə*] *n* término inapropiado o equivocado.

misogynist [mɪ'sɔdʒɪnɪst] *n* misógino.

misplace [mɪs'pleɪs] *vt* (*lose*) extraviar.

misprint ['mɪsprɪnt] *n* errata, error *m* de
imprenta.

Miss [mɪs] *n* Señorita.

miss [mɪs] *vt* (*train etc*) perder; (*fail to
hit: target*) no dar en; (*regret the absence of*): **I ~ him** (yo) le echo de menos *or* a faltar // *vi* fallar // *n* (*shot*) tiro
fallido *or* perdido; **to ~ out** *vt* (*Brit*)
omitir.

misshapen [mɪs'ʃeɪpən] *a* deforme.

missile ['mɪsaɪl] *n* (*AVIAT*) mísil *m*; (*object thrown*) proyectil *m*.

missing ['mɪsɪŋ] *a* (*pupil*) ausente;
(*thing*) perdido; (*MIL*) desaparecido; **to
be ~** faltar.

mission ['mɪʃən] *n* misión *f*; **~ary** *n*
misionero/a.

misspent ['mɪs'spent] *a*: **his ~ youth** su
juventud disipada.

mist [mɪst] *n* (*light*) neblina; (*heavy*) niebla; (*at sea*) bruma // *vi* (*also: ~ over,
~ up: weather*) nublarse; (: *Brit: win-
dows*) empañarse.

mistake [mɪs'teɪk] *n* error *m* // *vt* (*irg:
like* take) entender mal; **by ~** por equivocación; **to make a ~** equivocarse; **to ~
A for B** confundir A con B; **~n** *a* (*idea
etc*) equivocado; **to be ~n** equivocarse,
engañarse.

mister ['mɪstə*] *n* (*col*) señor *m*; *see* **Mr.**

mistletoe ['mɪsltəu] *n* muérdago.

mistook [mɪs'tuk] *pt of* **mistake.**

mistress ['mɪstrɪs] *n* (*lover*) amante *f*;
(*of house*) señora (de la casa); (*Brit: in
primary school*) maestra; (*in secondary
school*) profesora; *see* **Mrs.**

mistrust [mɪs'trʌst] *vt* desconfiar de.

misty ['mɪstɪ] *a* nebuloso, brumoso; (*day*)
de niebla; (*glasses*) empañado.

misunderstand [mɪsʌndə'stænd] (*irg:
like* understand) *vt*, *vi* entender mal;
~ing *n* malentendido.

misuse [mɪs'juːs] *n* mal uso; (*of power*)
abuso // *vt* [mɪs'juːz] abusar de; (*funds*)
malversar.

mitre, (*US*) **miter** ['maɪtə*] *n* mitra.

mitt(en) ['mɪt(n)] *n* manopla.

mix [mɪks] *vt* (*gen*) mezclar; (*combine*)
unir // *vi* mezclarse; (*people*) llevarse
bien // *n* mezcla; **to ~ up** *vt* mezclar;
(*confuse*) confundir; **~ed** *a* (*assorted*)
variado, surtido; (*school etc*) mixto;
~ed-up *a* (*confused*) confuso, revuelto;
~er *n* (*for food*) licuadora; (*person*):
he's a good ~er tiene don de gentes;
~ture *n* mezcla; **~-up** *n* confusión *f*.

mm *abbr* (= *millimetre*) mm.

moan [məun] *n* gemido // *vi* gemir; (*col:
complain*): **to ~ (about)** quejarse (de).

moat [məut] *n* foso.

mob [mɔb] *n* multitud *f*; (*pej*): **the ~** el
populacho // *vt* acosar.

mobile ['məubaɪl] *a* móvil // *n* móvil *m*;
~ home *n* caravana.

mock [mɔk] *vt* (*make ridiculous*) ridiculizar; (*laugh at*) burlarse de // *a* fingido;
~ery *n* burla.

mod [mɔd] *a see* **convenience.**

mode [məud] *n* modo.

model ['mɔdl] *n* (*gen*) modelo; (*ARCH*)
maqueta; (*person: for fashion, ART*) modelo *m/f* // *a* modelo // *vt* modelar // *vi*
ser modelo; **~ railway** ferrocarril *m* de
juguete; **to ~ clothes** pasar modelos, ser
modelo.

modem ['məudəm] *n* modem *m*.

moderate ['mɔdərət] *a*, *n* moderado/a
m/f // *vb* ['mɔdəreɪt] *vi* moderarse, calmarse // *vt* moderar.

modern ['mɔdən] *a* moderno; **~ize** *vt*
modernizar.

modest ['mɔdɪst] *a* modesto; **~y** *n* modestia.

modicum ['mɔdɪkəm] *n*: **a ~ of** un mínimo de.

modify ['mɔdɪfaɪ] *vt* modificar.

module ['mɔdjuːl] *n* (*unit, component,
SPACE*) módulo.

mogul ['məugəl] *n* (*fig*) magnate *m*.

mohair ['məuhɛə*] *n* mohair *m*.

moist [mɔɪst] *a* húmedo; **~en** ['mɔɪsn] *vt*
humedecer; **~ure** ['mɔɪstʃə*] *n* humedad
f; **~urizer** ['mɔɪstʃəraɪzə*] *n* crema hidratante.

molar ['məulə*] *n* muela.

molasses [məu'læsɪz] *n* melaza.

mold [məuld] n, vt (US) = **mould**.
mole [məul] n (animal) topo; (spot) lunar m.
molecule ['mɔlɪkjuːl] n molécula.
molest [məu'lest] vt importunar.
mollycoddle ['mɔlɪkɔdl] vt mimar.
molt [məult] vi (US) = **moult**.
molten ['məultən] a fundido; (lava) líquido.
mom [mɔm] n (US) = **mum**.
moment ['məumənt] n momento; at the ~ de momento, por ahora; ~**ary** a momentáneo; ~**ous** [-'mentəs] a trascendental, importante.
momentum [məu'mentəm] n momento; (fig) ímpetu m; to gather ~ cobrar velocidad.
mommy ['mɔmɪ] n (US) = **mummy**.
Monaco ['mɔnəkəu] n Mónaco.
monarch ['mɔnək] n monarca m/f; ~**y** n monarquía.
monastery ['mɔnəstərɪ] n monasterio.
Monday ['mʌndɪ] n lunes m inv.
monetary ['mʌnɪtərɪ] a monetario.
money ['mʌnɪ] n dinero; to make ~ ganar dinero; ~**lender** n prestamista m/f; ~ **order** n giro; ~-**spinner** n (col): to be a ~-spinner dar mucho dinero.
mongol ['mɔngəl] a, n (MED) mongólico.
mongrel ['mʌngrəl] n (dog) perro mestizo.
monitor ['mɔnɪtə*] n (SCOL) monitor m; (also: television ~) receptor m de control; (of computer) monitor m // vt controlar.
monk [mʌŋk] n monje m.
monkey ['mʌŋkɪ] n mono; ~ **nut** n (Brit) cacahuete m, maní (LAm); ~ **wrench** n llave f inglesa.
mono... [mɔnəu] pref: ~**chrome** a monocromo.
monocle ['mɔnɔkl] n monóculo.
monologue ['mɔnəlɔg] n monólogo.
monopoly [mə'nɔpəlɪ] n monopolio.
monotone ['mɔnətəun] n voz f (or tono) monocorde.
monotonous [mə'nɔtənəs] a monótono.
monotony [mə'nɔtənɪ] n monotonía.
monsoon [mɔn'suːn] n monzón m.
monster ['mɔnstə*] n monstruo.
monstrosity [mɔns'trɔsɪtɪ] n monstruosidad f.
monstrous ['mɔnstrəs] a (huge) enorme; (atrocious) monstruoso.
montage ['mɔntɑːʒ] n montaje m.
month [mʌnθ] n mes m; ~**ly** a mensual // ad mensualmente // n (magazine) revista mensual.
monument ['mɔnjumənt] n monumento; ~**al** [-'mentl] a monumental.
moo [muː] vi mugir.
mood [muːd] n humor m; to be in a good/bad ~ estar de buen/mal humor; ~**y** a (changeable) de humor variable; (sullen) malhumorado.

moon [muːn] n luna; ~**light** n luz f de la luna; ~**lighting** n pluriempleo; ~**lit** a: a ~**lit** night una noche de luna.
Moor [muə*] n moro/a.
moor [muə*] n páramo // vt (ship) amarrar // vi echar las amarras.
Moorish ['muərɪʃ] a moro; (architecture) árabe, morisco.
moorland ['muələnd] n páramo, brezal m.
moose [muːs] n, pl inv alce m.
mop [mɔp] n fregona; (of hair) greña, melena // vt fregar; to ~ **up** vt limpiar.
mope [məup] vi estar or andar deprimido.
moped ['məuped] n ciclomotor m.
moral ['mɔrl] a moral // n moraleja; ~**s** npl moralidad f, moral f.
morale [mɔ'rɑːl] n moral f.
morality [mə'rælɪtɪ] n moralidad f.
morass [mə'ræs] n pantano.
morbid ['mɔːbɪd] a (interest) morboso; (MED) mórbido.
more [mɔː*] ♦ a 1 (greater in number etc) más; ~ **people/work** than before más gente/trabajo que antes
2 (additional) más; do you want (some) ~ **tea?** ¿quieres más té?; is there any ~ **wine?** ¿queda vino?; it'll take a few ~ **weeks** tardará unas semanas más; it's 2 kms ~ **to the house** faltan 2 kms para la casa; ~ **time/letters than we expected** más tiempo del que/más cartas de las que esperábamos
♦ pron (greater amount, additional amount) más; ~ **than 10** más de 10; it cost ~ **than the other/than we expected** costó más que el otro/más de lo que esperábamos; is there any ~? ¿hay más?; **many/much** ~ mucho(a)/muchos(as) más
♦ ad más; ~ **dangerous/easily (than)** más peligroso/fácilmente (que); ~ **and** ~ **expensive** cada vez más caro; ~ **or less** más o menos; ~ **than ever** más que nunca.
moreover [mɔː'rəuvə*] ad además, por otra parte.
morgue [mɔːg] n depósito de cadáveres.
Mormon ['mɔːmən] n mormón/ona m/f.
morning ['mɔːnɪŋ] n (gen) mañana; (early ~) madrugada; **in the** ~ por la mañana; **7 o'clock in the** ~ las 7 de la mañana.
Moroccan [mə'rɔkən] a, n marroquí m/f.
Morocco [mə'rɔkəu] n Marruecos m.
moron ['mɔːrɔn] n imbécil m/f.
morose [mə'rəus] a hosco, malhumorado.
morphine ['mɔːfiːn] n morfina.
Morse [mɔːs] n (also: ~ **code**) (código) morse.
morsel ['mɔːsl] n (of food) bocado.
mortal ['mɔːtl] a, n mortal m; ~**ity** [-'tælɪtɪ] n mortalidad f.
mortar ['mɔːtə*] n argamasa; (imple-

ment) mortero.

mortgage ['mɔːgɪdʒ] *n* hipoteca // *vt* hipotecar; ~ **company** *n* (*US*) ≈ banco hipotecario.

mortify ['mɔːtɪfaɪ] *vt* mortificar, humillar.

mortuary ['mɔːtjuərɪ] *n* depósito de cadáveres.

mosaic [məu'zeɪɪk] *n* mosaico.

Moscow ['mɔskəu] *n* Moscú *m*.

Moslem ['mɔzləm] *a, n* = **Muslim**.

mosque [mɔsk] *n* mezquita.

mosquito [mɔs'kiːtəu], *pl* ~**es** *n* mosquito (*Sp*), zancudo (*LAm*).

moss [mɔs] *n* musgo.

most [məust] *a* la mayor parte de, la mayoría de // *pron* la mayor parte, la mayoría // *ad* el más (very) muy; **the** ~ (*also*: + *adjective*) el más; ~ **of them** la mayor parte de ellos; I saw the ~ yo vi el que más; **at the** (**very**) ~ a lo sumo, todo lo más; **to make the** ~ **of** aprovechar (al máximo); **a** ~ **interesting book** un libro interesantísimo; **a** ~ **interesting book** un libro interesantísimo; **~ly** *ad* en su mayor parte, principalmente.

MOT *n abbr* = *Ministry of Transport*): **the** ~ (**test**) *inspección (anual) obligatoria de coches y camiones.*

moth [mɔθ] *n* mariposa nocturna; (*clothes* ~) polilla; ~**ball** *n* bola de naftalina.

mother ['mʌðə*] *n* madre *f* // *a* materno // *vt* (*care for*) cuidar (como una madre); ~**hood** *n* maternidad *f*; ~**-in-law** *n* suegra; ~**ly** *a* maternal; ~**-of-pearl** *n* nácar *m*; ~**-to-be** *n* futura madre; ~ **tongue** *n* lengua materna.

motif [məu'tiːf] *n* motivo; (*theme*) tema *m*.

motion ['məuʃən] *n* movimiento; (*gesture*) ademán *m*, señal *f*; (*at meeting*) moción *f* // *vt, vi*: **to** ~ (**to**) **sb to do sth** hacer señas a uno para que haga algo; ~**less** *a* inmóvil; ~ **picture** *n* película.

motivated ['məutɪveɪtɪd] *a* motivado.

motive ['məutɪv] *n* motivo.

motley ['mɔtlɪ] *a* variado.

motor ['məutə*] *n* motor *m*; (*Brit*: *col*: *vehicle*) coche *m*, carro (*LAm*), automóvil *m* // *a* motor (*f*: motora, motriz); ~**bike** *n* moto *f*; ~**boat** *n* lancha motora; ~**car** *n* (*Brit*) coche *m*, carro (*LAm*), automóvil *m*; ~**cycle** *n* motocicleta; ~**cycle racing** *n* motociclismo; ~**cyclist** *n* motociclista *m/f*; ~**ing** *n* (*Brit*) automovilismo; ~**ist** *n* conductor(a) *m/f*, automovilista *m/f*; ~ **racing** *n* (*Brit*) carreras *fpl* de coches, automovilismo; ~ **scooter** *n* moto *f*; ~ **vehicle** *n* automóvil *m*; ~**way** *n* (*Brit*) autopista.

mottled ['mɔtld] *a* abigarrado, multicolor.

motto ['mɔtəu], *pl* ~**es** *n* lema *m*;

(*watchword*) consigna.

mould, (*US*) **mold** [məuld] *n* molde *m*; (*mildew*) moho // *vt* moldear; (*fig*) formar; ~**er** *vi* (*decay*) decaer; ~**ing** *n* moldura; ~**y** *a* enmohecido.

moult, (*US*) **molt** [məult] *vi* mudar (la piel/las plumas).

mound [maund] *n* montón *m*, montículo.

mount [maunt] *n* monte *m*; (*horse*) montura; (*for jewel etc*) engarce *m*; (*for picture*) marco // *vt* montar, subir a // *vi* (*also*: ~ **up**) subirse, montarse.

mountain ['mauntɪn] *n* montaña // *cpd* de montaña; ~**eer** [-'nɪə*] *n* alpinista *m/f*, andinista *m/f* (*LAm*); ~**eering** [-'nɪərɪŋ] *n* alpinismo, andinismo (*LAm*); ~**ous** *a* montañoso; ~**side** *n* ladera de la montaña.

mourn [mɔːn] *vt* llorar, lamentar // *vi*: **to** ~ **for** llorar la muerte de, lamentarse por; ~**er** *n* doliente *m/f*; dolorido/a; ~**ful** *a* triste, lúgubre; ~**ing** *n* luto // *cpd* (*dress*) de luto; **in** ~**ing** de luto.

mouse [maus], *pl* **mice** *n* ratón *m*; (*COMPUT*) ratón *m*; ~**trap** *n* ratonera.

mousse [muːs] *n* (*CULIN*) crema batida; (*for hair*) espuma (moldeadora).

moustache [məs'tɑːʃ] *n* bigote *m*.

mousy ['mausɪ] *a* (*person*) tímido; (*hair*) pardusco.

mouth [mauθ], *pl* ~**s** [-ðz] *n* boca; (*of river*) desembocadura; ~**ful** *n* bocado; ~ **organ** *n* armónica; ~**piece** *n* (*of musical instrument*) boquilla; (*spokesman*) portavoz *m/f*; ~**wash** *n* enjuague *m*; ~**watering** *a* apetitoso.

movable ['muːvəbl] *a* movible.

move [muːv] *n* (*movement*) movimiento; (*in game*) jugada; (: *turn to play*) turno; (*change of house*) mudanza // *vt* mover; (*emotionally*) conmover; (*POL*: *resolution etc*) proponer // *vi* (*gen*) moverse; (*traffic*) circular; (*also*: *Brit*: ~ **house**) trasladarse, mudarse; **to** ~ **sb to do sth** mover a uno a hacer algo; **to get a** ~ **on** darse prisa; **to** ~ **about** *or* **around** *vi* moverse; (*travel*) viajar; **to** ~ **along** *vi* avanzar, adelantarse; **to** ~ **away** *vi* alejarse; **to** ~ **back** *vi* retroceder; **to** ~ **forward** *vi* avanzar // *vt* adelantar; **to** ~ **in** *vi* (*to a house*) instalarse; **to** ~ **on** *vi* ponerse en camino; **to** ~ **out** *vi* (*of house*) mudarse; **to** ~ **over** *vi* apartarse; **to** ~ **up** *vi* subir; (*employee*) ser ascendido.

movement ['muːvmənt] *n* movimiento; (*TECH*) mecanismo.

movie ['muːvɪ] *n* película; **to go to the** ~**s** ir al cine; ~ **camera** *n* cámara cinematográfica.

moving ['muːvɪŋ] *a* (*emotional*) conmovedor(a); (*that moves*) móvil.

mow [məu], *pt* **mowed,** *pp* **mowed** *or* **mown** *vt* (*grass*) cortar; (*corn*: *also*: ~ **down**) segar; (*shoot*) acribillar; ~**er** *n* (*also*: **lawnmower**) cortacéspedes *m inv*.

MP *n abbr* = **Member of Parliament.**

m.p.h. *abbr* = *miles per hour* (*60 m.p.h.* = *96 k.p.h.*).

Mr, Mr. ['mɪstə*] *n*: ~ Smith (el) Sr. Smith.

Mrs, Mrs. ['mɪsɪz] *n*: ~ Smith (la) Sra. Smith.

Ms, Ms. [mɪz] *n* (= *Miss* or *Mrs*): ~ Smith (la) Sr(t)a. Smith.

M.Sc. *abbr* = **Master of Science.**

much [mʌtʃ] *a* mucho // *ad*, *n* or *pron* mucho; (*before pp*) muy; **how** ~ **is it?** ¿cuánto es?, ¿cuánto cuesta?; **too** ~ demasiado; **it's not** ~ no es mucho; **as** ~ **as** tanto como; **however** ~ **he tries** por mucho que se esfuerce.

muck [mʌk] *n* (*dirt*) suciedad *f*; (*fig*) porquería; **to** ~ **about** *or* **around** *vi* (*col*) perder el tiempo; (*enjoy o.s.*) entretenerse; **to** ~ **up** *vt* (*col*: *ruin*) arruinar, estropear; ~**y** *a* (*dirty*) sucio.

mucus ['mjuːkəs] *n* moco.

mud [mʌd] *n* barro, lodo.

muddle ['mʌdl] *n* desorden *m*, confusión *f*; (*mix-up*) embrollo, lío // *vt* (*also*: ~ **up**) embrollar, confundir; **to** ~ **through** *vi* salir del paso.

muddy ['mʌdɪ] *a* fangoso, cubierto de lodo.

mud: ~**guard** *n* guardabarros *m inv*; ~**-slinging** *n* injurias *fpl*, difamación *f*.

muff [mʌf] *n* manguito // *vt* (*chance*) desperdiciar; (*lines*) estropear.

muffin ['mʌfɪn] *n* mollete *m*.

muffle ['mʌfl] *vt* (*sound*) amortiguar; (*against cold*) embozar; ~**r** *n* (*US AUT*) silenciador *m*.

mug [mʌg] *n* (*cup*) taza grande (*sin platillo*); (*for beer*) jarra; (*col*: *face*) jeta; (: *fool*) bobo // *vt* (*assault*) asaltar; ~**ging** *n* asalto.

muggy ['mʌgɪ] *a* bochornoso.

mule [mjuːl] *n* mula.

mull [mʌl]: **to** ~ **over** *vt* meditar sobre.

mulled [mʌld] *a*: ~ **wine** vino caliente.

multifarious [mʌltɪ'fɛərɪəs] *a* múltiple.

multi-level [mʌltɪ'lɛvl] *a* (*US*) = **multi-storey.**

multiple ['mʌltɪpl] *a*, *n* múltiplo; ~ **sclerosis** *n* esclerosis *f* múltiple; ~ **store** *n* (*Brit*) (cadena de) grandes almacenes.

multiplication [mʌltɪplɪ'keɪʃən] *n* multiplicación *f*.

multiply ['mʌltɪplaɪ] *vt* multiplicar // *vi* multiplicarse.

multistorey [mʌltɪ'stɔːrɪ] *a* (*Brit*: *building, car park*) de muchos pisos.

multitude ['mʌltɪtjuːd] *n* multitud *f*.

mum [mʌm] *n* (*Brit*) mamá // *a*: **to keep** ~ mantener la boca cerrada.

mumble ['mʌmbl] *vt*, *vi* hablar entre dientes, refunfuñar.

mummy ['mʌmɪ] *n* (*Brit*: *mother*) ma-

má; (*embalmed*) momia.

mumps [mʌmps] *n* paperas *fpl*.

munch [mʌntʃ] *vt*, *vi* mascar.

mundane [mʌn'deɪn] *a* trivial.

municipal [mjuː'nɪsɪpl] *a* municipal; ~**ity** [-'pælɪtɪ] *n* municipio.

mural ['mjuərl] *n* (pintura) mural *m*.

murder ['mɜːdə*] *n* asesinato; (*in law*) homicidio // *vt* asesinar, matar; ~**er/** ~**ess** *n* asesino/a; ~**ous** *a* homicida.

murky ['mɜːkɪ] *a* (*water, past*) turbio; (*room*) sombrío.

murmur ['mɜːmə*] *n* murmullo // *vt*, *vi* murmurar.

muscle ['mʌsl] *n* músculo; **to** ~ **in** *vi* entrometerse; **muscular** ['mʌskjulə*] *a* muscular; (*person*) musculoso.

muse [mjuːz] *vi* meditar // *n* musa.

museum [mjuː'zɪəm] *n* museo.

mushroom ['mʌʃrum] *n* (*gen*) seta, hongo; (*small*) champiñón *m* // *vi* (*fig*) crecer de la noche a la mañana.

music ['mjuːzɪk] *n* música; ~**al** *a* melodioso; (*person*) musical // *n* (*show*) comedia musical; ~**al instrument** *n* instrumento musical; ~ **hall** *n* teatro de variedades; ~**ian** [-'zɪʃən] *n* músico/a.

Muslim ['mʌzlɪm] *a*, *n* musulmán/ana *m/f*.

muslin ['mʌzlɪn] *n* muselina.

mussel ['mʌsl] *n* mejillón *m*.

must [mʌst] *auxiliary vb* (*obligation*): **I** ~ **do it** debo hacerlo, tengo que hacerlo; (*probability*): **he** ~ **be there by now** ya debe (de) estar allí // *n*: **it's a** ~ es imprescindible.

mustard ['mʌstəd] *n* mostaza.

muster ['mʌstə*] *vt* juntar, reunir.

mustn't ['mʌsnt] = **must not.**

musty ['mʌstɪ] *a* mohoso, que huele a humedad.

mute [mjuːt] *a*, *n* mudo/a.

muted ['mjuːtɪd] *a* callado.

mutiny ['mjuːtɪnɪ] *n* motín *m* // *vi* amotinarse.

mutter ['mʌtə*] *vt*, *vi* murmurar.

mutton ['mʌtn] *n* carne *f* de cordero.

mutual ['mjuːtʃuəl] *a* mutuo; (*friend*) común; ~**ly** *ad* mutuamente.

muzzle ['mʌzl] *n* hocico; (*protective device*) bozal *m*; (*of gun*) boca // *vt* amordazar; (*dog*) poner un bozal a.

my [maɪ] *a* mi(s); ~ **house/brother/sisters** mi casa/mi hermano/mis hermanas; **I've washed** ~ **hair/cut** ~ **finger** me he lavado el pelo/cortado un dedo; **is this** ~ **pen or yours?** ¿es este bolígrafo mío o tuyo?

myriad ['mɪrɪəd] *n* (*of people, things*) miríada.

myself [maɪ'sɛlf] *pron* (*reflexive*) me; (*emphatic*) yo mismo; (*after prep*) mí (mismo); *see also* **oneself.**

mysterious [mɪs'tɪərɪəs] *a* misterioso.

mystery ['mɪstərɪ] *n* misterio.

mystify ['mɪstɪfaɪ] *vt* (*perplex*) dejar per-

plejo; (*disconcert*) desconcertar.
mystique |mɪsˈtiːk| *n* misterio (profesional *etc*).
myth |mɪθ| *n* mito; ~**ical** *a* mítico.

N

n/a *abbr* (= *not applicable*) ≈ no interesa.
nab |næb| *vt* (*col: grab*) coger (*Sp*), agarrar (*LAm*); (: *catch out*) pillar.
nag |næg| *n* (*pej: horse*) rocín *m* // *vt* (*scold*) regañar; (*annoy*) fastidiar; ~**ging** *a* (*doubt*) persistente; (*pain*) continuo // *n* quejas *fpl*.
nail |neɪl| *n* (*human*) uña; (*metal*) clavo // *vt* clavar; (*fig: catch*) coger (*Sp*), pillar; **to** ~ **sb down to doing sth** comprometer a uno a que haga algo; ~**brush** *n* cepillo para las uñas; ~**file** *n* lima para las uñas; ~ **polish** *n* esmalte *m* or laca para las uñas; ~ **polish remover** *n* quitaesmalte *m*; ~ **scissors** *npl* tijeras *fpl* para las uñas; ~ **varnish** *n* (*Brit*) = ~ **polish**.
naïve |naɪˈiːv| *a* ingenuo.
naked |ˈneɪkɪd| *a* (*nude*) desnudo; (*flame*) expuesto al aire.
name |neɪm| *n* (*gen*) nombre *m*; (*surname*) apellido; (*reputation*) fama, renombre *m* // *vt* (*child*) poner nombre a; (*appoint*) nombrar; **by** ~ de nombre; **in the** ~ **of** en nombre de; **what's your** ~? ¿cómo se llama?; **to give one's** ~ **and address** dar sus señas; ~**less** *a* anónimo, sin nombre; ~**ly** *ad* a saber; ~**sake** *n* tocayo/a.
nanny |ˈnænɪ| *n* niñera.
nap |næp| *n* (*sleep*) sueñecito, siesta; **to be caught** ~**ping** estar desprevenido.
napalm |ˈneɪpɑːm| *n* nápalm *m*.
nape |neɪp| *n*: ~ **of the neck** nuca, cogote *m*.
napkin |ˈnæpkɪn| *n* (*also*: **table** ~) servilleta.
nappy |ˈnæpɪ| *n* (*Brit*) pañal *m*; ~ **liner** *n* gasa; ~ **rash** *n* prurito.
narcissus |nɑːˈsɪsəs|, *pl* **-si** |-saɪ| *n* narciso.
narcotic |nɑːˈkɒtɪk| *a*, *n* narcótico.
narrative |ˈnærətɪv| *n* narrativa // *a* narrativo.
narrow |ˈnærəu| *a* estrecho, angosto // *vi* estrecharse, angostarse; (*diminish*) reducirse; **to have a** ~ **escape** escaparse por los pelos; **to** ~ **sth down** reducir algo; ~**ly** *ad* (*miss*) por poco; ~**minded** *a* de miras estrechas.
nasty |ˈnɑːstɪ| *a* (*remark*) feo; (*person*) antipático; (*revolting: taste, smell*) asqueroso; (*wound, disease etc*) peligroso, grave.
nation |ˈneɪʃən| *n* nación *f*.
national |ˈnæʃənl| *a*, *n* nacional *m/f*; ~

dress *n* vestido nacional; **N~ Health Service (NHS)** *n* (*Brit*) servicio nacional de salud pública; ≈ Insalud *m* (*Sp*); **N~ Insurance** *n* (*Brit*) seguro social nacional; ~**ism** *n* nacionalismo; ~**ist** *a*, *n* nacionalista *m/f*; ~**ity** |-ˈnælɪtɪ| *n* nacionalidad *f*; ~**ize** *vt* nacionalizar; ~**ly** *ad* (*nationwide*) en escala nacional; (*as a nation*) nacionalmente, como nación.
nationwide |ˈneɪʃənwaɪd| *a* en escala *or* a nivel nacional.
native |ˈneɪtɪv| *n* (*local inhabitant*) natural *m/f*, nacional *m/f*; (*in colonies*) indígena *m/f*, nativo/a // *a* (*indigenous*) indígena; (*country*) natal; (*innate*) natural, innato; **a** ~ **of Russia** un(a) natural *m/f* de Rusia; ~ **language** *n* lengua materna; **a** ~ **speaker of French** un hablante nativo de francés.
Nativity |nəˈtɪvɪtɪ| *n*: **the** ~ Navidad *f*.
NATO |ˈneɪtəu| *n* *abbr* (= *North Atlantic Treaty Organization*) OTAN *f*.
natural |ˈnætʃrəl| *a* natural; ~ **gas** *n* gas *m* natural; ~**ize** *vt*: **to become** ~**ized** (*person*) naturalizarse; (*plant*) aclimatarse; ~**ly** *ad* (*speak etc*) naturalmente; (*of course*) desde luego, por supuesto; (*instinctively*) por instinto, por naturaleza.
nature |ˈneɪtʃə*| *n* naturaleza; (*group, sort*) género, clase *f*; (*character*) carácter *m*, genio; **by** ~ por *or* de naturaleza.
naught |nɔːt| = **nought**.
naughty |ˈnɔːtɪ| *a* (*child*) travieso; (*story, film*) verde, escabroso, colorado (*LAm*).
nausea |ˈnɔːsɪə| *n* náusea; ~**te** |-sɪeɪt| *vt* dar náuseas a; (*fig*) dar asco a.
nautical |ˈnɔːtɪkl| *a* náutico, marítimo; (*mile*) marino.
naval |ˈneɪvl| *a* naval, de marina; ~ **officer** *n* oficial *m/f* de marina.
nave |neɪv| *n* nave *f*.
navel |ˈneɪvl| *n* ombligo.
navigate |ˈnævɪgeɪt| *vt* gobernar // *vi* navegar; **navigation** |-ˈgeɪʃən| *n* (*action*) navegación *f*; (*science*) náutica; **navigator** *n* navegador(a) *m/f*, navegante *m/f*.
navvy |ˈnævɪ| *n* (*Brit*) peón *m* caminero.
navy |ˈneɪvɪ| *n* marina de guerra; (*ships*) armada, flota; ~**(-blue)** *a* azul marino.
Nazi |ˈnɑːtsɪ| *n* nazi *m/f*.
NB *abbr* (= *nota bene*) nótese.
near |nɪə*| *a* (*place, relation*) cercano; (*time*) próximo // *ad* cerca // *prep* (*also*: ~ **to**: *space*) cerca de, junto a; (: *time*) cerca de // *vt* acercarse a, aproximarse a; ~**by** |nɪəˈbaɪ| *a* cercano, próximo // *ad* cerca; ~**ly** *ad* casi, por poco; **I** ~**ly fell** por poco me caigo; ~ **miss** *n* tiro cercano; ~**side** *n* (*AUT*) lado derecho; ~**-sighted** *a* miope, corto de vista.
neat |niːt| *a* (*place*) ordenado, bien cuidado; (*person*) pulcro; (*plan*) ingenioso;

(*spirits*) solo; ~**ly** *ad* (*tidily*) con esmero; (*skilfully*) ingeniosamente.

nebulous ['nɛbjuləs] *a* (*fig*) vago, confuso

necessarily ['nɛsɪsrɪlɪ] *ad* necesariamente.

necessary ['nɛsɪsrɪ] *a* necesario, preciso; he did all that was ~ hizo todo lo necesario.

necessity [nɪ'sɛsɪtɪ] *n* necesidad *f*; necessities *npl* artículos *mpl* de primera necesidad.

neck [nɛk] *n* (*ANAT*) cuello; (*of animal*) pescuezo // *vi* besuquearse; ~ **and** ~ parejos.

necklace ['nɛklɪs] *n* collar *m*.

neckline ['nɛklaɪn] *n* escote *m*.

necktie ['nɛktaɪ] *n* (*US*) corbata.

née [neɪ] *a*: ~ Scott de soltera Scott.

need [niːd] *n* (*lack*) escasez *f*, falta; (*necessity*) necesidad *f* // *vt* (*require*) necesitar; I ~ **to do it** tengo que *or* debo hacerlo; **you don't** ~ **to go** no hace falta que vayas.

needle ['niːdl] *n* aguja // *vt* (*fig*: col) picar, fastidiar.

needless ['niːdlɪs] *a* innecesario, inútil; ~ **to say** huelga decir que.

needlework ['niːdlwəːk] *n* (*activity*) costura, labor *f* de aguja.

needn't ['niːdnt] = **need not**.

needy ['niːdɪ] *a* necesitado.

negative ['nɛgətɪv] *n* (*PHOT*) negativo; (*LING*) negación *f* // *a* negativo.

neglect [nɪ'glɛkt] *vt* (*one's duty*) faltar a, no cumplir con; (*child*) descuidar, desatender // *n* (*state*) abandono; (*personal*) dejadez *f*; (*of duty*) incumplimiento.

negligee ['nɛglɪʒeɪ] *n* (*nightdress*) salto de cama.

negligence ['nɛglɪdʒəns] *n* negligencia, descuido.

negligible ['nɛglɪdʒɪbl] *a* insignificante, despreciable.

negotiate [nɪ'gəʊʃɪeɪt] *vt* (*treaty, loan*) negociar; (*obstacle*) franquear // *vi*: **to** ~ (**with**) negociar (con); **negotiation** [-'eɪʃən] *n* negociación *f*, gestión *f*.

Negress ['niːgrɪs] *n* negra.

Negro ['niːgrəʊ] *a*, *n* negro.

neigh [neɪ] *n* relincho // *vi* relinchar.

neighbour, (*US*) **neighbor** ['neɪbə*] *n* vecino/a; ~**hood** *n* (*place*) vecindad *f*, barrio; (*people*) vecindario; ~**ing** *a* vecino.

neither ['naɪðə*] *a* ni // *conj*: I didn't move **and** ~ **did John** no me he movido, ni Juan tampoco // *pron* ninguno; ~ **is true** ninguno/a de los/las dos es cierto/a // *ad*: ~ **good nor bad** ni bueno ni malo.

neon ['niːɔn] *n* neón *m*; ~ **light** *n* lámpara de neón.

nephew ['nevjuː] *n* sobrino.

nerve [nəːv] *n* (*ANAT*) nervio; (*courage*) valor *m*; (*impudence*) descaro, frescura;

a fit of ~**s** un ataque de nervios; ~**-racking** *a* desquiciante.

nervous ['nəːvəs] *a* (*anxious, ANAT*) nervioso; (*timid*) tímido, miedoso; ~ **breakdown** *n* crisis *f* nerviosa.

nest [nɛst] *n* (*of bird*) nido // *vi* anidar; ~ **egg** *n* (*fig*) ahorros *mpl*.

nestle ['nɛsl] *vi*: **to** ~ **down** acurrucarse.

net [nɛt] *n* (*gen*) red *f* // *a* (*COMM*) neto, líquido // *vt* coger (*Sp*) *or* agarrar (*LAm*) con red; (*SPORT*) marcar; ~**ball** *n* básquet *m*; ~ **curtain** *n* visillo.

Netherlands ['nɛðələndz] *npl*: **the** ~ los Países Bajos.

nett [nɛt] *a* = **not**.

netting ['nɛtɪŋ] *n* red *f*, redes *fpl*.

nettle ['nɛtl] *n* ortiga.

network ['nɛtwəːk] *n* red *f*.

neurosis [njuə'rəʊsɪs], *pl* -**ses** [-siːz] *n* neurosis *f inv*; **neurotic** [-'rɔtɪk] *a*, *n* neurótico/a *m/f*.

neuter ['njuːtə*] *a* (*LING*) neutro // *vt* castrar, capar.

neutral ['njuːtrəl] *a* (*person*) neutral; (*colour etc, ELEC*) neutro // *n* (*AUT*) punto muerto; ~**ity** [-'trælɪtɪ] *n* neutralidad *f*; ~**ize** *vt* neutralizar.

neutron ['njuːtrɔn] *n* neutrón *m*; ~ **bomb** *n* bomba de neutrones.

never ['nɛvə*] *ad* nunca, jamás; I ~ **went** no fui nunca; ~ **in my life** jamás en la vida; *see also* **mind**; ~**-ending** *a* interminable, sin fin; ~**theless** [nɛvəðə'lɛs] *ad* sin embargo, no obstante.

new [njuː] *a* nuevo; (*recent*) reciente; ~**born** *a* recién nacido; ~**comer** ['njuːkʌmə*] *n* recién venido/a *or* llegado/a; ~**fangled** *a* (*pej*) modernísimo; ~**found** *a* (*friend*) nuevo; (*enthusiasm*) recién adquirido; ~**ly** *ad* nuevamente, recién; ~**ly-weds** *npl* recién casados *mpl*; ~ **moon** *n* luna nueva.

news [njuːz] *n* noticias *fpl*; **a piece of** ~ una noticia; **the** ~ (*RADIO, TV*) las noticias *fpl*, telediario; ~ **agency** *n* agencia de noticias; ~**agent** *n* (*Brit*) vendedor(a) *m/f* de periódicos; ~**caster** *n* presentador(a) *m/f*, locutor(a) *m/f*; ~ **dealer** *n* (*US*) = ~**agent**; ~ **flash** *n* noticia de última hora; ~**letter** *n* hoja informativa, boletín *m*; ~**paper** *n* periódico, diario; ~**print** *n* papel *m* de periódico; ~**reader** *n* = ~**caster**; ~**reel** *n* noticiario; ~ **stand** *n* quiosco *or* puesto de periódicos.

newt [njuːt] *n* tritón *m*.

New Year *n* Año Nuevo; ~**'s Day** *n* Día *m* de Año Nuevo; ~**'s Eve** *n* Nochevieja.

New York [njuː'jɔːk] *n* Nueva York.

New Zealand [njuː'ziːlənd] *n* Nueva Zelanda; ~**er** *n* neozelandés/esa *m/f*.

next [nɛkst] *a* (*house, room*) vecino; (*bus stop, meeting*) próximo; (*page*) siguiente // *ad* después; **the** ~ **day** el día siguiente;

~ time la próxima vez; ~ year el año próximo or que viene; ~ door ad en la casa de al lado // a vecino, de al lado; ~-of-kin n pariente m más cercano; ~ to prep junto a, al lado de; ~ to nothing casi nada.

NHS n abbr = **National Health Service**.

nib [nɪb] n plumilla.

nibble ['nɪbl] vt mordisquear, mordiscar.

Nicaragua [nɪkə'ræɡjuə] n Nicaragua; ~n a, n nicaragüense m/f.

nice [naɪs] a (likeable) simpático; (kind) amable; (pleasant) agradable; (attractive) bonito, mono, lindo (LAm); (distinction) fino; ~-looking a guapo; ~ly ad amablemente; bien.

niche [niːʃ] n nicho.

nick [nɪk] n (wound) rasguño; (cut, indentation) mella, muesca // vt (col) birlar, robar; **in the ~ of time** justo a tiempo.

nickel ['nɪkl] n níquel m; (US) moneda de 5 centavos.

nickname ['nɪkneɪm] n apodo, mote m // vt apodar.

nicotine ['nɪkətiːn] n nicotina.

niece [niːs] n sobrina.

Nigeria [naɪ'dʒɪərɪə] n Nigeria; ~n a, n nigeriano/a m/f.

nigger ['nɪɡə*] n (col!: highly offensive) negro/a.

niggling ['nɪɡlɪŋ] a (trifling) nimio, insignificante; (annoying) molesto.

night [naɪt] n (gen) noche f; (evening) tarde f; **last ~** anoche; **the ~ before last** anteanoche; **at ~, by ~** de noche, por la noche; ~**cap** n (drink) bebida que se toma antes de acostarse; ~ **club** n cabaret m; ~**dress** n (Brit) camisón m; ~**fall** n anochecer m; ~**gown**, ~**ie** ['naɪtɪ] n (Brit) = ~**dress**.

nightingale ['naɪtɪŋɡeɪl] n ruiseñor m.

nightly ['naɪtlɪ] a de todas las noches // ad todas las noches, cada noche.

nightmare ['naɪtmɛə*] n pesadilla.

night: ~ **porter** n guardián m nocturno; ~ **school** n clase(s) f(pl) nocturna(s); ~ **shift** n turno nocturno or de noche; ~**-time** n noche f.

nil [nɪl] n (Brit SPORT) cero, nada.

Nile [naɪl] n: **the ~** el Nilo.

nimble ['nɪmbl] a (agile) ágil, ligero; (skilful) diestro.

nine [naɪn] num nueve; ~**teen** num diecinueve, diez y nueve; ~**ty** num noventa.

ninth [naɪnθ] a noveno.

nip [nɪp] vt (pinch) pellizcar; (bite) morder.

nipple ['nɪpl] n (ANAT) pezón m; (of bottle) tetilla.

nitrogen ['naɪtrədʒən] n nitrógeno.

no [nəu] ♦ ad (opposite of 'yes') no; **are you coming?** — ~ (**I'm not**) ¿vienes? — no; **would you like some more?** — ~ **thank you** ¿quieres más? — no gracias ♦ a (not any): **I have ~ money/time/books** no tengo dinero/tiempo/libros; **no other man would have done it** ningún otro lo hubiera hecho; '~ **entry**' 'prohibido el paso'; '~ **smoking**' 'prohibido fumar' ♦ n (pl ~es) no m.

nobility [nəu'bɪlɪtɪ] n nobleza.

noble ['nəubl] a noble.

nobody ['nəubədɪ] pron nadie.

nod [nɔd] vi saludar con la cabeza; (in agreement) decir que sí con la cabeza // vt: **to ~ one's head** inclinar la cabeza // n inclinación f de cabeza; **to ~ off** vi cabecear.

noise [nɔɪz] n ruido; (din) escándalo, estrépito; **noisy** a (gen) ruidoso; (child) escandaloso.

nominal ['nɔmɪnl] a nominal.

nominate ['nɔmɪneɪt] vt (propose) proponer; (appoint) nombrar; **nomination** [-'neɪʃən] n propuesta; nombramiento.

nominee [nɔmɪ'niː] n candidato/a.

non... [nɔn] pref no, des..., in...; ~**alcoholic** a no alcohólico; ~**-aligned** a no alineado.

nonchalant ['nɔnʃələnt] a indiferente.

non-committal ['nɔnkə'mɪtl] a (reserved) reservado; (uncommitted) evasivo.

nonconformist [nɔnkən'fɔːmɪst] a (attitude) heterodoxo; (person) inconformista m/f.

nondescript ['nɔndɪskrɪpt] a soso.

none [nʌn] pron ninguno/a // ad de ninguna manera; ~ **of you** ninguno de vosotros; **I've** ~ **left** no me queda ninguno/a; **he's** ~ **the worse for it** no está peor por ello.

nonentity [nɔ'nɛntɪtɪ] n cero a la izquierda, nulidad f.

nonetheless [nʌnðə'lɛs] ad sin embargo, no obstante.

non-existent [nɔnɪg'zɪstənt] a inexistente.

non-fiction [nɔn'fɪkʃən] n literatura no novelesca.

nonplussed [nɔn'plʌst] a perplejo.

nonsense ['nɔnsəns] n tonterías fpl, disparates fpl; ~! ¡qué tonterías!

non: ~**-smoker** n no fumador(a) m/f; ~**-stick** a (pan, surface) antiadherente; ~**-stop** a continuo; (RAIL) directo // ad sin parar.

noodles ['nuːdlz] npl tallarines mpl.

nook [nuk] n rincón m; ~**s and crannies** escondrijos mpl.

noon [nuːn] n mediodía m.

no-one ['nəuwʌn] pron = **nobody**.

noose [nuːs] n lazo corredizo.

nor [nɔː*] conj = **neither** // ad see **neither**.

norm [nɔːm] n norma.

normal ['nɔːml] *a* normal; **~ly** *ad* normalmente.

north [nɔːθ] *n* norte *m* // *a* del norte, norteño // *ad* al or hacia el norte; **N~ America** *n* América del Norte; **~-east** *n* nor(d)este *m*; **~erly** ['nɔːðəlɪ] *a* (*point, direction*) norteño; **~ern** ['nɔːðən] *a* norteño, del norte; **N~ern Ireland** *n* Irlanda del Norte; **N~ Pole** *n* Polo Norte; **N~ Sea** *n* Mar *m* del Norte; **~ward(s)** ['nɔːθwəd(z)] *ad* hacia el norte; **~-west** *n* nor(d)oeste *m*.

Norway ['nɔːweɪ] *n* Noruega; **Norwegian** [-'wiːdʒən] *a, n* noruego/a *m/f*.

nose [nəʊz] *n* (*ANAT*) nariz *f*; (*ZOOL*) hocico, (*sense of smell*) olfato // *vi*: to ~ **about** curiosear; **~bleed** *n* hemorragia nasal; **~-dive** *n* picado vertical; **~y** *a* curioso, fisgón/ona.

nostalgia [nɔs'tældʒɪə] *n* nostalgia.

nostril ['nɔstrɪl] *n* ventana de la nariz.

nosy ['nəʊzɪ] *a* = **nosey**.

not [nɔt] *ad* no; ~ that... no es que...; it's too late, isn't it? es demasiado tarde, ¿verdad or no?; ~ yet/now todavía/ahora no; why ~? ¿por qué no?; *see also* **all, only**.

notably ['nəʊtəblɪ] *ad* especialmente.

notary ['nəʊtərɪ] *n* notario/a.

notch [nɔtʃ] *n* muesca, corte *m*.

note [nəʊt] *n* (*MUS, record, letter*) nota; (*banknote*) billete *m*; (*tone*) tono // *vt* (*observe*) notar, observar; (*write down*) apuntar, anotar; **~book** *n* libreta, cuaderno; **~d** ['nəʊtɪd] *a* célebre, conocido; **~pad** *n* bloc *m*; **~paper** *n* papel *m* para cartas.

nothing ['nʌθɪŋ] *n* nada; (*zero*) cero; he does ~ no hace nada; ~ **new** nada nuevo; **for** ~ (*free*) gratis, sin pago; (*in vain*) en balde.

notice ['nəʊtɪs] *n* (*announcement*) anuncio; (*dismissal*) despido; (*resignation*) dimisión *f* // *vt* (*observe*) notar, observar; **to take** ~ **of** tomar nota de, prestar atención a; **at short** ~ con poca anticipación; **until further** ~ hasta nuevo aviso; **to hand in one's** ~ dimitir; **~able** *a* evidente, obvio; ~ **board** *n* (*Brit*) tablón *m* de anuncios.

notify ['nəʊtɪfaɪ] *vt*: to ~ **sb** (**of sth**) comunicar (algo) a uno.

notion ['nəʊʃən] *n* noción *f*, concepto; (*opinion*) opinión *f*; **~s** *n* (*US*) mercería.

notorious [nəʊ'tɔːrɪəs] *a* notorio.

notwithstanding [nɔtwɪθ'stændɪŋ] *ad* no obstante, sin embargo; ~ **this** a pesar de esto.

nougat ['nuːgɑː] *n* turrón *m*.

nought [nɔːt] *n* cero.

noun [naʊn] *n* nombre *m*, sustantivo.

nourish ['nʌrɪʃ] *vt* nutrir; **~ing** *a* nutritivo; **~ment** *n* alimento, sustento.

novel ['nɔvl] *n* novela // *a* (*new*) nuevo, original; (*unexpected*) insólito; **~ist**

novelista *m/f*; **~ty** *n* novedad *f*.

November [nəʊ'vembə*] *n* noviembre *m*.

novice ['nɔvɪs] *n* principiante *m/f*, novato/a; (*REL*) novicio/a.

now [naʊ] *ad* (*at the present time*) ahora; (*these days*) actualmente, hoy día // *conj*: ~ (**that**) ya que, ahora que; **right** ~ ahora mismo; **by** ~ ya; **just** ~: **I'll do it just** ~ ahora mismo lo hago; ~ **and then**, ~ **and again** de vez en cuando; **from** ~ **on** de ahora en adelante; **~adays** ['naʊədeɪz] *ad* hoy (en) día, actualmente.

nowhere ['nəʊwɛə*] *ad* (*direction*) a ninguna parte; (*location*) en ninguna parte.

nozzle ['nɔzl] *n* boquilla.

nuance ['njuːɑːns] *n* matiz *m*.

nuclear ['njuːklɪə*] *a* nuclear.

nucleus ['njuːklɪəs], *pl* **-lei** [-lɪaɪ] *n* núcleo.

nude [njuːd] *a, n* desnudo/a *m/f*; **in the** ~ desnudo.

nudge [nʌdʒ] *vt* dar un codazo a.

nudist ['njuːdɪst] *n* nudista *m/f*.

nudity ['njuːdɪtɪ] *n* desnudez *f*.

nuisance ['njuːsns] *n* molestia, fastidio; (*person*) pesado, latoso; **what a ~!** ¡qué lata!

nuke ['njuːk] (*col*) *n* bomba atómica // *vt* atacar con arma nuclear.

null [nʌl] *a*: ~ **and void** nulo y sin efecto.

numb [nʌm] *a* entumecido; (*fig*) insensible // *vt* entumecer, entorpecer.

number ['nʌmbə*] *n* número; (*numeral*) número, cifra // *vt* (*pages etc*) numerar, poner número a; (*amount to*) sumar, ascender a; **to be ~ed among** figurar entre; **a** ~ **of** varios, algunos; **they were ten in** ~ eran diez; ~ **plate** *n* (*Brit*) matrícula, placa.

numeral ['njuːmərəl] *n* número, cifra.

numerate ['njuːmərɪt] *a* competente en la aritmética.

numerical ['njuː'mɛrɪkl] *a* numérico.

numerous ['njuːmərəs] *a* numeroso, muchos.

nun [nʌn] *n* monja, religiosa.

nurse [nɜːs] *n* enfermero/a; (*nanny*) niñera // *vt* (*patient*) cuidar, atender; (*baby*: *Brit*) mecer; (: *US*) criar, amamantar.

nursery ['nɜːsərɪ] *n* (*institution*) guardería infantil; (*room*) cuarto de los niños; (*for plants*) criadero, semillero; ~ **rhyme** *n* canción *f* infantil; ~ **school** *n* parvulario, escuela de párvulos; ~ **slope** *n* (*Brit SKI*) cuesta para principiantes.

nursing ['nɜːsɪŋ] *n* (*profession*) profesión *f* de enfermera; (*care*) asistencia, cuidado; ~ **home** *n* clínica de reposo.

nurture ['nɜːtʃə*] *vt* (*child, plant*) alimentar, nutrir.

nut [nʌt] *n* (*TECH*) tuerca; (*BOT*) nuez *f*; **~crackers** *npl* cascanueces *m inv*; **~s**

a (*col*) loco.

nutmeg ['nʌtmeg] *n* nuez *f* moscada.

nutritious [nju:'trɪʃəs] *a* nutritivo, rico.

nutshell ['nʌtʃel] *n* cáscara de nuez; **in a ~ en** resumidas cuentas.

nylon ['naɪlən] *n* nilón *m* // *a* de nilón.

O

oak [əuk] *n* roble *m* // *a* de roble.

O.A.P. *abbr* = **old-age pensioner.**

oar [ɔ:*] *n* remo.

oasis [əu'eɪsɪs], *pl* **-ses** [-si:z] *n* oasis *m inv.*

oath [əuθ] *n* juramento; (*swear word*) palabrota; **on** (*Brit*) *or* **under ~ bajo juramento.**

oatmeal ['əutmi:l] *n* harina de avena.

oats [əuts] *n* avena.

obedience [ə'bi:dɪəns] *n* obediencia.

obedient [ə'bi:dɪənt] *a* obediente.

obey [ə'beɪ] *vt* obedecer; (*instructions, regulations*) cumplir.

obituary [ə'bɪtjuərɪ] *n* necrología.

object ['ɔbdʒɪkt] *n* (*gen*) objeto; (*purpose*) objeto, propósito; (*LING*) complemento // *vi* [əb'dʒɛkt]: **to ~ to** (*attitude*) protestar contra; (*proposal*) oponerse a; **expense is no ~** no importa cuánto cuesta; **I ~!** ¡yo protesto!; **to ~ that** objetar que; **~ion** [əb'dʒɛkʃən] *n* protesta; **I have no ~ion to...** no tengo inconveniente en que...; **~ionable** [əb'dʒɛkʃənəbl] *a* (*gen*) desagradable; (*conduct*) censurable; **~ive** *a, n* objetivo.

obligation [ɔblɪ'geɪʃən] *n* obligación *f*; (*debt*) deber *m*; **without ~** sin compromiso.

oblige [ə'blaɪdʒ] *vt* (*do a favour for*) complacer, hacer un favor a; **to ~ sb to do sth** forzar *or* obligar a uno a hacer algo; **to be ~d to sb for sth** estarle agradecido a uno por algo; **obliging** *a* servicial, atento.

oblique [ə'bli:k] *a* oblicuo; (*allusion*) indirecto.

obliterate [ə'blɪtəreɪt] *vt* borrar.

oblivion [ə'blɪvɪən] *n* olvido; **oblivious** [-ɪəs] *a*: **oblivious of** inconsciente de.

oblong ['ɔblɔŋ] *a* rectangular // *n* rectángulo.

obnoxious [əb'nɔkʃəs] *a* odioso, detestable; (*smell*) nauseabundo.

oboe ['əubəu] *n* oboe *m*.

obscene [əb'si:n] *a* obsceno.

obscure [əb'skjuə*] *a* oscuro // *vt* oscurecer; (*hide*: *sun*) esconder.

observance [əb'zɔ:vns] *n* observancia, cumplimiento; (*ritual*) práctica.

observant [əb'zɔ:vnt] *a* observador(a).

observation [ɔbzə'veɪʃən] *n* observación *f*; (*by police etc*) vigilancia; (*MED*) examen *m*.

observatory [əb'zɔ:vətrɪ] *n* observatorio.

observe [əb'zɔ:v] *vt* (*gen*) observar; (*rule*) cumplir; **~r** *n* observador(a) *m/f*.

obsess [əb'sɛs] *vt* obsesionar; **~ive** *a* obsesivo; obsesionante.

obsolescence [ɔbsə'lɛsns] *n* obsolescencia.

obsolete ['ɔbsəli:t] *a*: **to be ~** estar en desuso.

obstacle ['ɔbstəkl] *n* obstáculo; (*nuisance*) estorbo; **~ race** *n* carrera de obstáculos.

obstinate ['ɔbstɪnɪt] *a* terco, porfiado; (*determined*) tenaz.

obstruct [əb'strʌkt] *vt* (*block*) obstruir; (*hinder*) estorbar, obstaculizar; **~ion** [əb'strʌkʃən] *n* obstrucción *f*; estorbo, obstáculo.

obtain [əb'teɪn] *vt* (*get*) obtener; (*achieve*) conseguir; **~able** *a* asequible.

obtrusive [əb'tru:sɪv] *a* (*person*) importuno, entrometido; (*building etc*) demasiado visible.

obvious ['ɔbvɪəs] *a* (*clear*) obvio, evidente; (*unsubtle*) poco sutil; **~ly** *ad* evidentemente, naturalmente.

occasion [ə'keɪʒən] *n* oportunidad *f*, ocasión *f*; (*event*) acontecimiento // *vt* ocasionar, causar; **~al** *a* poco frecuente, ocasional; **~ally** *ad* de vez en cuando.

occupant ['ɔkjupənt] *n* (*of house*) inquilino/a; (*of car*) ocupante *m/f*.

occupation [ɔkju'peɪʃən] *n* (*of house*) tenencia; (*job*) trabajo; (: *calling*) oficio; **~al hazard** *n* riesgo profesional.

occupier ['ɔkjupaɪə*] *n* inquilino/a.

occupy ['ɔkjupaɪ] *vt* (*seat, post, time*) ocupar; (*house*) habitar; **to ~ o.s. with** *or* **by doing** (*as job*) dedicarse a hacer; (*to pass time*) pasar el tiempo haciendo.

occur [ə'kə:*] *vi* pasar, suceder; **to ~ to sb** ocurrírsele a uno; **~rence** [ə'kʌrəns] *n* acontecimiento.

ocean ['əuʃən] *n* océano; **~-going** *a* de alta mar.

ochre, (*US*) **ocher** ['əukə*] *n* ocre *m*.

OCR *n abbr* = **optical character recognition/reader.**

o'clock [ə'klɔk] *ad*: **it is 5 ~** son las 5.

octave ['ɔktɪv] *n* octava.

October [ɔk'təubə*] *n* octubre *m*.

octopus ['ɔktəpəs] *n* pulpo.

odd [ɔd] *a* (*strange*) extraño, raro; (*number*) impar; (*left over*) sobrante, suelto; **60 ~** 60 y pico; **at ~ times** de vez en cuando; **to be the ~ one out** estar de más; **~s and ends** *npl* minucias *fpl*; **~ity** *n* rareza; (*person*) excéntrico; **~ jobs** *npl* bricolaje *m*; **~ly** *ad* curiosamente, extrañamente; **~ments** *npl* (*Brit COMM*) retales *mpl*; **~s** *npl* (*in betting*) puntos *mpl* de ventaja; **it makes no ~s** da lo mismo; **at ~s** reñidos/as.

odometer [ɔ'dɔmɪtə*] *n* (*US*) cuentakilómetros *m inv.*

odour, (*US*) **odor** ['əudə*] *n* olor *m*;

(*perfume*) perfume *m*.

of *prep* 1 (*gen*) de; **a friend ~ ours** un amigo nuestro; **a boy ~ 10** un chico de 10 años; **that was kind ~ you** muy amable por *or* de tu parte
2 (*expressing quantity, amount, dates etc*) de; **a kilo ~ flour** un kilo de harina; **there were 3 ~ them** había tres; **3 ~ us** went tres de nosotros fuimos; **the 5th ~ July** el 5 de julio
3 (*from, out of*) de; **made ~ wood** (hecho) de madera.

off [ɔf] *a*, *ad* (*engine*) desconectado; (*light*) apagado; (*tap*) cerrado; (*Brit: food: bad*) pasado, malo; (: *milk*) cortado, (*cancelled*) cancelado // *prep* de; **to be ~** (*to leave*) irse, marcharse; **to be ~ sick** estar enfermo *or* de baja; **a day ~** un día libre *or* sin trabajar; **to have an ~ day** tener un día malo; **he had his coat ~** se había quitado el abrigo; **10% ~** (*COMM*) (con el) 10% de descuento; **5 km ~** (*the road*) a 5 km (de la carretera); **~ the coast** frente a la costa; **I'm ~ meat** (*no longer eat/like it*) paso de la carne; **on the ~ chance** por si acaso; **~ and on** de vez en cuando.

offal ['ɔfl] *n* (*Brit CULIN*) menudencias *fpl*.

off-colour [ɔf'kʌləʳ] *a* (*Brit: ill*) indispuesto.

offence, (*US*) **offense** [ə'fɛns] *n* (*crime*) delito; (*insult*) ofensa; **to take ~ at** ofenderse por.

offend [ə'fɛnd] *vt* (*person*) ofender; **~er** *n* delincuente *m/f*; (*against regulations*) infractor(a) *m/f*.

offensive [ə'fɛnsɪv] *a* ofensivo; (*smell etc*) repugnante // *n* (*MIL*) ofensiva.

offer ['ɔfəʳ] *n* (*gen*) oferta, ofrecimiento; (*proposal*) propuesta // *vt* ofrecer; (*opportunity*) facilitar; 'on ~' (*COMM*) 'en oferta'; **~ing** *n* ofrenda.

offhand [ɔf'hænd] *a* informal // *ad* de improviso.

office ['ɔfɪs] *n* (*place*) oficina; (*room*) despacho; (*position*) carga, oficio; **doctor's ~** (*US*) consultorio; **to take ~** entrar en funciones; **~ automation** *n* ofimática, buromática; **~ block**, (*US*) **~ building** *n* bloque *m* de oficinas; **~ hours** *npl* horas *fpl* de oficina; (*US MED*) horas *fpl* de consulta.

officer ['ɔfɪsəʳ] *n* (*MIL etc*) oficial *m/f*; (*of organization*) director(a) *m/f*; (*also: police officer*) agente *m/f* de policía.

office worker *n* oficinista *m/f*.

official [ə'fɪʃl] *a* (*authorized*) oficial, autorizado // *n* funcionario, oficial *m*; **~dom** *n* burocracia.

offing ['ɔfɪŋ] *n*: **in the ~** (*fig*) en perspectiva.

off: **~-licence** *n* (*Brit: shop*) bodega, tienda de vinos y bebidas alcohólicas; **~-line** *a*, *ad* (*COMPUT*) fuera de línea;

~-peak *a* (*holiday*) de temporada baja; (*electricity*) de banda económica; **~-putting** *a* (*Brit*) asqueroso; desalentador(a); **~-season** *a*, *ad* fuera de temporada.

offset ['ɔfsɛt] (*irg: like* set) *vt* (*counteract*) contrarrestar, compensar.

offshoot ['ɔfʃuːt] *n* (*fig*) ramificación *f*.

offshore [ɔf'ʃɔːʳ] *a* (*breeze, island*) costera; (*fishing*) de bajura.

offside ['ɔf'saɪd] *a* (*SPORT*) fuera de juego; (*AUT*) del lado izquierdo.

offspring ['ɔfsprɪŋ] *n* descendencia.

off: **~stage** *ad* entre bastidores; **~-the-peg**, (*US*) **~-the-rack** *ad* confecciona do; **~-white** *a* blanco grisáceo.

often ['ɔfn] *ad* a menudo, con frecuencia; **how ~ do you go?** ¿cada cuánto vas?

ogle ['əʊgl] *vt* comerse con los ojos a.

oh [əʊ] *excl* ¡ah!

oil [ɔɪl] *n* aceite *m*; (*petroleum*) petróleo // *vt* (*machine*) engrasar; **~can** *n* lata de aceite; **~field** *n* campo petrolífero; **~ filter** *n* (*AUT*) filtro de aceite; **~-fired** *a* que quema aceite combustible; **~ painting** *n* pintura al óleo; **~ rig** *n* torre *f* de perforación; **~skins** *npl* impermeables *mpl* de hule, chubasquero *sg*; **~ tanker** *n* petrolero; **~ well** *n* pozo (de petróleo); **~y** *a* aceitoso; (*food*) grasiento.

ointment ['ɔɪntmənt] *n* ungüento.

O.K., **okay** ['əʊ'keɪ] *excl* O.K., ¡está bien!, ¡vale! // *a* bien // *vt* dar el visto bueno a.

old [əʊld] *a* viejo; (*former*) antiguo; **how ~ are you?** ¿cuántos años tienes?, ¿qué edad tienes?; **he's 10 years ~** tiene 10 años; **~er brother** hermano mayor; **~ age** *n* vejez *f*; **~-age pensioner (O.A.P.)** *n* (*Brit*) jubilado(a); **~-fashioned** *a* anticuado, pasado de moda.

olive ['ɔlɪv] *n* (*fruit*) aceituna; (*tree*) olivo // *a* (*also*: **~-green**) verde oliva; **~ oil** *n* aceite *m* de oliva.

Olympic [əʊ'lɪmpɪk] *a* olímpico; **the ~ Games**, **the ~s** *npl* las Olimpiadas *fpl*.

omelet(te) ['ɔmlɪt] *n* tortilla, tortilla de huevo (*LAm*).

omen ['əʊmən] *n* presagio.

ominous ['ɔmɪnəs] *a* de mal agüero, amenazador(a).

omit [əʊ'mɪt] *vt* omitir.

on [ɔn] ♦ *prep* 1 (*indicating position*) en; sobre; **~ the wall** en la pared; **it's ~ the table** está sobre *or* en la mesa; **~ the left** a la izquierda
2 (*indicating means, method, condition etc*): **~ foot** a pie; **~ the train/plane** (*go*) en tren/avión; (*be*) en el tren/el avión; **~ the radio/television/telephone** por *or* en la radio/televisión/al teléfono; **to be ~ drugs** drogarse; (*MED*) estar a tratamiento; **to be ~ holiday/business es-**

tar de vacaciones/en viaje de negocios
3 (*referring to time*): ~ **Friday** el viernes; ~ **Fridays** los viernes; ~ **June 20th** el 20 de junio; **a week** ~ **Friday** del viernes en una semana; ~ **arrival** al llegar; ~ **seeing this** al ver esto
4 (*about, concerning*) sobre, acerca de; **a book** ~ **physics** un libro de or sobre física

♦ *ad* **1** (*referring to dress*): **to have one's coat** ~ tener or llevar el abrigo puesto; **she put her gloves** ~ se puso los guantes
2 (*referring to covering*): '**screw the lid** ~ **tightly**' 'cerrar bien la tapa'
3 (*further, continuously*): **to walk** etc ~ seguir caminando etc

♦ *a* **1** (*functioning, in operation: machine, radio, TV, light*) encendido/a, prendido/a (*LAm*); (: *tap*) abierto/a; (: *brakes*) echado/a, puesto/a; **is the meeting still** ~? (*in progress; not cancelled*) ¿todavía continúa la reunión?; **there's a good film** ~ **at the cinema** ponen una buena película en el cine
2: **that's not** ~! (*col : not possible*) ¡eso ni hablar!, ¡eso no está bien!; (: *not acceptable*) ¡eso no se hace!

once [wʌns] *ad* una vez; (*formerly*) antiguamente // *conj* una vez que; ~ **he had left/it was done** una vez que se había marchado/se hizo; **at** ~ en seguida, inmediatamente; (*simultaneously*) a la vez; ~ **a week** una vez por semana; ~ **more** otra vez; ~ **and for all** de una vez por todas; ~ **upon a time** érase una vez.

oncoming [ˈɒnkʌmɪŋ] *a* (*traffic*) que viene de frente.

one [wʌn] ♦ *num* un(o)/una; ~ **hundred and fifty** ciento cincuenta; ~ **by** ~ uno a uno

♦ *a* **1** (*sole*) único; **the** ~ **book which** el único libro que; **the** ~ **man who** el único que
2 (*same*) mismo/a; **they came in the** ~ **car** vinieron en un solo coche

♦ *pron* **1**: **this** ~ éste/ésta; **that** ~ ése/ésa; (*more remote*) aquél/aquella; **I've already got (a red** ~**)** ya tengo uno/a (rojo/a); ~ **by** ~ uno por uno/a
2: ~ **another** os (*Sp*), se (+ *el uno al otro, unos a otros etc*); **do you two ever see** ~ **another?** ¿vosotros dos os veis alguna vez? (*Sp*), ¿se ven ustedes dos alguna vez?; **the boys didn't dare look at** ~ **another** los chicos no se atrevieron a mirarse (el uno al otro); **they all kissed** ~ **another** se besaron unos a otros
3 (*impersonal*): ~ **never knows** nunca se sabe; **to cut** ~**'s finger** cortarse el dedo; ~ **needs to eat** hay que comer.

one: ~**-armed bandit** *n* máquina tragaperras; ~**-day excursion** *n* (*US*) billete *m* de ida y vuelta en un día; ~**-man** *a* (*business*) individual; ~**-man band** *n* hombre-orquesta *m*; ~**-off** *n* (*Brit col:*

event) acontecimiento único.

oneself [wʌnˈsɛlf] *pron* (*reflexive*) se; (*after prep*) sí; (*emphatic*) uno/a mismo/a; **to hurt** ~ hacerse daño; **to keep sth for** ~ guardarse algo; **to talk to** ~ hablar solo.

one: ~**-sided** *a* (*argument*) parcial; ~**-to-**~ *a* (*relationship*) de dos; ~**-upmanship** *n* arte *m* de aventajar a los demás.

ongoing [ˈɒngəʊɪŋ] *a* continuo.

onion [ˈʌnjən] *n* cebolla.

on-line [ˈɒnlaɪn] *a, ad* (*COMPUT*) en línea.

onlooker [ˈɒnlʊkə*] *n* espectador(a) *m/f*.

only [ˈəʊnlɪ] *ad* solamente, sólo // *a* único, solo // *conj* solamente que, pero; **an** ~ **child** un hijo único; **not** ~ ... **but also**... no sólo ... sino también...

onset [ˈɒnsɛt] *n* comienzo.

onshore [ˈɒnʃɔː*] *a* (*wind*) que sopla del mar hacia la tierra.

onslaught [ˈɒnslɔːt] *n* ataque *m*, embestida.

onto [ˈɒntu] *prep* = **on to**.

onus [ˈəʊnəs] *n* responsabilidad *f*.

onward(s) [ˈɒnwəd(z)] *ad* (*move*) (hacia) adelante.

ooze [uːz] *vi* rezumar.

opaque [əʊˈpeɪk] *a* opaco.

OPEC [ˈəʊpɛk] *n abbr* (= *Organization of Petroleum-Exporting Countries*) OPEP *f*.

open [ˈəʊpn] *a* abierto; (*car*) descubierto; (*road, view*) despejado; (*meeting*) público; (*admiration*) manifiesto // *vt* abrir // *vi* (*flower, eyes, door, debate*) abrirse; (*book etc: commence*) comenzar; **in the** ~ (*air*) al aire libre; **to** ~ **on to** *vt fus* (*subj: room, door*) dar a; **to** ~ **up** *vt* abrir; (*blocked road*) despejar // *vi* abrirse, empezar; ~**ing** *n* abertura, comienzo; (*opportunity*) oportunidad *f*; (*job*) puesto vacante, vacante *f*; ~**ly** *ad* abiertamente; ~**-minded** *a* imparcial; ~**-plan** *a*: ~**-plan office** gran oficina sin particiones.

opera [ˈɒpərə] *n* ópera; ~ **house** *n* teatro de la ópera.

operate [ˈɒpəreɪt] *vt* (*machine*) hacer funcionar; (*company*) dirigir // *vi* funcionar; (*drug*) hacer efecto; **to** ~ **on sb** (*MED*) operar a uno.

operatic [ɒpəˈrætɪk] *a* de ópera.

operating [ˈɒpəreɪtɪŋ] *a*: ~ **table/theatre** mesa/sala de operaciones.

operation [ɒpəˈreɪʃən] *n* (*gen*) operación *f*; (*of machine*) funcionamiento; **to be in** ~ estar funcionando or en funcionamiento; **to have an** ~ (*MED*) ser operado; ~**al** *a* operacional, en buen estado.

operative [ˈɒpərətɪv] *a* (*measure*) en vigor.

operator [ˈɒpəreɪtə*] *n* (*of machine*) maquinista *m/f*, operario/a; (*TEL*) operador(a) *m/f*, telefonista *m/f*.

ophthalmic [ɔfˈθælmɪk] a oftálmico.

opinion [əˈpɪnɪən] n (gen) opinión f; in my ~ en mi opinión, a mi juicio; ~ated a testarudo; ~ poll n encuesta, sondeo.

opponent [əˈpəunənt] n adversario/a, contrincante m/f.

opportunist [ɔpəˈtjuːnɪst] n oportunista m/f.

opportunity [ɔpəˈtjuːnɪtɪ] n oportunidad f; to take the ~ of doing aprovechar la ocasión para hacer.

oppose [əˈpəuz] vt oponerse a; to be ~d to sth oponerse a algo; as ~d to a diferencia de; **opposing** a (side) opuesto, contrario.

opposite [ˈɔpəzɪt] a opuesto, contrario a; (house etc) de enfrente // ad en frente // prep en frente de, frente a // n lo contrario.

opposition [ɔpəˈzɪʃən] n oposición f.

oppress [əˈprɛs] vt oprimir.

opt [ɔpt] vi: to ~ for optar por; to ~ to do optar por hacer; to ~ out of optar por no hacer.

optical [ˈɔptɪkl] a óptico; ~ character recognition/reader (OCR) n reconocimiento/lector m óptico de caracteres.

optician [ɔpˈtɪʃən] n óptico m/f.

optimist [ˈɔptɪmɪst] n optimista m/f; ~ic [-ˈmɪstɪk] a optimista.

optimum [ˈɔptɪməm] a óptimo.

option [ˈɔpʃən] n opción f; to keep one's ~s open (fig) mantener las opciones abiertas; ~al a facultativo, discrecional.

or [ɔː*] conj o; (before o, ho) u; (with negative): he hasn't seen ~ heard anything no ha visto ni oído nada; ~ else si no.

oracle [ˈɔrəkl] n oráculo.

oral [ˈɔːrəl] a oral // n examen m oral.

orange [ˈɔrɪndʒ] n (fruit) naranja // a color naranja.

orator [ˈɔrətə*] n orador(a) m/f.

orbit [ˈɔːbɪt] n órbita // vt, vi orbitar.

orchard [ˈɔːtʃəd] n huerto.

orchestra [ˈɔːkɪstrə] n orquesta; (US: seating) platea; ~l [-ˈkɛstrəl] a de orquesta.

orchid [ˈɔːkɪd] n orquídea.

ordain [ɔːˈdeɪn] vt (REL) ordenar, decretar; (decide) mandar.

ordeal [ɔːˈdiːl] n experiencia horrorosa.

order [ˈɔːdə*] n orden m; (command) orden f; (type, kind) clase f; (state) estado; (COMM) pedido, encargo // vt (also: put in ~) arreglar, poner en orden; (COMM) encargar, pedir; (command) mandar, ordenar; in ~ (gen) en orden; (of document) en regla; in (working) ~ en funcionamiento; in ~ to do para hacer; on ~ (COMM) pedido; to ~ sb to do sth mandar a uno hacer algo; ~ form n hoja de pedido; ~ly n (MIL) ordenanza m; (MED) enfermero/a (auxiliar) // a ordenado.

ordinary [ˈɔːdnrɪ] a corriente, normal; (pej) común y corriente; out of the ~ fuera de lo común.

ordnance [ˈɔːdnəns] n (MIL: unit) artillería.

ore [ɔː*] n mineral m.

organ [ˈɔːgən] n órgano; ~ic [ɔːˈgænɪk] a orgánico.

organization [ɔːgənaɪˈzeɪʃən] n organización f.

organize [ˈɔːgənaɪz] vt organizar; ~r n organizador(a) m/f.

orgasm [ˈɔːgæzəm] n orgasmo.

orgy [ˈɔːdʒɪ] n orgía.

Orient [ˈɔːrɪənt] n Oriente m; **oriental** [-ˈɛntl] a oriental.

origin [ˈɔrɪdʒɪn] n origen m; (point of departure) procedencia.

original [əˈrɪdʒɪnl] a original; (first) primero; (earlier) primitivo // n original m; ~ity [-ˈnælɪtɪ] n originalidad f; ~ly ad (at first) al principio; (with originality) con originalidad.

originate [əˈrɪdʒɪneɪt] vi: to ~ from, to ~ in surgir de, tener su origen en.

Orkneys [ˈɔːknɪz] npl: the ~ (also: 'the Orkney Islands) las Orcadas.

ornament [ˈɔːnəmənt] n adorno; (trinket) chuchería; ~al [-ˈmɛntl] a decorativo, de adorno.

ornate [ɔːˈneɪt] a muy ornado, vistoso.

orphan [ˈɔːfn] n huérfano/a // vt: to be ~ed quedar huérfano/a; ~age n orfanato.

orthodox [ˈɔːθədɔks] a ortodoxo; ~y n ortodoxia.

orthopaedic, (US) **orthopedic** [ɔːθəˈpiːdɪk] a ortopédico

oscillate [ˈɔsɪleɪt] vi oscilar; (person) vacilar.

ostensibly [ɔsˈtɛnsɪblɪ] ad aparentemente.

ostentatious [ɔstɛnˈteɪʃəs] a ostentoso.

osteopath [ˈɔstɪəpæθ] n osteópata m/f.

ostracize [ˈɔstrəsaɪz] vt hacer el vacío a.

ostrich [ˈɔstrɪtʃ] n avestruz m.

other [ˈʌðə*] a otro // pron: the ~ (one) el/la otro/a; ~s (~ people) otros; ~ than (apart from) aparte de; ~wise ad, conj de otra manera; (if not) si no.

otter [ˈɔtə*] n nutria.

ouch [autʃ] excl ¡ay!

ought [ɔːt], pt ought auxiliary vb: I ~ to do it debería hacerlo; this ~ to have been corrected esto debiera de haberse corregido; he ~ to win (probability) debe or debiera ganar.

ounce [auns] n onza (28.35g).

our [ˈauə*] a nuestro; see also my; ~s pron (el) nuestro/(la) nuestra etc; see also mine; ~selves pron pl (reflexive, after prep) nosotros; (emphatic) nosotros mismos; see also oneself.

oust [aust] vt desalojar.

out [aut] ad fuera, afuera; (not at home)

fuera (de casa); (*light, fire*) apagado; ~ there allí (fuera); he's ~ (*absent*) no está, ha salido; to be ~ in one's calculations equivocarse (en sus cálculos); to run ~ salir corriendo; ~ loud en alta voz; ~ of (*outside*) fuera de; (*because of: anger etc*) por; ~ of petrol sin gasolina; '~ of order' 'no funciona'; ~**-and-~** a (*liar, thief etc*) redomado, empedernido.

outback ['autbæk] n interior m.

outboard ['autbɔ:d] a: ~ motor (*motor m*) fuera borda m.

outbreak ['autbreik] n (*of war*) comienzo; (*of disease*) epidemia; (*of violence etc*) ola.

outburst ['autbə:st] n explosión f, arranque m.

outcast ['autka:st] n paria m/f.

outcome ['autkʌm] n resultado.

outcrop ['autkrɔp] n (*of rock*) afloramiento.

outcry ['autkrai] n protestas fpl.

outdated [aut'deitid] a anticuado, fuera de moda.

outdo [aut'du:] (*irg: like do*) vt superar.

outdoor [aut'dɔ:*] a, ~s ad al aire libre.

outer ['autə*] a exterior, externo; ~ space n espacio exterior.

outfit ['autfit] n equipo; (*clothes*) traje m; ~**ter's** n (*Brit*) sastrería.

outgoing ['autɡəuiŋ] a (*character*) extrovertido; ~s npl (*Brit*) gastos mpl.

outgrow [aut'ɡrəu] (*irg: like grow*) vt: he has ~n his clothes su ropa le queda pequeña ya.

outhouse ['authaus] n dependencia.

outing ['autiŋ] n excursión f, paseo.

outlandish [aut'lændiʃ] a estrafalario.

outlaw ['autlɔ:] n proscrito.

outlay ['autlei] n inversión f.

outlet ['autlet] n salida; (*of pipe*) desagüe m; (*US ELEC*) toma de corriente; (*for emotion*) desahogo; (*also*: retail ~) punto de venta.

outline ['autlain] n (*shape*) contorno, perfil m; in ~ (*fig*) a grandes rasgos.

outlive [aut'liv] vt sobrevivir a.

outlook ['autluk] n perspectiva; (*opinion*) punto de vista.

outlying ['autlaiiŋ] a remoto, aislado.

outmoded [aut'məudid] a anticuado, pasado de moda.

outnumber [aut'nʌmbə*] vt exceder en número.

out-of-date [autəv'deit] a (*passport*) caducado; (*clothes*) pasado de moda.

out-of-the-way [autəvðə'wei] a (*place*) apartado.

outpatient ['autpeiʃənt] n paciente m/f externo/a.

outpost ['autpəust] n puesto avanzado.

output ['autput] n (volumen m de) producción f, rendimiento; (*COMPUT*) salida.

outrage ['autreidʒ] n (*scandal*) escándalo; (*atrocity*) atrocidad f // vt ultrajar; ~**ous** [-'reidʒəs] a monstruoso.

outright [aut'rait] ad (*win*) de manera absoluta; (*be killed*) en el acto; (*completely*) completamente // a ['autrait] completo.

outset ['autset] n principio.

outside [aut'said] n exterior m // a exterior, externo // ad fuera // prep fuera de; (*beyond*) más allá de; at the ~ (*fig*) a lo sumo; ~ lane n (*AUT: in Britain*) carril m de la derecha; ~**-left/right** n (*FOOTBALL*) extremo izquierdo/derecho; ~ line n (*TEL*) línea (exterior); ~**r** n (*stranger*) extraño, forastero.

outsize ['autsaiz] a (*clothes*) de talla grande.

outskirts ['autskə:ts] npl alrededores mpl, afueras fpl.

outspoken [aut'spəukən] a muy franco.

outstanding [aut'stændiŋ] a excepcional, destacado; (*unfinished*) pendiente.

outstay [aut'stei] vt: to ~ one's welcome quedarse más de la cuenta.

outstretched [aut'stretʃt] a (*hand*) extendido.

outstrip [aut'strip] vt (*competitors, demand*) dejar atrás, aventajar.

out-tray ['auttrei] n bandeja de salida.

outward ['autwəd] a (*sign, appearances*) externo; (*journey*) de ida; ~**ly** ad por fuera.

outweigh [aut'wei] vt pesar más que.

outwit [aut'wit] vt ser más listo que.

oval ['əuvl] a ovalado // n óvalo.

ovary ['əuvəri] n ovario.

oven ['ʌvn] n horno; ~**proof** a resistente al horno.

over ['əuvə*] ad encima, por encima // a (or ad) (*finished*) terminado; (*surplus*) de sobra // prep (por) encima de; (*above*) sobre; (*on the other side of*) al otro lado de; (*more than*) más de; (*during*) durante; ~ here (por) aquí; ~ there (por) allí or allá; all ~ (*everywhere*) por todas partes; ~ and ~ (*again*) una y otra vez; ~ and above además de; to ask sb ~ invitar a uno a casa; to bend ~ inclinarse.

overall ['əuvərɔ:l] a (*length*) total; (*study*) de conjunto // ad [əuvər'ɔ:l] en conjunto // n (*Brit*) guardapolvo; ~s npl mono sg, overol msg (*LAm*).

overawe [əuvər'ɔ:] vt: to be ~d (by) quedar impresionado (con).

overbalance [əuvə'bæləns] vi perder el equilibrio.

overbearing [əuvə'bɛəriŋ] a autoritario, imperioso.

overboard ['əuvəbɔ:d] ad (*NAUT*) por la borda.

overbook [əuvə'buk] vt sobrereservar.

overcast ['əuvəka:st] a encapotado.

overcharge [əuvə'tʃa:dʒ] vt: to ~ sb co-

brar un precio excesivo a uno.
overcoat |'əuvəkəut| *n* abrigo, sobretodo.
overcome |əuvə'kʌm| (*irg*: *like come*)
vt (*gen*) vencer; (*difficulty*) superar.
overcrowded |əuvə'kraudɪd| *a* atestado
de gente; (*city, country*) superpoblado.
overdo |əuvə'duː| (*irg*: *like do*) *vt* exagerar; (*overcook*) cocer demasiado.
overdose |'əuvədəus| *n* sobredosis *f inv.*
overdraft |'əuvədrɑːft| *n* saldo deudor.
overdrawn |əuvə'drɔːn| *a* (*account*) en
descubierto.
overdue |əuvə'djuː| *a* retrasado; (*recognition*) tardío.
overestimate |əuvər'estɪmeɪt| *vt* sobreestimar.
overflow |əuvə'fləu| *vi* desbordarse // *n*
|'əuvəfləu| (*excess*) exceso; (*of river*)
desbordamiento; (*also:* ~ *pipe*) (cañería
de) desagüe *m.*
overgrown |əuvə'grəun| *a* (*garden*) invadido por la vegetación.
overhaul |əuvə'hɔːl| *vt* revisar, repasar //
n |'əuvəhɔːl| revisión *f.*
overhead |əuvə'hed| *ad* por arriba *or* encima // *a* |'əuvəhed| (*cable*) aéreo; (*railway*) elevado, aéreo // *n* (*US*) = ~**s**; ~**s**
npl gastos *mpl* generales.
overhear |əuvə'hɪə*| (*irg*: *like hear*) *vt*
oír por casualidad.
overheat |əuvə'hiːt| *vi* (*engine*) recalentarse.
overjoyed |əuvə'dʒɔɪd| *a* encantado, lleno de alegría.
overkill |'əuvəkɪl| *n*: that would be ~ eso
sería sobrepasarse.
overland |'əuvəlænd| *a, ad* por tierra.
overlap |əuvə'læp| *vi* traslaparse.
overleaf |əuvə'liːf| *ad* al dorso.
overload |əuvə'ləud| *vt* sobrecargar.
overlook |əuvə'luk| *vt* (*have view of*)
dar a, tener vistas a; (*miss*) pasar por
alto; (*forgive*) hacer la vista gorda a.
overnight |əuvə'naɪt| *ad* durante la noche; (*fig*) de la noche a la mañana // *a*
de noche; to stay ~ pasar la noche.
overpass |'əuvəpɑːs| *n* (*US*) paso superior.
overpower |əuvə'pauə*| *vt* dominar;
(*fig*) embargar; ~**ing** *a* (*heat*) agobiante; (*smell*) penetrante.
overrate |əuvə'reɪt| *vt* sobreestimar.
override |əuvə'raɪd| (*irg*: *like ride*) *vt*
(*order, objection*) no hacer caso de;
overriding *a* predominante.
overrule |əuvə'ruːl| *vt* (*decision*) anular;
(*claim*) denegar.
overrun |əuvə'rʌn| (*irg*: *like run*) *vt*
(*country*) invadir; (*time limit*) rebasar,
exceder.
overseas |əuvə'siːz| *ad* en ultramar;
(*abroad*) en el extranjero // *a* (*trade*) exterior; (*visitor*) extranjero.
overseer |'əuvəsɪə*| *n* (*in factory*) superintendente *m/f*; (*foreman*) capataz *m.*

overshadow |əuvə'ʃædəu| *vt* (*fig*) eclipsar.
overshoot |əuvə'ʃuːt| (*irg*: *like shoot*) *vt*
excederse.
oversight |'əuvəsaɪt| *n* descuido.
oversleep |əuvə'sliːp| (*irg*: *like sleep*) *vi*
quedarse dormido.
overspill |'əuvəspɪl| *n* exceso de población.
overstep |əuvə'step| *vt*: to ~ the mark
pasarse de la raya.
overt |əu'vəːt| *a* abierto.
overtake |əuvə'teɪk| (*irg*: *like take*) *vt*
sobrepasar; (*Brit AUT*) adelantar.
overthrow |əuvə'θrəu| (*irg*: *like throw*)
vt (*government*) derrocar.
overtime |'əuvətaɪm| *n* horas *fpl* extraordinarias.
overtone |'əuvətəun| *n* (*fig*) tono.
overture |'əuvətʃuə*| *n* (*MUS*) obertura;
(*fig*) preludio.
overturn |əuvə'təːn| *vt, vi* volcar.
overweight |əuvə'weɪt| *a* demasiado
gordo *or* pesado.
overwhelm |əuvə'welm| *vt* aplastar;
~**ing** *a* (*victory, defeat*) arrollador(a);
(*desire*) irresistible.
overwork |əuvə'wəːk| *n* trabajo excesivo
// *vi* trabajar demasiado.
overwrought |əuvə'rɔːt| *a* sobreexcitado.
owe |əu| *vt* deber; to ~ sb sth, to ~ sth
to sb deber algo a uno; **owing to** *prep*
debido a, por causa de.
owl |aul| *n* búho, lechuza.
own |əun| *vt* tener, poseer // *a* propio; a
room of my ~ una habitación propia; to
get one's ~ back tomar revancha; on
one's ~ solo, a solas; to ~ up *vi* confesar; ~**er** *n* dueño/a; ~**ership** *n* posesión
f.
ox |ɔks|, *pl* ~**en** |'ɔksn| *n* buey *m.*
oxtail |'ɔksteɪl| *n*: ~ soup sopa de rabo
de buey.
oxygen |'ɔksɪdʒən| *n* oxígeno; ~ **mask/
tent** *n* máscara/tienda de oxígeno.
oyster |'ɔɪstə*| *n* ostra.
oz. *abbr* = **ounce(s).**
ozone |'əuzəun| *n*: ~ **layer** capa de ozono *or* ozónica.

P

p |piː| *abbr* = **penny, pence.**
P.A. *n abbr* = **personal assistant; public address system.**
p.a. *abbr* = **per annum.**
pa |pɑː| *n* (*col*) papá *m.*
pace |peɪs| *n* paso; (*rhythm*) ritmo // *vi*:
to ~ up and down pasearse de un lado a
otro; to keep ~ with llevar el mismo
paso que; (*events*) mantenerse a la altura de *or* al corriente de; ~**maker** *n*
(*MED*) regulador *m* cardíaco, marcapa-

sos *m inv*.

pacific [pə'sɪfɪk] *a* pacífico // *n*: the P~ (Ocean) el (Océano) Pacífico.

pacify ['pæsɪfaɪ] *vt* (*soothe*) apaciguar; (*country*) pacificar.

pack [pæk] *n* (*packet*) paquete *m*; (*of hounds*) jauría; (*of thieves etc*) manada, bando; (*of cards*) baraja; (*bundle*) fardo; (*US: of cigarettes*) paquete *m* // *vt* (*wrap*) empaquetar; (*fill*) llenar; (*in suitcase etc*) meter, poner; (*cram*) llenar, atestar; (*fig: meeting etc*) llenar de partidarios; to ~ (one's bags) hacerse la maleta; to ~ sb off despachar a uno; ~ it in! (*col*) ¡déjalo!

package ['pækɪdʒ] *n* paquete *m*; (*bulky*) bulto; (*also:* ~ deal) acuerdo global; ~ tour *n* viaje *m* organizado.

packed lunch *n* almuerzo frío.

packet ['pækɪt] *n* paquete *m*.

packing ['pækɪŋ] *n* embalaje *m*; ~ case *n* cajón *m* de embalaje.

pact [pækt] *n* pacto.

pad [pæd] *n* (*of paper*) bloc *m*; (*cushion*) cojinete *m*; (*launching* ~) plataforma (de lanzamiento); (*col: flat*) casa // *vt* rellenar; ~ding *n* relleno; (*fig*) paja.

paddle ['pædl] *n* (*oar*) canalete *m*; (*US: for table tennis*) raqueta // *vt* impulsar con canalete // *vi* (*with feet*) chapotear; ~ steamer *n* vapor *m* de ruedas; **paddling pool** *n* (*Brit*) estanque *m* de juegos.

paddock ['pædək] *n* corral *m*.

paddy field ['pædɪ-] *n* arrozal *m*.

padlock ['pædlɒk] *n* candado.

paediatrics [piːdɪ'ætrɪks] *n* pediatría.

pagan ['peɪgən] *a, n* pagano/a *m/f*.

page [peɪdʒ] *n* (*of book*) página; (*of newspaper*) plana; (*also:* ~ boy) paje *m* // *vt* (*in hotel etc*) llamar por altavoz a.

pageant ['pædʒənt] *n* (*procession*) desfile *m*; (*show*) espectáculo; ~ry *n* pompa.

paid [peɪd] *pt, pp of* pay // *a* (*work*) remunerado; (*official*) asalariado; to put ~ to (*Brit*) acabar con.

pail [peɪl] *n* cubo, balde *m*.

pain [peɪn] *n* dolor *m*; to be in ~ sufrir; to take ~s over/to do sth tomarse grandes molestias con/en hacer algo; ~ed *a* (*expression*) afligido; ~ful *a* doloroso; (*difficult*) penoso; (*disagreeable*) desagradable; ~fully *ad* (*fig: very*) terriblemente; ~killer *n* analgésico; ~less *a* que no causa dolor; ~staking ['peɪnzteɪkɪŋ] *a* (*person*) concienzudo, esmerado.

paint [peɪnt] *n* pintura // *vt* pintar; to ~ the door blue pintar la puerta de azul; ~brush *n* (*artist's*) pincel *m*; (*decorator's*) brocha; ~er *n* pintor(a) *m/f*; ~ing *n* pintura; ~work *n* pintura.

pair [pɛə*] *n* (*of shoes, gloves etc*) par *m*; (*of people*) pareja; a ~ of scissors unas tijeras; a ~ of trousers unos pantalones, un pantalón.

pajamas [pɪ'dʒɑːməz] *npl* (*US*) pijama *msg*.

Pakistan [pɑːkɪ'stɑːn] *n* Paquistán *m*; ~i *a, n* paquistaní *m/f*.

pal [pæl] *n* (*col*) compinche *m/f*, compañero/a.

palace ['pæləs] *n* palacio.

palatable ['pælɪtəbl] *a* sabroso; (*acceptable*) aceptable.

palate ['pælɪt] *n* paladar *m*.

palatial [pə'leɪʃəl] *a* (*surroundings, residence*) suntuoso, espléndido.

palaver [pə'lɑːvə*] *n* (*fuss*) lío.

pale [peɪl] *a* (*gen*) pálido; (*colour*) claro // *n*: to be beyond the ~ pasarse de la raya; to grow ~ palidecer.

Palestine ['pælɪstaɪn] *n* Palestina; **Palestinian** [-'tɪnɪən] *a, n* palestino/a *m/f*.

palette ['pælɪt] *n* paleta.

paling ['peɪlɪŋ] *n* (*stake*) estaca; (*fence*) valla.

pall [pɔːl] *n* (*of smoke*) capa (de humo) // *vi* perder el sabor.

pallet ['pælɪt] *n* (*for goods*) pallet *m*.

pallor ['pælə*] *n* palidez *f*.

pallid ['pælɪd] *a* pálido.

palm [pɑːm] *n* (*ANAT*) palma; (*also:* ~ tree) palmera, palma // *vt*: to ~ sth off on sb (*Brit col*) encajar algo a uno; P~ Sunday *n* Domingo de Ramos.

palpable ['pælpəbl] *a* palpable.

palpitation [pælpɪ'teɪʃən] *n* palpitación *f*; to have ~s tener vahidos.

paltry ['pɔːltrɪ] *a* (*quantity*) irrisorio; (*person*) insignificante.

pamper ['pæmpə*] *vt* mimar.

pamphlet ['pæmflət] *n* folleto.

pan [pæn] *n* (*also:* sauce~) cacerola, cazuela, olla; (*also:* frying ~) sartén *m*; (*of lavatory*) taza // *vi* (*CINEMA*) tomar panorámicas.

panache [pə'næʃ] *n*: with ~ con estilo.

Panama ['pænəmɑː] *n* Panamá *m*; the ~ Canal el Canal de Panamá.

pancake ['pænkeɪk] *n* crepe *f*.

panda ['pændə] *n* panda *m*; ~ car *n* (*Brit*) coche *m* Z.

pandemonium [pændɪ'məunɪəm] *n*: there was ~ se armó un tremendo jaleo.

pander ['pændə*] *vi*: to ~ to complacer a.

pane [peɪn] *n* cristal *m*.

panel ['pænl] *n* (*of wood*) panel *m*; (*of cloth*) paño; (*RADIO, TV*) panel *m* de invitados; ~ling, (*US*) ~ing *n* paneles *mpl*.

pang [pæŋ] *n*: ~s of conscience remordimiento *sg*; ~s of hunger dolores *mpl* del hambre.

panic ['pænɪk] *n* (*terror m*) pánico // *vi* dejarse llevar por el pánico; ~ky *a* (*person*) asustadizo; ~-stricken *a* preso de pánico.

pansy ['pænzɪ] *n* (*BOT*) pensamiento;

(col: pej) maricón m.
pant [pænt] vi jadear.
panther ['pænθə*] n pantera.
panties ['pæntız] npl bragas fpl, pantis mpl.
pantihose ['pæntıhəuz] n (US) pantimedias fpl.
pantomime ['pæntəmaım] n (Brit) revista musical representada en Navidad, basada en cuentos de hadas.
pantry ['pæntrı] n despensa.
pants [pænts] n (Brit: underwear: woman's) bragas fpl; (: man's) calzoncillos mpl; (US: trousers) pantalones mpl.
papal ['peıpəl] a papal.
paper ['peıpə*] n papel m; (also: news~) periódico, diario; (study, article) artículo; (exam) examen m // a de papel // vt empapelar, tapizar (LAm); (identity) ~s npl papeles mpl, documentos mpl; ~back n libro de bolsillo; ~ bag n bolsa de papel; ~ clip n clip m; ~ hankie n pañuelo de papel; ~weight n pisapapeles m inv; ~work n trabajo administrativo; (pej) papeleo.
papier-mâché ['pæpıeı'mæʃeı] n cartón m piedra.
paprika ['pæprıkə] n pimienta húngara or roja.
par [pɑ:*] n par f; (GOLF) par m; to be on a ~ with estar a la par con.
parable ['pærəbl] n parábola.
parachute ['pærəʃu:t] n paracaídas m inv // vi lanzarse en paracaídas.
parade [pə'reıd] n desfile m // vt (gen) recorrer, desfilar por; (show off) hacer alarde de // vi desfilar; (MIL) pasar revista.
paradise ['pærədaıs] n paraíso.
paradox ['pærədɔks] n paradoja; ~ically [-'dɔksıklı] ad paradójicamente.
paraffin ['pærəfın] n (Brit): ~ (oil) parafina.
paragon ['pærəgən] n modelo.
paragraph ['pærəgrɑ:f] n párrafo.
Paraguay ['pærəgwaı] n Paraguay m.
parallel ['pærəlɛl] a en paralelo; (fig) semejante // n (line) paralela; (fig, GEO) paralelo.
paralysis [pə'rælısıs] n parálisis f inv.
paralyze ['pærəlaız] vt paralizar.
paramedic [pærəmɛdık] n (US) ambulanciero/a.
paramount ['pærəmaunt] a: of ~ importance de suma importancia.
paranoid ['pærənɔıd] a (person, feeling) paranoico.
paraphernalia [pærəfə'neılıə] n (gear) avíos mpl.
parasite ['pærəsaıt] n parásito/a.
parasol ['pærəsɔl] n sombrilla, quitasol m.
paratrooper ['pærətru:pə*] n paracaidista m/f.
parcel ['pɑ:sl] n paquete m // vt (also: ~

up) empaquetar, embalar.
parch [pɑ:tʃ] vt secar, resecar; ~ed a (person) muerto de sed.
parchment ['pɑ:tʃmənt] n pergamino.
pardon ['pɑ:dn] n perdón m; (LAW) indulto // vt perdonar; indultar; ~ me!, I beg your ~! ¡perdone usted!; (I beg your) ~?, (US) ~ me? ¿cómo?
parent ['pɛərənt] n: ~s npl padres mpl; ~al [pə'rɛntl] a paternal/maternal.
parenthesis [pə'rɛnθısıs], pl -theses [-θısi:z] n paréntesis m inv.
Paris ['pærıs] n París m.
parish ['pærıʃ] n parroquia.
parity ['pærıtı] n paridad f, igualdad f.
park [pɑ:k] n parque m // vt aparcar, estacionar // vi aparcar, estacionarse.
parking ['pɑ:kıŋ] n aparcamiento, estacionamiento; 'no ~' 'prohibido estacionarse'; ~ lot n (US) parking m; ~ meter n parquímetro; ~ ticket n multa de aparcamiento.
parlance ['pɑ:ləns] n lenguaje m.
parliament ['pɑ:ləmənt] n parlamento; (Spanish) Cortes fpl; ~ary [-'mɛntərı] a parlamentario.
parlour, (US) **parlor** ['pɑ:lə*] n sala de recibo, salón m, living (LAm).
parochial [pə'rəukıəl] a parroquial; (pej) de miras estrechas.
parody ['pærədı] n parodia.
parole [pə'rəul] n: on ~ libre bajo palabra.
parquet ['pɑ:keı] n: ~ floor(ing) parquet m.
parrot ['pærət] n loro, papagayo.
parry ['pærı] vt parar.
parsimonious [pɑ:sı'məunıəs] a tacaño.
parsley ['pɑ:slı] n perejil m.
parsnip ['pɑ:snıp] n chirivía.
parson ['pɑ:sn] n cura m.
part [pɑ:t] n (gen, MUS) parte f; (bit) trozo; (of machine) pieza; (THEATRE etc) papel m; (of serial) entrega; (US: in hair) raya // ad = **partly** // vt separar; (break) partir // vi (people) separarse; (roads) bifurcarse; (crowd) apartarse; (break) romperse; to take ~ in participar or tomar parte en; to take sth in good ~ tomar algo en buena parte; to take sb's ~ defender a uno; for my ~ por mi parte; for the most ~ en su mayor parte; (people) en su mayoría; to ~ with vt fus ceder, entregar; (money) pagar; (get rid of) deshacerse de; ~ exchange n (Brit): in ~ exchange como parte del pago.
partial ['pɑ:ʃl] a parcial; to be ~ to ser aficionado a.
participant [pɑ:'tısıpənt] n (in competition) concursante m/f.
participate [pɑ:'tısıpeıt] vi: to ~ in participar en; **participation** [-'peıʃən] n participación f.
participle ['pɑ:tısıpl] n participio.

particle ['pɑːtɪkl] n partícula; (of dust) grano; (fig) pizca.

particular [pə'tɪkjulə*] a (special) particular; (concrete) concreto; (given) determinado; (detailed) detallado, minucioso; (fussy) quisquilloso, exigente; ~s npl (information) datos mpl, detalles mpl; (details) pormenores mpl; in ~ en particular; ~ly ad especialmente, en particular.

parting ['pɑːtɪŋ] n (act of) separación f; (farewell) despedida; (Brit: in hair) raya f a de despedida.

partisan [pɑːtɪ'zæn] a, n partidario/a.

partition [pɑː'tɪʃən] n (POL) división f; (wall) tabique m.

partly ['pɑːtlɪ] ad en parte.

partner ['pɑːtnə*] n (COMM) socio/a; (SPORT, at dance) pareja; (spouse) cónyuge m/f; (friend etc) compañero/a // vt acompañar; ~ship n (gen) asociación f; (COMM) sociedad f.

partridge ['pɑːtrɪdʒ] n perdiz f.

part-time [pɑːt'taɪm] a, ad a tiempo parcial.

party ['pɑːtɪ] n (POL) partido; (celebration) fiesta; (group) grupo; (LAW) parte f, interesado // a (POL) de partido; (dress etc) de fiesta, de gala; ~ **line** n (TEL) línea compartida.

pass [pɑːs] vt (time, object) pasar; (place) pasar por; (exam) aprobar; (overtake, surpass) rebasar; (approve) aprobar // vi pasar; (SCOL) aprobar, ser aprobado // n (permit) permiso; (membership card) carnet m; (in mountains) puerto, desfiladero; (SPORT) pase m; (SCOL: also: ~ **mark**): to get a ~ in aprobar en; to ~ **sth through** sth pasar algo por algo; to make a ~ at sb (col) hacer proposiciones a uno; to ~ **away** vi fallecer; to ~ **by** vi pasar // vt (ignore) pasar por alto; to ~ **for** pasar por; to ~ **on** vt transmitir; to ~ **out** vi desmayarse; to ~ **up** vt (opportunity) renunciar a; ~able a (road) transitable; (tolerable) pasable.

passage ['pæsɪdʒ] n (also: ~way) pasillo; (act of passing) tránsito; (fare, in book) pasaje m; (by boat) travesía.

passbook ['pɑːsbuk] n libreta de banco.

passenger ['pæsɪndʒə*] n pasajero/a, viajero/a.

passer-by [pɑːsə'baɪ] n transeúnte m/f.

passing ['pɑːsɪŋ] a (fleeting) pasajero; in ~ de paso; ~ **place** n (AUT) apartadero.

passion ['pæʃən] n pasión f; ~ate a apasionado.

passive ['pæsɪv] a (also LING) pasivo.

Passover ['pɑːsəuvə*] n Pascua (de los judíos).

passport ['pɑːspɔːt] n pasaporte m; ~ **control** n control m de pasaporte.

password ['pɑːswɜːd] n contraseña.

past [pɑːst] prep (further than) más allá de; (later than) después de // a pasado; (president etc) antiguo // n (time) el pasado; (of person) antecedentes mpl; he's ~ **forty** tiene más de cuarenta años; for the ~ **few/3 days** durante los últimos días/últimos 3 días; to run ~ sb pasar a uno corriendo.

pasta ['pæstə] n pasta.

paste [peɪst] n (gen) pasta; (glue) engrudo // vt (stick) pegar; (glue) engomar.

pasteurized ['pæstəraɪzd] a pasteurizado.

pastille ['pæstl] n pastilla.

pastime ['pɑːstaɪm] n pasatiempo.

pastor ['pɑːstə*] n pastor m.

pastry ['peɪstrɪ] n (dough) pasta; (cake) pastel m.

pasture ['pɑːstʃə*] n (grass) pasto.

pasty ['pæstɪ] n empanada // a ['peɪstɪ] pastoso; (complexion) pálido.

pat [pæt] vt dar una palmadita a; (dog etc) acariciar.

patch [pætʃ] n (of material) parche m; (mended part) remiendo; (of land) terreno // vt (clothes) remendar; (to go through) a bad ~ (pasar por) una mala racha; to ~ **up** vt (mend temporarily) reparar; (quarrel) hacer las paces en; ~**work** n labor m de retazos; ~**y** a desigual.

pâté ['pæteɪ] n paté m.

patent ['peɪtnt] n patente f // vt patentar // a patente, evidente; ~ **leather** n charol m.

paternal [pə'tɜːnl] a paternal; (relation) paterno.

paternity [pə'tɜːnɪtɪ] n paternidad f.

path [pɑːθ] n camino, sendero; (trail, track) pista; (of missile) trayectoria.

pathetic [pə'θetɪk] a (pitiful) patético, lastimoso; (very bad) malísimo; (moving) conmovedor(a).

pathological [pæθə'lɒdʒɪkəl] a patológico.

pathology [pə'θɒlədʒɪ] n patología.

pathos ['peɪθɒs] n patetismo.

pathway ['pɑːθweɪ] n sendero, vereda.

patience ['peɪʃns] n paciencia; (Brit CARDS) solitario.

patient ['peɪʃnt] n paciente m/f // a paciente, sufrido.

patio ['pætɪəu] n patio.

patriotic [pætrɪ'ɒtɪk] a patriótico.

patrol [pə'trəul] n patrulla // vt patrullar por; ~ **car** n coche m patrulla; ~**man** n (US) policía m.

patron ['peɪtrən] n (in shop) cliente m/f; (of charity) patrocinador(a) m/f; ~ **of the arts** mecenas m; ~**ize** ['pætrənaɪz] vt (shop) ser cliente de; (look down on) condescender con.

patter ['pætə*] n golpeteo; (sales talk) labia // vi (rain) tamborilear.

pattern ['pætən] n (SEWING) patrón m; (design) dibujo.

paunch [pɔːntʃ] *n* panza, barriga.
pauper ['pɔːpə*] *n* pobre *m/f*.
pause [pɔːz] *n* pausa; (*interval*) intérvalo // *vi* hacer una pausa.
pave [peɪv] *vt* pavimentar; **to ~ the way for** preparar el terreno para.
pavement ['peɪvmənt] *n* (*Brit*) acera, vereda (*LAm*).
pavilion [pə'vɪlɪən] *n* pabellón *m*; (*SPORT*) caseta.
paving ['peɪvɪŋ] *n* pavimento, enlosado; **~ stone** *n* losa.
paw [pɔː] *n* pata; (*claw*) garra.
pawn [pɔːn] *n* (*CHESS*) peón *m*; (*fig*) instrumento // *vt* empeñar; **~ broker** *n* prestamista *m/f*; **~shop** *n* monte *m* de piedad.
pay [peɪ] *n* paga; (*wage etc*) sueldo, salario // (*vb: pt, pp* **paid**) *vt* pagar // *vi* pagar; (*be profitable*) rendir; **to ~ attention (to)** prestar atención (a); **to ~ back** *vt* (*money*) reembolsar; (*person*) pagar; **to ~ for** *vt* pagar; **to ~ in** *vt* ingresar; **to ~ off** *vt* liquidar // *vi* (*scheme, decision*) dar resultado; **to ~ up** *vt* pagar (de mala gana); **~able** *a* pagadero; **~ day** *n* día *m* de paga; **~ee** *n* portador(a) *m/f*; **~ envelope** *n* (*US*) = **~ packet**; **~ment** *n* pago; **advance ~ment** anticipo; **monthly ~ment** mensualidad *f*; **~ packet** *n* (*Brit*) sobre *m* (de paga); **~-phone** *n* teléfono público; **~roll** *n* nómina; **~ slip** *n* recibo de sueldo.
PC *n abbr* = **personal computer.**
p.c. *abbr* = **per cent.**
pea [piː] *n* guisante *m*, chícharo (*LAm*), arveja (*LAm*).
peace [piːs] *n* paz *f*; (*calm*) paz *f*, tranquilidad *f*; **~able** *a* pacífico; **~ful** *a* (*gentle*) pacífico; (*calm*) tranquilo, sosegado.
peach [piːtʃ] *n* melocotón *m*, durazno (*LAm*).
peacock ['piːkɔk] *n* pavo real.
peak [piːk] *n* (*of mountain: top*) cumbre *f*, cima; (: *point*) pico; (*of cap*) visera; (*fig*) cumbre *f*; **~ hours** *npl*, **~ period** *n* horas *fpl* punta.
peal [piːl] *n* (*of bells*) repique *m*; **~ of laughter** carcajada.
peanut ['piːnʌt] *n* cacahuete *m*, maní *m* (*LAm*).
pear [pɛə*] *n* pera.
pearl [pɜːl] *n* perla.
peasant ['pɛznt] *n* campesino/a.
peat [piːt] *n* turba.
pebble ['pɛbl] *n* guijarro.
peck [pɛk] *vt* (*also:* **~ at**) picotear; (*food*) comer sin ganas // *n* picotazo; (*kiss*) besito; **~ing order** *n* orden *m* de jerarquía; **~ish** *a* (*Brit col*): **I feel ~ish** tengo ganas de picar algo.
peculiar [pɪ'kjuːlɪə*] *a* (*odd*) extraño, raro; (*typical*) propio, característico; **~**

to propio de; **~ity** [pɪkjuːlɪ'ærɪtɪ] *n* peculiaridad *f*, característica.
pedal ['pɛdl] *n* pedal *m* // *vi* pedalear.
pedantic [pɪ'dæntɪk] *a* pedante.
peddler ['pɛdlə*] *n* vendedor(a) *m/f* ambulante.
pedestal ['pɛdəstl] *n* pedestal *m*.
pedestrian [pɪ'dɛstrɪən] *n* peatón/ona *m/f* // *a* pedestre; **~ crossing** *n* (*Brit*) paso de peatones.
pediatrics [piːdɪ'ætrɪks] *n* (*US*) = **paediatrics.**
pedigree ['pɛdɪgriː] *n* genealogía; (*of animal*) raza // *cpd* (*animal*) de raza, de casta.
pedlar ['pɛdlə*] *n* = **peddler.**
pee [piː] *vi* (*col*) mear.
peek [piːk] *vi* mirar a hurtadillas.
peel [piːl] *n* piel *f*; (*of orange, lemon*) cáscara; (: *removed*) peladuras *fpl* // *vt* pelar // *vi* (*paint etc*) desconcharse; (*wallpaper*) despegarse, desprenderse.
peep [piːp] *n* (*Brit: look*) mirada furtiva; (*sound*) pío // *vi* (*Brit*) piar; **to ~ out** *vi* asomar la cabeza; **~hole** *n* mirilla.
peer [pɪə*] *vi*: **to ~ at** esudriñar // *n* (*noble*) par *m*; (*equal*) igual *m*; **~age** *n* nobleza.
peeved [piːvd] *a* enojado.
peevish ['piːvɪʃ] *a* malhumorado.
peg [pɛg] *n* clavija; (*for coat etc*) gancho, colgadero; (*Brit: also:* **clothes ~**) pinza; (*tent ~*) estaca // *vt* (*prices*) fijar.
Peking [piː'kɪŋ] *n* Pekín.
pekinese [piːkɪ'niːz] *n* pequinés/esa *m/f*.
pelican ['pɛlɪkən] *n* pelícano; **~ crossing** *n* (*Brit AUT*) paso de peatones señalizado.
pellet ['pɛlɪt] *n* bolita; (*bullet*) perdigón *m*.
pelmet ['pɛlmɪt] *n* galería.
pelt [pɛlt] *vt*: **to ~ sb with sth** arrojarle algo a uno // *vi* (*rain*) llover a cántaros // *n* pellejo.
pen [pɛn] *n* pluma; (*for sheep*) redil *m*.
penal ['piːnl] *a* penal; **~ize** *vt* (*punish*: *SPORT*) castigar.
penalty ['pɛnltɪ] *n* (*gen*) pena; (*fine*) multa; (*SPORT*) castigo; **~ (kick)** *n* (*FOOTBALL*) penalty *m*.
penance ['pɛnəns] *n* penitencia.
pence [pɛns] *pl of* **penny.**
pencil ['pɛnsl] *n* lápiz *m*, lapicero (*LAm*); **~ case** *n* estuche *m*; **~ sharpener** *n* sacapuntas *m inv.*
pendant ['pɛndnt] *n* pendiente *m*.
pending ['pɛndɪŋ] *prep* antes de // *a* pendiente; **~ the arrival of ...** hasta que llegue ...
pendulum ['pɛndjuləm] *n* péndulo.
penetrate ['pɛnɪtreɪt] *vt* penetrar.
penfriend ['pɛnfrɛnd] *n* (*Brit*) amigo/a por carta.
penguin ['pɛŋgwɪn] *n* pingüino.
penicillin [pɛnɪ'sɪlɪn] *n* penicilina.

peninsula |pə'nınsjulə| n península.

penis ['pi:nıs] n pene m.

penitent ['penıtnt] a arrepentido; (REL) penitente.

penitentiary |penı'tenʃərı| n (US) cárcel f, presidio.

penknife ['pennaıf] n navaja.

pen name n seudónimo.

penniless ['penılıs] a sin dinero.

penny ['penı], pl **pennies** ['penız] or (Brit) **pence** [pens] n penique m; (US) centavo.

penpal ['penpæl] n amigo/a por carta.

pension ['penʃən] n (allowance, state payment) pensión f; (old-age) jubilación f; ~**er** n (Brit) jubilado/a.

pensive ['pensıv] a pensativo; (withdrawn) preocupado.

pentagon ['pentəgən] n: the P~ (US POL) el Pentágono.

Pentecost ['pentıkɔst] n Pentecostés m.

penthouse ['penthaus] n ático de lujo.

pent-up ['pentʌp] a (feelings) reprimido.

people ['pi:pl] npl gente f; (citizens) pueblo sg, ciudadanos mpl // n (nation, race) pueblo, nación f // vt poblar; **several** ~ came vinieron varias personas; ~ **say** that... dice la gente que... .

pep [pep] n (col) energía; **to** ~ **up** vt animar.

pepper ['pepə*] n (spice) pimienta; (vegetable) pimiento // a (fig) salpicar; ~**mint** n menta; (sweet) pastilla de menta.

peptalk ['peptɔ:k] n: **to give sb a** ~ darle a uno una inyección de ánimo.

per [pə:*] prep por; ~ **day/person** por día/persona; ~ **annum** ad al año; ~ **capita** a, ad per cápita.

perceive [pə'si:v] vt percibir; (realize) darse cuenta de.

per cent n por ciento.

percentage [pə'sentıdʒ] n porcentaje m.

perception [pə'sepʃən] n percepción f; (insight) perspicacia; **perceptive** [-'septıv] a perspicaz.

perch [pə:tʃ] n (fish) perca; (for bird) percha // vi posarse.

percolator ['pə:kəleıtə*] n cafetera de filtro.

perennial [pə'renıəl] a perenne.

perfect ['pə:fıkt] a perfecto // n (also: ~ tense) perfecto // vt [pə'fekt] perfeccionar; ~**ly** ad perfectamente.

perforate ['pə:fəreıt] vt perforar; **perforation** [-'reıʃən] n perforación f.

perform [pə'fɔ:m] vt (carry out) realizar, llevar a cabo; (THEATRE) representar; (piece of music) interpretar // vi (THEATRE) actuar; (TECH) funcionar; ~**ance** n (of task) realización f; (of a play) representación f; (of player etc) actuación f; (of car, engine) rendimiento; (of function) desempeño; ~**er** n (actor) actor m, actriz f; (MUS) intérprete

m/f; ~**ing** a (animal) amaestrado.

perfume ['pə:fju:m] n perfume m.

perfunctory [pə'fʌŋktərı] a superficial.

perhaps [pə'hæps] ad quizá(s), tal vez.

peril ['perıl] n peligro, riesgo.

perimeter [pə'rımıtə*] n perímetro.

period ['pıərıəd] n período; (HISTORY) época; (SCOL) clase f; (full stop) punto; (MED) regla // a (costume, furniture) de época; ~**ic** [-'ɔdık] a periódico; ~**ical** [-'ɔdıkl] n periódico; ~**ically** [-'ɔdıklı] ad de vez en cuando, cada cierto tiempo.

peripheral [pə'rıfərəl] a periférico // n (COMPUT) periférico, unidad f periférica.

perish ['perıʃ] vi perecer; (decay) echarse a perder; ~**able** a perecedero.

perjury ['pə:dʒərı] n (LAW) perjurio.

perk [pə:k] n extra m; **to** ~ **up** vi (cheer up) animarse; ~**y** a alegre, despabilado.

perm [pə:m] n permanente f.

permanent ['pə:mənənt] a permanente.

permeate ['pə:mıeıt] vi penetrar, trascender // vt penetrar, trascender a.

permissible [pə'mısıbl] a permisible, lícito.

permission [pə'mıʃən] n permiso.

permissive [pə'mısıv] a permisivo.

permit ['pə:mıt] n permiso, licencia // vt [pə'mıt] permitir; (accept) tolerar.

pernicious [pə:'nıʃəs] a nocivo; (MED) pernicioso.

perpetrate ['pə:pıtreıt] vt cometer.

perpetual [pə'petjuəl] a perpetuo.

perplex [pə'pleks] vt dejar perplejo.

persecute ['pə:sıkju:t] vt (pursue) perseguir; (harass) acosar.

perseverance [pə:sı'vıərəns] n perseverancia.

persevere [pə:sı'vıə*] vi persistir.

Persian ['pə:ʃən] a, n persa m/f; **the** (~) **Gulf** el Golfo Pérsico.

persist [pə'sıst] vi: **to** ~ (**in doing sth**) persistir (en hacer algo); ~**ence** n empeño; ~**ent** a persistente; (determined) porfiado; (continuing) constante.

person ['pə:sn] n persona; **in** ~ en persona; ~**able** a atractivo; ~**al** a personal; individual; (visit) en persona; (Brit TEL) persona a persona; ~**al assistant** (**P.A.**) n ayudante m/f personal; ~**al column** n anuncios mpl personales; ~**al computer** (**PC**) n computador m personal; ~**ality** [-'nælıtı] n personalidad f; ~**ally** ad personalmente; ~**ify** [-'sɔnıfaı] vt encarnar.

personnel [pə:sə'nel] n personal m.

perspective [pə'spektıv] n perspectiva.

Perspex ['pə:speks] n ® plexiglás m.

perspiration [pə:spı'reıʃən] n transpiración f.

persuade [pə'sweıd] vt: **to** ~ **sb to do sth** persuadir a uno para que haga algo.

pert [pə:t] a impertinente, fresco.

pertaining [pə:'teınıŋ]: ~ **to** prep relacionado con.

pertinent |'pɜ:tɪnənt| *a* pertinente, a propósito.

Peru |pə'ru:| *n* el Perú.

peruse |pə'ru:z| *vt* leer con detención, examinar.

Peruvian |pə'ru:vɪən| *a, n* peruano/a *m/f*.

pervade |pə'veɪd| *vt* impregnar, infundirse en.

perverse |pə'vɜ:s| *a* perverso; (*stubborn*) terco; (*wayward*) travieso.

pervert |'pɜ:vɜ:t| *n* pervertido/a // *vt* |pə'vɜ:t| pervertir.

pessimist |'pesɪmɪst| *n* pesimista *m/f*; **~ic** |-'mɪstɪk| *a* pesimista.

pest |pest| *n* (*insect*) insecto nocivo; (*fig*) lata, molestia.

pester |'pestə*| *vt* molestar, acosar.

pet |pet| *n* animal m doméstico; (*favourite*) favorito/a // *vt* acariciar // *vi* (*col*) besuquearse.

petal |'petl| *n* pétalo.

peter |'pi:tə*|: to ~ out *vi* agotarse, acabarse.

petite |pə'ti:t| *a* chiquito.

petition |pə'tɪʃən| *n* petición *f*.

petrified |'petrɪfaɪd| *a* horrorizado.

petrol |'petrəl| (*Brit*) *n* gasolina; (*for lighter*) bencina; **two/four-star ~** gasolina normal/súper; **~ can** *n* bidón *m* de gasolina.

petroleum |pə'trəʊlɪəm| *n* petróleo.

petrol: **~ pump** *n* (*Brit*) (*in car*) bomba de gasolina; (*in garage*) surtidor *m* de gasolina; **~ station** *n* (*Brit*) gasolinera; **~ tank** *n* (*Brit*) depósito (de gasolina).

petticoat |'petɪkəʊt| *n* enaguas *fpl*.

petty |'petɪ| *a* (*mean*) mezquino; (*unimportant*) insignificante; **~ cash** *n* dinero para gastos menores; **~ officer** *n* contramaestre *m*.

petulant |'petjʊlənt| *a* malhumorado.

pew |pju:| *n* banco.

pewter |'pju:tə*| *n* peltre *m*.

phantom |'fæntəm| *n* fantasma *m*.

pharmacist |'fɑ:məsɪst| *n* farmacéutico/a.

pharmacy |'fɑ:məsɪ| *n* farmacia.

phase |feɪz| *n* fase *f* // *vt*: to ~ sth in/out introducir/retirar algo por etapas.

Ph.D. *abbr* = **Doctor of Philosophy**.

pheasant |'feznt| *n* faisán *m*.

phenomenon |fə'nɒmɪnən|, *pl* **phenomena** |-nə| *n* fenómeno.

phial |'faɪəl| *n* ampolla.

philately |fɪ'lætəlɪ| *n* filatelia.

Philippines |'fɪlɪpi:nz|: the ~ las Filipinas.

philosopher |fɪ'lɒsəfə*| *n* filósofo/a.

philosophy |fɪ'lɒsəfɪ| *n* filosofía.

phlegm |flem| *n* flema; **~atic** |fleg'mætɪk| *a* flemático.

phobia |'fəʊbjə| *n* fobia.

phone |fəʊn| *n* teléfono // *vt* telefonear,

llamar por teléfono; **to be on the ~** tener teléfono; (*be calling*) estar hablando por teléfono; **to ~ back** *vt, vi* volver a llamar; **to ~ up** *vt, vi* llamar por teléfono; **~ book** *n* guía telefónica; **~ box** *or* **booth** cabina telefónica; **~ call** *n* llamada (telefónica); **~-in** *n* (*Brit RADIO, TV*) programa *m* de participación (telefónica).

phonetics |fə'netɪks| *n* fonética.

phoney |'fəʊnɪ| *a* falso // *n* (*person*) farsante *m/f*.

phonograph |'fəʊnəgræf| *n* (*US*) fonógrafo, tocadiscos *m* inv.

phosphate |'fɒsfeɪt| *n* fosfato.

photo |'fəʊtəʊ| *n* foto *f*.

photo... |'fəʊtəʊ| *pref*: **~copier** *n* fotocopiadora; **~copy** *n* fotocopia // *vt* fotocopiar; **~graph** *n* fotografía // *vt* fotografiar; **~grapher** |fə'tɒgrəfə*| *n* fotógrafo; **~graphy** |fə'tɒgrəfɪ| *n* fotografía.

phrase |freɪz| *n* frase *f* // *vt* expresar; **~ book** *n* libro de frases.

physical |'fɪzɪkl| *a* físico; **~ education** *n* educación *f* física; **~ly** *ad* físicamente.

physician |fɪ'zɪʃən| *n* médico/a.

physicist |'fɪzɪsɪst| *n* físico/a.

physics |'fɪzɪks| *n* física.

physiotherapy |fɪzɪəʊ'θerəpɪ| *n* fisioterapia.

physique |fɪ'zi:k| *n* físico.

pianist |'pi:ənɪst| *n* pianista *m/f*.

piano |pɪ'ænəʊ| *n* piano.

piccolo |'pɪkələʊ| *n* (*MUS*) flautín *m*.

pick |pɪk| *n* (*tool: also*: **~axe**) pico, piqueta // *vt* (*select*) elegir, escoger; (*gather*) coger (*Sp*), recoger (*LAm*); (*lock*) abrir con ganzúa; take your ~ escoja lo que quiera; the ~ of lo mejor de; **to ~ one's nose/teeth** hurgarse las narices/limpiarse los dientes; **to ~ pockets** ratear, ser carterista; **to ~ off** *vt* (*kill*) matar uno a uno; **to ~ on** *vt fus* (*person*) meterse con; **to ~ out** *vt* escoger; (*distinguish*) identificar; **to ~ up** *vi* (*improve: sales*) ir mejor; (: *patient*) reponerse; (: *FINANCE*) recobrarse // *vt* (*from floor*) recoger; (*buy*) comprar; (*find*) encontrar; (*learn*) aprender; **to ~ up speed** acelerarse; **to ~ o.s. up** levantarse.

picket |'pɪkɪt| *n* (*in strike*) piquete *m* // *vt* piquetear; **~ line** *n* piquete m.

pickle |'pɪkl| *n* (*also*: **~s**: *as condiment*) escabeche *m*; (*fig: mess*) apuro // *vt* encurtir; (*in vinegar*) envinagrar.

pickpocket |'pɪkpɒkɪt| *n* carterista *m/f*.

pickup |'pɪkʌp| *n* (*Brit: on record player*) pickup *m*; (*small truck*) furgoneta.

picnic |'pɪknɪk| *n* merienda // *vi* ir de merienda.

pictorial |pɪk'tɔ:rɪəl| *a* pictórico; (*magazine etc*) ilustrado.

picture |'pɪktʃə*| *n* cuadro; (*painting*) pintura; (*photograph*) fotografía; (*film*) película // vt pintar; **the** ~s (Brit) el cine; ~ **book** n libro de dibujos.

picturesque [pɪktʃə'rɛsk] a pintoresco.

pie [paɪ] n pastel m; (open) tarta; (small: of meat) empanada.

piece [piːs] n pedazo, trozo; (of cake) trozo; (item): a ~ of **furniture/advice** un mueble/un consejo // vt: **to ~ together** juntar; (TECH) armar; **to take to** ~s desmontar; ~**meal** ad poco a poco; ~**work** n trabajo a destajo.

pie chart n gráfico de sectores or tarta.

pier [pɪə*] n muelle m, embarcadero.

pierce [pɪəs] vt penetrar en; perforar.

piercing ['pɪəsɪŋ] a (cry) penetrante.

piety ['paɪətɪ] n piedad f.

pig [pɪg] n cerdo, puerco; (fig) cochino.

pigeon ['pɪdʒən] n paloma; (as food) pichón m; ~**hole** n casilla.

piggy bank ['pɪgɪbæŋk] n hucha (en forma de cerdito).

pigheaded ['pɪg'hɛdɪd] a terco, testarudo.

pigskin ['pɪgskɪn] n piel f de cerdo.

pigsty ['pɪgstaɪ] n pocilga.

pigtail ['pɪgteɪl] n (girl's) trenza; (Chinese, TAUR) coleta.

pike [paɪk] n (spear) pica; (fish) lucio.

pilchard ['pɪltʃəd] n sardina.

pile [paɪl] n (heap) montón m; (of carpet) pelo // (vb: also: ~ **up**) vt amontonar; (fig) acumular // vi amontonarse; **to ~ into** (car) meterse en.

piles [paɪlz] npl (MED) almorranas fpl, hemorroides mpl.

pile-up ['paɪlʌp] n (AUT) accidente m múltiple.

pilfering ['pɪlfərɪŋ] n ratería.

pilgrim ['pɪlgrɪm] n peregrino/a; ~**age** n peregrinación f, romería.

pill [pɪl] n píldora; **the** ~ la píldora.

pillage ['pɪlɪdʒ] vt pillar, saquear.

pillar ['pɪlə*] n (gen) pilar m; (concrete) columna; ~ **box** n (Brit) buzón m.

pillion ['pɪljən] n (of motorcycle) asiento trasero.

pillow ['pɪləu] n almohada; ~**case** n funda.

pilot ['paɪlət] n piloto // a (scheme etc) piloto // vt pilotar; (fig) guiar, conducir; ~ **light** n piloto.

pimp [pɪmp] n chulo, cafiche m (LAm).

pimple ['pɪmpl] n grano.

pin [pɪn] n alfiler m; (TECH) perno; (: wooden) clavija // vt prender (con alfiler); sujetar con perno; ~**s and needles** npl hormigueo sg; **to ~ sb down** (fig) hacer que uno concrete; **to ~ sth on sb** (fig) colgarle a uno el sambenito de algo.

pinafore ['pɪnəfɔː*] n delantal m; ~ **dress** n (Brit) mandil m.

pinball ['pɪnbɔːl] n fliper m.

pincers ['pɪnsəz] npl pinzas fpl, tenazas fpl.

pinch [pɪntʃ] n pellizco; (of salt etc) pizca // vt pellizcar; (col: steal) birlar // vi (shoe) apretar; **at a** ~ en caso de apuro.

pincushion ['pɪnkuʃən] n acerico.

pine [paɪn] n (also: ~ **tree**) pino // vi: **to ~ for** suspirar por; **to ~ away** vi morirse de pena.

pineapple ['paɪnæpl] n piña, ananás m.

ping [pɪŋ] n (noise) sonido agudo; ~**pong** n ® pingpong m ®.

pink [pɪŋk] a rosado, (color de) rosa // n (colour) rosa; (BOT) clavel m, clavellina.

pinnacle ['pɪnəkl] n cumbre f.

pinpoint ['pɪnpɔɪnt] vt precisar.

pint [paɪnt] n pinta (Brit = 0.57 l; US = 0.47 l); (Brit col: of beer) pinta de cerveza, ≈ jarra (Sp).

pioneer [paɪə'nɪə*] n pionero/a.

pious ['paɪəs] a piadoso, devoto.

pip [pɪp] n (seed) pepita; **the** ~s (Brit TEL) la señal.

pipe [paɪp] n tubo, caño; (for smoking) pipa // vt conducir en cañerías; ~s npl (gen) cañería sg; (also: **bag**~s) gaita sg; **to ~ down** vi (col) callarse; ~ **cleaner** n limpiapipas m inv; ~ **dream** n sueño imposible; ~**line** n tubería, cañería; (for oil) oleoducto; (for gas) gasoducto; ~**r** n (gen) flautista m/f; (with bagpipes) gaitero/a.

piping ['paɪpɪŋ] ad: **to be ~ hot** estar que quema.

piquant ['piːkənt] a picante.

pique [piːk] n pique m, resentimiento.

pirate ['paɪərət] n pirata m/f; ~ **radio** n (Brit) emisora pirata.

pirouette [pɪru'ɛt] n pirueta // vi piruetear.

Pisces ['paɪsiːz] n Piscis m.

piss [pɪs] vi (col) mear; ~**ed** a (col: drunk) borracho.

pistol ['pɪstl] n pistola.

piston ['pɪstən] n pistón m, émbolo.

pit [pɪt] n hoyo; (also: **coal** ~) mina; (in garage) foso de inspección; (also: **orchestra** ~) platea // vt: **to ~ A against B** oponer A a B; ~s npl (AUT) box msg.

pitch [pɪtʃ] n (throw) lanzamiento; (MUS) tono; (Brit SPORT) campo, terreno; (tar) brea; (in market etc) puesto // vt (throw) arrojar, lanzar // vi (fall) caer(se); (NAUT) cabecear; **to ~ a tent** montar una tienda (de campaña); ~**black** a negro como boca de lobo; ~**ed battle** n batalla campal.

pitcher ['pɪtʃə*] n cántaro, jarro.

pitchfork ['pɪtʃfɔːk] n horca.

piteous ['pɪtɪəs] a lastimoso.

pitfall ['pɪtfɔːl] n riesgo.

pith [pɪθ] n (of orange) médula; (fig) meollo.

pithy ['pɪθɪ] a jugoso.

pitiful ['pɪtɪful] a (touching) lastimoso, conmovedor(a); (contemptible) lamentable, miserable.

pitiless ['pitilis] *a* despiadado.

pittance ['pitns] *n* miseria.

pity ['piti] *n* compasión *f*, piedad *f* // *vt* compadecer(se de); **what a ~!** ¡qué pena!

pivot ['pivət] *n* eje *m*.

pizza ['pi:tsə] *n* pizza.

placard ['plæka:d] *n* (*in march etc*) pancarta.

placate [plə'keit] *vt* apaciguar.

place [pleis] *n* lugar *m*, sitio; (*rank*) rango; (*seat*) plaza, asiento; (*post*) puesto; (*home*): **at/to his ~** en/a su casa // *vt* (*object*) poner, colocar; (*identify*) reconocer; (*find a post for*) dar un puesto a, colocar; **to take ~** tener lugar; **to be ~d** (*in race, exam*) colocarse; **out of ~** (*not suitable*) fuera de lugar; **in the first ~** (*first of all*) en primer lugar; **to change ~s with sb** cambiarse de sitio con alguien.

placid ['plæsid] *a* apacible.

plague [pleig] *n* plaga; (*MED*) peste *f* // *vt* (*fig*) acosar, atormentar.

plaice [pleis] *n, pl inv* platija.

plaid [plæd] *n* (*material*) tartán *m*.

plain [plein] *a* (*clear*) claro, evidente; (*simple*) sencillo; (*frank*) franco, abierto; (*not handsome*) poco atractivo; (*pure*) natural, puro // *ad* claramente // *n* llano, llanura; **in ~ clothes** (*police*) vestido de paisano; **~ly** *ad* claramente, evidentemente; (*frankly*) francamente.

plaintiff ['pleintif] *n* demandante *m/f*.

plait [plæt] *n* trenza // *vt* trenzar.

plan [plæn] *n* (*drawing*) plano; (*scheme*) plan *m*, proyecto // *vt* (*think*) pensar; (*prepare*) proyectar, planificar // *vi* hacer proyectos; **to ~ to do** pensar hacer.

plane [plein] *n* (*AVIAT*) avión *m*; (*tree*) plátano; (*tool*) cepillo; (*MATH*) plano.

planet ['plænit] *n* planeta *m*.

plank [plæŋk] *n* tabla.

planner ['plænə*] *n* planificador(a) *m/f*.

planning ['plæniŋ] *n* planificación *f*; **family ~** planificación familiar; **~ permission** *n* permiso para realizar obras.

plant [pla:nt] *n* planta; (*machinery*) maquinaria; (*factory*) fábrica // *vt* plantar; (*field*) sembrar; (*bomb*) colocar.

plaque [plæk] *n* placa.

plaster ['pla:stə*] *n* (*for walls*) yeso; (*also: ~ of Paris*) yeso mate; (*Brit: also: sticking ~*) tirita, esparadrapo, curita (*LAm*) // *vt* enyesar; (*cover*): **to ~ with** llenar *or* cubrir de; **~ed** *a* (*col*) borracho; **~er** *n* yesero.

plastic ['plæstik] *n* plástico // *a* de plástico; **~ bag** *n* bolsa de plástico.

plasticine ['plæstisi:n] *n* (*Brit*) ® plastilina ®.

plastic surgery *n* cirugía plástica.

plate [pleit] *n* (*dish*) plato; (*metal, in book*) lámina; (*PHOT*) placa.

plateau ['plætəu], *pl* **~s** *or* **~x** [-z] *n* meseta, altiplanicie *f*.

plate glass *n* vidrio cilindrado.

platform ['plætfɔ:m] *n* (*RAIL*) andén *m*; (*stage*) plataforma; (*at meeting*) tribuna; (*POL*) programa *m* (*electoral*); **~ ticket** *n* (*Brit*) billete *m* de andén.

platinum ['plætinəm] *n* platino.

platitude ['plætitju:d] *n* lugar *m* común, tópico.

platoon [plə'tu:n] *n* pelotón *m*.

platter ['plætə*] *n* fuente *f*.

plausible ['plɔ:zibl] *a* verosímil; (*person*) convincente.

play [plei] *n* (*gen*) juego, (*THEATRE*) obra, comedia // *vt* (*game*) jugar; (*instrument*) tocar; (*THEATRE*) representar; (: *part*) hacer el papel de; (*fig*) desempeñar // *vi* jugar; (*frolic*) juguetear; **to ~ safe** ir a lo seguro; **to ~ down** *vt* quitar importancia a; **to ~ up** *vi* (*cause trouble to*) dar guerra; **~boy** *n* playboy *m*; **~er** *n* jugador(a) *m/f*; (*THEATRE*) actor *m*/actriz *f*; (*MUS*) músico/a; **~ful** *a* juguetón/ona; **~ground** *n* (*in school*) patio de recreo; **~group** *n* jardín *m* de niños; **~ing card** *n* naipe *m*, carta; **~ing field** *n* campo de deportes; **~mate** *n* compañero/a de juego; **~-off** *n* (*SPORT*) (partido de) desempate *m*; **~pen** *n* corral *m*; **~school** *n* = **~ group**; **~thing** *n* juguete *m*; **~wright** *n* dramaturgo/a.

plc *abbr* (= *public limited company*) S.A.

plea [pli:] *n* (*request*) súplica, petición *f*; (*excuse*) pretexto, disculpa; (*LAW*) alegato, defensa.

plead [pli:d] *vt* (*LAW*): **to ~ sb's case** defender a uno; (*give as excuse*) poner como pretexto // *vi* (*LAW*) declararse; (*beg*): **to ~ with sb** suplicar *or* rogar a uno.

pleasant ['plɛznt] *a* agradable; **~ries** *npl* (*polite remarks*) cortesías *fpl*.

please [pli:z] *vt* (*give pleasure to*) dar gusto a, agradar // *vi* (*think fit*): **do as you ~** haz lo que quieras; **~!** ¡por favor!; **~ yourself!** ¡haz lo que quieras!, ¡como quieras!; **~d** *a* (*happy*) alegre, contento; **~d** (*with*) satisfecho (de); **~d to meet you** ¡encantado!, ¡tanto gusto!; **pleasing** *a* agradable, grato.

pleasure ['plɛʒə*] *n* placer *m*, gusto; (*will*) voluntad *f*; 'it's a ~' el gusto es mío.

pleat [pli:t] *n* pliegue *m*.

pledge [plɛdʒ] *n* (*object*) prenda; (*promise*) promesa, voto // *vt* empeñar; prometer.

plentiful ['plɛntiful] *a* copioso, abundante.

plenty ['plɛnti] *n* abundancia; **~ of** mucho(s)/a(s).

pliable ['plaɪəbl] *a* flexible.

pliers ['plaɪəz] *npl* alicates *mpl*, tenazas *fpl*.

plight [plaɪt] *n* situación *f* difícil.

plimsolls ['plɪmsəlz] *npl* (*Brit*) zapatos *mpl* de tenis.

plinth [plɪnθ] *n* plinto.

plod [plɔd] *vi* caminar con paso pesado; (*fig*) trabajar laboriosamente; **~der** *n* trabajador(a) *m/f* diligente pero lento/a.

plonk [plɔŋk] (*col*) *n* (*Brit: wine*) vino peleón // *vt*: **to ~ sth down** dejar caer algo.

plot [plɔt] *n* (*scheme*) complot *m*, conjura; (*of story, play*) argumento; (*of land*) terreno, lote *m* (*LAm*) // *vt* (*mark out*) trazar; (*conspire*) tramar, urdir // *vi* conspirar; **~ter** *n* (*instrument*) trazador *m* de gráficos.

plough, (*US*) **plow** [plau] *n* arado // *vt* (*earth*) arar; **to ~ back** *vt* (*COMM*) reinvertir; **to ~ through** *vt fus* (*crowd*) abrirse paso por la fuerza por; (*book, work*) roer.

ploy [plɔɪ] *n* truco, estratagema.

pluck [plʌk] *vt* (*fruit*) coger (*Sp*), recoger (*LAm*); (*musical instrument*) puntear; (*bird*) desplumar // *n* valor *m*, ánimo; **to ~ up courage** hacer de tripas corazón; **~y** *a* valiente.

plug [plʌg] *n* tapón *m*; (*ELEC*) enchufe *m*, clavija; (*AUT: also:* **spark(ing) ~**) bujía // *vt* (*hole*) tapar; (*col: advertise*) dar publicidad a; **to ~ in** *vt* (*ELEC*) enchufar.

plum [plʌm] *n* (*fruit*) ciruela // *a*: **~ job** (*col*) puesto (de trabajo) muy codiciado.

plumb [plʌm] *a* vertical // *n* plomo // *ad* (*exactly*) exactamente, en punto // *vt* sondar; (*fig*) sondear.

plumber ['plʌmə*] *n* fontanero/a, plomero/a.

plumbing ['plʌmɪŋ] *n* (*trade*) fontanería; (*piping*) cañería.

plume [plu:m] *n* pluma.

plummet ['plʌmɪt] *vi*: **to ~ (down)** caer a plomo.

plump [plʌmp] *a* rechoncho, rollizo // *vt*: **to ~ sth (down) on** dejar caer algo en; **to ~ for** *vt fus* (*col: choose*) optar por.

plunder ['plʌndə*] *n* pillaje *m*; (*loot*) botín *m* // *vt* pillar, saquear.

plunge [plʌndʒ] *n* zambullida // *vt* sumergir, hundir // *vi* (*fall*) caer; (*dive*) saltar; (*person*) arrojarse; (*sink*) hundirse; **to take the ~** lanzarse; **~r** *n* émbolo; (*for drain*) desatascador *m*.

pluperfect [plu:'pə:fɪkt] *n* pluscuamperfecto.

plural ['pluərl] *n* plural *m*.

plus [plʌs] *n* (*also:* **~ sign**) signo más // *prep* más, y, además de; **ten/twenty ~** más de diez/veinte.

plush [plʌʃ] *a* de felpa.

plutonium [plu:'təunɪəm] *n* plutonio.

ply [plaɪ] *vt* (*a trade*) ejercer // *vi* (*ship*) ir y venir; (*for hire*) ofrecerse (para alquilar); **to ~ sb with drink** insistir en ofrecer a alguien muchas copas; **~wood** *n* madera contrachapada.

P.M. *abbr* = **Prime Minister**.

p.m. *ad abbr* (= *post meridiem*) de la tarde *or* noche.

pneumatic [nju:'mætɪk] *a* neumático; **~ drill** *n* martillo neumático.

pneumonia [nju:'məunɪə] *n* pulmonía.

poach [pəutʃ] *vt* (*cook*) escalfar; (*steal*) cazar/pescar en vedado // *vi* cazar/pescar en vedado; **~ed** *a* (*egg*) escalfado; **~er** *n* cazador(a) *m/f* furtivo/a; **~ing** *n* caza/pesca furtiva.

P.O. Box *n abbr* = **Post Office Box**.

pocket ['pɔkɪt] *n* bolsillo; (*of air*, *GEO*, *fig*) bolsa; (*BILLIARDS*) tronera // *vt* meter en el bolsillo; (*steal*) embolsar; (*BILLIARDS*) entronerar; **to be out of ~** salir perdiendo; **~book** *n* (*US: wallet*) cartera; **~ knife** *n* navaja; **~ money** *n* asignación *f*.

pod [pɔd] *n* vaina.

podgy ['pɔdʒɪ] *a* gordinflón/ona.

podiatrist [pɔ'di:ətrɪst] *n* (*US*) pedicuro/a.

poem ['pəuɪm] *n* poema *m*.

poet ['pəuɪt] *n* poeta *m/f*; **~ic** [-'ɛtɪk] *a* poético; **~ laureate** *n* poeta *m* laureado; **~ry** *n* poesía.

poignant ['pɔɪnjənt] *a* conmovedor(a).

point [pɔɪnt] *n* punto; (*tip*) punta; (*purpose*) fin *m*, propósito; (*use*) utilidad *f*; (*significant part*) lo significativo; (*also:* **decimal ~**): **2 ~ 3** (**2.3**) dos coma tres (2,3) // *vt* (*gun etc*): **to ~ sth at sb** apuntar algo a uno // *vi* señalar con el dedo; **~s** *npl* (*AUT*) contactos *mpl*; (*RAIL*) agujas *fpl*; **to be on the ~ of doing sth** estar a punto de hacer algo; **to make a ~ of** poner empeño en; **to get the ~** comprender; **to come to the ~** ir al meollo; **there's no ~ (in doing)** no tiene sentido (hacer); **to ~ out** *vt* señalar; **to ~ to** *vt fus* indicar con el dedo; (*fig*) indicar, señalar; **~-blank** *ad* (*also:* **at ~-blank range**) a quemarropa; **~ed** *a* (*shape*) puntiagudo, afilado; (*remark*) intencionado; **~edly** *ad* intencionadamente; **~er** *n* (*stick*) puntero; (*needle*) aguja, indicador *m*; **~less** *a* sin sentido; **~ of view** *n* punto de vista.

poise [pɔɪz] *n* (*of head, body*) porte *m*; (*calmness*) aplomo, elegancia.

poison ['pɔɪzn] *n* veneno // *vt* envenenar; **~ing** *n* envenenamiento; **~ous** *a* venenoso; (*fumes etc*) tóxico; (*fig*) pernicioso.

poke [pəuk] *vt* (*fire*) hurgar, atizar; (*jab with finger, stick etc*) empujar; (*put*): **to ~ sth in(to)** introducir algo en; **to ~ about** *vi* fisgonear.

poker ['pəukə*] *n* atizador *m*; (*CARDS*)

póker *m*; **~-faced** *a* de cara impasible.

poky ['pəukı] *a* estrecho.

Poland ['pəulənd] *n* Polonia.

polar ['pəulə*] *a* polar,

Pole [pəul] *n* polaco/a.

pole [pəul] *n* palo; (GEO) polo; (TEL) poste *m*; (*flag* ~) asta; (*tent* ~) mástil *m*; **~ bean** *n* (US) judía trepadora; **~ vault** *n* salto con pértiga.

police [pə'li:s] *n* policía // *vt* vigilar; **~ car** *n* coche-patrulla *m*; **~man** *n* policía *m*, guardia *m*; **~ state** *n* estado policial; **~ station** *n* comisaría; **~woman** *n* mujer *f* policía.

policy ['pɔlısı] *n* política; (*also:* **insurance** ~) póliza.

polio ['pəulıəu] *n* polio *f*.

Polish ['pəulıʃ] *a* polaco // *n* (LING) polaco.

polish ['pɔlıʃ] *n* (*for shoes*) betún *m*; (*for floor*) cera (de lustrar); (*for nails*) esmalte *m*; (*shine*) brillo, lustre *m*; (*fig:* refinement) educación *f* // *vt* (*shoes*) limpiar; (*make shiny*) pulir, sacar brillo a; (*fig: improve*) perfeccionar; **to ~ off** *vt* (*work*) terminar; (*food*) despachar; **~ed** *a* (*fig: person*) elegante.

polite [pə'laıt] *a* cortés, atento; (*formal*) correcto; **~ness** *n* cortesía.

politic ['pɔlıtık] *a* prudente; **~al** [pə'lıtıkl] *a* político; **~ian** [-'tıʃən] *n* político/a; **~s** *n* política.

polka ['pɔlkə] *n* polca; **~ dot** *n* lunar *m*.

poll [pəul] *n* (*votes*) votación *f*, votos *mpl*; (*also:* **opinion** ~) sondeo, encuesta // *vt* (*votes*) obtener.

pollen ['pɔlən] *n* polen *m*.

polling ['pəulıŋ] (*Brit*): **~ booth** *n* cabina de votar; **~ day** *n* día *m* de elecciones; **~ station** *n* centro electoral.

pollution [pə'lu:ʃən] *n* polución *f*, contaminación *f* del medio ambiente.

polo ['pəuləu] *n* (*sport*) polo; **~-neck** *a* de cuello vuelto.

polyester [pɔlı'estə*] *n* poliéster *m*.

polyethylene [pɔlı'εθıli:n] *n* (US) politeno.

Polynesia [pɔlı'ni:zıə] *n* Polinesia.

polystyrene [pɔlı'staırı:n] *n* poliestireno.

polytechnic [pɔlı'tεknık] *n* ≈ escuela de formación profesional.

polythene ['pɔlıθi:n] *n* (*Brit*) politeno.

pomegranate ['pɔmıgrænıt] *n* granada.

pomp [pɔmp] *n* pompa.

pompom ['pɔmpɔm], **pompon** ['pɔmpɔn] *n* borla.

pompous ['pɔmpəs] *a* pomposo.

pond [pɔnd] *n* (*natural*) charca; (*artificial*) estanque *m*.

ponder ['pɔndə*] *vt* meditar; **~ous** *a* pesado.

pong [pɔŋ] *n* (*Brit col*) hedor *m*.

pontoon [pɔn'tu:n] *n* pontón *m*; (*Brit:* card game) veintiuna.

pony ['pəunı] *n* poney *m*, jaca, potro

(*LAm*); **~tail** *n* cola de caballo; **~ trekking** *n* (*Brit*) excursión *f* a caballo.

poodle ['pu:dl] *n* caniche *m*.

pool [pu:l] *n* (*natural*) charca; (*pond*) estanque *m*; (*also:* **swimming** ~) piscina, alberca (*LAm*); (*billiards*) chapolín // *vt* juntar; typing ~ servicio de mecanografía; (**football**) **~s** *npl* quinielas *fpl*.

poor [puə*] *a* pobre; (*bad*) de mala calidad // *npl:* **the** ~ los pobres; **~ly** *a* mal, enfermo.

pop [pɔp] *n* (*sound*) ruido seco; (MUS) (música) pop *m*; (US: col: *father*) papá *m*; (*lemonade*) gaseosa // *vt* (*burst*) hacer reventar // *vi* reventar; (*cork*) saltar; **to ~ in/out** *vi* entrar/salir un momento; **to ~ up** *vi* aparecer inesperadamente; **~ concert** *n* concierto pop; **~corn** *n* palomitas *fpl*.

pope [pəup] *n* papa *m*.

poplar ['pɔplə*] *n* álamo.

poppy ['pɔpı] *n* amapola.

popsicle ['pɔpsıkl] *n* (US) polo.

populace ['pɔpjuləs] *n* pueblo, plebe *f*.

popular ['pɔpjulə*] *a* popular; **~ize** *vt* popularizar; (*disseminate*) vulgarizar.

population [pɔpju'leıʃən] *n* población *f*.

porcelain ['pɔːslın] *n* porcelana.

porch [pɔːtʃ] *n* pórtico, entrada.

porcupine ['pɔːkjupaın] *n* puerco *m* espín.

pore [pɔː*] *n* poro // *vi:* **to ~ over** engolfarse en.

pork [pɔːk] *n* carne *f* de cerdo *or* chancho (*LAm*).

pornography [pɔː'nɔgrəfı] *n* pornografía.

porous ['pɔːrəs] *a* poroso.

porpoise ['pɔːpəs] *n* marsopa.

porridge ['pɔrıdʒ] *n* gachas *fpl* de avena.

port [pɔːt] *n* (*harbour*) puerto; (NAUT: left side) babor *m*; (*wine*) vino de Oporto; **~ of call** puerto de escala.

portable ['pɔːtəbl] *a* portátil.

portent ['pɔːtent] *n* presagio, augurio.

porter ['pɔːtə*] *n* (*for luggage*) maletero; (*doorkeeper*) portero/a, conserje *m/f*.

portfolio [pɔːt'fəulıəu] *n* (*case, of artist*) cartera, carpeta; (POL, FINANCE) cartera.

porthole ['pɔːthəul] *n* portilla.

portion ['pɔːʃən] *n* porción *f*; (*helping*) ración *f*.

portly ['pɔːtlı] *a* corpulento.

portrait ['pɔːtreıt] *n* retrato.

portray [pɔː'treı] *vt* retratar; (*in writing*) representar.

Portugal ['pɔːtjugl] *n* Portugal *m*.

Portuguese [pɔːtju'gi:z] *a* portugués/esa // *n, pl inv* portugués/esa *m/f*; (LING) portugués *m*.

pose [pəuz] *n* postura, actitud *f*; (*pej*) afectación *f*, pose *f* // *vi* posar; (*pretend*): **to ~ as** hacerse pasar por // *vt* (*question*) plantear.

posh [pɒʃ] *a* (*col*) elegante, de lujo.

position [pə'zɪʃən] *n* posición *f*; (*job*) puesto // *vt* colocar.

positive ['pɒzɪtɪv] *a* positivo; (*certain*) seguro; (*definite*) definitivo.

posse ['pɒsɪ] *n* (*US*) pelotón *m*.

possess [pə'zɛs] *vt* poseer; **~ion** [pə'zɛʃən] *n* posesión *f*.

possibility [pɒsɪ'bɪlɪtɪ] *n* posibilidad *f*.

possible ['pɒsɪbl] *a* posible; as big as ~ lo más grande posible; **possibly**· *ad* (*perhaps*) posiblemente, tal vez; I cannot possibly come me es imposible venir.

post [pəust] *n* (*Brit: letters, delivery*) correo; (*job, situation*) puesto; (*pole*) poste *m* // *vt* (*Brit: send by post*) echar al correo; (*MIL*) apostar; (*bills*) fijar, pegar; (*Brit: appoint*): to ~ to enviar a; **~age** *n* porte *m*, franqueo; **~al** *a* postal, de correos; **~al order** *n* giro postal; **~box** *n* (*Brit*) buzón *m*; **~card** *n* tarjeta postal; **~code** *n* (*Brit*) código postal.

postdate [pəust'deɪt] *vt* (*cheque*) poner fecha adelantada a.

poster ['pəustə*] *n* cartel *m*.

poste restante [pəust'rɛstõnt] *n* (*Brit*) lista de correos.

posterior [pɒs'tɪərɪə*] *n* (*col*) culo, trasero.

postgraduate ['pəust'grædjuət] *n* posgraduado/a.

posthumous ['pɒstjuməs] *a* póstumo.

post: **~man** *n* cartero; **~mark** *n* matasellos *m inv*; **~master** *n* administrador · *m* de correos.

post-mortem [pəust'mɔːtəm] *n* autopsia.

post office *n* (*building*) (oficina de) correos *m*; (*organization*): the **P~** **O~** Administración *f* General de Correos; **P~** **O~** **Box (P.O. Box)** *n* apartado postal, casilla de correos (*LAm*).

postpone [pəs'pəun] *vt* aplazar.

postscript ['pəustskrɪpt] *n* posdata.

posture ['pɒstʃə*] *n* postura, actitud *f*.

postwar [pəust'wɔː*] *a* de la posguerra.

posy ['pəuzɪ] *n* ramillete *m* (de flores).

pot [pɒt] *n* (*for cooking*) olla; (*for flowers*) maceta; (*for jam*) tarro, pote *m*; (*col: marijuana*) costo // *vt* (*plant*) poner en tiesto; (*conserve*) conservar; to go to ~ (*col: work, performance*) irse al traste.

potato [pə'teɪtəu], *pl* **~es** *n* patata, papa (*LAm*); ~ **peeler** *n* pelapatatas *m inv*.

potent ['pəutnt] *a* potente, poderoso; (*drink*) fuerte.

potential [pə'tɛnʃl] *a* potencial, posible // *n* potencial *m*; **~ly** *ad* en potencia.

pothole ['pɒthəul] *n* (*in road*) bache *m*; (*Brit: underground*) gruta; **potholing** *n* (*Brit*): to go potholing dedicarse a la espeleología.

potion ['pəuʃən] *n* poción *f*, pócima.

potluck [pɒt'lʌk] *n*: to take ~ tomar lo que haya.

potshot ['pɒtʃɒt] *n*: to take a ~ at sth tirar a algo sin apuntar.

potted ['pɒtɪd] *a* (*food*) en conserva; (*plant*) en tiesto *or* maceta.

potter ['pɒtə*] *n* alfarero/a // *vi*: to ~ around, ~ about hacer trabajitos; **~y** *n* cerámica; alfarería.

potty ['pɒtɪ] *a* (*col: mad*) chiflado // *n* orinal *m* de niño.

pouch [pautʃ] *n* (*ZOOL*) bolsa; (*for tobacco*) petaca.

poultry ['pəultrɪ] *n* aves *fpl* de corral; (*dead*) pollos *mpl*.

pounce [pauns] *vi*: to ~ on precipitarse sobre

pound [paund] *n* libra (*weight = 453g, 16oz; money = 100 pence*); (*for dogs*) corral *m*; (*for cars*) depósito // *vt* (*beat*) golpear; (*crush*) machacar // *vi* (*beat*) dar golpes.

pour [pɔː*] *vt* echar; (*tea*) servir // *vi* correr, fluir; (*rain*) llover a cántaros; to ~ **away** *or* **off** *vt* vaciar, verter; to ~ **in/out** *vi* (*people*) entrar/salir en tropel // *vt* (*drink*) echar, servir; **~ing** *a*: **~ing rain** lluvia torrencial.

pout [paut] *vi* hacer pucheros.

poverty ['pɒvətɪ] *n* pobreza, miseria; **~stricken** *a* necesitado.

powder ['paudə*] *n* polvo; (*face* ~) polvos *mpl*; (*gun* ~) pólvora // *vt* polvorear; to ~ one's face ponerse polvos; ~ **compact** *n* polvera; **~ed milk** *n* leche *f* en polvo; ~ **puff** *n* borla; ~ **room** *n* aseos *mpl*.

power ['pauə*] *n* poder *m*; (*strength*) fuerza; (*nation, TECH*) potencia; (*drive*) empuje *m*; (*ELEC*) fuerza, energía // *vt* impulsar; to be in ~ (*POL*) estar en el poder; ~ **cut** *n* (*Brit*) apagón *m*; **~ed** *a*: **~ed by** impulsado por; ~ **failure** *n* = ~ **cut**; **~ful** *a* poderoso; (*engine*) potente; **~less** *a* impotente, ineficaz; ~ **point** *n* (*Brit*) enchufe *m*; ~ **station** *n* central *f* eléctrica.

p.p. *abbr* (= *per procurationem*): ~ J. Smith p.p. (por poder de) J. Smith.

PR *n abbr* = **public relations**.

practicable ['præktɪkəbl] *a* (*scheme*) factible.

practical ['præktɪkl] *a* práctico; **~ity** [-'kælɪtɪ] *n* (*of situation etc*) factibilidad *f*; ~ **joke** *n* broma pesada; **~ly** *ad* (*almost*) casi.

practice ['præktɪs] *n* (*habit*) costumbre *f*; (*exercise*) práctica, ejercicio; (*training*) adiestramiento; (*MED*) clientela // *vt, vi* (*US*) = **practise**; in ~ (*in reality*) en la práctica; out of ~ desentrenado.

practise, (*US*) **practice** ['præktɪs] *vt* (*carry out*) practicar; (*profession*) ejercer; (*train at*) practicar // *vi* ejercer; (*train*) practicar; **practising** *a* (*Christian etc*) practicante; (*lawyer*) que ejerce.

practitioner |præk'tɪʃənə*| n practicante m/f; (MED) médico/a.

prairie |'preərɪ| n (in N. America) pampa.

praise |preɪz| n alabanza(s) f(pl), elogio(s) m(pl); ~**worthy** a loable.

pram |præm| n (Brit) cochecito de niño.

prance |prɑːns| vi (horse) hacer cabriolas.

prank |præŋk| n travesura.

prawn |prɔːn| n gamba.

pray |preɪ| vi rezar.

prayer |preə*| n oración f, rezo; (entreaty) ruego, súplica; ~ **book** n devocionario, misal m.

preach |priːtʃ| vi predicar.

precaution |prɪ'kɔːʃən| n precaución f.

precede |prɪ'siːd| vt, vi preceder.

precedence |'presɪdəns| n precedencia; (priority) prioridad f.

precedent |'presɪdənt| n precedente m.

precinct |'priːsɪŋkt| n recinto; ~**s** npl contornos mpl; **pedestrian** ~ (Brit) zona peatonal; **shopping** ~ (Brit) centro comercial.

precious |'preʃəs| a precioso.

precipice |'presɪpɪs| n precipicio.

precipitate |prɪ'sɪpɪtɪt| a (hasty) precipitado // vt |prɪ'sɪpɪteɪt| precipitar.

precise |prɪ'saɪs| a preciso, exacto; ~**ly** ad exactamente, precisamente.

preclude |prɪ'kluːd| vt excluir.

precocious |prɪ'kəʊʃəs| a precoz.

precondition |priːkən'dɪʃən| n condición f previa.

predator |'predətə*| n animal m de rapiña.

predecessor |'priːdɪsesə*| n antecesor(a) m/f.

predicament |prɪ'dɪkəmənt| n apuro.

predict |prɪ'dɪkt| vt pronosticar; ~**able** a previsible.

predominantly |prɪ'dɒmɪnəntlɪ| ad en su mayoría.

preen |priːn| vt: **to** ~ **itself** (bird) limpiarse (las plumas); **to** ~ **o.s.** pavonearse.

prefab |'priːfæb| n casa prefabricada.

preface |'prefəs| n prefacio.

prefect |'priːfekt| n (Brit: in school) monitor(a) m/f.

prefer |prɪ'fəː*| vt preferir; ~**able** |'prefrəbl| a preferible; ~**ably** |'prefrəblɪ| ad de preferencia; ~**ence** |'prefrəns| n preferencia; (priority) prioridad f; ~**ential** |prefə'renʃəl| a preferente.

prefix |'priːfɪks| n prefijo.

pregnancy |'pregnənsɪ| n embarazo.

pregnant |'pregnənt| a embarazada.

prehistoric |'priːhɪs'tɒrɪk| a prehistórico.

prejudice |'predʒudɪs| n (bias) prejuicio; (harm) perjuicio // vt (bias) predisponer; (harm) perjudicar; ~**d** a (person) predispuesto; (view) parcial, interesado.

prelude |'prɛljuːd| n preludio.

premarital |'priː'mærɪtl| a premarital.

premature |'premətʃuə*| a prematuro.

premier |'premɪə*| a primero, principal // n (POL) primer(a) ministro/a.

première |'premɪeə*| n estreno.

premise |'premɪs| n premisa; ~**s** npl local msg; **on the** ~**s** en el lugar mismo.

premium |'priːmɪəm| n premio; (COMM) prima; **to be at a** ~ ser muy solicitado; ~ **bond** n (Brit) bono del estado que participa en una lotería nacional.

premonition |premə'nɪʃən| n presentimiento.

preoccupied |priː'ɒkjupaɪd| a (worried) preocupado; (absorbed) ensimismado.

prep |prep| n (SCOL: study) deberes mpl; ~ **school** n = **preparatory school**.

prepaid |priː'peɪd| a porte pagado.

preparation |prepə'reɪʃən| n preparación f; ~**s** npl preparativos mpl.

preparatory |prɪ'pærətərɪ| a preparatorio, preliminar; ~ **school** n escuela preparatoria.

prepare |prɪ'peə*| vt preparar, disponer // vi: **to** ~ **for** prepararse or disponerse para; (make preparations) hacer preparativos para; ~**d to** dispuesto a.

preposition |prepə'zɪʃən| n preposición f.

preposterous |prɪ'pɒstərəs| a absurdo, ridículo.

prerequisite |priː'rekwɪzɪt| n requisito.

prerogative |prɪ'rɒgətɪv| n prerrogativa.

preschool |'priː'skuːl| a preescolar.

prescribe |prɪ'skraɪb| vt prescribir; (MED) recetar.

prescription |prɪ'skrɪpʃən| n (MED) receta.

presence |'prezns| n presencia; (attendance) asistencia; ~ **of mind** aplomo.

present |'preznt| a (in attendance) presente; (current) actual // n (gift) regalo; (actuality) actualidad f, presente m // vt |prɪ'zent| (introduce) presentar; (expound) exponer; (give) presentar, dar, ofrecer; (THEATRE) representar; **to give sb a** ~ regalar algo a uno; **at** ~ actualmente; ~**able** |prɪ'zentəbl| a: **to make o.s.** ~**able** arreglarse; ~**ation** |-'teɪʃən| n presentación f; (gift) obsequio; (of case) exposición f; (THEATRE) rèpresentación f; ~**day** a actual; ~**er** |prɪ'zentə*| n (RADIO, TV) locutor(a) m/f; ~**ly** ad (soon) dentro de poco.

preservation |prezə'veɪʃən| n conservación f.

preservative |prɪ'zəːvətɪv| n conservante m.

preserve |prɪ'zəːv| vt (keep safe) preservar, proteger; (maintain) mantener; (food) conservar; (in salt) salar // n (for game) coto, vedado; (often pl: jam) conserva, confitura.

president |'prezɪdənt| n presidente m/f;

~**ial** |-'dɛnʃl| a presidencial.

press |prɛs| n (tool, machine, newspapers) prensa; (printer's) imprenta; (of hand) apretón m // vt (push) empujar; (squeeze) apretar; (grapes) pisar; (clothes: iron) planchar; (pressure) presionar; (insist): to ~ sth on sb insistir en que uno acepte algo // vi (squeeze) apretar; (pressurize) ejercer presión; we are ~ed for time tenemos poco tiempo; to ~ on vi avanzar; (hurry) apretar el paso; ~ **agency** n agencia de prensa; ~ **conference** n rueda de prensa; ~**ing** a apremiante; ~ **stud** n (Brit) botón m de presión; ~-**up** n (Brit) plancha.

pressure |'prɛʃə*| n presión f; ~ **cooker** n olla a presión; ~ **gauge** n manómetro; ~ **group** n grupo de presión; **pressurized** a (container) a presión.

prestige |prɛs'tiːʒ| n prestigio.

presumably |prɪ'zjuːməblɪ| ad es de suponer que, cabe presumir que.

presume |prɪ'zjuːm| vt presumir, suponer; to ~ to do (dare) atreverse a hacer.

presumption |prɪ'zʌmpʃən| n suposición f; (pretension) presunción f.

presumptuous |prɪ'zʌmptjuəs| a presumido.

pretence, (US) **pretense** |prɪ'tɛns| n (claim) pretensión f; (pretext) pretexto; (make-believe) fingimiento; on the ~ of bajo pretexto de.

pretend |prɪ'tɛnd| vt (feign) fingir // vi (feign) fingir; (claim): to ~ to sth pretender a algo.

pretense |prɪ'tɛns| n (US) = **pretence**.

pretension |prɪ'tɛnʃən| n (claim) pretensión f.

pretentious |prɪ'tɛnʃəs| a presumido; (ostentatious) ostentoso, aparatoso.

pretext |'priːtɛkst| n pretexto.

pretty |'prɪtɪ| a (gen) bonito, lindo (LAm) // ad bastante.

prevail |prɪ'veɪl| vi (gain mastery) prevalecer; (be current) predominar; (persuade): to ~ (up)on sb to do sth persuadir a uno para que haga algo; ~**ing** a (dominant) predominante.

prevalent |'prɛvələnt| a (dominant) dominante; (widespread) extendido; (fashionable) de moda.

prevent |prɪ'vɛnt| vt: to ~ (sb from doing sth) impedir (a uno hacer algo); ~**ive** a preventivo.

preview |'priːvjuː| n (of film) preestreno.

previous |'priːvɪəs| a previo, anterior; ~**ly** ad antes.

prewar |priː'wɔː*| a de antes de la guerra.

prey |preɪ| n presa // vi: to ~ on vivir a costa de; (feed on) alimentarse de.

price |praɪs| n precio // vt (goods) fijar el precio de; ~**less** a que no tiene precio; ~ **list** n tarifa.

prick |prɪk| n pinchazo; (sting) picadura // vt pinchar; picar; to ~ **up** one's ears aguzar el oído.

prickle |'prɪkl| n (sensation) picor m; (BOT) espina; (ZOOL) púa; **prickly** a espinoso; (fig: person) enojadizo; **prickly heat** n sarpullido causado por exceso de calor.

pride |praɪd| n orgullo; (pej) soberbia // vt: to ~ o.s. on enorgullecerse de.

priest |priːst| n sacerdote m; ~**ess** n sacerdotisa; ~**hood** n (practice) sacerdocio; (priests) clero.

prig |prɪg| n gazmoño/a.

prim |prɪm| a (demure) remilgado; (prudish) gazmoño.

primarily |'praɪmərɪlɪ| ad (above all) ante todo.

primary |'praɪmərɪ| a primario; (first in importance) principal; ~ **school** n (Brit) escuela primaria.

primate |'praɪmɪt| n (REL) primado // n |'praɪmeɪt| (ZOOL) primate m.

prime |praɪm| a primero, principal; (basic) fundamental; (excellent) selecto, de primera clase // n: in the ~ of life en la flor de la vida // vt (gun, pump) cebar; (fig) preparar; **P~ Minister (P.M.)** n primer(a) ministro/a.

primer |praɪmə*| n (book) texto elemental; (paint) imprimación f.

primeval |praɪ'miːvəl| a primitivo.

primitive |'prɪmɪtɪv| a primitivo; (crude) rudimentario.

primrose |'prɪmrəuz| n primavera, prímula.

primus (stove) |'praɪməs-| n ® (Brit) hornillo de camping.

prince |prɪns| n príncipe m.

princess |prɪn'sɛs| n princesa.

principal |'prɪnsɪpl| a principal, mayor // n director(a) m/f.

principle |'prɪnsɪpl| n principio; in ~ en principio; on ~ por principio.

print |prɪnt| n (impression) marca, impresión f; huella; (letters) letra de molde; (fabric) estampado; (ART) grabado; (PHOT) impresión f // vt (gen) imprimir; (on mind) grabar; (write in capitals) escribir en letras de molde; out of ~ agotado; ~**ed matter** n impresos mpl; ~**er** n (person) impresor(a) m/f; (machine) impresora; ~**ing** n (art) imprenta; (act) impresión f; (quantity) tirada; ~**out** n (COMPUT) impresión f.

prior |'praɪə*| a anterior, previo // n prior m; ~ **to doing** antes de hacer.

priority |praɪ'ɔrɪtɪ| n prioridad f.

prise |praɪz| vt: to ~ **open** abrir con palanca.

prison |'prɪzn| n cárcel f, prisión f // cpd carcelario; ~**er** n (in prison) preso/a; (under arrest) detenido/a; (in dock) acusado/a.

privacy |'prɪvəsɪ| n (seclusion) soledad f;

(*intimacy*) intimidad *f*.

private ['praivit] *a* (*personal*) particular; (*confidential*) secreto, confidencial; (*sitting etc*) a puertas cerradas // *n* soldado raso; '~' (*on envelope*) 'confidencial'; (*on door*) 'prohibido el paso'; **in** ~ en privado; ~ **enterprise** *n* la empresa privada; ~ **eye** *n* detective *m/f* privado/a; **~ly** *ad* en privado; (*in o.s.*) personalmente; ~ **property** *n* propiedad *f* privada; ~ **school** *n* colegio particular.

privet ['privit] *n* alheña.

privilege ['privilidʒ] *n* privilegio; (*prerogative*) prerrogativa.

privy ['privi] *a*: **to be** ~ **to** estar enterado de; **P~ Council** *n* Consejo del Estado.

prize [praiz] *n* premio // *a* (*first class*) de primera clase // *vt* apreciar, estimar; **~-giving** *n* distribución *f* de premios; **~winner** *n* premiado/a.

pro [prəu] *n* (*SPORT*) profesional *m/f*; **the ~s and cons** los pros y los contras.

probability [probə'biliti] *n* probabilidad *f*.

probable ['probəbl] *a* probable.

probably ['probəbli] *ad* probablemente.

probation [prə'beiʃən] *n*: **on** ~ (*employee*) a prueba; (*LAW*) en libertad condicional.

probe [prəub] *n* (*MED, SPACE*) sonda; (*enquiry*) encuesta, investigación *f* // *vt* sondar; (*investigate*) investigar.

problem ['probləm] *n* problema *m*.

procedure [prə'si:dʒə*] *n* procedimiento; (*bureaucratic*) trámites *mpl*.

proceed [prə'si:d] *vi* proceder; (*continue*): **to** ~ (**with**) continuar *or* seguir (con); **~s** ['prəusi:dz] *npl* ganancias *fpl*, ingresos *mpl*; **~ings** *npl* acto *sg*, actos *mpl*; (*LAW*) proceso *sg*; (*meeting*) función *fsg*; (*records*) actas *fpl*.

process ['prəuses] *n* proceso; (*method*) método, sistema *m* // *vt* tratar, elaborar; **in** ~ en curso; **~ing** *n* tratamiento, elaboración *f*.

procession [prə'seʃən] *n* desfile *m*; funeral ~ cortejo fúnebre.

proclaim [prə'kleim] *vt* proclamar; (*announce*) anunciar; **proclamation** [proklə'meiʃən] *n* proclamación *f*; (*written*) proclama.

procrastinate [prəu'kræstineit] *vi* demorarse.

procure [prə'kjuə*] *vt* conseguir

prod [prod] *vt* empujar.

prodigal ['prodigl] *a* pródigo.

prodigy ['prodidʒi] *n* prodigio.

produce ['prodju:s] *n* (*AGR*) productos *mpl* agrícolas // *vt* [prə'dju:s] producir; (*yield*) rendir; (*show*) presentar, mostrar; (*THEATRE*) presentar, poner en escena; (*offspring*) dar a luz; ~ **dealer** *n* (*US*) verdulero/a; **~r** *n* (*THEATRE*) director(a) *m/f*; (*AGR, CINEMA*) produc-

tor(a) *m/f*.

product ['prodʌkt] *n* producto; (*result*) fruto, producto.

production [prə'dʌkʃən] *n* (*act*) producción *f*; (*THEATRE*) presentación *f*; ~ **line** *n* línea de producción.

productive [prə'dʌktiv] *a* productivo; **productivity** [prodʌk'tiviti] *n* productividad *f*.

profane [prə'fein] *a* profano.

profession [prə'feʃən] *n* profesión *f*; **~al** *n* profesional *m/f* // *a* profesional; (*by profession*) de profesión.

professor [prə'fesə*] *n* (*Brit*) catedrático/a; (*US*) profesor(a) *m/f*.

proficiency [prə'fiʃənsi] *n* capacidad, habilidad *f*.

proficient [prə'fiʃənt] *a* experto, hábil.

profile ['prəufail] *n* perfil *m*.

profit ['profit] *n* (*COMM*) ganancia; (*fig*) provecho; **to make a** ~ obtener beneficios // *vi*: **to** ~ **by** *or* **from** aprovechar *or* sacar provecho de; **~ability** [-ə'biliti] *n* rentabilidad *f*; **~able** *a* (*ECON*) rentable; (*beneficial*) provechoso; **~eering** [-'tiəriŋ] *n* (*pej*) explotación *f*.

profound [prə'faund] *a* profundo.

profusely [prə'fju:sli] *ad* profusamente; **profusion** [-'fju:ʒən] *n* profusión *f*, abundancia.

progeny ['prodʒini] *n* progenie *f*.

programme, (*US*) **program** ['prəugræm] *n* programa *m* // *vt* programar; **~r**, (*US*) **programer** *n* programador(a) *m/f*; **programming**, (*US*) **programing** *n* programación *f*.

progress ['prəugres] *n* progreso; (*development*) desarrollo // *vi* [prə'gres] progresar, avanzar; desarrollarse; **in** ~ en curso; **~ive** [-'gresiv] *a* progresivo; (*person*) progresista.

prohibit [prə'hibit] *vt* prohibir; **to** ~ **sb from doing sth** prohibir a uno hacer algo.

project ['prodʒekt] *n* proyecto // (*vb*: [prə'dʒekt]) *vt* proyectar // *vi* (*stick out*) salir, sobresalir.

projectile [prə'dʒektail] *n* proyectil *m*.

projection [prə'dʒekʃən] *n* proyección *f*; (*overhang*) saliente *m*.

projector [prə'dʒektə*] *n* proyector *m*.

proletariat [prəuli'teəriət] *n* proletariado.

prologue ['prəulog] *n* prólogo.

prolong [prə'loŋ] *vt* prolongar, extender.

prom [prom] *n abbr* = **promenade**; (*US: ball*) baile *m* de gala.

promenade [promə'nɑ:d] *n* (*by sea*) paseo marítimo; ~ **concert** *n* concierto (en que parte del público permanece de pie).

prominence ['prominəns] *n* (*fig*) importancia.

prominent ['prominənt] *a* (*standing out*) saliente; (*important*) eminente, importante.

promiscuous [prə'mıskjuəs] a (sexually) promiscuo.

promise ['prɒmıs] n promesa // vt, vi prometer; **promising** a prometedor(a).

promontory ['prɒməntrı] n promontorio.

promote [prə'məut] vt promover; (new product) hacer propaganda por; (MIL) ascender; ~r n (of sporting event) promotor(a) m/f; **promotion** [-'məuʃən] n (advertising) promoción f; (in rank) ascenso.

prompt [prɒmpt] a (punctual) puntual; (quick) rápido // ad: at 6 o'clock ~ a las seis en punto // n (COMPUT) aviso // vt (urge) mover, incitar; (THEATRE) apuntar; to ~ sb to do sth instar a uno a hacer algo; ~ly ad puntualmente; rápidamente.

prone [prəun] a (lying) postrado; ~ to propenso a.

prong [prɒŋ] n diente m, punta.

pronoun ['prəunaun] n pronombre m.

pronounce [prə'nauns] vt pronunciar // ví: to ~ (up)on pronunciarse sobre; ~d a (marked) marcado; ~ment n declaración f.

pronunciation [prənʌnsı'eıʃən] n pronunciación f.

proof [pru:f] n prueba; 70° ~ graduación f del 70 por 100 // a: ~ against a prueba de.

prop [prɒp] n apoyo; (fig) sostén m // vt (also: ~ up) apoyar; (lean): to ~ sth against apoyar algo contra.

propaganda [prɒpə'gændə] n propaganda.

propel [prə'pel] vt impulsar, propulsar; ~ler n hélice f; ~ling pencil n (Brit) lapicero.

propensity [prə'pensıtı] n propensión f.

proper ['prɒpə*] a (suited, right) propio; (exact) justo; (apt) apropiado, conveniente; (timely) oportuno; (seemly) decente; (authentic) verdadero; (col: real) auténtico; ~ly ad (adequately) correctamente; (decently) decentemente; ~ noun n nombre m propio.

property ['prɒpətı] n propiedad f; (personal) bienes mpl muebles; (estate) finca; ~ owner n dueño/a de propiedades.

prophecy ['prɒfısı] n profecía.

prophesy ['prɒfısaı] vt profetizar; (fig) predecir.

prophet ['prɒfıt] n profeta m.

proportion [prə'pɔ:ʃən] n proporción f; (share) parte f; ~al a proporcional; ~ate a proporcionado.

proposal [prə'pəuzl] n propuesta; (offer of marriage) oferta de matrimonio; (plan) proyecto.

propose [prə'pəuz] vt proponer // vi declararse; to ~ to do sth tener intención de hacer algo.

proposition [prɒpə'zıʃən] n propuesta.

proprietor [prə'praıətə*] n propietario/a, dueño/a.

propriety [prə'praıətı] n decoro.

pro rata [prəu'ra:tə] ad a prorrateo.

prose [prəuz] n prosa; (SCOL) traducción f inversa.

prosecute ['prɒsıkju:t] vt (LAW) procesar; **prosecution** [-'kju:ʃən] n proceso, causa; (accusing side) acusación f; **prosecutor** n acusador(a) m/f; (also: **public prosecutor**) fiscal m.

prospect ['prɒspekt] n (view) vista; (outlook) perspectiva; (hope) esperanza // vb [prə'spekt] vt explorar // vi buscar; ~s npl (for work etc) perspectivas fpl; ~ing n prospección f; ~ive [prə'spektıv] a (possible) probable, eventual; (certain) futuro; ~or [prə'spektə*] n explorador(a) m/f.

prospectus [prə'spektəs] n prospecto.

prosper ['prɒspə*] vi prosperar; ~ity [-'sperıtı] n prosperidad f; ~ous a próspero.

prostitute ['prɒstıtju:t] n prostituta.

prostrate ['prɒstreıt] a postrado.

protagonist [prə'tægənıst] n protagonista m/f.

protect [prə'tekt] vt proteger; ~ion [-'tekʃən] n protección f; ~ive a protector(a).

protégé ['prəuteʒeı] n protegido/a.

protein ['prəuti:n] n proteína.

protest ['prəutest] n protesta // vb: [prə'test] vi protestar // vt (affirm) afirmar, declarar.

Protestant ['prɒtıstənt] a, n protestante m/f.

protester [prə'testə*] n manifestante m/f.

protracted [prə'træktıd] a prolongado.

protrude [prə'tru:d] vi salir, sobresalir.

proud [praud] a orgulloso; (pej) soberbio, altanero.

prove [pru:v] vt probar; (verify) comprobar; (show) demostrar // vi: to ~ correct resultar correcto; to ~ o.s. probar su valía.

proverb ['prɒvə:b] n refrán m.

provide [prə'vaıd] vt proporcionar, dar; to ~ sb with sth proveer a uno de algo; ~d (that) conj con tal de que, a condición de que; to ~ for vt fus (person) mantener a; (problem etc) tener en cuenta.

providing [prə'vaıdıŋ] conj a condición de que, con tal de que.

province ['prɒvıns] n provincia; (fig) esfera; **provincial** [prə'vınʃəl] a provincial; (pej) provinciano.

provision [prə'vıʒən] n provisión f; (supply) suministro, abastecimiento; ~s npl (food) comestibles mpl; ~al a provisional; (temporary) interino.

proviso [prə'vaızəu] n condición f, estipulación f.

provocative [prə'vɒkətıv] a provocativo.

provoke [prə'vəuk] vt (arouse) provocar, incitar; (anger) enojar.
prow [prau] n proa.
prowess ['prauıs] n destreza.
prowl [praul] vi (also: ~ about, ~ around) merodear // n: on the ~ de merodeo; ~er n merodeador(a) m/f.
proxy ['prɔksı] n poder m; (person) apoderado/a; by ~ por poderes.
prudence ['pru:dns] n prudencia.
prudent ['pru:dənt] a prudente.
prudish ['pru:dıʃ] a gazmoño.
prune [pru:n] n ciruela pasa // vt podar.
pry [praı] vi: to ~ into entrometerse en.
PS n abbr (= postscript) P.D.
psalm [sɑ:m] n salmo.
pseudo- [sju:dəu] pref seudo-; **pseudonym** n seudónimo.
psyche ['saıkı] n psique f.
psychiatric [saıkı'ætrık] a psiquiátrico.
psychiatrist [saı'kaıətrıst] n psiquiatra m/f.
psychiatry [saı'kaıətrı] n psiquiatría.
psychic ['saıkık] a (also: ~al) psíquico.
psychoanalysis [saıkəuə'nælısıs] n psicoanálisis m inv; **psychoanalyst** [-'ænəlıst] n psicoanalista m/f.
psychological [saıkə'lɔdʒıkl] a psicológico.
psychologist [saı'kɔlədʒıst] n psicólogo/a.
psychology [saı'kɔlədʒı] n psicología.
PTO abbr (= please turn over) sigue.
pub [pʌb] n abbr (= public house) pub m, taberna.
puberty ['pju:bətı] n pubertad f.
pubic ['pju:bık] a púbico.
public ['pʌblık] a, n público; in ~ en público; ~ **address system (P.A.)** n megafonía.
publican ['pʌblıkən] n tabernero/a.
publication [pʌblı'keıʃən] n publicación f.
public: ~ **company** n sociedad f anónima; ~ **convenience** n (Brit) aseos mpl públicos, sanitarios mpl (LAm); ~ **holiday** n día de fiesta, (día) feriado (LAm); ~ **house** n (Brit) bar m, pub m.
publicity [pʌb'lısıtı] n publicidad f.
publicize ['pʌblısaız] vt publicitar; (advertise) hacer propaganda para.
publicly ['pʌblıklı] ad públicamente, en público.
public: ~ **opinion** n opinión f pública; ~ **relations (PR)** n relaciones fpl públicas; ~ **school** n (Brit) escuela privada; (US) instituto; ~**-spirited** a que tiene sentido del deber ciudadano; ~ **transport** n transporte m público.
publish ['pʌblıʃ] vt publicar; ~**er** n (person) editor(a) m/f; (firm) editorial f; ~**ing** n (industry) industria del libro.
puce [pju:s] a de color pardo rojizo.
pucker ['pʌkə*] vt (pleat) arrugar;

(brow etc) fruncir.
pudding ['pudıŋ] n pudín m; (Brit: sweet) postre m; **black** ~ morcilla.
puddle ['pʌdl] n charco.
puff [pʌf] n soplo; (of smoke) bocanada; (of breathing, engine) resoplido // vt: to ~ one's pipe chupar la pipa // vi (gen) soplar; (pant) jadear; to ~ out smoke echar humo; ~**ed** a (col: out of breath) sin aliento.
puff pastry n hojaldre m.
puffy ['pʌfı] a hinchado.
pull [pul] n (tug): to give sth a ~ dar un tirón a algo; (influence) influencia // vt tirar de; (muscle) agarrotarse; (haul) tirar, arrastrar // vi tirar; to ~ to pieces hacer pedazos; to ~ one's punches (fig) no andarse con bromas; to ~ one's weight hacer su parte; to ~ o.s. together tranquilizarse; to ~ sb's leg tomar el pelo a uno; to ~ **apart** vt (take apart) desmontar; to ~ **down** vt (house) derribar; to ~ **in** vi (AUT: at the kerb) parar (junto a la acera); (RAIL) llegar a la estación; to ~ **off** vt (deal etc) cerrar; to ~ **out** vi irse, marcharse; (AUT: from kerb) salir // vt sacar, arrancar; to ~ **over** vi (AUT) hacerse a un lado; to ~ **through** vi salir adelante; (MED) recobrar la salud; to ~ **up** vi (stop) parar // vt (uproot) arrancar, desarraigar; (stop) parar.
pulley ['pulı] n polea.
pullover ['puləuvə*] n jersey m, suéter m.
pulp [pʌlp] n (of fruit) pulpa; (for paper) pasta.
pulpit ['pulpıt] n púlpito.
pulsate [pʌl'seıt] vi pulsar, latir.
pulse [pʌls] n (ANAT) pulso; (of music, engine) pulsación f; (BOT) legumbre f.
pummel ['pʌml] vt aporrear.
pump [pʌmp] n bomba; (shoe) zapatilla // vt sacar con una bomba; (fig: col) sonsacar; to ~ **up** vt inflar.
pumpkin ['pʌmpkın] n calabaza.
pun [pʌn] n juego de palabras.
punch [pʌntʃ] n (blow) golpe m, puñetazo; (tool) punzón m; (for paper) perforadora; (for tickets) taladro; (drink) ponche m // vt (hit): to ~ sb/sth dar un puñetazo or golpear a uno/algo; (make a hole in) punzar; perforar; ~**line** n palabras que rematan un chiste; ~**-up** n (Brit col) riña.
punctual ['pʌŋktjuəl] a puntual.
punctuation [pʌŋktju'eıʃən] n puntuación f.
puncture ['pʌŋktʃə*] (Brit) n pinchazo // vt pinchar.
pundit ['pʌndıt] n experto/a.
pungent ['pʌndʒənt] a acre.
punish ['pʌnıʃ] vt castigar; ~**ment** n castigo.
punk [pʌŋk] n (also: ~ **rocker**) punki m/

f; (*also:* ~ **rock**) música punk; (*US col: hoodlum*) rufián *m*.

punt |pʌnt| *n* (*boat*) batea.

punter |'pʌntə*| *n* (*Brit: gambler*) jugador(a) *m/f*.

puny |'pju:nɪ| *a* débil.

pup |pʌp| *n* cachorro.

pupil |'pju:pl| *n* alumno/a.

puppet |'pʌpɪt| *n* títere *m*.

puppy |'pʌpɪ| *n* cachorro, perrito.

purchase |'pə:tʃɪs| *n* compra // *vt* comprar; ~**r** *n* comprador(a) *m/f*.

pure |pjuə*| *a* puro.

purée |'pjuəreɪ| *n* puré *m*.

purely |'pjuəlɪ| *ad* puramente.

purge |pə:dʒ| *n* (*MED, POL*) purga // *vt* purgar.

purify |'pjuərɪfaɪ| *vt* purificar, depurar.

puritan |'pjuərɪtən| *n* puritano/a.

purity |'pjuərɪtɪ| *n* pureza.

purl |pə:l| *n* punto del revés.

purple |'pə:pl| *a* purpúreo; morado.

purport |pə:'pɔ:t| *vi:* **to** ~ **to** be/do dar a entender que es/hace.

purpose |'pə:pəs| *n* propósito; **on** ~ a propósito, adrede; ~**ful** *a* resuelto, determinado.

purr |pə:*| *vi* ronronear.

purse |pə:s| *n* monedero; (*US*) bolsa, cartera (*LAm*) // *vt* fruncir.

purser |'pə:sə*| *n* (*NAUT*) comisario/a.

pursue |pə'sju:| *vt* seguir; ~**r** *n* perseguidor(a) *m/f*.

pursuit |pə'sju:t| *n* (*chase*) caza; (*occupation*) actividad *f*.

purveyor |pə'veɪə*| *n* proveedor(a) *m/f*.

push |puʃ| *n* empuje *m*, empujón *m*; (*MIL*) ataque *m*; (*drive*) empuje *m* // *vt* empujar; (*button*) apretar; (*promote*) promover; (*thrust*): **to** ~ **sth** (**into**) meter algo a la fuerza (en) // *vi* empujar; (*fig*) hacer esfuerzos; **to** ~ **aside** *vt* apartar con la mano; **to** ~ **off** *vi* (*col*) largarse; **to** ~ **on** *vi* (*continue*) seguir adelante; **to** ~ **through** *vt* (*measure*) despachar; **to** ~ **up** *vt* (*total, prices*) hacer subir; ~**chair** *n* (*Brit*) sillita de ruedas; ~**er** *n* (*drug* ~*er*) traficante *m/f* de drogas; ~**over** *n* (*col*): it's a ~**over** está tirado; ~-**up** *n* (*US*) plancha; ~**y** *a* (*pej*) agresivo.

puss |pus|, **pussy(-cat)** |'pusɪ(kæt)| *n* minino.

put |put|, *pt, pp* **put** *vt* (*place*) poner, colocar; (~ *into*) meter; (*say*) expresar; (*a question*) hacer; **to** ~ **about** *vi* (*NAUT*) virar // *vt* (*rumour*) diseminar; **to** ~ **across** *vt* (*ideas etc*) comunicar; **to** ~ **away** *vt* (*store*) guardar; **to** ~ **back** *vt* (*replace*) devolver a su lugar; (*postpone*) aplazar; **to** ~ **by** *vt* (*money*) guardar; **to** ~ **down** *vt* (*on ground*) poner en el suelo; (*animal*) sacrificar; (*in writing*) apuntar; (*suppress: revolt etc*) sofocar; (*attribute*)

atribuir; **to** ~ **forward** *vt* (*ideas*) presentar, proponer; (*date*) adelantar; **to** ~ **in** *vt* (*application, complaint*) presentar; **to** ~ **off** *vt* (*postpone*) aplazar; (*discourage*) desanimar; **to** ~ **on** *vt* (*clothes, lipstick etc*) ponerse; (*light etc*) encender; (*play etc*) presentar; (*weight*) ganar; (*brake*) echar; **to** ~ **out** *vt* (*fire, light*) apagar; (*one's hand*) alargar; (*news, rumour*) hacer circular; (*tongue etc*) sacar; (*person: inconvenience*) molestar, fastidiar; **to** ~ **up** *vt* (*raise*) levantar, alzar; (*hang*) colgar; (*build*) construir; (*increase*) aumentar; (*accommodate*) alojar; **to** ~ **up with** *vt fus* aguantar.

putrid |'pju:trɪd| *a* podrido.

putt |pʌt| *vt* hacer un putt // *n* putt *m*, golpe *m* corto; ~**ing green** *n* green *m*; minigolf *m*.

putty |'pʌtɪ| *n* masilla.

puzzle |'pʌzl| *n* (*riddle*) acertijo; (*jigsaw*) rompecabezas *m inv*; (*also:* **crossword** ~) crucigrama *m*; (*mystery*) misterio // *vt* dejar perplejo, confundir // *vi:* **to** ~ **about** quebrar la cabeza por; **puzzling** *a* misterioso, extraño.

pyjamas |pɪ'dʒɑ:məz| *npl* (*Brit*) pijama *m*.

pylon |'paɪlən| *n* torre *f* de conducción eléctrica.

pyramid |'pɪrəmɪd| *n* pirámide *f*.

Pyrenees |pɪrə'ni:z| *npl:* **the** ~ los Pirineos.

python |'paɪθən| *n* pitón *m*.

Q

quack |kwæk| *n* (*of duck*) graznido; (*pej: doctor*) curandero/a.

quad |kwɒd| *n abbr* = **quadrangle; quadruplet.**

quadrangle |'kwɒdræŋgl| *n* (*Brit: courtyard: abbr:* **quad**) patio.

quadruple |kwɒ'drupl| *vt, vi* cuadruplicar.

quadruplet |kwɔ:'dru:plɪt| *n* cuatrillizo/a.

quagmire |'kwægmaɪə*| *n* lodazal *m*, cenegal *m*.

quail |kweɪl| *n* (*bird*) codorniz *f* // *vi* amedrentarse.

quaint |kweɪnt| *a* extraño; (*picturesque*) pintoresco.

quake |kweɪk| *vi* temblar // *n abbr* = **earthquake.**

Quaker |'kweɪkə*| *n* cuáquero/a.

qualification |kwɒlɪfɪ'keɪʃən| *n* (*ability*) capacidad *f*; (*requirement*) requisito; (*diploma etc*) título.

qualified |'kwɒlɪfaɪd| *a* (*trained, fit*) capacitado; (*professionally*) titulado; (*limited*) limitado.

qualify |'kwɒlɪfaɪ| *vt* (*LING*) calificar a; (*capacitate*) capacitar; (*modify*) modificar // vi (SPORT) clasificarse; to ~ (as) calificarse (de), graduarse (en); to ~ (for) reunir los requisitos (para).

quality ['kwɔlɪtɪ] n calidad f; (moral) cualidad f.

qualm [kwɑːm] n escrúpulo.

quandary ['kwɔndrɪ] n: to be in a ~ tener dudas.

quantity ['kwɔntɪtɪ] n cantidad f; ~ **surveyor** n aparejador(a) m/f.

quarantine ['kwɔrntiːn] n cuarentena.

quarrel ['kwɔrl] n riña, pelea // vi reñir, pelearse; ~**some** a pendenciero.

quarry ['kwɔrɪ] n (for stone) cantera; (animal) presa.

quart [kwɔːt] n cuarto de galón = 1.136 l.

quarter ['kwɔːtə*] n cuarto, cuarta parte f; (of year) trimestre m; (district) barrio // vt dividir en cuartos; (MIL: lodge) alojar; ~s npl (barracks) cuartel m; (living ~s) alojamiento sg; a ~ of an hour un cuarto de hora; ~ **final** n cuarto de final; ~**ly** a trimestral // ad cada 3 meses, trimestralmente; ~**master** n (MIL) comisario, intendente m militar.

quartet(te) [kwɔː'tɛt] n cuarteto.

quartz [kwɔːts] n cuarzo.

quash [kwɔʃ] vt (verdict) anular.

quasi- ['kweɪzaɪ] pref cuasi.

quaver ['kweɪvə*] n (Brit MUS) corchea // vi temblar.

quay [kiː] n (also: ~side) muelle m.

queasy ['kwiːzɪ] a: to feel ~ tener náuseas.

queen [kwiːn] n reina; (CARDS etc) dama; ~ **mother** n reina madre.

queer [kwɪə*] a (odd) raro, extraño // n (pej: col) maricón m.

quell [kwɛl] vt (feeling) calmar; (rebellion etc) sofocar.

quench [kwɛntʃ] vt (flames) apagar; to ~ one's thirst apagar la sed.

querulous ['kwɛruləs] a (person, voice) quejumbroso.

query ['kwɪərɪ] n (question) pregunta; (doubt) duda // vt dudar de.

quest [kwɛst] n busca, búsqueda.

question ['kwɛstʃən] n pregunta; (matter) asunto, cuestión f // vt (doubt) dudar de; (interrogate) interrogar, hacer preguntas a; **beyond** ~ fuera de toda duda; it's out of the ~ imposible; ni hablar; ~**able** a discutible; (doubtful) dudoso; ~ **mark** n punto de interrogación; ~**naire** [-'nɛə*] n cuestionario.

queue [kjuː] (Brit) n cola // vi hacer cola.

quibble ['kwɪbl] vi sutilizar.

quick [kwɪk] a rápido; (temper) vivo; (mind) listo; (eye) agudo // n: cut to the ~ (fig) herido en lo vivo; be ~! ¡date prisa!; ~**en** vt apresurar // vi apresurarse, darse prisa; ~**ly** ad rápidamente, de prisa; ~**sand** n arenas fpl movedizas; ~**-witted** a perspicaz.

quid [kwɪd] n, pl inv (Brit col) libra.

quiet ['kwaɪət] a tranquilo; (person) callado; (discreet) discreto // n silencio, tranquilidad f // vt, vi (US) = ~**en**; keep ~! ¡cállate!, ¡silencio!; ~**en** (also: ~en down) vi (grow calm) calmarse; (grow silent) callarse // vt calmar; hacer callar; ~**ly** ad tranquilamente; (silently) silenciosamente; ~**ness** n (silence) silencio; (calm) tranquilidad f.

quilt [kwɪlt] n (Brit) edredón m.

quin [kwɪn] n abbr = **quintuplet**.

quinine [kwɪ'niːn] n quinina.

quintet(te) [kwɪn'tɛt] n quinteto.

quintuplet [kwɪn'tjuːplɪt] n quintillizo/a.

quip [kwɪp] n pulla.

quirk [kwɜːk] n peculiaridad f.

quit [kwɪt], pt, pp **quit** or **quitted** vt dejar, abandonar; (premises) desocupar // vi (give up) renunciar; (go away) irse; (resign) dimitir.

quite [kwaɪt] ad (rather) bastante; (entirely) completamente; ~ a few of them un buen número de ellos; ~ (so)! ¡así es!, ¡exactamente!

quits [kwɪts] a: ~ (with) en paz (con); let's call it ~ dejémoslo en tablas.

quiver ['kwɪvə*] vi estremecerse

quiz [kwɪz] n (game) concurso; (: TV, RADIO) programa-concurso // vt interrogar; ~**zical** a burlón(ona).

quota ['kwəʊtə] n cuota.

quotation [kwəʊ'teɪʃən] n cita; (estimate) presupuesto; ~ **marks** npl comillas fpl.

quote [kwəʊt] n cita // vt (sentence) citar; (price) cotizar // vi: to ~ from citar de.

quotient ['kwəʊʃənt] n cociente m.

R

rabbi ['ræbaɪ] n rabino.

rabbit ['ræbɪt] n conejo; ~ **hutch** n conejera.

rabble ['ræbl] n (pej) chusma, populacho.

rabies ['reɪbiːz] n rabia.

RAC n abbr (Brit) = Royal Automobile Club.

race [reɪs] n carrera; (species) raza // vt (horse) hacer correr; (person) competir contra; (engine) acelerar // vi (compete) competir; (run) correr; (pulse) latir a ritmo acelerado; ~ **car** n (US) = **racing car**; ~ **car driver** n (US) = **racing driver**; ~**course** n hipódromo; ~**horse** n caballo de carreras; ~**track** n hipódromo; (for cars) autódromo.

racial ['reɪʃl] a racial; ~**ist** a, n racista m/f.

racing ['reɪsɪŋ] n carreras fpl; ~ **car** n (Brit) coche m de carreras; ~ **driver** n (Brit) corredor(a) m/f de coches.

racism ['reɪsɪzəm] n racismo; **racist**

[-sɪst] *a*, *n* racista *m/f*.

rack [ræk] *n* (*also*: **luggage ~**) rejilla; (*shelf*) estante *m*; (*also*: **roof ~**) baca, portaequipajes *m inv*; (*clothes ~*) percha // *vt* (*cause pain to*) atormentar; **to ~ one's brains** devanarse los sesos.

racket ['rækɪt] *n* (*for tennis*) raqueta; (*noise*) ruido, estrépito; (*swindle*) estafa, timo.

racquet ['rækɪt] *n* raqueta.

racy ['reɪsɪ] *a* picante, salado.

radar ['reɪdɑ:*] *n* radar *m*.

radiance ['reɪdɪəns] *n* brillantez *f*, resplandor *m*.

radiant ['reɪdɪənt] *a* brillante, resplandeciente.

radiate ['reɪdɪeɪt] *vt* (*heat*) radiar, irradiar // *vi* (*lines*) extenderse.

radiation [reɪdɪ'eɪʃən] *n* radiación *f*.

radiator ['reɪdɪeɪtə*] *n* radiador *m*.

radical ['rædɪkl] *a* radical.

radii ['reɪdɪaɪ] *npl of* **radius**.

radio ['reɪdɪəu] *n* radio *f*; **on the ~** por radio.

radio... [reɪdɪəu] *pref*: **~active** *a* radioactivo.

radio-controlled [reɪdɪəukən'trəuld] *a* teledirigido.

radiography [reɪdɪ'ɔgrəfɪ] *n* radiografía.

radiology [reɪdɪ'ɔlədʒɪ] *n* radiología.

radio station *n* emisora.

radiotherapy ['reɪdɪəuθerəpɪ] *n* radioterapia.

radish ['rædɪʃ] *n* rábano.

radius ['reɪdɪəs], *pl* **radii** [-ɪaɪ] *n* radio.

RAF *n abbr* = **Royal Air Force**.

raffle ['ræfl] *n* rifa, sorteo // *vt* rifar.

raft [rɑ:ft] *n* (*craft*) baba; (*also*: **life ~**) balsa salvavidas.

rafter ['rɑ:ftə*] *n* viga.

rag [ræg] *n* (*piece of cloth*) trapo; (*torn cloth*) harapo; (*pej*: *newspaper*) periodicucho; (*for charity*) actividades estudiantiles benéficas // *vt* (*Brit*) tomar el pelo a; **~s** *npl* harapos *mpl*; **~-and-bone man** *n* (*Brit*) = **~man**; **~ doll** *n* muñeca de trapo.

rage [reɪdʒ] *n* (*fury*) rabia, furor *m* // *vi* (*person*) rabiar, estar furioso; (*storm*) bramar; **it's all the ~** es lo último.

ragged ['rægɪd] *a* (*edge*) desigual, mellado; (*cuff*) roto; (*appearance*) andrajoso, harapiento.

ragman ['rægmæn] *n* trapero.

raid [reɪd] *n* (*MIL*) incursión *f*; (*criminal*) asalto; (*by police*) redada // *vt* invadir, atacar; asaltar; **~er** *n* invasor(a) *m/f*.

rail [reɪl] *n* (*on stair*) barandilla, pasamanos *m inv*; (*on bridge, balcony*) pretil *m*; (*of ship*) barandilla; (*for train*) riel *m*, carril *m*; **~s** *npl* vía *sg*; **by ~** por ferrocarril; **~ing(s)** *n(pl)* verja *sg*, enrejado *sg*; **~road** *n* (*US*) = **~way**; **~way** *n* (*Brit*) ferrocarril *m*, vía férrea; **~way line** *n* (*Brit*) línea (de fe-

rrocarril); **~wayman** *n* (*Brit*) ferroviario; **~way station** *n* (*Brit*) estación *f* de ferrocarril.

rain [reɪn] *n* lluvia // *vi* llover; **in the ~** bajo la lluvia; **it's ~ing** llueve, está lloviendo; **~bow** *n* arco iris; **~coat** *n* impermeable *m*; **~drop** *n* gota de lluvia; **~fall** *n* lluvia; **~y** *a* lluvioso.

raise [reɪz] *n* aumento // *vt* (*lift*) levantar; (*build*) erigir, edificar; (*increase*) aumentar; (*doubts*) suscitar; (*a question*) plantear; (*cattle, family*) criar; (*crop*) cultivar; (*army*) reclutar; (*funds*) reunir; (*loan*) obtener; **to ~ one's voice** alzar la voz.

raisin ['reɪzn] *n* pasa de Corinto.

rake [reɪk] *n* (*tool*) rastrillo; (*person*) libertino // *vt* (*garden*) rastrillar; (*fire*) hurgar; (*with machine gun*) barrer.

rally ['rælɪ] *n* (*POL etc*) reunión *f*, mitin *m*; (*AUT*) rallye *m*; (*TENNIS*) peloteo // *vt* reunir // *vi* reunirse; (*sick person, Stock Exchange*) recuperarse; **to ~ round** *vt fus* (*fig*) dar apoyo a.

RAM [ræm] *n abbr* (= *random access memory*) RAM *f*.

ram [ræm] *n* carnero; (*TECH*) pisón *m* // *vt* (*crash into*) dar contra, chocar con; (*tread down*) apisonar.

ramble ['ræmbl] *n* caminata, excursión *f* en el campo // *vi* (*pej*: *also*: **~ on**) divagar; **~r** *n* excursionista *m/f*; (*BOT*) trepadora; **rambling** *a* (*speech*) inconexo; (*BOT*) trepador(a).

ramp [ræmp] *n* rampa; **on/off ~** *n* (*US AUT*) vía de acceso/salida.

rampage [ræm'peɪdʒ] *n*: **to be on the ~** desmandarse.

rampant ['ræmpənt] *a* (*disease etc*): **to be ~** estar extendiéndose mucho.

rampart ['ræmpɑ:t] *n* terraplén *m*; (*wall*) muralla.

ramshackle ['ræmʃækl] *a* destartalado.

ran [ræn] *pt of* **run**.

ranch [rɑ:ntʃ] *n* (*US*) hacienda, estancia; **~er** *n* ganadero.

rancid ['rænsɪd] *a* rancio.

rancour, (US) rancor ['ræŋkə*] *n* rencor *m*.

random ['rændəm] *a* fortuito, sin orden; (*COMPUT, MATH*) aleatorio // *n*: **at ~** al azar.

randy ['rændɪ] *a* (*Brit col*) cachondo.

rang [ræŋ] *pt of* **ring**.

range [reɪndʒ] *n* (*of mountains*) cadena de montañas, cordillera; (*of missile*) alcance *m*; (*of voice*) registro; (*series*) serie *f*; (*of products*) surtido; (*MIL*: *also*: **shooting ~**) campo de tiro; (*also*: **kitchen ~**) fogón *m* // *vt* (*place*) colocar; (*arrange*) arreglar // *vi*: **to ~ over** (*wander*) recorrer; (*extend*) extenderse por; **to ~ from ... to...** oscilar entre ... y....

ranger [reɪndʒə*] *n* guardabosques *m inv*.

rank [ræŋk] n (row) fila; (MIL) rango; (status) categoría; (Brit: also: taxi ~) parada // vi: to ~ among figurar entre // a (stinking) fétido, rancio; the ~ and file (fig) la base.

rankle ['ræŋkl] vi (insult) doler.

ransack ['rænsæk] vt (search) registrar; (plunder) saquear.

ransom ['rænsəm] n rescate m; **to hold sb to ~** (fig) hacer chantaje a uno.

rant [rænt] vi divagar, desvariar.

rap [ræp] vt golpear, dar un golpecito en.

rape [reɪp] n violación f; (BOT) colza // vt violar; **~ (seed) oil** n aceite m de colza.

rapid ['ræpɪd] a rápido; **~s** npl (GEO) rápidos mpl; **~ity** [rə'pɪdɪtɪ] n rapidez f; **~ly** ad rápidamente.

rapist ['reɪpɪst] n violador m.

rapport [ræ'pɔ:*] n simpatía.

rapture ['ræptʃə*] n éxtasis m.

rare [rɛə*] a raro, poco común; (CULIN: steak) poco hecho.

rarely ['rɛəlɪ] ad pocas veces.

raring ['rɛərɪŋ] a: **to be ~ to go** (col) tener muchas ganas de empezar.

rarity ['rɛərɪtɪ] n rareza.

rascal ['rɑ:skl] n pillo, pícaro.

rash [ræʃ] a imprudente, precipitado // n (MED) salpullido, erupción f (cutánea).

rasher ['ræʃə*] n lonja.

raspberry ['rɑ:zbərɪ] n frambuesa.

rasping ['rɑ:spɪŋ] a: **a ~ noise** un ruido áspero.

rat [ræt] n rata.

rate [reɪt] n (ratio) razón f; (percentage) tanto por ciento; (price) precio; (: of hotel) tarifa; (of interest) tipo; (speed) velocidad f // vt (value) tasar; (estimate) estimar; **to ~ as** ser considerado como; **~s** npl (Brit) impuesto sg municipal; (fees) tarifa sg; **~able value** n (Brit) valor m impuesto; **~payer** n (Brit) contribuyente m/f.

rather ['rɑ:ðə*] ad: it's ~ expensive es algo caro; (too much) es demasiado caro; there's ~ a lot hay bastante; I would or I'd ~ go preferiría ir; or ~ mejor dicho.

ratify ['rætɪfaɪ] vt ratificar.

rating ['reɪtɪŋ] n (valuation) tasación f; (standing) posición f; (Brit NAUT: sailor) marinero.

ratio ['reɪʃɪəu] n razón f; **in the ~ of 100 to 1** a razón de 100 a 1.

ration ['ræʃən] n ración f; **~s** npl víveres mpl // vt racionar.

rational ['ræʃənl] a racional; (solution, reasoning) lógico, razonable; (person) cuerdo, sensato; **~e** [-'nɑ:l] n razón f fundamental; **~ize** vt (industry) reconvertir; (behaviour) justificar.

rationing ['ræʃnɪŋ] n racionamiento.

rat race n lucha incesante por la supervivencia.

rattle ['rætl] n golpeteo; (of train etc) traqueteo; (object: of baby) sonaja, sonajero; (: of sports fan) matraca // vi sonar, golpear; traquetear; (small objects) castañetear // vt hacer sonar agitando; **~snake** n serpiente f de cascabel.

raucous ['rɔ:kəs] a estridente, ronco.

ravage ['rævɪdʒ] vt hacer estragos en, destrozar; **~s** npl estragos mpl.

rave [reɪv] vi (in anger) encolerizarse; (with enthusiasm) entusiasmarse; (MED) delirar, desvariar.

raven ['reɪvən] n cuervo.

ravenous ['rævənəs] a hambriento.

ravine [rə'vi:n] n barranco.

raving ['reɪvɪŋ] a: **~ lunatic** loco de atar.

ravishing ['rævɪʃɪŋ] a encantador(a).

raw [rɔ:] a (uncooked) crudo; (not processed) bruto; (sore) vivo; (inexperienced) novato, inexperto; **~ deal** n injusticia; **~ material** n materia prima.

ray [reɪ] n rayo; **~ of hope** (rayo de) esperanza.

rayon ['reɪən] n rayón m.

raze [reɪz] vt arrasar.

razor ['reɪzə*] n (open) navaja; (safety ~) máquina de afeitar; **~ blade** n hoja de afeitar.

Rd abbr = **road**.

re [ri:] prep con referencia a.

reach [ri:tʃ] n alcance m; (BOXING) envergadura; (of river etc) extensión f entre dos recodos // vt alcanzar, llegar a; (achieve) lograr // vi extenderse; **within ~** al alcance (de la mano); **out of ~** fuera del alcance; **to ~ out for sth** alargar or tender la mano para tomar algo.

react [ri:'ækt] vi reaccionar; **~ion** [-'ækʃən] n reacción f.

reactor [ri:'æktə*] n reactor m.

read [ri:d], pt, pp **read** [rɛd] vi leer // vt leer; (understand) entender; (study) estudiar; **to ~ out** vt leer en alta voz; **~able** a (writing) legible; (book) leíble; **~er** n lector(a) m/f; (book) libro de lecturas; (Brit: at university) profesor(a) m/f adjunto/a; **~ership** n (of paper etc) (número de) lectores mpl.

readily ['rɛdɪlɪ] ad (willingly) de buena gana; (easily) fácilmente; (quickly) en seguida.

readiness ['rɛdɪnɪs] n buena voluntad; (preparedness) preparación f; **in ~** (prepared) listo, preparado.

reading ['ri:dɪŋ] n lectura; (understanding) comprensión f; (on instrument) indicación f.

readjust [ri:ə'dʒʌst] vt reajustar // vi (person): **to ~** reajustarse a.

ready ['rɛdɪ] a listo, preparado; (willing) dispuesto; (available) disponible // ad: **~-cooked** listo para comer // n: **at the ~** (MIL) listo para tirar; **to get ~** vi prepararse // vt preparar; **~-made** a confeccionado; **~ money** n dinero contante;

~ **reckoner** n libro de cálculos hechos; ~-**to-wear** a confeccionado.

real |rɪəl| a verdadero, auténtico; in ~ terms en términos reales; ~ **estate** n bienes mpl raíces; ~**istic** |-'lɪstɪk| a realista.

reality |ri:'ælɪtɪ| n realidad f.

realization |rɪəlaɪ'zeɪʃən| n comprensión f; realización f.

realize ['rɪəlaɪz] vt (understand) darse cuenta de; (a project; COMM: asset) realizar.

really ['rɪəlɪ] ad realmente; ~? ¿de veras?

realm |rɛlm| n reino; (fig) esfera.

realtor ['rɪəltɔː*] n (US) corredor(a) m/f de bienes raíces.

reap |ri:p| vt segar; (fig) cosechar, recoger.

reappear |ri:ə'pɪə*| vi reaparecer.

rear |rɪə*| a trasero // n parte f trasera // vt (cattle, family) criar // vi (also: ~ up) (animal) encabritarse; ~**guard** n retaguardia.

rearmament |ri:'ɑːməmənt| n rearme m.

rearrange |ri:ə'reɪndʒ| vt ordenar or arreglar de nuevo.

rear-view ['rɪəvjuː]: ~ **mirror** n (AUT) (espejo) retrovisor m.

reason |'ri:zn| n razón f // vi: to ~ with sb tratar de que uno entre en razón; it stands to ~ that es lógico que; ~**able** a razonable; (sensible) sensato; ~**ably** ad razonablemente; ~**ed** a (argument) razonado; ~**ing** n razonamiento, argumentos mpl.

reassurance |ri:ə'ʃuərəns| n consuelo.

reassure |ri:ə'ʃuə*| vt tranquilizar, alentar; to ~ sb that tranquilizar a uno asegurando que; **reassuring** a alentador(a).

rebate ['ri:beɪt] n (on product) rebaja; (on tax etc) descuento; (repayment) reembolso.

rebel ['rɛbl] n rebelde m/f // vi |rɪ'bɛl| rebelarse, sublevarse; ~**lion** |rɪ'bɛljən| n rebelión f, sublevación f; ~**lious** |rɪ'bɛljəs| a rebelde; (child) revoltoso.

rebound |rɪ'baund| vi (ball) rebotar // n ['ri:baund] rebote m.

rebuff |rɪ'bʌf| n desaire m, rechazo.

rebuild |ri:'bɪld| (irg: like build) vt reconstruir.

rebuke |rɪ'bju:k| vt reprender.

rebut |rɪ'bʌt| vt rebatir.

recalcitrant |rɪ'kælsɪtrənt| a reacio.

recall |rɪ'kɔːl| vt (remember) recordar; (ambassador etc) retirar // n recuerdo.

recant |rɪ'kænt| vi retractarse.

recap ['ri:kæp] vt, vi recapitular.

recapitulate |ri:kə'pɪtjuleɪt| vt, vi = recap.

rec'd abbr (= received) rbdo.

recede |rɪ'si:d| vi retroceder; **receding** a (forehead, chin) huidizo; **receding** hair-

line entradas fpl.

receipt |rɪ'si:t| n (document) recibo; (for parcel etc) acuse m de recibo; (act of receiving) recepción f; ~**s** npl (COMM) ingresos mpl.

receive |rɪ'si:v| vt recibir; (guest) acoger; (wound) sufrir; ~**r** n (TEL) auricular m; (RADIO) receptor m; (of stolen goods) perista m/f; (LAW) administrador m jurídico.

recent ['ri:snt] a reciente; ~**ly** ad recientemente; ~**ly** arrived recién llegado.

receptacle |rɪ'sɛptɪkl| n receptáculo.

reception |rɪ'sɛpʃən| n (gen) recepción f; (welcome) acogida; ~ **desk** n recepción f; ~**ist** n recepcionista m/f.

recess |rɪ'sɛs| n (in room) hueco; (for bed) nicho; (secret place) escondrijo; (POL etc: holiday) clausura; ~**ion** |-'sɛʃən| n recesión f.

recharge |ri:'tʃɑːdʒ| vt (battery) recargar.

recipe ['rɛsɪpɪ] n receta.

recipient |rɪ'sɪpɪənt| n recibidor(a) m/f; (of letter) destinatario/a.

recital |rɪ'saɪtl| n recital m.

recite |rɪ'saɪt| vt (poem) recitar; (complaints etc) enumerar.

reckless ['rɛkləs] a temerario, imprudente; (speed) peligroso; ~**ly** ad imprudentemente; de modo peligroso.

reckon ['rɛkən] vt (count) contar; (consider) considerar; I ~ that... me parece que...; to ~ on vt fus contar con; ~**ing** n (calculation) cálculo.

reclaim |rɪ'kleɪm| vt (land) recuperar; (: from sea) rescatar; (demand back) reclamar.

recline |rɪ'klaɪn| vi reclinarse; **reclining** a (seat) reclinable.

recluse |rɪ'kluːs| n recluso/a.

recognition |rɛkəg'nɪʃən| n reconocimiento; **transformed beyond** ~ irreconocible.

recognizable ['rɛkəgnaɪzəbl] a: ~ (by) reconocible (por).

recognize ['rɛkəgnaɪz] vt: to ~ (by/as) reconocer (por/como).

recoil |rɪ'kɔɪl| vi (person): to ~ from doing sth retraerse de hacer algo // n (of gun) retroceso.

recollect |rɛkə'lɛkt| vt recordar, acordarse de; ~**ion** |-'lɛkʃən| n recuerdo.

recommend |rɛkə'mɛnd| vt recomendar.

recompense ['rɛkəmpɛns] vt recompensar // n recompensa.

reconcile ['rɛkənsaɪl] vt (two people) reconciliar; (two facts) compaginar; to ~ o.s. to sth conformarse a algo.

recondition |ri:kən'dɪʃən| vt (machine) reacondicionar.

reconnaissance |rɪ'kɔnɪsns| n (MIL) reconocimiento.

reconnoitre, (US) **reconnoiter** |rɛkə'nɔɪtə*| vt, vi (MIL) reconocer.

reconsider [riːkən'sɪdə*] vt repensar.

reconstruct [riːkən'strʌkt] vt reconstruir.

record ['rekɔːd] n (MUS) disco; (of meeting etc) relación f; (register) registro, partida; (file) archivo; (also: police ~) antecedentes mpl; (written) expediente m; (SPORT) récord m // vt [rɪ'kɔːd] (set down) registrar; (relate) hacer constar; (MUS: song etc) grabar; **in ~ time** en un tiempo récord; **off the ~** a no oficial // ad confidencialmente; **~ card** n (in file) ficha; **~ed delivery** n (Brit POST) entrega con acuse de recibo; **~er** n (MUS) flauta de pico; (TECH) contador m; **~ holder** n (SPORT) actual poseedor(a) m/f del récord; **~ing** n (MUS) grabación f; **~ player** n tocadiscos m inv.

recount [rɪ'kaunt] vt contar.

re-count ['riːkaunt] n (POL: of votes) segundo escrutinio // vt [riː'kaunt] volver a contar.

recoup [rɪ'kuːp] vt: **to ~ one's losses** recuperar las pérdidas.

recourse [rɪ'kɔːs] n recurso.

recover [rɪ'kʌvə*] vt recuperar; (rescue) rescatar // vi (from illness, shock) recuperarse; (country) recuperar; **~y** n recuperación f; rescate m; (MED): **to make a ~y** restablecerse.

recreation [rekrɪ'eɪʃən] n (amusement, SCOL) recreo; **~al** a de recreo.

recruit [rɪ'kruːt] n recluta m/f // vt reclutar; (staff) contratar (personal); **~ment** n reclutamiento.

rectangle ['rektæŋgl] n rectángulo; **rectangular** [-'tæŋgjulə*] a rectangular.

rectify ['rektɪfaɪ] vt rectificar.

rector ['rektə*] n (REL) párroco; **~y** n casa del párroco.

recuperate [rɪ'kuːpəreɪt] vi reponerse, restablecerse.

recur [rɪ'kɔː*] vi repetirse; (pain, illness) producirse de nuevo; **~rence** [rɪ'kʌrens] n repetición f; **~rent** [rɪ'kʌrent] a repetido.

red [red] n rojo // a rojo; **to be in the ~** (account) estar en números rojos; (business) tener un saldo negativo; **to give sb the ~ carpet treatment** recibir a uno con todos los honores; **R~ Cross** n Cruz f Roja; **~currant** n grosella roja; **~den** vt enrojecer // vi enrojecerse; **~dish** a (hair) rojizo.

redeem [rɪ'diːm] vt (sth in pawn) desempeñar; (fig, also REL) rescatar; **~ing** a: **~ing feature** rasgo bueno or favorable.

redeploy [riːdɪ'plɔɪ] vt (resources) reorganizar.

red: **~-haired** a pelirrojo; **~-handed** a: **to be caught ~-handed** cogerse (Sp) or pillarse (LAm) con las manos en la masa; **~head** n pelirrojo/a; **~ herring** n (fig) pista falsa; **~-hot** a candente.

redirect [riːdaɪ'rekt] vt (mail) reexpedir.

red light n: **to go through a ~** (AUT) pasar la luz roja; **red-light district** n barrio chino.

redo [riː'duː] (irg: like do) vt rehacer.

redolent ['redələnt] a: **~ of** (smell) con fragancia a; **to be ~ of** (fig) recordar.

redouble [riː'dʌbl] vt: **to ~ one's efforts** intensificar los esfuerzos.

redress [rɪ'dres] n reparación f // vt reparar.

Red Sea n: **the ~** el mar Rojo.

redskin ['redskɪn] n piel roja m/f.

red tape n (fig) trámites mpl.

reduce [rɪ'djuːs] vt reducir; (lower) rebajar; **'~ speed now'** (AUT) 'reduzca la velocidad'; **at a ~d price** (of goods) (a precio) rebajado; **reduction** [rɪ'dʌkʃən] n reducción f; (of price) rebaja; (discount) descuento.

redundancy [rɪ'dʌndənsɪ] n desempleo.

redundant [rɪ'dʌndnt] a (Brit) (worker) parado, sin trabajo; (detail, object) superfluo; **to be made ~** quedar(se) sin trabajo.

reed [riːd] n (BOT) junco, caña.

reef [riːf] n (at sea) arrecife m.

reek [riːk] vi: **to ~ (of)** apestar (a).

reel [riːl] n carrete m, bobina; (of film) rollo // vt (TECH) devanar; (also: ~ in) sacar // vi (sway) tambalear(se).

ref [ref] n abbr (col) = **referee**.

refectory [rɪ'fektərɪ] n comedor m.

refer [rɪ'fɔː*] vt (send) remitir; (ascribe) referir a, relacionar con // vi: **to ~ to** (allude to) referirse a, aludir a; (apply to) relacionarse con; (consult) consultar.

referee [refə'riː] n árbitro; (Brit: for job application) valedor m; **to be a ~** (for job application) proporcionar referencias // vt (match) arbitrar en.

reference ['refrəns] n (mention) referencia; (for job application: letter) carta de recomendación; **with ~ to** con referencia a; (COMM: in letter) me remito a; **~ book** n libro de consulta; **~ number** n número de referencia.

refill [riː'fɪl] vt rellenar // n ['riːfɪl] repuesto, recambio.

refine [rɪ'faɪn] vt (sugar, oil) refinar; **~d** a (person, taste) fino; **~ment** n (of person) cultura, educación f.

reflect [rɪ'flekt] vt (light, image) reflejar // vi (think) reflexionar, pensar; **it ~s badly/well on him** le perjudica/le hace honor; **~ion** [-'flekʃən] n (act) reflexión f; (image) reflejo; (discredit) crítica; **on ~ion** pensándolo bien; **~or** n (AUT) captafaros m inv; (telescope) reflector m.

reflex ['riːfleks] a, n reflejo; **~ive** [rɪ'fleksɪv] a (LING) reflexivo.

reform [rɪ'fɔːm] n reforma // vt reformar; **the R~ation** [refə'meɪʃən] n la Reforma; **~atory** n (US) reformatorio; **~er** n reformador(a) m/f.

refrain [rɪ'freɪn] vi: **to ~ from doing** abstenerse de hacer // n estribillo.

refresh [rɪ'frɛʃ] vt refrescar; ~er course n (Brit) curso de repaso; ~ing a (drink) refrescante; (change etc) estimulante; ~ments npl (drinks) refrescos mpl.

refrigerator [rɪ'frɪdʒəreɪtə*] n nevera, refrigeradora (LAm).

refuel [riː'fjuəl] vi repostar (combustible).

refuge ['rɛfjuːdʒ] n refugio, asilo; to take ~ in refugiarse en.

refugee [rɛfjuˈdʒiː] n refugiado/a.

refund ['riːfʌnd] n reembolso // vt [rɪ'fʌnd] devolver, reembolsar.

refurbish [riːˈfɜːbɪʃ] vt restaurar, renovar.

refusal [rɪˈfjuːzəl] n negativa; to have first ~ on tener la primera opción a.

refuse ['rɛfjuːs] n basura // vb [rɪˈfjuːz] vt rechazar // vi negarse; (horse) rehusar; ~ collection recolección f de basuras.

regain [rɪˈɡeɪn] vt recobrar, recuperar.

regal ['riːɡl] a regio, real.

regalia [rɪˈɡeɪlɪə] n insignias fpl.

regard [rɪˈɡɑːd] n (esteem) respeto, consideración f // vt (consider) considerar; to give one's ~s to saludar de su parte a; 'with kindest ~s' 'con muchos recuerdos'; ~ing, as ~s, with ~ to prep con respecto a, en cuanto a; ~less ad a pesar de todo; ~less of sin reparar en.

régime [reɪˈʒiːm] n régimen m.

regiment ['rɛdʒɪmənt] n regimiento // vt reglamentar; ~al [-'mɛntl] a militar.

region ['riːdʒən] n región f; in the ~ of (fig) alrededor de; ~al a regional.

register ['rɛdʒɪstə*] n registro // vt registrar; (birth) declarar; (letter) certificar; (subj: instrument) marcar, indicar // vi (at hotel) registrarse; (sign on) inscribirse; (make impression) producir impresión; ~ed a (design) registrado; (Brit: letter) certificado; ~ed trademark n marca registrada.

registrar ['rɛdʒɪstrɑː*] n secretario/a (del registro civil).

registration [rɛdʒɪsˈtreɪʃən] n (act) declaración f; (AUT: also: ~ number) matrícula.

registry ['rɛdʒɪstrɪ] n registro; ~ office n (Brit) registro civil; to get married in a ~ office casarse por lo civil.

regret [rɪˈɡrɛt] n sentimiento, pesar m; (remorse) remordimiento // vt sentir, lamentar; (repent of) arrepentirse de; ~fully ad con pesar; ~table a lamentable; (loss) sensible.

regroup [riːˈɡruːp] vt reagrupar // vi reagruparse.

regular ['rɛɡjulə*] a regular; (soldier) profesional; (col: intensive) verdadero // n (client etc) cliente/a m/f habitual; ~ity [-'lærɪtɪ] n regularidad f; ~ly ad con regularidad.

regulate ['rɛɡjuleɪt] vt (gen) controlar; **regulation** [-'leɪʃən] n (rule) regla, reglamento; (adjustment) regulación f.

rehearsal [rɪˈhɜːsəl] n ensayo.

rehearse [rɪˈhɜːs] vt ensayar.

reign [reɪn] n reinado; (fig) predominio // vi reinar; (fig) imperar.

reimburse [riːɪmˈbɜːs] vt reembolsar.

rein [reɪn] n (for horse) rienda.

reindeer ['reɪndɪə*] n, pl inv reno.

reinforce [riːɪnˈfɔːs] vt reforzar; ~d concrete n hormigón m armado; ~ment n (action) refuerzo; ~ments npl (MIL) refuerzos mpl.

reinstate [riːɪnˈsteɪt] vt (worker) reintegrar (a su puesto).

reiterate [riːˈɪtəreɪt] vt reiterar, repetir.

reject ['riːdʒɛkt] n (thing) desecho // vt [rɪˈdʒɛkt] rechazar; (suggestion) descartar; ~ion [rɪˈdʒɛkʃən] n rechazo.

rejoice [rɪˈdʒɔɪs] vi: to ~ at or over regocijarse or alegrarse de.

rejuvenate [rɪˈdʒuːvəneɪt] vt rejuvenecer.

relapse [rɪˈlæps] n (MED) recaída.

relate [rɪˈleɪt] vt (tell) contar, relatar; (connect) relacionar // vi relacionarse; ~d a afín; (person) emparentado; ~d to (subject) relacionado con; **relating to** prep referente a.

relation [rɪˈleɪʃən] n (person) pariente/a m/f; (link) relación f; ~ship n relación f; (personal) relaciones fpl; (also: family ~ship) parentesco.

relative ['rɛlətɪv] n pariente/a m/f, familiar m/f // a relativo; ~ly ad (comparatively) relativamente.

relax [rɪˈlæks] vi descansar; (unwind) relajarse // vt relajar; (mind, person) descansar; ~ation [riːlækˈseɪʃən] n (rest) descanso; (entertainment) diversión f; ~ed a relajado; (tranquil) tranquilo; ~ing a relajante.

relay ['riːleɪ] n (race) carrera de relevos // vt (RADIO, TV, pass on) retransmitir.

release [rɪˈliːs] n (liberation) liberación f; (discharge) puesta en libertad f; (of gas etc) escape m; (of film etc) estreno // vt (prisoner) poner en libertad; (film) estrenar; (book) publicar; (piece of news) difundir; (gas etc) despedir, arrojar; (free: from wreckage etc) soltar; (TECH: catch, spring etc) desenganchar; (let go) soltar, aflojar.

relegate ['rɛləɡeɪt] vt relegar; (SPORT): to be ~d to bajar a.

relent [rɪˈlɛnt] vi ablandarse; ~less a implacable.

relevant ['rɛləvənt] a (fact) pertinente; relevant to relacionado con.

reliability [rɪlaɪəˈbɪlɪtɪ] n fiabilidad f; seguridad f; veracidad f.

reliable [rɪˈlaɪəbl] a (person, firm) de confianza, de fiar; (method, machine) seguro; (source) fidedigno; **reliably** ad: to

be reliably informed that... saber de fuente fidedigna que... .
reliance [rɪˈlaɪəns] n: ~ (on) dependencia (de).
relic [ˈrelɪk] n (REL) reliquia; (of the past) vestigio.
relief [rɪˈliːf] n (from pain, anxiety) alivio; (help, supplies) socorro, ayuda; (ART, GEO) relieve m.
relieve [rɪˈliːv] vt (pain, patient) aliviar; (bring help to) ayudar, socorrer; (burden) aligerar; (take over from: gen) sustituir; (: guard) relevar; to ~ sb of sth quitar algo a uno; to ~ o.s. hacer sus necesidades.
religion [rɪˈlɪdʒən] n religión f; **religious** a religioso.
relinquish [rɪˈlɪŋkwɪʃ] vt abandonar; (plan, habit) renunciar a.
relish [ˈrelɪʃ] n (CULIN) salsa; (enjoyment) entusiasmo // vt (food etc) saborear; to ~ doing gustar mucho de hacer.
relocate [riːləʊˈkeɪt] vt cambiar de lugar, mudar // vi mudarse.
reluctance [rɪˈlʌktəns] n renuencia; **reluctant** a renuente; **reluctantly** ad de mala gana.
rely [rɪˈlaɪ]: to ~ on vt fus confiar en, fiarse de; (be dependent on) depender de.
remain [rɪˈmeɪn] vi (survive) quedar; (be left) sobrar; (continue) quedar(se), permanecer; ~der n resto; ~ing a sobrante; ~s npl restos mpl.
remand [rɪˈmɑːnd] n: on ~ detenido (bajo custodia) // vt: to ~ in custody mantener bajo custodia; ~ home n (Brit) reformatorio.
remark [rɪˈmɑːk] n comentario // vt comentar; ~able a notable; (outstanding) extraordinario.
remarry [riːˈmærɪ] vi volver a casarse.
remedial [rɪˈmiːdɪəl] a: ~ education educación f de los niños atrasados.
remedy [ˈremədɪ] n remedio // vt remediar, curar.
remember [rɪˈmembə*] vt recordar, acordarse de; (bear in mind) tener presente; **remembrance** n: in remembrance of en conmemoración de.
remind [rɪˈmaɪnd] vt: to ~ sb to do sth recordar a uno que haga algo; to ~ sb of sth recordar algo a uno; she ~s me of her mother me recuerda a su madre; ~er n notificación f; (memento) recuerdo.
reminisce [remɪˈnɪs] vi recordar (viejas historias); ~nt a: to be ~nt of sth recordar algo.
remiss [rɪˈmɪs] a descuidado; it was ~ of him fue un descuido de su parte.
remission [rɪˈmɪʃən] n remisión f; (of sentence) disminución f de pena.
remit [rɪˈmɪt] vt (send: money) remitir, enviar; ~tance n remesa, envío.
remnant [ˈremnənt] n resto; (of cloth)

retazo; ~s npl (COMM) restos mpl de serie.
remorse [rɪˈmɔːs] n remordimientos mpl; ~ful a arrepentido; ~less a (fig) implacable; inexorable.
remote [rɪˈməʊt] a (distant) lejano; (person) distante; ~ control n telecontrol m; ~ly ad remotamente; (slightly) levemente.
remould [ˈriːməʊld] n (Brit: tyre) neumático or llanta (LAm) recauchutado/a.
removable [rɪˈmuːvəbl] a (detachable) separable.
removal [rɪˈmuːvəl] n (taking away) el quitar; (Brit: from house) mudanza; (from office: dismissal) destitución f; (MED) extirpación f; ~ van n (Brit) camión m de mudanzas.
remove [rɪˈmuːv] vt quitar; (employee) destituir; (name: from list) tachar, borrar; (doubt) disipar; (abuse) suprimir, acabar con; (TECH) retirar, separar; (MED) extirpar; ~rs npl (Brit: company) agencia de mudanzas.
Renaissance [rɪˈneɪsɒns] n: the ~ el Renacimiento.
render [ˈrendə*] vt (thanks) dar; (aid) proporcionar, prestar; (honour) dar, conceder; (assistance) dar, prestar; to ~ sth + a volver algo + a; ~ing n (MUS etc) interpretación f.
rendez-vous [ˈrɒndɪvuː] n cita.
renegade [ˈrenɪgeɪd] n renegado/a.
renew [rɪˈnjuː] vt renovar; (resume) reanudar; (extend date) prorrogar; ~al n renovación f; reanudación f; prórroga.
renounce [rɪˈnaʊns] vt renunciar a; (right, inheritance) renunciar.
renovate [ˈrenəveɪt] vt renovar.
renown [rɪˈnaʊn] n renombre m; ~ed a renombrado.
rent [rent] n alquiler m; (for house) arriendo, renta // vt alquilar; ~al n (for television, car) alquiler m.
renunciation [rɪnʌnsɪˈeɪʃən] n renuncia.
rep [rep] n abbr = **representative**; **repertory**.
repair [rɪˈpeə*] n reparación f, compostura // vt reparar, componer; (shoes) remendar; in good/bad ~ en buen/mal estado; ~ kit n caja de herramientas.
repartee [repɑːˈtiː] n réplicas fpl agudas.
repatriate [riːˈpætrɪeɪt] vt repatriar.
repay [riːˈpeɪ] (irg: like pay) vt (money) devolver, reembolsar; (person) pagar; (debt) liquidar; (sb's efforts) devolver, corresponder a; ~ment n reembolso, devolución f; (sum of money) recompensa.
repeal [rɪˈpiːl] n revocación f // vt revocar.
repeat [rɪˈpiːt] n (RADIO, TV) reposición f // vt repetir // vi repetirse; ~edly ad repetidas veces.
repel [rɪˈpel] vt (fig) repugnar; ~lent a

repugnante // n: insect ~lent crema/ loción f anti-insectos.

repent [rɪ'pɛnt] vi: to ~ (of) arrepentirse (de); ~ance n arrepentimiento.

repercussion [ri:pə'kʌʃən] n (consequence) repercusión f; to have ~s repercutir.

repertoire ['rɛpətwɑ:*] n repertorio.

repertory ['rɛpətərɪ] n (also: ~ theatre) teatro de repertorio.

repetition [rɛpɪ'tɪʃən] n repetición f.

repetitive [rɪ'pɛtɪtɪv] a repetitivo.

replace [rɪ'pleɪs] vt (put back) devolver a su sitio; (take the place of) reemplazar, sustituir; ~ment n (act) reposición f; (thing) recambio; (person) suplente m/f.

replay ['ri:pleɪ] n (SPORT) desempate m; (of tape, film) repetición f.

replenish [rɪ'plɛnɪʃ] vt (tank etc) rellenar; (stock etc) reponer.

replete [rɪ'pli:t] a repleto, lleno.

replica ['rɛplɪkə] n copia, reproducción f (exacta).

reply [rɪ'plaɪ] n respuesta, contestación f // vi contestar, responder; ~ coupon n cupón-respuesta m.

report [rɪ'pɔ:t] n informe m; (PRESS etc) reportaje m; (Brit: also: school ~) boletín m escolar; (of gun) estallido // vt informar de; (PRESS etc) hacer un reportaje sobre; (notify: accident, culprit) denunciar // vi (make a report) presentar un informe; (present o.s.): to ~ (to sb) presentarse (ante uno); ~ card n (US, Scottish) cartilla escolar; ~edly ad según se dice; ~er n periodista m/f.

repose [rɪ'pəuz] n: in ~ (face, mouth) en reposo.

reprehensible [rɛprɪ'hɛnsɪbl] a reprensible, censurable.

represent [rɛprɪ'zɛnt] vt representar; (COMM) ser agente de; ~ation [-'teɪʃən] n representación f; ~ations npl (protest) quejas fpl; ~ative a (gen) representante m/f; (US POL) diputado/a m/f // a representativo.

repress [rɪ'prɛs] vt reprimir; ~ion [-'prɛʃən] n represión f.

reprieve [rɪ'pri:v] n (LAW) indulto; (fig) alivio.

reprimand ['rɛprɪmɑ:nd] n reprimenda // vt reprender.

reprisal [rɪ'praɪzl] n represalia.

reproach [rɪ'prəutʃ] n reproche m // vt: to ~ sb with sth reprochar algo a uno; ~ful a de reproche, de acusación.

reproduce [ri:prə'dju:s] vt reproducir // vi reproducirse; **reproduction** [-'dʌkʃən] n reproducción f.

reproof [rɪ'pru:f] n reproche m.

reprove [rɪ'pru:v] vt: to ~ sb for sth reprochar algo a uno.

reptile ['rɛptaɪl] n reptil m.

republic [rɪ'pʌblɪk] n república; ~an a, n republicano/a m/f.

repudiate [rɪ'pju:dɪeɪt] vt (accusation) rechazar; (obligation) desconocer.

repulse [rɪ'pʌls] vt rechazar; **repulsive** a repulsivo.

reputable ['rɛpjutəbl] a (make etc) de renombre.

reputation [rɛpju'teɪʃən] n reputación f.

repute [rɪ'pju:t] n reputación f, fama; ~d a supuesto; ~dly ad según dicen or se dice.

request [rɪ'kwɛst] n solicitud f; petición f // vt: to ~ sth of or from sb solicitar algo a uno; ~ stop n (Brit) parada discrecional.

require [rɪ'kwaɪə*] vt (need: subj: person) necesitar, tener necesidad de; (: thing, situation) exigir; (want) pedir; (demand) insistir en que; ~ment n requisito; (need) necesidad f.

requisite ['rɛkwɪzɪt] n requisito // a necesario.

requisition [rɛkwɪ'zɪʃən] n: ~ (for) solicitud f (de) // vt (MIL) requisar.

rescind [rɪ'sɪnd] vt (LAW) abrogar; (contract, order etc) anular.

rescue ['rɛskju:] n rescate m // vt rescatar; to ~ from librar de; ~ party n expedición f de salvamento; ~r n salvador(a) m/f.

research [rɪ'sə:tʃ] n investigaciones fpl // vt investigar; ~er n investigador(a) m/ f.

resemblance [rɪ'zɛmbləns] n parecido.

resemble [rɪ'zɛmbl] vt parecerse a.

resent [rɪ'zɛnt] vt tomar a mal; ~ful a resentido; ~ment n resentimiento.

reservation [rɛzə'veɪʃən] n (area of land, doubt) reserva; (booking) reservación f; (Brit: also: central ~) mediana.

reserve [rɪ'zə:v] n reserva; (SPORT) suplente m/f // vt (seats etc) reservar; ~s npl (MIL) reserva sg; in ~ de reserva; ~d a reservado.

reservoir ['rɛzəvwɑ:*] n (for irrigation, etc) embalse m; (tank etc) depósito.

reshape [ri:'ʃeɪp] vt (policy) reformar, rehacer.

reshuffle [ri:'ʃʌfl] n: cabinet ~ (POL) remodelación f del gabinete.

reside [rɪ'zaɪd] vi residir, vivir.

residence ['rɛzɪdəns] n residencia; (formal: home) domicilio; (length of stay) permanencia; ~ permit n (Brit) permiso de permanencia.

resident ['rɛzɪdənt] n (of area) vecino/a; (in hotel) huésped(a) m/f // a (population) permanente; ~ial [-'dɛnʃəl] a residencial.

residue ['rɛzɪdju:] n resto; (CHEM, PHYSICS) residuo.

resign [rɪ'zaɪn] vt (gen) renunciar a // vi dimitir; to ~ o.s. to (endure) resignarse a; ~ation [rɛzɪg'neɪʃən] n dimisión f; (state of mind) resignación f; ~ed a resignado.

resilience [rɪ'zɪlɪəns] n (of material) elasticidad f; (of person) resistencia.
resilient [rɪ'aɪlɪənt] a (person) resistente.
resin ['rezɪn] n resina.
resist [rɪ'zɪst] vt resistir, oponerse a; **~ance** n resistencia.
resolute ['rezəluːt] a resuelto.
resolution [rezə'luːʃən] n resolución f.
resolve [rɪ'zɒlv] n resolución f // vt resolver // vi resolverse; **to ~ to do** resolver hacer; **~d** a resuelto.
resort [rɪ'zɔːt] n (town) centro turístico; (recourse) recurso // vi: **to ~ to** recurrir a; **in the last ~** como último recurso.
resound [rɪ'zaund] vi: **to ~ (with)** resonar (con); **~ing** a sonoro; (fig) clamoroso.
resource [rɪ'sɔːs] n recurso; **~s** npl recursos mpl; **~ful** a despabilado, ingenioso.
respect [rɪs'pekt] n (consideration) respeto; **~s** npl recuerdos mpl, saludos mpl // vt respetar **with ~ to** con respecto a; **in this ~** en cuanto a eso; **~able** a respetable; (large) apreciable; (passable) tolerable; **~ful** a respetuoso.
respective [rɪs'pektɪv] a respectivo; **~ly** ad respectivamente.
respite ['respaɪt] n respiro; (LAW) prórroga.
resplendent [rɪs'plendənt] a resplandeciente.
respond [rɪs'pɒnd] vi responder; (react) reaccionar; **response** [-'pɒns] n respuesta; reacción f.
responsibility [rɪspɒnsɪ'bɪlɪtɪ] n responsabilidad f.
responsible [rɪs'pɒnsɪbl] a (character) serio, formal; (job) de confianza; (liable): **~ (for)** responsable (de).
responsive [rɪs'pɒnsɪv] a sensible.
rest [rest] n descanso, reposo; (MUS) pausa, silencio; (support) apoyo; (remainder) resto // vi descansar; (be supported): **to ~ on** descansar sobre // vt (lean): **to ~ sth on/against** apoyar algo en or sobre/contra; **the ~ of them** (people, objects) los demás; **it ~s with him** depende de él.
restaurant ['restərɒn] n restorán m, restaurante m; **~ car** n (Brit RAIL) coche comedor m.
restful ['restful] a descansado, tranquilo.
rest home n residencia para jubilados.
restitution [restɪ'tjuːʃən] n: **to make ~ to sb for sth** indemnizar a uno por algo.
restive ['restɪv] a inquieto; (horse) rebelón(ona).
restless ['restlɪs] a inquieto.
restoration [restə'reɪʃən] n restauración f; devolución f.
restore [rɪ'stɔː*] vt (building) restaurar; (sth stolen) devolver; (health) restablecer.
restrain [rɪs'treɪn] vt (feeling) contener,

refrenar; (person): **to ~ (from doing)** disuadir (de hacer); **~ed** a (style) reservado; **~t** n (restriction) restricción f; (of manner) reserva.
restrict [rɪs'trɪkt] vt restringir, limitar; **~ion** [-kʃən] n restricción f, limitación f; **~ive** a restrictivo.
rest room n (US) aseos mpl.
result [rɪ'zʌlt] n resultado // vi: **to ~ in** terminar en, tener por resultado; **as a ~ of** a consecuencia de.
resume [rɪ'zjuːm] vt (work, journey) reanudar // vi (meeting) continuar.
résumé ['reɪzjuːmeɪ] n resumen m.
resumption [rɪ'zʌmpʃən] n reanudación f.
resurgence [rɪ'sɜːdʒəns] n resurgimiento.
resurrection [rezə'rekʃən] n resurrección f.
resuscitate [rɪ'sʌsɪteɪt] vt (MED) resucitar.
retail ['riːteɪl] n venta al por menor // cpd al por menor // vt vender al por menor; **~er** n detallista m/f; **~ price** n precio de venta al público.
retain [rɪ'teɪn] vt (keep) retener, conservar; (employ) contratar; **~er** n (servant) criado; (fee) anticipo.
retaliate [rɪ'tælɪeɪt] vi: **to ~ (against)** tomar represalias (contra); **retaliation** [-'eɪʃən] n represalias fpl.
retarded [rɪ'tɑːdɪd] a retrasado.
retch [retʃ] vi dársele a uno arcadas.
retentive [rɪ'tentɪv] a (memory) retentivo.
reticent ['retɪsnt] a reservado.
retina ['retɪnə] n retina.
retinue ['retɪnjuː] n séquito, comitiva.
retire [rɪ'taɪə*] vi (give up work) jubilarse; (withdraw) retirarse; (go to bed) acostarse; **~d** a (person) jubilado; **~ment** n (state) retiro; (act) jubilación f; **retiring** a (leaving) saliente; (shy) retraído.
retort [rɪ'tɔːt] n (reply) réplica // vi contestar.
retrace [riː'treɪs] vt: **to ~ one's steps** volver sobre sus pasos, desandar lo andado.
retract [rɪ'trækt] vt (statement) retirar; (claws) retraer; (undercarriage, aerial) replegar // vi retractarse.
retrain [riː'treɪn] vt reciclar; **~ing** n readaptación f profesional.
retread ['riːtred] n neumático or llanta (LAm) recauchutado/a.
retreat [rɪ'triːt] n (place) retiro; (MIL) retirada // vi retirarse; (flood) bajar.
retribution [retrɪ'bjuːʃən] n desquite m.
retrieval [rɪ'triːvəl] n recuperación f; information ~ recuperación f de datos.
retrieve [rɪ'triːv] vt recobrar; (situation, honour) salvar; (COMPUT) recuperar; (error) reparar; **~r** n perro cobrador.
retrograde ['retrəgreɪd] a retrógrado.

retrospect ['rɛtrəspɛkt] *n*: in ~ retrospectivamente; ~**ive** [-'spɛktɪv] *a* restrospectivo; (*law*) retroactivo.

return [rɪ'tɜːn] *n* (*going or coming back*) vuelta, regreso; (*of sth stolen etc*) devolución *f*; (*recompense*) recompensa; (*FINANCE: from land, shares*) ganancia, ingresos *mpl* // *cpd* (*journey*) de regreso; (*Brit: ticket*) de ida y vuelta; (*match*) de desquite // *vi* (*person etc: come or go back*) volver, regresar; (*symptoms etc*) reaparecer // *vt* devolver; (*favour, love etc*) corresponder a; (*verdict*) pronunciar; (*POL: candidate*) elegir; ~**s** *npl* (*COMM*) ingresos *mpl*; in ~ (for) en cambio (de); by ~ of post a vuelta de correo; **many happy ~s (of the day)!** ¡feliz cumpleaños!

reunion [riːˈjuːnɪən] *n* reunión *f*.

reunite [riːjuːˈnaɪt] *vt* reunir; (*reconcile*) reconciliar.

rev [rɛv] (*AUT*) *n abbr* (= *revolution*) revolución // (*vb: also*: ~ **up**) *vt* girar // *vi* (*engine*) girarse; (*driver*) girar el motor.

revamp [riːˈvæmp] *vt* (*company, organization*) reorganizar.

reveal [rɪˈviːl] *vt* (*make known*) revelar; ~**ing** *a* revelador(a).

reveille [rɪˈvælɪ] *n* (*MIL*) diana.

revel ['rɛvl] *vi*: **to ~ in sth/in doing sth** gozar de algo/con hacer algo.

revelry ['rɛvlrɪ] *n* jarana, juerga.

revenge [rɪˈvɛndʒ] *n* venganza; (*in sport*) revancha; **to take ~ on** vengarse de.

revenue ['rɛvənjuː] *n* ingresos *mpl*, rentas *fpl*.

reverberate [rɪˈvɜːbəreɪt] *vi* (*sound*) resonar, retumbar; **reverberation** [-ˈreɪʃən] *n* retumbo, eco.

revere [rɪˈvɪə*] *vt* venerar; ~**nce** ['rɛvərəns] *n* reverencia.

Reverend ['rɛvərənd] *a* (*in titles*): **the ~ John Smith** (*Anglican*) el Reverendo John Smith; (*Catholic*) el Padre John Smith; (*Protestant*) el Pastor John Smith.

reverie ['rɛvərɪ] *n* ensueño.

reversal [rɪˈvɜːsl] *n* (*of order*) inversión *f*; (*of policy*) cambio; (*of decision*) revocación *f*.

reverse [rɪˈvɜːs] *n* (*opposite*) contrario; (*back: of cloth*) revés *m*; (: *of coin*) reverso, (: *of paper*) dorso; (*AUT: also*: ~ **gear**) marcha atrás // *a* (*order*) inverso; (*direction*) contrario // *vt* (*decision, AUT*) dar marcha atrás a; (*position, function*) invertir // *vi* (*Brit AUT*) dar marcha atrás; ~-**charge call** *n* (*Brit*) llamada a cobro revertido; **reversing lights** *npl* (*Brit AUT*) luces *fpl* de marcha atrás.

revert [rɪˈvɜːt] *vi*: **to ~ to** volver a.

review [rɪˈvjuː] *n* (*magazine, MIL*) revista; (*of book, film*) reseña; (*US: exami-*

nation) repaso, examen *m* // *vt* repasar, examinar; (*MIL*) pasar revista a; (*book, film*) reseñar; ~**er** *n* crítico/a.

revile [rɪˈvaɪl] *vt* injuriar, vilipendiar.

revise [rɪˈvaɪz] *vt* (*manuscript*) corregir; (*opinion*) modificar; (*Brit: study: subject*) repasar; (*look over*) revisar; **revision** [rɪˈvɪʒən] *n* corrección *f*; modificación *f*; repaso; revisión *f*.

revitalize [riːˈvaɪtəlaɪz] *vt* revivificar.

revival [rɪˈvaɪvəl] *n* (*recovery*) reanimación *f*; (*POL*) resurgimiento; (*of interest*) renacimiento; (*THEATRE*) reestreno; (*of faith*) despertar *m*.

revive [rɪˈvaɪv] *vt* resucitar; (*custom*) restablecer; (*hope, interest*) despertar; (*play*) reestrenar // *vi* (*person*) volver en sí; (*from tiredness*) reponerse; (*business*) reactivarse.

revolt [rɪˈvəʊlt] *n* rebelión *f* // *vi* rebelarse, sublevarse // *vt* dar asco a, repugnar; ~**ing** *a* asqueroso, repugnante.

revolution [rɛvəˈluːʃən] *n* revolución *f*; ~**ary** *a*, *n* revolucionario/a *m/f*.

revolve [rɪˈvɒlv] *vi* dar vueltas, girar.

revolver [rɪˈvɒlvə*] *n* revólver *m*.

revolving [rɪˈvɒlvɪŋ] *a* (*chair, door etc*) giratorio.

revue [rɪˈvjuː] *n* (*THEATRE*) revista.

revulsion [rɪˈvʌlʃən] *n* asco, repugnancia.

reward [rɪˈwɔːd] *n* premio, recompensa // *vt*: **to ~ (for)** recompensar or premiar (por); ~**ing** *a* (*fig*) valioso.

rewire [riːˈwaɪə*] *vt* (*house*) renovar la instalación eléctrica de.

reword [riːˈwɜːd] *vt* expresar en otras palabras.

rewrite [riːˈraɪt] (*irg: like* write) *vt* reescribir.

rhapsody ['ræpsədɪ] *n* (*MUS*) rapsodia.

rhetoric ['rɛtərɪk] *n* retórica; ~**al** [rɪˈtɒrɪkl] *a* retórico.

rheumatism ['ruːmətɪzəm] *n* reumatismo, reúma *m*.

Rhine [raɪn] *n*: **the ~** el (río) Rin.

rhinoceros [raɪˈnɒsərəs] *n* rinoceronte *m*.

rhododendron [rəʊdəˈdɛndrn] *n* rododendro.

Rhone [rəʊn] *n*: **the ~** el (río) Ródano.

rhubarb ['ruːbɑːb] *n* ruibarbo.

rhyme [raɪm] *n* rima; (*verse*) poesía.

rhythm ['rɪðm] *n* ritmo.

rib [rɪb] *n* (*ANAT*) costilla // *vt* (*mock*) tomar el pelo a.

ribald ['rɪbəld] *a* escabroso.

ribbon ['rɪbən] *n* cinta; **in ~s** (*torn*) hecho trizas.

rice [raɪs] *n* arroz *m*; ~ **pudding** *n* arroz *m* con leche.

rich [rɪtʃ] *a* rico; (*soil*) fértil; (*food*) pesado; (: *sweet*) empalagoso; **the ~** *npl* los ricos; ~**es** *npl* riqueza *sg*; ~**ly** *ad* ricamente; ~**ness** *n* riqueza; fertilidad *f*.

rickets ['rɪkɪts] *n* raquitismo.

rickety ['rɪkɪtɪ] a (old) desvencijado; (shaky) tambaleante.

rickshaw ['rɪkʃɔː] n carro do culi.

ricochet ['rɪkəʃeɪ] n rebote m // vi rebotar.

rid [rɪd], pt, pp rid vt: to ~ sb of sth librar a uno de algo; to get ~ of deshacerse or desembarazarse de.

ridden ['rɪdn] pp of ride.

riddle ['rɪdl] n (puzzle) acertijo; (mystery) enigma m, misterio // vt: to be ~d with ser lleno or plagado de.

ride [raɪd] n (distance covered) viaje m, recorrido // (vb: pt rode, pp ridden) vi (horse: as sport) montar; (go somewhere: on horse, bicycle) dar un paseo, pasearse; (journey: on bicycle, motorcycle, bus) viajar // vt (a horse) montar a; (distance) recorrer; to ~ a bicycle andar en bicicleta; to ~ at anchor (NAUT) estar fondeado; to take sb for a ~ (fig) engañar a uno; ~r n (on horse) jinete/a m/f; (on bicycle) ciclista m/f; (on motorcycle) motociclista m/f.

ridge [rɪdʒ] n (of hill) cresta; (of roof) caballete m.

ridicule ['rɪdɪkjuːl] n irrisión f, burla // vt poner en ridículo, burlarse de; **ridiculous** [-'dɪkjuləs] a ridículo.

riding ['raɪdɪŋ] n equitación f; I like ~ me gusta montar a caballo; ~ school n escuela de equitación.

rife [raɪf] a: to be ~ ser muy común; to be ~ with abundar en.

riffraff ['rɪfræf] n gentuza.

rifle ['raɪfl] n rifle m, fusil m // vt saquear; ~ range n campo de tiro; (at fair) tiro al blanco.

rift [rɪft] n (fig: between friends) desavenencia; (: in party) ruptura f.

rig [rɪg] n (also: oil ~: on land) torre f de perforación; (: at sea) plataforma petrolera // vt (election etc) amañar; to ~ out vt (Brit) ataviar; to ~ up vt improvisar; ~ging n (NAUT) aparejo.

right [raɪt] a (true, correct) correcto, exacto; (suitable) indicado, debido; (proper) apropiado; (just) justo; (morally good) bueno; (not left) derecho // n (title, claim) derecho; (not left) derecha // ad (correctly) bien, correctamente; (straight) derecho, directamente; (not left) a la derecha; (to the ~) hacia la derecha // vt enderezar // excl ¡bueno!, ¡está bien!; to be ~ (person) tener razón; by ~s en justicia; on the ~ a la derecha; to be in the ~ tener razón; ~ now ahora mismo; ~ in the middle exactamente en el centro; ~ away en seguida; ~ **angle** n ángulo recto; ~**eous** ['raɪtʃəs] a justo, honrado; (anger) justificado; ~**ful** a (heir) legítimo; ~**handed** a (person) que usa la mano derecha; ~-**hand man** n brazo derecho; the ~-**hand side** n la derecha; ~**ly** ad

correctamente, debidamente; (with reason) con razón; ~ **of way** n (on path etc) derecho de paso; (AUT) prioridad f, ~-**wing** a (POL) derechista.

rigid ['rɪdʒɪd] a rígido; (person, ideas) inflexible; ~**ity** [rɪ'dʒɪdɪtɪ] n rigidez f; inflexibilidad f.

rigmarole ['rɪgmərəul] n galimatías m inv.

rigorous ['rɪgərəs] a riguroso.

rigour, (US) **rigor** ['rɪgə*] n rigor m, severidad f.

rile [raɪl] vt irritar.

rim [rɪm] n borde m; (of spectacles) aro; (of wheel) llanta.

rind [raɪnd] n (of bacon) corteza; (of lemon etc) cáscara; (of cheese) costra.

ring [rɪŋ] n (of metal) aro; (on finger) anillo; (also: wedding ~) alianza; (of people) corro; (of objects) círculo; (gang) banda; (for boxing) cuadrilátero; (of circus) pista; (bull ~) ruedo, plaza; (sound of bell) toque m; (telephone call) llamada // vb (pt rang, pp rung) vi (on telephone) llamar por teléfono; (large bell) repicar; (also: ~ out: voice, words) sonar; (ears) zumbar // vt (Brit TEL: also: ~ up) llamar, telefonear (esp LAm); (bell etc) hacer sonar; (doorbell) tocar; to ~ back vt (TEL) devolver la llamada; to ~ off vi (Brit TEL) colgar, cortar la comunicación; ~**ing** n (of large bell) repique m; (in ears) zumbido; ~**ing tone** n (TEL) tono de llamada; ~**leader** n (of gang) cabecilla m.

ringlets ['rɪŋlɪts] npl rizos mpl, bucles mpl.

ring road n (Brit) carretera periférica or de circunvalación.

rink [rɪŋk] n (also: ice ~) pista de hielo.

rinse [rɪns] vt (dishes) enjuagar; (clothes) aclarar; (hair) dar reflejos a.

riot ['raɪət] n motín m, disturbio // vi amotinarse; to run ~ desmandarse; ~**er** n amotinado/a; ~**ous** a alborotado; (party) bullicioso; (uncontrolled) desenfrenado.

rip [rɪp] n rasgón m, rasgadura // vt rasgar, desgarrar // vi rasgarse, desgarrarse; ~**cord** n cabo de desgarre.

ripe [raɪp] a (fruit) maduro; ~**n** vt madurar // vi madurarse.

rip-off ['rɪpɔf] n (col): it's a ~! ¡es una estafa!

ripple ['rɪpl] n onda, rizo; (sound) murmullo // vi rizarse // vt rizar.

rise [raɪz] n (slope) cuesta, pendiente f; (hill) altura; (increase: in wages: Brit) aumento; (: in prices, temperature) subida; (fig: to power etc) ascenso // vi (pt rose, pp risen ['rɪzn]) (gen) elevarse; (prices) subir; (waters) crecer; (river) nacer; (sun) salir; (person: from bed etc) levantarse; (also: ~ up: rebel) sublevarse; (in rank) ascender; to give ~ to dar lugar or origen a; **to ~** to the occasion ponerse a la altura de las circunstancias; **rising** a (increasing: number) creciente; (: prices) en aumento or alza; (tide) creciente; (sun, moon) naciente // n (uprising) sublevación f.

risk [rɪsk] n riesgo, peligro // vt arriesgar; (run the ~ of) exponerse a; **to take** or **run the ~ of** doing correr el riesgo de hacer; **at ~** en peligro; **at one's own ~** bajo su propia responsabilidad; **~y** a arriesgado, peligroso.

risqué [ˈriːskeɪ] a (joke) subido de color.

rissole [ˈrɪsəul] n croqueta.

rite [raɪt] n rito; **last ~s** exequias fpl.

ritual [ˈrɪtjuəl] a ritual // n ritual m, rito.

rival [ˈraɪvl] n rival m/f; (in business) competidor(a) m/f // a rival, opuesto // vt competir con; **~ry** n rivalidad f, competencia.

river [ˈrɪvə*] n río // cpd (port, fish) de río; (traffic) fluvial; **up/down ~** río arriba/abajo; **~bank** n orilla (del río); **~bed** n lecho, cauce m.

rivet [ˈrɪvɪt] n roblón m, remache m // vt remachar; (fig) captar.

Riviera [rɪvɪˈeərə] n: **the** (French) **~** la Costa Azul (francesa); **the Italian ~** la Riviera italiana.

road [rəud] n (gen) camino; (motorway etc) carretera; (in town) calle f; **major/minor ~** carretera principal/secundaria; **~block** n barricada; **~hog** n loco/a del volante; **~ map** n mapa m de carreteras; **~ safety** n seguridad f vial; **~side** n borde m (del camino) // cpd al lado de la carretera; **~sign** n señal f de tráfico; **~ user** n usuario/a de la vía pública; **~way** n calzada; **~works** npl obras fpl; **~worthy** a (car) en buen estado para circular.

roam [rəum] vi vagar // vt vagar por.

roar [rɔː*] n (of animal) rugido, bramido; (of crowd) rugido; (of vehicle, storm) estruendo; (of laughter) carcajada // vi rugir, bramar; hacer estruendo; **to ~ with laughter** reírse a carcajadas; **to do a ~ing trade** hacer buen negocio.

roast [rəust] n carne f asada, asado // vt (meat) asar; (coffee) tostar; **~ beef** n rosbif m.

rob [rɔb] vt robar; **to ~ sb of sth** robar algo a uno; (fig: deprive) quitar algo a uno; **~ber** n ladrón/ona m/f; **~bery** n robo.

robe [rəub] n (for ceremony etc) toga; (also: bath ~) bata.

robin [ˈrɔbɪn] n petirrojo.

robot [ˈrəubɔt] n robot m.

robust [rəuˈbʌst] a robusto, fuerte.

rock [rɔk] n (gen) roca; (boulder) peña, peñasco; (Brit: sweet) ≈ pirulí // vt (swing gently: cradle) balancear, mecer; (: child) arrullar; (shake) sacudir // vi mecerse, balancearse; sacudirse; **on**

the **~s** (drink) con hielo; (marriage etc) en ruinas; **~ and roll** n rocanrol m; **~-bottom** n (fig) punto más bajo // a: **at ~-bottom prices** a precios regalados; **~ery** n cuadro alpino.

rocket [ˈrɔkɪt] n cohete m.

rocking [ˈrɔkɪŋ]: **~ chair** n mecedora; **~ horse** n caballo de balancín.

rocky [ˈrɔkɪ] a (gen) rocoso; (unsteady: table) inestable.

rod [rɔd] n vara, varilla; (TECH) barra; (also: fishing ~) caña.

rode [rəud] pt of ride.

rodent [ˈrəudnt] n roedor m.

roe [rəu] n (species: also: ~ deer) corzo; (of fish): **hard/soft ~** hueva/lecha.

rogue [rəug] n pícaro, pillo.

role [rəul] n papel m, rol m.

roll [rəul] n rollo; (of bank notes) fajo; (also: bread ~) panecillo; (register) lista, nómina; (sound: of drums etc) redoble m; (movement: of ship) balanceo // vt hacer rodar; (also: ~ up: string) enrollar; (: sleeves) arremangar; (cigarettes) liar; (also: ~ out: pastry) aplanar // vi (gen) rodar; (drum) redoblar; (in walking) bambolearse; (ship) balancearse; **to ~ about** or **around** vi (person) revolcarse; **to ~ by** vi (time) pasar; **to ~ in** vi (mail, cash) entrar a raudales; **to ~ over** vi dar una vuelta; **to ~ up** vi (col: arrive) aparecer // vt (carpet) arrollar; **~ call** n: **to take a ~ call** pasar lista; **~er** n rodillo; (wheel) rueda; **~er coaster** n montaña rusa; **~er skates** npl patines mpl de rueda.

rolling [ˈrəulɪŋ] a (landscape) ondulado; **~ pin** n rodillo (de cocina); **~ stock** n (RAIL) material m rodante.

ROM [rɔm] n abbr (= read only memory) ROM f.

Roman [ˈrəumən] a, n romano/a m/f; **~ Catholic** a, n católico/a m/f (romano/a).

romance [rəˈmæns] n (love affair) amor m; (charm) lo romántico; (novel) novela de amor.

Romania [ruːˈmeɪnɪə] n = **Rumania**.

Roman numeral n número romano.

romantic [rəˈmæntɪk] a romántico.

Rome [rəum] n Roma.

romp [rɔmp] n retozo, juego // vi (also: ~ about) jugar, brincar.

rompers [ˈrɔmpəz] npl pelele m.

roof [ruːf], pl **~s** n (gen) techo; (of house) techo, tejado; (of car) baca // vt techar, poner techo a; **the ~ of the mouth** el paladar; **~ing** n techumbre f; **~ rack** n (AUT) baca, portaequipajes m inv.

rook [ruk] n (bird) graja; (CHESS) torre f.

room [ruːm] n (in house) cuarto, habitación f, pieza (esp LAm); (also: bed~) dormitorio; (in school etc) sala; (space) sitio, cabida; **~s** npl (lodging) aloja-

miento *sg*; '~s to let', (*US*) '~s for rent'
'se alquilan pisos *or* cuartos'; **single/
double** ~ habitación individual/doble *or*
para dos personas; **~ing house** *n* (*US*)
pensión *f*; **~mate** *n* compañero/a de
cuarto; ~ **service** *n* servicio de habitaciones; **~y** *a* espacioso.

roost [ru:st] *n* percha // *vi* pasar la noche.

rooster ['ru:stə*] *n* gallo.

root [ru:t] *n* (*BOT. MATH*) raíz *f* // *vi*
(*plant, belief*) arraigarse; **to** ~ **about**
vi (*fig*) buscar y rebuscar; **to** ~ **for** *vt
fus* apoyar a; **to** ~ **out** *vt* desarraigar.

rope [rəup] *n* cuerda; (*NAUT*) cable *m* //
vi (*box*) atar *or* amarrar con (una) cuerda; (*climbers: also:* ~ **together**) encor-
darse; **to** ~ **sb in** (*fig*) persuadir a uno a
tomar parte; **to know the ~s** (*fig*) conocer los trucos (del oficio); ~ **ladder** *n*
escala de cuerda.

rosary ['rəuzərɪ] *n* rosario.

rose [rəuz] *pt of* rise // *n* rosa; (*also:*
~**bush**) rosal *m*; (*on watering can*) rose-
ta // *a* color de rosa.

rosé ['rəuzeɪ] *n* vino rosado.

rose: ~**bud** *n* capullo de rosa; ~**bush** *n*
rosal *m*.

rosemary ['rəuzmərɪ] *n* romero.

rosette [rəu'zɛt] *n* escarapela.

roster ['rɔstə*] *n*: **duty** ~ lista de deberes.

rostrum ['rɔstrəm] *n* tribuna.

rosy ['rəuzɪ] *a* rosado, sonrosado; **the future looks** ~ el futuro parece promete-
dor.

rot [rɔt] *n* (*fig: pej*) tonterías *fpl* // *vt, vi*
pudrirse; **it has** ~ está podrido.

rota ['rəutə] *n* lista (de tandas).

rotary ['rəutərɪ] *a* rotativo.

rotate [rəu'teɪt] *vt* (*revolve*) hacer girar,
dar vueltas a; (*change round: crops*)
cultivar en rotación; (: *jobs*) alternar //
vi (*revolve*) girar, dar vueltas; **rotating**
a (*movement*) rotativo.

rote [rəut] *n*: **by** ~ maquinalmente, de
memoria.

rotten ['rɔtn] *a* (*decayed*) podrido; (*dishonest*) corrompido; (*col: bad*) pésimo;
to feel ~ (*ill*) sentirse muy mal.

rouge [ru:ʒ] *n* colorete *m*.

rough [rʌf] *a* (*skin, surface*) áspero;
(*terrain*) quebrado; (*road*) desigual;
(*voice*) bronco; (*person, manner:
coarse*) tosco, grosero; (*weather*) bo-
rrascoso; (*treatment*) brutal; (*sea*) bravo; (*cloth*) basto; (*plan*) preliminar;
(*guess*) aproximado; (*violent*) violento
// *n* (*GOLF*) ~; **in the** ~ en las hierbas altas; **to** ~ **it** vivir sin comodidades; **to
sleep** ~ (*Brit*) pasar la noche al raso; ~
age *n* fibra(s) *f(pl)*; ~**-and-ready** *a*
improvisado; ~**cast** *n* mezcla gruesa; ~
copy *n*, ~ **draft** *n* borrador *m*; ~**en** *vt*
(*a surface*) poner áspero; ~**ly** *ad* (*han-

dle*) torpemente; (*make*) toscamente;
(*approximately*) aproximadamente.

roulette [ru:'lɛt] *n* ruleta.

Roumania [ru:'meɪnɪə] *n* = **Rumania**.

round [raund] *a* redondo // *n* círculo en
(*Brit: of toast*) rodaja; (*of policeman*)
ronda; (*of milkman*) recorrido; (*of doctor*) visitas *fpl*; (*game: of cards, in competition*) partida; (*of ammunition*) cartucho; (*BOXING*) asalto; (*of talks*) ronda //
vt (*corner*) doblar // *prep* alrededor de //
ad: **all** ~ por todos lados; **the long way**
~ por el camino menos directo; **all the
year** ~ durante todo el año; **it's just** ~
the corner (*fig*) está a la vuelta de la esquina; ~ **the clock** *ad* las 24 horas; **to go**
~ **to sb's (house)** ir a casa de uno; **to go**
~ **the back** pasar por atrás; **to go** ~ **a
house** visitar una casa; **enough to go** ~
bastante (para todos); **to go the** ~**s**
(*story*) circular; **a** ~ **of applause** una
salva de aplausos; **a** ~ **of drinks/
sandwiches** una ronda de bebidas/
bocadillos; **to** ~ **off** *vt* (*speech etc*) acabar, poner término a; **to** ~ **up** *vt* (*cattle*) acorralar; (*people*) reunir; (*prices*)
redondear; ~**about** *n* (*Brit: AUT*) isleta; (: *at fair*) tiovivo // *a* (*route, means*)
indirecto; ~**ers** *n* (*Brit: game*) juego similar al béisbol; ~**ly** *ad* (*fig*) rotunda-
mente; ~**-shouldered** *a* cargado de espaldas; ~ **trip** *n* viaje *m* de ida y vuelta; ~**up** *n* rodeo; (*of criminals*) redada.

rouse [rauz] *vt* (*wake up*) despertar;
(*stir up*) suscitar; **rousing** *a* (*applause*)
caluroso; (*speech*) conmovedor(a).

rout [raut] *n* (*MIL*) derrota.

route [ru:t] *n* ruta, camino; (*of bus*) recorrido; (*of shipping*) derrota; ~ **map** *n*
(*Brit: for journey*) mapa *m* de carreteras.

routine [ru:'ti:n] *a* (*work*) rutinario // *n*
rutina; (*THEATRE*) número.

roving ['rəuvɪŋ] *a* (*wandering*) errante;
(*salesman*) ambulante.

row [rəu] *n* (*line*) fila, hilera; (*KNITTING*)
pasada; [rau] (*noise*) escándalo; (*dispute*) bronca, pelea; (*fuss*) jaleo;
(*scolding*) regaño // *vi* (*in boat*) remar;
[rau] reñir(se) // *vt* (*boat*) conducir re-
mando; **4 days in a** ~ 4 días seguidos;
~**boat** *n* (*US*) bote *m* de remos.

rowdy ['raudɪ] *a* (*person: noisy*) ruidoso;
(: *quarrelsome*) pendenciero; (*occasion*)
alborotado // *n* pendenciero.

row houses (*US*) casas *fpl* adosadas.

rowing ['rəuɪŋ] *n* remo; ~ **boat** *n* (*Brit*)
bote *m* de remos.

royal ['rɔɪəl] *a* real; **R~ Air Force
(RAF)** *n* Fuerzas Aéreas Británicas *fpl*;
~**ty** *n* (~ *persons*) familia real; (*payment to author*) derechos *mpl* de autor.

rpm *abbr* (= *revs per minute*) r.p.m.

R.S.V.P. *abbr* (= *répondez s'il vous
plait*) SRC.

Rt.Hon. abbr (Brit: = Right Honourable) título honorífico de diputado.

rub [rʌb] vt (gen) frotar; (hard) restregar // n (gen) frotamiento; (touch) roce m; **to ~ sb up** or (US) **~ sb the wrong way** entrarle uno por mal ojo; **to ~ off** vi borrarse; **to ~ off on** vt fus influir en; **to ~ out** vt borrar.

rubber ['rʌbə*] n caucho, goma; (Brit: eraser) goma de borrar; **~ band** n goma, gomita; **~ plant** n ficus m; **~y** a elástico.

rubbish ['rʌbɪʃ] n (Brit) (from household) basura; (waste) desperdicios mpl; (fig: pej) tonterías fpl; (trash) pacotilla; **~ bin** n cubo or bote m (LAm) de la basura; **~ dump** n (in town) vertedero, basurero.

rubble ['rʌbl] n escombros mpl.

ruby ['ru:bɪ] n rubí m.

rucksack ['rʌksæk] n mochila.

ructions ['rʌkʃənz] npl lío sg.

rudder ['rʌdə*] n timón m.

ruddy ['rʌdɪ] a (face) rubicundo; (col: damned) condenado.

rude [ru:d] a (impolite: person) mal educado; (: word, manners) grosero; (indecent) indecente.

rueful ['ru:ful] a arrepentido.

ruffian ['rʌfɪən] n matón m, criminal m.

ruffle ['rʌfl] vt (hair) despeinar; (clothes) arrugar; **to get ~d** (fig: person) alterarse.

rug [rʌg] n alfombra; (Brit: for knees) manta.

rugby ['rʌgbɪ] n (also: **~ football**) rugby m.

rugged ['rʌgɪd] a (landscape) accidentado; (features) robusto.

rugger ['rʌgə*] n (Brit col) rugby m.

ruin ['ru:ɪn] n ruina // vt arruinar; (spoil) estropear; **~s** npl ruinas fpl, restos mpl.

rule [ru:l] n (norm) norma, costumbre f; (regulation) regla; (government) dominio // vt (country, person) gobernar; (decide) disponer // vi gobernar; (LAW) fallar; **as a ~** por regla general; **to ~ out** vt excluir; **~d** a (paper) rayado; **~r** n (sovereign) soberano; (for measuring) regla; **ruling** a (party) gobernante; (class) dirigente // n (LAW) fallo, decisión f.

rum [rʌm] n ron m.

Rumania [ru:'meɪnɪə] n Rumania; **~n** a, n rumano/a m/f.

rumble ['rʌmbl] vi retumbar, hacer un ruido sordo; (stomach, pipe) sonar.

rummage ['rʌmɪdʒ] vi: **to ~** (in or among) revolver (en).

rumour, (US) **rumor** ['ru:mə*] n rumor m // vt: **it is ~ed that...** se rumorea que...

rump [rʌmp] n (of animal) ancas fpl, grupa; **~ steak** n filete m de lomo.

rumpus ['rʌmpəs] n (col) lío, jaleo;

(quarrel) pelea, riña.

run [rʌn] n (SPORT) carrera; (outing) paseo, excursión f; (distance travelled) trayecto; (series) serie f; (THEATRE) temporada; (SKI) pista; (in tights, stockings) carrera; // vb (pt ran, pp run) vt (operate: business) dirigir; (: competition, course) organizar; (: hotel, house) administrar, llevar; (COMPUT) ejecutar; (to pass: hand) pasar; (bath): **to ~ a bath** llenar la bañera // vi (gen) correr; (work: machine) funcionar, marchar; (bus, train: operate) circular, ir; (: travel) ir; (continue: play) seguir; (: contract) ser válido; (flow: river, bath) fluir; (colours, washing) desteñirse; (in election) ser candidato; **there was a ~ on (meat, tickets)** hubo mucha demanda de; **in the long ~** a la larga; **on the ~** en fuga; **I'll ~ you** to the station te llevaré a la estación en coche; **to ~ a risk** correr un riesgo; **to ~ about** or **around** vi (children) correr por todos lados; **to ~ across** vt fus (find) dar or topar con; **to ~ away** vi huir; **to ~ down** vi (clock) parar // vt (production) ir reduciendo; (factory) ir restringiendo la producción de; (AUT) atropellar; (criticize) criticar; **to be ~ down** (person: tired) estar debilitado; **to ~ in** vt (Brit: car) rodar; **to ~ into** vt fus (meet: person, trouble) tropezar con; (collide with) chocar con; **to ~ off** vt (water) dejar correr // vi huir corriendo; **to ~ out** vi (person) salir corriendo; (liquid) irse; (lease) caducar, vencer; (money) acabarse; **to ~ out of** vt fus quedar sin; **to ~ over** vt (AUT) atropellar // vt fus (revise) repasar; **to ~ through** vt fus (instructions) repasar; **to ~ up** vt (debt) contraer; **to ~ up against** (difficulties) tropezar con; **~away** a (horse) desbocado; (truck) sin frenos; (inflation) galopante.

rung [rʌŋ] pp of **ring** // n (of ladder) escalón m, peldaño.

runner ['rʌnə*] n (in race: person) corredor/a m/f; (: horse) caballo; (on sledge) patín m; (wheel) ruedecilla; **~ bean** n (Brit) judía escarlata; **~-up** n subcampeón/ona m/f.

running ['rʌnɪŋ] n (sport) atletismo; (race) carrera // a (water, costs) corriente; (commentary) continuo; **to be in/out of the ~ for sth** tener/no tener posibilidades de ganar algo; **6 days ~** 6 días seguidos.

runny ['rʌnɪ] a derretido.

run-of-the-mill ['rʌnəvðə'mɪl] a común y corriente.

runt [rʌnt] n (also pej) redrojo, enano.

run-up ['rʌnʌp] n: **~ to** (election etc) período previo a.

runway ['rʌnweɪ] n (AVIAT) pista de aterrizaje.

rupee |ruː'piː| n rupia.
rupture |'rʌptʃə*| n (MED) hernia // vt: to ~ o s causarse una hernia.
rural |'ruərl| a rural.
ruse |ruːz| n ardid m.
rush |rʌʃ| n ímpetu m; (hurry) prisa; (COMM) demanda repentina; (BOT) junco; (current) corriente f fuerte, ráfaga // vt apresurar; (work) hacer de prisa; (attack: town etc) asaltar // vi correr, precipitarse; ~ **hour** n horas fpl punta.
rusk |rʌsk| n bizcocho tostado.
Russia |'rʌʃə| n Rusia; ~**n** a, n ruso/a m/f.
rust |rʌst| n herrumbre f, moho // vi oxidarse.
rustic |'rʌstɪk| a rústico.
rustle |'rʌsl| vi susurrar // vt (paper) hacer crujir; (US: cattle) hurtar, robar.
rustproof |'rʌstpruːf| a inoxidable.
rusty |'rʌstɪ| a oxidado.
rut |rʌt| n surco; (ZOOL) celo; **to be in a ~** ser esclavo de la rutina.
ruthless |'ruːθlɪs| a despiadado.
rye |raɪ| n centeno; ~ **bread** n pan de centeno.

S

sabbath |'sæbəθ| n domingo; (Jewish) sábado.
sabotage |'sæbətɑːʒ| n sabotaje m // vt sabotear.
saccharin(e) |'sækərɪn| n sacarina.
sachet |'sæʃeɪ| n sobrecito.
sack |sæk| n (bag) saco, costal m // vt (dismiss) despedir; (plunder) saquear; **to get the ~** ser despedido; ~**ing** n (material) arpillera.
sacred |'seɪkrɪd| a sagrado, santo.
sacrifice |'sækrɪfaɪs| n sacrificio // vt sacrificar.
sacrilege |'sækrɪlɪdʒ| n sacrilegio.
sacrosanct |'sækrəʊsæŋkt| a sacrosanto.
sad |sæd| a (unhappy) triste; (deplorable) lamentable.
saddle |'sædl| n silla (de montar); (of cycle) sillín m // vt (horse) ensillar; **to be ~d with sth** (col) quedar cargado con algo; ~**bag** n alforja.
sadistic |sə'dɪstɪk| a sádico.
sadness |'sædnɪs| n tristeza.
s.a.e. abbr (= stamped addressed envelope) sobre con las propias señas de uno y con sello.
safari |sə'fɑːrɪ| n safari m.
safe |seɪf| a (out of danger) fuera de peligro; (not dangerous, sure) seguro; (unharmed) ileso; (trustworthy) digno de confianza // n caja de caudales, caja fuerte; ~ **and sound** sano y salvo; (just) **to be on the ~ side** para mayor seguridad; ~**conduct** n salvoconducto; ~**deposit** n (vault) cámara acorazada;

(box) caja de seguridad; ~**guard** n protección f, garantía // vt proteger, defender; ~**keeping** n custodia; ~**ly** ad seguramente, con seguridad; **to arrive ~ly** llegar bien.
safety |'seɪftɪ| n seguridad f // a de seguridad; ~ **first!** ¡precaución!; ~ **belt** n cinturón m (de seguridad); ~ **pin** n imperdible m, seguro (LAm).
saffron |'sæfrən| n azafrán m.
sag |sæg| vi aflojarse.
sage |seɪdʒ| n (herb) salvia; (man) sabio.
Sagittarius |sædʒɪ'teərɪəs| n Sagitario.
Sahara |sə'hɑːrə| n: **the ~** (Desert) el (desierto del) Sáhara.
said |sed| pt, pp of **say.**
sail |seɪl| n (on boat) vela // vt (boat) gobernar // vi (travel: ship) navegar; (: passenger) pasear en barco; (set off) zarpar; **to go for a ~** dar un paseo en barco; **they ~ed into Copenhagen** arribaron a Copenhague; **to ~ through** vt fus (exam) no tener problemas para aprobar; ~**boat** n (US) velero, barco de vela; ~**ing** n (SPORT) balandrismo; **to go ~ing** salir en balandro; ~**ing ship** n barco de vela // ~**or** n marinero, marino.
saint |seɪnt| n santo; ~**ly** a santo.
sake |seɪk| n: **for the ~ of** por.
salad |'sæləd| n ensalada; ~ **bowl** n ensaladera; ~ **cream** n (Brit) (especie de) mayonesa; ~ **dressing** n aliño.
salary |'sælərɪ| n sueldo.
sale |seɪl| n venta; (at reduced prices) liquidación f, saldo; **'for ~'** 'se vende'; **on ~** en venta; **on ~ or return** (goods) venta por reposición // n sala de subastas; ~**s assistant,** (US) ~**s clerk** n dependiente/a m/f; **salesman/woman** n vendedor/a m/f; (in shop) dependiente/a m/f; (representative) viajante m/f.
salient |'seɪlɪənt| a sobresaliente.
saliva |sə'laɪvə| n saliva.
sallow |'sæləʊ| a cetrino.
salmon |'sæmən| n, pl inv salmón m.
salon |'sælɔn| n salón m.
saloon |sə'luːn| n (US) bar m, taberna; (Brit AUT) (coche m de) turismo; (ship's lounge) cámara, salón m.
salt |sɔlt| n sal f // vt salar; (put ~ on) poner sal en; **to ~ away** vt (col: money) ahorrar; ~ **cellar** n salero; ~**water** a de agua salada; ~**y** a salado.
salutary |'sæljutərɪ| a saludable.
salute |sə'luːt| n saludo; (of guns) salva // vt saludar.
salvage |'sælvɪdʒ| n (saving) salvamento, recuperación f; (things saved) objetos mpl salvados // vt salvar.
salvation |sæl'veɪʃən| n salvación f; **S~ Army** n Ejército de Salvación.
same |seɪm| a mismo // pron: **the ~** el/la mismo/a, los/las mismos/as; **the ~ book as** el mismo libro que; **at the ~ time** (at

the ~ moment) al mismo tiempo; (*yet*) sin embargo; **all** *or* **just the ~** sin embargo, aun así; **to do the ~** (as sb) hacer lo mismo (que uno); **the ~ to you!** ¡igualmente!

sample ['sɑːmpl] *n* muestra // *vt* (*food, wine*) probar.

sanatorium [sænə'tɔːriəm], *pl* **-ria** [-riə] *n* (*Brit*) sanatorio.

sanction ['sæŋkʃən] *n* sanción *f* // *vt* sancionar.

sanctity ['sæŋktiti] *n* (*gen*) santidad *f*; (*inviolability*) inviolabilidad *f*.

sanctuary ['sæŋktjuəri] *n* santuario; (*refuge*) asilo, refugio; (*for wildlife*) reserva.

sand [sænd] *n* arena // *vt* (*also:* **~ down**) lijar.

sandal ['sændl] *n* sandalia; **~wood** *n* sándalo.

sand: **~box** *n* (*US*) = **~pit**; **~castle** *n* castillo de arena; **~ dune** *n* duna; **~paper** *n* papel *m* de lija; **~pit** *n* (*for children*) cajón *m* de arena; **~stone** *n* piedra arenisca.

sandwich ['sændwitʃ] *n* bocadillo (*Sp*), sandwich *m* (*LAm*) // *vt* (*also:* **~ in**) intercalar; **~ed between** apretujado entre; **cheese/ham ~** sandwich de queso/jamón; **~ board** *n* cartelón *m*; **~ course** *n* (*Brit*) curso de medio tiempo.

sandy ['sændi] *a* arenoso; (*colour*) rojizo.

sane [sein] *a* cuerdo, sensato.

sang [sæŋ] *pt of* **sing**.

sanitarium [sæni'tɛəriəm] *n* (*US*) = **sanatorium**.

sanitary ['sænitəri] *a* (*system, arrangements*) sanitario; (*clean*) higiénico; **~ towel**, (*US*) **~ napkin** *n* paño higiénico, compresa.

sanitation [sæni'teiʃən] *n* (*in house*) servicios *mpl* higiénicos; (*in town*) servicio de desinfección; **~ department** *n* (*US*) departamento de limpieza y recogida de basuras.

sanity ['sæniti] *n* cordura; (*of judgment*) sensatez *f*.

sank [sæŋk] *pt of* **sink**.

Santa Claus [sæntə'klɔːz] *n* San Nicolás, Papá Noel.

sap [sæp] *n* (*of plants*) savia // *vt* (*strength*) minar, agotar.

sapling ['sæpliŋ] *n* árbol nuevo *or* joven.

sapphire ['sæfaiə*] *n* zafiro.

sarcasm ['sɑːkæzm] *n* sarcasmo.

sardine [sɑː'diːn] *n* sardina.

Sardinia [sɑː'diniə] *n* Cerdeña.

sash [sæʃ] *n* faja.

sat [sæt] *pt, pp of* **sit**.

Satan ['seitn] *n* Satanás *m*.

satchel ['sætʃl] *n* (*child's*) cartera, mochila (*LAm*).

sated ['seitid] *a* (*appetite, person*) saciado.

satellite ['sætəlait] *n* satélite *m*.

satin ['sætin] *n* raso // *a* de raso.

satire ['sætaiə*] *n* sátira.

satisfaction [sætis'fækʃən] *n* satisfacción *f*.

satisfactory [sætis'fæktəri] *a* satisfactorio.

satisfy ['sætisfai] *vt* satisfacer; (*convince*) convencer; **~ing** *a* satisfactorio.

saturate ['sætʃəreit] *vt*: **to ~ (with)** empapar *or* saturar (de).

Saturday ['sætədi] *n* sábado.

sauce [sɔːs] *n* salsa; (*sweet*) crema; **~pan** *n* cacerola, olla.

saucer ['sɔːsə*] *n* platillo.

saucy ['sɔːsi] *a* fresco, descarado.

Saudi ['saudi]: **~ Arabia** *n* Arabia Saudí *or* Saudita; **~ (Arabian)** *a*, *n* saudí *m/f*, saudita *m/f*.

sauna ['sɔːnə] *n* sauna.

saunter ['sɔːntə*] *vi*: **to ~ in/out** entrar/salir sin prisa.

sausage ['sɔsidʒ] *n* salchicha; **~ roll** *n* empanadita de salchicha.

sautéed ['səuteid] *a* salteado.

savage ['sævidʒ] *a* (*cruel, fierce*) feroz, furioso; (*primitive*) salvaje // *n* salvaje *m/f* // *vt* (*attack*) embestir.

save [seiv] *vt* (*rescue*) salvar, rescatar; (*money, time*) ahorrar; (*put by*) guardar; (*COMPUT*) salvar (*y* guardar); (*avoid: trouble*) evitar // *vi* (*also:* **~ up**) ahorrar // *n* (*SPORT*) parada // *prep* salvo, excepto.

saving ['seiviŋ] *n* (*on price etc*) economía // *a*: **the ~ grace** of el único mérito de; **~s** *npl* ahorros *mpl*; **~s account** *n* cuenta de ahorros; **~s bank** *n* caja de ahorros.

saviour, (*US*) **savior** ['seivjə*] *n* salvador(a) *m/f*.

savour, (*US*) **savor** ['seivə*] *n* sabor *m*, gusto // *vt* saborear; **~y** *a* sabroso; (*dish: not sweet*) salado.

saw [sɔː] *pt of* **see** // *n* (*tool*) sierra // *vt* (*pt* **sawed**, *pp* **sawed** *or* **sawn**) serrar; **~dust** *n* (a)serrín *m*; **~mill** *n* aserradero; **~n-off shotgun** *n* escopeta de cañones recortados.

saxophone ['sæksəfəun] *n* saxófono.

say [sei] *n*: **to have one's ~** expresar su opinión; **to have a** *or* **some ~ in sth** tener voz *or* tener que ver en algo // *vt* (*pt, pp* **said**) decir; **to ~ yes/no** decir que sí/no; **that is to ~** es decir; **that goes without ~ing** ni que decir tiene; **~ing** *n* dicho, refrán *m*.

scab [skæb] *n* costra; (*pej*) esquirol *m*.

scaffold ['skæfəuld] *n* (*for execution*) cadalso; **~ing** *n* andamio, andamiaje *m*.

scald [skɔːld] *n* escaldadura // *vt* escaldar.

scale [skeil] *n* (*gen, MUS*) escala; (*of fish*) escama; (*of salaries, fees etc*) escalafón *m* // *vt* (*mountain*) escalar; (*tree*) trepar; **~s** *npl* (*small*) balanza *sg*; (*large*) báscula *sg*; **on a large ~** en gran escala; **~ of charges** tarifa, lista de precios; **to ~ down** *vt* reducir a escala; **~ model** *n* modelo a escala.

scallop ['skɔləp] *n* (*ZOOL*) venera; (*SEWING*) festón *m*.

scalp [skælp] *n* cabellera // *vt* escalpar.

scalpel ['skælpl] *n* bisturí *m*.

scamper ['skæmpə*] *vi*: **to ~ away**, **~ off** irse corriendo.

scampi ['skæmpɪ] *npl* gambas *fpl*.

scan [skæn] *vt* (*examine*) escudriñar; (*glance at quickly*) dar un vistazo a; (*TV, RADAR*) explorar, registrar.

scandal ['skændl] *n* escándalo; (*gossip*) chismes *mpl*.

Scandinavia [skændɪ'neɪvɪə] *n* Escandinavia; **~n** *a, n* escandinavo/a *m/f*.

scant [skænt] *a* escaso; **~y** *a* (*meal*) insuficiente; (*clothes*) ligero.

scapegoat ['skeɪpgəut] *n* cabeza de turco, chivo expiatorio.

scar [skɑ:] *n* cicatriz *f*.

scarce [skɛəs] *a* escaso; **~ly** *ad* apenas; **scarcity** *n* escasez *f*.

scare [skɛə*] *n* susto, sobresalto; (*panic*) pánico // *vt* asustar, espantar; **to ~ sb stiff** dar a uno un susto de muerte; **bomb ~** amenaza de bomba; **~crow** *n* espantapájaros *m inv*; **~d** *a*: **to be ~d** estar asustado.

scarf [skɑ:f], *pl* **scarves** [skɑ:vz] *n* (*long*) bufanda; (*square*) pañuelo.

scarlet ['skɑ:lɪt] *a* escarlata; **~ fever** *n* escarlatina.

scarves [skɑ:vz] *pl of* **scarf**.

scathing ['skeɪðɪŋ] *a* mordaz.

scatter ['skætə*] *vt* (*spread*) esparcir, desparramar; (*put to flight*) dispersar // *vi* desparramarse; dispersarse; **~brained** *a* ligero de cascos.

scavenger ['skævəndʒə*] *n* (*person*) basurero/a; (*ZOOL: animal*) animal *m* de carroña; (: *bird*) ave *f* de carroña.

scenario [sɪ'nɑ:rɪəu] *n* (*THEATRE*) argumento; (*CINEMA*) guión *m*; (*fig*) escenario.

scene [si:n] *n* (*THEATRE, fig etc*) escena; (*of crime, accident*) escenario; (*sight, view*) panorama *m*; (*fuss*) escándalo; **~ry** *n* (*THEATRE*) decorado; (*landscape*) paisaje *m*; **scenic** *a* (*picturesque*) pintoresco.

scent [sɛnt] *n* perfume *m*, olor *m*; (*fig: track*) rastro, pista; (*sense of smell*) olfato.

sceptic, (*US*) **skeptic** ['skɛptɪk] *n* escéptico/a; **~al** *a* escéptico; **~ism** ['skɛptɪsɪzm] *n* escepticismo.

sceptre, (*US*) **scepter** ['sɛptə*] *n* cetro.

schedule ['ʃɛdju:l] *n* (*of trains*) horario; (*of events*) programa *m*; (*list*) lista // *vt* (*visit*) fijar la hora de; **to arrive on ~** llegar a la hora debida; **to be ahead of/behind ~** estar adelantado/en retraso;

~d flight *n* vuelo regular.

schematic [skɪ'mætɪk] *a* (*diagram etc*) esquemático.

scheme [ski:m] *n* (*plan*) plan *m*, proyecto; (*method*) esquema *m*; (*plot*) intriga; (*trick*) ardid *m*; (*arrangement*) disposición *f*; (*pension ~ etc*) sistema *m* // *vt* proyectar // *vi* (*plan*) hacer proyectos; (*intrigue*) intrigar; **scheming** *a* intrigante.

schism ['skɪzəm] *n* cisma *m*.

scholar ['skɔlə*] *n* (*learned person*) sabio/a, erudito/a; **~ly** *a* erudito; **~ship** *n* erudición *f*; (*grant*) beca.

school [sku:l] *n* (*gen*) escuela, colegio; (*in university*) facultad *f* // *vt* (*animal*) amaestrar; **~ age** *n* edad *f* escolar; **~book** *n* libro de texto; **~boy** *n* alumno; **~ children** *npl* alumnos *mpl*; **~days** *npl* años *mpl* del colegio; **~girl** *n* alumna; **~ing** *n* enseñanza; **~master/mistress** *n* (*primary*) maestro/a; (*secondary*) profesor(a) *m/f*; **~teacher** *n* (*primary*) maestro/a; (*secondary*) profesor(a) *m/f*.

schooner ['sku:nə*] *n* (*ship*) goleta.

sciatica [saɪ'ætɪkə] *n* ciática.

science ['saɪəns] *n* ciencia; **~ fiction** *n* ciencia-ficción *f*; **scientific** [-'tɪfɪk] *a* científico; **scientist** *n* científico/a.

scintillating ['sɪntɪleɪtɪŋ] *a* brillante, ingenioso.

scissors ['sɪzəz] *npl* tijeras *fpl*; **a pair of ~** unas tijeras.

scoff [skɔf] *vt* (*Brit col: eat*) engullir // *vi*: **to ~ (at)** (*mock*) mofarse (de).

scold [skəuld] *vt* regañar.

scone [skɔn] *n* pastel de pan.

scoop [sku:p] *n* cucharón *m*; (*for flour etc*) pala; (*PRESS*) exclusiva; **to ~ out** *vt* excavar; **to ~ up** *vt* recoger.

scooter ['sku:tə*] *n* (*motor cycle*) moto *f*; (*toy*) patinete *m*.

scope [skəup] *n* (*of plan, undertaking*) ámbito; (*reach*) alcance *m*; (*of person*) competencia; (*opportunity*) libertad *f* (de acción).

scorch [skɔ:tʃ] *vt* (*clothes*) chamuscar; (*earth, grass*) quemar, secar; **~ing** *a* abrasador(a).

score [skɔ:*] *n* (*points etc*) puntuación *f*; (*MUS*) partitura; (*reckoning*) cuenta; (*twenty*) veintena // *vt* (*goal, point*) ganar; (*mark*) rayar // *vi* marcar un tanto; (*FOOTBALL*) marcar (un) gol; (*keep score*) llevar el tanteo; **on that ~** en lo que se refiere a eso; **to ~ 6 out of 10** obtener una puntuación de 6 sobre 10; **to ~ out** *vt* tachar; **~board** *n* marcador *m*; **~r** *n* marcador *m*; (*keeping score*) tanteador(a) *m/f*.

scorn [skɔ:n] *n* desprecio // *vt* despreciar; **~ful** *a* desdeñoso, despreciativo.

Scorpio ['skɔ:pɪəu] *n* Escorpión *m*.

scorpion ['skɔ:pɪən] *n* alacrán *m*.

Scot [skɔt] *n* escocés/esa *m/f*.

scotch [skɔtʃ] *vt* (*rumour*) desmentir; (*plan*) abandonar; **S~** *n* whisky *m* escocés; **S~ tape** *n* ® (*US*) cinta adhesiva, celo, scotch *m* (*LAm*).

scot-free [skɔt'friː] *ad*: **to get off ~** (*unpunished*) salir impune.

Scotland ['skɔtlənd] *n* Escocia.

Scots [skɔts] *a* escocés/esa; **~man/woman** *n* escocés/esa *m/f*; **Scottish** ['skɔtiʃ] *a* escocés/esa.

scoundrel ['skaundrl] *n* canalla *m/f*, sinvergüenza *m/f*.

scour ['skauə*] *vt* (*clean*) fregar, estregar; (*search*) recorrer, registrar.

scourge [skɔːdʒ] *n* azote *m*.

scout [skaut] *n* (*MIL, also: boy ~*) explorador *m*; **to ~ around** *vi* reconocer el terreno.

scowl [skaul] *vi* fruncir el ceño; **to ~ at** sb mirar con ceño a uno.

scrabble ['skræbl] *vi* (*claw*): **to ~ (at)** arañar; (*also: to ~ around: search*) revolver todo buscando // *n*: **S~** ® Scrabble *m* ®.

scraggy ['skrægɪ] *a* flaco, descarnado.

scram [skræm] *vi* (*col*) largarse.

scramble ['skræmbl] *n* (*climb*) subida (difícil); (*struggle*) pelea // *vi*: **to ~ out/through** salir/abrirse paso con dificultad; **to ~ for** pelear por; **~d eggs** *npl* huevos *mpl* revueltos.

scrap [skræp] *n* (*bit*) pedacito; (*fig*) pizca; (*fight*) riña, bronca; (*also: ~ iron*) chatarra, hierro viejo // *vt* (*discard*) desechar, descartar // *vi* reñir, armar (una) bronca; **~s** *npl* (*waste*) sobras *fpl*, desperdicios *mpl*; **~book** *n* álbum *m* de recortes; **~ dealer** *n* chatarrero/a.

scrape [skreɪp] *n*: **to get into a ~** meterse en un lío // *vt* raspar; (*skin etc*) rasguñar; (*~ against*) rozar // *vi*: **to ~ through** (*exam*) aprobar por los pelos; **~r** *n* raspador *m*.

scrap: **~ heap** *n* (*fig*): **to be on the ~ heap** estar acabado; **~ merchant** *n* (*Brit*) chatarrero/a; **~ paper** *n* pedazos *mpl* de papel.

scratch [skrætʃ] *n* rasguño; (*from claw*) arañazo // *a*: **~ team** equipo improvisado // *vt* (*record*) rayar; (*with claw, nail*) rasguñar, arañar // *vi* rascarse; **to start from ~** partir de cero; **to be up to ~** cumplir con los requisitos.

scrawl [skrɔːl] *n* garabatos *mpl* // *vi* hacer garabatos.

scrawny ['skrɔːnɪ] *a* (*person, neck*) flaco.

scream [skriːm] *n* chillido // *vi* chillar.

scree [skriː] *n* cono de desmoronamiento.

screech [skriːtʃ] *vi* chirriar.

screen [skriːn] *n* (*CINEMA, TV*) pantalla; (*movable*) biombo; (*wall*) tabique *m*; (*also: wind~*) parabrisas *m inv* // *vt* (*conceal*) tapar; (*from the wind etc*) proteger; (*film*) proyectar; (*candidates*

etc) investigar a; **~ing** *n* (*MED*) investigación *f* médica; **~play** *n* guión *m*.

screw [skruː] *n* tornillo; (*propeller*) hélice *f* // *vt* atornillar; **to ~ up** *vt* (*paper etc*) arrugar; (*col: ruin*) fastidiar; **to ~ up one's eyes** arrugar el entrecejo; **~driver** *n* destornillador *m*.

scribble ['skrɪbl] *n* garabatos *mpl* // *vt* escribir con prisa.

script [skrɪpt] *n* (*CINEMA etc*) guión *m*; (*writing*) escritura, letra.

Scripture ['skrɪptʃə*] *n* Sagrada Escritura.

scroll [skrəul] *n* rollo.

scrounge [skraundʒ] *vt* (*col*): **to ~ sth off or from sb** obtener algo de uno de gorra // *vi*: **to ~ on sb** vivir a costa de uno; **~r** *n* gorrón/ona *m/f*.

scrub [skrʌb] *n* (*clean*) fregado; (*land*) maleza // *vt* fregar, restregar; (*reject*) cancelar, anular.

scruff [skrʌf] *n*: **by the ~ of the neck** por el pescuezo.

scruffy ['skrʌfɪ] *a* desaliñado, piojoso.

scrum(mage) ['skrʌm(mɪdʒ)] *n* (*RUGBY*) melée *f*.

scruple ['skruːpl] *n* escrúpulo.

scrutinize ['skruːtɪnaɪz] *vt* escudriñar; (*votes*) escrutar.

scrutiny ['skruːtɪnɪ] *n* escrutinio, examen *m*.

scuff [skʌf] *vt* (*shoes, floor*) rayar.

scuffle ['skʌfl] *n* refriega.

scullery ['skʌlərɪ] *n* trascocina.

sculptor ['skʌlptə*] *n* escultor(a) *m/f*.

sculpture ['skʌlptʃə*] *n* escultura.

scum [skʌm] *n* (*on liquid*) espuma; (*pej: person*) canalla *m*.

scupper ['skʌpə*] *vt* (*plans*) dar al traste con.

scurrilous ['skʌrɪləs] *a* difamatorio, calumnioso.

scurry ['skʌrɪ] *vi*: **to ~ off** escabullirse.

scuttle ['skʌtl] *n* (*also: coal ~*) cubo, carbonera // *vt* (*ship*) barrenar // *vi* (*scamper*): **to ~ away, ~ off** escabullirse.

scythe [saɪð] *n* guadaña.

SDP *n abbr* (*Brit*) = *Social Democratic Party*.

sea [siː] *n* mar *m* // *cpd* de mar, marítimo; **by ~** (*travel*) en barco; **on the ~** (*boat*) en el mar; (*town*) junto al mar; **to be all at ~** (*fig*) estar despistado; **out to or at ~** en alta mar; **~board** *n* litoral *m*; **~ breeze** *n* brisa de mar; **~food** *n* mariscos *mpl*; **~ front** *n* paseo marítimo; **~gull** *n* gaviota.

seal [siːl] *n* (*animal*) foca; (*stamp*) sello // *vt* (*close*) cerrar; (: *with ~*) sellar; **to ~ off** *vt* (*area*) acordonar.

sea level *n* nivel *m* del mar.

seam [siːm] *n* costura; (*of metal*) juntura; (*of coal*) veta, filón *m*.

seaman ['siːmən] *n* marinero.

seamy ['siːmɪ] *a* sórdido.
seance ['seɪɔns] *n* sesión *f* de espiritismo.
sea plane ['siːpleɪn] *n* hidroavión *m*.
seaport ['siːpɔːt] *n* puerto de mar.
search [səːtʃ] *n* (*for person, thing*) busca, búsqueda; (*of drawer, pockets*) registro; (*inspection*) reconocimiento // *vt* (*look in*) buscar en; (*examine*) examinar; (*person, place*) registrar // *vi*: to ~ for buscar; in ~ of en busca de; to ~ through *vt fus* registrar; ~ing *a* penetrante; ~light *n* reflector *m*; ~ party *n* pelotón *m* de salvamento; ~ warrant *n* mandamiento (judicial).
sea: ~shore *n* playa, orilla del mar; ~sick *a* mareado; ~side *n* playa, orilla del mar; ~side resort *n* playa.
season ['siːzn] *n* (*of year*) estación *f*; (*sporting etc*) temporada; (*gen*) época, período // *vt* (*food*) sazonar; ~al *a* estacional; ~ed *a* (*fig*) experimentado; ~ing *n* condimento, aderezo; ~ ticket *n* abono.
seat [siːt] *n* (*in bus, train: place*) asiento; (*chair*) silla; (*PARLIAMENT*) escaño; (*buttocks*) culo, trasero; (*of government*) sede *f* // *vt* sentar; (*have room for*) tener cabida para; to be ~ed sentarse; ~ belt *n* cinturón *m* de seguridad.
sea: ~ water *n* agua del mar; ~weed *n* alga marina; ~worthy *a* en condiciones de navegar.
sec. *abbr* = **second(s)**.
secluded [sɪˈkluːdɪd] *a* retirado.
second ['sɛkənd] *a* segundo // *ad* (*in race etc*) en segundo lugar // *n* (*gen*) segundo; (*AUT: also:* ~ **gear**) segunda; (*COMM*) artículo con algún desperfecto // *vt* (*motion*) apoyar; ~ary *a* secundario; ~ary school *n* escuela secundaria; ~class *a* de segunda clase // *ad* (*RAIL*) en segunda; ~hand *a* de segunda mano, usado; ~ hand *n* (*on clock*) segundero; ~ly *ad* en segundo lugar; ~ment [sɪˈkɔndmənt] *n* (*Brit*) traslado temporal; ~rate *a* de segunda categoría; ~ thoughts *npl*: to have ~ thoughts cambiar de opinión; on ~ thoughts *or* (*US*) thought pensándolo bien.
secrecy ['siːkrəsɪ] *n* secreto.
secret ['siːkrɪt] *a, n* secreto; in ~ *ad* en secreto.
secretarial [sɛkrɪˈtɛərɪəl] *a* de secretario.
secretary ['sɛkrətərɪ] *n* secretario/a; S~ of State (for) (*Brit POL*) Ministro (de).
secretion [sɪˈkriːʃən] *n* secreción *f*.
secretive ['siːkrətɪv] *a* reservado, sigiloso.
secretly ['siːkrɪtlɪ] *ad* en secreto.
sect [sɛkt] *n* secta; ~arian [-ˈtɛərɪən] *a* sectario.
section ['sɛkʃən] *n* sección *f*; (*part*) parte *f*; (*of document*) artículo; (*of opinion*) sector *m*.
sector ['sɛktə*] *n* sector *m*.

secular ['sɛkjulə*] *a* secular, seglar.
secure [sɪˈkjuə*] *a* (*free from anxiety*) seguro; (*firmly fixed*) firme, fijo // *vt* (*fix*) asegurar, afianzar; (*get*) conseguir.
security [sɪˈkjuərɪtɪ] *n* seguridad *f*; (*for loan*) fianza; (: *object*) prenda.
sedan [sɪˈdæn] *n* (*US AUT*) sedán *m*.
sedate [sɪˈdeɪt] *a* tranquilo; // *vt* tratar con sedantes.
sedation [sɪˈdeɪʃən] *n* (*MED*) sedación *f*.
sedative ['sɛdɪtɪv] *n* sedante *m*, sedativo.
seduce [sɪˈdjuːs] *vt* (*gen*) seducir; **seduction** [-ˈdʌkʃən] *n* seducción *f*; **seductive** [-ˈdʌktɪv] *a* seductor(a).
see [siː] (*pt* saw, *pp* seen) *vt* (*gen*) ver; (*understand*) ver, comprender // *vi* ver // *n* (*arz*)obispado; to ~ sb to the door acompañar a uno a la puerta; to ~ that (*ensure*) asegurar que; ~ you soon! ¡hasta pronto!; to ~ about *vt fus* atender a, encargarse de; to ~ off *vt* despedir; to ~ through *vt fus* calar // *vt* (*plan*) llevar a cabo; to ~ to *vt fus* atender a, encargarse de.
seed [siːd] *n* semilla; (*in fruit*) pepita; (*fig*) germen *m*; (*TENNIS*) preseleccionado/a; to go to ~ (*plant*) granar; (*fig*) descuidarse; ~ling *n* planta de semillero; ~y *a* (*shabby*) desaseado, raído.
seeing ['siːɪŋ] *conj*: ~ (that) visto que, en vista de que.
seek [siːk], *pt, pp* sought *vt* (*gen*) buscar; (*post*) solicitar.
seem [siːm] *vi* parecer; there seems to be... parece que hay; ~ingly *ad* aparentemente, según parece.
seen [siːn] *pp* of **see**.
seep [siːp] *vi* filtrarse.
seesaw ['siːsɔː] *n* balancín *m*, columpio.
seethe [siːð] *vi* hervir; to ~ with anger estar furioso.
see-through ['siːθruː] *a* transparente.
segregate ['sɛgrɪgeɪt] *vt* segregar.
seize [siːz] *vt* (*grasp*) agarrar, asir; (*take possession of*) secuestrar; (: *territory*) apoderarse de; (*opportunity*) aprovecharse de; to ~ (up)on *vt fus* aprovechar; to ~ up *vi* (*TECH*) agarrotarse.
seizure ['siːʒə*] *n* (*MED*) ataque *m*; (*LAW*) incautación *f*.
seldom ['sɛldəm] *ad* rara vez.
select [sɪˈlɛkt] *a* selecto, escogido // *vt* escoger, elegir; (*SPORT*) seleccionar; ~ion [-ˈlɛkʃən] *n* selección *f*, elección *f*; (*COMM*) surtido.
self [sɛlf] *n* (*pl* selves) uno mismo; the ~ el yo // *pref* auto...; ~-assured *a* seguro de sí mismo; ~-catering *a* (*Brit*) con cocina; ~-centred, (*US*) ~-centered *a* egocéntrico; ~-coloured, (*US*) ~-colored *a* de color natural; (*of one colour*) de un color; ~-confidence *n* confianza en sí mismo; ~-conscious *a*

cohibido; **~-contained** a (gen) autónomo; (Brit: flat) con entrada particular; **~-control** n autodominio; **~-defence**, (US) **~-defense** n defensa propia; **~-discipline** n autodisciplina; **~-employed** a que trabaja por cuenta propia; **~-evident** a patente; **~-governing** a autónomo; **~-indulgent** a autocomplaciente; **~-interest** n egoísmo; **~-ish** a egoísta; **~ishness** n egoísmo; **~less** a desinteresado; **~-made** a: **~-made man** hombre m que se ha hecho a sí mismo; **~-pity** n lástima de sí mismo; **~-portrait** n autorretrato; **~-possessed** a sereno, dueño de sí mismo; **~-preservation** n propia conservación f; **~-reliant** a independiente, autosuficiente; **~-respect** n amor m propio; **~-righteous** a santurrón/ona; **~-sacrifice** n abnegación f; **~-satisfied** a satisfecho de sí mismo; **~-service** a de autoservicio; **~-sufficient** a autosuficiente; **~-taught** a autodidacta.

sell [sɛl], pt, pp **sold** vt vender // vi venderse; to ~ at or for £10 venderse a 10 libros; to ~ off vt liquidar; to ~ out vi transigir, transar (LAm); **~-by date** n fecha de caducidad; **~er** n vendedor(a) m/f; **~ing price** n precio de venta.

sellotape ['sɛləuteɪp] n ® (Brit) cinta adhesiva, celo, scotch m (LAm).

sellout ['sɛlaut] n traición f; it was a ~ (THEATRE etc) fue un éxito de taquilla.

selves [sɛlvz] pl of **self**.

semaphore ['sɛməfɔ:*] n semáforo.

semblance ['sɛmbləns] n apariencia.

semen ['si:mən] n semen m.

semester [sɪ'mɛstə*] n (US) semestre m.

semi... [sɛmɪ] pref semi..., medio...; **~-circle** n semicírculo; **~-colon** n punto y coma; **~-conductor** n semiconductor m; **~-detached (house)** n (casa) semi-separada; **~-final** n semi-final m.

seminar ['sɛmɪna:*] n seminario.

seminary ['sɛmɪnərɪ] n (REL) seminario.

semiskilled ['sɛmɪskɪld] a (work, worker) semi-cualificado.

senate ['sɛnɪt] n senado; **senator** n senador(a) m/f.

send [sɛnd], pt, pp **sent** vt mandar, enviar; to ~ away vt (letter, goods) despachar; to ~ away for vt fus pedir; to ~ back vt devolver; to ~ for vt fus mandar traer; to ~ off vt (goods) despachar; (Brit SPORT: player) expulsar; to ~ out vt (invitation) mandar; (signal) emitir; to ~ up vt (person, price) hacer subir; (Brit: parody) parodiar; **~er** n remitente m/f; **~-off** n: a good **~-off** una buena despedida.

senior ['si:nɪə*] a (older) mayor, más viejo; (: on staff) de más antigüedad; (of higher rank) superior // n mayor m; ~ **citizen** n persona de la tercera edad; **~ity** [-'ɔrɪtɪ] n antigüedad f.

sensation [sɛn'seɪʃən] n sensación f; **~al** a sensacional.

sense [sɛns] n (faculty, meaning) sentido; (feeling) sensación f; (good ~) sentido común, juicio // vt sentir, percibir; ~ of humour sentido del humor; **it makes** ~ tiene sentido; **~less** a estúpido, insensato; (unconscious) sin conocimiento.

sensibility [sɛnsɪ'bɪlɪtɪ] n sensibilidad f; **sensibilities** npl susceptibilidades fpl.

sensible ['sɛnsɪbl] a sensato; (reasonable) razonable, lógico.

sensitive ['sɛnsɪtɪv] a sensible; (touchy) susceptible.

sensual ['sɛnsjuəl] a sensual.

sensuous ['sɛnsjuəs] a sensual.

sent [sɛnt] pt, pp of **send**.

sentence ['sɛntns] n (LING) oración f; (LAW) sentencia, fallo // vt: to ~ sb to death/to 5 years condenar a uno a muerte/a 5 años de cárcel.

sentiment ['sɛntɪmənt] n sentimiento; (opinion) opinión f; **~al** [-'mɛntl] a sentimental.

sentry ['sɛntrɪ] n centinela m.

separate ['sɛprɪt] a separado; (distinct) distinto // vb ['sɛpəreɪt] vt separar; (part) dividir // vi separarse; **~s** npl (clothes) coordinados mpl; **~ly** ad por separado; **separation** [-'reɪʃən] n separación f.

September [sɛp'tɛmbə*] n se(p)tiembre m.

septic ['sɛptɪk] a séptico; ~ **tank** n fosa séptica.

sequel ['si:kwl] n consecuencia, resultado; (of story) continuación f.

sequence ['si:kwəns] n sucesión f, serie f; (CINEMA) secuencia.

serene [sɪ'ri:n] a sereno, tranquilo.

sergeant ['sa:dʒənt] n sargento.

serial ['sɪərɪəl] n (TV) telenovela, serie f televisiva; ~ **number** n número de serie.

series ['sɪəri:z] n, pl inv serie f.

serious ['sɪərɪəs] a serio; (grave) grave; **~ly** ad en serio; (ill, wounded etc) gravemente; **~ness** n seriedad f; gravedad f.

sermon ['sə:mən] n sermón m.

serrated [sɪ'reɪtɪd] a serrado, dentellado.

serum ['sɪərəm] n suero.

servant ['sə:vənt] n (gen) servidor(a) m/f; (house ~) criado/a.

serve [sə:v] vt servir; (customer) atender; (subj: train) pasar por; (apprenticeship) hacer; (prison term) cumplir // vi (also TENNIS) sacar; to ~ as/for/to do servir de/para/para hacer // n (TENNIS) saque m; it ~s him right se lo merece, se lo tiene merecido; to ~ out, ~ up vt (food) servir.

service ['sə:vɪs] n (gen) servicio; (REL) misa; (AUT) mantenimiento; (of dishes) juego // vt (car, washing machine) man-

tener; (: *repair*) reparar; **the S~s** las
fuerzas armadas; **to be of ~ to sb** ser
útil a uno; **~able** *a* sérvible, utilizable;
~ area *n* (*on motorway*) servicios *mpl*;
~ charge *n* (*Brit*) servicio; **~man** *n*
militar *m*; **~ station** *n* estación *f* de
servicio.

serviette [sə:vɪ'et] *n* (*Brit*) servilleta.

session ['sɛʃən] *n* (*sitting*) sesión *f*; **to be
in ~** estar en sesión.

set [sɛt] *n* juego; (*RADIO*) aparato; (*TV*)
televisor *m*; (*of utensils*) batería; (*of
cutlery*) cubierto; (*of books*) colección *f*;
(*TENNIS*) set *m*; (*group of people*) grupo; (*CINEMA*) plató *m*; (*THEATRE*) decorado; (*HAIRDRESSING*) marcado // *a*
(*fixed*) fijo; (*ready*) listo; (*resolved*) resuelto, decidido // *vb* (*pt, pp* **set**) *vt*
(*place*) poner, colocar; (*fix*) fijar; (*adjust*) ajustar, arreglar; (*decide: rules etc*)
establecer, decidir // *vi* (*sun*) ponerse;
(*jam, jelly*) cuajarse; (*concrete*) fra-
guar; **to be ~ on doing sth** estar empeñado en hacer algo; **to ~ to music** poner
música a; **to ~ on fire** incendiar, poner
fuego a; **to ~ free** poner en libertad; **to
~ sth going** poner algo en marcha; **to ~
sail** zarpar, hacerse a la vela; **to ~
about** *vt fus*: **to ~ about doing sth** ponerse a hacer algo; **to ~ aside** *vt* poner
aparte, dejar de lado; **to ~ back** *vt*: **to
~ back (by)** retrasar (por); **to ~ off** *vi*
partir // *vt* (*bomb*) hacer estallar;
(*cause to start*) poner en marcha; (*show
up well*) hacer resaltar; **to ~ out** *vi*: **to
~ out to do sth** proponerse hacer algo //
vt (*arrange*) disponer; (*state*) exponer;
to ~ up *vt* (*organization*) establecer;
~back *n* (*hitch*) revés *m*, contratiempo;
~ menu *n* menú *m*.

settee [se'ti:] *n* sofá *m*.

setting ['sɛtɪŋ] *n* (*scenery*) marco; (*of
jewel*) engaste *m*, montadura.

settle ['sɛtl] *vt* (*argument, matter*) resolver; (*accounts*) ajustar, liquidar; (*land*)
colonizar; (*MED*: *calm*) calmar, sosegar
// *vi* (*dust etc*) depositarse; (*weather*) serenarse; (*also*: **~ down**) instalarse; tranquilizarse; **to ~ for sth** convenir en aceptar algo; **to ~ on sth** decidirse por algo;
to ~ up with sb ajustar cuentas con uno;
to ~ in *vi* instalarse; **~ment** *n* (*payment*) liquidación *f*; (*agreement*) acuerdo, convenio; (*village etc*) pueblo; **~r** *n*
colono/a, colonizador(a) *m/f*.

setup ['sɛtʌp] *n* sistema *m*.

seven ['sɛvn] *num* siete; **~teen** *num*
diez y siete, diecisiete; **~th** *a* séptimo;
~ty *num* setenta.

sever ['sɛvə*] *vt* cortar; (*relations*) romper.

several ['sɛvərl] *a, pron* varios/as *m/fpl*,
algunos/as *m/fpl*; **~ of us** varios de nosotros.

severance ['sɛvərəns] *n* (*of relations*)

ruptura; **~ pay** *n* pago de despedida.

severe [sɪ'vɪə*] *a* severo; (*serious*) grave; (*hard*) duro; (*pain*) intenso; **severity** [sɪ'vɛrɪtɪ] *n* severidad *f*; gravedad *f*;
intensidad *f*.

sew [səu], *pt* **sewed**, *pp* **sewn** *vt, vi* coser; **to ~ up** *vt* coser, zurcir.

sewage ['su:ɪdʒ] *n* aguas *fpl* residuales.

sewer ['su:ə*] *n* alcantarilla, cloaca.

sewing ['səuɪŋ] *n* costura; **~ machine** *n*
máquina de coser.

sewn [səun] *pp of* **sew**.

sex [sɛks] *n* sexo; **to have ~ with sb** tener
relaciones (sexuales) con uno; **~ist** *a, n*
sexista *m/f*.

sexual ['sɛksjuəl] *a* sexual.

sexy ['sɛksɪ] *a* sexy.

shabby ['ʃæbɪ] *a* (*person*) desharrapado;
(*clothes*) raído, gastado.

shack [ʃæk] *n* choza, chabola.

shackles ['ʃæklz] *npl* grillos *mpl*, grilletes *mpl*.

shade [ʃeɪd] *n* sombra; (*for lamp*) pantalla; (*for eyes*) visera; (*of colour*) matiz
m, tonalidad *f* // *vt* dar sombra a; **in the
~** en la sombra; **a ~ of** un poquito de; **a
~ smaller** un poquito menor.

shadow ['ʃædəu] *n* sombra // *vt* (*follow*)
seguir y vigilar; **~ cabinet** *n* (*Brit
POL*) gabinete paralelo formado por el
partido de oposición; **~y** *a* oscuro;
(*dim*) indistinto.

shady ['ʃeɪdɪ] *a* sombreado; (*fig: dishonest*) sospechoso; (: *deal*) turbio.

shaft [ʃɑ:ft] *n* (*of arrow, spear*) astil *m*;
(*AUT, TECH*) eje *m*, árbol *m*; (*of mine*)
pozo; (*of lift*) hueco, caja; (*of light*)
rayo.

shaggy ['ʃægɪ] *a* peludo.

shake [ʃeɪk] *vb* (*pt* **shook**, *pp* **shaken**) *vt*
sacudir; (*building*) hacer temblar; (*bot-
tle, cocktail*) agitar // *vi* (*tremble*) temblar // *n* (*movement*) sacudida; **to ~
one's head** (*in refusal*) negar con la cabeza; (*in dismay*) mover o menear la
cabeza, incrédulo; **to ~ hands with sb** estrechar la mano a uno; **to ~ off** *vt* sacudirse; (*fig*) deshacerse de; **to ~ up**
vt agitar; **shaky** *a* (*hand, voice*) trémulo; (*building*) inestable.

shall [ʃæl] *auxiliary vb*: **I ~ go** iré; **~ I
help you?** ¿quieres que te ayude?; **I'll
buy three, ~ I?** compro tres, ¿no te parece?

shallow ['ʃæləu] *a* poco profundo; (*fig*)
superficial.

sham [ʃæm] *n* fraude *m*, engaño // *a* falso, fingido // *vt* fingir, simular.

shambles ['ʃæmblz] *n* confusión *f*.

shame [ʃeɪm] *n* vergüenza; (*pity*) lástima // *vt* avergonzar; **it is a ~ that/to do**
es una lástima que/hacer; **what a ~!**
¡qué lástima!; **~faced** *a* avergonzado;
~ful *a* vergonzoso; **~less** *a* descarado.

shampoo [ʃæm'pu:] *n* champú *m* // *vt* lavar con champú; ~ **and set** *n* lavado y marcado.

shamrock ['ʃæmrɔk] *n* trébol *m* (*emblema nacional irlandés*).

shandy ['ʃændɪ], (*US*) **shandygaff** ['ʃændɪgæf] *n* mezcla de cerveza con gaseosa.

shan't [ʃɑːnt] = **shall not.**

shanty town ['ʃæntɪ-] *n* barrio de chabolas.

shape [ʃeɪp] *n* forma // *vt* formar, dar forma a; (*sb's ideas*) formar; (*sb's life*) determinar // *vi* (*also*: ~ **up**) (*events*) desarrollarse; (*person*) formarse; **to take** ~ tomar forma; ~**d** *suffix*: **heart**-~**d** en forma de corazón; ~**less** *a* informe, sin forma definida; ~**ly** *a* bien formado *or* proporcionado.

share [ʃeə*] *n* (*part*) parte *f*, porción *f*; (*contribution*) cuota; (*COMM*) acción *f* // *vt* dividir; (*have in common*) compartir; **to** ~ **out** (*among or between*) repartir (*entre*); ~**holder** *n* (*Brit*) accionista *m/f*.

shark [ʃɑːk] *n* tiburón *m*.

sharp [ʃɑːp] *a* (*razor, knife*) afilado; (*point*) puntiagudo; (*outline*) definido; (*pain*) intenso; (*MUS*) desafinado; (*contrast*) marcado; (*voice*) agudo; (*person: quick-witted*) astuto; (: *dishonest*) poco escrupuloso // *n* (*MUS*) sostenido // *ad*: **at 2 o'clock** ~ a las 2 en punto; ~**en** *vt* afilar; (*pencil*) sacar punta a; (*fig*) aguzar; ~**ener** *n* (*also*: **pencil** ~**ener**) sacapuntas *m inv*; ~**-eyed** *a* de vista aguda; ~**ly** *ad* (*turn, stop*) bruscamente; (*stand out, contrast*) claramente; (*criticize, retort*) severamente.

shatter ['ʃætə*] *vt* hacer añicos *or* pedazos; (*fig: ruin*) destruir, acabar con // *vi* hacerse añicos.

shave [ʃeɪv] *vb* (*pt* shaved, *pp* shaved *or* shaven) *vt* afeitar, rasurar // *vi* afeitarse // *n*: **to have a** ~ afeitarse; ~**r** *n* (*also*: **electric** ~**r**) máquina de afeitar (eléctrica).

shaving ['ʃeɪvɪŋ] *n* (*action*) el afeitarse, rasurado; ~**s** *npl* (*of wood etc*) virutas *fpl*; ~ **brush** *n* brocha (de afeitar); ~ **cream** *n* crema (de afeitar).

shawl [ʃɔːl] *n* chal *m*.

she [ʃiː] *pron* ella; ~**-cat** *n* gata; *NB: for ships, countries follow the gender of your translation.*

sheaf [ʃiːf], *pl* **sheaves** [ʃiːvz] *n* (*of corn*) gavilla; (*of arrows*) haz *m*; (*of papers*) fajo.

shear [ʃɪə*] *vb* (*pt* sheared, *pp* sheared *or* shorn) *vt* (*sheep*) esquilar, trasquilar; ~**s** *npl* (*for hedge*) tijeras *fpl* de jardín; **to** ~ **off** *vi* romperse.

sheath [ʃiːθ] *n* vaina; (*contraceptive*) preservativo.

sheaves [ʃiːvz] *pl of* **sheaf.**

shed [ʃed] *n* cobertizo // *vt* (*pt, pp* shed)

(*skin*) mudar; (*tears*) derramar.

she'd [ʃiːd] = **she had; she would.**

sheen [ʃiːn] *n* brillo, lustre *m*.

sheep [ʃiːp] *n, pl inv* oveja; ~**dog** *n* perro pastor; ~**ish** *a* tímido, vergonzoso; ~**skin** *n* piel *f* de carnero.

sheer [ʃɪə*] *a* (*utter*) puro, completo; (*steep*) escarpado; (*material*) diáfano // *ad* verticalmente.

sheet [ʃiːt] *n* (*on bed*) sábana; (*of paper*) hoja; (*of glass, metal*) lámina.

sheik(h) [ʃeɪk] *n* jeque *m*.

shelf [ʃelf], *pl* **shelves** *n* estante *m*.

shell [ʃel] *n* (*on beach*) concha; (*of egg, nut etc*) cáscara; (*explosive*) proyectil *m*, obús *m*; (*of building*) armazón *f* // *vt* (*peas*) desenvainar; (*MIL*) bombardear.

she'll [ʃiːl] = **she will; she shall.**

shellfish ['ʃelfɪʃ] *n, pl inv* crustáceo; (*pl: as food*) mariscos *mpl*.

shelter ['ʃeltə*] *n* abrigo, refugio // *vt* (*aid*) amparar, proteger; (*give lodging to*) abrigar; (*hide*) esconder // *vi* abrigarse, refugiarse; ~**ed** *a* (*life*) protegido; (*spot*) abrigado.

shelve [ʃelv] *vt* (*fig*) aplazar; ~**s** *pl of* **shelf.**

shepherd ['ʃepəd] *n* pastor *m* // *vt* (*guide*) guiar, conducir; ~**'s pie** *n* pastel de carne y patatas.

sherry ['ʃerɪ] *n* jerez *m*.

she's [ʃiːz] = **she is; she has.**

Shetland ['ʃetlənd] *n* (*also*: **the** ~**s, the** ~ **Isles**) las Islas *fpl* de Zetlandia.

shield [ʃiːld] *n* escudo; (*TECH*) blindaje *m* // *vt*: **to** ~ (**from**) proteger (de).

shift [ʃɪft] *n* (*change*) cambio; (*at work*) turno // *vt* trasladar; (*remove*) quitar // *vi* moverse; (*change place*) cambiar de sitio; ~**less** *a* (*person*) perezoso; ~ **work** *n* (*Brit*) trabajo por turno; ~**y** *a* tramposo; (*eyes*) furtivo.

shilling ['ʃɪlɪŋ] *n* (*Brit*) chelín *m*.

shilly-shally ['ʃɪlɪʃælɪ] *vi* titubear, vacilar.

shimmer ['ʃɪmə*] *n* reflejo trémulo // *vi* relucir.

shin [ʃɪn] *n* espinilla.

shine [ʃaɪn] *n* brillo, lustre *m* // (*vb: pt, pp* shone) *vi* brillar, relucir // *vt* (*shoes*) lustrar, sacar brillo a; **to** ~ **a torch on** sth dirigir una linterna hacia algo.

shingle ['ʃɪŋgl] *n* (*on beach*) guijarras *fpl*; ~**s** *n* (*MED*) herpes *mpl or fpl*.

shiny ['ʃaɪnɪ] *a* brillante, lustroso.

ship [ʃɪp] *n* buque *m*, barco // *vt* (*goods*) embarcar; (*oars*) desarmar; (*send*) transportar *or* enviar por vía marítima; ~**building** *n* construcción *f* de buques; ~**ment** *n* (*act*) embarque *m*; (*goods*) envío; ~**per** *n* exportador(a) *m/f*; ~**ping** *n* (*act*) embarque *m*; (*traffic*) buques *mpl*; ~**shape** *a* en buen orden; ~**wreck** *n* naufragio // *vt*: **to be** ~**wrecked** naufragar; ~**yard** *n* astillero.

shire ['ʃaɪə*] n (Brit) condado.

shirk [ʃəːk] vt eludir, esquivar; (obligations) faltar a.

shirt [ʃəːt] n camisa; **in ~ sleeves** en mangas de camisa.

shit [ʃɪt] excl (col!) ¡mierda! (!)

shiver ['ʃɪvə*] vi temblar, estremecerse; (with cold) tiritar.

shoal [ʃəul] n (of fish) banco.

shock [ʃɔk] n (impact) choque m; (ELEC) descarga (eléctrica); (emotional) conmoción f; (start) sobresalto, susto; (MED) postración f nerviosa // vt dar un susto a; (offend) escandalizar; ~ **absorber** n amortiguador m; ~**ing** a (awful) espantoso; (improper) escandaloso.

shod [ʃɔd] pt, pp of **shoe**.

shoddy ['ʃɔdɪ] a de pacotilla.

shoe [ʃuː] n zapato; (for horse) herradura; (brake ~) zapata // vt (pt, pp shod) (horse) herrar; ~**brush** n cepillo para zapatos; ~**horn** n calzador m; ~ **lace** n cordón m; ~ **polish** n betún m; ~**shop** n zapatería; ~**string** n (fig): **on a ~string** con muy poco dinero.

shone [ʃɔn] pt, pp of **shine**.

shoo [ʃuː] excl ¡fuera!

shook [ʃuk] pt of **shake**.

shoot [ʃuːt] n (on branch, seedling) retoño, vástago // vt (pt, pp shot) disparar; (kill) matar a tiros; (execute) fusilar; (film) rodear, filmar // vi (FOOTBALL) chutar; **to ~ (at)** tirar (a); **to ~ down** vt (plane) derribar; **to ~ in/out** vi entrar corriendo/salir disparado; **to ~ up** vi (prices) dispararse; ~**ing** n (shots) tiros mpl; (HUNTING) caza con escopeta; ~**ing star** n estrella fugaz.

shop [ʃɔp] n tienda; (workshop) taller m // vi (also: **go ~ping**) ir de compras; ~ **assistant** n (Brit) dependiente/a m/f; ~ **floor** n (Brit fig) taller m, fábrica; ~**keeper** n (Brit) tendero/a; ~**lifting** n mechería; ~**per** n comprador(a) m/f; ~**ping** n (goods) compras fpl; ~**ping bag** n bolsa (de compras); ~**ping centre**, (US) ~**ping center** n centro comercial; ~**soiled** a (Brit) usado; ~ **steward** n (Brit INDUSTRY) enlace m sindical; ~ **window** n escaparate m, vidriera (LAm); ~**worn** a (US) usado.

shore [ʃɔː*] n (of sea, lake) orilla // vt: **to ~ (up)** reforzar.

shorn [ʃɔːn] pp of **shear**.

short [ʃɔːt] a (not long) corto; (in time) breve, de corta duración; (person) bajo; (curt) brusco, seco // n (also: ~ film) cortometraje m; (a pair of) ~**s** (unos) pantalones mpl cortos; **to be ~ of sth** estar falto de algo; **in ~** en pocas palabras; ~ **of doing...** fuera de hacer...; **everything ~ of...** todo menos...; **it is ~ for** es la forma abreviada de; **to cut ~** (speech, visit) interrumpir, terminar inesperadamente; **to fall ~ of** no alcanzar; **to stop ~** parar en seco; **to stop ~ of** detenerse antes de; ~**age** n escasez f, falta; ~**bread** n especie de mantecada; ~**change** vt no dar el cambio completo a; ~**circuit** n cortocircuito // vt poner en cortocircuito // vi ponerse en cortocircuito; ~**coming** n defecto, deficiencia; ~**(crust) pastry** n (Brit) pasta quebradiza; ~**cut** n atajo; ~**en** vt acortar; (visit) interrumpir; ~**fall** n déficit m; ~**hand** n (Brit) taquigrafía; ~**hand typist** n (Brit) taquimecanógrafo/a; ~ **list** n (Brit: for job) lista de candidatos escogidos; ~**ly** ad en breve, dentro de poco; ~**sighted** a (Brit) corto de vista, miope; (fig) imprudente; ~**staffed** a falto de personal; ~ **story** n cuento; ~**tempered** a enojadizo; ~**term** a (effect) a corto plazo; ~**wave** n (RADIO) onda corta.

shot [ʃɔt] pt, pp of **shoot** // n (sound) tiro, disparo; (person) tirador(a) m/f; (try) tentativa; (injection) inyección f; (PHOT) toma, fotografía; **like a ~** (without any delay) como un rayo; ~**gun** n escopeta.

should [ʃud] auxiliary vb: **I ~ go now** debo irme ahora; **he ~ be there now** debe de haber llegado (ya); **I ~ go if I were you** yo en tu lugar me iría; **I ~ like to** me gustaría.

shoulder ['ʃəuldə*] n hombro; (Brit: of road) hard ~ andén m // vt (fig) cargar con; ~ **blade** n omóplato; ~ **strap** n tirante m.

shouldn't ['ʃudnt] = should not.

shout [ʃaut] n grito // vt gritar // vi gritar, dar voces; **to ~ down** vt hundir a gritos; ~**ing** n griterío.

shove [ʃʌv] n empujón m // vt empujar; (col: put): **to ~ sth in** meter algo a empellones; **to ~ off** vi (NAUT) alejarse del muelle; (fig: col) largarse.

shovel ['ʃʌvl] n pala; (mechanical) excavadora // vt mover con pala.

show [ʃəu] n (of emotion) demostración f; (semblance) apariencia; (exhibition) exposición f; (THEATRE) función f, espectáculo // vb (pt showed, pp shown) vt mostrar, enseñar; (courage etc) mostrar, manifestar; (exhibit) exponer; (film) proyectar // vi mostrarse; (appear) aparecer; **on ~** (exhibits etc) expuesto; **to ~ in** vt (person) hacer pasar; **to ~ off** vi (pej) presumir // vt (display) lucir; (pej) hacer gala de; **to ~ out** vt: **to ~ sb out** acompañar a uno a la puerta; **to ~ up** vi (stand out) destacar; (col: turn up) aparecer // vt descubrir; (unmask) desenmascarar; ~ **business** n el mundo del espectáculo; ~**down** n enfrentamiento (final).

shower ['ʃauə*] n (rain) chaparrón m, chubasco; (of stones etc) lluvia; (also: ~**bath**) ducha, regadera (LAm) // vi llover // vt: to ~ sb with sth colmar a uno de algo; ~**proof** a impermeable.

showing ['ʃəuɪŋ] n (of film) proyección f.

show jumping n hipismo.

shown [ʃəun] pp of **show**.

show: ~-**off** n (col: person) presumido/a; ~**piece** n (of exhibition etc) objeto cumbre; ~**room** n sala de muestras.

shrank [ʃræŋk] pt of **shrink**.

shrapnel ['ʃræpnl] n metralla.

shred [ʃrɛd] n (gen pl) triza, jirón m // vt hacer trizas; (CULIN) desmenuzar; ~**der** n (vegetable ~der) picadora; (document ~der) trituradora (de papel).

shrewd [ʃruːd] a astuto.

shriek [ʃriːk] n chillido // vt, vi chillar.

shrill [ʃrɪl] a agudo, estridente.

shrimp [ʃrɪmp] n camarón m.

shrine [ʃraɪn] n santuario, sepulcro.

shrink [ʃrɪŋk], pt **shrank**, pp **shrunk** vi encogerse; (be reduced) reducirse // vt encoger; to ~ from doing sth no atreverse a hacer algo; ~**age** n encogimiento; reducción f; ~**wrap** vt empaquetar al vacío.

shrivel ['ʃrɪvl] (also: ~ up) vt (dry) secar; (crease) arrugar // vi secarse; arrugarse.

shroud [ʃraud] n sudario // vt: ~ed in mystery envuelto en el misterio.

Shrove Tuesday ['ʃrəuv-] n martes m de carnaval.

shrub [ʃrʌb] n arbusto; ~**bery** n arbustos mpl.

shrug [ʃrʌg] n encogimiento de hombros // vt, vi: to ~ (one's shoulders) encogerse de hombros; **to ~ off** vt negar importancia a.

shrunk [ʃrʌŋk] pp of **shrink**.

shudder ['ʃʌdə*] n estremecimiento, escalofrío // vi estremecerse.

shuffle ['ʃʌfl] vt (cards) barajar; to ~ (one's feet) arrastrar los pies.

shun [ʃʌn] vt rehuir, esquivar.

shunt [ʃʌnt] vt (RAIL) maniobrar.

shut [ʃʌt], pt, pp **shut** vt cerrar // vi cerrarse; **to ~ down** vt, vi cerrar; **to ~ off** vt (supply etc) interrumpir, cortar; **to ~ up** vi (col: keep quiet) callarse // vt (close) cerrar; (silence) callar; ~**ter** n contraventana; (PHOT) obturador m.

shuttle ['ʃʌtl] n lanzadera; (also: ~ service: AVIAT) puente m aéreo.

shuttlecock ['ʃʌtlkɔk] n volante m.

shy [ʃaɪ] a tímido; ~**ness** n timidez f.

sibling ['sɪblɪŋ] n hermano/a.

Sicily ['sɪsɪlɪ] n Sicilia.

sick [sɪk] a (ill) enfermo; (nauseated) mareado; (humour) negro; to be ~ (Brit) vomitar; to feel ~ tener náuseas; to be ~ of (fig) estar harto de; ~ **bay** n enfermería; ~**en** vt dar asco a // vi enfermar; ~**ening** a (fig) asqueroso.

sickle ['sɪkl] n hoz f.

sick: ~ **leave** n baja por enfermedad; ~**ly** a enfermizo; (taste) empalagoso; ~**ness** n enfermedad f, mal m; (vomiting) náuseas fpl; ~ **pay** n subsidio de enfermedad.

side [saɪd] n (gen) lado; (of body) costado; (of lake) orilla; (team) equipo; (of hill) ladera // cpd (door, entrance) lateral // vi: to ~ with sb tomar el partido de uno; by the ~ of al lado de; ~ by ~ juntos/as; from all ~s de todos lados; to take ~s (with) tomar partido (con); ~**board** n aparador m; ~**boards** (Brit), ~**burns** npl patillas fpl; ~ **effect** n efecto secundario; ~**light** n (AUT) luz f lateral; ~**line** n (SPORT) línea lateral; (fig) empleo suplementario; ~**long** a de soslayo; ~**saddle** ad a mujeriegas, a la inglesa; ~ **show** n (stall) caseta; ~**step** vt (fig) esquivar; ~ **street** n calle f lateral; ~**track** vt (fig) desviar (de su propósito); ~**walk** n (US) acera; ~**ways** ad de lado.

siding ['saɪdɪŋ] n (RAIL) apartadero, vía muerta.

sidle ['saɪdl] vi: to ~ up (to) acercarse furtivamente (a).

siege [siːdʒ] n cerco, sitio.

sieve [sɪv] n colador m // vt cribar.

sift [sɪft] vt cribar; (fig: information) escudriñar.

sigh [saɪ] n suspiro // vi suspirar.

sight [saɪt] n (faculty) vista; (spectacle) espectáculo; (on gun) mira, alza // vt divisar; in ~ a la vista; out of ~ fuera de (la) vista; ~**seeing** n excursionismo, turismo; to go ~**seeing** hacer turismo.

sign [saɪn] n (with hand) señal f, seña; (trace) huella, rastro; (notice) letrero; (written) signo // vt firmar; to ~ sth over to sb firmar el traspaso de algo a uno; **to ~ on** vi (MIL) alistarse; (as unemployed) registrarse como desempleado // vt (MIL) alistar; (employee) contratar; **to ~ up** vi (MIL) alistarse // vt (contract) contratar.

signal ['sɪgnl] n señal f // vi (AUT) hacer señales // vt (person) hacer señas a; (message) comunicar por señales; ~**man** n (RAIL) guardavía m.

signature ['sɪgnətʃə*] n firma; ~ **tune** n sintonía de apertura de un programa.

signet ring ['sɪgnət-] n anillo de sello.

significance [sɪg'nɪfɪkəns] n significado; (importance) trascendencia.

significant [sɪg'nɪfɪkənt] a significativo; trascendente.

signify ['sɪgnɪfaɪ] vt significar.

signpost ['saɪnpəust] n indicador m.

silence ['saɪlns] n silencio // vt hacer callar; (guns) reducir al silencio; ~**r** n (on gun, Brit AUT) silenciador m.

silent ['saɪlnt] a (gen) silencioso; (not speaking) callado; (film) mudo; to remain ~ guardar silencio; ~ **partner** n

(*COMM*) socio/a comanditario/a.
silhouette [sɪluː'et] *n* silueta.
silicon chip ['sɪlɪkən-] *n* plaqueta de silicio.
silk [sɪlk] *n* seda // *cpd* de seda; **~y** *a* sedoso.
silly ['sɪlɪ] *a* (*person*) tonto; (*idea*) absurdo.
silo ['saɪləu] *n* silo.
silt [sɪlt] *n* sedimento.
silver ['sɪlvə*] *n* plata; (*money*) moneda suelta // *cpd* de plata; **~ paper** *n* (*Brit*) papel *m* de plata; **~-plated** *a* plateado; **~smith** *n* platero/a; **~ ware** *n* plata; **~y** *a* plateado.
similar ['sɪmɪlə*] *a*: **~ to** parecido *or* semejante a; **~ly** *ad* del mismo modo.
simile ['sɪmɪlɪ] *n* símil m.
simmer ['sɪmə*] *vi* hervir a fuego lento.
simpering ['sɪmpərɪŋ] *a* afectado; (*foolish*) bobo.
simple ['sɪmpl] *a* (*easy*) sencillo; (*foolish, COMM: interest*) simple; **simplicity** [-'plɪsɪtɪ] *n* sencillez *f*; **simplify** ['sɪmplɪfaɪ] *vt* simplificar.
simply ['sɪmplɪ] *ad* (*live, talk*) sencillamente; (*just, merely*) sólo.
simultaneous [sɪməl'teɪnɪəs] *a* simultáneo; **~ly** *ad* simultáneamente.
sin [sɪn] *n* pecado // *vi* pecar.
since [sɪns] *ad* desde entonces, después // *prep* desde // *conj* (*time*) desde que; (*because*) ya que, puesto que; **~ then** desde entonces.
sincere [sɪn'sɪə*] *a* sincero; **~ly** *ad*: **yours ~ly**, (*US*) **~ly yours** (*in letters*) le saluda atentamente; **sincerity** [-'serɪtɪ] *n* sinceridad *f*.
sinew ['sɪnjuː] *n* tendón m.
sinful ['sɪnful] *a* (*thought*) pecaminoso; (*person*) pecador/a.
sing [sɪŋ], *pt* **sang**, *pp* **sung** *vt* cantar // *vi* cantar.
Singapore [sɪŋə'pɔː*] *n* Singapur m.
singe [sɪndʒ] *vt* chamuscar.
singer ['sɪŋə*] *n* cantante m/f.
singing ['sɪŋɪŋ] *n* (*gen*) canto; (*songs*) canciones *fpl*.
single ['sɪŋgl] *a* único, solo; (*unmarried*) soltero; (*not double*) simple, sencillo // *n* (*Brit: also:* **~ ticket**) billete m sencillo; (*record*) sencillo, single m; **~s** *npl* (*TENNIS*) individual *msg*; **to ~ out** *vt* (*choose*) escoger; **~ bed** *n* cama individual; **~-breasted** *a* (*jacket, suit*) recto; **single-file** *n*: **in ~ file** en fila de uno; **~-handed** *ad* sin ayuda; **~-minded** *a* resuelto, firme; **~ room** *n* cuarto individual.
singlet ['sɪŋglɪt] *n* camiseta.
singly ['sɪŋglɪ] *ad* uno por uno.
singular ['sɪŋgjulə*] *a* (*odd*) raro, extraño; (*LING*) singular // *n* (*LING*) singular m.
sinister ['sɪnɪstə*] *a* siniestro.

sink [sɪŋk] *n* fregadero // *vb* (*pt* **sank**, *pp* **sunk**) *vt* (*ship*) hundir, echar a pique; (*foundations*) excavar; (*piles etc*): **to ~ sth into** hundir algo en // *vi* (*gen*) hundirse; **to ~ in** *vi* (*fig*) penetrar, calar.
sinner ['sɪnə*] *n* pecador(a) m/f.
sinus ['saɪnəs] *n* (*ANAT*) seno.
sip [sɪp] *n* sorbo // *vt* sorber, beber a sorbitos.
siphon ['saɪfən] *n* sifón m; **to ~ off** *vt* desviar.
sir [sə*] *n* señor m; **S~ John Smith** Sir John Smith; **yes ~** sí, señor.
siren ['saɪərn] *n* sirena.
sirloin ['səːlɔɪn] *n* solomillo.
sissy ['sɪsɪ] *n* (*col*) marica m.
sister ['sɪstə*] *n* hermana; (*Brit: nurse*) enfermera jefe; **~-in-law** *n* cuñada.
sit [sɪt], *pt, pp* **sat** *vi* sentarse; (*be sitting*) estar sentado; (*assembly*) reunirse // *vt* (*exam*) presentarse a; **to ~ down** *vi* sentarse; **to ~ in on** *vt fus* asistir a; **to ~ up** *vi* incorporarse; (*not go to bed*) velar.
sitcom ['sɪtkɔm] *n* abbr (= *situation comedy*) comedia de situación.
site [saɪt] *n* sitio; (*also:* **building ~**) solar m // *vt* situar.
sit-in ['sɪtɪn] *n* (*demonstration*) ocupación *f*.
sitting ['sɪtɪŋ] *n* (*of assembly etc*) sesión *f*; (*in canteen*) turno; **~ room** *n* sala de estar.
situated ['sɪtjueɪtɪd] *a* situado.
situation [sɪtju'eɪʃən] *n* situación *f*; '**~s vacant**' (*Brit*) 'ofrecen trabajo'.
six [sɪks] *num* seis; **~teen** *num* diez y seis, dieciséis; **~th** *a* sexto; **~ty** *num* sesenta.
size [saɪz] *n* (*gen*) tamaño; (*extent*) extensión *f*; (*of clothing*) talla; (*of shoes*) número; **to ~ up** *vt* formarse una idea de; **~able** *a* importante, considerable.
sizzle ['sɪzl] *vi* crepitar.
skate [skeɪt] *n* patín m; (*fish: pl inv*) raya // *vi* patinar; **~board** *n* monopatín m; **~r** *n* patinador(a) m/f; **skating** *n* patinaje m; **skating rink** *n* pista de patinaje.
skeleton ['skelɪtn] *n* esqueleto; (*TECH*) armazón *f*; (*outline*) esquema m; **~ key** *n* llave *f* maestra; **~ staff** *n* personal m reducido.
skeptic ['skeptɪk] *etc* (*US*) = **sceptic**.
sketch [sketʃ] *n* (*drawing*) dibujo; (*outline*) esbozo, bosquejo; (*THEATRE*) sketch m // *vt* dibujar; esbozar; **~ book** *n* libro de dibujos; **~y** *a* incompleto.
skewer ['skjuːə*] *n* broqueta.
ski [skiː] *n* esquí m // *vi* esquiar; **~ boot** *n* bota de esquí.
skid [skɪd] *n* patinazo // *vi* patinar.
ski: ~er *n* esquiador(a) m/f; **~ing** *n* esquí m; **~ jump** *n* salto con esquís.
skilful ['skɪlful] *a* diestro, experto.

ski lift n telesilla m, telesquí m.

skill [skɪl] n destreza, pericia; ~**ed** a hábil, diestro; (worker) cualificado.

skim [skɪm] vt (milk) desnatar; (glide over) rozar, rasar // vi: **to ~ through** (book) hojear; ~**med milk** n leche f desnatada.

skimp [skɪmp] vt (work) chapucear; (cloth etc) escatimar; ~**y** a (meagre) escaso; (skirt) muy corto.

skin [skɪn] n (gen) piel f; (complexion) cutis m // vt (fruit etc) pelar; (animal) despellejar; ~**deep** a superficial; ~ **diving** n buceo; ~**ny** a flaco; ~**tight** a (dress etc) muy ajustado.

skip [skɪp] n brinco, salto; (container) cuba // vi brincar; (with rope) saltar a la comba // vt (pass over) omitir, saltar.

ski pants npl pantalones mpl de esquí.

ski pole n bastón m de esquiar.

skipper ['skɪpə*] n (NAUT, SPORT) capitán m.

skipping rope ['skɪpɪŋ-] n (Brit) cuerda (de saltar).

skirmish ['skə:mɪʃ] n escaramuza.

skirt [skə:t] n falda, pollera (LAm) // vt (surround) ceñir, rodear; (go round) ladear.

ski suit n traje m de esquiar.

skit [skɪt] n sátira, parodia.

skittle ['skɪtl] n bolo; ~**s** n (game) boliche m.

skive [skaɪv] vi (Brit col) gandulear.

skulk [skʌlk] vi esconderse.

skull [skʌl] n calavera; (ANAT) cráneo.

skunk [skʌŋk] n mofeta.

sky [skaɪ] n cielo; ~**light** n tragaluz m, claraboya; ~**scraper** n rascacielos m inv.

slab [slæb] n (stone) bloque m; (flat) losa; (of cake) trozo.

slack [slæk] a (loose) flojo; (slow) de poca actividad; (careless) descuidado; ~**s** npl pantalones mpl; ~**en** (also: ~en off) vi aflojarse // vt aflojar; (speed) disminuir.

slag [slæg] n escoria, escombros mpl; ~ **heap** n escorial m, escombrera.

slain [sleɪn] pp of **slay**.

slam [slæm] vt (throw) arrojar (violentamente); **to ~ the door** dar un portazo // vi cerrarse de golpe.

slander ['slɑ:ndə*] n calumnia, difamación f // vt calumniar, difamar.

slang [slæŋ] n argot m; (jargon) jerga.

slant [slɑ:nt] n sesgo, inclinación f; (fig) interpretación f; ~**ed** a parcial; ~**ing** a inclinado.

slap [slæp] n palmada; (in face) bofetada // vt dar una palmada/bofetada a // ad (directly) exactamente, directamente; ~**dash** a descuidado; ~**stick** n: ~**stick comedy** comedia de golpe y porrazo; ~**up** a: a ~**up meal** (Brit) un banquetazo, una comilona.

slash [slæʃ] vt acuchillar; (fig: prices) quemar.

slat [slæt] n tablilla, listón m.

slate [sleɪt] n pizarra // vt (Brit: fig: criticize) criticar duramente.

slaughter ['slɔ:tə*] n (of animals) matanza; (of people) carnicería // vt matar; ~**house** n matadero.

Slav [slɑ:v] a eslavo.

slave [sleɪv] n esclavo/a // vi (also: ~ away) sudar tinta; ~**ry** n esclavitud f.

slay [sleɪ], pt **slew**, pp **slain** vt matar.

SLD n abbr = Social and Liberal Democrats.

sleazy ['sli:zɪ] a de mala fama.

sled [slɛd] n (US) trineo.

sledge [slɛdʒ] n (Brit) trineo; ~**hammer** n mazo.

sleek [sli:k] a (shiny) lustroso.

sleep [sli:p] n sueño // vi (pt, pp slept) dormir; **to go to ~** quedarse dormido; **to ~ in** vi (oversleep) quedarse dormido; ~**er** n (person) durmiente m/f; (Brit RAIL: on track) traviesa; (: train) coche-cama m; ~**ing bag** n saco de dormir; ~**ing car** n coche-cama m; ~**ing pill** n somnífero; ~**less** a: a ~**less night** una noche en blanco; ~**walker** n sonámbulo/a; ~**y** a soñoliento.

sleet [sli:t] n nevisca.

sleeve [sli:v] n manga; (TECH) manguito.

sleigh [sleɪ] n trineo.

sleight [slaɪt] n: ~ **of hand** escamoteo.

slender ['slɛndə*] a delgado; (means) escaso.

slept [slɛpt] pt, pp of **sleep**.

slew [slu:] vi (veer) torcerse // pt of **slay**.

slice [slaɪs] n (of meat) tajada; (of bread) rebanada; (of lemon) rodaja; (utensil) pala // vt cortar (en tajos); rebanar.

slick [slɪk] a (skilful) hábil, diestro // n (also: oil ~) marea negra.

slide [slaɪd] n (in playground) tobogán m; (PHOT) diapositiva; (Brit: also: **hair ~**) pasador m // vb (pt, pp slid) vt correr, deslizar // vi (slip) resbalarse; (glide) deslizarse; ~ **rule** n regla de cálculo; **sliding** a (door) corredizo; **sliding scale** n escala móvil.

slight [slaɪt] a (slim) delgado; (frail) delicado; (pain etc) leve; (trivial) insignificante; (small) pequeño // n desaire m // vt (offend) ofender, desairar; **not in the ~est** en absoluto; ~**ly** ad ligeramente, un poco.

slim [slɪm] a delgado, esbelto // vi adelgazar.

slime [slaɪm] n limo, cieno.

slimming ['slɪmɪŋ] n adelgazamiento.

sling [slɪŋ] n (MED) cabestrillo; (weapon) honda // vt (pt, pp slung) tirar, arrojar.

slip [slɪp] n (slide) resbalón m; (mistake) descuido; (underskirt) combinación f; (of paper) papelito // vt (slide) deslizar //

vi (*slide*) deslizarse; (*stumble*) resbalar(se); (*decline*) decaer; (*move smoothly*): **to ~ into/out of** (*room etc*) introducirse en/salirse de; **to give sh the ~**: eludir a uno; **a ~ of the tongue** un lapsus; **to ~ sth on/off** ponerse/quitarse algo; **to ~ away** *vi* escabullirse; **to ~ in** *vt* meter // *vi* meterse; **to ~ out** *vi* (*go out*) salir (un momento); **~ped disc** *n* vértebra dislocada.

slipper ['slɪpə*] *n* zapatilla, pantufla.

slippery ['slɪpərɪ] *a* resbaladizo.

slip: **~ road** *n* (*Brit*) carretera de acceso; **~shod** *a* descuidado; **~up** *n* (*error*) desliz *m*; **~way** *n* grada, gradas *fpl*.

slit [slɪt] *n* raja; (*cut*) corte *m* // *vt* (*pt, pp* **slit**) rajar, cortar.

slither ['slɪðə*] *vi* deslizarse.

sliver ['slɪvə*] *n* (*of glass, wood*) astilla; (*of cheese etc*) raja.

slob [slɒb] *n* (*col*) patán/ana *m/f*.

slog [slɒg] (*Brit*) *vi* sudar tinta; **it was a ~** costó trabajo (hacerlo).

slogan ['sləugən] *n* eslogan *m*, lema *m*.

slop [slɒp] *vi* (*also*: **~ over**) derramarse, desbordarse // *vt* derramar, verter.

slope [sləup] *n* (*up*) cuesta, pendiente *f*; (*down*) declive *m*; (*side of mountain*) falda, vertiente *m* // *vi*: **to ~ down** estar en declive; **to ~ up** inclinarse; **sloping** *a* en pendiente; en declive.

sloppy ['slɒpɪ] *a* (*work*) descuidado; (*appearance*) desaliñado.

slot [slɒt] *n* ranura // *vt*: **to ~ into** encajar en.

sloth [sləuθ] *n* (*laziness*) pereza.

slot machine *n* (*Brit*: *vending machine*) aparato vendedor, distribuidor *m* automático; (*for gambling*) máquina tragaperras.

slouch [slautʃ] *vi*: **to ~ about** (*laze*) gandulear.

slovenly ['slʌvənlɪ] *a* (*dirty*) desaliñado, desaseado; (*careless*) descuidado.

slow [sləu] *a* lento; (*watch*): **to be ~** atrasarse // *ad* lentamente, despacio // *vi, vi* (*also*: **~ down, ~ up**) retardar; **'~'** (*road sign*) 'disminuir velocidad'; **~ down** *n* (*US*) huelga de manos caídas; **~ly** *ad* lentamente, despacio; **slow motion** *n*: **in ~ motion** a cámara lenta.

sludge [slʌdʒ] *n* lodo, fango.

slug [slʌg] *n* babosa; (*bullet*) posta; **~gish** *a* (*slow*) lento; (*lazy*) perezoso.

sluice [slu:s] *n* (*gate*) esclusa; (*channel*) canal *m*.

slum [slʌm] *n* casucha.

slumber ['slʌmbə*] *n* sueño.

slump [slʌmp] *n* (*economic*) depresión *f* // *vi* hundirse.

slung [slʌŋ] *pt, pp of* **sling**.

slur [slə:*] *n* calumnia // *vt* calumniar, difamar; (*word*) pronunciar mal.

slush [slʌʃ] *n* nieve *f* a medio derretir; **~**

fund *n* caja negra (*fondos para sobornar*).

slut [slʌt] *n* (*sloppy*) marrana.

sly [slaɪ] *a* astuto.

smack [smæk] *n* (*slap*) manotada; (*blow*) golpe *m* // *vt* dar una manotada a; golpear con la mano // *vi*: **to ~ of** saber a, oler a.

small [smɔ:l] *a* pequeño; **~ ads** *npl* (*Brit*) anuncios *mpl* por palabras; **~ change** *n* suelto, cambio; **~holder** *n* (*Brit*) granjero/a, parcelero/a; **~ hours** *npl*: **in the ~ hours** en las altas horas (de la noche); **~pox** *n* viruela; **~ talk** *n* cháchara.

smart [smɑ:t] *a* elegante; (*clever*) listo, inteligente; (*quick*) rápido, vivo // *vi* escocer, picar; **to ~en up** *vi* arreglarse // *vt* arreglar.

smash [smæʃ] *n* (*also*: **~-up**) choque *m* // *vt* (*break*) hacer pedazos; (*car etc*) estrellar; (*SPORT*: *record*) batir // *vi* hacerse pedazos; (*against wall etc*) estrellarse; **~ing** *a* (*col*) cojonudo.

smattering ['smætərɪŋ] *n*: **a ~ of** Spanish algo de español.

smear [smɪə*] *n* mancha; (*MED*) frotis *m inv* // *vt* untar; (*fig*) calumniar, difamar.

smell [smɛl] *n* olor *m*; (*sense*) olfato // (*pt, pp* **smelt** *or* **smelled**) *vt, vi* oler; **it ~s good/of garlic** huele bien/a ajo; **~y** *a* maloliente.

smile [smaɪl] *n* sonrisa // *vi* sonreír; **smiling** *a* sonriente.

smirk [smə:k] *n* sonrisa falsa *or* afectada.

smith [smɪθ] *n* herrero; **~y** ['smɪðɪ] *n* herrería.

smock [smɒk] *n* blusa; (*children's*) delantal *m*; (*US*: *overall*) guardapolvo.

smog [smɒg] *n* esmog *m*.

smoke [sməuk] *n* humo // *vi* fumar; (*chimney*) echar humo // *vt* (*cigarettes*) fumar; **~d** *a* (*bacon, glass*) ahumado; **~r** *n* (*person*) fumador(a) *m/f*; (*RAIL*) coche *m* fumador; **~ screen** *n* cortina de humo; **~ shop** *n* (*US*) estanco, tabaquería (*LAm*); **smoking** *n*: '**no smoking**' 'prohibido fumar'; **smoky** *a* (*room*) lleno de humo.

smolder ['sməuldə*] *vi* (*US*) = **smoulder**.

smooth [smu:ð] *a* liso; (*sea*) tranquilo; (*flavour, movement*) suave; (*person*: *pej*) meloso // *vt* alisar; (*also*: **~ out**: *creases, difficulties*) allanar.

smother ['smʌðə*] *vt* sofocar; (*repress*) contener

smoulder, (*US*) **smolder** ['sməuldə*] *vi* arder sin llama.

smudge [smʌdʒ] *n* mancha // *vt* manchar.

smug [smʌg] *a* presumido.

smuggle ['smʌgl] *vt* pasar de contrabando; **~r** *n* contrabandista *m/f*; **smuggling** *n* contrabando.

smutty ['smʌtɪ] *a* (*fig*) verde, obsceno.
snack [snæk] *n* bocado; ~ **bar** *n* cafetería.
snag [snæg] *n* problema *m*.
snail [sneɪl] *n* caracol *m*.
snake [sneɪk] *n* (*gen*) serpiente *f*; (*harmless*) culebra; (*poisonous*) víbora.
snap [snæp] *n* (*sound*) chasquido; golpe *m* seco; (*photograph*) foto *f* ‖ *a* (*decision*) instantáneo ‖ *vt* (*fingers etc*) castañetear; (*break*) quebrar; (*photograph*) tomar una foto de ‖ *vi* (*break*) quebrarse; (*fig: person*) contestar bruscamente; **to ~ shut** cerrarse de golpe; **to ~ at** *vt fus* (*subj: dog*) intentar morder; **to ~ off** *vi* (*break*) partirse; **to ~ up** *vt* agarrar; ~ **fastener** *n* (*US*) botón *m* de presión; ~**py** *a* (*col: answer*) instantáneo; (*slogan*) conciso; **make it ~py!** (*hurry up*) ¡date prisa!; ~**shot** *n* foto *f* (instantánea).
snare [snɛə*] *n* trampa ‖ *vt* cazar con trampa; (*fig*) engañar.
snarl [snɑːl] *n* gruñido ‖ *vi* gruñir.
snatch [snætʃ] *n* (*fig*) robo; ~**es of** trocitos *mpl* de ‖ *vt* (~ *away*) arrebatar; (*grasp*) coger (*Sp*), agarrar.
sneak [sniːk] *vi*: **to ~ in/out** entrar/salir a hurtadillas ‖ *n* (*col*) soplón/ona *m/f*; ~**ers** *npl* (*US*) zapatos *mpl* de lona; ~**y** *a* furtivo.
sneer [snɪə*] *vi* sonreír con desprecio.
sneeze [sniːz] *vi* estornudar.
sniff [snɪf] *vi* sorber (por la nariz) ‖ *vt* husmear, oler.
snigger ['snɪgə*] *vi* reírse con disimulo.
snip [snɪp] *n* (*piece*) recorte *m*; (*bargain*) ganga ‖ *vt* tijeretear.
sniper ['snaɪpə*] *n* francotirador(a) *m/f*.
snippet ['snɪpɪt] *n* retazo.
snivelling ['snɪvlɪŋ] *a* llorón/ona.
snob [snɔb] *n* (e)snob *m/f*; ~**bery** *n* (e)snobismo; ~**bish** *a* (e)snob.
snooker ['snuːkə*] *n* especie de billar.
snoop [snuːp] *vi*: **to ~ about** fisgonear.
snooty ['snuːtɪ] *a* (e)snob.
snooze [snuːz] *n* siesta ‖ *vi* echar una siesta.
snore [snɔː*] *vi* roncar; **snoring** *n* ronquidos *mpl*.
snorkel ['snɔːkl] *n* (tubo) respirador *m*.
snort [snɔːt] *n* bufido ‖ *vi* bufar.
snout [snaut] *n* hocico, morro.
snow [snəu] *n* nieve *f* ‖ *vi* nevar; ~**ball** *n* bola de nieve; ~**bound** *a* bloqueado por la nieve; ~**drift** *n* ventisquero; ~**drop** *n* campanilla; ~**fall** *n* nevada; ~**flake** *n* copo de nieve; ~**man** *n* figura de nieve; ~**plough**, (*US*) ~**plow** *n* quitanieves *m inv*; ~**shoe** *n* raqueta (de nieve); ~**storm** *n* nevada, nevasca.
snub [snʌb] *vt*: **to ~ sb** desairar a alguien ‖ *n* desaire *m*, repulsa; ~**-nosed** *a* chato.
snuff [snʌf] *n* rapé *m*.

snug [snʌg] *a* (*cosy*) cómodo; (*fitted*) ajustado.
snuggle ['snʌgl] *vi*:. **to ~ up to sb** arrimarse a uno.
so [səu] ♦ *ad* **1** (*thus, likewise*) así, de este modo; **if ~** de ser así; **I like swimming — ~ do I** a mí me gusta nadar — a mí también; **I've got work to do — ~ has Paul** tengo trabajo que hacer — Paul también; **it's 5 o'clock — ~ it is!** son las cinco — ¡pues es verdad!; **I hope/think ~** espero/creo que sí; ~ **far** hasta ahora; (*in past*) hasta este momento
2 (*in comparisons etc: to such a degree*) tan; ~ **quickly (that)** tan rápido (que); ~ **big (that)** tan grande (que); **she's not ~ clever as her brother** no es tan lista como su hermano; **we were ~ worried** estábamos preocupadísimos
3: ~ **much** *a* tanto/a ‖ *ad* tanto; ~ **many** tantos/as
4 (*phrases*): **10 or ~** unos 10, 10 o así; ~ **long!** (*col: goodbye*) ¡hasta luego!
♦ *conj* **1** (*expressing purpose*): ~ **as to do** para hacer; ~ **(that)** para que + *subjun*
2 (*expressing result*) así que; ~ **you see, I could have gone** así que ya ves, (yo) podría haber ido.
soak [səuk] *vt* (*drench*) empapar; (*put in water*) remojar ‖ *vi* remojarse, estar a remojo; **to ~ in** *vi* penetrar; **to ~ up** *vt* absorber.
so-and-so ['səuənsəu] *n* (*somebody*) fulano/a de tal.
soap [səup] *n* jabón *m*; ~**flakes** *npl* escamas *fpl* de jabón; ~ **opera** *n* telenovela; ~ **powder** *n* jabón *m* en polvo; ~**y** *a* jabonoso.
soar [sɔː*] *vi* (*on wings*) remontarse; (*building etc*) elevarse.
sob [sɔb] *n* sollozo ‖ *vi* sollozar.
sober ['səubə*] *a* (*moderate*) moderado; (*not drunk*) sobrio; (*colour, style*) discreto; **to ~ up** *vi* pasársele a uno la borrachera.
so-called ['səu'kɔːld] *a* así llamado.
soccer ['sɔkə*] *n* fútbol *m*.
social ['səuʃl] *a* social ‖ *n* velada, fiesta; ~ **club** *n* club *m*; ~**ism** *n* socialismo; ~**ist** *a*, *n* socialista *m/f*; ~**ize** *vi*: **to ~ize (with)** alternar (con); ~**ly** *ad* socialmente; ~ **security** *n* seguridad *f* social; ~ **work** *n* asistencia social; ~ **worker** *n* asistente/a *m/f* social.
society [sə'saɪətɪ] *n* sociedad *f*; (*club*) asociación *f*; (*also*: **high ~**) buena sociedad.
sociologist [səusɪ'ɔlədʒɪst] *n* sociólogo/a.
sociology [səusɪ'ɔlədʒi] *n* sociología.
sock [sɔk] *n* calcetín *m*, media (*LAm*).
socket ['sɔkɪt] *n* (*ELEC*) enchufe *m*.
sod [sɔd] *n* (*of earth*) césped *m*; (*col!*) cabrón/ona *m/f* (!).
soda ['səudə] *n* (*CHEM*) sosa; (*also*: ~

water) soda; (*US: also:* ~ **pop**) gaseosa.
sodden ['sɔdn] *a* empapado.
sodium ['səʊdɪəm] *n* sodio.
sofa ['səʊfə] *n* sofá *m*.
soft [sɒft] *a* (*not hard, lenient*) blando; (*gentle, not loud*) suave; (*stupid*) bobo; ~ **drink** *n* bebida no alcohólica; ~**en** ['sɒfn] *vt* ablandar; suavizar // *vi* ablandarse; suavizarse; ~**ly** *ad* suavemente; (*gently*) delicadamente, con delicadeza; ~**ness** *n* blandura; suavidad *f*; ~**ware** *n* (*COMPUT*) software *m*.
soggy ['sɔgɪ] *a* empapado.
soil [sɔɪl] *n* (*earth*) tierra, suelo // *vt* ensuciar; ~**ed** *a* sucio.
solace ['sɔlɪs] *n* consuelo.
sold [səʊld] *pt, pp of* sell; ~ **out** *a* (*COMM*) agotado.
solder ['səʊldə*] *vt* soldar // *n* soldadura.
soldier ['səʊldʒə*] *n* (*gen*) soldado; (*army man*) militar *m*.
sole [səʊl] *n* (*of foot*) planta; (*of shoe*) suela; (*fish: pl inv*) lenguado // *a* único.
solemn ['sɔləm] *a* solemne.
solicit [sə'lɪsɪt] *vt* (*request*) solicitar // *vi* (*prostitute*) importunar.
solicitor [sə'lɪsɪtə*] *n* (*Brit: for wills etc*) ≈ notario/a; (: *in court*) ≈ abogado/a.
solid ['sɔlɪd] *a* sólido; (*gold etc*) macizo // *n* sólido.
solidarity [sɔlɪ'dærɪtɪ] *n* solidaridad *f*.
solitaire [sɔlɪ'tɛə*] *n* (*game, gem*) solitario.
solitary ['sɔlɪtərɪ] *a* solitario, solo; ~ **confinement** *n* incomunicación *f*.
solitude ['sɔlɪtjuːd] *n* soledad *f*.
solo ['səʊləʊ] *n* solo; ~**ist** *n* solista *m/f*.
solution [sə'luːʃən] *n* solución *f*.
solve [sɔlv] *vt* resolver, solucionar.
solvent ['sɔlvənt] *a* (*COMM*) solvente // *n* (*CHEM*) solvente *m*.
sombre, (*US*) **somber** ['sɔmbə*] *a* sombrío.
some [sʌm] ♦ *a* 1 (*a certain amount or number of*): ~ **tea/water/biscuits** té/agua/(unas) galletas; **there's** ~ **milk in the fridge** hay leche en el frigo; **there were** ~ **people outside** había algunas personas fuera; **I've got** ~ **money, but not much** tengo algo de dinero, pero no mucho
2 (*certain: in contrasts*) algunos/as; ~ **people say that ...** hay quien dice que ...; ~ **films were excellent, but most were mediocre** hubo películas excelentes, pero la mayoría fueron mediocres
3 (*unspecified*): ~ **woman was asking for you** una mujer estuvo preguntando por ti; **he was asking for** ~ **book (or other)** pedía un libro; ~ **day** algún día; ~ **day next week** un día de la semana que viene
♦ *pron* 1 (*a certain number*): **I've got** ~ (*books etc*) tengo algunos/as
2 (*a certain amount*) algo; **I've got** ~

(*money, milk*) tengo algo; **could I have** ~ **of that cheese?** ¿me puede dar un poco de ese queso?; **I've read** ~ **of the book** he leído parte del libro
♦ *ad*: ~ **10 people** unas 10 personas, una decena de personas
somebody ['sʌmbədɪ] *pron* = **someone**.
somehow ['sʌmhaʊ] *ad* de alguna manera; (*for some reason*) por una u otra razón.
someone ['sʌmwʌn] *pron* alguien.
someplace ['sʌmpleɪs] *ad* (*US*) = **somewhere**.
somersault ['sʌməsɔːlt] *n* (*deliberate*) salto mortal; (*accidental*) vuelco // *vi* dar un salto mortal; dar vuelcos.
something ['sʌmθɪŋ] *pron* algo; **would you like** ~ **to eat/drink?** ¿te gustaría cenar/tomar algo?
sometime ['sʌmtaɪm] *ad* (*in future*) algún día, en algún momento; ~ **last month** durante el mes pasado.
sometimes ['sʌmtaɪmz] *ad* a veces.
somewhat ['sʌmwɔt] *ad* algo.
somewhere ['sʌmwɛə*] *ad* (*be*) en alguna parte; (*go*) a alguna parte; ~ **else** (*be*) en otra parte; (*go*) a otra parte.
son [sʌn] *n* hijo.
song [sɔŋ] *n* canción *f*.
sonic ['sɔnɪk] *a* (*boom*) sónico.
son-in-law ['sʌnɪnlɔː] *n* yerno.
sonnet ['sɔnɪt] *n* soneto.
sonny ['sʌnɪ] *n* (*col*) hijo.
soon [suːn] *ad* pronto, dentro de poco; ~ **afterwards** poco después; *see also* as; ~**er** *ad* (*time*) antes, más temprano; **I would** ~**er do that** preferiría hacer eso; ~**er or later** tarde o temprano.
soot [sʊt] *n* hollín *m*.
soothe [suːð] *vt* tranquilizar; (*pain*) aliviar.
sophisticated [sə'fɪstɪkeɪtɪd] *a* sofisticado.
sophomore ['sɔfəmɔː*] *n* (*US*) estudiante *m/f* de segundo año.
soporific [sɔpə'rɪfɪk] *a* soporífero.
sopping ['sɔpɪŋ] *a*: ~ (*wet*) empapado.
soppy ['sɔpɪ] *a* (*pej*) bobo, tonto.
soprano [sə'prɑːnəʊ] *n* soprano *f*.
sorcerer ['sɔːsərə*] *n* hechicero.
sore [sɔː*] *a* (*painful*) doloroso, que duele; (*offended*) resentido // *n* llaga; ~**ly** *ad*: **I am** ~**ly tempted to** estoy muy tentado a.
sorrow ['sɔrəʊ] *n* pena, dolor *m*.
sorry ['sɔrɪ] *a* (*regretful*) arrepentido; (*condition, excuse*) lastimoso; ~! ¡perdón!, ¡perdone!; **to feel** ~ **for sb** tener lástima a uno; **I feel** ~ **for him** me da lástima.
sort [sɔːt] *n* clase *f*, género, tipo // *vt* (*also:* ~ **out:** *papers*) clasificar; (: *problems*) arreglar, solucionar; ~**ing office** *n* sala de batalla.

SOS *n abbr* (= *save our souls*) SOS *m*.
so-so ['sausau] *ad* regular, así así.
soufflé ['su:fleɪ] *n* suflé *m*.
sought [sɔ:t] *pt, pp of* **seek**.
soul [saul] *n* alma *f*; **~-destroying** *a* (*work*) deprimente; **~ful** *a* lleno de sentimiento.
sound [saund] *a* (*healthy*) sano; (*safe, not damaged*) en buen estado; (*reliable: person*) digno de confianza; (*sensible*) sensato, razonable // *ad*: ~ **asleep** profundamente dormido // *n* (*noise*) sonido, ruido; (*GEO*) estrecho // *vt* (*alarm*) sonar; (*also*: ~ **out**: *opinions*) consultar, sondear // *vi* sonar, resonar; (*fig: seem*) parecer; **to** ~ **like** sonar a; ~ **barrier** *n* barrera del sonido; ~ **effects** *npl* efectos *mpl* sonoros; **~ing** *n* (*NAUT etc*) sondeo; **~ly** *ad* (*sleep*) profundamente; (*beat*) completamente; **~proof** *a* insonorizado; **~track** *n* (*of film*) banda sonora.
soup [su:p] *n* (*thick*) sopa; (*thin*) caldo; **in the** ~ (*fig*) en apuros; ~ **plate** *n* plato sopero; **~spoon** *n* cuchara sopera.
sour ['saua*] *a* agrio; (*milk*) cortado; it's just ~ **grapes**! (*fig*) ¡están verdes!
source [sɔ:s] *n* fuente *f*.
south [sauθ] *n* sur *m* // *a* del sur // *ad* al sur, hacia el sur; **S~ Africa** *n* África del Sur; **S~ African** *a, n* sudafricano/a; **S~ America** *n* América del Sur, Sudamérica; **S~ American** *a, n* sudamericano/a *m/f*; **~-east** *n* sudeste *m*; **~erly** ['sʌðəlɪ] *a* sur; (*from the* ~) del sur; **~ern** ['sʌðən] *a* del sur, meridional; **S~ Pole** *n* Polo Sur; **~ward(s)** *ad* hacia el sur; **~-west** *n* suroeste *m*.
souvenir [su:vəˈnɪə*] *n* recuerdo.
sovereign ['sɔvrɪn] *a, n* soberano/a *m/f*.
soviet ['səuvɪət] *a* soviético; **the S~ Union** la Unión Soviética.
sow [sau] *n* cerda, puerca // *vt* ([səu], *pt* sowed, *pp* sown [səun]) (*gen*) sembrar.
soya ['sɔɪə], (*US*) **soy** [sɔɪ] *n* soja.
spa [spa:] *n* balneario.
space [speɪs] *n* espacio; (*room*) sitio // *vt* (*also*: ~ **out**) espaciar; **~craft** *n* nave *f* espacial; **~man/woman** *n* astronauta *m/f*, cosmonauta *m/f*; **~ship** *n* = ~**craft**; **spacing** *n* espaciamiento.
spacious ['speɪʃəs] *a* amplio.
spade [speɪd] *n* (*tool*) pala, laya; **~s** *npl* (*CARDS: British*) picos *mpl*; (: *Spanish*) espadas *fpl*.
spaghetti [spəˈgetɪ] *n* espaguetis *mpl*, fideos *mpl*.
Spain [speɪn] *n* España.
span [spæn] *n* (*of bird, plane*) envergadura; (*of hand*) palmo; (*of arch*) luz *f*; (*in time*) lapso // *vt* extenderse sobre, cruzar; (*fig*) abarcar.
Spaniard ['spænjəd] *n* español(a) *m/f*.
spaniel ['spænjəl] *n* perro de aguas.
Spanish ['spænɪʃ] *a* español(a) // *n*

(*LING*) español *m*, castellano; **the** ~ *npl* los españoles.
spank [spæŋk] *vt* zurrar.
spanner ['spænə*] *n* (*Brit*) llave *f* (inglesa).
spar [spa:*] *n* palo, verga // *vi* (*BOXING*) entrenarse.
spare [spɛə*] *a* de reserva; (*surplus*) sobrante, de más // *n* (*part*) pieza de repuesto // *vt* (*do without*) pasarse sin; (*afford to give*) tener de sobra; (*refrain from hurting*) perdonar; (*details etc*) ahorrar; **to** ~ (*surplus*) sobrante, de sobra; ~ **part** *n* pieza de repuesto; ~ **time** *n* tiempo libre; ~ **wheel** *n* (*AUT*) rueda de recambio.
sparing ['spɛərɪŋ] *a*: **to be** ~ **with** ser parco en; **~ly** *ad* poco; con moderación.
spark [spa:k] *n* chispa; ~ **plug,** (*Brit*) **~ing plug** *n* bujía.
sparkle ['spa:kl] *n* centelleo, destello // *vi* centellear; (*shine*) relucir, brillar; **sparkling** *a* centelleante; (*wine*) espumoso.
sparrow ['spærəu] *n* gorrión *m*.
sparse [spa:s] *a* esparcido, escaso.
spartan ['spa:tən] *a* (*fig*) espartano.
spasm ['spæzəm] *n* (*MED*) espasmo; (*fig*) arranque *m*, ataque *m*.
spastic ['spæstɪk] *n* espástico/a.
spat [spæt] *pt, pp of* **spit**.
spate [speɪt] *n* (*fig*): ~ **of** torrente *m* de; **in** ~ (*river*) crecido.
spatter ['spætə*] *vt*: **to** ~ **with** salpicar de.
spawn [spɔ:n] *vi* desovar, frezar // *n* huevas *fpl*.
speak [spi:k], *pt* **spoke,** *pp* **spoken** *vt* (*language*) hablar; (*truth*) decir // *vi* hablar; (*make a speech*) intervenir; **to** ~ **to sb/of** *or* **about sth** hablar con uno/de *or* sobre algo; ~ **up!** ¡habla fuerte!; **~er** *n* (*in public*) orador(a) *m/f*; (*also*: **loud~er**) altavoz *m*; (*for stereo etc*) bafle *m*; (*POL*): **the S~er** (*Brit*) el Presidente de la Cámara de los Comunes; (*US*) el Presidente del Congreso.
spear [spɪə*] *n* lanza; (*for fishing*) arpón *m* // *vt* alancear; arponear; **~head** *vt* (*attack etc*) encabezar.
spec [spek] *n* (*col*): **on** ~ como especulación.
special ['speʃl] *a* especial; (*edition etc*) extraordinario; (*delivery*) urgente; **~ist** *n* especialista *m/f*; **~ity** [speʃɪˈælɪtɪ] *n* (*Brit*) especialidad *f*; **~ize** *vi*: **to** ~**ize** (**in**) especializarse (en); **~ly** *ad* sobre todo, en particular; **~ty** *n* (*US*) = **~ity**.
species ['spi:ʃi:z] *n* especie *f*.
specific [spəˈsɪfɪk] *a* específico; **~ally** *ad* específicamente.
specify ['spesɪfaɪ] *vt, vi* especificar, precisar.
specimen ['spesɪmən] *n* ejemplar *m*; (*MED: of urine*) espécimen *m* (: *of*

blood) muestra.

speck [spɛk] *n* grano, mota.

speckled ['spɛkld] *a* moteado.

specs [spɛks] *npl* (*col*) gafas *fpl* (*Sp*), anteojos *mpl*.

spectacle ['spɛktəkl] *n* espectáculo; **~s** *npl* (*Brit*) gafas *fpl* (*Sp*), anteojos *mpl*; **spectacular** [-'tækjulə*] *a* espectacular; (*success*) impresionante.

spectator [spɛk'teɪtə*] *n* espectador(a) *m/f*.

spectre, (*US*) **specter** ['spɛktə*] *n* espectro, fantasma *m*.

spectrum ['spɛktrəm], *pl* **-tra** [-trə] *n* espectro.

speculation [spɛkju'leɪʃən] *n* especulación *f*.

speech [spiːtʃ] *n* (*faculty*) habla; (*formal talk*) discurso; (*words*) palabras *fpl*; (*manner of speaking*) forma de hablar; lenguaje *m*; **~less** *a* mudo, estupefacto.

speed [spiːd] *n* velocidad *f*; (*haste*) prisa; (*promptness*) rapidez *f*; at full or top **~** a máxima velocidad; **to ~ up** *vi* acelerarse // *vt* acelerar; **~boat** *n* lancha motora; **~ily** *ad* rápido, rápidamente; **~ing** *n* (*AUT*) exceso de velocidad; **~ limit** *n* límite *m* de velocidad, velocidad *f* máxima; **~ometer** [spɪ'dɒmɪtə*] *n* velocímetro; **~way** *n* (*SPORT*) pista de carrera; **~y** *a* (*fast*) veloz, rápido; (*prompt*) pronto.

spell [spɛl] *n* (*also*: **magic ~**) encanto, hechizo; (*period of time*) rato, período; (*turn*) turno // *vt* (*pt*, *pp* **spelt** (*Brit*) or **spelled**) (*also*: **~ out**) deletrear; (*fig*) anunciar, presagiar; **to cast a ~ on sb** hechizar a uno; **he can't ~** no sabe escribir bien, sabe poco de ortografía; **~bound** *a* embelesado, hechizado; **~ing** *n* ortografía.

spend [spɛnd], *pt*, *pp* **spent** [spɛnt] *vt* (*money*) gastar; (*time*) pasar; (*life*) dedicar; **~thrift** *n* derrochador(a) *m/f*, pródigo/a.

sperm [spəːm] *n* esperma.

spew [spjuː] *vt* vomitar, arrojar.

sphere [sfɪə*] *n* esfera.

spice [spaɪs] *n* especia.

spick-and-span ['spɪkən'spæn] *a* aseado, (bien) arreglado.

spider ['spaɪdə*] *n* araña.

spike [spaɪk] *n* (*point*) punta; (*ZOOL*) pincho, púa; (*BOT*) espiga.

spill [spɪl], *pt*, *pp* **spilt** or **spilled** *vt* derramar, verter // *vi* derramarse; **to ~ over** desbordarse.

spin [spɪn] *n* (*revolution of wheel*) vuelta, revolución *f*; (*AVIAT*) barrena; (*trip in car*) paseo (en coche) // *vb* (*pt*, *pp* **spun**) *vt* (*wool etc*) hilar; (*wheel*) girar // *vi* girar, dar vueltas; **to ~ out** *vt* alargar, prolongar.

spinach ['spɪnɪtʃ] *n* espinaca; (*as food*) espinacas *fpl*.

spinal ['spaɪnl] *a* espinal; **~ cord** *n* columna vertebral.

spindly ['spɪndlɪ] *a* (*leg*) zanquivano.

spin-dryer [spɪn'draɪə*] *n* (*Brit*) secador *m* centrífugo.

spine [spaɪn] *n* espinazo, columna vertebral; (*thorn*) espina.

spinning ['spɪnɪŋ] *n* (*of thread*) hilado; (*art*) hilandería; **~ top** *n* peonza; **~ wheel** *n* rueca, torno de hilar.

spin-off ['spɪnɒf] *n* derivado, producto secundario.

spinster ['spɪnstə*] *n* soltera.

spiral ['spaɪərl] *n* espiral *f* // *a* en espiral; **~ staircase** *n* escalera de caracol.

spire ['spaɪə*] *n* aguja, chapitel *m*.

spirit ['spɪrɪt] *n* (*soul*) alma *f*; (*ghost*) fantasma *m*; (*attitude*) espíritu *m*; (*courage*) valor *m*, ánimo; **~s** *npl* (*drink*) alcohol *msg*, bebidas *fpl* alcohólicas; **in good ~s** alegre, de buen ánimo; **~ed** *a* enérgico, vigoroso; **~ level** *n* nivel *m* de aire.

spiritual ['spɪrɪtjuəl] *a* espiritual.

spit [spɪt] *n* (*for roasting*) asador *m*, espetón *m* // *vi* (*pt*, *pp* **spat**) escupir; (*sound*) chisporrotear.

spite [spaɪt] *n* rencor *m*, ojeriza // *vt* causar pena a, mortificar; **in ~ of** a pesar de, pese a; **~ful** *a* rencoroso, malévolo.

spittle ['spɪtl] *n* saliva, baba.

splash [splæʃ] *n* (*sound*) chapoteo; (*of colour*) mancha // *vt* salpicar de // *vi* (*also*: **~ about**) chapotear.

spleen [spliːn] *n* (*ANAT*) bazo.

splendid ['splɛndɪd] *a* espléndido.

splint [splɪnt] *n* tablilla.

splinter ['splɪntə*] *n* (*of wood*) astilla; (*in finger*) espigón *m* // *vi* astillarse, hacer astillas.

split [splɪt] *n* hendedura, raja; (*fig*) división *f*; (*POL*) escisión *f* // *vb* (*pt*, *pp* **split**) *vt* partir, rajar; (*party*) dividir; (*work*, *profits*) repartir // *vi* (*divide*) dividirse, escindirse; **to ~ up** *vi* (*couple*) separarse; (*meeting*) acabarse.

splutter ['splʌtə*] *vi* chisporrotear; (*person*) balbucear.

spoil [spɔɪl], *pt*, *pp* **spoilt** or **spoiled** *vt* (*damage*) dañar; (*ruin*) estropear, echar a perder; (*child*) mimar, consentir; **~s** *npl* despojo *sg*, botín *msg*; **~ed** *a* (*US*: *food*: *bad*) pasado, malo; (: *milk*) cortado; **~sport** *n* aguafiestas *m inv*.

spoke [spəuk] *pt* of **speak** // *n* rayo, radio.

spoken ['spəukn] *pp* of **speak**.

spokesman ['spəuksmən] *n*, **spokeswoman** [-wumən] *n* vocero *m/f*, portavoz *m/f*.

sponge [spʌndʒ] *n* esponja // *vt* (*wash*) lavar con esponja // *vi*: **to ~ off** or **on sb** vivir a costa de uno; **~ bag** *n* (*Brit*) esponjera; **~ cake** *n* bizcocho.

sponsor ['spɒnsə*] *n* (*RADIO*, *TV*) patrocinador(a) *m/f*; (*for membership*) padrino/madrina; (*COMM*) fiador(a) *m/f* // *vt* patrocinar; apadrinar; (*idea etc*) presentar, promover; **~ship** *n* patrocinio.

spontaneous [spɔn'teɪnɪəs] *a* espontáneo.

spooky ['spu:kɪ] *a* espeluznante, horripilante.

spool [spu:l] *n* carrete *m*; (*of sewing machine*) canilla.

spoon [spu:n] *n* cuchara; **~-feed** *vt* dar de comer con cuchara a; (*fig*) tratar como a un niño a; **~ful** *n* cucharada.

sport [spɔ:t] *n* deporte *m*; (*person*): to be a good ~ ser muy majo; **~ing** *a* deportivo; to give sb a ~ing chance darle a uno una (buena) oportunidad; **~s car** *n* coche *m* sport; **~s jacket**, (*US*) ~ **jacket** *n* chaqueta deportiva; **~sman** *n* deportista *m*; **~smanship** *n* deportividad *f*; **~swear** *n* trajes *mpl* de deporte *or* sport; **~swoman** *n* deportista; **~y** *a* deportivo.

spot [spɔt] *n* sitio, lugar *m*; (*dot: on pattern*) punto, mancha; (*pimple*) grano; (*small amount*): a ~ of un poquito de // *vt* (*notice*) notar, observar; on the ~ en el acto, acto seguido; ~ **check** *n* reconocimiento rápido; **~less** *a* perfectamente limpio; **~light** *n* foco, reflector *m*; (*AUT*) faro auxiliar; **~ted** *a* (*pattern*) de puntos; **~ty** *a* (*face*) con granos.

spouse [spauz] *n* cónyuge *m/f*.

spout [spaut] *n* (*of jug*) pico; (*pipe*) caño // *vi* chorrear.

sprain [spreɪn] *n* torcedura // *vt*: to ~ one's ankle torcerse el tobillo.

sprang [spræŋ] *pt of* **spring**.

sprawl [sprɔ:l] *vi* tumbarse.

spray [spreɪ] *n* rociada; (*of sea*) espuma; (*container*) atomizador *m*; (*of paint*) pistola rociadora; (*of flowers*) ramita // *vt* rociar; (*crops*) regar.

spread [spred] *n* extensión *f*; (*of idea*) diseminación *f*; (*food*) pasta para untar // *vb* (*pt, pp* **spread**) *vt* extender; diseminar; (*butter*) untar; (*wings, sails*) desplegar; (*scatter*) esparcir // *vi* extenderse; diseminarse; untarse; desplegarse; esparcirse; **~-eagled** *a* a pata tendida; **~sheet** *n* (*COMPUT*) hoja electrónica *or* de cálculo.

spree [spri:] *n*: to go on a ~ ir de juerga.

sprightly ['spraɪtlɪ] *a* vivo, enérgico.

spring [sprɪŋ] *n* (*season*) primavera; (*leap*) salto, brinco; (*coiled metal*) resorte *m*; (*of water*) fuente *f*, manantial *m* // *vi* (*pt* **sprang**, *pp* **sprung**) (*arise*) brotar, nacer; (*leap*) saltar, brincar; to ~ **up** *vi* (*problem*) surgir; **~board** *n* trampolín *m*; **~-clean** *n* (*also*: **~-cleaning**) limpieza general; **~time** *n* primavera; **~y** *a* elástico; (*grass*) muelle.

sprinkle ['sprɪŋkl] *vt* (*pour*) rociar; to ~ water *etc* on, ~ with water *etc* rociar *or* salpicar de agua *etc*; **~r** *n* (*for lawn*) rociadera; (*to put out fire*) aparato de rociadura automática.

sprint [sprɪnt] *n* esprint *m* // *vi* esprintar.

sprout [spraut] *vi* brotar, retoñar; **(Brussels) ~s** *npl* coles *fpl* de Bruselas.

spruce [spru:s] *n* (*BOT*) pícea // *a* aseado, pulcro.

sprung [sprʌŋ] *pp of* **spring**.

spry [spraɪ] *a* ágil, activo.

spun [spʌn] *pt, pp of* **spin**.

spur [spə:*] *n* espuela; (*fig*) estímulo, aguijón *m* // *vt* (*also*: ~ **on**) estimular, incitar; on the ~ of the moment de improviso.

spurious ['spjuərɪəs] *a* falso.

spurn [spə:n] *vt* desdeñar, rechazar.

spurt [spə:t] *n* chorro; (*of energy*) arrebato // *vi* chorrear.

spy [spaɪ] *n* espía *m/f* // *vi*: to ~ on espiar a // *vt* (*see*) divisar, lograr ver; **~ing** *n* espionaje *m*.

sq. *abbr* = **square**.

squabble ['skwɔbl] *vi* reñir, pelear.

squad [skwɔd] *n* (*MIL*) pelotón *m*; (*POLICE*) brigada; (*SPORT*) equipo.

squadron ['skwɔdrn] *n* (*MIL*) escuadrón *m*; (*AVIAT, NAUT*) escuadra.

squalid ['skwɔlɪd] *a* vil, miserable.

squall [skwɔ:l] *n* (*storm*) chubasco; (*wind*) ráfaga.

squalor ['skwɔlə*] *n* miseria.

squander ['skwɔndə*] *vt* (*money*) derrochar, despilfarrar; (*chances*) desperdiciar.

square [skwɛə*] *n* cuadro; (*in town*) plaza // *a* cuadrado; (*col: ideas, tastes*) trasnochado // *vt* (*arrange*) arreglar; (*MATH*) cuadrar // *vi* cuadrar, conformarse; all ~ igual(es); to have a ~ meal comer caliente; 2 metres ~ 2 metros en cuadro; a ~ metre un metro cuadrado; **~ly** *ad* (*fully*) de lleno.

squash [skwɔʃ] *n* (*Brit: drink*): lemon/orange ~ zumo (*Sp*) *or* jugo (*LAm*) de limón/naranja; (*SPORT*) squash *m*, frontenis *m* // *vt* aplastar.

squat [skwɔt] *a* achaparrado // *vi* agacharse, sentarse en cuclillas; **~ter** *n* persona que ocupa ilegalmente una casa.

squawk [skwɔ:k] *vi* graznar.

squeak [skwi:k] *vi* (*hinge, wheel*) chirriar, rechinar; (*shoe, wood*) crujir.

squeal [skwi:l] *vi* chillar, dar gritos agudos.

squeamish ['skwi:mɪʃ] *a* delicado, remilgado.

squeeze [skwi:z] *n* presión *f*; (*of hand*) apretón *m*; (*COMM*) restricción *f* // *vt* (*lemon etc*) exprimir; (*hand, arm*) apretar; to ~ **out** *vt* exprimir; (*fig*) excluir.

squelch [skweltʃ] *vi* chapotear.

squid [skwɪd] *n* calamar *m*.

squiggle ['skwɪgl] n garabato.

squint [skwɪnt] vi bizquear, ser bizco // n (MED) estrabismo; **to ~ at** sth mirar algo de soslayo.

squire ['skwaɪə*] n (Brit) terrateniente m.

squirm [skwə:m] vi retorcerse, revolverse.

squirrel ['skwɪrəl] n ardilla.

squirt [skwə:t] vi salir a chorros.

Sr abbr = **senior**.

St abbr = **saint**; **street**.

stab [stæb] n (of pain) pinchazo; **to have a ~ at (doing)** sth (col) intentar (hacer) algo // vt apuñalar.

stable ['steɪbl] a estable // n cuadra, caballeriza

stack [stæk] n montón m, pila // vt amontonar, apilar.

stadium ['steɪdɪəm] n estadio.

staff [sta:f] n (work force) personal m, plantilla; (Brit SCOL) cuerpo docente; (stick) bastón m // vt proveer de personal.

stag [stæg] n ciervo, venado.

stage [steɪdʒ] n escena; (point) etapa; (platform) plataforma; **the ~** el escenario, el teatro // vt (play) poner en escena, representar; (organize) montar, organizar; (fig: perform: recovery etc) efectuar; **in ~s** por etapas; **~coach** n diligencia; **~ door** n entrada de artistas; **~ manager** n director(a) m/f de escena.

stagger ['stægə*] vi tambalear // vt (amaze) asombrar; (hours, holidays) escalonar.

stagnant ['stægnənt] a estancado.

stagnate [stæg'neɪt] vi estancarse.

stag night, stag party n despedida de soltero.

staid [steɪd] a (clothes) serio, formal.

stain [steɪn] n mancha; (colouring) tintura // vt manchar; (wood) teñir; **~ed glass window** n vidriera de colores; **~less** a (steel) inoxidable; **~ remover** n quitamanchas m inv.

stair [stɛə*] n (step) peldaño, escalón m; **~s** npl escaleras fpl; **~case, ~way** n escalera.

stake [steɪk] n estaca, poste m; (BETTING) apuesta // vt apostar; **to be at ~** estar en juego.

stale [steɪl] a (bread) duro; (food) pasado.

stalemate ['steɪlmeɪt] n tablas fpl (por ahogado); **to reach ~** (fig) estancarse.

stalk [stɔ:k] n tallo, caña // vt acechar, cazar al acecho; **to ~ off** irse airado.

stall [stɔ:l] n (in market) puesto; (in stable) casilla (de establo) // vt (AUT) parar // vi (AUT) pararse; (fig) buscar evasivas; **~s** npl (Brit: in cinema, theatre) butacas fpl.

stallion ['stælɪən] n semental m.

stalwart ['stɔ:lwət] n partidario/a incondicional.

stamina ['stæmɪnə] n resistencia.

stammer ['stæmə*] n tartamudeo // vi tartamudear.

stamp [stæmp] n sello, estampilla (LAm); (mark, also fig) marca, huella; (on document) timbre m // vi (also: ~ one's foot) patear // vt patear, golpear con el pie; (letter) poner sellos en; (with rubber ~) marcar con sello; **~ album** n álbum m para sellos; **~ collecting** n filatelia.

stampede [stæm'pi:d] n estampida.

stance [stæns] n postura.

stand [stænd] n (attitude) posición f, postura; (for taxis) parada; (SPORT) tribuna; (at exhibition) stand m // vb (pt, pp stood) vi (be) estar, encontrarse; (be on foot) estar de pie; (rise) levantarse; (remain) quedar en pie // vt (place) poner, colocar; (tolerate, withstand) aguantar, soportar; **to make a ~** resistir; (fig) mantener una postura firme; **to ~ for parliament** (Brit) presentarse (como candidato) a las elecciones; **to ~ by** vi (be ready) estar listo // vt fus (opinion) aferrarse a; **to ~ down** vi (withdraw) ceder el puesto; **to ~ for** vt fus (signify) significar; (tolerate) aguantar, permitir; **to ~ in for** vt fus suplir a; **to ~ out** vi (be prominent) destacarse; **to ~ up** vi (rise) levantarse, ponerse de pie; **to ~ up for** vt fus defender; **to ~ up to** vt fus hacer frente a.

standard ['stændəd] n patrón m, norma; (flag) estandarte m // a (size etc) normal, corriente, estándar; **~s** npl (morals) valores mpl morales; **~ lamp** n (Brit) lámpara de pie; **~ of living** n nivel m de vida.

stand-by ['stændbaɪ] n (alert) alerta, aviso; **to be on ~** estar sobre aviso; **~ ticket** n (AVIAT) (billete m) standby m.

stand-in ['stændɪn] n suplente m/f; (CINEMA) doble m/f.

standing ['stændɪŋ] a (upright) derecho; (on foot) de pie, en pie // n reputación f; **of many years'** ~ que lleva muchos años; **~ order** n (Brit: at bank) orden f de pago permanente; **~ orders** npl (MIL) reglamento sg general; **~ room** n sitio para estar de pie.

stand: ~offish a reservado, poco afable; **~point** n punto de vista; **~still** n: **at a ~still** (industry, traffic) paralizado; (car) parado; **to come to a ~still** quedar paralizado; pararse.

stank [stæŋk] pt of **stink**.

staple ['steɪpl] n (for papers) grapa // a (food etc) básico // vt engrapar; **~r** n grapadora.

star [sta:*] n estrella; (celebrity) estrella, astro // vi: **to ~ in** ser la estrella or el astro de.

starboard ['stɑːbəd] n estribor m.

starch [stɑːtʃ] n almidón m.

stardom ['stɑːdəm] n estrellato.

stare [stɛə*] n mirada fija // vi: to ~ at mirar fijo.

starfish ['stɑːfɪʃ] n estrella de mar.

stark [stɑːk] a (bleak) severo, escueto // ad: ~ naked en cueros.

starling ['stɑːlɪŋ] n estornino.

starry ['stɑːrɪ] a estrellado; ~-eyed a (innocent) inocentón/ona, ingenuo.

start [stɑːt] n (beginning) principio, comienzo; (of race) salida; (sudden movement) salto, sobresalto // vt émpezar, comenzar; (cause) causar; (found) fundar; (engine) poner en marcha // vi (begin) comenzar, empezar; (with fright) asustarse, sobresaltarse; (train etc) salir; to ~ doing or to do sth empezar a hacer algo; to ~ off vi empezar, comenzar; (leave) salir, ponerse en camino; to ~ up vi comenzar; (car) ponerse en marcha // vt comenzar; (car) poner en marcha; ~er n (AUT) botón m de arranque; (SPORT: official) juez m/f de salida; (: runner) corredor(a) m/f; (Brit CULIN) entrada; ~ing point n punto de partida.

startle ['stɑːtl] vt asustar, sobrecoger; **startling** a alarmante.

starvation [stɑː'veɪʃən] n hambre f.

starve [stɑːv] vi pasar hambre; to ~ to death morir de hambre // vt hacer pasar hambre; (fig) privar de; I'm starving estoy muerto de hambre.

state [steɪt] n estado // vt (say, declare) afirmar; (a case) presentar, exponer; to be in a ~ estar agitado; the S~s los Estados Unidos; ~ly a majestuoso, imponente; ~ment n afirmación f; (LAW) declaración f; ~sman n estadista m.

static ['stætɪk] n (RADIO) parásitos mpl // a estático; ~ electricity n estática.

station ['steɪʃən] n (gen) estación f; (RADIO) emisora; (rank) posición f social // vt colocar, situar; (MIL) apostar.

stationary ['steɪʃnərɪ] a estacionario, fijo.

stationer ['steɪʃənə*] n papelero/a; ~'s (shop) n (Brit) papelería; ~y [-nərɪ] n papel m de escribir, artículos mpl de escritorio.

station master n (RAIL) jefe m de estación.

station wagon n (US) furgoneta.

statistic [stə'tɪstɪk] n estadística; ~s n (science) estadística; ~al a estadístico.

statue ['stætjuː] n estatua.

status ['steɪtəs] n estado; (reputation) estatus m; ~ symbol n símbolo de prestigio.

statute ['stætjuːt] n estatuto, ley f; **statutory** a estatutario.

staunch [stɔːntʃ] a leal, incondicional.

stave [steɪv] vt: to ~ off (attack) recha-

zar; (threat) evitar.

stay [steɪ] n (period of time) estancia // vi (remain) quedar(se); (as guest) hospedarse; to ~ put seguir en el mismo sitio; to ~ the night/5 days pasar la noche/estar 5 días; to ~ behind vi quedar atrás; to ~ in vi (at home) quedarse en casa; to ~ on vi quedarse; to ~ out vi (of house) no volver a casa; to ~ up vi (at night) velar, no acostarse; ~ing power n aguante m.

stead [stɛd] n: in sb's ~ en lugar de uno; to stand sb in good ~ ser muy útil a uno.

steadfast ['stɛdfɑːst] a firme, resuelto.

steadily ['stɛdɪlɪ] ad (improve, grow) constantemente; (work) sin parar; (gaze) fijamente.

steady ['stɛdɪ] a (fixed) firme, fijo; (regular) regular; (person, character) sensato, juicioso // vt (hold) mantener firme; (stabilize) estabilizar; (nerves) calmar; to ~ o.s. on or against sth afirmarse en algo.

steak [steɪk] n (gen) filete m; (beef) bistec m.

steal [stiːl], pt **stole**, pp **stolen** vt, vi robar.

stealth [stɛlθ] n: by ~ a escondidas, sigilosamente; ~y a cauteloso, sigiloso.

steam [stiːm] n vapor m; (mist) vaho, humo // vt (CULIN) cocer al vapor // vi echar vapor; (ship): to ~ along avanzar, ir avanzando; to ~ up vt empañar; ~ engine n máquina de vapor; ~er n (buque m de) vapor m; ~roller n apisonadora; ~ship n = ~er; ~y a (room) lleno de vapor; (window) empañado.

steel [stiːl] n acero // cpd de acero; ~works n acería.

steep [stiːp] a escarpado, abrupto; (stair) empinado; (price) exorbitante, excesivo // vt empapar, remojar.

steeple ['stiːpl] n aguja.

steer [stɪə*] vt (car) conducir (Sp), manejar (LAm); (person) dirigir // vi conducir; ~ing n (AUT) dirección f; ~ing wheel n volante m.

stem [stɛm] n (of plant) tallo; (of glass) pie m; (of pipe) cañón m // vt detener; (blood) restañar; to ~ from vt fus ser consecuencia de.

stench [stɛntʃ] n hedor m.

stencil ['stɛnsl] n (typed) cliché m, clisé m; (lettering) plantilla // vt hacer un cliché de.

stenographer [stɛ'nɔgrəfə*] n (US) taquígrafo/a.

step [stɛp] n paso; (sound) paso, pisada; (on stair) peldaño, escalón m // vi: to ~ forward dar un paso adelante; ~s npl (Brit) = ~ladder; to be in/out of ~ with estar acorde con/estar en disonancia con; to ~ down vi (fig) retirarse; to ~ off vt fus bajar de; to ~ up vt (increase) aumentar; ~brother n hermanastro; ~**daughter** n hijastra; ~**father** n padrastro; ~**ladder** n escalera doble or de tijera; ~**mother** n madrastra; ~**ping stone** n pasadera; (fig) trampolín m; ~**sister** n hermanastra; ~**son** n hijastro.

stereo ['stɛrɪəu] n estéreo // a (also: ~**phonic**) estéreo, estereofónico.

sterile ['stɛraɪl] a estéril; **sterilize** ['stɛrɪlaɪz] vt esterilizar.

sterling ['stə:lɪŋ] a (silver) de ley // n (ECON) (libras fpl) esterlinas fpl; a **pound** ~ una libra esterlina.

stern [stə:n] a severo, austero // n (NAUT) popa.

stethoscope ['stɛθəskəup] n estetoscopio.

stew [stju:] n cocido, estofado, guisado (LAm) // vt estofar, guisar; (fruit) cocer.

steward ['stju:əd] n (Brit: AVIAT, NAUT, RAIL) camarero; ~**ess** n azafata.

stick [stɪk] n palo; (as weapon) porra; (walking ~) bastón m // vb (pt, pp **stuck**) vt (glue) pegar; (col: put) meter; (: tolerate) aguantar, soportar // vi pegarse; (come to a stop) quedarse parado; to ~ sth into clavar or hincar algo en; to ~ **out**, to ~ **up** vi sobresalir; to ~ **up for** vt fus defender; ~**er** n (label) etiqueta engomada; (with slogan) pegatina; ~**ing plaster** n (Brit) esparadrapo.

stickler ['stɪklə*] n: to be a ~ for insistir mucho en.

stick-up ['stɪkʌp] n asalto, atraco.

sticky ['stɪkɪ] a pegajoso; (label) engomado; (fig) difícil.

stiff [stɪf] a rígido, tieso; (hard) duro; (difficult) difícil; (person) inflexible; (price) exorbitante; ~**en** vt hacer más rígido; (limb) entumecer // vi endurecerse; (grow stronger) fortalecerse; ~ **neck** n torticolis m inv; ~**ness** n rigidez f, tiesura.

stifle ['staɪfl] vt ahogar, sofocar; **stifling** a (heat) sofocante, bochornoso.

stigma ['stɪgmə], pl (BOT, MED, REL) ~**ta** [-tə], (fig) ~**s** n estigma m.

stile [staɪl] n escalera (para pasar una cerca).

stiletto [stɪ'lɛtəu] n (Brit: also: ~ **heel**) tacón m de aguja.

still [stɪl] a inmóvil, quieto // ad (up to this time) todavía; (even) aun; (nonetheless) sin embargo, aun así; ~**born** a nacido muerto; ~ **life** n naturaleza muerta.

stilt [stɪlt] n zanco; (pile) pilar m, soporte m.

stilted ['stɪltɪd] a afectado.

stimulate ['stɪmjuleɪt] vt estimular.

stimulus ['stɪmjuləs], pl **-li** [-laɪ] n estímulo, incentivo.

sting [stɪŋ] n (wound) picadura; (pain)

escozor m, picazón f; (organ) aguijón m // vb (pt, pp **stung**) vt picar // vi picar, escocer.

stingy ['stɪndʒɪ] a tacaño.

stink [stɪŋk] n hedor m, tufo // vi (pt **stank**, pp **stunk**) heder, apestar; ~**ing** a hediondo, fétido; (fig: col) horrible.

stint [stɪnt] n tarea, destajo // vi: to ~ on escatimar; to do one's ~ hacer su parte.

stir [stə:*] n (fig: agitation) conmoción f // vt (tea etc) remover; (move) agitar; (fig: emotions) provocar // vi moverse; to ~ **up** vt excitar; (trouble) fomentar.

stirrup ['stɪrəp] n estribo.

stitch [stɪtʃ] n (SEWING) puntada; (KNITTING) punto; (MED) punto (de sutura); (pain) punzada // vt coser; (MED) suturar.

stoat [stəut] n armiño.

stock [stɔk] n (COMM: reserves) existencias fpl, stock m; (: selection) surtido; (AGR) ganado, ganadería; (CULIN) caldo; (FINANCE) capital m; (: shares) acciones fpl // a (fig: reply etc) clásico // vt (have in ~) tener existencias de; (supply) proveer, abastecer; ~**s** npl cepo sg; in ~ en existencia or almacén; out of ~ agotado; to take ~ of (fig) asesorar, examinar; ~**s and shares** acciones y valores; to ~ **up with** vt fus abastecerse de.

stockbroker ['stɔkbrəukə*] n agente m/f or corredor(a) m/f de bolsa.

stock cube n pastilla de caldo.

stock exchange n bolsa.

stocking ['stɔkɪŋ] n media.

stock: ~**holder** n (US) accionista m/f; ~**ist** n (Brit) distribuidor(a) m/f; ~ **market** n bolsa (de valores); ~ **phrase** n cliché m; ~**pile** n reserva // vt acumular, almacenar; ~**taking** n (Brit COMM) inventario.

stocky ['stɔkɪ] a (strong) robusto; (short) achaparrado.

stodgy ['stɔdʒɪ] a indigesto, pesado.

stoke [stəuk] vt atizar.

stole [stəul] pt of **steal** // n estola.

stolen ['stəuln] pp of **steal**.

stolid ['stɔlɪd] a (person) imperturbable, impasible.

stomach ['stʌmək] n (ANAT) estómago; (abdomen) vientre m // vt tragar, aguantar; ~**ache** n dolor m de estómago.

stone [stəun] n piedra; (in fruit) hueso; (Brit: weight) = 6.348kg; 14 pounds // cpd de piedra // vt apedrear; ~**cold** a helado; ~**deaf** a sordo como una tapia; ~**work** n (art) cantería.

stood [stud] pt, pp of **stand**.

stool [stu:l] n taburete m.

stoop [stu:p] vi (also: have a ~) ser cargado de espaldas.

stop [stɔp] n parada, alto; (in punctuation) punto // vt parar, detener; (break *off*) suspender; (*block*) tapar, cerrar; (*also*: put a ~ to) poner término a // *vi* pararse, detenerse; (*end*) acabarse; to ~ doing sth dejar de hacer algo; to ~ dead pararse en seco; **to ~ off** *vi* interrumpir el viaje; **to ~ up** (*hole*) tapar; **~gap** *n* (*person*) interino/a; **~lights** *npl* (*AUT*) luces *fpl* de detención; **~over** *n* parada; (*AVIAT*) rescala.

stoppage ['stɔpɪdʒ] *n* (*strike*) paro; (*temporary stop*) interrupción *f*; (*of pay*) suspensión *f*; (*blockage*) obstrucción *f*.

stopper ['stɔpə*] *n* tapón *m*.

stop press *n* noticias *fpl* de última hora.

stopwatch ['stɔpwɔtʃ] *n* cronómetro.

storage ['stɔːrɪdʒ] *n* almacenaje *m*; (*COMPUT*) almacenamiento; **~ heater** *n* acumulador *m*.

store [stɔː*] *n* (*stock*) provisión *f*; (*depot*; *Brit*: *large shop*) almacén *m*; (*US*) tienda; (*reserve*) reserva, repuesto // *vt* almacenar; (*keep*) guardar; **~s** *npl* víveres *mpl*; **to ~ up** *vt* acumular; **~keeper** *n* (*US*) tendero/a; **~room** *n* despensa.

storey, (*US*) **story** ['stɔːrɪ] *n* piso.

stork [stɔːk] *n* cigüeña.

storm [stɔːm] *n* tormenta; (*wind*) vendaval *m* // *vi* (*fig*) rabiar // *vt* tomar por asalto; **~y** *a* tempestuoso.

story ['stɔːrɪ] *n* historia; (*joke*) cuento, chiste *m*; (*US*) = **storey**; **~book** *n* libro de cuentos; **~teller** *n* cuentista *m/f*.

stout [staut] *a* (*strong*) sólido; (*fat*) gordo, corpulento // *n* cerveza negra.

stove [stəuv] *n* (*for cooking*) cocina; (*for heating*) estufa.

stow [stəu] *vt* meter, poner; (*NAUT*) estibar; **~away** *n* polizón/ona *m/f*.

straddle ['strædl] *vt* montar a horcajadas.

straggle ['strægl] *vi* (*lag behind*) rezagarse; **~r** *n* rezagado.

straight [streɪt] *a* recto, derecho; (*frank*) franco, directo // *ad* derecho, directamente; (*drink*) sin mezcla; **to put or get sth ~** dejar algo en claro; **~ away, ~ off** (*at once*) en seguida; **~en** *vt* (*also*: **~en out**) enderezar, poner derecho; **~-faced** *a* serio; **~forward** *a* (*simple*) sencillo; (*honest*) honrado, franco.

strain [streɪn] *n* (*gen*) tensión *f*; (*MED*) torcedura // *vt* (*back etc*) torcerse; (*tire*) cansar; (*stretch*) estirar; (*filter*) filtrar // *vi* esforzarse; **~s** *npl* (*MUS*) son *m*; **~ed** *a* (*muscle*) torcido; (*laugh*) forzado; (*relations*) tenso; **~er** *n* colador *m*.

strait [streɪt] *n* (*GEO*) estrecho; **~-jacket** *n* camisa de fuerza; **~-laced** *a* mojigato, gazmoño.

strand [strænd] *n* (*of thread*) hebra; (*of hair*) trenza; **~ed** *a* (*person*: *without money*) desamparado; (: *transport*) col-

gado.

strange [streɪndʒ] *a* (*not known*) desconocido; (*odd*) extraño, raro; **~r** *n* desconocido/a; (*from another area*) forastero/a.

strangle ['stræŋgl] *vt* estrangular; **~hold** *n* (*fig*): **to have a ~hold on sth** dominar algo completamente.

strap [stræp] *n* correa; (*of slip, dress*) tirante *m* // *vt* atar con correa.

strapping ['stræpɪŋ] *a* robusto, fornido.

stratagem ['strætɪdʒəm] *n* estratagema.

strategic [strə'tiːdʒɪk] *a* estratégico.

strategy ['strætɪdʒɪ] *n* estrategia.

straw [strɔː] *n* paja; (*drinking ~*) caña, pajita; **that's the last ~!** ¡eso es el colmo!

strawberry ['strɔːbərɪ] *n* fresa, frutilla (*LAm*).

stray [streɪ] *a* (*animal*) extraviado; (*bullet*) perdido // *vi* extraviarse, perderse.

streak [striːk] *n* raya; (*fig*: *of madness etc*) vena // *vt* rayar // *vi*: **to ~ past** pasar como un rayo.

stream [striːm] *n* riachuelo, arroyo; (*jet*) chorro; (*flow*) corriente *f*; (*of people*) oleada // *vt* (*SCOL*) dividir en grupos por habilidad // *vi* correr, fluir; **to ~ in/out** (*people*) entrar/salir en tropel.

streamer ['striːmə*] *n* serpentina.

streamlined ['striːmlaɪnd] *a* aerodinámico; (*fig*) racionalizado.

street [striːt] *n* calle *f* // *cpd* callejero; **~car** *n* (*US*) tranvía *m*; **~ lamp** *n* farol *m*; **~ plan** *n* plano; **~wise** *a* (*col*) que tiene mucha calle.

strength [streŋθ] *n* fuerza; (*of girder, knot etc*) resistencia; **~en** *vt* fortalecer, reforzar.

strenuous ['strenjuəs] *a* (*tough*) arduo; (*energetic*) enérgico.

stress [stres] *n* (*force, pressure*) presión *f*; (*mental strain*) estrés *m*; (*accent*) acento; (*TECH*) tensión *f*, carga // *vt* subrayar, recalcar.

stretch [stretʃ] *n* (*of sand etc*) trecho; (*of road*) tramo // *vi* estirarse // *vt* extender, estirar; (*make demands of*) exigir el máximo esfuerzo a; **to ~ to or as far as** extenderse hasta; **to ~ out** *vi* tenderse // *vt* (*arm etc*) extender; (*spread*) estirar.

stretcher ['stretʃə*] *n* camilla.

strewn [struːn] *a*: **~ with** cubierto *or* sembrado de.

stricken ['strɪkən] *a* (*person*) herido; (*city, industry etc*) condenado; **~ with** (*disease*) afligido por.

strict [strɪkt] *a* estricto; **~ly** *ad* estrictamente; (*totally*) terminantemente.

stride [straɪd] *n* zancada, tranco // *vi* (*pt* **strode**, *pp* **stridden** ['strɪdn]) dar zancadas, andar a trancos.

strident ['straɪdnt] *a* estridente; (*colour*) chillón/ona.

strife [straɪf] n lucha.
strike [straɪk] n huelga; (of oil etc) descubrimiento; (attack) ataque m; (SPORT) golpe m // vb (pt, pp **struck**) vt golpear, pegar; (oil etc) descubrir; (obstacle) topar con // vi declarar la huelga; (attack) atacar; (clock) dar la hora; on ~ (workers) en huelga; **to ~ a match** encender un fósforo; **to ~ down** vt derribar; **to ~ out** vt borrar, tachar; **to ~ up** vt (MUS) empezar a tocar; (conversation) entablar; (friendship) trabar; **~r** n huelguista m/f; (SPORT) delantero; **striking** a llamativo; (obvious: resemblance) notorio.
string [strɪŋ] n (gen) cuerda; (row) hilera // vt (pt, pp **strung**): **to ~ together** encartar; **to ~ out** extenderse; **the ~s** npl (MUS) los instrumentos de cuerda; **to pull ~s** (fig) mover palancas; **~ bean** n judía verde, habichuela; **~(ed) instrument** n (MUS) instrumento de cuerda.
stringent ['strɪndʒənt] a riguroso, severo.
strip [strɪp] n tira; (of land) franja; (of metal) cinta, lámina // vt desnudar; (also: ~ **down**: machine) desmontar // vi desnudarse; **~ cartoon** n tira cómica, historieta (LAm).
stripe [straɪp] n raya; (MIL) galón m; **~d** a a rayas, rayado.
strip lighting n alumbrado fluorescente.
stripper ['strɪpə*] n artista m/f de striptease.
strive [straɪv], pt **strove**, pp **striven** ['strɪvn] vi: **to ~ to do sth** esforzarse o luchar por hacer algo.
strode [strəud] pt of **stride**.
stroke [strəuk] n (blow) golpe m; (MED) apoplejía; (caress) caricia // vt acariciar; **at a ~** de un solo golpe.
stroll [strəul] n paseo, vuelta // vi dar un paseo o una vuelta; **~er** n (US: for child) sillita de ruedas.
strong [strɔŋ] a fuerte; **they are 50 ~** son 50; **~box** n caja fuerte; **~hold** n fortaleza; (fig) baluarte m; **~ly** ad fuertemente, con fuerza; (believe) firmemente; **~room** n cámara acorazada.
strove [strəuv] pt of **strive**.
struck [strʌk] pt, pp of **strike**.
structure ['strʌktʃə*] n estructura; (building) construcción f.
struggle ['strʌgl] n lucha // vi luchar.
strum [strʌm] vt (guitar) rasguear.
strung [strʌŋ] pt, pp of **string**.
strut [strʌt] n puntal m // vi pavonearse.
stub [stʌb] n (of ticket etc) talón m; (of cigarette) colilla; **to ~ one's toe** dar con el dedo (del pie) contra algo; **to ~ out** vt apagar.
stubble ['stʌbl] n rastrojo; (on chin) barba (incipiente).
stubborn ['stʌbən] a terco, testarudo.
stucco ['stʌkəu] n estuco.
stuck [stʌk] pt, pp of **stick** // a (jammed)

atascado; **~-up** a engreído, presumido.
stud [stʌd] n (shirt ~) corchete m; (of boot) taco; (of horses) caballeriza; (also: ~ **horse**) caballo semental // vt (fig): **~ded with** salpicado de.
student ['stju:dənt] n estudiante m/f // cpd estudiantil; ~ **driver** n (US AUT) aprendiz(a) m/f.
studio ['stju:dɪəu] n estudio; (artist's) taller m; ~ **flat**, (US) ~ **apartment** n estudio.
studious ['stju:dɪəs] a estudioso; (studied) calculado; **~ly** ad (carefully) con esmero.
study ['stʌdɪ] n estudio // vt estudiar; (examine) examinar, investigar // vi estudiar.
stuff [stʌf] n materia; (cloth) tela; (substance) material m, sustancia; (things, belongings) cosas fpl // vt llenar; (CULIN) rellenar; (animals) disecar; **~ing** n relleno; **~y** a (room) mal ventilado; (person) de miras estrechas.
stumble ['stʌmbl] vi tropezar, dar un traspié; **to ~ across** (fig) tropezar con; **stumbling block** n tropiezo, obstáculo.
stump [stʌmp] n (of tree) tocón m; (of limb) muñón m // vt: **to be ~ed for an answer** no saber qué contestar.
stun [stʌn] vt dejar sin sentido.
stung [stʌŋ] pt, pp of **sting**.
stunk [stʌŋk] pp of **stink**.
stunning ['stʌnɪŋ] a (news) pasmoso; (fabulous) sensacional.
stunt [stʌnt] n (AVIAT) vuelo acrobático; (publicity ~) truco publicitario; **~ed** a enano, achaparrado; **~man** n especialista m.
stupefy ['stju:pɪfaɪ] vt dejar estupefacto.
stupendous [stju:'pɛndəs] a estupendo, asombroso.
stupid ['stju:pɪd] a estúpido, tonto; **~ity** [-'pɪdɪtɪ] n estupidez f.
sturdy ['stə:dɪ] a robusto, fuerte.
stutter ['stʌtə*] vi tartamudear.
sty [staɪ] n (for pigs) pocilga.
stye [staɪ] n (MED) orzuelo.
style [staɪl] n estilo; (fashion) moda; **stylish** a elegante, a la moda; **stylist** n (hair stylist) peluquero/a.
stylus ['staɪləs] n (of record player) aguja.
suave [swɑ:v] a cortés; (pej) zalamero.
sub... [sʌb] pref sub...; **~conscious** a subconsciente // n subconsciente m; **~contract** vt subcontratar; **~divide** vt subdividir.
subdue [səb'dju:] vt sojuzgar; (passions) dominar; **~d** a (light) tenue; (person) sumiso, manso.
subject ['sʌbdʒɪkt] n súbdito; (SCOL) tema m, materia // vt [səb'dʒɛkt]: **to ~ sb to sth** someter a uno a algo; **to be ~ to** (law) estar sujeto a; (subj: person) ser propenso a; **~ive** [-'dʒɛktɪv] a subje-

tivo; ~ **matter** n materia; (content) contenido.

subjunctive [səb'dʒʌŋktɪv] a, n subjuntivo.

sublet [sʌb'lɛt] vt subarrendar.

submachine gun ['sʌbmə'ʃiːn-] n metralleta.

submarine [sʌbmə'riːn] n submarino.

submerge [səb'mɜːdʒ] vt sumergir; (flood) inundar // vi sumergirse.

submissive [səb'mɪsɪv] a sumiso.

submit [səb'mɪt] vt someter // vi someterse.

subnormal [sʌb'nɔːməl] a subnormal.

subordinate [sə'bɔːdɪnət] a, n subordinado/a m/f.

subpoena [səb'piːnə] (LAW) n citación f // vt citar.

subscribe [səb'skraɪb] vi suscribir; **to ~ to** (opinion, fund) suscribir, aprobar; (newspaper) suscribirse a; **~r** n (to periodical, telephone) abonado/a.

subscription [səb'skrɪpʃən] n (to club) abono; (to magazine) suscripción f.

subsequent ['sʌbsɪkwənt] a subsiguiente, posterior; **~ly** ad posteriormente, más tarde.

subside [səb'saɪd] vi hundirse; (flood) bajar; (wind) amainar; **~nce** [-'saɪdns] n hundimiento; (in road) socavón m.

subsidiary [səb'sɪdɪərɪ] n sucursal f, filial f.

subsidize ['sʌbsɪdaɪz] vt subvencionar.

subsidy ['sʌbsɪdɪ] n subvención f.

substance ['sʌbstəns] n sustancia; (fig) esencia.

substantial [səb'stænʃl] a sustancial, sustancioso; (fig) importante.

substantiate [səb'stænʃɪeɪt] vt comprobar.

substitute ['sʌbstɪtjuːt] n (person) suplente m/f; (thing) sustituto // vt: **to ~ A for B** sustituir B por A, reemplazar A por B.

subtitle ['sʌbtaɪtl] n subtítulo.

subtle ['sʌtl] a sutil; **~ty** n sutileza.

subtract [səb'trækt] vt restar; sustraer; **~ion** [-'trækʃən] n resta; sustracción f.

suburb ['sʌbəːb] n suburbio; **the ~s** las afueras (de la ciudad); **~an** [sə'bəːbən] a suburbano; (train etc) de cercanías; **~ia** [sə'bəːbɪə] n barrios mpl residenciales.

subway ['sʌbweɪ] n (Brit) paso subterráneo or inferior; (US) metro.

succeed [sək'siːd] vi (person) tener éxito; (plan) salir bien // vt suceder a; **to ~ in doing** lograr hacer; **~ing** a (following) sucesivo.

success [sək'sɛs] n éxito; **~ful** a (venture, person) exitoso; (business) próspero; **to be ~ful (in doing)** lograr (hacer); **~fully** ad con éxito.

succession [sək'sɛʃən] n sucesión f, serie f.

successive [sək'sɛsɪv] a sucesivo, consecutivo.

succinct [sək'sɪŋkt] a sucinto.

such [sʌtʃ] a tal, semejante; (of that kind): ~ **a book** tal libro; (so much): ~ **courage** tanto valor // ad tan; ~ **a long trip** un viaje tan largo; ~ **a lot of** tanto(s)/a(s); ~ **as** (like) tal como; a **noise** ~ **as** to un ruido tal que; **as** ~ ad como tal; **~-and~** a tal o cual.

suck [sʌk] vt chupar; (bottle) sorber; (breast) mamar; **~er** n (BOT) serpollo; (ZOOL) ventosa; (col) bobo, primo.

suction ['sʌkʃən] n succión f.

Sudan [su'dæn] n Sudán m.

sudden ['sʌdn] a (rapid) repentino, súbito; (unexpected) imprevisto; **all of a** ~ ad de repente; **~ly** ad de repente.

suds [sʌdz] npl espuma sg de jabón.

sue [suː] vt demandar.

suede [sweɪd] n ante m, gamuza (LAm).

suet ['suɪt] n sebo.

Suez ['suːɪz] n: **the** ~ **Canal** el Canal de Suez.

suffer ['sʌfə*] vt sufrir, padecer; (tolerate) aguantar, soportar // vi sufrir; **~er** n víctima; (MED) enfermo/a; **~ing** n sufrimiento; (pain) dolor m.

suffice [sə'faɪs] vi bastar, ser suficiente.

sufficient [sə'fɪʃənt] a suficiente, bastante; **~ly** ad suficientemente, bastante.

suffocate ['sʌfəkeɪt] vi ahogarse, asfixiarse.

suffrage ['sʌfrɪdʒ] n sufragio.

suffused [sə'fjuːzd] a: ~ **with** bañado de.

sugar ['ʃugə*] n azúcar m // vt echar azúcar a, azucarar; ~ **beet** n remolacha; ~ **cane** n caña de azúcar; **~y** a azucarado.

suggest [sə'dʒɛst] vt sugerir; (recommend) aconsejar; **~ion** [-'dʒɛstʃən] n sugerencia.

suicide ['suɪsaɪd] n suicidio; (person) suicida m/f.

suit [suːt] n (man's) traje m; (woman's) conjunto; (LAW) pleito; (CARDS) palo // vt convenir; (clothes) sentar a, ir bien a; (adapt): **to ~ sth to** adaptar or ajustar algo a; **well ~ed** (well matched: couple) hechos el uno para el otro; **~able** a conveniente; (apt) indicado; **~ably** ad convenientemente; en forma debida.

suitcase ['suːtkeɪs] n maleta, valija (LAm).

suite [swiːt] n (of rooms, MUS) suite f; (furniture): **bedroom/dining room** ~ (juego de) dormitorio/comedor m.

suitor ['suːtə*] n pretendiente m.

sulfur ['sʌlfə*] n (US) = **sulphur**.

sulk [sʌlk] vi estar de mal humor; **~y** a malhumorado.

sullen ['sʌlən] a hosco, malhumorado.

sulphur, (US) **sulfur** ['sʌlfə*] n azufre m.

sultana [sʌl'tɑːnə] n (fruit) pasa de Esmirna.

sultry ['sʌltrɪ] *a* (*weather*) bochornoso.

sum [sʌm] *n* suma; (*total*) total *m*; **to ~ up** *vt* resumir // *vi* hacer un resumen.

summarize ['sʌmɘraɪz] *vt* resumir.

summary ['sʌmɘrɪ] *n* resumen *m* // *a* (*justice*) sumario.

summer ['sʌmɘ*] *n* verano // *cpd* de verano; **~house** *n* (*in garden*) cenador *m*, glorieta; **~time** *n* (*season*) verano; **~ time** *n* (*Brit: by clock*) hora de verano.

summit ['sʌmɪt] *n* cima, cumbre *f*; **~ (conference)** *n* (conferencia) cumbre *f*.

summon ['sʌmɘn] *vt* (*person*) llamar; (*meeting*) convocar; (*LAW*) citar; **to ~ up** *vt* (*courage*) armarse de; **~s** *n* llamamiento, llamada // *vt* citar, emplazar.

sump [sʌmp] *n* (*Brit AUT*) cárter *m*.

sumptuous ['sʌmptjuɘs] *a* suntuoso.

sun [sʌn] *n* sol *m*.

sunbathe ['sʌnbeɪð] *vi* tomar el sol.

sunburn ['sʌnbɘ:n] *n* (*painful*) quemadura; (*tan*) bronceado.

Sunday ['sʌndɪ] *n* domingo; **~ school** *n* catequesis *f* dominical.

sundial ['sʌndaɪɘl] *n* reloj *m* de sol.

sundown ['sʌndaun] *n* anochecer *m*.

sundry ['sʌndrɪ] *a* varios/as, diversos/as; **all and ~** todos sin excepción; **sundries** *npl* géneros *mpl* diversos.

sunflower ['sʌnflauɘ*] *n* girasol *m*.

sung [sʌŋ] *pp* of **sing**.

sunglasses ['sʌnglɑ:sɪz] *npl* gafas *fpl* or anteojos *mpl* (*LAm*) de sol.

sunk [sʌŋk] *pp* of **sink**.

sun: **~light** *n* luz *f* del sol; **~lit** *a* iluminado por el sol; **~ny** *a* soleado; (*day*) de sol; (*fig*) alegre; **~rise** *n* salida del sol; **~ roof** *n* (*AUT*) techo corredizo; **~set** *n* puesta del sol; **~shade** *n* (*over table*) sombrilla; **~shine** *n* sol *m*; **~stroke** *n* insolación *f*; **~tan** *n* bronceado; **~tan oil** *n* aceite *m* bronceador.

super ['su:pɘ*] *a* (*col*) bárbaro.

superannuation [su:pɘrænju'eɪʃɘn] *n* cuota de jubilación.

superb [su:'pɘ:b] *a* magnífico, espléndido.

supercilious [su:pɘ'sɪlɪɘs] *a* altanero.

superfluous [su'pɘ:fluɘs] *a* superfluo, de sobra.

superhuman [su:pɘ'hju:mɘn] *a* sobrehumano.

superimpose ['su:pɘrɪm'pɘuz] *vt* sobreponer.

superintendent [su:pɘrɪn'tɛndɘnt] *n* director(a) *m/f*; (*police* **~**) subjefe/a *m/f*.

superior [su'pɪɘrɪɘ*] *a* superior; (*smug*) desdeñoso // *n* superior *m*; **~ity** [-'ɔrɪtɪ] *n* superioridad *f*; desdén *m*.

superlative [su'pɘ:lɘtɪv] *a*, *n* superlativo.

superman ['su:pɘmæn] *n* superhombre *m*.

supermarket ['su:pɘmɑ:kɪt] *n* supermercado.

supernatural [su:pɘ'nætʃɘrɘl] *a* sobrena-

tural.

superpower ['su:pɘpauɘ*] *n* (*POL*) superpotencia.

supersede [su:pɘ'si:d] *vt* suplantar.

supersonic ['su:pɘ'sɔnɪk] *a* supersónico.

superstitious [su:pɘ'stɪʃɘs] *a* supersticioso.

supertanker ['su:pɘtæŋkɘ*] *n* superpetrolero.

supervise ['su:pɘvaɪz] *vt* supervisar; **supervision** [-'vɪʒɘn] *n* supervisión *f*; **supervisor** *n* supervisor(a) *m/f*.

supper ['sʌpɘ*] *n* cena; **to have ~** cenar.

supplant [sɘ'plɑ:nt] *vt* suplantar.

supple ['sʌpl] *a* flexible.

supplement ['sʌplɪmɘnt] *n* suplemento // *vt* [sʌplɪ'mɛnt] suplir; **~ary** [-'mɛntɘrɪ] *a* suplementario.

supplier [sɘ'plaɪɘ*] *n* suministrador(a) *m/f*; (*COMM*) distribuidor(a) *m/f*.

supply [sɘ'plaɪ] *vt* (*provide*) suministrar; (*information*) facilitar; (*equip*): **to ~ (with)** proveer (de) // *n* provisión *f*; (*gas, water etc*) suministro // *cpd* (*Brit: teacher etc*) suplente; **supplies** *npl* (*food*) víveres *mpl*; (*MIL*) pertrechos *mpl*.

support [sɘ'pɔ:t] *n* (*moral, financial etc*) apoyo; (*TECH*) soporte *m* // *vt* apoyar; (*financially*) mantener; (*uphold*) sostener; **~er** *n* (*POL etc*) partidario/a; (*SPORT*) aficionado/a.

suppose [sɘ'pɘuz] *vt*, *vi* suponer; (*imagine*) imaginarse; **to be ~d to do sth** deber hacer algo; **~dly** [sɘ'pɘuzɪdlɪ] *ad* según cabe suponer; **supposing** *conj* en caso de que.

suppress [sɘ'prɛs] *vt* suprimir; (*yawn*) ahogar.

supreme [su'pri:m] *a* supremo.

surcharge ['sɘ:tʃɑ:dʒ] *n* sobretasa, recargo.

sure [ʃuɘ*] *a* seguro; (*definite, convinced*) cierto; **to make ~ of sth/that** asegurarse de algo/asegurar que; **~!** (*of course*) ¡claro!, ¡por supuesto!; **~ enough** efectivamente; **~ly** *ad* (*certainly*) seguramente.

surety ['ʃuɘrɘtɪ] *n* fianza; (*person*) fiador(a) *m/f*.

surf [sɘ:f] *n* olas *fpl*.

surface ['sɘ:fɪs] *n* superficie *f* // *vt* (*road*) revestir // *vi* salir a la superficie; **~ mail** *n* vía terrestre.

surfboard ['sɘ:fbɔ:d] *n* plancha (de surf).

surfeit ['sɘ:fɪt] *n*: **a ~ of** un exceso de.

surfing ['sɘ:fɪŋ] *n* surf *m*.

surge [sɘ:dʒ] *n* oleada, oleaje *m* // *vi* avanzar a tropel.

surgeon ['sɘ:dʒɘn] *n* cirujano/a.

surgery ['sɘ:dʒɘrɪ] *n* cirugía; (*Brit: room*) consultorio; **to undergo ~** operarse; **~ hours** *npl* (*Brit*) horas *fpl* de consulta.

surgical ['sɘ:dʒɪkl] *a* quirúrgico; **~ spir-**

it *n* (*Brit*) alcohol *m* de 90°.

surly ['sə:lɪ] *a* hosco, malhumorado.

surmount [sə:'maunt] *vt* superar, vencer.

surname ['sə:neɪm] *n* apellido.

surpass [sə:'pɑ:s] *vt* superar, exceder.

surplus ['sə:pləs] *n* excedente *m*; (*COMM*) superávit *m* // *a* excedente, sobrante.

surprise [sə'praɪz] *n* sorpresa // *vt* sorprender; **surprising** *a* sorprendente; **surprisingly** *ad* (*easy, helpful*) de modo sorprendente.

surrender [sə'rɛndə*] *n* rendición *f*, entrega // *vi* rendirse, entregarse.

surreptitious [sʌrəp'tɪʃəs] *a* subrepticio.

surrogate ['sʌrəgɪt] *n* sucedáneo; **~ mother** *n* madre *f* portadora.

surround [sə'raund] *vt* rodear, circundar; (*MIL etc*) cercar; **~ing** *a* circundante; **~ings** *npl* alrededores *mpl*, cercanías *fpl*.

surveillance [sə:'veɪləns] *n* vigilancia.

survey ['sə:veɪ] *n* inspección *f*, reconocimiento; (*inquiry*) encuesta // *vt* [sə:'veɪ] examinar, inspeccionar; (*look at*) mirar, contemplar; (*make inquiries about*) hacer una encuesta de; **~or** *n* (*Brit*) agrimensor(a) *m/f*.

survival [sə'vaɪvl] *n* supervivencia.

survive [sə'vaɪv] *vi* sobrevivir; (*custom etc*) perdurar // *vt* sobrevivir a; **survivor** *n* superviviente *m/f*.

susceptible [sə'sɛptəbl] *a*: **~ (to)** (*disease*) susceptible (a); (*flattery*) sensible (a).

suspect ['sʌspɛkt] *a, n* sospechoso/a *m/f* // *vt* [səs'pɛkt] sospechar.

suspend [səs'pɛnd] *vt* suspender; **~ed sentence** *n* (*LAW*) libertad *f* condicional; **~er belt** *n* portaligas *m inv*; **~ers** *npl* (*Brit*) ligas *fpl*; (*US*) tirantes *mpl*.

suspense [səs'pɛns] *n* incertidumbre *f*, duda; (*in film etc*) suspense *m*.

suspension [səs'pɛnʃən] *n* (*gen, AUT*) suspensión *f*; (*of driving licence*) privación *f*; **~ bridge** *n* puente *m* colgante.

suspicion [səs'pɪʃən] *n* sospecha; (*distrust*) recelo; (*trace*) traza; **suspicious** [-ʃəs] *a* (*suspecting*) receloso; (*causing* **~**) sospechoso.

sustain [səs'teɪn] *vt* sostener, apoyar; (*suffer*) sufrir, padecer; **~ed** *a* (*effort*) sostenido.

sustenance ['sʌstɪnəns] *n* sustento.

swab [swɔb] *n* (*MED*) algodón *m*; (*for specimen*) frotis *m inv*.

swagger ['swægə*] *vi* pavonearse.

swallow ['swɔləu] *n* (*bird*) golondrina // *vt* tragar; **to ~ up** *vt* (*savings etc*) consumir.

swam [swæm] *pt of* **swim**.

swamp [swɔmp] *n* pantano, ciénaga // *vt*: **to ~ (with)** abrumar (de), agobiar (de); **~y** *a* pantanoso.

swan [swɔn] *n* cisne *m*.

swap [swɔp] *vt*: **to ~ (for)** canjear (por).

swarm [swɔ:m] *n* (*of bees*) enjambre *m*; (*fig*) multitud *f* // *vi*: **to ~ (with)** pulular (de).

swarthy ['swɔ:ðɪ] *a* moreno.

swastika ['swɔstɪkə] *n* esvástika, cruz *f* gamada.

swat [swɔt] *vt* aplastar.

sway [sweɪ] *vi* mecerse, balancearse // *vt* (*influence*) mover, influir en.

swear [swɛə*], *pt* **swore**, *pp* **sworn** *vi* jurar; **to ~ to sth** declarar algo bajo juramento; **~word** *n* taco, palabrota.

sweat [swɛt] *n* sudor *m* // *vi* sudar.

sweater ['swɛtə*], **sweatshirt** ['swɛtʃə:t] *n* suéter *m*.

sweaty ['swɛtɪ] *a* sudoroso.

Swede [swi:d] *n* sueco/a.

swede [swi:d] *n* (*Brit*) nabo.

Sweden ['swi:dn] *n* Suecia.

Swedish ['swi:dɪʃ] *a* sueco // *n* (*LING*) sueco.

sweep [swi:p] *n* (*act*) barrido; (*of arm*) manotazo; (*curve ~*) curva, alcance *m*; (*also: chimney ~*) deshollinador(a) *m/f* // *vb* (*pt, pp* **swept**) *vt, vi* barrer; **to ~ away** *vt* barrer; (*rub out*) borrar; **to ~ past** *vi* pasar majestuosamente; **to ~ up** *vi* barrer; **~ing** *a* (*gesture*) dramático; (*generalized*) generalizado.

sweet [swi:t] *n* (*candy*) dulce *m*, caramelo; (*Brit: pudding*) postre *m* // *a* dulce; (*sugary*) azucarado; (*fig*) dulce, amable; **~corn** *n* maíz *m*; **~en** *vt* (*person*) endulzar; (*add sugar to*) poner azúcar a; **~heart** *n* novio/a; **~ness** *n* (*gen*) dulzura; **~ pea** *n* guisante *m* de olor.

swell [swɛl] *n* (*of sea*) marejada, oleaje *m* // *a* (*US: col: excellent*) estupendo, fenomenal // *vb* (*pt* **swelled**, *pp* **swollen** *or* **swelled**) *vt* hinchar, inflar // *vi* hincharse, inflarse; **~ing** *n* (*MED*) hinchazón *f*.

sweltering ['swɛltərɪŋ] *a* sofocante, de mucho calor.

swept [swɛpt] *pt, pp of* **sweep**.

swerve [swə:v] *vi* desviarse bruscamente.

swift [swɪft] *n* (*bird*) vencejo // *a* rápido, veloz; **~ly** *ad* rápidamente.

swig [swɪg] *n* (*col: drink*) trago.

swill [swɪl] *n* bazofia // *vt* (*also:* **~ out**, **~ down**) lavar, limpiar con agua.

swim [swɪm] *n*: **to go for a ~** ir a nadar *or* a bañarse // *vb* (*pt* **swam**, *pp* **swum**) *vi* nadar; (*head, room*) dar vueltas // *vt* pasar *or* cruzar a nado; **~mer** *n* nadador(a) *m/f*; **~ming** *n* natación *f*; **~ming cap** *n* gorro de baño; **~ming costume** *n* bañador *m*, traje *m* de baño; **~ming pool** *n* piscina, alberca (*LAm*); **~suit** *n* = **~ming costume**.

swindle ['swɪndl] *n* estafa // *vt* estafar.

swine [swaɪn] *n, pl inv* cerdos *mpl*, puercos *mpl*; (*col!*) canalla *sg* (!).

swing [swiŋ] n (in playground) columpio; (movement) balanceo, vaivén m; (change of direction) viraje m; (rhythm) ritmo // vb (pt, pp **swung**) vt balancear; (on a ~) columpiar; (also: ~ round) voltear, girar // vi balancearse, columpiarse; (also: ~ round) dar media vuelta; **to be in full** ~ estar en plena marcha; ~ **bridge** n puente m giratorio; ~ **door**, (US) **~ing door** n puerta giratoria.

swingeing [swindʒiŋ] a (Brit) abrumador(a).

swipe [swaip] vt (hit) golpear fuerte; (col: steal) guindar.

swirl [swə:l] vi arremolinarse.

swish [swiʃ] a (col: smart) elegante // vi chasquear.

Swiss [swis] a, n, pl inv suizo/a m/f.

switch [switʃ] n (for light, radio etc) interruptor m; (change) cambio // vt (change) cambiar de; **to ~ off** vt apagar; (engine) parar; **to ~ on** vt encender, prender (LAm); (engine, machine) arrancar; **~board** n (TEL) centralita (de teléfonos), conmutador m (LAm).

Switzerland [switsələnd] n Suiza.

swivel [swivl] vi (also: ~ round) girar.

swollen [swəulən] pp of **swell**.

swoon [swu:n] vi desmayarse.

swoop [swu:p] n (by police etc) redada // vi (also: ~ **down**) calarse.

swop [swɒp] = **swap**.

sword [sɔ:d] n espada; **~fish** n pez m espada.

swore [swɔ:*] pt of **swear**.

sworn [swɔ:n] pp of **swear**.

swot [swɒt] (Brit) vt, vi empollar.

swum [swʌm] pp of **swim**.

swung [swʌŋ] pt, pp of **swing**.

sycamore [sikəmɔ:*] n sicomoro.

syllable [siləbl] n sílaba.

syllabus [siləbəs] n programa m de estudios.

symbol [simbl] n símbolo.

symmetry [simitri] n simetría.

sympathetic [simpə'θɛtik] a compasivo; (understanding) comprensivo.

sympathize [simpəθaiz] vi: **to ~ with sb** compadecerse de uno; **~r** n (POL) simpatizante m/f.

sympathy [simpəθi] n (pity) compasión f; (understanding) comprensión f; **with our deepest** ~ nuestro más sentido pésame.

symphony [simfəni] n sinfonía.

symposium [sim'pəuziəm] n simposio.

symptom [simptəm] n síntoma m, indicio.

synagogue [sinəgɔg] n sinagoga.

syndicate [sindikit] n (gen) sindicato; (of newspapers) agencia (de noticias).

syndrome [sindrəum] n síndrome m.

synonym [sinənim] n sinónimo.

synopsis [si'nɒpsis], pl **-ses** [-si:z] n sinopsis f inv.

syntax [sintæks] n sintaxis f inv.

synthesis [sinθəsis], pl **-ses** [-si:z] n síntesis f inv.

synthetic [sin'θɛtik] a sintético.

syphilis [sifilis] n sífilis f.

syphon [saifən] = **siphon**.

Syria [siriə] n Siria; **~n** a, n sirio/a m/f.

syringe [si'rindʒ] n jeringa.

syrup [sirəp] n jarabe m, almíbar m.

system [sistəm] n sistema m; (ANAT) organismo; **~atic** [-'mætik] a sistemático; metódico; ~ **disk** n (COMPUT) disco del sistema; **~s analyst** n analista m/f de sistemas.

T

ta [tɑ:] excl (Brit col) ¡gracias!

tab [tæb] n lengüeta; (label) etiqueta; **to keep ~s on** (fig) vigilar.

tabby [tæbi] n (also: ~ **cat**) gato atigrado.

table [teibl] n mesa; (of statistics etc) cuadro, tabla // vt (Brit: motion etc) presentar; **to lay or set the** ~ poner la mesa; **~cloth** n mantel m; ~ **of contents** n índice m de materias; ~ **d'hôte** [tɑ:bl'dəut] n menú m; ~ **lamp** n lámpara de mesa; **~mat** n salvamantel m; **~spoon** n cuchara grande; (also: **~spoonful:** as measurement) cucharada.

tablet [tæblit] n (MED) pastilla, comprimido; (for writing) bloc m; (of stone) lápida.

table tennis n ping-pong m, tenis m de mesa.

table wine n vino de mesa.

tabloid [tæbloid] n periódico popular sensacionalista; **the ~s** la prensa amarilla.

tabulate [tæbjuleit] vt disponer en tablas.

tacit [tæsit] a tácito.

tack [tæk] n (nail) tachuela; (stitch) hilván m; (NAUT) bordada // vt (nail) clavar con tachuelas; (stitch) hilvanar // vi virar.

tackle [tækl] n (gear) equipo; (fishing ~, for lifting) aparejo; (RUGBY) placaje m // vt (difficulty) enfrentar; (grapple with) agarrar; (RUGBY) placar.

tacky [tæki] a pegajoso.

tact [tækt] n tacto, discreción f; **~ful** a discreto, diplomático.

tactical [tæktikl] a táctico.

tactics [tæktiks] n, npl táctica sg.

tactless [tæktlis] a indiscreto.

tadpole [tædpəul] n renacuajo.

taffy [tæfi] n (US) melcocha.

tag [tæg] n (label) etiqueta; **to ~ along with sb** acompañar a uno.

tail [teil] n cola; (of shirt, coat) faldón m

// *vt* (*follow*) vigilar a; **to ~ away, ~ off** *vi* (*in size, quality etc*) ir disminuyendo; **~back** *n* (*Brit AUT*) cola; **~ coat** *n* frac *m*; **~ end** *n* cola, parte *f* final; **~gate** *n* (*AUT*) puerta trasera.

tailor ['teɪlə*] *n* sastre *m*; **~ing** *n* (*cut*) corte *m*; **~-made** *a* (*also fig*) hecho a la medida.

tailwind ['teɪlwɪnd] *n* viento de cola.

tainted ['teɪntɪd] *a* (*water, air*) contaminado; (*fig*) manchado.

take [teɪk], *pt* **took**, *pp* **taken** *vt* tomar; (*grab*) coger (*Sp*), agarrar (*LAm*); (*gain: prize*) ganar; (*require: effort, courage*) exigir; (*support weight of*) aguantar; (*hold: passengers etc*) tener cabida para; (*accompany, bring, carry*) llevar; (*exam*) presentarse a; **to ~ sth from** (*drawer etc*) sacar algo de; (*person*) coger (*Sp*) *or* tomar (*LAm*) algo a; **I ~ it that...** supongo que...; **to ~ after** *vt fus* parecerse a; **to ~ apart** *vt* desmontar; **to ~ away** *vt* (*remove*) quitar; (*carry off*) llevar; **to ~ back** *vt* (*return*) devolver; (*one's words*) retractar; **to ~ down** *vt* (*building*) derribar; (*letter etc*) apuntar; **to ~ in** *vt* (*Brit: deceive*) engañar; (*understand*) entender; (*include*) abarcar; (*lodger*) acoger, recibir; **to ~ off** *vi* (*AVIAT*) despegar // *vt* (*remove*) quitar; (*imitate*) imitar; **to ~ on** *vt* (*work*) aceptar; (*employee*) contratar; (*opponent*) desafiar; **to ~ out** *vt* sacar; (*remove*) quitar; **to ~ over** *vt* (*business*) tomar posesión de // *vi*: **to ~ over from sb** reemplazar a uno; **to ~ to** *vt fus* (*person*) coger cariño a (*Sp*), encariñarse con (*LAm*); (*activity*) aficionarse a; **to ~ up** *vt* (*a dress*) acortar; (*occupy: time, space*) ocupar; (*engage in: hobby etc*) dedicarse a; **~away** *a* (*Brit: food*) para llevar; **~home pay** *n* salario neto; **~off** *n* (*AVIAT*) despegue *m*; **~over** *n* (*COMM*) absorción *f*.

takings ['teɪkɪŋz] *npl* (*COMM*) ingresos *mpl.*

talc [tælk] *n* (*also: ~um powder*) talco.

tale [teɪl] *n* (*story*) cuento; (*account*) relación *f*; **to tell ~s** (*fig*) chismear.

talent ['tælnt] *n* talento; **~ed** *a* talentoso.

talk [tɔːk] *n* charla; (*gossip*) habladurías *fpl*, chismes *mpl*; (*conversation*) conversación *f* // *vi* (*speak*) hablar; (*chatter*) charlar; **~s** *npl* (*POL etc*) conversaciones *fpl*; **to ~ about** hablar de; **to ~ sb into doing sth** convencer a uno para que haga algo; **to ~ sb out of doing sth** disuadir a uno de que haga algo; **to ~ shop** hablar del trabajo; **to ~ over** *vt* discutir; **~ative** *a* hablador(a); **~ show** *n* programa *m* magazine.

tall [tɔːl] *a* alto; (*tree*) grande; **to be 6 feet ~** ≈ medir 1 metro 80, tener 1 metro 80 de alto; **~boy** *n* (*Brit*) cómoda alta;

~ story *n* cuento chino.

tally ['tælɪ] *n* cuenta // *vi*: **to ~ (with)** corresponder (con).

talon ['tælən] *n* garra.

tambourine [tæmbə'riːn] *n* pandereta.

tame [teɪm] *a* (*mild*) manso; (*tamed*) domesticado; (*fig: story, style*) mediocre.

tamper ['tæmpə*] *vi*: **to ~ with** tocar, andar con.

tampon ['tæmpən] *n* tampón *m*.

tan [tæn] *n* (*also: sun~*) bronceado // *vt* broncear // *vi* ponerse moreno // *a* (*colour*) marrón.

tang [tæŋ] *n* sabor *m* fuerte.

tangent ['tændʒənt] *n* (*MATH*) tangente *f*; **to go off at a ~** (*fig*) salirse por la tangente.

tangerine [tændʒə'riːn] *n* mandarina.

tangle ['tæŋgl] *n* enredo; **to get in(to) a ~** enredarse.

tank [tæŋk] *n* (*water ~*) depósito, tanque *m*; (*for fish*) acuario; (*MIL*) tanque *m*.

tanker ['tæŋkə*] *n* (*ship*) buque *m* cisterna; (*truck*) camión *m* cisterna.

tanned [tænd] *a* (*skin*) moreno, bronceado.

tantalizing ['tæntəlaɪzɪŋ] *a* tentador(a).

tantamount ['tæntəmaunt] *a*: **~ to** equivalente a.

tantrum ['tæntrəm] *n* rabieta.

tap [tæp] *n* (*Brit: on sink etc*) grifo, canilla (*LAm*); (*gentle blow*) golpecito; (*gas ~*) llave *f* // *vt* (*table etc*) tamborilear; (*shoulder etc*) palmear; (*resources*) utilizar, explotar; (*telephone*) intervenir; **on ~** (*fig: resources*) a mano; **~-dancing** *n* zapateado.

tape [teɪp] *n* cinta; (*also: magnetic ~*) cinta magnética; (*sticky ~*) cinta adhesiva // *vt* (*record*) grabar (en cinta); **~ measure** *n* cinta métrica, metro.

taper ['teɪpə*] *n* cirio // *vi* afilarse.

tape recorder *n* grabadora.

tapestry ['tæpɪstrɪ] *n* (*object*) tapiz *m*; (*art*) tapicería.

tar [tɑː] *n* alquitrán *m*, brea.

target ['tɑːgɪt] *n* (*gen*) blanco; **~ practice** *n* tiro al blanco.

tariff ['tærɪf] *n* tarifa.

tarmac ['tɑːmæk] *n* (*Brit: on road*) alquitranado; (*AVIAT*) pista (de aterrizaje).

tarnish ['tɑːnɪʃ] *vt* deslustrar.

tarpaulin [tɑː'pɔːlɪn] *n* alquitranado.

tart [tɑːt] *n* (*CULIN*) tarta; (*Brit col: pej: woman*) puta // *a* (*flavour*) agrio, ácido; **to ~ up** *vt* (*room, building*) dar tono a.

tartan ['tɑːtn] *n* tartán *m*, escocés *m* // *a* de tartán.

tartar ['tɑːtə*] *n* (*on teeth*) sarro; **~(e) sauce** *n* salsa tártara.

task [tɑːsk] *n* tarea; **to take to ~** reprender; **~ force** *n* (*MIL, POLICE*) grupo de operaciones.

tassel ['tæsl] *n* borla.

taste [teɪst] *n* sabor *m*, gusto; (*also:*

after~) dejo; (*sip*) sorbo; (*fig: glimpse,
idea*) muestra, idea // *vt* probar // *vi*: **to
~ of** *or* **like** (*fish etc*) saber a; **you can ~
the garlic** (in it) se nota el sabor a ajo;
can I have a ~ of this wine? ¿puedo pro
bar este vino?; **to have a ~ for sth** ser
aficionado a algo; **in good/bad ~** de
buen/mal gusto; **~ful** *a* de buen gusto;
~less *a* (*food*) soso; (*remark*) de mal
gusto; **tasty** *a* sabroso, rico.

tatters ['tætəz] *npl*: **in ~** (*also*: **tattered**)
hecho jirones.

tattoo [tə'tuː] *n* tatuaje *m*; (*spectacle*)
espectáculo militar // *vt* tatuar.

tatty ['tætɪ] *a* (*Brit col*) raído.

taught [tɔːt] *pt, pp of* **teach**.

taunt [tɔːnt] *n* burla // *vt* burlarse de.

Taurus ['tɔːrəs] *n* Tauro.

taut [tɔːt] *a* tirante, tenso.

tawdry ['tɔːdrɪ] *a* de mal gusto.

tax [tæks] *n* impuesto // *vt* gravar (con un
impuesto); (*fig: test*) poner a prueba (:
patience) agotar; **~able** *a* (*income*) imponible; **~ation** [-'seɪʃən] *n* impuestos
mpl; **~ avoidance** *n* evasión *f* de impuestos; **~ collector** *n* recaudador(a)
m/f; **~ disc** *n* (*Brit AUT*) pegatina del
impuesto de circulación; **~ evasion** *n*
evasión *f* fiscal; **~-free** *a* libre de impuestos.

taxi ['tæksɪ] *n* taxi *m* // *vi* (*AVIAT*) rodar
por la pista; **~ driver** *n* taxista *m/f*;
(*Brit*) **~ rank, ~ stand** *n* parada de
taxis.

tax: **~ payer** *n* contribuyente *m/f*; **~ relief** *n* desgravación *f* fiscal; **~ return** *n*
declaración *f* de ingresos.

TB *n abbr* = **tuberculosis**.

tea [tiː] *n* té *m*; (*Brit: snack*) merienda;
high ~ (*Brit*) merienda-cena; **~ bag** *n*
bolsita de té; **~ break** *n* (*Brit*) descanso
para el té.

teach [tiːtʃ], *pt, pp* **taught** *vt*: **to ~ sb
sth, ~ sth to sb** enseñar algo a uno // *vi*
enseñar; (*be a teacher*) ser profesor(a);
~er *n* (*in secondary school*) profesor(a)
m/f; (*in primary school*) maestro/a;
~ing *n* enseñanza.

tea cosy *n* cubretetera *m*.

teacup ['tiːkʌp] *n* taza para el té.

teak [tiːk] *n* (madera de) teca.

team [tiːm] *n* equipo; (*of animals*) pareja; **~work** *n* trabajo en equipo.

teapot ['tiːpɒt] *n* tetera.

tear [tɛə*] *n* rasgón *m*, desgarrón *m* // *n*
[tɪə*] lágrima // *vb* (*pt* **tore**, *pp* **torn**) *vt*
romper, rasgar // *vi* rasgarse; **in ~s** llorando; **to ~ along** *vi* (*rush*) precipitarse; **to ~ up** *vt* (*sheet of paper etc*)
romper; **~ful** *a* lloroso; **~ gas** *n* gas *m*
lacrimógeno.

tearoom ['tiːruːm] *n* salón *m* de té, cafetería.

tease [tiːz] *n* bromista *m/f* // *vt* tomar el
pelo a.

tea: **~ set** *n* servicio de té; **~spoon** *n*
cucharita; (*also*: **~spoonful**: *as measurement*) cucharadita.

teat [tiːt] *n* (*of bottle*) tetina.

teatime ['tiːtaɪm] *n* hora del té.

tea towel *n* (*Brit*) paño de cocina.

technical ['tɛknɪkl] *a* técnico; **~ity**
[-'kælɪtɪ] *n* detalle *m* técnico.

technician [tɛk'nɪʃn] *n* técnico/a.

technique [tɛk'niːk] *n* técnica.

technological [tɛknə'lɒdʒɪkl] *a* tecnológi-
co.

technology [tɛk'nɒlədʒɪ] *n* tecnología.

teddy (bear) ['tɛdɪ-] *n* osito de felpa.

tedious ['tiːdɪəs] *a* pesado, aburrido.

tee [tiː] *n* (*GOLF*) tee *m*.

teem [tiːm] *vi*: **to ~ with** rebosar de; **it is
~ing** (**with rain**) llueve a mares.

teenage ['tiːneɪdʒ] *a* (*fashions etc*) juvenil; **~r** *n* adolescente *m/f*.

teens [tiːnz] *npl*: **to be in one's ~** ser
adolescente.

tee-shirt ['tiːʃəːt] *n* = **T-shirt**.

teeter ['tiːtə*] *vi* balancearse.

teeth [tiːθ] *npl of* **tooth**.

teethe [tiːð] *vi* echar los dientes.

teething ['tiːðɪŋ]: **~ ring** *n* mordedor
m; **~ troubles** *npl* (*fig*) dificultades *fpl*
iniciales.

teetotal ['tiː'təutl] *a* (*person*) abstemio.

telegram ['tɛlɪɡræm] *n* telegrama *m*.

telegraph ['tɛlɪɡrɑːf] *n* telégrafo.

telepathy [tə'lɛpəθɪ] *n* telepatía.

telephone ['tɛlɪfəun] *n* teléfono // *vt* llamar por teléfono, telefonear; **~ booth**,
(*Brit*) **~ box** *n* cabina telefónica; **~
call** *n* llamada (telefónica); **~ directory** *n* guía (telefónica); **~ number** *n*
número de teléfono; **telephonist**
[tə'lɛfənɪst] *n* (*Brit*) telefonista *m/f*.

telephoto ['tɛlɪ'fəutəu] *a*: **~ lens** teleob-
jetivo.

telescope ['tɛlɪskəup] *n* telescopio.

televise ['tɛlɪvaɪz] *vt* televisar.

television ['tɛlɪvɪʒən] *n* televisión *f*; **~
set** *n* televisor *m*.

telex ['tɛlɛks] *n* télex *m* // *vt, vi* enviar un
télex (a).

tell [tɛl], *pt, pp* **told** *vt* decir; (*relate:
story*) contar; (*distinguish*): **to ~ sth
from** distinguir algo de // *vi* (*talk*): **to ~
(of)** contar; (*have effect*) tener efecto;
to ~ sb to do sth mandar a uno hacer
algo; **to ~ off** *vt*: **to ~ sb off** regañar a
uno; **~er** *n* (*in bank*) cajero/a; **~ing** *a*
(*remark, detail*) revelador(a); **~tale** *a*
(*sign*) indicador(a).

telly ['tɛlɪ] *n* (*Brit col*) tele *f*.

temp [tɛmp] *n abbr* (*Brit*: = **temporary**)
temporero/a // vi trabajar de interino/a.

temper ['tɛmpə*] *n* (*mood*) humor *m*;
(*bad ~*) (mal) genio; (*fit of anger*) ira;
(*of child*) rabieta // *vt* (*moderate*) moderar; **to be in a ~** estar furioso; **to lose
one's ~** enfadarse, enojarse (*LAm*).

temperament ['tɛmprəmənt] *n* (*nature*) temperamento.

temperate ['tɛmprət] *a* moderado; (*climate*) templado.

temperature ['tɛmprətʃə*] *n* temperatura; **to have** *or* **run a ~** tener fiebre.

tempest ['tɛmpɪst] *n* tempestad *f*.

template ['tɛmplɪt] *n* plantilla.

temple ['tɛmpl] *n* (*building*) templo; (*ANAT*) sien *f*.

temporarily ['tɛmpərərɪlɪ] *ad* temporalmente.

temporary ['tɛmpərərɪ] *a* provisional, temporal; (*passing*) transitorio; (*worker*) temporero.

tempt [tɛmpt] *vt* tentar; **to ~ sb into doing sth** tentar *or* inducir a uno a hacer algo; **~ation** [-'teɪʃən] *n* tentación *f*; **~ing** *a* tentador(a).

ten [tɛn] *num* diez.

tenable ['tɛnəbl] *a* sostenible.

tenacity [tə'næsɪtɪ] *n* tenacidad *f*.

tenancy ['tɛnənsɪ] *n* alquiler *m*; (*of house*) inquilinato.

tenant ['tɛnənt] *n* (*rent-payer*) inquilino/a; (*occupant*) habitante *m/f*.

tend [tɛnd] *vt* cuidar // *vi*: **to ~ to do sth** tener tendencia a hacer algo.

tendency ['tɛndənsɪ] *n* tendencia.

tender ['tɛndə*] *a* (*meat*) tierno; (*sore*) sensible; (*affectionate*) tierno, cariñoso // *n* (*COMM: offer*) oferta; (*money*): **legal ~** moneda de curso legal // *vt* ofrecer; **~ness** *n* ternura; (*of meat*) blandura.

tenement ['tɛnəmənt] *n* casa de pisos *or* vecinos (*Sp*).

tenet ['tɛnət] *n* principio.

tennis ['tɛnɪs] *n* tenis *m*; **~ ball** *n* pelota de tenis; **~ court** *n* cancha de tenis; **~ player** *n* tenista *m/f*; **~ racket** *n* raqueta de tenis; **~ shoes** *npl* zapatillas *fpl* de tenis.

tenor ['tɛnə*] *n* (*MUS*) tenor *m*.

tense [tɛns] *a* (*moment, atmosphere*) tenso; (*stretched*) tirante; (*stiff*) rígido, tieso; (*person*) nervioso // *n* (*LING*) tiempo.

tension ['tɛnʃən] *n* tensión *f*.

tent [tɛnt] *n* tienda (de campaña), carpa (*LAm*).

tentacle ['tɛntəkl] *n* tentáculo.

tenterhooks ['tɛntəhuks] *npl*: **on ~** sobre ascuas.

tenth [tɛnθ] *a* décimo.

tent peg *n* clavija, estaca.

tent pole *n* mástil *m*.

tenuous ['tɛnjuəs] *a* tenue.

tenure ['tɛnjuə*] *n* (*of land*) tenencia; (*of job: period*) ejercicio.

tepid ['tɛpɪd] *a* tibio.

term [təːm] *n* (*COMM: time limit*) plazo; (*word*) término; (*period*) período; (*SCOL*) trimestre *m* // *vt* llamar; **~s** *npl* (*conditions*) condiciones *fpl*; **in the short/long ~** a corto/largo plazo; **to be on good ~s with sb** llevarse bien con uno; **to come to ~s with** (*problem*) adaptarse a.

terminal ['təːmɪnl] *a* (*disease*) mortal // *n* (*ELEC*) borne *m*; (*COMPUT*) terminal *m*; (*also:* **air ~**) terminal *f*; (*Brit: also:* **coach ~**) (estación *f*) terminal *f*.

terminate ['təːmɪneɪt] *vt* terminar // *vi*: **to ~ in** acabar por.

terminus ['təːmɪnəs], *pl* **-mini** [-mɪnaɪ] *n* término, (estación *f*) terminal *f*.

terrace ['tɛrəs] *n* terraza; (*Brit: row of houses*) hilera de casas adosadas; **the ~s** (*Brit SPORT*) las gradas *fpl*; **~d** *a* (*garden*) colgante; (*house*) adosado.

terrain [tɛ'reɪn] *n* terreno.

terrible ['tɛrɪbl] *a* terrible, horrible; (*fam*) atroz; **terribly** *ad* terriblemente; (*very badly*) malísimamente.

terrier ['tɛrɪə*] *n* terrier *m*.

terrific [tə'rɪfɪk] *a* fantástico, fenomenal; (*wonderful*) maravilloso.

terrify ['tɛrɪfaɪ] *vt* aterrorizar.

territory ['tɛrɪtərɪ] *n* territorio.

terror ['tɛrə*] *n* terror *m*; **~ism** *n* terrorismo; **~ist** *n* terrorista *m/f*; **~ize** *vt* aterrorizar.

terse [təːs] *a* (*style*) conciso; (*reply*) brusco.

Terylene ['tɛrəliːn] *n* ® (*Brit*) terylene *m* ®.

test [tɛst] *n* (*trial, check*) prueba, ensayo; (: *of goods in factory*) control *m*; (*of courage etc, CHEM*) prueba; (*MED*) examen *m*; (*exam*) examen *m*, test *m*; (*also:* **driving ~**) examen *m* de conducir // *vt* probar, poner a prueba; (*MED*) examinar.

testament ['tɛstəmənt] *n* testamento; **the Old/New T~** el Antiguo/Nuevo Testamento.

testicle ['tɛstɪkl] *n* testículo.

testify ['tɛstɪfaɪ] *vi* (*LAW*) prestar declaración; **to ~ to sth** atestiguar algo.

testimony ['tɛstɪmənɪ] *n* (*LAW*) testimonio, declaración *f*.

test: **~ match** *n* (*CRICKET, RUGBY*) partido internacional; **~ pilot** *n* piloto/mujer piloto *m/f* de pruebas; **~ tube** *n* probeta; **~ tube baby** *n* niño/a probeta.

tetanus ['tɛtənəs] *n* tétano.

tether ['tɛðə*] *vt* atar (con una cuerda) // *n*: **to be at the end of one's ~** no aguantar más.

text [tɛkst] *n* texto; **~book** *n* libro de texto.

textiles ['tɛkstaɪlz] *npl* textiles *mpl*, tejidos *mpl*.

texture ['tɛkstʃə*] *n* textura.

Thai [taɪ] *a, n* tailandés/esa *m/f*; **~land** *n* Tailandia.

Thames [tɛmz] *n*: **the ~** el (río) Támesis.

than [ðæn] *conj* (*in comparisons*): **more ~ 10/once** más de 10/una vez; **I have more/less ~ you/Paul** tengo más/menos que tú/Paul; **she is older ~ you think** es mayor de lo que piensas.

thank [θæŋk] *vt* dar las gracias a, agradecer; ~ **you (very much)** muchas gracias; ~**s** *npl* gracias *fpl* // *excl* ¡gracias!; ~**s to** *prep* gracias a; ~**ful** *a*: ~**ful (for)** agradecido (por); ~**less** *a* ingrato; **T~sgiving (Day)** *n* día *m* de Acción de Gracias.

that [ðæt] ♦ *a* (*demonstrative*: *pl* those) ese/a, *pl* esos/as; (*more remote*) aquel/aquella, *pl* aquellos/as; **leave those books on the table** deja esos libros sobre la mesa; ~ **one** ése/ésa; (*more remote*) aquél/aquélla; ~ **one over there** ése/ésa de ahí; aquél/aquélla de allí
♦ *pron* **1** (*demonstrative*: *pl* those) ése/a, *pl* ésos/as; (*neuter*) eso; (*more remote*) aquél/aquélla, *pl* aquéllos/as; (*neuter*) aquello; **what's** ~? ¿qué es eso (*or* aquello)?; **who's** ~? ¿quién es ése/a (*or* aquél/aquélla)?; **is** ~ **you?** ¿eres tú?; **will you eat all** ~? ¿vas a comer todo eso?; ~**'s my house** ésa es mi casa; ~**'s what he said** eso es lo que dijo; ~ **is** (*to say*) es decir
2 (*relative*: *subject, object*) que; (*with preposition*) (el/la) que *etc*, el/la cual *etc*; **the book** (~) **I read** el libro que leí; **the books** ~ **are in the library** los libros que están en la biblioteca; **all** (~) **I have** todo lo que tengo; **the box** (~) **I put it in** la caja en la que *or* donde lo puse; **the people** (~) **I spoke to** la gente con la que hablé
3 (*relative*: *of time*) que; **the day** (~) **he came** el día (en) que vino
♦ *conj* que; **he thought** ~ **I was ill** creyó que estaba enfermo
♦ *ad* (*demonstrative*): **I can't work** ~ **much** no puedo trabajar tanto; **I didn't realise it was** ~ **bad** no creí que fuera tan malo; ~ **high** así de alto.

thatched [θætʃt] *a* (*roof*) de paja; ~ **cottage** casita con tejado de paja.

thaw [θɔː] *n* deshielo // *vi* (*ice*) derretirse; (*food*) descongelarse // *vt* (*food*) descongelar.

the [ðiː, ðə] *definite article* **1** (*gen*) el, *f* la, *pl* los, *fpl* las (*NB* = **el** *immediately before* f *noun beginning with stressed* (*h*)*a*; *a* + **el** = **al**; *de* + **el** = **del**); ~ **boy/girl** el chico/la chica; ~ **books/flowers** los libros/las flores; **to** ~ **postman/from** ~ **drawer** al cartero/del cajón; **I haven't** ~ **time/money** no tengo tiempo/dinero
2 (+ *adjective to form noun*) los; lo; ~ **rich and** ~ **poor** los ricos y los pobres; **to attempt** ~ **impossible** intentar lo imposible
3 (*in titles*): **Elizabeth** ~ **First** Isabel primera; **Peter** ~ **Great** Pedro el Grande
4 (*in comparisons*): ~ **more he works** ~ **more he earns** cuanto más trabaja más gana.

theatre, (*US*) **theater** [ˈθɪətə*] *n* teatro; ~**goer** *n* aficionado/a al teatro.

theatrical [θɪˈætrɪkl] *a* teatral.

theft [θeft] *n* robo.

their [ðɛə*] *a* su; ~**s** *pron* (el) suyo/(la) suya *etc*; *see also* **my, mine.**

them [ðɛm, ðəm] *pron* (*direct*) los/las; (*indirect*) les; (*stressed, after prep*) ellos/ellas; *see also* **me.**

theme [θiːm] *n* tema *m*; ~ **song** *n* tema *m* (musical).

themselves [ðəmˈselvz] *pl pron* (*subject*) ellos mismos/ellas mismas; (*complement*) se; (*after prep*) sí (mismos/as); *see also* **oneself.**

then [ðen] *ad* (*at that time*) entonces; (*next*) pues; (*later*) luego, después; (*and also*) además // *conj* (*therefore*) en ese caso, entonces // *a*: **the** ~ **president** el entonces presidente; **from** ~ **on** desde entonces.

theology [θɪˈɒlədʒɪ] *n* teología.

theoretical [θɪəˈretɪkl] *a* teórico.

theory [ˈθɪərɪ] *n* teoría.

therapist [ˈθerəpɪst] *n* terapeuta *m/f.*

therapy [ˈθerəpɪ] *n* terapia.

there [ˈðɛə*] *ad* **1**: ~ **is,** ~ **are** hay; ~ **is no-one here/no bread left** no hay nadie aquí/no queda pan; ~ **has been an accident** ha habido un accidente
2 (*referring to place*) ahí; (*distant*) allí; **it's** ~ está allí; **put it in/on/up/down** ~ ponlo ahí dentro/encima/arriba/abajo; **I want that book** ~ quiero ese libro de ahí; ~ **he is!** ¡ahí está!
3: ~, ~ (*esp to child*) ea, ea.

there: ~**abouts** *ad* por ahí; ~**after** *ad* después; ~**by** *ad* así, de ese modo; ~**fore** *ad* por lo tanto; ~**'s** = ~ **is;** ~ **has.**

thermal [ˈθɜːml] *a* termal; (*paper*) térmico; ~ **printer** *n* termoimpresora.

thermometer [θəˈmɒmɪtə*] *n* termómetro.

Thermos [ˈθɜːməs] *n* ® (*also:* ~ **flask**) termo.

thermostat [ˈθɜːməustæt] *n* termostato.

thesaurus [θɪˈsɔːrəs] *n* tesoro.

these [ðiːz] *pl a* estos/as // *pl pron* éstos/as.

thesis [ˈθiːsɪs], *pl* -**ses** [-siːz] *n* tesis *f inv.*

they [ðeɪ] *pl pron* ellos/ellas; (*stressed*) ellos (mismos)/ellas (mismas); ~ **say that...** (*it is said that*) se dice que...; ~**'d** = **they had, they would;** ~**'ll** = **they shall, they will;** ~**'re** = **they are;** ~**'ve** = **they have.**

thick [θɪk] *a* (*liquid, smoke*) espeso; (*wall, slice*) grueso; (*vegetation, beard*) tupido; (*stupid*) torpe // *n*: **in the** ~ **of the battle** en lo más reñido de la batalla; **it's 20 cm** ~ tiene 20 cm de espesor; ~**en** *vi* espesarse // *vt* (*sauce etc*) espesar; ~**ness** *n* espesor *m*, grueso; ~**set** *a* fornido; ~**skinned** *a* (*fig*) insensible.

thief [θiːf], pl **thieves** [θiːvz] n ladrón/ona m/f.

thigh [θaɪ] n muslo.

thimble ['θɪmbl] n dedal m.

thin [θɪn] a (person, animal) flaco; (material) delgado; (liquid) poco denso; (soup) aguado; (fog) ligero; (crowd) escaso // vt: to ~ (down) (sauce, paint) diluir.

thing [θɪŋ] n cosa; (object) objeto, artículo; (contraption) chisme m; ~s npl (belongings) efectos mpl (personales); the best ~ would be to... lo mejor sería...; how are ~s? ¿qué tal?

think [θɪŋk], pt, pp **thought** vi pensar // vt pensar, creer; what did you ~ of them? ¿qué te parecieron?; to ~ about sth/sb pensar en algo/uno; I'll ~ about it lo pensaré; to ~ of doing sth pensar en hacer algo; I ~ so/not creo que sí/no; to ~ well of sb tener buen concepto de uno; to ~ over vt reflexionar sobre, meditar; to ~ up vt imaginar; ~ tank n gabinete m de estrategia.

third [θəːd] a tercer(a) // n tercero/a; (fraction) tercio; (Brit SCOL: degree) de tercera clase; ~ly ad en tercer lugar; ~ party insurance n (Brit) seguro contra terceros; ~-rate a (de calidad) mediocre; the T~ World el Tercer Mundo.

thirst [θəːst] n sed f; ~y a: to be ~y tener sed.

thirteen ['θəː'tiːn] num trece.

thirty ['θəːtɪ] num treinta.

this [ðɪs] ♦ a (demonstrative: pl these) este/a; pl estos/as; (neuter) esto; ~ man/woman este hombre/esta mujer; these children/flowers estos chicos/estas flores; ~ one (here) éste/a, esto (de aquí)
♦ pron (demonstrative: pl these) éste/a; pl éstos/as; (neuter) esto; who is ~? ¿quién es éste/ésta?; what is ~? ¿qué es esto?; ~ is where I live aquí vivo; ~ is what he said esto es lo que dijo; ~ is Mr Brown (in introductions) le presento al Sr. Brown; (photo) éste es el Sr. Brown; (on telephone) habla el Sr. Brown
♦ ad (demonstrative): ~ high/long etc así de alto/largo etc; ~ far hasta aquí.

thistle ['θɪsl] n cardo.

thong [θɒŋ] n correa.

thorn [θɔːn] n espina.

thorough ['θʌrə] a (search) minucioso; (knowledge, research) profundo; ~bred a (horse) de pura sangre; ~fare n calle f; 'no ~fare' 'prohibido el paso'; ~ly ad minuciosamente; profundamente, a fondo.

those [ðəuz] pl pron ésos/ésas; (more remote) aquéllos/as // pl a esos/esas; aquellos/as.

though [ðəu] conj aunque // ad sin embargo.

thought [θɔːt] pt, pp of **think** // n pensa-

miento; (opinion) opinión f; (intention) intención f; ~ful a pensativo; (considerate) atento; ~less a desconsiderado.

thousand ['θauzənd] num mil; two ~ dos mil; ~s of miles de; ~th a milésimo.

thrash [θræʃ] vt apalear; (defeat) derrotar; to ~ about vi revolcarse; to ~ out vt discutir a fondo.

thread [θrɛd] n hilo; (of screw) rosca // vt (needle) enhebrar; ~bare a raído.

threat [θrɛt] n amenaza; ~en vi amenazar // vt: to ~en sb with sth/to do amenazar a uno con algo/con hacer.

three [θriː] num tres; ~-dimensional a tridimensional; ~-piece suit n traje m de tres piezas; ~-piece suite n tresillo; ~-ply a (wool) triple; ~-wheeler n (car) coche m cabina.

thresh [θrɛʃ] vt (AGR) trillar.

threshold ['θrɛʃhəuld] n umbral m.

threw [θruː] pt of **throw**.

thrifty ['θrɪftɪ] a económico.

thrill [θrɪl] n (excitement) emoción f // vt emocionar; to be ~ed (with gift etc) estar encantado; ~er n película/novela de suspense.

thrilling ['θrɪlɪŋ] a emocionante.

thrive [θraɪv], pt **thrived** or **throve** [θrəuv], pp **thrived** or **thriven** ['θrɪvn] vi (grow) crecer; (do well) prosperar; **thriving** a próspero.

throat [θrəut] n garganta; to have a sore ~ tener dolor de garganta.

throb [θrɒb] vi (heart) latir; (engine) vibrar; (with pain) dar punzadas.

throes [θrəuz] npl: in the ~ of en medio de.

throne [θrəun] n trono.

throng [θrɒŋ] n multitud f, muchedumbre f // vt agolparse en.

throttle ['θrɒtl] n (AUT) acelerador m // vt estrangular.

through [θruː] prep por, a través de; (time) durante; (by means of) por medio de, mediante; (owing to) gracias a // a (ticket, train) directo // ad completamente, de parte a parte; de principio a fin; to put sb ~ to sb (TEL) poner or pasar a uno con uno; to be ~ (TEL) tener comunicación; (have finished) haber terminado; 'no ~ road' (Brit) 'calle sin salida'; ~out prep (place) por todas partes de, por todo; (time) durante todo // ad por or en todas partes.

throve [θrəuv] pt of **thrive**.

throw [θrəu] n tiro; (SPORT) lanzamiento // vt (pt **threw**, pp **thrown**) tirar, echar; (SPORT) lanzar; (rider) derribar; (fig) desconcertar; to ~ a party dar una fiesta; to ~ away vt tirar; to ~ off vt deshacerse de; to ~ out vt tirar; to ~ up vi vomitar; ~away a para tirar, desechable; ~-in n (SPORT) saque m.

thru [θruː] (US) = **through**.

thrush [θrʌʃ] n zorzal m, tordo.

thrust [θrʌst] n (TECH) empuje m // vt (pt, pp thrust) empujar; (push in) introducir.

thud [θʌd] n golpe m sordo.

thug [θʌg] n gamberro/a.

thumb [θʌm] n (ANAT) pulgar m // vt: to ~ a lift hacer autostop; to ~ through vt fus (book) hojear; ~tack n (US) chincheta, chinche m (LAm).

thump [θʌmp] n golpe m; (sound) ruido seco or sordo // vt, vi golpear.

thunder [ˈθʌndə*] n trueno; (of applause etc) estruendo // vi tronar; (train etc): to ~ past pasar como un trueno; ~bolt n rayo; ~clap n trueno; ~storm n tormenta; ~y a tormentoso.

Thursday [ˈθəːzdɪ] n jueves m inv.

thus [ðʌs] ad así, de este modo.

thwart [θwɔːt] vt frustrar.

thyme [taɪm] n tomillo.

thyroid [ˈθaɪrɔɪd] n tiroides m inv.

tiara [tɪˈɑːrə] n tiara, diadema.

tic [tɪk] n tic m.

tick [tɪk] n (sound: of clock) tictac m; (mark) palomita; (ZOOL) garrapata; (Brit col): in a ~ en un instante // vi hacer tictac // vt marcar; to ~ off vt marcar; (person) reñir; to ~ over vi (engine) girar en marcha lenta; (fig) ir tirando.

ticket [ˈtɪkɪt] n billete m, tíquet m, boleto (LAm); (for cinema etc) entrada, boleto (LAm); (in shop: on goods) etiqueta; (for library) tarjeta; ~ collector n revisor(a) m/f; ~ office n (THEATRE) taquilla, boletería (LAm); (RAIL) despacho de billetes or boletos (LAm).

tickle [ˈtɪkl] n: to give sb a ~ hacer cosquillas a uno // vt hacer cosquillas a; **ticklish** a (person) cosquilloso.

tidal [ˈtaɪdl] a de marea; ~ wave n maremoto.

tidbit [ˈtɪdbɪt] (US) = titbit.

tiddlywinks [ˈtɪdlɪwɪŋks] n juego infantil de habilidad con fichas de plástico.

tide [taɪd] n marea; (fig: of events) curso, marcha; high/low ~ marea alta/baja.

tidy [ˈtaɪdɪ] a (room) ordenado; (drawing, work) limpio; (person) (bien) arreglado // vt (also: ~ up) poner en orden.

tie [taɪ] n (string etc) atadura; (Brit: neck~) corbata; (fig: link) vínculo, lazo; (SPORT: draw) empate m // vt atar // vi (SPORT) empatar; to ~ in a bow atar con un lazo; to ~ a knot in sth hacer un nudo en algo; to ~ down vt atar; (fig): to ~ sb down to obligar a uno a; to ~ up vt (parcel) envolver; (dog) atar; (boat) amarrar; (arrangements) concluir; to be ~d up (busy) estar ocupado.

tier [tɪə*] n grada; (of cake) piso.

tiger [ˈtaɪgə*] n tigre m.

tight [taɪt] a (rope) tirante; (clothes, budget) ajustado; (programme) apreta-

do; (bend) cerrado; (col: drunk) borracho // ad (squeeze) muy fuerte; (shut) herméticamente; ~s npl (Brit) pantimedias fpl; ~en vt (rope) estirar; (screw) apretar // vi apretarse; estirarse; ~fisted a tacaño; ~ly ad (grasp) muy fuerte; ~rope n cuerda floja.

tile [taɪl] n (on roof) teja; (on floor) baldosa; (on wall) azulejo; ~d a embaldosado.

till [tɪl] n caja (registradora) // vt (land) cultivar // prep, conj = until.

tiller [ˈtɪlə*] n (NAUT) caña del timón.

tilt [tɪlt] vt inclinar // vi inclinarse.

timber [ˈtɪmbə*] n (material) madera; (trees) árboles mpl.

time [taɪm] n tiempo; (epoch: often pl) época; (by clock) hora; (moment) momento; (occasion) vez f; (MUS) compás m // vt calcular or medir el tiempo de; (race) cronometrar; (remark etc) elegir el momento para; a long ~ mucho tiempo; 4 at a ~ 4 a la vez; for the ~ being de momento, por ahora; from ~ to ~ de vez en cuando; in ~ (soon enough) a tiempo; (after some time) con el tiempo; (MUS) al compás; in a week's ~ dentro de una semana; in no ~ en un abrir y cerrar de ojos; any ~ cuando sea; on ~ a la hora; 5 ~s 5 5 por 5; what ~ is it? ¿qué hora es?; to have a good ~ pasarlo bien, divertirse; ~ bomb n bomba de efecto retardado; ~ lag n desfase m; ~less a eterno; ~ly a oportuno; ~ off n tiempo libre; ~r n (~ switch) interruptor m; (in kitchen etc) programador m horario; ~ scale n escala de tiempo; ~ switch n (Brit) interruptor m (horario); ~table n horario; ~ zone n huso horario.

timid [ˈtɪmɪd] a tímido.

timing [ˈtaɪmɪŋ] n (SPORT) cronometraje m; the ~ of his resignation el momento que eligió para dimitir.

timpani [ˈtɪmpənɪ] npl tímpanos mpl.

tin [tɪn] n estaño; (also: ~ plate) hojalata; (Brit: can) lata; ~foil n papel m de estaño.

tinge [tɪndʒ] n matiz m // vt: ~d with teñido de.

tingle [ˈtɪŋgl] vi sentir hormigueo.

tinker [ˈtɪŋkə*] n calderero/a; (gipsy) gitano/a; to ~ with vt fus jugar con, tocar.

tinkle [ˈtɪŋkl] vi tintinear.

tinned [tɪnd] a (Brit: food) en lata, en conserva.

tin opener [-ˈəupnə*] n (Brit) abrelatas m inv.

tinsel [ˈtɪnsl] n oropel m.

tint [tɪnt] n matiz m; (for hair) tinte m; ~ed a (hair) teñido; (glass, spectacles) ahumado.

tiny [ˈtaɪnɪ] a minúsculo, pequeñito.

tip [tɪp] n (end) punta; (gratuity) propina; (*Brit: for rubbish*) vertedero; (*advice*) consejo // *vt* (*waiter*) dar una propina a; (*tilt*) inclinar; (*empty: also* ~ out) vaciar, echar; **to ~ over** *vt* volcar // *vi* volcarse; **~-off** *n* (*hint*) advertencia; **~ped** *a* (*Brit: cigarette*) con filtro.

tipsy ['tɪpsɪ] *a* alegre, mareado.

tiptoe ['tɪptəu] *n* (*Brit*): **on ~** de puntillas.

tiptop ['tɪp'tɔp] *a*: **in ~ condition** en perfectas condiciones.

tire ['taɪə*] *n* (*US*) = **tyre** // *vt* cansar // *vi* (*gen*) cansarse; (*become bored*) aburrirse; **~d** *a* cansado; **to be ~d of sth** estar harto de algo; **~less** *a* incansable; **~some** *a* aburrido; **tiring** *a* cansado.

tissue ['tɪʃuː] *n* tejido; (*paper handkerchief*) pañuelo de papel, kleenex *m* ®; **~ paper** *n* papel *m* de seda.

tit [tɪt] *n* (*bird*) herrerillo común; **to give ~ for tat** dar ojo por ojo.

titbit ['tɪtbɪt], (*US*) **tidbit** *n* (*food*) golosina; (*news*) pedazo.

titillate ['tɪtɪleɪt] *vt* estimular, excitar.

titivate ['tɪtɪveɪt] *vt* emperejilar.

title ['taɪtl] *n* título; **~ deed** *n* (*LAW*) título de propiedad; **~ role** *n* papel *m* principal.

titter ['tɪtə*] *vi* reírse entre dientes.

titular ['tɪtjulə*] *a* (*in name only*) nominal.

TM *abbr* (= *trademark*) marca de fábrica.

to [tuː, tə] ♦ *prep* **1** (*direction*) a; **to go ~ France/London/school/the station** ir a Francia/Londres/al colegio/a la estación; **to go ~ Claude's/the doctor's** ir a casa de Claude/al médico; **the road ~ Edinburgh** la carretera de Edimburgo **2** (*as far as*) hasta, a; **from here ~ London** de aquí a or hasta Londres; **to count ~ 10** contar hasta 10; **from 40 ~ 50 people** entre 40 y 50 personas **3** (*with expressions of time*): **a quarter/twenty ~ 5** las 5 menos cuarto/veinte **4** (*for, of*): **the key ~ the front door** la llave de la puerta principal; **she is secretary ~ the director** es la secretaria del director; **a letter ~ his wife** una carta a or para su mujer **5** (*expressing indirect object*) a; **to give sth ~ sb** darle algo a alguien; **to talk ~ sb** hablar con alguien; **to be a danger ~ sb** ser un peligro para alguien; **to carry out repairs ~ sth** hacer reparaciones en algo **6** (*in relation to*): **3 goals ~ 2** 3 goles a 2; **30 miles ~ the gallon** ≈ 9,4 litros a los cien (kms) **7** (*purpose, result*): **to come ~ sb's aid** venir en auxilio or ayuda de alguien; **to sentence sb ~ death** condenar a uno a muerte; **~ my great surprise** con gran sorpresa mía ♦ *with vb* **1** (*simple infinitive*): **~ go/eat**

ir/comer **2** (*following another vb*): **to want/try/start ~ do** querer/intentar/empezar a hacer; *see also relevant verb* **3** (*with vb omitted*): **I don't want ~** no quiero **4** (*purpose, result*) para; **I did it ~ help you** lo hice para ayudarte; **he came ~ see you** vino a verte **5** (*equivalent to relative clause*): **I have things ~ do** tengo cosas que hacer; **the main thing is ~ try** lo principal es intentarlo **6** (*after adjective etc*): **ready ~ go** listo para irse; **too old ~ ...** demasiado viejo (como) para ... ♦ *ad*: **pull/push the door ~** tirar de/empujar la puerta

toad [təud] *n* sapo; **~stool** *n* hongo venenoso.

toast [təust] *n* (*CULIN: also*: **piece of ~**) tostada; (*drink, speech*) brindis *m* // *vt* (*CULIN*) tostar; (*drink to*) brindar; **~er** *n* tostador *m*.

tobacco [tə'bækəu] *n* tabaco; **~nist** *n* estanquero/a, tabaquero/a (*LAm*); **~nist's (shop)** *n* (*Brit*) estanco, tabaquería (*LAm*); **~ shop** *n* (*US*) = **~nist's (shop)**.

toboggan [tə'bɔgən] *n* tobogán *m*.

today [tə'deɪ] *ad, n* (*also: fig*) hoy *m*.

toddler ['tɔdlə*] *n* niño/a (que empieza a andar).

toddy ['tɔdɪ] *n* ponche *m*.

to-do [tə'duː] *n* (*fuss*) lío.

toe [təu] *n* dedo (del pie); (*of shoe*) punta; **to ~ the line** (*fig*) conformarse; **~nail** *n* uña del pie.

toffee ['tɔfɪ] *n* caramelo.

together [tə'gɛðə*] *ad* juntos; (*at same time*) al mismo tiempo, a la vez; **~ with** *prep* junto con.

toil [tɔɪl] *n* trabajo duro, labor *f*.

toilet ['tɔɪlət] *n* (*Brit: lavatory*) servicios *mpl*, wáter *m*, sanitario (*LAm*) // *cpd* (*soap etc*) de aseo; **~ bag** *n* esponjera; **~ bowl** *n* taza (de retrete); **~ paper** *n* papel *m* higiénico; **~ries** *npl* artículos *mpl* de aseo; (*make-up etc*) artículos *mpl* de tocador; **~ roll** *n* rollo de papel higiénico; **~ water** *n* (agua de) colonia.

token ['təukən] *n* (*sign*) señal *f*, muestra; (*souvenir*) recuerdo; (*voucher*) vale *m*; (*disc*) ficha; **book/record ~** (*Brit*) vale *m* para comprar libros/discos.

Tokyo ['təukjəu] *n* Tokio, Tokío.

told [təuld] *pt, pp of* **tell**.

tolerable ['tɔlərəbl] *a* (*bearable*) soportable; (*fairly good*) pasable.

tolerance ['tɔlrns] *n* (*also: TECH*) tolerancia.

tolerant ['tɔlərnt] *a*: **~ of** tolerante con.

tolerate ['tɔləreɪt] *vt* tolerar.

toll [təul] *n* (*of casualties*) número de víctimas; (*tax, charge*) peaje *m* // *vi* (*bell*) doblar.

tomato [tə'mɑːtəu], pl ~es n tomate m.

tomb [tuːm] n tumba.

tomboy ['tɒmbɔɪ] n marimacho.

tombstone ['tuːmstəun] n lápida.

tomcat ['tɒmkæt] n gato.

tomorrow [tə'mɒrəu] ad, n (also: fig) mañana; **the day after** ~ pasado mañana; ~ **morning** mañana por la mañana; **a week** ~ de mañana en ocho (días).

ton [tʌn] n tonelada (Brit = 1016 kg; US = 907 kg); (metric ~) tonelada métrica; ~s of (col) montones de.

tone [təun] n tono // vi armonizar; **to** ~ **down** vt (criticism) suavizar; (colour) atenuar; **to** ~ **up** vt (muscles) tonificar; ~-**deaf** a que no tiene oído musical.

tongs [tɒŋz] npl (for coal) tenazas fpl; (for hair) tenacillas fpl.

tongue [tʌŋ] n lengua; ~ **in cheek** ad irónicamente; ~-**tied** a (fig) mudo; ~-**twister** n trabalenguas m inv.

tonic ['tɒnɪk] n (MED) tónico; (MUS) tónica; (also: ~ **water**) (agua) tónica.

tonight [tə'naɪt] ad, n esta noche.

tonnage ['tʌnɪdʒ] n (NAUT) tonelaje m.

tonsil ['tɒnsl] n amígdala; ~**litis** [-'laɪtɪs] n amigdalitis f.

too [tuː] ad (excessively) demasiado; (also) también; ~ **much** ad, a demasiado; ~ **many** a demasiados/as; ~ **bad!** ¡mala suerte!

took [tuk] pt of **take**.

tool [tuːl] n herramienta; ~ **box** n caja de herramientas.

toot [tuːt] vi (with car horn) tocar la bocina.

tooth [tuːθ], pl **teeth** n (ANAT, TECH) diente m; (molar) muela; ~**ache** n dolor m de muelas; ~**brush** n cepillo de dientes; ~**paste** n pasta de dientes; ~**pick** n palillo.

top [tɒp] n (of mountain) cumbre f, cima; (of head) coronilla; (of ladder) lo alto; (of cupboard, table) superficie f; (lid: of box, jar) tapa; (: of bottle) tapón m; (of list etc) cabeza; (toy) peonza // a de arriba; (in rank) principal, primero; (best) mejor // vt (exceed) exceder; (be first in) encabezar; **on** ~ of sobre, encima de; **from** ~ **to bottom** de pies a cabeza; **to** ~ **up**, (US) **to** ~ **off** vt llenar; ~ **floor** n último piso; ~ **hat** n sombrero de copa; ~-**heavy** a (object) descompensado en la parte superior.

topic ['tɒpɪk] n tema m; ~**al** a actual.

top: ~**less** a (bather etc) topless; ~**level** a (talks) al más alto nivel; ~**most** a más alto.

topple ['tɒpl] vt volcar, derribar // vi caerse.

top-secret ['tɒp'siːkrɪt] a de alto secreto.

topsy-turvy ['tɒpsɪ'tɜːvɪ] a, ad patas arriba.

torch [tɔːtʃ] n antorcha; (Brit: electric) linterna.

tore [tɔː*] pt of **tear**.

torment ['tɔːment] n tormento // vt [tɔː'ment] atormentar; (fig: annoy) fastidiar.

torn [tɔːn] pp of **tear**.

torrent ['tɔrnt] n torrente m.

torrid ['tɒrɪd] a (fig) apasionado.

tortoise ['tɔːtəs] n tortuga; ~**shell** ['tɔːtʃəfel] a de carey.

torture ['tɔːtʃə*] n tortura // vt torturar; (fig) atormentar.

Tory ['tɔːrɪ] a, n (Brit POL) conservador(a) m/f.

toss [tɒs] vt tirar, echar; (head) sacudir; **to** ~ **a coin** echar a cara o cruz; **to** ~ **up for sth** jugar a cara o cruz algo; **to** ~ **and turn** (in bed) dar vueltas.

tot [tɒt] n (Brit: drink) copita; (child) nene/a m/f.

total ['təutl] a total, entero // n total m, suma // vt (add up) sumar; (amount to) ascender a.

totalitarian [təutælɪ'tɛərɪən] a totalitario.

totally ['təutəlɪ] ad totalmente.

totter ['tɒtə*] vi tambalearse.

touch [tʌtʃ] n tacto; (contact) contacto; (FOOTBALL): **to be in** ~ estar fuera de juego // vt tocar; (emotionally) conmover; **a** ~ **of** (fig) una pizca or un poquito de; **to get in** ~ **with sb** ponerse en contacto con uno; **to lose** ~ (friends) perder contacto; **to** ~ **on** vt fus (topic) aludir (brevemente); **to** ~ **up** vt (paint) retocar; ~-**and-go** a arriesgado; ~**down** n aterrizaje m; (on sea) amerizaje m; (US FOOTBALL) ensayo; ~**ed** a conmovido; (col) chiflado; ~**ing** a conmovedor(a); ~**line** n (SPORT) línea de banda; ~**y** a (person) quisquilloso.

tough [tʌf] a (meat) duro; (difficult) difícil; (resistant) resistente; (person) fuerte // n (gangster etc) gorila m; ~**en** vt endurecer.

toupée ['tuːpeɪ] n peluca.

tour ['tuə*] n viaje m, vuelta; (also: **package** ~) viaje m todo comprendido; (of town, museum) visita // vt viajar por; ~**ing** n viajes mpl turísticos, turismo.

tourism ['tuərɪzm] n turismo.

tourist ['tuərɪst] n turista m/f // cpd turístico; ~ **office** n oficina de turismo.

tournament ['tuənəmənt] n torneo.

tousled ['tauzld] a (hair) despeinado.

tout [taut] vi: **to** ~ **for business** solicitar clientes // n (also: **ticket** ~) revendedor(a) m/f.

tow [təu] vt remolcar; 'on or (US) in ~' (AUT) 'a remolque'.

toward(s) [tə'wɔːd(z)] prep hacia; (of attitude) respecto a, con; (of purpose) para.

towel ['tauəl] n toalla; ~**ling** n (fabric)

felpa; ~ **rail**, (US) ~ **rack** n toallero.
tower ['tauə*] n torre f; ~ **block** n
(Brit) torre f (de pisos); ~**ing** a muy
alto, imponente.
town [taun] n ciudad f; **to go to ~** ir a la
ciudad; (fig) echar los bofes por; ~
centre n centro de la ciudad; ~ **clerk** n
secretario/a del ayuntamiento; ~ **council** n ayuntamiento, consejo municipal;
~ **hall** n ayuntamiento; ~ **plan** n plano
de la ciudad; ~ **planning** n urbanismo.
towrope ['təurəup] n cable m de remolque.
tow truck n (US) camión m grúa.
toy [tɔɪ] n juguete m; **to ~ with** vt fus
jugar con; (idea) acariciar; ~**shop** n
juguetería.
trace [treɪs] n rastro // vt (draw) trazar,
delinear; (locate) encontrar; **tracing
paper** n papel m de calco.
track [træk] n (mark) huella, pista;
(path: gen) camino, senda; (: of bullet
etc) trayectoria; (: of suspect, animal)
pista, rastro; (RAIL) vía; (SPORT) pista;
(on record) canción f // vt seguir la pista
de; **to keep ~ of** mantenerse al tanto de,
seguir; **to ~ down** vt (person) locali-
zar; (sth lost) encontrar; ~**suit** n chan-
dal m.
tract [trækt] n (GEO) región f; (pamphlet) folleto.
traction ['trækʃən] n (AUT, power) tracción f; **in ~** (MED) en tracción.
tractor ['træktə*] n tractor m.
trade [treɪd] n comercio; (skill, job) oficio // vi negociar, comerciar; **to ~ in sth**
comerciar en algo; **to ~ in** vt (old car
etc) ofrecer como parte del pago; ~ **fair**
n feria comercial; ~**in price** n valor de
un objeto usado que se descuenta del
precio de otro nuevo; ~**mark** n marca
de fábrica; ~ **name** n marca registrada; ~**r** n comerciante m/f; ~**sman** n
(shopkeeper) tendero; ~ **union** n sindicato; ~ **unionist** n sindicalista m/f;
trading n comercio; **trading estate** n
(Brit) zona comercial.
tradition [trə'dɪʃən] n tradición f; ~**al** a
tradicional.
traffic ['træfɪk] n (gen, AUT) tráfico, circulación f, tránsito (LAm); **air ~** tránsito aéreo // vi: **to ~ in** (pej: liquor,
drugs) traficar en; ~ **circle** n (US) glorieta de tráfico; ~ **jam** n embotellamiento; ~ **lights** npl semáforo sg; ~
warden n guardia m/f de tráfico.
tragedy ['trædʒədɪ] n tragedia.
tragic ['trædʒɪk] a trágico.
trail [treɪl] n (tracks) rastro, pista;
(path) camino, sendero; (dust, smoke)
estela // vt (drag) arrastrar; (follow) seguir la pista de; (follow closely) vigilar
// vi arrastrarse; **to ~ behind** vi quedar a la zaga; ~**er** n (AUT) remolque
m; (caravan) caravana; (CINEMA) trai-

ler m, avance m; ~ **truck** n (US) trailer m.
train [treɪn] n tren m; (of dress) cola;
(series) serie f // vt (educate) formar;
(teach skills to) adiestrar; (sportsman)
entrenar; (dog) amaestrar; (point: gun
etc): **to ~ on** apuntar a // vi (SPORT) entrenarse; (be educated) formarse; **one's
~ of thought** razonamiento de uno; ~**ed**
a (worker) cualificado; (animal) amaestrado; ~**ee** [treɪ'niː] n aprendiz(a) m/f;
~**er** n (SPORT) entrenador(a) m/f; (of
animals) domador(a) m/f; ~**ing** n formación f; entrenamiento; **to be in ~ing**
(SPORT) estar entrenando; (: fit) estar
en forma; ~**ing college** n (gen) colegio
de formación profesional; (for teachers)
escuela normal; ~**ing shoes** npl zapatillas fpl (de deporte).
traipse [treɪps] vi andar penosamente.
trait [treɪt] n rasgo.
traitor ['treɪtə*] n traidor(a) m/f.
tram [træm] n (Brit: also: ~**car**) tranvía
m.
tramp [træmp] n (person) vagabundo/a;
(col: offensive: woman) puta // vi andar
con pasos pesados.
trample ['træmpl] vt: **to ~ (underfoot)** pisotear.
trampoline ['træmpəliːn] n trampolín m.
tranquil ['træŋkwɪl] a tranquilo; ~**lizer** n
(MED) tranquilizante m.
transact [træn'zækt] vt (business) tramitar; ~**ion** [-'zækʃən] n transacción f,
operación f.
transcend [træn'send] vt rebasar.
transcript ['trænskrɪpt] n copia; ~**ion**
[-'skrɪpʃən] n transcripción f.
transfer ['trænsfə*] n transferencia;
(SPORT) traspaso; (picture, design) cal-
comanía // vt [træns'fə:*] trasladar, pasar; **to ~ the charges** (Brit TEL) llamar
a cobro revertido.
transform [træns'fɔ:m] vt transformar.
transfusion [træns'fju:ʒən] n transfusión
f.
transient ['trænzɪənt] a transitorio.
transistor [træn'zɪstə*] n (ELEC) transistor m; ~ **radio** n transistor m.
transit ['trænzɪt] n: **in ~** en tránsito.
transitive ['trænzɪtɪv] a (LING) transiti-
vo.
translate [trænz'leɪt] vt traducir; **translation** [-'leɪʃən] n traducción f; **translator** n traductor(a) m/f.
transmission [trænz'mɪʃən] n transmisión f.
transmit [trænz'mɪt] vt transmitir; ~**ter**
n transmisor m; (station) emisora.
transparency [træns'peərnsɪ] n (Brit
PHOT) diapositiva.
transparent [træns'pærnt] a transparente.
transpire [træns'paɪə*] vi (turn out) resultar; (happen) ocurrir, suceder; **it ~d**

that ... se supo que ...

transplant [træns'plɑːnt] *vt* transplantar // *n* ['trænsplɑːnt] (*MED*) transplante *m*.

transport ['trænspɔːt] *n* transporte *m* // *vt* [-'pɔːt] transportar; **~ation** [-'teɪʃən] *n* transporte *m*; (*of prisoners*) deportación *f*; **~ café** *n* (*Brit*) bar-restaurant *m* de carretera.

trap [træp] *n* (*snare, trick*) trampa; (*carriage*) cabriolé *m* // *vt* coger (*Sp*) or agarrar (*LAm*) en una trampa; (*immobilize*) bloquear; (*jam*) atascar; **~ door** *n* escotilla.

trapeze [trə'piːz] *n* trapecio.

trappings ['træpɪŋz] *npl* adornos *mpl*.

trash [træʃ] *n* (*pej: goods*) pacotilla; (*nonsense*) tonterías *fpl*; **~ can** *n* (*US*) cubo *or* balde *m* (*LAm*) de la basura.

travel ['trævl] *n* viaje *m* // *vi* viajar // *vt* (*distance*) recorrer; **~ agency** *n* agencia de viajes; **~ agent** *n* agente *m/f* de viajes; **~ler**, (*US*) **~er** *n* viajero/a; **~ler's cheque**, (*US*) **~er's check** *n* cheque *m* de viajero; **~ling**, (*US*) **~ing** *n* los viajes *mpl*, el viajar; **~ sickness** *n* mareo.

travesty ['trævəstɪ] *n* parodia.

trawler ['trɔːlə*] *n* pesquero de arrastre.

tray [treɪ] *n* (*for carrying*) bandeja; (*on desk*) cajón *m*.

treachery ['tretʃərɪ] *n* traición *f*.

treacle ['triːkl] *n* (*Brit*) melaza.

tread [tred] *n* (*step*) paso, pisada; (*sound*) ruido de pasos; (*of tyre*) banda de rodadura // *vi* (*pt* trod, *pp* trodden) pisar; **to ~ on** *vt fus* pisar.

treason ['triːzn] *n* traición *f*.

treasure ['treʒə*] *n* tesoro // *vt* (*value*) apreciar, valorar.

treasurer ['treʒərə*] *n* tesorero/a.

treasury ['treʒərɪ] *n*: **the T~**, (*US*) **the T~ Department** el Ministerio de Hacienda.

treat [triːt] *n* (*present*) regalo; (*pleasure*) placer *m* // *vt* tratar; **to ~ sb to sth** invitar a uno a algo.

treatise ['triːtɪz] *n* tratado.

treatment ['triːtmənt] *n* tratamiento.

treaty ['triːtɪ] *n* tratado.

treble ['trebl] *a* triple // *vt* triplicar // *vi* triplicarse; **~ clef** *n* (*MUS*) clave *f* de sol.

tree [triː] *n* árbol *m*.

trek [trek] *n* (*long journey*) expedición *f*; (*tiring walk*) caminata.

trellis ['trelɪs] *n* enrejado.

tremble ['trembl] *vi* temblar.

tremendous [trɪ'mendəs] *a* tremendo; (*enormous*) enorme; (*excellent*) estupendo.

tremor ['tremə*] *n* temblor *m*; (*also*: **earth ~**) temblor *m* de tierra.

trench [trentʃ] *n* zanja; (*MIL*) trinchera.

trend [trend] *n* (*tendency*) tendencia; (*of events*) curso; (*fashion*) moda; **~y** *a* de

moda.

trepidation [trepɪ'deɪʃən] *n* inquietud *f*.

trespass ['trespəs] *vi*: **to ~ on** entrar sin permiso en; 'no **~ing**' 'prohibido el paso'.

tress [tres] *n* trenza.

trestle ['tresl] *n* caballete *m*; **~ table** *n* mesa de caballete.

trial ['traɪəl] *n* (*LAW*) juicio, proceso; (*test: of machine etc*) prueba; (*hardship*) desgracia; **by ~ and error** a fuerza de probar.

triangle ['traɪæŋgl] *n* (*MATH. MUS*) triángulo.

tribe [traɪb] *n* tribu *f*.

tribunal [traɪ'bjuːnl] *n* tribunal *m*.

tributary ['trɪbjutərɪ] *n* (*river*) afluente *m*.

tribute ['trɪbjuːt] *n* homenaje *m*, tributo; **to pay ~** to rendir homenaje a.

trice [traɪs] *n*: **in a ~** en un santiamén.

trick [trɪk] *n* trampa; (*conjuring ~, deceit*) truco; (*joke*) broma; (*CARDS*) baza // *vt* engañar; **to play a ~ on sb** gastar una broma a uno; **that should do the ~** a ver si funciona así; **~ery** *n* engaño.

trickle ['trɪkl] *n* (*of water etc*) chorrito // *vi* gotear.

tricky ['trɪkɪ] *a* difícil; delicado.

tricycle ['traɪsɪkl] *n* triciclo.

trifle ['traɪfl] *n* bagatela; (*CULIN*) dulce de bizcocho borracho, gelatina, fruta y natillas // *ad*: **a ~ long** un poquito largo; **trifling** *a* insignificante.

trigger ['trɪgə*] *n* (*of gun*) gatillo; **to ~ off** *vt* desencadenar.

trill [trɪl] *n* (*of bird*) gorjeo.

trim [trɪm] *a* (*elegant*) aseado; (*house, garden*) en buen estado; (*figure*) de talle esbelto // *n* (*haircut etc*) recorte *m* // *vt* (*neaten*) arreglar; (*cut*) recortar; (*decorate*) adornar; (*NAUT: a sail*) orientar; **~mings** *npl* (*extras*) accesorios *mpl*; (*cuttings*) recortes *mpl*.

trinket ['trɪŋkɪt] *n* chuchería, baratija.

trip [trɪp] *n* viaje *m*; (*excursion*) excursión *f*; (*stumble*) traspié *m* // *vi* (*stumble*) tropezar; (*go lightly*) andar a paso ligero; **on a ~** de viaje; **to ~ up** *vi* tropezar, caerse // *vt* hacer tropezar *or* caer.

tripe [traɪp] *n* (*CULIN*) callos *mpl*; (*pej: rubbish*) bobadas *fpl*.

triple ['trɪpl] *a* triple.

triplets ['trɪplɪts] *npl* trillizos/as *m/fpl*.

triplicate ['trɪplɪkət] *n*: **in ~** por triplicado.

tripod ['traɪpɔd] *n* trípode *m*.

trite [traɪt] *a* trillado.

triumph ['traɪʌmf] *n* triunfo // *vi*: **to ~ (over)** vencer.

trivia ['trɪvɪə] *npl* trivialidades *fpl*.

trivial ['trɪvɪəl] *a* insignificante, trivial.

trod [trɔd], **trodden** ['trɔdn] *pt*, *pp* of **tread**.

trolley ['trɒlı] n carrito.
trombone [trɒm'bəun] n trombón m.
troop [tru:p] n grupo, banda; ~s npl
(MIL) tropas fpl; **to** ~ **in/out** vi
entrar/salir en tropel; ~**er** n (MIL) soldado (de caballería); ~**ing the colour**
n (ceremony) presentación f de la bandera.
trophy ['trəufı] n trofeo.
tropic ['trɒpık] n trópico; ~**al** a tropical.
trot [trɒt] n trote m // vi trotar; **on the** ~
(Brit fig) seguidos/as.
trouble ['trʌbl] n problema m, dificultad
f; (worry) preocupación f; (bother, effort) molestia, esfuerzo; (unrest) inquietud f; (MED): **stomach** ~ problemas
mpl gástricos // vt molestar; (worry)
preocupar, inquietar // vi: **to** ~ **to do sth**
molestarse en hacer algo; ~**s** npl (POL
etc) conflictos mpl; **to be in** ~ estar en
un apuro; **to go to the** ~ **of doing sth** tomarse la molestia de hacer algo; **what's
the** ~? ¿qué pasa?; ~**d** a (person)
preocupado; (epoch, life) agitado; ~**-
maker** n agitador(a) m/f; ~**shooter** n
(in conflict) conciliador(a) m/f; ~**some**
a molesto, inoportuno.
trough [trɒf] n (also: **drinking** ~) abre-
vadero; (also: **feeding** ~) comedero;
(channel) canal m.
troupe [tru:p] n grupo.
trousers ['trauzəz] npl pantalones mpl;
short ~ pantalones mpl cortos.
trousseau ['tru:səu], pl ~**x** or ~**s** [-z] n
ajuar m.
trout [traut] n, pl inv trucha.
trowel ['trauəl] n paleta.
truant ['truənt] n: **to play** ~ (Brit) hacer
novillos.
truce [tru:s] n tregua.
truck [trʌk] n (US) camión m; (RAIL) vagón m; ~ **driver** n camionero; ~ **farm**
n (US) huerto de hortalizas.
truculent ['trʌkjulənt] a agresivo.
trudge [trʌdʒ] vi caminar penosamente.
true [tru:] a verdadero; (accurate) exacto; (genuine) auténtico; (faithful) fiel.
truffle ['trʌfl] n trufa.
truly ['tru:lı] ad (genuinely, emphatic:
very) realmente; (faithfully) fielmente.
trump [trʌmp] n triunfo; ~**ed-up** a in-
ventado.
trumpet ['trʌmpıt] n trompeta.
truncheon ['trʌntʃən] n (Brit) porra.
trundle ['trʌndl] vt, vi: **to** ~ **along** rodar
haciendo ruido.
trunk [trʌŋk] n (of tree, person) tronco;
(of elephant) trompa; (case) baúl m;
(US AUT) maletero; ~**s** npl (also: **swimming** ~s) bañador m; ~ **call** n (Brit
TEL) llamada interurbana.
truss [trʌs] n (MED) braguero; **to** ~
(up) vt atar; (CULIN) espetar.
trust [trʌst] n confianza; (COMM) trust
m; (LAW) fideicomiso // vt (rely on) te-

ner confianza en; (entrust): **to** ~ **sth to
sb** confiar algo a uno; ~**ed** a de confianza; ~**ee** [trʌs'ti:] n (LAW) fideicomisa-
rio; ~**ing** a confiado; ~**worthy** a
digno de confianza.
truth [tru:θ], pl ~**s** [tru:ðz] n verdad f;
~**ful** a (person) veraz.
try [traı] n tentativa, intento; (RUGBY)
ensayo // vt (LAW) juzgar, procesar;
(test: sth new) probar, someter a prueba; (attempt) intentar; (strain: patience) hacer perder // vi probar; **to** ~ **to
do sth** intentar hacer algo; **to** ~ **on** vt
(clothes) probarse; **to** ~ **out** vt probar,
poner a prueba; ~**ing** a cansado; (person) pesado.
T-shirt ['ti:ʃə:t] n camiseta.
T-square ['ti:skwɛə*] n regla en T.
tub [tʌb] n cubo (Sp), balde m (LAm);
(bath) tina, bañera.
tuba ['tju:bə] n tuba.
tubby ['tʌbı] a regordete.
tube [tju:b] n tubo; (Brit: underground)
metro.
tuberculosis [tjubə:kju'ləusıs] n tuberculosis f inv.
tubing ['tju:bıŋ] n tubería (Sp), cañería;
a piece of ~ un trozo de tubo.
tubular ['tju:bjulə*] a tubular.
TUC n abbr (Brit: = Trades Union Congress) federación nacional de sindicatos.
tuck [tʌk] n (SEWING) pliegue m // vt
(put) poner; **to** ~ **away** vt esconder;
to ~ **in** vt meter dentro; (child) arropar // vi (eat) comer con apetito; **to** ~
up vt (child) arropar; ~ **shop** n
(SCOL) tienda de golosinas.
Tuesday ['tju:zdı] n martes m inv.
tuft [tʌft] n mechón m; (of grass etc)
manojo.
tug [tʌg] n (ship) remolcador m // vt remolcar; ~**-of-war** n lucha de tiro de
cuerda.
tuition [tju:'ıʃən] n (Brit) enseñanza; (:
private ~) clases fpl particulares; (US:
school fees) matrícula.
tulip ['tju:lıp] n tulipán m.
tumble ['tʌmbl] n (fall) caída // vi caerse, tropezar; **to** ~ **to sth** (col) caer en la
cuenta de algo; ~**down** a destartalado;
~ **dryer** n (Brit) secadora.
tumbler ['tʌmblə*] n vaso.
tummy ['tʌmı] n (col) barriga, vientre
m.
tumour, (US) **tumor** ['tju:mə*] n tumor
m.
tuna ['tju:nə] n, pl inv (also: ~ **fish**) atún
m.
tune [tju:n] n (melody) melodía // vt
(MUS) afinar; (RADIO, TV, AUT) sintonizar; **to be in/out of** ~ (instrument) estar
afinado/desafinado; (singer) cantar
afinadamente/desafinar; **to** ~ **in** (to) (RA-
DIO, TV) sintonizar (con); **to** ~ **up** vi
(musician) afinar (su instrumento);

~**ful** a melodioso; ~**r** n (radio set) sintonizador m; **piano** ~**r** afinador(a) m/f de pianos.

tunic ['tjuːnɪk] n túnica.

tuning ['tjuːnɪŋ] n sintonización f; (MUS) afinación f; ~ **fork** n diapasón m.

Tunisia [tjuːˈnɪzɪə] n Túnez m.

tunnel ['tʌnl] n túnel m; (in mine) galería // vi construir un túnel/una galería.

turban ['təːbən] n turbante m.

turbine ['təːbaɪn] n turbina.

turbulence ['təːbjuləns] n (AVIAT) turbulencia.

tureen [təˈriːn] n sopera.

turf [təːf] n césped m; (clod) tepe m // vt cubrir con césped; **to ~ out** vt (col) echar a la calle.

turgid ['təːdʒɪd] a (prose) pesado.

Turk [təːk] n turco/a.

Turkey ['təːkɪ] n Turquía.

turkey ['təːkɪ] n pavo.

Turkish ['təːkɪʃ] a turco.

turmoil ['təːmɔɪl] n desorden m, alboroto.

turn [təːn] n turno; (in road) curva; (THEATRE) número; (MED) ataque m // vt girar, volver; (collar, steak) dar la vuelta a; (change): **to ~ sth into** convertir algo en // vi volver; (person: look back) volverse; (reverse direction) dar la vuelta; (milk) cortarse; (change) cambiar; (become) convertirse en; **a good ~** un favor; it gave me quite a ~ me dio un susto; '**no left** ~' (AUT) 'prohibido girar a la izquierda'; it's your ~ te toca a ti; **in** ~ por turnos; **to take** ~**s** turnarse; **to ~ away** vi apartar la vista; **to ~ back** vi volverse atrás; **to ~ down** vt (refuse) rechazar; (reduce) bajar; (fold) doblar; **to ~ in** vi (col: go to bed) acostarse // vt (fold) doblar hacia dentro; **to ~ off** vi (from road) desviarse // vt (light, radio etc) apagar; (engine) parar; **to ~ on** vt (light, radio etc) encender, prender (LAm); (engine) poner en marcha; **to ~ out** vt (light, gas) apagar // vi: **to ~ out to be...** resultar ser...; **to ~ over** vi (person) volverse // vt (object) dar la vuelta a; (page) volver; **to ~ round** vi volverse; (rotate) girar; **to ~ up** vi (person) llegar, presentarse; (lost object) aparecer // vt (gen) subir; ~**ing** n (in road) vuelta; ~**ing point** n (fig) momento decisivo.

turnip ['təːnɪp] n nabo.

turnout ['təːnaut] n concurrencia.

turnover ['təːnəuvə*] n (COMM: amount of money) facturación f; (: of goods) movimiento.

turnpike ['təːnpaɪk] n (US) autopista de peaje.

turnstile ['təːnstaɪl] n torniquete m.

turntable ['təːnteɪbl] n plato.

turn-up ['təːnʌp] n (Brit: on trousers) vuelta.

turpentine ['təːpəntaɪn] n (also: **turps**) trementina.

turquoise ['təːkwɔɪz] n (stone) turquesa // a color turquesa.

turret ['tʌrɪt] n torreón m.

turtle ['təːtl] n galápago; ~**neck (sweater)** n (jersey m de) cuello cisne.

tusk [tʌsk] n colmillo.

tussle ['tʌsl] n lucha, pelea.

tutor ['tjuːtə*] n profesor.a m/f; ~**ial** [-'təːrɪəl] n (SCOL) seminario.

tuxedo [tʌkˈsiːdəu] n (US) smóking m, esmoquin m.

TV [tiːˈviː] n abbr (= television) tele f.

twang [twæŋ] n (of instrument) punteado; (of voice) timbre m nasal.

tweezers ['twiːzəz] npl pinzas fpl (de depilar).

twelfth [twelfθ] a duodécimo.

twelve [twelv] num doce; **at** ~ **o'clock** (midday) a mediodía; (midnight) a medianoche.

twentieth ['twentɪɪθ] a vigésimo.

twenty ['twentɪ] num veinte.

twice [twaɪs] ad dos veces; ~ **as much** dos veces más.

twiddle ['twɪdl] vt, vi: **to** ~ **(with) sth** dar vueltas a algo; **to** ~ **one's thumbs** (fig) estar mano sobre mano.

twig [twɪg] n ramita // vi (col) caer en la cuenta.

twilight ['twaɪlaɪt] n crepúsculo.

twin [twɪn] a, n gemelo/a m/f // vt hermanar; ~**-bedded room** n habitación f con camas gemelas.

twine [twaɪn] n bramante m // vi (plant) enroscarse.

twinge [twɪndʒ] n (of pain) punzada; (of conscience) remordimiento.

twinkle ['twɪŋkl] vi centellear; (eyes) parpadear.

twirl [twəːl] n giro // vt dar vueltas a // vi piruetear.

twist [twɪst] n (action) torsión f; (in road, coil) vuelta; (in wire, flex) doblez f; (in story) giro // vt torcer, retorcer; (roll around) enrollar; (fig) deformar // vi serpentear.

twit [twɪt] n (col) tonto.

twitch [twɪtʃ] // vi moverse nerviosamente.

two [tuː] num dos; **to put** ~ **and** ~ **together** (fig) atar cabos; ~**-door** a (AUT) de dos puertas; ~**-faced** a (pej: person) falso; ~**fold** ad: **to increase** ~**fold** doblarse; ~**-piece (suit)** n traje m de dos piezas; ~**-piece (swimsuit)** n dos piezas m inv, bikini m; ~**-seater plane/car** n avión m/coche m de dos plazas; ~**some** n (people) pareja; ~**-way** a: ~**-way traffic** circulación f de dos sentidos.

tycoon [taɪˈkuːn] n: (business) ~ magnate m/f.

type [taɪp] n (category) tipo, género; (model) modelo; (TYP) tipo, letra // vt (*letter etc*) escribir a máquina; ~-**cast** *a* (*actor*) encasillado; ~**face** *n* tipo; ~**script** *n* texto mecanografiado; ~**writer** *n* máquina de escribir; ~**written** *a* mecanografiado.

typhoid ['taɪfɔɪd] *n* tifoidea.

typical ['tɪpɪkl] *a* típico.

typing ['taɪpɪŋ] *n* mecanografía.

typist ['taɪpɪst] *n* mecanógrafo/a.

tyranny ['tɪrənɪ] *n* tiranía.

tyrant ['taɪərnt] *n* tirano/a.

tyre, (*US*) **tire** ['taɪə*] *n* neumático, llanta (*LAm*); ~ **pressure** *n* presión *f* de los neumáticos.

U

U-bend ['juː'bend] *n* (*AUT, in pipe*) recodo.

udder ['ʌdə*] *n* ubre *f*.

UFO ['juːfəu] *n abbr* = (*unidentified flying object*) OVNI *m*.

ugh [əːh] *excl* ¡uf!

ugly ['ʌglɪ] *a* feo; (*dangerous*) peligroso.

UK *n abbr* = **United Kingdom.**

ulcer ['ʌlsə*] *n* úlcera.

Ulster ['ʌlstə*] *n* Ulster *m*.

ulterior [ʌl'tɪərɪə*] *a* ulterior; ~ **motive** segundas intenciones *fpl*.

ultimate ['ʌltɪmət] *a* último, final; (*authority*) más alto; ~**ly** *ad* (*in the end*) por último, al final; (*fundamentally*) *a* or en fin de cuentas.

ultrasound [ʌltrə'saund] *n* (*MED*) ultrasonido.

umbilical cord [ʌm'bɪlɪkl-] *n* cordón *m* umbilical.

umbrella [ʌm'brelə] *n* paraguas *m inv*.

umpire ['ʌmpaɪə*] *n* árbitro.

umpteen [ʌmp'tiːn] *a* enésimos/as; for the ~th time por enésima vez.

UN *n abbr* = **United Nations (Organization).**

unable [ʌn'eɪbl] *a*: to be ~ to do sth no poder hacer algo.

unaccompanied [ʌnə'kʌmpənɪd] *a* no acompañado.

unaccountably [ʌnə'kauntəblɪ] *ad* inexplicablemente.

unaccustomed [ʌnə'kʌstəmd] *a*: to be ~ to no estar acostumbrado a.

unanimous [juː'nænɪməs] *a* unánime; ~**ly** *ad* unánimemente.

unarmed [ʌn'ɑːmd] *a* desarmado.

unassuming [ʌnə'sjuːmɪŋ] *a* modesto, sin pretensiones.

unattached [ʌnə'tætʃt] *a* (*person*) sin pareja; (*part etc*) suelto.

unattended [ʌnə'tendɪd] *a* (*car, luggage*) sin atender.

unauthorized [ʌn'ɔːθəraɪzd] *a* no autorizado.

unavoidable [ʌnə'vɔɪdəbl] *a* inevitable.

unaware [ʌnə'weə*] *a*: to be ~ of igno-

rar; ~**s** *ad* de improviso.

unbalanced [ʌn'bælənst] *a* desequilibrado; (*mentally*) trastornado.

unbearable [ʌn'beərəbl] *a* insoportable.

unbeknown(st) [ʌnbɪ'nəun(st)] *ad*: ~ to me sin saberlo yo.

unbelievable [ʌnbɪ'liːvəbl] *a* increíble.

unbend [ʌn'bend] (*irg: like* **bend**) *vi* (*fig: person*) relajarse // *vt* (*wire*) enderezar.

unbiased [ʌn'baɪəst] *a* imparcial.

unborn [ʌn'bɔːn] *a* que va a nacer.

unbreakable [ʌn'breɪkəbl] *a* irrompible.

unbroken [ʌn'brəukən] *a* (*seal*) intacto; (*series*) continuo; (*record*) no batido; (*spirit*) indómito.

unbutton [ʌn'bʌtn] *vt* desabrochar.

uncalled-for [ʌn'kɔːldfɔː*] *a* gratuito, inmerecido.

uncanny [ʌn'kænɪ] *a* extraño, extraordinario.

unceasing [ʌn'siːsɪŋ] *a* incesante.

unceremonious ['ʌnserɪ'məunɪəs] *a* (*abrupt, rude*) brusco, hosco.

uncertain [ʌn'sɔːtn] *a* incierto; (*indecisive*) indeciso; ~**ty** *n* incertidumbre *f*.

unchecked [ʌn'tʃekt] *a* desenfrenado.

uncivilized [ʌn'sɪvɪlaɪzd] *a* (*gen*) inculto; (*fig: behaviour etc*) bárbaro.

uncle ['ʌŋkl] *n* tío.

uncomfortable [ʌn'kʌmfətəbl] *a* incómodo; (*uneasy*) inquieto.

uncommon [ʌn'kɔmən] *a* poco común, raro.

uncompromising [ʌn'kɔmprəmaɪzɪŋ] *a* intransigente.

unconcerned [ʌnkən'sɔːnd] *a* indiferente, despreocupado.

unconditional [ʌnkən'dɪʃənl] *a* incondicional.

unconscious [ʌn'kɔnʃəs] *a* sin sentido; (*unaware*) inconsciente // *n*: the ~ el inconsciente; ~**ly** *ad* inconscientemente.

uncontrollable [ʌnkən'trəuləbl] *a* (*temper*) indomable; (*laughter*) incontenible.

unconventional [ʌnkən'venʃənl] *a* poco convencional.

uncouth [ʌn'kuːθ] *a* grosero, inculto.

uncover [ʌn'kʌvə*] *vt* (*gen*) descubrir; (*take lid off*) destapar.

undecided [ʌndɪ'saɪdɪd] *a* (*character*) indeciso; (*question*) no resuelto, pendiente.

under ['ʌndə*] *prep* debajo de; (*less than*) menos de; (*according to*) según, de acuerdo con // *ad* debajo, abajo; ~ there allí abajo; ~ **construction** bajo construcción.

under... ['ʌndə*] *pref* sub; ~-**age** *a* menor de edad; ~**carriage** *n* (*Brit AVIAT*) tren *m* de aterrizaje; ~**charge** *vt* cobrar menos de la cuenta; ~**clothes** *npl* ropa *sg* interior *or* íntima (*LAm*); ~**coat** *n* (*paint*) primera mano; ~**cover** *a* clandestino; ~**current** *n* corriente *f* submarina; (*fig*) tendencia oculta; ~**cut**

vt irg vender más barato que; **~developed** *a* subdesarrollado; **~dog** *n* desvalido/a; **~done** *a* (*CULIN*) poco hecho; **~estimate** *vt* subestimar; **~exposed** *a* (*PHOT*) subexpuesto; **~fed** *a* subalimentado; **~foot** *ad*: it's wet **~foot** el suelo está mojado; **~go** *vt irg* sufrir; (*treatment*) recibir; **~graduate** *n* estudiante *m/f*; **~ground** *n* (*Brit*: *railway*) metro; (*POL*) movimiento clandestino // *a* subterráneo; **~growth** *n* maleza; **~hand** *a* (*fig*) socarrón; **~lie** *vt irg* (*fig*) ser la razón fundamental de; **~line** *vt* subrayar; **~ling** ['ʌndəlɪŋ] *n* (*pej*) subalterno/a; **~mine** *vt* socavar, minar; **~neath** [ʌndə'niːθ] *ad* debajo // *prep* debajo de, bajo; **~paid** *a* mal pagado, **~pants** *npl* calzoncillos *mpl*; **~pass** *n* (*Brit*) paso subterráneo; **~privileged** *a* desvalido; **~rate** *vt* menospreciar, subestimar; **~shirt** *n* (*US*) camiseta; **~shorts** *npl* (*US*) calzoncillos *mpl*; **~side** *n* parte *f* inferior, revés *m*; **~skirt** *n* (*Brit*) enaguas *fpl*.

understand [ʌndə'stænd] (*irg: like* stand) *vt, vi* entender, comprender; (*assume*) tener entendido; **~able** *a* comprensible; **~ing** *a* comprensivo // *n* comprensión *f*, entendimiento *f*; (*agreement*) acuerdo.

understatement ['ʌndəsteɪtmənt] *n* subestimación *f*; (*modesty*) modestia (excesiva).

understood [ʌndə'stud] *pt, pp of* **understand** // *a* entendido; (*implied*): it is ~ that se sobreentiende que.

understudy ['ʌndəstʌdɪ] *n* suplente *m/f*.

undertake [ʌndə'teɪk] (*irg: like* take) *vt* emprender; **to ~ to do sth** comprometerse a hacer algo.

undertaker ['ʌndəteɪkə*] *n* director(a) *m/f* de pompas fúnebres.

undertaking ['ʌndəteɪkɪŋ] *n* empresa; (*promise*) promesa.

undertone ['ʌndətəun] *n*: **in an ~** en voz baja.

underwater [ʌndə'wɔːtə*] *ad* bajo el agua // *a* submarino.

underwear ['ʌndəwɛə*] *n* ropa interior *or* íntima (*LAm*).

underworld ['ʌndəwəːld] *n* (*of crime*) hampa, inframundo.

underwriter ['ʌndəraɪtə*] *n* (*INSURANCE*) asegurador/a *m/f*.

undies ['ʌndɪz] *npl* (*col*) ropa interior *or* íntima (*LAm*).

undo [ʌn'duː] (*irg: like* do) *vt* deshacer; **~ing** *n* ruina, perdición *f*.

undoubted [ʌn'dautɪd] *a* indudable; **~ly** *ad* indudablemente, sin duda.

undress [ʌn'drɛs] *vi* desnudarse.

undue [ʌn'djuː] *a* indebido, excesivo.

undulating ['ʌndjuleɪtɪŋ] *a* ondulante.

unduly [ʌn'djuːlɪ] *ad* excesivamente, demasiado.

unearth [ʌn'əːθ] *vt* desenterrar.

unearthly [ʌn'əːθlɪ] *a* (*hour*) inverosímil.

uneasy [ʌn'iːzɪ] *a* intranquilo; (*worried*) preocupado.

uneducated [ʌn'ɛdjukeɪtɪd] *a* ignorante, inculto.

unemployed [ʌnɪm'plɔɪd] *a* parado, sin trabajo // *n*: **the ~** los parados.

unemployment [ʌnɪm'plɔɪmənt] *n* paro, desempleo.

unending [ʌn'ɛndɪŋ] *a* interminable.

unerring [ʌn'əːrɪŋ] *a* infalible.

uneven [ʌn'iːvn] *a* desigual; (*road etc*) quebrado.

unexpected [ʌnɪk'spɛktɪd] *a* inesperado; **~ly** *ad* inesperadamente.

unfailing [ʌn'feɪlɪŋ] *a* (*support*) indefectible; (*energy*) inagotable.

unfair [ʌn'fɛə*] *a*: ~ (**to sb**) injusto (con uno).

unfaithful [ʌn'feɪθful] *a* infiel.

unfamiliar [ʌnfə'mɪlɪə*] *a* extraño, desconocido.

unfashionable [ʌn'fæʃnəbl] *a* pasado *or* fuera de moda.

unfasten [ʌn'fɑːsn] *vt* desatar.

unfavourable, (*US*) **unfavorable** [ʌn'feɪvərəbl] *a* desfavorable.

unfeeling [ʌn'fiːlɪŋ] *a* insensible.

unfinished [ʌn'fɪnɪʃt] *a* inacabado, sin terminar.

unfit [ʌn'fɪt] *a* indispuesto, enfermo; (*incompetent*) incapaz; ~ **for work** no apto para trabajar.

unfold [ʌn'fəuld] *vt* desdoblar; (*fig*) revelar // *vi* abrirse; revelarse.

unforeseen ['ʌnfɔː'siːn] *a* imprevisto.

unforgettable [ʌnfə'gɛtəbl] *a* inolvidable.

unforgivable [ʌnfə'gɪvəbl] *a* imperdonable.

unfortunate [ʌn'fɔːtʃnət] *a* desgraciado; (*event, remark*) inoportuno; **~ly** *ad* desgraciadamente.

unfounded [ʌn'faundɪd] *a* infundado.

unfriendly [ʌn'frɛndlɪ] *a* antipático.

ungainly [ʌn'geɪnlɪ] *a* (*walk*) desgarbado.

ungodly [ʌn'gɔdlɪ] *a*: **at an ~ hour** a una hora inverosímil.

ungrateful [ʌn'greɪtful] *a* ingrato.

unhappiness [ʌn'hæpɪnɪs] *n* tristeza.

unhappy [ʌn'hæpɪ] *a* (*sad*) triste; (*unfortunate*) desgraciado; (*childhood*) infeliz; ~ **with** (*arrangements etc*) poco contento con, descontento de.

unharmed [ʌn'hɑːmd] *a* (*person*) ileso.

unhealthy [ʌn'hɛlθɪ] *a* (*gen*) malsano; (*person*) enfermizo.

unheard-of [ʌn'həːdɔv] *a* inaudito, sin precedente.

unhook [ʌn'huk] *vt* desenganchar; (*from wall*) descolgar; (*undo*) desabrochar.

unhurt [ʌn'həːt] *a* ileso.

uniform ['ju:nɪfɔ:m] n uniforme m // a uniforme; ~ity [-'fɔ:mɪtɪ] n uniformidad f.

unify ['ju:nɪfaɪ] vt unificar, unir.

uninhabited [ʌnɪn'hæbɪtɪd] a desierto.

unintentional [ʌnɪn'tɛnʃənəl] a involuntario.

union ['ju:njən] n unión f; (also: trade ~) sindicato // cpd sindical; U~ Jack n bandera del Reino Unido.

unique [ju:'ni:k] a único.

unison ['ju:nɪsn] n: in ~ (speak, reply) al unísono; in ~ with junto con.

unit ['ju:nɪt] n unidad f; (team, squad) grupo; kitchen ~ módulo de cocina.

unite [ju:'naɪt] vt unir // vi unirse; ~d a unido; U~d Kingdom (UK) n Reino Unido; U~d Nations (Organization) (UN, UNO) n Naciones fpl Unidas (ONU f); U~d States (of America) (US, USA) n Estados mpl Unidos (EE.UU.).

unit trust n (Brit) bono fiduciario.

unity ['ju:nɪtɪ] n unidad f.

universal [ju:nɪ'vɜ:sl] a universal.

universe ['ju:nɪvɜ:s] n universo.

university [ju:nɪ'vɜ:sɪtɪ] n universidad f.

unjust [ʌn'dʒʌst] a injusto.

unkempt [ʌn'kɛmpt] a descuidado; (hair) despeinado.

unkind [ʌn'kaɪnd] a poco amable; (comment etc) cruel.

unknown [ʌn'nəun] a desconocido.

unlawful [ʌn'lɔ:ful] a ilegal, ilícito.

unleash [ʌn'li:ʃ] vt desatar.

unless [ʌn'lɛs] conj a menos que; ~ he comes a menos que venga; ~ otherwise stated salvo indicación contraria.

unlike [ʌn'laɪk] a distinto // prep a diferencia de.

unlikely [ʌn'laɪklɪ] a improbable.

unlisted [ʌn'lɪstɪd] a (US TEL) que no consta en la guía.

unload [ʌn'ləud] vt descargar.

unlock [ʌn'lɔk] vt abrir (con llave).

unlucky [ʌn'lʌkɪ] a desgraciado; (object, number) que da mala suerte; to be ~ tener mala suerte.

unmarried [ʌn'mærɪd] a soltero.

unmistakable [ʌnmɪs'teɪkəbl] a inconfundible.

unmitigated [ʌn'mɪtɪgeɪtɪd] a rematado, absoluto.

unnatural [ʌn'nætʃrəl] a (gen) antinatural; (manner) afectado; (habit) perverso.

unnecessary [ʌn'nɛsəsərɪ] a innecesario, inútil.

unnoticed [ʌn'nəutɪst] a: to go ~ pasar desapercibido.

UNO ['ju:nəu] n abbr = United Nations Organization.

unobtainable [ʌnəb'teɪnəbl] a inconseguible; (TEL) inexistente.

unobtrusive [ʌnəb'tru:sɪv] a discreto.

unofficial [ʌnə'fɪʃl] a no oficial.

unpack [ʌn'pæk] vi deshacer las maletas, desempacar (LAm).

unpalatable [ʌn'pælətəbl] a (truth) desagradable.

unparalleled [ʌn'pærəlɛld] a (unequalled) sin par; (unique) sin precedentes.

unpleasant [ʌn'plɛznt] a (disagreeable) desagradable; (person, manner) antipático.

unplug [ʌn'plʌg] vt desenchufar, desconectar.

unpopular [ʌn'pɔpjulə*] a poco popular.

unprecedented [ʌn'prɛsɪdəntɪd] a sin precedentes.

unpredictable [ʌnprɪ'dɪktəbl] a imprevisible.

unprofessional [ʌnprə'fɛʃənl] a: ~ conduct negligencia.

unqualified [ʌn'kwɔlɪfaɪd] a sin título, no cualificado; (success) total, incondicional.

unquestionably [ʌn'kwɛstʃənəblɪ] ad indiscutiblemente.

unravel [ʌn'rævl] vt desenmarañar.

unreal [ʌn'rɪəl] a irreal.

unrealistic [ʌnrɪə'lɪstɪk] a poco realista.

unreasonable [ʌn'ri:znəbl] a irrazonable; (demand) excesivo.

unrelated [ʌnrɪ'leɪtɪd] a sin relación; (family) no emparentado.

unreliable [ʌnrɪ'laɪəbl] a (person) informal; (machine) poco fiable.

unremitting [ʌnrɪ'mɪtɪŋ] a constante.

unreservedly [ʌnrɪ'zə:vɪdlɪ] ad sin reserva.

unrest [ʌn'rɛst] n inquietud f, malestar m; (POL) disturbios mpl.

unroll [ʌn'rəul] vt desenrollar.

unruly [ʌn'ru:lɪ] a indisciplinado.

unsafe [ʌn'seɪf] a peligroso.

unsaid [ʌn'sɛd] a: to leave sth ~ dejar algo sin decir.

unsatisfactory ['ʌnsætɪs'fæktərɪ] a poco satisfactorio.

unsavoury, (US) **unsavory** [ʌn'seɪvərɪ] a (fig) repugnante.

unscathed [ʌn'skeɪðd] a ileso.

unscrew [ʌn'skru:] vt destornillar.

unscrupulous [ʌn'skru:pjuləs] a sin escrúpulos.

unsettled [ʌn'sɛtld] a inquieto; (situation) inestable; (weather) variable.

unshaven [ʌn'ʃeɪvn] a sin afeitar.

unsightly [ʌn'saɪtlɪ] a feo.

unskilled [ʌn'skɪld] a: ~ workers mano fsg de obra no cualificada.

unspeakable [ʌn'spi:kəbl] a indecible; (awful) incalificable.

unstable [ʌn'steɪbl] a inestable.

unsteady [ʌn'stɛdɪ] a inestable.

unstuck [ʌn'stʌk] a: to come ~ despegarse; (fig) fracasar.

unsuccessful [ʌnsək'sɛsful] a (attempt) infructuoso; (writer, proposal) sin éxito;

to be ~ (in attempting sth) no tener éxito, fracasar; ~ly ad en vano, sin éxito.
unsuitable [ʌn'suːtəbl] a inapropiado; (time) inoportuno.
unsure [ʌn'ʃuə*] a inseguro, poco seguro.
unsympathetic [ʌnsɪmpə'θɛtɪk] a poco comprensivo.
untapped [ʌn'tæpt] a (resources) sin explotar.
unthinkable [ʌn'θɪŋkəbl] a inconcebible, impensable.
untidy [ʌn'taɪdɪ] a (room) desordenado, en desorden; (appearance) desaliñado.
untie [ʌn'taɪ] vt desatar.
until [ən'tɪl] prep hasta // conj hasta que; ~ he comes hasta que venga; ~ now hasta ahora; ~ then hasta entonces.
untimely [ʌn'taɪmlɪ] a inoportuno; (death) prematuro.
untold [ʌn'təʊld] a (story) nunca contado; (suffering) indecible; (wealth) incalculable.
untoward [ʌntə'wɔːd] a (behaviour) impropio; (event) adverso.
unused [ʌn'juːzd] a sin usar.
unusual [ʌn'juːʒuəl] a insólito, poco común.
unveil [ʌn'veɪl] vt (statue) descubrir.
unwavering [ʌn'weɪvərɪŋ] a inquebrantable.
unwelcome [ʌn'wɛlkəm] a (at a bad time) inoportuno.
unwell [ʌn'wɛl] a: to feel ~ estar indispuesto.
unwieldy [ʌn'wiːldɪ] a difícil de manejar.
unwilling [ʌn'wɪlɪŋ] a: to be ~ to do sth estar poco dispuesto a hacer algo; ~ly ad de mala gana.
unwind [ʌn'waɪnd] (irg: like wind) vt desenvolver // vi (relax) relajarse.
unwise [ʌn'waɪz] a imprudente.
unwitting [ʌn'wɪtɪŋ] a inconsciente.
unworkable [ʌn'wəːkəbl] a (plan) impráctico.
unworthy [ʌn'wəːðɪ] a indigno.
unwrap [ʌn'ræp] vt deshacer.
unwritten [ʌn'rɪtn] a (agreement) tácito; (rules, law) no escrito.
up [ʌp] ♦ prep: to go/be ~ sth subir/estar subido en algo; he went ~ the stairs/the hill subió las escaleras/la colina; we walked/climbed ~ the hill subimos la colina; they live further ~ the street viven más arriba en la calle; go ~ that road and turn left sigue por esa calle y gira a la izquierda
♦ ad 1 (upwards, higher) más arriba; ~ in the mountains en lo alto (de la montaña); put it a bit higher ~ ponlo un poco más arriba or alto; ~ there ahí or allí arriba; ~ above en lo alto, por encima, arriba
2: to be ~ (out of bed) estar levantado;

(prices, level) haber subido
3: ~ to (as far as) hasta; ~ to now hasta ahora or la fecha
4: to be ~ to (depending on): it's ~ to you depende de ti; he's not ~ to it (job, task etc) no es capaz de hacerlo; his work is not ~ to the required standard su trabajo no da la talla; (col: be doing): what is he ~ to? ¿que estará tramando?
♦ n: ~s and downs altibajos mpl.
up-and-coming [ʌpənd'kʌmɪŋ] a prometedor(a).
upbringing ['ʌpbrɪŋɪŋ] n educación f.
update [ʌp'deɪt] vt poner al día.
upheaval [ʌp'hiːvl] n trastornos mpl; (POL) agitación f.
uphill [ʌp'hɪl] a cuesta arriba; (fig: task) penoso, difícil // ad: to go ~ ir cuesta arriba.
uphold [ʌp'həʊld] (irg: like hold) vt sostener.
upholstery [ʌp'həʊlstərɪ] n tapicería.
upkeep ['ʌpkiːp] n mantenimiento.
upon [ə'pɒn] prep sobre.
upper ['ʌpə*] a superior, de arriba // n (of shoe: also: ~s) pala; ~-class a de clase alta; ~ hand n: to have the ~ hand tener la sartén por el mango; ~most a el más alto; what was ~most in my mind lo que me preocupaba más.
upright ['ʌpraɪt] a vertical; (fig) honrado.
uprising ['ʌpraɪzɪŋ] n sublevación f.
uproar ['ʌprɔː*] n tumulto, escándalo.
uproot [ʌp'ruːt] vt desarraigar.
upset ['ʌpsɛt] n (to plan etc) revés m, contratiempo; (MED) trastorno // vt [ʌp'sɛt] (irg: like set) (glass etc) volcar; (spill) derramar; (plan) alterar; (person) molestar, perturbar // a [ʌp'sɛt] molesto, perturbado; (stomach) revuelto.
upshot ['ʌpʃɒt] n resultado.
upside-down ['ʌpsaɪd'daʊn] ad al revés.
upstairs [ʌp'stɛəz] ad arriba // a (room) de arriba // n el piso superior.
upstart ['ʌpstɑːt] n advenedizo/a.
upstream [ʌp'striːm] ad río arriba.
uptake ['ʌpteɪk] n: he is quick/slow on the ~ es muy listo/torpe.
uptight [ʌp'taɪt] a tenso, nervioso.
up-to-date ['ʌptə'deɪt] a moderno, actual.
upturn ['ʌptəːn] n (in luck) mejora; (COMM: in market) resurgimiento económico.
upward ['ʌpwəd] a ascendente; ~(s) ad hacia arriba.
urban ['əːbən] a urbano.
urbane [əː'beɪn] a cortés, urbano.
urchin ['əːtʃɪn] n pilluelo, golfillo.
urge [əːdʒ] n (force) impulso; (desire) deseo // vt: to ~ sb to do sth animar a uno a hacer algo.
urgency ['əːdʒənsɪ] n urgencia.

urgent ['ɔːdʒənt] *a* urgente.

urinate ['juərɪneɪt] *vi* orinar.

urine ['juərɪn] *n* orina, orines *mpl*.

urn [ɜːn] *n* urna; (*also:* tea ~) *cacharro metálico grande para hacer té.*

Uruguay ['juerəgwaɪ] *n* el Uruguay; ~**an** *a, n* uruguayo/a *m/f*.

us [ʌs] *pron* nos; (*after prep*) nosotros/as; *see also* me.

US, USA *n abbr* = **United States (of America).**

usage ['juːzɪdʒ] *n* (*LING*) uso; (*utilization*) utilización *f*.

use [juːs] *n* uso, empleo; (*usefulness*) utilidad *f* // *vt* [juːz] usar, emplear; she ~**d** to do it (ella) solía *or* acostumbraba hacerlo; in ~ en uso; out of ~ en desuso; to be of ~ servir; it's no ~ (*pointless*) es inútil; (*not useful*) no sirve; to be ~**d** to estar acostumbrado a, acostumbrar; to ~ **up** *vt* agotar; ~**d** *a* (*car*) usado; ~**ful** *a* útil; ~**fulness** *n* utilidad; ~**less** *a* inútil; ~**r** *n* usuario/a; ~**r-friendly** *a* (*computer*) amistoso.

usher ['ʌʃə*] *n* (*at wedding*) ujier *m*; (*in cinema etc*) acomodador *m*; ~**ette** [-'rɛt] *n* (*in cinema*) acomodadora.

USSR *n abbr*: the ~ la URSS.

usual ['juːʒuəl] *a* normal, corriente; as ~ como de costumbre; ~**ly** *ad* normalmente.

utensil [juː'tɛnsl] *n* utensilio; **kitchen** ~**s** batería *sg* de cocina.

uterus ['juːtərəs] *n* útero.

utilitarian [juːtɪlɪ'tɛərɪən] *a* utilitario.

utility [juː'tɪlɪtɪ] *n* utilidad *f*; ~ **room** *n* trascocina.

utilize ['juːtɪlaɪz] *vt* utilizar.

utmost ['ʌtməust] *a* mayor // *n*: to do one's ~ hacer todo lo posible.

utter ['ʌtə*] *a* total, completo // *vt* pronunciar, proferir; ~**ance** *n* palabras *fpl*, declaración *f*; ~**ly** *ad* completamente, totalmente.

U-turn ['juː'tɜːn] *n* viraje *m* en U.

V

v. *abbr* = **verse; versus; volt;** (= *vide*) véase.

vacancy ['veɪkənsɪ] *n* (*Brit: job*) vacante *f*; (*room*) cuarto libro.

vacant ['veɪkənt] *a* desocupado, libre; (*expression*) distraído; ~ **lot** *n* (*US*) solar *m*.

vacate [və'keɪt] *vt* (*house, room*) desocupar; (*job*) dejar (vacante).

vacation [və'keɪʃən] *n* vacaciones *fpl*; ~**er** *n* (*US*) turista *m/f*.

vaccinate ['væksɪneɪt] *vt* vacunar.

vaccine ['væksiːn] *n* vacuna.

vacuum ['vækjum] *n* vacío; ~ **bottle** *n* (*US*) = ~ **flask**; ~ **cleaner** *n* aspiradora; ~ **flask** (*Brit*) *n* termo; ~**-packed**

a empaquetado al vacío.

vagina [və'dʒaɪnə] *n* vagina.

vagrant ['veɪgrnt] *n* vagabundo/a.

vague [veɪg] *a* vago; (*blurred: memory*) borroso; (*ambiguous*) impreciso; (*person*) distraído; ~**ly** *ad* vagamente.

vain [veɪn] *a* (*conceited*) presumido; (*useless*) vano, inútil; in ~ en vano.

valentine ['væləntaɪn] *n* (*also:* ~ **card**) tarjeta del Día de los Enamorados.

valet ['væleɪ] *n* ayuda *m* de cámara.

valiant ['væljənt] *a* valiente.

valid ['vælɪd] *a* válido; (*ticket*) valedero; (*law*) vigente.

valley ['vælɪ] *n* valle *m*.

valour, (*US*) **valor** ['vælə*] *n* valor *m*, valentía.

valuable ['væljuəbl] *a* (*jewel*) de valor; (*time*) valioso; ~**s** *npl* objetos *mpl* de valor.

valuation [væljuˈeɪʃən] *n* tasación *f*, valuación *f*.

value ['væljuː] *n* valor *m*; (*importance*) importancia // *vt* (*fix price of*) tasar, valorar; (*esteem*) apreciar; ~ **added tax** (**VAT**) *n* (*Brit*) impuesto sobre el valor añadido (IVA *m*); ~**d** *a* (*appreciated*) apreciado.

valve [vælv] *n* (*ANAT, TECH*) válvula.

van [væn] *n* (*AUT*) furgoneta, camioneta (*LAm*); (*Brit RAIL*) furgón *m* (de equipajes).

vandal ['vændl] *n* vándalo/a; ~**ism** *n* vandalismo; ~**ize** *vt* dañar, destruir.

vanilla [və'nɪlə] *n* vainilla.

vanish ['vænɪʃ] *vi* desaparecer, esfumarse.

vanity ['vænɪtɪ] *n* vanidad *f*; ~ **case** *n* neceser *m*.

vantage point ['vɑːntɪdʒ-] *n* (*for views*) punto panorámico.

vapour, (*US*) **vapor** ['veɪpə*] *n* vapor *m*; (*on breath, window*) vaho.

variable ['vɛərɪəbl] *a* variable; (*person*) voluble.

variance ['vɛərɪəns] *n*: to be at ~ (**with**) estar en desacuerdo (con).

variation [vɛərɪ'eɪʃən] *n* variación *f*.

varicose ['værɪkəus] *a*: ~ **veins** varices *fpl*.

varied ['vɛərɪd] *a* variado.

variety [və'raɪətɪ] *n* variedad *f*; ~ **show** *n* espectáculo de variedades.

various ['vɛərɪəs] *a* varios/as, diversos/as.

varnish ['vɑːnɪʃ] *n* barniz *m* // *vt* barnizar; (*nails*) pintar (con esmalte).

vary ['vɛərɪ] *vt* variar; (*change*) cambiar // *vi* variar.

vase [vɑːz] *n* florero.

Vaseline ['væsɪliːn] *n* ® Vaselina ®.

vast [vɑːst] *a* enorme; (*success*) abrumador(a).

VAT [væt] *n* (*Brit*) *abbr* = **value added tax.**

vat [væt] n tina, tinaja.
Vatican ['vætɪkən] n: the ~ el Vaticano.
vault [vɔ:lt] n (of roof) bóveda; (tomb) panteón m; (in bank) cámara acorazada // vt (also: ~ over) saltar (por encima de).
vaunted ['vɔ:ntɪd] a: much ~ cacareado, alardeada.
VCR n abbr = **video cassette recorder.**
VD n abbr = **venereal disease.**
VDU n abbr = **visual display unit.**
veal [vi:l] n ternera.
veer [vɪə*] vi (ship) virar.
vegetable ['vedʒtəbl] n (BOT) vegetal m; (edible plant) legumbre f, hortaliza // a vegetal; ~s npl (cooked) verduras fpl.
vegetarian [vedʒɪ'tɛərɪən] a, n vegetariano/a m/f.
vehement ['vi:mənt] a vehemente, apasionado.
vehicle ['vi:ɪkl] n vehículo.
veil [veɪl] n velo // vt velar.
vein [veɪn] n vena; (of ore etc) veta.
velocity [vɪ'lɒsɪtɪ] n velocidad f.
velvet ['vɛlvɪt] n terciopelo.
vending machine ['vɛndɪŋ-] n distribuidor m automático.
vendor ['vɛndə*] n vendedor(a) m/f.
veneer [və'nɪə*] n chapa, enchapado; (fig) barniz m.
venereal [vɪ'nɪərɪəl] a: ~ disease (VD) enfermedad f venérea.
Venetian blind [vɪ'ni:ʃən-] n persiana.
Venezuela [vɛnɪ'zweɪlə] n Venezuela; ~n a, n venezolano/a m/f.
vengeance ['vɛndʒəns] n venganza; with a ~ (fig) con creces.
venison ['vɛnɪsn] n carne f de venado.
venom ['vɛnəm] n veneno.
vent [vɛnt] n (opening) abertura; (airhole) respiradero; (in wall) rejilla (de ventilación) // vt (fig: feelings) desahogar.
ventilate ['vɛntɪleɪt] vt ventilar; **ventilator** n ventilador m.
ventriloquist [vɛn'trɪləkwɪst] n ventrílocuo/a.
venture ['vɛntʃə*] n empresa // vt arriesgar; (opinion) ofrecer // vi arriesgarse, lanzarse.
venue ['vɛnju:] n lugar m de reunión.
veranda(h) [və'rændə] n terraza; (with glass) galería.
verb [və:b] n verbo; ~al a verbal.
verbatim [və:'beɪtɪm] a, ad palabra por palabra.
verbose [və:'bəus] a prolijo.
verdict ['və:dɪkt] n veredicto, fallo; (fig) opinión f, juicio.
verge [və:dʒ] n (Brit) borde m; to be on the ~ of doing sth estar a punto de hacer algo; **to ~ on** vt fus rayar en.
verify ['vɛrɪfaɪ] vt comprobar, verificar.
veritable ['vɛrɪtəbl] a verdadero, auténtico.

vermin ['və:mɪn] npl (animals) bichos mpl; (insects, fig) sabandijas fpl.
vermouth ['və:məθ] n vermut m.
versatile ['və:sətaɪl] a (person) polifacético; (machine, tool etc) versátil.
verse [və:s] n versos mpl, poesía; (stanza) estrofa; (in bible) versículo.
versed [və:st] a: (well-)~ in versado en.
version ['və:ʃən] n versión f.
versus ['və:səs] prep contra.
vertebra ['və:tɪbrə], pl ~e [-bri:] n vértebra.
vertical ['və:tɪkl] a vertical.
vertigo ['və:tɪgəu] n vértigo.
verve [və:v] n brío.
very ['vɛrɪ] ad muy // a: the ~ book which el mismo libro que; the ~ last el último de todos; at the ~ least al menos; ~ much muchísimo.
vessel ['vɛsl] n (ANAT) vaso; (ship) barco; (container) vasija.
vest [vɛst] n (Brit) camiseta; (US: waistcoat) chaleco; ~ed interests npl (COMM) intereses mpl creados.
vestibule ['vɛstɪbju:l] n vestíbulo.
vestige ['vɛstɪdʒ] n vestigio, rastro.
vestry ['vɛstrɪ] n sacristía.
vet [vɛt] n abbr = **veterinary surgeon** // vt repasar, revisar.
veteran ['vɛtərn] n veterano.
veterinary ['vɛtrɪnərɪ] a veterinario; ~ **surgeon**, (US) **veterinarian** n veterinario/a m/f.
veto ['vi:təu], pl ~es n veto // vt prohibir, vedar.
vex [vɛks] vt fastidiar; ~ed a (question) controvertido.
VHF abbr (= very high frequency) muy alta frecuencia.
via ['vaɪə] prep por, por vía de.
vibrate [vaɪ'breɪt] vi vibrar.
vicar ['vɪkə*] n párroco (de la Iglesia Anglicana); ~**age** n parroquia.
vicarious [vɪ'kɛərɪəs] a indirecto.
vice [vaɪs] n (evil) vicio; (TECH) torno de banco.
vice- [vaɪs] pref vice-; ~**chairman** n vicepresidente m.
vice versa ['vaɪsɪ'və:sə] ad viceversa.
vicinity [vɪ'sɪnɪtɪ] n vecindad f; in the ~ (of) cercano (a).
vicious ['vɪʃəs] a (remark) malicioso; (blow) fuerte; ~ **circle** n círculo vicioso.
victim ['vɪktɪm] n víctima; ~**ize** vt (strikers etc) tomar represalias contra.
victor ['vɪktə*] n vencedor(a) m/f.
victory ['vɪktərɪ] n victoria.
video ['vɪdɪəu] cpd video // n (~ film) videofilm m; (also: ~ **cassette**) videocassette f; (also: ~ **cassette recorder**) videograbadora; ~ **tape** n cinta de vídeo.
vie [vaɪ] vi: to ~ with competir con.
Vienna [vɪ'ɛnə] n Viena.
Vietnam [vjɛt'næm] n Vietnam m.
view [vju:] n vista, perspectiva; (land-

scape) paisaje *m*; (*opinion*) opinión *f*, criterio // *vt* (*look at*) mirar; (*examine*) examinar; **on ~** (*in museum etc*) expuesto; **in full ~** (**of**) en plena vista (de); **in ~ of the fact that** en vista del hecho de que; **~er** *n* (*small projector*) visionadora; (*TV*) televidente *m/f*; **~finder** *n* visor *m* de imagen; **~point** *n* punto de vista.

vigil ['vɪdʒɪl] *n* vigilia.

vigorous ['vɪgərəs] *a* enérgico, vigoroso.

vigour, (*US*) **vigor** ['vɪgə*] *n* energía, vigor *m*.

vile [vaɪl] *a* (*action*) vil, infame; (*smell*) asqueroso.

vilify ['vɪlɪfaɪ] *vt* vilipendiar.

villa ['vɪlə] *n* (*country house*) casa de campo; (*suburban house*) chalet *m*.

village ['vɪlɪdʒ] *n* aldea; **~r** *n* aldeano/a.

villain ['vɪlən] *n* (*scoundrel*) malvado/a; (*criminal*) maleante *m/f*.

vindicate ['vɪndɪkeɪt] *vt* vindicar, justificar.

vindictive [vɪn'dɪktɪv] *a* vengativo.

vine [vaɪn] *n* vid *f*.

vinegar ['vɪnɪgə*] *n* vinagre *m*.

vineyard ['vɪnjɑːd] *n* viña, viñedo.

vintage ['vɪntɪdʒ] *n* (*year*) vendimia, cosecha; **~ wine** *n* vino añejo.

vinyl ['vaɪnl] *n* vinilo.

viola [vɪ'əulə] *n* (*MUS*) viola.

violate ['vaɪəleɪt] *vt* violar.

violence ['vaɪələns] *n* violencia.

violent ['vaɪələnt] *a* (*gen*) violento; (*pain*) intenso.

violet ['vaɪələt] *a* violado, violeta // *n* (*plant*) violeta.

violin [vaɪə'lɪn] *n* violín *m*; **~ist** *n* violinista *m/f*.

VIP *n abbr* (= *very important person*) VIP *m*.

viper ['vaɪpə*] *n* víbora.

virgin ['vɜːdʒɪn] *n* virgen *f* // *a* virgen.

Virgo ['vɜːgəu] *n* Virgo.

virile ['vɪraɪl] *a* viril.

virtually ['vɜːtjuəlɪ] *ad* prácticamente.

virtue ['vɜːtjuː] *n* virtud *f*; **by ~ of** en virtud de.

virtuous ['vɜːtjuəs] *a* virtuoso.

virus ['vaɪərəs] *n* virus *m*.

visa ['viːzə] *n* visado, visa (*LAm*).

vis-à-vis [viːzə'viː] *prep* con respecto a.

visibility [vɪzɪ'bɪlɪtɪ] *n* visibilidad *f*.

visible ['vɪzəbl] *a* visible.

vision ['vɪʒən] *n* (*sight*) vista; (*foresight*, *in dream*) visión *f*.

visit ['vɪzɪt] *n* visita // *vt* (*person*) visitar, hacer una visita a; (*place*) ir a, (ir a) conocer; **~ing hours** *npl* (*in hospital etc*) horas de visita; **~or** *n* (*in museum*) visitante *m/f*; (*tourist*) turista *m/f*; **to have ~ors** (*at home*) tener visita; **~ors' book** *n* libro de visitas.

visor ['vaɪzə*] *n* visera.

vista ['vɪstə] *n* vista, panorama.

visual ['vɪzjuəl] *a* visual; **~ aid** *n* medio visual; **~ display unit (VDU)** *n* unidad *f* de presentación visual (UPV); **~ize** *vt* imaginarse; (*foresee*) prever.

vital ['vaɪtl] *a* (*essential*) esencial, imprescindible; (*dynamic*) dinámico **~ly ad**: **~ly important** de primera importancia; **~ statistics** *npl* (*fig*) medidas *fpl* vitales.

vitamin ['vɪtəmɪn] *n* vitamina.

vivacious [vɪ'veɪʃəs] *a* vivaz, alegre.

vivid ['vɪvɪd] *a* (*account*) gráfico; (*light*) intenso; (*imagination*) vivo; **~ly ad** (*describe*) gráficamente; (*remember*) como si fuera hoy.

V-neck ['viːnɛk] *n* cuello de pico.

vocabulary [vəu'kæbjulərɪ] *n* vocabulario.

vocal ['vəukl] *a* vocal; (*articulate*) elocuente; **~ chords** *npl* cuerdas *fpl* vocales.

vocation [vəu'keɪʃən] *n* vocación *f*; **~al** *a* profesional.

vociferous [və'sɪfərəs] *a* vociferante.

vodka ['vɔdkə] *n* vodka *m*.

vogue [vəug] *n* boga, moda.

voice [vɔɪs] *n* voz *f* // *vt* (*opinion*) expresar.

void [vɔɪd] *n* vacío; (*hole*) hueco // *a* (*invalid*) nulo, inválido; (*empty*): **~ of** carente *or* desprovisto de.

volatile ['vɔlətaɪl] *a* volátil.

volcano [vɔl'keɪnəu], *pl* **-es** *n* volcán *m*.

volition [və'lɪʃən] *n*: **of one's own ~** de su propia voluntad.

volley ['vɔlɪ] *n* (*of gunfire*) descarga; (*of stones etc*) lluvia; (*TENNIS etc*) volea; **~ball** *n* vol(e)ibol *m*.

volt [vəult] *n* voltio; **~age** *n* voltaje *m*.

voluble ['vɔljubl] *a* locuaz, hablador(a).

volume ['vɔljuːm] *n* (*gen*) volumen *m*; (*book*) tomo.

voluntarily ['vɔləntrɪlɪ] *ad* libremente, voluntariamente.

voluntary ['vɔləntərɪ] *a* voluntario; (*statement*) espontáneo.

volunteer [vɔlən'tɪə*] *n* voluntario/a // *vi* ofrecerse (de voluntario); **to ~ to do** ofrecerse a hacer.

vomit ['vɔmɪt] *n* vómito // *vt*, *vi* vomitar.

vote [vəut] *n* voto; (*votes cast*) votación *f*; (*right to ~*) derecho de votar; (*franchise*) sufragio // *vt* (*chairman*) elegir // *vi* votar, ir a votar; **~ of thanks** voto de gracias; **~r** *n* votante *m/f*; **voting** *n* votación *f*.

vouch [vautʃ]: **to ~ for** *vt fus* garantizar, responder de.

voucher ['vautʃə*] *n* (*for meal*, *petrol*) vale *m*.

vow [vau] *n* voto // *vi* jurar.

vowel ['vauəl] *n* vocal *f*.

voyage ['vɔɪdʒ] *n* (*journey*) viaje *m*; (*crossing*) travesía.

vulgar ['vʌlgə*] *a* (*rude*) ordinario, gro-

sero; (*in bad taste*) de mal gusto; ~**ity**
[-'gærɪtɪ] *n* grosería; mal gusto.
vulnerable ['vʌlnərəbl] *a* vulnerable.
vulture ['vʌltʃə*] *n* buitre *m*.

W

wad [wɔd] *n* (*of cotton wool, paper*) bolita; (*of banknotes etc*) fajo.
waddle ['wɔdl] *vi* anadear.
wade [weɪd] *vi*: to ~ through (*water*) caminar por; (*fig: a book*) leer con dificultad; **wading pool** *n* (*US*) piscina para
niños.
wafer ['weɪfə*] *n* (*biscuit*) galleta, barquillo; (*COMPUT, REL*) oblea.
waffle ['wɔfl] *n* (*CULIN*) gofre *m* // *vi* dar
el rollo.
waft [wɔft] *vt* llevar por el aire // *vi* flotar.
wag [wæg] *vt* menear, agitar // *vi* moverse, menearse.
wage [weɪdʒ] *n* (*also*: ~s) sueldo, salario
// *vt*: to ~ war hacer la guerra; ~ **earn-**
er *n* asalariado/a; ~ **packet** *n* sobre *m*
de paga.
wager ['weɪdʒə*] *n* apuesta // *vt* apostar.
waggle ['wægl] *vt* menear, mover.
wag(g)on ['wægən] *n* (*horse-drawn*) -ca-
rro; (*Brit RAIL*) vagón *m*.
wail [weɪl] *n* gemido // *vi* gemir.
waist [weɪst] *n* cintura, talle *m*; ~**coat** *n*
(*Brit*) chaleco; ~**line** *n* talle *m*.
wait [weɪt] *n* espera; (*interval*) pausa //
vi esperar; to lie in ~ for acechar a; I
can't ~ to (*fig*) estoy deseando; to ~ for
esperar (a); to ~ **behind** *vi* quedarse;
to ~ **on** *vt fus* servir a; ~**er** *n* camarero; ~**ing** *n*: 'no ~**ing**' (*Brit AUT*) 'prohibido estacionarse'; ~**ing list** *n* lista de
espera; ~**ing room** *n* sala de espera;
~**ress** *n* camarera.
waive [weɪv] *vt* suspender.
wake [weɪk] *vb* (*pt* **woke** *or* **waked**, *pp*
woken *or* **waked**) *vt* (*also*: ~ **up**) despertar // *vi* (*also*: ~ **up**) despertarse // *n* (*for*
dead person) vela, velatorio; (*NAUT*) estela; ~**n** *vt, vi* = **wake.**
Wales [weɪlz] *n* País *m* de Gales.
walk [wɔːk] *n* (*stroll*) paseo; (*hike*) excursión *f* a pie, caminata; (*gait*) paso,
andar *m*; (*in park etc*) paseo, alameda //
vi andar, caminar; (*for pleasure, exer-*
cise) pasearse // *vt* (*distance*) recorrer a
pie, andar; (*dog*) pasear; **10 minutes'** ~
from here a 10 minutos de aquí andando;
people from all ~**s of life** gente de todas
las esferas; **to walk out on** *vt fus*
(*col*) abandonar; ~**er** *n* (*person*) pa-
seante *m/f*, caminante *m/f*; ~**ie-talkie**
['wɔːkɪ'tɔːkɪ] *n* walkie-talkie *m*; ~**ing** *n*
el andar; ~**ing shoes** *npl* zapatos *mpl*
para andar; ~**ing stick** *n* bastón *m*;
~**out** *n* (*of workers*) huelga; ~**over** *n*

(*col*) pan *m* comido; ~**way** *n* paseo.
wall [wɔːl] *n* pared *f*; (*exterior*) muro;
(*city* ~ *etc*) muralla; ~**ed** *a* (*city*)
amurallado; (*garden*) con tapia.
wallet ['wɔlɪt] *n* cartera, billetera
(*LAm*).
wallflower ['wɔːlflauə*] *n* alhelí *m*; **to be**
a ~ (*fig*) comer pavo.
wallop ['wɔləp] *vt* (*col*) zurrar.
wallow ['wɔləu] *vi* revolcarse.
wallpaper ['wɔːlpeɪpə*] *n* papel *m* pintado.
wally ['wɔlɪ] *n* (*Brit: col*) palurdo/a.
walnut ['wɔːlnʌt] *n* nuez *f*; (*tree*) nogal
m.
walrus ['wɔːlrəs], *pl* ~ *or* ~ **es** *n* morsa.
waltz [wɔːlts] *n* vals *m* // *vi* bailar el
vals.
wan [wɔn] *a* pálido.
wand [wɔnd] *n* (*also*: **magic** ~) varita
(mágica).
wander ['wɔndə*] *vi* (*person*) vagar;
deambular; (*thoughts*) divagar; (*get*
lost) extraviarse // *vt* recorrer, vagar
por.
wane [weɪn] *vi* menguar.
wangle ['wæŋgl] *vt* (*Brit col*): to ~ sth
agenciarse algo.
want [wɔnt] *vt* (*wish for*) querer, desear;
(*need*) necesitar; (*lack*) carecer de // *n*:
for ~ **of** por falta de; ~**s** *npl* (*needs*) necesidades *fpl*; to ~ to do querer hacer;
to ~ **sb** to do sth querer que uno haga
algo; ~**ing**: to be found ~**ing** no estar a
la altura de las circunstancias.
wanton ['wɔntn] *a* (*playful*) juguetón/
ona; (*licentious*) lascivo.
war [wɔː*] *n* guerra; to make ~ hacer la
guerra.
ward [wɔːd] *n* (*in hospital*) sala; (*POL*)
distrito electoral; (*LAW: child*) pupilo/a;
to ~ **off** *vt* (*blow*) desviar, parar; (*at-*
tack) rechazar.
warden ['wɔːdn] *n* (*Brit: of institution*)
director(a) *m/f*; (*of park, game reserve*)
guardián/ana *m/f*; (*Brit: also*: **traffic** ~)
guardia *m/f*.
warder ['wɔːdə*] *n* (*Brit*) guardián/ana
m/f, carcelero/a.
wardrobe ['wɔːdrəub] *n* armario, guardarropa, ropero (*esp LAm*).
warehouse ['wɛəhaus] *n* almacén *m*, depósito.
wares [wɛəz] *npl* mercancías *fpl*.
warfare ['wɔːfɛə*] *n* guerra.
warhead ['wɔːhɛd] *n* cabeza armada.
warily ['wɛərɪlɪ] *ad* con cautela, cautelo-
samente.
warm [wɔːm] *a* caliente; (*thanks*) efusivo; (*clothes etc*) abrigado; (*welcome,*
day) caluroso; it's ~ hace calor; I'm ~
tengo calor; **to** ~ **up** *vi* (*room*) calentarse; (*person*) entrar en calor; (*ath-*
lete) hacer ejercicios de calentamiento;
(*discussion*) acalorarse // *vt* calentar;

~-hearted *a* afectuoso; **~ly** *ad* afectuosamente; **~th** *n* calor *m*.

warn [wɔ:n] *vt* avisar, advertir; **~ing** *n* aviso, advertencia; **~ing light** *n* luz *f* de advertencia; **~ing triangle** *n* (AUT) triángulo señalizador.

warp [wɔ:p] *vi* (*wood*) combarse // *vt* combar; (*mind*) pervertir.

warrant ['wɔrnt] *n* (LAW: *to arrest*) orden *f* de detención; (: *to search*) mandamiento de registro.

warranty ['wɔrəntɪ] *n* garantía.

warren ['wɔrən] *n* (*of rabbits*) madriguera; (*fig*) laberinto.

warrior ['wɔrɪə*] *n* guerrero/a.

Warsaw ['wɔ:sɔ:] *n* Varsovia.

warship ['wɔ:ʃɪp] *n* buque *m* o barco de guerra.

wart [wɔ:t] *n* verruga.

wartime ['wɔ:taɪm] *n*: in ~ en tiempos de guerra, en la guerra.

wary ['wɛərɪ] *a* cauteloso.

was [wɔz] *pt of* **be**.

wash [wɔʃ] *vt* lavar // *vi* lavarse // *n* (*clothes etc*) lavado; (*bath*) baño; (*of ship*) estela; to have a ~ lavarse; **to ~ away** *vt* (*stain*) quitar lavando; (*subj: river etc*) llevarse; (*fig*) limpiar; **to ~ off** *vt* quitar lavando; **to ~ up** *vi* (*Brit*) fregar los platos; (US) lavarse; **~able** *a* lavable; **~basin**, (US) **~bowl** *n* lavabo; **~cloth** *n* (US) manopla; **~er** *n* (TECH) arandela; **~ing** *n* (*dirty*) ropa sucia; (*clean*) colada; **~ing machine** *n* lavadora; **~ing powder** *n* (*Brit*) detergente *m* (en polvo); **~ing-up** *n* fregado, platos *mpl* (para fregar); **~ing-up liquid** *n* líquido lavavajillas; **~-out** *n* (*col*) fracaso; **~room** *n* servicios *mpl*.

wasn't ['wɔznt] = **was not**.

wasp [wɔsp] *n* avispa.

wastage ['weɪstɪdʒ] *n* desgaste *m*; (*loss*) pérdida; **natural ~** desgaste natural.

waste [weɪst] *n* derroche *m*, despilfarro; (*misuse*) desgaste *m*; (*of time*) pérdida; (*food*) sobras *fpl*; (*rubbish*) basura, desperdicios *mpl* // *a* (*material*) de desecho; (*left over*) sobrante // *vt* (*squander*) malgastar, derrochar; (*time*) perder; (*opportunity*) desperdiciar; **~s** *npl* (*area of land*) tierras *fpl* baldías; **to lay ~** devastar, arrasar; **to ~ away** *vi* consumirse; **~ disposal unit** *n* (*Brit*) triturador *m* de basura; **~ful** *a* derrochador(a); (*process*) antieconómico; **~ ground** *n* (*Brit*) terreno baldío; **~paper basket** *n* papelera; **~ pipe** *n* tubo de desagüe.

watch [wɔtʃ] *n* reloj *m*; (MIL: *guard*) centinela *m*; (: *spell of duty*) guardia // *vt* (*look at*) mirar, observar; (: *match, programme*) ver; (*spy on, guard*) vigilar; (*be careful of*) cuidarse de, tener cuidado de // *vi* ver, mirar; (*keep guard*) montar guardia; **to keep ~ on sb** mantener a uno bajo vigilancia; **to ~**

out *vi* cuidarse, tener cuidado; **~dog** *n* perro guardián; **~ful** *a* vigilante, sobre aviso; **~maker** *n* relojero/a; **~man** *n* guardián *m*; (*also*: **night ~man**) sereno, vigilante *m* (LAm); (*in factory*) vigilante *m* nocturno; **~ strap** *n* pulsera (de reloj).

water ['wɔ:tə*] *n* agua // *vt* (*plant*) regar // *vi* (*eyes*) hacerse agua; in British **~s** en aguas británicas; **to ~ down** *vt* (*milk etc*) aguar; **~ closet** *n* wáter *m*; **~colour** *n* acuarela; **~cress** *n* berro; **~fall** *n* cascada, salto de agua; **~ heater** *n* calentador *m* de agua; **~ing can** *n* regadera; **~ level** *n* nivel *m* del agua; **~ lily** *n* nenúfar *m*; **~line** *n* (NAUT) línea de flotación; **~logged** *a* (*boat*) anegado; (*ground*) inundado; **~ main** *n* cañería del agua; **~mark** *n* (*on paper*) filigrana; **~melon** *n* sandía; **~ polo** *n* polo acuático; **~proof** *a* impermeable; **~shed** *n* (GEO) cuenca; (*fig*) momento crítico; **~skiing** *n* esquí *m* acuático; **~ tank** *n* depósito de agua; **~tight** *a* hermético; **~way** *n* vía fluvial *or* navegable; **~works** *npl* central *f* depuradora; **~y** *a* (*colour*) desvaído; (*coffee*) aguado; (*eyes*) lloroso.

watt [wɔt] *n* vatio,

wave [weɪv] *n* ola; (*of hand*) señal *f* con la mano; (RADIO, *in hair*) onda; (*fig*) oleada // *vi* agitar la mano; (*flag*) ondear // *vt* (*handkerchief, gun*) agitar; **~length** *n* longitud *f* de onda.

waver ['weɪvə*] *vi* (*flame etc*) oscilar; (*confidence*) disminuir; (*faith*) flaquear.

wavy ['weɪvɪ] *a* ondulado.

wax [wæks] *n* cera // *vt* encerar // *vi* (*moon*) crecer; **~ paper** *n* (US) papel apergaminado; **~works** *npl* museo *sg* de cera.

way [weɪ] *n* camino; (*distance*) trayecto, recorrido; (*direction*) dirección *f*, sentido; (*manner*) modo, manera; (*habit*) costumbre *f*; **which ~? — this ~** ¿por dónde?, ¿en qué dirección? — por aquí; **on the ~** (*en route*) en (el) camino; **to be on one's ~** estar en camino; **to be in the ~** bloquear el camino; (*fig*) estorbar; **to go out of one's ~ to do sth** desvirse por hacer algo; **to lose one's ~** extraviarse; **in a ~** en cierto modo *or* sentido; **by the ~** a propósito; **'~ in'** (*Brit*) 'entrada'; **'~ out'** (*Brit*) 'salida'; **the ~ back** el camino de vuelta; **give ~'** (*Brit* AUT) 'ceda el paso'; **no ~!** (*col*) ¡ni pensarlo!

waylay [weɪ'leɪ] (*irg*: *like* lay) *vt*: I was waylaid (by) me entretuve (con).

wayward ['weɪwəd] *a* díscolo; caprichoso.

W.C. ['dʌblju'si:] *n* (*Brit*) wáter *m*.

we [wi:] *pl pron* nosotros/as.

weak [wi:k] *a* débil, flojo; (*tea*) claro; **~en** *vi* debilitarse; (*give way*) ceder //

vt debilitar; **~ling** *n* debilucho/a;
~ness *n* debilidad *f*; *(fault)* punto débil.
wealth [wɛlθ] *n (money, resources)* riqueza; *(of details)* abundancia; **~y** *a* rico.
wean [wiːn] *vt* destetar.
weapon [ˈwɛpən] *n* arma.
wear [wɛə*] *n (use)* uso; *(deterioration through use)* desgaste *m*; *(clothing)*: **sports/baby~** ropa de deportes/de niños // *vb (pt* **wore***, pp* **worn***) vt (clothes)* llevar; *(shoes)* calzar; *(damage: through use)* gastar, usar // *vi (last)* durar; *(rub through etc)* desgastarse; **evening ~** *(man's)* traje *m* de etiqueta; *(woman's)* traje *m* de noche; **to ~ away** *vt* gastar // *vi* desgastarse; **to ~ down** *vt* gastar; *(strength)* agotar; **to ~ off** *vi (pain etc)* pasar, desaparecer; **to ~ out** *vt* desgastar; *(person, strength)* agotar; **~ and tear** *n* desgaste *m*.
weary [ˈwɪərɪ] *a (tired)* cansado; *(dispirited)* abatido.
weasel [ˈwiːzl] *n (ZOOL)* comadreja.
weather [ˈwɛðə*] *n* tiempo // *vt (storm, crisis)* hacer frente a; **under the ~** *(fig: ill)* indispuesto, pachucho; **~-beaten** *a* curtido; **~cock** *n* veleta; **~ forecast** *n* boletín *m* meteorológico; **~ vane** *n* = **~cock**.
weave [wiːv], *pt* **wove***, pp* **woven** *vt (cloth)* tejer; *(fig)* entretejer; **~r** *n* tejedor(a) *m/f*.
web [wɛb] *n (of spider)* telaraña; *(on foot)* membrana; *(network)* red *f*.
wed [wɛd], *pt, pp* **wedded** *vt* casar // *vi* casarse.
we'd [wiːd] = **we had; we would**.
wedding [ˈwɛdɪŋ] *n* boda, casamiento; **silver/golden ~ anniversary** bodas *fpl* de plata/de oro; **~ day** *n* día *m* de la boda; **~ dress** *n* traje *m* de novia; **~ present** *n* regalo de boda; **~ ring** *n* alianza.
wedge [wɛdʒ] *n (of wood etc)* cuña; *(of cake)* trozo // *vt* acuñar; *(push)* apretar.
wedlock [ˈwɛdlɔk] *n* matrimonio.
Wednesday [ˈwɛdnzdɪ] *n* miércoles *m* *inv*.
wee [wiː] *a (Scottish)* pequeñito.
weed [wiːd] *n* mala hierba, maleza // *vt* escardar, desherbar; **~killer** *n* herbicida *m*; **~y** *a (person)* debilucho.
week [wiːk] *n* semana; **a ~ today/on Friday** de hoy/del viernes en ocho días; **~day** *n* día *m* laborable; **~end** *n* fin *m* de semana; **~ly** *ad* semanalmente, cada semana // *a* semanal // *n* semanario.
weep [wiːp], *pt, pp* **wept** *vi, vt* llorar; **~ing willow** *n* sauce *m* llorón.
weigh [weɪ] *vt, vi* pesar; **to ~ anchor** levar anclas; **to ~ down** *vt* sobrecargar; *(fig: with worry)* agobiar; **to ~ up** *vt* pesar.
weight [weɪt] *n* peso; *(metal ~)* pesa; **to lose/put on ~** adelgazar/engordar; **~ing**

n (allowance): **(London)~ing** *dietas fpl (por residir en Londres)*; **~ lifter** *n* levantador(a) *m/f* de pesas; **~y** *a* pesado.
weir [wɪə*] *n* presa.
weird [wɪəd] *a* raro, extraño.
welcome [ˈwɛlkəm] *a* bienvenido // *n* bienvenida // *vt* dar la bienvenida a; *(be glad of)* alegrarse de; **thank you — you're ~** gracias — de nada.
weld [wɛld] *n* soldadura // *vt* soldar.
welfare [ˈwɛlfɛə*] *n* bienestar *m*; *(social aid)* asistencia social; **W~** *n (US)* subsidio de paro; **~ state** *n* estado del bienestar; **~ work** *n* asistencia social.
well [wɛl] *n* fuente *f*, pozo // *ad* bien // *a*: **to be ~** estar bien *(de salud)* // *excl* ¡vaya!, ¡bueno!; **as ~** también; **as ~ as** además de; **~ done!** ¡bien hecho!; **get ~ soon!** ¡que te mejores pronto!; **to do ~** *(business)* ir bien; *(in exam)* salir bien; **to ~ up** *vi* brotar.
we'll [wiːl] = **we will; we shall**.
well: ~-behaved *a* modoso; **~-being** *n* bienestar *m*; **~-built** *a (person)* fornido; **~-deserved** *a* merecido; **~-dressed** *a* bien vestido; **~-heeled** *a (col: wealthy)* rico.
wellingtons [ˈwɛlɪŋtənz] *npl (also: wellington boots)* botas *fpl* de goma.
well: ~-known *a (person)* conocido; **~-mannered** *a* educado; **~-meaning** *a* bienintencionado; **~-off** *a* acomodado; **~-read** *a* leído; **~-to-do** *a* acomodado; **~-wisher** *n* admirador(a) *m/f*.
Welsh [wɛlʃ] *a* galés/esa // *n (LING)* galés *m*; **the ~** *npl* los galeses; **~man/woman** *n* galés/esa *m/f*; **~ rarebit** *n* pan *m* con queso tostado.
went [wɛnt] *pt of* **go**.
wept [wɛpt] *pt, pp of* **weep**.
were [wɔː*] *pt of* **be**.
we're [wɪə*] = **we are**.
weren't [wɔːnt] = **were not**.
west [wɛst] *n* oeste *m* // *a* occidental, del oeste // *ad* al *or* hacia el oeste; **the W~** *n* el Oeste, el Occidente; **the W~ Country** *n (Brit)* el suroeste de Inglaterra; **~erly** *a (wind)* del oeste; **~ern** *a* occidental // *n (CINEMA)* película del oeste; **W~ Germany** *n* Alemania Occidental; **W~ Indian** *a, n* antillano/a *m/f*; **W~ Indies** *npl* Antillas *fpl*; **~ward(s)** *ad* hacia el oeste.
wet [wɛt] *a (damp)* húmedo; *(~ through)* mojado; *(rainy)* lluvioso; **to get ~** mojarse; '**~ paint**' 'recién pintado'; **~ blanket** *n*: **to be a ~ blanket** *(fig)* ser un/una aguafiestas; **~ suit** *n* traje *m* de buzo.
we've [wiːv] = **we have**.
whack [wæk] *vt* dar un buen golpe a.
whale [weɪl] *n (ZOOL)* ballena.
wharf [wɔːf], *pl* **wharves** [wɔːvz] *n* muelle *m*.
what [wɔt] ♦ *a* **1** *(in direct/indirect ques-*

tions) qué; ~ **size** is he? ¿qué talla usa?; ~ **colour/shape** is it? ¿de qué color/forma es?
2 (*in exclamations*): ~ **a mess!** ¡qué desastre!; ~ **a fool I am!** ¡qué tonto soy!
♦ *pron* **1** (*interrogative*) qué; ~ **are you doing?** ¿qué haces *or* estás haciendo?; ~ **is happening?** ¿qué pasa *or* está pasando?; ~ **is it called?** ¿cómo se llama?; ~ **about me?** ¿y yo qué?; ~ **about doing ...?** ¿qué tal si hacemos ...?
2 (*relative*) lo que; **I saw** ~ **you did/was on the table** vi lo que hiciste/había en la mesa
♦ *excl* (*disbelieving*) ¡cómo!; ~, **no coffee!** ¡que no hay café!

whatever [wɒtˈɛvə*] *a*: ~ **book you choose** cualquier libro que elijas // *pron*: **do** ~ **is necessary** haga lo que sea necesario; **no reason** ~ *or* **whatsoever** ninguna razón sea la que sea; **nothing** ~ nada en absoluto.

wheat [wiːt] *n* trigo.

wheedle [ˈwiːdl] *vt*: **to** ~ **sb into doing sth** engatusar a uno para que haga algo; **to** ~ **sth out of sb** sonsacar algo a uno.

wheel [wiːl] *n* rueda; (*AUT: also:* **steering** ~) volante *m*; (*NAUT*) timón *m* // *vt* (*pram etc*) empujar // *vi* (*also:* ~ **round**) dar la vuelta, girar; ~**barrow** *n* carretilla; ~**chair** *n* silla de ruedas; ~ **clamp** *n* (*AUT*) cepo.

wheeze [wiːz] *vi* resollar.

when [wɛn] ♦ *ad* cuando; ~ **did it happen?** ¿cuándo ocurrió?; **I know** ~ **it happened** sé cuándo ocurrió
♦ *conj* **1** (*at, during, after the time that*) cuando; **be careful** ~ **you cross the road** ten cuidado al cruzar la calle; **that was** ~ **I needed you** fue entonces que te necesité
2 (*on, at which*): **on the day** ~ **I met him** el día en que le conocí
3 (*whereas*) cuando.

whenever [wɛnˈɛvə*] *conj* cuando; (*every time*) cada vez que.

where [wɛə*] *ad* dónde // *conj* donde; **this is** ~ aquí es donde; ~**abouts** *ad* dónde // *n*: **nobody knows his** ~**abouts** nadie conoce su paradero; ~**as** *conj* visto que, mientras; ~**by** *pron* por lo cual; ~**upon** *conj* con lo cual, después de lo cual; ~**ver** [-ˈɛvə*] *ad* dondequiera que; (*interrogative*) dónde; ~**withal** *n* recursos *mpl*.

whet [wɛt] *vt* estimular.

whether [ˈwɛðə*] *conj* si; **I don't know** ~ **to accept or not** no sé si aceptar o no; ~ **you go or not** vayas o no vayas.

which [wɪtʃ] ♦ *a* **1** (*interrogative: direct, indirect*) qué; ~ **picture(s) do you want?** ¿qué cuadro(s) quieres?; ~ **one?** ¿cuál?
2: in ~ **case** en cuyo caso; **we got there at 8 pm, by** ~ **time** the cinema was full llegamos allí a las 8, cuando el cine esta-

ba lleno
♦ *pron* **1** (*interrogative*) cual; **I don't mind** ~ el/la que sea
2 (*relative: replacing noun*) que; (*: replacing clause*) lo que; (*: after preposition*) (el/la) que *etc*, el/la cual *etc*; **the apple** ~ **you ate/~ is on the table** la manzana que comiste/que está en la mesa; **the chair on** ~ **you are sitting** la silla en la que estás sentado; **he said he knew,** ~ **is true/I feared** dijo que lo sabía, lo cual *or* lo que es cierto/me temía.

whichever [wɪtʃˈɛvə*] *a*: **take** ~ **book you prefer** coja el libro que prefiera; ~ **book you take** cualquier libro que coja.

whiff [wɪf] *n* bocanada.

while [waɪl] *n* rato, momento // *conj* durante; (*whereas*) mientras; (*although*) aunque; **for a** ~ durante algún tiempo; **to** ~ **away the time** pasar el rato.

whim [wɪm] *n* capricho.

whimper [ˈwɪmpə*] *vi* (*weep*) lloriquear; (*moan*) quejarse.

whimsical [ˈwɪmzɪkl] *a* (*person*) caprichoso.

whine [waɪn] *vi* (*with pain*) gemir; (*engine*) zumbar.

whip [wɪp] *n* látigo; (*POL: person*) encargado/a de la disciplina partidaria en el parlamento // *vt* azotar; (*snatch*) arrebatar; (*US: CULIN*) batir; ~**ped cream** *n* nata *or* crema montada; ~**round** *n* (*Brit*) colecta.

whirl [wəːl] *vt* hacer girar, dar vueltas a // *vi* girar, dar vueltas; (*leaves, water etc*) arremolinarse; ~**pool** *n* remolino; ~**wind** *n* torbellino.

whirr [wəː*] *vi* zumbar.

whisk [wɪsk] *n* (*Brit: CULIN*) batidor *m* // *vt* (*Brit: CULIN*) batir; **to** ~ **sb away** *or* **off** llevar volando a uno.

whisker [ˈwɪskə*] *n*: ~**s** (*of animal*) bigotes *mpl*; (*of man: side* ~**s**) patillas *fpl*.

whisky, (*US, Ireland*) **whiskey** [ˈwɪskɪ] *n* whisky *m*.

whisper [ˈwɪspə*] *vi* cuchichear, hablar bajo // *vt* decir en voz muy baja.

whistle [ˈwɪsl] *n* (*sound*) silbido; (*object*) silbato // *vi* silbar.

white [waɪt] *a* blanco; (*pale*) pálido // *n* blanco; (*of egg*) clara; ~ **coffee** *n* (*Brit*) café *m* con leche; ~-**collar worker** *n* oficinista *m/f*; ~ **elephant** *n* (*fig*) maula; ~ **lie** *n* mentirilla; ~**ness** *n* blancura; ~ **noise** *n* sonido blanco; ~ **paper** *n* (*POL*) libro rojo; ~**wash** *n* (*paint*) jalbegue *m*, cal *f* // *vt* (*also fig*) encubrir.

whiting [ˈwaɪtɪŋ] *n*, *pl inv* (*fish*) pescadilla.

Whitsun [ˈwɪtsn] *n* (*Brit*) pentecostés *m*.

whittle [ˈwɪtl] *vt*: **to** ~ **away**, ~ **down** ir reduciendo.

whizz [wɪz] *vi*: **to** ~ **past** *or* **by** pasar a toda velocidad; ~ **kid** *n* (*col*) prodigio.

who [hu:] *pron* **1** (*interrogative*) quién;
~ is it?, ~'s there? ¿quién es?; ~ are
you looking for? ¿a quién buscas?; I
told her ~ I was le dije quién era yo
2 (*relative*) que; the man/woman ~
spoke to me el hombre/la mujer que habló conmigo; those ~ can swim los que
saben *or* sepan nadar.

whodun(n)it [hu:'dʌnɪt] *n* (*col*) novela
policíaca.

whoever [hu:'ɛvə*] *pron*: ~ finds it cualquiera *or* quienquiera que lo encuentre;
ask ~ you like pregunta a quien quieras;
~ he marries no importa con quién se
case.

whole [həul] *a* (*not broken*) intacto;
(*all*): the ~ of the town toda la ciudad,
la ciudad entera // *n* (*total*) total *m*;
(*sum*) conjunto; on the ~, as a ~ en general; ~hearted *a* sincero, cordial;
~meal *a* integral; ~sale *n* venta al por
mayor // *a* al por mayor; (*destruction*)
sistemático; ~saler *n* mayorista *m/f*;
~some *a* sano; ~wheat *a* = ~meal;
wholly *ad* totalmente, enteramente.

whom [hu:m] *pron* **1** (*interrogative*): ~
did you see? ¿a quién viste?; to ~ did
you give it? ¿a quién se lo diste?; tell
me from ~ you received it dígame de
quién lo recibí
2 (*relative*): *direct object*) que; to ~ a
quien(es); of ~ de quien(es), del/de la
que *etc*; the man ~ I saw/to ~ I wrote el
hombre que vi/a quien escribí; the lady
about/with ~ I was talking la señora de/
con quien *or* (la) que hablaba.

whooping cough ['hu:pɪŋ-] *n* tos *f* ferina.

whore [hɔ:*] *n* (*col: pej*) puta.

whose [hu:z] ♦ *a* **1** (*possessive: interrogative*): ~ book is this?, ~ is this
book? ¿de quién es este libro?; ~ pencil
have you taken? ¿de quién es el lápiz
que has cogido?; ~ daughter are you?
¿de quién eres hija?
2 (*possessive: relative*) cuyo/a, *pl*
cuyos/as; the man ~ son you rescued el
hombre cuyo hijo rescataste; those ~
passports I have aquellas personas cuyos
pasaportes tengo; the woman ~ car was
stolen la mujer a quien le robaron el coche
♦ *pron* de quién; ~ is this? ¿de quién es
esto?; I know ~ it is sé de quién es.

why [waɪ] ♦ *ad* por qué; ~ not? ¿por qué
no?; ~ not do it now? ¿por qué no lo haces (*or* hacemos *etc*) ahora?
♦ *conj*: I wonder ~ he said that me pregunto por qué dijo eso; that's not ~ I'm
here no es por eso (por lo) que estoy
aquí; the reason ~ la razón por la que
♦ *excl* (*expressing surprise, shock, annoyance*) ¡hombre!, ¡vaya! (*explaining*): ~,
it's you! ¡hombre, eres tú!; ~, that's impossible! ¡pero sí eso es impossible!

wick [wɪk] *n* mecha.

wicked ['wɪkɪd] *a* malvado, cruel.

wicker ['wɪkə*] *n* (*also*: ~work) artículos
mpl de mimbre // *cpd* de mimbre.

wicket ['wɪkɪt] *n* (*CRICKET*) palos *mpl*.

wide [waɪd] *a* ancho; (*area, knowledge*)
vasto, grande; (*choice*) grande // *ad*: to
open ~ abrir de par en par; to shoot ~
errar el tiro; ~-angle lens *n* objetivo
granangular; ~-awake *a* bien despierto; ~ly *ad* (*differing*) muy; it is ~ly be-
lieved that... hay una convicción general
de que...; ~n *vt* ensanchar; ~ open *a*
abierto de par en par; ~spread *a* (*belief etc*) extendido, general.

widow ['wɪdəu] *n* viuda; ~ed *a* viudo;
~er *n* viudo.

width [wɪdθ] *n* anchura; (*of cloth*) ancho.

wield [wi:ld] *vt* (*sword*) manejar; (*power*) ejercer.

wife [waɪf], *pl* wives [waɪvz] *n* mujer *f*,
esposa.

wig [wɪg] *n* peluca.

wiggle ['wɪgl] *vt* menear // *vi* menearse.

wild [waɪld] *a* (*animal*) salvaje; (*plant*)
silvestre; (*rough*) furioso, violento;
(*idea*) descabellado; ~s *npl* regiones *fpl*
salvajes, tierras *fpl* vírgenes; ~erness
['wɪldənɪs] *n* desierto; ~-goose chase *n*
(*fig*) búsqueda inútil; ~life *n* fauna; ~ly
ad (*roughly*) violentamente; (*foolishly*)
locamente; (*rashly*) descabelladamente.

wilful ['wɪlful] *a* (*action*) deliberado;
(*obstinate*) testarudo.

will [wɪl] ♦ *auxiliary vb* **1** (*forming future
tense*): I ~ finish it tomorrow lo termina-
ré *or* voy a terminar mañana; I ~ have
finished it by tomorrow lo habré terminado para mañana; ~ you do it? — yes I
~/no I won't ¿lo harás? — sí/no
2 (*in conjectures, predictions*): he ~ *or*
he'll be there by now ya habrá *or* debe
(de) haber llegado; that ~ be the post-
man será *or* debe ser el cartero
3 (*in commands, requests, offers*): ~
you be quiet! ¿quieres callarte?; ~ you
help me? ¿quieres ayudarme?; ~ you
have a cup of tea? ¿te apetece un té?; I
won't put up with it! ¡no lo soporto!
♦ *vt* (*pt, pp* willed): to ~ sb to do sth
desear que alguien haga algo; he ~ed
himself to go on con gran fuerza de voluntad, continuó
♦ *n* voluntad *f*; (*testament*) testamento.

willing ['wɪlɪŋ] *a* (*with goodwill*) de buena voluntad; complaciente; he's ~ to do
it está dispuesto a hacerlo; ~ly *ad* con
mucho gusto; ~ness *n* buena voluntad.

willow ['wɪləu] *n* sauce *m*.

will power *n* fuerza de voluntad.

willy-nilly ['wɪlɪ'nɪlɪ] *ad* quiérase o no.

wilt [wɪlt] *vi* marchitarse.

wily ['waɪlɪ] *a* astuto.

win [wɪn] *n* (*in sports etc*) victoria, triunfo // vb (pt, pp won) vt ganar; (obtain) conseguir, lograr // vi ganar; **to ~ over**, (Brit) ~ **round** vt convencer a.

wince [wins] vi encogerse.

winch [wintʃ] n torno.

wind [wind] n viento; (MED) gases mpl // vb (pt, pp **wound**) vt enrollar; (wrap) envolver; (clock, toy) dar cuerda a // vi (road, river) serpentear // vt [wind] (take breath away from) dejar sin aliento a; **to ~ up** vt (clock) dar cuerda a; (debate) concluir, terminar; **~fall** n golpe m de suerte; **~ing** a (road) tortuoso; **~ instrument** n (MUS) instrumento de viento; **~mill** n molino de viento.

window ['windəu] n ventana; (in car, train) ventanilla; (in shop etc) escaparate m, vitrina (LAm), vidriera (LAm); ~ **box** n jardinera de ventana; ~ **cleaner** n (person) limpiacristales m inv; ~ **ledge** n alféizar m, repisa (LAm); ~ **pane** n cristal m; **~sill** n alféizar m, repisa (LAm).

windpipe ['windpaip] n tráquea.

windscreen ['windskrin], (US) **windshield** ['windfi:ld] n parabrisas m inv; ~ **washer** n lavaparabrisas m inv; ~ **wiper** n limpiaparabrisas m inv.

windswept ['windswept] a azotado por el viento.

windy ['windi] a de mucho viento; it's ~ hace viento.

wine [wain] n vino; ~ **cellar** n bodega; ~ **glass** n copa (para vino); ~ **list** n lista de vinos; ~ **merchant** n vinatero; ~ **tasting** n degustación f de vinos; ~ **waiter** n escanciador m.

wing [wiŋ] n ala; (Brit AUT) aleta; **~s** npl (THEATRE) bastidores mpl; **~er** n (SPORT) extremo.

wink [wiŋk] n guiño, pestañeo // vi guiñar, pestañear; (light etc) parpadear.

winner ['winə*] n ganador(a) m/f.

winning ['winiŋ] a (team) ganador(a); (goal) decisivo; **~s** npl ganancias fpl; ~ **post** n meta.

winter ['wintə*] n invierno // vi invernar; ~ **sports** npl deportes mpl de invierno.

wintry ['wintri] a invernal.

wipe [waip] n: to give sth a ~ pasar un trapo sobre algo // vt limpiar; **to ~ off** vt limpiar con un trapo; **to ~ out** vt (debt) liquidar; (memory) borrar; (destroy) destruir; **to ~ up** vt limpiar.

wire ['waiə*] n alambre m; (ELEC) cable m (eléctrico); (TEL) telegrama m // vt (house) instalar el alambrado en; (also: ~ **up**) conectar.

wireless ['waiəlis] n (Brit) radio f.

wiring ['waiəriŋ] n alambrado.

wiry ['waiəri] a enjuto y fuerte.

wisdom ['wizdəm] n sabiduría, saber m; (good sense) cordura; ~ **tooth** n muela del juicio.

wise [waiz] a sabio; (sensible) juicioso.

...wise [waiz] suffix: time~ en cuanto a or respecto al tiempo.

wisecrack ['waizkræk] n broma.

wish [wiʃ] n (desire) deseo // vt desear; (want) querer; **best ~es** (on birthday etc) felicidades fpl; **with best ~es** (in letter) saludos mpl, recuerdos mpl; **to ~ sb goodbye** despedirse de uno; **he ~ed me well** me deseó mucha suerte; **to ~ to do/ sb to do sth** querer hacer/que alguien haga algo; **to ~ for** desear; **~ful** n: it's **~ful thinking** eso sería soñar.

wishy-washy ['wiʃiwɔʃi] a (col: colour, ideas) desvaído.

wisp [wisp] n mechón m; (of smoke) voluta.

wistful ['wistful] a pensativo.

wit [wit] n (wittiness) ingenio, gracia; (intelligence; also: **~s**) inteligencia; (person) chistoso/a.

witch [witʃ] n bruja.

with [wið, wiθ] prep **1** (accompanying, in the company of) con (con + mí, ti, sí = conmigo, contigo, consigo); I **was ~ him** estaba con él; **we stayed ~ friends** nos hospedamos en casa de unos amigos; I'm (not) **~ you** (understand) (no) te entiendo; **to be ~ it** (col: person: up-to-date) estar al tanto; (: alert) ser despabilado

2 (descriptive, indicating manner etc) con; de; **a room ~ a view** una habitación con vistas; **the man ~ the grey hat/blue eyes** el hombre del sombrero gris/de los ojos azules; **red ~ anger** rojo/a de ira; **to shake ~ fear** temblar de miedo; **to fill sth ~ water** llenar algo de agua.

withdraw [wiθ'drɔ:] (irg: like draw) vt retirar, sacar // vi retirarse; (go back on promise) retractarse; **to ~ money** (from the bank) retirar fondos (del banco); **~al** n retirada; **~n** a (person) reservado, introvertido.

wither ['wiðə*] vi marchitarse.

withhold [wiθ'həuld] (irg: like hold) vt (money) retener; (decision) aplazar; (permission) negar; (information) ocultar.

within [wið'in] prep dentro de // ad dentro; ~ **reach** al alcance de la mano; ~ **sight of** a la vista de; ~ **the week** antes de acabar la semana.

without [wið'aut] prep sin.

withstand [wiθ'stænd] (irg: like stand) vt resistir a.

witness ['witnis] n (person) testigo m/f; (evidence) testimonio // vt (event) presenciar; (document) atestiguar la veracidad de; ~ **box**, (US) ~ **stand** n tribuna de los testigos.

witticism ['witisizm] n occurrencia.

witty ['witi] a ingenioso.

wives [waivz] npl of **wife**.

wizard ['wizəd] n hechicero.

wk *abbr* = **week**.
wobble ['wɔbl] *vi* tambalearse; (*chair*) ser poco firme.
woe [wəu] *n* desgracia.
woke [wəuk], **woken** ['wəukən] *pt, pp of* **wake**.
wolf [wulf], *pl* **wolves** [wulvz] *n* lobo.
woman ['wumən], *pl* **women** *n* mujer *f*; ~ **doctor** *n* médica; **women's lib** *n* (*pej*) la liberación de la mujer; ~**ly** *a* femenino.
womb [wu:m] *n* (*ANAT*) matriz *f*, útero.
women ['wimin] *npl of* **woman**.
won [wʌn] *pt, pp of* **win**.
wonder ['wʌndə*] *n* maravilla, prodigio; (*feeling*) asombro // *vi*: to ~ **whether** preguntarse si; to ~ **at** asombrarse de; to ~ **about** pensar sobre *or* en; it's no ~ that no es de extrañarse que + *subjun*; ~**ful** *a* maravilloso; ~**fully** *ad* maravillosamente, estupendamente.
won't [wəunt] = **will not**.
woo [wu:] *vt* (*woman*) cortejar.
wood [wud] *n* (*timber*) madera; (*forest*) bosque *m*; ~ **alcohol** *n* (*US*) alcohol *m* desnaturalizado; ~ **carving** *n* tallado en madera; ~**ed** *a* arbolado; ~**en** *a* de madera; (*fig*) inexpresivo; ~**pecker** *n* pájaro carpintero; ~**wind** *n* (*MUS*) instrumentos *mpl* de viento de madera; ~**work** *n* carpintería; ~**worm** *n* carcoma.
wool [wul] *n* lana; to **pull the** ~ **over sb's eyes** (*fig*) dar a uno gato por liebre; ~**len**, (*US*) ~**en** *a* de lana; ~**lens** *npl* géneros *mpl* de lana; ~**ly**, (*US*) ~**y** *a* lanudo, de lana; (*fig: ideas*) confuso.
word [wə:d] *n* palabra; (*news*) noticia; (*promise*) palabra (de honor) // *vt* redactar; **in other** ~**s** en otras palabras; to **break/keep one's** ~ faltar a la palabra/ cumplir la promesa; ~**ing** *n* redacción *f*; ~ **processing** *n* proceso de textos; ~ **processor** *n* procesador *m* de palabras.
wore [wɔ:*] *pt of* **wear**.
work [wə:k] *n* trabajo; (*job*) empleo, trabajo; (*ART, LITERATURE*) obra // *vi* trabajar; (*mechanism*) funcionar, marchar; (*medicine*) ser eficaz, surtir efecto // *vt* (*shape*) trabajar; (*stone etc*) tallar; (*mine etc*) explotar; (*machine*) manejar, hacer funcionar; to **be out of** ~ estar parado, no tener trabajo; ~**s** *n* (*Brit: factory*) fábrica // *npl* (*of clock, machine*) mecanismo *sg*; to ~ **loose** *vi* (*part*) desprenderse; (*knot*) aflojarse; ~ **on** *vt fus* trabajar en, dedicarse a; (*principle*) basarse en; to ~ **out** *vi* (*plans etc*) salir bien, funcionar // *vt* (*problem*) resolver; (*plan*) elaborar; it ~**s out at £100** suma 100 libras; to ~ **up** *vt*: to **get** ~**ed up** excitarse; ~**able** *a* (*solution*) práctico, factible; **workaholic** *n* trabajador(a) obsesivo/a *m/f*; ~**er** *n* trabajador(a) *m/f*, obrero/a; ~**force** *n*

mano *f* de obra; ~**ing class** *n* clase *f* obrera; ~**ing-class** *a* obrero; ~**ing order** *n*: **in** ~**ing order** en funcionamiento; ~**man** *n* obrero; ~**manship** *n* (*art*) hechura, arte *m*; (*skill*) habilidad *f*, trabajo; ~**mate** *n* compañero/a de trabajo; ~**sheet** *n* hoja de trabajo; ~**shop** *n* taller *m*; ~ **station** *n* puesto *or* estación *f* de trabajo; ~**-to-rule** *n* (*Brit*) huelga de brazos caídos.
world [wə:ld] *n* mundo // *cpd* (*champion*) del mundo; (*power, war*) mundial; to **think the** ~ **of sb** (*fig*) tener un concepto muy alto de uno; ~**ly** *a* mundano; ~**wide** *a* mundial, universal.
worm [wə:m] *n* gusano; (*earth* ~) lombriz *f*.
worn [wɔ:n] *pp of* **wear** // *a* usado; ~**out** *a* (*object*) gastado; (*person*) rendido, agotado.
worried ['wʌrid] *a* preocupado.
worry ['wʌri] *n* preocupación *f* // *vt* preocupar, inquietar // *vi* preocuparse; ~**ing** *a* inquietante.
worse [wə:s] *a, ad* peor // *n* lo peor; **a change for the** ~ un empeoramiento; ~**n** *vt, vi* empeorar; ~ **off** *a* (*fig*): you'll be ~ **off this way** de esta forma estarás peor que nunca.
worship ['wə:ʃip] *n* (*organized* ~) culto; (*act*) adoración *f* // *vt* adorar; **Your W**~ (*Brit: to mayor*) señor alcalde; (: *to judge*) señor juez.
worst [wə:st] *a* el/la peor // *ad* peor // *n* lo peor; **at** ~ en lo peor de los casos.
worsted ['wustid] *n*: (**wool**) = estambre *m*.
worth [wə:θ] *n* valor *m* // *a*: to **be** ~ valer; it's ~ it vale *or* merece la pena; to **be** ~ **one's while** (to do) merecer la pena (hacer); ~**less** *a* sin valor; (*useless*) inútil; ~**while** *a* (*activity*) que merece la pena; (*cause*) loable.
worthy ['wə:ði] *a* (*person*) respetable; (*motive*) honesto; ~ **of** digno de.
would [wud] *auxiliary vb* **1** (*conditional tense*): **if you asked him he** ~ **do it** si se lo pidieras, lo haría; **if you had asked him he** ~ **have done it** si se lo hubieras pedido, lo habría *or* hubiera hecho **2** (*in offers, invitations, requests*): ~ **you like a biscuit?** ¿quiere(s) una galleta?; (*formal*) ¿querría una galleta?; ~ **you ask him to come in?** ¿quiere(s) hacerle pasar?; ~ **you open the window please?** ¿quiere *or* podría abrir la ventana, por favor? **3** (*in indirect speech*): **I said I** ~ **do it** dije que lo haría **4** (*emphatic*): **it WOULD have to snow today!** ¡tenía que nevar precisamente hoy! **5** (*insistence*): **she** ~**n't behave** no quiso comportarse bien **6** (*conjecture*): **it** ~ **have been midnight** sería medianoche; **it** ~ **seem so** parece

ser que sí
7 (*indicating habit*): **he ~ go there on
Mondays** iba allí los lunes.
would-be ['wudbiː] *a* (*pej*) presunto.
wouldn't ['wudnt] = **would not**.
wound [waund] *pt*, *pp of* **wind** // *n*
[wuːnd] herida // *vt* herir.
wove [wəuv], **woven** ['wəuvən] *pt*, *pp of*
weave.
wrangle ['ræŋgl] *n* riña // *vi* reñir.
wrap [ræp] *n* (*stole*) chal *m* // *vt* (*also:*
~ **up**) envolver; **~per** *n* (*Brit: of book*)
sobrecubierta; **~ping paper** *n* papel *m*
de envolver.
wrath [rɔθ] *n* cólera.
wreak [riːk] *vt*: **to ~ havoc (on)** hacer
estragos (en); **to ~ vengeance (on)** vengarse (de).
wreath [riːθ], *pl* **~s** [riːðz] *n* (*funeral ~*)
corona; (*of flowers*) guirnalda.
wreck [rɛk] *n* (*ship: destruction*) naufragio; (: *remains*) restos *mpl* del barco;
(*pej: person*) ruina // *vt* (*ship*) hundir;
(*fig*) arruinar; **~age** *n* (*remains*) restos
mpl; (*of building*) escombros *mpl*.
wren [rɛn] *n* (ZOOL) reyezuelo.
wrench [rɛntʃ] *n* (TECH) llave *f* inglesa;
(*tug*) tirón *m* // *vt* arrancar; **to ~ sth
from sb** arrebatar algo violentamente a
uno.
wrestle ['rɛsl] *vi*: **to ~ (with sb)** luchar
(con *or* contra uno); **~r** *n* luchador(a)
m/f (de lucha libre); **wrestling** *n* lucha
libre.
wretched ['rɛtʃid] *a* miserable.
wriggle ['rɪgl] *vi* serpentear.
wring [rɪŋ], *pt*, *pp* **wrung** *vt* torcer, retorcer; (*wet clothes*) escurrir; (*fig*): **to
~ sth out of sb** sacar algo por la fuerza a
uno.
wrinkle ['rɪŋkl] *n* arruga // *vt* arrugar //
vi arrugarse.
wrist [rɪst] *n* muñeca; **~ watch** *n* reloj
m de pulsera.
writ [rɪt] *n* mandato judicial.
write [raɪt], *pt* **wrote**, *pp* **written** *vt*, *vi*
escribir; **to ~ down** *vt* escribir; (*note*)
apuntar; **to ~ off** *vt* (*debt*) borrar
(como incobrable); (*fig*) desechar por
inútil; **to ~ out** *vt* escribir; **to ~ up**
vt redactar; **~-off** *n* pérdida total; **the
car is a ~-off** el coche quedó para chatarra; **~r** *n* escritor(a) *m/f*.
writhe [raɪð] *vi* retorcerse.
writing ['raɪtɪŋ] *n* escritura; (*hand-~*) letra; (*of author*) obras *fpl*; **in ~** por escrito; **~ paper** *n* papel *m* de escribir.
written ['rɪtn] *pp of* **write**.
wrong [rɔŋ] *a* (*wicked*) malo; (*unfair*)
injusto; (*incorrect*) equivocado, incorrecto; (*not suitable*) inoportuno, inconveniente // *ad* mal; equivocadamente // *n*
mal *m*; (*injustice*) injusticia // *vt* ser injusto con; (*hurt*) agraviar; **you are ~ to
do it** haces mal en hacerlo; **you are ~**

about that, **you've got it ~** en eso estás
equivocado; **to be in the ~** no tener razón, tener la culpa; **what's ~?** ¿qué
pasa?; **to go ~** (*person*) equivocarse;
(*plan*) salir mal; (*machine*) estropearse;
~ful *a* injusto; **~ly** *ad* injustamente.
wrote [rəut] *pt of* **write**.
wrought [rɔːt] *a*: **~ iron** hierro forjado.
wrung [rʌŋ] *pt*, *pp of* **wring**.
wry [raɪ] *a* irónico.
wt. *abbr* = **weight**.

X

Xmas ['ɛksməs] *n abbr* = **Christmas**.
X-ray [eks'reɪ] *n* radiografía; **~s** *npl* ra-
yos *mpl* X.
xylophone ['zaɪləfəun] *n* xilófono.

Y

yacht [jɔt] *n* yate *m*; **~ing** *n* (*sport*) ba-
landrismo; **~sman/woman** *n* balan-
drista *m/f*.
Yank [jæŋk], **Yankee** ['jæŋkɪ] *n* (*pej*)
yanqui *m/f*.
yap [jæp] *vi* (*dog*) aullar.
yard [jɑːd] *n* patio; (*measure*) yarda;
~stick *n* (*fig*) criterio, norma.
yarn [jɑːn] *n* hilo; (*tale*) cuento, historia.
yawn [jɔːn] *n* bostezo // *vi* bostezar;
~ing *a* (*gap*) muy abierto.
yd(s). *abbr* = **yard(s)**.
yeah [jɛə] *ad* (*col*) sí.
year [jɪə*] *n* año; **to be 8 ~s old** tener 8
años; **an eight-~-old child** un niño de
ocho años (de edad); **~ly** *a* anual // *ad*
anualmente, cada año.
yearn [jən] *vi*: **to ~ for sth** añorar algo,
suspirar por algo; **~ing** *n* ansia, añoranza.
yeast [jiːst] *n* levadura.
yell [jɛl] *n* grito, alarido // *vi* gritar.
yellow ['jɛləu] *a*, *n* amarillo.
yelp [jɛlp] *n* aullido // *vi* aullar.
yeoman ['jəumən] *n*: **Y~ of the Guard**
alabardero de la Casa Real.
yes [jes] *ad*, *n* sí *m*; **to say/answer ~**
decir/contestar que sí.
yesterday ['jɛstədɪ] *ad*, *n* ayer *m*; **~
morning/evening** ayer por la mañana/
tarde; **all day ~** todo el día de ayer.
yet [jɛt] *ad* todavía // *conj* sin embargo, a
pesar de todo; **it is not finished ~** todavía no está acabado; **the best ~** el/la mejor hasta ahora; **as ~** hasta ahora, todavía.
yew [juː] *n* tejo.
yield [jiːld] *n* producción *f*; (AGR) cosecha; (COMM) rendimiento // *vt* producir,
dar; (*profit*) rendir // *vi* rendirse, ceder;
(US AUT) ceder el paso.
YMCA *n abbr* (= *Young Men's Christian*

Association) Asociación *f* de Jóvenes
Cristianos.
yoga ['jəugə] *n* yoga *m*.
yog(h)ourt, yog(h)urt ['jəugət] *n* yogur
m.
yoke [jəuk] *n* yugo.
yolk [jəuk] *n* yema (de huevo).
yonder ['jɔndə*] *ad* allá (a lo lejos).
you [ju:] *pron* **1** (*subject: familiar*) tú, *pl*
vosotros/as (*Sp*), ustedes (*LAm*); (*po-
lite*) usted, *pl* ustedes; ~ **are very kind**
eres/es *etc* muy amable; ~ **French enjoy**
your food a vosotros (*or* ustedes) los
franceses os (*or* les) gusta la comida; ~
and I will go iremos tú y yo
2 (*object: direct: familiar*) te, *pl* os
(*Sp*), les ((*LAm*); (*polite*) le, *pl* les, *f* la,
pl las; **I know** ~ te/le *etc* conozco
3 (*object: indirect: familiar*) te, *pl* os
(*Sp*), les (*LAm*); (*polite*) le, *pl* les; **I**
gave the letter to ~ **yesterday** te/os *etc*
di la carta ayer
4 (*stressed*): **I told you to do it** te dije a
ti que lo hicieras, es a ti a quien dije que
lo hicieras; *see also* **3, 5**
5 (*after prep: NB:* **con** + **ti** = **contigo:**
familiar) ti, *pl* vosotros/as (*Sp*), ustedes
(*LAm*); (: *polite*) usted, *pl* ustedes; **it's**
for ~ es para ti/vosotros *etc*.
6 (*comparisons: familiar*) tú, *pl* voso-
tros/as (*Sp*), ustedes (*LAm*); (: *polite*)
usted, *pl* ustedes; **she's younger than** ~
es más joven que tú/vosotros *etc*
7 (*impersonal: one*): **fresh air does** ~
good el aire puro (te) hace bien; ~ **ne-**
ver know nunca se sabe; ~ **can't do**
that! ¡eso no se hace!
you'd [ju:d] = **you had, you would**.
you'll [ju:l] = **you will, you shall**.
young [jʌŋ] *a* joven // *npl* (*of animal*)
cría *sg*; (*people*): **the** ~ los jóvenes, la
juventud *sg*; ~**er** *a* (*brother etc*) menor;
~**ster** *n* joven *m/f*.
your [jɔ:*] *a* tu; (*pl*) vuestro; (*formal*)
su; *see also* **my**.
you're [juə*] = **you are**.
yours [jɔ:z] *pron* tuyo; (: *pl*) vuestro;
(*formal*) suyo; *see also* **faithfully, mine,**
sincerely.
yourself [jɔ:'sɛlf] *pron* (*reflexive*) tú

mismo; (*complement*) te; (*after prep*)
tí (mismo); (*formal*) usted mismo; (:
complement) se; (: *after prep*) sí (mismo); **yourselves** *pl pron* vosotros mismos; (*after prep*) vosotros (mismos);
(*formal*) ustedes (mismos); (: *complement*) se; (: *after prep*) sí mismos;
see also **oneself**.
youth [ju:θ] *n* juventud *f*; (*young man:*
pl ~**s** [ju:ðz]) joven *m*; ~ **club** *n* club *m*
juvenil; ~**ful** *a* juvenil; ~ **hostel** *n* albergue *m* de juventud.
you've [ju:v] = **you have**.
YTS *n abbr* (*Brit:* = *Youth Training*
Scheme) plan de inserción profesional juvenil.
Yugoslav ['ju:gəsla:v] *a*, *n*
yugo(e)slavo/a *m/f*.
Yugoslavia [ju:gəu'sla:vɪə] *n* Yugoslavia.
yuppie ['jʌpɪ] (*col*) *a*, *n* yuppie *m/f*.
YWCA *n abbr* (= *Young Women's*
Christian Association) Asociación *f* de
Jóvenes Cristianas.

Z

zany ['zeɪnɪ] *a* estrafalario.
zap [zæp] *vt* (*COMPUT*) borrar.
zeal [zi:l] *n* celo, entusiasmo.
zebra ['zi:brə] *n* cebra; ~ **crossing** *n*
(*Brit*) paso de peatones.
zenith ['zɛnɪθ] *n* cénit *m*.
zero ['zɪərəu] *n* cero.
zest [zɛst] *n* ánimo, vivacidad *f*.
zigzag ['zɪgzæg] *n* zigzag *m*.
zinc [zɪŋk] *n* cinc *m*, zinc *m*.
zip [zɪp] *n* (*also:* ~ **fastener,** (*US*) ~**per**)
cremallera, cierre *m* (*LAm*) // *vt* (*also:*
~ **up**) cerrar la cremallera de; ~ **code**
n (*US*) código postal.
zodiac ['zəudɪæk] *n* zodíaco.
zone [zəun] *n* zona.
zoo [zu:] *n* (jardín *m*) zoológico.
zoologist [zu'ɔlədʒɪst] *n* zoólogo/a.
zoology [zu:'ɔlədʒɪ] *n* zoología.
zoom [zu:m] *vi*: **to** ~ **past** pasar zumban-
do; ~ **lens** *n* zoom *m*.
zucchini [zu:'ki:nɪ] *n*(*pl*) (*US*) calaba-
cín(ines) *m*(*pl*).

SPANISH VERBS

1 Gerund *2* Imperative *3* Present *4* Preterite *5* Future *6* Present subjunctive *7* Imperfect subjunctive *8* Past participle *9* Imperfect. *Etc* indicates that the irregular root is used for all persons of the tense, e.g. **oír** *6* oiga *etc* = oigas, oigamos, oigáis, oigan. Forms which consist of the unmodified verb root + verb ending are not shown, e.g. acertamos, acertáis.

acertar *2* acierta *3* acierto, aciertas, acierta, aciertan *6* acierte, aciertes, acierte, acierten

acordar *2* acuerda *3* acuerdo, acuerdas, acuerda, acuerdan *6* acuerde, acuerdes, acuerde, acuerden

advertir *1* advirtiendo *2* advierte *3* advierto, adviertes, advierte, advierten *4* advirtió, advirtieron *6* advierta, adviertas, advierta, advirtamos, advirtáis, adviertan *7* advirtiera *etc*

agradecer *3* agradezco *6* agradezca *etc*

aparecer *3* aparezco *6* aparezca *etc*

aprobar *2* aprueba *3* apruebo, apruebas, aprueba, aprueban *6* apruebe, apruebes, apruebe, aprueben

atravesar *2* atraviesa *3* atravieso, atraviesas, atraviesa, atraviesan *6* atraviese, atravieses, atraviese, atraviesen

caber *3* quepo *4* cupe, cupiste, cupo, cupimos, cupisteis, cupieron *5* cabré *etc* *6* quepa *etc* *7* cupiera *etc*

caer *1* cayendo *3* caigo *4* cayó, cayeron *6* caiga *etc* *7* cayera *etc*

calentar *2* calienta *3* caliento, calientas, calienta, calientan *6* caliente, calientes, caliente, calienten

cerrar *2* cierra *3* cierro, cierras, cierra, cierran *6* cierre, cierres, cierre, cierren

COMER *1* comiendo *2* come, comed *3* como, comes, come, comemos, coméis, comen *4* comí, comiste, comió, comimos, comisteis, comieron *5* comeré, comerás, comerá, comeremos, comeréis, comerán *6* coma, comas, coma, comamos, comáis, coman *7* comiera, comieras, comiera, comiéramos, comierais, comieran *8* comido *9* comía, comías, comía, comíamos, comíais, comían

conocer *3* conozco *6* conozca *etc*

contar *2* cuenta *3* cuento, cuentas, cuenta, cuentan *6* cuente, cuentes, cuente, cuenten

costar *2* cuesta *3* cuesto, cuestas, cuesta, cuestan *6* cueste, cuestes, cueste, cuesten

dar *3* doy *4* di, diste, dio, dimos, disteis, dieron *7* diera *etc*

decir *2* di *3* digo *4* dije, dijiste, dijo, dijimos, dijisteis, dijeron *5* diré *etc* *6* diga *etc* *7* dijera *etc* *8* dicho

despertar *2* despierta *3* despierto, despiertas, despierta, despiertan *6* despierte, despiertes, despierte, despierten

divertir *1* divirtiendo *2* divierte *3* divierto, diviertes, divierte, divierten *4* divirtió, divirtieron *6* divierta, diviertas, divierta, divirtamos, divirtáis, diviertan *7* divirtiera *etc*

dormir *1* durmiendo *2* duerme *3* duermo, duermes, duerme, duermen *4* durmió, durmieron *6* duerma, duermas, duerma, durmamos, durmáis, duerman *7* durmiera *etc*

empezar *2* empieza *3* empiezo, empiezas, empieza, empiezan *4* empecé *6* empiece, empieces, empiece, empecemos, empecéis, empiecen

entender *2* entiende *3* entiendo, entiendes, entiende, entienden *6* entienda, entiendas, entienda, entiendan

ESTAR *2* está *3* estoy, estás, está, están *4* estuve, estuviste, estuvo, estuvimos, estuvisteis, estuvieron *6* esté, estés, esté, estén *7* estuviera *etc*

HABER *3* he, has, ha, hemos, han *4* hube, hubiste, hubo, hubimos, hubisteis, hubieron *5* habré *etc* *6* haya *etc* *7* hubiera *etc*

HABLAR *1* hablando *2* habla, hablad *3* hablo, hablas, habla, hablamos, habláis, hablan *4* hablé, hablaste, habló, hablamos, hablasteis, hablaron *5* hablaré, hablarás, hablará, hablaremos, hablaréis, hablarán *6* hable, hables, hable, hablemos, habléis, hablen *7* hablara, hablaras, hablara, habláramos, hablarais, hablaran *8* hablado *9* hablaba, hablabas, hablaba, hablábamos, hablabais, hablaban

hacer *2* haz *3* hago *4* hice, hiciste, hizo, hicimos, hicisteis, hicieron *5* haré *etc* *6* haga *etc* *7* hiciera *etc* *8* hecho

instruir *1* instruyendo *2* instruye *3* instruyo, instruyes, instruye, instruyen *4* instruyó, instruyeron *6* instruya *etc* *7* instruyera *etc*

ir *1* yendo *2* ve *3* voy, vas, va, vamos, vais, van *4* fui, fuiste, fue, fuimos, fuisteis, fueron *6* vaya, vayas, vaya, vayamos, vayáis, vayan *7* fuera *etc* *8* iba, ibas, iba, íbamos, ibais, iban

jugar *2* juega *3* juego, juegas, juega, juegan *4* jugué *6* juegue *etc*

leer *1* leyendo *4* leyó, leyeron *7* leyera *etc*

morir *1* muriendo *2* muere *3* muero, mueres, muere, mueren *4* murió, murieron *6* muera, mueras, muera, muramos, muráis, mueran *7* muriera *etc* *8* muerto

mostrar *2* muestra *3* muestro, muestras, muestra, muestran *6* muestre, muestres, muestre, muestren

mover *2* mueve *3* muevo, mueves, mueve, mueven *6* mueva, muevas, mueva, muevan

negar *2* niega *3* niego, niegas, niega, niegan *4* negué *6* niegue, niegues, niegue, neguemos, neguéis, nieguen

ofrecer *3* ofrezco *6* ofrezca *etc*

oír *1* oyendo *2* oye *3* oigo, oyes, oye, oyen *4* oyó, oyeron *6* oiga *etc* *7* oyera *etc*

oler *2* huele *3* huelo, hueles, huele, huelen *6*

huela, huelas, huela, huelan

parecer *3* parezco *6* parezca *etc*

pedir *1* pidiendo, *2* pide *3* pido, pides, pide, piden *4* pidió, pidieron *6* pida *etc* *7* pidiera *etc*

pensar *2* piensa *3* pienso, piensas, piensa, piensan *6* piense, pienses, piense, piensen

perder *2* pierde *3* pierdo, pierdes, pierde, pierden *6* pierda, pierdas, pierda, pierdan

poder *1* pudiendo *2* puede *3* puedo, puedes, puede, pueden *4* pude, pudiste, pudo, pudimos, pudisteis, pudieron *5* podré *etc* *6* pueda, puedas, pueda, puedan *7* pudiera *etc*

poner *2* pon *3* pongo *4* puse, pusiste, puso, pusimos, pusisteis, pusieron *5* pondré *etc* *6* ponga *etc* *7* pusiera *etc* *8* puesto

preferir *1* prefiriendo *2* prefiere *3* prefiero, prefieres, prefiere, prefieren *4* prefirió, prefirieron *6* prefiera, prefieras, prefiera, prefiramos, prefiráis, prefieran *7* prefiriera *etc*

querer *2* quiere *3* quiero, quieres, quiere, quieren *4* quise, quisiste, quiso, quisimos, quisisteis, quisieron *5* querré *etc* *6* quiera, quieras, quiera, quieran *7* quisiera *etc*

reír *2* ríe *3* río, ríes, ríe, ríen *4* rio, rieron *6* ría, rías, ría, riamos, riáis, rían *7* riera *etc*

repetir *1* repitiendo *2* repite *3* repito, repites, repite, repiten *4* repitió, repitieron *6* repita *etc* *7* repitiera *etc*

rogar *2* ruega *3* ruego, ruegas, ruega, ruegan *4* rogué *6* ruegue, ruegues, ruegue, roguemos, roguéis, rueguen

saber *3* sé *4* supe, supiste, supo, supimos, supisteis, supieron *5* sabré *etc* *6* sepa *etc* *7* supiera *etc*

salir *2* sal *3* salgo *5* saldré *etc* *6* salga *etc*

seguir *1* siguiendo *2* sigue *3* sigo, sigues, sigue, siguen *4* siguió, siguieron *6* siga *etc* *7* siguiera *etc*

sentar *2* sienta *3* siento, sientas, sienta, sien-

tan *6* siente, sientes, siente, sienten

sentir *1* sintiendo *2* siente *3* siento, sientes, siente, sienten *4* sintió, sintieron *6* sienta, sientas, sienta, sintamos, sintáis, sientan *7* sintiera *etc*

SER *2* sé *3* soy, eres, es, somos, sois, son *4* fui, fuiste, fue, fuimos, fuisteis, fueron *6* sea *etc* *7* fuera *etc* *9* era, eras, era, éramos, erais, eran

servir *1* sirviendo *2* sirve *3* sirvo, sirves, sirve, sirven *4* sirvió, sirvieron *6* sirva *etc* *7* sirviera *etc*

soñar *2* sueña *3* sueño, sueñas, sueña, sueñan *6* sueñe, sueñes, sueñe, sueñen

tener *2* ten *3* tengo, tienes, tiene, tienen *4* tuve, tuviste, tuvo, tuvimos, tuvisteis, tuvieron *5* tendré *etc* *6* tenga *etc* *7* tuviera *etc*

traer *1* trayendo *3* traigo *4* traje, trajiste, trajo, trajimos, trajisteis, trajeron *6* traiga *etc* *7* trajera *etc*

valer *2* val *3* valgo *5* valdré *etc* *6* valga *etc*

venir *2* ven *3* vengo, vienes, viene, vienen *4* vine, viniste, vino, vinimos, vinisteis, vinieron *5* vendré *etc* *6* venga *etc* *7* viniera *etc*

ver *3* veo *6* vea *etc* *8* visto *9* veía *etc*

vestir *1* vistiendo *2* viste *3* visto, vistes, viste, visten *4* vistió, vistieron *6* vista *etc* *7* vistiera *etc*

VIVIR *1* viviendo *2* vive, vivid *3* vivo, vives, vive, vivimos, vivís, viven *4* viví, viviste, vivió, vivimos, vivisteis, vivieron *5* viviré, vivirás, vivirá, viviremos, viviréis, vivirán *6* viva, vivas, viva, vivamos, viváis, vivan *7* viviera, vivieras, viviera, viviéramos, vivierais, vivieran *8* vivido *9* vivía, vivías, vivía, vivíamos, vivíais, vivían

volver *2* vuelve *3* vuelvo, vuelves, vuelve, vuelven *6* vuelva, vuelvas, vuelva, vuelvan *8* vuelto

222

VERBOS IRREGULARES EN INGLÉS

present	pt	pp	present	pt	pp
arise	arose	arisen	fly (flies)	flew	flown
awake	awoke	awaked	forbid	forbade	forbidden
be (am, is,	was, were	been	forecast	forecast	forecast
are;			forego	forewent	foregone
being)			foresee	foresaw	foreseen
bear	bore	born(e)	foretell	foretold	foretold
beat	beat	beaten	forget	forgot	forgotten
become	became	become	forgive	forgave	forgiven
begin	began	begun	forsake	forsook	forsaken
behold	beheld	beheld	freeze	froze	frozen
bend	bent	bent	get	got	got, (US)
beset	beset	beset			gotten
bet	bet, betted	bet, betted	give	gave	given
bid	bid, bade	bid, bidden	go (goes)	went	gone
bind	bound	bound	grind	ground	ground
bite	bit	bitten	grow	grew	grown
bleed	bled	bled	hang	hung,	hung,
blow	blew	blown		hanged	hanged
break	broke	broken	have (has;	had	had
breed	bred	bred	having)		
bring	brought	brought	hear	heard	heard
build	built	built	hide	hid	hidden
burn	burnt,	burnt,	hit	hit	hit
	burned	burned	hold	held	held
burst	burst	burst	hurt	hurt	hurt
buy	bought	bought	keep	kept	kept
can	could	(been able)	kneel	knelt,	knelt,
cast	cast	cast		kneeled	kneeled
catch	caught	caught	know	knew	known
choose	chose	chosen	lay	laid	laid
cling	clung	clung	lead	led	led
come	came	come	lean	leant, leaned	leant, leaned
cost	cost	cost	leap	leapt, leaped	leapt, leaped
creep	crept	crept	learn	learnt,	learnt,
cut	cut	cut		learned	learned
deal	dealt	dealt	leave	left	left
dig	dug	dug	lend	lent	lent
do (3rd	did	done	let	let	let
person;			lie (lying)	lay	lain
he/she/it			light	lit, lighted	lit, lighted
does)			lose	lost	lost
draw	drew	drawn	make	made	made
dream	dreamed,	dreamed,	may	might	—
	dreamt	dreamt	mean	meant	meant
drink	drank	drunk	meet	met	met
drive	drove	driven	mistake	mistook	mistaken
dwell	dwelt	dwelt	mow	mowed	mown,
eat	ate	eaten			mowed
fall	fell	fallen	must	(had to)	(had to)
feed	fed	fed	pay	paid	paid
feel	felt	felt	put	put	put
fight	fought	fought	quit	quit, quitted	quit, quitted
find	found	found	read	read	read
flee	fled	fled	rid	rid	rid
fling	flung	flung	ride	rode	ridden

223

present	pt	pp	present	pt	pp
ring	rang	rung	spoil	spoiled,	spoiled,
rise	rose	risen		spoilt	spoilt
run	ran	run	spread	spread	spread
saw	sawed	sawn	spring	sprang	sprung
say	said	said	stand	stood	stood
see	saw	seen	steal	stole	stolen
seek	sought	sought	stick	stuck	stuck
sell	sold	sold	sting	stung	stung
send	sent	sent	stink	stank	stunk
set	set	set	stride	strode	stridden
shake	shook	shaken	strike	struck	struck,
shall	should	—			stricken
shear	sheared	shorn,	strive	strove	striven
		sheared	swear	swore	sworn
shed	shed	shed	sweep	swept	swept
shine	shone	shone	swell	swelled	swollen,
shoot	shot	shot			swelled
show	showed	shown	swim	swam	swum
shrink	shrank	shrunk	swing	swung	swung
shut	shut	shut	take	took	taken
sing	sang	sung	teach	taught	taught
sink	sank	sunk	tear	tore	torn
sit	sat	sat	tell	told	told
slay	slew	slain	think	thought	thought
sleep	slept	slept	throw	threw	thrown
slide	slid	slid	thrust	thrust	thrust
sling	slung	slung	tread	trod	trodden
slit	slit	slit	wake	woke, waked	woken, waked
smell	smelt,	smelt,	waylay	waylaid	waylaid
	smelled	smelled	wear	wore	worn
sow	sowed	sown, sowed	weave	wove,	woven,
speak	spoke	spoken		weaved	weaved
speed	sped,	sped,	wed	wedded, wed	wedded, wed
	speeded	speeded	weep	wept	wept
spell	spelt,	spelt,	win	won	won
	spelled	spelled	wind	wound	wound
spend	spent	spent	withdraw	withdrew	withdrawn
spill	spilt, spilled	spilt, spilled	withhold	withheld	withheld
spin	spun	spun	withstand	withstood	withstood
spit	spat	spat	wring	wrung	wrung
split	split	split	write	wrote	written

LOS NÚMEROS

NUMBERS

un, uno(a)	1	one
dos	2	two
tres	3	three
cuatro	4	four
cinco	5	five
seis	6	six
siete	7	seven
ocho	8	eight
nueve	9	nine
diez	10	ten
once	11	eleven
doce	12	twelve
trece	13	thirteen
catorce	14	fourteen
quince	15	fifteen
dieciséis	16	sixteen
diecisiete	17	seventeen
dieciocho	18	eighteen
diecinueve	19	nineteen
veinte	20	twenty
veintiuno	21	twenty-one
veintidós	22	twenty-two
treinta	30	thirty
treinta y uno(a)	31	thirty-one
treinta y dos	32	thirty-two
cuarenta	40	forty
cuarenta y uno(a)	41	forty-one
cincuenta	50	fifty
sesenta	60	sixty
setenta	70	seventy
ochenta	80	eighty
noventa	90	ninety
cien, ciento	100	a hundred, one hundred
ciento uno(a)	101	a hundred and one
doscientos(as)	200	two hundred
doscientos(as) uno(a)	201	two hundred and one
trescientos(as)	300	three hundred
trescientos(as) uno(a)	301	three hundred and one
cuatrocientos(as)	400	four hundred
quinientos(as)	500	five hundred
seiscientos(as)	600	six hundred
setecientos(as)	700	seven hundred
ochocientos(as)	800	eight hundred
novecientos(as)	900	nine hundred
mil	1 000	a thousand
mil dos	1 002	a thousand and two
cinco mil	5 000	five thousand
un millón	1 000 000	a million

LOS NÚMEROS

NUMBERS

primer, primero(a), 1º, 1ᵉʳ (1ª, 1ᵉʳᵃ)	first, 1st
segundo(a) 2º (2ª)	second, 2nd
tercer, tercero(a), 3º (3ª)	third, 3rd
cuarto(a), 4º (4ª)	fourth, 4th
quinto(a), 5º (5ª)	fifth, 5th
sexto(a), 6º (6ª)	sixth, 6th
séptimo(a)	seventh
octavo(a)	eighth
noveno(a)	ninth
décimo(a)	tenth
undécimo(a)	eleventh
duodécimo(a)	twelfth
decimotercio(a)	thirteenth
decimocuarto(a)	fourteenth
decimoquinto(a)	fifteenth
decimosexto(a)	sixteenth
decimoséptimo(a)	seventeenth
decimoctavo(a)	eighteenth
decimonoveno(a)	nineteenth
vigésimo(a)	twentieth
vigésimo(a) primero(a)	twenty-first
vigésimo(a) segundo(a)	twenty-second
trigésimo(a)	thirtieth
centésimo(a)	hundredth
centésimo(a) primero(a)	hundred-and-first
milésimo(a)	thousandth

Números Quebrados etc

Fractions etc

un medio	a half
un tercio	a third
dos tercios	two thirds
un cuarto	a quarter
un quinto	a fifth
cero coma cinco, 0,5	(nought) point five, 0.5
tres coma cuatro, 3,4	three point four, 3.4
diez por cien(to)	ten per cent
cien por cien	a hundred per cent

Ejemplos

Examples

va a llegar el 7 (de mayo)	he's arriving on the 7th (of May)
vive en el número 7	he lives at number 7
el capítulo/la página 7	chapter/page 7
llegó séptimo	he came in 7th

N.B. In Spanish the ordinal numbers from 1 to 10 are commonly used; from 11 to 20 rather less; above 21 they are rarely written and almost never heard in speech. The custom is to replace the forms for 21 and above by the cardinal number.

LA HORA

THE TIME

¿qué hora es?	*what time is it?*
es/son	*it's* o *it is*

medianoche, las doce (de la noche)	midnight, twelve p.m.
la una (de la madrugada)	one o'clock (in the morning), one (a.m.)
la una y cinco	five past one
la una y diez	ten past one
la una y cuarto *or* quince	a quarter past one, one fifteen
la una y veinticinco	twenty-five past one, one twenty-five
la una y media *or* treinta	half-past one, one thirty
las dos menos veinticinco, la una treinta y cinco	twenty-five to two, one thirty-five'
las dos menos veinte, la una cuarenta	twenty to two, one forty
las dos menos cuarto, la una cuarenta y cinco	a quarter to two, one forty-five
las dos menos diez, la una cincuenta	ten to two, one fifty
mediodía, las doce (de la tarde)	twelve o'clock, midday, noon
la una (de la tarde)	one o'clock (in the afternoon), one (p.m.)
las siete (de la tarde)	seven o'clock (in the evening), seven (p.m.)

¿a qué hora?	*(at) what time?*

a medianoche	at midnight
a las siete	at seven o'clock

en veinte minutos	in twenty minutes
hace quince minutos	fifteen minutes ago